AMERICAN POLITICAL

AND SOCIAL HISTORY

CROFTS AMERICAN HISTORY SERIES

DIXON RYAN FOX, GENERAL EDITOR

AMERICAN POLITICAL

AND SOCIAL HISTORY

By

HAROLD UNDERWOOD FAULKNER

Smith College

FOURTH EDITION

F. S. CROFTS & CO.   NEW YORK

1945

973

A WARTIME BOOK
THIS COMPLETE EDITION IS PRODUCED
IN FULL COMPLIANCE WITH THE GOVERN-
MENT'S REGULATIONS FOR CONSERVING
PAPER AND OTHER ESSENTIAL MATERIALS

PRINTED IN THE UNITED STATES OF AMERICA

TO

PAMELA

AND

SHIRLEY

EDITOR'S FOREWORD

Presumably every American college student some time in his young life has had a course in the history of his country. Possibly it has been partial, sketchy, and perfunctory, but more likely it has been a fairly comprehensive survey so far as great events and outstanding personalities are concerned. In most schools, certainly, American history is taught as thoroughly and intelligently as most other subjects; the college freshman has a right to feel that he has already grasped the rudiments of the subject. This could not be said of many college students in philosophy or psychology, economics or Italian, or a large number of other subjects. Whatever the uncertainties may be in other fields, those in charge of American history find it difficult to decide just what to teach in college. While high schools are accused now and then of trying to present a college program, colleges do not want to be repeating high-school education. Surely their students resent any such confusion and are quick to make their resentment known. At the same time a large number desire to "go on" with American history.

There seem to be three ways out of the difficulty; all three are used, and each is a good way. First, one may forego any attempt to review the whole development of the American nation and its people, and, rather, cover a limited phase or period with all possible thoroughness; abandoning the responsibility of a general course, one converts a special course into a fundamental course, perhaps prerequisite to others, since it offers the primary training in methods of investigation and criticism usually appurtenant to a beginning course in college. Second, one may use a two- or three-volume series, aggregating fifteen hundred or two thousand pages, as a text; this procedure seeks an ordered understanding of our whole development, but, with the practical requirements of time, the understanding, so far as it is gained from books, must be gained almost exclusively from the text. Third, one may choose a single volume, which starts at the beginning and comes down to yesterday, which has a quality of freshness and a quality of wisdom, which builds its story with discriminating care as to proportion, which has that complex value known as "teachability," generally developed from an author's long experience in the classroom, and which supposes a considerable amount of concurrent reading in the library.

In the present text Professor Faulkner has sought, steadily and conscientiously, to meet the demand last indicated. Having taught American history to college classes for more than twenty years, he (unfortunately) knows that it is better not to assume at the start their acquaintance with the main facts. Teachers of solid geometry can make some such assumptions as to plane geometry, but for some mysterious reason an analogous proceeding with American history has not generally been justified. Consequently, the author is obliged to repeat a number of facts that undoubtedly have been seen before in the high-school textbook. But, inasmuch as he writes out of his own inquiries, most of these facts appear with a meaning enlarged and altered in some degree. Beyond these in the author's treatment of political history there is a wealth of new material not previously exploited in a textbook at any level. A glance at the table of contents will reveal that more than a third of the book is given to phases of American life that have not generally had attention in a general course on our history. And yet it is vitally interesting to all of us to know our backgrounds in the means and habits of getting a living and enjoying leisure, in the various arts of expression, in scientific thought and social custom. The chapter titles will also indicate, or at least suggest, however, that this social history has not been kept by itself; rather it has been used throughout to interpret our political action. We have here, not several books intermingled, but one book on the whole experience of America so far as the author can see its interrelations.

As to the wisdom of the book, it is not likely that everyone will agree in all particulars. That would be impossible where any attempt is made at interpretation. Professor Faulkner has been bold enough to think about the material that he has accumulated and pertinacious enough to keep thinking about it. His observation has made him a liberal, and he writes from what may be called a liberal point of view. It is soon apparent that he is somewhat more on Jefferson's side of thought than on Hamilton's side. Since the majority of college teachers in the social studies lean in the same direction—perhaps unconsciously as a balancing corrective to the majority of college students, who tend to lean in the other direction—the slight "tendency" of the book should awaken and sustain an interesting discussion in the classroom. Ours would be a dull world, certainly ours would be a dull classroom, if we all had to agree; there are such worlds and classrooms. It is a merit of this book, as a college text, that it contains some discussable propositions. We who study history need not look with impotent envy on those who study law and philosophy and sociology, in whose classrooms lively discussion is almost inevitable. The history with which we are concerned is not what actually happened, but what we believe happened and what we think were the causes of it. Happily in these matters there are grounds for disagreement, yet no one would maintain that disagreement is the purpose of discussion. Clouds of disagreement are dissolved by the clarifying light of evidence. The value of disagreement is to stimulate inquiry.

Though a one-volume text may leave the student time for inquiry, that is to say outside reading, he appreciates some guidance as to where pertinent reading may be found when he gets to the library. Professor Faulkner has supplied this need in two ways. To each chapter he has appended a note suggesting a few books that will usefully amplify the text and make classroom discussion far more fruitful. He has purposely kept within a fairly narrow range, so that these books may be kept on reference shelves, or some of them, better still when possible, be purchased by the student. This supplementary reading, if followed at all systematically, will greatly enrich the student's understanding and incidentally destroy the queer delusion to be found in many students' minds that all essential knowledge is to be gained from textbooks.

A good course, however, may well offer more than this sort of supplementary reading; this, like many other good textbooks, is equipped with a bibliographical chapter at the end calling attention to hundreds of general and special works on the development of America, most of them characterized in brief but helpful comment. The library habit is one of the best that a student can carry away from college, whatever his future life may be. A bibliographical chapter, simply in itself, will do very little in encouraging such an acquirement; but if, under the stimulation of good teaching, the chapter is actually used, it will be an important aid.

DIXON RYAN FOX

Union College

ACKNOWLEDGMENTS

The manuscript, with the exception of the last chapter, was read by Professor Merle E. Curti of Columbia University and Professor Louis C. Hunter of the American University. For their kindness and numerous helpful suggestions the author is very grateful. He is also appreciative of aid rendered in various ways by Mr. Tyler Kepner, Director of Social Studies, Brookline, Massachusetts. The author is likewise under obligation for many courtesies extended by the staffs of the Forbes Library of Northampton, Massachusetts, and the Smith College Library.

H. U. F.

NOTE TO THE FOURTH EDITION

The fourth edition has been concerned chiefly with revision of the material since 1932, an extension of our history to the spring of 1945, and an effort to bring certain of the bibliographies up to date. The author is particularly grateful to those of his colleagues who have pointed out errors or shortcomings in earlier editions. All have helped to improve the book.

H. U. F.

Northampton, Mass.
March 21, 1945

CONTENTS

COLONIAL CIVILIZATION

EMERGENCE OF A NEW NATION

LIST OF ILLUSTRATIONS

LIST OF MAPS

AMERICAN POLITICAL

AND SOCIAL HISTORY

COLONIAL CIVILIZATION

Chapter I

THE BACKGROUND OF COLONIZATION

What if wise men had, as far back as Ptolemy,
Judged that the earth like an orange was
    round?
None of them ever said, Come along, follow me,
Sail to the West, and the East will be found.

ARTHUR HUGH CLOUGH

EUROPE ON THE EVE OF EXPANSION

History is largely a study of causes and effects. Nothing happens without cause, and nothing happens without leaving behind some results. The business of the historian, therefore, is the eternal search for the facts that may explain a historical event and the constant effort to place that event in its true perspective with regard to the events that follow. The American historian, as a consequence, must begin his story, not in America, but in other lands, whatever they may have been, whose adventurers first peopled the American continents. For the moment then, we turn our eyes to Europe in an endeavor to unravel some of those tangled threads that finally led to the epochal voyage of Columbus.

In the fifteenth century Europe was fast preparing itself for the age of discovery and expansion. The collapse of the Roman Empire, the disappearance of Roman culture, and the disintegration of the highly developed Roman system of communication had all tended to throw Europe backward into a period of cultural decline. Politically Europe broke up into innumerable territorial units ruled over by nobles of greater or less degree under whose protection gathered the retainers and serfs who fought the wars and tilled the fields. Much romance has grown up around the age of feudalism, but it was in reality a period of confusion and insecurity. The noble, who lived in his castle and occupied himself chiefly with the interminable warfare of the Middle Ages, afforded his subjects some protection in return for service. The masses, nevertheless, lived in constant uncertainty and danger, and eked out a marginal existence on the primitive agriculture of the period. Art and learning had almost disappeared; poverty and ignorance were virtually universal. The one integrating influence of these centuries was the Christian Church, which provided a common belief, attempted to keep alive the flickering lamp of knowledge, and, by instilling the fear of God into the hearts of ignorant and superstitious nobles, helped to prepare the way for a better day.

The first great influence tending to break this stalemate was that of the crusades. Aroused by a stirring call from Pope Urban II at the Council of Clermont and by the itinerant preaching of Peter the Hermit, the First Crusade, undertaken to rescue the holy places of Palestine from the desecrating hands of the Turks, swept across Europe in 1096, followed by other expeditions, at frequent though irregular intervals, for almost two hundred years. Torn from the rudest parts of a half-savage Europe, tens of thousands were suddenly confronted with a civilization that in culture and art was far superior to their own. Europe was again introduced to the luxuries of the East, and the old trade routes were reopened to take care of the increasing eastern trade. Of all civilizing influences, none is more potent than commerce. Cities began to grow along the routes of trade, and in these cities there developed a class of merchants and bankers whose accumulated wealth was in time to sustain a renascence of art and learning. Revival of commerce meant larger ships, an increase in geographical knowledge, and improved methods of navigation.

Of what, then, did this important eastern trade consist? First of all were the spices that helped to preserve and make palatable the monotonous food of those times, when, of course, refrigeration was quite unknown—pepper from the Malabar coast of India, cloves, cinnamon, and nutmegs from the Moluccas, and sugar from Arabia and Persia. From Asia came most of the important drugs used by the medieval apothecaries and the precious stones that adorned the persons of the wealthy. For the textile industry came various dyes and also alum for fixing the colors, and from Asia Minor and the Far East came many manufactured products of material and workmanship impossible to obtain in Europe—glass and cutlery from Damascus, Samarkand, and Bagdad; silk, linen, and woolens from Asia Minor; and procelain from China. The names of many of these commodities indicate their origin: for example, damask (cloth of Damascus), muslin (cloth of Mosul), Cashmere shawls, taffeta silk, and japanned ware. In exchange Europe had little besides woolen goods and metals to offer, but wool and the less valuable metals were too heavy and bulky for the long journey, and to make up for the unfavorable balance of trade Europe was forced continually to export gold and silver, a process that was draining the West of the precious metals.

Three main trade routes were used in this European-Asiatic commerce: the northern, which led from the back doors of India and China by land to Asia Minor; the second, across the Indian Ocean, through the Persian Gulf, and by land to the Mediterranean; and the third, across the Indian Ocean to the Red Sea, overland to the Nile, and down that river to Alexandria. European merchants, chiefly from Italy, congregated at the various ports along the eastern shore of the Mediterranean, purchased the goods from the Orient, and distributed them throughout Europe, either overland through the Alpine passes into central Europe, or by sea through the Straits of Gibraltar to London or Bruges, where the merchants of the Hanseatic League completed the distribution. Although the routes were about as short as could be found, they were extremely expensive. Restricted by commercial regulations and customs tolls, and harassed by robbers, Oriental trade would be able to expand only if cheaper sea routes were opened up.

Extensive as was the commerce carried on over these ancient trade routes, little was known in Europe of the great continent of Asia. True, an occasional missionary, adventurer, or trader had penetrated the unknown continent and returned with stories of strange civilizations and enormous wealth to stir the interest and whet the avarice of merchant and prince. Some of these tales, copied and recopied, as that of the famous Venetian, Marco Polo, were important contributions to the geographical knowledge of Europe; but, speaking broadly, Asia, as late as the fifteenth century, was a closed book. To Europe it was a mythical, fabulously wealthy land from which came innumerable commodities for which there was an insatiable demand.

The disadvantages of the old trade routes, combined with the desire for Oriental wealth, undoubtedly gave the greatest impetus to the age of discovery.[1] Certainly the draining of precious metals from the West brought an insistent need for economies in transportation. Other motives, nevertheless, related to religion, conquest, and adventure, played an important part. Love of adventure, zeal for religion, desire for wealth were the great human motives behind the intrepid explorers who opened new routes to the East at the end of the fifteenth century, but other factors contributed to make this possible. After 1300 there was a continual improvement in the maps and sailing charts (*portolani*) of the known world. By 1400 the compass to tell direction and the astrolabe to determine latitude were in use, and, before many years had passed, mariners were in possession of tables and chronometers by which longitude could be figured.

---

[1] The old theory that the age of discovery was largely promoted by the Turkish conquests in Asia Minor and Africa, which were supposed to have interfered with trade over the ancient routes, has been largely discredited. No serious interference with trade and no rise in the prices of Eastern goods appear to have followed these conquests. See A. H. Lybyer, "The Influence of the Ottoman Turks upon the Routes of Oriental Trade," *Annual Report,* American Historical Association, 1914, I, 125–133.

Besides these aids to navigation, there was the growing certainty on the part of educated astronomers that the earth was round. "I have always read that the world," said Columbus, "comprising the land and the water, is spherical, as is testified by the investigations of Ptolemy and others, who have proved it by the eclipses of the moon and other observations made from east to west as well as by the observations from north to south."

In addition to all this, there were the growing wealth of the trading class, ever anxious for increased commerce, the envy of the Italian monopoly of eastern trade, and the encouragement offered by the rulers of the rising national states of western Europe, who saw in extended commerce an opportunity not alone to increase the wealth of their domains but also to build up a powerful trading class to offset the strength of the feudal lords. In short, many influences were at work to bring about this age of discovery and the great expansion of Europe. In one sense it was a part of that great revival of learning often called the Renaissance, a movement characterized by dissatisfaction with the old order and by an eagerness to extend the knowledge of the world in all directions.

THE COMMERCIAL REVOLUTION

From the dawn of history the center of European wealth, power, and culture had lain on the shores of the Mediterranean Sea. Certainly in the Middle Ages this pre-eminence rested almost wholly upon control of the eastern trade routes. In the latter part of the fifteenth century new trade routes with the East were discovered, and with startling suddenness the center of the world's commerce shifted from the Mediterranean basin to the Atlantic Ocean, and with the shift of commerce went a shift in power and culture. We are dealing, moreover, not alone with a commercial revolution but with one of the great turning points in history, for the search for new routes to the Orient brought the discovery of America.

Whatever may have been the innumerable economic and social forces leading to the age of discovery and expansion, the drama of history, after all, is played by human beings. Of the many actors who passed across this stage, two are particularly important, Prince Henry of Portugal and Christopher Columbus. It was Prince Henry "the Navigator" (1394–1460), more than any other person, who stimulated interest and activity in navigation and exploration during the fifteenth century. Endowed with rare business ability, a burning zeal for Christianity, and a consuming desire to open up new worlds, Prince Henry established at Sagres on the southern tip of Portugal a great maritime school for map-makers and navigators. Under his inspiration Portuguese navigators gradually pushed farther and farther south along the coast of Africa, passing Cape Blanco in

1441 and Cape Verde in 1445. The work so well begun by Henry continued without interruption after his death. In 1486 Bartholomew Diaz discovered what he called the Cape of Storms, but which King John II of Portugal, with more vision, christened the Cape of Good Hope, and ten years later Vasco da Gama rounded the tip of Africa, turned the prow of his ship northward, and in 1498 reached India. The long-sought routes to the East had been discovered.[2]

Six years before da Gama's epochal voyage to India, Christopher Columbus had also attempted, by sailing due west into an unknown sea, to discover the fabled lands of Cathay and the Indies. The shores of Asia he never saw, but his voyage opened for Europe a new world. Columbus, concerning whose early life little is known, was probably born in Genoa about 1446. He went to sea early, became a skilled sailor and an expert map-maker, and eventually found himself in Portugal, the natural meeting place of fifteenth-century mariners. In some manner he became convinced that the world was round and that by sailing west one might reach the East. There was nothing original in this conception, which was held by all educated astronomers of the time; the greatness of Columbus was rather in the courage that he displayed in venturing into an unknown sea to prove the validity of his thesis and in his pertinacity in the pursuit of his project.

Without resources to fit out an expedition alone, he pressed for aid at the courts of England, France, Portugal, and Spain. Hope long deferred was finally fulfilled when the Spanish sovereigns, Ferdinand and Isabella, gave their support, commissioned him admiral and governor of the new lands he might discover, and granted him a tenth part of "all the pearls, precious stones, gold, silver, spices, and other merchandise" he might find. Starting out on August 3, 1492, with his three tiny ships and about one hundred men, Columbus set his course due west until, on the night of October 11, one of his men saw a light "like a small wax candle that was being hoisted and raised." The next day he landed on one of the inhabited islands of the Bahamas and took possession in the name of the sovereigns of Spain. After cruising for several weeks among the islands of the West Indies, he returned to carry the great tidings to Europe.

Until the end of his days Columbus was convinced that he had discovered the outlying islands of Asia. He returned to continue his explorations and establish colonies in 1493, 1498, and 1502, on his third trip sight-

---

[2] The significance of eastern trade routes has persisted into modern times. The opening of the Suez Canal in 1869 greatly shortened the sea routes. In the early years of the twentieth century Germany by means of the Berlin-Bagdad railway attempted further to shorten the route and, incidentally, to assume control. Two decades later Britain's "life line" was again threatened when Italy, anxious to dominate the Mediterranean, entered the Second World War to break British control of Gibraltar, Egypt, and the Suez Canal.

ing the northern coast of South America and on his fourth skirting the coast of Central America. Instead of the wealth he expected, Columbus met with continued disappointment, and he passed away in 1506 in obscurity and poverty. But the work of the great admiral, like that of Prince Henry, went on after his death.[3] For over a century skillful mariners pursued the quest for a western route to the Indies. Already in 1497 a Genoese navigator, John Cabot, sailing for the King of England, had touched the coast of Canada and laid the basis for the subsequent claims of England to the continent of North America. Even after the Spanish adventurer, Balboa, had discovered the western ocean (1513), and a Portuguese seaman in the service of Spain, Ferdinand Magellan, had sailed around the world (1519–1522) in the greatest feat of exploration of all time,[4] other navigators continued to seek for channels that might penetrate the continent and lead more quickly to the East. Verrazano, sailing for the King of France, skirted the coast from North Carolina to Nova Scotia (1524); Jacques Cartier on his second voyage sailed up the Saint Lawrence to the rapids; the Englishmen, Martin Frobisher (1576–1578) and John Davis (1585–1587), sought vainly to reach the Indies by a northwest passage, and finally Henry Hudson, under the flag of the Dutch East India Company, sailed up the Hudson to the head of navigation. No passage to the Indies was found, but mighty rivers were discovered, and much coastland was explored. The quest of these navigators was to find fruition only when the hand of man three centuries later cut an artificial route across the Isthmus of Panama.

Any attempt to appraise the results of this age of exploration would lead the student into the tangled maze of modern world history. To describe the immediate results of the discovery of new trade routes and the American continents, historians have used the term "Commercial Revolution." By this they imply the breaking of the Italian monopoly of

[3] Columbus did not even give his name to the continents. The term "America" comes from the first name of Amerigo Vespucci, an Italian business man who went to Spain as the commercial agent of the Medici. According to his own account, he made four voyages to America. An account of the first, which Vespucci claims was made in 1497 (thus antedating the discovery by Columbus of the South American continent in 1498), but which may have taken place in 1499, was published in 1507 and was the first account of the discovery of the mainland to be printed. Later Martin Waldseemüller, a German professor of geography at St. Die, France, first suggested in a book the use of the name "America" and placed it on an accompanying map.

[4] Magellan met death at the hands of natives in the Philippines; his ship, the *Vittoria,* completed the journey in a little over three years. In 1872 Jules Verne, the French novelist, stirred interest with a romance entitled *Around the World in Eighty Days.* In 1889 Joseph Pulitzer, owner of the New York *World,* sent a reporter to prove it might be done; she made the trip in 72 days, 6 hours, and 11 minutes. In 1924 the circumnavigation by airplane was accomplished by army fliers in 175 days; seven years later Wiley Post and Harold Gatty girdled the globe in 8 days, 15 hours, and 51 minutes. Post, flying alone, reduced the record in 1933 to 7 days, 18 hours, and 49 minutes.

Oriental trade, the shifting of the center of world commerce from the Mediterranean to the Atlantic seaboard, the development of new trade routes, the cheapening of Eastern products, the introduction into Europe of many new commodities, such as tea, coffee, Indian corn, and tobacco, and a stimulation to maritime activity that resulted in larger and faster ships. But this is simply the beginning of the story. The shift of commerce to the Atlantic brought new wealth to the nations facing the ocean and gave a tremendous impetus to the development of the national state. The explorers were making known to Europe the bare outlines at least of Africa, Asia, and the two American continents, and upon the new highways of commerce were planted colonies and trading posts. The expansion of commerce was quickly followed by migrations of Europeans to the new-found lands and by the introduction of European civilization to the far corners of the world. The profits were too great for any one nation to enjoy peaceably, and the centuries that followed were characterized by long wars for commercial and imperial domination. Maritime supremacy came first to Portugal, which first discovered the routes to the Indies and established her colonies in the Far East. But the golden age of Portugal was brief. Spain, growing suddenly rich and powerful from the spoils of Mexico and Peru, absorbed the Portuguese empire, only to have her proud position challenged by the Dutch and then by the English. The victory in the end was to fall to Great Britain as the great commercial and colonial power, but the achievement and maintenance of that position meant three centuries of intermittent warfare, first with Spain, then with Holland, then with France, and finally with the rising German Empire.

Upon the economic and social life of Europe the effect of the discoveries was profound. The flood of precious metals from America reversed the movement of gold and silver, brought a revolution in prices, and upset existing economic conditions. Increased commerce stimulated the development of manufacturing to provide commodities for the new trade routes, and incidentally gave an impetus to agriculture as new crops were introduced and more food produced for the growing population. Upon social classes the effect of all this was epochal. The power of the trading class or bourgeoisie (city dwellers), which had been growing in the late Middle Ages, now developed rapidly, and, as the middle class grew in power, the aristocracy declined. Just as the aristocracy waned in the face of the rising bourgeoisie, so feudalism retreated before advancing capitalism.

THE GEOGRAPHIC BACKGROUND

The great drama of history may be played by human beings, but the stage upon which it is set is the world of geography. To no small extent man is a creature of his environment; he has never been a free agent. "Thus," says the great historian, Buckle, "we have man modifying nature, and nature modifying man; while out of this reciprocal modification all events must necessarily spring." The history of civilization is the story of how man has conquered nature, and how nature in turn has reacted upon man. Physical environment, as scientists have often asserted, ranks with biological variations as an essential determinant in tracing the evolution of human capacities, occupations, and general progress. In other words, if we are to trace the course of history, we must look beyond mankind to consider such factors as climate, rainfall, soil, land contour, natural transportation facilities, and other geographic factors that determine how human beings live.

Properly, history should begin in remote geological ages in an effort to account for the physical environment in which people later found themselves. Thousand of years before the white man came to America glaciers time and again covered the Laurentian highlands of Canada, pressing southward to scoop out the Great Lakes, turn the courses of rivers, smooth off the mountains, and mix the soil in a manner to affect future agriculture. Six times the continental glaciers advanced and retreated across the central region of the United States, mixing the subsoil with the surface soil to produce those rich limestone areas where productivity reaches its highest point. Absence or presence of glacial action may determine, thousands of years later, the course of civilization.

The first white men who landed on the shores of the present United States sought sudden wealth in gold and spices. This they did not find, but they did discover a land ideally fitted for settlement by the races of Europe. First of all, access to the land was easy. In the South innumerable little rivers, navigable to the small boats of the colonial period, facilitated settlement and commerce. In the North, where the rivers were not so numerous, excellent harbors indented the coast and provided a rendezvous for trade and commerce. Except in New England there were no high mountains close to the eastern shore to cut off the movement inland, as there were on the Pacific. Not only was the American continent extremely accessible, but it was endowed with an excellent climate. The United States lies between the lines of forty and seventy degrees average annual temperature, which represents a climate similar to that of the parts of Europe producing the most energetic and civilized races. For the development of a high civilization, many scientists believe, the temperature must not be extremely hot or extremely cold, or too humid, and it must be subject to frequent and rapid changes. Such a climate is typical of the region covered by most of the present United States. Quite as fundamental

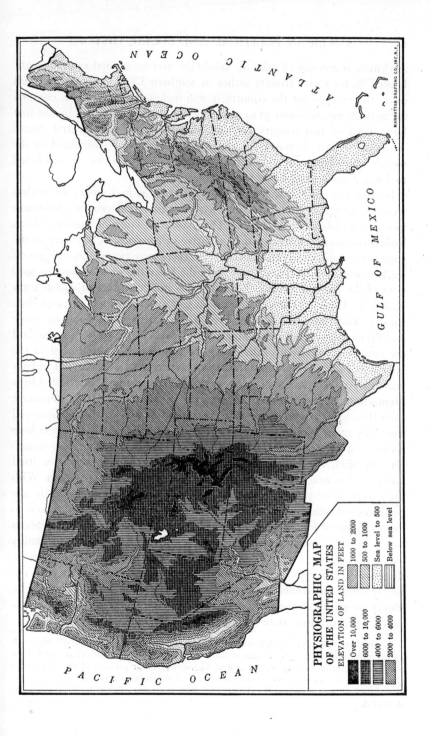

PHYSIOGRAPHIC MAP
OF THE UNITED STATES
ELEVATION OF LAND IN FEET

1000 to 2000
500 to 1000
Sea level to 500
Below sea level

Over 10,000
6000 to 10,000
4000 to 6000
2000 to 4000

as climate is amount of rainfall. While the average annual rainfall in the United States varies from 5 inches in southern Utah to 60 on the Gulf coast, the average for the country is 26.6 inches. As 20 inches is essential for agriculture and from 30 to 50 for ideal soil moisture, it is obvious that large areas of this country are suitable for agriculture. Central North America, in fact, contains the choicest large block of homeland in the world; soil, climate, minerals, and transportation facilities are combined to form a great productive region.

Because the climate was essentially the same as in Europe, the settlers were not obliged to acquire a new agriculture or undergo an adjustment to a totally different food supply. The main food crops of Europe, wheat, barley, rye, and oats, were found to thrive in America, as did most of the garden vegetables and fruits. In addition there were two plants indigenous to American soil, the potato and corn, the latter the most important food crop of the colonial period. Tobacco (also indigenous) and cotton grew well here. Thus the United States soon had a richer variety of crops than Europe. The scarcity of food suffered by the early colonists at Jamestown and Plymouth was but temporary, for the forest swarmed with game, and the streams teemed with fish. The great forests that covered most of the land were more of a nuisance to the first settlers than a benefit, but in later years they were a source of great wealth. There was little demanded by a premachine civilization that did not exist in abundance. More important than this, time was to prove that the United States was better equipped than any other nation in the world with those essentials of a machine civilization—water power, oil, iron, copper—and with many other minerals.[5] In brief, the United States comprises an economic world in itself and comes as near being a self-sufficing unit as any nation on earth. With the exception of rubber, coffee, tin, and one or two minor minerals, she produces everything necessary for her own consumption and much to export. Some students have attributed the greatness of the United States to the peculiar excellence of its political institutions or the high quality of its population. These are undoubtedly important, but certainly an indispensable factor in our tremendous development and present power is the amount and combination of our national resources. Only man's inability to use these resources more wisely has prevented a sounder economic progress and more widespread contentment.

[5] During the late 1920s the United States produced 70 per cent of the world's oil, nearly 50 per cent of the copper, 38 per cent of the lead, 42 per cent of the zinc, 42 per cent of the coal, 46 per cent of the iron, 54 per cent of the cotton, and 62 per cent of the corn, and it possessed 36 per cent of the developed horsepower of the world; yet it contained only 6 per cent of the land area of the world and 6 per cent of the population. *Commerce Yearbook, 1930,* II, Part II.

THE ROLE OF THE INDIAN

When the white man reached America, he found the land already inhabited. Where these people came from, how they came here, and how long they had been in America, no one knows, but the generally accepted belief is that they came from Asia, probably by way of Alaska, and that they had been here for thousands of years. While there is some unity in the general characteristics of the Indians, as the white man called them, there are many striking variations. In Yucatan the Spaniards found a race no taller than the Japanese, dwelling in great cities with highly carved public buildings, exquisitely chiseled ornaments, a system of writing, and a calendar more accurate than that of Europe. Quite different from the Mayans of Yucatan were the Indians encountered by the English in the region of the present United States. Here were natives living with a primitive type of agriculture and in houses that varied from wigwams and tepees to the "long houses" of the Iroquois and the pueblos of the Southwest. The Indians varied in height, in color, in civilization, in their love of war, and in their ability to oppose the white invader. More important for present history, of course, is the great variation in the extent to which Indian blood and Indian culture have persisted in various parts of the American continents.

At the time of the first white settlements there were probably not more than 1,000,000 Indians in the region north of Mexico. They were divided into hundreds of tribes and represented in the United States some fifty-nine families of languages. Although they knew how to raise corn, tobacco, and a number of vegetables, their agriculture was primitive, they had domesticated no animal but the dog, and they were hardly out of the hunting and fishing stage of cultural development. All these facts help to account for the sparsity of their population. Scanty as was the Indian population, there were probably 40,000 fighting men in the region east of the Mississippi, who, if they had concentrated, could easily have disposed of the handful of white settlers. Such concentration of power, however, was never consummated. Two centuries before the English learned how to conquer India by setting one Indian nation against another, Hernando Cortez with a handful of Spanish adventurers had played the same game in Mexico.

The relations between whites and Indians may be noted in three fields, the military, the religious, and the economic. It was the fortune of the Spaniards to find in Mexico and Peru rich but decaying civilizations, which they succeeded in conquering and subjecting to a hierarchy of officials and priests. The Indian in Latin America was reduced to serfdom, was forced to pay homage to the white man's God and to devote his life to enriching the relatively few Spaniards who migrated to the New World. But it was an extremely thin veneer of European civilization that the Spaniards spread over the millions of Indians dwelling in the vast territory from California to Cape Horn. That region remains today an Indian's rather than a white man's country,[6] and today American diplomacy and American economic penetration are concerned with seventeen different Indian nations.

In Latin America the Indian was not destroyed,[7] but he was reduced to serfdom and made to subserve the economic interests of the conqueror. In British North America the history was far different. Occupation of the land was too slow and the Indians were too scattered to make possible a sudden conquest. It was a process of dispossessing the Indian and pushing him ever onward that lasted for three centuries. It was an economic conflict in which the English farm pressed against the Indian hunting ground, and English land exploitation replaced Indian animal exploitation. A basic economic conflict such as this could only mean warfare. The North American Indian was a hard and ruthless fighter, and the advancing frontier has been well called "a red line of cruelty." The early clashes, like the Pequot War in New England, were little more than isolated skirmishes between the Indians and the first white settlers. Then came attacks by confederations of tribes, as in King Philip's War, and then alliances between the Indians and one group of white men to fight another group, as in the French and Indian wars or in the Indians' alliance with the English against the colonists during the Revolution. The final stage was the series of frontier wars in the last half of the nineteenth century, resulting in defeat, destruction, or concentration upon reservations. Like the Spaniards and the French, the English made some effort to bring to the Indian the consolation of Christianity; Dartmouth College, for example, was founded as an Indian school. But the economic clash overpowered other considerations. To Cotton Mather the Indian was a "tawney serpent," and to generations of frontiersmen the "only good Indian was a dead Indian." As far as the "red man" was concerned, the Puritan was more interested in his scalp than in his soul.

Since the Indian was thus ruthlessly pushed aside before the white man's advance, what, then, is his significance in American history? That the Indians delayed—for good or ill—the movement toward the west there can be no doubt, but it is also true that the Indian trails were those first

---

[6] Except in Argentina, Uruguay, and southern Brazil.

[7] In the West Indies, ruthless exploitation of Indian labor and the white man's diseases virtually eliminated the Indian. On only one of the islands, Dominica, are there any of the natives left. Their place was taken by negro slaves imported from Africa.

followed by the white man and that it was the missionary and fur trader who first made known these trails. In the early period of settlement the fur trade was always an important economic interest, and the Indian hunter was the medium through which the furs were collected. Beyond this the Indian made a real contribution to agriculture. It was the Indian who introduced the settler to tobacco, the economic backbone of the colonial South, and corn, the principal food of the early pioneer days. The New England farm, cleared by tree girdling, with its rows of corn twined with bean vines, interspersed with squash and pumpkin and protected by scarecrows, was a close replica of the Indian field. There are today possibly almost as many Indians in the United States as when the white man first arrived, but they are largely concentrated in reservations, exploited by the white men, scourged by trachoma and tuberculosis, and their power broken. Their role in American history, however, has not been without significance, and in the realm of international relations it is far from ended.

Although overemphasizing the influence of the Turks in promoting exploration, E. P. Cheney, *The European Background of American History*, American Nation Series, Chaps. I–IV, VII, VIII, is still valuable for the background of discovery and settlement. More recent are the excellent Chaps. I–IV in Curtis Nettels, *The Roots of American Civilization*. The physiographic background is interpreted in E. C. Semple, *American History and Its Geographic Conditions*, Chaps. I–III, in A. M. Schlesinger, *New Viewpoints in American History*, Chaps. I–III, and is briefly described in H. U. Faulkner, *American Economic History*, 5th ed., Chap. I. A. B. Hulbert, *Soil: Its Influence on the History of the United States*, Chaps. II–IV, is a significant study. In Ellsworth Huntington, *The Red Man's Continent* (Chronicles of America), pre-Columbian Indian culture is also briefly covered. C. M. Andrews, *The Colonial Period in American History*, Chap. I, is an excellent brief survey of the age of discovery. The bibliography that has just been given comprises merely a few selected readings designed particularly for students. A more complete bibliography on this and succeeding chapters will be found at the conclusion of this book.

COLONIAL CIVILIZATION

Chapter II

THE SETTLEMENT OF AMERICA

*If you touche him [Philip of Spain] in the
Indies, you touche the apple of his eye; for take
away his treasure, which is* neruus belli, *and
which he has almost oute of his West Indies,
his olde bandes of souldiers will soone be dissolved, his purposes defeated, his powr and
strengthe diminished, his pride abated, and his
tyranie utterly suppressed.*

Richard Hakluyt (1584)

THE SPANISH SETTLEMENTS

A century before the Pilgrim fathers landed on the bleak shores of
Massachusetts Bay, Hernando Cortez and his band of Spanish adventurers
marched into the City of Mexico (November 8, 1519). Precious metals, they
discovered, existed in abundance, and with incredible speed and ruthless cruelty the Spaniards extended their conquests during the next decade
from northern Mexico to southern Peru. If rich civilizations were to be
found in Mexico and Peru, why not in other parts of America? Spain and
the "Indies" were full of brave but impecunious soldiers, and it was not
long before the quest of wealth and glory led one expedition after another
into the region of the present United States. Instead of rich cities, however,
they found squalid Indian villages, and instead of glory only disappointment and death. In 1521 Ponce de León, in search of the fountain of youth,
led a company of two hundred men to the Florida peninsula, but he was
attacked by the natives and driven back to Cuba, mortally wounded. Five
years later Ayllon, with a band of five hundred, attempted to found a settlement on the Carolina coast, but after two years of bitter hardship the
survivors returned to Santo Domingo. Pánfilo de Narváez, succeeding to
the patent of de León, organized in Spain a colony of six hundred persons
and in 1528 reached Florida. After weeks of exploration and Indian fighting, the expedition arrived at the coast near St. Marks Bay, constructed a
fleet of crazy ships, and set sail for the west. Eight years later Cabeza de
Vaca and three companions, the only survivors, reached the Spanish settle-

14

ments in Sinaloa, with one of the most amazing tales of adventure known to man.

The lure of Florida still dominated the Spanish mind, and, nothing daunted, Hernando de Soto landed on the peninsula in 1539. Trained in the school of Cortez and Pizarro and in command of "the most distinguished company of would-be Indian killers and robbers that had come together on Spanish soil since 1493," de Soto led his followers for three years through the southern forests; when he died, he was buried secretly in the Mississippi lest the Indians learn that the great white leader had gone. The expedition, now under the leadership of Luis de Moscoso, attempted to reach Mexico by marching overland through Arkansas and Texas, gave up the attempt, returned to the Mississippi, and sailed down the river, reaching the Spanish settlement of Panuco in the autumn of 1543. After four years of exploration in an unknown country and almost constant warfare with hostile Indians, half of the original six hundred survived, a testimonial to the hardihood and courage of this remarkable band.

Despite these and subsequent failures, the desire to occupy Florida continued. The route of merchant ships lay through the Bahama channel, and a port was needed where they might seek refuge from storms and pirates. When the French built Fort Caroline on the St. Johns River, the Spaniards were spurred to renewed efforts. Pedro Menéndez in September, 1565, founded St. Augustine and a few days later captured Fort Caroline, slew most of the defenders, and left a Spanish garrison. Two years later the French returned, surprised the Spaniards, and hanged the prisoners, but, however satisfying as an act of revenge, the deed had no other effect. Florida was now definitely in the hands of the Spaniards, who established forts and settlements, from which went out expeditions and missionaries to the north and west. In the meantime, through de Vaca and others, there filtered into New Spain rumors of Indian cities to the northwest. Fray Marcos, a Franciscan missionary, was sent on to reconnoiter, and upon his return, in 1540, an elaborate expedition under Francisco Coronado set out. But the fabled Seven Cities of Cíbola proved to be only the pueblos of the Zuñi Indians, and Coronado's expedition is famous chiefly as the first white exploration of New Mexico, Oklahoma, and Kansas. About the time that Coronado returned to Mexico another expedition, under Cabrillo, set out from Mexico by sea to explore the western coast of the continent as far north as Oregon. From these interesting expeditions came little of importance for several decades. It was not until 1598 that Juan de Oñate entered New Mexico with a colony of settlers and 1609 that Santa Fé was founded. By 1680 more than 2500 Spaniards had occupied the region and practically subjected the Indians.

As in the case of Florida, it was French exploration that stirred the

Spaniards to occupy Texas. Shortly after the Frenchman, La Salle, tried unsuccessfully to plant his colonies near the mouth of the Mississippi, the Spaniards founded their first missions in Texas (1690). Abandoning the region temporarily, they came back in 1716 and founded San Antonio. A military expedition under the Marquis of Aguayo (1720–1722) clinched the hold of Spain on Texas, and in the next century the Spanish boundaries in Texas were extended in all directions. A half century later the Russian menace on the Pacific stirred the Spaniards to action. A joint expedition by land and sea under Governor Portola was sent north into upper California in 1769. In that year San Diego was founded, in 1770 Monterey, and the year of the Declaration of Independence of the United States saw the beginnings of San Francisco. When Washington was inaugurated President, all the land now encompassed by the United States was under the control either of the infant American republic or of Spain, with England and Russia disputing the northern boundary line.

Despite the fact that two thirds of the territory of the United States was at one time under Spanish control, the culture of Spain has but slightly affected the region north of the Rio Grande. It did, however, dominate the lands to the south, and, as the world grows smaller, our contacts with that culture become more intimate. The main features of this Spanish empire, which was to last for three centuries,[1] were apparent by the time the first English settlers had reached America. By 1600 it was an empire based upon the labor of 5,000,000 Indians ruled over by some 200,000 Spaniards—miners, merchants, ranchers, soldiers, and, most important of all, some 4000 *encomenderos* or lords of Indian serfs. With lavish hand the land of New Spain had been divided into great estates or *encomiendas,* which carried with them the services of the Indians, who were forced to till the soil, work the mines, and tend the cattle. As in Europe in the Middle Ages, the economic system was based upon great estates of overlords and serfs, with an occasional town where some industrial life existed, and with but little change this economic system, in which labor was based upon peonage for debt, has continued until the twentieth century.

No nation of the world was more firmly attached than Spain to the theory that colonies existed merely for the benefit of the home country. Those products needed at home were encouraged, those which came in competition with Spain were debarred. In the colonies the culture of olives, grapes, tobacco, and hemp was forbidden. The mining of the precious metals was, of course, encouraged, and it is estimated that the

---

[1] Between 1810, when revolt against Spanish rule began at Caracas, and the revolutionary victory on the battlefield of Ayocucho (December 9, 1824), the mainland colonies of Spain from Mexico to Patagonia achieved their independence. In the meantime (1822) Brazil severed her allegiance to Portugal.

total production of the mines of New Spain between 1690 and 1818 amounted to 1,500,000,000 pesos. Silver and gold, with indigo, vanilla, cocoa, cochineal, and other agricultural products, formed the bases of the export trade, for which in return the colonists took back the luxuries and manufactured products of Europe. In Spain this trade was strictly supervised by the Council of the Indies, through its subsidiary, the *casa de contratación;* it was largely conducted through the single port of Seville and was maintained by huge fleets of merchant vessels, which set out once a year, under the protection of warships, to distribute their cargoes, chiefly from Vera Cruz on the Mexican seacoast and Porto Bello on the Isthmus of Panama. Restrictions on trade routes, combined with tariffs and with monopolies granted by the king to his favorites on such important commodities as African slaves, gunpowder, salt, tobacco, and quicksilver, made the commerce of Spain exceedingly artificial and expensive. For much less than this the English colonists revolted from the mother country. Like their English cousins to the north, the Spanish settlers broke every commercial regulation imposed from Europe and finally separated from Spain, but despite these restrictions the imperial system of Spain worked with reasonable success. Before a single Englishman had settled in the New World there existed in Spanish America a colorful civilization, based on the wealth of mine, ranch, and farm, which had built beautiful churches, established schools and universities, and provided an honored place for authors, scholars, and artists.

THE FRENCH IN AMERICA

When the first Frenchmen reached America, we do not know. Certainly by 1500 Breton fishermen were frequenting the banks of Newfoundland in search of fish. In comparison with the flow of wealth from Spanish America, the modest profits from the fisheries hardly satisfied the imaginative mind of the French, and for a century spasmodic but unsuccessful efforts at exploration and colonization were made. French Huguenots attempted settlements in Brazil (1555) and Florida (1564), but were ousted by the Portuguese and Spaniards, and the efforts to establish permanent settlements on the banks of the St. Lawrence were equally futile. In the sixteenth century the energies of France were absorbed by civil and religious wars; the seventeenth century saw the erection of a strong central government and a powerful national state, and at the same time a renewed effort toward empire-building.

By 1600 it was evident that in the region of the St. Lawrence great profits might be made in furs, and for the next three quarters of a century a succession of commercial companies, chartered by the king, explored the country, attempted to colonize Nova Scotia and the St. Lawrence valley, and exploited the fur trade. The directing genius of these early years was Samuel de Champlain, who in 1608 established at Quebec the first permanent French settlement, discovered in 1609 the lake that bears his name, and in subsequent expeditions explored the Ottawa River, Georgian Bay, and Lake Ontario. When Champlain passed from the scene in 1635, the colony at Quebec was firmly established. French power in Canada, nevertheless, was not impressive, for probably not more than two hundred white men held the line from Acadia to the Great Lakes. With much greater success had the French operated in the West Indies. Beginning with an expedition to St. Kitts in 1625, they could boast by 1665 of domination over fourteen Caribbean islands, which, with a population of over 15,000 whites and as many negro slaves, included the rich sugar islands of Guadeloupe and Martinique.

Important as was the economic significance of their West Indian possessions, the great drive for empire was to come from the tiny and unpromising settlements in Canada. After Colbert, the able counselor of Louis XIV, became director general of finances in 1662, he began aggressively the task of empire-building in Canada, ending company control in 1674 and putting the government directly under royal administration. About the same time there arrived in Canada the Comte de Frontenac (governor from 1672 to 1682 and again from 1689 to 1698), the ablest administrator in the annals of New France. With tireless energy he pushed westward and southward the outposts of empire. In 1671 St. Lusson in an elaborate ceremony at Sault Ste. Marie took possession of the gateway between Huron and Superior. Two years later the fur trader, Louis Joliet, and the Jesuit priest, Father Marquette, floated their canoes down the mighty Mississippi as far south as the Arkansas River.

Before the decade was over, the greatest of the French explorers, the Sieur de La Salle, was exploring the Illinois country and the upper reaches of the Mississippi. In 1682 he descended the Mississippi to its mouth, took possession of the whole valley for France, and named it Louisiana in honor of his sovereign, Louis XIV. But the dream of La Salle went far beyond the mere erection of trading posts or even the conversion of heathen Indians; he envisaged an entire continent under the rule of France. The next step was to plant a colony at the mouth of the Mississippi, but the expedition from France that he led missed the mouth of the river (1685) and landed on the coast of Texas, where it speedily went to pieces, La Salle himself being murdered by one of his mutinous companions. Other brave Frenchmen continued the work of La Salle, including Le Moyne d'Iberville, who established the first permanent French settlement on the Gulf at Biloxi in 1699, until by the middle of the eighteenth century the

French empire was represented by a string of forts and trading posts running from the mouth of the St. Lawrence along the Lakes and south by the Illinois and Mississippi Rivers to New Orleans.

Grandiose as was the scheme of empire and brilliant as was the work of explorers and Jesuit missionaries, the great dream of La Salle was to dissolve before cold economic reality. Not enough Frenchmen ever came to New France to hold it against the aggression of the more numerous English to the south. Inducements of various kinds were made to entice emigrants to Canada, but the French were reluctant to try their fortunes in the New World. The industrious Huguenots, persecuted at home, might have come, but they were denied admittance. The climate was severe and the soil stubborn, and it was a long time before the colonists established prosperous communities. Agriculture, furthermore, was always in competition with the more lucrative fur trade, which was the primary economic interest of New France and which occupied the attention of a third of the colonial population. The government, by offering titles of nobility and land grants, attempted to establish an agricultural feudalism, but the system never prospered. Instead of the compact feudal village of Europe, the "habitants" preferred to set up their farms in long strips with a few rods' frontage along the rivers and lakes, so that their villages sometimes stretched for miles along the shore. Sometimes the seigneur was prosperous, but generally his rents were small and his economic condition was little better than that of his tenants. The more energetic and venturesome quickly turned to the fur trade. As eastern Canada was not rich in peltries, the traders had to push into the recesses of the wilderness in search of furs, which accounts in part for the rapidity of the upstream movement and the vast region over which the French exercised some sort of control. The furs were largely obtained by the Indians and collected by the French fur men, *coureurs de bois,* who loaded their imported French commodities in canoes and traveled far inland to exchange their wares for the coveted furs. Many of them intermarried with the Indians. This type of trade was expensive, but the intimate relationship between Frenchmen and Indians enabled the former to compete successfully with the English traders, who covered less mileage and traded with cheaper colonial products.

Despite the competition of the fur trade, the artificial restraints of feudalism, and the lack of agricultural markets, life in New France was not devoid of reasonable comforts in the eighteenth century. One traveler (La Hontin) remarked that the "boors of the manours" lived with greater comfort "than an infinity of the gentry in France," while the Swedish traveler, Peter Kalm, testified to the general air of contentment. The French population of New France did not exceed 80,000 when Canada came under English rule (1763), but the race has held on so tenaciously that French language and customs persist in those regions where they originally settled. Exceedingly prolific, this race has increased from about 30,000 at the end of the seventeenth century to more than 3,000,000 today, a portion of which, through immigration, comprises an important element in the population of New England. That part of our racial stock that is French in origin comes mainly from Canada rather than directly from France.

THE DUTCH AND THE SWEDES

The occupation of the Hudson Valley was but an incident in the golden age of Holland, when the Dutch established commercial outposts on every continent of the globe. As distributors since 1500 in northern Europe of the products of the Orient, the people of Holland had grown prosperous and powerful. Goaded by economic restrictions and religious persecution, they rose in revolt against Spain during the latter half of the sixteenth century and eventually secured a virtual independence in 1609. When Philip II, during the revolt, closed to them the port of Lisbon (1585), the Dutch immediately began to open direct trade with the Far East. In 1602 the States General of Holland chartered the Dutch East India Company, one of whose captains, Henry Hudson, in search of a shorter route to the Indies, sailed up the Hudson in 1609 to the head of navigation. Annual visits of fur traders followed, exploration of the coast continued, and trading posts were established on Manhattan Island and near the site of the present Albany (1614). In that year the Amsterdam Company was chartered, and in 1621 its successor, the more famous West India Company. Directed by a powerful organization, the Dutch thrust to the west was now pushed aggressively. Colonies were planted in Brazil, in Guiana on the northern coast of South America, and in Curaçao and several other West Indian islands. For a moment there were possibilities that the Caribbean might be a Dutch rather than a Spanish lake. Engaged as it was in extensive schemes of colonization, interested in gold, slaves, and tropical products, and supporting scores of privateers to prey upon the commerce of Spain and Portugal, the Dutch West India Company considered its settlements on the Hudson River as but a small item in its widespread operations. This the company clearly intimated in a remonstrance to the States General against peace with Spain, when they declared that their object was not "trifling trade with the Indians nor the tardy cultivation of uninhabited regions" but "acts of hostility against the ships and property of the King of Spain and his subjects."

What interest the company had in New Netherland was primarily in the fur trade, and only spasmodically were efforts made to build up the population. Of these efforts the best-known was that of 1629, when any member of the company who would bring over fifty families at his own expense was offered a grant of land sixteen miles long on one bank of the Hudson or eight miles on each side with no limit as to width. Some of the Hudson valley was taken over by patroons, who were granted with the land certain feudal rights, but the plan failed to bring any large influx of settlers, and other inducements were later offered. When New Netherland was captured without a blow by the English in 1664, there were not more than 10,000 people in the colony, only a part of whom were Dutch. At that time, it is asserted, nineteen languages were spoken in the already cosmopolitan New Amsterdam.

Neglected as was the colony at home and small as was the population, New Netherland did not lack a certain vitality. The fur trade was pushed aggressively until the outposts of Dutch empire extended from the Mohawk on the north to the Connecticut on the east and the Delaware on the south. Such governors as William Kieft and Peter Stuyvesant were undoubtedly tactless, quarrelsome, and offensively paternalistic, but they struggled with dogged pertinacity to uphold the interests of the company. All this involved Indian wars, continued friction with the English, and the conquest of the near-by Swedish settlements.

Sweden, as well as Holland, rose for a brief period in the seventeenth century to the position of a first-rate power. Inspired by the Dutchman, William Usselincx, who had earlier been the chief figure in the formation of the Dutch West India Company, several Swedish companies were organized, which between 1637 and 1654 set up various trading posts on the lower Delaware. This encroachment on the fur preserves of the Dutch ended in 1655, when Stuyvesant sent a Dutch fleet to the Delaware and forced the surrender of the Swedish forts. In less than a decade a similar drama was enacted on the Hudson, when New Netherland succumbed to the English during one of the commercial wars between England and Holland. Driven like a wedge between the English colonies and thwarting their territorial and commercial expansion, New Netherland proved too weak to withstand the first test of real strength on the part of the English. Brief as the regime of the Dutch on the Hudson, their population and culture have continued parts of the heritage of that region. More significant in our history was the long warfare waged by the Dutch against Spain, which contributed to undermine the power of the Spanish empire and thus ease the path for British colonization and domination in North America.

THE COMING OF THE ENGLISH

Of all the European nations that sought wealth and power through colonial expansion, England proved the most successful. The reasons for this, as we look back over the centuries, are not difficult to discover. Her geographic position, which isolated her from the Continent, saved her from the inroads of foreign armies and allowed her to develop her political institutions and economic life with comparative freedom. After 1066 she was disturbed by no foreign invasion. Her protection, it was evident, must rest not upon an army but upon naval strength, and a great navy is the *sine qua non* of an aggressive imperialism. Along with this essential factor must be reckoned the earlier integration of her own political life and the continued chaos on the Continent. The War of the Roses, which ended in 1485, was the last great feudal disturbance in England. From it emerged a strong central government under Tudor monarchs whose policy was to destroy the military strength of the feudal aristocracy and undermine the political and economic power of the church. In this process came the erection of an English state church, the confiscation of monastic wealth, and the creation of a new nobility.

While this was being accomplished in England, the Continent struggled in political chaos and was deluged with the blood of civil and religious warfare. In such a situation it needed no great amount of political acumen for English statesmen to plot an advantageous course. The enemy of England became the Continental nation that for the moment displayed the greatest power on the sea, and her policy was to lend aid and comfort to whoever challenged that nation. In the three centuries that followed her own emergence as a sea power she played in turn the Dutch against the Spaniards and the French, the French against the Dutch, the Prussians against the French, and finally the French against the rising colonial ambitions of Germany. After each major conflict she appeared with greater colonial possessions and added commerce.[2]

England's success, however, was due not alone to geographical position and a fortuitous political situation, but also to economic conditions. With the possible exception of the Dutch, no other people in Europe was so free from the domination of church and noble as was the English by 1600. The breakdown of feudalism had freed commerce and industry, had separated large numbers of agricultural proletariat from the land, and had allowed the development of a strong class of yeomen or small farmers. The Continental wars had brought skillful immigrants to England ready to take an active part in the development of industrial life. The disintegration of the old nobility had opened the way for wealthy bourgeois to push into

[2] For further discussion of this see Chapter V.

the titled ranks, men whose minds were occupied with the problems of trade and commerce. England was becoming a business nation with surplus wealth to expend in foreign trade, and with an independent, self-reliant population eager for gain and commercial development. Not the least among the advantages of England was the fact that the development of nationalism and the growth in strength of the national government were not accompanied, as in France and Spain, by the loss of popular representative agencies. England retained her Lords and Commons, whose power developed during the constitutional conflicts with the Stuarts and whose ranks were increasingly filled with the leaders of commerce and industry intent on the enlargement of England's economic position. In brief, the development of English imperialism was not imposed by an autocratic paternalistic government, but rather came as a natural urge of the whole nation.

All this and more become evident as we read the sixteenth-century propaganda for colonization and trace the growth of the British empire in America. In the arguments for colonization we find political, religious, and economic motives closely interwoven. England was interested in restraining the power, in the earlier decades, of Spain, and, in later years, of France. The "plantinge of twoo or three strong fortes upon some goodd havens (whereof there is greate store) betweene Florida and Cape Briton," said that great advocate of imperialism, Richard Hakluyt, in 1584, "woulde be a matter in shorte space of greater domage as well to his [the King of Spain's] flete as to his westerne Indies," for with such bases for attack the "Spanishe empire falles to the grounde, and the Spanishe kinge shall be lefte bare as Aesops proude crowe." In the days when politics and religion were so closely united it was hardly likely that the religious aspect would be neglected. Of "the countruys lying north of Florida," said Sir Humphrey Gilbert, "God hath reserved the same to be reduced unto Christian civilty by the English nation," while the managers of the Virginia Company stated that the *"Principal and Maine Endes"* of their enterprise "were first to preach and baptize into the *Christian Religion,* and by propagation of the *Gospell,* to recover out of the arms of the Divell, a number of poore and miserable soules, wrapt up unto death, in almost invincible ignorance." In the actual colonization the saving of Indian souls receded into the background, but the hope of English Puritans, Quakers, and Catholics, of finding relief from persecution, proved an important impetus.

Of the motives for colonization the economic were the strongest. No less than the Spaniards, the English longed for great wealth. They also sought for shorter routes to the Indies, and they also dreamed of Virginia as a land where "gold is more plentiful than copper with us" and where "for rubies and diamonds they go forth on holidays and gather 'em by the seashore to hang on their children's coats." A little actual contact with the new land dispelled such dreams, and the emphasis turned to the more prosaic possibilities of America as a source of raw materials, a market for manufactured products, and an opportunity to put idle hands to work. That the problem of unemployment has not been limited to the period since the Industrial Revolution is but too well confirmed by a study of sixteenth-century England. The breakdown of feudalism, the dissolution of the monasteries and the inclosure of farm land into sheep pastures, all combined to set adrift thousands from their customary occupations. Not only would commerce with colonies employ the men, said Sir George Peckham (1582), "but also children of twelve or fourteene yeeres of age, or vnder, may bee kept from idlenesse, in making a thousand kindes of trifling things, which wil be good merchandise for that country," and moreover, "our idle women (which the Realme may well spare) shall also be employed in divers manufacturing." Not only would "many decayed towns" be thus repaired, but the colonies might prove an outlet for the "rogues, vagabonds and sturdy beggars" with which England was "exceedingly pestered" and which the Elizabethan poor laws did not eradicate. In the colonies, said another pamphleteer, we may be rid of "our multitudes of such as lie at home, pestering the land with pestilence and penury, and infecting one another with vice and villany worse than the plague itself."

Powerful as were these arguments, they made little impression on the English monarchs. For the founding of colonies they contributed no money, simply a charter and their blessing, which cost them nothing. The foundations of English colonization in America were laid by private initiative and by the risking of private fortunes. Barring the voyage of Cabot, England's contact with America to the end of the sixteenth century was largely of a commercial or piratical nature, and her interest was in striking at Spain directly rather than in settling colonists. One of the first of the famous English sea captains to roam the Spanish Main was Sir John Hawkins.[3] Instructing his crew to "serve God daily" and "love one another," he filled his ship with African slaves, sailed for the West Indies, and forced the Spaniards to buy them at the point of a gun. Risky and profitable as this might be, it did not satisfy his nephew, Francis Drake, who between 1572 and 1574 carried on a private warfare in the Spanish Main, capturing treasure ships and sacking towns for the glory of God and of England and, incidentally, for his private fortune. Setting sail in 1577 with five vessels and 150 men, he fought and plundered his way around the world. Instead of confiscating his booty, as the Spanish ambassador demanded, Queen Elizabeth knighted him on his own quarter-

---

[3] His father, William Hawkins, had carried slaves to Brazil as early as 1528.

deck. This open baiting in American waters and the secret aid given to his enemies in Europe finally aroused Philip to a supreme effort to crush the growing power of the upstart Protestant nation. Gathering together a mighty armada, he dispatched it in 1588 for the conquest of England. To men like Hawkins and Drake, however, the Spanish navy held no terrors. In brilliant defensive fighting they destroyed one ship after another; unfavorable winds and bad storms did the rest; and what was left of the great Armada limped back to Spain. The defeat of the Armada broke the morale of the Spanish seamen and marked the end of Spanish imperial expansion. From then until her last vestige of empire was destroyed at Santiago in 1898, her power declined. For England the victory in 1588 marked her emergence as a sea power and cleared the way for imperial expansion.

The decade that witnessed the defeat of the Armada saw also the first English attempts to colonize America. Securing in 1578 a patent for exploration and settlement, that model knight, Sir Humphrey Gilbert, twice set out for America. His first expedition was scattered by a storm, and on his second, in 1583, his frail bark disappeared. Gilbert's half brother, Sir Walter Raleigh, now took up the task and spent the remainder of his life and his large fortune in an effort to plant a settlement. His first expedition (1584) brought back glowing reports of the coast of Virginia, a second sent over the next year to plant a colony returned in discouragement, and a third, left stranded on the island of Roanoke, disappeared from history, leaving as the only clue the word "Croatoan" carved on a tree. With his fortune exhausted, Raleigh retired from active colonization, but he remained until his death an ardent proponent of English expansion. His expeditions helped to familiarize Englishmen with the coast of America, and they also proved that colonization in its initial stages was beyond the resources of a single individual, needing the combined financial backing of many if it was to be successful.

Such resources were finally to come through a commercial corporation, one of the many chartered during the sixteenth and seventeenth centuries by European monarchs to trade with the lands beyond the seas. In 1606, James I granted to the Virginia Company a charter that provided for two subordinate companies known as the London and Plymouth Companies. To "certain Knights, Gentlemen, Merchants, and other Adventurers, of our city of London and elsewhere," was given the right to trade and colonize between parallels 34 and 41, and to "Sundry Knights, Gentlemen, Merchants, and other Adventurers, of our cities of Bristol and Exeter, and of our town of Plymouth," similar rights between parallels 38 and 45, providing that the region between 38 and 41 be open to either on condition that neither settle within one hundred miles of the other. While these charters granted wide powers for economic exploitation, the king reserved to himself the control of government. A royal council was established in London to rule the colonies beyond the sea, with additional councils for each company, and a resident council in each colony, all appointed by the king. To the settlers, however, he granted "all liberties, Franchises, and Immunities . . . as if they had been abiding and born, within this our Realm of *England,* or any other of our said Dominions." Under this charter both companies attempted colonization, the Plymouth Company unsuccessfully at the mouth of the Kennebec River in Maine, and the London Company on the James River in Virginia.

In early May of 1607, after a weary voyage of four months, three ships with 104 men landed at a point thirty-two miles from the mouth of the James and planted the first permanent English colony in America. The early years were an unrelieved story of suffering and misfortune. The site of Jamestown was marshy and unhealthful, the Indians were a constant source of trouble, the English supplies were poor and inadequate, and the settlers proved incapable of fending for themselves when faced by starvation. The colonists, themselves, were mostly servants and laborers of the company, who were expected to work for a term of years in return for maintenance. What little initiative they might have had was ruined by sickness and by the mismanagement and quarrels of the leaders. Concerning these early days, one of the survivors wrote, "there were never Englishmen left in a foreign country in such miserie as we were in this new discovered Virginia. . . . If there were conscience in men, it would make their hearts bleed to heare the pitiful murmurings and outcries of our sick men without reliefe, every night and day for the space of sixe weekes; in the morning their bodies being trailed out of their cabins like Dogges, to be buried." New recruits came in January, 1608, but their lot was little better than that of the first expedition. Only the effective leadership of Captain John Smith, the only surviving member of the original local council, kept the colony from perishing during the first two years. Barely one fourth of the first two expeditions survived.

Discouraged by lack of progress, the investors of the London Company demanded a reorganization. The king was favorable and granted a new charter to a group now known as the Virginia Company, which was given the direct management of its own affairs. Under aggressive leadership the enterprise was pushed with renewed vigor. Government by council in the colony was abolished, and a one-man dictatorship was established. Sickness and Indian conflicts continued to decimate the settlers; yet, under the businesslike but ruthlessly cruel rule of Sir Thomas Dale, some order was brought out of chaos, and the colony began to prosper. In addition to the enthusiasm and large financial expenditure of the Virginia Company, three factors undoubtedly contributed to the saving of Virginia to the British Empire. The first was the policy begun by Dale, and extended by Governor Yeardley, of modifying the company-and-servant conception of the colony by granting to the settlers stock in the company and individual allotments of land that they might work for their own benefit. The second was the discovery by John Rolfe, in 1612, that tobacco could be grown profitably in Virginia. For this product there was a ready market in Europe, and by 1617 even the streets of Jamestown were sown with tobacco. The third was the grant by the company, in 1619, of a representative assembly, the first representative government to exist in America.

For the stockholders in England the Virginia Company represented only a heavy financial loss, but in world history its role was important, for it laid the foundation of the English world empire and the American nation. In the history of empire-building its leaders, Sir Thomas Smythe and Sir Edwin Sandys, must rank high. Despite its great contribution, James had determined to abolish the company. Through court action, in 1624, he revoked the charter, and Virginia became a royal province under the direct rule of a governor appointed by the king, but with the old representative assembly still maintained. This form of government became the usual type as one royal province after another was later established.

Virginia was founded by a commerical company primarily interested in profits; Plymouth, the next permanent English settlement, was established by a band of Protestant dissenters in search of religious freedom and economic betterment. Like other nations of Europe, England for a century had been torn by the religious conflicts following the Protestant revolt. Under Henry VIII England broke away from Catholicism and established her own state church with a form of religion midway between Catholicism and extreme Protestantism. Under his three children the nation vacillated: it moved toward extreme Protestantism under Edward, back to Catholicism under Mary, and then back again under Elizabeth to the middle ground of Henry. In such a period of kaleidoscopic change innumerable variations of religious thought were bound to arise; the difficulty lay in the fact that each government expected the people to conform to the particular brand that it favored. When James I came to the throne in 1603, England seemed definitely committed to Protestantism, but what form Protestantism might take was doubtful. A large element, the Puritans, were dissatisfied with the compromise of Henry and Elizabeth and were anxious to "purify" the English church of those forms of Catholic worship and belief that still remained. Most of the Puritans believed that this could be done by working within the church, but the more radical, considering that this was hopeless, determined to separate from the Church of England. It was from this group, the Separatists, that the Pilgrim fathers came. From James such reformers could expect nothing. "No Bishop, no King," he declared, and "If this is all your party hath to say, I will make them conform or harry them out of the land."

To "conform" was the last thing in the mind of the Separatist, and one group from Scrooby in Nottinghamshire under the lead of their pastor, John Robinson, fled to Holland. But life in a strange country was hard, and a natural desire to maintain their own language and traditions turned their eyes to America. From the Virginia Company they secured a patent to settle in America and from seventy London merchants £7000 to finance the expedition. The expedition was, in reality, a joint-stock enterprise, in which the merchants risked the capital and the Separatists their lives and labor. Each share of stock was worth £10, and every emigrant over sixteen was entitled to one share, or two if he outfitted himself or paid for his transportation. For seven years the labor of the colonists was to go into the common store from which they were to be provided with the necessities of life.[4] Under this arrangement 102 men, women, and children sailed from Plymouth on the *Mayflower* in September, 1620, arriving off Provincetown, on Cape Cod, November 12.[5] Finding themselves beyond the bounds of the Virginia Company, they had no charter of government and no title to the land upon which they might settle. In this predicament they drew up the Mayflower Compact, in which they pledged themselves to obey "such just and equall laws as shall be thought most meete and convenient for ye generell good of the colonie" and which was signed by forty-one of the male settlers. John Carver was elected governor.

Having drawn up this famous agreement, sometimes called the "first pure democracy in America," they determined on Plymouth as the site of their settlement and in the middle of December began to construct their huts. Almost half of their number died during this first terrific winter, but not one of the survivors returned to England when their ship sailed back in the spring. In 1621 they secured from the Council for New England a patent to the land [6] and in 1627 bought out, for £1800, the London merchants who had financed them. Under the wise leadership of William Bradford, governor (with the exception of five years) from 1621 until his death in 1657, the colony established amicable relations with the Indians and slowly extended its settlements along the coast. With but little help from England, the Pilgrim fathers in a few years had established themselves in a new land, become economically self-sufficient, and set up a

---

[4] This system was modified in 1623, when individual land allotments were made.

[5] Not more than a dozen were from the original Scrooby congregation, and not more than a third from Leyden.

[6] A second patent in 1630 more clearly delimited their territory. The Council for New England was a body of merchant adventurers, survivors of the old Plymouth Company, to whom the king in 1621 granted land from parallel 40 to 48 from "sea to sea."

simple but effective form of popular government. It was a precedent that innumerable bands of pioneers were to follow in the coming years as the movement of population spread westward.

The civilization of the Spanish, French, and Dutch settlements is described by H. I. Priestly, *The Coming of the White Man* (History of American Life, Vol. I). Of Jamestown and Plymouth the treatments in Edward Channing, *A History of the United States,* Vol. I, Chaps. VI–VIII, X, XI, and C. M. Andrews, *The Colonial Period in American History,* Vol. I, Chaps. V–VIII, XII, XIII, are adequate. Constitutional documents are in H. S. Commager, *Documents of American History,* Vol. I, 5–18.

Period in American History, Vol. I, Chaps. V–VIII, XII, XIII, are excellent. The economic aspect is stressed in Curtis Nettels, *The Roots of American Civilization,* Chaps. V, VI, VIII. Constitutional documents are in H. S. Commager, *Documents of American History,* Vol. I, 5–18.

COLONIAL CIVILIZATION

Chapter III

COLONIAL DEVELOPMENT

The inhabitants of the plantations are generally educated in republican principles; upon republican principles all is conducted. Little more than a shadow of royal authority remains in the Northern Colonies.

Reply to the Representation of the
New York Assembly of May 19, 1747

THE EXPANSION OF NEW ENGLAND

It was at Jamestown and Plymouth that England established her first footholds on the continent of America. But, like the Spanish, Dutch, and French, the English were intrigued by the rich sugar islands to the south. Before Plymouth was settled, a commercial company had established a prosperous colony in Bermuda (1612), and during the next twenty years various proprietors succeeded in planting settlements on the islands of St. Kitts, Nevis, Barbados, and other West Indian islands. The years 1620–1642, indeed, marked the great period of early English migration, when at least 65,000 Englishmen, mainly for economic reasons, came to the New World. Of all the English colonies then established, that of Massachusetts Bay grew with the greatest rapidity, for religious as well as economic motives contributed to its development. Despite the hostility of James I, Puritanism had grown rapidly in England during his reign. With the advent of his successor, Charles I (1625–1649), the prospects became darker, and Puritan leaders began looking toward America as a haven for their persecuted followers. Under grants from the Council for New England various tiny settlements already existed on the New England seacoast north of Plymouth. One of these, at Salem, came under the control of a group of adventurers, who obtained a grant of land from the mouth of the Merrimac to the mouth of the Charles and sent John Endicott and a body of colonists in 1628 to establish their authority. In 1629 this company came under the control of Puritans, its title was reaffirmed by a royal charter, its name was changed to "the Governor and Company of Massachusetts

Bay in New England," and it became the instrument of a great Puritan migration to New England.

On the face of it the Massachusetts Bay Company was a commercial corporation directed by officers annually elected by the stockholders, who were to meet four times a year and make laws not contrary to those of England. Certain Puritan leaders, the most prominent of whom was John Winthrop, agreed to migrate if the charter and government were transferred to America. This the company voted in 1629, thereby paving the way for a religious commonwealth in Massachusetts.[1] John Winthrop was elected governor and Thomas Dudley deputy governor, and under the leadership of these men 840 immigrants arrived off the coast of Massachusetts in the late spring and early summer of 1630. Finding the land around Salem inadequate for their support, they spread southward, planting settlements at Dorchester, Boston, Newtowne (now Cambridge), and elsewhere. Half of the 1630 migration either died or returned to England during the first year, but the rest held on doggedly, and their numbers were soon augmented by a heavy migration that brought 15,000 to Massachusetts in the next ten years.

Desire for economic betterment and the longing for religious freedom, which impelled thousands to seek the shores of Massachusetts, were the very motives that led many eventually to leave the jurisdiction of that colony. To Winthrop and the dominant faction Massachusetts Bay was to be no indiscriminate haven of refuge to the persecuted of other lands. Only those who conformed to their own idea of a Bible commonwealth were welcomed; the rest might keep out. The first to incur the wrath of the Puritan fathers and incidentally to win a glorious name in American history was Roger Williams, pastor of the Salem church. Bradford characterized Williams as "a man godly & zealous, having many precious parts, but very unsettled in judgmente." By the latter he undoubtedly meant that Williams had certain ideas extremely disturbing to the rulers of Massachusetts. Among these were the beliefs that the land belonged to the Indians and not to the king, that church and state should be separated, and that the state had no right to interfere with the religious life of an individual. Before the magistrates could banish him to England, Williams fled southward, obtained a title of land from the Indians, and founded a settlement at Providence (1636).

Hardly was Williams out of the way before Massachusetts Bay was rocked by another religious controversy. In this case it was a woman, Mrs. Anne Hutchinson, the spiritual mother in America of a long line of intellectual and independent women. To Winthrop she was a woman "of a haughty and fierce carriage, of a nimble wit and active spirit, and a very

[1] For a discussion of the political aspect, see pages 36-37.

voluble tongue, more bold than a man, though in understanding and judgment inferior to many women." Be that as it may, she aroused the authorities by holding meetings at her house at which she discussed the Sunday sermons, criticized certain of the local divines, and suggested that true religion must be founded on personal revelation rather than on any set of doctrines officially promulgated by the clergy. Banished from Massachusetts, she fled to Providence and later with a group of friends founded Portsmouth (1638). Other emigrants followed, settlements were established at Newport and elsewhere, and in 1643 Williams obtained a patent for the land from the Long Parliament, the title of which was later reaffirmed by Charles II (1663).

Although discontent with the political and religious narrowness of Massachusetts Bay played a part, the chief impetus in the migration to the Connecticut valley was the desire for more fertile land. After some friction with the authorities, Thomas Hooker, pastor of the Newtowne church, obtained permission to leave the colony and in June of 1636 led a group of his congregation to found Hartford. Some had preceded him, and others quickly followed, so that by the end of 1636 eight hundred people were living in Hartford, Windsor, and Wethersfield. In the next year came the war with the Pequot Indians, but the destruction of the Indians opened the way for the rapid settlement of the most fertile land in New England. The Indians were hardly subdued before the Reverend John Davenport and Theophilus Eaton arrived with a strong band of immigrants, who founded New Haven (1638) and other towns along the coast. Neither the Hartford nor the New Haven settlers had a patent to the land. A charter, however, was obtained in 1662, which, to the disgust of New Haven, incorporated that colony under the same jurisdiction as the Connecticut River settlements. From Connecticut as a base English settlers in the succeeding years pushed north into Vermont and west into New York and crossed the sound to Long Island.

In the meantime were laid the foundations of the white dominion in northern New England. Under grants from the Council for New England the region of Maine, New Hampshire, and Vermont came into the possession of Ferdinando Gorges and John Mason, later to be divided, Gorges taking Maine, and Mason New Hampshire. Both attempted to colonize their respective regions but with indifferent success. Most of the settlers were northward-moving immigrants from Massachusetts, as, for example, the group under the leadership of the Reverend John Wheelwright (brother-in-law to Anne Hutchinson and like her expelled for his religious views), which founded Exeter. By a far-fetched interpretation of her charter, Massachusetts claimed the region to the north and gradually extended her jurisdiction over these weak settlements. In 1679

Charles II gave independence and a new charter to New Hampshire, but Maine remained a part of Massachusetts until 1820, when Massachusetts consented to a separation.

THE PROPRIETARY COLONIES

Virginia and Massachusetts, as we have seen, as well as New Netherland and New Sweden, were founded by commercial companies, while Plymouth was financed by a group of London investors. The way having been blazed, it became possible for single individuals again to undertake colonization. Gilbert and Raleigh had attempted it in earlier years and had failed, and little more success had attended the efforts of Gorges and Mason. In the case of Maryland we find a different story. To George Calvert, Lord Baltimore, a man long interested in colonization, Charles I granted in 1632 the region between the Potomac and the fortieth parallel. Before the charter was signed, George Calvert died, and it passed to his son, Cecilius, who hoped that Maryland might prove a refuge for his persecuted fellow Catholics. Under the leadership of his brother Leonard, the first group of immigrants arrived in February, 1634, picked a site on the St. George, a tributary of the Potomac, and founded St. Mary's. The Calverts were wise administrators. Cecilius granted religious toleration —any other course for a Catholic proprietor would have been suicidal— and a share in the government, and his brother saw to it that the settlers wasted no time in search of gold or a passage to the Indies. The site selected was healthful, the crops immediately planted proved abundant, and Maryland escaped the "starving time" that decimated the Jamestown settlers. In spite of excellent climate, economic prosperity, and wise rule, Maryland for some years grew slowly. Her colonial history is largely a story of religious conflict between Catholics and Protestants, friction between proprietors and settlers, and disputes with her neighbors over boundary lines. As a result of the English revolution of 1689, the Calverts lost their political rights in Maryland, but when the fifth Lord Baltimore became a Protestant in 1715, they were restored.

With the restoration of the Stuarts under Charles II in 1660, a new era of English colonization opened. This was due not to any great desire on the part of the king to settle America but rather to his desire to reward as cheaply as possible those noblemen who had aided in the restoration. To eight of these men he granted in 1663 land south of Virginia, the boundaries of which were soon extended to include all the region between Virginia and Spanish Florida. Interested primarily in financial exploitation, these proprietors never gave to their possession intelligent or adequate supervision. True, they engaged the famous philosopher, John Locke, to draw up a feudal form of government, the "Fundamental Constitutions of Carolina," but its elaborate and highly artificial social and political institutions hardly fitted a howling wilderness, and it was never put into operation. Two centers of population developed, one around Albemarle Sound, composed chiefly of Virginia frontiersmen discontented with life in the Old Dominion, and the other around Charleston, founded in 1670 and soon joined by French Huguenots, who settled on the Santee River, and by planters from Barbados. In 1719 the southern group petitioned the king to end the inefficient rule of the proprietors. This he did in 1729, when he bought out their rights and at the same time divided the region into two colonies.

In the meantime occurred one of the most important events in American colonial history. In 1664 Charles II granted to his brother, the Duke of York, the land between the Connecticut and the Delaware. The purpose of the king was primarily to weaken the commercial power of Holland, and an expedition was immediately dispatched for the capture of New Amsterdam. Not only was Dutch rule in North America ended, but by the establishment of a continuous stretch of English territory along the seacoast the way was prepared for eventual unification. The name of the newly won territory was changed to New York, proprietary government was established, and almost immediately a part of the territory, New Jersey,[2] was conferred upon Lord John Berkeley and Sir George Carteret, two of the Carolina proprietors. The proprietors of New Jersey soon lost interest; Berkeley sold his share, known as West New Jersey, to a wealthy Quaker (1674), and in 1682 the Carteret heirs disposed of East New Jersey. Both sections came under the control of William Penn and his Quaker associates, who held them until 1702, when they surrendered their rights to the king.

Of all the Englishmen interested in American colonization William Penn was the most successful, and his personality is perhaps the most engaging. Son of the famous and wealthy Admiral Penn, he had thrown in his lot with the small and despised religious group known as the Quakers. Anxious to find a refuge for his persecuted fellow Quakers, Penn asked for a grant of land from Charles II in consideration of the contributions that his father had made to the monarchy. A charter to land west of the Delaware, which the king called Pennsylvania, was given him in 1681, and in the following year the Delaware region was added.[3] Penn, with the first group of colonists, arrived in October, 1682, and founded

---

[2] Named after the Island of Jersey in the English Channel, which Carteret as governor had at one time bravely defended.

[3] The boundaries of Pennsylvania were in dispute for almost a century. It was not until 1767 that the famous Mason and Dixon line was drawn between Maryland and Pennsylvania.

Philadelphia. The colony prospered from the start. Penn, who was a good business man, spread his advertising propaganda far and wide, and it was not long before a continuous stream of settlers from England, Germany, and Ireland had set in for Pennsylvania. Not only Quakers but the persecuted of all religions were welcome. "My prison shall be my grave," said Penn, "before I will budge one jot, for I owe obedience of my conscience to no mortal man," and the freedom that Penn demanded for himself he was willing that others should have. Similarly, he granted participation in the government. "Any government," said he, "is free to the people under it (whatever be the frame) where the laws rule and the people are a party to those laws; and more than that is tyranny, oligarchy and confusion." The liberal common sense of Penn bore quick fruits. Within three years after the founding, Penn could truthfully say, "I have led the greatest colony into America that ever man did upon a private credit, and the most prosperous beginnings that were ever in it are to be found among us." And the "holy experiment," as he called it, was to grow in power and prosperity as the years went on. The Delaware region was separated from Pennsylvania in 1712 and given its own legislature, but both colonies continued to be supervised by the same governor, appointed by the Penn family.

Under the influence of the soldier-philanthropist, James Oglethorpe, Georgia, the last of the thirteen colonies, was founded in 1733. Oglethorpe hoped that Georgia might provide a new chance for English debtors, consigned to prison under the barbarous laws of the time, and might also be a refuge for the persecuted Protestant sects of Germany. On the theory that Georgia might become a buffer state against the imperialistic ambitions of the Spanish in Florida, the British government looked upon the project with favor and backed it financially. That it might the more effectively serve the latter purpose, the government was to be under the complete power of a board of trustees for twenty-one years, after which the colony was to be a royal province. Slavery was at first forbidden, and for the purpose of establishing compact settlements a limit was placed upon the amount of land that might be acquired. In the face of economic necessity, regulations such as these soon broke down, and the trustees in 1752 surrendered their authority to the crown. Except for clashes with the Spaniards to the south, the early years of the colony were uneventful.

POLITICAL FOUNDATIONS

Like other aspects of American civilization, our political institutions were based upon European precedent, modified as the years went on by the pressure of local conditions. In the case of Virginia we have seen how the king at first attempted to participate directly in the rule of the colony, then in a second charter (1609) turned the government over to the Virginia Company, then took it back in 1624, when he revoked the charter and made the colony a royal province. The needs of the situation and the liberality of the company led to the granting in 1619 of an assembly, composed of two representatives from each local unit, which was continued after the charter was revoked. From 1624 until the Revolution the Virginia government was made up of this representative assembly or House of Burgesses, as it was called, which acted as a lower house, and of a governor and six councilors, appointed by the king, who acted as the executive, the high court of justice, and the upper house of the legislature. The assembly might make laws, subject to the veto of the king, that were not contrary to those of England. Local government followed English precedent. In general this was the government followed in the other royal provinces that were gradually established.

When the Pilgrims reached Cape Cod, they found themselves without any government and were forced to establish one. This they did in the simplest manner possible by choosing a governor and promising to obey "such just and equal laws" as seemed necessary for the general good of the colony. These laws, as time went on, were made in town meeting by those members of the community who were accepted as citizens. As the Plymouth colony expanded, so simple a government became impossible, and an assembly of representatives from the various towns met to make laws for the colony. The Plymouth colony maintained its separate identity until 1691, when by royal decree it was joined to the more powerful Massachusetts Bay to the north.

Like that of Virginia, the government of Massachusetts Bay was originally determined by a charter granted to a joint-stock company. Under this charter a "general court" of the freemen was to meet four times a year, elect a governor, a deputy governor, and eighteen assistants, and make laws not contrary to those of England. As Massachusetts Bay was chartered as a commercial company, this organization was not unlike that of a modern business corporation, the governor representing the president, the deputy governor the vice-president, the assistants the board of directors, and the freemen the stockholders. By the end of 1630 over 2000 had migrated to Massachusetts Bay, but the freemen numbered a scant dozen, including the governor, the deputy governor, and five or six assistants. These men had migrated to establish a Puritan commonwealth, and they had no intention of relinquishing power or opening the door to all kinds and all faiths. Their aim was to establish an oligarchy of the righteous, a theocratic state. As a consequence, and without authority of the charter, they conferred upon the officers and assistants the power to make laws, and then, again in violation of the charter, began to levy taxes. This aroused immediate opposition, and the General Court, fearful that the discontented might migrate elsewhere, admitted 118 to the company as freemen, but limited their rights merely to the election of assistants. When the famous Watertown Protest of 1631 against taxation without representation was presented, Governor Winthrop and his group granted each town (1632) the right to send two representatives to the General Court to confer on taxation and extended the power of the freemen to the election of the governor and assistants, as the charter had always provided. Two years later, when representatives from fourteen towns repaired to Boston and demanded a view of the charter, Winthrop capitulated, and a representative assembly was established with power to make laws and levy taxes.

The attempt of Winthrop and his fellow leaders to establish autocratic rule broke down because it was impossible for a few men without military backing to exert their will over the great mass of settlers. They did, however, by limiting the franchise to church members and by granting new lands only to acceptable, God-fearing Puritans, maintain their theocratic state unimpaired for many years. The first break came under Charles II in 1684, when the charter was revoked. The new charter granted by William in 1691 made property-holding rather than church membership the basis for the franchise. In that year Massachusetts became a royal province with the governor appointed by the king, but unlike the government of other royal provinces, the upper house or governor's council was not appointed by the crown but was nominated by the assembly or General Court and approved by the governor.

When New Hampshire became a royal province in 1680, the typical government of a royal province, such as we have seen in Virginia, was established. In Connecticut, on the other hand, we find a government much like that of Massachusetts before 1691. Under the inspiration of Hooker the settlers adopted a constitution, called the "fundamental orders," providing for the election of a governor, six assistants, and a law-making assembly. Suffrage was extended to all accepted by a majority of the township in which they lived. This did not specifically make church membership a requirement, but in actual practice it often amounted to that. The charter that the settlers got in 1662 confirmed this government, and they managed to hold it throughout the colonial period. The same was true of Rhode Island, where all officials were elected and where home rule was maintained. Unlike the other New England colonies, Rhode Island had separated church and state.

Somewhat different from the government in the royal colonies and in the self-governing colonies of Connecticut and Rhode Island was that of the proprietary colonies. Here the model adopted by the king was that of the County Palatine of Durham in northern England, where the Bishop of Durham had in his own territory the powers of the king. *Quicquid Rex habet extra, Episcopus habet intra,* ran the old law. To Lord Baltimore the king not only gave the land outright but also granted political, military, and judicial authority. The king renounced his right to levy taxes in the colony and made no provision for submission of laws to him or for appeals to the English courts. Almost the only limitation to the powers of the proprietors [4] was the provision that the laws must not be contrary to those of England, that they must be made with the "advice, assent, and approbation of the freemen or the major part of them or their representatives," and that the settlers should enjoy "all the privileges, franchises, and liberties which other English subjects enjoyed." In general this was the type of charter granted to the proprietary rulers,[5] but the broad feudal rights granted to Calvert and Penn were modified in general practice by the humanitarian principles of the founders and their anxiety to promote prosperous colonies. Calvert gave his settlers a representative lower house, but appointed his own governor and council. Penn granted his colonists the right to elect both houses,[6] and Pennsylvania enjoyed almost complete home rule under the governors appointed by the Penn family. In the Carolinas the proprietary grant was made to a group of proprietors, and in Georgia to a board of trustees, but the powers were like those of Penn and Calvert.

Such were the general forms of colonial government almost from the beginning. In all the colonies (except New York until 1691) there existed some form of popular assembly through which the colonists could make known their desires, express their grievances, and counteract the ambitions of crown or proprietor. The new state constitutions of the Revolutionary period and the later federal Constitution did not spring from the void, full-fledged and ready to function. Behind them was a century and a half of valuable political experience. During this long period each of the colonies had its own political history, too detailed for close examination here, but a history in which we see the clash of local with imperial interests and the reaction of world events. The Fathers of the Revolution were trained in a school of politics in which provincial problems and international events were often inextricably tied together.

On the face of it colonial society was fairly homogeneous and the government reasonably democratic. Closer scrutiny, however, reveals a dif-

[4] Except the Duke of York, to whom nothing was said about participation by the colonists.

[5] The Pennsylvania charter provided for royal veto and supremacy of Parliament.

[6] Under a new arrangement (1701) Penn reserved the right to appoint the councilors but the councilors or upper house gave up participation in legislation. As a result Pennsylvania, unlike the other colonies, had but one legislative body.

ferent situation. In the South, particularly in Virginia, government was controlled by the large plantation-owners, in Pennsylvania the wealthy eastern counties had more than their fair share of representation, and in most of New England the power rested in a minority composed largely of powerful adherents of the state church. Generally speaking, there was throughout the colonies a continual conflict between the enfranchised and the unenfranchised, between the frontiersman and the more wealthy merchant, capitalist, or plantation-owner in the East, and between the adherents of the state church and the dissenting sects rapidly growing powerful on the frontiers. Property qualifications for the franchise kept the poorer classes of the towns in check, and large counties on the frontier served the same purpose there.

Examples of sectional and economic conflicts during the colonial period are common. One of the most famous was Bacon's Rebellion (1676) in Virginia. Here economic distress, high taxes, and the failure of Governor Berkeley aggressively to prosecute the Indian war, led the frontiersmen and small planters to rise under Nathaniel Bacon, gain possession of the legislature, and pass a series of laws aimed to strengthen the local democracy. With the death of Bacon the rebellion collapsed and the king revoked the laws, and the whole episode strengthened for the time being arbitrary rule in Virginia. A somewhat similar uprising was that of the Regulators (1768–1771) in North Carolina. Unjust taxation, inequitable representation, difficulties in obtaining legal redress, and other causes led the frontiersmen to take up arms, but they were defeated by the lowland militia in the bloody battle of the Alamance. In the political field alone there was ample cause for discontent. In South Carolina one fifth of the population living in the lowlands controlled the state; in Virginia, wrote Jefferson, "the 19,000 men below the falls gave law to more than 30,000 living in other parts of the state, and appoint all of their chief offices, executive and judiciary." The frontiersmen in Pennsylvania protested (1764) that the three counties of Chester, Bucks, and Philadelphia elected twenty-six delegates to the Pennsylvania legislature, while the five frontier counties elected only ten. Attempts of the frontiersmen to escape the political control of the East can be seen in the efforts during the 1770s to establish the new states of Franklin, Transylvania, and Vermont.

The political conflicts, of course, were but the reflection of the more deep-seated clash of economic interests between the sections. The colonial frontier, like every American frontier, was populated by a debtor class, poor men seeking to better their economic condition. Money on the frontier was rare, and the struggle to pay taxes and interest on debts was a hard one. The demand for cheap money was continuous, and the complaints against absentee landlords and moneylenders were loud. This is well brought out in the unforgettable Deerfield petition of 1678 to the Massachusetts General Court: "You may be pleased to know that the very principle & best of the land; the best for soile; the best for situation; as lying in ye center & midle of the town: & as to quantity, nere half, belongs unto eight or 9 proprietors each and every of which, are never likely to come to a settlement amongst us, which we have formerly found grievous & doe Judge for the future will be found intollerable if not altered." Men who bore the brunt of Indian warfare and the rigors of frontier life, and at the same time found themselves discriminated against in the laws and in political representation, could hardly be expected to view with tolerance the economic interests of those who profited from their hardships.

In addition to the internal clash of economic and class interests, colonial legislatures were busy in maintaining their own interests against those of Great Britain. In the thirteen colonies Britain was concerned with the problems of commercial regulation, imperial defense, and political supervision, and all these phases of imperial activity were a fruitful cause of friction. With respect to the long list of British trade regulations, the colonists obeyed when they were advantageous and violated them when they were injurious (Chapter VI), and in the matter of enforcement the crown received but little help from colonial legislatures. Likewise, there were opposing points of view with respect to imperial defense. The British government, viewing the American colonies only with reference to the problem of world imperialism, bestirred itself to the defense of the colonists only when it seemed advantageous to fight on the American frontier, and then complained because of lack of co-operation. The colonists, on the other hand, who for a century had to withstand the force of French aggression, naturally resented having their lives and property subordinated to the wider needs of British imperialism. The chief business of the colonial legislatures, however, was concerned with the daily contact between the king's officials and themselves, for in eight of the colonies by the time of the Revolution there were royal governors, and in the rest there were customs officials and other representatives of the crown.

Throughout this period the British government was primarily interested in enforcing the imperial laws and in securing a stronger imperial control. This was the business of its representatives. A few of these royal governors were able administrators, but, unfortunately for Great Britain, the typical English official was a place-hunter chiefly interested in lining his own pockets during his enforced exile in the American wilderness. With some exaggeration Bancroft describes America as "the hospital of Great Britain for its decayed members of Parliament and abandoned courtiers," where they might quickly mend their fortunes and provide sinecures for their friends. Profitable as these positions may have been, they were no beds of roses, one of the governors complaining bitterly that "I have to steer between Scylla and Charybdis, to please the king's ministers at home and a touchy people here; to luff for one and bear away for the other." Fortunately for American destiny, the colonial legislatures held the purse strings, and like the Parliament in England, they maintained a spirited resistance against the financial ambitions of the king's placemen and their desire to establish arbitrary rule. Not only did the provincial legislatures vote the salaries, but in several of the states the legislatures got control of the treasury. "Let us keep the dogs poore," said one member of the New Jersey legislature, "and we'll make them do what we please."

The progress of colonial self-government reflected in certain respects a similar movement in England and was influenced by it. The rule of the first Stuarts, James I (1603–1625) and Charles I (1625–1649), was characterized by persecution of nonconformists and attempts to rule without Parliament. The growing autocracy of Charles I and his evident leaning toward Catholicism brought civil war (1642–1649) and the establishment of a Puritan commonwealth under Oliver Cromwell. The return of the Stuarts in the person of the easygoing Charles II (1660–1685) did not restore arbitrary rule, but it took a second revolution (the "Glorious Revolution") in 1688 to eliminate the unpopular James II and clinch the time-honored rights of Englishmen. When the crown was offered to the Protestant prince, William of Orange, and his wife, Mary, they agreed to the "Bill of Rights," which established the financial control of Parliament. During the period of political conflict and civil war, it was hardly possible to maintain a consistent policy in the colonies, nor under such circumstances were a people 3000 miles away likely to relinquish their rights without a struggle. Fortunately, the "Glorious Revolution" brought comparative political peace in England and greater political stability in the colonies. In Virginia the long period of encroachments on the liberties of the colonists by the arbitrary Stuart governors came to an end. In Maryland religious dissension was quieted by the victory of the Protestants and by a brief period (1692–1715) when that colony became a royal province. The political confusion in England did not break the proprietorship of Penn, but it strengthened the opposition to proprietary rule. When James II, proprietor of New York, became king, that colony became a royal province and continued so after the revolution of 1688. As a result of the "Glorious Revolution," New York finally in 1691 obtained an elective assembly.

Of all the sections perhaps New England was to be most affected by the political convulsions of the mother country. During the civil wars and the ascendancy of the Puritans she was left undisturbed, but with the restoration of the Stuarts there ensued a bitter struggle with the authority of the crown. Continuous complaints reached England of the arbitrary rule of the Massachusetts governors, of their denial of civil rights to others than Puritans, of violations of the charter, of failure to obey imperial laws, and of encroachments on New Hampshire and Maine. The charges were sifted by a royal commission and examined into by a special agent, and Massachusetts was warned to mend her ways. When she failed to do this, Charles revoked her charter in 1684. In the next year Maine, New Hampshire, Massachusetts, and a part of Rhode Island were put under one governnor, and in 1686 Sir Edmund Andros arrived with instructions to rule over all New England, New York, and New Jersey. Connecticut and Rhode Island refused to surrender their charters, but all submitted reluctantly to the rule of Andros.

But the Dominion of New England was of brief duration. Massachusetts opposed the new governor in every way, and Andros, in disgust, dismissed the assembly, abolished the courts, collected taxes without consent, arbitrarily arrested citizens, introduced the Anglican form of worship, and in every way outraged the feelings of the colony. News of the revolution in England brought quick revenge. Andros and his advisers were clapped into prison, and Massachusetts awaited a new dispensation. This came in the form of a new charter, which separated New Hampshire but added Plymouth and made the colony a royal province (page 37). Rhode Island and Connecticut quietly brought their charters out of hiding and continued their old form of government undisturbed.

Such is the bare outline of the story of the rise and fall of the Dominion of New England. Fundamentally, the episode marks the most important effort of the British government to tighten and consolidate her colonial administration in America. In the colonies the effort was complicated by a simultaneous conflict between the old theocracy, which would maintain the *status quo,* and the new commercial aristocracy, which desired certain political and economic reforms.

The development of colonial self-government and self-consciousness was likewise made possible by the somewhat impersonal and decentralized control exercised from England. The final authority rested in the Privy Council, but the actual task of supervising colonial administration was carried on by committees or specially constituted boards. In 1660 the king appointed a Privy Council Committee for Foreign Plantations, but, finding this inadequate, established in 1675 a standing committee of twenty-four of the Privy Council known as the Lords of Trade. The Lords of Trade lasted until 1696, when a new body, the Commissioners of Trade and Plantation, independent of the Privy Council, was created. The business of these boards was to collect information, draft instructions, suggest appointments to colonial offices, hear colonial complaints, review colonial laws, and in general act as a directing and supervising body. Imperial control was strengthened by the Navigation Act of 1696, which subjected the governors of the chartered colonies to royal approval and authorized the establishment wherever necessary of customs houses and admiralty courts directed from England. In the meantime, however, the administration had become less centralized as new agencies of control had developed. The Treasury Board had control of finances, and its subordinate, the Customs Board, attempted to enforce the navigation acts and collect the duties levied under these acts. The Admiralty Board was expected to protect commerce and prosecute smugglers, the War Office to deal with internal military protection, the law officers to examine colonial laws, and the Bishop of London to supervise the affairs of the Anglican Church in the colonies. As the cabinet system gradually developed, it took over some of the work of the Privy Council, and the Secretary of State for the Southern Department became its agent in colonial affairs. This array of bureaucrats appeared more formidable than it was, for there were much overlapping and waste motion. By holding the purse strings, colonial legislatures effectively weakened imperial control, while their own agents in London were ever ready to present the colonial point of view and counteract the complaints of discontented royal governors. In practice, imperial control was ineffective, and the colonies enjoyed a freedom without precedent in colonial administration, a freedom that was reflected in a general prosperity.

THE GROWTH OF RELIGIOUS LIBERTY

No aspect of colonial development is more pleasant for the historian to recount than the growth of religious toleration. Most people migrate because of dissatisfaction with conditions at home, and there is no question but that religious persecution was an important cause of colonial migration. It was important in bringing the Separatists to Plymouth, the Puritans to Massachusetts, the Catholics to Maryland, the Huguenots to South Carolina, German Protestant sects to Pennsylvania, and "Scotch-Irish" Presbyterians to many of the colonies. Against this deluge of dissenting sects religious despotism could not indefinitely survive. There was also an economic background. If king, proprietor, or provincial land speculator would people the country, he could hardly close the door to available immigrants. In Europe every country had its state church, supported by taxation and generally commanding the compulsory allegiance of all citizens. As European civilization moved to America, it was quite normal that such a system should be established here. Different conditions on the American scene prevented this in some of the colonies, an excellent example of how civilization becomes modified in transit.

At the end of the colonial period we find the Anglican or Episcopalian Church established in the five southern states of Georgia, North Carolina, South Carolina, Virginia, and Maryland and in the four southern counties of New York. In Massachusetts, New Hampshire, and Connecticut the Congregational Church was the official established denomination, but no attempt was ever made to establish a state church in Rhode Island, Pennsylvania, and Delaware, nor was the effort ever successful in New Jersey. Without separation of church and state and equality before the law of all denominations there could be no complete religious liberty, but there could be religious toleration, and that was eventually established everywhere. The first recognition of toleration was in Maryland when the proprietor, anxious to open the colony to persecuted Catholics, granted toleration to both Catholics and Protestant dissenters. As the Protestants outnumbered the Catholics almost from the start, friction quickly developed until in 1649 the famous Toleration Act was passed, providing that those "professing to believe in Jesus Christ shall not henceforth be anyways troubled, molested, or discountenanced for, or in respect of, his or her religion, nor in the free exercise thereof within this province." [7] In liberal Pennsylvania only Christians could participate in the government, but anyone was welcomed who acknowledged "one Almighty and Eternal God" to be the "Creator, Upholder, and Ruler of the World" and who conducted himself decently and refrained from work on Sunday. Even in these two states religious liberty did not exist, for only Christians could vote.

Although strict laws regarding church attendance were passed in early Virginia, and in all colonies where established churches existed there was discrimination, it was in the Puritan colonies that the greatest religious intolerance existed. Here we find a form of worship and organization like that advocated by the Separatists—separation from the Church of England, rejection of many forms of worship that the Anglican Church had taken over from Catholicism, abolition of the bishop's office, and the substitution for it of congregational control. In spite of local autonomy, the religious and civil administrations were closely tied together, as we have noted, in the admittance of church members only to the franchise. Not only did they demand absolute religious conformity, but the Puritan divines were obsessed by an urge to regulate the private lives of those living in their community. The harshness of the so-called "blue laws" has

[7] When Maryland became a royal province (1692–1715), the Anglican Church was established and continued as the state church until the Revolution.

been much exaggerated, but there was no small amount of regulation. Such extreme conformity brought quick reaction. The expulsion of Roger Williams and Anne Hutchinson resulted in the establishment of Rhode Island, the one and only colony where complete religious liberty existed. Positive as the fiery Roger Williams may have been in his own convictions, he insisted that all others also enjoy freedom of thought and expression. In Rhode Island there were no religious tests for voting,[8] no taxes for the support of the church, and no compulsory church attendance. Thirteen years before the Toleration Act of Maryland, Williams gave to America and the world a model of a free commonwealth. Strong religious convictions, it appears, might result in complete freedom as well as complete conformity. Although the established church continued in the other New England colonies until long after the Revolution, the power of the church, where an establishment existed, was rapidly undermined during the eighteenth century.

Brief accounts of the expansion of New England are C. M. Andrews, *The Fathers of New England* (Chronicles of America), and Edward Channing, *A History of the United States,* Vol. I, Chaps. XII–XV. For New Jersey, Pennsylvania, and Delaware read S. G. Fisher, *The Quaker Colonies* (Chronicles of America), and for the South, O. P. Chitwood, *A History of Colonial America,* Chaps. IV, V, XI, XVI. On political development, see C. M. Andrews, *The Colonial Background of the American Revolution,* Chap. I or Curtis Nettels, *The Roots of American Civilization,* Chap. VII. For pertinent sources see H. S. Commager, *Documents of American History,* Vol. I, 19–42.

[8] Except apparently for Catholics between 1719 and 1783. See Channing, *A History of the United States,* II, 426–427.

COLONIAL CIVILIZATION

Chapter IV

COLONIAL LIFE

> *Yet the thirteen colonies, in which was involved the futurity of our race, were feeble settlements in the wilderness, fringed along the coast of a continent, little connected with each other, little heeded by their metropolis, almost unknown in the world. They were bound together only as British America, that part of the western hemisphere which the English mind had appropriated.*
>
> GEORGE BANCROFT

THE PEOPLE

If there is one fact that stands out clear-cut in our social history, it is the heterogeneity of the American people. From England have come our language and the predominant influence in our legal, political, religious, and social institutions, but our people have been drawn from many parts of the world. In addition to the English there were in the seventeenth century Spanish, Dutch, Swedes, Welsh, Germans, and French in America, to say nothing of the Indians already here and the Negroes imported as slaves. Many attempts have been made to estimate the sources of colonial population, and a spirited battle has been waged on this point by social historians. Using the names of heads of families as they appear on the census of rolls of five states in 1790, the directors of the twelfth census estimated that at least four fifths of the population in 1790 were of English descent.[1] From the historians of other racial stocks, however, these

[1] *A Century of Population Growth 1790–1900* (1909) gives (page 121) the following estimate for 1790 (nationality as indicated by personal name):

	Number	Per Cent
	3,172,444	*100*
English	2,605,699	82.1
Scotch	221,562	7.0
Irish	61,534	1.9
Dutch	78,959	2.5
French	17,619	.6
German	176,407	5.6
All Others	10,664	.3

46

conclusions brought only ridicule. Although this analysis probably over-estimated the English strain, it is clear enough that the immigrants from England and their descendants comprised a large majority of the colonial population. But it is also clear that by the end of the colonial period the number of immigrants from other nations composed a much larger proportion of the population than is generally supposed.

Although historians quite naturally emphasize the early settlements, the great period of immigration was the eighteenth century. It is doubtful if there were more than 250,000 settlers in the colonies in 1700, but this number had grown to between 2,500,000 and 3,000,000 by the time of the Revolution. As in all other periods in our history, this growth came from natural increase and from immigration. The great period of colonial migration was in the eighteenth rather than in the seventeenth century, and it came primarily from Germany and Ireland rather than from England. It is also evident that it came chiefly to the middle colonies. The great German migration that settled portions of the Hudson and Mohawk valleys and eastern and central Pennsylvania was composed chiefly of various Protestant sects from the Rhineland who came to escape religious persecution and the terrible wars that decimated Germany for a century. From 1683, when the first group of Mennonites under Francis Daniel Pastorius left their Palatine homes to found the village of Germantown near Philadelphia, until the Revolution, well over 100,000 Germans came to the American colonies. Although most of the Germans remained in the region of their first settlements, perhaps a fourth pushed on to the frontiers of Maryland and the colonies to the south. Frugal, honest, religious, and home-loving, they exemplified those virtues making for permanency, and their hold on the regions that they so early occupied has never been broken.

More numerous than the Germans were the immigrants from Ireland. The most numerous of these were the North Irish Protestants from Ulster, the so-called "Scotch-Irish," so famous in American history, but there was also a large migration of southern Irish, greater than has been generally conceded. The history of "Scotch-Irish" migration goes back to the early seventeenth century, when the English government, to ensure control of Ireland, promoted the migration of Scotch and English to North Ireland, where they were settled on confiscated Irish land.[2] In spite of incessant border warfare and the hostility of the natives, these settlers held on to their land and created prosperous agricultural and industrial

---

[2] The term "Scotch-Irish" is not quite accurate. Many of the settlers in North Ireland were English; those from Scotland were mainly from the lowlands and might have been English as well as Scotch. In colonial America they were almost invariably known as "Irish." In spite of heavy migration, Ulster remains today Protestant and outside the Irish republic.

communities. This prosperity was severely threatened toward the end of the century by English trade laws that closed the markets of Scotland and England. At the same time these "Scotch-Irish" Presbyterians resented paying taxes to support the English state church. As a result of these causes, religious and economic, there started the movement to America that continued throughout the eighteenth century. How extensive it was can only be surmised. Arthur Young noted in 1776 that for many years the migration from Belfast had been at the rate of 2000 a year, while a committee of the House of Commons reported in 1775 that the vicissitudes of the linen trade had caused a migration of not less than 10,000 within two or three years. Arriving in America, these immigrants found the coast lands taken up, and were forced to move on to the frontier. As colonial frontiersmen they played their great role in early American history, their settlements running from Maine (Belfast) and New Hampshire (Londonderry) through western Massachusetts and Pennsylvania and along the backlands of the southern colonies. Trained in the rough school of Irish frontier warfare, brave, resourceful, and intelligent, they became the frontiersmen *par excellence,* the founders and defenders of frontier towns, the vanguard of civilization. Their arrival in such numbers aroused mingled feelings in colonial authorities. When Penn's agent, James Logan, wanted them to settle on some dangerous frontier, he described them as "good sober people came in from Ireland," but later asserted they settled Penn's land in an "audacious and disorderly manner," alleging that it "was against the laws of God and nature, that so much land should be idle while so many Christians wanted it to labour on and raise their bread," and again that "the settlement of five families from Ireland give more trouble than fifty of any other people." However they may have settled Pennsylvania, we must agree with their historians that they have contributed more than their proportion of leaders to the religious, political, military, and intellectual life of the nation.

Heavy as was the eighteenth-century immigration, it is estimated that in 1763 two thirds of the inhabitants were descendants of early comers rather than recently arrived immigrants. The key to the reasons for rapid population increase is made clearly evident by the Swedish traveler, Peter Kalm. "It does not seem difficult," said he, "to find out the reasons, why people multiply more here than in Europe. As soon as a person is old enough, he may marry in these provinces, without any fear of poverty, for there is such a tract of good ground yet uncultivated, that a new-married man can, without difficulty, get a spot of ground, where he may sufficiently subsist with his wife and children. The taxes are very low, and he need not be under any concern on their account." He might have added that under such conditions in an agricultural civilization children were an economic asset. Certainly early marriages and large families were the rule. He notes a Mrs. Sarah Tuthel of Ipswich, Massachusetts, who "had brought sixteen children into the world; and from seven of them only, she had seen one hundred and twenty-seven grandchildren and great-grandchildren," and another New England woman, who, when she died in the hundredth year of her age, "could count altogether five hundred children, grandchildren, great-grandchildren and great-great-grandchildren," two hundred and fifty-eight of whom were alive, with a granddaughter of hers already a "grandmother near fifteen years."

Much laborious effort has been wasted by genealogists in attempting to prove the aristocratic ancestry of the colonial settlers. American immigrants came almost entirely from the middle and poor classes of society, for whom life at home held out few opportunities. This was just as true of aristocratic Virginia as it was of more plebeian colonies. The "great Cavalier exodus" to Virginia stressed by Fiske and other historians never took place, and but few of the English nobility, or even gentry, found their way to that colony. Where an aristocratic class developed, it arose from within the colony among those individuals who had pushed upward in the economic struggle—the great plantation owners in Virginia, rich merchants in the seaport towns of New England and the middle colonies, great landholders everywhere. Although a small wage-earning class of citizens and unskilled laborers existed in the towns, the typical colonist was a small farmer. While the political life was undoubtedly dominated by the local aristocracy, society was not stabilized. The immigrant who came as an indentured servant (page 54) might look forward to the ownership of a farm and even to the possibility of rising into the ruling class.

COLONIAL ECONOMY

As is usual in new countries, the economic life of the American colonies was based primarily upon agriculture and the production of raw materials. Even in New England, where the development of industry and commerce had gone furthest, nine tenths of the people were farmers. Agriculture differed somewhat in the various colonies as it was influenced by soil, climate, natural products, and English trade regulations, but it was everywhere similar in that it was exceedingly crude and wasteful. The seventeenth century had not yet seen the dawn of scientific farming. Today we know that the fertility of soil may be renewed by rotation of crops, by artificial fertilizer, or by letting the land lie fallow, but the Europe of the Middle Ages knew little beyond the last method. The great improvements in English agriculture that led to the introduction of turnips, clovers, and better grasses, to the more scientific rotation of crops, and to the abandonment of the three-field system did not come until the eighteenth century. In America two great influences delayed even these improvements—scarcity of labor and a limitless supply of cheap fertile land. "In Europe," said Jefferson, "the object is to make the most of their land, labor being abundant: here it is to make the most of our labor, land being abundant." As a consequence "land butchery" was universally practiced. European observers commented on both the fertility of the soil and the careless husbandry. "They had nothing to do," says Kalm of the New Jersey farmers, "but cut down the wood, put it into heaps, and clear the dead leaves away. They could then immediately proceed to ploughing, which in such loose ground is very easy; and having sown their corn, they get a most plentiful harvest. This easy method of getting a rich crop has spoiled the English and other European inhabitants, and induced them to adopt the same method of agriculture which the Indians make use of, that is, to sow uncultivated grounds, as long as they will produce a crop without manuring, but to turn them into pastures as soon as they can bear no more and to take in hand new spots of ground, covered since time immemorial with woods, which have been spared by fire or the hatchet ever since the creation." Even worse was their treatment of livestock. Another observer insisted that, in all that concerned cattle, the New England farmers were "the most negligent ignorant set of men in the world. Nor do I know any country in which animals are worse treated." Some of the Virginians, it is said, held that to house or milk cows in the winter would be the death of them.

In spite of unscientific agriculture and the unbelievably bad treatment of livestock, the colonial farmer was one of the most prosperous in the world. Livestock deteriorated under frontier conditions, it is true, but nevertheless increased rapidly. Even in New England, where soil and climate were not propitious for large farms or great surpluses, there was an abundance of food. Some of the surplus went to support the commercial and fishing population of the seaport towns; some of it was exported to the West Indies. Like that of New England, the agriculture of the middle colonies was diversified, but, unlike that of New England, it provided a large exportable surplus. From these "bread colonies" went large quantities of flour, wheat, and packed meat to the West Indies and southern Europe. As we move south, we encounter the large plantation growing a staple crop for export, tobacco in Maryland and Virginia, rice and indigo in the Carolinas. As these commodities could be best raised on large plantations, and as the chief cost was labor, their production tended to concentrate in the hands of the more wealthy planters. Labor on the great plantations in the seventeenth century was largely furnished by white indentured servants, but these gave way in the eighteenth to Negro

The Lowell House (Elmwood), Cambridge, Massachusetts.

The Ver Plank House, Fishkill, New York.

COLONIAL EXTERIORS

The William Gibbes House, Charleston, South Carolina. (Reproduced from *Great Georgian Houses of America* by permission of the Architects Emergency Committee and Dwight James Baum, who did the restoration work on this house.)

COLONIAL INTERIORS

Above—John Ward House, Salem, Massachusetts
Below—Colonel Willoughby Tebbs House, Dumfries, Virginia. (Reproduced from *Colonial Interiors* by Leigh French by permission of William Helburn, Inc., publishers)

slaves. Even in the South nine tenths of the farms were small, but it was the large plantation owners that dominated the political life and gave the tone to the civilization. Novelists have given us an engaging picture of the luxury and gaiety of life on those colonial plantations. Certainly, in comfort and luxury, it was on a par with that of the English country gentry, but it was often more prosperous in appearance than in fact. The one-crop system that rapidly wore out the land, the declining prices of tobacco, the rising cost of land, and the excessive duties levied by England all contributed to make it exceedingly difficult during the eighteenth century for many tobacco planters to operate at a profit.

While colonial civilization was primarily agricultural, a certain amount of industry existed. Colonial commerce was essentially on a barter rather than on a money economy. The average colonist lived on a self-sufficing farm; he possessed little ready money and was unable to purchase his manufactured goods from Europe. He either manufactured them himself on his farm or bought them with his produce from the blacksmith, shoemaker, cabinetmaker, and other craftsmen who found work in the villages and towns. As a consequence, a large amount of domestic and small-shop manufacturing was carried on. As time went on, household manufacturing in some cases developed from manufacturing merely for the family to manufacturing for the general market, and the product of the artisan changed from custom work to goods for general sale. That much of this work was capably and artistically done is evident from the thriving business carried on today in antique furnishings.

Quite as important as domestic needs in the development of industry was the stimulation of foreign commerce. The collection and preparation of furs were important occupations, particularly in the seventeenth century, for there was always a ready market in Europe. There was likewise a large market for the products of the forest both in America and in Europe. Naval supremacy necessitated a supply of ships, masts, tar, pitch, rosin, and turpentine, and these commodities England desired to obtain from her colonies rather than from foreign countries. Bounties were offered to stimulate their production, and laws were passed to ensure that British commerce be carried only in ships built in England or in the colonies. In New England the surveyor general even marked with the "broad arrow" trees of size suitable for the royal navy. As important as the English market was that of the West Indies, where there was a constant demand for lumber for ships and buildings and for staves, hoops, and headings for the manufacture of the hogsheads and barrels used as containers for tobacco, sugar, molasses, rum, and other commodities. For lumber of all kinds there was, of course, much demand at home, particularly in New England, where the fishing industry and the manufacture of rum also demanded hogsheads and barrels. As iron existed in all the colonies and copper in some sections, and as it was cheaper to produce them at home than to import them, a mining industry developed, and the manufacture of metal commodities began. The fuel used in the colonial period for the smelting of iron was charcoal, and, as the forests of England were rapidly disappearing, the English government to save their own forests encouraged the production of iron ore in the colonies.

English colonial policy, as we shall see (Chapter VI), was based on the economic doctrine of mercantilism, a theory that promoted national self-sufficiency and a favorable balance of trade. That nation was the most prosperous that bought the least and sold the most. The colonies must not compete with the products produced at home, but were expected to supply those things that the home country did not have. English tariffs, as a consequence, favored naval stores, crude iron, tobacco, and tropical products, but debarred those foodstuffs that came in competition with the British farmer. This policy, speaking broadly, favored the southern colonies but worked disadvantageously in the middle colonies and New England. Fortunately, these regions found a way out. In the West Indies and southern Europe a market was developed where the farmers of the middle colonies could dispose of their surplus foodstuffs, and where New Englanders could sell their fish and derive profits from the carrying trade. Despite the finely spun theories of mercantilism, commerce somehow tends to balance, and the triangular trade routes of the colonial period provide a striking example. To southern Europe the New England and middle colonies sent their grain, meat, lumber, and fish, traded them for wine and fruit, exchanged the latter commodities in England for manufactured goods, which they brought back home. A second triangular route was from New England and the middle colonies to the West Indies, where the same foodstuffs and lumber were exchanged for sugar, molasses, and fruit, the latter taken to England and exchanged for manufactured goods to be brought home. A special trade route profitable to New England was that which involved the export of rum and other commodities to Africa to be exchanged for slaves, the latter being brought to the West Indies and exchanged for molasses and coin. The molasses was then distilled into rum, which was sold in the domestic market or used in the slave trade. By means of these trade routes the colonists not only disposed of their surplus and developed a prosperous economic life, but were thus enabled to benefit England through the purchase of large quantities of manufactured goods. This Benjamin Franklin made clear to a committee of the House of Commons during the controversy over the Stamp Act, when he explained how Pennsylvania could import yearly £500,000

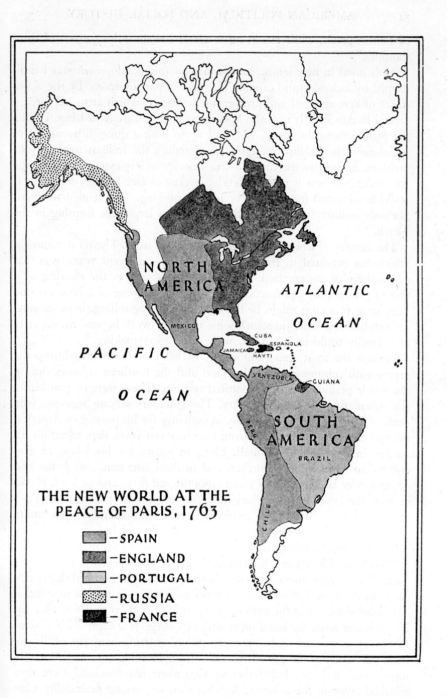

NORTH
AMERICA

ATLANTIC

OCEAN

PACIFIC

OCEAN

MEXICO

CUBA
ESPAÑOLA
JAMAICA
HAYTI

VENEZUELA

GUIANA

SOUTH
AMERICA

PERU

BRAZIL

CHILE

THE NEW WORLD AT THE
PEACE OF PARIS, 1763

— SPAIN
— ENGLAND
— PORTUGAL
— RUSSIA
— FRANCE

of British goods, while exporting to Great Britain only £40,000 of commodities.

As is usual in new lands, American economic development was handicapped by lack of liquid capital. This was in part overcome by the abundance of raw material and prosperous commerce, which attracted foreign capital to America. It was also handicapped by a scarcity of labor. Unlike the Spaniards to the south, who had to do with a quite different native population, the English were unable to reduce the Indians to slavery or serfdom, or even to use them as free laborers to any extent except in the fur trade. Nor was it easy to develop a class of free laborers where land could be obtained for nothing or next to nothing. This tended to retard not only industry but also the development of large-scale farming in the North.

The scarcity of labor was met in a number of ways. The most common, which has persisted in frontier communities into recent years, was that of community co-operation. The launching of a ship, the clearing of a plot of ground, the construction of a road, the building of a house, or the harvesting of a crop might be the occasion of a log-rolling, house-raising, or corn-husking "bee," in which some necessary work beyond the capacity of a family could be combined with social merrymaking.

Perhaps the most important source of labor in the South during the seventeenth century and in Maryland and the northern colonies during the whole period was the indentured servants. These were of two kinds, the voluntary and the involuntary. The voluntary servant was one who came of his own volition and who, in exchange for his passage to America, sold his labor for a period of from four to seven years, depending on his success in disposing of himself. Here, in return for his labor, he was entitled to food, clothing, shelter, and medical attention, and at the end of his service he was usually given an outfit and fifty acres of land. Harsh as were the laws governing servitude, the system was not without its advantages. It enabled poor but ambitious men to reach a land of opportunity and provided in America a much needed supply of labor.

A darker side of this picture has to do with those who came against their will, particularly those children and adults kidnaped by professional "spirits" or crimps and sold to shipmasters. Although the English government made some half-hearted attempts to put a stop to this practice, it flourished throughout the period, many in high stations profiting thereby. There is one amazing scene on record, of George Jeffries, himself famous in history as a cruel and obnoxious judge, ordering a mayor of Bristol from the bench to the prisoners' dock and upbraiding him as a "kidnaping rogue." It is the belief that in 1670 alone ten thousand were thus whisked away to the colonies. Another class of varying desirability were those who had run counter to the law. The barbarity of the English criminal code, which provided the death penalty for some three hundred offenses, was mitigated by allowing the prisoner to elect transportation rather than other punishment. Many who thus came were political prisoners or had committed minor offenses and were as good as or better than the voluntary indentured servant; others were a burden to the colonies. At all events "His Majesty's Seven Year Passengers" were far from welcome. Massachusetts "earnestly desired to be excused from entertaining criminals transported to America," and other colonies vigorously protested, but the practice continued to the end of the period. The lot of the indentured servant, whether voluntary or involuntary, was a hard one, and many died before the term of service was up, but the fact remains that the indentured servant made up a larger part of colonial immigration than is generally supposed. To Virginia alone there came annually between 1635 and 1705 from 1500 to 2000. "This system of immigration," says Wertenbaker, "was the foundation of the economic life of the tobacco colonies for almost a century."

Negro slavery existed in America from the arrival of the first Spaniards. It was introduced in the English colonies in 1619, when a Dutch man-of-war visited Jamestown and sold the settlers twenty Negroes. Great as was the need for laborers, Negro slavery was not popular at first and grew slowly. Toward the end of the century, however, the importation of Negroes increased rapidly. The Anglo-Dutch war of 1665–1667 broke the Dutch control, and the trade was thrown open when the monopoly of the Royal African Company was ended in 1697. It was then that the New Englanders entered aggressively into the trade, and it was then that the importation took a jump. About the same time the tobacco planters came to the conclusion that the Negro slave was more profitable than the white indentured servant, who was barely trained when his time was up, while the indigo and rice planters found white labor utterly unadapted to their crops.[3] Although slavery existed in all the colonies, it developed most rapidly in the region of large plantations. As late as 1670 the slaves numbered but five per cent of the population of Virginia; by 1756 the Negroes numbered 120,000 and the white population 173,000. By 1760 there were twice as many blacks as whites in the province of South Carolina. By that date there were around 400,000 Negroes in America, three fourths of whom were in the South, where they comprised two fifths of the population.[4] So large was their number that colonial legislation attempted to

[3] It seems also probable that the unemployment situation in Great Britain had eased somewhat, thus checking the flow of white servants to the colonies.

[4] The first census (1790) recorded a colored population of 757,208, of whom 697,624 were slaves. It put the total population at 3,929,214.

discourage the traffic in slaves, but the vested interests in the slave trade, it was discovered, were strong enough to influence the British government to disallow such colonial laws. While Negro slavery solved in a manner the problem of labor scarcity, the general effect was unfortunate. Slave competition lowered the status of the white laborer and small farmer and "transformed Virginia," says Wertenbaker, "from a land of hard-working, independent peasants, to a land of slaves and slave holders."

EVERYDAY LIFE

Physical survivals in sufficient numbers exist for us to visualize with reasonable accuracy the life of our forefathers. Like other aspects of American cultural life, colonial architecture was the outgrowth of European influence modified by American environment. The first dwelling was likely to be a crude log cabin of one room, the typical abode of the pioneer for almost three centuries. These were but temporary, giving way to more comfortable and commodious houses as the Indian menace passed and as prosperity increased. Generalizing roughly, colonial houses were usually built of the material at hand. In Virginia, where wood was abundant and other materials scarce, the typical house was a simple structure of clapboard. This was true of New England in spite of an abundance of stone. On the other hand, the settlers in the middle colonies loved to duplicate their European homes. "Almost all the houses hereabouts," said Kalm of Pennsylvania (about 1749) "were built either of stones or bricks, but those of stone were more numerous. Germantown, which is about two English miles long, had no other house, and the country houses thereabouts were all built of stone." As the eighteenth century progressed, the more wealthy colonists attempted to follow the prevailing mode in England, the so-called Georgian architecture, an ornate and somewhat artificial classical style, which, grafted on to prevailing colonial styles, sometimes produced results of dignity and beauty. In New England it can be seen executed in wood, plain without but decorative within, in such houses as the Royall house in Medford, the Lee mansion in Marblehead, and in New York in the Jumel house. It can be seen in Pennsylvania in the stone mansion of Cliveden in Germantown, and it reached its consummation in Virginia in the brick structures at Shirley and Westover on the James. Architecture as a profession hardly existed in colonial days, but the builders somehow so neatly adapted the designs in English books to fit the needs of the people and the demands of environment, that modern architects have striven to recapture the style and beauty of these early homes. Today the New England farmhouse, the Dutch homestead with its gambrel roof, and the Pennsylvania stone or brick house has again come into its own, to the great improvement of American suburban architecture.

The central feature of colonial architecture was the fireplace, which provided facilities for cooking and warmth in the winter, and around which the life of the family centered. There were hung the heavy utensils that made cooking an onerous task, and close at hand were the spinning wheel and weaving frame, the constant companions of the industrious housewife. Needless to say, the kitchen was also the dining room, and the wooden platters and highly polished pewter from which the family ate occupied near-by shelves. As life became more commodious in the eighteenth century, other fireplaces were added, more rooms were used, paper was added to the walls, and china was often substituted for pewter. Forks, of which the first settlers were innocent, were added to the tableware. For the first crude handmade furniture there were often substituted the more ornate and delicate Chippendales or Sheratons of the late eighteenth century. Light was furnished by bayberry, spermaceti, or tallow candles or by little metal vessels in which was burned oil of varying kinds. That the homes of the prosperous merchant and planter class were comfortably and even luxuriously furnished, often with imported commodities, there can be no doubt. Not long before the Revolution Josiah Wedgwood, the father of the English porcelain industry, wrote that the British consumption of white stoneware was "very trifling in comparison with what is sent abroad; and the principal of these markets are the Continent and Islands of North America. To the Continent we send an amazing quantity of white stoneware and some of the finer kinds; but for the Islands we cannot make anything too rich or costly." The typical continental colonist, it must be remembered, was not a wealthy planter or merchant, but a poor or middle-class farmer who hardly aspired to imported mahogany or chinaware.

As with house furnishings, so also in the diet there was a difference between rich and poor. Many accounts have come down of the lavish hospitality and the groaning boards of the wealthy, loaded down with many varieties of imported foods and wines. The diet of the common man, however, was much more monotonous, particularly in the winter, when corn bread and salt meat or fish formed the staple for his table. The colonial housewife, nevertheless, was proficient in the preservation of food, and the products of the garden and the results of the hunting trip gave seasonal variation. The strenuous outdoor life of the colonist made him a heavy eater, and the lack of other amusements tended to emphasize the delights of the table. These causes and the wide use of salt meat also help to explain the universal and heavy consumption of alcoholic beverages. Imported claret, port, Madeira, and other wines were widely used by the wealthy, while the less affluent, as in the days of the recent experiment in prohibition, satisfied themselves with homemade drinks—cider and various kinds of brandy and beer. The cheapest, the most common, and undoubtedly the most injurious of the "hard liquors" consumed was rum. Some of it was imported from the West Indies, but most was made in New England, where distilleries were established to supply the demand of the fishing fleet and the slave trade. In North Carolina, if we are to believe Byrd, "most of the rum in this country comes from New England, and is so bad and unwholesome that it is not improperly called kill-devil. It is distilled from foreign molasses, which, if skillfully managed, yields near gallon for gallon." In the amount of liquor consumed there was but little difference between the various colonies or between the classes of people. We learn that "Gen'l Washington notwithstanding his perfect regularity and love of decorum could bear to drink more wine than most people," and that John Adams, "an early and earnest wisher for temperance reform," to the end of his life drank a large tankard of hard cider each morning upon arising.

While drinking itself provided relaxation and was the invariable accompaniment of all social gatherings, it was far from being the only colonial amusement. The vast amount of work needed in the early years to clear the land and make it habitable left little time for sport and undoubtedly explains the origin of that glorification of work that is part of our American philosophy of life. This was accentuated in New England by Puritan seriousness and by the desire "to prevent the Heathenish Popish observation of Dayes, Moneths and Yeares, that they may be forgotten among the people of the Land." Orthodox Puritans, at the end of the seventeenth century, still frowned upon the observation of Christmas Day. But even in New England the Sabbath service and the Thursday lecture hardly satisfied the desire for a respite from work. Militia training gave opportunity for holidays, when the training was followed by much eating, drinking, and outdoor sports, while the raising of a home, the launching of a ship, or other forms of communal effort provided a chance for revelry as well as hard work. From our modern point of view, life in seventeenth-century New England may have been somewhat drab, but there was certainly much boisterous pleasure in later years. Judge Sewall, whose diary is as valuable for Boston life as that of Pepys is for English society, complains in 1686 of several of his friends who, after a drinking party near Roxbury, returned to Boston singing and swearing "to the great disturbance of the Town and the grief of good people. Such high-handed wickedness has hardly been heard of before in Boston." But this and much more soon became common enough. Although not all as gay as Boston, eighteenth-century New England was hardly the gloomy place that some have pictured.

In all the colonies hunting and fishing were universal outdoor sports. In the South, horse-racing and cock-fighting, next to hunting, provided amusements for the wealthy and were followed enthusiastically. Cock-fighting, which has disappeared except among the more degraded element, was then, if we are to believe Josiah Quincy, "a very predominant passion." In Maryland, he says, "I spent yesterday chiefly with young men of fortune: they were gamblers and cock-fighters, hound-breeders and horse-jockies. To hear them converse, you would think that the grand point of all science was properly to fix a gaff and touch with dexterity the tail of a cock while in combat." Turning from outdoor to indoor amusements, we discover what Professor Andrews calls "the representative colonial vices," namely, drinking, smoking, and gambling. Hard drinking has already been noted. Tobacco was sometimes chewed, but usually taken as snuff or smoked in a pipe. The cigar did not come in until about 1800, and the cigarette is a comparatively modern invention, but pipe-smoking in colonial days was widespread among women as well as men. Except among the strict Puritans, the Quakers, and other serious religious sects, gambling was an enthusiastic accompaniment of all games and was indulged in by both sexes. "The ladies of New York," says Eggleston, "were considered virtuous above many others of their sex because of the moderation of their gambling."

Despite all this, colonial amusement was generally harmless enough. Of all forms perhaps the most common and popular was dancing. "Dancing," says one traveler of the people of the Carolinas, "they are all fond of, especially when they can get a Fiddle, or Bag-pipe; at this they will continue Hours together, nay, so attached are they to this darling, Amusement, that if they can't procure music, they will sing for themselves," and this was true of all the colonies in the eighteenth century. The more formal dances were long-drawn-out affairs, and it was not unusual to have the same partner for the entire evening. One author tells of a wedding dance at Norwich, Connecticut, at which there were recorded ninety-two jigs, fifty-two country dances, forty-five minuets, and seventeen hornpipes.

The study of crime and punishment in any age is a discouraging and gloomy task. An examination of colonial court records makes evident the fact that there were relatively few cases of vagrancy, theft, and homicide. The population was too scanty, the people too dependent upon one another, and the economic opportunities too great to foster this sort of crime. On the other hand, we find the courts cluttered with cases involving all types of sexual lapses, and this in spite of harsh laws, a high ideal of conduct upheld by church and state, and early marriage. The coarse sensuality of the seventeenth and eighteenth centuries, the low character of many of the immigrants, the strenuous life combined with the lack of recreational outlets, and the morbid publicity given to such crimes undoubtedly contributed to their prevalence. The age was a cruel one, our ancestors were callous to suffering, and the lesser punishments were freely enforced. These included whipping, exposure in the stocks (sometimes with the ear nailed to the post), branding, mutilation, wearing the scarlet letter, ducking, and imprisonment. The existence of other types of punishment and the scarcity of labor made imprisonment rare, but where prisons existed they were incredibly filthy and cruel.

Although the English common law formed the basis of American legal codes, capital punishment was fortunately less common. While three hundred crimes in England were punishable by death, the Massachusetts Body of Liberties listed only ten,[5] and in some of the other states there were fewer. Nevertheless, capital punishment was frequently invoked; we find examples in the hanging of Quakers on Boston Common, the putting to death of twenty victims of the famous Salem witchcraft delusion of 1692, and the burning at the stake of rebellious Negroes in New York. Colonial justice was characterized not only by greater cruelty than at present, but, as we have seen, by greater publicity. Public executions, exhibiting the culprit in the stocks, and public confession in the church, all to the supposed edification of the populace, hardly conform to our more scientific conception of the administration of justice.

Our discussion of colonial life so far has been largely concerned with the economic and political phase. The task of subduing a wilderness gave little time to devote to the intellectual life, and, except for the ministry, the professions developed slowly. This was particularly true in the field of medicine, where the physician combined the practice of medicine with perhaps a half dozen other occupations. It was just as well, for medical knowledge was so limited that the physician usually did more harm than good. Cathartics and bleeding, or, to use the quaint language of the time, "purging the belly" and "breathing the veins," were the stock remedies prescribed for all ailments. If the patient survived this, which he quite often did not, there was a whole array of curious concoctions, which might contain anything from ground rubies to pulverized butterflies, grasshoppers, or toad powder. The brain of the shark was believed beneficial in obstetric cases; the brain of the screech owl was recommended for

---

[5] Heresy or idolatory, blasphemy, murder, poisoning, bestiality, sodomy, adultery, man-stealing, and treason. At various times up to 1701 laws in the four New England colonies made thirty crimes punishable by death, including kidnaping, piracy, robbery, rioting, and selling arms to Indians, but the laws were frequently not enforced.

headache and spiderweb pills for the ague. The seventeenth-century physician believed that the human body consisted of four elements—earth, air, fire and water—and similarly that it contained four humors or liquids—bile or choler, blood, melancholy or black bile, and phlegm. Disease was caused by an excess of one humor or by a humor's being too hot, too dry, or too moist, and it was for these wrongly tempered humors that the strange mixtures were designed. In addition to the perils of medicine, the colonist was affected with amazing ideas of hygiene. John Locke, one of the most intelligent men of his generation, in his *Thoughts Concerning Education* advised for children "especially the head and feet kept cold, and the feet often used to cold water and exposed to wet." It is not surprising that infant mortality was high and the span of life short. One important medical advance, however, can be recorded. Of all the colonial diseases that have since been brought under control, smallpox was the most virulent. Experiments with inoculation were being made in England, and the knowledge of this was introduced by Zabdiel Boylston in 1721–1722 into Massachusetts, where, in spite of opposition, the practice became general long before it did so in Great Britain.

As the physician combined his practice with other occupations, so the lawyer was likely to be also a farmer and a politician. Against him there was much prejudice until increasing commerce made him necessary. His legal business was largely concerned with suits over conflicting land claims, but between this and politics he often enjoyed a lucrative income and attained a powerful position. Literature, on the other hand, never attained the dignity of a profession. A printing press was established in Cambridge as early as 1639, and books, more than one might expect in a new and undeveloped land, were written, but all were by-products of a busy life in other fields, and the majority had to do with theological controversy. Here colonial divines sometimes reached a high plane, as with Jonathan Edwards's *Freedom of the Will* (1754), which proved not only a literary landmark in America but the first American book to exert profound influence in either America or Europe. Today we are more concerned with the diaries, journals, and histories that some colonists found time to write, and of these William Bradford's immortal *History of Plimoth Plantation* is the most important. Outside architecture and cabinet-making, artistic development is to be seen chiefly in the work of the silversmiths and in portrait-painting, which occupied the full time of a few men.

Like other professions, the clergy eked out their income by teaching, and sometimes, especially in the South, by farming and commerce. Their influence varied with the section. In theocratic New England they were all-powerful in religion and exerted a tremendous influence in the political life. Towering above their congregations in education and intellectual equipment, respected for their piety and devotion, they were unquestionably the natural leaders and aristocracy of the New England commonwealths. Pious and learned divines were to be found in the other colonies, but their influence was spiritual rather than political. In the South, if we are to believe the comments of travelers, the clergy of the established church had fallen to a low estate. Appointed chiefly through political or personal influence, they were likely to be the social companions of their parishioners rather than their intellectual or spiritual guides. Unlike New England, the South usually regarded Sunday as a day of pleasure and amusement.

Whatever may have been the spiritual influence of the clergy, they played a major part in colonial education, and this was true both of the educational efforts that sprang from the missionary activity in England and of those that originated in the colonies. Private tutors or teachers of parochial schools supplied the backbone of education in the middle colonies and the South, and religious influence was behind the attempts at public education in New England, while the hand of the clergy is seen in the founding of the colonial colleges. Especially interesting are the first attempts in New England to establish universal public education. As early as 1642 the Massachusetts General Court directed officials to insist that parents see to it that their children were taught to read. Asserting in the more famous law of 1647 that it was "one chief project of ye ould deluder, Satan, to keep men from the knowledge of ye Scriptures," they ordered that every town having fifty householders appoint a teacher of reading and writing whose wages might be paid by the parents or inhabitants in general in whatever way the town might desire, and that every town having one hundred householders must set up a grammar or Latin school to fit youths for the university. For the first time among English-speaking people, the right of the state was established to require communities to set up and maintain schools. With the exception of Rhode Island, the system of compulsory instruction in the rudiments was followed in other New England colonies. But beyond the rudiments few went, even in New England. Except for reading and writing, education for girls hardly existed, and throughout the colonies illiteracy was widespread.

The influence of religion can be seen also in the colleges. "After God had carried us safe to New England," said a contemporary writer, "and we had builded our houses, provided necessaries for our livelihood, reared convenient places for God's worship, and settled the Civill Government, one of the next things we longed for and looked after was to advance Learning and perpetuate it to Posterity; dreading to leave an illiterate ministry to the churches, when our present Ministers shall lie in the Dust." Chiefly to educate ministers, Harvard was founded in 1636, and for the same reason the clergy in Connecticut founded Yale (1701), the Presbyterians the College of New Jersey (now Princeton) in 1746, the Baptists Rhode Island College (now Brown) in 1764, and the adherents of the Dutch Reformed Rutgers (1766). Dartmouth (1769) was an outgrowth of Eleazer Wheelock's missionary work with the Indians in New Hampshire. The second of the colonial colleges to be founded, William and Mary in Virginia (1693), was largely the work of Dr. James Blair, a Scotch Anglican clergyman, who went to England to solicit money and a charter. The Episcopalians founded Kings College, now Columbia (1754), but Pennsylvania (1749), the inspiration for which came from Franklin, was free of direct sectarian control from the start and closer than the others to the scientific spirit of later days. In all of them the equipment was inadequate, the work elementary, and the curriculum dominated by the classics and by the fact that most of the students were training for the ministry.

Colleges, however, touched the lives of but very few colonists. Books, except the Bible, were not common among the masses, and their chief intellectual stimulation from reading came from the newspapers. The first newspaper, if we omit the short-lived *Public Occurrences,* which appeared in Boston in 1690, was the Boston *News Letter,* founded in 1704. Gradually their number increased until the larger towns in all the colonies usually boasted of some sort of weekly paper. Judged by modern standards, they were poor affairs, made up of advertising, a few local items, and stale news from Europe. Handicapped by lack of facilities for news-gathering and transportation, newspapers were also often impeded by government censorship. But American journalism was well sired, and the editors fought back. The arrest of John Peter Zenger in 1734 for criticizing the government resulted in a famous trial, the acquittal of Zenger, and a mighty blow for the freedom of the press. It was in journalism that the Boston-born editor of the *Pennsylvania Gazette* and the founder of one of the earliest American magazines first won wealth and fame. Benjamin Franklin, whom some have described as the "first civilized American," not only played a part in the history of American education and journalism, but through his experiments and interest in science, and by his work in improving the mail service as one of the two postmasters general (1753–1774) [6] in charge of the American colonies, made important contributions to American intellectual development.

On economic life, see H. U. Faulkner, *American Economic History,* Chaps. III–V; or E. C. Kirkland, *A History of American Economic Life,* Chaps. II, III, and, for

[6] Franklin, after independence was declared, was invited by Congress again to assume the position of Postmaster General.

contemporary material, G. S. Callender, *Selections from the Economic History of the United States,* 29–84. The best brief survey of the social history is C. M. Andrews, *Colonial Folkways* (Chronicles of America). A more nearly complete treatment is T. J. Wertenbaker, *The First Americans,* Chaps. II–XIII, and J. T. Adams, *Provincial* Society, Chaps. II–VIII, X, XI (both volumes in the History of American Life series). Also excellent are O. P. Chitwood, *A History of Colonial America,* Chaps. XX–XXVIII and Curtis Nettels, *The Roots of American Civilization,* Chaps. IX, X, XII, XIII, XV–XVIII. F. R. Dulles, *America Learns to Play,* Chaps. I–III, deals with recreation.

COLONIAL CIVILIZATION

Chapter V

THE BATTLE FOR EMPIRE

*Up to our own day American history has been
in a large degree the history of the colonization of
the Great West. The existence of an area of free
land, its continuous recession, and the advance of
American settlement westward, explain American development.*

FREDERICK JACKSON TURNER (1893)

*Are you ignorant of the difference between the
king of England and the king of France? Go see
the forts our king has established and you will
see that you can still hunt under their very walls.
. . . The English, on the contrary, are no sooner
in possession of a place than the game is driven
away. The forest falls before them as they advance, and the soil is laid bare so that you can
scarce find the wherewithal to erect a shelter for
the night.*

GOVERNOR DUQUESNE TO THE IROQUOIS

THE SIGNIFICANCE OF THE FRONTIER

If there is one factor above all others that has dominated American history, it is the movement of population toward the west. Unlike western
Europe, where dense populations press against one another, America
throughout her history exhibits rather a picture of population pressing on
land as the settlers moved forward to search for furs, clear the land for
agriculture, and exploit the mineral resources. It began with the first
settlers and has continued almost to our own day. Essentially economic as
was this process, its effects can be seen in every aspect of our life. For one
thing, it has prevented a stabilized condition. The continued movement
of people torn away from their early environment has produced a restless and fluid civilization that has inevitably influenced American psychology. Frontier life attracted not only the restless, but the energetic,
practical, buoyant, and optimistic spirits. Natural resources existed in

65

abundance; opportunities were everywhere at hand. One false start was but an incident; another gamble might bring success and wealth. In such conditions the economic theory of *laissez faire* was bound to persist. Frontier life was also favorable to democracy. Whatever men's condition in Europe or the East, on the frontier they must meet the same elemental struggle with nature. In the face of these stern frontier realities, as Turner has so well pointed out,[1] the settlers, no matter what their origin or race, tended to fuse into a composite type. Environment mastered the settler, and a distinct American civilization evolved, not a New France, a New Netherland, a New Spain, or even a New England, but a new nation and a new civilization. As the frontier pressed ever westward, the influence, the ties, even the prejudices of Europe were weakened and the way prepared for political freedom.

As American history unfolds, the influence of the westward movement will be apparent everywhere. The opening of new land created great sections with their own economic interests, which came in conflict with other and older sections, these conflicts often resulting in great political struggles and in one case in civil war. From Bacon's Rebellion of 1676 (page 39) to the farmers' strikes of 1933, these economic and political struggles have been continuously evident. The needs of the West have been the chief influence in the development of American transportation, which has sought to keep pace with, or precede, the frontier movement. Industrial history shows a constant westward movement of factory production, while labor history exhibits the influence of free land in preventing a surplus of labor and in maintaining wage scales. The struggle between the debtor West, with its demand for inflation and easy money, and the creditor East, with its insistence upon a stable currency, comprises at least nine tenths of the history of American currency and banking. From the West also has come the chief influence in the effort to control big business and in the willingness to experiment with democratic innovations. Finally, and this story will be partly told in the latter part of this chapter, the effect of the westward movement of population has inevitably precipitated clashes with northward moving Spaniards and with the southward moving French.

THE EARLY WESTWARD MOVEMENT

Historians have noted a certain regularity in the stages of westward advance. First come the hunter and trader in quest of furs and the missionary in search of converts. Typical of the fur men were Daniel Boone, who wandered through Kentucky before the advent of settlers, and the trappers of the Hudson's Bay Company who explored Oregon. Typical of

[1] F. J. Turner, *The Frontier in American History* (1921).

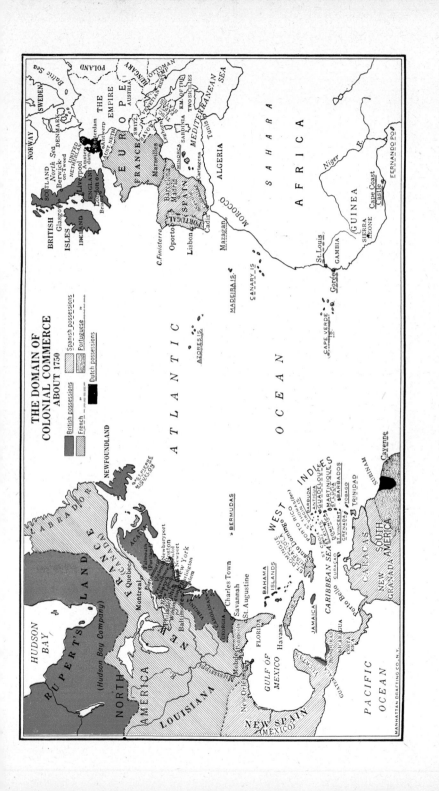

he missionaries were the Jesuit priests who labored with the Indians of he lake regions and the Franciscan friars who headed the Spanish advance n the Southwest. After the hunter and the missionary comes the rancher. Of all frontier products, livestock in the days before the railroad was the easiest to transport, and, from the "cow-pens" of the colonial South to the famous ranchers' frontier of the 1870s, a cattle industry is discernible on he edge of settlement. After the rancher come the farmer and, finally, with the development of towns and industry, the capitalist or industrialist. While these stages were typical, they were not inevitable, and many a frontier community saw representatives of all of these groups appearing simultaneously. There was also a certain regularity in the routes taken by he pioneers, for where possible the advance followed the navigable streams, and the first settlements were made on the fertile bottom lands of the rivers.

Although the westward movement commenced with the first settlers, it was almost a century before population had penetrated a hundred miles inland. By 1700, however, the land had been largely occupied to the "fall line" or head of navigation of the streams flowing into the Atlantic. With this preliminary work done, the westward movement was speeded during he eighteenth century as the wave of immigration set in from Germany and Ireland. It was in these years that the "Old West" was settled—the back country of New England, the Mohawk valley of New York, the counties of central Pennsylvania, the Shenandoah valley of Virginia and he piedmont region of the whole South. Finding the coast lands pre-empted, these immigrants moved on to the frontier. Pennsylvania caught he greatest number, but for many their abode here was temporary, as hey soon pushed south along the mountain valleys, where they were joined by westward moving frontiersmen from Virginia and the Carolinas. By the eve of the Revolution these sturdy settlers in the piedmont were ready to break through the mountain passes of the Alleghenies and descend upon the fertile lands of the Tennessee and Ohio valleys. It was in 1774 that James Harrod from Pennsylvania led a band of pioneers into Kentucky to establish the first permanent settlement in that region and on April 1, 1775, a few days before the battle of Lexington, that Daniel Boone and his followers began to build their cabins at Boonesboro.

Since American history is so largely written in terms of the westward movement, the methods under which the land was occupied and the terms under which it was granted are of great importance. In the New England colonies the ownership and with it the right to dispose of the land were transferred by the king to the holders of the charter, which, with reservation in New Hampshire, meant the colonial legislature. Colonization was ordinarily carried on by a group, rather than by individuals, and under

the supervision of the legislature. A group desiring to move west petitioned
the legislature for a grant of land. If the petition was favorably received
the surveyors laid out the bounds of a township, and the settlers distributed
the land among themselves. The site of a church was fixed, the boundary
of the common was determined, the house lots around the common were
assigned, and the remainder of the land was distributed among the settlers
each receiving a share in the upland, the meadow land, and the marsh
land and rights in the common. Reminiscent as were these towns of the
villages of medieval England, they differed in that ownership of part of
the land was absolute (fee simple). That part owned in common eventually gave way to individual ownership. This method of colonization had
the great advantage of promoting compact settlement on the frontier when
protection against the Indians was necessary. It also had the advantage
of careful regulation and lessened the disputes over land tenure. It had
the disadvantage of favoring only those persons who were religiously
and morally acceptable to the legislature, often powerful individuals who
were interested in land speculation and often never settled themselves
(page 39). This method of group or congregational settlement broke
down in the eighteenth century as land speculation became more rife
and as the legislatures became more anxious to settle the frontiers as a
protection against Indians and the claims of other colonies. In 1760, for
example, Governor Wentworth of New Hampshire laid out 130 towns
west of the Connecticut River (later Vermont) and sold them for cash to
speculators. In similar manner Massachusetts in 1762 auctioned off a group
of townships in the Berkshires to the highest bidders, when, says Turner
"the transfer from the social-religious to the economic conception was
complete, and the frontier was deeply influenced by the change to 'land
mongering.'"

Except in the chartered colonies of New England, the land was held
by some form of tenure from the king or from a proprietor to whom the
king had granted it. It found its way to the actual settler either by sale or
by grant, the latter usually carrying with it some form of quitrent.[2] As
the proprietors and royal governors were anxious to settle the land, the
grants were liberal and the quitrents small. Ordinarily any immigrant
who would come and settle was granted land, and he could usually obtain
more on payment of a small fee or by paying the passage of another immigrant. Whatever the laws were, they usually broke down before the
need for more room for expansion or before the speculative greed of
wealthy colonists. Though the typical farm in the middle and southern
colonies was small, much of the best land in the eighteenth century came

---

[2] A quitrent was a form of rent originating in Europe and was ordinarily a fixed amount of
money payable in commutation of certain feudal services.

under the control of large landowners, who in turn let it out under a
quitrent. This system had the advantage of promoting quick and easy occupation, but it had the disadvantage of enabling the wealthy through
favoritism or actual fraud to obtain large blocks. Three quarters of the
best land in New York, it was asserted, had been granted to thirty persons largely by a single governor, while examples of huge holdings in
other sections are found in the Morris estate in New Jersey, the Carroll
grants in Maryland, the Fairfax lands in Virginia, and the Granville
holdings in the Carolinas. This system also lacked the supervision and
regularity of that of New England.

A considerable proportion of frontiersmen were mere squatters on the
land, who had no title and who refused to pay quitrents. Small as the
quitrents might be, they seemed unjust and onerous to the settler who had
braved the hardships of frontier life, and attempts to collect them often
resulted in violent resistance. Many of the laws governing landholding,
including quitrents, primogeniture, and entails, disappeared, as we shall
see, with the Revolution, but the whole practice gave a background for the
later land system under which the vast public domain found its way into
private hands.

IMPERIAL RIVALRY

Even before the great eighteenth-century migration had occupied the
piedmont region of the English colonies, evidences were at hand of the
coming conflict between the empires of France and England in America.
By 1700 the French had established their long line of trading posts from
the mouth of the St. Lawrence westward along the Great Lakes and down
the Mississippi to its mouth. This vast inland empire, if it could be successfully established and maintained, would eventually close the interior
to the westward moving English. For the moment this was not a pressing
problem, for the English settlements were as yet hugging the seacoast.
Their fur traders, however, had already clashed with the *coureurs de bois,*
and the rivalry for furs was to become more intense. French trade and
power were to no small extent dependent on Indian allies who peopled
the region of the Great Lakes and Mississippi. Unfortunately the French
had won the enmity of the Iroquois and their dependent tribes, who occupied a wide band from the upper Hudson to Lake Erie, the best route
to the west, and who projected like a wedge into the territory that France
was anxious to dominate. The friendship of the Iroquois the English
soon learned to cherish and thus were enabled to tap the fur trade of the
inland regions. The rivalry for furs, however, was a phenomenon of
America; the long conflict with France, as far as this continent was concerned, was an imperial struggle primarily for control of the Ohio and

Mississippi valleys. In its large aspect it was part of a great world conflict for empire and trade, which was to extend from 1689 to the close of the Napoleonic wars in 1815. In America this conflict involved Spain as well as France, for the northward advance of Spain had brought clashes with the settlers of the Carolinas and Georgia and with the English fur traders of the South. Spain was also irritated by the piracy and smuggling rampant on the Spanish Main, much of which she attributed to the English.

Against this background of colonial friction must be placed the great European drama, where national rivalries, the problem of the "balance of power," the question of succession to the Spanish throne, the ambitions of Louis XIV or Frederick the Great, and innumerable other causes, major and minor, provided dynamite for the "Second Hundred Years' War." [3] Whatever may have been the immediate causes of each conflict, historians now assert that behind them all was a dominating rivalry between England and France for world empire, colonial commerce, and control of the seas. One of this long series of wars actually began in America, but wherever they began, America was inevitably drawn into the world struggle.

Events both in America and in Europe during the latter decades of the seventeenth century brought this inevitable clash. Under the Count of Frontenac, greatest of the French governors (1672–1682 and 1689–1698), the expansion of New France was pushed so rapidly that the English could hardly fail to see the handwriting on the wall. In England the reign of the Stuarts, subservient to the French king, came to an end with the "Glorious Revolution" of 1688 and the accession of William of Orange. William, who had headed the desperate defense of the Dutch against the aggression of Louis XIV, was delighted to continue the conflict in his new position, and, when the armies of Louis invaded the Rhenish Palatinate in 1689, England quickly joined a coalition against him. In this first war, known in America as King William's War, 1689–1697, both France and England were too busy fighting in Europe to pay much attention or lend much aid to their colonies in America, but the struggle here quickly took on the characteristics of the later colonial wars. In many ways the English had a distinct advantage; they outnumbered the French twelve to one and far surpassed them in the diversity and wealth of their economic

3	*Europe*		*America*
War of the League of Augsburg,	1689–1697		King William's War
War of the Spanish Succession,	1701–1713		Queen Anne's War, 1702–1713
War of the Austrian Succession,	1744–1748		King George's War
Seven Years' War,	1756–1763		French and Indian War, 1754–176.
War of the American Revolution,	1775–1783		Revolutionary War
War of the French Revolution,	1792–1802		
Napoleonic wars,	1803–1815		War of 1812

resources. They were also aided in the later phases of the struggle by the increasing interest taken by the home country in the colonial aspect. While France had her eyes fixed steadily on the possibility of European aggrandizement, England came even more clearly to see the struggle in terms of world empire. The French on the other hand had the advantages of a greater number of Indian allies, a more integrated government, and a more clear-cut plan of operations. The impossibility of co-ordinating the operations of thirteen colonial governments, to say nothing of effecting a smooth co-operation between the home government and the colonies, tended to offset the numerical and economic superiority of the English settlements.

All this the brilliant Frontenac clearly saw. His plan was to use his Indian allies in sudden attacks upon the scattered frontier settlements and by spreading a reign of terror hold back the English advance. With ruth-less severity the French and their savage allies ravaged during King William's War the frontier from Schenectady, New York, to Haverhill, Massachusetts, and Fort Loyal (now Portland), Maine. In retaliation the English organized expeditions against the French strongholds. Port Royal, Acadia, was captured in 1690, but an expedition by sea against Quebec and one by land against Montreal were disastrous failures. The treaty of Ryswick (1697) settled nothing, and within four years war broke out again (Queen Anne's War, 1702–1713). The French and Indians again raided the frontier towns, notably Deerfield, Massachusetts (1704), while the Spaniards, now allied with the French, attacked the frontier of the Carolinas. As in the previous war, the English responded by expeditions against Canada. The first against Quebec ran on the rocks at the mouth of the St. Lawrence; the second, composed of New England militiamen and British marines, again captured Port Royal, this time not to be returned. The treaty of Utrecht (1713), which closed the war, was the first of the great treaties by which England extended her colonial empire. From Spain she received Gibraltar and the island of Minorca, by which she might guard her Mediterranean commerce, and the exclusive privilege of supply-ing the Spanish-American colonies with slaves for thirty years. From France she received Acadia, Newfoundland, and the Hudson Bay region, a boon to English fur traders and New England fishermen. Important as the treaty of Utrecht obviously was, it did not settle the important question as to which nation was to dominate the continent. Nor did the third conflict, King George's War (1744–1748), which was promptly rec-ognized as indecisive.[4] After the loss of Acadia, France built the great fort of Louisburg on Cape Breton Island, off the mouth of the St. Lawrence,

[4] War between England and Spain (War of Jenkins's Ear) had begun in 1739, and there had been fighting on the Georgia frontier several years before France came into the struggle.

as an eastern outpost of her empire. As a rendezvous of French privateersmen, it was a constant menace to New England. To the amazement of both England and France, a New England expedition under William Pepperell captured it (1745). The capture of Louisburg was the most brilliant military stroke yet delivered by the colonies, and the return of the fort to France at the conclusion of the war aroused keen resentment in New England.

By the end of the third war two facts were evident. Handicapped by a sparse population spread over an immense area, the French were unable to withstand a carefully planned and well-executed effort directed at any single point of their possessions. This was clear from the ease with which the English had captured Port Royal and Louisburg. On the other hand, it was obvious that unless better co-operation could be achieved among the English colonies, the French menace might continue indefinitely. Such co-operation was difficult, for provincial jealousies, religious differences, and economic rivalries kept them apart. It had, nevertheless, once been achieved in the New England Confederation (1643–1684), when Connecticut, New Haven, Plymouth, and Massachusetts, in the face of Indian danger, had formed "a firme and perpetual league of friendship and amity for offense and defense, mutual advice and succor." Nor was England blind to the need, as is evident from her effort to join the colonies north of Pennsylvania into the short-lived Dominion of New England (page 42). In June of 1754, upon instructions from the British government, the governors of seven colonies met at Albany to negotiate an agreement with the Iroquois. At this famous Albany Congress, Benjamin Franklin proposed a scheme of colonial union that provided for a federal congress with powers to maintain a colonial army, deal with the Indians, control public lands, and levy necessary taxes for the general welfare. Accepted by the congress, the plan was rejected by the colonies, which were loath to surrender any of their power, and was coolly received by the British government, which feared to increase colonial strength in this way. It was significant, nevertheless, as a forerunner and model of the later Continental Congresses, which were to direct the Revolution against Great Britain.

THE FINAL STROKE

The Albany Congress had not yet adjourned when hostilities again broke out in America. The treaty of Aix-la-Chapelle, which closed King George's War, proved to be merely a truce, and in the succeeding years both nations attempted to strengthen their position in the debatable regions on the frontier. In 1749 Céloron de Bienville passed south from Lake Erie to the Great Miami burying leaden plates proclaiming the authority of

France, and four years later (1753) Governor Duquesne sent an expedition to occupy the Ohio valley. From Presque Isle, now Erie, Pennsylvania, the French built a series of forts south to the Allegheny, and ousted the English traders from Venango (now Franklin, Pennsylvania).[5] Under instructions from England, Governor Dinwiddie of Virginia sent the young Virginian surveyor, George Washington, to warn them off, and early in 1754 dispatched a body of backwoodsmen to build a fort at the forks of the Ohio. These were quickly ousted by the French, who completed the work and called it Fort Duquesne. An expedition of Virginia militia, the advance guard under Washington, started west, surprised a French scouting party at Great Meadows, and killed or captured them all, but were themselves captured shortly after, when a larger body of Frenchmen forced their surrender of Fort Necessity. Thus in the wilderness of western Pennsylvania there began one phase of a struggle that was soon to involve many European nations and to be fought on three continents.[6] England did not declare war on France until 1756, but that did not prevent active campaigning in America. In 1755 expeditions were launched against Crown Point on Lake Champlain, against Niagara, and against Fort Duquesne. The first two failed to accomplish their object, while the third, under General Braddock, was ambushed within seven miles of Duquesne and barely escaped annihilation. The only British accomplishment of the year was the removal of the Acadians and their distribution among the thirteen colonies. Fear of Canadian loyalty to the French led to this unnecessary cruelty.

In 1756 there arrived in America the Marquis de Montcalm, the greatest French soldier ever to fight on American soil. He quickly ousted the British from their most advanced post at Oswego and in the next year captured Fort William Henry at the southern end of Lake George. Four years of uninterrupted defeats in America, to say nothing of failure in India, finally brought the British government to a realization of the task, and to the head of the war office came the "great commoner" William Pitt. To Pitt the war was no mere defense of colonial frontiers; he saw it as a struggle for a continent, in fact, a struggle for world empire, successful only if the French were driven from America. His enthusiasm brought new energy into the British war machine and greater co-operation from

[5] Not only were English fur traders operating in this region, but land speculators were proposing to move into the Ohio valley. The Ohio Company, in which the Washingtons were interested, and the Walpole Company (Grand Ohio Company), in which Franklin and other Pennsylvanians were involved, had already received grants.

[6] In Europe the struggle was known as the Seven Years' War, with Frederick the Great of Prussia, aided by England, endeavoring to hold his conquest of Silesia against a coalition of France, Austria, Russia, Sweden, and many smaller German states. Spain, in a family alliance with France, was drawn in (1762).

colonial governments, as the resources of both England and America were
brought to bear on the struggle. By 1758 the new spirit was evident, and
the campaign was pushed on all fronts. Jeffrey Amherst with an adequate
force captured Louisburg, never again to be returned, and General Forbes
after cautiously cutting a road across Pennsylvania, reached Duquesne but
found it deserted. A British attempt to invade Canada along the Cham
plain-Richelieu route, however, was stopped by Montcalm at Ticonderoga
The year 1758, however, had brought into British hands the French out
posts on Cape Breton and the Ohio and had prepared the way for a con
centration the following year on the St. Lawrence valley.

With the summer of 1759, the struggle approached its climax. Three
main expeditions were planned. Wolfe with a fleet was to attack Quebec
by way of the St. Lawrence; Amherst with a strong force was to move
against the same stronghold by way of Lake Champlain; and a third con
tingent was to capture Fort Niagara and then come east along Ontario
and the river. Under this concentrated attack Montcalm was forced to
relinquish his outlying posts, and Niagara, Crown Point, and Ticonderoga
were captured during the summer. In the meantime Wolfe had for two
months unsuccessfully besieged Quebec. Finally, unobserved by the
French, he landed 4500 troops on the night of September 12, scaled the
cliffs above the town, and stood ready at daybreak on the Plains o
Abraham for the assault. In the ensuing battle both commanders lost thei
lives, but victory went to the British, who managed to hold Quebec dur
ing the winter. With the capture of Montreal by Amherst during the nex
summer, the whole of Canada was in British hands.

Although French rule in Canada was ended, the war continued ove
two years longer. The British fleet captured Cuba and the Philippine
from Spain and Martinique from France. In the treaty of Paris (1763)
which closed the long conflict, France ceded to Great Britain Canad
and all her claims east of the Mississippi except the Island of Orleans an
two little islands (St. Pierre and Miquelon) off the coast of Newfound
land, upon which her fishermen might dry their fish. To Spain she cede
New Orleans and her claims west of the Mississippi in compensation fo
the loss of Florida, which Spain ceded to Great Britain. Cuba was re
stored to Spain and the rich islands of Martinique and Guadaloupe t
France. So important were the sugar islands considered during the eight
eenth century that many were in favor of retaining the French West Indie
and returning Canada; but better counsel prevailed. The effect of this wa
was far-reaching. Except for a brief attempted revival under Napoleon
the treaty of Paris marked the end of the French empire on the continen
of North America, and it also ended the possibility of French control o
India. It freed the thirteen colonies from the menace of the French, opene

the way for a more rapid movement to the west, and set the stage for the Revolution. "They will not fail to shake off their dependence," predicted the French minister, Choiseul, "the moment Canada is ceded." Above all, it marked the emergence of England as the leading colonial and naval power of the world. Her history since that time has been largely an effort to maintain that position.

On the significance of the frontier the most important reading is in the brilliant essays of F. J. Turner, *The Frontier in American History,* Chaps. I–III. The westward movement of the colonial period is briefly surveyed in H. U. Faulkner, *American Economic History,* Chap. VI. For the French and Indian wars read G. M. Wrong, *The Conquest of New France* (Chronicles of America), or Curtis Nettels, *The Roots of American Civilization,* Chaps. XIV, XXI. The flavor of Parkman can be obtained in *Montcalm and Wolfe,* Chaps. XVIII ("Pitt"), XXIV ("Wolfe"), XXVII ("The Heights of Abraham"), XXVIII ("The Fall of Quebec").

COLONIAL CIVILIZATION

Chapter VI

THE CLASH OF INTERESTS

One single Act of Parliament has set people a-thinking, in six months, more than they have done in their whole life before.

JAMES OTIS

These worthy New Englanders ever feel as old Englanders ought to do.

LORD CHATHAM

THE ECONOMIC BACKGROUND

No simple formula explains the American Revolution. Why should the American colonies, enjoying under British rule a general economic prosperity and a political liberty far beyond what was usual in the eighteenth century, rise in revolution and fight a long war to establish their freedom? A simple answer would be that this economic prosperity and political freedom were endangered by the new British policy after 1763, but this does not take into consideration the long decades of friction between colony and crown, the innumerable laws passed by colonial legislatures that were nullified by the British government, and the subordination of colonial interests to those of Great Britain. It does not take into consideration many aspects of the American scene—the racial heterogeneity of the colonial people, the conflict of classes in the colonies, the independence engendered by frontier life, religious strains and stresses, and even the personality of the revolutionary propagandists. These and many other causes must be woven into the general pattern of the revolutionary scene before any clear picture can be obtained. "The Revolution," as John Adams asserted many years after the event, "was effected before the war commenced." It was "in the minds and hearts of the people."

As we reconstruct the background of the Revolution, the most important element is the economic relations between England and the colonies. As in other imperial nations of the seventeenth and eighteenth centuries, English statesmen, as we have already noted (page 52), were dominated by the theory of mercantilism—the questionable doctrine that if a nation was

76

to be great and powerful it must achieve, as far as possible, economic self-sufficiency and a favorable balance of trade. For this purpose—particularly to obtain commodities not available at home—colonies should be established, and, where necessary, their economic interests should be subordinated to those of the home country. The groundwork of English mercantilism was laid in three famous navigation acts passed by Parliament in the middle of the seventeenth century. The act of 1651 provided that all goods from Asia, Africa, and America imported into England or her dominions must be in ships of which the proprietor, the master, and the major portion of the crew were English, and that all goods from Europe imported into England or her dominions must come either in English ships or in those of the nation where the goods were produced. This measure of Cromwell was strengthened in 1660 by a new law providing that goods carried to and from England must be transported in ships that not only were owned and manned by Englishmen but had also been built in England or her colonies. These two strokes of policy not only sought to strengthen the English merchant marine and to keep the profits of the carrying trade in English (or colonial) hands, but also added a new feature—the insistence that certain colonial products be shipped only to England. These "enumerated articles" began with sugar, tobacco, cotton-wool, indigo, ginger, fustic, and other dyeing woods, but in later legislation naval stores, furs, molasses, and many other products were added. The unenumerated articles, chief of which were fish, grain, and rum, could be exported anywhere until 1766, but after that date only to the nations south of Cape Finisterre.

By another act, of 1663, England sought to monopolize the handling of imports into the colonies by placing high duties upon all European goods destined for the colonies unless they were brought *via* England and in British (including colonial) built and manned ships. In addition to these acts governing commerce, there were laws of Parliament that attempted to restrain the type of colonial manufacturing that came in competition with British industry. Such laws forbade the exportation of wool, the exportation of hats, and the erection of slitting or rolling mills or of furnaces for making steel. Particularly irritating to the colonists were the laws forbidding the establishment of mints and the issuance of paper money, the latter first applied to New England in 1751 and extended to the other colonies in 1764. Because of the unequal balance of trade between England and the colonies (page 52), the small amount of specie that found its way to the colonies was quickly drained out to England. Furthermore, this lack of adequate currency accentuated the inequality of trade by keeping the real price of colonial exports low and that of imports high. It also hindered the development in the colonies of a diversified economic life.

Ignoring a real need for paper currency, Parliament seemed interested merely in prolonging this situation favorable to England and in protecting the English creditor against possible inflation.

Students of colonial history have long debated the question of the extent of damage inflicted upon the economic life of the colonies by the British mercantile system. One school holds that little harm was done. America, they point out, was a new country, and, as such, her normal interests were in agriculture and in the extractive industries. Many of the English laws, they contend, were of great benefit to the colonies, as, for example, the bounties offered on naval stores, the monopoly of the English market reserved to certain colonial products, and the navigation acts that stimulated colonial shipbuilding. The English tariff laws, which shut out colonial foodstuffs, were, they admit, injurious, but the colonists eventually found other markets. The Molasses Act of 1733, passed at the behest of British sugar planters, which put prohibitive duties on molasses imported from other than the English islands and which would have seriously injured the New England rum industry, was evaded. The whole application of the laws in the colonies during the first half of the eighteenth century was rather lax, as England followed the lead of Robert Walpole and his policy *Quieta non movere* ("Let sleeping dogs lie"). Finally, they insist, the colonists should have been willing to make some sacrifices for the protection that they obtained from the British fleet. All this may be conceded, but the colonists were less likely to dwell upon the benefits than upon the injuries of British mercantilism. They knew that they were regarded as a source of cheap raw materials but at the same time as a market for high-priced manufactured goods. They knew that the navigation and trade acts affected freight rates and prices to their detriment, and they understood the hardships caused by the currency legislation. Many saw clearly that their prosperity depended upon breaking the British laws. Above all they realized that their interests were always secondary to those of England, a realization brought home by a century and a half of friction and by the vetoing of numerous bills passed by colonial legislatures. Historians have often likened the friction to a clash between metropolis and colony. It was the same sort of economic conflict that can be seen today between agriculture and industry, between city and country.

THE END OF "SALUTARY NEGLECT"

Great Britain emerged from the French and Indian War heavily in debt and confronted with new imperial problems. From the experience of the war the British government was convinced that the whole colonial system should be put on a more systematic basis, that the empire should be

strengthened and unified, and that the colonies should contribute according to their ability to the defenses of the empire. Colonial contribution,
particularly in the early years of the war, had been dilatory and ineffective;
none of the colonies, with the exception of Massachusetts, had made financial or other contributions in accord with their ability. Colonial legislatures had often seemed interested in winning victories over royal or
proprietary governors rather than over the French, while many private
citizens had no hesitancy in illegally trading with the enemy if profits
were to be made. The colonists, wrote one British general to Pitt, were "a
lawless set of smugglers, who continually supply the Enemy with what
provisions they want." Pitt, himself, asserted that the war had lasted three
years longer than necessary because American smugglers had frustrated
the work of the British navy. Hardly had the treaty of peace been signed
when a great Indian uprising under Pontiac laid waste the frontier of
the Northwest and necessitated a definite English policy with respect to
Indian control. These facts rather than any concerted plan to establish
British tyranny or increase the royal prerogative explain the legislation
and administrative policy that preceded the Revolution.

The first move of the British government was in the form of the Proclamation of 1763. Besides providing for the government of the new provinces (Quebec, East Florida, and West Florida), it laid down the policy
to be pursued with reference to the Indians and western land. Indian trade
was to be placed under imperial control and the traders licensed. Colonial governors were forbidden to warrant surveys or grant patents "for
any lands beyond the heads or sources of any of the rivers which fall
into the Atlantic Ocean from the west or northwest," nor was there to
be any private purchase of land from the Indians or settlement beyond
this line. This proclamation was undoubtedly an honest effort to solve
the Indian problem, but it was exceedingly irritating to speculators dream ·
ing of fortunes in western land and to frontiersmen who had already extended their settlements to the limits of the coastal slope and were ready
to move into the region beyond the mountains. It also aroused the opposition of powerful colonists, particularly in Virginia and Maryland, as
well as that of poverty-stricken frontiersmen. It was significant also in
that it involved imperial policing of the new provinces and the frontier.
Ten thousand soldiers, at a cost of £220,000 a year, it was estimated,
would be the added burden of this imperial policy to a nation already
heavily taxed.

To take care of this added burden the British government proposed to
tax the colonies. To British officials it seemed perfectly fair that the colonists should pay for their own defense, and Tory landowners and Whig
merchants both accepted with alacrity the proposals for heavier colonial

taxation. What both failed to realize was that the colonies, now relieved of the French menace, saw less need than ever for added taxation and were more ready than ever before to oppose it. The first of the new legislation, the Sugar Act of 1764, reduced the import duties on foreign molasses from sixpence to threepence a gallon. On the face of it this seemed more liberal than the act of 1733, but the new act the British government intended to enforce. British naval officers were to collect the customs duties, and cases arising from indictments for smuggling were to be tried by British Admiralty courts. The trade in molasses upon which the rum and slave business was built was an important part of the West Indian commerce, and any interference with it would be a serious blow to the economic life of the northern colonies. As the British West Indies supplied hardly one eighth of the needs of the colonists and at a price much higher than that of the French islands, colonial merchants for decades had smuggled in their molasses. Merchants who believed that even a tax of threepence would ruin their business were now thoroughly aroused. The act also placed duties on wines from the Azores and Madeira and upon white sugar, coffee, pimiento, and indigo from the foreign islands of the West Indies, significant because these commodities, wines especially, were important items in colonial trade. Just as the extraordinary prosperity of the war years was subsiding, along came the Sugar Act to accentuate the hard times.

The Sugar Act affected only the commercial colonies of the north and the merchants and manufacturers interested in molasses; the Stamp Act, however, which came in the next year, was to touch the pocketbook of all the colonies and all classes of people. It provided that all newspapers, pamphlets, and legal documents and many instruments of business should pay a stamp tax, and that the revenue should be expended exclusively for the purpose of "defending, protecting, and securing" the colonies. While the tax was in preparation, colonial agents strenuously objected, but, as they could offer no substitute except the old system of requisitions, the Grenville ministry proceeded with its plan. The act passed in March of 1765 with but little opposition. "Nothing of note in Parliament, but one slight day on the American taxes" was the contemporary comment of Horace Walpole.

The work of this "slight day," however, was to have immediate reverberations. Patrick Henry, after a fiery speech in the Virginia House of Burgesses, introduced resolutions, one of which declared "that the general assembly of this colony have the only and sole exclusive right and power to lay taxes and impositions upon the inhabitants of this colony." In Massachusetts the House of Representatives issued a call for a meeting of delegates to be held in New York to formulate a united opposition.

Throughout the colonies an organization known as the Sons of Liberty staged demonstrations and intimidated stamp agents, their activities in Massachusetts culminating in the destruction of the home of the conservative Lieutenant-Governor Hutchinson. Merchants agreed to buy no more goods from England until the Stamp Act was repealed. When the intercolonial congress met in October, it took the definite position that, as conditions made impossible their representation in the House of Commons, taxes never had been and never could be constitutionally imposed on the colonies, except by their respective legislatures. In the face of this unexpected and almost universal colonial opposition, which made the Stamp Tax a dead letter, and in the face of protests from British merchants, whose trade had been curtailed, Parliament succumbed, repealing the Stamp Act in 1766 and revising the Sugar Act downward. In spite of the opposition of Pitt and other British liberals, repeal was accompanied by a declaratory act asserting that Parliament "had, hath, and of a right ought to have full power and authority to make laws and statutes of sufficient force and validity to bind the colonies and people of *America,* subjects to the crown of Great Britain, in all cases whatsoever."

In their joy over the repeal of the Stamp Act, the colonists failed to give attention to this sweeping declaration. English conservatives, however, did not! A coalition cabinet headed by William Pitt had taken office soon after the repeal of the Stamp Act, but Pitt's illness had thrown the leadership into the hands of Charles Townshend, the brilliant, aggressive, but superficial Chancellor of the Exchequer. The hope of relieving British taxpayers at the expense of the colonies did not die easily, and Townshend determined to try again. Remembering that in the controversy over the Stamp Tax the colonists had differentiated between internal and external taxes, objecting to the Stamp Tax on the ground that it was an internal tax and a new departure by the British government, Townshend determined to follow the beaten paths. Tariff duties were placed on painters' colors, paper, glass, lead, and tea. Although not high, these taxes were on articles of common use and raised the cost of living. Far more dangerous than the taxes were other features of the Townshend acts (1767), which called for a reorganization of the customs service, with courts of admiralty established in the colonies to expedite cases of smuggling, and provided that the money raised was to be used to pay the expenses of the civil government. The latter provision was particularly obnoxious in that it would have removed from the colonies their chief weapon in their conflict with British officials. A special act suspended the New York assembly because it had refused to comply with a law of 1765 that had called for the adequate quartering of soldiers in the colonies. Irritating also was that part of one of the acts that reaffirmed the legality of writs of assistance—general warrants permitting customs officials to enter private premises in search of smuggled goods. Such general warrants might be effective in preventing smuggling, but they were also exceedingly dangerous to personal liberty. Great Britain had first used them in the colonies in an effort to curtail trading with the enemy during the French and Indian War. The colonists had immediately protested, and James Otis had thundered against them so eloquently (1761) that John Adams later called his speech the "opening gun of the Revolution."

The purport of all this was not lost on the colonies. Encouraged by the success of their opposition to the Stamp Act, they organized a similar resistance to the Townshend acts. Nonconsumption and nonimportation agreements were made by the citizens and merchants both in the North and in the South, and recalcitrant merchants were threatened or treated to a coat of tar and feathers. Radical politicians kept opposition at a white heat, while more conservative lawyers and publicists were not slow in pointing to the danger of these acts. John Dickinson, for example, in his *Letters from a Farmer in Pennsylvania,* while he urged that the colonists "behave like dutiful children," pointed out clearly that, if England maintained her right to tax imports, "the tragedy of American liberty is finished." The economic boycott of 1768–1769 was more than a voluntary movement; it was backed and encouraged by legislative bodies. British imports into New England and the middle colonies dropped from £1,-363,000 in 1768 to £504,000 in 1769, and created on the part of British merchants a strong backfire against the act in England. Once again the British government backed down; in April, 1770, all duties of the Townshend acts were repealed except that on tea, which was retained as a matter of principle to assert the power of the crown to tax the colonies.

Such in bare outline is a survey of the economic background of the American Revolution. In 1760 the American colonists were reasonably contented and loyal subjects of the British crown; a decade and a half later a proportion of them were in armed rebellion. As far as the economic causes of the Revolution are concerned, they lie primarily in the fact that the mercantile policy of the British government, which caused little annoyance in the seventeenth century, worked progressively in the eighteenth to restrict the operation of colonial merchant capitalism and so to imperil the economic prosperity of the mainland colonies as to lead directly to rebellion. The strengthening of the acts of trade and navigation and the currency acts relative to paper money, the promulgation of the proclamation of 1763, and the increasing interference with economic life all sacrificed the colonial merchant capitalist and land speculator to British interests. Since the well-being of laborers, mechanics, and fishermen was closely tied to the prosperity of the merchant capitalist, the participation of these groups in revolutionary activity is readily explained. In the South, British mercantilism operated to the detriment of plantation-owners, who must sell their commodities in the British market at low prices and purchase needed commodities at high prices. Few of them escaped crushing debt, and, when the Proclamation of 1763 blasted the hope of re-establishing their fortunes through the usual method of land speculation, Southern planters easily took the leadership in rebellion.[1]

THE POLITICAL ASPECT OF THE REVOLUTION

It is relatively simple to note the causes of economic discontent and to point out the specific pieces of legislation that aroused opposition in the colonies. The general political story is more complicated. Famous English Whig historians, and they have been often followed in America, have pictured the struggle as a great battle for human liberty, in which the British king and the Tory party were intent upon abridging the freedom of Englishmen and in restoring the royal prerogative, while Whig statesmen and the American colonies were fighting to preserve this hard-won liberty. Such an interpretation hardly bears close scrutiny. It is true enough that George III was tired of the long domination of Parliament by the Whigs and was active in building through political patronage a new Tory party in which he might take an active part, but there was never any question in England of the restoration of divine-right monarchy. Nor was there any noticeable difference between the Whigs and the Tories regarding the legislation that concerned the American colonies. Both parties took the point of view that it was perfectly legal for Parliament to legislate for the colonies in any way it saw fit, to impose navigation laws and new taxes, if necessary, and for the crown to veto colonial laws. These prerogatives the English government had been exercising for a century and a half, and the legislation that preceded the Revolution was simply a continuation of such practice. With respect to taxation, there was nothing new in the legislation except the Stamp Tax, and that was repealed within a year.

Nor was the policy toward America directed by George III through subservient ministers. The king seems to have had some influence in the passage of the Declaratory Act, and undoubtedly approved of the general policy, but the leaders of both parties believed in the authority of Parliament. When acts were repealed and leniency shown, it was for reasons of practical policy and in no way a surrender of theoretical rights. George Grenville, who originated the policy of more effective imperial control,

---

[1] L. M. Hacker, "The First American Revolution," *Columbia University Quarterly*, XXVII, No. 3, 259–295.

was an efficient administrator, who rose to power through his own ability and was cordially hated by the king. Lord Rockingham, head of the government that repealed the Stamp Act but *also* passed the Declaratory Act, was a Whig, as was Charles Townshend, whose policies were more far-reaching than Grenville's. Townshend, it is interesting to note, was Chancellor of the Exchequer in a cabinet headed by Pitt, who was famous as a friend of leniency toward the colonies. The government during these years of controversy was generally headed by coalition cabinets, whose policies looked toward greater imperial integration but whose acts were dominated by the interests of British taxpayers and merchants rather than by colonial desires. In general, the politicians who surrounded George III were above the average in ability, and any desire to establish tyranny in America was far from their minds. As a rule, they were industrious but unimaginative bureaucrats who took their work seriously. "Grenville lost America," said a contemporary official, "because he read the American dispatches, which none of his predecessors had done."

In America the political situation and the constitutional arguments of political leaders were even less clear-cut than in England. The long clash of interests between the colonists and the representatives of the British government had developed a spirit of antagonism that quickly came to a head with the imposition of the Stamp Tax and the Townshend duties. Opposition to these acts seems to have been almost universal. During the agitation against British legislation, wealthy merchants and political leaders had called upon the poor and unenfranchised, and these classes, having tasted power, were not to be denied. Throughout the whole controversy between England and the colonies it is possible also to see a struggle in the colonies between social and economic groups. "The Revolution," as one authority has well said, "was not merely a question of 'home rule'; it was also a question who should rule at home." The unenfranchised found ready leaders in men like Samuel Adams and Patrick Henry, and it is possible to discern the political ambitions of radical leaders playing an important part in colonial discontent. The "mobish turn" of the people of Boston, which Governor Shirley had early noticed, explains in part a conservative reaction that produced many Tories when the break finally came.

During the years previous to the break with Great Britain, the cry of "No taxation without representation!" was often raised—an excellent example of the influence of economics upon politics. It was, however, not taxation without representation that the colonies objected to; it was taxation by anybody at any time. From the time of first settlement, America had been taxed without representation. Except in theory the British Parliament of the eighteenth century was not a representative body, and American agitators knew that there was but slight likelihood that American representation would ever be achieved. Objection to the enforcement of old taxes and the imposition of new ones simply brought forward whatever constitutional arguments seemed effective at the moment. A recent student [2] has maintained that the colonials held at different times three different constitutional theories in defense of their rights. Before 1765 they based their arguments on the privileges granted to them by their charters. From 1765 to 1774 they were inclined to follow the theory that Parliament had authority to legislate for the colonies but in the exercise of such authority was restricted in the colonies, as it was in England, by the legal precedents of the English constitution and by the higher law of natural rights. In other words, Americans, regardless of their charters, were entitled to all the rights of Englishmen "by the law of God and nature, by the common law, and by act of Parliament." As such a theory was inconsistent with their opposition to much that was in no way a violation of "natural rights" or common law, the constitutional arguments finally came to rest on the principle that Great Britain had no right through the Parliament to interfere in any way with the internal affairs of the colonies. Colonial legislatures, in other words, were coequal with the British Parliament in a British commonwealth of nations. Governor Bernard saw this clearly when he wrote: "In Britain the American governments are considered as Corporations empowered to make by-laws, existing only during the Pleasure of Parliament. . . . In America they claim to be perfect states, not otherwise dependent upon Great Britain than by having the same King." No clear-cut chronological development, of course, can be traced. All these arguments were being used during all this period.

THE CLIMAX APPROACHES

Whatever the constitutional arguments may have been, they meant little unless specific acts of the British government were sufficiently onerous to arouse protest. The Townshend acts had been so considered, and the reaction had been immediate. The quartering of troops in Boston in 1768 to lend aid in the enforcement of law was also considered an example of tyranny and was bitterly resented. Eighteen months of continual friction between citizens and soldiery culminated (March 5, 1770) in the "Boston Massacre," when a group of soldiers, goaded beyond endurance, fired into a mob, killing five and wounding several. Distorted accounts of this event spread throughout the colonies and did much to inflame the popular mind. Despite the Boston Massacre and the fact that the most objectionable and tyrannical aspects of the Townshend acts, including the

[2] C. H. McIlwain, *The American Revolution: A Constitutional Interpretation* (1923).

tax on tea, still remained on the statute books, opposition to British policy collapsed rapidly after 1770. Nonimportation broke down, trade was resumed on a large scale, and prosperity returned. Although the theory of Parliamentary taxation had been established, there were few complaints. Radical political leaders were deserted by the prosperous merchants, who were making money in spite of import duties and who were beginning both to dread the activities of the mobs that they had so freely used in previous years and to fear the rising consciousness of the poorer classes. The more conservative American patriots, including men like Franklin, advised quiet, on the theory that England, unless forced to meet the issue, would go no farther, and that the increasing wealth and population in America would eventually and inevitably settle the dispute in America's favor.

During this period of conservative reaction there were many evidences that at least a temporary *rapprochement* with the British government might be effected. It was prevented by two influences—the activities of revolutionary agitators and the stupidity of the British government and its American agents. In Massachusetts Samuel Adams seized every opportunity to maintain a running fight with the governor in an effort to keep the revolutionary spirit alive. He denounced the attitude of the conservatives as a "tame opposition to an unjust imposition" and answered their arguments by the statement, "When our liberty is gone, history and civilization alike will teach us that an increase in inhabitants will be but an increase in slaves." In 1772 he carried a vote in a Boston town meeting to create a Committee of Correspondence to exchange views and information with other towns in the colony. Hutchinson described the Boston Committee of Correspondence as in part composed of "deacons" and "atheists" and "blackhearted fellows whom one would not chose to meet in the dark," but they did their work well, and it was not long before every town of importance in the colony had its committee. In the following year the Virginia House of Burgesses, through the influence of Thomas Jefferson and Patrick Henry, carried a resolution to appoint a committee for Virginia to correspond with similar committees elsewhere on matters of common welfare. Other colonies followed Virginia, and the movement of colonial opposition took on new life. Not only so, but the committees gave a strong impetus toward a colonial integration that later made possible a united resistance. "Massachusetts," says Bancroft, "organized a Province; Virginia promoted a confederacy. Were the several Committees but to come together, the world would see an American Congress."

The business man's truce was also imperiled by royal governors, particularly Hutchinson of Massachusetts, whose acts, often unwise and illegal, were forcing the issue and giving strength to the radicals. There was likewise enough friction between customs officials and colonial importers to keep the issue alive. In Rhode Island the tactless and unpleasantly officious commander of the British naval ship *Gaspée* aroused the ire of the merchant class, and, when the *Gaspée* unluckily ran aground on the night of June 9, 1772, she was boarded by eight boatloads of armed men, who took possession and burned her to the water's edge. A special royal commission was sent to investigate the affair, but, in spite of the fact that everyone in Rhode Island knew who the culprits were, little evidence was collected, and no convictions followed.

It was the British government, however, that unwittingly ended the truce, with the help, of course, of Adams and Hutchinson. That famous and much favored corporation, the East India Company, which had long exploited without interference the great riches of India, had, through bad management and extravagance, fallen upon evil days. Its bankruptcy would drag down with it a horde of English capitalists and politicians, and such an event must be forestalled. The company had 17,000,000 pounds of surplus tea stored in its warehouses, and among the measures adopted to save the company was one that gave it the right to sell directly to America and remitted the customary shilling-a-pound tax on all tea transshiped to the colonies. This would help the company find a market and at the same time provide the colonists with cheaper tea than they had ever enjoyed. Before the Tea Act of 1773 the colonists paid four profits—to the East India Company, the English middleman, the American middleman or importer, and the local shopkeeper. Allowing the East India Company to import directly into the colonies eliminated two groups of middlemen as well as two profits. Furthermore, such an arrangement would inevitably give the East India Company a monopoly on the importation of tea into the colonies. If the company could be given a monopoly on tea, why not on other commodities that it transported from India? If a monopoly could be conferred upon the East India Company, a similar monopoly on other commodities might be granted to any company. Obviously, other principles besides that of taxation were involved. Instantly the most powerful class in the seaport towns was aroused. Merchants like Hancock, who had been importing and paying the duty on tea, now strenuously opposed the Tea Act, and their opposition, in conjunction with the activities of the radical politicians, led directly to the break with Great Britain.

By the time the tea ships arrived, the colonists were ready for them. So much opposition had developed that the agents in New York, Philadelphia, and Charleston had resigned, and, when the tea arrived, there was no one to receive it. At New York a vigilance committee dumped the tea of one vessel into the harbor but allowed a second vessel to return without unloading; at Charleston the cargo was landed, stored in a government warehouse, and some years later sold at auction for the benefit of the patriot cause. At Annapolis the tea ship, *Peggy Stewart,* with its cargo, was burned at the behest of the patriots.[3] Under Samuel Adams the opposition in Boston speedily took form when a town meeting refused to allow the tea to be landed. The ship arrived on November 28, 1773, and the unpopular Governor Hutchinson, whose two sons were among the company's agents, refused to allow the ships to return to England. The deadlock continued until the night of December 16, when Adams rose at a large mass meeting in the Old South Church and said, "This meeting can do nothing more to save the country." Whether this was a signal for action is unknown, but immediately a body of citizens disguised as Indians boarded the vessels and dumped the cargo of 342 chests of tea into the water.

The "Boston tea party" was a direct challenge to British authority, as Adams meant it to be, and the results were momentous. British public opinion was aroused against the colonists, particularly Massachusetts, and the die-hard conservatives in the British government were convinced that punishment should be swift and severe. Many American patriots regretted the incident, and firm friends of the colonies in England felt that the act was quite unjustified. The British government, now under the leadership of Lord North, responded immediately with four coercive measures or "intolerable acts," as they were called in the colonies. The first, the Boston Port Bill, to go into effect in June, 1774, transferred the capital of the colony and the customs house of Boston from Boston to Salem and closed the port of Boston to all commercial navigation until the tea, valued at around £18,000, should be paid for. The second, the Massachusetts Government Act, lessened the power of the people by providing that the governor's councilors, hitherto nominated by the assembly, should be appointed solely by the crown, that minor judicial and executive officers should be appointed and not elected, and that town meetings must not meet, except for election of officers, without the consent of the governor. The third, the Administration of Justice Act, gave the governor power to send officials charged with capital offenses to England for trial. The fourth, which applied to all the colonies of North America, revived the old Quartering Act of 1765 and authorized the governors to requisition certain buildings for the use of British troops, "a reasonable allowance for the same" being made. It was not without sig-

[3] Marylanders take pride in the fact that the disposition of the *Peggy Stewart* tea was not done in secrecy or disguise but discussed openly in popular assembly, the owners of the tea and vessel forced to apologize, and the vessel finally fired at the hand of its owner, Anthony Stewart.

nificance that Hutchinson was removed and that General Gage, commander of the British troops in North America, was appointed governor of Massachusetts.

A fifth act, the Quebec Act, which came in the same year and which aroused much opposition in the colonies, had nothing to do wth the situation in Boston, being simply the result of a long study as to the best method of handling the problem of Canadian administration. New France was organized into the Province of Quebec, and to it was attached the region between the Ohio and the Great Lakes. The Catholic Church was established by law; French law, which meant trial without jury, was to be used in civil cases, and the government was to be under a royal council with no elective assembly. Although the Quebec Act ended the restrictions of the Proclamation of 1763 for the region north of the Ohio, it was resented by many because Virginia, New York, Connecticut, and Massachusetts all had claims upon some parts of that territory. The recognition of the Catholic Church—indeed, the British government's establishment of any church—offended the religious sensibilities of the New Englanders, and the establishment of autocratic government was considered a dangerous precedent by the liberty-loving Englishmen in the thirteen colonies.

In organizing the spirit of opposition to British laws, the committees of correspondence had done their work well. From New Hampshire to South Carolina came sympathy and aid to the distraught people of Boston. Conservative merchants were willing to pay for the tea, but public sentiment was too strong for them. There had been some talk of a continental congress in the letters of the committees of correspondence, and during May the suggestion for calling such a body came from many quarters. The Virginia House of Burgesses set aside June 1, the day when the Boston Port Bill was to go into effect, as a day of prayer and fasting, and for this was dissolved by the governor. Meeting unofficially at the famous Raleigh Tavern in Williamsburg, it sent out a summons for a congress to consider the "united interests of America." The Massachusetts legislature, behind locked doors, and while the royal secretary stood outside reading the governor's order dissolving it, voted to send representatives. In only three of the colonies were the legislatures in session, but elsewhere (except in Georgia) conventions were called, which elected delegates.

The body that convened September 5 at Philadelphia contained many of the ablest colonial leaders and represented a fair cross section of the opposition to British policy in America. In its councils sat John and Samuel Adams and Elbridge Gerry of Massachusetts, Roger Sherman of Connecticut, John Jay and Philip Livingston of New York, John Dickinson and Joseph Galloway of Pennsylvania, George Washington and Patrick Henry of Virginia, and the Rutledges of South Carolina. The body was about equally divided between those who advocated an active resistance to British policy and those who favored conciliation, but the former, led by the Adamses of Massachusetts and Henry of Virginia, proved the more skillful and aggressive and won the day. "Government," said Henry, "is dissolved . . . the distinctions between Virginians, Pennsylvanians, and New Englanders, are no more. I am not a Virginian, but an American."

The more radical group secured the endorsement of the "Resolves" adopted by Suffolk County, Massachusetts, declaring no obedience must be rendered to the "Coercive Acts" and advocating forcible resistance. They succeeded in defeating by the narrow margin of one vote the conservative proposal of Joseph Galloway that the colonies form a union much like the one advocated earlier by Franklin at Albany (page 72) and thus establish their rights within the empire. The congress then adopted a nonintercourse agreement, recommending that after December 1, 1774, no goods be imported from Great Britain, and that after September 10, 1775, no exports be shipped except rice to the British West Indies. A "Declaration of Rights and Grievances" was drawn up, setting forth the political theory of the colonists, a petition to the king was framed, and addresses were sent to the people of Great Britain, Quebec, and the thirteen colonies. Although the delegates affirmed their loyalty to the king, there was no doubt that the more radical element had gained control. Said one conservative delegate from Maryland: "Adams with his crew, and the haughty Sultans of the South, juggled the whole conclave of the delegates." The congress adjourned in late October to meet again in the following May if their grievances were not redressed.

Before the next congress could assemble, however, the controversy had passed from petitions and addresses to the field of battle. General Gage, a mild and conciliatory officer who had married an American woman, arrived in Boston in May of 1774 with instructions to enforce the acts of Parliament. His efforts to handle an extremely difficult situation were to prove futile before the carefully organized opposition and the rising bitterness of the colonists. Urged on by the government, but against his better judgment, Gage determined on a military demonstration. Hearing that military stores were being collected at Concord, he dispatched an expedition of about 1000 men on the night of April 18 to destroy them. The patriots, waiting for such a move, quickly sent out the alarm, and, when the British reached Lexington at daybreak, they encountered a band of militia on the common. A brief skirmish ensued, which left eight of the minute men killed and ten wounded. Pressing on to Concord, the British destroyed what stores had not been removed, and after a fight at Concord bridge commenced the long retreat to Boston. By now the countryside was thoroughly aroused, and the militia were swarming from all directions and directing a deadly fire at the British regulars from behind rock, fence, and tree. With the aid of reinforcements, the British finally reached Boston, followed by the minute men, who closed in around the city to commence a siege that was to result eleven months later in the evacuation of the British. Long years of controversy had culminated in the clash of arms, and the fighting was to continue until independence was achieved.

THE CAUSES OF REBELLION SUMMARIZED

Concerning the causes of the American Revolution enough has been said to make it evident that the easy explanations of earlier days are hardly sufficient. It did not come because an English king sought to regain a lost power. English history disproves that. It did not come because of "taxation without representation." From the beginning of their history the colonies had been taxed without Parliamentary representation. There was nothing new in the British taxation after 1763 except the Stamp Tax, and that was quickly discontinued. Even the sounder theory that the rebellion came because of the adverse economic effect of the British navigation and trade acts hardly satisfies the careful student. Nor was the situation wholly covered by the explanation of an aged veteran, who many years after the event was asked by a student of history:

"Captain Preston, why did you go to the Concord fight, the 19th of April, 1775?" The old man, bowed beneath the weight of years, raised himself upright, and turning to me said: "Why did I go?" "Yes," I replied: "My histories tell me that you men of the Revolution took up arms against 'intolerable oppressions.'" "What were they? Oppressions? I didn't feel them." "What, were you not oppressed by the Stamp Act?" "I never saw one of those stamps, and always understood that Governor Bernard put them all in Castle William. I am certain I never paid a penny for one of them." "Well, what then about the tea-tax?" "Tea-tax! I never drank a drop of the stuff; the boys threw it all overboard." "Then I suppose you had been reading Harrington or Sidney and Locke about the eternal principles of liberty." "Never heard of 'em. We read only the Bible, the Catechism, Watts's Psalms and Hymns and the Almanack." "Well, then, what was the matter? and what did you mean in going to the fight?" "Young man, what we meant in going for those red-coats was this: we always had governed ourselves, and we always meant to. They didn't mean we should." [4]

The American Revolution was not a sudden outbreak; its root causes run back through the whole length of colonial history. First must be noted the clash of economic interests. The acts of Parliament that attempted to

[4] Mellen Chamberlain, *John Adams, the Statesman of the American Revolution* (1898), 248–249.

control colonial navigation, commerce, manufacturing, and finance were in some ways advantageous to the colonies, and certain disadvantages were overcome by smuggling or by the fortunate exploitation of the West Indian market. There was, nevertheless, throughout the whole period a definite subordination of colonial economic interests to those of the home country, which often worked a real hardship and was a constant cause of friction and irritation. In the second place, there was the long controversy between the colonial legislatures intent upon maintaining or increasing their own power and the agents of proprietor or crown. The activities of these turbulent legislatures and their conflicts with British officials mirror with great accuracy the growing divergence of interests between crown and colony and gave rise to the various schools of political theory upon which the colonists based their demand for home rule. In the third place we note a gradual growing apart as a new civilization developed in America and an increasing lack of understanding between the colonies and the homeland. The problems faced by the settlers in the new land were not those of England, and they were determined to meet them in their own way.

There was, for example, friction on religious grounds. Many of the colonists had migrated to America to escape religious persecution; they were dissenters from the established churches, and some of them, as the Plymouth Separatists and the German Protestant sects, were dissenters from dissenters. Religious rebels are not likely to submit tamely to what they may consider political tyranny. The population, it must be remembered, was far from homogeneous. By the time of the Revolution at least one fourth of the white population had come, not from England, but from Holland, Sweden, Germany, and Ireland, many of the latter with an inherited hostility to Great Britain. The older stock was largely English, but even in New England the bulk of the people, comments a contemporary historian, "knew little of the mother country, having only heard of her as a distant Kingdom, the rulers of which had, in the preceding century, persecuted and banished their ancestors to the woods of America." Innumerable economic, political, and social forces were driving the two peoples apart.

Finally, there was the immediate train of events that prefaced the break with England. Other English colonies—Canada, Australia, New Zealand, South Africa—have found their interests also at odds with the home country but have remained within the empire. Britain's willingness to bow to their wishes and grant virtual home rule in part explains this continuing loyalty. In the American colonies an attempt to tighten imperial supervision at an inopportune moment, coupled with specific legislative acts obnoxious to the colonists, was sufficient to cause the break.

With all these causes the rebellion might never have come without the increasing efforts of revolutionary agitators of the type of Samuel Adams and Patrick Henry, men skillful in organizing discontent, full of confidence in the destiny of America, and ever alert to try the issue with the British government.

Perhaps the most brilliant single chapter on the causes of the Revolution is in Charles and Mary Beard, *The Rise of American Civilization,* Chap. V. In C. H. Van Tyne, *The Causes of the War of Independence,* Chaps I–III, XIV, the political is emphasized; in H. U. Faulkner, *American Economic History,* Chap. VII, and in Curtis Nettels, *The Roots of American Civilization,* Chap. XXII, the economic. A. M. Schlesinger, *New Viewpoints in American History,* Chap. VII, is an excellent summary, while H. E. Egerton, *The Causes and Character of the American Revolution,* Chaps. I–V, gives an Englishman's interpretation. Many of the most important documents are in H. S. Commager, *Documents of American History,* Vol. I, 42–90, and in S. E. Morison, *Sources and Documents Illustrating the American Revolution 1764–1788,* 1–148.

Chapter VII

REVOLUTION

Let them know that while every colony honors the mother city so long as it is well treated, yet that if wronged, it becomes alienated; for colonists are not sent out to be slaves of those who are left behind, but to be their equals.

THUCYDIDES

THE DIE IS CAST

The news of Lexington spread rapidly, strengthening everywhere the spirit of revolt. In Vermont Ethan Allen on his own initiative raised a company of "Green Mountain Boys" and captured Ticonderoga, May 10, 1775, and Crown Point two days later. A gathering of militiamen in Mecklenburg County, North Carolina, declared the existing civil and military commissions null and void, and established a local government "until laws shall be provided for us by the Congress"—an action that was virtually a declaration of independence. In the meantime the siege of Boston was pushed vigorously. To oust the British it would be necessary to occupy and hold the heights behind Boston, either at Charlestown or at Dorchester, and, on the night of June 16, Colonel Prescott occupied Breed's Hill in Charlestown.[1] Against the bombardment of the British fleet the colonials held their position throughout the morning of the June 17. In the afternoon Gage ordered Sir William Howe to storm the position. Twice the British regulars advanced only to be driven back by the withering fire of the militia. On the third attempt the Americans, their ammunition exhausted, retreated. The British held Breed's Hill, which enabled them to remain in Boston, but their loss of over 1000 killed or wounded was so severe and the fighting qualities displayed by the American militia so great that the colonials considered the battle as good as a victory.

On the day that Ethan Allen captured the fortress of Ticonderoga the second Continental Congress met at Philadelphia. Its powers, if it had

[1] Prescott's objective was Bunker Hill, which has given its name to the battle, but he occupied Breed's Hill by mistake and here the battle was fought.

any, were extremely vague; it represented, said Bancroft, "nothing more than the unformed opinion of an unformed people." But no abler group of representatives has probably ever assembled on the American continent, and, confronted by a war actually existing, they speedily took charge of the situation. On the request of Massachusetts they assumed responsibility for the troops around Boston, appointed George Washington as commander-in-chief of the continental army, and authorized an expedition against Canada. Massachusetts and New Hampshire, asking for advice respecting the formation of a new government, were urged to proceed "until a governor of his Majesty's appointment shall consent to govern the province according to its charter." From the pens of John Dickinson and Thomas Jefferson came a stirring Declaration of the Causes and Necessity of Taking up Arms, and upon the advice of Dickinson another petition was addressed to the king.

Despite the actions of the Congress and the fact that war actually existed, independence, except in the minds of the extreme radicals, seemed far from the thoughts of the delegates. "We have not raised armies with ambitious designs of separating from Great Britain, and establishing independent states," said the Declaration of Causes, and this must be accepted as sober truth. "It is well known," said Jefferson in 1782, "that in July, 1775, a separation from Great Britain and the establishment of a Republican Government had not yet entered any person's mind." As late as the autumn of that year the legislatures of at least five states were on record against independence, and in January, 1776, the king's health was still being toasted at the officer's mess presided over by Washington. Whatever may have been the feeling of the majority of the delegates, events had gone too far for an amicable settlement. The king refused to receive the petition addressed to him by Congress. In August he issued a proclamation declaring the colonies in a state of rebellion, and in September he hired 20,000 Hessians to put down the revolt. During the following month the British navy, without provocation, burned Falmouth Harbor (Portland, Maine), and in January it burned Norfolk, Virginia. On December 22, 1775, an act of Parliament forbade all trade and intercourse with the colonies. "It throws thirteen colonies out of the royal protection," said John Adams when he received news of this act, "and makes us independent in spite of supplications and entreaties."

He was right. Both sides had gone too far to turn back. Not satisfied with a mere defense of their rights at home, the American colonists had launched an expedition against Canada. One column under Montgomery captured Montreal and proceeded toward Quebec, where it was joined by a second force under Arnold. On the last day of the year, in a blinding snowstorm, the combined forces attempted unsuccessfully to storm the town. Failure to capture Quebec necessitated retreat, but Arnold so effectively disputed the way that the British forces in Canada were prevented from co-operating with their fellow countrymen on the lower Hudson during the campaign of 1776. By summer the South had also experienced the clash of arms. Whigs and Tories of North Carolina had engaged in sharp battle at Moore's Creek in February, and in June the British fleet unsuccessfully attempted to occupy Charleston. Throughout the winter Washington had tightened his lines around Boston. Determined to end the siege, he seized and held Dorchester Heights in March, with the result that Howe, who had succeeded Gage in command, evacuated the city and sailed for Halifax with some 1000 Boston loyalists.

A year had elapsed since that fateful morning at Lexington, and much had happened to solidify the patriot cause and strengthen the desire for independence. No influence was more potent than the powerful pen of that radical English immigrant, Thomas Paine. His pamphlet *Common Sense,* published in January and read everywhere throughout the colonies, was a ringing denunciation of British legislation, of monarchical rule, and of George III, "the Royal Brute of Great Britain," and was a clarion call to separate from the mother country. "The sun," said Paine, "never shined on a cause of greater worth. . . . 'Tis not the concern of a day, a year, or an age; posterity are virtually involved in the contest, and will be more or less affected even to the end of time. . . . Freedom hath been hunted around the Globe. Asia and Africa have long expelled her.—Europe regards her like a stranger, and England hath given her warning to depart. O! receive the fugitive, and prepare in time an asylum for mankind."

The growing sentiment toward independence led Congress on May 15 to advise the colonies to establish themselves into states with reorganized governments based upon the consent of the people. Virginia had already called a convention and on the same day declared herself independent. One of her delegates to Congress, Richard Henry Lee, pursuant to instructions from his home state, rose on June 7 and moved that "these United Colonies are, and of right ought to be, free and independent states; that they are absolved from all allegiance to the British crown; and that all political connection between them and the state of Great Britain is, and ought to be, totally dissolved." The radical Whigs were not yet strong enough to secure immediate adoption, and it was not until July 2 that Lee's resolution was accepted. In the meantime a committee was appointed to propose a declaration, which was adopted on July 4, 1776.

The Declaration of Independence, almost entirely the work of Jefferson, divides itself into three parts. The first is a statement of the radical philosophy of the seventeenth century: "that all men are created equal, that they are endowed by their Creator with certain unalienable Rights, that among these are Life, Liberty and the pursuit of Happiness—that to secure these rights, Governments are instituted among Men, deriving their just powers from the Consent of the governed,—That whenever any Form of Government becomes destructive to these ends, it is the Right of the People to alter or abolish it, and to institute new Government." The second part of the Declaration is a list of twenty-seven grievances against the British king, and the third is the formal declaration of independence.

Viewed from the high point of twentieth-century historical and ethnological research, the Declaration is not wholly convincing. Only in a limited sense, if at all, have men ever been created equal, nor are they endowed with any rights except those they can obtain and hold, nor were governments, in spite of certain American precedents, originated to secure these "unalienable rights." The twenty-seven grievances, in the opinion of Morison and Commager, "are scarcely those which appeal to the student of that period as fundamental; examined in the candid light of history many seem distorted, others inconsequential, some unfair." [2]

To place the grievances entirely upon the head of George III is obviously unfair, as has already been pointed out (page 83), and seems to have been done because colonial political theory in the last phases of the revolutionary movement was contending that Parliament had no right to interfere with the internal affairs of the colonies and that therefore the blame rested upon the king rather than upon Parliament. But the Declaration was not written as a closely reasoned analysis of political theory nor as a strictly impartial statement of the controversy between Great Britain and her American colonies. Essentially a document of propaganda, it was a recapitulation of well-known grievances, an appeal to the liberal thought of Europe, and a call to arms at home. It meant the final break with England and a notice to the world that a new nation had been born. Its stirring phrases have become immortal not alone because it fathered American freedom but also because of its influence in the revolutionary movements of nineteenth-century Europe.

WHIGS AND TORIES

Owing to the fact that the colonial legislatures by the summer of 1776 were largely in the hands of the radical or Whig group, the delegates of all colonies signed the Declaration of Independence. This does not mean that the American people were at all unanimous in their desire for independence. At the opening of the conflict probably a majority of the people were loyalists, and it was the belief of John Adams that one third continued to be "deluded" throughout the struggle. Much evidence points

[2] S. E. Morison and H. S. Commager, *The Growth of the American Republic*, 76.

to the fact that only in Massachusetts and Virginia were the masses in favor of revolution, and that the regions of New York, Pennsylvania, and New Jersey until after the coming of the Hessians were almost hostile territory to Washington's army.[3] Dr. Flick, in a detailed study of the important Tory province of New York, divides the loyalists into seven groups: (1) the royal officials and their hangers-on, (2) the large landed proprietors and their tenants, (3) a large proportion of the professional classes, (4) the wealthy commercial classes of the towns whose interests were adversely affected by civil war, (5) conservative farmers, prosperous under English rule but injured by edicts of Congress and by the war, (6) certain politicians who followed the king's cause for mercenary reasons, and finally (7) the conservative masses of all ranks who "through loyalty, religion, interest or influence disapproved of independence." "Thus it appears," concludes Flick, "that the loyalists of New York had within their ranks persons of all social positions from that of the poor emigrant but recently come to America, to the oldest and wealthiest family in the colony, that it included most of the leaders in culture, religion and society, many of the solid business men and also much of the brawn and muscle of the common people."[4] Flick's description of the Tories in New York applies with some modifications to most of the other provinces. Virginia, however, had probably a higher proportion of the wealthy classes enrolled in the patriot cause than the other colonies. Here the rich planters, heavily in debt to England and deeply engaged in land speculation beyond the proclamation line, suffered under the existing system, and were quick to resent any encroachments upon their political power.

Generalizing broadly, it would be safe to say that the most cultivated, influential, and wealthy inhabitants of the coast towns were likely to be loyalists, and that the loyalists and rebels were divided roughly along economic and social lines. "After the Revolution passed the bounds of peaceful resistance," says Van Tyne, "it was distinctly a movement of the lower and middle classes." It is true enough that among the patriot leaders there were wealthy merchants like Hancock, able bankers like Morris, and influential planters of the type of Washington, but, except in Virginia, the typical patriot leader came for the most part from the middle class. The Revolution was at first chiefly the work of an earnest minority composed principally of mechanics, sailors, small shopkeepers, and small farmers, led by able young lawyers and discontented importers, the group as a whole representing the various elements that were not prospering

---

[3] The British historian, Lecky, asserted correctly that "the American Revolution, like most others, was the work of an energetic minority who succeeded in committing an undecided and fluctuating majority to causes for which they had little love and leading them step by step to a position from which it was impossible to recede."

[4] A. C. Flick, *Loyalism in New York During the Revolution*, 35, 36.

under the existing political and economic regime. The warm adherence of the majority of frontiersmen to the patriot cause has led some historians to see in the struggle a challenge both to a waning feudalism and to a rising capitalism.

With Tories and Whigs somewhat evenly divided, as was the case in certain provinces, and with a class cleavage often to be discerned, it is not surprising to find in the conflict between Tory and Whig the most unlovely aspect of the Revolution. Where the Whigs were in power, the Tories suffered severely. Since they were disfranchised politically, discriminated against in the courts, forced to accept depreciated colonial currency in payment of debts, often exiled and their lands confiscated, it is hardly surprising that over 1000 of them sailed with Howe to Halifax in 1776 and 3000 with Clinton from Philadelphia in 1778. At least 60,000 Tories migrated to Canada during the war, there to lay the foundations for a new English commonwealth, while thousands of others sailed for England or the British West Indies. The Tories contributed 30,000 to 50,000 men to the British army, almost as many troops as there were in the American army at any one time. Loyalist militia aided Burgoyne in New York, co-operated with the Indians in the cruel border warfare that culminated in the Wyoming and Cherry Valley massacres and comprised the expedition under Tryon, in July, 1779, which laid Fairfield and Norwalk in ashes. But considering the size of the Tory party, the comparatively small influence of this group is astonishing. It was due to the British authorities' lack of appreciation of the value of loyalists, to British lack of tact and sense in dealing with the whole problem, and in part to the aggressive action of the patriots. With an exaggerated opinion of the power of Great Britain, the Tories were slow to act. At the same time the Whigs, by means of committees of correspondence, had integrated their movement and were prepared to strike swiftly. There was, as a contemporary historian well put it, "an animation in the friends of Congress which was generally wanting in the advocates for royal government."

More amazing than the success of the Whig minority in precipitating a revolution was their fortune in winning eventual independence, for in this struggle they encountered not only Tory opposition at home but the power of the British Empire. Many factors made success almost impossible. The jealousy and conflicting interests of thirteen separate provinces prevented close political or military co-operation. The Continental Congress, which directed the war, had little power. It might raise armies and borrow from abroad, but it had no power of taxation, and its requisitions upon the states were more frequently ignored than honored. When danger threatened, a state might call the militia and vote supplies, but its support of the Continental army was intermittent and often lukewarm. Hatred of taxation had been an important cause of the Revolution, and few state legislatures had the hardihood to increase taxes to support the war. Parliamentary acts, it will be remembered, had forbidden the colonial governments to issue bills of credit. An opportunity to issue them had finally come, and the Continental Congress during the war authorized forty-two emissions of paper money to the amount of $191,552,380, and in addition eleven states authorized close to $246,366,941. This currency quickly depreciated until "not worth a continental" became a synonym of worthlessness. Certificates of indebtedness issued by quartermasters, domestic and foreign loans, gifts from abroad, and other small amounts obtained in various ways, along with state contributions, enabled Congress to keep the war going, but the funds were always inadequate to the task at hand.

Washington's army was continually in need of food, clothing, munitions, and medicines; Valley Forge was only the most spectacular episode in over six years of suffering due to inadequate popular support. As late as 1782 General Greene declared, "Our men are almost naked for want of overalls and sheets and the greater part of the army barefoot." Nor was it all the fault of Congress, which did everything possible to finance the war. As always in time of war, there were many who were quite willing to profit from the public need. "Such a dearth of public spirit," said Washington in 1775, "and want of virtue, such stock-jobbing and fertility in all the low arts to obtain advantage of one kind or another . . . I never saw before, and I pray God I may never be a witness to again. . . . Such a dirty mercenary spirit pervades the whole that I should not be at all surprised at any disaster that may happen."

Under such circumstances it is not surprising that the number of soldiers, militia and regulars, in the American army was always small in comparison to the man power of the country.[5] Only upon exceptional occasions did the total American forces reach thirty or forty thousand. Including the sick and ineffectives, Washington never had more than 16,000 in the summer of 1776, and just before Trenton his force had sunk to but 5000. There were times when he could barely put two or three thousand in the field. The majority of the American forces were always militia, and for these Washington had almost as much contempt as the British, a feeling that was far from being justified, for these same militia had given a good account of themselves at Bunker Hill, Saratoga, and many another critical battle in the Revolution. In letters to Congress Washington frequently complained of his "want of confidence in the

---

[5] "Taking the highest estimate of three million as the total population of the continental colonies in 1775," says Professor Channing, "and regarding forty per cent as militant revolutionists, this would be twelve hundred thousand, of whom one-fifth would be men of military age, or two hundred and fifty thousand at the outside." *History of the United States,* III, 221.

generality of the troops" and of the militia that they "come in, you cannot tell how; go, you cannot tell when, and act you cannot tell where, consume your provisions, exhaust your stores, and leave you at last at a critical moment."

Washington continually urged the enlargement of the regular army that Congress had established, but there were relatively few who were willing to submit to the harsh discipline that he had established in imitation of the European military system. The efficiency of the army was also weakened by the inexperience of the officers. A few, including Washington, had received some taste of military life in the border struggles of the French and Indian War, but many, who later proved to be his ablest officers, soldiers like Arnold and Greene, had come from civilian life, with little, if any, military experience. Nor did Washington always obtain from his army its maximum strength. The typical American volunteer was a farmer, usually a crack shot who excelled in individual fighting, guerrilla warfare, and quick action, yet Washington with the help of foreign officers attempted to whip them into a military machine to function after the European fashion. He was obsessed with the importance of artillery and failed to appreciate the value of cavalry for the open warfare usual in America. His victories, it will be noted, were won when surprise and quickness of action were the major factors; his defeats came when, in a stand-up battle, he threw his troops against the British regulars.

In spite of divided opinion at home, a loose and ineffective union of the provinces,[6] inadequate financial backing, and a small army, the colonists won their independence from the British Empire. Certain factors help to explain this result: (1) the geographical nature of the problem, (2) the inefficiency of the British war office and of most of its generals in America, (3) aid from France, (4) the harassing of British commerce on the seas, and (5) the unfailing courage and dogged persistence of Washington and his soldiers, who kept up the apparently unequal struggle for over six long and dreary years against overwhelming odds and under the most discouraging circumstances. The strategy of the British, with the strongest navy in the world, was to blockade the American coast, occupy the seaport towns, cut off New England from the rest of the colonies, and then, with Tory aid, conquer piecemeal the various sections. The conflict, however, was carried on 3000 miles from their base; the expected Tory aid was in no way as effective as they had hoped, and an efficient blockade, especially after the entrance of the French, proved more difficult than expected. With the exception of Boston, the British eventually occupied the seaport towns without great difficulty, but their army was

---

[6] The war was carried on until 1781 by the Continental Congress; then the new states came together in a formal union under the Articles of Confederation.

far too small to possess successfully the vast area included in the rebelling states. As soon as their army ventured into the interior, it was harassed by the colonial forces until it became evident enough that British authority existed only in those spots occupied by their army. Burgoyne, surrounded and overwhelmed in the forests of New York, was forced to capitulate, and Cornwallis, cornered on the York peninsula, surrendered when the British navy for a brief period lost control of the coasts. In general, the Americans waged a defensive war with nature as their ally.

But nature was not the only ally. The British war office was guilty of stupidity and inefficiency. Its hiring of Hessians did much to make reconciliation impossible; it was in part responsible for the bungling of the Saratoga campaign; and it was unwise in its appointments to the higher military positions. Sir William Howe, who succeeded Gage in 1776 and continued in command until 1778, was a Whig who opposed the measures that brought on the war and who much preferred the luxuries of town life to active campaigning. Sir Henry Clinton, who succeeded him, was a man of small military talents, slow to move, ignorant of American conditions of warfare, and without realization of the difficulty of the task. With but little modification the same can be said of Burgoyne and Cornwallis. More important than British military ineffectiveness was the aid rendered by France. Confined at first to financial gifts secretly made and to the occasional enlistment of an ardent young Frenchman like Lafayette, it developed after the victory of Saratoga into a declaration of war by France against Great Britain, military and naval co-operation with the American forces, and loans of almost $8,000,000.

THE ORDEAL OF BATTLE

Since the British were without the resources to attack the colonies simultaneously along the whole front, the Revolution was in reality a succession of wars waged first in New England, then in the middle colonies, and finally in the South. Of the campaigns most significant in the final outcome three stand out: (1) the operations of 1776 culminating in the victory of Trenton, (2) the capture of Burgoyne at Saratoga in 1777, and (3) the movements of 1781 ending in the victory of Yorktown.

After the evacuation of Boston in March, 1776, Washington, judging correctly that the next British objective would be New York, moved to the defense of that city. Washington's occupation of New York undoubtedly strengthened the position of the Whigs in that province, but the campaign was poorly conceived and executed, and but for the dilatory tactics of the British the patriot cause might have been doomed at the start. Time and again during the next few months Howe could have destroyed the American army, but just as often he allowed it to escape. Against the army of 32,000 that Howe landed in June and the strong fleet under the command of his brother, Lord Howe, an attempt to hold Manhattan Island was foolhardy in the extreme. Washington made his position even more dangerous by dividing his forces and placing part of them across the East River on Brooklyn Heights. Here, on the morning of August 27, Howe surprised and badly shattered the American force, but, instead of pushing home his victory, he allowed them to escape across the river on the night of August 29. The Howes, anxious to end the dispute without more bloodshed, now asked for a conference. The Americans through Franklin, their spokesman, refused to negotiate except on the basis of independence, and, as the British commanders could offer only clemency in return for a cessation of fighting, the war went on. Howe easily seized New York and flanked Washington from the East River, and the American commander had no option but to retreat, fighting a rear-guard action at Harlem and a major battle at White Plains (October 22). To protect New Jersey, Washington again unwisely divided his force, moving with the main body into New Jersey and leaving the remainder on the New York side under General Charles Lee, a vainglorious if not treacherous officer. Fort Washington on the east bank of the Hudson was left exposed, and Howe captured it with 2600 of the best men in the American army. Lee failed to co-operate in the defense of New Jersey, and Washington, with his force reduced to a bare 3000, retreated rapidly until he had safely placed the remnant of his army south of the Delaware.

Flushed with easy success, Howe believed the war all but over. He issued a proclamation of pardon to all who would submit, and many accepted. The American army was rapidly disintegrating, and time seemed on the side of England. The war never looked more hopeless or the cause more desperate. In the words of Paine, it was indeed a time to try men's souls. To push home the final blow, Cornwallis was detailed to clear the Americans out of New Jersey, and his vanguard arrived in Trenton as Washington's last soldiers escaped across the river. Congress, fleeing from Philadelphia, gave Washington authority to carry on the war as he saw fit, and its confidence was soon justified. Turning suddenly, he recrossed the river on Christmas night, marched eight miles through a blinding storm of sleet, and fell upon the 1400 Hessians at Trenton, capturing 1000. Aroused to action, Cornwallis quickly concentrated his army at Trenton to destroy the Americans, but Washington, leaving his camp-fires brightly burning to deceive the enemy, slipped away and administered a severe defeat to three British regiments caught at Princeton (January 3, 1777) beyond supporting distance from the main army. Within a few days the entire aspect was changed. Despair had turned to hope, and a cause that had seemed all but lost was suddenly revived. "All our hopes," lamented Germain, the British colonial secretary, "were blasted by that unhappy affair at Trenton." Washington now established winter head-quarters at Morristown, New Jersey, from which point he so effectively harassed the line of communication of the British that they retired to New York. Located but thirty miles from that city, Washington's small force of 4000 might not have survived until spring but for the British inaction. Dilatory as usual and with an antipathy to winter fighting, Howe allowed another opportunity to slip from his grasp.

In the summer of 1777 came the turning point of the Revolution. In far-away England the lords of the war board again determined upon an expedition from Canada to cut in two the area of colonial resistance. Burgoyne, with 8000 men, was to proceed south from Canada along the Champlain route and effect a juncture with Howe at Albany, while Colonel St. Leger, with a small force, was to come through the woodland from Oswego and join Burgoyne on the Hudson. On paper it was a beautiful plan, but factors of which the British strategists were little aware made it extremely hazardous. Carleton, it will be remembered, had at-tempted a similar feat in 1776, but had been stopped by the shattered remnants of Arnold's force. Success in this second effort was prevented from the start by the overconfidence of Burgoyne and the British war office, who were certain that the expedition could reach Albany without aid from Howe. As a result, Howe turned south to occupy Philadelphia, expecting to effect a juncture with Burgoyne after the latter had reached Albany and after his own campaign had been completed.

In the meantime the British movement from the north got under way according to schedule. St. Leger got as far as Fort Stanwix (Rome, New York) on the upper Mohawk, where he was forced to lay siege. To aid the beleaguered fort came General Herkimer with a body of frontier Germans, who, with the aid of the garrison, inflicted such damage upon the British at Oriskany that St. Leger allowed himself to be misled as to his enemies' strength and, deserted by his Indian allies, retreated head-long into Canada. Burgoyne, a former member of Parliament, a play-wright, and a man who had won some distinction in European warfare but who was quite ignorant of American conditions and geography, reached Ticonderoga with little difficulty by early July, only to find the fort abandoned. From then on, however, his advance was slow and beset with difficulties. To replenish his diminishing stores, he detached a body of 500 Hessians for a foraging expedition into Vermont, but John Stark and the militia from around Bennington surrounded and destroyed them (August 16) and defeated a British detachment sent to give reinforce-ment. Heartened by the victories at Oriskany and near Bennington, the

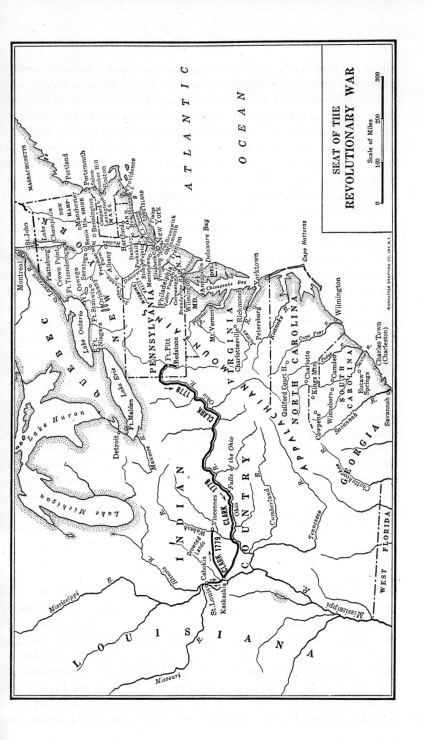

SEAT OF THE
REVOLUTIONARY WAR

Scale of Miles
0   100   200   300

militia of New York and New England were soon swarming around
Burgoyne's army to the number of 20,000. General Philip Schuyler, who
had skillfully impeded the advance of the British, was unpopular with
the New England troops, and his place was given to Horatio Gates, an
incompetent professional soldier but a favorite of Congress. The credit for
the victory that was soon to come must go chiefly to his subordinates,
Arnold, Lincoln, and Morgan. At Bemis Heights on the Hudson, about
fifteen miles north of Troy, Burgoyne reached on September 19 the farth-
est point of his advance. With his provisions exhausted and his troops
deserting and heavily outnumbered by the Americans, Burgoyne retreated
to Saratoga, near Schuylerville, where he surrendered his army (October
17, 1777).

While Burgoyne's army was floundering to defeat in the forests of
northern New York, Howe sailed for Philadelphia. Washington, surprised
that he had not moved northward to co-operate with Burgoyne, hastened
south to impede the occupation of Philadelphia. Outnumbered and out-
maneuvered, the Continentals fought gallantly throughout the day at
Brandywine Creek (September 11), only to retreat in the night and allow
Howe two weeks later to enter Philadelphia. A surprise attack on the
main British army at Germantown (October 4) proved unsuccessful.
While the British established themselves comfortably at Philadelphia,
Washington moved his defeated army to Valley Forge to spend the dreary
winter of 1777-1778.

The sufferings of the Continentals during the trying winter at Valley
Forge have made it easy to believe that these months marked the lowest
ebb of American fortunes. Such is far from the truth. Washington and
his army had gone into headquarters with the knowledge that by keeping
Howe occupied they had helped in the victory at Saratoga, and Saratoga
was to prove the decisive blow of the war. It was decisive because it
brought France officially into the conflict. France had already given much
aid secretly; nine tenths of the munitions used at Saratoga had come from
abroad, and it is doubtful if the American armies could have been kept
in the field without French supplies.

Yet the names of the two men chiefly responsible for this are little
known in American history. Early in 1776 Congress sent Silas Deane to
France to secure aid for the colonies, and there he worked closely with
the famous playwright, Beaumarchais, whose fanatical zeal for American
independence finally won the cautious French ministry to a policy of
secret help. Through a dummy company, Hortalez et Cie, organized by
Beaumarchais, the financial contributions and loans of the French and
Spanish governments were turned into munitions of war and shipped to
America. Arthur Lee and Franklin were later sent to aid Deane, but

Deane eventually retired, broken by the slanders of the jealous Lee and the suspicions of John Adams. The American cause, however, was ably promoted by the popular Franklin; after Saratoga France entered the war against Great Britain (late spring of 1778) and was joined in 1779 by Spain. The motives of both nations seem to have been chiefly revenge for the defeat of the Seven Years' War and a desire to strengthen or enlarge their colonial possessions [7] by means of a successful war. To safeguard neutral trade, Catherine II of Russia organized in 1780 a League of Armed Neutrality to maintain the freedom of the seas, and in the same year England forced the Netherlands into the war. The conflict that had started between Britain and a faction of discontented colonists had grown into an international struggle with Great Britain at war with three European nations and eyed coldly by many others.

Except for loans and the necessity of Great Britain to guard her possessions elsewhere, the entrance of France had little effect for some time upon colonial fortunes. The French fleet hovered intermittently off the American coast, but it was not until the Yorktown campaign three years later that there was effective co-operation. It was then that French sea power proved the decisive factor. In the meantime the war dragged out its weary course. In the spring of 1778 Howe withdrew from Philadelphia. Washington tried to intercept him at Monmouth, New Jersey, and might have prevented his movement but for the incapacity of Charles Lee. Monmouth was the last major battle in the North; the scene thereafter shifts largely to the West and the South.

At the opening of the Revolution frontiersmen, beginning to push across the mountains, found themselves exposed to constant Indian attacks. Behind the Indian hostility was seen the influence of England, and in 1778 George Rogers Clark, with a commission from Patrick Henry, Governor of Virginia, set out with a small force of militia to break the power of England in the Northwest. Descending the Ohio, he captured the old French forts, now held by the British, at Kaskaskia and Cahokia on the Mississippi and Vincennes on the Wabash. Driven out of Vincennes in December by Lieutenant-Governor Hamilton of Canada, Clark returned two months later (February, 1779) and surprised and captured the garrison. This brilliant exploit left the Northwest in American hands at the end of the war. Although it seems likely that this occupation was

---

[7] The liberal enthusiasm existing among many of the French aristocracy may also have influenced that nation. The entrance of France into the war was preceded by two treaties (signed February 6, 1788) with the American states, one to promote better commercial relations and the other a defensive alliance, the only alliance in which the United States has ever engaged, which provided for mutual help in case France should be involved in war with England, arrangements concerning the disposition of conquered territories, and the promise that neither party would conclude peace without the consent of the other.

known to the American peace commissioners, there is nothing to show that it had any influence in the award of this territory to the United States. It was in this same year (1779) that the British with their Indian allies let loose the horrors of war upon the frontier settlements at Cherry Valley in central New York and in the Wyoming valley of Pennsylvania.

In the North the war was a stalemate; the British held the land their troops actually occupied and little more, and from these posts it seemed impossible to oust them. Believing that a demonstration in the South, where the Tories were supposed to be strong would recover the southern colonies, the British seized Savannah (December, 1778), captured Charleston (May, 1780), and spent the next year and a half marching through South Carolina, North Carolina, and Virginia in an effort to strike terror into the hearts of the patriots. Against this marauding, Sumter, Marion, Pickens, and other leaders kept up a guerrilla warfare until Congress sent Gates with an army of regulars to aid the southern militia. Gates's incapacity was evident when his army was defeated at Camden, South Carolina (August 16, 1780), and his command was later turned over to Greene, who was, next to Washington, the ablest of the American generals. In the meantime the British received their first check in the South when the militia from the back country of the Carolinas destroyed a band of 1000 Tories at Kings Mountain (October 7). With great skill Greene now directed the American defense. During the nine months of marching and countermarching through the Carolinas, he lost four battles but gained his ultimate objective, the retirement of the British to the seacoast. Their long campaign had gained them nothing but a few seacoast towns.

Cornwallis, in command of the main British army in the South, now transferred his operations to Virginia, where he was eventually maneuvered by Lafayette [8] into a position on the Yorktown peninsula. The great opportunity had come, and Washington saw it. Seven thousand French troops, who had been lying inactive at Newport, Rhode Island, under General Rochambeau, joined Washington before New York. Making a feint at New York to deceive the British commander, the American and French armies quickly moved south to the Chesapeake and embarked for the Yorktown peninsula. In the meantime the French fleet had sailed north from the West Indies and stood guard at the head of the bay while the army closed in around the unfortunate Cornwallis. Caught in an inescapable trap, he surrendered his army of 7000 on October 19, 1781.

[8] The Marquis de Lafayette, a young French liberal, had joined the American cause in 1777, won the friendship of Washington, and attained high command. His chief importance was as a liaison officer between the French and American armies and governments.

Perfect co-ordination between French and Americans and brief control of the sea had made possible this victory.

Although the treaty of Paris was not signed until 1783, military operations in the colonies were over. The British offered to the Americans all that they had ever asked for except independence and tried to detach the French from the alliance by offering concessions in India, but neither government accepted. Less scrupulous than the French and in violation of the treaty of 1778, the American negotiators, Franklin, Adams, and Jay, made a separate treaty with Great Britain when that nation finally offered independence. Fear that France would support Spanish designs on the territory between the Alleghenies and the Mississippi and the British belief that the region was less dangerous in the weak hands of the American confederation than in the stronger hands of Spain led to the separate negotiation. The treaty signed September 3, 1783, recognized independence, placed the western boundary line at the Mississippi, and granted the Americans a share in the Newfoundland fisheries. The British demand for the payment of debts owed by America to British subjects at the opening of the war and for the restoration of confiscated Tory property was refused, and a meaningless phrase was inserted that Congress would recommend restoration and would not hinder the British from collecting debts through the courts. The terms were all that the Americans could desire, but the problem of British debts, the treatment of the Tories, and the uncertainty of boundary lines provided causes for subsequent friction that led to much ill-feeling. The only part of the treaty that was absolutely clear was that recognizing independence, but that was the most important.

ECONOMIC AND SOCIAL ASPECTS

Considering the length of the struggle, the effect of the Revolution upon agriculture, industry, and commerce was not as great as might have been expected. The economic life of America at the end of the war was much as it had been at the beginning. Except where immediate danger threatened there was widespread apathy, and the campaigns of the militia were spasmodic and brief. But a small minority were under arms at any time, and agriculture went on much as usual. After the first few months New England was hardly touched by the war. In the middle states, where the conflict chiefly centered, the farmers profited from the demands of the commissaries of both armies. The last two years of the war saw the destruction of property and the confiscation of slaves in the South, but there too, during the rest of the struggle, agriculture went on much as usual. The loss of the bounties on indigo was a blow, but the exportation of tobacco and rice continued, while the nonimportation agreements and the British blockade stimulated the development of cotton culture. The knowledge of European improvements in agriculture was spread by foreigners whom the war brought into the country and resulted in an aroused interest in scientific agriculture and in the founding of our first agricultural societies in the 1780s.

Industry was, perhaps, more definitely affected than agriculture. The nonimportation agreements before the war and the British blockade during the struggle stimulated domestic manufacturing, forcing even the wealthy to use American-made goods. This artificial stimulation of industry was further aided by the setting aside of the Parliamentary legislation restricting manufacturing. The war, of course, promoted the manufacture of munitions and other military necessities, to which the states by bounties and other aid gave encouragement. Congress, itself, in 1778 founded works in Springfield, Massachusetts, where cannon were cast, the predecessor of the national armory established there in 1794. Some industries, as shipbuilding, were adversely affected, but there can be no doubt that the war, even in this primitive agricultural society, gave a distinct impetus to manufacturing.

Nonimportation agreements and the British blockade were a severe blow to the commercial life of the colonies, but there were compensating features that operated to save American commerce. The Revolution ended, of course, the British Navigation acts as they applied to the colonies. This was not entirely advantageous, as the new nation was soon to see, for it greatly restricted American trade with Great Britain and her colonies. Elsewhere, of course, Americans might trade where they pleased, and, as they developed means of avoiding the blockade, a thriving commerce was opened with the continental nations of Europe. After 1777 there was little lack of foreign merchandise. Even during the war the Virginian planters sent their tobacco to England by a roundabout route to obscure its origin. More important than the legitimate commerce was the large-scale privateering. To Massachusetts vessels alone 626 letters of marque were issued by the Continental Congress and a thousand more by the General Court. In Rhode Island, where privateering became so popular that the assembly attempted to check it and pass laws to limit the size of the crews, nearly two hundred commissions were issued. There was scarcely a seacoast town of any size in New England or Long Island that did not have its privateers searching the seas for British merchantmen and incidentally lining the pockets of shipowners and crews with fat profits. "Probably as many as ninety-thousand Americans were, first and last," says Jameson, "engaged in these voyages, a number of men almost as great as served in the army, and greater than that of the army in any single year but one." [9] The losses to the English merchant class were stupendous and undoubtedly increased the unpopularity of the war in England. To American commerce privateering was important for holding capital and labor in an industry that was to thrive mightily in the seventy-five years following the close of the conflict.

Overshadowed by the great fact that the Revolution brought political independence, historians have but recently realized the tremendous social results of the struggle. The Revolution not only removed the political domination of Great Britain but also enabled the colonies to throw off a great burden of economic disabilities and to shake themselves free from a mass of feudal barbarities, legal walls, and social customs inherited and artificially imposed from without. The exodus of thousands of Tories removed in the North a considerable part of the old ruling class. The confiscation of their lands, which Congress recommended in 1777, and their sale to numerous individuals in small lots, effected a change in agrarian economics similar to that of the French Revolution of 1789. As in France, during its revolution, "country lawyers and newly rich merchants swarmed over the seats of the once proud aristocracy, so in the United States during and after the cataclysm a host of groundlings, fresh from the plow and counting house, surged over the domains of the Jessups, De Lanceys and Morrises." [10] This agrarian change consisted not merely in the confiscation and breaking up of large estates and the elimination of the Penns and Calverts, but also in a more democratic land tenure. The system of quitrents quickly disappeared; entail in all but two states was abolished by 1786; and within five years more primogeniture had gone. These acts, as Jefferson well said, "laid the axe to the root of pseudo-aristocracy."

Not alone in the change of land laws can the results of the Revolution be seen. Whatever was not indigenous to American soil was bound to be weakened by the upheaval. Conservative as were the new state constitutions, they revealed in their bills of rights the surge of the new democracy that was to grow stronger in the years to come. Continual discussion of the "rights of man" could not help bearing fruit in the social as well as in the political field. The first antislavery society was organized in Philadelphia in 1775, and during the next ten years Rhode Island and Pennsylvania passed acts looking toward the abolition of slavery. Before the close of the century at least two of the states softened their criminal codes, and the first prison-reform society was organized in Philadelphia in 1776. Even in religion the effect of the war was seen. The Methodist and Episcopal churches, branches of these denominations in England,

9 J. F. Jameson, *The American Revolution Considered as a Social Movement,* 103.
10 C. A. and M. Beard, *The Rise of American Civilization,* I, 294.

were separated and organized as American churches. More important, the idea of the established church was dealt a death blow in America. By 1786, the year when Jefferson's Statute of Virginia for Religious Freedom was finally passed, the church had been disestablished in every state of the union except Massachusetts, New Hampshire, and Connecticut. The movement for these reforms was merely released by the Revolution; many of them were consummated in the years to follow. The penetrating mind of the great Philadelphia physician, Benjamin Rush, clearly discerned this fact. "There is nothing more common," said he, "than to confound the terms of the American Revolution with those of the late American war. The American war is over; but this is far from being the case with the American revolution. On the contrary, nothing but the first act of the great drama is closed."

On the military history, see Edward Channing, *A History of the United States,* Vol. III, Chaps. VI–XII. Most valuable on the social and economic effects is J. F. Jameson, *The Revolution Considered as a Social Movement.* This phase is also dealt with in H. U. Faulkner, *American Economic History,* 132–141, in A. M. Schlesinger, *New Viewpoints in American History,* Chap. VII, and in C. and M. Beard, *The Rise of American Civilization,* Chap. V. Merle Curti, *The Growth of American Thought,* Chap. VI, discusses the intellectual effect of the Revolution. On the diplomatic, see S. F. Bemis, *A Diplomatic History of the United States,* Chaps. I–IV or T. A. Bailey, *A Diplomatic History of the American People,* Chaps. II, III. G. S. Callender, *Selections from the Economic History of the United States,* 142–180, gives source material on the economic, while H. S. Commager, *Documents of American History,* Vol. I, 91–119, and S. E. Morison, *Sources and Documents, Illustrating the American Revolution 1764–1788,* 149–203, do the same for the political.

Chapter VIII

A NEW NATION

*Some men look at Constitutions with sancti-
monious reverence, and deem them, like the ark
of the covenant, too sacred to be touched. They
ascribe to the men of the preceding age a wisdom
more than human, and suppose what they did
to be beyond amendment. I knew that age well;
I belonged to and labored with it. It deserved
well of its country. It was very like the present,
but without the experience of the present; and
forty years of experience in Government is worth
a century of book-reading; and this they would
say themselves, were they to rise from the dead.
I am certainly not an advocate for frequent and
untried changes in laws and Constitutions. I
think moderate imperfections had better be borne
with; because, when once known, we accom-
modate ourselves to them, and find practical
means of correcting their ill effects. But I know,
also, that laws and institutions must go hand
in hand with the progress of the human mind.
As that becomes more developed, more enlightened, as new discoveries are made, new truths
disclosed, and manners and opinions change with
the change of circumstances, institutions must advance also and keep pace with the times.*

THOMAS JEFFERSON

THE SCARS OF WAR

Despite the fact that the Revolution was fought on American soil, the
war years were characterized by a certain amount of prosperity. Artificial
stimulation of agriculture and industry, higher wage scales, widespread
smuggling, and the high profits of privateering, all contributed to an
active economic life. With the coming of peace, Americans looked hopefully for an even greater prosperity. Their expectations were not fulfilled;
the years from the close of the war to the end of 1786 marked a period of
economic stagnation and social and political discontent. Labor and capital

during the war had been diverted from agriculture and legitimate trade to manufacturing and privateering, and time was needed for a readjustment to a peace-time basis. Colonial prosperity had been based on the exportation of raw materials and on an active commerce. Both were curtailed by the coming of peace. The old navigation acts, which had aided and protected American commerce as well as hindered it, were now applied against the American confederation just as against any other foreign nation. Certain American raw materials were allowed importation into England without payment of alien duties even when imported in American ships, but the West Indies were absolutely closed to American vessels. British ships might take American lumber and foodstuffs to the sugar islands, but not the products of the sea. France and Spain, which had accorded to the rebellious Americans special commercial privileges during the war, now largely revoked them.

Under such restrictions American commerce was in a far worse condition than before the Revolution. Only by resort to the long-tried methods of legal evasion was the American merchant marine able to survive. In need of American commodities, France and Spain opened some West Indian ports to American vessels, and the English planters, unable to compete without the same cheap foodstuffs and lumber, connived at the evasion of the law. Even so, the trade was restricted, and prices at home fell to disastrous levels, bringing ruin to many. What was true of agriculture was also characteristic of industry. A real development had taken place in manufacturing during the war only to be temporarily halted by the influx of cheaper British goods that were released at the conclusion of the conflict and now crammed the warehouses.

Earlier historians have tended to overemphasize the disastrous effect upon the economic life of the political conditions of the period. The situation just described was a natural result of the war and not of politics. It is true, nevertheless, that the impotence of the federal government and the jealousies of state governments often accentuated the economic difficulties. The thirteen states, as we shall presently point out, had bound themselves in 1781 into a loose confederation, but Congress under the Confederation had no power to establish tariffs or levy taxes. The absence of such power weakened its authority at home and its standing abroad. England openly flouted the treaty of 1783 by refusing to surrender the posts in the Northwest; Spain intrigued in the Southwest to stir up rebellion along the frontier; and the Barbary pirates levied blackmail on American merchant ships. For three years John Adams remained in England attempting without success to negotiate a commercial treaty. Of the European nations only Sweden (1783) and Prussia (1785) made treaties guaranteeing reciprocal commercial privileges; the others refused to negotiate or else signed treaties on unequal terms.

The inability of the federal government to secure commercial concessions from foreign nations led certain of the states to act. Beginning with the erection of tariff walls against British goods, it was not long before they were discriminating against one another in a bitter economic warfare. The absurd lengths to which this was sometimes carried is illustrated by the act of New York in 1787 levying import duties upon farm products from New Jersey and Connecticut, which had formerly supplied the New York market. New Jersey retaliated by placing a tax of $1800 upon a lighthouse recently purchased by New York and essential to the safety of the harbor, and a mass meeting of New London business men pledged themselves for a period of a year not to send goods to New York. Ill feeling between the states was accentuated by boundary-line disputes, particularly in the Wyoming valley, where Pennsylvania carried on petty war against Connecticut settlers, who claimed that their holdings were covered by the ancient charters of their native state, and on the eastern shores of Lake Champlain, where the inhabitants fought off New York landlords and were intent upon erecting an independent state.

The economic distress that culminated in 1786 brought insistent demands from the debtor class for currency inflation. The wealthy and conservative, in defense of their own interests, opposed the demands and in six of the states [1] prevented the further emission of paper money. This class struggle resulted in much bitterness and some violence. In New Hampshire a mob, crying out for paper money, surrounded the meeting house at Exeter where the legislature was assembled and were dispersed only by the calling of the militia. In Rhode Island the controversy over paper money resulted in one of the famous legal cases in our history. Against the opposition of the merchants a paper-money law was carried through the legislature. The merchants closed their shops and refused to accept the scrip. One of them, a certain John Weeden, a butcher, was haled into court, where the law was declared unconstitutional. The legislature in anger called the judges before it, browbeat them, and later dismissed four, but the decision stood.[2] In Massachusetts embittered agrarians under Daniel Shays rose in rebellion, demanding paper money, a scaling-down of the state debts, and a revision of the constitution to eliminate the special privileges of property. It took an army of militia and the effusion of blood to end the rebellion.

[1] New Hampshire, Massachusetts, Connecticut, Delaware, Maryland, and Virginia.
[2] Trevett v. Weeden, 1786. This is the most important of early cases in American history when the judiciary attempted to annul a legislative act.

Beginning with 1787, the economic situation brightened. Some portion of the old West Indian trade had been regained. To take the place of what was lost, Yankee skippers, ever ready to adapt themselves to changing conditions, were opening new markets, particularly in the Far East. It was in 1785 that the *Empress of China* returned to New York from Canton and in 1787 that the *Grand Turk* sailed into Salem from the same port. It was during these years that the first New England traders reached the Northwest in search of furs, the beginning of a new three-cornered commerce, in which the New Englanders traded manufactured commodities to the Northwest Indians for furs and exchanged the furs in China for Oriental goods to be brought back to the states. Here and there tiny factories were again appearing, and inventors like John Fitch and James Rumsey were successfully experimenting with steam engines for water transportation. There was every indication in the late eighties that the nation was experiencing a normal but rapid economic recovery. "The defects of the old confederation," as Callender well says, "were then in no way responsible for the hard times. It had not produced them, nor could the best government in the world have removed them." [3] The people themselves realized that the situation could be remedied easily in only two ways: one was to open some of the old markets or discover new ones, and the other was to stop consuming foreign commodities and produce at home. They attempted both with some success, and this success was creating prosperity.

THE "CRITICAL PERIOD"

About a half century ago the historian-philosopher, John Fiske, wrote a popular account of the 1780s, which he entitled *The Critical Period*, a term that has since been used by numerous writers as they have played with many variations upon the theme "darkness before dawn." That it was a time of difficult problems, like every period of reconstruction following a war, there can be no doubt. On the other hand, a real economic prosperity was being achieved, and this in spite of a weak central government, currency chaos, and class friction. The common man had made distinct political and social progress, and he was in no haste to strengthen the federal government. To the farmers and planters, laden with debt, inflated currency and cheap foreign goods were no hardship. For other groups, however, the situation, while not "critical," was certainly difficult. The manufacturer who needed a protective tariff, the shipowner who needed protection on the high seas and an opportunity to trade in foreign ports, the capitalist who wanted a stable currency and protection against

[3] G. S. Callender, *Selections from the Economic History of the United States 1765–1860*. 182.

the debtor class, with their legislation for stay laws and paper money, the owner and speculator in continental securities who hoped for their payment in full, and the speculators in western land, could all see the advantages of a central authority with adequate power to protect their interests. It was from this group that the movement for a new constitution developed, and with returning prosperity their influence grew stronger.

THE ARTICLES OF CONFEDERATION

From 1775 to 1781 a group of delegates from thirteen sovereign states (the Continental Congress) acted as a central committee to carry on the war. The necessity of a stronger union was obvious and a committee of the Congress, of which John Dickinson was the leading spirit, drafted the Articles of Confederation. In the enthusiasm following Burgoyne's surrender these articles were submitted to the states, and by the midsummer of 1778 ten had ratified. Maryland, the last state to ratify, withheld her consent until March 1, 1781, so that the Articles of Confederation did not go into effect until that year.

Maryland's refusal to ratify for three years was a tremendous benefit to the cause of national unity. She took the position as early as 1779 "that a country unsettled at the commencement of this war, claimed by the British crown, and ceded to it by the Treaty of Paris, if wrested from the common enemy by the blood and treasure of thirteen States, should be considered as common property, subject to be parcelled out by Congress into free, convenient, and independent governments, in such manner and at such times as the wisdom of the assembly shall hereafter direct." The inclusive early charters of Georgia, the Carolinas, Virginia, Connecticut, and Massachusetts granted indefinite westward expansion, and New York by Indian treaties also claimed western land. Other states, Maryland, Pennsylvania, Delaware, New Jersey, New Hampshire, and Rhode Island, had little or no claim to the western region, and the relative positions of these states in the new confederation would be imperiled by the great size of the rest. Furthermore, the region north of the Ohio was in dispute between several states, and it was the part of wisdom to follow the suggestion of Maryland. New York, whose claims were vague, led the way in 1780, and Virginia, whose claims were greatest, made the sacrifice in 1781. Others promised to do the same, although it was not until 1802 that Georgia, the last state, turned over her western lands to Congress.

It has been all too easy for students to emphasize the weakness of the Articles of Confederation and to forget its important contributions toward national unity. It is true that the Articles conferred upon Congress no power to tax or regulate commerce and that it failed to set up a national judiciary. It did, however, give Congress power to declare war, borrow money, administer Indian affairs and the post office, regulate the value of metallic coins, fix the standard of weights and measures, and settle certain disputes between the states. In the exercise of certain of these powers nine states must agree, but the student of history cannot but be amazed at the powers granted rather than at those withheld. Certainly the people of the time felt that they had gone far in endowing the central body with the powers of government, the exercise of which by Great Britain they had objected to. It was not necessary to proceed much further to set up an authority greater than that ever exercised by the mother country.

Nor was the government under the Articles of Confederation an utterly weak instrument, as some have pictured it. It was responsible for laying the foundations of our public-land policy [4] and for determining the government and procedure by which the new western states might seek admission to the union. The settlement of the West demanded action, and in 1787 the famous Northwest Ordinance, besides prohibiting slavery in the region north of the Ohio, provided (1) that not less than three nor more than five states be erected out of the territory; (2) that at first the territory should be ruled by a governor and three judges appointed by Congress, who determined local officers and adopted laws subject to veto by Congress; (3) that, after the population numbered 5000 free male inhabitants, the territory might have a two-house legislature and a representative in Congress with the right to debate but not to vote; and (4) that, when any of the proposed states had 60,000 free inhabitants, it might form a government with a constitution and, if Congress approved, its delegates might be admitted to Congress "on an equal footing with the original States in all respects whatever." This ordinance, says a noted Swiss historian, "has been called one of the most important laws of the United States (from the point of view of world history it is perhaps the most important). . . . Thus the principle was abandoned that the welfare of the colonies ought to be subordinated to that of the mother country; rather was the principle established that colonies which are settled by a people are to be regarded as an extension of the mother country and one to be put on an equal footing in every respect."

DRAFTING A CONSTITUTION

Important as were the Articles of Confederation in our constitutional history, they failed to provide the strong cohesive force necessary for the growth of national unity. The states, as the years went by, seemed to be drifting apart. Congress had fallen into such low estate that many of the

[4] To be discussed in Chapter XIV.

most capable leaders refused membership in it, and for months in 1786–1787 not even a quorum could be gathered. The famous Ordinance of 1787 was passed with only eighteen of a possible ninety-one members present. This decline in the part played by Congress was undoubtedly due to the strong feeling of state sovereignty and to the absence of any critical situation demanding united action, but to strong nationalists it was the sign of portending doom. "I do not conceive we can exist long as a nation," wrote Washington in 1786, "without having lodged some where a power, which will pervade the whole Union in as energetic a manner as the authority of the State governments extends over the several states." Hamilton was even more emphatic. "We may . . . be said to have reached almost the last stage of national humiliation," he asserted in 1787. "There is scarcely anything that can wound the pride, or degrade the character, of an independent people, which we do not experience. . . . The delinquencies of the states have . . . at length arrested all the wheels of the national government. . . . The frail and tottering edifice seems ready to fall upon our heads, and to crush us beneath its ruins." Grounded in political science by study and experience, such leaders knew that a much more centralized and "energetic" government was necessary if a nation was to be organized—and they were for organizing a nation.

As this feeling grew among a minority of leaders, it was inevitable that further efforts would be made to strengthen the union. A dispute between Maryland and Virginia over the use of the Potomac and Chesapeake came to a head in 1785 when representatives of the two states met at Mount Vernon to settle their differences. When it developed that Pennsylvania and Delaware also were interested, Virginia issued a call to all the states for a trade convention to meet at Annapolis in 1786. Nine states appointed delegates, but representatives from only five appeared. Under the circumstances little could be done, and the delegates adopted a report of Hamilton calling for another convention to meet in Philadelphia in May, 1787, to consider "the situation of the United States, to devise such further provisions as shall appear to them necessary to render the constitution of the federal goverment adequate to the exigencies of the Union." Congress issued the call, being careful to restrict the business of the convention to the "sole and express purpose of revising the Articles of Confederation," and providing that the finished work be reported to Congress and accepted by the legislatures of the states.

That the advocates of a stronger central government were alert to the opportunity is evidenced by the quickness with which all the states but Rhode Island appointed these delegates. Of the sixty-two delegates appointed, fifty-five attended the sessions and thirty-nine signed the final draft. It was a distinguished group, representing, as it did, many of the ablest leaders of the states. From Virginia came George Mason; Edmund Randolph, the governor; James Madison, "Father of the Constitution"; and George Washington, who was to preside over the sessions. New York sent Alexander Hamilton; Delaware, the constitutional lawyer, John Dickinson; New Jersey, the able William Paterson; Connecticut, Roger Sherman and Oliver Ellsworth; Massachusetts, Rufus King and Elbridge Gerry; South Carolina, John Rutledge and the two Pinckneys. Second to none was the delegation from Pennsylvania, including the many-sided Franklin, the distinguished jurist, James Wilson, the brilliant Gouverneur Morris, and the able financier, Robert Morris. Among them were many who had played an important part in the revolutionary movement and were destined for distinguished places in the future government. Able and distinguished the group undoubtedly was, but it was also conservative. It represented the right wing of the revolutionary movement and was composed, says one historian, "of practical men of affairs—holders of state and continental bonds, money lenders, merchants, lawyers, speculators in the public land—who could speak with knowledge and feeling about the disabilities they had suffered under the Articles of Confederation." Of those in attendance, more than half were either investors or speculators in public securities. Virtually all represented the privileged and wealthy classes; the common man was without a hearing. Notably absent were the left-wing revolutionary radicals. Thomas Jefferson was then American minister at Paris; Thomas Paine was deep in the revolutionary movement in Europe; Patrick Henry refused to attend because, as he said, he "smelt a rat"; and Samuel Adams was not elected.

Unlike the Constituent Assembly of France, which was soon to formulate its constitution under the eyes and in the presence of the tumultuous populace of Paris, the fathers of the American Constitution held their meetings behind closed doors and in secret. But for the scanty notes of a few members, particularly James Madison, posterity would be quite ignorant of what happened. When the fragmentary information is pieced together, one fact stands out clearly. The delegates were practically unanimous in the belief that the central government should be strengthened by giving it power to lay and collect taxes, regulate commerce, control the issue of currency, assume the financial obligations of the confederation, and prevent the impairment of contracts. If the new constitution failed "to do justice to the public creditors and retrieve the national character," insisted Washington, the states might as well continue under the old confederation. The delegates were also in general agreement as to the dangers of democracy and the necessity of preventing their development. The object of the delegates, said Madison, was "to secure the public good and private rights against the danger of such a faction and at the same time preserve the spirit and form of popular government." The differences of opinion, which almost wrecked the convention, and which historians have made so much of, were differences as to method or detail and not as to purpose.

The fathers of the Constitution were not without experience for the task that they had at hand. During the revolutionary period all the states but Connecticut and Rhode Island had erected new frames of government. Some of the delegates to the constitutional convention had participated in constitution-making; others had been delegates to Congress under the Articles of Confederation. All were students of government or had had practical political experience. They had seen constitutions appear in America—written documents that took the form of social contracts, documents that stressed the rights of man and the belief that through checks and balances rulers should be carefully controlled. To what extent would these principles, emphasized in the state constitutions, be carried over into the new federal instruments?

Early in the convention the delegates threw over the idea of amending the Articles of Confederation and determined that a "national government ought to be established consisting of a supreme legislative, executive, and judiciary." The chief conflict in the convention now arose over the power in the new government of the large and small states, which, in the light of a century and a half of experience, seems a waste of time. Virginia proposed a lower house elected by the people and an upper elected by the lower house, the legislature to choose a single executive and the judiciary. The smaller states, led by Paterson of New Jersey, offered a counterproposal (the New Jersey plan) calling for a single legislature based upon states regardless of population with a plural executive elected by Congress and a judiciary appointed by the executive. A deadlock between the larger and smaller states was finally broken by a compromise establishing the system under which we are now governed.

The sectional difference between the commercial North and the agricultural South brought other compromises. After the convention had granted Congress the power to levy direct taxes and had provided for a lower house elected according to population, the question of slavery arose. The slaves, said the North, should be counted as property in levying direct taxes, but not as people in determining the basis of representation. The result of the debates was the "three-fifths compromise," providing that three fifths of the slaves be counted for purposes of both representation and taxation. Other compromises were effected between the slaveholding, free-trade South and the North. Congress was not to interfere with the slave trade for twenty years and could lay no import tax in excess of $10 a slave. While Congress might regulate commerce, it might not levy export taxes, and the ratification of all treaties required a two thirds vote of the Senate. These and less important compromises were finally hammered out, and on September 17 thirty-nine of the forty-two delegates affixed their signatures. The document, which seems to have been largely based on the Articles of Confederation, the New Jersey plan, and specific precedents provided in state constitutions, was not satisfactory to any delegate, but they considered it the best that they could agree upon and referred it to Congress with the provision that it be submitted to state conventions for ratification.

THE FIGHT FOR RATIFICATION

By the masses of the people, the Constitution was greeted with anything but enthusiasm. Some pointed out that the delegates had failed to follow instructions in not revising the Articles of Confederation and in submitting it to conventions rather than to the legislatures. Others opposed the sacrifice of state powers to the strengthening of the federal government. Others resented the fact that the Constitution seemed interested solely in safeguarding the rights of property and made no reference to the "rights of man," so prominent in the revolutionary philosophy of the period. Yet others complained that the federal government was essentially undemocratic. The lower house, to be sure, was popularly elected, but it was to be balanced against an indirectly elected senate, and both were to be balanced against a president, whose election the framers believed they had removed from popular control. Yet another agency had been established that might negate the work of both the legislative and the administrative branches, namely, a federal judiciary appointed (not elected) for life, the most conservative of all. The Constitution nowhere authorized the judiciary to declare the laws of Congress null and void, but there appears to be no doubt that many of the framers looked upon such a possibility with favor. It did say that "The judicial Power shall extend to all Cases, in Law and Equity arising under the Constitution, the Laws of the United States, and treaties made," and there were, of course, the precedents of judicial review in the states, as in the case of Trevett v. Weeden. The whole was a system of checks and balances designed to keep the power out of the hands of the democratic and turbulent masses.

The most amazing result of the whole situation, and this point was not lost upon all, was that the Constitution aimed to restore much the same sort of authority that the colonists had fought a long war to abolish. State acts must conform to the Constitution; federal courts, analogous to the British judiciary, might invalidate local legislation and determine disputes between states; a central body, with powers like those of Parliament, might

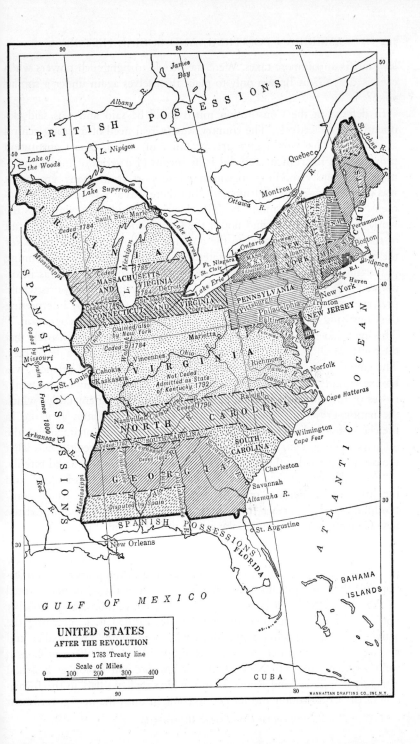

UNITED STATES
AFTER THE REVOLUTION
━━━━ 1783 Treaty line
Scale of Miles
0   100   200   300   400

levy tariffs and impose taxes. Were the people to fight such powers when exercised by Great Britain only to place themselves again under a similar yoke?

In defense of the Constitution much could be said and was said eloquently and effectively. The country was in real need of a strong central government that would give greater unity of action. The Constitution provided the instrument and did it by means of a series of nice compromises sufficiently soothing to command support from many groups. It was never intended to be democratic, but there was a possibility of amendment, difficult as that might be. The doctrine of judicial review was the work of the later courts and not of the Constitution, and it was the fault of the electorate, if, opposed to the doctrine, it allowed it to develop. For the failure to include the usual statement of the rights of man Channing offers this explanation: "The real reason why no such feature was incorporated in the document was the belief that the United States courts would preserve the people from executive and legislative tyranny by interpreting the Constitution in the light of the Common Law and the rules of reason." [5] This may have been so, but there were many at the time who felt that the courts might also thwart the perfectly legitimate desires of a democracy. The government, as planned, with its numerous checks and balances, was an exceedingly cumbersome affair, but it did obviate many of the weaknesses of the old confederation and provided an instrument under which the nation grew and prospered. If it protected the creditor, as it did in the clause forbidding any state to pass laws *ex post facto* or impairing the obligation of contract, it happened that protection of the creditor was what the country needed at the time if business enterprise was to proceed rapidly.

"From the ocean to the American outposts nearest the Mississippi," said the historian, Bancroft, "one desire prevailed for a closer connection." Nothing could be farther from the truth. When Congress submitted the new Constitution to the states, the people quickly divided into two groups, the Federalists, who favored the new Constitution, and the Antifederalists, who opposed it. What proportion of the people were in favor of the new instrument it is impossible to determine. Owing to the property qualifications for the franchise, not more than one fourth of the adult males voted in the election for delegates to the ratifying conventions, and probably not more than one sixth of the adult males ratified it. Concerning the activities of the ratifying conventions we know more. The smaller and weaker states were generally overwhelmingly in favor of the new Constitution. Exceptions were New Hampshire, whose convention at first had a majority opposed, and Rhode Island, which took no part in the formation of the Constitution and refused to come in until the new government

[5] E. Channing, *A History of the United States,* III, 515–516.

was formed. On the other hand, the larger states found their conventions about evenly divided and ratified only after long and bitter fights. North Carolina, in fact, like Rhode Island, delayed ratification until economic pressure brought her in.

Delaware, the first state to ratify, voted approval unanimously December 7, 1787. Five days later Pennsylvania, after a much more stubborn opposition than would be supposed from the prompt result, by a vote of 46 to 23 also ratified. The New Jersey convention, after a week's debate, gave unanimous approval, as did Georgia on January 2, 1788. Connecticut followed within a few days by a vote of three to one. So far it had been clear sailing, but most of the larger states without whose acceptance there could be no union were yet to be heard from. The Massachusetts convention, which met early in January, appeared to have a majority opposed, including Elbridge Gerry, who had refused to sign his endorsement. Ratification depended in no small degree upon the attitude of John Hancock and Samuel Adams. Adams at first opposed. The tradesmen of Boston, however, were strongly in favor, and no politician could ignore their wish. Hancock appears to have been finally won over by promises of political preferment, and Adams consented when ratification was accompanied by a demand, like that in Pennsylvania, for nine amendments largely in the nature of a bill of rights. The final vote was 187 to 168 for ratification (February 6). Maryland approved in April and South Carolina in May. The New Hampshire convention had met in February, but, when it was discovered that the opponents had a majority, the Federalists secured an adjournment until June. By that time Massachusetts had ratified, and New Hampshire followed with a vote of 57 to 46.

The requisite nine states had now ratified, but two of the largest, Virginia and New York, had as yet made no decision. In Virginia the struggle was hard fought and uncertain till the end. The prestige of Washington, Madison, and Marshall strengthened the cause of adoption, but the opposition was led by men of almost equal influence, such as Patrick Henry and George Mason. Approval finally came (June 25) by a vote of 89 to 79 on the understanding that amendments were to be added. To obtain ratification in New York was extremely difficult, for the Antifederalists had captured two thirds of the convention. Federalist success seems to have been due chiefly to the untiring efforts of Hamilton and to the fact that ten other states had already accepted the new Constitution. In an effort to win the support of the educated classes, Hamilton, Madison, and Jay published a series of eighty-five essays in defense of the Constitution, which have since been known as *The Federalist*. What influence they may have had on the situation is unknown, but they remain today our best authority as to the nature and purpose of the Constitution. New York finally fell in line by a vote of 30 to 27 (July 26), with a recommendation for amendments. It was not until the first Congress under the new Constitution brought economic pressure to bear by means of a tariff on foreign goods that North Carolina (November 21, 1789) and Rhode Island (May 29, 1790) saw the light.

The Constitution was adopted in most of the larger states only by the narrowest margin and by the cleverest political manipulation. What proportion of the people desired it no one can know, but it is doubtful if a direct submission to the people would have brought ratification. "Indeed," commented John Marshall a decade after the event, "it is scarcely to be doubted that in some of the adopting states, a majority of the people were in the opposition. In all of them the numerous amendments proposed, demonstrate the reluctance with which the new government was accepted; and that a dread of dismemberment, not an approbation of the particular system under consideration, had induced an acquiescence in it." "I believe it to be a fact," said Patrick Henry, "that the great body of yeomanry are in decided opposition to it." Certainly the opposition came mostly from the agricultural districts and the debtor areas, while the movement for ratification was centered in the propertied classes, whose economic well-being was endangered by the inability of the old government to redeem its financial obligations and to protect commerce, industry, and speculation. Speaking broadly, and here we note the exception of Rhode Island, the regions of the coast were generally in favor, and the back country opposed. The success of the conservative Federalists in 1787 and 1788, like the success of the radicals in 1776, was due to an active, powerful, and well-integrated minority, concentrated in the towns and represented in each state. As Professor Beard has well said, "The Constitution was not created by 'the whole people,' as the jurists have said; neither was it created by 'the states,' as Southern nullifiers long contended; but it was the work of a consolidated group whose interests knew no state boundaries and were truly national in their scope." [6]

"Governments are instituted among men," insisted Jefferson in the Declaration of Independence, to secure "certain unalienable Rights, that among these are Life, Liberty and the pursuit of Happiness." Madison, twelve years later, arguing for ratification in the tenth number of the *Federalist,* asserted that "the first object of government" was the protection of "the diversity of the faculties of men, from which the rights of property originate," and held that the "principal task of modern legislation" was the regulation of conflicting economic interests. It was a far call from the high idealism of Jefferson to the stern realism of Madison, but not all had forgotten the political precepts of the revolutionary era. Massachusetts,

[6] C. A. Beard, *An Economic Interpretation of the Constitution,* 325.

New York, Pennsylvania, and Virginia, to name but four of seven, had ratified the Constitution only on the virtual promise that it would be amended to protect the "rights of man." As a consequence, the first session of the first Congress submitted twelve amendments to the states, ten of which, known as the Bill of Rights, were duly ratified. They guaranteed such fundamental rights as liberty of speech, press, and assembly, religious liberty, jury trial, and protection against unreasonable searches and seizures and against excessive bail and punishments, while the ninth and tenth amendments were blanket protection against usurpations by the federal government of the rights of citizens and states. With the adoption of these amendments, it seemed that human rights as well as property had been covered in the Constitution, but scarcely a decade passed before it was evident that phrases in a constitution, no matter how confidently they had been placed there, might acquire unexpected meaning as interpreted by the courts.

These years are ably interpreted in A. M. Schlesinger, *New Viewpoints in American History*, Chap. VIII, and in C. and M. Beard, *The Rise of American Civilization*, Chap. VII. C. A. Beard, *An Economic Interpretation of the Constitution of the United States*, Chaps. II, III, VI, X, XI, is fundamental to an understanding of that document. Scholarly but conventional is Edward Channing, *A History of the United States*, Vol. III, Chaps. XIII–XVIII. W. E. Binkley, *American Political Parties*, Chap. I, discusses the political background. For social history read H. J. Carman, *Social and Economic History of the United States*, Vol. I, Chap. VI. Foreign relations are discussed in T. A. Bailey, *A Diplomatic History of the American People*, Chap. IV. Source materials are in G. S. Callender, *Selections from the Economic History of the United States*, 180–235; H. S. Commager, *Documents of American History*, Vol. I, 119–150; and S. E. Morison, *Sources and Documents*, 204 ff.

Chapter IX

FEDERALIST DOMINATION

> *"You are afraid," says Mr. Oswald today, "of being made the tools of the powers of Europe." "Indeed I am," says I. "What powers?" said he. "All of them," said I. "It is obvious that all the powers of Europe will be continually manoeuvering with us, to work us into their real or imaginary balances of power. They will wish to make us a make-weight candle, when they are weighing out their pounds. Indeed, it is not surprising; for we shall often, if not always, be able to turn the scale. But I think it ought to be our rule not to meddle."*
>
> JOHN ADAMS, *Works*, III, 316

STARTING THE MACHINERY

Among the last acts of the expiring Congress under the Articles of Confederation was the passing of a group of laws for the establishment of the new government. Following these directions, the first Congress under the Constitution was elected, and the President and the Vice-President were chosen. As to the choice for the presidency, there could be no uncertainty. The tall and dignified Virginian, who during the dark days of the Revolution had led the patriot cause, held first place in the hearts of his countrymen and was unanimously chosen. Although but fifty-seven years of age, Washington accepted the post reluctantly. Friends of the new government were convinced that his unique position at home and his prestige abroad were absolutely essential if success was to be achieved, and he bowed to the imperative call of duty. The vice-presidency naturally went to the North and was given to John Adams of Massachusetts, who had just returned from his post as minister to Great Britain and had recently published his *Defence of the Constitutions of Government of the United States of America*. On April 30, 1789, before a wildly enthusiastic throng, Washington took the oath of office on the balcony of Federal Hall, New York, and immediately after delivered his inaugural address in the Senate chamber.

The new nation had been born, but would it outlast the early days of infancy? No taxes had yet been levied to support it, and no administrative machinery had been created through which it might function. North Carolina and Rhode Island had not yet entered the Union; the people of Vermont had actually been negotiating at London for recognition as an independent state, while the trans-Allegheny settlers were wavering between secession and adherence. No tradition or organized public opinion was behind the new government, and even its ardent supporters were dubious of its success. Hamilton called it a "frail and worthless fabric," and John Adams doubted if it would outlast his day.

On the other hand, there were encouraging factors. Prosperity was rapidly returning, soon to be augmented by the increase of foreign commerce resulting from European wars. So important was this that recent students have been inclined to believe that the success of the new Constitution was due primarily to this factor.[1] Furthermore, the new government had the backing of a favorable press and hopeful public opinion. Even opponents like Patrick Henry and lukewarm adherents like Samuel Adams and Thomas Jefferson were determined to support it. Their support won over many distrustful citizens, as did the adoption of the first ten amendments. Important also was the fact that the new government was in the hands of its friends. With the exception of the Attorney General, Edmund Randolph, whose attitude had been wavering, and Thomas Jefferson, Secretary of State, officials of the new government were ardent adherents of a strong central government. Washington was not concerned with rewarding loyalty or building a party machine. He attempted to choose men of capacity, integrity, and eminence, with due consideration to sectional representation, but, with the exceptions noted, his principal appointees were all strong Federalists. This was true not only of Hamilton, the Secretary of the Treasury, and Henry Knox, Secretary of War, but of all the judges soon to be chosen. To the first Congress only one who had been an opponent of the new Constitution was elected. Of the twenty-four senators, eleven had helped draft the instrument, and in the House there was a strong group of framers and ratifiers led by James Madison.[2] The new government was in no sense a coalition. It was anxious that the Constitution should be a success, and it pressed forward aggressively and withal intelligently to accomplish this object.

The problems confronting the administration, naturally difficult, were

[1] Washington, himself, writing to Lafayette, June 18, 1788, suggested another interpretation: "And then, I expect that blessings will be attributed to our new government, which are now taking their rise from that industry and frugality, into the produce of which the people have been forced from necessity."

[2] Twenty-six of the thirty-nine signers of the Constitution were represented in some branch of the new government.

made more so by the realization that any act might mean the establishment of a precedent and that a single false move might doom the new system of government. Congress debated for days as to the best method of addressing the President, and much time was spent in determining points of etiquette regarding the relationship between various branches of government. Washington, surrounded by aristocrats, many of whom were not unfavorable to monarchy, and by nature extremely punctilious himself, was careful not to arouse democratic antagonism by too much mimicry of royal majesty. Regarding his own powers he had to tread with a careful step, for the first Congress was not inclined to relinquish any powers to the strengthening of the executive. "An attempt to define the Presidency as Roosevelt or Wilson administered it," says one historian, "would have been considered plain tyranny in 1788."

Three primary tasks confronted the first Congress. First was the problem of amendments to make the Constitution more palatable. This was taken up immediately, and by the end of 1791 the first ten had been added to the Constitution, although the contemptuous and unreasoned opposition of many Federalist leaders, as Schouler suggests, "marked the Federalist Party for division and early ruin." Second was the task of creating the machinery of government, in a sense, completing the work of the constitutional convention. A post office already existed, but the judiciary and the departments of war, state, and the treasury must be established. The most important of the laws bearing on this problem was the Judiciary Act of 1789, which, in addition to creating the office of Attorney General, established a Supreme Court with a chief justice and five associates,[3] circuit courts, and district courts. The act gave to the federal courts the power to review the findings of state courts regarding the constitutionality of state or federal legislation.[4] Thus began in our federal system the theory of judicial review, which, enlarged and strengthened by Marshall in later years, was to make the judiciary the final and determining power in our government.

With the exception of a formal statute with reference to the taking of oaths, the first law enacted was the Tariff Act of July 4, 1789. Upon eighty-one enumerated articles specific or *ad valorem* rates were levied, and upon all other imports a flat 5-per-cent duty was placed. Although the act was designed primarily for revenue, a very definite effort was made to place many of the duties where they would give protection. Upon goods imported in American ships a discount of 10 per cent of the

---

[3] John Jay was appointed Chief Justice. The associate justices were James Wilson of Pennsylvania, John Rutledge of South Carolina, John Blair of Virginia, William Cushing of Massachusetts, and James Iredell of North Carolina.

[4] See the Constitution, Article III, Section 2 (1).

tariff was allowed, and to encourage the China trade an even larger discount was given to imports of tea. A few days later another act on the tonnage duties paid upon entering port discriminated heavily in favor of American ships; at the same time it provided that American vessels in the coastwise trade should pay duty only once a year, while foreign ships must pay it at every entry. It was not for nothing that the manufacturing and mercantile interests had supported the Constitution. Their recompense was immediate.

HAMILTONIANISM VERSUS JEFFERSONIANISM

If Washington's was the guiding hand of the first administration, the policies were those of Hamilton. Born in the West Indies in 1757 of a Scotch father and a French Huguenot mother, Hamilton had come to the mainland at the age of fifteen in search of education and fortune. Precocious, ambitious, ever alert to the main chance, he distinguished himself while at King's College in New York as an ardent advocate of revolution and served in the war as the secretary and trusted confidant of Washington, adding to his military reputation by leading the New York troops in an assault at Yorktown. His marriage into the powerful Schuyler family of New York only confirmed his reverence for tradition and his instinctive preference for control by the competent few. As a delegate to the constitutional convention, he advocated a government so thoroughly centralized and aristocratic that even that conservative body was not impressed, and his influence was slight. Small as was his faith in the document as it was finally written, his labors in its behalf appear to have been the chief influence in securing its adoption in New York. Hamilton has left his imprint upon American history through the sheer force of his intellect. His practical mind saw clearly how the new government might be strengthened and stabilized through financial reorganization, and his earnestness and his tight logic bore down the opposition. A master of finance and government, his genius, as one biographer insists, like that of most, was "three-fourths hard work." Restless energy, great moral courage, extraordinary mental capacity, and an intensity of application extraordinary in any age account for his influence and power. More than any other, perhaps, Hamilton was responsible for launching the new nation upon a successful career, but his own weaknesses were also in part responsible for the development of an opposition to his policies that was soon to destroy the Federalist Party. His egotism and vanity, his dictatorial manner, his failure in the management of men, and his lack of political judgment continually handicapped his efforts. With little understanding of the American mind and spirit, and the least American of the great men of his day, he had, nevertheless, a patriotism that on more than one occasion saved the new nation from irreparable damage.

The tariff and tonnage acts had been passed before Hamilton assumed the treasury post, but for subsequent financial legislation he was largely responsible. One of the last acts of the first Congress was to request him to make a report on the state of the finances, and in compliance he submitted four reports: the first dealing with the public debt, the second recommending an excise, the third urging a national bank, and the fourth, his famous report on manufacturing. Though he strongly believed, on the ground of economic soundness, in the measures he advocated, it was evident from these reports that the measures were also political. His economic policies had in them the primary motive of political centralization and stabilization. All of them were designed to establish the financial solvency and credit of the federal government and thus increase its strength at home and abroad, and secure the backing of the monied classes.

Hamilton estimated the foreign debt to France, Spain, and Holland with arrears of interest at $11,710,378, the domestic debt with interest at $42,414,185, and the state debts incurred in aid of the Revolution at about $25,000,000. The latter, he urged, should be assumed by the federal government, and all should be refunded at par. Against the payment of the foreign debt there was little to be said, and all were agreed that some part of the federal domestic debt should be paid. On the other hand, there was bitter opposition to the payment of the domestic debt at par and to the assumption of the state debts. In the hard times following the war much of the original Continental paper had passed out of the hands of the original owners and had found its way into those of speculators. As the terms of Hamilton's plan leaked out, wealthy speculators scoured the back country for securities. "I call not at a single house or go into any company," wrote the Republican senator, Maclay, in his diary, "but traces of speculation in certificates appear," and he added, a few days later, "Hawkins, of North Carolina, said as he came up he passed two expresses with very large sums of money on their way to North Carolina for purposes of speculation in certificates. Wadsworth has sent off two small vessels for the Southern States, on the errand of buying up certificates. I really fear the members of Congress are deeper in this business than any others." [5] Madison, leading the opposition, failed to effect a compromise, and Hamilton's bill, which may have been expedient—indeed necessary—if not just, finally passed.

To the assumption of state debts an even greater opposition developed.

[5] E. S. Maclay, editor, *Journal of William Maclay* (1890), 177–179.

Hamilton pleaded for it on the ground of political unity. "If all the public creditors," he urged, "receive their dues from one source, distributed with an equal hand, having the same interests, they will unite in support of the fiscal arrangements of the government." In support of the measure were the capitalists, the speculators, and the states having large debts; in opposition were the small farmer and the states that by taxation, payment in land grants, and other means had comparatively small debts. Assumption seemed doomed, and only clever political manipulation secured the enactment of the bill. Pleading eloquently with Jefferson that the whole fate of the union depended on his bill, Hamilton won the support of the man who was soon to become his chief political opponent. At a dinner at Jefferson's house, a deal was made with the Virginia representatives whereby, in return for the location of the national capital on the Potomac, enough Virginians were to vote for assumption to carry the measure. Thus two controversial issues were settled, and thus the national capital was set up on the banks of the Potomac. Two years later Jefferson wrote disgustedly to Washington that he was "duped" into this "by the Secretary of the Treasury, and made a tool for forwarding his schemes, not then sufficiently understood by me; and of all the errors of my political life, this has occasioned me the deepest regret." "I was most ignorantly and innocently made to hold the candle," he bitterly complained. In the heat of subsequent political strife, the canny Virginian was probably assuming an innocence hardly warranted by his activity at the time.

Hamilton in his third report advocated the establishment of a national bank modeled somewhat after the Bank of England, arguing that it would provide a much needed paper currency, benefit the government and private business by providing banking facilities for carrying on commercial transactions, and act as a depository for public funds and as a fiscal agency for the government. Such a bank was eventually chartered in 1791 for twenty years with a capital of $10,000,000, one fifth of which was to be subscribed by the government, the subscription to be one fourth in specie and three fourths in government bonds. The notes of the bank were limited to the amount of the capital stock and were to be receivable in taxes as long as they were redeemable in specie. For such a bank there was a real need, but the bill to establish it aroused the bitter opposition of the group that opposed further federal centralization and feared the control of the government by the monied interests.

Jefferson, who had approved of the payment of the federal debt and somewhat reluctantly backed assumption, threw himself into the fight against the bank, while Madison assumed the leadership of the opposition in the House. Disturbed by the heat of the controversy, Washington asked for opinions from his cabinet. Hamilton's reply was a closely reasoned argument for a highly nationalistic, "loose-construction" interpretation of the Constitution, in which he urged that "If the *end* be clearly comprehended within any of the specified powers, and if the measure have an obvious relation to that *end,* and is not forbidden by any particular provision of the Constitution, it may safely be deemed to come within the compass of the national authority." In subsequent years this argument was to be the framework of many of Marshall's nationalistic decisions, particularly in the famous case of McCulloch *v.* Maryland. Jefferson and Randolph, on the other hand, presented the theories of the states' rights "strict-construction" school, asserting that "laws necessary and proper" did not mean laws merely convenient. Convinced by the Hamiltonian logic, Washington signed the bill. In general the vote was sectional; the North favored it, the South opposed.

On the same day that Hamilton had presented his report urging the United States bank, he offered another recommending excise taxes. His motive here was not merely to secure revenue, but to extend the operations of the federal government throughout the nation so that even the most remote frontiersman might know that a strong central authority had been established. His purpose was but too well accomplished, for the backwoodsmen of Pennsylvania, whose grain had to be reduced to whisky if it was to be profitably transported to the market, rose in rebellion in the summer of 1794. The President's proclamation calling out the militia of four states not only ended the Whisky Rebellion, but furnished an excellent opportunity to demonstrate the authority of the new government. Less successful for the moment was Hamilton's fourth report, on manufactures, in which he urged the promotion of industry by protective tariffs. It was an able argument for protection—in fact, the primary classic of that doctrine—but its influence upon a Congress representing the mercantile and agrarian classes was slight. It took the nationalism of the War of 1812, the rising strength of the manufacturing interests, and the subsequent arguments of economists and statesmen to develop the movement for protection.

The American Constitution had made no provision for government by political parties. The formation of parties, however, could not long be delayed. Men differed too radically in their philosophy of the powers and function of the national government, economic interests developed conflicting points of view, and personal ambitions and animosities produced friction. These elements can all be seen in the fight over the adoption of the Constitution and in the conflicting philosophies of the Federalists and Antifederalists. The latter had generally opposed the financial measures of Hamilton, and they were joined by many who had advocated adoption but now opposed the tendency toward centralization or mistrusted the financial group benefited by the Hamiltonian program. Of these the ablest was Jefferson. Thoroughly aroused by the bank bill, and fearful of the monarchical leanings of Hamilton and his followers, Jefferson took upon himself the task of organizing the opposition, which soon became known as the Republican Party.[6] In 1791, with Madison, he took a trip to New York, ostensibly a botanizing expedition in the Hudson valley, but actually for the purpose of "lining up" the powerful Clinton and Livingston families, whose power in New York politics for the moment was overshadowed by the Schuylers and other aristocrats who had backed the Constitution. With this group he later united the radicals of Pennsylvania, whose ablest leader was Albert Gallatin, soon to rank with Hamilton among the nation's great financial statesmen. To undermine the prestige of Hamilton, an opposition paper was established in Philadelphia under the editorship of Philip Freneau, whose vituperative attacks upon Hamilton and the administration can hardly be matched in modern journalism and would be unthinkable if inspired by a member of the cabinet today. In Congress, under the leadership of Jefferson's two lieutenants, James Madison and William B. Giles of Virginia, an incessant attack was maintained against Hamilton's measures and conduct of the treasury. To all this Hamilton replied in kind, easily vindicating his honesty and efficiency; but the strategy of Jefferson was successfully building up a party that in 1800 was to overthrow the ascendancy of the Federalists.

This bitter conflict in Washington's official family could not continue interminably. Jefferson, convinced that Washington was entirely under the influence of Hamilton in both domestic and foreign policy, resigned in December, 1793; Hamilton, unwilling to resign while under Congressional attack, remained until January, 1795. In the meantime Washington, worn out by factional controversy and the cares of office, had opposed standing for re-election in 1792, but finally yielded to the urging of both Jefferson and Hamilton that his leadership was necessary to establish firmly the new government. Having acquiesced in the candidacy of Washington, the followers of Jefferson, who were gradually assuming the name of the Republican Party, could not manifest their true strength. They gave George Clinton fifty votes for the vice-presidency, but John Adams received seventy-seven and was re-elected.

[6] The term "Federalist" is self-evident. The term "Republican" was used to designate a party opposed to monarchy, aristocracy, and privilege. Its enemies dubbed its adherents Democratic-Republicans as the most opprobrious term they could think of, but "Democratic" was soon dropped and was not used again until Jackson's time. If parties today may be said to have ancestors, the Democratic Party would find its origin in the Republican Party of Jefferson's time, and the Republican Party of recent years in the Hamiltonian Federalists.

FOREIGN COMPLICATIONS

Wars involving all Europe, with tremendous political and economic implications, have occurred three times since the American republic was founded. In the first two of these wars the United States was eventually drawn into the conflict, and in both cases her future was affected in important ways. Almost a century and a half has elapsed since the French Revolution set the match to the first conflagration, and it is now possible to discern its influence upon American history. American historians are still searching to determine the full effects of the World War of 1914–1918.

Five days after Washington had taken the oath of office the Estates General of France met for the first time in more than 150 years. Called together to save France from impending bankruptcy, they succeeded in establishing a limited monarchy and in sweeping away many of the absurdities and abuses of an antiquated feudalism. The long-delayed process of reform having started, power quickly passed to the more radical groups. Foreign war broke out in 1792, the king was beheaded, and a republic was established. In the turmoil of revolution and war, power was eventually grasped by the dictator, Napoleon, who gave France sixteen years of comparative quiet at home but incessant wars of conquest abroad. In their early stage the wars resulting from the French Revolution were a conflict between political democracy (liberty, equality, fraternity) and monarchical despotism; in their later stage they became imperial conflicts in which the two leading nations, France and England, struggled for colonial empire and the domination of Europe.

Nowhere was the French Revolution more joyfully acclaimed than in America. Ardent liberals wore liberty caps, set up liberty poles, and organized clubs similar to the revolutionary political clubs of Paris, and when France became involved in war, many believed that we should fulfill the treaty of 1778 to the letter and actively aid our former ally. On the other hand, the democratic swing of the Revolution and the excesses of the Reign of Terror turned the more conservative classes against France and, when war broke out between that nation and Great Britain, Americans were sharply divided in their sympathies. The Anglo-men, as Jefferson called them, were influenced not only by their horror of democracy but also by the fact that the merchant and shipping classes were closely affiliated with London bankers and exporters. By the Anglo-men the sympathizers of France were denounced as Jacobins and atheists. It was not long before this conflict of opinion was injected into the already overheated political situation. Political and economic interests naturally in

:lined the Federalists toward England, the Antifederalists or Jeffersonian Republicans toward France.

With feeling running high, the more reckless partisans advocated war on one side or the other. The cautious Washington, however, clearly saw the danger of foreign entanglements to the infant republic, and his opinion was strengthened by both Hamilton and Jefferson. Working against almost insuperable difficulties, when a single false step might have meant war, Washington brought his administration to a peaceful conclusion. Under similar odds, as we shall see, Adams and Jefferson continued his policy, and it was not until the administration of Madison that the rising West precipitated an armed conflict with Great Britain. The whole question of foreign relations, furthermore, was not made less difficult by the fact that the territory of the United States was surrounded on three sides by the possessions of foreign nations and that neither England nor France was content to abide by the decisions of the treaty of 1783.

On April 20, 1792, France declared war on Austria, a war that was soon to involve all Europe and to continue with but two short interruptions until 1815. In February, 1793, she declared war against Great Britain. The French government assumed that the treaty of alliance of 1778, which bound the United States to help defend the West Indies and to open her ports to ships captured by the French, was still in force and that this country would inevitably be drawn into the conflict. Washington, however, issued on April 22 a proclamation of neutrality.

Two weeks earlier there had arrived at Charleston, South Carolina, Edmond Charles Genêt, first minister of the new French republic to the United States. Young in years, but experienced in diplomacy, Genêt had been instructed to use the United States as a base for privateering and to recruit forces for the conquest of Florida and Louisiana. Ignoring Washington's proclamation, he made contacts with frontier leaders for expeditions against Spanish territory, fitted out privateers to prey upon British commerce, and, when he found it impossible to send captured prizes to France, set up French prize courts on American soil. All this was in violation of neutrality, but Genêt's head had been turned by the enthusiastic reception accorded him in the southern and middle states. His mission was to use the United States in France's war against Britain, and he carried out his instructions with no more ardor than had Franklin and Deane when they pursued a similar purpose in France during the Revolution. When Genêt arrived in Philadelphia, Washington received him with cold formality, while Jefferson put an end to his illegal activities. After the French minister had appealed to the people over the heads of the government, Washington requested his recall, and Genêt's public career was ended.

Genêt's high-handed conduct undoubtedly injured the French party in America. It was further weakened by the French decree authorizing her navy to seize foodstuffs and private property of English citizens even on neutral ships. This decree was soon withdrawn but not before it had done much damage to American shipping in French ports. Claims for this damage were pressed by our strongly pro-French minister, James Monroe, but he accomplished little and was soon recalled.

While the Washington administration was straining desperately to escape entanglement in the European imbroglio, it was exerting its best efforts to iron out controversies with Spain concerning four problems: the right of free navigation of the Mississippi [7]; the "right of deposit" or of transshipment of goods to seagoing vessels at New Orleans without payment of duty; the policy of Spain in inciting the Indians of the Southwest against American settlers; and, finally, the question of the boundary line between the United States and Florida. The last problem arose over a clause in the provisional treaty of 1782 (not included in the final ratified draft of 1783), which stated that, if England retained Florida, the boundary should be 32° 28′, but, if Florida was ceded to Spain, it should be 31°. Of this arrangement Spain promptly announced its defiance.

These problems involved the economic prosperity of the western settlers and even the stability of the infant republic. Products of the frontier found a market by way of the Mississippi, and westward expansion could go on only if the Spanish menace was removed. Taking advantage of this obvious anxiety, emissaries of France, Spain, and England were constantly intriguing with frontier leaders in an effort to separate the new settlements from the American union. "The western states," said Washington, ". . . stand as it were upon a pivot. A touch of a feather would turn them either way." In this controversy complete success finally attended American diplomacy. The turn of European events and the fear that the United States was drawing closer to England led Spain, to the gratification of our representative, Thomas Pinckney, to sign a treaty (1795) that granted free navigation, the right of deposit, the 31° boundary, and a promise to restrain the Indians.

Less successful were the negotiations carried on with Great Britain. The treaty that Adams, Franklin, and Jay had signed in 1783 was a victory for American diplomacy, but it left open more questions than it settled. The boundary between Canada and the United States, it was soon discovered, was anything but definite. More pressing at the moment, however, were

[7] The right of free navigation had been obtained by England in 1763. This right she granted to the United States in the treaty of 1783, although her power to do so was questionable.

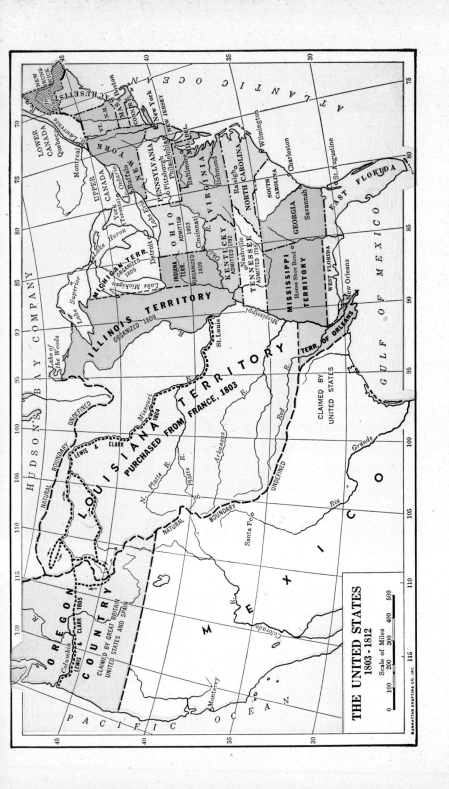

THE UNITED STATES
1803 - 1812

Scale of Miles
0   100   200   300   400   500

MANHATTAN DRAFTING CO. INC.

the questions concerning the restoration of Tory property, the payment of debts owed by Americans to British subjects at the opening of the Revolution, the rights of Americans to fish off the Canadian coast, and the unwillingness of Great Britain to surrender the forts and trading posts on American soil. The shipping interests were anxious to open up the lucrative trade with the British West Indies that had been closed after the Revolution by the British navigation acts and to reach an understanding with Great Britain concerning the right of neutrals on the high seas. Hardly had the war with France commenced when Great Britain began the obnoxious practice of impressing American seamen and confiscating American property. During the French and Indian War, the British government had promulgated a decree known as the rule of 1756, to the effect that trade illegal in time of peace was illegal in time of war. When American shippers, after the war had started, began to trade freely with the French West Indies and to carry the products of these islands to France, Britain enforced this rule and confiscated scores of American ships and cargoes.

Regardless of the efforts of France to involve us in a war with England, there were obviously enough points of controversy existing between Great Britain and the United States to precipitate a conflict. War, in fact, seemed inevitable, and it was prevented only by the firm conviction of the administration that it must be avoided at any cost. Some of the problems could wait; a half century was to pass before the boundary line was straightened out, and it was not until 1910 that the question of the fisheries was settled. The problems that pressed for immediate solution were those of neutral rights, the northwest posts, and the debts to British subjects. Concerning Tory property, the treaty stipulated that "Congress earnestly recommend to the legislatures of the respective states" the restitution of confiscated property, while another article said that creditors "shall meet with no lawful impediment to the recovery of the full value in sterling money." To say that Tories and British merchants had achieved scant success in obtaining restitution would be to put it mildly. It was too great a strain on human nature to expect the states willingly to indemnify the Tories or to expect the debt-ridden Southern planters who had shaken off their obligations by means of revolution to assume them voluntarily again. Until the debts were paid, the British government made it clear, the posts in American soil would not be relinquished. In reality this was an excuse, for the British held on to protect a fur trade estimated at £100,000 a year and to intrigue with the Indians to hold back the westward movement of population.

To conciliate these differences, John Adams had been sent to England during the period of the confederation, but he had achieved no success.

In a desperate effort to prevent war, Washington now dispatched John Jay with instructions to join with the northern powers of Europe in a league of armed neutrality if his msision failed. Jay's position was not without strength, for the United States was Great Britain's largest customer, and the developing European situation made it extremely undesirable for the British nation to push the United States into the ranks of her enemies. A man of integrity and ability, Jay obtained much less than was hoped for by the aggressive young republic. By the Jay treaty Great Britain agreed to evacuate all posts on American territory, but British subjects were to be allowed to carry on the fur trade on American soil. Mixed commissions were to be established to determine the Maine boundary line, the amount of the debts owed to British subjects, which the United States was to assume, and the losses inflicted by the illegal capture of vessels and cargoes of the two countries.[8] Reciprocal commercial relations (limited to ten years) were established between Great Britain, East India, and the United States, and trade with the West Indies was opened under conditions so harsh and exacting that the article was struck out before the treaty was accepted. Nothing was said concerning impressment, and the treaty acquiesced in the claim of Great Britain that she might confiscate enemy goods on American ships and seize contraband of war.

The treaty satisfied no one. Washington, however, anxious to preserve peace, sent it to the Senate, where the Federalists supported it and finally passed it by a bare two-thirds vote after debating it in secret session for sixteen days. Feeling ran so high that S. T. Mason of Virginia, in violation of Senate secrecy, gave the treaty to the press. Public reaction was instant; Jay was burned in effigy in many of the towns of the country, and Hamilton was stoned by a mob when he attempted to defend the treaty in New York. So hateful was the new engagement "that some of our respectable men," moaned Senator Cabot of Massachusetts, "have joined the Jacobins." Jefferson asserted bitterly that it was "really nothing more than a treaty of alliance between England and the Anglo-men of this country against the Legislature and people of the United States." The treaty, nevertheless, by establishing commissions, set an important precedent for the arbitration of differences between this country and Great Britain, which was valuable, and secured the evacuation of the northwestern posts, which was important, but it failed to establish the rights of neutrals on the sea at the opening of a long European war.

[8] The first commission decided that the Shodiac was the river meant by the negotiators of 1783 under the name of St. Croix, but this was only a beginning of the eventual boundary-line settlement. The second commission could not agree, but a convention in 1802 annulled Article VI of the treaty and set a figure of $2,664,000, which the United States paid. The third ordered the payment of $5,849,082 to Americans and $143,428 to British subjects (1804).

ADAMS AND THE DOWNFALL OF FEDERALISM

In retrospect Washington's policy regarding the Jay treaty seems wise enough, but his signing of it was the most unpopular act of his life, and he finished his second term under a storm of abuse and criticism. Not opposed to a third term on principle, but utterly wearied with the trials of office, Washington gave notice to his countrymen in a farewell address that he would retire at the end of the term. Wrung from eight bitter years of experience, the address closed with an admonition to avoid foreign entanglements, a restatement in a sense of the foreign policy of his own administration.

> The great rule of conduct for us [he urged], in regard to foreign nations, is, in extending our commercial relations, to have with them as little *political* connection as possible. . . .
>
> Europe has a set of primary interests, which to us have none, or a very remote relation. Hence she must be engaged in frequent controversies, the causes of which are essentially foreign to our concerns. Hence, therefore, it must be unwise in us to implicate ourselves, by artificial ties in the ordinary vicissitudes of her politics, or the ordinary combinations and collisions of her friendships, or enmities. . . .
>
> It is our true policy to steer clear of permanent alliances, with any nation of the foreign world. . . .[9]

Washington's retirement left the field to other candidates. The Federalists favored John Adams and Thomas Pinckney, and the Republicans Jefferson and Aaron Burr. Hamilton, who heartily disliked Adams, worked strenuously to bring about the election of Pinckney, but was prevented by eighteen New England Federalists who scattered their second vote among minor candidates. This also helped to elect the Republican Jefferson Vice-President, a curious situation, a repetition of which the twelfth amendment (1804) was in part designed to prevent. Brusque, tactless, and devoid of personal graces, Adams was a man of scholarly tastes, wide experience in diplomacy, and strong force of character. His knowledge of governments ancient and modern, as displayed in his books, is the admiration of modern political scientists; his long and able services in the trying years after 1775 command the respect of historians. As a politician, however, he was doomed from the start. Long an advocate of aristocratic government, he was distrusted by the Republicans for his conservatism, while the Federalists were alienated by the coldness of his manner. The enmity of Hamilton, the intellectual leader of the Federalist Party, handicapped his administration throughout and contributed greatly to the Federalist decline.

[9] J. D. Richardson, *Messages and Papers of the Presidents*, I, 214–215.

Even more than that of Washington, the administration of Adams was dominated by the European war. His policy was essentially that of Washington, fortified by an intimate knowledge of European diplomacy, which harbored not the slightest illusion. But the efforts of Adams to maintain peace and neutrality encountered even greater difficulties than those of his predecessor. The French Directory, convinced that the Jay treaty was a violation of the treaties of 1778 and that it marked the beginning of an Anglo-American entente, refused to receive Charles C. Pinckney, the new American minister sent by Washington to succeed Monroe, and turned loose the French navy upon American shipping. By June of 1797 over three hundred American ships and their cargoes had been confiscated.

In America this situation deepened the party cleavage. The Republicans, bitterly hostile to the Jay treaty and sympathetic with France, were inclined to justify French depredations. They failed to realize that France had passed the idealistic stage of the Revolution, that her government was fast approaching a dictatorship under the control of ambitious and corrupt officials, and that the nation was now more interested in attaining the military supremacy of Europe than in spreading the doctrines of liberty, equality, and fraternity. Nor did they comprehend that the policy of France toward the United States was to resent any close relationships with Great Britain and that her ambition was to obtain Louisiana, Florida, and Canada and thus surround the young republic with French territory. The Federalists, on the other hand, whose ships were being confiscated, clamored for retaliatory action against France.

Hoping to reconcile the differences, Adams proposed that a peace mission be sent to France. For this he picked the Republican, Elbridge Gerry, and the two Federalists, John Marshall and C. C. Pinckney. In Paris strange treatment awaited the American negotiators. Talleyrand, the French foreign minister, refused to receive them officially but carried on informal negotiations through three agents. As a preliminary to further negotiations, these agents demanded an apology for the remarks of Adams in his message to Congress of May, 1797, a loan to the French government, and a bribe of $250,000 to the members of the Directory.[10] After months of this type of diplomacy the mission broke up. Adams sent their report to Congress, substituting for the names of the French agents the letters X, Y, and Z, and informed Congress that he would "never send another minister to France without assurances that he will be received, respected,

---

[10] When, during the discussions, one of the French agents exclaimed, "Gentlemen, you do not speak to the point. It is money; we expect you to offer money," Pinckney stated his answer: "It is no; no, not a sixpence." This reply was soon transformed into "Millions for defense, but not a cent for tribute."

and honored as the representative of a free, powerful, and independent nation."

The picture of French diplomacy, as revealed by the XYZ papers, was a disillusioning experience for the Republicans, and they heartily co-operated in plans for retaliation. Congress abrogated the treaties of 1778, created a navy department, ordered the purchase or construction of twelve new vessels, authorized the President to issue letters of marque and re-prisal against France, and provided for the raising of a military force of 10,000 men. Thus, without declaration, commenced in 1798 what was virtually a war against France. By the end of that year two hundred privateers and fourteen men-of-war were at sea, and within two years what was left of French commerce in the West Indies had been destroyed.

The Federalists hopefully expected that this would lead to a declaration of war by France. Adams was willing to fight France if necessary, but his purpose was to bring that nation to terms without a formal declaration, and in this he was supported by most of the Republicans. The Directory was wabbling, and Talleyrand was too wise to embark deliberately on an unnecessary war or to drive the United States into the arms of Great Britain. Prompted by Jefferson, he gave evidence of pacific intentions by ordering French officials to respect American ships, by issuing an official explanation of the XYZ affair, and by intimating that a minister would be received with respect. As the months went on, the war ardor began to cool, enlistments came in slowly, and the Republicans became suspicious of the purpose of the new army as they saw all important commissions given to Federalists. A bitter factional fight that developed between Adams and Hamilton regarding the appointment of major generals set Adams at odds with his cabinet. Convinced that the time was ripe to begin open negotiations, Adams, in March, 1799, suddenly sent to the Senate the nomination of a minister to France. The Republicans were overjoyed, the Federalists stricken with dismay. The latter finally gave in, and Adams compromised by a commission instead of a single envoy. Napoleon, now First Consul, received the commission cordially, but refused to recognize any claims for spoliations unless the United States would abide by the treaties of 1778. The commission returned with no indemnities, but with a treaty (1800) in which France agreed to the abrogation of the earlier alliance and promised to respect the rights of neutrals (free ships make free goods).

The troubles with France, which for the moment had increased the strength of the Federalists and had enabled them to win their last political victory in the congressional elections of 1798–1799, was in the end to prove their undoing. Taking advantage of the war furore and the temporary weakening of the Republicans, they pushed through Congress in 1788 four acts known collectively as the alien and sedition acts. A Naturalization Act lengthened the period of residence necessary for citizenship from five to fourteen years, while two alien acts gave the President the power to expel from the country aliens judged dangerous to the peace and safety of the United States and in time of war to expel or restrain aliens as he deemed wise. The alien acts were not enforced, but the accompanying Sedition Act, which made it a crime under penalty of fine or imprisonment to write or publish "any false, scandalous or malicious" statement condemning the President or either house of Congress or bringing them into "contempt or disrepute," was enforced. War might have given a partial excuse for some of this legislation, but the Republicans had a well-grounded suspicion that it was aimed at them rather than at the enemies of the republic. Many French aliens were residents in America, and with few exceptions they were active in Republican politics. Of some twenty-five persons arrested and ten convicted under the Sedition Act, most, it was noticeable, were Republican editors or politicians, thus conveniently eliminated.

The Sedition Act, however, was a boomerang. Wise leaders of the Federalist Party, such as Hamilton and Marshall, had advised against it but with no success. The Republicans, who considered the acts directly aimed at their party and who hailed everyone convicted as a martyr, actively opposed them, and Republican leaders decided to make a direct appeal to the states. Madison drew up resolutions that were passed by the Virginia legislature and Jefferson the resolutions passed by Kentucky. Both the Virginia and the Kentucky resolutions (1798) embodied the theory of states' rights or the "compact theory" of government so often to be revived in succeeding years. The federal government, they insisted, was a voluntary compact of equal and sovereign states, which retained their right to judge when the federal government had transcended its powers. If the federal government assumed undelegated authority, its acts were null and void. The Kentucky resolutions called upon the other states to concur in declaring the alien and sedition acts void and to unite in requesting their repeal. Both resolutions insisted that Congress had violated the first amendment, and in this they were quite correct.

Important as are the Virginia and Kentucky resolutions in the history of American political theory as the first platform of the states' rights movement, their immediate purpose was largely that of a political thrust at Federalism. But the day of the Federalists was almost ended. The temporary patching of the differences with France undermined their prestige, factional fights weakened their position, taxation imposed in preparation for war aroused opposition, the alien and sedition acts were unpopular, and the common man distrusted the party of the "rich and well born." Above all else the clever political activity of Jefferson and his lieutenants had created a strong party to compete for power. The Federalists, in organizing and firmly establishing the new government, had made their contribution to American development, but their party, top-heavy with brilliant and able leaders, had lost touch with the common man and the rising frontier democracy. The united and well-disciplined Republicans carried the elections of 1800, but the House had the task of deciding whether Jefferson or Burr should be President.[11] That the nation was finished with the Federalists there could be no doubt, nor was there any question as to their first choice for the presidency. A considerable part of the Federalists, nevertheless, believed Burr the lesser of two evils, and fought strenuously to elect him President. Only the unselfish efforts of Hamilton, who correctly judged the two men, made possible the victory of Jefferson on the thirty-sixth ballot.

C. and M. Beard, *The Rise of American Civilization*, Chap. VIII, is interpretative. H. J. Ford, *Washington and his Colleagues* (Chronicles of America), is brief but spirited. Edward Channing, *A History of the United States*, Vol. IV, Chaps. I–VIII, is dependable. In L. M. Sears, *George Washington*, Chaps. XXIII–XXIX, the story of Washington during his presidency is told in detail. W. E. Binkley, *American Political Parties*, Chap. II, interprets political Federalism. Although Jefferson is interpreted to the disadvantage of Hamilton, A. J. Nock, *Jefferson*, Chap. V, is suggestive. For the diplomatic, see S. F. Bemis, *A Diplomatic History of the United States*, Chap. V or T. A. Bailey, *A Diplomatic History of the American People*, Chaps. V, VI, and for sources, H. S. Commager, *Documents of American History*, Vol. I, 151–186.

[11] Under the method of casting electoral votes then used both received 73 votes, Adams 65, and Pinckney 64. It was this tie vote for the presidency of two men of the same political party that was in part responsible for the twelfth amendment (superseding Article II, Section 1, Clause 3). The movement for the admendment was also strengthened by the election of 1796, when Adams, a Federalist, was elected President, and Jefferson, a Republican, was elected Vice-President (page 141).

Chapter X

JEFFERSONIAN REPUBLICANISM

> *Democracy is a troubled spirit fated never to rest, and whose dreams if it sleep, present only visions of hell.*
>
> FISHER AMES

> *The Gothic idea that we are to look backwards instead of forwards for the improvement of the human mind, and to recur to the annals of our ancestors for what is most perfect in government, in religion, and in learning, is worthy of those bigots in religion and government by whom it has been recommended, and whose purpose it would answer.*
>
> JEFFERSON TO JOSEPH PRIESTLEY
> (January 27, 1800)

JEFFERSON AND HIS PHILOSOPHY

On the morning of March 4, 1801, Thomas Jefferson, leader of the victorious Republican Party,[1] walked from his boarding house to the capitol and took the oath of office. Six feet two and a half inches in height, his face freckled from exposure to the sun but with features clear-cut and benign, he appeared to an English observer "a tall, large-boned farmer." A farmer, if not a very successful one, he was indeed, for next to his country, his interests and affection centered in his beautiful home and estate in the foothills of Virginia. "No occupation is so delightful to me," he said, "as the culture of the earth, and no culture comparable to that of the garden." Although he was the most astute politician of his time, his political leadership came to him through the failure of other men to create an opposition to Federalism rather than through his love of public life. A philosopher and lover of peace, he was happiest when his mind could play upon the problems of art, science, or religion, and when he could communicate and debate his ideas or discoveries with men of

---

[1] Not to be confused with the Republican Party of today. See footnote 6, page 135.

similar minds. He worked out a mathematical formula that still governs the shape of plowshares, made calculations for the hour lines on a horizontal sundial, "conferred an unintended benefit upon the bureaucracies" by inventing the swivel chair, devised a leather buggy top still in use, and drew the plans for the University of Virginia, the most beautiful grouping of buildings on a college campus in America. His restless and inquisitive mind was ever on the search for new facts that might benefit his countrymen and oblivious to any pecuniary advantages that might come to himself. His own estimate of his greatest contributions he wrote for an epitaph to be carved on his tombstone: "Here lies Thomas Jefferson, Author of the Declaration of Independence, of the Statute of Virginia for Religious Freedom, and Father of the University of Virginia."

Like many philosophers, Jefferson's statements of his own political and economic philosophy are often rambling and diffuse, but there is no missing the heart of his position. He was, says Channing, "an idealist who was in politics from a sincere desire to save the nation from those whom he termed monocrats and monopolists." [2] Virginian aristocrat as he was, he very definitely represented an economic class interest. Government, he believed, should rest in the hands of the producing class, that is, in the great majority who applied labor and capital directly to natural resources for the production of wealth. "His instincts," says one of his biographers, "reacted like the reflex action of an eyelid against anything that menaced that interest." [3] Unlike most other political leaders of his day, he had no financial interest in any speculative undertaking, never even acquiring a foot of land for speculative purposes. His philosophy, closely akin to that of the economic physiocrats,[4] made it easy to become a doctrinaire democrat. To him the intelligence, sanity, and genius of America rested in the ranks of the producing masses; to them must be extended the franchise and the control of government. True democratic progress could be attained by the simple formula of extending and preserving political and economic liberty, religious freedom, and educational privileges. Do this, and the better nature of man could then assert itself, and the golden day be achieved.

REPUBLICANISM AT THE HELM

Jefferson always believed that the Republican victory of 1800 ushered in a second great revolution in America. Certainly the Federalists believed

[2] Edward Channing, *The Jeffersonian System*, 4.

[3] A. J. Nock, *Jefferson*, 192.

[4] A system of economic thought, developed in France in the eighteenth century, emphasizing agriculture as the primary form of labor and wealth, land as the primary form of private property, and a system based upon the belief in natural laws that must be followed if men are to achieve their highest well-being.

this was true, and not a few agreed with President Dwight of Yale, who prophesied that, if Jefferson was elected, the Bible would be cast into a bonfire, our holy worship changed into a dance of Jacobin "phrensy," our wives and daughters dishonored, and our sons converted into disciples of Voltaire and the dragoons of Marat.[5] After the election was over, another member of the illustrious Dwight family again expressed Federalist sentiments with the words: "We have now reached the consummation of democratic blessedness. We have a country ruled by blockheads and knaves."

But there was nothing revolutionary in Jefferson's inaugural address, which was designed to conciliate political opponents. Many Americans have been separated, he insisted, by difference of opinion rather than by difference of principle. "We have called by different names brethren of the same principle. We are all Republicans, we are all Federalists." This sentiment may have dismayed ardent partisans, but it was not without truth. Few of either party could take exception to his principles—"equal and exact justice to all"; "peace, commerce and friendship with all nations, entangling alliances with none"; "support of State governments in all their rights"; "preservation of the General Government in its whole constitutional vigor"; "jealous care of the right of election"; "a well-disciplined militia"; "honest payment of our debts"; "encouragement of agriculture, and of commerce as its handmaid"; "diffusion of information"; "freedom of religion; freedom of the press, and freedom of person under the right of the habeas corpus, and trial by juries impartially selected." "These principles," said Jefferson, "form the bright constellation which has gone before us and guided our steps through an age of revolution and reformation." There was little here but the old eighteenth-century liberal political theory upon which supposedly our nation had been founded.

The problems confronting the Jefferson administration were substantially the same as those that troubled Washington and Adams. Some of them were attacked from a different point of view, but in the dominating problem of foreign affairs Jefferson held to the course of his predecessors. The most obvious immediate change was the introduction of "Republican simplicity" in official routine. Gone was the stiff and stately formality of the Federalist court. Gone were the weekly levees at which Washington and Adams received their callers with dignified formality. The President's house was open to anyone at any time of day, which led John Quincy

---

[5] While Jefferson was thus being stigmatized and pious old ladies buried their Bibles for fear they would be confiscated, Jefferson was spending his time at home during the campaign in a codification of the "morals of Jesus." The clergy hated him for his deism and his advocacy of the separation of church and state.

Adams to remark that Jefferson's "whole eight years was a levee." He even received the British ambassador in slippers and morning undress. In social functions official precedence was banned; his theory was that "all persons when brought together in society are perfectly equal, whether foreign or domestic, tilled or untilled, in or out of office." In his relations with Congress he substituted written messages for the annual "speech from the throne," and he expected no formal answers.

The first years of the Jefferson administration were the most fortunate and peaceful of the twenty-five years of Republican domination. Abroad the treaty of Amiens gave Europe a temporary cessation from war (March, 1802–May, 1803), allowing the new administration to concentrate on domestic problems. At home the Republicans had control of both houses of Congress, and had not held power long enough to split into factional controversy. Jefferson's cabinet worked harmoniously; his Secretary of State, James Madison, who saw eye to eye with his friend and chief, was an industrious and able executive; his Secretary of the Treasury, the Swiss-born immigrant, Albert Gallatin, was a financier of the first order. The stage seemed auspiciously set for a favorable testing of Republican principles, but circumstances over which Jefferson and his party had no control were soon to push them into assuming Federalist principles, while the Federalists found themselves upholding Republican policies. Jefferson had spoken more truly than he realized when he said, "We are all Republicans, we are all Federalists."

Working closely with Congress and taking an active part in the framing of legislation, Jefferson proceeded to undo what he considered some of the worst abuses of Federalist rule. The Naturalization Act (page 144) was repealed and the five-year period necessary for citizenship restored. The alien and sedition acts having expired in 1801, Jefferson pardoned persons convicted under them. The Judiciary Act of 1801 was repealed and the "midnight judges" ousted from their positions. This act, which had provided for a much needed reorganization of the federal courts, had been passed during the closing weeks of the last Federalist Congress and had provided for sixteen new judges with an added number of attorneys, marshals, and clerks. Even during his last night in office Adams was busy filling all available positions with Federalists. That party might lose the legislative and executive branches, but in this manner it sought to hold power in what was destined to be the most important branch. Such flagrant abuse of party power aroused the ire of Jefferson and developed in him a strong desire to curb the judiciary. Nothing had contributed to the early development of the Republican Party more than the financial legislation of the Federalists. Much of this could not now be undone. The Bank of the United States was allowed to finish its course, but the hated excise tax, which Gallatin had strongly opposed at the time of the Whisky Rebellion, was repealed. The Republicans, furthermore, were pledged to a reduction not only of taxes but also of the public debt, which now amounted to about $80,000,000. Drastic retrenchment in the military and naval establishments and in the civil and diplomatic services, combined with increasing tariff income, enabled Gallatin by 1810 to reduce the debt to $27,500,000, and this in spite of the cost of the Tripolitan War and the purchase of Louisiana.

To Jefferson military establishments were but the symbol of aristocratic power and were always dangerous to the liberty of mankind. In a letter offering the navy post in his cabinet to one of his followers, he wrote that he would be chagrined if he could not lay up the seven larger men-of-war on the eastern bank of the Potomac, where they would be under the immediate eye of the department and would require but "one set of plunderers to take care of them."

Avowed and ardent pacifist that he was, Jefferson could strike when necessary. In spite of the cry, "millions for defense, but not a cent for tribute," the American government, following the practice of European nations, had paid some $2,000,000 to the Barbary states of northern Africa to purchase immunity for our merchant marine trading in the Mediterranean. Jefferson had scarcely taken office when news arrived that the pirates were not satisfied with their tribute and had commenced to capture American ships and imprison American seamen. Levying a special import tax to provide revenue, the administration sent one squadron after another to the Mediterranean to retaliate. Four years of war brought the pirates to terms, established peace for ten years, practically ended the tributes, and won new laurels for the navy that Jefferson would have been only too glad to keep inactive. To Federalist shipowners, who believed the agrarian Republicans had no interest in the prosperity of the merchant marine, this came as a revelation, and it undoubtedly strengthened the Republicans in New England.

THE WEST AND THE LOUISIANA PURCHASE

The most important event of the Jefferson administration was the purchase of Louisiana, the first and the largest addition to the original territory of the United States. In one sense it was logical for it to happen under Republican auspices. Federalism, with its interests centered primarily upon commerce and the sea, was a party of the seacoast; the inland farmers were usually Republicans. Toward the west had gone the political and religious radicals, the unenfranchised and the discontented, and the new territories and states forming in the great trans-Allegheny region gave natural allegiance to the principles of Jefferson. Jefferson, himself, had formulated the policies that had been followed years before in the framing of the famous ordinances of 1785 and 1787, under which the Northwest had been settled and governed (Chapters VIII and XIV), and few statesmen of the time had a keener perception of western problems. The generous terms of the Pinckney treaty had for the moment solved the problem of western trade, but, as settlers by the thousands swarmed into the western territories, friction with Spain was inevitable.

While Louisiana and Florida remained in the hands of the declining Spanish Empire, the situation was not serious, but the entrance again of France upon the scene radically changed the situation. Although France had ceded Louisiana to Spain in 1763, she had never lost her interest in that province, and under successive French governments repeated efforts had been made to regain it. Success finally came in 1800, when Spain, by the treaty of San Ildefonso, agreed to exchange Louisiana for a kingdom in Italy, which Napoleon had promised to erect for the son-in-law of the Spanish king. Napoleon's interest in Louisiana was based upon his hope of reviving the French colonial empire in America. In Santo Domingo, the richest of the West Indian Islands, a Negro slave revolt under Toussaint L'Ouverture had shaken off French rule. Santo Domingo, as the key of his American empire, must be reconquered, and Louisiana must be annexed as a granary for the French West Indies.

The treaty of San Ildefonso and the news of the French expedition to Santo Domingo stirred Jefferson to action. Instructing the American minister to France, Robert R. Livingston, to press for the cession of Florida and the island of Orleans, he declared: "The day that France takes possession of N. Orleans fixes the sentence which is to restrain her forever within her low water mark. . . . From that moment we must marry ourselves to the British fleet and nation." Securing a grant of $2,000,-000 from Congress, he sent James Monroe as minister extraordinary to France and Spain to act with Livingston. For months Livingston sought with no success to detach the territory around the mouth of the Mississippi from the new French possessions. Suddenly Bonaparte changed his plans and offered to sell the whole of Louisiana. Failure of the French adventure in Santo Domingo, the need of money to defray a new war soon to break out, and undoubtedly the realization that in case of war England might conquer the newly acquired territory led to the offer. The price for the vast region was approximately 80,000,000 francs ($15,000,000), and tradition has it that, as Livingston and Monroe affixed their names to the treaty, Livingston remarked, "We have lived long, but this is the noblest work of our lives. . . . From this day the United States take their place among the powers of first rank."

Jefferson, who had hoped for but a small area of land to protect the interests of the West, had now acquired quite unexpectedly the entire territory of Louisiana. Strict constructionist as he was, he could find nothing in the Constitution authorizing any such purchase. Twice he proposed that a constitutional amendment be submitted to validate his action, but his followers had no such scruples. Fearing that delay might be dangerous, he submitted the treaty to Congress, where it was ratified (October 21, 1803) in spite of the strong opposition of New England Federalists, who rightly foresaw that the accession of this vast new territory would diminish the economic importance and political influence of their section. By a sudden turn of events the Hamiltonian loose constructionists found themselves in the opposite camp.

By the same turn of events the doctrinaire democrat, Jefferson, found himself the autocratic ruler of the new province. The treaty stated that the inhabitants of the territory were to be "incorporated into the union." They expected immediate statehood, but Congress divided the province into the two territories of Orleans at the south and Louisiana at the north, and, until the usual territorial government was granted in 1805, ruled the inhabitants by appointed officers. One of Jefferson's great interests in Louisiana was now scientific. Months before the purchase had been consummated, he had secured from Congress an appropriation for a scientific exploration of the region. This expedition, under Meriwether Lewis and William Clark, left St. Louis in the spring of 1804, reached the mouth of the Columbia in the summer of 1805, and returned to St. Louis in 1806 with a vast amount of information as well as misinformation concerning the region.

Nothing is more apparent in American history than the insatiable land hunger of the West. Rarely, if ever, have the American people answered in the negative when the question of continental extension has been squarely presented to them. The intent in 1803 had been to acquire New Orleans and the Floridas, and the instructions of Monroe and Livingston to do this had been explicit. Instead, they had purchased Louisiana, and no one knew what the boundaries of that province were. The treaty did not describe them except to say that Louisiana was to be of "the same extent that it now has in the hands of Spain,[6] and that it had when France possessed it." When Livingston pressed Talleyrand for a description of the eastern boundaries, he would only say, "You have made a noble bargain for yourselves, and I suppose you will make the most of it." Transfers and retransfers of territory had made the statement of the treaty anything but definite, but there seems to be no doubt that the French be-

[6] France did not take formal possession until November 30, 1803, twenty days before she turned the territory over to the United States.

lieved that the Louisiana they had briefly regained included Texas but not the Floridas. By a curious train of reasoning which a psychologist could describe only as the result of "wishful thinking," Livingston and Monroe came to the conclusion that the purchase included West Florida, and by the same process Jefferson agreed. Negotiations, however, were opened for the purchase of this region, but any hope of success was halted by the Mobile Act of 1804, which erected West Florida as far as the Perdido into a customs district and annexed it to Mississippi Territory. The customs house was located north of the Florida line to prevent immediate clash, but the purpose of the United States was clear, and it was but the first act of the drama that was to close in 1821 with the annexation of Spanish Florida. The desire of succeeding administrations to attach Spanish Florida to the United States was little less than a mania.

THE TURN OF JEFFERSON'S FORTUNES

The fortuitous purchase of Louisiana marked the apex of Republican success, and in the months following Jefferson was at the height of his popularity. His first administration had indeed been a successful one. The debt had been reduced, taxes lowered, the Tripolitan pirates brought to terms, a more liberal land policy adopted, and Louisiana purchased. European wars had helped make the nation prosperous, and Jefferson had been extraordinarily successful in weakening the power of the Federalists. His more enlightened opponents could not fail to see that the federal structure was safe in his hands; the more irreconcilable had failed miserably in their intrigues to disrupt the union. Dismayed by the rising tide of Republicanism, Timothy Pickering and other leaders of the Essex Junto of Massachusetts, along with Roger Griswold and certain Federalist leaders of Connecticut, sought means to disrupt the union by organizing a northeastern confederacy. To be successful it must attach New York, but Hamilton refused to be a party to such treasonable plots. Believing that Vice-President Burr would be sympathetic, the Federalist intriguers succeeded in nominating him for governor on the Republican ticket, with the intention of throwing Federalist support behind him. Burr was defeated largely through the efforts of Hamilton, and Federalism received a blow from which it never recovered. The episode also ended Hamilton's brilliant career. His patriotism had twice thwarted the ambitions of Burr, and, in the duel that followed, Burr's bullet ended the life of the great statesman.

The success of the first administration was reflected in the election of 1804, when Jefferson and George Clinton of New York easily defeated their opponents, Charles C. Pinckney and Rufus King, carrying every state in the union but Connecticut and Delaware. It was with pardonable if undue optimism that Jefferson in his second inaugural address congratulated his fellow countrymen that "not a cloud appeared on the horizon." Clouds, nevertheless, dark and portentous, were rapidly gathering, foreboding ill to his own political theories, to the harmony of his party, and to the peace and prosperity of his country. An important check to his own political philosophy, although he may not have realized it at the moment, had come four days earlier when the Senate failed to convict Justice Samuel Chase.

Of all the "trappings of Federalism," nothing irritated the Republicans more than the exaltation of the judiciary. That branch, thoroughly Federalist in its make-up and sympathy, the Republicans determined to weaken. Having eliminated some of their opponents by repealing the Judiciary Act of 1801, the Republicans set out to rid themselves of other Federalist judges. Judge John Pickering of the federal district court of New Hampshire, who was really insane, was impeached for gross misconduct and removed. Justice Chase of the Supreme Court was next impeached, and it was believed that his conviction would be followed by impeachment of Chief Justice Marshall. Chase was badly biased, his political diatribes were obnoxious, and he was no fit man to serve in a judicial capacity, but the most strenuous political maneuvers of the administration to secure conviction failed. Whether for good or for ill, the failure to convict Chase ended the efforts to change the political complexion of the Supreme Court by impeachment proceedings and incidentally to bring it under the close control of the legislative branch. The proceedings, however, undoubtedly served one good purpose in helping to convince the judiciary that its activities should be more largely divorced from politics. Quite as important as the failure of this attack upon the judiciary was the decision of the Supreme Court in the famous case of Marbury v. Madison (1803), the full import of which was later to be realized.

One of the "midnight appointments" of President Adams under the Judiciary Act of 1801 had been that of William Marbury to be justice of the peace in the District of Columbia. Madison, the new Secretary of State, refused to deliver the commission, and Marbury sought from the Supreme Court a writ of mandamus to compel delivery. Stating the opinion of the court, Chief Justice Marshall held that Marbury had a right to his commission and that Madison's action was in plain violation of the plaintiff's rights. From the Supreme Court, however, he could obtain no redress, for, said Marshall, Section 13 of the Judiciary Act of 1789, which authorized the Supreme Court to issue writs of mandamus to public officers, appeared not warranted in the Constitution. With clear and convincing logic Marshall asserted the supremacy of the Constitution over all departments of the government and held that "a legislative act contrary to the Constitution is not law." "The particular phraseology of the Constitution of the United States," he held, "confirms and strengthens the principle, supposed to be essential to all written constitutions, that a law repugnant to the Constitution is void; and that *courts,* as well as other departments, are bound by that instrument." This might all be true enough, but the question was still an open one as to where the power rested to decide on the constitutionality of a law. The Constitution did not say; Jefferson and Madison in the Kentucky and Virginia resolutions had already laid down the principle that the states might decide. In Marshall's mind, however, there was no question but that the power resided in the judiciary. His arguments in the Marbury case and his declaration that part of the Judiciary Act was unconstitutional were the first important statements by the Supreme Court of the doctrine of judicial supremacy. If the doctrine could be maintained, the idea of the American government as an organization with power evenly balanced between three departments was ended, though it is quite possible that the federal union might be more secure under this doctrine than it would have been under the theory of the Virginia and Kentucky resolutions. This was indeed a political revolution that boded ill for the Jeffersonian democracy and the Jeffersonian economics. "The Constitution on this hypothesis," exclaimed Jefferson, "is a mere thing of wax in the hands of the judiciary which may twist and shape it into any form they please." But Marshall stuck by his guns. If the Supreme Court could declare an act of Congress unconstitutional, it could certainly declare acts of state legislatures unconstitutional, and this it frequently did as the years went on.

The failure to weaken the judiciary was but the first of many setbacks that Jefferson was to experience. Before his second administration was a year old, his own party was badly split. The first trouble arose over the complicated Yazoo land claims, a question involving the region west of the present state of Georgia, which was claimed at one time or another by Georgia, South Carolina, and the United States. Believing that the land was hers, Georgia in 1785 had disposed of large tracts to various groups of speculators, then in 1795 had sold much of the same land to other companies, and finally, as a result of popular protests, had rescinded the contracts of 1795. The United States, asserting her authority in 1798, created the Territory of Mississippi and provided for a commission to settle the dispute. This commission, composed of Levi Lincoln, Madison, and Gallatin, agreed to pay Georgia $1,250,000 and the proceeds from the sale of 5,000,000 acres to the grantees of the land, and a bill to authorize this agreement came before Congress in 1805. Randolph and others, convinced that it was a political deal favoring northern land speculators, attacked the bill savagely, and Congress quickly split into the Yazoo and anti-Yazoo men, the latter mostly Southerners. The matter was not finally adjusted until 1814, but in the meantime the question had given Marshall, in the famous case of Fletcher *v.* Peck (1810), a chance to declare unconstitutional, as a violation of contract, the act of Georgia that had nullified the 1795 grants.

While the Yazoo controversy was splitting his party, Jefferson aroused further animosity by his Florida policy. In the annual message of 1805 Jefferson spoke of the Florida question in terms that suggested the possibility of war. Southern Republicans had no hesitancy in fighting Spain to gain Florida, but, when it became evident, from a secret message sent to Congress, that all Jefferson wanted was $2,000,000 to bribe Napoleon to extort West Florida from Spain, the disgust of Randolph and his cohorts knew no bounds. Jefferson got the money, but the Spanish affair proved a fiasco in international diplomacy as well as damaging to his prestige at home.

Unfortunate also was the episode of the Burr conspiracy. Hated by the Federalists for causing the death of their great leader, and distrusted by the Republicans for equivocal conduct in the New York state election, Burr, like many another before and since, turned to the West to repair his shattered fortunes. On a preliminary trip in 1805 he talked with political leaders and adventurers of various sorts, spinning a web of intrigue wherever he went. What his plan was, if any had been definitely formed, no one knows. It may have been the separation of the West from the Union, an attack on the Spanish possessions, a filibustering expedition into Mexico, or merely a venture in western land speculation. With different men he talked, as it were, different languages. To the British minister he offered to detach the West from the Union for $500,000, and from the Spanish minister he actually obtained $10,000 for the purpose of protecting the Spanish possessions.

Whatever his purpose, he repaired again to the West in 1806, collected men and supplies at Blennerhasset's Island on the Ohio, and informed General Wilkinson, governor of Louisiana Territory, that his expedition was ready to depart. Wilkinson, who was deep in the intrigues of Burr, suddenly deserted the adventurer and informed Jefferson that there was a "deep, dark and widespread conspiracy" afoot to dismember the Union. Jefferson immediately issued a proclamation warning the West of the conspiracy and ordering the arrest of Burr. The latter deserted his followers and made a dash for Florida, but was apprehended and returned east for trial. The trial was ostensibly to determine the treason of Burr; actually it was a bitter political conflict with Federalists and anti-Jefferson

Republicans arrayed against Jefferson and his followers. Marshall, who presided at the trial, and Randolph, who acted as foreman of the jury, were both intent on acquitting Burr, while the legal talent appearing for the prosecution and defense were also divided on political lines. Marshall's rulings made conviction impossible, and Burr was acquitted, although all knew that he was responsible for what had happened. One episode of the trial was of more than passing importance. Marshall summoned Jefferson to appear before the court with certain papers, but Jefferson ignored the summons on the ground that the President was not at the command of the federal courts. His action, combined with a similar stand taken earlier by Adams, set some limit to the pretensions of the judiciary.

ECONOMIC BOYCOTT

Despite interference from British warships, French privateers, and Tripolitan pirates, the period of the European wars had been one of extraordinary prosperity for American agriculture and commerce. Engaged in a life-and-death struggle, Europe needed food and raw materials of all kinds, and the prices paid for American commodities rose steadily. With her merchantmen driven from the seas, France depended upon American ships to carry the imports from her own possessions. As a result of all this, American exports increased from $19,000,000 in 1792 to over $108,000,000 in 1807 and imports from $29,000,000 to almost $247,000,000. Registered tonnage engaged in foreign trade mounted from 123,893 tons in 1789 to 810,163 in 1807, while the proportion of trade (import and export) carried in American ships jumped from 23.6 per cent in 1789 to 92 per cent in 1807. Such was the harvest of neutrality, a harvest not unlike that of the first two and a half years of the World War (1914-17). Under trying circumstances, as we have seen, the administrations of Washington and Adams had avoided formal war with either France or England, to the great benefit of American commerce. Jefferson's first five years were relatively free from foreign complications, but the old problems of neutral rights again rose to plague the remainder of his administration. In 1805 came the battle of Austerlitz, which left Napoleon master of the Continent, and the battle of Trafalgar, which made England mistress of the seas. As the great conflict approached its climax in the following years, neutral rights received but slight consideration.

With the French navy and commerce destroyed, it was natural that the friction should be mainly with Great Britain. This friction, as it developed, concerned chiefly the problems of impressment and neutral trade. Life in the British navy for the common seamen was cruelly difficult, and desertions were frequent, but the navy must be maintained at full strength, and for two centuries England had resorted to impressment in order to keep her ships at fighting strength. The British government never claimed the right to impress native-born Americans, but, as the years went on, her officers gave little concern to this question. The problem was complicated by the fact that Great Britain and other nations at that time did not recognize the right of expatriation—"once an Englishman, always an Englishman." The United States, on the other hand, made up of immigrants and their descendants, had naturalization laws and was continually naturalizing foreigners. The expansion of American trade and the growth of the American merchant marine had been so rapid that the labor market could not supply enough seamen. Wages rose from $8 to $24 a month, and British sailors, attracted by high wages and better working conditions, deserted from many of the merchantmen and frigates that entered our ports. "Once safe on our shores," says McMaster, "an American name was assumed, an American protection purchased, and Jack, thus disguised as an American citizen, was soon on the deck of an American merchantman on his way to San Domingo or Martinique." At Norfolk the crew of a British vessel quit in a body and shipped for a cruise on an American sloop of war. So far had British impressment and desertions gone that the king's battles were often fought by Americans, and American trade carried on by Englishmen. Captain Bainbridge, during the Tripolitan War, admitted that "the greater part of our crew consists of English subjects not naturalized in America." In a crew of 419 on the frigate *Constitution* there were at one time 149 avowed British subjects.

On this question both sides were at fault. British sailors were encouraged to desert, were naturalized without fulfillment of the legal residence requirements, and were often supplied with forged papers. On their side British boarding officers laughed at certificates of citizenship and took away with them any likely looking sailor that pleased their fancy. British warships lay off the American coast and even entered ports to search for deserters. The United States had first taken the position that the flag covered the man, but had later abandoned this and ordered collectors of the ports to issue certificates of citizenship. On the basis that holders of these certificates were exempted from seizure, negotiations with Great Britain were unsuccessfully pressed. The climax came in June, 1807. The British admiral, hearing that deserters had enlisted for service on the newly built *Chesapeake,* ordered all commanders to search the ship if it was discovered on the high seas. The *Chesapeake,* many of her guns not yet mounted, her decks strewn with timber, and her crew untrained, set sail to join the Mediterranean squadron. Off Chesapeake Bay she was overhauled by the British man-of-war *Leopard,* and the demand was made to search her for deserters. The American commander refused, stating that the only British deserters aboard were three Americans formerly illegally impressed by the British. Whereupon the *Leopard* poured three broadsides into the *Chesapeake,* killing three and wounding eighteen. The American commander struck his flag, and the British removed the three Americans and a British subject [7] whom they found aboard. When the *Chesapeake* limped back to Norfolk, the nation was aroused as it had not been since the Revolution. "For the first time in their history," said Henry Adams, "the people of the United States learned, in June, 1807, the feeling of true national emotion." Jefferson could have had war at once, and it would have been a popular one, but he contented himself with demanding an apology and reparation, ordering all British war vessels to leave American waters, and calling Congress in special session in October. By that time the war spirit might cool.

Until the *Chesapeake-Leopard* affair Federalist shipowners had not been greatly concerned over impressment, claiming that the extent of it had been greatly exaggerated. After all, the practice concerned only human rights, and, as long as profits were maintained, it might be winked at. But now the rights of neutral commerce were again endangered, and this was another story. The opening of the conflict between England and France (page 137) was signalized by the effort of England to enforce the "Rule of 1756" forbidding during time of war trade that was illegal in time of peace. France had retaliated by ordering that all neutrals be treated by France in just such manner as they suffered England to treat them. American losses had been high, but diplomatic negotiations, coupled with the economic necessities of Europe, brought a toleration for most of the commerce on American ships. The situation was also temporarily improved by British admiralty court decisions in the case of the *Immanuel* (1799) and the *Polly* (1800), which decreed that enemy goods landed at a neutral port became, after the payment of customs duties, neutral goods and as such immune to capture if transshipped. This gave an opening, and it was not long before half the commerce carried on American ships was concerned with the "broken voyage." The favorable situation changed in the summer of 1805, when in the case of the *Essex* the British court reversed itself, asserting that the landing of enemy goods on American soil and the payment of duties did not neutralize them.

Without avail Jefferson used his best diplomatic efforts to secure a reversal of the *Essex* decision. By this time both Great Britain and France had come to the conclusion that only through economic boycott could victory be accomplished. Already in 1804 British orders in council had

---

[7] The presence of this man, who was later hanged by the British, was unknown to Commodore Barron, commander of the *Chesapeake.*

declared under blockade French ports from Ostend to the Seine, and in 1806 the blockade was extended to include the coast from the Elbe to Brest.[8] Napoleon, recently victorious over Prussia, answered with his Berlin Decree, declaring the British Isles under blockade. Great Britain retaliated by another order in council (1807), declaring that no neutral vessel might trade at any port of France or her allies without first stopping and paying duties at an English port. Napoleon answered this order with the Milan Decree (1807), stating that any vessel sailing to or from Great Britain or her colonies was liable to seizure, as was any vessel that submitted to the orders in council of 1807. On the high seas Napoleon's decrees were merely a paper blockade, for his navy had been driven from the ocean; but he now controlled the entire Continent except Russia, and there he could enforce his "Continental System." The orders and decrees, if carried out, meant the virtual elimination of American ships from the European trade. Often evaded, and but inadequately enforced, these orders and decrees resulted, nevertheless, in the capture of 1600 American ships and the loss of $60,000,000 in property.

International law, if any such thing exists in time of war, had been ruthlessly violated by both England and France to the great detriment of American interests. Action was essential, but war seemed as inadvisable as during the administrations of Washington and Adams. To Jefferson, philosopher and lover of peace, it was particularly repugnant. The policy he formulated was one of "peaceable coercion." If England and France could attempt an economic boycott, why not he? "Our commerce is so valuable to them," he wrote, "that they will be glad to purchase it, when the only price we ask is to do us justice." Jefferson's policy was far from being as impractical as many historians have insisted. Europe badly needed American goods, and, if the boycott could have been adequately enforced, it might have succeeded. What Jefferson apparently did not realize was that the European struggle had reached a stage where neutral rights no longer counted and that Great Britain also was anxious to cripple the trade of the United States, her greatest commercial rival. Nor did he realize that American shipowners would bitterly oppose his policy. His first move was to secure from Congress, early in 1806, the Nonintercourse Act, providing that certain goods could not be imported from Great Britain after November of that year,[9] and with this as a weapon he sent a diplomatic mission to England with instructions to secure indemnity for captures since the *Essex* decision, an end to impressments, and restoration of trade with French colonies. The treaty that Monroe and William Pinkney sent

[8] Extended further in 1807 to include all places and ports of France and her allies, including colonies.

[9] The act did not actually go into effect until December, 1807.

back secured none of these, and Jefferson refused to submit it to the Senate. On his advice Congress, in December, 1807, passed the Embargo Act, prohibiting American vessels from sailing to foreign ports and allowing coastwise trade only if the owner gave bonds double the value of the cargo that the cargo be relanded in the United States.

Instead of bringing England to terms, the embargo appeared only to ruin American commerce. Exports dropped from $108,343,000 in 1807 to $22,431,000 in 1808 and imports from $138,500,000 to $56,990,000. New York, commented a British traveler at that time, "was full of shipping, but they were dismantled and laid up. Their decks were cleared, their hatches fastened down, and scarcely a sailor was to be found on board. Not a box, bale, cask, barrel or package, was to be seen upon the wharves. . . . The streets near the waterside were almost deserted; the grass had begun to grow upon the wharves." McMaster estimates that during the embargo 55,000 sailors and 100,000 mechanics and laborers were thrown out of work, ships lost $12,500,000 in net earnings, and customs revenues fell from $16,000,000 to a few thousand. Upon Massachusetts the blow fell with especial force, and some of the ports, such as Newburyport, Salem, and Plymouth, never recovered. The old cry that the Republicans were trying to ruin New England commerce was raised, and declining Federalism was given a new lease of life. If this was not so, inquired the Federalists, why had Jefferson also put a ban on the trade with China and the East Indies? From a hundred towns came resolutions against the embargo. Methods to evade the act were soon found, and American goods reached England *via* Canada and Florida. Napoleon even confiscated American ships on the plea that he was helping Jefferson enforce the embargo and that American ships in French harbors must be British ships in disguise.

The presidential election of 1808 came while the opposition to the embargo was rapidly increasing. Although the Republican Party was rent with faction, Jefferson held his machine together long enough to elect his favorite, James Madison, by an electoral vote of 176 to 54.[10] The Federalists, however, had recaptured New England (except Vermont) and increased their representation in both houses of Congress. In spite of rising opposition, Congress, in January, 1809, passed the Force Act, allowing federal officials without warrant to seize goods under suspicion of foreign destination. This was too much for New England, where legislatures now talked the same language as that of the Virginia and Kentucky resolutions and advocated resistance. Jefferson's Republican adherents from New England even predicted civil war. His followers in the South, on the other

[10] George Clinton of New York, a rival candidate for the presidency, was elected Vice-President. The Federalist candidates were the same as in 1804, Charles C. Pinckney—for the Federalists had not entirely lost their following in the tidewater South—and Rufus King.

hand, were opposed to a war with Great Britain that might only benefit New England through a conquest of Canada. Their markets also were ruined, and there was widespread distress in the South. Enough Republicans broke with the administration to secure repeal of the Embargo Act, and Jefferson, with a heavy heart, signed the repeal three days before he retired from office. For the embargo was substituted the Nonintercourse Act prohibiting trade only with Great Britain and France and their possessions.

The collapse of Jefferson's embargo policy should in no way obscure the contributions of one of the greatest of American statesmen. As the Federalists under Washington and Hamilton had largely created and solidified the new national government, so the Republican Party, of which Jefferson was the builder and leader, helped to restore and preserve the ideals of democracy and human liberty and the dignity of the common man. His creation of the Republican Party and his leadership of that party to success in 1800 is clear proof of his great political ability; the eventual splits in his party and the development of opposition to his policies were due after all more to circumstances over which he had no control than to mistakes in his own political strategy. More important in gauging his stature as a political leader was his sincere liberalism, his tolerance of opponents in an age of the bitterest and most personal political enmities, and his belief in evolution by reason rather than by force. With the exception of Lincoln, it is doubtful if any American better combined political sagacity and high statesmanship. In a material way Jefferson's most important contribution to his country was the Louisiana purchase, but the greatest heritage that he left was in the realm of the spirit—his faith in political democracy, in liberty of thought, in the efficacy of reason, and in the future of mankind. His last great effort as President—the maintenance of peace through an economic boycott—was a demonstration of high idealism combined with stern realism, which was not the least of his great contributions.

Brief introductions are C. and M. Beard, *The Rise of American Civilization*, Chap. IX; Allen Johnson, *Jefferson and His Colleagues* (Chronicles of America); and Edward Channing, *A History of the United States*, Vol. IV, Chaps. IX–XIV. In Henry Adams, *A History of the United States During the Administration of Thomas Jefferson*, Vol. I, Chap. VII, the student may obtain a bowing acquaintance with the most important book on the Jefferson administration, written by one of America's great historians. On Jefferson read A. J. Nock, *Jefferson*, Chap. VI, or F. W. Hirst, *Life and Letters of Thomas Jefferson*, Book IV, Chaps. I, II. For his economic and political philosophy read C. A. Beard, *The Economic Origins of the Jeffersonian Democracy*, Chap. XIV. See also W. E. Binkley, *American Political Parties*, Chaps. III–IV. On the diplomatic, see Bemis, *A Diplomatic History of the United States*, Chaps. VII–IX or T. A. Bailey, *A Diplomatic History of the American People*, Chaps. VII, VIII. Source material is in H. S. Commager, *Documents of American History*, Vol. I, 186–205, and G. S. Callender, *Selections from the Economic History of the United States*, 239–260.

Chapter XI

RESURGENT NATIONALISM

> *The long, exciting and splendid panorama of revolution and war, which for twenty-five years absorbed the world's attention and dwarfed all other interests, vanished more quickly in America than in Europe, and left fewer elements of disturbance. . . . In a single day, almost in a single instant, the public turned from interests and passions that had supplied its thought for a generation, and took up a class of ideas that had been unknown or but vaguely defined before.*
>
> HENRY ADAMS

AGRARIAN IMPERIALISM

A scholar and a thoroughly competent Secretary of State, James Madison, as President, lacked the political capacity, the large vision, and the force in execution that characterized his predecessors. No better description of him has been left us than that of Sir Augustus Foster, the British minister:

I thought Mr. Jefferson more of a statesman and man of the world than Mr. Madison, who was rather too much the disputatious pleader; yet the latter was better informed, and moreover a social, jovial, and good-humored companion, full of anecdote, sometimes rather of a loose description, but oftener of a political and historical interest. He was a little man with small features, rather wizened when I saw him, but occasionally lit up with a good-natured smile. He wore a black coat, stockings with shoes buckled, and had his hair powdered, with a tail.

His first cabinet, with the exception of Gallatin, was distinctly mediocre; it was strengthened, however, in later years by the appointment of Monroe as Secretary of State. Madison, himself, was unable to impose his leadership upon Congress, and drifted weakly with the current. The early months of his administration, nevertheless, opened auspiciously. With the British minister, Erskine, he concluded a treaty by which Great Britain was to exempt American vessels from the orders in council on condition that the United States revoke all commercial interdicts against Great Britain and forbid trade with France. Great rejoicing followed as Madison suspended nonintercourse with Great Britain, and trade rapidly revived. But Erskine had gone beyond his instructions, and Canning, the British foreign minister, repudiated the agreement. Congress, without presidential leadership and at a loss as to what to do, replied by passing Macon's Bill No. 2 (May 1, 1810), which restored commercial intercourse with both England and France but provided that as soon as one of these nations withdrew its decrees against our shipping the Nonintercourse Act would be revived against the other. England ignored the act, but Napoleon announced the repeal of his decrees. Although the French emperor continued to seize and confiscate American shipping, Madison fatuously took him at his word and announced in November that nonintercourse would be revived against Britain if in three months' time she did not revoke the orders in council.

The commercial complications were no worse than they had been for years, but two events had taken place that were soon to drive the nation into a second war with England. The first was the revival of Indian war on the northwestern frontier; the second the war spirit of the twelfth Congress, elected in 1810. By this time Ohio had achieved statehood (1803), and frontiersmen were aggressively pushing into Indiana Territory and other portions of the Northwest. Plied with whisky and overwhelmed with oratory, the demoralized Indians made nine cessions of territory after the treaty of Greenville (1795), in which they had alienated 50,000,000 acres, before they again rose in desperation. Led by two able chiefs, Tecumseh and his brother, the Prophet, the Indian tribes organized a confederacy, determined to dispute the legality of the last cession of territory, and made a settlement on Tippecanoe Creek, a tributary of the Wabash. While Tecumseh was absent in an effort to obtain the adherence of the Creeks, William Henry Harrison, governor of Indiana Territory, set out to destroy the Indian settlement. Near Tippecanoe he was suddenly attacked by the Indians but beat them off after a costly battle (November 7, 1811). Retiring southwest, Harrison learned to his great surprise that he had won a victory, for the Indians, demoralized after the battle, had lost faith in Tecumseh and retreated to Canada. The result made Harrison a frontier hero and many years later was an important factor in winning for him the presidency. Harrison and every western settler with him believed that England was responsible for the Indian uprising. British agents, it is true, had encouraged the confederacy, and the Indians fought with arms and munitions largely obtained from Canada, but the Indian war was primarily a frontier conflict between the advancing white man and the Indian hopelessly struggling to retain his land. It was the same old struggle that had begun with the Jamestown settlement and was to end only with the defeat of the Apaches in 1886. In all this the outstanding feature was not the treachery of the red man but the ruthless greed of the settler backed by the ever ready guns of the regulars.

The Congress elected in 1810 was quite different from the inept legislature that had passed Macon's Bill. Half the former Congress had failed of re-election, and the new House contained many who were to play a leading part in the years to come. The new generation of statesmen included Henry Clay of Kentucky, Sevier and Felix Grundy of Tennessee, Lowndes, Cheves, and Calhoun of South Carolina, and Peter B. Porter of New York. Taking possession of Congress, the young "Warhawks," mostly from the West, elected Clay to the speakership and demanded war. Carried along by the younger and more radical elements of his party and convinced that war was inevitable, Madison sent to Congress on June 1, 1812, his war message. The wrongs, as recapitulated in the message, were violations of the flag on the high seas, confiscation of ships, illegal impressment, blockade of our shores, the obnoxious orders in council, and inciting of the Indians against our borders. A few days later (June 18) war was declared in the House by a vote of 79 to 49 and in the Senate by a close vote of 19 to 13. The war, as we shall see, accomplished little, if anything, and, in spite of innumerable wrongs, was unnecessary. If Madison had followed the milder elements of his party and had sent a minister to Great Britain, he would have learned that the embargo and nonintercourse acts had had their effect upon Great Britain, that British merchants were clamoring for a reopening of trade, and that the British ministry had moved in May for a repeal of the orders in council. On June 23, four days after Madison's proclamation of war, the orders were repealed. Jefferson's "economic boycott" had accomplished its purpose; modern cables might have prevented the war.

There are many other curious aspects of the War of 1812. Madison in his war message stressed the violation of maritime rights, and only once, when he suggested England's part in the Indian uprising, did he approach the heart of the subject. The Northeast, the section that suffered most from British depredations, opposed the war. Certain New England governors refused to allow their militia to go beyond the boundaries of their own states, New England capitalists refused to subscribe to war loans, and Federalist leaders inaugurated a movement that squinted toward secession. Convinced that the Republicans sought to ruin its commerce and closely bound to England by economic ties, New England Federalism looked upon Napoleon as Anti-Christ, and, like their pro-Ally descendants a century later, echoed Pickering's famous toast, "The world's last hope—

Briton's fast-anchored isle." It was not the commercial section that advocated war, which might destroy their remaining commerce and add more
farmers and planters to the already overwhelming Republican majority,
but the young Warhawks of the West, anxious to end the menace of the
Indians and inflamed with dreams of annexing Florida and Canada. It
was along the border from Vermont to Kentucky that the war fever was
rising. "Is it nothing to us," cried Henry Clay, "to extinguish the torch that
lights up savage warfare? Is it nothing to acquire the entire fur trade
connected with that country?" "The waters of the St. Lawrence and the
Mississippi," asserted another member of the House hopefully, "interlock
in a number of places; and the great Disposer of Human Events intended
those two rivers should belong to the same people." While the northern
frontiersmen kept their eyes on Canada, the South was equally interested
in Florida. After an American uprising in West Florida, Madison had
already (1810) annexed that region as far east as the Pearl. Spain was now
an ally of England, and war might provide an opportunity to secure the
whole of Florida. The antiwar Republican, John Randolph, who felt that
the war would result only in creating "a preponderating northern influence," penetrated to the heart of the matter. "Agrarian cupidity," he
cried scornfully, "not maritime right, urges the war. Ever since the report
of the Committee on Foreign Relations came into the House we have
heard but one word,—like the whip-poor-will, but one eternal monotonous
tone—Canada! Canada! Canada!"

While the Indian menace and agricultural imperialism help explain the
votes cast by many Congressmen for the war with Great Britain, more
fundamental was the economic depression that had hit both the eastern
and the western farmer as a result of British orders and French decrees.
High prices of agricultural products had brought prosperity to the farmers
of the Ohio and Mississippi valleys, as well as to those in the East, which
reached its peak in 1805. Recession began in 1806, became general in 1808,
and continued, with but temporary relief in 1809 and 1810, until the outbreak of war. The western farmer quite logically attributed his distress to
interference with commerce. Great Britain's command of the seas made
her the chief aggressor, and this, combined with traditional frontier hatred
of Britain, made it easy to lay the blame upon that nation rather than
upon France. At all odds the West supported the retaliatory legislation of
the Jefferson administration, and, when that did not seem effective, supported war. "The true question in controversy," insisted Felix Grundy,
". . . is the right of exporting the products of our own soil and industry
to foreign markets." [1]

[1] The causes of the War of 1812 have been discussed at length in J. W. Pratt, *Expansionists
of 1812* (1925). While he conclusively proves the overwhelming desire to conquer Canada, he

THE "SECOND WAR OF INDEPENDENCE"

"The conquest of Canada is in your power," declared Clay in the House in 1810. "I trust I shall not be presumptuous when I state that I verily believe that the militia of Kentucky are alone competent to place Montreal and Upper Canada at your feet." Such was the ill-grounded optimism of the war-makers of 1812. As a matter of fact, the country was almost totally unprepared for war. Although war had been impending since 1806, no preparations had been made. The army numbered but 6700, poorly equipped and officered by old men of petty experience. Eustis, the Secretary of War at the opening of the conflict, was a shiftless politician incapable of choosing officers or planning a campaign. Dearborn, the senior major general, left the collectorship of Boston at 61 to take command of the army; Thomas Pinckney, the junior major general, who had had his only military experience in the guerrilla warfare of Marion and Sumter, was 63; James Wilkinson, the senior brigadier general, was insubordinate and negligent if not traitorous; William Hull, the junior brigadier general, was later court-martialed and convicted of cowardice and neglect of duty. The militia, if we are to believe Amos Kendall, "were without order, and apparently without officers—mean, dirty, ugly, and in every respect contemptible." The navy consisted of about twelve vessels, the largest of which was a 44-gun frigate, and some two hundred gun-boats useless even for coast defense. Fortunately, the tiny navy had had some experience in the Tripolitan War and was manned by many excellent officers.

Military unpreparedness was not the sole handicap. Shortly before the declaration of war Congress had authorized the enlargement of the regular army to 25,000 men, the enlistment of 50,000 volunteers, and a loan of $11,000,000, but then had adjourned without providing taxes to support their act. The financing of the war was made even more difficult by Congress's refusal, against the advice of Gallatin and the administration, to recharter the first Bank of the United States when its charter ran out in 1811. More serious than all this, however, was the fact that the struggle was a partisan, a class, and a sectional war. The Federalists, almost to a man, as well as a considerable number of Republicans, voted against the declaration. In general, agrarians favored the war, while merchants and ship-owners opposed it. Antiwar demonstrations were frequent in the early months of the war. New England, as we have noted, was opposed from the beginning. "Organize a *peace party* throughout your Country," re-

attributes the reason to an anxiety to eradicate the Indian menace rather than to mere "land hunger." He fails, however, to take into adequate consideration the influence of the agricultural depression, but fortunately this has since been done by George R. Taylor in "Agrarian Discontent in the Mississippi Valley Preceding the War of 1812," *Journal of Political Economy,* XXXIX, No. 4 (August, 1931), 471–505.

solved the Massachusetts House of Representatives; "let the sound of your disapprobation of this war be loud and deep . . . let there be no volunteers except for defensive war." "To sabotage the war, in the interest of early peace," says Morison, "became the declared policy of maritime Massachusetts." [2]

Unprepared for war and with a large section of the population opposed, the United States had entered the lists against the wealthiest nation in the world, in command of a large army well trained in Continental wars and at the height of its efficiency, a nation with a navy of over eight hundred war vessels, two hundred and thirty of which were larger than any American warship. The struggle, of course, was not as unequal as first appeared. The American navy might be small, but there was a reserve of the most expert seamen in the world to man the privateers. The chief energies of Great Britain were employed in the European war; the American phase was merely a side issue. Above all else, America was saved, as in the Revolution, by her geographical position and by the fact that England was again fighting France. "The attempts of England," says one historian, "to penetrate into the great interior would be like the blows of a sledgehammer struck into a bin of wheat: a few kernels would be bruised or destroyed, but the iron would soon bury itself harmlessly just under the surface of the mass." [3]

The military operations of the War of 1812 may be briefly summarized. The main objective during the three years of the war was Canada. In 1812 General William Hull advanced to Detroit in preparation for invasion. Stupidly he allowed his baggage to be captured and then ignominiously surrendered his army to Brock, the skillful and courageous British general. With the surrender of Detroit, the Northwest was temporarily in British hands. An attempt of Dearborn to invade Canada by the Champlain route was frustrated by the tardy arrival of the militia and their refusal to leave the country. On the Niagara an American invasion was halted by Brock at Queenstown, the American defeat with a loss of 1000 men due again to the failure of the New York militia to support the regulars. The campaign of 1813 opened disastrously in the West with the annihilation of an American force at Frenchtown on the Raisin River, but closed successfully with the reoccupation of Detroit. The way was opened by Oliver H. Perry, who defeated a British fleet (September 10, 1813) and cleared the enemy from Lake Erie. William Henry Harrison, now in command of the West, pushed on to Detroit, but found it deserted and the British in retreat. Pursuing them into Canada, he dealt them a severe defeat in the battle of the Thames, a victory that detached the western Indians from

[2] S. E. Morison, *Maritime History of Massachusetts,* 198.
[3] K. C. Babcock, *The Rise of American Nationality,* 82.

the British cause. In the meantime an American army at Sackett's Harbor under Wilkinson and another on Lake Champlain under Wade Hampton, who were to co-operate in an advance on Montreal, failed miserably, owing chiefly to Wilkinson's ineffectiveness. The year 1813 ended, therefore, with Canada cleared of American troops, but with Detroit regained by the Americans. The recapture of Detroit was important in preventing a flanking movement from the west.

Having cornered Napoleon at last and packed him off to Elba, England was prepared in 1814 to assume the initiative in the American war. Her plan was to invade the United States at Niagara and along Lake Champlain in the North and at New Orleans in the South, at the same time raiding the coast under cover of a strict blockade. By 1814 the American army was under the command of abler officers who had won their position through meritorious service, and the regular army was disciplined by two years of campaigning. Before the Niagara expedition could get under way, Generals Brown and Scott had crossed into Canada, defeated the British advance guard at Chippewa (July 5), and fought, three weeks later, the severest battle of the war at Lundy's Lane. Neither side gained the victory, but the battle ended the British invasion at Niagara. With heavy reinforcements from England, another British army in the meantime had advanced toward Lake Champlain. While the British halted before the strong fortifications at Plattsburg, Commodore MacDonough destroyed their fleet (September 11) in what was perhaps the decisive battle of the war. On the following day the British marched back to Canada, and the second invasion had failed.

The third British expeditionary force, that against the South, did not reach New Orleans until December, and found the Americans ready for it. The Southwest had already produced a leader in the Tennessee frontiersman, Andrew Jackson, who had broken the power of the southwestern Indians at Horseshoe Bend in 1814 and then had swept into Spanish Florida to put a stop to the British intrigues with the refugee Creeks. Hastening to New Orleans, Jackson gathered what troops were available and strongly fortified the approaches. With customary British contempt of the American militia, Sir Edward Pakenham landed 6000 European veterans and attempted to storm the American works by a frontal attack. The result was complete defeat; Pakenham and 2000 of his seasoned troops were killed before the army withdrew to the fleet. The victory had no effect on the war, for the treaty of peace had been signed two weeks before, but it had a tremendous effect in raising the morale of the people of the Southwest.

Against the dark background of inefficiency and failure that characterized the military operations during the first years of the war were the

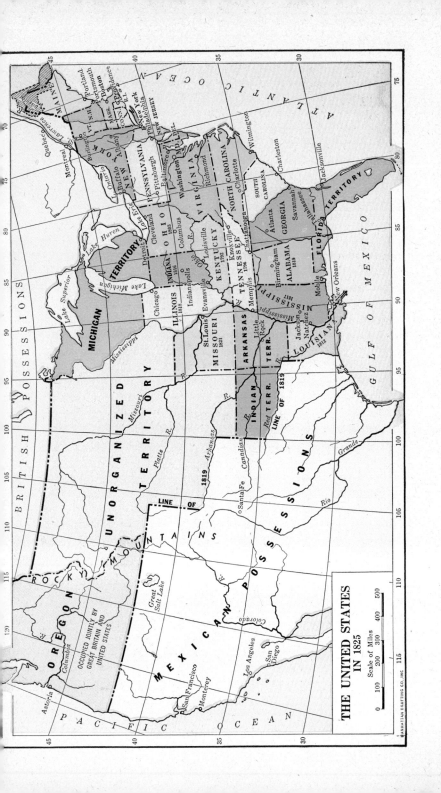

THE UNITED STATES
IN 1825

Scale of Miles
0   100   200   300   400   500

brilliant exploits of the American navy. The victories of Perry on Lake Erie and MacDonough on Lake Champlain were important. On the sea the *Constitution* and her sister frigates destroyed a half dozen of the proud warships of the British line before they themselves were either destroyed or bottled up in American harbors by the overwhelming blockading squadron of Great Britain. Important as were the victories of the warships on the high seas in maintaining the morale of the American people, their contribution was hardly as important as that of the 492 privateers commissioned by the federal government, which captured over 1300 British ships with an estimated value of $39,000,000. Their operations were chiefly in European and Asiatic waters, for the British blockade in America restricted their movements near the American coast. The strong blockading fleet enabled the British to raid the American coast almost at will, but their most important foray was on the Chesapeake in August, 1814. Brushing aside the militia with little trouble, the British occupied Washington and burned the White House, the department buildings, and the capitol.[4] Returning to their ships, they sailed for Baltimore, but found the city well prepared. After two sharp battles with the militia and a futile bombardment, the attempt to capture the city was given up.[5]

Inefficient as was the federal government in its conduct of the war, its operations, it is only fair to note, were badly impeded by the antiwar party. In all wars of the American republic there has been a minority that on one ground or another has opposed.[6] In none, however, has the opposition been relatively so large, so determined, and so vocal as in that of 1812. Opposed to the war from the start, New England by 1814 determined to take active steps to bring it to a conclusion. Connecticut and Massachusetts withdrew their militia from federal service, and in October the Massachusetts legislature issued an invitation to the other New England states to send delegates to Hartford to confer upon "their public grievances and concerns" and to take measures, if necessary, to call a convention of all of the states to revise the Constitution. Ardent Federalists of the Essex Junto, led by Timothy Pickering and John Lowell, hoped that the Hartford convention would demand a revision of the Constitution that would protect the interests of New England, and, if that failed, they hoped that New England would make a separate peace. Unfortunately for them, the convention, composed of delegates from Massachusetts, Connecticut, and Rhode Island, came under the control of the conservative group. The

---

[4] A rain storm saved the rest of the city. As an excuse for this wanton destruction, the British pointed to the equally unnecessary destruction by the Americans of the government buildings at York (later Toronto) in April, 1813.

[5] It was during this bombardment that Francis Scott Key wrote *The Star Spangled Banner*.

[6] American opposition to war has been fully told by Merle Curti in *The American Peace Crusade, 1815–1860* (1929) and in *Peace or War* (1936).

chairman was George Cabot, whose theory of political action was summed up in a question to Pickering: "Why can't you and I let the world ruin itself in its own way?" After a secret session the convention recommended seven amendments to the Constitution, suggested several ways by which the interests of New England might be better safeguarded, and hinted that, if these recommendations went unheeded, a second convention would be called with secession as a possible objective. A committee was sent to Washington to lay these demands before federal authorities, but news of the victory at New Orleans and the successful progress of the peace negotiations made their mission ridiculous and gave those in charge of the government a chance to cover their own inefficiency by accusing New England of treason.

The American war aroused little enthusiasm in Great Britain. For twenty years that nation had been fighting France; taxes were extremely burdensome; the public debt was stupendous; and the people were heartily sick of it all. In America, the Warhawks, sobered by two years of failure, were also willing to end it. Informal negotiations looking toward peace started almost immediately after war was declared, but it was not until January, 1814, that Monroe learned that Britain was willing to treat. A commission of five, including Albert Gallatin, Henry Clay, and John Quincy Adams, was instructed to demand the abandonment of impressment, a clear definition of the rights of neutrals, restoration of territory in British hands, and indemnities for certain seizures of merchant vessels. The British commissioners, three men of mediocre talents, were instructed to insist upon a buffer Indian state in the West, cessions of American territory, surrender of the inshore fisheries off the Canadian coasts, and equally harsh demands. The demands of the two sides were so far apart that an agreement seemed impossible, and Adams urged that the commission depart. Clay, however, who knew nothing of the tactics of international diplomacy, but who was thoroughly conversant with the ways of men, was convinced that England was playing for larger stakes at Vienna and wanted peace, and that a waiting game would produce results. He was right. MacDonough's victory at Plattsburg improved the American position, and England agreed to peace on the basis of the *status quo ante bellum*. The treaty of Ghent (December 24, 1814) made no mention of neutral rights, impressment, or blockades; it merely restored peace and provided for four commissions to settle the disputed Canadian boundary.

Seemingly so indecisive, the War of 1812 had results for the United States of the greatest magnitude. While it rudely ended for many years the dream of annexing Canada, it also put an end to British hopes of an Indian buffer state, and to British intrigues with the Indians. The war gave Harrison the opportunity to break the power of the Indians in the

Northwest and Jackson the opportunity to smash the Creeks in the Southwest, incidentally providing two war heroes for the presidency. It opened the West to rapid settlement and made the annexation of Florida a natural if not inevitable consequence. In addition to promoting western settlement, it had important economic results, particularly in the Northeast, the section so strongly opposed to the war. New England, in fact, received the chief benefit. Not only did her shipping revive after the war, but the embargo, the nonintercourse acts, and the war itself brought a development of manufacturing, which was soon to receive protection in the tariff of 1816. The financial interests were also benefited by the creation in the same year of the second Bank of the United States, which the Republicans were forced to establish to aid in handling the war debt. A war brought on by agrarians had redounded to the benefit of industrialists and capitalists. Politically, the war dealt the final blow to Federalism; at the Hartford convention that party committed political suicide. It was now the Republicans who were the ardent nationalists.

REPUBLICAN NATIONALISM

The close of the war opened a new era in American history. For the first time in twenty years the American people could turn their attention from Europe and devote their energies to domestic problems. In the stress of war the people had elected some of the most vigorous and able men of the generation, and the fourteenth Congress, which convened in 1816, tackled the major problems of peace with a sureness that had been sadly lacking in preceding Congresses. In a patriotic surge of nationalism, sectional differences seemed for the moment to be pushed into the background. Madison,[7] forgetting his earlier Republican principles, took the lead in his message of 1815 by advocating "liberal provision" for defense, an enlarged navy, protection to manufactures, new national roads and canals, and a militia under the effective control of the federal government, while Dallas, his Secretary of the Treasury, urged the creation of a new national bank as the best means by which the government might regain control of the currency. Shades of Hamilton and Washington! What more could any Federalist ask?

Nothing loath, the Republicans, overwhelmingly in control of Congress, responded with vigor. Introduced by Lowndes of South Carolina and supported by Calhoun, Clay, and the old contingent of Warhawks, the first

---

[7] Madison had been re-elected in 1812 with Elbridge Gerry of Massachusetts as Vice-President by an electoral vote of 128 to 89. The Federalists supported De Witt Clinton of New York, a conservative Republican, for the presidency and Jared Ingersoll of Pennsylvania for the vice-presidency.

protective tariff (1816) was passed. With duties ranging from 7.5 to 30 per cent *ad valorem,* it gave special protection to cottons, woolens, iron, and other manufactured commodities that had been stimulated by the recent war. These early protectionists, curiously enough, were from the agricultural sections, but their theory, as expressed in the "American system" of Clay, looked toward reciprocal benefits to agriculture as manufacturing developed (page 254). These would come through improvement in transportation between the agricultural and the industrial sections, and, in line with this, appropriations were voted in succeeding years to push the Cumberland Road west to the Mississippi.

The refusal of the Republicans to recharter the Bank of the United States in 1811 had severely handicapped the prosecution of the war and had left the currency situation in chaos. With the restraining influence of the first Bank of the United States eliminated, the number of state banks had increased from 88 to 246 in the five years 1811–1816, and their note issues from approximately $50,000,000 to $100,000,000, an inflation that resulted in the suspension of specie payments after the British had captured Washington. During the war the government had issued $80,000,000 in bonds, for which they obtained but $34,000,000 measured in specie, while the public debt had increased from $45,200,000 to $127,334,000. The Republicans were in a quandary. Either they must make terms with northern bankers who had opposed the war, or they must take the situation in hand and create their own bank. They chose the latter, and men like Clay, who had voted against a recharter in 1811, now strongly urged a second Bank of the United States, while Madison, who had denounced Hamilton's bank as unconstitutional, signed in 1816 the bill creating a similar institution.[8] The second Bank of the United States was chartered for twenty years, one fifth of the $35,000,000 capital was to be subscribed by the federal government, and five of the twenty-five directors were to be appointed by the President. Like the earlier bank, its notes were to be receivable for all money due to the government and were to be payable on demand in specie. On its part the government agreed to create no other bank (except in the District of Columbia) and to deposit its funds in the bank, while the bank was to make loans to the government up to $500,000 and pay a bonus of $1,500,000 for the charter. Within a few weeks the stock was completely subscribed, mostly by capitalists from the middle states. Stephen Girard of Philadelphia alone took the last three million, and the Republicans, like the Federalists a quarter of a century earlier, found themselves allied with eastern capital and supported by eastern wealth.

The idealistic nationalism that swept the nation in the decade following

---

[8] This action of the Republicans was far from being unanimous. The great Democratic theorist, John Taylor—and his was not a lone voice—opposed the recharter and the new bank.

the war was bound to disintegrate before stronger forces of economic sectionalism. Before it subsided, however, the new nationalism had been written into constitutional law, chiefly by the dominating personality of Chief Justice Marshall. Appointed Chief Justice by Adams, Marshall remained on the bench for thirty-four years, handing down nationalistic decisions in season and out. Republican Presidents filled vacancies with states' rights Republicans, but all of them, even the able Justice Story, soon fell under the spell of Marshall's ideas. In the thirty-four years, Marshall dissented from the majority only eight times and wrote 519 of 1106 opinions handed down. Marshall was no fair-weather Federalist; he held consistently to his original course while members of his own party were turning to the doctrine of states' rights. In American judicial history Marshall occupies a place similar to that of Hamilton in American financial history. This place he attained not because of legal learning, but because of very definite opinions regarding the function of state and national governments, an ability to state these beliefs clearly and logically, and the strength to carry his associates with him. He wrote his opinions as one might compose an essay on constitutional government and then handed them to more learned men to justify them. "Brother Story," he is reputed to have said on one occasion, "will add the citations."

Upon American legal and constitutional history Marshall left his imprint primarily along three lines. In the first place, he was responsible more than any other in establishing the doctrine of judicial supremacy. There were precedents for this in the state courts, but it was Marshall who applied it to the national system. In Marbury v. Madison (1803), it will be remembered (page 154), he declared an act of the federal Congress unconstitutional. If the federal government was bound by the Constitution, he held, so were the states, and in many notable decisions he voided acts of state legislatures. In Fletcher v. Peck (1810) he informed the state of Georgia that it was not sovereign but part of a large empire and of a union that had a Constitution, "which imposes limits to the legislation of the several states." In Dartmouth College v. Woodward (1819) he declared an act of the New Hampshire legislature unconstitutional on the ground that it had infringed a charter that was a contract, a violation of which the Constitution forbade.

In the second place, he gave judicial sanction to the doctrine of the centralization of federal powers at the expense of the states. This is seen in the cases already cited, in which acts of the state legislatures were declared unconstitutional, and in many other notable decisions.[9] Among the most famous of his decisions was that in McCollough v. Maryland (1819),

---

[9] Years before Marshall became Chief Justice, the Federalist Supreme Court had commenced this process in Chisholm v. Georgia (1793), when it held that a state might be sued by a citizen

which arose from an attempt of the state of Maryland to destroy a branch of the second Bank of the United States by levying a tax upon its notes. The questions at issue were: (1) Did the Constitution give Congress the right to charter a bank? (2) Had Maryland the right to tax it? The purpose of the bank, said Marshall, was legitimate and constitutional, and Congress under the Constitution had power to pass "all laws which shall be necessary and proper for carrying into execution" a thoroughly constitutional object. What the federal government has the power to create, no state has the power to destroy, for the nation is "an indestructable union of indestructable states." The power to tax is the power to destroy, therefore in this case unconstitutional. Quite as important was the decision in Gibbons *v*. Ogden (1824), involving an act of the New York legislature conferring upon certain parties a monopoly of steamboat navigation on New York waters. Here Marshall interpreted the word "commerce" in the Constitution in the broadest sense, and annulled the act of the New York legislature on the ground that it violated the power of the central government to regulate commerce. Particularly interesting is the case of Cohens *v*. Virginia, which the Cohen brothers, after conviction by the state courts for selling lottery tickets, appealed to the Supreme Court. The eleventh amendment had been passed with the intention, supposedly, of keeping such cases out of the federal courts, but Marshall accepted appellate jurisdiction on the ground that the eleventh amendment did not apply to a case in which the state was the original plaintiff, thereby cutting about three fourths of the meaning out of the amendment. Marshall called upon the Virginia authorities to appear before the court, and the Virginia legislature replied by a resolution denying the right of the Supreme Court to do this.

Finally, Marshall's decisions were important in their use of the federal Constitution to protect property rights from state legislatures. This is obvious in the Peck case and the Dartmouth College case, where acts were declared unconstitutional because they violated, in his opinion, the sanctity of contracts. It is also seen in one of his last decisions, Craig *v*. Missouri (1830), when he held an act of Missouri authorizing the emission of bills of credit unconstitutional as violating Article I, Section 10. Although Marshall's decisions were in line with nineteenth-century economic development and with the brief surge of nationalism after 1815, they were often bitterly opposed by the masses of the democracy. In the constitutional conflict between federal authority and states' rights and in the economic conflict between the rich and the poor, the victory was to rest with Mar-

of another state, a decision that so angered the country that the eleventh amendment was passed to prevent such action.

shall rather than with Jefferson, champion of the individual and the agrarian, or with Jackson, champion of the masses.

THE ERA OF GOOD FEELING

While occupied with the important nationalistic legislation of 1816, the Republican members of Congress paused long enough to nominate James Monroe for the presidency. Monroe was the last of the Virginia dynasty and the last of the older generation of Presidents who had been active in the days of the Revolution. As the outstanding member of the rapidly changing cabinets of Madison's closing years, he was the natural heir to the presidency, but his choice was due to expediency rather than to personal popularity. Possessed of many fine qualities, Monroe lacked the ability of his predecessors, nor was he the intellectual equal of many of the younger generation of statesmen who were pressing to the fore. His administration was a period of transition from the old to the new America, and Monroe was a political stop-gap until the new generation could find itself. Nomination was tantamount to election. The Federalists, it is true, nominated Rufus King, their brilliant senator from New York, but he was heavily defeated by an electoral vote of 183 to 34.[10] So far had party divisions disappeared that Monroe's cabinet was headed by John Quincy Adams, son of the Federalist President against whom the older Republicans had hurled their harshest criticism. Two of the ablest of the younger statesmen also found places in the cabinet, William H. Crawford as Secretary of the Treasury and John C. Calhoun as Secretary of War. When Monroe, in 1817, made a tour of New England, the Boston *Centinel*, bursting out in a paean of praise, heralded his administration as the "Era of Good Feeling." In comparison with earlier and later periods, there was justification for this phrase;[11] actually it was a far from accurate description.

The harmony and peace that characterized the domestic situation at the opening of the administration could not last long. The years following the conclusion of the war had seen a rapid revival of commerce and agriculture. Settlers were flocking to the West and opening new lands on the easy credit of the wild-cat banks that had sprung up like mushrooms after the passing in 1811 of the first Bank of the United States. Eastern manufacturers, encouraged by the tariffs of 1816 and by increased markets, were constructing plants beyond the needs of the nation. The same sort of over-

---

[10] King carried but three states, Massachusetts, Connecticut, and Delaware.

[11] In 1820 the Federalist Party, practically extinct, offered no candidate, and Monroe received all electoral votes but one. A single vote was cast for J. Q. Adams.

expansion as followed the Civil War and the World War resulted in a similar and inevitable collapse in 1819, when the second Bank of the United States, in a sudden panic for its own safety, demanded that the state banks redeem their obligations to it in specie. Immediately arose the cry, so often heard before and since, of the western debtor against the eastern creditor. "All the flourishing cities of the West," cried Benton of Missouri, "are mortgaged to this money power. They may be devoured at any minute. They are in the jaws of the Monster." Economic sectionalism, as seen in the conflict between the western farmer and the eastern banker, was stirring again. The panic resulted in an investigation and reorganization of the bank. It brought the Land Act of 1820, which abolished the system of purchasing public lands on credit, liberalized the land policy by reducing the amount of land that must be purchased from 160 to 80 acres, and lowered the price from $2 an acre to $1.25. All these changes were important improvements on the Harrison Act of 1800 and at the same time provided a safety valve for the depression. The typical frontiersman was too poor to afford as much as 160 acres at the earlier price, and the credit system had promoted speculation and overexpansion. For the distressed manufacturers the friends of protection attempted to pass a higher tariff in 1820, but consideration in the Senate was postponed. The votes, however, showed the Northwest, where manufacturing was now well started, solid for protection, the South and Southwest almost solid against it, and the Northeast divided.

The panic of 1819 had unmistakably uncovered a double basis for economic sectionalism in (1) the conflict between the western debtor and the eastern creditor and (2) the controversy over the tariff. Another conflict, destined to be more serious, the problem of slavery as against free labor, suddenly pushed to the front. In February, 1819, the Territory of Missouri, which had been cut from the Louisiana purchase, petitioned for admission to the Union. To the amazement of southern members of the House, John Talmadge of New York offered an amendment to the bill prohibiting further introduction of slavery and requiring the freeing of all children born after admission to the Union when they reached the age of twenty-five. The whole question of slavery, which had been quiescent for years, arose again to plague the nation. In the debate that followed, northern representatives attacked the institution with a barrage of argument to which subsequent controversy added little. Southern representatives, failing to justify slavery on moral grounds, recognized it as a necessary evil that could not be avoided, argued that its evils would be mitigated by a wide diffusion, and asserted that Congress had not the power to ban it from the Louisiana purchase. For the latter argument they pointed to the fact that slavery had existed under Spanish and French rule and that the purchase treaty had guaranteed that the inhabitants would be protected in their liberty, property, and religion.

The question of slavery, however, was not primarily a moral issue; it was one that involved the economic prosperity and the political strength of the South. By 1820 the North had a population of 5,152,000, with 105 members in the House; the South had a population of 4,485,000, with 81 members. Thus early the free states had control of the lower branch of the legislature. In the Senate, on the other hand (after the admission of Alabama in 1819), the representation of free and slave states was equal. If the new states to be created from the Louisiana purchase should be free, this equilibrium would be upset forever. Northern politicians saw an opportunity to create a solid North that might put an end to the domination of the South, while southern politicians saw clearly that the political position of the South in the federal structure was at stake. From that time the slavery issue had also a political basis.

The amended bill for admission passed the House but failed in the Senate, and the controversy was continued in the press and the state legislatures. In the meantime Maine had separated from Massachusetts, with the latter's consent, and now also petitioned for admission. This opened a way to settlement. When Congress convened again, both Maine and Missouri were admitted, thus maintaining an equal representation in the Senate. To the admission of Missouri as a slave state a compromise amendment was added, providing for the prohibition of slavery in the Louisiana purchase north of 36° 30′ (the southern boundary of Missouri). At the moment it seemed a fair compromise, and it was successful in shelving the slavery issue for twenty years. The South had gained its immediate objective; the possibility of the creation of other states in the northern region of the Louisiana purchase seemed at that time remote, while the admission of Arkansas and Florida as slave states was eventually inevitable. It seemed like a southern victory, but the North had maintained its position that Congress might determine the status of slavery in the territories, and it had gained the greater part of the unsettled area in dispute. Fortunate as was the compromise, far-sighted statesmen sensed the significance of the issue. The compromise, said John Quincy Adams, was "a mere preamble"; Jefferson described it as "a reprieve only, not a final sentence." "This momentous question," said he, "like a fire bell in the night, awakened and filled me with terror." It is the "most portentous" question "which has ever yet threatened our Union. In the gloomiest hour of the Revolutionary War, I never had any apprehensions equal to those which I feel from this source."

MONROE AND HIS DOCTRINE

The aggressive confidence and optimism displayed in nationalistic legislation was also reflected in international relations during the later years of Madison and the administration of Monroe. A combination of fortunate circumstances made it a period of successful diplomacy. Lord Castlereagh, the British foreign minister, sensing perhaps that American expansion would be toward the west rather than toward the north, reversed the traditional policy of the British foreign office, treated the United States as an equal among nations, and did his part in straightening out the differences between the two countries. At the same time John Quincy Adams, an ardent nationalist and an aggressive if not a polished diplomat, dominated the foreign policy of the Monroe administration to the great benefit of American interests. Finally, the European situation and the revolutions in Central and South America played into the hands of the United States.

With England important progress was made in settling the boundary-line controversy with Canada. The treaty of Ghent (1814), it will be remembered, provided for several commissions to take up this problem. One decided where the eastern line should run in Passamaquoddy Bay; a second failed to determine the northern boundary of Maine, and it was not until 1842 that the question was finally settled; a third carried the line from parallel 45 through the St. Lawrence and the Great Lakes to where Huron and Superior meet. By the convention of 1818 the two nations agreed that the line should extend from the northwestern corner of the Lake of the Woods due south to parallel 49 and then due west to the "Great Stony Mountains," thus rectifying an impossible boundary laid down in the treaty of 1783. No agreement could be reached regarding the Oregon boundary, and the commission provided for joint occupation for ten years. By this agreement the Canadian boundary was now settled except in Maine and Oregon. Quite as significant was the agreement, arrived at in 1817 by Secretary of State Richard Rush and the British minister Sir Charles Bagot, that both nations should maintain on the Great Lakes only such vessels as were necessary to police the waterways. The Rush-Bagot agreement, promoted by the desire for amity and economy, accomplished both purposes and gave the world the amazing spectacle of a 3000-mile boundary absolutely undefended.

While boundary disputes with Great Britain were progressing favorably, the Florida controversy approached its climax. From the moment that Jefferson had purchased Louisiana and had convinced himself that the purchase included West Florida, the desire to obtain all Florida had grown with the years. Land hunger, desire for an outlet to the Gulf for Mississippi and Alabama, and the hope of establishing natural boundary lines explain the tenacity with which succeeding administrations held to the purpose of annexation. Some justification for the American desire can be found in the fact that Florida was a refuge for runaway slaves, for marauding bands of Indians, and for smugglers, pirates, and other lawbreakers. Spain, in the Pinckney treaty, had promised protection from Indian attacks but was too weak to make good her pledge. The frontiersmen of the Southwest would have conquered the region at the drop of the hat, but Jefferson preferred diplomacy. When this failed, Jefferson erected the region around Mobile into a customs district (page 153). In the following years American settlers moved into West Florida; they revolted from Spain in 1810 and demanded annexation. Madison responded with alacrity and annexed West Florida to the Pearl River. In 1813 West Florida from the Pearl to the Perdido was added to the Territory of Mississippi. Madison defended his action on the ground that the Spanish Empire was breaking up and that he could not "without serious inquietude" see this neighboring territory "pass from the hands of Spain into those of any other foreign power."

The acquisition of West Florida was but a preliminary to further annexation. Already in 1811 Congress had authorized Madison to take temporary possession of East Florida if any foreign nation attempted to occupy it. Madison sent two agents in the spring of 1812 to organize a filibustering expedition; but after they had captured Amelia Island, Madison, with a British war impending, disavowed their acts. During the war came Jackson's invasion of Florida (1814) to prevent the British from seizing Pensacola. In 1818, asserting that he had received authorization from the federal government, he again invaded East Florida, to put down outrages of the Seminole Indians. On this expedition he not only thoroughly chastised the Indians and captured the Spanish forts at St. Marks and Pensacola, but also executed two Englishmen, Ambrister and Arbuthnot, accused of supplying arms to the Indians. Jackson's expedition made him again a hero in the West, but it also made war with England and Spain possible. Monroe and all of his cabinet but Adams believed that the expedition should be disavowed, but Adams finally won them over. The administration supported Jackson and addressed a strong note to the Spanish government, demanding either adequate policing of Florida or the cession of that province to the United States. Castlereagh, who declared that England would have declared war "if the ministry had but held up a finger," avoided rupture by taking the position that the two Englishmen summarily executed by Jackson had so acted as to put themselves beyond the protection of their government.

Spain, unable to handle the situation, decided to sell before the territory was seized. The result was the treaty of 1819, by which Spain ceded to the United States all her land east of the Mississippi in return for the assumption by the United States of the claims of her citizens against Spain for damages to commerce during the Napoleonic wars and the relinquishment by the United States of claims to Texas. By the treaty the boundary of Louisiana was placed, on the west, at the Sabine River, thence north and west to parallel 42, and then west to the Pacific. There were not a few in Congress who were unwilling "to trade Texas for Florida," but the treaty was finally ratified in 1821.

The ease with which Florida was acquired was in large part due to the declining strength of the Spanish Empire and to its difficulties with its other colonies in America. Spanish America during the colonial period had suffered under a system of mercantilism far more severe than that imposed on the British colonies. When Napoleon invaded Spain in 1808 and deposed the Bourbon monarch, the Spanish colonies set up provisional governments and abolished the rigid commercial system, at the same time continuing their allegiance to Spain. When the Bourbons were restored in 1814 and attempted to revive their old trade regulations, the colonies revolted, and by 1822 Spanish America from California to Cape Horn had won its freedom. By that time it was obvious enough that Spain was incapable alone of winning back her American colonies, and she sought aid from her fellow members of the Holy Alliance. Russia and France were willing enough to intervene in her behalf. The co-operation of Great Britain, whose navy controlled the sea, was necessary to success, but this they failed to get. The British government had no sympathy for countries that had revolted against their "legitimate monarchs," but Great Britain had profited handsomely from the opening of Spanish-American trade, and this commerce she had no intention of losing. Her policy was to promote reconciliation but to refuse military intervention.

The heroic struggle of the Spanish colonies for freedom was followed with interest and sympathy in the United States. The new nations quite naturally expected immediate recognition by this country, and idealistic nationalists, led by Henry Clay, demanded that we give it. The policy of Monroe and Adams, however, during these years was distinctly realistic if not selfish. Hasty recognition might involve us in a European war and imperil the negotiations for the acquisition of Florida, and the administration warily avoided all overtures of England, the Holy Alliance, and the revolutionists that might involve us in any way. But action of some kind could not indefinitely be postponed. The administration proposed to Great Britain a joint recognition of independence, but the British government refused.

In 1821 the tsar issued a ukase extending Alaska to parallel 51, thus encroaching on the Oregon region, jointly claimed by Great Britain and the United States, and warned all foreign ships to keep clear of the Russian-

American coast. Here was danger from another quarter, and, as the administration feared that the results in Spanish America might result in monarchies rather than republics, the United States, on March, 1822, accorded recognition to Argentina, Chile, Peru, Colombia, and Mexico. In 1823 France invaded Spain to deliver the Bourbon king from the liberal constitution that he had been forced to accept, and fears were aroused that this would be followed by a Franco-Spanish expedition against the states of Spanish America. While England exerted successful pressure upon France to renounce any such intention, Canning proposed to Richard Rush, the American minister, that the two nations join in a public declaration to the Holy Alliance against "any forcible enterprize for reducing the colonies to subjugation," but with the understanding that neither Great Britain nor the United States would take Spanish-American territory. Rush agreed to join in a declaration if Great Britain would recognize the independence of the Spanish-American states, but Canning refused.

When Canning's proposal reached America, Monroe was in a quandary. Personally he thought it should be accepted, and in this position he had the support of Jefferson and Madison—strange advice from two old Republicans long opposed to European entanglements and strongly anti-British. It was John Quincy Adams, a younger and perhaps wiser statesman, who prevailed. Thoroughly convinced that there was no danger of intervention, he strongly urged, "It would be more candid, as well as more dignified, to avow our principles explicitly to Great Britain and France, than to come in as a cockboat in the wake of the British man-of-war," and eventually won over Monroe and his cabinet. The British offer was declined, and Monroe in his annual message of 1823 (in words expressing the ideas of Adams) stated the American position in what has since been known as the Monroe Doctrine. He first reminded Russia "that the American continents, by the free and independent condition which they have assumed and maintain, are henceforth not to be considered as subjects for future colonization by any European powers." To those powers about to intervene in South America, he said:

> We owe it, therefore, to candor, and to the amicable relations existing between the United States and those European powers, to declare that we should consider any attempt on their part to extend their system to any portion of this hemisphere as dangerous to our peace and safety. With the existing colonies or dependencies of any European power we have not interfered and shall not interfere. But with the Governments who have declared their independence, . . . and whose independence we have . . . acknowledged, we could not view any interposition . . . by any European power, in any other light than as the manifestation of an unfriendly disposition towards the United States.

Finally, he intimated that we intended to mind our own business, for "Our policy in regard to Europe . . . is not to interfere in the internal concerns of any of its powers [but] to cultivate friendly relations with it, submitting to injuries from none."

Obviously the Monroe Doctrine stemmed from many sources. New England commercial and fur interests were as hostile to Russian pretensions in the Northwest as the most ardent theoretical nationalist. The old idea of American interests as separate from those of Europe was now being reinforced by a new nationalism and by the idea that as a Republic we had a mission to encourage other Republics, no matter how far away they might be. Madison, for example, went as far as to urge a declaration in favor of Greek freedom. And, of course, there was the western desire to find markets for agricultural goods in Latin American countries *via* New Orleans by winning the friendship of peoples to the south. Nor was the United States even this early without a very definite interest in the fate of Cuba.

Whatever the reasons, the President's message was a ringing warning against Russian ambitions in Oregon and against European interference to upset the *status quo*, and a striking indication of the rising power of the American nation and its new nationalism. In a bold statement the young republic had announced to the world that she would determine her own foreign policies.

A full account is in Edward Channing, *A History of the United States,* Vol. IV, Chaps. XV–XX. On politics see W. E. Binkley, *American Political Parties,* Chap. V. J. W. Pratt, *The Expansion of 1812,* Introduction and Chaps. I, II, is excellent on the causes of the war. Henry Adams, *A History of the United States During the Administrations of Jefferson and Madison,* Vol. IX, Chaps. I, II, discusses the treaty of Ghent. On the Monroe Doctrine read either Dexter Perkins, *The Monroe Doctrine, 1823–1826,* Chap. III, or D. Y. Thomas, *One Hundred Years of the Monroe Doctrine,* Chaps. I–IV. On foreign affairs, see S. F. Bemis, *A Diplomatic History of the United States,* Chaps. X–XII and T. A. Bailey, *A Diplomatic History of the American People,* Chaps. IX–XIII. See also Commager, *Documents of American History,* Vol. I, 207–242.

Chapter XII

JACKSONIAN DEMOCRACY

*The election of General Jackson was a triumph
of democratic principle, and an assertion of the
people's right to govern themselves.*

THOMAS HART BENTON

The reign of King "Mob" seemed triumphant.

JOSEPH STORY

To the victors belong the spoils.
WILLIAM LEARNED MARCY

THE ERA OF HARD FEELING

Despite the stirrings of sectionalism, the administration of Monroe had
been a peaceful one and satisfactory to the great majority of the people.
Even old John Adams once called it an administration "without a fault."
The disappearance of the Federalist Party from national politics had
opened the way to the political ambitions of Republican leaders, and the
last four years of Monroe were characterized politically by the efforts of
various Republican statesmen to achieve the presidency. The campaign of
1824 was a sort of elimination contest, a "scrub race for the presidency," as
Woodrow Wilson called it. As early as 1818 John Quincy Adams had observed that the aspirants were preparing "not for the next Presidential
election, but for the one after." Besides Adams, there were four candidates
in 1824, Crawford, Calhoun, Clay, and Jackson. William H. Crawford, a
wealthy plantation-owner of Georgia, had been minister to France, United
States Senator, Secretary of War, and Secretary of the Treasury. An astute
politician rather than a statesman of high order, he had secured the nomination of the now discredited congressional caucus, which probably did
him more harm than good. From the lower South came the second con-
testant, John C. Calhoun, then forty-two years of age. Born in South
Carolina of "Scotch-Irish" ancestry and educated in New England, he had
behind him a service of fourteen years in state and federal legislatures and
had been Secretary of War during Monroe's two terms. Burgess describes

him as "grave, pure, and patriotic as Adams himself, and almost as puritanic," as an able administrator, and as a man "fascinating in conversation, kind and generous in his feelings, . . . a personality to be looked up to with reverence, admiration, and confidence."

The candidate of the Northwest was Henry Clay of Kentucky, then in the prime of manhood, leader of the Warhawks of 1812, and Speaker of the House almost continuously since 1811. There was nothing of the Puritan about Clay. Irresistible in conversation, an entrancing orator, and a prince of good fellows, Clay throughout his career was the most popular of the great political figures who occupied the stage of the middle period. Lacking the learning of Calhoun and the wide diplomatic experience of Adams, he left his imprint upon his time as a pacifier of sectional disputes and as the upholder of what came to be called the "American system." Contesting with Clay for the support of the West was Andrew Jackson, conqueror of the Creeks, hero of New Orleans, and in 1824 senator from Tennessee. Violent in temper and notably lacking in tact in his only administrative office, the territorial governorship of Florida, "Old Hickory" was popular with the masses as the plain and honest frontiersman rather than as a professional office-seeker.

Never before or since has the American people had a chance to choose among a more appealing or abler group of candidates. Calhoun finally withdrew from the race, accepting the nomination for Vice-President and throwing his support to Jackson. The campaign, characterized by much personal bitterness, resulted in 99 electoral votes for Jackson, 84 for Adams, 41 for Crawford, and 37 for Clay. For the second and last time in our history the choice for the presidency was thrown into the House. Clay as the fourth man was eliminated, and Crawford, physically incapacitated by a paralytic stroke, was out of consideration. The choice now lay between Jackson and Adams, with the attitude of Clay the determining factor. Personal interest and reasoned judgment led him to throw his support to Adams,[1] and the second member of that famous family assumed the presidency in March, 1825. With a long, successful, and distinguished public career behind him, John Quincy Adams was superior in training to any of his rivals, but his four years in office were a long martyrdom. Like his father, Adams lacked personal magnetism and in his daily contacts was cold, taciturn, and tactless. His burning patriotism, his high political idealism, and the almost morbid conscientiousness with which he devoted himself to public duty counted for nothing in the eyes of the disappointed politicians who had failed in 1824 and who began immediately to prepare for the next election. Their tactics were centered on breaking

[1] Adams received the vote of thirteen states, Jackson of seven, and Crawford of four.

Adams politically, and for four years Adams fought back like a man at bay. His appointment of Clay as head of the Department of State brought forth the cry, "corrupt bargain," the charge that Adams had conferred this position upon Clay in return for the presidency. In Congress amendments were continuously proposed demanding abolition of the choice of the President by the House and exclusion of members of Congress from appointment to executive office during their term of service.

The difficulties of Adams were due not alone to his political opponents. His beliefs ran counter to the developing sectionalism and to the political ideas of the time. In his inaugural address he transcended even the nationalism of Hamilton, urging increased appropriations for internal improvement, an enlarged navy, and national institutions of learning and research. Old Republicans of the states' rights variety were aroused, and Jefferson even suggested that the Virginia legislature pass resolutions similar to those of 1798. It was a call for aggressive nationalism at a time when sectional differences were again coming to the front. By a judicious manipulation of federal patronage Adams might have strengthened his political position, but the technique of the politician was foreign to his nature. Fitness for position was his sole criterion; he retained even in his own cabinet two men known to be loyal to the opposition. Wide application of the "spoils system" he left to his successor. As nothing was selfishly to be gained by working for him, his following soon disintegrated, and in the midterm elections he lost the slender margin by which he had controlled the House.

The opposition to Adams first coalesced over the question of sending delegates to the ill-fated Panama Congress. In 1825 Simón Bolívar proposed a congress of American nations to meet the following year to consider their common interests. Contrary to the desire of Bolívar, Mexico and Colombia invited the United States to participate. Clay, who saw an opportunity for his country to establish a leadership in Latin-American affairs, eagerly approved; but Adams, fearful of entangling alliances, hesitated. Finally convinced of the wisdom of the move, Adams in December asked the Senate to confirm the nomination of two delegates. The debate lasted until March before the nominations were confirmed—too late to be of any value. One of the delegates died on the way; the other reached Panama after the congress had adjourned. The debate over participation at Panama brought out many objections. Northern representatives feared that it might lead to embarrassing alliances; southern representatives wanted no part in a congress that would undoubtedly consider plans for the freeing of Cuba and Puerto Rico from Spain and for the abolition of slavery in those islands. The real nature of the opposition, however, was political. "They have beaten us," said Van Buren, "by a few votes, after a hard battle, but if they had only taken the other side, and refused the mission, we should have had them."

More serious than the political opposition to participation in the Panama Congress was the developing sectionalism displayed in the controversy over the tariff of 1828. Here economic sectionalism and political opportunism were curiously intertwined. Failure in 1824 to increase the tariff brought renewed efforts. The woolen manufacturers of the middle states, with their plants overexpanded and unable to meet the competition of English woolen goods, led the movement. A bill raising duties on both raw and finished wool passed the House in 1827 and was defeated in the Senate only by the vote of Calhoun, who had now definitely allied himself with the free-trade South. In the following year a new tariff bill that gave added protection not alone to woolens but to glass, iron, flax, and other commodities was introduced. It was supported by the iron interests of Pennsylvania, the wool-growers of Ohio and the middle states, and manufacturers everywhere, but it increased the hostility of the shipping interests of the North and the cotton-growers of the South. The bill, as it came before Congress, far from being an honest effort to promote the economic well-being of the nation, bore all the earmarks of an intrigue to promote the political ambitions of the Jacksonian politicians.

Sure of the South in the next presidential election, their aim was to defeat the tariff but at the same time allow the Jackson men of the middle and western states to pose as the friends of industry. By putting the rates obnoxiously high on raw materials used by New England manufacturers they expected that New England would join with the South in defeating the bill, while the Jackson men from the protectionist states could vote for it. "The bill," said John Randolph disgustedly, "referred to manufactures of no sort or kind, but the manufacture of a President of the United States." To the surprise of the authors of this well-laid scheme, the New Englanders voted for the bill,[2] and the "tariff of abominations," as it was popularly called, became law.

In the South the tariff of 1828 was greeted with bitter and widespread opposition. Vice-President Calhoun, who had been deep in the political plot to prevent its passage, now offered to the South, through a committee of the South Carolina legislature, a document in which he developed the Southern position on the tariff and a new doctrine of states' rights, the doctrine of nullification. In this famous "Exposition and Protest" Calhoun maintained first that the Constitution gave Congress the power to enact

---

[2] The support of New England is evidence of the rapid growth of manufacturing in that section and the relative decline of shipping. It is seen in the vote of Daniel Webster, who opposed the tariff of 1824 but favored that of 1828.

a tariff for revenue alone and not for protection. Not only was a protective tariff unconstitutional, he insisted, but it very clearly operated seriously to injure the economic interests of the South, a region engaged in the production and export of agricultural products. If a protective tariff was both unconstitutional and injurious, there must be a remedy. "Universal experience," he asserted, "in all ages and countries . . . teaches that power can only be restrained by power, and not by reason and justice." The remedy that he offered and the method of restraining a power illegally assumed by the federal government were in a state convention called to act on a specific question. "If the question be decided in the affirmative," he wrote, "the Convention will then determine in what manner the acts of Congress ought to be declared null and void within the limits of the State; which solemn declaration, based on her rights as a member of the Union, would be obligatory, not only on her own citizens but on the General Government itself; and thus place the violated rights of the State under the shield of the Constitution." Here was the old states' rights doctrine of the Virginia and Kentucky resolutions and the Hartford convention carried a step farther in designating the specific method whereby a single state might act. Only the doctrine of secession needed to be added to give any section an economic argument and a political method for the destruction of the Union. For the moment the South rested on this protest, suspending action until after the election of 1828, when a change of administration, it was expected, would rectify the unpopular tariff.

THE ASCENDANCY OF KING ANDREW

Outwardly the Republican Party was still intact in the election of 1824, which appeared to be simply a battle between leaders of the same party, whose views on national problems were much the same. Actually the party was already disintegrating, and this was evident enough by 1828. On the one hand were the conservative business interests of the East and the ardent nationalists in other sections who had picked up the old Federalist doctrines. On the other hand were agricultural interests and the upholders of states' rights, the backbone of the early Jeffersonian Republicans. The latter began to call themselves Democrats to distinguish themselves from their more conservative party colleagues. Into the ranks of the Democrats naturally gravitated the "common man," who had been enfranchised by the new western state constitutions and by revisions of the eastern constitutions, which had largely eliminated or modified the property qualification for voting. The electorate of 1828 was far different from that of Washington's day, when not more than one seventh of the adult males had the right to vote. The "rise of the common man" was to have its effects upon national politics.

The campaign to elect Andrew Jackson had been pushed continuously for six years, and the failure in 1824 had merely spurred his political backers to increased activity. By 1828 the Crawford and Calhoun factions in the South had been won over, while in the North his fortunes were in the capable hands of such men as Martin Van Buren of New York, the cleverest politician of the middle period, and James Buchanan of Pennsylvania, destined like Van Buren later to win the presidency. The southern aristocracy had no love for the common man and no faith in the hot-headed hero of the West, but they hated the tariff and feared the nationalism of the Adams group. The Northwest deserted Clay, resenting his advocacy of the bank, and swung naturally to Jackson because of the Old Hero's well-known policy of eliminating the Indian menace. Since 1825 the Jackson managers had drummed into the ears of the masses the cry of "bargain and corruption" and "stolen election." Adams had been constitutionally elected, they admitted, but Jackson had received the greater number of popular votes, and the people had been defrauded. A continuation of these factors plus clever political manipulation gave Jackson and his party the victory in 1828 by an electoral vote of 178 to 83. Adams carried New England, but Jackson won the entire South and West, the state of Pennsylvania, and twenty of the thirty-six votes in New York.

The masses who had voted for Jackson believed that his election was the triumph of an honest man over a decadent group of aristocratic and corrupt politicians. In this they were wrong. The election, nevertheless, was far more of a political revolution than that of 1800. For the first, and perhaps the only, time in American history, the democratic masses had put their man in the White House. This was symbolized by the motley crowd that descended upon Washington for the inauguration and swarmed over the White House at the reception, upsetting pails of orange punch, breaking glasses, and standing with muddy boots on the damask-covered chairs in their eagerness to see the new President and press his hand. What the opinions of Jackson might be on national questions no one knew, for he had kept discreetly silent during the campaign, but the democratic masses had every confidence that a new day had dawned. Jackson himself was a typical son of the frontier. Born in 1767 in North Carolina, he had migrated to Tennessee in early manhood, studied law and held prominent local offices, and then served in both houses of the national legislature. His national fame had come from his exploits as a military leader in expeditions against the Indians and in the defense of New Orleans. His education was meager, his tastes uncultivated, and his opinions often hastily formed and dominated by prejudice, but he was a born leader of men who could act decisively, and in his state papers he expressed his ideas clearly and forcibly. Under the crude frontier conditions of his early life he had acquired self-discipline and dignity of manner; his sincerity was undoubted and his private life beyond reproach.

How this son of the West would handle his new responsibility was not long in doubt. With an exalted conception of the presidential office and a certainty that the people were behind him, he assumed a leadership that he expected other branches of the government to follow. His cabinet positions were distributed to personal friends among the factions that had supported him, but in his mind they were little more than chief clerks. Van Buren, the Secretary of State, was the only person of outstanding ability. His real advisers, soon known as the "Kitchen Cabinet," were a half dozen newspaper editors who had been brought on to Washington and given government jobs. Although Jackson in earlier years had expressed himself against partisan appointments to office, he firmly held to the theory of rotation and the belief that any honest man with ordinary ability could satisfactorily fulfill the duties of public office. The importunities of office-seekers and the popular demand that the old crowd be eliminated led to widespread removal, and the test of fitness was loyalty to Jackson. The "clean sweep" was not nearly as thorough as was popularly supposed. The judicial branch and the diplomatic service were barely touched, and not more than a third of the other office-holders were removed. The "spoils system" was, of course, not new, for it was already firmly established in state politics and not unknown in national politics, but Jackson must in part bear the responsibility for its wider practice. In this he was not wholly at fault, for, says McMaster, "The people, not the leaders, were to blame." After a six-year struggle it was more than human nature could stand to allow the old bureaucracy that had supported their enemies to remain in power. For the substitution of new blood after a political upheaval much can be said, but there seems to be no doubt that the system of supporting political parties by a careful distribution of salary spoils and with it the creation of an office-seeking class gained their first real foothold in America under Jackson.

With a following drawn from so many diverse factions, there was little likelihood that Jackson's administration would be a peaceful one. Western Democrats wanted cheap land, extermination or dislodgment of the Indian, internal improvements at government expense, and protection from the money monopolists of the East. Southern Democrats wanted a reduction of the tariff. In the Northeast, on the other hand, the Democrats generally favored protection and were in many respects opposed to the demands of the West. How successfully could Jackson meet the desires of these conflicting sections? The hope of the West that the federal government would liberally aid in promoting internal improvements was given a severe blow in 1830 by the veto of the Maysville Road Bill, which provided for government aid in the construction of a link (from Maysville to Lexington, Kentucky) in a proposed turnpike between the Cumberland Road at Zanesville, Ohio, and Florence, Alabama. Jackson justified his action on constitutional grounds, pointing out that this road was a local project entirely within the boundaries of Kentucky,[3] and insisted that the chief business of the government was to pay the public debt before embarking on local and private transportation projects. Jackson was not rabid on the question of internal improvements at government expense where there was no constitutional objection, and Congress during his administration appropriated four times the amount expended under Adams for rivers and harbors and construction of roads in the territories. The Maysville and subsequent vetoes, however, were extremely significant in that they halted federal participation in transportation projects at the opening of the railroad era, and threw the burden upon the states and private individuals.

On the other hand, Jackson saw eye to eye with the West on the Indian problem. During his administration he concluded ninety-four treaties with the Indians, thereby opening for settlement millions of acres of land. When the Indians failed to move speedily enough, Jackson was quick to side with the settlers and push the Indians forcibly toward the west. When a handful of Illinois Indians under their chief, Black Hawk, attempted in 1832 to hold on to enough of their ancestral lands to raise a little corn, many were ruthlessly massacred and the rest chased into Wisconsin. In Florida, when the majority of the Seminoles repudiated a treaty signed by a few chiefs and calling for their removal, a war ensued that lasted until 1842 and resulted in virtual extermination of these Indians. The Creek, Chickasaw, and Choctaw Indians of the Old Southwest were removed to Indian territory beyond the Mississippi, but with the Cherokees of western Georgia difficulties arose. When Georgia ceded her western lands to the federal government in 1802, it was stipulated that the United States should extinguish the Indian claims "as early as they can be peaceably obtained on reasonable terms." By a series of treaties obtained with great difficulty, the federal government had forced the Indians by 1826 to relinquish about all of the 60,000,000 acres originally held except a narrow strip on the western border. But this was not enough for the state of Georgia, which, in violation of federal treaties, annexed the Cherokee lands and decreed that after June 1, 1830, the Cherokees were subject to

[3] Federal aid to construct interstate highways has been continuously granted since the authorization of the Cumberland Road in 1806.

the laws of the state. The case came before the Supreme Court in Worcester *v.* Georgia (1832). Marshall upheld the position of the Cherokees and declared the Georgia statute unconstitutional. Jackson, who was determined that the Cherokees also should be removed to the region beyond the Mississippi, reproved the Supreme Court, remarking, so it is said, "John Marshall has made his decision, now let him enforce it." The Indians departed and Georgia won, but Jackson's stand in this controversy was influenced by his own frontier attitude toward the Indian problem rather than by his belief in states' rights. His attitude toward South Carolina's attempt at nullification in the same year, as we shall see, was quite different.

To his own surprise, Jackson's veto of the Maysville Road Bill was for the most part popular. So also was his Indian policy. At the same time, however, the political situation in his own party was anything but satisfactory. The trouble that arose to plague the Old Hero came from the women of his official family. His Secretary of War, Eaton, had married a young widow, in her girlhood Peggy O'Neill, the daughter of a Washington tavern-keeper. Stories reflecting on her early life were circulated, and, led by Mrs. Calhoun, the cabinet wives made it evident that she was socially undesirable. Jackson remembered that his own wife, who had died just before inauguration, and about whom unkind remarks had been made, had received Mrs. Eaton socially and he gallantly supported her. He brought the matter to the attention of his cabinet, but, when they refused to interfere, he ceased calling them into consultation. About the same time Jackson discovered that it was Calhoun and not Adams that had advocated his arrest and trial for insubordination at the time of the Florida invasion (page 181). Jackson called upon him for an explanation and, when it was not satisfactorily forthcoming, broke political and social relations with Calhoun. The latter finally resigned from the vice-presidency (1832) and returned to Washington as senator for South Carolina. During the O'Neill affair Van Buren, a widower, had won Jackson's heart by his chivalrous attitude toward Mrs. Eaton; Van Buren now suggested that he and Eaton resign from the cabinet and thus give Jackson the opportunity of asking for the resignations of other members. This was done, and Van Buren was nominated minister to Great Britain. The Senate defeated the nomination, but Van Buren was satisfied. The Calhoun faction was eliminated from Jackson's favor, and Van Buren rather than Calhoun became the heir apparent to the presidency. Jackson reconstructed his cabinet with Edward Livingston as Secretary of State, Lewis Cass, an able representative of the Northwest, in Eaton's place, Louis McLane as Secretary of the Treasury, and Roger B. Taney of Maryland, soon to succeed Marshall, as Attorney General. The O'Neill affair is of importance not alone because it determined the successor of Jackson, but also because it hastened the sectional differences and hardened the lines of conflict that were rapidly forming.

THE END OF THE BANK

While Jackson alienated the support of the powerful Calhoun faction, his political opponents of the National Republican Party [4] fortunately presented him with an issue upon which he could fight the campaign of 1832. From the beginning of his administration Jackson had eyed the second Bank of the United States with a suspicion that reflected his western origin. To him it seemed a money monopoly dominated by wealthy eastern capitalists who profited from this monopoly given them by the government. He also had a personal animus that came from his belief that the bank had interfered politically to oppose his election in 1828. In successive messages he questioned both the constitutionality and the expediency of the bank, asserting that it had failed in the great end of establishing a uniform and sound currency. The constitutionality, in spite of Marshall's numerous opinions upholding it, might be a matter of opinion, but the assertion that the bank had failed to accomplish its purpose was without foundation. The enmity to it was in no small part due to the fact that it had succeeded only too well in providing a stable currency and in restraining the inflationary tendencies of the state banks. Committees in both houses investigated the bank and reported favorably, while Jackson on his part stated in his message of 1831 that he held to his former view, but left the question for the people and their representatives to settle.

It was the friends of the bank rather than Jackson, however, who precipitated its ruin. Henry Clay, now leader of the National Republicans, scented an issue for the coming campaign and convinced Nicholas Biddle that the bank should apply immediately for a recharter, although the existing charter would not run out until 1836. The bill to recharter passed both houses but was returned by Jackson with a resounding veto. He pointed to the fact that $8,000,000 worth of stock was owned in Europe and that most of the rest was held in the East. The bank, he believed, was not "consistent with the rights of the States or the liberties of the people," since "most of the state banks exist by its forbearance." "It is easy to conceive," he asserted, "that great evils to our country and its institutions might flow from such a concentration of power in the hands of a few

---

[4] This was the name assumed by the nationalistic followers of Clay and Webster in the middle twenties. In 1834 the opposition to Jacksonian Democracy consolidated under the name "Whigs." The name "National Republican" was dropped.

men irresponsible to the people." "Each public officer," insisted Jackson, "who takes an oath to support the Constitution swears that he will support it as he understands it, and not as it is understood by others. . . . The opinion of the judges has no more authority over Congress than the opinion of Congress over the judges, and, on that point, the President is independent of both." The economic arguments of the veto message were so weak that the bank distributed copies wholesale. If Europe and the East had surplus wealth that the West needed, it was an advantage to have a sound agency through which this surplus might find its way to the West, and unsound money in the long run would injure the West as well as the East. The bank, however, failed to appreciate the political strength of the message or to realize that the masses cared but little for the constitutional aspect of the question.

By this time the bank, which had attempted to steer its course on sound business lines through the maze of politics, was driving ahead as incautiously as Jackson. Political pressure of all kinds was exerted; Webster was on its payroll, and Clay and other National Republicans received convenient loans. It is also established that the bank called loans for the purpose of bringing economic distress in the hope of crushing political opposition. Under such circumstances it is not surprising that the bank was the leading issue in the campaign of 1832. Politically the campaign is interesting in that it marked the end of the caucus system of nominating presidential candidates. A sudden outburst of hostility toward secret societies led to the short existence of a third party, the Anti-Masons, whose representatives gathered at Baltimore in the first nominating convention of our history to choose a presidential candidate. Since, as a new organization, they had no legislators to form a caucus, they chose this method, which had already been tried in some of the states. The National Republicans, following their lead, also called a convention, which nominated Clay, and the Democrats in similar fashion nominated Jackson and Van Buren and at the same time originated the "two-thirds rule" for a choice, which was followed in their conventions until 1936.[5] Despite the desertion of Calhoun, Jackson won easily.[6] Essentially, the election of 1832 was a personal victory, but it was also undoubtedly an endorsement of Jackson's policies.

Thoroughly outraged over the political opposition of the bank and convinced that his victory was a mandate from the people to destroy the

---

[5] The Democratic nominating convention of 1936 voted to end the two-thirds rule, the method of nominating by majority to begin in 1940.

[6] Jackson received 219 electoral votes, Clay 49, and William Wirt, Anti-Mason, 7. South Carolina, piqued over the treatment of Calhoun, threw her 11 votes away by casting them for John Floyd of Virginia.

"money monster," Jackson determined to continue his war upon the bank without waiting for its charter to run out. The sudden termination of the bank, with the attendant contraction of currency and loans, might easily result in widespread financial disaster, and Jackson hoped to avoid this by gradually contracting its operations. This might be done by depositing no more federal funds and drawing out what was already deposited as needed for government expenses. The law provided that the government money might be deposited elsewhere if so directed by the Secretary of the Treasury, who should submit his reasons at the next session of Congress. To find a secretary who would do this caused Jackson no little trouble. Livingston was sent as minister to France so that McLane, a friend of the bank, might be advanced from the treasury to the premier post of the cabinet. When William J. Duane, the new Secretary of the Treasury, would not issue the necessary orders, he was dismissed, and the post was given to Roger B. Taney.

Twenty-three state banks, soon known as "pet banks," were chosen to receive the money. Aroused at what they believed to be Jackson's high-handed action, the Senate publicly censured him, charging that he "assumed upon himself authority and power not conferred by the constitution and laws, but in derogation of both." Jackson characterized the action of the Senate as "unauthorized by the constitution" and "contrary to its spirit" and suggested that if he had acted with unlawful or corrupt intent, as they had insinuated, the proper course was impeachment. Senator Benton, Jackson's friend, announced that he would introduce a resolution in every succeeding session until the censure was expunged from the minutes, and this was accomplished in 1837. Thus the severest political conflict that the nation had yet experienced ended with a victory for Jackson. Although the services of the second Bank of the United States had been valuable, one cannot help feeling that there was soundness in Jackson's position. The charter did confer valuable monopolistic rights upon private individuals, who thereby profited from their connection with the government, and the bank during its later years had used its power to play politics in a thoroughly unscrupulous manner.

THE TARIFF AND NULLIFICATION

More important than the problem of the bank in its implications of future changes in the nation was the question of states' rights arising from the conflict of economic sections. Having made known her position through Calhoun's "Exposition and Protest," South Carolina awaited developments. In the first session of Congress under Jackson the opportunity came to express her theories before a national audience. In December, 1829, Senator Foot of Connecticut introduced a resolution requesting the Committee on Public Lands to inquire into the expediency of limiting for a period the sales of public lands to those already on the market. To the westerners eager for expansion and anxious to settle under the easiest terms possible, this seemed like a deliberate effort on the part of the East to restrain them. In truth the East, both North and South, was dismayed at the rapidity of the westward advance, which was depopulating eastern areas, pushing down the price of land, and at the same time increasing the cost of labor. Quite naturally Foot's resolution was met by united opposition from the western representatives, and in this they were unexpectedly joined by representatives from the Old South. The seaboard South, strongly opposed to a protective tariff, was too weak politically to prevent it without an alliance with the West, and it now became the policy of southern politicians to promote such an alliance. Senator Robert Y. Hayne of South Carolina, one of the ablest debaters in the Senate, saw the opportunity and entered the fray in behalf of the West. Denouncing the attitude of the Northeast as selfish and sectional, he pictured the economic needs of the South and West as alike and invited the West to join the Old South in a political alliance. He virtually offered southern support for cheap lands in return for western support of a tariff for revenue only.

As Hayne continued his speech, he shifted the subject from public lands to the danger of centralization and to the economic hardship occasioned by the use of federal authority for the benefit of a single section. This gave him the opportunity to expound at length the doctrine of state sovereignty as enunciated by Jefferson, Madison, and Calhoun. Hayne's attack on New England brought Webster into the debate, and, as the long forensic conflict progressed, less was said about public lands and more concerning the nature of the Union. Webster denied that the union was a compact of states, stoutly maintaining that it was a union of people; it is "the people's Constitution, the people's government, made for the people, made by the people, and answerable to the people." Against Calhoun's argument that a state might interpose its authority to nullify a law, Webster had no difficulty in making clear the anarchy and chaos that would ensue if such a position were carried to its logical conclusion. If differences arose or abuses occurred, there were remedies, he urged, in judicial interpretations, in constitutional amendments, and in frequent elections. In a brilliant peroration, dear to the hearts of generations of schoolboy orators, he closed his plea for the union with the memorable words, "liberty *and* union, now and forever, one and inseparable!" Hayne was far nearer the historical truth than Webster when he asserted that the Union was a compact of sovereign states rather than a compact of the people, but Webster (in spite of the fact that in the war days he had talked the language of Hayne) was more in line with the growing strength of the federal government and the integrating force of the Industrial Revolution.

The Webster-Hayne debate marked the reopening of the conflict between federal supremacy and state sovereignty, which was eventually to be settled on the field of battle. The South had stated its position and was anxious to carry the controversy further. Much hung on the question whether Jackson would follow Webster or Calhoun. To determine this, careful preparations were made for the annual dinner on Jefferson's birthday, at which Jackson would be present and at which the nullifiers were to express their views in toasts and speeches. The Old Hero might believe in states' rights when it came to ousting the Indians from Georgia, but he was no friend to any move that might imperil the Union. When his turn came to give his toast, he was prepared. Looking straight at the nullifiers, he said clearly, "Our Federal Union—it must be preserved." Calhoun, who followed him, tried to save the situation by his toast, "The Union—next to our liberty the most dear," but the occasion was a severe disappointment to the upholders of states' rights.

These were but preliminary skirmishes for the real battle over the tariff. Jackson was not greatly interested in the question; his messages showed a desire to eliminate the iniquities of the act of 1828 but no opposition to a protective tariff on constitutional grounds. An overflowing treasury led Congress in 1832 to enact a new tariff that greatly reduced the revenue and eliminated some of the "abominations" of 1828, but maintained the theory of protection. There was an air of permanency about the tariff of 1832 that stirred South Carolina to action. Immediately after its passage the members of Congress from that state issued an address to their fellow citizens asserting that "all hope of relief from Congress is irrevocably gone." The state election fought on the question of nullification was won by the states' rights party; a state convention was immediately called (in line with the Calhoun formula), and the Ordinance of Nullification was passed, declaring the tariffs of 1828 and 1832 null and void in the state of South Carolina. If the federal government persists in enforcing the tariffs, the ordinance declared, South Carolina must secede from the Union. Jackson was not a man whose authority one might easily question. In good old frontier fashion he threatened to "hang the first man of them I can get my hands on to the first tree I can find." He then strengthened the federal forces in South Carolina and prepared for action. In more measured language he issued a proclamation that said, in part, "I consider the power to annul a law of the United States, assumed by one State, incompatible with the existence of the Union, contradicted expressly by the letter of the Constitution, unauthorized by its spirit, inconsistent with every principle upon which it is founded, and destructive of the great object for which it was formed."

Before the issue could reach a final test, the compromisers stepped in. Calhoun, who at this point had resigned from the vice-presidency, wavered as to the consequences and looked about for a way out. Clay and Van Buren responded, and the controversy for the time being was set at rest. In response to Jackson's demand, Congress passed the Force Bill, empowering the President to use the army and navy to enforce the execution of laws in South Carolina, and on the same day it passed the Compromise Tariff of 1833, which provided for a gradual reduction of rates over a nine-year period until by 1842 a maximum of 20 per cent would be reached. Unable to win the support of other southern states, South Carolina repealed the Ordinance of Nullification and as a parting shot nullified the Force Act. Her immediate objective, the securing of a lower tariff, South Carolina had won, but the question of state sovereignty as opposed to federal authority was as unsettled as ever.

OTHER ISSUES

Although the controversy over the bank and the tariff dominated the eight years of the Jackson administration, other problems of more or less importance presented themselves. The destruction of the second Bank of the United States brought a short period of economic distress during 1833, but this was followed by a period of extraordinary prosperity, in part due to the inflation that followed when the restraining influence of the bank was lifted. Jackson had little understanding of the world of finance, but he realized the chaotic condition of the currency and the danger of the speculation that had followed inflation, particularly in western land. At first he attempted a remedy by promoting the minting of gold coins and urging the states to restrict the issuance of bank notes, but to little avail. In an effort to restrain speculation in public land, he issued in 1836 his Specie Circular, which directed that payments for public land must be in specie. This not only halted speculation, but was an important cause of the panic of 1837, which was soon to engulf the nation.

The prosperity of the Jackson years as well as the inordinate land speculation increased the income of the government to such an extent that in 1835 the public debt was extinguished and for two years the nation enjoyed the unique experience of freedom from financial obligation. This situation naturally gave rise to a demand for further tariff reduction and strengthened the demand of the West that the public land be either reduced in price or given freely to the states and settlers. Few politicians wanted to touch the tariff again; that troublesome question had just been settled by the Compromise Tariff of 1833. Likewise, the East was unfavorable to meeting the western demand for free or cheaper land. Again the great compromiser, Clay, thought he saw a way whereby the surplus might be taken care of, the West mollified, and the break between the manufacturing East and the agricultural West prevented. He proposed that proceeds of the sale of public lands be distributed among the states according to the ratio of their representation in Congress. When the bill first passed Congress in 1833, it was vetoed by Jackson, but a second bill three years later, providing that all government surplus over $5,000,000 be distributed to the states in the form of a loan, became law. Distribution began early in 1837, but the panic of that year soon ended this generous "hand-out."

Untrained as he was in the art of diplomacy, Jackson proved unexpectedly successful in his handling of foreign relations. Ever since the Revolution successive administrations had attempted without success to prevail upon Great Britain to open again the lucrative West Indian trade to American shippers. Soon after inauguration Jackson again took up the task, and this time American overtures were received with attention. Economic conditions in Great Britain were rapidly shifting in the early decades of the nineteenth century as she changed from an agricultural to a manufacturing nation. Her desire was now to obtain cheap raw materials and to extend her markets for manufactured goods, and the exclusion from the American coastwise trade injured her prospects. When Jackson offered to open American ports on reciprocal terms if Great Britain would open the West Indian ports to American produce and ships, she accepted, and legitimate trade, which had been closed for half a century, was again opened in 1830. With France there remained the old spoliation claims for seizures and confiscations under the Napoleonic decrees.[7] In exchange for a reduction of duties on French wines and a promise by the United States to assume certain claims for French losses under the Louisiana purchase, France agreed to pay the United States $25,000,000. The treaty was so unpopular in France that the Chamber of Deputies failed to appropriate the money, whereupon Jackson urged Congress to authorize reprisals upon French property. France broke off diplomatic relations, but the money was eventually voted on condition that Jackson offer "satisfactory explanation" for his message to Congress. Jackson with characteristic heat refused to apologize, but later stated that he had not intended to "menace or insult the government of France." England offered mediation, the differences were patched up, and the money

---

[7] Similar claims against Great Britain, it will be remembered, had been in part settled in 1804 under terms of the Jay treaty. Subsequent claims had been one cause of the War of 1812, but the treaty of Ghent made no provision for adjustment.

was paid. Jackson's forthright actions, the skill of his subordinates, and world economic conditions brought success where better-trained diplomats had failed.

A more difficult problem in foreign affairs was that of the relation between the United States and the newly established Texan republic. As early as 1821 American settlers had commenced to trickle into Texas, and by 1836 there were 30,000 there. Differences in social and political ideals and in economic interests inevitably brought on revolution in 1835 and the achievement of an independent republic in 1836. From the United States Texas wanted immediate recognition and eventual annexation. The problem presented many difficulties foreign and domestic, and Jackson, unwilling to disturb further the harmony of his party, delayed action until after the election of 1836. He then placed the burden on Congress and upon their recommendation recognized the new republic in March, 1837.[8]

VAN BUREN AND THE PANIC OF 1837

The opposition to the Jacksonian democracy was much stronger in 1836 than it had been four years earlier, but it was not yet well organized or united. In 1834 the anti-Jackson group had taken the name of Whigs, a party that was to "bridge the chasm between the decadent Federalism of the first quarter of the century and the principled Republicanism of the fifties."[9] Throughout its history it was a curious hodge-podge of dissatisfied elements, a party that was to be successful in the elections of 1840 and 1848, but never to be effective in establishing or maintaining a clear-cut political or economic program. In general, it represented men of property and social position, particularly in the North, the nationalists and protectionists of the Adams-Clay school. In 1836 it included not only this group but also the former Anti-Masons and various factions dissatisfied with Jackson's policies. The cement that seemed to bind the factions in that year was opposition to what they considered the gross usurpations of the executive. The Democrats, on the other hand, stood generally for strict construction of the Constitution, the maintenance of states' rights, the enlargement of popular suffrage, direct participation of the people in the choice of public officials, and opposition to monopolies and special privilege. Despite opposition from many quarters, Jackson was never more popular with the masses than in 1836. He had been notably successful in his foreign and domestic policy, and the common man sensed the fact that Jackson had generally been right on important questions. In a last

---

[8] The early history of Texas and her relations with the United States will be more fully recounted in Chap. XVIII.

[9] William Macdonald, *Jacksonian Democracy*, 295.

political victory he forced a recalcitrant convention to nominate his friend and adviser, Van Buren, for the presidency.

The Whig strategy was to nominate a number of candidates in the hope of preventing Van Buren from obtaining a majority in the electoral college and thus throwing the decision into the House of Representatives. As a consequence, Webster was nominated by the legislature of Massachusetts, Senator Hugh L. White by the legislatures of Tennessee and Alabama, and William H. Harrison of Tippecanoe fame by Pennsylvania. Less than 30,000 separated the popular vote of Van Buren from that of the combined Whig candidates, but he received a majority of the electoral vote.[10] In reality it was a victory of Jackson rather than of Van Buren, and "Old Hickory" had the satisfaction of returning home with the belief that his policies would be continued. There he died, June 8, 1845. Jackson's limitations were many, but he was undoubtedly the most forceful and influential political figure in American politics between Jefferson and Lincoln. He was more than that, however, for he personified the new democracy. Unlike the Jeffersonian leaders, Jackson represented a democracy not afraid of a strong central government and one that insisted that the people should rule as well as vote. In the victory of the Jacksonian democracy the great dream of Jefferson, as expressed in the Declaration of Independence, moved perceptibly toward realization.

The new President was a man under medium height, with a quick eye, pleasing features, and courteous manners. A man of strong convictions, he sought to accomplish his purpose by political diplomacy rather than by the mailed fist. As leader of the dominant faction of the Democratic Party in New York, he had risen through the medium of machine politics and by his own genius as a political organizer to be governor of New York, United States Senator, Secretary of State, and Vice-President. The striking personality of his predecessor and his misfortune in occupying the presidency during the depression following the panic of 1837 have obscured his merits and prevented posterity from according him his just due. As with Herbert Hoover almost a century later, Van Buren's administration was dominated by one outstanding event, the panic of 1837 and the subsequent depression.

Like all American panics of the nineteenth century, that of 1837 was primarily due to overexpansion and overspeculation in the development of land and transportation facilities. With the mania for canal-building, which had commenced in the early twenties and reached its climax in the late thirties, had gone a corresponding speculation in land, which meant

---

[10] For the only time in our history no vice-presidential candidate received a majority of votes, and the election was thrown into the Senate. There Richard M. Johnson of Kentucky, Van Buren's "running-mate" on the Democratic ticket, was chosen.

an inevitable economic collapse. It was presaged by the failure of important business houses in London, which had invested heavily in American securities, and by crop failures in 1835 and 1837, which prevented farmers from meeting their obligations, reduced exports, and caused a flow of specie from the United States. While the collapse was inevitable, it was undoubtedly precipitated by Jackson's financial policy. The smashing of the second Bank of the United States and the distribution of public money among the state banks encouraged speculation. Then, when inordinate speculation was at its height, it was suddenly halted by Jackson's Specie Circular of 1836, and the condition of the banks was made more difficult by the withdrawal of federal funds to distribute among the states under the Distribution Act. By May of 1837 every bank in the country had suspended specie payments; the banknote circulation contracted from $149,000,000 in 1837 to $58,000,000 in 1843, and the income from the sale of public lands fell from $20,000,000 in 1836 to $1,000,000 in 1841. Most states, which had borrowed heavily to promote internal improvements, were thrown into bankruptcy.

America was suffering her first major economic depression. In the summer of 1837 the editor, Horace Greeley, asserted that "one-fourth of all connected with mercantile and manufacturing interests are out of business with dreary prospects for the winter," and a few months later it was said that nine tenths of the factories in the eastern states were closed. Philip Hone, merchant and later mayor of New York, wrote in his diary in 1840: "Business of all kinds is completely at a stand . . . and the whole body politic sick and infirm, and calling aloud for a remedy." The effects of the panic were long drawn out; as late as 1845 it was estimated that in New York "there are at no time less than twenty thousand persons vainly seeking work in this city." [11]

The science of economics (if such a thing exists) was still in its infancy, and no one in 1837 understood the terrific forces let loose by the Industrial Revolution. A few obvious things, nevertheless, were done to meet the situation. Van Buren called a special session of Congress, which stopped further distribution of the surplus, authorized loans to take care of the treasury deficit, and passed a bankruptcy bill under the terms of which 39,000 people canceled $441,000,000 worth of debt. Following Jackson's theory that the federal government should be divorced from private banking, and believing that he had a safe method of bringing order out of chaos in the deposit and currency systems, Van Buren proposed to Congress an independent treasury system. Under this plan the government should take charge of its own funds instead of depositing them in state

[11] Samuel Reznek, "The Social History of an American Depression, 1837–1843," *American Historical Review*, XL, No. 4, 662–687 (July, 1935).

banks or a national bank, and the money taken in and paid out should be in specie. This, he believed, would keep public funds safe and prevent their use for speculation. The Whigs, particularly the groups that had profited from the use of public money, fought the proposal bitterly, but an act authorizing the establishment of an independent treasury was passed in 1840; it was repealed by the next administration in 1841, reestablished without the specie feature by the Democrats in 1846, and destined to last until abolished by an act of 1920.

Handicapped by the panic of 1837 and the necessity of bearing the brunt of the results of certain of Jackson's policies, the Van Buren administration was doomed from the start. Van Buren had skillfully sidestepped the Texas question and with considerable force and ability prevented serious complications on the Canadian border during a revolution in Canada, but this had only created further dissatisfaction with the administration. Whig victories were common in 1838, notably in New York state, where the Whigs elected William H. Seward as governor, thereby ending the long control of the Van Buren Democrats known as the Albany Regency. In high hopes, therefore, the divergent Whig elements coalesced in 1840 and nominated William Henry Harrison and John Tyler. The Democrats unanimously nominated Van Buren, and a new party, an antislavery element known as the Liberty Party, nominated James G. Birney. The Whigs had no platform and contented themselves with merely attacking Van Buren. A Baltimore newspaper unwittingly gave them an issue when it quoted a disgusted politician, who had remarked that, if Harrison were given a pension of $2000 a year, a barrel of cider, and a log cabin, he would be content to forget the presidency and retire to his cabin. Immediately the prosperous Harrison became the log-cabin candidate, and Whigs paraded the streets drinking hard cider, displaying banners emblazoned with a log cabin, and singing:

> Let Van from his coolers of silver drink wine,
> And lounge on his cushioned settee.
> Our man on his buckeye bench can recline,
> Content with hard cider is he,
> The iron-armed soldier, the true-hearted soldier,
> The gallant old soldier of Tippecanoe.

With the Whigs denouncing Van Buren and the Jacksonian Democrats for their wealth, and the Democrats sneering at Harrison for his supposed poverty, it is obvious that politics knows no consistency, and that campaigns are often devoid of serious or important issues. With a majority of less than 150,000 out of a total vote of 2,400,000, Harrison was victorious by an electoral vote of 294 to 60 and secured a majority of both houses of

Congress. Van Buren's defeat brought to an end a political era; the Democratic Party that was soon to dominate national politics again would be very different from the simple democracy of the Jacksonian period.

For a general interpretation, read C. and M. Beard, *The Rise of American Civilization*, Chap. XII. A brief review of the administration is F. A. Ogg, *The Reign of Andrew Jackson* (Chronicles of America), and a more recent summary is F. J. Turner, *The United States, 1830–1850*, Chap. IX. J. S. Bassett, *Andrew Jackson*, Chap. XXXII, deals with Jackson's personality; William MacDonald, *Jacksonian Democracy*, Chap. XVIII, appraises his work. For financial history see D. R. Dewey, *Financial History of the United States*, Chaps. VIII–X; for sources, H. S. Commager, *Documents of American History*, Vol. I, 242–291.

Chapter XIII

AMERICAN LIFE AT THE BEGINNING OF THE NINETEENTH CENTURY

> *While the republics of North America are new, the ideas of the people are old. While these republics were colonies, they contained an old people, living under old institutions, in a new country. Now they are a mixed people, infant as a nation, with a constant accession of minds from old countries, living in a new country, under institutions newly combined out of old elements . . . the Americans have no national character yet; nor can have for a length of years.*
>
> HARRIET MARTINEAU

TOWN AND COUNTRY

Life in America at the beginning of the nineteenth century was essentially rural and primitive. The first census (1790) gave the population of the new nation as 3,929,000 and that of 1800 as 5,308,000, a population considerably smaller than that of the city of New York in 1930. Only five towns, Philadelphia, New York, Baltimore, Boston, and Charleston, boasted of over 20,000, and their combined population was but slightly over 200,000; in 1800 but 4 per cent of the people lived in towns of 8000 or more. Virginia, the state with the largest population, had within its borders but 880,000, while Delaware, the state with the smallest, had slightly over 64,000. The character of the economic life was appropriate to the size and distribution of population. Under an act of Congress passed in 1789, a survey for the purpose of direct taxation was made. This showed the value of lands (not including houses, which amounted to $140,000,000 in addition) to be approximately $479,293,000. Certainly the wealth of the whole nation at the opening of the century, according to the money values then existing, was considerably under $1,000,000,000. The valuation of New York state for direct taxation in 1799 was $100,000,000 and of Massachusetts but $84,000,000. The exports from New York in 1800 amounted to but $14,000,000, and Henry Adams believed that in that year the gross exports and imports of the nation may have balanced at about $75,000,000. The nominal capital of all the banks in the country, including the Bank of the United States, was less than $29,000,000, and the debt of the nation, considered then as staggering, was about $80,000,000. With the exception of state and federal bonds and the paper of a few banks, insurance offices, transportation companies, and land companies, stocks and bonds hardly existed. Although speculation in land was widespread, there was not enough business in other types of securities to support a stock exchange.

Life in the cities of 1800 would today be considered mean and uncomfortable. Except in Philadelphia, which had been laid out with foresight and where the prosperous townsmen had made some effort to pave the streets, the highways were either unpaved or the cobbles so badly laid as to make travel with a wheeled vehicle very uncomfortable. In Boston and New York wooden and brick houses intermingled along crooked and narrow alleys. Oil lamps for street lighting were just beginning to come into existence, but were not lighted when the moon shone and rarely on rainy nights, for the inhabitants retired early. Few ventured forth at night, for the poorly paved, narrow, and crooked streets, with an occasional watchman but without police protection as we know it now, were neither safe nor pleasant places in which to roam. When street lighting by gas was adopted in Boston in 1822, in New York in 1823, and in Philadelphia in 1837, urban life was affected in an important way. It was not until 1845 that the old and inefficient night watch, which lit the lamps, cried out the hours of night, and gave alarms for fires, was superseded in New York by an organization of day and night watchmen more nearly resembling the police force of today. The modern police system, in fact, extends back hardly more than eighty years.

Conveniences for living within doors were as meager as those without. Although Franklin and other American inventors had applied themselves to the development of a stove for cooking and heating, the old-fashioned fireplace in 1800 was still the only means available for indoor heat. The existence of anthracite coal was known in the eighteenth century, and shipments were made to Philadelphia as early as 1805, but its application to home heating did not begin until after 1815. Its extensive use was, of course, delayed by absence of transportation facilities and by the expense of installing grates and stoves; when the transportation problem was in a measure overcome, fireplaces, in the larger centers, were gradually bricked up and stoves substituted. By 1860 the manufacture of stoves was one of the leading iron industries, and their use in the cities was general. A further impetus to the use of coal and to more comfortable living came with the invention of the furnace for indirect heating. Inventors by 1850 had conceived the idea of dropping the stove to the cellar, and by that time practical furnaces for central heating were on the market. The drudgery of housekeeping was lightened not only by the introduction of the stove but also by the use of tinware, which was gradually supplanting some of the heavier iron and copper utensils that in earlier years had hung around the fireplaces.

More pressing than the problem of heating was that of the water supply. Until well into the century city dwellers obtained their water from cisterns, house pumps, or various community pumps scattered about the towns. In 1799 water from the Schuylkill River was raised by steam pumps and distributed through wooden pipes to a small section of Philadelphia. This system was improved in 1822 by the opening of the Fairmount Waterworks, which conveyed the water by iron pipes through the entire city, a pioneer project in America and one of immense importance to the well-being of the citizens. The first effort to supply New York with water from a central reservoir was undertaken by the Manhattan Water Company, a concern created by a legislative bill proposed by Aaron Burr. In reality this company was a banking corporation disguised as a water company to compete with Hamilton's bank in New York, but it started the movement toward a better water supply. Wooden pipes supplying the lower city gave way to iron pipes, and eventually an adequate supply was obtained when the Croton reservoir was constructed in 1842. By that year the larger cities were supplied with water by artificial distribution. It was well that this was so, for no adequate sewage disposal had yet been laid out in any American city, and the close proximity of the water supply to the refuse drains resulted in frequent epidemics of sickness and a high rate of mortality. Domestic animals, including swine, roamed at will through the streets, adding refuse and filth to that already existing in profusion, but at the same time acting as scavengers.

Of American cities in 1800, Philadelphia, with a population of 70,000, was the largest as well as the most prosperous and beautiful. "Philadelphia is not only the finest city in the United States," wrote the Duc de Liancourt, "but may be deemed one of the most beautiful in the world." In truth, Philadelphia had made the most of its resources. Backed by a rich agricultural hinterland and enjoying an active commerce, its prosperous burghers lived in an affluence unrivaled in other towns. Decimated repeatedly by yellow fever, Philadelphia had pioneered in efforts to secure adequate water supply and sewage disposal. Her streets, as we have noted, were cleaner and better paved than elsewhere. As the seat of the Continental Congress and later for some years as the capital of the nation, she enjoyed a prestige that was augmented by her leadership in what little America could boast of in the way of literature and science. New

York, whose commerce and prosperity had been ruined by the Revolution, had now recovered, and with a population in 1800 of 60,000 had commenced the expansion that was soon to make her the leading American city. The city proper occupied the tip of Manhattan Island and barely extended beyond the present City Hall Park. Although it was chiefly supported by commerce, its leading citizens still derived their wealth from land. It already had the most cosmopolitan and perhaps the most aggressive population of all American cities and had taken on many of its later characteristics. Fourth in size was Boston, for decades almost at a standstill, but now stirring with new life as a result of the European wars. Its narrow, crooked streets, inadequately paved with cobbles and winding around the three hills upon which it was built, aroused no enthusiasm among travelers, to whom it seemed like a second-rate provincial English market town. South of Philadelphia only Baltimore and Charleston had reached urban size and character. Baltimore had found not only new prosperity on the sea but large extension in inland trade and had suddenly developed a population and commerce greater than those of Boston. Charleston, whose white population was the equal in wealth and cultivation of any group of similar size in the Union, was the export center of rice and of the rapidly developing cotton production, and was closer to the new towns of the Southwest and the rich West Indian commerce than other centers. There appeared in 1800 no reason why it should not enjoy as brilliant a future as that of any seaboard city. Washington, to which the government removed in 1800, boasted only a single row of brick houses, two department buildings, an unfinished White House, and a Capitol with the two unjoined wings still in course of construction.

Few as were city conveniences in 1800, life in the country, where over nine tenths of the people lived, was much more primitive. A hundred miles inland probably half of the houses were log cabins, most of which did not boast the luxury of a glass window. The furniture was likely to be homemade, and the clothing almost surely homespun. Agricultural methods had not yet profited from the new scientific experiments that gentlemen farmers in England were making known. "The plough," says Adams, "was crude and clumsy; the sickle as old as Tubal Cain, and even the cradle not in general use; the flail was unchanged since the Aryan exodus; in Virginia, grain was still commonly trodden out by horses." [1] Just as in the colonial period, grain was sowed by hand, rotation of crops was rarely practiced, the use of fertilizer was hardly known, and the ignorance concerning the care of livestock was incredible. Cheap and fertile land quickly demoralized any habits of careful hus-

[1] Henry Adams, *History of the United States*, I, 17.

bandry that earlier immigrants had brought with them. Nevertheless, William Cobbett, a thoroughly competent observer, certified that good farmhouses in America were better than the general run in England, particularly on the inside, but the farm itself and outside buildings were not so "neat and tight."

Although country districts were rarely swept by the epidemics that periodically decimated the city population, the hardships of pioneer life took heavy toll. European travelers of this period often remarked on the laziness of Americans, but in general rural life was one of unremitting toil and monotony. Only an occasional newspaper found its way to the country farmer, and the receipt of a letter from the outside world was almost a village event. Farmers desisted from their labor and tavern loafers from their gossip to crowd around the post rider to gather what few crumbs of news he might be willing and able to dispense. While intercourse with the outside world was inevitably slight under existing conditions, rural life in other respects seemed unnecessarily monotonous. On well-established farms, for example, there was an abundance of food, yet salt pork and Indian corn usually appeared on the table three times a day to provide the staff of life. Whisky, rapidly becoming the national drink, was freely used and added its part to make dyspepsia the national disease.

Except on the frontier, where elemental conditions reduced life to a sameness, it is as difficult to paint a picture of early American civilization in broad strokes as it would be to depict that of any nation. In the farming regions of the more settled northern states the differences in economic and social status were, perhaps, not as pronounced as in later decades. Far different was the South, where the wealthy and often cultured plantation-owner of the Virginia tidewater was as far removed in his standard of living from the poor white of the Carolina uplands as an industrial magnate of today is from an unskilled proletarian worker. Certainly, in the northern cities of 1800, the difference was as great as today. On the one hand we have a picture of a merchant like Hancock, dining from imported china, drinking the choicest of European wines, and clothed, according to contemporary description, in a red velvet cap, a blue damask gown lined with velvet, a white stock, a white satin embroidered waistcoat, black satin small-clothes, white silk stockings, and red morocco slippers. On the other is the unforgettable picture that McMaster draws of the laboring class:

Sand sprinkled on the floor did duty as a carpet. There was no glass on his table, there was no china in his cupboard, there were no prints on his wall. What a stove was he did not know, coal he had never seen, matches he had never heard of. . . . He rarely tasted fresh meat as often as once in a week, and paid for it a much higher price than his posterity. . . .

If the food of an artisan would now be thought coarse, his clothes would be thought abominable. A pair of yellow buckskin or leathern breeches, a checked shirt, a red flannel jacket, a rusty felt hat cocked up at the corners, shoes of neat's-skin set off with huge buckles of brass, and a leathern apron, comprised his scanty wardrobe. The leather he smeared with grease to keep it soft and flexible. His sons followed in his footsteps or were apprenticed to neighboring tradesmen. His daughter went out to service.[2]

TRAVEL AND COMMUNICATION

Except for those who tore themselves from their homes to start life anew in the West, few Americans in 1800 had ever traveled more than a score of miles from their place of birth. Roads, if such they can be called, connected the towns along the seacoast and penetrated in such places perhaps fifty miles inland, but they were generally execrably bad, deep with mud in the fall and spring and dusty in the summer. Bridges were few, and the danger from fallen trees, swollen rivers, and uncertain fords made a long journey a disagreeable and hazardous experience, to be undertaken only upon urgent necessity. Nor had the means of travel been marked by any advances since the days of the Roman Empire. On land one journeyed by horseback or in a wheeled vehicle drawn by animal power; on water the traveler was dependent upon variable winds. As far as comfort and speed were concerned, there was little to choose; a trip by water from New York to Providence might consume a week, from New York to London from six to sixteen weeks. As long as Americans lived close to the seacoast or upon the numerous rivers running into the Atlantic, the problem of communication was not insoluble, but America was moving westward and needed other facilities for inland transportation. The great expanse of territory, the high cost of labor, and the scarcity of capital, rather than any lack of need, had prevented the building of more and better roads.

Despite the poor roads, the government by 1800 had established a mail route from Maine to Georgia, with branches leading westward as far as Canandaigua (New York), Lexington (Kentucky), and Nashville (Tennessee). Contracts required a daily service (except Sundays) between Portsmouth (New Hampshire) and Petersburg (Virginia), with delivery three times a week south of that point. The postage for a letter weighing a quarter of an ounce for not more than thirty miles was eight cents, with added cost for a greater distance. Even so the movement was

[2] J. B. McMaster, *History of the People of the United States*, I, 96–97.

slow and the mails insecure; public men often wrote in cipher to prevent the contents of their letters from becoming known. The eighteenth century was the great age of letter-writing, a time when men of affairs had the leisure to discuss in their letters problems of science and politics, but the gross receipts of the postal service, amounting to only $320,000 for the year ending October 1, 1801, makes it clear that the luxury of letter-writing was limited to a small portion of the population. The mail was ordinarily carried by post riders on horseback; regular stagecoach traffic for passengers was limited to a few stretches of the better roads between the larger centers. The few stagecoach routes established before the Revolution had been disrupted by the war, but were operating again by 1800. Passengers between New York and Boston might set out three times a week and cover the distance in from three days to a week. Between New York and Philadelphia, the two most populous cities of the country, a daily service was maintained, but it took two days to cover the ninety miles. A similar service operated from Philadelphia to Baltimore, but south of that point travel was exceedingly difficult. Except for a stagecoach between Charleston and Savannah, there appears to have been no regular service in any of the three southernmost states.

Even under the best of circumstances travel was an arduous experience. The vehicles were ordinarily open wagons without springs, hung with curtains of leather or wool. The cost, including tavern bills, averaged about ten cents a mile. Although de Warville wrote in 1788 that the stagecoaches sometimes ran ninety-six miles a day, the ordinary coach was lucky if it exceeded five miles an hour. The time consumed on a journey made the matter of tavern accommodations an important one, and here foreign travelers found little to praise. There might be sufficient food and drink, but the hostelries were seldom noted for their cleanliness, and the traveler might have to share his room with a dozen others crowded into as many beds as the room would hold. Wansey, for example, who stayed at the best hotels in Boston and Philadelphia, complained of his "old tormentors, the bugs." The indifferent accommodations of larger towns, however, were a luxury in comparison to those in the less settled regions. On the Carolina frontier, says Bernard, "you might always know an ordinary, on emerging from the woods, by an earthen jug suspended by a handle from a pole; the pipe of the chimney never rising above the roof; or a score of black hogs luxuriating in the sunshine and mud before the door." [3] His description of the interior and the accommodations is similar to that left by the great ornithologist, Alexander Wilson. "The taverns," said he, "are the most desolate and beggarly imaginable,—bare, bleak and dirty walls: one or two old broken

---

[3] Quoted by Allan Nevins, *American Social History as Recorded by British Travellers*, 43.

chairs, and a bench, form all the furniture. The white females seldom make their appearance and everything must be transacted through the medium of negroes. At supper, you sit down to a meal, the sight of which is sufficient to deaden the most eager appetite, and you are surrounded by half a dozen dirty, half naked blacks, male and female, whom any man with common scent might smell a quarter of a mile off. The house itself is raised upon props four or five feet, and the space below is left open for the hogs, with whose charming vocal performance the weary traveler is serenaded the whole night long. . . . " [4] While this undoubtedly represented American taverns at their worst, there was little to be said for them throughout the South. Travelers, if possible, avoided them and took advantage of the lavish hospitality of the planters, who were willing, indeed anxious, to entertain them for the news of the outside world that they brought. Some planters were known to post a Negro on the road at the inn to watch for wayfarers and invite them to their master's house.

No better description of American travel in the last decade of the eighteenth century can be found than Josiah Quincy's account of a journey over one of the most frequented highways of the continent:

> I set out from Boston the end of December, 1794, or the beginning of January, 1795, in the line of stages lately established by an enterprising Yankee, Pease by name, which at that day was considered a method of transportation of wonderful expedition. The journey to New York took up a week. The carriages were old and shackling and much of the harness made of ropes. One pair of horses carried the stage eighteen miles. We generally reached our resting-place for the night, if no accident intervened, at ten o'clock, and, after a frugal supper, went to bed with a notice that we should be called at three the next morning,—which generally proved to be half past two. Then, whether it snowed or rained, the traveller must arise and make ready by the help of a horn lantern and a farthing candle, and proceed on his way over bad roads,—sometimes with a driver showing no doubtful symptoms of drunkenness, which good-hearted passengers never failed to improve at every stopping-place by urging upon him the comfort of another glass of toddy. Thus we travelled, eighteen miles a stage, sometimes obliged to get out and help the coachman lift the coach out of a quagmire or rut, and arrived at New York after a week's hard travelling, wondering at the ease as well as expedition with which our journey was effected.

EDUCATION AND THE ARTS

In many respects American society at the opening of the century seemed stagnant. Enervation had followed the turmoil of the Revolution and

[4] Alexander Wilson, *American Ornithology* (1832), I, xiii.

the "critical years" that culminated in the adoption of the federal Constitution. Intellectual energy had been chiefly expended in the political field; interest in art, literature, and science lagged. With the death of Franklin there passed from the scene the only scientist of international repute; in the world of letters there was no figure of primary importance. Only in political theory could America boast of great thinkers or expositors in a galaxy of great minds that included John Taylor, George Mason, James Wilson, Madison, Adams, Jefferson, and Hamilton. To the casual observer it was only in the restless progress toward the setting sun that the American people gave an inkling of that burst of energy and genius that was so soon to display itself in many fields.

Elementary education, which had received an impetus in New England by the Massachusetts laws of 1642 and 1647, had fallen into decline. The demoralizing effects of the war years, the breaking up of old communities, the dispersal of the people along the westward moving frontier, and the lowering of intellectual standards by the environment and preoccupation of the frontier all injured the development of education. In the simple agricultural life of the time there was no great economic impetus for universal education, for only the professions felt the need of anything beyond the "three Rs." Public education, where it persisted, was found chiefly in New England and those regions of the West where immigrants from that section had settled. Later, of course, it spread elsewhere. School districts, subdivisions of towns or counties, elected trustees and provided ungraded schools where reading, writing, arithmetic, and occasionally other subjects were taught. The terms were short, the textbooks woefully inadequate,[5] the discipline severe, and the teachers often little less ignorant than the pupils. The salaries of teachers were small, and they were ordinarily paid in part by being "boarded around." The best of the teachers were college students earning a pittance to continue their own education.

Education at the opening of the century was for the classes rather than for the masses, and for boys rather than for girls. The wealthy families hired tutors, while the more prosperous middle class sent their children to the private academies now to be found in every state. Before the first two decades had passed, a half dozen of these academies or seminaries had been established for girls. To the nine colleges of the colonial period fifteen more were added by 1800, but they were small in size and elementary in the work they gave. Harvard, the oldest and one of the largest, had about three hundred students in the early part of the

[5] The beginnings of American textbook writing may be placed in these years with the appearance of Noah Webster's *American Spelling Book* (1783), Jedediah Morse's *Geography* (1784), and Lindley Murray's *Grammar* (1795).

century and usually graduated between sixty and seventy. Princeton had about seventy students, and "from their appearance," said the English traveler, Weld, "and the course of studies they seemed to be engaged in like all the other American colleges I saw, it better deserves the title of a grammar-school than of a college. The library which we were shown is most wretched, consisting for the most part of old theological books not even arranged with any regularity." At Harvard, in 1800, the president, the professor of Hebrew, the professor of theology, the professor of mathematics, and four tutors comprised the entire instructing staff. As far as the range of subject matter was concerned, this small faculty was probably enough, since the curriculum as yet consisted chiefly of Latin, Greek, rhetoric, mathematics, philosophy, ethics, logic, and metaphysics. Although the instruction was of indifferent quality and the work elementary, the students as a rule lived plainly and worked conscientiously. Going to college was a serious business, not to be disturbed by social clubs or intercollegiate athletics. The colonial colleges were founded primarily to educate for the ministry, a fact that in part explains the type of curriculum and its essential conservatism. By 1800, however, an increasing proportion of graduates were entering other professions. Harvard, in fact, had founded a medical school in 1783, which had three professors and graduated two or three students each year.

Although elementary education had been declining in the last quarter of the eighteenth century and the nature of college instruction had changed but little during these years, there were evidences by 1800 of an awakening interest in education. This was in part stimulated by eighteenth-century liberalism, which emphasized democracy and the perfectibility of man, and by the responsibility that many leaders of the new nation felt for improving the educational standards of its citizens. Many leaders, both Federalist and Republican, advocated a great national university where public officers might be trained, scientific endeavor promoted, and nationalism strengthened. Both Washington and Jefferson favored such an institution, but eventually the competition of state colleges and the predominance of state over federal interests prevented its foundation. Nevertheless, Congress did much for education. When the Northwest was opened, not only was one section in each township granted for schools, but a donation of two townships was made to the Ohio Company to found a university, thus establishing the original endowment of Ohio University. When Ohio became a state in 1803, Congress likewise granted a township to found Miami University for the settlers around Cincinnati. As each new state was added to the Union, similar grants were made, with the result that seventeen state universities were in existence by 1860.

Widespread interest and discussion were aroused in the 1790s when the American Philosophical Society offered a prize for "the best system of liberal education and literary instruction adapted to the genius of the government of the United States." The plans submitted were interesting and surprisingly modern in that they emphasized the need of a system of national education, urged the study of the sciences rather than the classics, and stressed the need of utilitarian subjects. Among the foremost advocates of educational innovations was Jefferson, who believed that merit rather than wealth should determine the educational opportunities of youth. Public education, commencing with the primary school and closing with the university, should be open to anyone whose abilities warranted these opportunities. To Jefferson the classics and philosophy were not enough; he would add science, history, law, political economy, and modern languages. Having failed to introduce his scheme in full measure at his own college, William and Mary, he succeeded in founding in 1819 (opened 1825) the University of Virginia, which in its early years stood at the forefront of progressive college education. The educational ideas of Jefferson and others are important, not so much for what they immediately accomplished as for the fact that they pointed to the way that American education was to follow in the future.

Since the nation was as yet too poor to support widespread education and too backward for the masses to appreciate its necessity, it was hardly likely that the fine arts would be better supported. The colonial period had produced three painters of merit, but their productive years, with the exception of Stuart, had been largely spent in Europe. Benjamin West, born in Pennsylvania of Quaker stock, had early gone to England, where he pioneered in realistic historical painting, executed portraits, aided and encouraged American students, and from 1792 until his death was president of the Royal Academy. John Singleton Copley and Gilbert Stuart went to England on the outbreak of the Revolution, but Stuart later returned to paint the portraits of many famous Americans. Artists could scarcely hope for remuneration except in portrait painting, and America, after the desertion of Copley and Stuart, could boast for fifteen years of but one well-known portrait painter, Charles Wilson Peale, and Peale had to eke out a living as a harness-maker, silversmith, watch-maker, and dentist. Peale was an excellent artist whose portraits are impressive for their simplicity and sincerity, and his difficulty in making ends meet was typical of the state of the arts in America. Not only as a painter does Peale deserve remembrance but also as the founder of the Museum of Natural History in Philadelphia (1784) and as one of the founders of the Pennsylvania Academy of Fine Arts (1805).

As the resources of the nation expanded, painters found greater opportunities. John Trumbull, who had been an officer in the Revolution, returned from his studies abroad to paint revolutionary episodes in the grand manner, while Washington Allston, a South Carolinian by birth, and other American painters who found their way to European training followed the classical style of the period. Able artists of the early decades of the nineteenth century, notably the "Hudson River school," devoted their talents to painting American landscapes. While the art of painting improved and with the years increased in amount, sculpture languished. William Rush, a skillful woodcarver, was the pioneer, but it was not until many years later that much of note was accomplished. Important statues existing in America, such as Houdon's Washington at the Virginia state capitol, were the work of imported sculptors.

If Americans painted few pictures and chiseled even fewer statues, they built houses with great rapidity. It is an open question, however, whether the architecture of the early republic was an improvement over that of the colonial period. Colonial builders were generally without formal training in architecture and seldom possessed a textbook, but somehow they adapted European models to American needs so skillfully that modern architects have sought to recreate the spirit and beauty of these early homes. The well-proportioned New England farmhouse built of wood, with its barns and sheds connected with the main building, the low Dutch dwelling with its gambrel roof, the Pennsylvania stone house, the southern-border architecture in the Spanish style all seemed perfectly at home in the American environment. While the frontiersmen continued to construct the usual log-cabin and citizens of humble means continued to live in dwellings simple and unadorned, new influences from Europe were to be seen in the more wealthy and populous districts.

The Greek revolution and new archeological discoveries turned the attention of the world again to the early civilizations of the Mediterranean, and buildings with Greek and Roman columns began to dot the landscape. Some of this building, as in the central portion of the Capitol at Washington and in the state house at Boston, was successful and effective. Sometimes, as in the main building of Girard College at Philadelphia, a replica of a Greek temple was erected so accurately that Greece seemed transported to the New World. Greek architecture was indeed one of the glorious creations of human intellect and might fittingly be used in public buildings, but, as exemplified in private dwellings, it seemed out of place in the American environment and hardly fitted to the needs of the American family. The "Greek revival" was followed by the "Gothic revival," stimulated by the medieval romances of Sir Walter Scott and other novelists, but the Gothic structures, reminiscent of medieval castles, seemed no more indigenous to American civilization than did the Greek temples.

THE PROFESSIONS

The position of the theater in 1800 was hardly more favorable than that of the fine arts. Except for the amateur productions of British army officers, play-acting had largely ceased during the Revolution. Congress in 1774 had urged the colonists to discourage shows, plays, and other entertainments during the emergency and in 1778 had passed even stronger regulations. There was little or no opposition to the theater in the southern states, and strolling players could usually command an audience in the larger towns. In Philadelphia, New York, and Boston, however, there was strong opposition to the revival of the drama, and the question was debated in newspapers and legislative halls. In the end the friends of the theater were successful, and by 1800 theaters had been built in all the leading cities. Many of the best actors were Englishmen, and most of the plays were imported, but there were a few American playwrights. Of these the most notable was William Dunlap, "Father of the American Drama," theatrical manager and playwright, who not only wrote, translated, or adapted over sixty plays, but in 1832 published his invaluable *History of the American Theatre.*

Of far wider effect than the theater in appealing to the masses were the newspapers, which had already commenced their double role in America as a chief source of recreation and education. From forty at the close of the Revolution the number had increased to over 350 by 1810, and of these at least thirty were dailies. Some of them were frankly political organs, as *The Evening Post* of New York, established by Hamilton and other Federalists in 1801 under the editorship of William Coleman, or *The National Gazette* of Philadelphia, established by Jefferson and his Republican friends and edited by Philip Freneau. Only by a stretch of the imagination could these four-page sheets be called newspapers. They were chiefly vehicles for advertising matter and political propaganda, the latter appearing usually in letters signed by assumed names; it was not at all unusual for men in high political position to use such a medium to blast their enemies and expound their theories. The typical newspaper of 1800 might contain news of Congress several weeks old, extracts of European letters months old, a letter or so on moral or political philosophy, and various advertisements, but so hungry were the people for any type of news that the journalist rapidly became an influential figure and newspaper-publishing a prosperous industry.

Less numerous than the newspapers and less influential in forming public opinion were the various magazines, of which the most important example was *The American Museum,* founded by Mathew Carey. Some of the magazines had a definite political point of view, but most were concerned with establishing a circulation through articles covering a wide field in science, art, and literature. As the years went on, the more prosperous began to include engravings. The most famous of the early magazines were *The Port Folio,* founded by Joseph Dennie at Philadelphia in 1801, which commanded the support of the ablest pens of the time, and *The North American Review* of Boston, established in 1815 and supported by the *literati* of that city.

Although, aside from the political writing, little that appeared in America at the turn of the century is now read, except by historians or antiquarians, America was not without its literary figures who drew their characters and inspiration from the American scene. Royall Tyler, in *The Contrast,* satirized many phases of American life; Hugh H. Brackenridge, in his widely read novel of the back-country, *Modern Chivalry,* took a similar fling at the crudities of those early years; and Charles Brockden Brown, our most important novelist of the period and a dreamer indoctrinated with radical eighteenth-century philosophy, wrote ardently in behalf of women's rights and of rationalism as a cure for the ills of the time. More strongly than the novelists, the poets of the period were influenced by the political struggles. The "Hartford Wits," including such men as Timothy Dwight, Joel Barlow, and John Trumbull, "the literary old guard of the eighteenth century," attempted epic poems of seemingly endless length in defense of Federalist philosophy. Barlow, perhaps the ablest of them, later went over to Republicanism and in a revision of *The Columbiad* attempted to prove that "all good morals, as well as good government and hopes of permanent peace" must be founded on "republican principle." Philip Freneau, Jefferson's partisan editor, wrote the most beautiful lyrics in America of his day, but his political attacks upon Federalism won him the undying hatred of his political opponents.

Until the last years of the colonial period, the science and practice of medicine had made but slight progress. The chief remedies for most diseases in 1800 were still the bleeding of the patient and the administration of heroic doses of physic. In many quarters the innumerable useless and loathsome medicines concocted during the colonial period were still supposed to effect a cure (page 60). The outlook, however, was improving as medical schools were founded, notably that of the University of Pennsylvania in 1765, of Columbia in 1767, and of Harvard in 1783. In these schools the medical knowledge of Europe was taught, but the classes numbered a mere handful, and the facilities for study were inadequate. Only by robbing graveyards or begging the dead bodies of criminals from the authorities could subjects for dissection be obtained. The typical doctor of 1800 had never seen the inside of a medical school; his training had been secured as an apprentice to some practicing physician, from whom he had learned how to grind powder, mix pills, bandage wounds, and bleed patients. If the doctor was intelligent and observing, his career, despite the inadequacy of medical knowledge, might be beneficial to the community; if he was an ignoramus, he did more harm than good. It was not until 1798 that vaccination was made known,[6] and the discovery of anesthetics waited until 1846. While epidemics of smallpox, yellow fever, and other deadly diseases periodically swept the cities, physicians without the knowledge of the simplest remedies for the commonest ailments could do next to nothing. By the end of the eighteenth century, however, dispensaries had been opened in the principal cities, and careful case records were being compiled.

Although the legal profession was far from popular with the masses of the people in the years following the Revolution, it attracted many as a quick road to wealth and political preferment. As land was then the chief form of wealth, the typical lawyer was chiefly concerned with cases involving real estate, a fact that helps to explain his great unpopularity with the debt-ridden farmer. Like the doctor, he learned the rudiments of his profession as an apprentice in the office of an older and established practitioner, and his success was dependent upon native cleverness and personal industry rather than upon adequate schooling. King's College established the first professorship of law in 1773, but instruction was not actually begun until after the Revolution. Jefferson succeeded in prevailing upon the college of William and Mary to set up a chair of law in 1779, and James Wilson, one of the leading authorities on the Constitution, expounded public and private law at the University of Pennsylvania after 1790. Before these professorships of law in the larger colleges developed into university law schools, several private schools had been founded. Of these the most famous was that at Litchfield, Connecticut, established by Judge Tapping Reeve, where, in 1784, in a tiny frame building, the first special law course in the United States was held. Like the physician, the law student was handicapped by lack of books. If he had a copy of Blackstone's *Commentaries, Coke upon Littleton,* and Bacon's *Abridgement,* he was lucky, but as specialization in law had not yet developed, any education or information that the young lawyer could pick up was grist to his mill. The gradual development of bar associations tended to raise the ethical and educational standards of the profession, but the economic and social fluidity of a rapidly expanding nation long made America a "happy hunting ground" for the untrained and unscrupulous attorney.

THE CLERGY AND RELIGION

The Revolution, as already noted, had an important influence upon American Christianity. Except in three New England states (page 112),

---

[6] Inoculation against smallpox, on the other hand, had been known much earlier (page 61).

it speedily disestablished the church throughout the confederation; in accordance with these precedents the federal government was forbidden to set up an official church by Amendment I of the new Constitution. Just as the political bonds between Great Britain and her colonies were broken by war, so religious supervision from Great Britain ended. The Protestant Episcopal Church in 1789 formally commenced its separate existence in America, and five years earlier the Methodist Episcopal Church, under the leadership of Francis Asbury, had taken a similar step. The Revolution likewise severed the connection of American Catholics with England, the termination being officially recognized by the Pope in appointing John Carroll as Superior of the Mission of the Thirteen States of North America. Other churches severed their close connection with parent bodies—the Dutch Reformed, the Moravian, the Lutheran—while the Presbyterians, in the 1780s, completed the reorganization of their church on a national basis. Although the Revolution disturbed the even flow of religious life and disrupted the earlier religious organization, the disestablishment of the church promoted tolerance. The nationalizing of American religious bodies likewise instilled a new life and enthusiasm into the various church organizations.

During this period of reorganization orthodox religion found itself confronted by eighteenth-century rationalism. Stirred by the scientific advance of that century, many of the greatest intellects were convinced that mankind was only on the threshold of its possibilities, that man was a rational being, and that, given an encouraging environment, there was no limit to his progress. This optimistic philosophy, which had undermined the sacredness of divine-right monarchy and prepared the way for democracy in government, was even more critical of orthodox religion. If man was a rational being, how could he be a depraved creature, cursed by original sin, predestined to punishment unless saved by the grace of God through the instrumentality of a church? To eighteenth-century philosophers organized religion seemed fantastic; an all-wise God might be the center of the universe, but individuals, they believed, must determine their own basis for a rational morality. The popular name given to these ideas was deism, and no one was more influential in spreading them in America than Thomas Paine in his *Age of Reason,* which first appeared here in 1794. "I believe in one God, and no more"; said Paine, "and I hope for happiness beyond this life. I believe in the equality of man, and I believe that religious duties consist in doing justice, loving mercy, and endeavoring to make our fellow creatures happy." While Deism made rapid progress among the educated and wealthy, who might follow the trend of European intellectual life, and was extremely popular among the faculty and students of the colleges, it hardly touched the masses. In Calvinistic New England there had long been a revolt among some of the abler clergymen against the older doctrines; deism lent a helping hand, and by the turn of the century Unitarianism had made important inroads. After Henry Ware, a Unitarian, became Hollis Professor of Divinity at Harvard in 1805, the Calvinists established a theological seminary of their own at Andover in 1808, and, from then until the American Unitarian Association was founded in 1825, the battle between these two schools of thought was unceasing.

While deism and a general religious skepticism spread rapidly among the educated classes, and the clergy were denouncing the colleges as "dens of infidelity," the inevitable reaction came. A revival of religious interest swept in, coming first where conditions seemed the least propitious. The pioneers who poured through the mountain passes into the Ohio and Mississippi valleys represented all denominations, but the poor backwoods Presbyterians, Baptists, and Methodists predominated. Whatever their connections in the East, pioneer environment with its poverty and thinly scattered population made it difficult to preserve any form of organized Christianity. Congregationalists, Presbyterians, and Baptists sent out home missionaries and resident pastors, who labored to hold the backwoodsmen to Christianity, while the Methodists organized the efficient system of circuit-riding. In Logan County, Kentucky, one of the most typical pioneer communities, and at the same time one of the least religious, there was evident in 1797, under the ministrations of a Presbyterian minister, James McGready, a spiritual quickening. This became more pronounced in 1799, and for six years a religious revival like a prairie fire swept up and down the western frontier. It was during this revival that the camp meetings originated, and it was in these gatherings, which lasted for days, that frontier ministers and circuit-riders whipped their congregations into unbelievable frenzies of emotion and aroused in many a hardened sinner a realization of his danger. The cause of this sudden burst of religious activity is difficult to determine; a natural reaction from years of spiritual barrenness, a craving for social intercourse and emotional excitement, which the camp meeting provided, and the ready co-operation of ministers of different sects may all have helped. Whatever the causes, the results were firmly to establish religion on the middle western frontier, to throw the region into the power of Presbyterians, Baptists, and Methodists, and to establish for a long period certain religious agencies, of which the camp meeting was the most important. The backwash in the East of this tremendous religious revival, coupled with the sustained but quiet efforts of many clergymen, gradually effected a similar spiritual awakening in the seaboard states.

While the Mississippi valley was being won to Christianity by the sturdy pioneer pastors and the tireless circuit-riders, religion in the East was undergoing significant development. The spiritual awakening of the early years of the century quickly developed a crusading spirit and an evangelistic drive the effects of which were felt in all corners of the world. It was in 1798 that the Missionary Society of Connecticut was formed "to christianize the heathen of North America, and to promote Christian knowledge in the new settlements within the United States," [7] and it was in the summer of 1800 that its first missionary, David Bacon, set out for the wilderness southwest of Lake Erie. Ten years later the American Board of Commissioners for Foreign Missions was constituted, and, having failed to secure co-operation from the London Missionary Society, sent, in 1812, five young clergymen to India, the first American missionaries to sail for a foreign land. For twenty-seven years the American Board was the common organ of foreign missionary operations of the Congregationalists, Presbyterians, Dutch Reformed, and German Reformed churches. Eventually the missionary activities of these churches were separated, and in the meantime the Baptists, the Episcopalians, the Methodists, and other denominations had caught the desire to evangelize other nations. The American Home Missionary Society was organized in 1826 to co-ordinate the work of the Congregationalists and Presbyterians in caring for the New England westward migration, and other denominations soon followed with similar organizations. The social effect of these missionary enterprises was felt not alone on the American frontier and in foreign lands, but likewise in every church and hamlet where a branch organization existed. Church fairs, socials, and sewing societies, organized to provide funds or fill the missionary barrels, provided not only opportunity for rural recreation but also, particularly among women, a vent for religious and humanitarian impulses.

Some very excellent social history has been done on this period. No student should miss J. B. McMaster, *A History of the People of the United States,* Vol. I, 1–50, for a picture of conditions in the 1780s, a pioneer effort in social history. The description of social America at the opening of the Jefferson administration in Henry Adams, *A History of the United States During the Administration of Thomas Jefferson,* Vol. I, Chaps. I–VI, is as notable as any part of the work, and his chapters on conditions sixteen years later, *A History of the United States During the Administration of James Madison,* Book IX, Chaps. VII–X, are also important. More nearly exhaustive than McMaster and Adams is F. J. Turner's description of American sections about 1830, *The United States, 1830–1850,* Chaps. I–VIII. Other important works are Merle Curti, *The Growth of American Thought,* Chaps. VII–XI; J. A. Krout and D. R. Fox, *The Completion of Independence 1790–1830;* and H. J. Carman, *A Social and Economic History of the United States,* Vol. I, Chap. VII.

[7] The Massachusetts Home Missionary Society started in 1803, and similar organizations in New Hampshire in 1801, in Rhode Island in 1803, in Maine in 1807, and in Vermont in 1818, all later becoming auxiliaries of the American Home Missionary Society.

NATIONALISM AND SECTIONALISM

Chapter XIV

AMERICA MOVES WESTWARD

America was bred in a cabin.

MORRIS BIRKBECK

*If the cause of the happiness of this country
was examined into, it would be found to arise as
much from the great plenty of land in proportion
to the inhabitants which their citizens enjoyed
as from the wisdom of their political institutions.
It is because the poor man has been able always
to attain his portion of the land.*

ALBERT GALLATIN

THE INFLUENCE OF THE WESTWARD MOVEMENT

When Professor Frederick Jackson Turner, almost a half century ago,
called attention in a brilliant essay to the significance of the frontier, he
handed to American historians the key by which they might more adequately interpret the history of their nation. Historians, following his lead,
have shown how the existence for almost three centuries of an expanding
frontier not only has influenced the psychology and the philosophy of the
American people but has tremendously affected, as suggested in an earlier
chapter, the economic and political history of the nation (page 66). It has,
for example, until recent years, made agriculture and the production of
raw materials the major concerns of the American people. At the same time
the continued existence of a supply of fresh land has also perpetuated wasteful methods of agriculture. While labor was scarce, land was to be obtained
in abundance, with the result that agricultural improvements took the
form of labor-saving machinery rather than of land-saving methods. The
continued exodus to the West produced at times a scarcity of labor in the
East and kept the wage scale higher than it otherwise might have been. On
the other hand, the expanding market for manufactured commodities in the
West was an impetus for industrial development, and it was not long before the factory system began to move westward to touch more closely the
source of raw materials and the new market. The history of American

transportation is largely the history of the problem of keeping up with the expanding West and providing facilities for the movement of products and population. Excellent as are the natural transportation facilities of the American continent, they generally follow a direction from north to south. The movement of commerce, on the other hand, has been in an easterly-westerly direction, and artificial transportation facilities—roads, canals, and railroads—have been built in this direction. In the history of finance the influence of the debtor West has been ever present, exerting a pressure for easy banking laws and currency inflation.

If our economic development has been so largely dominated by a frontier West, it is obvious that political history, which is primarily a reflection of economic influences, must likewise have been similarly influenced. The political influence of the expanding West appears to have operated primarily along two lines—the extension of democracy and the development of nationalism. Suspicious of the economic groups sponsoring the Constitution, and distrustful of the undemocratic government proposed by that instrument, the small farmers of the West generally opposed it. As the new western state constitutions were subsequently drawn up, they led the way in the movement toward universal manhood suffrage and other democratic innovations. Certainly the backbone of the Jeffersonian democracy and of the Jacksonian democracy was the frontier West, and its leadership has continued until the twentieth century with the movement toward the initiative, the referendum, the recall, direct election of senators, woman suffrage, and the primary system, all democratic innovations first welcomed in America in the western states.

Although sectional economic interests often brought the frontier in conflict with the East and thus promoted sectionalism, the influence of the West on the whole has been to stimulate nationalism. It was the young Warhawks of the West who precipitated the War of 1812; it was Henry Clay, "Harry of the West," who advocated the "American system" with its dual policy of protective tariffs and internal improvements. It was the West rather than the East that enthusiastically favored the territorial expansion of the forties. The West, financially poor and laden with debt, needed the aid of a strong government to handle foreign affairs, to protect it from the Indians, and to provide aid in the development of transportation facilities, and the westerner by necessity looked toward the national rather than toward the state governments.

THE DEVELOPMENT OF A LAND POLICY

In earlier chapters attention has been called to the westward movement of the colonial period—how the pioneers, by means of head rights, proprietary grants, or group settlement under the New England plan, had occupied by 1700 the coastal plain and during the eighteenth century had pushed their settlements into the piedmont (pages 66–69). By the opening of the Revolution, the Old West, as it is called, was largely occupied, and the most advanced of the frontiersmen were ready to break through the Appalachian barrier into the great plains of the Mississippi valley. Although James Harrod, with a few others, had established a settlement and built a fort in 1774 at Harrodsburg, Kentucky, the first exodus of importance into that region came the following year, when Judge Richard Henderson of North Carolina obtained by the treaty of Sycamore Shoals a huge grant of land from the Indians, and his agent, Daniel Boone, cut a road northwest from Cumberland Gap and founded Boonesboro. The spearpoint of the movement into the Old Southwest was the little settlements on the Watauga River in the northeastern corner of the present state of Tennessee. It was from there that Boone recruited his followers in 1775 and that James Robertson led his band in 1779 into middle Tennessee to found the settlement at Nashville. It was from the settlers of this region that John Sevier in 1784 was to organize the short-lived state of Franklin. Against constant Indian attacks the pioneers of Kentucky and Tennessee held on during the Revolution. By 1792 Kentucky had enough population to join the Union, and four years later it was followed by Tennessee.

The movement of settlers into the trans-Appalachian region brought to a head the conflicting claims of various states to western land, the question of Indian relations, and the problem of land disposal. Fortunately, as we have seen, these problems were transferred to the Federal government during the period of the Confederation (page 117), when the states with claims to western land transferred them to Congress. Although the question of western land was far from being the only problem confronting the Confederation, it was the one dealt with most constructively. A committee headed by Jefferson and reporting in 1784 had divided the Northwest into tracts and provided for a system of government. Adopted as the Ordinance of 1784, it was later superseded by the more famous Ordinance of 1787. In the meantime Congress enacted the Land Ordinance of 1785, which laid the basis for the subsequent land system, just as the Ordinance of 1787 provided for government. The legislation of 1785 was a compromise between the New England system of disposal by township and the southern system of individual grants. It provided that surveyors were first to mark off a base line running from east to west. Across this base line at six-mile intervals meridians were laid down. Between the meridians rows of townships, known as ranges, were surveyed, each township being thirty-six square miles. The townships were to be divided into sections, each of one square mile, and each section might be divided into a half section of 320 acres, a quarter section of 160 acres, and so on. Following an early New England custom, section 16 was to be reserved for the support of schools. In this ordinance is to be found the basis of the subsequent land policy of the federal government—base lines, boundaries carefully run and marked according to a uniform plan, the six-mile township, and the section. It had the advantage of simplicity and undoubtedly saved endless litigation.

The method of survey was far from being the only problem arising from the necessity of disposing of the public land. There was also the question of the size of the tract to be sold. The typical frontiersman was too poor to buy much land even at the first price of $1 an acre, yet the breaking of the land into small lots would tend to scatter the settlers, raise the cost of surveys, and result in selling only the good land. On the other hand, the sale of large tracts would encourage large-scale speculation to the detriment of *bona fide* settlers. The question of price was important, for upon it rested the decision as to whether western land was to be sold primarily for the benefit of the settler or for the treasury of the United States. Other problems had to do with settlement requirements, the location of the land offices and auction sales, and the question whether the land should be sold for cash or for credit. It took several decades of experience before any final policy could be determined.

Six years after a report on the status of public lands by Hamilton, to which Congress had paid but little attention, the new federal government finally passed an act in 1796 raising the minimum price to $2 an acre, making 640 acres the smallest unit that could be purchased, and allowing credit for one year on half of the purchase price. Unsuccessful because $1280 was beyond the wildest dreams of the average frontiersman, the law was changed in 1800, chiefly through the influence of William Henry Harrison, then serving in Congress as the delegate of the Northwest Territory. Under the act of 1800 the size of tracts was reduced from 640 acres to 320, and, although the minimum price was still $2 an acre, the credit system was greatly extended so that but one quarter of the purchase price had to be paid at once. In 1804 the credit system was further liberalized and the size of the tract purchasable cut to 160 acres. Although considerable land was taken up under these early acts, they were far from successful either as a source of revenue for the federal treasury or in promoting the interests of the settlers. The credit feature had promoted inordinate speculation, which had its inevitable result in the panic of 1819. As a compromise, Congress in 1820 abolished the credit system but at the same time reduced the price to $1.25 an acre and the size of the tracts to 80 acres.

Whatever might have been the original purposes of the framers of the land legislation, it seems clear enough that by 1820 the interests of the West had become the predominant influence in the situation. By that year

Ohio (1803), Indiana (1816), Mississippi (1817), Illinois (1818), and Alabama (1819) had attained statehood, and settlers were moving into the outlying territories. The population of the Old Northwest already numbered approximately 800,000. The West was rapidly becoming the most important element in the national legislature and achieving power to secure its ends. Although the land acts had been liberalized steadily to meet western desires, the frontiersmen had long demanded the right of pre-emption and were already asserting that the government should give away its land rather than sell it. Pre-emption was settling on land before it was purchased or even before it was surveyed, and then buying it afterward. With that ability to evade unpopular laws in which Americans became so expert, pre-emption was widely practiced. Settlers would gather at the public-land office, and woe betide any interloper who attempted to bid in a tract upon which a settlement had already been made. The Preemption Act of 1830, therefore, recognized an existing situation when it allowed settlers to occupy 160 acres and buy the land later at the minimum price free from competitive bids. A few years later (1841) this act was amended to allow settlers to pre-empt their land even before the government surveyors had laid it out.

The agitation for free land was an effort to restore an old system rather than to establish something new. Much land had been given away free in the colonial days. The township grants of New England were free, as were the head-right grants of the crown colonies. The grants of the proprietary colonies carried quitrents, but the difficulty of collecting them made many of the grants for all practical purposes free. In general, the policy of free land had ended with the establishment of the federal government, but, as a matter of fact, Congress after 1842 had given away to settlers in Florida, Oregon, Washington, and elsewhere much land in recompense for possible military protection of the settlements from Indian attacks. Much land had also been donated for transportation facilities, education, and other purposes. Free land had early found advocates in Congress, notably Senator Thomas Hart Benton of Missouri. In the forties the question seriously entered politics when the Free Soil Party put in a strong plank advocating it, and during the fifties bills were repeatedly presented in Congress to make it possible. In general, free land was opposed by the Northeast and Southeast and favored by the West. Opponents asserted that such a measure would be unconstitutional, that it would entail loss of revenue to the federal government, that it would raise wages in the East and depress the value of eastern land. In the late fifties, however, the chief opposition came from the South, where it was believed that free land would so speed the movement of small farmers to the West that it would aid the abolition movement and prevent the extension of slavery. Advocates argued that it would stimulate the rapid occupation of the West and indirectly benefit the whole nation, and they talked much of the God-given right of everyone to participate in this great bounty that Providence had conferred upon the American people.

Finally, in 1860, a bill that got around any possible constitutional objection by retaining a nominal price of 25 cents an acre passed both houses of Congress, but was vetoed by Buchanan, whose policies were dominated by the South. In that year the newly formed Republican Party, looking for a program that would appeal to the West, made the bill a part of its platform, and the election of Lincoln presaged a more liberal land policy. During his administration large grants were made for the promotion of a transcontinental railroad and for the founding of schools of agriculture and mechanical arts (Morrill Act). Most important was the passing of the Homestead Act of 1862, which granted 160 acres to *bona fide* settlers after a preliminary period of occupation. The ultimate goal of free land had been established. There remained only to enlarge and liberalize the legislation of 1862.

THE SETTLEMENT OF THE OLD NORTHWEST

While Congress under the Articles of Confederation was laying the foundation for a public land policy, settlers were preparing to move into the region north of the Ohio. Virginia, to compensate her revolutionary veterans, had reserved a tract of 6000 square miles, the Virginia Military District, between the Scioto and the Little Miami. In similar manner Connecticut, to compensate her citizens who had suffered from British raids during the Revolution and to insure an outlet for her population, reserved a tract (the Connecticut Western Reserve) some 120 miles wide along the shore of Lake Erie. The rest was at the disposal of Congress, and the first cessions were to land companies. In 1787 there arrived in New York the Reverend Manasseh Cutler, representing a group of Massachusetts veterans who had pooled their depreciated Continental certificates and were anxious to settle in the Ohio country. Though he was trained first for the bar and then for the ministry, Cutler's "true calling," says McMaster, "was politics."[1] Immediately he became the center of activity, intrigue, and legislation. Congress was delighted to have a picked group of men establish a frontier outpost and at the same time relieve the government of some of its debts. To speed this project the Ordinance of 1787 was pushed through, and Cutler is believed to have influenced it greatly. Cutler wanted only a million and a half acres, but to obtain this land he was forced to ask for several million acres above his requirements, which were to be turned over later to another company, the Scioto Company, com-

[1] He was also the leading botanist of New England.

posed of a group of powerful politicians. "By this ordinance," says Cutler in his *Journal,* "we obtained the grant of over five millions of acres of land, amounting to three millions and a half of dollars; one million and a half of acres for the Ohio Company, and the remainder for a private specu-lation, in which many of the principal characters of America are concerned. Without connecting this speculation, similar terms and advantages could not have been obtained for the Ohio Company." Thus was the first great land job of the republic consummated.[2]

In December of 1787 the first settlers of the Ohio Company, under the leadership of General Rufus Putnam, set out from Ipswich, Massachusetts, and in the spring of the following year founded Marietta where the Mus-kingum joins the Ohio. The year that Marietta was founded saw a group of New Jersey and Pennsylvania veterans and land speculators under Judge John Cleves Symmes purchase from Congress the region between the Great and Little Miamis and establish Cincinnati as the center of their colony. As the years went by, settlers in increasing numbers followed these pio-neers, occupying the Virginia bounty lands, the Western Reserve, and other parts of Ohio. The movement of settlers along the lake shore be-gan in the summer of 1796, when Moses Cleaveland, in the employ of the Connecticut Land Company, led a party to the Western Reserve and picked out a site for the settlement that was to develop into the largest of the Ohio cities. Although New Englanders settled around Marietta and in the Western Reserve, the early population of Ohio was chiefly recruited from the middle states and the South. New England was still settling her own northern frontier and spending her expansive energy in opening western New York. The census of 1790 showed scarcely a thousand people in western New York, but in the following decade settlers from Pennsylvania and New Jersey followed the Susquehanna and Tioga north to Seneca Lake, where they were joined by New Englanders pushing westward along the Mohawk and Genesee. Before many years had elapsed, towns and cities whose names harked back to classic Greece and Rome were springing up in this western wilderness.

Once well started, the movement into the Old Northwest proceeded rapidly. Across New York the settlers came along the Mohawk and Genesee turnpikes or along the Catskill turnpike from the Hudson to the headwaters of the Allegheny. Across Pennsylvania they came by the old Forbes Road and up from Maryland along the Cumberland Road. Re-ligious and political unrest in the East, economic distress during the period of the embargo, the War of 1812, and the postwar depression (as well as

---

[2] The Scioto Company, which was supposed to get the rest of the land, had a short and disreputable history. Its agent, Joel Barlow, sold land in France to a few hundred French emi-grants, for whom Congress eventually had to make provision.

subsequent economic depressions) provided an impetus to drive thousands westward, while the lure of greater economic opportunities aided in tearing many from their homes. And there was always propaganda of various kinds, particularly that of the land speculator. An observer at Robbstown, Westmoreland County, Pennsylvania, on the highway to Pittsburgh announced that in one month toward the end of 1810 he saw 236 wagons, with men, women, and children, and 600 merino sheep pass through on their way to the Ohio. During the winter of 1814

> Old settlers in central New York declared they had never seen so many teams and sleighs loaded with women, children, and household goods travelling westward, bound for Ohio, which was then but another name for the West. One account describes the roads passing through Auburn as thronged all winter long "with flitting families from the Eastern States." Another, from Newburg, in New York, declares that during one day in July six wagons with seventy persons, all from Massachusetts, entered and left the village for the Ohio, and that scarcely a week passed without its citizens "witnessing more or less emigration of this sort." [3]

"Old America seems to be breaking up and moving westward," wrote the English observer, Morris Birkbeck, in 1817, as he journeyed along the National Pike. "We are seldom out of sight, as we travel this grand track toward the Ohio, of family groups behind and before us." [4] Testimony such as this from many places and covering a period of years shows how the population of Ohio could increase from 230,000 in 1810 to 581,000 in 1820, how Indiana could increase from 24,000 to 147,000 in the same years, and the whole Northwest from a few thousand in 1800 to almost 7,000,000 in 1860.

THE SETTLEMENT OF THE OLD SOUTHWEST

The settlement of the Old Southwest, which began during the Revolution with Boone's settlement in Kentucky and the exodus of Robertson and his band into Tennessee, preceded that of the Northwest. The heavy immigration of the eighteenth century had gone chiefly to Pennsylvania, whence it had naturally followed the mountain valleys southwestward until it broke through Cumberland Gap. Like the migration into the Northwest, the movement into the Southwest was surprisingly large. Two fifths of the inhabitants of South Carolina, it is estimated, one third of those of North Carolina and Virginia, and one fourth of those of Georgia moved across the mountains to form almost the entire population of the Southwest and the predominating element in the Northwest. As in the North-

---

[3] J. B. McMaster, *History of the People of the United States,* IV, 383.
[4] *Notes on a Journey in America,* etc. (1818), 31.

west, this early migration was composed almost entirely of the typical pioneer farmer. With the turn of the century, however, the complexion of
southern migration changed. The invention of the cotton gin, the rapid
development of cotton as the staple crop in the South, and the competition
of richer land to the west soon brought the rich plantation-owners hurrying
westward after the pioneer farmer.

> By the side of the picture of the advance of the pioneer farmer [says
> Turner] bearing his household goods in his canvas-covered wagon to his
> new home across the Ohio, must therefore be placed the picture of the south-
> ern planter crossing through forests of western Georgia, Alabama, and Mis-
> sissippi, or passing over the free state of Illinois to the Missouri Valley, in
> his family carriage, with servants, packs of hunting dogs, and a train of
> slaves, their nightly camp fires lighting up the wilderness where so recently
> the Indian hunter held possession.[5]

Such a party the English traveler, Captain Basil Hall, encountered as
late as 1829.

> During the morning's drive, we overtook several bodies of migrants . . .
> —farmers errant, proceeding with all their worldly goods, according to the
> usual tide of these matters in this country from East to West, or rather, to be
> quite correct, from North-east to South-west—from Virginia and Maryland
> to Florida, Georgia, and Alabama.
>
> The first party consisted of a planter and his wife, accompanied by his
> brother-in-law and family, a whole troop of their children—some forty or
> fifty slaves of all ages and sizes. The wanderers were encamped near a creek,
> as it is called in America, or what we should term a brook, or burn, on the
> grassy banks of which they were scattered, over a space of several hundred
> yards, on both sides of the road, under the shade of several sycamore-trees.
> The travelling equipage consisted of three wagons and one open carriage,
> under the lee of which some of the party were busy cooking the dinner when
> we came up.

The migration in large numbers of wealthy plantation-owners was a
new phenomenon in the history of the westward movement. Unable to
refuse the higher prices that this new type of immigrant was able to pay
for the land and unable to compete with slave labor, the pioneer farmers
retreated to the marginal soil of the mountains and became the "poor
whites" and mountaineers of the South or else moved northward or westward across the Ohio or Mississippi and became again the founders of new
towns and commonwealths. As the slave-owning planters took possession
of the rich black soil of Alabama and Mississippi, the center of cotton culture shifted to the Southwest and with it the center of southern wealth and

[5] F. J. Turner, *The Rise of the New West*, 92.

power. By the decade of the thirties King Cotton had established his throne
west of the mountains. The profits of cotton culture, as we shall see, came
primarily from the exploitation of virgin soil rather than from the excellence of slave labor, and the necessity of a continual access to fresh soil
helps explain the rapidity of the southern advance, the desire for Florida,
the movement into Texas, and the anxiety of the South to preserve as much
territory as possible for slave labor. Although the whole process by which
the Southwest was opened to settlement and cultivation was extremely
wasteful, it was highly efficient in its main objective—the rapid increase
of cotton production for the markets of Europe and the northern states.
The pioneer farmer bore the brunt of Indian warfare and the first drudgery
of clearing the wilderness; the capitalist plantation-owner followed quickly
to exploit the land.

THE BIRTH OF AN AMERICAN COMMUNITY

Just as it is possible to draw a fairly accurate picture of the founding of
a New England town in the colonial period, so it is possible to sketch with
reasonable accuracy the early stages of thousands of villages springing up
all over the West during the first half of the nineteenth century. Let this
be done by Morris Birkbeck, an intelligent observer who traveled through
the West in 1817 in search of a fitting place for a group of his fellow
countrymen to settle.

On any spot where a few settlers cluster together, attracted by ancient
neighbourhood, or the goodness of the soil, or vicinity to a mill, or by whatever cause, some enterprising proprietor finds in his section what he deems
a good site for a town: he has it surveyed and laid out in lots, which he
sells, or offers for sale by auction.

The new town then assumes the name of its founder:—a storekeeper
builds a little framed store, and sends for a few cases of goods; and then a
tavern starts up, which becomes the residence of a doctor and a lawyer, and
the boarding-house of a storekeeper, as well as the resort of the weary traveller: soon follow a black-smith and other handicraftsmen in useful succession: a schoolmaster who is also the minister of religion, becomes an
important accession to this rising community. Thus the town proceeds, if it
proceeds at all, with accumulating force, until it becomes the metropolis of
the neighbourhood. Hundreds of these speculations may have failed, but
hundreds prosper; and thus trade begins and thrives as population grows
around these lucky spots; imports and exports maintaining their just proportion. One year ago the neighbourhood of this very town of Princeton
was clad in "buckskin," now the men appear at church in good blue cloth,
and the women in fine calicoes and straw bônnets.

The town being fairly established, a cluster of inhabitants, small as it may be, acts as a stimulus on the cultivation of the neighbourhood: redundancy of supply is the consequence, and this demands a vent. Water mills, or in defect of water power, steam mills rise on the nearest navigable stream, and thus an effectual and constant market is secured for the increasing surplus of produce. Such are the elements of that accumulating mass of commerce, in exports, and consequent imports, which will render the Mississippi the greatest thoroughfare in the world.[6]

The pioneer who opened a new community hoped, of course, that he had chosen his location wisely and that the economic development would proceed much as Birkbeck described it. The future, however, could not be foretold. It often depended upon the existence of natural resources, but more often upon the development of trade routes. Many a settlement, like the Ohio town in which Mark Hanna was born, had enjoyed unusual prosperity in its early years because of its location on a much frequented turnpike, but declined later as the new railroads passed it by.[7] The typical pioneer, however, who was as much of a land speculator as a farmer, rarely looked into the distant future. He was likely to sell his holdings to the next wave of settlers and again strike into the wilderness to found a new community. Observers of the westward movement have discerned a certain rhythm in the process, nowhere better described than by J. M. Peck in *A New Guide for Emigrants to the West,* published in Boston in 1837.

Generally, in all the western settlements, three classes, like the waves of the ocean, have rolled one after the other. First comes the pioneer, who depends for the subsistence of his family chiefly upon the natural growth of vegetation, called the "range," and the proceeds of hunting. His implements of agriculture are rude, chiefly of his own make, and his efforts directed mainly to a crop of corn, and a "truck patch." The last is a rude garden for growing cabbage, beans, corn for roasting ears, cucumbers and potatoes; a log cabin, and, occasionally, a stable and corn-crib, and a field of a dozen acres, the timber girdled or "deadened" and fenced, are enough for his occupancy. It is quite immaterial whether he ever becomes the owner of the soil. He is the occupant for the time being, pays no rent, and feels as independent as the "lord of the manor." With a horse, cow, and one or two breeders of swine, he strikes into the woods with his family, and becomes the founder of a new county, or perhaps State. He builds his cabin, gathers around him a few other families of similar taste and habits, and occupies till the range is somewhat subdued, and hunting a little precarious; or, which is more frequently the case, till neighbors crowd around, roads, bridges, and fields annoy him, and he lacks elbow room. The preemption law enables him to dispose of his cabin and corn-field to the next class of emigrants, and, to employ his own figures, he "breaks for the high timber," "clears out for

[6] Morris Birkbeck, *op. cit.,* 103–105.
[7] Herbert Croly, *Marcus Alonzo Hanna* (1912), IV.

the New Purchase," or migrates to Arkansas or Texas, to work the same process over.

The next class of emigrants purchase the lands, add field to field, clear out the roads, throw rough bridges over the streams, put up hewn log houses, with glass windows, and brick or stone chimneys, occasionally plant orchards, build mills, school houses, court houses, &c., and exhibit the picture and forms of plain, frugal, civilized life.

Another wave rolls on. The men of capital and enterprise come. The "settler" is ready to sell out and take the advantage of the rise of property—push farther into the interior, and become, himself, a man of capital and enterprise in turn. The small village rises to a spacious town or city; substantial edifices of brick, extensive fields, orchards, gardens, colleges and churches are seen. Broadcloths, silks, leghorns, crapes, and all the refinements, luxuries, elegancies, frivolities and fashions, are in vogue. Thus wave after wave is rolling westward:—the real *el dorado* is still farther on.

A portion of the two first classes remain stationary amidst the general movement, improve their habits and condition, and rise in the scale of society.

The writer has traveled much amongst the first class, the real pioneers. He has lived many years in connection with the second grade; and now the third wave is sweeping over large districts of Indiana, Illinois, and Missouri. Migration has become almost a habit in the West. Hundreds of men can be found, not over 50 years of age, who have settled for the fourth, fifth, or sixth time on a new spot. To sell out and remove only a few hundred miles makes up a portion of the variety of backwoods life and manners.

While this economic rhythm was typical enough in those communities that advanced to more prospperous days, it was far from being inevitable. There were communities in which the pioneer, the more stable farmer, and the capitalist or industrialist arrived simultaneously and co-operated in the development of a new community.[8] There were many communities that never got beyond the pioneering stage. Furthermore, in the great "Cotton Kingdom" of the Old Southwest the rhythm was often quite different. Here the first stage, in which the pioneer farmer cleared the forest and commenced cultivation, was the same as that described by Peck. With the coming of the slave-owning planter the development differed. Dispossessing the pioneer and consolidating his fields, the development of large plantations prevented the growth of towns and villages, creating a civilization in which the white population was often smaller than during the pioneer stage. The second phase, a period of prosperous cotton plantations, often ended with the exhaustion of the soil under the crude agricultural methods of the time, ignorant slave labor, and the one-crop system. With cotton profits depending primarily upon the exploitation of virgin soil,

[8] C. W. Alvord, *Mississippi Valley Historical Review*, VII, 403–407 (March, 1921).

the exhaustion of the soil meant an exodus to new lands and a general economic decline.

> In 1825 [said a prominent citizen of Alabama in 1855] Madison county cast about 3,000 votes; now she cannot cast exceeding 2,300. In traversing that county one will discover numerous farm houses, once the abode of industrious and intelligent freemen, now occupied by slaves, or tenantless, deserted, and dilapidated; he will observe fields, once fertile, now unfenced, abandoned, and covered with those evil harbingers—fox-tail and broomsedge; he will see the moss growing on the mouldering walls of once thrifty villages; and will find "one only master grasps the whole domain" that once furnished happy homes for a dozen white families. Indeed, a county in its infancy, where, fifty years ago scarce a forest tree had been felled by the axe of the pioneer, is already exhibiting the sign of senility and decay, apparent in Virginia and the Carolinas; the freshness of its agricultural glory is gone; the vigor of its youth is extinct, and the spirit of desolation seems brooding over it.[9]

The movement to the West sometimes appeared more like the progress of a devastating army than the ripening of a new civilization, and its effects were not limited to the West. The exodus of hundreds of thousands and the competition of richer lands as transportation facilities brought the agricultural products of the West to the eastern markets eliminated from cultivation many eastern farms, particularly in New England and the South. By the middle of the century the deserted farm in New England was a common sight. In the older South, where the whole increase of the slave and white population was migrating westward, the effects were more striking. "In some counties of the seaboard states, such as Virginia," says Dodd, "the population decreased by half in one or two decades, and everywhere the lands and houses of well-to-do people declined in value. Jefferson's magnificent home sold in 1821 for about $3000; Madison struggled manfully but in vain to avoid selling his family slaves; and John Randolph talked of running away from his plantation to avoid bankruptcy."[10]

THE TRANS-MISSISSIPPI WEST

At the time of the Louisiana purchase not a few had argued that it might be centuries before the American people would have need of the land west of the Mississippi. The purchase, however, made occupation inevitable, and it came in a surprisingly short time. A handful of French at St. Louis and New Orleans comprised almost the only white population in 1803, but

[9] F. L. Olmsted, *A Journey in the Seaboard Slave States* (1856), 577.

[10] From W. E. Dodd, *The Cotton Kingdom,* Volume 27, The Chronicles of America, 9. Copyright Yale University Press.

by 1812 the white population of Louisiana was sufficient for its admission as a state, and by 1817 Missouri was demanding admission. The frontier line in 1830 cut across the center of Missouri to its western boundary and similarly had advanced in Arkansas and Louisiana to their western bounds. By 1860 pioneers had pushed into Minnesota (admitted 1858) and Iowa (1846), were penetrating the territories of Nebraska and Kansas, and had advanced halfway across Texas (annexed 1846). Although the frontier line in that year zigzagged irregularly from central Minnesota to the Gulf of Mexico, it was not far from meridian 95.

The migration of the pioneer farmer and plantation-owner into the trans-Mississippi West was preceded by the usual stage of exploration and hunting. The most famous of the expeditions of exploration was that (1804–1806) of Meriwether Lewis and William Clark (page 152). In the latter year Lieutenant Zebulon M. Pike traced the Mississippi practically to its source and subsequently explored the Arkansas and Red Rivers, penetrating to the Rockies and discovering the mountain that bears his name. Hunting parties, with their center at St. Louis, and less famous explorers penetrated the region during the following years, discovering mountain passes and pointing the routes to the West that Frémont, "the Pathfinder" but not the discoverer, was to make widely known.

Five new aspects of the frontier movement are to be noted during the period from 1840 to 1860. In the first place came the artificial stimulation given to the settlement of Texas by the Texas revolution and the annexation of that state to the Union. Secondly there was the stimulation given to the settlement of Kansas by the struggle for control between abolitionists and proslavery Southerners and by the inducements to settle offered by emigrant-aid societies, particularly those of the North. In the third place, propaganda for the settlement of Oregon speeded a movement to the Far West. A fourth aspect was the Mormon exodus to Utah, and finally came the discovery of gold in California, which caused the frontier line suddenly to jump a thousand miles to the Pacific coast, there to create a new frontier, which, in the succeeding decades, was to move eastward.

The first American penetration into Texas, in the early twenties, had been a normal movement of pioneer farmers, led by Stephen F. Austin to settle on lands granted by the Mexican government. By 1836 fully 20,-000 small farmers, ranchers, cotton-growers, and adventurers of all sorts had swarmed into Texas, colliding with Mexican ranchers and becoming restless under the rule of a foreign power. Friction over questions of taxation, customs duties, slavery, political representation, and home rule brought an inevitable revolution, independence for a decade as the Republic of Texas, annexation by the United States, and finally the Mexican War, which added a new Southwest to the American nation. Later (1853) the Gadsden purchase was consummated primarily to provide a southern route for a transcontinental railway.

Quite different is the history of how the United States secured the Oregon region. American interest in that country goes back to the voyages of Captains Gray and Kendrick in 1788 in search of furs for the China trade and to the discovery by Gray in 1792 of the Columbia River. The famous expedition of Lewis and Clark kept interest alive, and in 1811 the American Fur Company of John Jacob Astor established the fur post of Astoria on the Columbia as the basis of operations. In the meantime two English companies, the Hudson's Bay Company and the Northwest Company, had commenced to exploit this region; during the War of 1812 Astor's agent sold out to the Northwest Company, and the Americans retired. The Northwest Company was soon absorbed by the Hudson's Bay Company, and for the next quarter of a century that organization, through its local agent, the able and benevolent Dr. John McLaughlin, dominated the Oregon country. Although Americans had been ousted from the fur trade, the land was technically held under joint occupation. In 1818 British and American commissions, unable to reach a decision on the boundary line, had provided for joint occupation for ten years, and in 1827 this agreement had been revived for an indefinite period, either party having the right to terminate it upon a year's notice. In the meantime a new interest had developed in the Oregon region, this time on the part of prospective settlers rather than fur traders. A New England schoolmaster and engineer, Hall J. Kelley, convinced of the importance of Oregon, wrote pamphlets urging settlement,[11] organized a colonization society, and journeyed there in the early thirties. Business men, such as Nathaniel J. Wyeth of Cambridge, Massachusetts, who led an expedition to Oregon in 1832, were beginning again to dream of the commercial possibilities of the Oregon region. Missionaries of the Methodist Church and the Presbyterian Missionary Society, especially Marcus Whitman, helped to advertise Oregon in the East, as did Washington Irving's account of the adventures of Captain Bonneville. Only a handful of Americans were in the Oregon region during the thirties, but this propaganda and advertising, as well as the depression after the panic of 1837, set in motion in the early forties a migration that brought Oregon under the control of American settlers and resulted in a boundary settlement (1846) that gave the valuable Columbia basin to the United States. Fur traders, explorers, missionaries, propagandists, pioneer farmers,

[11] *A Geographical Sketch of that Part of North America called Oregon* (1829, 1830) and *General Circular to all Persons of Good Character who wish to emigrate to the Oregon Territory* (1831).

FOUR STAGES OF THE FRONTIER

(From O. Turner, *Pioneer History of Holland Land Purchase of Western New York*, 1850)

international diplomacy—all the influences that might stimulate occupation and possession are found in the story of Oregon.

While the covered wagons of the early settlers were creaking their way over the weary miles of the Oregon trail, another thrust into the Far West was being planned. Persecuted in the East, driven out of Missouri, subjected to mob violence in Illinois, and the founder of their religion murdered, the members of the Mormon church determined to move again. This time they would go far enough to be unmolested and, if need be, settle on Mexican territory. Their leader, Brigham Young, first sighted the Great Salt Lake in July of 1847, and to this promised land he brought his buffeted followers. Like the Puritans of an earlier century, the Mormons had the integrating force of a religious purpose. Combining skillful leadership, sobriety, and industry, the immigrants quickly turned a desert into a land of plenty. Mormon missionaries made new converts in Europe and the East, who were enabled to reach Utah by a "Perpetual Emigration Fund" that paid their expenses and was later reimbursed by the immigrants. Like Puritan Massachusetts, Utah was a theocratic state; church and state were closely joined, and the economic life was minutely dominated by the government. Much criticism was later directed against the Mormon practice of plural marriages, and Utah was kept from statehood until 1896, but American history bears no record of more successful group migration than that of the Mormons to Utah.

Hardly had the Mormons established themselves on the basin of the Great Salt Lake and the war with Mexico ended, when a new impetus for the settlement of the West was given by the discovery of gold on the mill-race of John Sutter some sixty miles from Sacramento. California was not entirely unknown to Americans before this. Frémont and other explorers had traveled the country, Yankee hide ships had visited the coast,[12] and a few American settlers had trickled in and obtained grants from the Mexican government. That California had already become an objective for pioneers was dramatically illustrated by the effort of the Donner party to reach California in 1846, the incredible tale of whose hardships is hardly equaled in American history. As the news of the discovery of gold leaked out, white settlers on the western coast swarmed to the diggings, and in the following year their numbers were recruited from every corner of the East. Along the overland trails, around the Horn, and across the Isthmus of Panama came the forty-niners, chanting variations of

> O, don't you cry Susanna!
> O, don't you cry for me!

[12] The story of the California hide trade in the thirties has been told in R. H. Dana, *Two Years Before the Mast* (1840), one of the classics of the sea.

I'm going to Californy
With a wash bowl on my knee.

O, don't you cry, for I am told
In that land where we're bound
They pick the great big lumps of gold
In chunks right off the ground!

Probably 35,000 found their way to California by land in that year and 42,000 by sea, while thousands of others left their bones to bleach on the long overland trails or in the disease-infested forests of Panama. Such a migration was made possible by the fact that the early gold-seekers sought the precious metal from the mountain washings on the bottoms of rivers and creeks, and for this only a pickax, a cradle, and plenty of brawn and optimism were necessary. Only a handful of the forty-niners ever secured wealth from the yellow metal; the early fortunes were usually made by the hotelkeeper, the gambling-house proprietor, and the transportation company. The gold fever, however, laid the foundation for California's subsequent development and brought enough people in a single year to raise the demand for statehood. The fever aroused by the discovery of gold was not to subside for many years. A decade later silver was discovered in the regions of the present Colorado, Arizona, Nevada and elsewhere, and just before the outbreak of the Civil War prospectors were swarming over the Rockies from Canada to the Mexican line, preparing the way for permanent settlements and laying the foundations for a half dozen mountain states.

C. and M. Beard, *The Rise of American Civilization*, Chaps. XI, XIII, is written with sweep and spirit. On the various topics concerned with the westward movement there are usually one or more chapters in F. L. Paxson, *A History of the American Frontier 1763–1895*. On the Old Northwest, F. J. Turner, *The Frontier in American History*, Chap. IV, is an interesting essay, while B. W. Bond, *The Civilization of the Old Northwest*, Chaps. I, II, X, and elsewhere, treats many phases of that region. S. E. White, *The Forty Niners* (Chronicles of America), writes interestingly of the settlement of California. Other treatments of the westward movement are Edward Channing, *A History of the United States*, Vol. V, Chap. II, and J. B. McMaster, *A History of the People of the United States*, Vol. II, 144 ff.; III, 100–142, 459–496; IV, 381–428; V, 160 ff. Nothing better has been done on this subject than some parts of McMaster. One important aspect is discussed in A. B. Hulbert, *Soil: Its Influence on the History of the United States*, Chaps. VII–XXI. For contemporary material see G. S. Callender, *Selections from the Economic History of the United States*, 597–690, and F. Flügel and H. U. Faulkner, *Readings in the Economic and Social History of the United States*, 379–397.

Chapter XV

THE INDUSTRIAL REVOLUTION

The transition from mother and daughter power to water and steam-power is a great one, greater by far than many have as yet begun to conceive—one that is to carry with it a complete revolution of domestic life and social manners.

HORACE BUSHNELL (1851)

THE COMING OF THE FACTORY SYSTEM

Although the American Revolution brought political independence, its effect upon the general economic life of America was slight. The United States continued to be essentially a mercantile and agricultural nation—a producer of foodstuffs and raw materials for export to the outside world. This does not mean that manufacturing did not exist. The typical small farmer or frontiersman, living on his self-sufficing farm, lacked the means to purchase imported manufactured goods and continued to make his own commodities or to secure them from local craftsmen. "Until about 1850," say the editors of the twelfth census, "the bulk of general manufacturing done in the United States was carried on in the shop and the household, by the labor of the family or individual proprietors, with apprentice assistants, as contrasted with the present system of factory labor, compensated by wages, and assisted by power." A glance at American industrial life at the opening of the national period reveals all those types of manufacturing that economic historians have found also in Europe at the dawn of the Industrial Revolution. There existed hardly a family but possessed its spinning wheel and weaving loom and whose men were not able to construct the crude farming implements that they used. Household manufacturing for the general market was also quite common, and we discover in some sections the merchant capitalist distributing raw materials to be finished in the home and then collected and sold. In the more settled communities it was possible to support manufacturing artisans—blacksmiths, leather workers, cabinetmakers, and others, who devoted their entire time to their craft, producing custom work on order and often manufacturing goods for

242

From the Old to the New World

German Emigrants Embarking on a Hamburg Steamer for New York (*Harper's Weekly*, November 7, 1874)

WESTERN IMMIGRATION

Covered Wagons Advancing into the Rocky Mountains

general sale. There was hardly a community that did not support a saw-mill, a grist mill or even a fulling mill.

The transition from this type of manufacturing to the factory system was far from sudden. The Industrial Revolution was delayed by lack of liquid capital, lack of an adequate currency, absence of satisfactory trans-portation facilities, and the rivalry of agriculture and maritime interests for labor and capital. It may also have been delayed at the start by the high cost of labor, although in the end this difficulty undoubtedly stimulated inventors to design labor-saving machinery and producers to buy such products. Likewise, it was delayed by competition from Great Britain, where the Industrial Revolution had a half-century start, where wages were low, and where capital, labor, and transportation facilities had achieved an integration that enabled them to handle production and dis-tribution. Great Britain also had a monopoly of the early technical im-provements that had given birth to the factory system, a monopoly that she tried to maintain by laws forbidding the emigration of skilled workmen and the export of machinery. This monopoly had come to Great Britain through a fortuitous combination of economic conditions that had brought epoch-making improvements in the manufacture of textiles and in the operation of steam engines. Beginning with John Kay's flying shuttle (1738) and coming down through James Hargreaves's spinning jenny (1770), Richard Arkwright's water frame (1769), Samuel Crompton's mule (1779), and Edmund Cartwright's power loom (1785), spinning and weaving had been largely removed from the home to the factory and water power substituted for hand power. When a Scotch scientist, James Watt, patented in 1769 an improved and practical steam engine, manufac-turers were freed from water power, and the way was prepared for new developments in transportation to speed the distribution of factory-made goods.

The speed and cheapness by which textiles could be produced through these revolutionary inventions were so obvious that the new machinery was bound to find its way to other parts of the world. As a consequence, the Industrial Revolution came first in America in the textile industry just as it had in Great Britain. Little mills in which the jenny was used appeared in America in the 1780s, but the first successful Arkwright water frame was erected at Pawtucket, Rhode Island, in 1791, by an English emigrant, Samuel Slater, who had served an apprenticeship in one of Arkwright's factories at Belper.[1] Slater's Pawtucket mill, where the machines, tended by nine little children, turned out satisfactory yarn, marks the real begin-

[1] At least, Slater's mill was the most famous of the early attempts. Broadus Mitchell has found evidences of power-driven machinery in the South that seems to antedate Slater, notably at Stateburg on the Santee River. *The Rise of Cotton Mills in the South*, 13–14.

nings of the American factory system, but the first systematic attempt to develop extensive water power for general manufacturing purposes was probably that of a company organized by Alexander Hamilton in 1791 for the manufacture of textiles at Passaic, New Jersey. Although America possessed an abundance of cheap raw materials, ingenious mechanics, and a rapidly expanding market that would have made the development of large-scale manufacturing inevitable, there is no doubt that it was given artificial stimulation by the embargo and nonintercourse acts, the War of 1812, and the subsequent protective tariffs. It was in the decade following 1807 that the factory system gained its first strong foothold in America.

To the textile industry the Yankee inventor, Eli Whitney, had already made an important contribution in the cotton gin, which made it possible for the cotton-producer to keep pace with the new textile machinery. The first successful power loom in America was set up by the Boston merchant, Francis Cabot Lowell, who, on a trip to England, 1810–1812, studied the operation of textile machinery and upon his return constructed, with the aid of a mechanical genius, Paul Moody, a new set of spinning machinery and a power loom. With the financial aid of a few relatives and friends, this machinery was put in operation at Waltham, Massachusetts, in 1814, where, it is believed, for the first time in the world all the processes of spinning and weaving were brought together under one roof. The operation of textile machinery having started, numerous American inventors made important contributions until Americans were able to produce high-grade textile machinery at home for a variety of purposes. The most famous of these was perhaps Elias Howe, who invented in 1846 a sewing machine that was to revolutionize the clothing and shoe industries.

Although Americans by 1860 were producing all types of textiles from machine-made lace to carpets, the greatest early success was in cotton. This fiber never supported independent homespun employment because it could be manufactured by the family only in combination with flax or wool. Cotton-manufacturing, as a consequence, was a new industry with no handicraft traditions to overcome. Its problem was to displace flax as the most common material for clothing, and, when this was accomplished, the success of cotton was assured. Machinery for the production of woolen yarn was set up as early as that for cotton, but the growth of the woolen industry was much slower. Severe foreign competition, frequent changes of style, and scarcity of skilled workmen and high-grade wool all handicapped it. The census of 1860, nevertheless, found over 1900 woolen factories with 49,000 employees.

Unlike textiles, the smelting of iron had never been a household industry, but had been carried on in colonial days close to the supplies of bog iron and ordinarily in conjunction with the manufacture of iron utensils.

Like textiles, however, it had received a strong impetus from the embargo and the War of 1812 and grew rapidly with the development of the Industrial Revolution and the expansion of the country. Added impetus to iron-production was given when iron ore was successfully smelted with anthracite coal in 1830, and when William Kelly of Kentucky independently discovered in 1851 the principle of the Bessemer method of decarbonizing molten metal by forcing air through it. Primarily the development of the iron industry came with a widening demand. Iron for the machinery of the expanding textile industry and for the new steam engines that Americans like Fitch, Rumsey, Evans, Stevens, and Fulton had done so much to develop was in constant demand.

More important was the coming of new agricultural machinery, notably the iron plow, first patented by Charles Newbold in 1797 and later improved by John Lane of Chicago with his steel moldboard (1833), and James Oliver of South Bend, Indiana, with his chilled-steel construction (1869). The expanding use of practical reaping machines, first put on the market in the early thirties by Obed Hussey and Cyrus McCormick, is also typical of agriculture's demand for iron. Another important market was found after 1840 in the manufacture of stoves, which were rapidly supplanting the old-fashioned fireplace for cooking and heating. During the same years the building of railroads was to supply a new but constantly growing demand. Throughout all these years the manufacture of firearms was an important metal industry, and it was in this industry that America made one of the most important contributions to the Industrial Revolution when Eli Whitney, in 1807, first applied in this country the principle of standardization of parts and interchangeable mechanism.[2] As the textile mills tended to center near the supply of water power in New England and the middle states, the metal industries concentrated chiefly around the source of raw materials. Important exceptions to this, however, are to be seen in the manufacture of certain smaller metal commodities, for which skilled labor, because of the labor time consumed, was the chief element of cost. Connecticut early came to be a center of tin manufacture, brass products, and clocks, while other New England towns, such as Providence, specialized in cheap jewelry and other novelties.

THE EXPANSION OF TRANSPORTATION

As a carrier of raw materials for export, adequate transportation has been extremely important to this country, and it became increasingly

[2] The idea was suggested even earlier in Europe, but Whitney seems to have been the first person to realize its possibilities. Victor Clark, *History of Manufactures in the United States,* I, 420.

so as population extended beyond the Appalachians. With the coming of the Industrial Revolution the Northeast turned definitely to manufacturing, thus accentuating the necessity of improved transportation, by means of which the machine-made goods of the East might be exchanged for the foodstuffs and raw materials of the West. The American transportation problem, however, has not been concerned merely with the exchange of commodities; the value of western land has been so dependent upon nearness to transportation facilities that transportation development and real-estate speculation have gone hand in hand.

Up to the Civil War American transportation history falls rather definitely within three periods: (1) the era of turnpikes and improved roads, (2) the era of canal-building, and (3) the coming of railroads. Throughout these three early periods there developed simultaneously the river steamboat and an active river commerce. Hardly had the national government been organized when the new nation was swept by a widespread interest in road-building. It began with the construction between 1792 and 1794 of an excellent 66-mile macadam turnpike between Philadelphia and Lancaster. Built with private capital and financially successful, it was the signal for similar projects in all the states. Pennsylvania, for example, during the next thirty years, chartered eighty-six companies, which built 2200 miles of road, and New York, by 1811, had chartered 137 companies, which constructed about 1400 miles. The building of toll bridges by private capital followed naturally the construction of toll roads. While privately owned toll roads have almost entirely disappeared, toll bridges still exist to arouse the ire of the motorist.

The widespread interest in transportation projects that developed during the turnpike era resulted eventually in pressure upon the federal government to lend its aid. This demand led in 1808 to a statesmanlike and now famous report on internal improvements, in which the author, Albert Gallatin, recommended that a great turnpike be built along the Atlantic coast from Maine to Georgia, that the peninsulas jutting into the Atlantic be cut by canals to reduce the distance and the dangers of coastwise commerce, that the headwaters of navigable streams running into the Atlantic be joined by roads with those running into the Mississippi, and that the rivers at various points be made navigable by canals. The cost, he believed, might be met by the sales of public lands. Gallatin's far-seeing plans have now been largely consummated, but the immediate result of the agitation for federal aid was the authorization by Congress in 1806 of the construction of a national road from Cumberland, Maryland, across the mountains into Ohio. The first contract was let in 1811, and in the succeeding years the road was pushed westward, reaching Wheeling (West Virginia) in 1818, Columbus (Ohio) in 1833, and

Vandalia (Illinois) in 1852. As it was gradually finished the 834 miles of the Cumberland Road or the "National Pike," as it came to be called, furnished one of the chief avenues to the West, crowded daily with immigrants and western commerce. "As many as twenty four-horse coaches have been counted in line at one time on the road," says one historian, "and large, broad-wheeled wagons, covered with white canvas stretched over bows laden with merchandise and drawn by six Conestoga horses, were visible all the day long at every point, and many times till late in the evening, besides innumerable caravans of horses, mules, cattle, hogs and sheep. It looked more like the leading avenue of a great city than a road through rural districts." [3]

While the National Pike was the most important federal transportation project during the first half of the century, federal aid was extended in one way or another to various enterprises, particularly during the period of strong nationalism in the years following the War of 1812. So ardent were the friends of federal aid that not less than 111 surveys and plans for roads, canals, and railroads were before Congress in 1830 when Jackson called a halt by his veto of the Maysville Road Bill (page 192).

While the building of new roads undoubtedly facilitated the movement of population and commerce over short distances, turnpikes fell far short of solving the problem of east-west transportation. Toll charges and other costs made the freight rates prohibitive on bulky commodities for long distances. In the twenties and thirties this problem was in part overcome by a large-scale building of canals. England, while the Industrial Revolution was developing, had added important links to her transportation system by means of canals, and their success had stimulated much interest in the United States. Although several small canals had been built here during the early years of the century, the era of canal-building really opened with the construction of the Erie Canal. After a quarter century of agitation, and taking advantage of the easiest route through the Appalachians to the West, New York authorized in 1817 a canal to connect the Hudson with Lake Erie. When, on October 26, 1825, cannon stationed at intervals along the canal announced the opening of the entire length and the departure of the first boats, a new chapter was begun in the history of American transportation. The success of the Erie Canal was instant and beyond the expectations of its most ardent backers. Tolls exceeded interest charges before it was finished and amounted during the first nine years to more than the original cost. Besides providing a new route to the West and making possible the long-distance shipment of freight, the canal stimulated tremendously the settlement of western New York and the economic life of that state. Utica, Syracuse, and Rochester

[3] T. B. Searight, *The Old Pike*, 16.

quickly became thriving cities, while the terminals, Buffalo, Albany, and New York, took on new life. New York doubled its population in a decade and wrested from Philadelphia the position of America's leading city.

With the success of the Erie a veritable mania for canal-building swept the country. Not to be outdone by New York and determined to hold her western trade, Philadelphia also developed (1826–1834) a system of canals and portages from the Delaware to the Ohio. The Pennsylvania Canal and its connecting railways was larger than the Erie, and the difficulties and expense were greater because of the higher elevations that had to be surmounted, but the canal served its purpose in retaining for Philadelphia its share in the western trade. Not to be outdone by their northern neighbors, Maryland and Virginia, in 1828, commenced construction of the Chesapeake and Ohio, but it was never pushed beyond the mountains, and its usefulness was limited. Many other shorter but temporarily important canals were built in the East, notably two across New Jersey: one, the Morris Canal between Jersey City and Phillipsburg on the Delaware, to bring coal from the anthracite regions of Pennsylvania to New York City; the other, the Delaware and Raritan from Bordentown on the Delaware to New Brunswick on the Raritan, to provide an inland water route from New York to Philadelphia. Of considerable economic importance were also those canals in the Old Northwest designed to establish connections between the Great Lakes and the Ohio and Mississippi Rivers. Of these Ohio built two, the Ohio and Erie from Cleveland to Portsmouth, and the Miami and Erie from Cincinnati to Toledo. Connecting with the last-named canal, Indiana built the Wabash and Erie, which ran southwest across the state to Evansville on the Ohio. Illinois constructed the Illinois and Michigan, which connected Lake Michigan with the Mississippi by an artificial waterway to the head of navigation on the Illinois.

This feverish construction of canals led directly to the panic of 1837 (page 202). Approximately 3000 miles of canals had been built in the two decades preceding 1837, an amount far in excess of the ability of the new regions to support them. Private capital proving inadequate, the states with but few exceptions had pledged their credit, with the result that, when the crash came, several repudiated their debts wholly or in part. This unfortunate experience led most of the states to sell out their internal improvements to private concerns and retire from the transportation business, while the citizens, turning to the opposite extreme, forbade in the new state constitutions the use of government credit for internal improvements. This halt in what might have been a normal development of government-owned transportation came just at a time when a new and

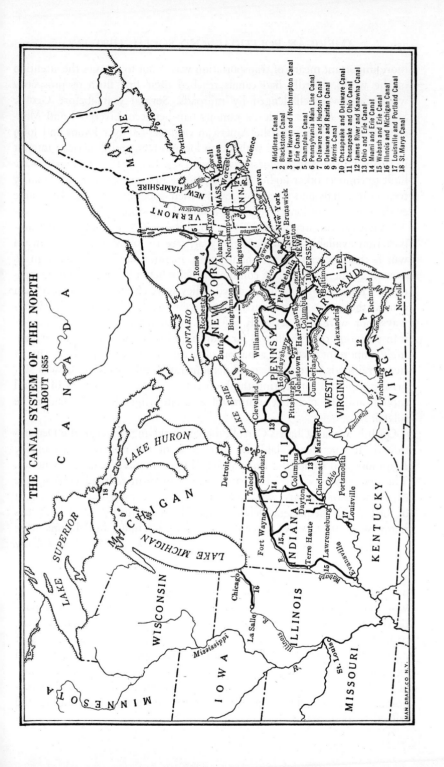

THE CANAL SYSTEM OF THE NORTH
ABOUT 1855

1 Middlesex Canal
2 Blackstone Canal
3 New Haven and Northampton Canal
4 Erie Canal
5 Champlain Canal
6 Pennsylvania Main Line Canal
7 Delaware and Hudson Canal
8 Delaware and Raritan Canal
9 Morris Canal
10 Chesapeake and Delaware Canal
11 Chesapeake and Ohio Canal
12 James River and Kanawha Canal
13 Ohio and Erie Canal
14 Miami and Erie Canal
15 Wabash and Erie Canal
16 Illinois and Michigan Canal
17 Louisville and Portland Canal
18 St. Marys Canal

more important means of transportation was about to capture the attention of the world. Hardly had canals reached their first flush of prosperity when they were challenged by railroads. Several years before George Stephenson's *Rocket* made its famous trip between Liverpool and Manchester, in October, 1829, the American engineers, Oliver Evans and John Stevens, had experimented with steam locomotives, and American interest in steam railroads was widespread after 1830. Just as the first canals were built to connect other bodies of water, so the first railroads were primarily feeders to canals and rivers, but, when their superiority to canals became evident, it was not long before they assumed a position of keen rivalry.

"What the country needed," says one historian, "was a means of transportation available throughout the year, free to follow the paths toward which the interests of merchants most inclined, and cheap enough to encourage the exchange of common articles between points widely separated." This need the railroads filled. They were cheaper to construct than canals; they were not confined to relatively low land, as were the waterways, nor were they seriously affected by changes of season. Moreover, transportation over them was far more rapid than over canals, an exceedingly important factor in a nation of great distances. The superiority of steam railroads over canals once demonstrated, they were built with surprising rapidity, considering the high cost of labor, the scarcity of liquid capital, and the fact that innumerable engineering difficulties had to be solved.

On July 4, 1828, Charles Carroll, the last surviving signer of the Declaration of Independence, laid the first stone of the railroad track of the Baltimore and Ohio, the first railroad in the modern sense in America. The first steam locomotive to run on an American railroad (barring the experiments of Stevens) was an imported 9-horsepower engine on a part of the track of the present Delaware and Hudson. During the early thirties many short stretches of track were laid and famous initial runs were made, including that of the *De Witt Clinton* in 1831 between Albany and Schenectady. Cities like Boston, Baltimore, Charleston, and Savannah, which had lost out in the scramble for western trade during the canal-building era, sought now to recover their positions by western railroads, while New York and Philadelphia endeavored to strengthen their positions in the same way. By 1860 the East had a skeleton railway system, the primary passes of the Alleghenies had been penetrated, 30,000 miles of rails had been laid at an expenditure of $1,250,000,000, and the railroad age had dawned. Like the canals, the railroads had stimulated the flow of goods from east to west and had an important political as well as economic significance in binding the Northwest to the East during the critical years of Southern secession.

Important as were canals and railroads in solving the needs of American transportation, it must be remembered that until after the Civil War rivers continued to provide the main links in the transportation system. Despite the great number and varied type of river craft, the continuance of large-scale river transportation for some time after the coming of railroads was undoubtedly due to the invention of the steamboat, which had preceded by some years that of the steam locomotive. Although a number of engineers in both Europe and America [4] had experimented with the idea of propelling a boat by means of a steam engine, it was left to the American, Robert Fulton, first to demonstrate that steam navigation might be commercially successful, when, in August, 1807, he drove the 160-ton side-wheeler, *Clermont,* from New York to Albany, a distance of 150 miles, in thirty-two hours.

> My steamboat voyage to Albany and back [wrote Fulton] has turned out better than I had calculated. The distance from New York to Albany is one hundred and fifty miles. I ran it up in thirty-two hours, and down in thirty. I had a light breeze against me the whole way, both going and coming; and the voyage has been performed wholly by the power of the steam-engine. I overtook many sloops and schooners beating to windward and parted with them. The power of propelling boats by steam is now fully proved. The morning I left New York there were not perhaps thirty persons in the city who believed that the boat would ever move one mile an hour or be of the least utility; and while we were putting off from the wharf, which was crowded with spectators, I heard a number of sarcastic remarks. This is the way in which ignorant men compliment what they call philosophers and projectors.

Fulton's voyage inaugurated the great age of the river steamboat, and it was not long before little steamboats equipped with wood-burning engines were belching forth smoke on every navigable river and speeding enormously the transportation of passengers and freight, particularly on the voyage upstream. When New York granted a monopoly of steam navigation on her waters to Livingston and Fulton, there was danger that the expansion of steamboat transportation might be delayed, but Marshall's far-seeing decision in Gibbons *v.* Ogden (1824) cleared the way for a normal development (page 176). Although the river steamboat was to be seen in all sections, it was upon the western waters that it achieved its highest development. As early as 1816 Henry M. Shreve, the most famous of the river navigators, throwing precedents aside, built a flat-bottomed side-wheeler with two decks, a design that combined maximum carrying space with minimum water displacement and that was particularly suited to overcome the dangers of navigating the shallow rivers.

[4] Including the Americans, Oliver Evans, John Fitch, James Rumsey, and John Stevens.

In spite of the fact that the widespread development of steamboat navigation came first on American waters, Americans were slow to adopt steam for ocean transportation. During the early decades of the century American shippers had developed a merchant marine that in size and importance was second only to that of Great Britain. There were at least twelve years between 1795 and 1827 when the proportion of imports and exports carried in American vessels was 90 per cent or more of the total trade, while there was scarcely a trading port of any importance where the Stars and Stripes were not to be seen. In addition to the second-largest mechant marine in the world, the United States supported an active fishing industry and at least three fourths of the world's total whaling fleet. This expansion of the merchant marine had been due not alone to the ability of the Yankee seamen and the enterprise of merchant capitalists, but also to the skill of American shipbuilders. Generations of skilled workmen and ingenious designers climaxed their work in the forties and fifties in the famous clipper ships. While Donald McKay and other great designers were turning out the fastest sailing ships that the world has ever seen, the possibilities of steam were neglected.

The utilization of coal in the production of steam and the invention of the screw propeller, both in the thirties, and the gradual substitution of iron for wood in ship construction made ocean steam transportation both practical and inevitable. With iron and coal in close proximity and near the ocean, with skilled mechanics and cheap labor, and with the foresight to comprehend the future, English steamship lines, heavily subsidized by the government, quickly turned to this type of transportation. The decline of the American merchant marine from its once proud position, however, was due not so much to this as to the fact that Americans found greater return for their capital and energy in the opening of the West, the development of inland transportation facilities, and the production of raw materials. A decline already apparent was speeded by the Civil War, which brought losses from Confederate cruisers, a rise in insurance rates, and the rivalry of the rapidly growing manufacturing industry. Within a quarter of a century after the Civil War, the ocean carrying trade, which had been a major American industry for a century and a half, had sunk to a position of relative unimportance. The coasting trade, however, continued to afford a large outlet for maritime enterprise.

FINANCING THE INDUSTRIAL REVOLUTION

Important as were sound and adequate systems of currency and banking in the centuries following the Commercial Revolution, they became even more necessary in the rapidly expanding economic processes of the

Industrial Revolution. Fortunately, at the suggestion of Jefferson, the Congress of the Confederation had adopted the decimal system of coinage, which was continued after the formation of the new government. Following the system generally in vogue in Europe at the time, Congress determined to establish a free and unlimited bimetallic coinage at a ratio of 15:1, the American gold dollar to have 24.75 grains of gold (the value of the Spanish milled dollar) and the silver dollar 15 times that or 371.25 grains of silver. From the start, however, it was found impossible to maintain both metals at a parity. At the ratio 15:1 silver was slightly overvalued, and under the operation of Gresham's law [5] the coinage of gold was discouraged. Special influences at the time caused the silver dollar also to disappear,[6] so that, except for subsidiary coins, American currency was largely limited to banknotes. In the hope of restoring metallic currency, Congress in 1834 changed the ratio to 15.98+ or approximately 16 to 1, at the same time reducing the weight of the gold dollar to 23.22 grains of pure gold. Under the new ratio gold was overvalued and came into circulation again, while silver failed to appear. Fortunately gold discoveries, particularly in California in 1848, provided sufficient metal for monetary needs until the nation suspended specie payment during the Civil War.

The chaotic condition of the currency, contends one economic historian, was "probably the most serious bar to the full development of our manufacturers between the time of Washington and Lincoln."[7] During part of this period, however, it was perhaps inadequacy rather than chaos that was the outstanding feature. Hamilton's first Bank of the United States (page 133) supplied during the two decades 1791–1811 a sound issue of banknotes and, by refusing to accept the notes of state banks unless they were redeemable in specie, exerted a salutary influence upon both currency and banking. The years between 1811, when the charter of the first Bank of the United States ran out, and 1816, when the second Bank of the United States was chartered, were years of chaos in both currency and banking, but after the panic of 1819, when the second Bank of the United States got into satisfactory operation, the situation was fairly satisfactory until that institution was destroyed by Jackson in the middle thirties. As it was tacitly assumed, up to the Civil War, that Congress had no constitutional power to issue federal paper money, and as politics and the western desire for inflation had ended the first and second banks, the currency needs from 1836 to the Civil War were met by federal metallic

[5] When two currencies of the same face value but of different intrinsic value exist, the tendency is for the more valuable to be hoarded and the less valuable to remain in use and determine the value of the circulating medium.

[6] The coinage of the silver dollar was suspended from 1806 to 1836.

[7] Malcolm Keir, *Manufacturing,* 110.

currency and the issues of state banks. The state laws on banking varied greatly and were usually quite inadequate to maintain sound note issues; it was extremely difficult to determine the value of the notes. When every banknote received in trade had to be scrutinized with care and accepted only after its value had been determined by consultation with books on the subject, it requires no imagination to picture the difficulties under which business was conducted.[8]

Although American panics have been chiefly due to overexpansion in transportation facilities and overspeculation in public lands, other factors, particularly the situation in currency and banking, have contributed. The panic of 1819 came in part because of a too rapid commercial expansion and a too rapid manufacturing development during the war years and thereafter, but the mismanagement of the second Bank of the United States during its early years contributed. It was not alone the building of canals and western land speculation that were responsible for the panic of 1837, but also the destruction of the second Bank of the United States, the rapid expansion of state banks and banknote issues, and Jackson's ill-timed effort to stop land speculation by his specie circular of 1836, which directed that payments for public lands be in specie. In one sentence the historian James Schouler has vividly described certain causes of the panic of 1857: "Premature railroads of the West had fostered premature cities, teeming with a premature traffic for a premature population; and while canals and railroads had conspired to reduce the mileage rate of transportation, the dispersion of American farmers over a vastly wider area counterbalanced that advantage." But along with these causes were the great increase in the amount of currency and the rise in prices due to the gold discovery of 1848, which fostered the boom.

Capital for the financing of the American Industrial Revolution came in part from local accumulations and in part from Europe. The disruption of commerce during the embargo and the War of 1812 led many merchants and shipowners, like Francis Cabot Lowell, to shift their capital from commerce to manufacturing. The decline of commerce in Salem led to a shift of capital to textiles and in Providence to textiles and metals, while the decline of whaling in New Bedford led to a similar shift to textile-manufacturing. As the Industrial Revolution developed, groups of capitalists appeared in the larger centers who were responsible for establishing little factories in country districts where water power existed, and these factories often resulted in the growth of large manufacturing

---

8 "It was estimated," said A. Barton Hepburn in speaking of the early years of the Civil War, "that there were 7,000 kinds and denominations of notes and fully 4,000 spurious or altered varieties were reported." *History of Coinage and Currency in the United States*, 177. This estimate is more likely too low than too high.

cities. Probably the majority of industrial establishments, however, originated from small shops or mills whose owners reinvested the profits until good-sized factories developed. More than in manufacturing, capital for transportation was obtained from abroad. Europeans invested heavily in canals, particularly in the canal bonds sponsored by the credit of the states. Speedily forgetting their misfortunes after the panic of 1837, Europeans again participated in the building of railroads. The latter were also helped in some cases by state credit, and by counties and towns competing with other counties and towns for railroad facilities. Like the farmers and merchants along the proposed routes, who also subscribed, the towns looked forward to increased prosperity from the coming of railroads rather than to profits from ownership of stocks or bonds.

That the coming of the Industrial Revolution was stimulated by the artificial conditions produced by the embargo and the War of 1812 there can be no doubt. It is more difficult to speak with accuracy concerning the American tariff system. The first tariff (1789), although it had recognized the principle of protection, was primarily for revenue, and this continued to be the case until 1816. Hamilton in his *Report on Manufactures,* submitted in 1791, had given classic expression to the doctrine of protection, but Hamilton's effort to establish in America the system of mercantilism aroused little interest among a commercial and agricultural people. The Industrial Revolution, as a consequence, received its early encouragement from other sources. The development of textiles during the war years, however, brought a demand for protection, and the ardent young nationalists who had advocated the war now acquiesced in the demand. The tariff of 1816, which is often said to mark the beginning of the protective system in this country, was primarily a revenue tariff, but it was protective in that it placed higher duties on cottons, woolens, iron goods, and other commodities that had been stimulated during the war.

The period from 1816 to 1828 marks, certainly, the first important protective movement in this country. The textile-manufacturers of New England, the iron-workers of Pennsylvania, and the industrialists generally wanted protection against the flood of European goods that poured in after the war, and their agitation was now reinforced by large elements of the agricultural population. Owing to poor harvests in Europe, the exportation of agricultural products had held up until the panic of 1819, but European recovery, corn laws, and other factors thereafter so cut down agricultural exports that the farmers felt the necessity of new markets. Many hoped to find these new markets in an urban manufacturing population built up by a protective tariff. The leader of this group was Henry Clay of Kentucky, who advocated what he termed the "American system," a policy that included not only the creation of home markets by means of a protective tariff but also the enthusiastic development of roads and canals ("internal improvements") to facilitate the exchange of manufactured for agricultural goods in the domestic market. A tariff bill calling for a general increase in rates failed of passage in 1820 by one vote; the first important legislative fruit of the "American system" was the tariff of 1824. This bill not only took care of the cotton, woolen, iron, and other manufacturers but also granted protection to producers of such raw materials as hemp and wool, thus enlisting some agricultural support. The regional divisions on the tariff of 1824 are interesting. The South, which in the postwar enthusiasm had supported the bill of 1816, now turned against protection, a position that she has more or less consistently held to the present day. New England was divided, the manufacturers favoring and the shipping interests opposing, while the middle and western states of those days—New York, New Jersey, Pennsylvania, Ohio, and Kentucky—were strongly in favor.

The high-water mark of the early protective movement, as we have intimated (page 188), was reached in the tariff of 1828, a bill preceded by a manufacturers' convention at Harrisburg and much agitation on the part of the woolen-manufacturers. Although a considerable amount of sentiment for a higher tariff had been aroused by this time, it is difficult to determine either its extent or its trend, for the tariff of 1828 was so preeminently a "political" measure that the whole question was clouded. Opposition to it was strong, and in 1832 most of the worst features were removed and the rates practically restored to the level of 1824. The South, however, now decidedly antiprotectionist, was thoroughly aroused, and South Carolina, as we have seen, passed a nullification ordinance declaring the tariff law of 1828 and the amendment thereto of 1832 to be null and void. Tariff duties had been a chief cause of the war of independence, and now they threatened to dissolve the young republic in revolution, but Jackson's uncompromising stand for national unity and the willingness of Congress to compromise delayed the revolt for another thirty years.

The compromise tariff of 1833 called for a reduction of all duties exceeding 20 per cent in the tariff of 1832, the reduction to be gradual until 1842, when a uniform rate of 20 per cent was to be established. Like the bill of 1828, it was essentially a political measure; its purpose was to mollify the South rather than to establish scientific rates. In this it was successful, but the tariff of 1833 is significant also in that it inaugurated a period of low tariffs. Although the protective feature was never lost sight of, the trend, with the exception of a higher tariff from 1842 to 1846, was downward. There was little interest in the tariff in 1842 or demand for change on the part of the general public, and Calhoun was not far wrong when he asserted that the act of that year was passed not at the demand of the manufacturers but rather because the politicians wanted an issue. The act of 1846 (Walker tariff), which lasted until 1857, brought radical reductions; at the same time it inaugurated *ad valorem* duties on a wide scale and introduced the warehousing system of storing goods until the duty was paid, an innovation permanently retained. An overflowing treasury was the cause of the next tariff (1857), which further lowered the duties, and, for a few years, says Taussig, "there is as near an approach to free trade as the country has had since 1816."

Whatever the currency system and the federal legislation regarding the tariff, the Industrial Revolution was financed in the first instance by the capital and savings of individual investors and entrepreneurs. Most of the early factories were owned by individuals, partnerships, or small groups of stockholders. Eventually the advantages of the corporate form of organization, particularly in raising funds, led many of the mills to apply for state charters. In this they were simply following the course already adopted by banks and transportation companies. Either because of the amount of capital involved or because the state itself was unwilling to enter these fields, charters conferring certain privileges upon groups of private individuals had been granted. Similar charters were now freely given to manufacturing establishments. The usual dangers that come from absentee ownership and the concentration of wealth and power in the hands of a few individuals were already apparent before the Civil War, and the growth of corporations was met by widespread protest and was challenged in the platforms of labor parties. Their development, however, undoubtedly facilitated and speeded the Industrial Revolution.

THE HUMAN ELEMENT

Three groups stand out in the development of the Industrial Revolution in America—the entrepreneurs, the inventors, and the workmen. America in the first half of the nineteenth century was particularly prolific of able and successful business men. The most famous, perhaps, were Francis Cabot Lowell, Patrick Tracy Jackson, Nathan Appleton, Abbott Lawrence, and their satellites of Boston, who developed Waltham, Lowell, Lawrence, and other towns; but there were many others, including Edmund Dwight, who played a similar role in Chicopee and Holyoke, and William Gregg of Graniteville, South Carolina. Other industrial centers besides Boston produced enterprising capitalists influential in their sections, such as the Browns of Providence and the Phelps family of New York, and there was hardly a manufacturing town that did not have its local families who, often without the aid of outside capital, developed important industries.

The American entrepreneur did not appear from the void; behind him was a century or more of land speculation and maritime shipping, enterprises in which the risks were great and profits often long delayed. Hand in hand with the entrepreneur was the inventor, behind whose resourcefulness and fertility were often to be found generations of hard-working and practical Yankee farmers. Men like Eli Whitney, Elias Howe, John Stevens, Robert Fulton, Paul Moody, and Charles Goodyear were but the most famous of this remarkable group that made possible industrial development. There was not an industry that did not have its inventors who originated new devices or improved on English models. In the days of small-scale industry many of these inventors themselves became also entrepreneurs and capitalists.

Although unskilled laborers existed in America from the earliest settlements, their number was relatively small because of the ease of attaining independence through landownership. Unlike that in Europe, where the differentiation of class was already sharply marked, the Industrial Revolution in America accentuated class differences and created a large laboring class. As in Europe, the factory system in America quickly separated thousands from the land and created a landless proletariat. Fortunately, the immediate effects of the factory system upon labor in America were not so deplorable as in Europe. Cotton-weaving did not exist here as a separate industry, while the spinning and weaving of woolens were carried on by women in the household as part of their general work. No large class of male textile workers was thrown out of work by the Industrial Revolution, but, on the contrary, a new opportunity of employment was offered to the farm girls and young men. Factory work, as a consequence, was not looked upon as a last resort, but rather as an opportunity. As the employer had to search the countryside for labor to man his mills, wages were higher than in Europe and working conditions were far better.

Knowing but too well the horrible conditions that attended the coming of the Industrial Revolution in England, European observers were amazed at the high type of girls found in the American mill and the general comfort of their life. To Anthony Trollope the young city of Lowell was a "commercial utopia," where the operatives were "taken in, as it were, to a philanthropic manufacturing college, and then looked after and regulated more as girls and lads at a great seminary, than as hands by whose industry profit is made out of capital." Dickens spoke of the green plants in the factory windows "trained to shade the glass," of how the factories contained "as much fresh air, cleanliness, and comfort as the nature of the occupation would possibly admit of," and how he could not "recall or separate one young face that gave me a painful impression." In quite as glowing terms the brilliant English woman, Harriet

THE MISSISSIPPI—LOW WATER

THE MISSISSIPPI—HIGH WATER

(Currier and Ives)

IMPROVEMENTS IN TRAVEL AND TRANSPORTATION ILLUSTRATED.

EVOLUTION OF TRANSPORTATION

Martineau, who visited Waltham in 1835, commented on the houses of the factory workers, "some with piazzas, and green venetian blinds; and all neat and sufficiently spacious." She wrote too of the library and of the lyceum with its lectures, "the best that money can procure."

This idyllic picture by English travelers quickly fades when subjected to close scrutiny. Child labor was widely prevalent and existed from Slater's first mill of 1791 (run by nine little children) throughout the whole history of the textile industry. This was particularly true in southern New England, where the entire family was accustomed to work in the mills. In New England, in the twenties, about half of the cotton-mill workers were children, and a labor paper, speaking of conditions around Philadelphia in the thirties, asserted that it was a "well known fact" that the principal part of the help of cotton mills were children "confined to steady employment during the longest days of the year from daylight until dark." The ordinary work day, in fact, ran from sun to sun, varying during most of the year from twelve to fifteen hours. Besides child labor and long hours, there were the old-fashioned mills with their small windows, bad air, and lack of sanitary appliances, while outside working hours labor was often subjected to a paternalism that today would be considered intolerable.

The Industrial Revolution not only created an industrial proletariat but, by drawing the workers together around the new factories, made possible the organization of labor. Only 3.3 per cent of the people in 1790 lived in cities of 8000 or over; in 1860 the percentage had risen to 16.1. While urbanization provided conditions favorable to unionization, other strong influences tended to delay it: (1) the existence of unoccupied western land to which factory workers could escape, (2) the optimism resulting from the unbounded opportunities of a new country, and (3) the fact that wages, measured by the standards of the time, were not intolerable. Nevertheless, local craft unions are to be found as early as the 1790s, and the history of labor organization can be traced from that time on. Particularly in the decade preceding the panic of 1837 can union activity be discerned in the organization of city trades associations and in several national unions. This early period of union prosperity was halted by the panic and its energy drawn off in various humanitarian movements that delayed the growth of strict unionism. Whatever may have been the condition of the girl operatives in the early years of the Industrial Revolution, the situation had changed by the forties. Overproduction of commodities, competition from immigration and overcrowding in the cities had reduced the standard of living so that the economic condition of the wage-earning class in America had never been worse. The terrible conditions of the forties made the need of unionization evident, while the improved economic situation in the fifties made it possible. In that decade labor had a new awakening, and by 1860 more than twenty trades had national organizations.

THE SIGNIFICANCE OF THE INDUSTRIAL REVOLUTION

Although the development of the factory system was rapid from the start, it was not until the later years of the nineteenth century that the United States became primarily an industrial nation and not until the twentieth that the full effects of the Industrial Revolution were felt. If the student compares the economic life of today with that of his great-grandfather, the effect of the Industrial Revolution will be apparent. It is the difference between the tallow candle and the electric light, between the hand scythe and the reaper, between the old-fashioned spinning wheel and the whirring shuttles of a great factory, between the lumbering stage-coach and the fast-moving airplane. In a period of only a century, it is the difference between an ancient and a modern civilization. The primary effect of the Industrial Revolution was to shift the production of goods from the hand to the machine and from the home to the factory; all else flows from this change. Machine-made goods can be produced more quickly than handmade and much more cheaply. The old craftsman might turn out a few pairs of shoes a day; the modern factory worker can produce five hundred pairs. When the construction of Cologne Cathedral was resumed in 1870, two men with a crane lifted as much stone as 360 men by hand during the Middle Ages. The greatly enhanced productiveness of the average worker meant, of course, that he could produce wealth more rapidly than before and make it possible for more people to live. The population of Great Britain increased from approximately 16,000,000 in 1800 to 49,000,000 in 1930, that of Germany from 23,000,000 in 1800 to 67,790,000 in 1914, and that of the United States from 4,000,000 in 1790 to 123,000,000 in 1930. This growth in population and in production of wealth was speeded, of course, by the cumulative effect of the Industrial Revolution. Only 276 patents were issued by the United States government in the decade 1790–1800, and in 1833 the head of the Patent Office, believing that the height of invention had been reached and passed, asked that his resignation be accepted; today approximately 2,000,000 patents have been issued, with the greatest total for one year exceeding 55,000.

Besides making possible a livelihood for additional millions, the chief effect of the Industrial Revolution upon population was to draw workers close to the factories and produce an urban civilization. The number of towns of 8000 or over in the United States increased from six in 1790 to 1208 in 1930. Quite as important was the effect of the new machinery upon the distribution of wealth. While the mill girl might produce wealth five hundred times more rapidly than her mother sitting before the spinning wheel, the wealth went not to the girl but to the owner of the machinery. The worker was now a mere wage-earner employed to create wealth for the owner of the machine—capital to build more machines for use in production and distribution. Without doubt the machinery created by the Industrial Revolution solved the problem of the production and distribution of commodities, but it did not solve the problem of markets or the distribution of wealth. When the home market for commodities was glutted, manufacturers sought markets abroad, and when the home market for capital was oversupplied, capitalists lent abroad. One result of capital export was to duplicate abroad the productive machinery of home and thus reduce the market for commodities made at home. As foreign markets for capital and commodities became more constricted, competition became keener, economic imperialism more dangerous, and the possibility of imperialist wars ever greater.

The ability to produce and distribute in unlimited amounts, in combination with the fact that business was conducted for profit, led producers periodically to manufacture more than the purchasing power of the market could absorb and to bring the disastrous panics and depressions under which the world has struggled since the coming of the Industrial Revolution. The number and intensity of the panics were, of course, increased by the unequal distribution of wealth, which kept the masses from consuming goods that they normally needed. That the Industrial Revolution has undoubtedly raised the general standard of living and made it possible for mankind to enjoy the use of more commodities, there can be no doubt, but it has also produced economic and social problems of extreme difficulty.

C. and M. Beard, *The Rise of American Civilization,* Chap. XIV, is an excellent introduction to be followed by H. U. Faulkner, *American Economic History,* Chaps. XIII, XIV, XV, or Edward Kirkland, *A History of American Economic Life,* Chaps. VIII, IX. The early days of the steamboat are recounted in A. B. Hulbert, *The Paths of Inland Commerce* (Chronicles of America); the condition of labor as affected by the Industrial Revolution in N. J. Ware, *The Industrial Worker, 1840–1860,* Chaps. IV–X; financing in D. R. Dewey, *Financial History of the United States,* Chaps. III–XI, and F. W. Taussig, *A Tariff History of the United States,* Part I. On industry read L. C. Hunter, "Heavy Industries Before 1860," and Constance M. Green, "Light Manufactures and the Beginnings of Precision Manufacture Before 1861," Chaps. XI and XII in H. F. Williamson, ed., *The Growth of the American Economy.* Also consult G. S. Callender, *Selections from the Economic History of the United States,* Chaps. VII–XI, 727–735.

Chapter XVI

THE MARCH OF THE HUMAN MIND

We are all a little wild here with numberless projects of social reform, not a reading man but has a draft of a new community in his waistcoat pocket.

EMERSON TO CARLYLE

THE HUMANITARIAN REVOLT

The Industrial Revolution brought epochal transformations in the economic processes and changed tremendously the material surroundings in which men lived. It speeded the conquest of a continent and the development of the unsurpassed resources of America. Men turned with new interest to the exploitation of unbounded wealth and with an enthusiasm that made many superficial observers believe that the outstanding char- acteristic of American life was the pursuit of the dollar. Yet the very years that saw the introduction of the factory system and the application of steam to transportation saw also an extraordinary spiritual and intellectual awakening. Men in all walks of life and of all degrees of education searched their hearts for the meaning of the new day that seemed to be dawning and turned with tremendous enthusiasm to the development of a better civilization. Literature and science felt the force of the great awakening, while many optimistically embarked on experiments in de- mocracy, education, religion, humanitarianism, and socialism. All sorts of extravagant fads and "crack-brained" schemes were born, found fol- lowers, and flourished for a brief period. In most cases they aimed in the right direction; in few instances did they do real harm. Much worth- while enthusiasm was, of course, spent upon schemes of doubtful value, but the reforming spirit of the period effected a change almost as re- markable, if not as spectacular, as the Industrial Revolution.

The humanitarian revolt against the callousness and cruelty of eight- eenth-century civilization was delayed by the dominance of the *laissez- faire* philosophy, and in America by the optimism engendered by the abundance of raw materials and the opportunities for material advance- ment. Many aspects of American life, however, called so loudly for reform that they could no longer be ignored. In spite of the much-heralded opportunities of America, destitution and pauperism were widespread in the eastern cities in the years after the War of 1812. When, in New York City, for example, the Society for the Prevention of Pauperism was organized in 1817 and proceeded to survey the situation, it found 15,000 of the population of the city living on charity and concluded that the outstanding causes were drink, the economic depression, lotteries, pawnbrokers, and charitable institutions, but seven eighths was ascribed to intemperance. The society drew up a comprehensive program of reform, which supplied a goal for later humanitarians. In 1821 Josiah Quincy submitted a *Report on the Pauper Laws of Massachusetts,* suggesting many reforms, and in 1835, under the influence of Joseph Tuckerman, the Society for the Prevention of Pauperism of Boston was established. Almshouses had long been established in the cities, and a well-established system of county almshouses existed in the older states. It is evident that by the decade of the forties government and private charity had developed to a considerable extent, and on the part of the latter there was already evident an appreciation of the necessity of applying scientific principles to the distribution of aid and of centralizing agencies.

The humanitarian impulse was also making itself felt with regard to punishments and the criminal code. Gradually imprisonment and fines were substituted for branding, whipping, mutilation, sitting in the stocks, and other forms of colonial punishment. In the forties a considerable movement against capital punishment arose, and, before it had subsided, most of the states had limited the crimes punishable by death to murder, treason, arson, and rape, and in the succeeding years this list was generally reduced to murder and treason. Several of the states went so far as entirely to abolish capital punishment.[1] Along with this curtailment went the elimination of public executions. It had been maintained that public executions acted as a deterrent to crime, but instead they were often an excuse for a noisy holiday for a whole countryside. Beginning with New Jersey and New York in 1835, one state after another put an end to these brutalizing spectacles.

No laws cried louder for reformation than those governing imprisonment for debt. At the opening of the century in most of the states a person could be thrown into the most filthy and abominable prison for the most trivial debt; there he was obliged to stay until his debt was paid, and there he subsisted, if he lived at all, on charity. The sheriff of New York certified in 1816 that of the 1984 debtors confined in that city, 1129 were imprisoned for debts of less than $25 and that every one of them would have starved but for the kindness of the Humane Society. Protests against these condi-

[1] Maine in 1837, Michigan in 1847, Rhode Island in 1852, and Wisconsin in 1853.

tions arose early in the century; by 1830 many states had passed laws to restrict imprisonment for debt, and the new state constitutions of the West sought to curtail it. In the thirties the outcry against this barbarous system blazed forth anew. Beginning with Kentucky in 1821 and New York in 1831, the movement swept through the country until by the Civil War the whole system of imprisonment for debt had gone by the board.

With the reformation in the criminal codes and the abolition of imprisonment for debt came a much needed improvement in the prison system. Until the nineteenth century prisons had been looked upon simply as places of detention for those owing money and for criminals awaiting trial; they were not considered primarily as means of punishment or as instruments of reformation. Partly as a consequence of this the condition of the prisons was pitifully neglected. The city prisons were dirty, disease-ridden, overcrowded, and without the slightest comfort—sometimes with not even straw to sleep on. Ordinarily the men and women prisoners were separated, and in some jails an effort was made to separate the insane, the criminal, and the debtor, but usually classification by sex was all that was attempted. Into these pest holes the minor debtor, the juvenile delinquent, the insane, and the hardened criminal were indiscriminately thrown, and there, not infrequently, the filthy, half-starved wretches were robbed and beaten by cruel keepers.

To a few, at least, of our ancestors this system seemed unwise and unjust; unwise in that it promoted rather than decreased crime; unjust, in that it treated all classes of defectives and delinquents in the same manner. For years criminologists like the great Italian, Beccaria, and humanitarians like the Englishman, John Howard, had been questioning the existing system. In America the lead for reform was taken by the Pennsylvania Quakers, who by 1784 had succeeded in abolishing capital punishment for all crimes but murder in the first degree and in establishing a state prison in which the "more hardened and atrocious" offenders should be confined in solitary cells. The old Walnut Street jail in Philadelphia was soon overcrowded, and in 1818 and 1821 respectively the western and eastern state penitentiaries were built. In these penitentiaries in 1829 there was established the "Pennsylvania system" of solitary confinement at hard labor. The prisoners, it was believed, might be reformed by the contemplation of their evil deeds that would be promoted by absolute solitude. As the cells were lighted, heated, and drained, the Pennsylvania system provided greater bodily comfort than the old prisons, but the mental cruelty inflicted by solitary confinement was greater than before. Simultaneously (1821) New York state commenced an experiment at Auburn, where the prisoners were confined in solitude at night, but, instead of working in solitude in their cells during the day, labored in gangs in absolute silence.

The Auburn system of gang work by day was necessarily accompanied by the strictest discipline, enforced by corporal punishment for the slightest offense. A specially constructed prison of five tiers of open cells, easily supervised by the guards, made escape virtually impossible, while the prisoners, terrorized into submission, lock-stepped to meals and to work under the guns of their keepers. For years prison societies and prison reformers argued pro and con the merits of the two systems. In the end both were found to be inhuman, and the austerity of both was relaxed. More visitors, books, and recreation were allowed, and the silence imposed by the two systems was lifted. Though both the Pennsylvania and the Auburn systems left much to be desired, they were better than the old congregate method of housing, and they served as the basis for later development in prison administration.

While these efforts at improving the prison systems were under way, a beginning was also made in the establishment of reformatories for juvenile delinquents. Likewise were to be seen the beginnings of some efforts toward crime prevention, particularly in the case of orphan children. The most famous example was Girard College, founded in Philadelphia in 1848 through the generosity of the banker, Stephen Girard, who some years before left a large part of a great fortune to educate and care for as many poor white male orphans as the income from the endowment would support.

While certain reformers were concerned with the problem of the handling of delinquents or of preventing delinquency, others were turning their attention to various groups of defectives. The condition of no class of unfortunates was more pitiful than that of the insane. In the colonial period they were cared for in private houses, and, if they became violent, were chained in an outhouse or cellar. With the rise of the almshouse the insane were sometimes cared for there, but the usual procedure was to turn them over to the prisons for safekeeping. There they were thrown into the cellar or kept in separate cells, where they existed in unbelievable misery. The Boston Discipline Society, after an investigation in 1827, reported finding one lunatic who had existed for nine years in a den that had nothing in it but a "heap of filthy straw" and who was clothed only in a "wreath of rags." The faint beginning of reform in the handling of the insane is to be discerned among the Philadelphia Quakers in the eighteenth century, and during the early decades of the next century some improvement is to be seen in eastern cities. The greatest advance, however, came in the forties, and then primarily through the ceaseless efforts of Dorothea Lynde Dix, who presented the plight of the insane to one state legislature after another, securing from many of them funds for state asylums. She even prevailed upon Congress to grant 10,000,000 acres for the indigent insane, only to lose it by the veto of President Pierce. As a result of her work and that of others, the insane were taken from the prisons and put into asylums, and the belief spread that many could be cured and taught a useful trade. Considering the recent emancipation from utter barbarity as respects the treatment of the insane and the ignorance of the medical profession regarding lunacy, these early insane asylums were often conducted with humanity and intelligence. In the state asylum at South Boston in 1842, if we are to believe Charles Dickens's account of it, there existed conditions that for the time must have been ideal.

One of the great reformers of this period was Dr. Samuel G. Howe of Boston, and of his many reforming interests none was more productive of good than his work for the blind. In 1832 he succeeded in establishing a school in Boston to which Colonel Thomas H. Perkins, a Boston merchant, donated his Pearl Street mansion on condition that the public raise $50,000, and the school developed into the famous Perkins Institution for the Blind. Here Dr. Howe experimented with musical instruments and with raised alphabets and other paraphernalia for instructing the blind, and here he educated Laura Bridgman, one of the most interesting and brilliant students to be trained in such an institution. Similar schools were soon established in New York and Philadelphia, and by 1864 there were no less than twenty-four such institutions for the blind. Even before Howe had commenced his work for the blind, the Reverend Thomas H. Gallaudet, with the aid of private subscription and state and congressional donations, had established his famous New England Asylum for the Deaf and Dumb at Hartford (1817), the forerunner of similar institutions that were to appear in other parts of the country.

Humanitarian interest in the defective and delinquent brought a realization of the influence of strong drink in promoting poverty and crime, and led to an important movement for temperance and prohibition. As in the colonial period, the universal consumption of alcohol was characteristic of the early nineteenth century. Every gathering for business or pleasure provided an excuse for drinking, and the habit was indulged in by those of both sexes and all ages. "No keel of a vessel could be laid," said a contemporary temperance pamphlet, "no frame of a house or barn reared, in any of the Atlantic States; no log house be put together west of the mountains, without the presence of several gallons of New England Rum, Jamaica Spirits, or Western Whiskey. . . . If young people met to dance; if grave men to be assessors, or jurors, or arbitrators; if a bench of judges to hold a court; if laborers to work on the highways; if Congregational divines and deacons to sit in Council; . . . if legislators to enact laws for the Commonwealth or Nation; all, all thought it important to have strong drink for refreshment." [2] There had been some agitation for temperance since the latter years of the eighteenth century, but until the decade of the twenties it had been without organization. In 1826 there was formed in Boston the American Society for the Promotion of Temperance. Hundreds of similar organizations now sprang up, particularly in New England and New York, and in 1833, at the call of the American Society, a great temperance convention was held in Philadelphia, where the United States Temperance Union was formed.[3] In succeeding years other organizations of a fraternal nature, such as the Independent Order of Rechabites (1841), the Order of the Sons of Temperance (1842), and the Order of Good Templars (1851), which boasted of hundreds of thousands of members, spread throughout the country. Reformed drunkards, led by John B. Gough, began to agitate with evangelistic fervor (in the "Washingtonian movement"), and a temperance literature rapidly appeared. Of this Timothy S. Arthur's *Ten Nights in a Bar-Room* (1854) was the most famous work. Dramatized immediately, it had an influence hardly less than that exerted later by *Uncle Tom's Cabin*. So powerful had the temperance movement become that when the famous British temperance agitator, Father Theobald Mathew, visited America in 1849, he was banqueted by President Taylor and honored with an invitation to visit the Senate chamber—an honor previously shown to but one foreigner, General Lafayette.

The strength of this early movement was so great that the agitation for temperance soon extended to prohibition and resulted in legislation. Neal Dow, a political leader in Maine, influenced the legislature of that state to pass in 1851 the first liquor-prohibition law in our history, a law that, except for two years (1856–1858), remained on the statute books until changed in 1933. A wave of legislation followed. Taking the Maine law as their model, thirteen states, all north of Mason and Dixon's line, attempted to restrict in some degree the sale of spirituous liquors. The movement, however, had been more rapid and the legislation more far-reaching than the preparation of the people. Everywhere popular opposition, just as during the period of the eighteenth amendment, made enforcement a difficult and hazardous matter. Except in Maine, New Hampshire, and Vermont, early temperance by legislation collapsed. Although the early prohibition movement subsided in the fifties and was almost obliterated by the Civil War, it arose in new strength toward the end of the century to achieve even greater victories.

[2] P. S. White and E. S. Ely, *Vindication of the Order of the Sons of Temperance*, 9.
[3] Called the American Temperance Union three years later, after the inclusion of Canada.

EXPERIMENTS IN LIVING

While reformers of all kinds were attacking innumerable aspects of American civilization and offering their favorite remedies to promote the happiness of mankind, others insisted that only through a fundamental reorganization of society on a basis of co-operative living could much of value be accomplished. So many of these projects were started that the United States, although probably the most individualistic nation in the world, has seen more experiments in communistic living than any other country. America, it appears, was the land of opportunity not only for the individualist but also for the collectivist, and the reasons are not hard to find—the existence of cheap and easily acquired land, somewhat removed from the corrupting influence of individualistic society, and the political and religious liberty existing in America, which made such experiments possible.

Of the various experiments in communistic living, those of the religious societies were the most successful. In America they date back to the short-lived German Pietist establishment of 1694 near Philadelphia and are seen in the Dunker community at Ephrata, Pennsylvania, founded in 1732, among the Moravians of Bethlehem and other Pennsylvania towns founded a decade later, among the Shakers, who established under Ann Lee their first community in 1776, among the Rappites in Pennsylvania and Indiana, among the German Separatists at Zoar, Ohio (1817), and among the Amana Society in Iowa, which came to America in the forties and whose communities were not disbanded until 1931. All these communities except those of the Shakers, whose first community was composed of English immigrants, were founded by German religious sects, and they had, of course, the cohesive force of a common religious purpose. The only sectarian community of purely American origin was that at Oneida, New York, organized by John Humphrey Noyes, a native of Vermont, a Dartmouth graduate, and a student of theology at Yale and Andover. Evolving a set of religious teachings, known as Perfectionism, Noyes gathered round him his relatives and friends and founded the Oneida Community. Economic success at Oneida came only after years of bitter struggle, but dearly won experience and superior products enabled them in the end to prosper. Dissolution came in 1880 and was caused not by internal friction or economic failure, but by outside agitation against their system of "complex marriage." In that year communism was given up and the resources of the members thrown into a joint-stock company, which continues to do a large business.

Less successful than the religious communities were those carried out under secular auspices. There were at least three waves of communistic activity during this period: the first, 1825–1830, which derived its inspiration from the idealism and energy of Robert Owen; the second, 1840–1850, founded on the teachings of Charles Fourier; and the third at the end of the decade of the forties and in the early fifties, which sought to found communities after the manner of another Frenchman, Étienne Cabet. Convinced from his own experiments, carried on in his mill town of New Lanark, Scotland, of the fundamental influence of environment upon human character, Robert Owen came to America in 1824, purchased the Rappite village of New Harmony, Indiana, with its 30,000 acres of land, and invited "the industrious and well disposed of all nations" to join him. Owen's success at New Lanark had made him a world figure, and his extensive lecture tour in America had thoroughly advertised his views. As a consequence, eight hundred responded to his call within six weeks, and, as the apparatus for living already existed, the community was quickly established. No test of qualification or motives had been set up, and the members of the community were a variegated lot; at one extreme were leading American philanthropists and scientists, and at the other were adventurers and idlers. Owen called his village New Harmony, but the name was anything but appropriate. No less than seven forms of government and constitutions were attempted during the two years of its existence. As long as Owen could give the project his full attention, and as long as his money held out, there was a chance for success, but in the end there was not sufficient binding force to hold the heterogeneous crowd together. The New Harmony experiment, nevertheless, excited great interest, and at least eleven other communities came into existence at that time.

The interest in Owenistic communism had barely subsided when a new wave of interest was aroused by Horace Greeley's and Albert Brisbane's explanations in the New York *Tribune* of the scheme for co-operative organization advanced by the Frenchman, Charles Fourier. Unlike Owen, who stressed the overwhelming importance of environment to the character of mankind, Fourier emphasized the economy and efficiency that would result if mankind could be organized into groups of from 300 to 1800 people (phalanxes), who would live in a large central building (phalanstery) that would contain also the workshop and granaries. The central building would be surrounded by a farm, and it was expected that an economic unit largely self-sufficing would be established and that each inhabitant would engage in the type of work that he enjoyed most. Fourier believed that a common workshop, granary, and dining hall, with one large farm efficiently managed, would be more economical than scores of little duplications and would result in greater happiness and prosperity.

Over thirty of these phalanxes were established in the various states, the most famous being that at Brook Farm near Boston. Originating among the members of the Transcendental Club of Boston, it included among its members George Ripley, Nathaniel Hawthorne, Charles A. Dana, and other well-known leaders of the New England intellectuals. It began as the Brook Farm Institute for Agriculture and Education, one of its purposes being "to substitute a system of brotherly co-operation for one of selfish competition." Part of the day was spent in labor and part in social and intellectual recreation. Although farming was done, the institute chiefly supported itself by the excellent school that it maintained. Declaring itself a phalanx in 1844, it became the center of Fourieristic propaganda. Destruction by fire of their phalanstery in 1846, just as it was being completed, lack of capital and business acumen, outside opposition, and the decline of the general movement spelled the end of Brook Farm in 1847.

The last wave of interest in communal life emanated from Étienne Cabet, one of the leading rebels of the revolution of 1830, who in 1839 published a novel, *A Voyage to Icaria,* in which he described a communistic utopia. His book, riding the wave of discontent swelling in France between the revolutions of 1830 and 1848, met with immense popularity, and Cabet spent the rest of his life in endeavoring to establish "Icarian communities." Purchasing a million acres in Texas from a group of dishonest land speculators, Cabet himself led a group of several hundred Icarians to America in 1848. The first settlement did not prosper, and in the next year they moved to the deserted Mormon village at Nauvoo, Illinois. Internal dissensions brought secessions and the founding of other communities in Missouri, California, and Iowa, the last of which continued until 1895.

"Basing our estimates on the fragmentary accounts . . . ," says Morris Hillquit, "we may safely assume that several hundred communities existed in different parts of the United States during the last century, and that the number of persons who at one time or another participated in the experiments ran into the hundred thousands." [4] In the end practically all failed. Their failure, however, was not caused by the stock reasons advanced by opponents of socialism. Communal life did not stifle industry or initiative. As a rule, the members of the communities were more industrious than their neighbors, and quite as resourceful in manufacturing and agriculture. Their schools were usually superior to the average, their morality almost invariably better, and general contentment and happiness as evident. While various factors contributed to the failure of the separate communities, the underlying cause was the inability long to maintain patches of communism in a strongly individualistic society, especially in

---

[4] Morris Hillquit, *Socialism in the United States,* 23.

a new country richly endowed with natural wealth and offering the widest temptations and allurements to the ambitious and talented. The sectarian societies lasted longest, not alone because they had the cohesive force of religion, but also because they were composed of simple, hardworking German peasants, who were content with the comparative opulence of their communities and did not long to build fortunes. Modern socialists have forsaken the idea of changing society by erecting individual utopias, but the story of these early attempts throws valuable light upon man as a co-operative individual.

EDUCATION FOR THE MASSES

Of the various reforms agitated during these years, the one that eventually captured most completely the American mind was universal public education. Many decades were to elapse before the ideal was realized, but by 1860 the principle of a free, tax-supported public-school system covering all stages of education from elementary to collegiate had been generally accepted. Many important influences were at work to promote public education: the development of urban life, which necessitated a new system; the increase of crime and pauperism in the rapidly growing cities, which, it was believed, might be prevented by education; the extension of the franchise, which gave the voters an opportunity of achieving their demands; the possibility in the new states of endowing education from the public lands; and, finally, the belief that a democracy could survive only if the masses were educated. De Witt Clinton, who fought as valiantly for a public-school system in New York as he had fought for a canal to the west, expressed a widely held opinion when he said in his message of 1827: "The bulwark of republican government is the cultivation of education; for the right of suffrage cannot be exercised in a salutary manner without intelligence."

Strong as were the arguments for a tax-supported public-school system, the movement was generally opposed by the wealthy taxpayer, by the proprietors of private schools, and by certain religious denominations that had established schools and wanted to control the education of their own children. The movement, nevertheless, made rapid headway with the lead taken by the states of the Northeast. In Massachusetts James G. Carter and Horace Mann aroused popular interest and then directed the movement with sanity. Mann succeeded in establishing normal schools for the training of teachers and in welding the local units into a state system. What Mann did for Massachusetts, Henry Barnard, "the scholar of the awakening," did for Connecticut and Rhode Island. Educational journals to promote their ideas were started by both men, of which the

American Journal of Education, founded by Barnard, was the most famous. These are but the best-known of a score of educational leaders who laid the foundations during these years of the American public-school system.

It was during these foundation years of the public-school system that the private seminaries and academies reached the height of their influence. Over 6000 were in existence in 1850, some of them functioning under endowments, some operated for private gain, and many supported by religious denominations. Almost every conference of the Methodist Church, for example, supported its seminary, and the work of many of these schools was not far below that of the colleges. The beginning of the American public high school goes back to a Massachusetts law of 1827, but not more than three hundred or four hundred were in existence by 1860. Their great development was to come after the Civil War and with it the decline in relative importance of the private school. Amazing also was the rapid development of collegiate education. To the nine colleges of the colonial period, fifteen were added by 1800 and 229 more by the end of 1860. Of these about twenty were state institutions; most of the remainder were denominational. The impetus for their founding came among other things from the rise of a national spirit, the intellectual awakening of the thirties and forties, the optimism of the West, and the desire of the churches to train a ministry to look after their rapidly growing constituencies. The Dartmouth College decision undoubtedly stimulated this expansion; on the one hand, it gave a sense of security to private endowments, and, on the other, it stimulated the establishment of state universities that might be controlled by the whole people. Another impetus, as we have seen, came from the public land endowments of the federal government to the early settlers of Ohio. Similar grants were made to other states as they entered the Union, until a climax was reached in the Morrill Act of 1862, by which the federal government granted to each state public land (30,000 acres for each representative and senator) to found mechanical and agricultural schools.

Although many of these early institutions could be called colleges only by courtesy, one thing was certain—the new democracy intended to have colleges of some kind and was willing to start them in regions that had not yet passed beyond frontier conditions. "It is but five or six years," said a frontier lawyer in 1834, "since we attended a meeting at Jacksonville—then a hamlet of log houses—held in an unfurnished building, where the company stood among the carpenter's chips and shavings, and when an institution was organized and called Illinois College. From this small beginning has arisen a valuable institution having a faculty consisting of a president and four other gentlemen, and a list of eighty-two students. The buildings are commodious and their prospects charming."

The influence of the public-school system and the newly founded colleges was to be in the future; for the moment other forms of education were more important. One of the great educational forces of the second quarter of the century was undoubtedly the lyceum. Where the idea originated is unknown, but the immediate father was Josiah Holbrook of Darby, Connecticut, who in 1826 contributed to the *American Journal of Education* an article on the subject of "associations of adults for the Purpose of Mutual Education." To illustrate his ideas he organized in the same year, in Millbury, Massachusetts, "Millbury Lyceum, No. 1, Branch of the American Lyceum." Within a few months fifteen near-by villages had responded to his lead, by 1834 at least 3000 lyceums had been established with state boards, and in 1839 there was even a national convention. In New England there was hardly a village of any size but boasted its lyceum. Upon their circuits the greatest intellects of the time gave their best thought to the masses. Especially were the lyceums valuable as a means for the wider dissemination of new scientific knowledge—platforms where the brilliant Benjamin Silliman of Yale lectured on chemistry, and Edward Hitchcock of Amherst and the famous Louis Agassiz on geology. Although political controversy and the Civil War destroyed fully 90 per cent of the lyceums, they left a legacy in the form of literary societies, lecture bureaus, Chautauquas, and such permanent foundations as Cooper Union in New York, the Peabody Institutes in Baltimore and Boston, and the Lowell Institute in the last-named city.

More important, perhaps, than the lyceum were the newspapers, which began to take on the characteristics of the modern daily and to reduce their price to an amount within the range of the masses. After several dailies had failed to support themselves by selling at one cent, the New York *Sun* not only succeeded in 1833 but became the first of the modern newspapers. Instead of stale news from Europe and abusive political tirades, it filled its columns with live and interesting accounts of local happenings. The New York *Herald,* founded in 1835 by James Gordon Bennett, became even more successful as the first to print financial news, report social affairs, and discuss the theater. Fortunately for American journalism, this period of rapid expansion and changing form was influenced by some of America's greatest editors. William Cullen Bryant, the poet, became editor of the New York *Evening Post* in 1828; Horace Greeley in 1841 founded the New York *Tribune,* soon to become the most influential paper in America, and in 1851 the New York *Times* was established under Henry J. Raymond. In the meantime famous newspapers and able editors appeared in the rising cities of the Middle West. Of all the provincial newspapers, probably the Springfield *Republican* (founded 1824), under the three Samuel Bowleses (1824–1915), proved the most influential. As the facilities for gathering and printing news improved at the same time that the cost to the public declined, it was not long before the newspaper provided the chief reading matter for the average citizen.

THE GROWTH OF DEMOCRACY

By breaking up the large landed estates of the Tories, by destroying the power of the former aristocratic class in many sections, and by bringing into being new and more equitable land laws, the American Revolution gave a distinct impetus to the development of democracy. All the new states, it will be remembered, with the exception of Connecticut and Rhode Island, drew up new constitutions, which in their bills of rights reflected the revolutionary philosophy of the eighteenth century. Here we find reference to certain "unalienable rights," such as life, liberty, and the pursuit of happiness; freedom of conscience, speech, the press, and petition; trial by jury; the right of *habeas corpus;* the prohibition of *ex post facto* laws; the subordination of the military to the civil authority; and the safeguarding of the home and private property. In spite of these bold assertions regarding the rights of man, the actual steps toward political democracy as yet were feeble and faltering. At the time of Washington's inauguration all the states had a property qualification of some kind for voting. Not only was this true, but thousands of men who might vote were still ineligible to hold office, for in all the states there were higher property qualifications for officeholding. When Vermont entered the Union as the fourteenth state in 1791, it was the only state recognizing universal manhood suffrage; in the others property qualification, religious opinions, a tax receipt, or a combination of these determined who should vote.

Six years of warfare, followed by several years of economic depression and social unrest, brought a conservative reaction. In an atmosphere charged by such disturbances as Shays's Rebellion, it was not surprising to find Gerry asserting that "the evils we experience flow from the excess of democracy" or John Adams observing that "a hereditary first magistrate at once would perhaps be preferable to elections by legislative representatives" or Hamilton in a burst of passion calling the people "a great beast." The chief fruits of this reactionary wave were the federal Constitution, the Federalist Party, and the growth in the power of the Supreme Court under Marshall. With the coming of the French Revolution, the rapid extension of the frontier, and the victory of the Jeffersonian

Republicans in 1800, the pendulum began to swing again toward democracy. Already the Ordinance of 1787 had forbidden slavery in the Northwest Territory, and only age, residence, and ownership of land were demanded of voters and officers. In the succeeding years the westward movement was carving out new states beyond the Alleghenies; by 1821 eleven new states and by 1848 seventeen had been added to the original thirteen. All except Maine and Vermont, where frontier conditions also existed, were in the West. With the exception of Ohio (1802), where an exceedingly democratic constitution had been adopted, and New Jersey (1807), where the property qualification had been eliminated but the franchise restricted to white males, the decade 1800–1810 had been barren of accomplishment.

In the second decade, however, the advance of democracy on the frontier had been irresistible, as can readily be seen in the constitutions of Louisiana (1810), Indiana (1816), Mississippi (1817), Illinois (1818), Alabama (1819), and Maine (1820). In these and subsequent constitutions property qualifications for voters were set aside and election of the governor was provided for.[5] The old distrust of the executive, which had developed during the revolutionary period, was passing away, and in all these constitutions his appointing power was enlarged, and he was given the power to veto, to pardon all offenses except treason, and to remit fines and forfeitures. On the other hand, confidence in the legislature as the safeguard of the liberties of the people had been broken. Experience had proved that the welfare of the state was not always safe in the hands of the legislature, and the constitution-makers were careful to put in specific directions regarding charters, banks, lotteries, and schools. Though the fear of the executive had waned, that of the judiciary had appeared with renewed force, and at least three of these states made it part of their constitutions that judges must be removed by the governor on address by the legislature.

What had taken place in the West with little opposition was achieved in the East only after a bitter fight. Between 1810 and 1826 Maryland, South Carolina, and New York adopted white manhood suffrage, and Connecticut in 1818 removed all restrictions except the requirement of taxpaying or military service. The Connecticut government under the old charter was so antiquated that a new constitution was obviously needed, but only a severe struggle secured it. The New York constitution, as it existed before its revision in 1821, was a veritable bulwark of upper-class control and was an instrument that facilitated corruption and inefficiency. The conservative element in New York was led by Chancellor Kent, who

---

[5] Louisiana and Mississippi restricted the vote to free white males who paid state or county taxes.

prayed that the convention would "not carry desolation through all the departments of the fabric erected by our fathers" and made his last stand upon a freehold qualification for electors of members of the senate. Kent and his followers in the end succumbed before the rising democracy led by Martin Van Buren, and New York submitted to a thoroughgoing revision. Massachusetts in 1820 reformed her constitution, abolishing the property qualification for voters but retaining that for senators. Daniel Webster, Joseph Story, and the aged John Adams all united stubbornly to oppose a wider extension of the franchise, but their efforts availed little in the face of public demand. The same was true of Virginia, where Madison, Monroe, Marshall, and Randolph all struggled vainly against the rising tide. Rhode Island hung on to her old charter until 1842 and then capitulated, but only after rebellion had broken out and a rival state government had been set up under a "People's Constitution" with Thomas W. Dorr as "governor."

The discussion of democracy so far has been largely concerned with the political rights of men. It was long after the Civil War before the political, economic, and legal position of women approached that of men. Nowhere in America had suffrage been extended to women; when a woman married, title to her property passed to her husband. A girl was lucky if she received the rudiments of an education; only a few radicals had as yet advocated the same curriculum for both boys and girls or the higher education for women. The agitation for "women's rights" commenced in America with the visit in 1820 of a young Scotchwoman, Frances Wright, who appeared on the platform in advocacy of many reforms. As the first woman to deliver public lectures, she painfully shocked the conservatives, but her work was an object lesson to women on the possibilities open to them to influence public opinion. Many noble women, who had been actively engaged in various reforms, now sought the lecture platform. Among them were Ernestine Rose, a Polish exile who attained great influence; Lydia Maria Child and Margaret Fuller, representing the finest product of intellectual New England womanhood; Angelina and Sara Grimke of South Carolina, among the most famous of Southern antislavery agitators; Mrs. Lucretia Mott, a Quakeress reformer of Philadelphia; and Mrs. Elizabeth Cady Stanton of New York.

It was the refusal of the World's Antislavery Convention meeting in London in 1840 to seat eight American women delegates that led two of them, Lucretia Mott and Elizabeth Cady Stanton, eight years later to call together the first Women's Rights Convention at Seneca Falls, New York. Here a "Declaration of Sentiments" was drawn up, declaring that "all men and women were created equal" and launching a seventy years' battle for the suffrage. Other women reformers would carry the emancipation of women further. Lucy Stone asserted that married women should keep their maiden names; Amelia Jenks Bloomer advocated a more sensible clothing and designed a costume consisting of loose Turkish trousers gathered at the ankle with an elastic band, a skirt that came below the knees, a short jacket, and a straw hat. Modern students of style are scarcely impressed by this costume, but all will admit that from the point of view of comfort and hygiene it was a step in advance over the tight corsets and hoop skirts of the day. All this began to have its reaction on education with the opening and development of seminaries for young ladies, notably that of Emma Willard at Troy, New York, in 1821, and that of Mary Lyon at South Hadley, Massachusetts (Mount Holyoke Seminary), in 1836. While these seminaries did not approach the standard of education in the leading men's colleges, they marked an important step toward the higher education of women. The honor of establishing coeducation in an American college goes to Oberlin, founded in 1834. It was followed by Antioch, founded by Horace Mann in 1853, and soon by most of the state universities. The whole women's rights movement lent itself easily to ridicule, and the smug respectability of the time agreed thoroughly with *Harper's New Monthly Magazine,* which asserted in November, 1853, that the movement had an "intimate connection with all the radical and infidel movements of the day. . . . It is avowedly opposed to the most time-honored proprieties of social life; it is opposed to nature; it is opposed to revelation. . . . In this respect no kindred movement is so decidedly infidel, so rancorously and avowedly antibiblical." With such language are great movements for reform usually greeted.

THE GOLDEN DAY

It would be impossible for a spiritual and intellectual awakening such as that experienced in America during the first half of the nineteenth century not to leave its imprint upon the literature of the period. Political, economic, and even intellectual dependence upon England had characterized the colonial period, but the Revolutionary War had snapped the political dependence, the Industrial Revolution was breaking the economic bonds, and new forces within were creating a national literature. Many factors had contributed to retard this development—the crudeness of a new land, the mighty task of conquering a vast continent, the inordinate pride in things American, and the knowledge that wealth was the key not only to comfort but to social and political preferment. On the other hand, there were influences conducive to literary development—a certainty in the high destiny of America that gave a feeling of self-confidence, and a growing realization that there was in America much to write about.

The East was old enough for history and traditions to have grown, and the dramatic episodes of colonial New England and New York were soon woven into essays, fiction, and poetry. The rebirth of the public school, the numerous newspapers and magazines, the lyceum lectures, and the universal interest in the projects of reform all stimulated a reading public. Although rudimentary education was not universal, as it is now, the reading public was as intelligent. The public library was still in its infancy, but the purchase of books was widespread.

Mention has been made in an earlier chapter of the literary output of the years immediately after the Revolution. In the early decades of the nineteenth century New York became the center of what literary activities existed, and here developed the first purely American school of literature. Outstanding in this group were Washington Irving, James Fenimore Cooper, and William Cullen Bryant. Irving's best work dealt with the history and traditions of the Hudson valley, but his pen was later busy with Spanish and English themes. He was the first American man of letters to catch the ear of Europe, and he did much to interpret for each continent the life of the other. Cooper had little of the urbanity and humor of Irving, but he caught the spirit of the vastness of the American wilderness and the lure of the mighty ocean, and presented them so vividly that Europe and America realized more acutely the romance of the New World. Bryant spent the first thirty years of his life in the mountains of western Massachusetts and then fifty-four years in New York City. Although his fame rests upon a few poems written in early manhood, his literary work was voluminous, and his contribution to the culture of his time through his half-century editorship of the New York *Evening Post* was notable. Besides Bryant, there drifted to New York writers from other sections, notably Edgar Allan Poe, the greatest American poet of his time and the first American to master the art of the short story. In later years the literary center shifted to Boston, but even at the height of the New England renascence there remained one native New Yorker of great genius, Herman Melville, whose *Moby Dick* remains today one of the greatest novels of the sea.

It was in New England that the *Aufklärung* bore its richest literary fruits. Here the finest products of two centuries of Puritan culture burst the shackles of an old order and stood forth as champions of free thought or of humanitarian reform. Here it was that William Ellery Channing and his followers created New England Unitarianism and by its reaction profoundly changed the outlook of Puritan Congregationalism. Here it was that Ralph Waldo Emerson struck fiercely at American materialism and American subserviency to Europe, and preached anew the age-old doctrine of the need of a high spiritual life to make the most of each passing day. Here it was that that stark individualist, Henry Thoreau, wove his transcendental philosophy into his charming nature studies of New England, models for much subsequent writing. The same little town (Concord) that nurtured Emerson and Thoreau gave Louisa M. Alcott materials for her novels for children and stimulated Nathaniel Hawthorne to conceive some of his immortal stories. It was in near-by Boston and Cambridge that three professors, Henry Wadsworth Longfellow, Oliver Wendell Holmes, and James Russell Lowell, glorified the commonplace in simple and unpretentious poetry, while in Amesbury, a few miles to the north, the Quaker poet, John Greenleaf Whittier, was devoting his pen to the antislavery movement. It was also not far from what Holmes playfully called the "hub of the Solar System" that Jared Sparks and George Bancroft laid the foundations of American historical writing and that William Hickling Prescott, John Lathrop Motley, and Francis Parkman developed grand themes with sound scholarship and fascinating style. This period marked the golden age of American literature, and seldom had any nation in any age witnessed such an outpouring.

In the realm of art the "Golden Day" was largely limited to literature. Portrait-painting did not reach the level of the revolutionary era, and, except for the work of the Hudson River school of landscape-painters, there was little painting of importance. Sculpture was on an even lower level than painting. The most famous single piece of these years was Hiram Powers's *Greek Slave*, but the high praise showered upon it illustrates the paucity of general accomplishment rather than the excellence of this particular work. Music fared a little better, for here we find Stephen C. Foster adapting Negro folk music, Lowell Mason adapting the music of the classic composers to psalms and hymns, and Louis M. Gottschalk, a prolific composer and perhaps the first American to show signs of musical genius, performing brilliantly in hundreds of concerts throughout the country.

In the realm of science Americans during these years were laying a foundation for great future developments. Interest was particularly keen in the fields of physiography and geology. Perhaps the earliest government department interested in science was the Coast and Geodetic Survey, which established an excellent reputation under the direction of Alexander Dallas Bache, a grandson of Benjamin Franklin, who was superintendent from 1843 to 1867. In co-operation with this work the government repeatedly used the army and navy to carry on exploration, as in the explorations of Lieutenant Charles Wilkes on the northwest coast and in the antarctic (1838–1842) and the more famous expeditions of John C. Frémont. It was in geology and zoology that Louis Agassiz, a French Swiss and an influential immigrant of these years, carried on his work. As early as 1840, the American Society of Geologists was founded, the first great society devoted to a particular science. Among other scientists of these years whose work is not forgotten were Professor Asa Gray of Harvard, who classified a large number of American plants and through his published works stimulated many successors to an interest in botany, and J. J. Audubon, a Frenchman trained in art by David, who came to Louisiana as a young man and spent much of his life in wandering through the southern forests, studying, describing, and painting the native birds with extraordinary exactness.

More typical, perhaps, of American science than the work of the scientists was the practical work of the many famous inventors who helped to usher in the modern age. Especially to be noted here are the significant applications of electricity to communication—the invention of the telegraph in the thirties by Samuel F. B. Morse and Joseph Henry and its subsequent use in the first transatlantic cable, laid in 1866 by Cyrus W. Field after repeated failures. Americans also made at least one outstanding contribution to the field of medicine in the years before the Civil War. In 1844 a Hartford dentist, Dr. Horace Wells, demonstrated that nitrous oxide gas might be used as an anesthetic to deaden pain. Two years earlier a Georgia physician, Dr. Crawford W. Long, had successfully experimented with ether, but it was not until 1846, when a Boston dentist, Dr. W. T. G. Morton, successfully etherized a patient for a surgical operation, that the possibilities of the discovery were apparent. The developing interest in science brought the founding in 1824 by Stephen Van Rensselaer at Troy, New York, of the first school in the United States devoted entirely to science and engineering. Five years later a great impetus was given to American science by the Englishman, James Smithson, who bequeathed an immense sum for that day, over $500,000, to found an establishment "for the increase and diffusion of knowledge among men." Chartered by Congress in 1846 as the Smithsonian Institution, it subsequently was liberally subsidized by the government and became a great center for scientific research.

C. and M. Beard, *The Rise of American Civilization*, Chap. XVI, is an excellent introduction. In the History of American Life series, J. A. Krout and D. R. Fox, *The Completion of Independence*, C. R. Fish, *The Rise of the Common Man*, Chaps. VII, IX–XII, and A. C. Cole, *The Irrepressible Conflict*, Chaps. I, IV–X, cover this period. E. P. Cubberley, *Public Education in the United States*, Chaps. IV–VII, gives the history of education, while educational philosophy is discussed in M. E. Curti, *The Social Ideas of American Educators*, Chaps. II, III. In Lewis Mumford, *The Golden Day*, Chaps. III, IV, are stimulating essays in literary history. Important on this period is Merle Curti, *The Growth of American Thought*, Chaps. XIII–XVI.

Chapter XVII

THE OLD SOUTH

They are not moral, but economical circum-
stances: they relate not to vice and virtue, but to
production. They are the circumstances, in which
one man finds it difficult or impossible to get
other men to work under his direction for wages.
They are the circumstances . . . which stand
in the way of combination and constancy of la-
bor, and which all civilized nations, in a certain
stage of their advance from barbarism, have en-
deavoured to counteract, and have in some meas-
ure counteracted, by means of some kind of
slavery.

EDWARD GIBBON WAKEFIELD

SOUTHERN DEVELOPMENT

The last chapter has dealt largely with conditions in the North. Let
us now turn to a consideration of the region south of the Mason and
Dixon line and of the Ohio River. The first census, taken in 1790, reported
a total for this region of 1,902,078, of whom 1,225,080 were white and 676,-
998 were Negro, the latter comprising 35.6 per cent of the Southern population. The South in that year contained nearly nine tenths of all the
Negroes, taken together with the whites about half the population of the
country. Geographically, the people were almost entirely located east of
the mountains, and the majority below the fall line. The civilization was
essentially rural, Charleston with 16,359 inhabitants and Baltimore with
13,503 being the only towns of any size. Racially, the people were predominantly English, although groups of Huguenots were to be found in
the tidewater sections of South Carolina, settlements of Scotch in the back
country of North Carolina, a considerable number of "Scotch-Irish" and
Germans, who had followed the mountain valleys south, in the frontier
counties of Virginia and the Carolinas, and, of course, descendants of the
French settlers in Louisiana. Economically, the wealth of the population
was primarily in land and slaves, the best land and most of the slaves

being occupied chiefly in raising tobacco and rice. As in almost all civilizations, this wealth was largely owned by a small group, perhaps one tenth of the white population, who comprised the tobacco- and rice-planting aristocracy. The remaining nine tenths of the whites were scattered on the poorer soil of the tidewater region or had been forced to the piedmont frontier in order to obtain land. Unable to compete with the planters in growing the great staples, they had naturally turned to self-sufficing agriculture similar to that of the northern small farmer. Although the Jeffersonian democracy had brought the ballot to the poorer whites, the section was politically dominated by the aristocracy.

Undoubtedly the most influential feature in the economic and social history of the South was the development of cotton-culture. The raising of cotton had made but little progress during the colonial period, for superior profits from tobacco, a lack of market, and other factors discouraged its production. The Revolution, however, by interrupting the importation of foreign fabrics, turned the attention of the planters to the possibilities of cotton, and the Industrial Revolution provided an insatiable market. At the same time the declining profits from the worn-out tobacco fields made the planters willing to experiment with new crops. The impetus for cotton-culture was present; all that held back its development was the difficulty of separating the seed from the fiber, and this problem had been solved in the nineties by the resourceful Yankee, Eli Whitney (page 244).

With the invention of the cotton gin many planters, especially south of Virginia, turned from tobacco to cotton, and, except in the embargo year 1808 and the war years 1812–1814, the spread of the new crop was rapid. Production increased from 4000 bales of five hundred pounds each in 1790 to 3,841,416 bales in 1860. By that year the value of the cotton exported amounted to over $333,000,000, comprising in value 57 per cent of the nation's exports, and it had long since become not only the largest single export of the country but the greatest commercial crop of the South. At the same time the cotton gin fastened slavery upon the South. Distinctly on the decline in the years after the Revolution and subject to the caustic criticism of most of the Southern leaders, slavery seemed to be doomed. Cotton-culture, however, was ideally suited to the crude and wasteful methods of ignorant slave labor, and the black man, whose economic value had been on the decline, suddenly took on new importance.

Not only did the cotton gin give to the South a great staple crop and fasten slavery upon that region, but it hastened at an astonishing pace the occupation of the Southwest. Slavery lived by exploiting the soil, and the land-hungry planters, gathering together their slaves and possessions, pushed over the mountains into the fertile valleys of the Chattahoochee, the Alabama, and the Tombigbee. Brushing aside the cattle ranger, the

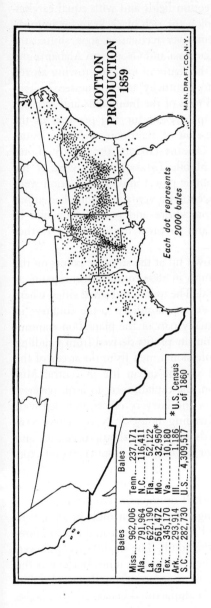

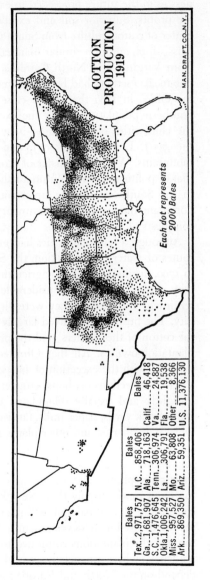

small pioneer farmer, and the Indian, with wanton ruthlessness they destroyed the timber to make way for cotton fields and with equal carelessness as to the future proceeded to exploit the rich black loam for immediate profits. Superior soil and excellent river navigation soon shifted the center of cotton-culture from South Carolina and Georgia to Alabama and Mississippi, and in a similar manner the center of tobacco-growing moved from Virginia and North Carolina to Kentucky and Tennessee. In 1790 but 109,000 settlers had been reported west of the mountains and south of the Ohio; in 1860 there were close to 6,950,000, or 57.3 per cent of the Southern population. With the exception of Baltimore and Charleston, the chief cities of the South—New Orleans (168,700 people), St. Louis (160,700), Louisville (68,000), and Mobile (41,000)—were west of the mountains. With the transfer of economic power and of population went that of political power. Within a half century a veritable empire had arisen in the Southwest, resting upon cotton-culture and powerful enough to dominate the national government and to press insistently for further conquests of fresh land.

Although a few small cities had grown up at the strategic points on the routes of water transportation, the South in 1860 continued to remain, as in 1790, distinctly rural and agricultural. The towns and small cities, where they existed, were to a considerable extent subsidiary to the country; in sentiment and interest they were virtually part of the plantation community. The business men lived largely on the profits derived from handling the cotton of the planters, and the professional men from the needs of the plantation-owners. All that Olmsted saw of urban life in central Mississippi "with the exception of Jackson, the capital, were forlorn, poverty-stricken collections of shops, groceries and lawyers' offices, mingled with unsightly and usually dilapidated dwelling houses." Nevertheless, sawmills, brick yards, paper mills, tan yards, blacksmith shops, turpentine and whisky distilleries, and other plants for primary and frontier manufacturing were to be found. Even cotton mills had been set up in South Carolina and Georgia, and already in 1852 the Saluda Mills at Columbia, with their 5000 spindles and 120 looms worked by slaves, were producing cotton cloth more cheaply than New England. Southern mills in 1860 were consuming 200,000 bales of cotton, and acute observers could already foresee the future textile development of the South. The small farms and even some of the plantations continued to be self-sufficing units, but it was the tendency, where financially possible, to concentrate on the staples and depend on the North and Europe for manufactured goods. Above all else it was climate or, more specifically, the length of the summers that dominated the economic life of the South. "The growing season," as Professor Phillips points out, "lasts on an average six months at Baltimore, Louisville and St. Louis; seven at Norfolk, Atlanta and Memphis; eight at Columbia, Montgomery and Dallas, and nine at Charleston, New Orleans and Galveston. The climate has fostered the cultivation of tobacco in the first zone, cotton in the second and third, and rice and sugar cane in the fourth." [1]

The white stock in the South continued as late as the Civil War to be largely the descendants of the prerevolutionary settlers. A few Northerners had gone south before 1860 to try their fortunes, but a comparatively small number of European immigrants had settled there. Although there were over 4,000,000 foreign-born in America in 1860, in a population of 27,489,000 whites, only five southern states showed a foreign-born population of over 5 per cent, Missouri (13.59), Louisiana (11.44), Maryland (11.24), Texas (17.19), and Kentucky (5.17). Of these, three were border states that contained large cities where foreign population centered.

THE PLANTER ARISTOCRACY

At the top of the social, economic, and political structure of the antebellum South were the great plantation-owners—the tobacco-planters, the rice magnates of South Carolina, and the cotton-growers of the lower South. Their number was comparatively small. The census of 1860 put the white population of the slave states at 8,099,760 and the slaves at 3,953,580; the slaves were owned by only 384,000 whites, of whom 107,957 owned more than ten, 10,781 owned fifty or more, and but 1733 owned 100 or more. More than two thirds of the white population had no direct interest in slavery, and but a handful of the remainder gained much wealth from the system. The concentration of wealth, as revealed in the ownership of slaves, was naturally seen in incomes. Around 1850, believes Dodd, a thousand families received $50,000,000 a year, while the remaining 666,000 families received only about $60,000,000, a concentration of wealth and income hardly surpassed in the most advanced stage of an industrialized society.

The disproportionate wealth that flowed into the coffers of this small number of families came chiefly from the proceeds of cotton, the great marketable crop. Wealth, and as a consequence social prestige and political power, rested with those who owned the type of property that would produce cotton, namely, land and slaves. For many years there was land in abundance, and the best of it went to the class having the ready cash to obtain it. Under the wasteful system of exploitation land was likely at last to decline in value. This was not true of slave property. The increase in the number of slaves was not sufficiently rapid to keep pace with

[1] Ulrich B. Phillips, *Life and Labor in the Old South*, 3.

the opening of fresh land to cotton, and the demand for slave labor was greater than the supply. Between 1845 and 1855 the price of cotton advanced 40 per cent and with that went a 100-per-cent increase in the value of slaves. An able-bodied field hand who sold for $300 before the invention of the cotton gin or $750 in 1845 might bring from $1500 to $2000 in 1860. Slaves seemed to be the one type of property that inevitably increased in value; a slave-owner had but to devote reasonable care to his slaves, and his wealth would expand. This rise in the value of slaves was a boon to the rapidly fading tidewater aristocracy of Virginia, who managed by selling their surplus Negroes to ward off ruin. Certainly there was little intentional breeding of slaves in the border states to "sell south"; it was primarily economic pressure that forced such a disposal of surplus Negroes. As early as 1832 Professor Dew of William and Mary asserted that Virginia was "a *negro* raising State for other States; she produces enough for her own supply and six thousand for sale," while Olmsted estimated that in the ten years preceding 1860 the annual export of Negroes from the border states was about 25,000. Cairnes, the English economist, emphasized the relative decline of Negro population in such border states as Virginia, Maryland, and Kentucky,[2] due in part to the draining off of the slave population.

The social and economic unit of the old South was the plantation, and here the planter magnates ruled in all their glory. Although imposing mansions with Grecian pillars and other adornments were scattered widely throughout the South, the average planter's home was a modest house of ten or twelve rooms, commodious in a rambling fashion, but with no great distinction without, nor great luxury within. Here the master and mistress, descendants of the prerevolutionary aristocracy or of more recent accessions from the middle class, attended to the multifarious duties of the estate and entered as actively as possible into the social life of the neighborhood. The isolation of plantation life emphasized the home and family, for neither felt any competition from theaters, clubs, or other urban institutions. Dependence upon themselves or neighbors likewise developed hospitality. There was little of grandeur about plantation life; it was in general a careless, easygoing existence, with the working hours taken up in the rather tiresome and often sordid details of production through slave labor. Wealth was displayed not so much by luxurious surroundings as by a galaxy of servants. The somewhat disorderly and easy-

---

[2] The percentage of increase in population for the decade ending 1850 showed:

STATE	WHITES	SLAVES
Virginia	20.77	5.21
Maryland	31.34	.70
Kentucky	28.99	15.75

going profusion of plantation life is caught from Olmsted's description of a meal at a Virginia planter's home:

> Although Mr. W. was very wealthy (or, at least, would be considered so anywhere at the North), and was a gentleman of education, his style of living was very farmer-like, and thoroughly Southern. On their plantations, generally, the Virginia gentlemen seem to drop their full-dress and constrained town-habits, and to live a free, rustic, shooting-jacket life. We dined in a room that extended out, rearwardly, from the house, and which, in a Northern establishment would have been the kitchen. The cooking was done in a detached log-cabin, and the dishes brought some distance, through the open air, by the servants. The outer door was left constantly open, though there was a fire in an enormous old fire-place, large enough, if it could have been distributed sufficiently, to have lasted a New York seamstress the best part of the winter. By the door, there was indiscriminate admittance of negro-children and fox-hounds, and, on an average, there were four of these, grinning or licking their chops, on either side of my chair, all the time I was at the table. A stout woman acted as head waitress, employing two handsome little mulatto boys as her aids in communicating with the kitchen, from which relays of hot cornbread, of an excellence quite new to me, were brought at frequent intervals. There was no other bread, and but one vegetable served—sweet potatoes, roasted in ashes, and this, I thought, was the best sweet potato, also, that I had ever eaten; but there were four preparations of swine's flesh, besides fried fowls, fried eggs, cold roast turkey, and opossum, cooked, I know not how, but it somewhat resembled baked sucking-pig. The only beverages on the table were milk and whiskey.[3]

The same traveler gives us a glimpse of another plantation and another meal at the other end of the South, in the home of an owner of forty Negroes, who had held his property for twenty years:

> We stopped one night at the house of a planter, now twenty years settled in Eastern Texas. He was a man of some education and natural intelligence, and had, he told us, an income from the labor of his slaves, of some $4,000. His residence was one of the largest we had seen in Texas. It had a second story, two wings and a long gallery. Its windows had once been glazed, but now, out of eighty panes that originally filled the lower windows, thirty only remained unbroken. Not a door of the house had been ever furnished with a latch or even a string; when they were closed, it was necessary to *claw* or to ask some one inside to push open. (Yet we happened to hear a neighbor expressing serious admiration of the way these doors fitted.) The furniture was of the rudest description. . . .
>
> On the supper-table was nothing but the eternal fry, pone and coffee. Butter, of dreadful odor, was here added by exception. Wheat flour was never used. It was "too much trouble."

[3] F. L. Olmsted, *Seaboard Slave States* (1904 edition), I, 101–103.

We were waited upon by two negro girls, dressed in short-waisted, twilled-cotton gowns, once white, now looking as though they had been drawn through a stove pipe in spring. The water for the family was brought in tubs upon the heads of these two girls from a creek, a quarter of a mile distant, this occupation filling nearly all their time.[4]

The southern planter was an outdoor man, skilled in horsemanship and keen for the hunt, but little drawn to books or learning. Given to strong drink and often to gambling, he was courteous in demeanor, but imperious in temper, and was quick to resent a wrong or punish an infringement of discipline. The excessive power that he enjoyed was as likely to encourage a lack of restraint as a sense of responsibility. The mistress of the plantation house, having been educated by a governess or at a girls' finishing school, divided her time between details of domestic supervision and social activities. The male children, after playing in their tender years with slaves of their own age, were sent, if they aspired to advanced education, to a southern or northern college, quite as often to the latter as to the former.

On the larger plantations white overseers supervised the labor of the slaves and relieved the owner of the details of management. This allowed the master and mistress to spend long periods at the state capital or at fashionable watering places, but it brought in its train the usual evils of absentee ownership. The planters of more limited means, and these comprised the greater number, were forced to give their personal attention to their plantations. In spite of the tradition of luxury and grandeur that surrounds the prewar plantation, there was, in fact, a certain economic precariousness and instability about the whole situation, and that notwithstanding the increase in the value of slaves and the relative stability of land as a form of wealth. The dependence upon a single crop, upon unreliable and ineffective slave labor, upon wasteful and often dishonest overseers, and upon land butchery, led frequently to bankruptcy. Combined often with a certain thriftlessness and inefficiency and with the disrupting influence of the lure of western land, there existed an economic restlessness characteristic of other sections of the country. Life on the plantations, however, was relatively uneventful. The routine was broken only by hunting trips, plantation celebrations, country parties, and an occasional trip to the city. For the wealthy planters it was an easygoing existence, but for the great mass of middle-class planters it was a life full of work and worry. The romance that has come to surround it emanates chiefly from the day dreams of reminiscing story-tellers.

[4] F. L. Olmsted, *A Journey Through Texas* (1857 edition), 115–116.

Historians and economists have been chiefly concerned with the large plantation-owner, but it should be remembered that nine tenths of the southern whites were small farmers. The small farmer included a number of types. Among them were the small planters with three or four slaves, who raised a few bales of cotton and whose incomes amounted to several hundred dollars a year, men who seldom attempted the role of gentleman farmer, but with their sons worked side by side with the slaves in the field. A second type was the tenant farmer or small landholder, who owned no slaves and raised one or two bales of cotton, a few hogs, and an acre or so of corn. "I think that two bales of cotton a year is as much as is generally made by people who do not own negroes," said one southern observer. "They are doing well if they net over fifty dollars a year from their labor, besides supplying themselves with corn." Still lower in the economic and social scale were the squatters and mountain whites, who dragged out a thin existence on the outskirts of civilization. Finally should be noted the relatively small number of poor and middle-class whites of the cities, and the economic white dependents of the great planters, the slave-dealers, overseers, rural mechanics, and the like.

Like the great planters, the poorer whites were composed of various racial strains and varied widely in ability. There were the "Scotch-Irish" (like the McCormicks), who had moved southwest into the piedmont of the seaboard states, and there were the sturdy yeoman farmers of the colonial tidewater region, who had moved westward to open up new lands. There was also a large group of descendants of the inefficient, low-type servant imported during the colonial period, who undoubtedly made up a proportion of the piney-woods squatters of Mississippi, the "pine-landers," "crackers," or "hill-billies" of northern Georgia and north-central Alabama, and the "clay-eaters" and "sand-hillers" of the Carolinas. The lowest of these, the "po-white trash" whom even the Negroes despised, were very likely brought to their low estate not only by congenital inefficiency but by malaria, hookworm, and the poor soil upon which they were marooned. Although there were examples in every section of the South of wealthy planters who had risen from the poor whites, the climb was a difficult one. The lack of urban life limited the ambitious chiefly to agriculture. The open sesame to improvement in economic condition was the ownership of slaves, and for this ready money was necessary. White labor was more efficient than black, but the slave-owner did not need it. Whites sometimes hired out at harvest time, but that was not general. Some of the more energetic obtained positions as overseers and in time accumulated enough to buy slaves and become small planters.

If the scale of living of the average planter was far from luxurious, that of the small farmer and poor white was decidedly wretched. Gregg spoke of him as existing "in a state but one step in advance of the Indian of the forest," [5] and Olmsted, to whom we are chiefly indebted for what knowledge we have of the poor and middle-class southern farmer of the antebellum period, asserted with possibly some exaggeration that "there is no part of Georgia which equals in poverty of natural resources, Cape Cod, in Massachusetts," yet "there is hardly a poor woman's cow on the Cape that is not better housed and more comfortably provided for than a majority of the white people of Georgia." [6] The same author describes a dwelling belonging to a white "by no means of the lowest class" in the back country of Mississippi:

> The house was all compressed in a single room, twenty-eight by twenty-five feet in area, and open to the roof above. There was a large fireplace at one end and a door at each side—no windows at all. Two bedsteads, a spinning-wheel, a packing case, which served as a bureau, a cupboard, made of rough hewn slabs, two or three deerskin-seated chairs, a Connecticut clock, and a large poster of Jayne's patent medicines, constituted all the visible furniture either useful or ornamental in purpose. [7]

Here the traveler slept in a bed while the family slept on the floor, and ate, as was the custom, bacon and corn bread.

With respect to the poor whites, the great Southern editor, De Bow, saw the situation clearly:

> In the more southern portion of this region [the Southwest] the non-slaveholders possess, generally, but small means, and the land which they possess is almost universally poor, and so sterile that a scarcity subsistence is all that can be derived from its cultivation; and the more fertile soil, being in the possession of the slave holder, must ever remain out of the power of those who have none. . . . And I lament to say that I have observed of late years that an evident deterioration is taking place in this part of the population, the younger portion of it being less industrious, and in every point of view less respectable than their ancestors. [8]

THE SLAVE SYSTEM

Just as ownership of machinery or of the agencies of distribution was the key to wealth in the North after the coming of the Industrial Revolu-

[5] Quoted by Helper, *Impending Crisis,* 377. William Gregg was a well-known advocate of Southern manufactures and built large cotton mills at Graniteville, South Carolina.

[6] F. L. Olmsted, *Seaboard Slaves States* (1904 edition), II, 179.

[7] F. L. Olmsted, *Back Country* (1907 edition), I, 220.

[8] J. D. B. De Bow, *Industrial Resources of the Southern and Western States,* II, 107.

tion, so the ownership of slave labor marked in the South the difference between affluence and poverty. This system, which was to color the whole economic life of the South and leave behind it a permanent racial problem, commenced in the English colonies, it will be remembered, when the Dutch in 1619 sold the Jamestown settlers a ship-load of slaves. In competition during the seventeenth century with indentured servants and free labor, slave labor was not adopted enthusiastically until the next century (page 55). Valuable as it proved to be on the tobacco plantations of Virginia and on the indigo and rice fields of the Carolinas, the slave system by the close of the Revolution had generally become unprofitable. Exhaustion of the soil, losses in the Revolution, and the competition that tobacco was meeting in other parts of the world led many to question the value of slavery and to predict its extinction in no distant future.

Just as the doom of slavery was being pronounced, it was saved, as we have seen, by the Industrial Revolution and the invention of the cotton gin, which made it possible to grow profitably the short-fibered upland cotton. Cotton, in truth, seemed wholly suited to slave labor. Its culture is simple; few tools and little equipment are needed, and its cultivation extends over a large part of the year. Women and children can be employed as well as men, while the labor of all can be compactly massed under the supervision of an overseer, an extremely important factor where overseers were expensive but absolutely necessary.

The adaptability of cotton to slave labor, however, was not the only influence favorable to slavery. In one sense slavery tends to perpetuate itself by eliminating competition. Free immigrants from Europe, in their desire to avoid competition with slave labor, largely avoided the agricultural South, while the poor white was being driven on to the poorer lands, into the mountains, or north of the Ohio. Slavery was also strengthened by the abundance of fresh land, which made it possible to waste the soil under a one-crop system with crude and ignorant slave labor and then move on to butcher another piece of land in the same way. Despite appearances, slave labor was expensive. If to the initial cost, interest, insurance, maintenance, and the expense of sickness and old age are added, accurate cost accounting shows that slave labor was often more costly than free, besides being usually more inefficient. As the margin of profits on cotton tended to grow smaller with the expanding cotton crop, most cotton-growers grew prosperous, it seems evident, not, as they believed, because of slave labor, but in spite of it. Actually it was the fertility of the virgin soil ruthlessly exploited that brought the profits. More than anything else the increase over the years of the value of slaves fastened the system upon the South and convinced the Southerners of its value. Land might wear out and decline in value, the price of cotton might decline as it did in the five years preceding the Civil War, but the value of slaves kept on climbing. The reason, obviously enough, was that the Southwest was being opened to cotton more rapidly than the labor market could supply the necessary slaves. As long as this situation continued, profits could be made with slave labor. When the cotton kingdom ceased to expand, slavery was doomed, and the end of this expansion was in sight in 1860.[9]

The 4,000,000 slaves of 1860 were roughly divided into two classes, the house servants and the field hands. The former, often with a mixture of white blood, were the most intelligent and were on the whole well used. The field hands, who did the bulk of the work on the tobacco, cotton, rice, and sugar plantations, were generally worked as hard as was consistent with health and productivity. They usually lived in rows of huts or tenements at the rear of the master's house and in many cases were allowed in their spare time to raise poultry, pigs, and garden truck. Holidays, gifts, and festivities were common, and all contributed to develop contentment and prevent truancy and sabotage. That cruelty existed on some plantations there can be no doubt. It was inevitable under a slave system and was accentuated by absentee ownership, by the low quality of overseers, and by frequent attempts of slaves to run away. One of the worst features of the whole system was the auction block, the "selling south," the separation of slave families. This was worst in the border states, just where it was most likely to fall under the eyes of the abolitionist.

Unfortunate as were certain aspects of the slave system, the treatment of the slaves was generally much better than was conceded in abolitionist literature. After all, the slave was the most valuable property that the Southerner possessed, and it was contrary to his interests to overwork or injure such property. "The theory of rigid coercion and complete exploitation," says Professor Phillips, "was as strange to the bulk of the planters as the doctrine and practice of moderation was to those who viewed the régime from afar and with the mind's eye." Slaveholders were not slow in asserting that the economic condition of the Negro slave in the South was better than that of the "wage slave" of the northern factory, and the argument had real point. Instances are numerous enough of Southerners hiring white immigrant laborers to do dangerous and unhealthful work rather than risk valuable slaves at such labor.

[9] Certain theories suggested in this paragraph and generally held by economists have been recently challenged sharply by A. O. Craven and W. E. Dodd, and particularly by Lewis C. Gray. Dr. Gray contends that slavery was often economically profitable on large plantations raising staple crops, that slaves were not economically less efficient than free white labor, that slavery did not inevitably result in soil exhaustion, and that there was no danger in 1860 of slavery's dying out because of a dearth of fresh land. L. C. Gray, *History of Agriculture in the Southern United States to 1860*, especially Volume I, Chapter 20.

It was not alone the exaggerations of abolition agitators that made the solution of the slavery question a difficult one; it was the confidence that the slaveholding Southerner had in the economic future of his region. Until just before the Civil War the market for cotton seemed insatiable, and during most of the antebellum period it could be raised at a profit. Between 1850 and 1860 the annual cotton crop increased from 2,500,000 bales to 5,000,000, more than doubling the wealth of the planters. If one had wealth to start with (land and slaves), all that was necessary was to ride the wave of prosperity and one inevitably grew richer. It was no wonder that King Cotton commanded the allegiance of his subjects and that they became enthusiastic supporters of the slave system.

As slavery appeared to be profitable, it was not long before economists and philosophers developed elaborate arguments in its favor. The best presentations of the Southern side, those offered by Chancellor William Harper of the Supreme Court of South Carolina, by Governor James H. Hammond of South Carolina, by William Gilmore Simms, poet and novelist, and by Thomas R. Dew, president of William and Mary, were fortunately collected in the *Pro-Slavery Argument* (1852) and are therefore easily accessible. Slavery is here defended from both the theoretical and the practical point of view; historical, Biblical, moral, and economic arguments are presented to justify it, and the specific criticisms of the abolitionists ably answered. Men like Dew, and particularly Harper, in their comprehensive defense, repudiated democracy, upheld the caste system, and threw the halo of moral and philosophical justification over the glaring economic inequality among the whites and the domination of the whole society by a few aristocrats. Frankly resting on the contemporary teaching of Carlyle, they stressed the natural inequality of mankind and the advantages that slavery offered to the achievement of an ideal and well-ordered social system. Southern leaders were convinced of the justice and necessity of slavery, and the rest of the white population accepted their point of view.

There was, nevertheless, a certain artificiality about the prosperity of the Cotton Kingdom. In the first place, the South tended to develop an excessively one-sided economic life. The slaveholder's motto, wrote one observer, was "Let us buy more negroes to raise more cotton, to buy more negroes; and so on *ad infinitum*. To raise more cotton the planters must also buy more land. Small farmers are induced to sell out to them, and move further west." In the concentration on cotton, the South had largely neglected industry and finance. Its exports were large, but its imports relatively small, the difference being consumed by the tariffs, freights, commissions, and profits that the Southerners had to pay. "Thus, while the planters monopolized the cotton industry," says Dodd, "drew to themselves the surplus of slaves, and apparently increased their wealth enormously, they were really but custodians of these returns, administrators of the wealth of Northern men who really ultimately received the profits of Southern plantations and Southern slavery." [10]

The same idea is expressed in a different way by Hinton R. Helper, a middle-class white of North Carolina, who produced the most scathing indictment to come from the pen of a Southerner:

> In one way or another we are more or less subservient to the North every day of our lives. In infancy we are swaddled in Northern muslin; in childhood we are humored with Northern gewgaws; in youth we are instructed out of Northern books; at the age of maturity we sow our "wild oats" on Northern soil; in middle life we exhaust our wealth, energies and talents in the dishonorable vocation of entailing our dependence on our children and on our children's children, and, to the neglect of our own interests and the interests of those around us, in giving aid and succor to every department of Northern power; in the decline of life we remedy our eyesight with Northern spectacles, and support our infirmities with Northern canes; in old age we are drugged with Northern physic; and, finally, when we die, our inanimate bodies, shrouded in Northern cambric, are stretched upon the bier, borne to the grave in a Northern carriage, entombed with a Northern spade, and memorized with a Northern slab. [11]

Cotton and slavery were not alone producing a one-sided civilization but were contributing to a rapid destruction of fertile soil and to an undermining of the economic foundations of Southern agriculture. The percentage of unused and exhausted land was high in the seaboard states and increasing in the Southwest. [12] In some regions the progress of King Cotton seemed rather like the advance of a devastating army. Even in Texas, before it had been ten years under cotton cultivation, the spectacle that was so familiar in the older slave states, says Olmsted, was already frequently seen by the traveler—"an abandoned plantation of 'worn-out' fields with its little village of dwellings, now a home only for wolves and vultures." Enthralled by the riches of King Cotton, the South had deliberately turned its back on manufacturing. Only in transportation had the South awakened to its needs and opportunities, but in 1860 railroad mileage in the southern states was but 9500 out of approximately 30,000 for the country as a whole. By the decade of the fifties it was evident that a diversified economic life and free labor had enabled the North to push ahead. Although the population of the two sections had been about even

---

[10] From W. E. Dodd, *The Cotton Kingdom,* Volume 27, The Chronicles of America, 29–30. Copyright Yale University Press.

[11] H. R. Helper, *The Impending Crisis of the South,* 22–23.

[12] See the quotation on page 236.

in 1800, the North had a population in 1860 of over 19,000,000 against 12,-315,000 in the South. Of the real and personal property of the country, amounting to $16,159,000,000 (1859), the northern states were credited with $10,957,000,000. Of the $3,736,000,000 of wealth produced in 1859, northern farms and factories contributed $2,818,000,000.

The northern states were rapidly forging ahead of the South not only in population and wealth but also in cultural facilities. When the two sections were compared in the number of public schools and colleges, the number and excellence of newspapers and magazines, the amount and quality of literature produced and scientific efforts made, there was every evidence in the South of a cultural lag. If slavery, as many contended, made possible the development on the part of the whites of a high general culture, there was little to prove it. This was perhaps more important than economic conditions in forcing a reconsideration of the beneficence of slavery.

THE POLITICAL SOUTH

If the slaveholding plantation-owners dominated the economic life in the South, their political position was even more impregnable. They made the laws of their states, controlled the higher courts, picked governors and congressmen, and dominated all the churches. "There was never in America," asserts Dodd, "a more perfect oligarchy of business men than that which ruled in the time of Jefferson Davis and Alexander Stephens." It is, of course, a fact that Jeffersonian democracy, to which the South had long given lip service, had widely extended the franchise in the East and established universal manhood suffrage in the new states of the Southwest, but it was rare for a poor or middle-class Southerner to achieve a prominent political career. Indeed, there have been few societies in world history in which such a small group has so easily held the reins of power and more completely dominated society. This was due not entirely to the persistence of property qualifications for officeholding in some of the eastern states or to the ease by which the wealthy could generally maintain control, but also to the leisure that the slave system gave to the planters, to the fact that practical politics and political philosophy comprised the chief, almost the only, intellectual interest of the wealthy Southerner, and to the necessity of cultivating politics in order to maintain their power in the federal government against the rapidly rising economic strength of the North and the developing antislavery agitation. Although slavery was ruinous to the poor and middle-class white, he was convinced of its necessity and blindly followed the political leadership of the slaveholding oligarchy.

While the Southern oligarchy was firmly committed to the slave system, it was not committed to any single party. As the Jeffersonian Republicans became safe and conservative, Southern Federalists deserted their early allegiance for its folds. The rise of the Democratic Party under Jackson split the South; the Westerners and small farmers flocked to its banners, but the wealthy planters of the old Federalist areas and the black belt of the lower South for some years gave their allegiance to the more conservative and respectable Whig Party of Clay. Unhappy as the wealthy slaveholder might be in associating with the common herd who followed the leadership of the Jacksonian politicians, in the end he had no other course. The Whigs stood for nationalism, while the South was increasingly turning to states' rights; the Whigs carried on the old Federalist tradition of protective tariffs as the South became more committed to free trade, and the Whigs in 1850 failed to take a definite stand on slavery. In the meantime, as we shall see, the Democratic Party became the advocate of the territorial expansion that was essential to slavery, while the Whigs were lukewarm or opposed. With the exception of the mountain region of western Virginia, where an area of nonslaveholders penetrated the South, and the small-farming region of North Carolina, the South by the fifties was closely integrated politically under the Democratic Party.

Not only had the Democratic Party assumed control of the South, but with two short intermissions it dominated the federal government from the days of Jackson to the election of Lincoln. Politically able as were the Southern oligarchy and certain of the policy which they should pursue, they were numerically too weak to control the federal government except with outside help. This they obtained by an alliance with the West and with the Democratic Party of the North. Western and Northern Democrats might be elected to the presidency and other important offices, but the directing hand was in the Southern Democracy. The primary strategy, however, was an alliance between the Western farmer and the Southern planter, which began in the days of Jackson and Hayne and lasted until broken by shifting trade routes and the rise of the Republican Party. This hegemony of agriculture under the Democratic Party was achieved despite Clay and his Western following and the strong appeal that his "American system" had in the Northwest. It was achieved by a common frontier desire for inflation, opposition to the second Bank of the United States, distrust of the money power of the East, and, above all, the market that the Western farmer found for his grain and pork on the plantations of the Southwest.

This unity of interest between the small farmer of the Northwest and the planter of the Cotton Kingdom was gradually broken by canals and railroads, which were drawing western products to eastern ports and weaving the North and West into a single economic pattern. To re-establish the old trade routes, Stephen A. Douglas projected a "Lakes to Gulf" railway, and the federal government donated large areas of the public domain for the Illinois Central Railroad, but the effort came too late. When the Republican Party, with its opposition to further extension of slavery, with its demand for free land and a transcontinental railway, won over the Northwest, the political control of the slaveholders was doomed. There remained only political defeat or secession.

An introductory chapter is W. B. Hesseltine, *A History of the South,* Chap. XII. One of the best of the Chronicles of America and the work of a life-long student of the Old South is W. E. Dodd, *The Cotton Kingdom.* U. B. Phillips, *Life and Labor in the Old South,* Chaps. XI–XV, is the work of a Southern historian who wrote with fine literary style and reasonable objectivity. His *American Negro Slavery,* Chaps. XI–XX, provides an excellent introduction to the subject. Slavery from the point of view of a careful Northern historian is in J. F. Rhodes, *A History of the United States,* Vol. I, Chap. IV. An excellent job of condensation is J. G. Randall, *The Civil War and Reconstruction,* Chaps. I, II. On the social history of the South read A. C. Cole, *The Irrepressible Conflict,* Chaps. II, III (History of American Life), and Merle Curti, *The Growth of American Thought,* Chap. XVII. Contemporary material is in G. S. Callender, *Selections from the Economic History of the United States,* Chap. XV, and in F. Flügel and H. U. Faulkner, *Readings in the Economic and Social History of the United States,* 415–447.

NATIONALISM AND SECTIONALISM

Chapter XVIII

AGRICULTURAL IMPERIALISM

And yet after all, unanswerable as is the demonstration of our legal title to Oregon—and the whole of Oregon, if a rood!—we have a still better title than any that can be constructed out of all these antiquated materials of old black-letter international law. . . . And that claim is by right of our manifest destiny to overspread and to possess the whole of the continent which Providence has given us for the development of the great experiment of liberty and federative self-government entrusted to us.

THE NEW YORK *Morning News*
(December 27, 1845)

HARRISON AND TYLER

The log-cabin and hard-cider campaign of 1840, which Andrew D. White many years later aptly described as "an apotheosis of tomfoolery," was a fitting commencement to four years of Whig humiliation and disappointment. Worn out by the swarm of office-seekers who encamped in his hotel corridors by night and besieged him throughout the day, the honest and kindly Harrison passed away on April 4, 1841, after one month in office. His successor was John Tyler, an independent Democrat of Virginia, who had received the Whig nomination for the vice-presidency because he was a friend of the defeated Clay and because he represented a large group of Democrats discontented with Jackson and Van Buren. The Whigs had taken a long gamble and lost; the discontented Democrats for whose votes they were angling were opposed to Jackson because of the nationalistic tendency that he had shown in the nullification controversy and because both Jackson and Van Buren at critical moments, as it seemed to them, tended toward the Whigs. Typical of this group was Tyler, a man obstinate and politically ambitious, with a mind high and narrow.

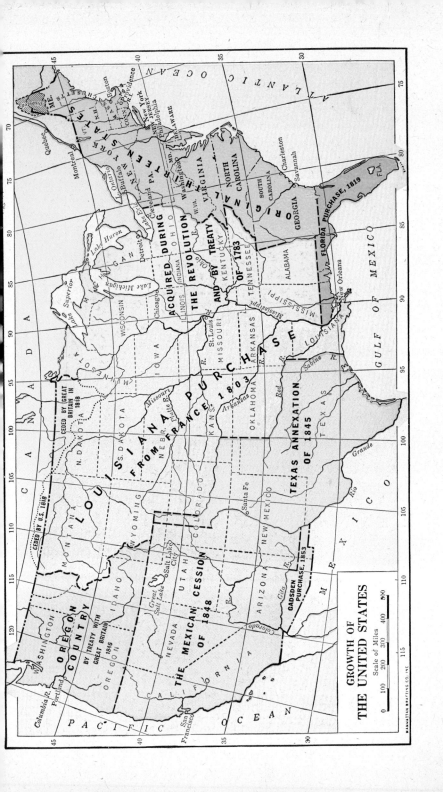

GROWTH OF
THE UNITED STATES

Scale of Miles
0   100   200   300   400   500

MANHATTAN DRAFTING CO. INC.

Harrison had offered the Department of State to Clay; upon his refusal he conferred it upon Webster, but with four of Clay's intimate friends
in the remaining positions. Tyler for the moment retained this cabinet.
When Congress met in special session, Tyler in his message advised that
the subtreasury be eliminated and its place taken by a "suitable fiscal
agent," that the proceeds of the public-land sales be distributed among the
states to help rehabilitate their credit, and that the tariff for the present
be left alone. Clay, who had expected to be the power behind the throne of
the Harrison administration, had no intention of resigning the leadership
to Tyler, and, before the session was a week old, he offered resolutions
incorporating the Whig program of the session: repeal of the Independent
Treasury Act, establishment of a new national bank, higher tariffs distribution among the states of the proceeds of public-land sales, passage of
needed appropriation bills, and an improvement of the banking system of
the District of Columbia. This was both a belated Whig program and a
notification to all that Clay intended to assume leadership.

On the repeal of the Treasury Act there was no difference of opinion
between Tyler and the Whig leaders, and it was speedily accomplished.
But with the way now clear for new bank legislation, the trouble commenced. Clay was all for a bank similar to that destroyed by Jackson, but
with this the states' rights and antibank Tyler refused to agree. Twice the
Whig Congress modified its bill to suit the supposed wishes of Tyler, and
twice he vetoed it. Accusing the President of treachery, a Whig congressional caucus now repudiated Tyler with the words, "all political connection between them and John Tyler was at an end." All members of the
cabinet except Webster, who was involved in delicate negotiations with
Great Britain regarding the Maine boundary, resigned, while Clay himself resigned from the Senate to devote his entire time to reorganizing the
party and isolating Tyler and Webster, who most Whigs believed had
deserted the party. Tyler in his second veto of the bank measure complained that he had concurred in all the important Whig legislation except this, and there was much truth in his contention. The urgent needs
of the treasury had been met by a loan, banking facilities in the District
of Columbia had been improved, and the navy had been strengthened.
After devious negotiations, an emasculated distribution bill had been
passed (1841), providing for distribution on condition that the tariff
should not be increased beyond the 20-per-cent level fixed by the Compromise Tariff of 1833. The distribution feature, however, failed to mate-
rialize, for the needs of the treasury made it necessary in 1842 to raise the
tariff beyond the 20-per-cent level, and further efforts to keep the distribution principle alive met executive veto.

THE CANADIAN BOUNDARY LINE

Whatever uncertainties might exist regarding Tyler's political theories or domestic policies, his conduct of foreign relations was consistently and aggressively imperialistic. In this policy his Secretaries of State, Webster, Upshur, and Calhoun, all co-operated with enthusiasm. Webster, with his New England background and ever on the alert to take care of the commercial interests of his section, sent Caleb Cushing to China after the Opium War, where the latter succeeded in obtaining (1844) a treaty that put the United States on the "most-favored-nation" basis and granted the principle of extraterritoriality. This concession gave Americans charged with civil or criminal offenses against Chinese laws the right to be tried in their own courts, and thus opened the way for foreign groups to reside in China almost independent of local authority. Throughout the entire administration the government assumed toward Mexico an aggressive, if not truculent, attitude. While American warships hung on the coast of California, ready to swoop down in case of war, the administration at Washington hammered the Mexican government with claims, demands, and proposals of various kinds.

The chief contribution of Webster, however, was his progress in solving the disputes over the Canadian boundary line. When he assumed office, three parts of the Canadian boundary remained to be determined—that which separated Maine from New Brunswick and Quebec, that between Lake Superior and the Lake of the Woods, and the Oregon line. The problem of the Oregon boundary was becoming more acute, as American immigrants in the early forties were pointing toward the Northwest, but the settlement of the controversy was to wait upon the next administration. The other boundary controversies were in no way simplified by the difficulties that had arisen between Great Britain and the United States during the Van Buren administration. American citizens had participated in the Canadian rebellion of 1837, and the insurrectionists had used American soil as the basis of operations.[1] At the same time citizens of New Brunswick and Maine were in armed conflict over the Aroostook valley ("Aroostook War"). British newspapers and British publicists were never more critical of American civilization or more hostile toward the United States than in the late thirties and early forties, but fortunately concilia-

---

[1] The *Caroline*, an American steamer in the rebel service, had been captured by Canadian militia and an American citizen killed. A Canadian citizen, Alexander McLeod, boasted in a New York saloon that he "had killed the American." Upon his arrest, the British government demanded his release on the ground that he had acted under orders. The federal government asserted that it could not interfere with a state court. The incident was closed when McLeod was acquitted, but Webster in 1841 secured an act of Congress providing that a foreign citizen on trial in a state court could be removed to a federal court on a writ of *habeas corpus*.

tory influences were also at work. Most important of all was the growing reliance of Great Britain upon American wheat and cotton.

Through negotiations conducted with Lord Ashburton, the Maine boundary line, in dispute since the treaty of Paris of 1783, was finally compromised, as was also the line between Superior and the Lake of the Woods. Of the territory in dispute in Maine, the United States obtained 7000 of the 12,000 square miles, including the fertile Aroostook valley, which has in recent years become the most important potato region of the East. The circumstances surrounding the eventual agreement were not without touches of humor. An American historian had discovered in the official French archives a map, believed to have been prepared by Franklin for the French foreign office, which supported the extreme English claims. Concealing this from the English, Webster showed it to the senators from Maine, and the treaty was ratified. At the same time a map formerly belonging to George III was discovered in the British Museum; on it the line, as described by the British peace commissioners of 1783, supported the extreme American claims, and this map was produced in Parliament when the treaty was attacked there. In this "battle of the maps" each side held the information most needed by the other, and in the compromise the United States was fortunate in securing the most valuable land.

TEXAS AND THE CAMPAIGN OF 1844

American penetration of Texas and the inevitable friction between Anglo-Saxon settlers and the Mexican authorities, led, as we have seen, to revolution and to the establishment under the leadership of Sam Houston of the Lone Star Republic (page 237). Although American settlers, aided by American adventurers, had consummated Texan independence, Jackson, unwilling that the Texan question should in any way complicate the campaign of 1836, withheld recognition of the new Republic until the last day but one of his administration (March 3, 1837). It was quickly evident, however, that Texas preferred annexation by the United States to independence. In fact, it was extremely uncertain whether independence could be maintained. Mexico refused to recognize the new republic, and it seemed probable that, if a nation of six million should seriously attempt to reduce one of 50,000, it would be successful. The hope of Texas lay either in annexation to the United States or in a guarantee of independence by France and England.

During the latter months of 1837 and the early months of 1838 Texas pressed for annexation. The time was unpropitious, for slavery was again becoming a national issue. Although agitation against the slave system had existed since the days of the Revolution and an American Colonization Society, sponsored by such men as Henry Clay and John Randolph, had been founded in 1816 to return Negroes to Africa, the late twenties found a general apathy regarding the problem of slavery. This situation was not to last long. The influence of antislavery advocates like Benjamin Lundy, who had been publishing since 1821 the *Genius of Universal Emancipation,* was beginning to have its effect. Lundy was honest and devoted to his cause, but courteous in the tone of his argument. His assistant editor, William Lloyd Garrison, however, issued on January 1, 1831, the first number of the *Liberator,* with the challenge: "I am in earnest—I will not equivocate—I will not excuse—I will not retreat a single inch—and I will be heard." To Whig business men who desired friendly and profitable economic relations with the South and to the "respectable" elements generally, the fanatical agitation of Garrison and his kind was anathema. Garrison himself was dragged through the streets of Boston with a rope around his neck and was saved from a worse fate only by the interference of the police. Two years later Elijah P. Lovejoy, editor of an antislavery paper in Alton, Illinois, was murdered by a mob. Despite popular disapproval, Garrison rapidly gained converts. In 1832 the New England Anti-slavery Society was formed and in the following year the American Anti-slavery Society, which within seven years boasted 2000 branch societies and 200,000 members. So rapid was this growth that the milder element, who would proceed through constitutional channels, organized the Liberty Party and nominated for the presidency in 1840 James G. Birney, a former slaveholder of Alabama.

As the antislavery movement spread Congress was bombarded with petitions for the abolition of the slave trade in the District of Columbia. Incensed by this interference with their cherished system, Southern congressmen succeeded in passing a "gag resolution" (1836) to table all petitions having to do with slavery. John Quincy Adams, now back in Washington representing his district in the House, was no abolitionist, but he regarded the "gag resolution" as unconstitutional and tyrannical, and fought session after session until it was repealed in 1844. It was during the early years of the battle over the "gag resolution" that Texas pressed for admission as a slave state and a resolution to admit her was introduced in Congress. Influenced by a Lundy pamphlet called *The War in Texas* and by a speech of John Quincy Adams, which at the rate of an hour a day took three weeks to deliver, Northern opponents of slavery became convinced that the whole Texan episode was a deep-dyed plot of the slaveholding South to add to its power. Although reputable historians have given countenance to this abolitionist belief, there seems to be no historical foundation for it. The movement into Texas was a normal advance of the frontier, in which the majority of the pioneers were naturally Southerners, and the revolution and request for annexation were quite as inevitable.

Whether the charge was true or not made little difference. Enough Northerners believed it to kill the resolution (July, 1838) and to prevent annexation for almost a decade. "Sooner perish! Sooner our name be blotted out from the record of nations!" than that Texas be annexed, cried William E. Channing, while Garrison called for secession if Texas with her slaves was admitted. On her part, the Lone Star State, realizing the situation, ceased further agitation for annexation, and Van Buren was able to sidestep the issue for the remainder of his term. Slaveholding Democrats, however, had no intention of letting the matter drop and were whipped into renewed activity during the Tyler administration by rumors that Texas was negotiating for British protection and that Great Britain had offered help on condition of the abolition of slavery. Upshur, who became Tyler's Secretary of State after the retirement of Webster in 1843, began negotiations for a treaty of annexation, and after his death Calhoun continued them. As neither party at the moment cared to assume the responsibility for annexation, the Senate in 1844 rejected the treaty.

The responsibility that the Senate had evaded was boldly assumed by the Democratic Party in the presidential election of that year. Casting aside Van Buren, whose position on the annexation of Texas was equivocal, the nominating convention chose James K. Polk of Tennessee and came out flat-footedly for "the reoccupation of Oregon and the reannexation of Texas." [2] The Whigs gave their great leader, Henry Clay, his third nomination, but the same reason that prevented Van Buren from receiving the Democratic nomination prevented the popular Clay from being elected. Before nomination Clay had opposed annexation, but during the campaign, under pressure from the South, he trimmed his sails, writing that he had no objection to annexation "without dishonor, without war, with the common consent of the union, on just and fair terms." Although Texas could never have come in under such conditions, this statement, it was said, aroused antislavery voters in New York state to cast their ballots for James G. Birney, again nominated by the Liberty Party, thus throwing the state to the Democrats and giving them the national election. By cleverly linking Oregon with Texas, the Democrats had shifted the emphasis from slavery to expansion. The issues were as clear-cut as they are ever likely to be in an American election, and the decision was in favor of expansion. "Manifest destiny" must be fulfilled.

The results of the election were sufficient for the politicians. Without

[2] Although the boundaries of the Louisiana purchase were indefinite, it was believed by many at the time of the purchase that the territory included Texas. Whether or not this was so, claims to Texas were given up by the Florida treaty of 1821 (page 182).

waiting for the next administration, Tyler and Calhoun took up the Texas question and, to avoid the possibility of defeat, obtained annexation by a joint resolution rather than by treaty, which would have required a two-thirds vote. Even so the vote was close, the Senate approving 27 to 25 and the House 132 to 76. It was the belief of many at the time, including the financier Jay Cooke, that Northern opposition to the annexation of Texas was overcome sufficiently to bring about this vote only by the influence of Northern holders of Texas bonds, who hoped in this way to revive their sinking securities. Be that as it may, the joint resolution provided that Texas be admitted as a state, that four additional states with her consent might be made from her territory, that Texas assume her own debt and surrender her fortifications on land and water, that the principle of the Missouri compromise apply to the new region, and that negotiations over boundary-line disputes be conducted by the United States.

MANIFEST DESTINY

James K. Polk, whose name was hardly known to the nation before the campaign of 1844, proved to be a man of commonplace mind but of great industry. His program was definite—re-establish the independent treasury, lower the tariff, and fulfill the expansionist planks in the Democratic platform. In the end he came closer to fulfilling his program than many a more brilliant man who has occupied the same exalted position. The independent treasury was restored in 1846, and the Walker tariff of the same year started the tariff rate downward again. Only on the Oregon question did Polk fail to achieve complete success. The Democrats had talked glibly of "the whole of Oregon or none," and "fifty-four forty or fight" had been a popular campaign slogan. Polk believed we should have the whole of Oregon, but war with Mexico seemed probable, and even the most ardent expansionist hesitated to contemplate a simultaneous conflict with Great Britain and Mexico. Southern Democrats, furthermore, had only an academic interest in Oregon. As a consequence, Polk instructed Buchanan, his Secretary of State, to renew an earlier American offer to compromise at parallel 49. The British refused, whereupon Polk, with Congressional sanction, gave Great Britain the one year's notice (page 238) for terminating the joint agreement of occupation. A few months later Great Britain accepted the compromise that she had repeatedly refused, except that she insisted upon retaining Vancouver Island. The Senate agreeing, such a treaty was consummated in June, 1846. As in the Maine compromise four years earlier, the United States came off with the lion's share, for the Columbia valley, the most valuable part of the disputed territory, went to the United States. After two years of haggling, Congress created Oregon as a free territory, and Polk signed the bill (1848) on the ground that Oregon was north of the Missouri Compromise line. Whether free or slave, American territory for the first time faced the Pacific, a fact of momentous importance.

Regarding the antecedents of the Mexican War there exist two schools of historians. One asserts that it was a war of outright imperialism premeditated and provoked by the United States to gain California and the Southwest. The other school holds that Mexico provoked the war and that the United States had no choice. Mexico had never recognized the independence of Texas, and in 1843 President Santa Anna had warned that "the Mexican government will consider equivalent to a declaration of war . . . the passage of an act for the incorporation of Texas into the territory of the United States." When such action was taken, Mexico broke off diplomatic relations. The Mexican Congress increased the army, and the Mexican government prepared for war. Texas having been annexed by joint resolution, Polk had nothing to do but defend this action from any aggression on the part of Mexico. As an ardent expansionist, he was prepared not only to do this but also to press for the annexation of California and the Southwest. Upon promise that a minister would be received, Polk sent John Slidell to Mexico in an effort to establish friendly relations with that nation, to reach a decision regarding Texas, and, if possible, to settle American claims by a further cession of territory. With many Mexicans clamoring for war and the existing government facing a revolution, Slidell was not received. Polk, having satisfied his conscience that an honest effort had been made to achieve the object of American ambitions without war, was now prepared in the spring of 1846 to force a war on his own part. Just as he was on the point of asking Congress for a declaration of war, Mexico struck the first blow and gave him an opportunity of placing on her shoulders the onus of commencing the struggle.

Although the Mexican government insisted that the Sabine River marked the northern boundary of Mexico, the more realistic Mexicans knew that Texas was gone for good. Even this group, however, insisted that the Nueces and not the Rio Grande was the southern boundary of Texas, and their position rested upon sound claims. Into this disputed territory between the two rivers Polk nevertheless ordered General Taylor and an American army. On April 24, 1846, a Mexican force crossed the Rio Grande and engaged a detachment of American cavalry, killing several and capturing the rest. News of this was received by Polk on the evening of May 9, and his war message went to Congress two days later. "The cup of forbearance," declared the President, "had been exhausted . . . now, after reiterated menaces, Mexico has passed the boundary of the United

States, has invaded our territory and shed American blood upon the American soil. . . . War exists, and notwithstanding all our efforts to avoid it, exists by the act of Mexico herself." Inasmuch as the clash had been provoked by the sending of American troops into disputed territory, this statement seems to be a little far-fetched, but it satisfied a majority of Congress, and war was declared on May 13. One man that it did not satisfy was Abraham Lincoln, an Illinois lawyer serving his only term in the House, who introduced in 1847 the "spot resolution" questioning whether the spot on which Taylor's scouts had been killed was our own soil. In a letter to his law partner Lincoln expressed what came to be a typical Whig position toward the war when he insisted that it was "unnecessarily and unconstitutionally commenced by the President."

If some of the Whigs, particularly in New England, were opposed to the war, the abolitionists condemned it with the utmost bitterness. With Lowell's castigation in the *Biglow Papers* they utterly agreed:

> They just want this Californy
> So's to lug new slave-states in
> To abuse ye, an' to scorn ye,
> An' to plunder ye like sin.

Nevertheless, the war was greeted with enthusiasm, especially in the South and West, and amazingly well conducted considering the fact that it was fought entirely on foreign soil and far from the base of supplies. To the embarrassment of the administration, both ranking generals were Whigs, who were eyed by Polk with coldness if not with suspicion, and who did not always receive the heartiest co-operation from Washington.

The history of the war logically divides itself into a description of three campaigns: that in northern Mexico under General Taylor, the advance from Vera Cruz under General Winfield Scott, and the conquest of California by Colonel Stephen Kearny. An aggressive frontier fighter, "Old Rough and Ready" Taylor, without waiting for a declaration of war, crossed the Rio Grande, defeated the Mexicans in several minor engagements, and after a three days' battle captured Monterey (September 23, 1846). Wisely deciding that a conquest of Mexico from the north was impossible, the administration ordered Taylor to send half of his force of 10,000 to Scott. Complaining of lack of support, Taylor disgustedly complied, but continued south as far as Buena Vista, where he defeated Santa Anna (February 22–23, 1847) and a force four times as large as his own. Buena Vista closed the northern campaign; the scene then shifted to the south.

A month later Scott, with some 9000 troops, captured Vera Cruz and started (March 27) on the 250-mile march to Mexico City over the route taken by Cortez three centuries earlier. Scott was a somewhat vain and swashbuckling soldier ("Fuss and Feathers," his soldiers called him), but he was an able officer, and his army contained many brilliant and dependable subalterns—Lee, Grant, and McClellan, for example—who in the years to come were to achieve fame on their own account. After clearing the Mexicans from the difficult mountain pass of Cerro Gordo (April 17-18) and winning stiff fights at Contreras and Churubusco (August 7-20), Scott was ready to move on Mexico City when Santa Anna consented to an armistice to discuss terms of peace. The real instigator of the armistice was one Nicholas P. Trist, chief clerk of the State Department, who, like the "deputies on mission" during the French Revolution, had been sent by Polk to keep his eye on Scott and negotiate a treaty of peace. Not daring to make peace on the terms proposed by Trist, the wily Santa Anna used the respite to prepare for further defense. Operations were resumed, and, after a severe engagement at Molino del Rey (September 8) and the storming of the fortified castle of Chapultepec (September 13), Mexico City surrendered (September 17). ·

Months before the American troops had quartered themselves in the "Halls of the Montezumas" to await a Mexican government that dared to make a treaty, Kearny had completed the conquest of California.[3] Setting out with 1800 men (June, 1846) from Fort Leavenworth, Kearny soon captured Santa Fé without a blow. After setting up a government under the American flag, he pressed on by way of the Gila valley to California. When he arrived in December, he found the conquest all but completed. Aided and abetted by Captain Frémont, then engaged in an exploratory expedition in the West, and by Commodores Sloat and Stockton of the navy, American settlers had risen in the "Bear Flag Revolt" and had already cut off the tenuous authority of the Mexican government.

After the occupation of Mexico City the American army remained four months before a Mexican government had the courage to accede to the harsh terms imposed by Scott and Trist. The latter had been recalled after the August armistice, but, disobeying instructions, remained with the army and negotiated the treaty of Guadalupe Hidalgo (February 2, 1848).

[3] The first white exploration of California was by Juan Rodriguez Cabrillo, 1542–1543, but it was not until 1769, when the Franciscans established a mission at San Diego, that white penetration of California may be said to have begun. The missionaries converted the natives and taught them some of the arts of civilization. Gradually a few Spaniards from the south trickled in, and eventually came whites of other nationalities. The economic life of this early period was based primarily upon ranching. In the meantime the mission lands had become secularized, and, after the revolution against Spain, California became a province of Mexico. Outside trade, at first forbidden, grew, bringing contacts with the outside world and an increasing non-Spanish element in the population. At the time of the Mexican War the Mexicans still outnumbered the foreign whites by at least three to one, but the latter were the most aggressive element in the population. Under the circumstances, a severance from Mexico was probably inevitable.

Polk was furious when he received this unauthorized treaty, but, as it accorded roughly with his original instructions to Trist, he decided to send it to the Senate, where it was ratified (March, 1848) by a vote of 38 to 14. By it the United States received the Rio Grande boundary for Texas, together with New Mexico and Upper California, in return assuming the claims of American citizens against Mexico and paying, in addition, $15,-000,000. This seemed like adequate booty for a short and relatively inexpensive war,[4] but there were many, including Secretary of State Buchanan, who advised annexing all of Mexico. To the clamor of the superexpansionists Polk wisely turned a deaf ear, and, except for the Gadsden purchase of 1853, the present continental boundary lines of the United States were achieved by the Guadalupe Hidalgo treaty.

THE WILMOT PROVISO AND THE ELECTION OF 1848

In view of the antislavery opposition to the annexation of Texas, it was hardly to be expected that the slavery issue would be quiescent during the war. It blazed forth with renewed vigor on August 8, 1846, when, in reply to Polk's appeal to Congress for $2,000,000 to buy additional territory from Mexico, David Wilmot of Pennsylvania introduced in the House an amendment to an appropriation bill:

> That, as an express and fundamental condition to the acquisition of any territory from the Republic of Mexico by the United States, by virtue of any treaty which may be negotiated between them, and to the use by the Executive of the moneys herein appropriated, neither slavery nor involuntary servitude shall ever exist in any part of said territory, except for crime, whereof the party shall first be duly convicted.

The Wilmot Proviso was written by Jacob Brinkerhoff of Ohio and appears to have originated among Northern Democrats in retaliation against the Southern wing of the party for failure to consummate the Democratic campaign pledge regarding Oregon. However it may have originated, it was significant as providing a rallying principle for the moderate antislavery forces and as pointing the way to a new political alignment of those in the North and Northwest who were opposed to the further extension of slavery. Although endorsed by ten free-state legislatures, the proviso failed to pass the Senate.

Slavery and the Mexican War dominated the campaign of 1848. Utterly

[4] Professor J. H. Smith, pointing out that an exact figure as to the cost of the war is impossible, says, "as a very bold guess one may suggest a hundred millions." This would include the excess expenditures of the army and navy, which appear to have been $63,605,621, the $12,000,000 later paid to Mexico, the claims against Mexico of which she was relieved, expenses of bounty lands, pensions, and so forth.

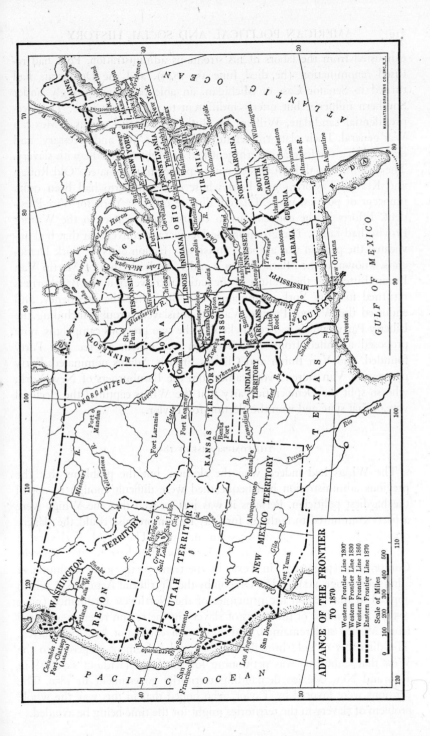

ADVANCE OF THE FRONTIER
TO 1870

Western Frontier Line 1800
Western Frontier Line 1830
Western Frontier Line 1860
Eastern Frontier Line 1870

Scale of Miles
0   100 200 300 400 500

exhausted from the labors of his strenuous administration, Polk had refused renomination (he died June 15, 1849), and the Democrats had turned to Senator Cass of Michigan, an able politician strongly under Southern influence but utterly indifferent to the slavery issue. The vice-presidential candidate, William O. Butler of Kentucky, was a Mexican War general. Their platform defended the war as "just and necessary" and declared that the federal government had no right to meddle with slavery. The Whigs, who did not bother with a platform, nominated "Old Rough and Ready" Taylor, a war hero whose career hitherto had been quite innocent of politics, with Millard Fillmore of New York for Vice-President. Efforts in the conventions to commit both parties to the Wilmot Proviso had failed. The group in the Democratic convention that had advocated the proviso was a liberal antislavery faction of New York Democrats, known as the "Barnburners," under the leadership of Martin Van Buren. Bitter over their failure at the national convention, the Barnburners returned to New York, nominated Van Buren for the presidency, and endorsed the Wilmot Proviso. Various antislavery groups, including the Liberty Party, which had run tickets in the two previous campaigns, now proposed a united front. A convention was called, a Free Soil Party founded, and Van Buren and Charles Francis Adams nominated. Forty per cent of Van Buren's vote came from the Barnburners of New York, who so split the Democratic Party that the Whigs captured the electoral vote of that state and won the election for Taylor.

THE COMPROMISE OF 1850

The Whigs had indeed won the election, but the problems that the previous administration had bequeathed were difficult enough to appall the hardiest politician. Perhaps it was just as well that the Whigs were a party committed to nothing, for only by compromise could the slavery question be settled without secession and war. The status of slavery, it will be recalled, was settled in the Louisiana purchase by the Missouri Compromise (page 179), in Texas by the terms of the joint resolution of admission (page 304), and in Oregon by the Territorial Act of 1848, which applied to that region the principles of the Northwest Ordinance (page 305). The problem of the status of slavery in the region recently acquired from Mexico still remained, and a solution could not long be delayed. The discovery of gold brought such a rapid movement of people to the West that California was petitioning for statehood (without slavery) in 1849 and New Mexico demanding territorial government in 1850. The petitions were favored by Taylor, who hoped that in this way the whole problem of slavery in the territories might for the time being be avoided.

The slavery issue, however, had become too tense for any such easy solution, and there were too many conflicting views to reconcile in this simple manner. One group, including Polk, believed that the easiest solution was to extend the Missouri Compromise line to the Pacific. A second group, composed of adherents of the Wilmot Proviso, would exclude slavery from all territories. A third group, representing Southern extremists of the Calhoun-Davis type, denied the power of Congress to prohibit slavery in federal territories. A fourth group, led by Cass and Stephen A. Douglas, advocated "popular sovereignty" or the right of the settlers to decide the issue for themselves. Wrangling over these conflicting solutions, the session of Congress of 1848–1849 accomplished nothing except to make clear that the slavery controversy included the question of fugitive slaves, the Mexican cession, and the status of slavery in the District of Columbia as well as in the territories.

The growing tension and threats of disunion aroused the political giants of the nationalist school, Clay, Webster, and Benton, to a last struggle to save the Union. Clay, who decades earlier had won fame as a strategist of compromise, again played the leading role. On January 29, 1850, he introduced eight resolutions, later incorporated into the "Omnibus Bill" and eventually known as the Compromise of 1850. They provided for the admission of California as a free state, territorial organization in the rest of the Mexican cession with no restrictions regarding slavery, relinquishment by Texas of her claims to New Mexico, assumption by the federal government of the Texan debt contracted before annexation, and a more stringent fugitive-slave law. For the next eight months Congress gave its chief attention to the subject matter of these resolutions.

Clay began the debate on February 5, 1850, with an eloquent plea for compromise and conciliation. He was followed a month later by Calhoun, the second of the great triumvirate. He was too ill to stand, and his carefully prepared speech was read by his friend Mason of Virginia. Unlike that of Clay, his speech was no plea for compromise. Recognizing the growing economic and political preponderance of the North, Calhoun insisted that the South had no redress against the grievances and oppression that it had suffered from the North. The Union, said he, could be saved—not by compromise by the weaker party, but by concessions from the stronger. If the North would cease agitation, enforce the laws regarding fugitive slaves, and grant to the South equal rights in the territories, all would be well. Otherwise, "let the States . . . agree to separate and part in peace." Calhoun was correct in pointing out the growing strength of the North, but quite wrong in attributing the failure of the South to hostile legislatio... On the contrary, the federal government until 1860 was almost continuously dominated by the South. It was the tragedy of the South that its greatest leader never grasped fully the economic significance of the life of his section.

Three days after Calhoun had sounded his note of despair, Webster rose to speak. Contrary to the expectations of the antislavery group, his famous "Seventh of March Speech" was a plea for compromise. New Mexico, he insisted, would in all likelihood be free by "an ordinance of nature," and it was folly to taunt the South with a Wilmot Proviso. He questioned the usefulness of abolition societies and insisted that the South was right in demanding a more stringent fugitive-slave law, but he ridiculed the possibility of "peaceable secession." "Sir," said he, "your eyes and mine are never destined to see that miracle." To the antislavery group in the North Webster was now anathema, and his eminently sane and statesmanlike position was savagely attacked. These irreconcilables of the North must also have their say, and William H. Seward of New York was their chief spokesman. The Constitution, said he, might tolerate slavery, but there was "a higher law than the constitution." Legislative compromises, he insisted, were all "radically wrong and essentially vicious."

Although Clay's original bills failed to pass, they were later rewritten by Stephen A. Douglas, accepted by Congress, and signed by Fillmore, who had become President after the death of Taylor (July 9, 1850) and who favored the compromise. The nation had not yet lost its sense of balance and was not yet ready to accept the ultimate results of fanatics who repudiated compromise and talked glibly of the "higher law." Natural differences of opinion among men as to what the "higher law" might be had already plunged the world into innumerable orgies of blood, and was destined to do it again in America. In the wave of prosperity that was rising rapidly after the gold discoveries of 1848, responsible men made a last desperate effort to direct attention from the slavery issue and to calm the troubled waters of sectional animosity. And this was true of the South [5] as well as of the North: men like Crittenden of Kentucky and Stephens, Cobb, and Toombs of Georgia worked earnestly to allay secessionist sentiment and to counteract the efforts of extremists of the type of Governor Quitman of Mississippi and William L. Yancey of Alabama.

In August and September the various acts comprising the Compromise of 1850 were passed. California was to be admitted as a free state (giving the North the balance of power in the Senate, 16–15); the remainder of the Mexican cession was to be divided into the two territories of Utah and New Mexico, which were to be admitted "with or without slavery as their Constitution may prescribe"; a new western boundary line was to reduce

[5] A convention called by Southern radicals in June, 1850, for the purpose of denouncing compromise and urging secession, found that the South as a whole was opposed to such drastic procedure, and the convention adjourned to await the results of congressional action.

the area of Texas, but the United States was to pay Texas $10,000,000 in compensation; the slave trade was abolished in the District of Columbia; and a drastic fugitive-slave law was enacted. While the compromise was satisfactory to few, and on the whole favored the North, it was an honest effort to solve the slavery problem, for some provision had now been made for every part of the Union. In the end it failed, but by postponing an armed conflict for ten years it so strengthened the North that the Union could not be broken beyond repair.

THE CAMPAIGN OF 1852

That the country was fairly well satisfied with the compromise, and that the majority were anxious to turn to other business, there is ample evidence. In Congress Clay and forty-four others pledged "their intention to maintain the said settlement inviolate . . . unless by the general consent of the friends of the measures." So anxious were the politicians to avoid the issue in the congressional session of 1850–1851 that they got no further than the passing of "pork-barrel" legislation. The campaign of 1852 was dominated by the question of the compromise just as that of 1848 had been by the Wilmot Proviso. The Democrats, unable to decide among their chief candidates, Douglas, Buchanan, and Marcy, finally nominated Franklin Pierce of New Hampshire, a handsome and urbane gentleman with respectable if not distinguished talents. "The Democratic party of the Union," said their platform, ". . . will abide by, and adhere to, a faithful execution of the acts known as the 'compromise' measures settled by the last Congress" and "will resist all attempts at renewing in Congress or out of it, the agitation of the slavery question." The Whigs also endorsed the compromise, but they passed over Fillmore and Webster, known adherents of the compromise, and nominated General Winfield Scott, who personally accepted the compromise but was known as the candidate of the Seward Whigs, who did not. Nathaniel Hawthorne, a college friend of Pierce, wrote his campaign biography, but even "the most graceful pen" in America could not make the candidate appear a great man. There was little enthusiasm for Pierce, but the nation was tired of the slavery question, and the merest suspicion that Scott and the Whigs were not sufficiently committed to the compromise enabled the Democrats to win by an electoral vote of 254–44. Scott carried only four states.

MORE MANIFEST DESTINY

While economic sectionalism, intensified by the slavery issue, was driving the nation to civil war, "manifest destiny" had still to play out its role.

Both the Oregon boundary and the treaty of Guadalupe Hidalgo were compromises that hardly satisfied the most ardent expansionists. This was particularly so after the rapid settlement of California made imperative the building of a transcontinental railroad and southern statesmen discovered that the best southern route would run through Mexican territory. The Gila–Rio-Grande line, which had been specified in the treaty and which seemed reasonable enough as a river boundary, was now disputed by the United States government. In the meantime, Santa Anna was pressing exaggerated claims for Indian depredations. To straighten out the dispute Pierce sent James Gadsden with instructions to purchase the land necessary for building the railroad. Gadsden sent back a treaty by which the United States for $15,000,000 was to obtain another block of land and secure relief both from Mexican claims and from a former pledge to restrain Indian raids. Congress, interested primarily in cutting down the cost of the transaction, refused to ratify on these terms. As a result the amount of territory was reduced to meet merely the needs of railroad construction, and the price was cut to $10,000,000. Congress ratified, but it was the old story of "penny wise and pound foolish." The original cession would have given the United States the entire Colorado River, thus simplified the problem of later irrigation projects, and secured for us control of the Gulf of California, important in any consideration of the nation's defense.

The agricultural imperialism of the forties and fifties was not confined to Oregon and Mexico. In 1846 the United States, dreaming of an interoceanic canal, had signed a treaty with New Granada (Colombia), obtaining a right of way across Panama for either a canal or a railroad, and in return had guaranteed the "perfect neutrality" of the isthmus. Conflicting interests of Great Britain and the United States in Central America had resulted two years later in the Clayton-Bulwer treaty, by which both nations agreed not to seek an exclusive control over any canal route or to establish dominion over any part of Central America. This might seem to be a renunciation of American ambitions, but, when it is realized that Great Britain was already established in British Honduras and attempting to extend her power, it is evident that the treaty was not one-sided. Not all Americans were satisfied with such a treaty. One of them, William Walker, a professional filibuster, descended upon Nicaragua in 1856 and secured control of the government. Eventually overthrown, he made a second attempt, but was seized and returned home by the American navy.

Nicaragua might be left to private initiative, but Cuba, the "Pearl of the Antilles," received the constant attention of proslavery governments. California and New Mexico might be free by "an ordinance of nature" and the "will of God," as Webster pointed out, but such was not the case with Cuba, which seemed to offer a logical next step in the extension of slavery. "It is our destiny to have Cuba," declared Douglas in 1858, "and it is folly to debate the question. It naturally belongs to the American continent." Thus the conception of "manifest destiny" was already extended beyond the continental boundaries. Beginning in 1848, filibustering expeditions instigated from the United States kept Cuba in a state of unrest, and our minister to Spain, Pierre Soulé, attempted to precipitate a war between the United States and Spain over the seizure of the *Black Warrior,* an American merchant vessel. As Marcy, Pierce's Secretary of State, refused to support the American minister, the threatening clouds blew over. Soon after, however, Soulé, along with John Y. Mason and James Buchanan, our ministers to France and Great Britain, gathered at Ostend, Belgium, and treated the world in the "Ostend Manifesto" to one of the most brazen bits of "shirt-sleeve diplomacy" on record.

"In the progress of human events the time has arrived," said the manifesto, "when the vital interests of Spain are as seriously involved in the sale as those of the United States in the purchase. . . . After we shall offer Spain a price for Cuba . . . and this shall have been refused . . . we shall be justified in wresting it from Spain, if we possess the power." That these sentiments were not far from those of the Pierce administration there can be no doubt, but the language was a little too honest and straightforward for international diplomacy, and the administration immediately repudiated it. Before Cuba could be annexed, the Civil War intervened, and Cuba's reduction to the status of an American protectorate was postponed until after the Spanish War, a half century later.

While the agricultural imperialism of the South looked abroad for new territory, the commercial and industrial interests of the North achieved a signal victory. For a half century American traders had trafficked with China, American whalers had scoured the Pacific, and the American merchant marine had penetrated the trading centers of the Pacific isles. Only Japan, on the direct route to Asia, remained closed to outside intercourse, and the world was becoming too small for such an incongruous situation. In 1853 Commodore Matthew C. Perry (younger brother of Oliver H. Perry, hero of Lake Erie) appeared with a strong fleet in Japanese waters, where, by a display of some of the interesting products of Western civilization, combined with a judicious mixture of force and tact, he secured a treaty that opened two ports to American trade. Through the influence of Townsend Harris, the first American consul in Japan and one of the ablest men who have ever represented American interests abroad, more liberal treaties were obtained. The question of opening Japan to foreign intercourse became intimately involved in the domestic politics of Japan and produced a period of unrest there. A joint naval demonstration in 1863 by Great Britain and the United States was necessary before Japan turned her face to the outside world and decided to modernize her ways.

A brief but well-written account of the Mexican War is N. W. Stephenson, *Texas and the Mexican War* (Chronicles of America). On the treaty of peace and on politics during the war read J. H. Smith, *The War With Mexico*, Vol. II, Chaps. XXXII–XXXIV. There is a good sketch of Polk in the Introduction to Allan Nevins, editor, *Polk: The Diary of a President,* and interesting material on the war as viewed by official Washington in Chap. IV. Relations with the Pacific and the Far East are reviewed in S. F. Bemis, *Diplomatic History of the United States,* Chap. XX. Foreign relations are ably recounted in T. A. Bailey, *A Diplomatic History of the American People,* Chaps. XIV–XX. For the philosophy of expansion, A. K. Weinberg, *Manifest Destiny,* Chap. I ff. Bernard De Voto, *The Year of Decision,* is accurate history written with spirit and imagination. Important sources are in H. S. Commager, *Documents of American History,* Vol. I, 306–314.

Chapter XIX

THE IRREPRESSIBLE CONFLICT

"A house divided against itself cannot stand."
I believe this government cannot endure perma-
nently half slave and half free. I do not expect
the Union to be dissolved—I do not expect the
house to fall—but I do expect it will cease to be
divided.

ABRAHAM LINCOLN (June 16, 1858)

The fault of the Free States in the eyes of the
South is not one that can be atoned for by any
yielding of special points here and there. . . .
Their crime is the census of 1860. Their increase
in number, wealth, and power is a standing ag-
gression. It would not be enough to please the
Southern States that we should stop asking them
to abolish slavery,—what they demand of us is
nothing less than that we should abolish the spirit
of the age.

JAMES RUSSELL LOWELL

THE PROSPEROUS FIFTIES

Conservatives both in the North and in the South hoped that the Compromise of 1850 would end the slavery controversy as a disturbing element in American politics. The discovery of gold in California had pushed prices upward and inaugurated a new era of prosperity, which the business interests were anxious to exploit. Except for a minor setback in 1854 and a more serious panic in 1857, the decade was one of extraordinary economic development. This development, without doubt, rested primarily upon the expansion of transportation facilities. The decade opened in a "plank road fever" that resulted in the building throughout the Middle West of thousands of miles of these transient highways. On the Mississippi and its tributaries the river steamboat enjoyed its golden age, when the gorgeous palaces of the rival companies vied with one another in comfort and speed, and owners accumulated fortunes in transporting the foodstuffs of Northern farmers and the cotton of Southern planters.

Through the plains and mountains of the Far West the government made heroic efforts to establish routes for communication and transportation. After an unsuccessful experiment with imported camels, the Postmaster General, in 1857, awarded to John Butterfield of the Overland Mail Company a contract for a semiweekly mail service between the Mississippi and the Pacific coast, and during the following year regular stagecoach and mail service, which covered the distance in twenty-five days or less, was established over both the northern and the southern routes to California. In 1860 the freighting company of Russell, Majors, and Waddell inaugurated the famous pony express, which carried letters from St. Joseph to Sacramento in the incredibly short period of ten days. The pony express marked the spectacular perfection of the overland service, but it was a losing venture and came to an end when the Western Union Telegraph Company completed construction of its transcontinental wires in October, 1861. The overland coaches and the pony express were but the most striking aspects of the Far Western transportation and communication. More important was the great freighting business on the overland trails, which by 1860 employed over 6000 wagons and 75,000 oxen.

More significant than all this was the rapid development of railroad transportation, which was soon to become the primary means of communication. Mileage increased during the decade from about 9000 to over 30,000, with the greatest expansion in the Northwest. Atlantic seaports, in bitter rivalry for western trade, pushed their lines west of the mountains. The local lines across New York state, which were consolidated in 1853 into the New York Central, found immediate competition in the Erie, completed to Dunkirk on Lake Erie in 1851, in the Pennsylvania, completed to Pittsburgh in 1852, in the Baltimore and Ohio, which reached Wheeling in 1853, and in the Grand Trunk, which joined Portland and Montreal in the same year. Hardly less important than these trans-Allegheny roads was the network in the Middle West centering in Chicago. By 1860 fifteen railroads reached that city, giving the rising rail metropolis of the West communication with the Mississippi at many points as well as with eastern seaports. In the South 8000 miles were built during the decade, affording that region communication between the Atlantic and the Mississippi and between the Gulf and the Great Lakes.

Although much American traffic was slipping into the hands of European shipowners, and England was establishing her pre-eminence in iron ships powered with steam, the American shipbuilders and the American merchant marine had achieved a position in the fifties second to none. Stimulated by the California traffic, by the repeal of British navigation acts, and by the Crimean War, the tonnage of the American merchant marine increased during the decade from 1,500,000 to nearly 2,500,000, while considerable tonnage was sold abroad. It was during these years, as we have seen, that the sailing ship reached its highest development in the famous American clippers (page 252).

This notable development of transportation facilities was in part a result and in part a cause of a similar development of industrial life. Immigration, which during the early forties had averaged less than 100,000 a year, had jumped in 1850 to over 350,000, providing labor for economic development and stimulating the westward movement. In spite of the low tariff, textile production advanced in the Northeast, and the ready-made-clothing and shoe industries were made possible by the invention of the sewing machine in the forties. The rapidly expanding agricultural domain provided a market for agricultural machinery, while railroads and factories created a growing market for iron, steel, and other metals. The number of factories increased during the decade by 17,000 and the number of employees by over 350,000, while the capital invested and the value of the raw materials consumed almost doubled.

Prosperity such as this brought the inevitable panic, and, like most American panics, it was primarily caused by overexpansion and overspeculation in transportation facilities and real estate. That there was much prematureness about the expansion there can be no doubt, but the general economic life was not essentially unhealthy. The panic was primarily financial, affecting chiefly the financial centers and speculative railroad investments. Rural sections, particularly the South, were little affected, a fact that strengthened the conviction of the Southerners that theirs was a superior civilization. At any rate, recovery was quick, and by the opening of the Civil War the nation was definitely on the upgrade of a new cycle of prosperity.

UPSETTING THE COMPROMISES

It is hardly surprising that, under the circumstances, conservative politicians strove to push the slave issue into the background. But the business man's truce was unfortunately destined to a speedy and inglorious end. One cause of the failure of compromise was undoubtedly the passing from the scene of the older statesmen, those able political leaders who had risen to power in the nationalistic era following the War of 1812. Van Buren had retired from national politics, and Benton had lost his seat in the Senate in 1851. Clay died in June of 1852 and Webster in October of the same year. Compromisers anxious to preserve the Union were still to be found in national politics, such men as Douglas of Illinois, Cass of Michigan, Marcy of New York, Bell of Tennessee, and Crittenden of Kentucky, but in the end it was the radicals of the North and South who were to prevail. Among the younger and ardent antislavery politicians of the North were Charles Sumner of Massachusetts, William H. Seward, formerly Whig governor of New York, and Salmon P. Chase of Ohio. Opposed to them were Southern secessionists of the type of Barnwell Rhett of South Carolina and J. A. Quitman and A. G. Brown of Mississippi, who were joined in the late fifties by such former Unionists as Jefferson Davis of Mississippi and Robert Toombs of Georgia.

In the North the most irritating part of the Compromise of 1850 was the Fugitive-Slave Law. To reclaim a fugitive slave, the master or agent had merely to present an affidavit before a United States judge or commissioner, whose fee was doubled if he decided in favor of the claimant. Testimony of the alleged fugitive was not admitted, and heavy penalties were imposed for hindering an arrest or aiding in the escape. The bill struck terror into the Negroes of the North whether fugitive or free and dealt a staggering blow to the "underground railroad" by which slaves had escaped to Canada. Resentment against the act took the form of mob violence, when Negroes were rescued from the authorities by abolition sympathizers. This type of opposition was climaxed in May, 1854, when a Boston mob, led by a Unitarian minister, attempted to rescue from the courthouse a hotel waiter, one Anthony Burns. It took the police and several thousand soldiers to put Burns aboard ship, and he was the last Negro returned from Massachusetts. In the same year Joshua Glover, a Negro arrested under the act in Wisconsin, was rescued by a mob and shipped to Canada. A newspaper editor, accused of inciting the mob, was tried, and the Wisconsin Supreme Court was given an opportunity to declare the Fugitive-Slave Act unconstitutional. Taney and the Supreme Court reversed the state court in a strongly nationalistic decision, which outdid Marshall himself, but the action of the Wisconsin court, in conjunction with the "personal-liberty laws" passed in several of the states to counteract the federal law, made evident to all the growing unpopularity of that part of the compromise.

Whether the Compromise of 1850 could have shelved the slavery issue long enough to make possible a solution without civil war no one can say. Historians sympathetic with the economic interpretation insist that slavery was becoming increasingly unprofitable, and that, when Southern slaveholders realized this, they would have taken measures to end it. Other students hold that a belief in the necessity of perpetuating the "peculiar institution" had become such an integral part of Southern psychology that the demand for more stringent safeguards would have continued until the inevitable break came. Whatever possibility existed of avoiding secession and civil war was ended when the Compromise of 1850 was thrown aside. Chiefly through the leadership of Stephen A. Douglas, aided by every political weapon that the Pierce administration could wield, the Kansas-Nebraska Bill was driven through the Senate in March of 1854 and through the House in May. It subdivided the Nebraska territory into two territories, divided at parallel 40, and stated that the restriction on slavery introduced by the Missouri Compromise "was superseded by the principles of the legislation of 1850, commonly called the compromise measures, and is hereby declared inoperative."

In defense of the measure Douglas had argued the principle of "squatter sovereignty," the same principle that the Compromise of 1850 applied to Utah and New Mexico, and had asserted his belief that physiographic limitations would actually prevent slavery from gaining a foothold in Kansas. It was evident, however, that supporters of the bill expected Kansas would become a slave state, and opponents fought the bill on this supposition. While the South as a whole did not initiate the bill, it naturally supported it. In the North the Kansas-Nebraska Act again opened up the whole slavery question and made the issue more vital than ever before. The attitude in that section was not far different from that expressed in *The Appeal of Independent Democrats of Congress to the People of the United States,* a document signed by the Free Soil members of Congress and largely written by Sumner, Salmon P. Chase, and J. R. Giddings of Ohio. In it the bill was condemned "as a gross violation of a sacred pledge; as part and parcel of an atrocious plot to exclude from a vast unoccupied region immigrants from the Old World and free laborers from our own States, and convert it into a dreary region of despotism inhabited by masters and slaves."

"I passed the Kansas-Nebraska Act myself," said Douglas, and upon him must rest the chief onus for the legislation. People of the time and many subsequent historians have attributed his action to his presidential aspirations. If this was so, he blundered badly, but there is little evidence upon which to base such an accusation. The act, in the form it took and as far as Douglas was interested in it, seems to have originated from a sincere desire to organize territorially the region west of Missouri on any terms that could be made. Southern politicians opposed territorial organization because they opposed new free states and because they were planning a southern railroad to the Pacific. The latter had already been made possible by the Gadsden purchase, and such a road would have had the advantage of running entirely through organized territory. Douglas, a heavy speculator in Illinois real estate and ardently desirous that any transcontinental road should terminate in Chicago, had, as chairman of the Committee on Territories, been striving for years to secure organization of this region, but bills providing for it had been checked by the South. The Kansas-Nebraska Act was fundamentally a bribe to the South to permit territorial organization to prepare the way for a northern transcontinental railroad. Needless to say, Douglas found his strongest backer in Senator Atchison of Missouri, a slave state that also aspired to be the eastern terminus of a transcontinental railway. One of the best biographers of Douglas also suggests that the Illinois senator was motivated by the belief that the Democratic Party had no longer a unifying principle and that the doctrine of "squatter sovereignty" would provide this.[1] In any case it seems evident that the interests of finance, transportation, and business played in many ways a larger role than slavery in the backstairs politics of the Kansas-Nebraska Bill.

SLAVERY AND THE TERRITORIES

Whatever may have been the motives of Douglas, the repeal proved a colossal blunder. The question of slavery was again opened to contention and this time was not to be closed without civil war. From the halls of Congress the struggle quickly shifted to the plains of Kansas. Douglas might orate that nature had destined Kansas to be free, but proslavery politicians had no intention that it should become so. When the territory was organized and elections held in November, 1854, for a territorial delegate to Congress and in March, 1855, for a territorial legislature, hundreds of armed men, organized in "Blue Lodges," poured in from Missouri and carried the elections for the slave candidates. Fraud was so evident that the territorial governor (Reeder) ordered supplementary elections in some districts, but the free-soil men elected were not seated, and the legislature enacted laws to protect slavery, even providing a penalty of two years at hard labor for anyone who denied the right of persons to hold slaves in the territory. In the meantime small farmers from the Northwest and immigrants from New England, the latter aided by Eli Thayer's New England Emigrant Aid Society, were staking their claims in Kansas and rapidly outnumbering the immigrants from the slave states. In October of 1855 the free-soilers called a convention at Topeka, drafted a constitution forbidding the entrance of slaves, and a month later chose a legislature and governor. The answer of the slave settlers was a descent, May 21, 1856, upon the free-state headquarters at Lawrence and the burning and pillaging of a number of buildings. In retaliation John Brown led a small band to Osawatomie Creek and murdered in cold blood five proslavery men.[2]

While the practical outcome of squatter sovereignty was civil war on the plains of Kansas, the Supreme Court injected itself into the slavery con-

---

[1] Allen Johnson, *Stephen A. Douglas* (1908), 236–237.
[2] The attack on Lawrence had been preceded by the murder of two abolitionists.

troversy and made the solution even more difficult. Years earlier a Negro slave, Dred Scott, had been taken by his master into the state of Illinois, land made free by the Northwest Ordinance, then into the northern part of the Louisiana purchase, territory made free by the Missouri Compromise, and finally back to Missouri, a slave state. On the ground that residence in free territory had made him a free man, Dred Scott sued for his freedom in 1846 in the Missouri courts. The Superior Court of the state ruled that, whatever his status might have been in a free territory, his return to Missouri made him again a slave. A new suit instituted in the United States Circuit Court brought the same result. When the case was carried to the Supreme Court on a writ of error, that body could easily have avoided any larger issue by refusing jurisdiction.

This seems to have been the original intention, but it was prevented by Justice McLean, a strong antislavery man with political aspirations, who announced his intention of filing a dissenting opinion, and by Justice Curtis, a Northerner, who also insisted upon dealing with the larger issues. The result was an opinion by Chief Justice Taney, upheld by the majority, in which Dred Scott's citizenship was denied. Furthermore, the court insisted that since the Constitution recognized slave property, Dred Scott's status was determined by the law of Missouri and not by that of Illinois, and that Congress, which held territories simply as a "trustee" of the states, had no right to discriminate between the property of the citizens of various states while it was in the territories. The latter contention, which made the Missouri Compromise unconstitutional, was an *obiter dictum,* and, like most of the decision, had no foundation in history or legal precedent, a fact that Justice Curtis in a dissenting opinion had no difficulty in making clear. The decision, if maintained, not only declared the Missouri Compromise unconstitutional, but, by denying the authority of Congress to legislate concerning slave property, upheld the most extreme views of the South and dealt a terrific blow at the newly formed Republican Party, which was founded on the thesis that the further extension of slavery might be prevented by congressional action.

Never was a Supreme Court decision more unpopular, and never was the fallacy that the judiciary is uninfluenced by economic or political views more strikingly exposed. Upon the Kansas situation, however, it had little effect. Pierce, by sending federal troops, had quieted the civil war in the territory, and Buchanan, who assumed the presidency in 1857, sent a new governor, Robert J. Walker, with the assurance that he would be supported in an impartial policy. Walker called for an election for a new constitutional convention, but the free-soil advocates refused to vote. Shortly after they changed front and elected a free-soil legislature. The constitutional convention meeting at Lecompton now drew up a document guaranteeing the property in slaves that was already in Kansas, and drafted a special clause that would have denied the prospective state both the power to emancipate slaves without consent of the owners and the power to forbid the entrance of slaves. This clause was the only one submitted to the voters, who theoretically were to vote on the "constitution with slavery" or the "constitution without slavery." As slavery remained in any case, the election was denounced as a trick by the free-state men, who refused to vote. The administration, nevertheless, now completely under Southern domination, upheld the Lecompton constitution and insisted that the Democratic Party admit Kansas as a slave state. In spite of the opposition of Douglas, who denounced the procedure as a burlesque on popular sovereignty, admission was voted in the Senate. The House refused to concur, but later (under the English Act) Kansas had an opportunity to obtain immediate admission by accepting the Lecompton constitution. She rejected it, and thus the situation remained until 1861, when she joined the Union as a free state.

THE HOUSE DIVIDED

The presidential campaign of 1852 had been dominated by the Compromise of 1850 and the pledge of both parties to uphold it. Within two years the sectional truce was destroyed; as a result the picture of American politics changed with amazing swiftness. Within six years the Whig Party entirely disappeared, the Democratic Party was split in twain, and a new political organization, the Republican Party, won a national election. As the Whig Party, with little to bind it together, disintegrated under the impact of the slavery controversy, and as free-soil Democrats became fighting mad over the Kansas-Nebraska Bill, the demand for the organization of a new antislavery party became widespread. A nonpartisan meeting in February, 1854, at Ripon, Wisconsin, demanded the organization of a party dedicated to the principle of no further extension of slavery, and the name "Republican" was suggested. In July, at Jackson, Michigan, such a party actually came into existence when a full slate of state officers were nominated, demanding the repeal of the Kansas-Nebraska Act and the Fugitive-Slave Law and the abolition of slavery in the District of Columbia. Similar organizations were effected in a few other states, but the only state victory of 1854 was in Ohio, where the new party won by a majority of 75,000.

The advance of the Republican Party was temporarily halted by the simultaneous appearance of another organization, the Know-Nothing Party, representing one of those curious antiforeign, anti-Catholic movements that have appeared more or less periodically in our history. Secret at first, the party took its name from the answer, "I know nothing," obediently given by its adherents to questions seeking information concerning its principles. As the Irish-Catholic immigrants were chiefly Democrats, the new organization obtained most of its adherents from the disintegrating Whig Party. Especially strong in the Northeast, during its brief career it captured Massachusetts in 1854, and Connecticut, New Hampshire, and Rhode Island in 1855. Its presidential candidate, Fillmore, carried in 1856 only the state of Maryland, and the party quickly disappeared.

Repelled by the fanaticism of the Know-Nothings, discerning Whig leaders in the East watched with interest during 1854 the rising Republican movement in the Middle West. By 1856 it seemed clear that their future lay with this new party. The Whig enterprise was spent, that of the Know-Nothings was splitting on the slavery issue, and the Democratic strength in the North was rapidly declining. The Republican Party, on the other hand, offered an opportunity for the "Conscience Whigs" of the North and the antislavery group of the Know-Nothings and Democrats to coalesce on the issue of slavery.

Acting on this theory, a national organization was perfected and a call issued for a nominating convention. In an effort to find a candidate acceptable to the many diverse elements of the new party, older politicians were sidetracked and the nomination given to John C. Frémont, a younger man unknown to politics, but a man whose western explorations had captured the imagination of the people. The platform demanded the immediate admission of Kansas on the basis of the Topeka constitution, opposed the further extension of slavery, and again raised the old war cry of the Free-Soilers of 1848, "free soil, free speech, free labor, and free men." Reaffirming their belief in squatter sovereignty, the Democrats, nevertheless, did not dare renominate Pierce, who had signed the Kansas-Nebraska Act. Instead, they chose an experienced and conservative politician, James Buchanan of Pennsylvania, whose chief claim to nomination rested in the fact that he came from a doubtful state and had been absent as ambassador to Great Britain during the Kansas controversy. The Know-Nothings nominated ex-President Fillmore.

The Republicans made Kansas the main issue of the campaign; the Democrats countered by stressing the Union, pointing out the sectional character of the Republican Party, and prophesying the break-up of the Union if Frémont was elected. While conservatives might have been glad to keep the Kansas issue in the background, it was quite impossible. On the eve of the nominating conventions had come the "sack of Lawrence," John Brown's atrocities at Osawatomie Creek, and the vicious assault in the Senate chamber upon Charles Sumner by Preston Brooks, a representative from South Carolina. Considering the fact that it was their first presidential election, the new party made an amazing showing. Buchanan, to be sure, won the election,[3] but it was closely fought, and he was the last Democrat to win the presidency for twenty-four years. Conservative business interests in the North, anxious to preserve peace, had been the deciding factor.

Encouraged by their showing in 1856, the Republicans looked forward hopefully to the next campaign, and their cause was strengthened by the Dred Scott decision and by the obvious fact that the Buchanan administration was completely under Southern domination. The weak cabinet that Buchanan gathered about him contained four Southerners but no prominent representative of the Douglas Democrats. Northern business interests lost confidence as the incapacity of the administration was repeatedly evidenced in the Kansas issue, the panic of 1857, and other problems confronting the nation. On the other hand, there seemed to be less enthusiasm for Republican principles in 1858 than there had been in 1856. As it became clear that Kansas would never accept a slave constitution, "squatter sovereignty" did not look so bad. Douglas's break with the administration over Kansas demonstrated his sincerity and again won for him much of his old-time popularity in the North. Some prominent Republicans, including the erratic Greeley of the New York *Tribune,* even advocated a coalition of antiadministration forces under his leadership. Ardent free-soilers, however, could not swallow the indifference of Douglas to slavery ("I care not whether it is voted down or voted up") and could not forget the part he had played in the passage of the Kansas-Nebraska Act. It was the Republicans of his own state who decided the future by refusing to endorse his candidacy for re-election to the Senate and by nominating Abraham Lincoln to oppose him.

The campaign of 1858 was significant in more ways than one. It meant, in the first place, that the Republican Party would carry on in spite of the Dred Scott decision and Douglas's break with the administration. It made Lincoln a national figure, and it served, as we shall see, to split hopelessly the Democratic Party. The Republican nominee for the Senate was then forty-nine years of age and approaching the apex of his intellectual powers. Born in a Kentucky log cabin, he had been taken by his parents to the Northwest and there in the rough frontier environment had achieved through his own efforts an education far beyond the average of that region. Beginning in 1834, he served several terms in the Illinois legislature and as a Whig was elected in 1846 to a single term in Congress, where he opposed the Mexican War, introduced the "spot resolution," and proposed a bill for compensated emancipation in the District of Columbia.

[3] The electoral vote was Buchanan 174, Frémont 114, Fillmore 8. The Democrats polled 1,838,169, the Republicans 1,324,264, and the Know-Nothings 874,534. Buchanan carried his home state by a majority of 1025 votes out of a total of 460,404.

Retiring from politics, he soon became a leader of the Illinois bar, where he was engaged in important and lucrative practice when the Kansas-Nebraska Act stirred him again to take an active part in the politics of his state. He was slow, easygoing, and lethargic by nature, but his fine intellect could be stirred under pressure to great activity. Neither his honesty nor his ability could be questioned. Of the shystering trickery so common in law courts Lincoln was amazingly free, and he was known to be a man who would not accept a case unless he was convinced his client was in the right. "He is," said Douglas, "a strong man of his party— full of wit, facts, dates—and the best stump-speaker, with his droll ways and dry jokes, in the West. He is as honest as he is shrewd; if I beat him, my victory will be hard won."

To the amazement of the nation, who knew Douglas as the ablest debater in the Senate, Lincoln challenged the "Little Giant" to a series of debates in the various election districts of the state. In Illinois, where Lincoln was known, the citizens flocked by the thousands to the great outdoor gatherings to hear these historic debates. In the second debate, at Freeport, Lincoln's opportunity came. "Can the people of a United States territory, in any lawful way, against the wishes of any citizen of the United States," asked Lincoln, "exclude slavery from its limits prior to the formation of the state constitution?" Put more concretely, what he demanded of Douglas was whether the latter adhered to his pet theory of "squatter sovereignty" or to the doctrine enunciated in the Dred Scott decision. A repudiation of "squatter sovereignty" would ruin him politically in the North, while a repudiation of the Supreme Court decision would end his political career in the South. In his attempt to reconcile the two Douglas supported the Dred Scott decision in theory, but insisted— and in this he was both sensible and quite realistic—that in actual practice slavery could only exist when supported by "police regulations . . . established by local legislatures." This "Freeport doctrine" of Douglas may have won him the election in Illinois,[4] but it aroused intense hostility in the South and two years later split the Democratic Party and prevented his election to the presidency.

Lincoln lost the election, but his party registered large gains.[5] The Democratic losses of 1858 were undoubtedly due in part to the panic of 1857, but, after we discount this influence, it is obvious that the policies of the Southern Democracy were being viewed with increasing dissatisfaction. In the short congressional session of 1858–1859 the South countered

---

[4] The Lincoln candidates polled about 190,000 votes to 170,000 for Douglas, but a Democratic "gerrymander" made the election of Douglas possible by 8 votes in the Illinois legislature.

[5] The election of 1856 had resulted in a house containing 131 Democrats, 92 Republicans, 14 Know-Nothings; that of 1858 gave 109 Republicans, 86 Democrats, 13 Anti-Lecompton Democrats, and 22 Know-Nothings.

with a proposal for the appropriation of $30,000,000 to purchase Cuba, but the bill failed.

Before Congress could meet again, an event occurred that was to stir anew the fires of the slavery controversy to white heat. With the financial aid of a few ardent abolitionists, old John Brown, long a spectacular figure in the civil war in Kansas, conceived the idea of invading Virginia with an armed band and establishing a position somewhere in the mountains from which he might descend upon the farming communities to free the slaves. His idea seems to have been to make slavery so insecure in this manner that masters would dispose of their remaining slaves. Collecting arms and a few followers at a farm near Harpers Ferry, he set out with a band of eighteen men on the night of October 16, captured the government arsenal at that point, and commenced freeing slaves. Two days later, surrounded by Virginia militia and a detachment of marines under Colonel Robert E. Lee, his band was dispersed, and he himself, with four of his men, was captured. If ever a crack-brained scheme was evolved, such a one was John Brown's raid. The actions of a man long brooding over the iniquity of the slave system, convinced that he was an instrument in the hands of God, and undoubtedly afflicted with congenital insanity, are easy to explain. More difficult is it to find excuses for the wealthy and prominent abolitionists, Gerritt Smith, Theodore Parker, Thomas Wentworth Higginson, and others, who financially aided this hopeless and criminal undertaking. The intensity of the antislavery crusade, however, and Brown's truly heroic bearing and speech during his last few days established him as a martyr, but the only result of the raid was to intensify the bitterness over slavery and to keep the country on edge as Brown went to trial in October and was executed on December 2.

Three days after Brown swung from a Virginia gallows, the thirty-sixth Congress assembled. In the House the choice of Speaker became immediately involved in the slavery issue. The Republican candidate, John Sherman of Ohio, it was discovered, had endorsed as a campaign document an abbreviated edition of Helper's *Impending Crisis of the South* (page 294). This picture of the economic and cultural backwardness of the slave states was (and still is) resented by Southerners as biased and unfair. In consequence, it was almost two months before a conservative Republican was elected, and in the overcharged atmosphere, said Senator Hammond of South Carolina somewhat extravagantly, "every man in both houses is armed with a revolver—some with two—and a bowie knife." Under such conditions there was little likelihood that much legislation of importance would be passed, and the session of Congress was little more than a preparation for the next presidential campaign.

With this in view, Jefferson Davis, representing the Southern wing of the Democratic Party, introduced resolutions (subsequently passed by the Democratic Senate) reaffirming the doctrine of state sovereignty, upholding the Dred Scott decision, denouncing the "Freeport doctrine" of Douglas, and calling on Congress to protect slavery in the territories. The Davis resolutions and the debates that followed made clear the growing schism in the Democratic ranks.

1860 AND SECESSION

When the nominating convention of the Democratic Party met in April, two factions struggled for domination—the radical group, who took an uncompromising position behind the Davis resolutions, and the conservatives, mostly Northerners, who backed Douglas and his doctrine of "squatter sovereignty." Fear of secession, returning prosperity, and other factors had greatly increased during the previous year the strength of Douglas and had provided a compromise program upon which the Union might have been saved. Nevertheless, the Committee on Resolutions introduced a majority report based on the Senate resolutions of Davis. When the convention refused to accept it and voted in favor of the minority report approving the stand of Douglas, William L. Yancey of Alabama led his delegation from the hall and was followed by the delegates of the other seven states of the lower South. Failure to nominate a candidate led the convention to adjourn to Baltimore, where it later nominated Douglas for President and Herschel V. Johnson of Georgia for Vice-President. The seceders, reconvening in the same city, nominated John C. Breckinridge of Kentucky and Joseph Lane of Oregon.

With the Democrats badly split, only hopeless bungling would prevent a Republican victory, and the practical politicians, who foregathered at Chicago, had no intention of committing any tactical errors. By stressing a protective tariff, free land for settlers, and a Pacific railroad, and reaffirming their earlier opposition to the extension of slavery, the Republican platform held out a beckoning hand to the conservative business interests of the Northeast, to the pioneer farmers of the West, and to the antislavery idealists who had founded the party. From the viewpoint of practical politics the platform was almost perfect. Would the presidential candidate be equally acceptable? When the convention met, the nomination was generally conceded to William H. Seward, the best-known leader of the party, but his well-known affiliations with the moneyed interests of New York, his friendliness to Catholic immigrants, and his radical opposition to slavery weakened his position. By clever political manipulation and lavish promises, the opposition to Seward was consolidated behind Lincoln, who received the nomination on the third ballot.[6] As a prominent railroad lawyer, Lincoln was satisfactory to big business; as an honest but not fanatical free-soil advocate, he appealed to the common man. In the meantime another party, the Constitutional Unionists, was organized for the campaign and nominated John Bell of Tennessee and Edward Everett of Massachusetts. Its brief platform calling for "the Constitution of the country, the Union of the states, and the enforcement of the laws," might inspire only ridicule from ardent partisans, but it was a sincere gesture toward saving the Union.

In the election the Republicans were as fortunate as in the nominating convention. By stressing the tariff in Pennsylvania and other manufacturing centers and the homestead plank in the Northwest, and by soft-pedaling slavery generally, Lincoln won an electoral vote of 180 against 72 for Breckinridge, 39 for Bell, and 12 for Douglas. In the final analysis Lincoln's victory was due to the shift of the Old Northwest from the Democratic column to that of the Republicans. For two decades an alliance between the planters of the South and the farmers of the Northwest had kept the Democrats in power; that alliance Lincoln had broken, and with it, at least for the time being, went the power of the Democrats in the national government.[7] As far as popular votes went, however, Lincoln was a minority President. His popular vote of 1,866,452 was but 40 per cent of the total; the rest was divided as follows: Douglas 1,376,957, Breckinridge 849,781, and Bell, 588,879. The combined Democratic vote exceeded that for Lincoln by over 360,000. Although the Davis Democrats took the election results as a signal for secession, there was little in them to warrant any such move. The combined vote of the antisecessionist candidates amounted to 80 per cent. Even in the southern states as a whole Breckinridge polled less than 50 per cent of the votes. Nor did the election of Lincoln mean Republican control. If the southern states had not se-

---

[6] The promises made by Judge David Davis, Lincoln's campaign manager, were made in violation of instructions, but Lincoln later made them good. The nomination for the vice-presidency went to Hannibal Hamlin of Maine.

[7] William E. Dodd, in his well-known article, "The Fight for the Northwest, 1860," *American Historical Review*, XVI, 774–788 (July, 1911), sums up his findings as follows: "It seems, therefore, fair to conclude that the flood-tide of Republican idealism was reached in 1856–58, that the able and well-organized aristocracy of the South came near to winning their point—an election in the House, that the property and religious influences of the Northwest compelled Lincoln and his advisers to recede from the high ground of 1856–58; and finally that the contest was won only on a narrow margin by the votes of the foreigners whom the railroads poured in great numbers into the contested region. The election of Lincoln and, as it turned out, the fate of the Union were thus determined not by native Americans but by the voters who knew least of American history and institutions."

Now is the time for those who would serve their Country.

THE
CLINTON RIFLES

Having been accepted, as the FIRST REGIMENT, under the new call,

A FEW RECRUITS ARE WANTED
TO FILL UP VACANCIES.

Rations commence as soon as Roll is signed,

The pay of a Soldier is $15 a month, on a discharge $100 Bounty, besides a Land Warrant.

The Uniform is Handsome, well made, and will not drop off after two week's wear.

Come all who would RESCUE our Glorious Union from Rebels and Traitors, and remember the Government needs every Man at the present time.

THE REGIMENT IS ENCAMPED AT THE

FIRST LANDING, STATEN ISLAND,
THE FINEST CAMP GROUND IN THE STATE.

For the whole Union, and may God Speed the Right,

CIVIL WAR RECRUITING POSTER

(Courtesy of the New York Historical Society)

WHAT THE ADMINISTRATION HAS DONE.

MAP SHOWING THE PROGRESS OF THE NATIONAL ARMIES DURING THE YEARS 1861, 1862, 1863 AND 1864.

THE TRUE ISSUE OR "THATS WHATS THE MATTER".

CAMPAIGN POSTER AND CARTOON, 1864

Above—Part of Union Party Campaign Poster (Courtesy of the New York Historical Society.)

Below—Currier and Ives Campaign Cartoon.

ceded, there would have been an antiadministration majority in both houses.

The frequent threats made during the campaign that the election of a "Black Republican" would mean secession were to be realized. Four days after Lincoln's election the South Carolina legislature called for a convention to meet on December 17 to consider the relation of South Carolina to the Union. On December 20, by a unanimous vote, this convention passed the Ordinance of Secession, declaring that "the Union now subsisting between South Carolina and the other states under the name of the United States of America is hereby dissolved." Commissioners were dispatched to Washington to treat regarding federal property, and urgent messages were sent to other states advising similar action. Although considerable Union sentiment was to be found in some of the southern states, elections to state conventions showed secessionist majorities, and by February 1, 1861, Mississippi, Florida, Alabama, Georgia, and Louisiana had followed South Carolina in seceding from the Union. They were joined by Texas on February 23, 1861. This movement for secession had undoubtedly been aided by the unwillingness of President Buchanan to do anything to halt it and by his belief, as stated in his annual message of December 4, that he had no power under the Constitution to prevent it.

In addition to Buchanan's weak-kneed indecision there was evidently a strong Northern opposition to an arbitrament by arms. Southern planters, it was estimated, owed to northern mercantile interests close to $300,-000,000. Prosperity was returning, and innumerable projects for economic development were in the air. The mayor of New York even suggested that the metropolis secede in order to carry on its business with the South. In addition to the economic interests there were many abolitionists who evidently believed the Union would be as well off without the slave states. "If the cotton states shall decide that they can do better out of the Union than in it," said Greeley in December, "we shall insist on letting them go in peace," and this sentiment was echoed by Wendell Phillips and Henry Ward Beecher.

As a consequence, sincere efforts were made at reconciliation. The one that received the most serious consideration was the Crittenden Compromise, introduced by Senator Crittenden of Kentucky. In addition to four resolutions, it proposed six unamendable amendments, the most important of which was the exclusion of slavery north of the 36° 30′ line and the establishment of it with federal protection south of that line.[8]

---

[8] Other amendments forbade Congress to interfere with slavery in the states where it was legal or to interfere with the domestic slave trade. By another the United States was to compensate the owners of fugitive slaves when arrests were prevented by force. Slavery was to be

With the exception of this amendment, Republicans were inclined to favor the compromise, but the restoration of slavery in all regions south of 36° 30′ was not only in violation of their campaign pledge but definitely opposed by Lincoln. If the failure of the Crittenden Compromise made war inevitable, no one was more responsible for the conflict than Lincoln, but its acceptance in all probability would have provided merely a respite and not a permanent solution. In any case it is quite improbable that South Carolina would have returned to the Union. One other important effort at reconciliation was made in the gathering of a "peace convention" of 150 delegates from twenty-one of the thirty-three states, which met on February 4 under the chairmanship of ex-President Tyler. Sessions continued for a month, but the solution proposed by the convention received only seven votes in the Senate.

On the day the peace convention met, delegates from six states, meeting at Montgomery, Alabama, established a provisional constitution (superseded by a permanent constitution March 11) for the "Confederate States of America," elected Jefferson Davis of Mississippi president and Alexander H. Stephens of Georgia, who had earlier opposed secession, vice-president. The Confederate constitution, while modeled on that of the United States, differed in many respects. Slavery was to be protected in the territories, and Congress was forbidden to deny or impair the right of property in slaves, but the importation of slaves was forbidden. Import duties were prohibited, and the executive was limited to one term of six years. In the belief of many the new constitution was an improvement over that of the United States in that it provided for an executive budget, empowered the president to veto special items in an appropriation bill, and empowered the congress to admit cabinet officers to either branch to discuss legislation pertaining to their respective departments. Having drawn up a new constitution, authorized an army of 100,000 men, and voted a bond issue of $15,000,000 to support it, the delegates had made secession an accomplished fact.

AN APPRAISAL OF SECESSION

Historians of an earlier generation were almost unanimous in attributing the secession of the South to the question of slavery. As recently as 1913 the eminent historian of the controversy, James Ford Rhodes, stated categorically that "of the American Civil War it may safely be asserted that there was a single cause, slavery." [9] Surely, as we glance back over

abolished in the District of Columbia only with the consent of the inhabitants of Virginia, Maryland, and the District.

[9] James Ford Rhodes, *Lectures on the American Civil War*, 2.

the political history of the two decades preceding secession, there is much to countenance that belief. Certainly Whig opposition to the Mexican War was influenced in part by opposition to the extension of slavery. The Wilmot Proviso was a dominant influence in the campaign of 1848, as was the Compromise of 1850 in that of 1852. The Kansas-Nebraska Act did more than anything else to smash the Whigs and bring into being the Republican Party in 1854, and, along with the "bleeding Kansas" that it created, it played a leading role in the campaign of 1856. The same was true of 1858. It was slavery that split the Democrats in 1860 and made possible the election of Lincoln, and it was the election of Lincoln that precipitated secession. With such a succession of events, how could a student arrive at any other interpretation?

Nevertheless, historians in recent years have been inclined to minimize slavery and to stress the conflicting economic interests of the two sections as the essential cause. Slavery was the surface issue; the real conflict went deeper. Twice before in our history nullification had been attempted with veiled threats of secession, by New England during the second war with England and by South Carolina in 1832. In neither case was slavery an issue; rather, it was the belief that local economic interests had been unjustly injured. In short, secession would have been quite possible if Negro slavery had never existed. On the one hand were the northern states, growing rapidly in wealth, in population, and in the development of economic resources, and turning increasingly to industry. The economic forces let loose by the Industrial Revolution were finding full play and were beating irresistibly upon a one-sided and rather static civilization in the South. In the words of Seward, it was an "irrepressible conflict," and in such an economic battle at such a period in world history there could be but one result—a victory for free labor, *laissez faire,* and industrialization. In spite of the general prosperity of its staple crops, the South, as Helper pointed out (page 294), was becoming economically subservient to the North.

On many fronts the economic struggle was carried on. Said a Southern writer in *De Bow's Review* in 1847: "A contest has been going on between the North and South not limited to slavery or no slavery—to abolition or no abolition, nor to the politics of either whigs or democrats as such, but a contest for the wealth and commerce of the great valley of the Mississippi —a contest tendered by our Northern brethren, whether the growing commerce of the great West shall be thrown upon New Orleans or given to the Atlantic cities." This rivalry was but one phase of a gigantic struggle between economic sections and economic systems. The struggle can be seen in the conflict over the protective tariff, territorial expansion, and the land system.

Although the South was losing in the economic struggle, her political power continued almost unbroken until 1860. Territorial expansion she had obtained, and, when she felt that further liberalization of the land law would strengthen the North, she prevented the establishment of a free land system. The tariff she had started on a downward course in 1833 and had kept it low. Throughout these years the South had controlled the executive and judicial branches and had been strong enough to prevent detrimental legislation. This political power, in conjunction with the recognized importance of "King Cotton," undoubtedly inflated the South's confidence in her economic system. When her political power was broken in 1860, she was certain that only secession could save her economic system. "It is not humanity," said Jefferson Davis to the North, "that influences you in the position which you now occupy before the country. . . . It is that you may have an opportunity of cheating us that you want to limit slave territory within circumscribed bounds. It is that you may have a majority in the Congress of the United States and convert the government into an engine of northern aggrandizement. It is that your section may grow in power and prosperity upon treasures unjustly taken from the South, like the vampire bloated and gorged with the blood which it has secretly sucked from its victim." Admittedly slavery was an important element in the economic life of the South, but it had also become a symbol of an economic system.

The economic causes are reviewed in H. U. Faulkner, *American Economic History*, Chap. XVI, and the political story in Jesse Macy, *The Anti-Slavery Crusade* (Chronicles of America), Edward Channing, *A History of the United States*, Vol. VI, Chaps. I–X, and W. E. Binkley, *American Political Parties*, Chaps. VIII–IX. All phases are skillfully interwoven in J. G. Randall, *The Civil War and Reconstruction*, Chaps. IV, V. A. C. Cole, *The Irrepressible Conflict*, Chap. I, summarizes the fifties, and Chaps. XI–XII develop the causes leading to the conflict. For the Kansas-Nebraska Bill see J. F. Rhodes, *A History of the United States*, Vol. I, Chap. V, or G. F. Milton, *The Eve of Conflict*, Chaps. VII–X. For legislation, debates, platforms, the Dred Scott decision, and other important material, see H. S. Commager, *Documents of American History*, Vol. I, 319–388.

NATIONALISM AND SECTIONALISM

Chapter XX

CLASH OF ECONOMIC SECTIONS

> *Without firing a gun, without drawing a
> sword, should they make war on us, we could
> bring the whole world to our feet. . . . No, you
> dare not make war on cotton. No power on earth
> dares make war upon it. Cotton is King.*
>
> SENATOR J. H. HAMMOND OF SOUTH CAROLINA

> *My paramount object in the struggle is to save
> the Union, and it is not either to save or destroy
> Slavery.*
>
> ABRAHAM LINCOLN

RESORT TO ARMS

Although Lincoln, in his public utterances, had maintained a discreet silence regarding the existing crisis, he had made his position in private correspondence quite clear. On the one hand, he insisted that he had not the slightest intent to interfere with slavery where it lawfully existed, but on the other, he asserted without equivocation his belief that "no State can in any way lawfully get out of the Union without the consent of the others." This position he reiterated in his inaugural address, but in words so restrained and conciliatory that many misconstrued it as uncertain and weak. His choice of cabinet members was dominated by the crisis and by political exigencies.[1] Four of them,—Seward, Chase, Cameron, and Bates —had been rivals for the presidential nomination, and Welles had been a Douglas Democrat; Bates and Blair were from loyal slave-holding states. With the exception of Cameron, who was inefficient if not corrupt and who was replaced by Edwin Stanton in 1862, the cabinet was much above the average, and under the skillful direction of Lincoln it worked capably if not harmoniously. Seward, the outstanding member, evidently believed

---

[1] In the first cabinet were William H. Seward, New York (State); Salmon P. Chase, Ohio (Treasury); Simon Cameron, Pennsylvania (War); Edward Bates, Missouri (Attorney General); Caleb B. Smith, Indiana (Interior); Montgomery Blair, Maryland (Postmaster General) and Gideon Welles, Connecticut (Navy).

that he represented the brains of the administration and that his would be the guiding hand. He intimated as much to the President and proposed the wild scheme of restoring the union of contending sections by means of a popular foreign war. After Lincoln had tactfully put him in his place, Seward became one of the most valuable members of the administration and handled foreign affairs with ability and energy. Picking of a cabinet, however, was simple in comparison with handling the horde of office-seekers of the new party. "I seem like one sitting in a palace," said Lincoln, "assigning apartments to importunate applicants, while the structure is on fire and likely soon to perish in ashes." Later the necessity of weeding Southern sympathizers from civil service proved an even more difficult task.

Unused to executive work, a stranger to the intricacies of Washington politics, overwhelmed by office-seekers, and confronted by problems of a magnitude greater than any American executive had yet faced, there is little wonder that Lincoln during the early months of his administration seemed at times to be indecisive and to lack mastery of the situation. Even then, however, his insistence on keeping slavery in the background and emphasizing the one principle that the Union must be preserved did more than all else to preserve the Union. As with Buchanan, his immediate problem was to avoid any action that would drive the eight remaining slave states into the Confederacy, but, try as he might, decisive action could not long be delayed.

All federal arsenals and fortifications in the seceding states had been taken over by the Confederate government, with the exception of four forts along the seacoast; Fort Sumter in Charleston harbor was the most important of the fortifications still in federal hands. Without provisions and reinforcements, Major Anderson and his small garrison could not hold it against an attack, but South Carolina and the Confederate government made no effort to reduce it, in the belief, reinforced by an unauthorized promise of Seward, that it would be surrendered. When Lincoln on April 6 announced his intention to dispatch an expedition to relieve the garrison, the Confederate government, although fully aware that lack of provisions would force a surrender within a few days, ordered an immediate attack on the fort. Anderson, when surrender was demanded, replied that, if help or instructions to the contrary were not forthcoming within three days, he would abandon the fort peaceably. In spite of virtual assurance of possession without resort to arms, the attack was begun, and after a 34-hour bombardment Anderson surrendered.

Controversial historians are often inclined to waste energy in an effort to determine who must bear the technical responsibility for precipitating the war. To the Southerner it seems clear that the responsibility was assumed by Lincoln when he decided to relieve Sumter. To the Northerner the unnecessary attack on Sumter was responsible. The controversy is futile; it is enough that Sumter commenced the war between the states, a conflict that in the number of men engaged and in economic cost was greater than any the world had previously experienced. When Davis issued his fateful order to reduce the fort, his Secretary of State, Toombs, protested, "It is suicide, murder, and will lose us every friend in the North." He was right. The day after Sumter fell, Lincoln issued his first call for 75,000 volunteers and called Congress to meet in special session. "That first gun at Sumter," wrote Lowell, "brought all the free States to their feet as one man."

STRATEGY, POLITICAL AND MILITARY

If Sumter electrified the North and put an end to indecision, its effect upon the South was equally momentous. To the seven states already in the Confederacy four more were added: Virginia on April 17, Arkansas on May 6, North Carolina on May 20, and Tennessee on June 8. To save the border slave states now became the major problem of the federal administration, and the cautious but decisive skill with which Lincoln accomplished it proved his leadership. Delaware made the decision without hesitation, but Maryland was saved only by convening the legislature at Frederick instead of Annapolis, by arresting secessionist leaders, and by stationing troops at the polls to ensure a Union vote. Kentucky, which had at first intended to remain neutral, was saved by skillful politics and by the resentment aroused by the invasion of Southern troops. In Missouri, where the majority favored the Union, the activities of the secessionist governor were stopped by the raising of several regiments of union sympathizers who were able to control the situation.

In the states that had joined the Confederacy after Sumter, there had been strong Union minorities. This was particularly true in Virginia, where the mountain counties in the western part of the state were economically dependent upon the Ohio River and northern railroads. When Virginia seceded from the Union, these counties, with encouragement from Washington and under the protection of federal troops, seceded from Virginia, organized themselves into the state of West Virginia, and obtained admission to the Union in 1863. As for the southern states that had seceded, Lincoln hoped to win back their loyalty and restore them to the Union as quickly as possible. In line with this policy he issued, December 8, 1863, a proclamation granting pardon and the restoration of property to Confederates (with certain exceptions) who would take a prescribed oath to uphold the Constitution and comply with executive proclamations and congressional acts regarding slavery. If 10 per cent of the voting population of 1860 would do this, a government might be organized that the President would accept. By 1864 governments organized under this proclamation had been set up in Arkansas, Louisiana, and Tennessee.

Except for a blockade of the South, proclaimed April 19, and the necessity of saving the border states, the military strategy of the North had hardly been formulated during the early months of the war. One of the outstanding characteristics, in fact, of those early days was the general unpreparedness in both North and South. "Not one man in America," wrote Henry Adams with a touch of exaggeration, "wanted the Civil War or expected or intended it." During the first year of the war there was no lack of volunteers on either side; the difficulty was in supplying them with arms and accouterments. To the governors of states begging for arms and munitions Secretary of War Cameron could only reply: "The government finds itself unable to furnish at once the uniforms and clothing demanded by the large force suddenly brought into service." An official report of July 1, 1861, gave the Union army at 186,000, but there were probably a bare 30,000 fit for service. Although organization in the South during the early stages was undoubtedly more effective, it was not sufficient to deal a determining blow. The general unpreparedness prevented either side from winning a decision during the early months and, by delaying the result, gave the ultimate victory to the North, whose economic superiority was bound to tell in a long conflict.

Before many months had elapsed, the seriousness of the struggle was evident to the far-seeing. It was particularly so after Bull Run, the first large-sized battle of the war. As the short-term volunteers poured into Washington during the spring of 1861, political leaders and the Northern press demanded that a decisive blow be struck before the enlistments expired. Although inadequately prepared for field operations, the army [2] deferred to the wishes of the administration, and in July General McDowell began the invasion of Virginia. On July 21 at Bull Run the Union army met that of the Confederates under Beauregard and Jackson,[3] turned their flank, and apparently had administered a severe defeat when Confederate reinforcements arrived. At this point the victorious Unionists, suddenly seized with panic, broke ranks and retreated toward Washington, a confused and utterly demoralized mob. Only the exhaustion and lack of experience of the Confederates saved the Union army from utter destruction.

The first battle of Bull Run was a bitter disappointment to the Union-

---

[2] The commander-in-chief was the aged Winfield Scott, who retired in October in favor of General George B. McClellan.

[3] It was here that Thomas J. Jackson won the nickname "Stonewall," which he carried to his death.

ists, but the North rallied at once. The idea that the war could be ended overnight was gone. "What we need," said General Sherman to Lincoln, "is cool, thoughtful, hard-fighting soldiers—no more hurrahing, no more humbug." Congress also saw the point. The day after Bull Run it authorized 500,000 three-year volunteers and voted loans adequate to take care of them. As far as Congress could do it, the North from that time never lacked resources for the struggle. As the North settled down to a long war, the strategy developed. It became a twofold effort to strangle the South economically and to defeat her on the field of battle. This "anaconda policy" of economic constriction was carried on in the first place by a blockade of southern ports, and in the second by military invasions, designed in the West to split the Confederate states by gaining possession of the Mississippi and then tightening the grip as the Union armies moved south and east. Except for a few ships built in Europe, the Confederate navy was a negligible factor, and the blockade became more effective as the war progressed. It was disastrous to the South particularly because of her one-sided economic organization, whose prosperity depended on exporting agricultural staples and importing manufactured commodities.

Although the Union army in the East, invading Virginia each summer in the hope of capturing the Confederate capital at Richmond,[4] failed dismally until 1865, better success attended Union arms in the West. There abler officers more quickly achieved command, and there the four years of war were a succession of significant and almost uninterrupted victories. For four years the war in the East was a stalemate. It was Union success in the West that made inevitable the collapse of the Confederacy.

Against the Union strategy of strangulation the Confederate states could only defend themselves and fight back. That with inferior resources they could maintain the war so long is evidence enough of the stamina and devotion of their people. Although blockade-running was developed to a high degree of efficiency, the only important Confederate effort to break the blockade was in March, 1862, when the *Merrimac*, covered with four inches of iron and equipped with a cast-iron ram, steamed forth and destroyed two federal frigates. Her career was stopped the next day by another ironclad, the *Monitor*, which had a hull built low in the water and a revolving turret with two powerful guns. Besides its failure to break the blockade, the chief significance of this historic encounter was again to demonstrate to the world that the days of the wooden battleship were numbered. On land the South on more than one occasion strove to take the war out of a purely defensive status. Twice the Army of Virginia attempted to invade the North in the hope both that it might encourage the

---

[4] After Virginia joined the Confederacy, the capital was shifted from Montgomery, Alabama, to Richmond.

antiwar spirit in the northern states and force a peace. The first invasion was halted at Antietam Creek in September, 1862, and the second at Gettysburg in July of the following year.

In the terrific struggle both sides could claim advantages. The South, first of all, was fighting on the defensive and on inside lines, a fact that helped to neutralize the Northern superiority in population and economic resources. Although a minority in every Confederate state was opposed to secession, and estimates of the number of white Southerners fighting in the Union army are put at around 300,000, there is no doubt but that the Confederate states as a whole were more integrated in their stand and more united in their enthusiasm for the war than the North. With their officers accustomed to positions of authority and the men with few exceptions inured to outdoor life, the Confederates during the early months of the struggle seemed to fight better than the Union soldiers. Their exaggerated belief that one Confederate could lick at least three Yankees gave them confidence even if later encounters did little to confirm such a faith. The South was particularly fortunate in the fact that its ablest commanders—Albert Sidney Johnston, Joseph E. Johnston, Thomas J. (Stonewall) Jackson, Robert E. Lee—were discovered immediately and given positions of authority, whereas it took years of bitter experience for the North to recognize the merit of officers of equal caliber. Another early advantage possessed by the South was a President who had been both a soldier and Secretary of War. In the end Lincoln proved superior to Davis both as a war President and in his comprehension of military strategy, but at the beginning the Southern executive understood better the problems that he faced.

Offsetting Southern advantages, the North had an overwhelming preponderance of man power and economic strength. Against a Northern population of 22,000,000, the seceding states of the South had but 9,000,000, of whom 3,500,000 were blacks. The latter were in no way to be discounted, for they continued as the labor force on farm and plantation, but even so the numerical preponderance of the North is evident enough. Quite as important was the many-sided civilization of the North. While the South struggled desperately to supply her needs by importing through the blockade and gradually establishing munition factories, the industries of the North were quickly geared to meet the war needs. As the South was being beaten into economic ruin, the North grew in wealth and prosperity.

THE WESTERN WAR

In the East, as we shall presently see, little was accomplished for four years. The Union generals were outclassed by Lee, Johnston, and Jackson, and the Union army did little beyond holding Maryland and keeping the Confederate Army of Virginia occupied. In the West, on the other hand, good Union generals appeared early—Buell, Thomas, Grant, and Sherman. Progress was slow, but it was steady, and Fort Donelson, Vicksburg, Chattanooga, Lookout Mountain, Atlanta, and Sherman's march to the sea marked significant milestones in Union success. This was fortunate, for the strength of the Confederacy lay in the Cotton Kingdom and the granaries of the Southwest. When this region was captured, the power of the South was broken, and collapse was inevitable.

Although the western campaign did not begin in earnest until 1862, the year 1861 was not without important events. Missouri and Kentucky were saved to the Union, and by occupying Cairo and Paducah the Union army forced the Confederates to establish their first line of defense along the northern border of Tennessee at Island No. 10 on the Mississippi, at Fort Henry on the Tennessee, and at Fort Donelson on the Cumberland. At the end of 1861 the army of the West was composed of two divisions, that of the Ohio under the command of General Don Carlos Buell, an excellent disciplinarian, whose business it was to invade Kentucky and relieve the Union sympathizers in eastern Tennessee, and that of the region west of the Cumberland Mountains under the command of Henry W. Halleck, a regular army officer who had achieved wide reputation as a military theoretician, but whose field operations were dilatory and often indecisive. His orders were to clear the enemy from the Mississippi.

Fortunately for Halleck, one of his brigadiers proved to be the military genius of the North, and to Grant, along with Buell, Sherman, and Thomas, must go the credit for the western success. A graduate of West Point and a veteran of the Mexican War, Ulysses S. Grant had never developed a liking for either war or army discipline. Forced to resign from the army rather than stand court-martial for drunkenness, he had tried his hand without success at farming, at selling real estate, and at tanning. When the war came, he was almost thirty-nine and a clerk in his father's store. Offering his services with some diffidence, he showed a skill in organizing raw recruits that gained him a brigadier's commission. Convinced that the Confederate line could be broken, Grant obtained Halleck's permission to make the attempt, and in co-operation with Commodore Foote and a flotilla of gunboats he proceeded against Henry and Donelson. Fort Henry capitulated after most of the garrison had escaped (February 6, 1862), and ten days later Donelson also surrendered after its garrison had failed to fight their way out.[5] The capture of Donelson broke the first

---

[5] When Floyd, the Confederate commander, asked Grant for terms of capitulation, the latter answered, "No terms except unconditional and immediate surrender can be accepted. I

Confederate line, saved Kentucky, caused the evacuation of Nashville, and resulted in a Union advance of more than two hundred miles. The victory was sorely needed in the North and heartened the Union cause. It was important also because it made Grant famous. "Judged by its moral and strategical result," wrote Ropes, "it was one of the turning points of the war."

After Donelson, Albert Sidney Johnston, the Confederate commander, retreated to Corinth, Mississippi, where he established a new line of defense. Grant followed him down the Tennessee River, expecting to push the campaign as soon as he was joined by Buell with the Army of the Ohio. Convinced that the Confederates were demoralized, and underestimating his opponent, Grant with inexcusable carelessness spread out his army around Pittsburg Landing to await Buell. To his utter surprise, Johnston attacked on April 6. In a bloody all-day battle around Shiloh Meeting House the Union forces were gradually driven back, but the South suffered an irretrievable loss in the death of its leader. During the night fresh troops under Buell arrived, and the Union army took the offensive the next day. After another hard day's battle the Confederates retreated, finally establishing themselves fifty miles south of Corinth at Tupelo, Mississippi. The campaign in western Tennessee had left the northern Mississippi ports open. Forts Pillow and Memphis were captured, and, at the south, Admiral Farragut, in a daring and brilliant move, destroyed the Confederate ships defending New Orleans and sailed past the Confederate forts to occupy the city. With the exception of Forts Hudson and Vicksburg, the Mississippi by the end of 1862 was in Union hands.

Failure of the Union army to push home its victory after the Confederate retreat from Shiloh gave the Southern forces, now under the command of General Braxton Bragg, a chance to launch a counteroffensive. Gathering an army of 35,000 at Chattanooga, Bragg marched them rapidly into Kentucky, followed by Buell. Cincinnati and other river towns were in a high state of tension before Buell got between Bragg and the Ohio and stopped the northwest advance at the stiff battle of Perryville (October 8). Bragg retreated rapidly, but Buell's pursuit was so slow that he was removed from command. Rosecrans, who succeeded him, was no more anxious than Buell to advance recklessly into enemy territory. He did, however, halt a counterattack in two severe engagements at Murfreesboro (December 31 and January 2), after which Bragg retired to Chattanooga. The year 1862 ended with all Kentucky and western and central Tennessee in Union hands, as well as the entire Mississippi except the stretch between Fort Hudson and Vicksburg.

propose to move immediately upon your works." To his admirers the general became from that moment "Unconditional Surrender Grant."

Important as were the western operations in 1862, they were but a preliminary to the great objectives of 1863—the capture of Chattanooga, the key to the Southwest, and of Vicksburg, the strongest Confederate position on the Mississippi. The capture of Vicksburg would mean Union control of the river and the cutting off of Louisiana sugar, Texas beef, and Mexican arms from the Confederates. For that reason the South must hold it at all costs. While one Union army under Rosecrans occupied the attention of Bragg at Chattanooga, Grant, now in command of the West,[6] moved slowly in the late fall to the attack of Vicksburg. To oppose him the Confederates sent Joseph E. Johnston, next to Lee their ablest officer. Grant was faced with two armies, one under Johnston and one under Pemberton, the commander at Vicksburg, as well as almost unconquerable geographic disadvantages. The winter had been rainy, the Mississippi was high, and the region around Vicksburg was badly flooded.

In the face of these difficulties Grant performed the most brilliant feat of his military career. "Moving with extraordinary rapidity," says Rhodes, "and throwing upon each detachment of the Confederates a superior force, Grant defeated them in detail and cleared the way to his final objective point. In 19 days [April 30–May 18] he had crossed the great river, into the enemy's territory, had marched one hundred and eighty miles through a very difficult country, skirmishing constantly, had fought and won five distinct battles, inflicting a greater loss upon the enemy than he himself sustained and capturing many cannon and field-pieces, had taken the capital of the State and destroyed its arsenals and military manufactories, had been for ten days without communication with any base or his government and was now in the rear of Vicksburg."[7] It was Grant at his best, quick, persistent, resourceful. "To find a parallel in military history to the deeds of those eighteen days," wrote Fiske, "we must go back to the first Italian campaign of Napoleon in 1796." The Union army now settled down to a siege of the fort, which lasted from May 22 to July 4. The day that Lincoln published the news of the victory at Gettysburg came the long awaited surrender of Vicksburg. Five days later Fort Hudson, which had been closely besieged for weeks, surrendered, and the Mississippi, in the words of Lincoln, flowed "unvexed to the sea."

While Grant was besieging Vicksburg, Rosecrans, after long delay, moved against Chattanooga. After skillfully maneuvering Bragg out of southeastern Tennessee, he succeeded in occupying Chattanooga (September 9). Believing Bragg in full retreat, the Union general started pur-

---

[6] Halleck had been called east and put in command of the entire army. This position he held until superseded by Grant, who became a lieutenant general February 27, 1864.

[7] J. F. Rhodes, *History of the Civil War 1861–1865*, 253–254. By permission of The Macmillan Company, publishers.

suit, but Bragg turned at Chickamauga and in a bitter two days' battle (September 18–19) forced the Union army back into Chattanooga. Only the bold stand of George H. Thomas, the "Rock of Chickamauga," who with the left wing of the Union army held off the persistent Confederate attacks during the long afternoon of the second day, saved the Union force from complete destruction. The terrific casualties sustained in many of these Civil War battles can be illustrated by the fact that the Confederates at Chickamauga lost 19,500 in killed, wounded, and captured (of whom 1500 were captured), and the Union army 16,000 (5000 captured). Following the Union army to Chattanooga, the Confederates fortified Missionary Ridge and Lookout Mountain and prepared to lay siege. This was the situation that confronted Grant when he arrived to take command (October 23). Replacing Rosecrans with Thomas, Grant began operations to relieve the beleaguered army from scarcity of supplies and to break the Confederate siege. In a month he was ready for the final stroke. In the last days of November the Confederates were driven from both Missionary Ridge and Lookout Mountain in spectacular battles, and the Union army was left unmolested at Chattanooga. The second great strategic point in the Confederacy was now in Union hands.

The Union objective in the West during 1864 was Atlanta, Georgia, a railroad center where the South had developed important manufacturing in the belief that the city was so far from the field of military operations that it could never be molested. Grant, who had been raised to the rank of lieutenant general and put in command of all the Northern armies, left for the East, placing Sherman in command of the West. The western campaign of 1864 therefore got under way in early May as Sherman commenced his march toward Atlanta. From then until Atlanta was taken on September 2 there were continued campaigning and numerous engagements. The length of the campaign was due to the brilliant Fabian tactics of Johnston, who had replaced the incapable Bragg, and whose campaign of defense was faultless. But Jefferson Davis, dissatisfied because Johnston had not halted Sherman, removed him on July 17 and put in command J. B. Hood, "a man who would fight." No one was more relieved than Sherman. Fighting was now more frequent and progress more rapid, and Atlanta soon fell. After Atlanta the ultimate success of the Union could hardly be in doubt, and this feeling was reflected in the critical elections of that autumn.

Unable to dislodge Sherman, Hood turned his back on the Union army and started for Tennessee in the hope that the threat of a northern invasion would force the recall of Sherman. The imperturbable Sherman, however, refused to be disturbed. Detaching the efficient Thomas with a strong force to follow Hood, he himself conceived the bold plan of cutting loose from his base of supplies and marching southeast from Atlanta to Savannah. His purpose was to cut a swath of destruction across the rich farm lands of Georgia in the belief that it would hasten the collapse of the Confederacy. Far from convinced of the wisdom of the plan, Lincoln and Grant finally gave their consent, and on November 12 Sherman cut his communications and set out with 62,000 picked men on his famous march to the sea. About a month later (December 10) he was before Savannah, and on December 20 he was able to telegraph Lincoln, "I beg to present you as a Christmas gift the city of Savannah, with one hundred and fifty guns and plenty of ammunition, and also about twenty-five thousand bales of cotton." From Atlanta to the sea, a distance of 300 miles, he had left a 60-mile swath of burned bridges, wrecked railroads, and ruined crops. No opposition was met, and it was little more than a picnic for the soldiers. With a maximum of looting and a minimum of discipline, it was the sort of campaign that most soldiers dream of, but few realize. Except for the destruction, atrocities were rare. "No army," said Dodge, "ever enjoyed such freedom or kept within such bounds." [8] One of the most amazing aspects of Sherman's campaign, at least to the military strategist, was the spectacle of two hostile armies, those under Sherman and Hood, "marching in opposite directions, each in the full belief that it was achieving a final and conclusive result in the great war." Hood's advance, in fact, worried the North for a brief period when, after a desperate fight at Franklin (November 30), the Northern troops fell back to Nashville. Here (December 15) Thomas inflicted the most complete defeat that a Confederate army had yet experienced and ended Confederate military power in the West.

THE WAR IN THE EAST

Leaving Sherman in Savannah, let us return to 1861 and trace the conflict on the eastern front. The day after Bull Run, Lincoln summoned General George B. McClellan to Washington and put him in command of the Army of the Potomac. A graduate of West Point, a veteran of the Mexican War, and later a railroad engineer, McClellan, although but thirty-four years of age, had already enjoyed a distinguished military and civil career. A man of arrogant self-confidence but of great personal magnetism, he was popular with his soldiers, who had complete faith in his capacity. As a drillmaster and organizer he was without peer; he could whip an army into shape in half the time it took an ordinary general. Nor was he without skill as a strategist. His weaknesses were overcaution and an inability to co-operate with his superiors. He quarreled with Scott and Stanton and insulted Lincoln. For six months after Bull Run, McClellan

[8] T. A. Dodge, *Bird's Eye View of Our Civil War*, 290.

remained in Washington reorganizing and drilling his army. The North, anxious for decisive action, complained bitterly over the delay. In spite of growing criticism, Lincoln stood behind him even to the extent of making him general-in-chief of all the armies on November 1. But even the matchless patience of Lincoln was finally worn down, and on February 22 he ordered an advance of all the armies. Two weeks later he took the supreme command from McClellan, leaving him only the Army of the Potomac, gave Stanton direction of the campaign, and detached part of the army from McClellan's command. In the resulting campaign there was frequent interference by Stanton and Lincoln, which contributed to its failure. It has been the habit of historians to join with the civilian population of the time in severely criticizing the delay and excess caution of McClellan. It should be noted, nevertheless, that McClellan's policy of delay and preparation was fundamentally correct. A single notable Northern victory, even if it could be won, was not likely to end the war. Every day of delay increased the Northern strength and in like manner made Southern success less likely. It was the South that needed a quick and decisive victory, and it might have obtained it but for the policy of defense and delay that Davis unwisely advocated.

McClellan's plan was to attack Richmond by moving his troops by sea and advancing up the York Peninsula. Lincoln consented, if McDowell with 40,000 men were left to defend Washington. The latter, if the campaign progressed successfully, was eventually to co-operate with McClellan. Concentrating over 100,000 men on the peninsula, McClellan allowed the Confederate fortification at Yorktown to delay him for a month. This delay enabled Johnston to detach Jackson, who in a series of brilliant strokes managed to keep the Union armies busy in the Shenandoah while he made a feint at Washington and drew McDowell far enough away to prevent his operating in the Richmond campaign.

By May 16 McClellan was within a day's march of Richmond. The Confederate government was prepared to evacuate, but on the advice of Lee it was decided to risk a battle to give Jackson a chance to complete his work. The result was the battle of Fair Oaks (May 31), which stopped McClellan's advance and held up the Union army for another month. At Fair Oaks Johnston had been severely wounded, and the command was given to Lee. Just as McClellan was ready for a renewed offensive, Lee called Jackson back from the Shenandoah and in brilliantly planned movements launched a major attack against the Union forces. In the Seven Days' Battle (June 26 to July 2) McClellan was forced to retreat and reform his troops along a new line. He was, however, in no way defeated. The casualties inflicted upon the enemy were greater than his own, he still had the largest and best-equipped army yet gathered in America, he outnumbered the Confederates, and his men were still full of fight. Although he begged to continue the campaign along the same line that Grant followed three years later, he had lost the confidence of the administration and was ordered to withdraw from the peninsula. McClellan's failure to strike aggressively, politics at Washington, and the advice of Halleck, now general-in-chief, combined to render futile this important campaign.

As the peninsula campaign came to an inglorious end, General John Pope, an officer who had won some minor successes in the West, was given command of the Army of Virginia with orders to concentrate and advance against Richmond by land. A dashing and boastful soldier, Pope had little military ability. Confident that because of his superior force he would not be attacked, he took few precautions. Lee, however, who feared brains rather than strength, sent Jackson swinging round to Pope's rear, launched a surprise attack at the second battle of Bull Run (August 29–30, 1862), and hurled the Union force severely defeated back toward Washington.

In many ways, the days after Bull Run were the best the Confederacy experienced. The South appeared invincible, the North was bitterly disappointed, and Europe seemed on the point of recognizing the Confederate states. The Lincoln administration was battered with criticism, particularly by the radicals, who demanded the abolition of slavery. One more decisive stroke and the South might win. With all this in mind Lee determined to invade the North. Such a move, if successful, he believed, would attach Maryland to the Confederacy, break the North in two by severing rail communication in Pennsylvania, and make it possible to dictate a peace after capturing Philadelphia, Baltimore, or Washington. By September 5 he was crossing the Potomac and invading Maryland. Three days earlier, against the opposition of most of his administration, Lincoln restored McClellan to command of the Army of the Potomac. Immediately broken morale was restored, and with unaccustomed speed McClellan set out to intercept Lee. Capturing Southern dispatches, he realized that the armies of Lee and Jackson were separated, and with more action he might have crushed them separately. The best he could do was to halt their combined strength at Antietam Creek (September 17) and force a retreat. He might have pursued, with a second chance of destroying Lee's army, but he did not, and Lee escaped.

McClellan's failure to pursue the Confederates aggressively again cost him his command. He had, nevertheless, by restoring the morale of the army and turning back the invasion, rendered invaluable service. Antietam gave Lincoln his opportunity to issue the Emancipation Proclamation and to attach the liberal sentiment of Europe to the side of the North. After Antietam, Burnside, a fair corps commander but a third-rate army general, was given command of the Army of the Potomac.[9] Moving South, he found Lee prepared to check his advance at Fredericksburg on the south bank of the Rappahannock. With reckless bravery but without success his men repeatedly charged the entrenched Confederates (December 13). The useless slaughter at Fredericksburg cost the Federals 12,653 men and sent the army northward in demoralized retreat. The battle also ended the eastern campaign of 1862, a campaign that had involved almost continuous operations for ten months. Four major battles had been fought, with terrific losses to both sides, but with the general military situation in the East little changed.

With Vicksburg and Chattanooga in the West and Gettysburg in the East, 1863 proved the critical year of the war. After Fredericksburg the Army of the Potomac was given to "Fighting Joe" Hooker, a boastful but mediocre officer, who commenced the operations of 1863. Moving southward with some initiative, he lost his aggressive attitude when confronted by Lee at Chancellorsville, allowed Jackson by a forced march to surprise and smash his right wing (May 2–4), and then retired across the Rappahannock utterly beaten and bewildered. Chancellorsville was the last important Confederate victory, a fact that may have been due to the loss of "Stonewall" Jackson, mistakenly shot by his own men in the dusk of the first day's battle.

Within a month after Chancellorsville Lee had set his army in motion for a second invasion of the North. Decisive action, he felt, was necessary. It was obvious that Vicksburg would soon surrender, and something was necessary to counteract the effect of this coming defeat. The North was tired of the war, and the resources of the South were failing. "Our resources in men are constantly diminishing," he wrote to Davis, "and the disproportion in this respect between us and our enemies, if they continue united in their efforts to subjugate us, is steadily augmenting. . . . No means of dividing and weakening our enemies should be neglected."

If the necessity of conquering a peace was evident in 1862, it was much more so in the following summer. During the last two weeks of June Lee moved his army rapidly across Maryland and into Pennsylvania, his advance cavalry actually getting within three miles of Harrisburg. Lee's early movements were well protected by his cavalry under Jeb Stuart, but when Stuart foolishly started upon one of his daring raids toward Washington, the Confederate movements were uncovered, and the Union army started in pursuit. Hooker, unable to get along with either the administration or his fellow officers, resigned, and his place was taken by General

[9] This change was a great relief to Lee, who considered McClellan the ablest opponent faced by him during the war. A recent historian, S. E. Morison, calls McClellan's removal "the greatest mistake Lincoln ever made."

George Gordon Meade, a responsible and capable if not brilliant soldier. On July 1 Meade's advance cavalry came in contact with a Confederate corps just outside Gettysburg, and the three-day battle began. All that day and during the following night the Confederates rapidly concentrated on the town along the roads leading from the north and west, while the Union soldiers approached from the east and south, and, as each regiment arrived, it swung into battle. During the first day the Federals were driven back through the town, but General Hancock, arriving in the afternoon, hastily fortified the strong position on Cemetery Ridge south of the town and held it until reinforcements arrived with Meade during the night.

On the second day of the battle (July 2), and before half of the Union army was yet in line, Lee attacked on the right, where he captured Culps Hill, and on the left, where he failed to take Little Round Top. The losses had been heavy, but Meade hung on and prepared for an attack upon his center, which he believed would come the next day. This took place dramatically, a little after three o'clock. A deafening artillery battle, then silence. Suddenly there emerged from the Confederate lines 15,000 picked men led by Pickett's famous brigade. Charging across the open fields and exposed to a deadly artillery and rifle fire, they were only a handful when they reached the Union breastworks. It was a glorious spectacle of reckless bravery, but it was as futile as secession itself. Lee's overconfidence, his errors in judgment, and the failure of Longstreet to obey orders more promptly, along with the brave Union defense, had brought defeat. Gettysburg was the greatest battle of the war, and as Lee, with the flower of his army destroyed, turned southward, it was evident that the days of the Confederacy were numbered. The end might have come sooner if Meade had pushed home his victory, but he allowed the Confederates to escape across the Potomac, and spent the rest of the summer in unsuccessfully attempting to outmaneuver Lee in northern Virginia. Four months after the battle, Lincoln journeyed to Gettysburg to dedicate the battlefield as a national cemetery and there he restated the Union purpose in immortal language.

Early in 1864 Congress revived the commission of lieutenant general, and on March 9 Lincoln gave to Grant the command of the armies. In contrast to the glitter of earlier officers, this "ordinary, scrubby-looking man with a slightly seedy look" [10] took control with quick confidence and personally directed the campaigns in Virginia. While Sherman in the West began his movement toward Atlanta, Grant crossed the Rapidan on May 3 and began the movement toward Richmond. Lee opposed him (May 5 and 6) in the severe battles of the Wilderness, after which Grant attempted a flanking movement but found his opponent entrenched at

[10] C. F. Adams, *Richard Henry Dana*, II, 271.

Spottsylvania Court House, where continuous fighting ensued (May 8–21). It was after the terrific losses at Spottsylvania that Grant with his superior resources believed that he could wear the enemy down by mere attrition, if in no other way, and wrote his famous dispatch, "I propose to fight it out on this line, if it takes all summer." By continual flanking movements he finally reached Cold Harbor, six miles from Richmond, where Lee awaited him behind strong defenses. In the hope of ending the campaign, Grant ordered an assault (June 3) on impregnable defenses, which resulted in a loss of between 8000 and 9000 men. Shortly after he shifted his base to McClellan's old position on the James, and after wasting 10,000 lives in futile attempts at Petersburg, Grant sat down to a nine months' siege. From the Rapidan to the James his losses had numbered about 55,000 men, and it was necessary to create what amounted to a new army. He was no nearer Richmond than McClellan had got in 1862 with hardly the loss of a man, but he had inflicted a loss of 30,000 upon Lee, which was important at this stage of the war.

In the hope of drawing Grant away from Petersburg, Lee dispatched Early to clear the Shenandoah valley and threaten Washington. This was done so effectively that in June 11 he was before Washington and with a little more speed might have captured the city. To end further trouble in this direction, Grant in September ordered Sheridan into the valley with instructions to oust the Confederates and destroy everything that might be of use to the enemy. Early was defeated at Winchester (October 19), and Grant's orders were so effectively carried out that "a crow flying over the country would need to carry his rations." Winchester, following a few weeks after the capture of Atlanta, helped to counteract the discouragement over Grant's failure to destroy Lee and helped to prepare the way for a Lincoln victory in the autumn elections of 1864.

With the Confederates driven from the Shenandoah and Grant tightening his grip on Richmond, Sherman, opposed by Johnston, began late in January to move northward. With the end of the Confederacy fast approaching, friends of peace engineered a conference at Hampton Roads (February 3, 1865). Lincoln offered peace on two conditions: restoration of the Union and emancipation, with the promise that he would ask Congress to compensate the slaveholders for their loss. As Davis would agree to nothing without independence, the war continued. Facing an army three times the size of his own, Lee realized that Richmond could not be saved and, in the hope of effecting a juncture with Johnston, extended his lines toward Lynchburg. To intercept this plan, Sheridan with a large force fell upon Lee's right at Five Forks (April 1) and administered such a blow that on the following day both Petersburg and Richmond were evacuated. With Grant pressing him from behind and Sheridan blocking his retreat to Johnston, Lee got as far as Appomattox Court House some eighty miles west of Richmond, where he surrendered on April 9, 1865. At the memorable meeting, Grant, unkempt after a rapid march, appeared in a private's blouse, Lee in a new full-dress uniform with jewel-studded sword. Here, after some informal talk of early army days, Grant offered his liberal terms—surrender of arms and material except officers' side arms and the horses and mules that the men would need for spring plowing.

In the meantime, Sherman, late in January, had started north from Savannah. Between then and April 26, when Johnston surrendered to him, he had marched some 450 miles to Goldsboro, North Carolina, repeating the devastation of Georgia. Hindered by rain, mud, swampy rivers, and constant obstruction by the enemy, this march was in certain aspects the most notable movement of the war. In admiration Johnston wrote to Lee, "I made up my mind, there had been no such Army since the day of Julius Caesar."

POLITICS DURING WAR TIME

Although Lincoln was elected as a minority President, his political position was greatly strengthened by the Southern secession, which gave him an administration majority in Congress. Nevertheless, his political position during the war was an exceedingly trying one. His own party was badly divided over the slavery question. The regular Republicans, of whom Lincoln was typical, were first and foremost Unionists. Their opposition to slavery might be mild or strong, but in any case it was subordinated to saving the Union. In opposition were the ardent abolitionists, who made emancipation the primary objective. This group, led by Senators Wade, Chandler, and Trumbull from the Old Northwest, and backed by Greeley and the New York *Tribune,* kept up an incessant criticism of the administration. Their objective, says Channing, was "to have all the slaves freed at once, to hang Jeff Davis and as many other rebels as could be caught, to seize all the property of traitors and keep it forever, and to bring the war to a short and successful conclusion by intrusting the chief command to Butler or Frémont." [11] Although the Radical Republicans criticized the administration and the conduct of the war to the end, their demands regarding slavery were finally met, but only when Lincoln became convinced that such action would be of value. When Greeley, in August, 1862, addressed an open letter to the President under the title, "The Prayer of Twenty Millions," complaining "that the Union cause has suffered and

[11] Benjamin F. Butler of Massachusetts was the typical political general, and his incapacity was frequently evident. Frémont, the Republican candidate in 1856 and the darling of the abolitionists, was both erratic and incapable. Lincoln gave him two opportunities to prove himself and finally accepted his resignation with relief.

is now suffering immensely from your mistaken deference to slavery," Lincoln replied in clear-cut language:

> As to the policy I "seem to be pursuing," as you say, I have not meant to leave any one in doubt. . . . My paramount object in this struggle *is* to save the Union, and is *not* either to save or destroy Slavery. If I could save the Union without freeing *any* slave, I would do it; and if I could save it by freeing *all* the slaves, I would do it; and if I could do it by freeing some and leaving others alone, I would also do that. What I do about Slavery and the colored race, I do because I believe it helps to save this Union; and what I forbear, I forbear, because I do *not* believe it would help to save the Union.

Lincoln, however, had determined to move against slavery and had already written the first draft of the Emancipation Proclamation. He awaited only an opportune moment, which came after the battle of Antietam. Without constitutional authority to interfere with slavery in any state, Lincoln, in exercise of his power as commander-in-chief and to weaken the war power of the Confederacy, proclaimed (September 22, 1862) that after January 1 "all persons held as slaves within any state or designated part of a state the people whereof shall be in rebellion against the United States shall be then, thenceforward, and forever free." As the proclamation applied only to Confederate states not yet conquered, it did not for the moment free a single slave. It simply announced a policy for the future. That it helped to pacify the abolitionists and win friendship abroad there can be no doubt.

Secession and civil war also deepened the split in the Northern Democrats. The large majority, headed by Douglas (who unfortunately died June 3, 1861), supported the war. Some, like Stanton and Johnson, supported Lincoln; others, like McClellan, opposed him. While the majority, the "War Democrats," supported the policy of crushing secession by force of arms, many others, popularly known as "Copperheads," professed loyalty but had no hesitancy in tying the hands of the government and in demanding the end of hostilities. Against the Copperheads Lincoln acted vigorously. Without constitutional authority, for Congress alone can do this, Lincoln suspended the privilege of *habeas corpus*. Congress later backed the President, and during the war federal agents arbitrarily arrested at least 13,535 persons, and there were thousands of others confined in state prisons for whom no federal records are to be found. It is also estimated that between three hundred and four hundred papers were suppressed for longer or shorter periods, to say nothing of occasional interference with elections in the border states.

This abrogation of ordinary civil rights may have helped win the war, but it aroused bitter resentment and was undoubtedly a primary cause for the heavy Republican losses in the elections of 1862. In that election six important states (New York, Pennsylvania, Ohio, Indiana, Illinois, and Wisconsin), which had voted Republican in 1860, shifted to the Democrats. In Ohio two men imprisoned by Lincoln were actually elected to Congress. It is the belief of one of the most scholarly of recent students that it was Lincoln's arbitrary policy and the opposition to it by a few able men that saved the Democratic Party in the North from extinction. Their slogan in 1862 was "the Constitution as it is and the Union as it was," and one of the results of the elections was the freeing of practically all the political prisoners.

Shaken by the reverses of 1862, the administration approached the campaign of 1864 with many misgivings. Lincoln's political instincts for once failed him, and, in the midst of gloomy forebodings, he prepared a "memorandum" stating that it was his duty to co-operate with the President-elect to save the Union between election day and March 4, for after that it would be impossible. There was, indeed, much war weariness in the North, and the military results of the summer of 1864 were discouraging. Furthermore, the Radical Republicans were particularly vocal in their criticisms and were concentrating upon the nomination of Salmon P. Chase, who had long been their representative in the cabinet. Chase was a willing candidate, but, when his own state would not endorse him, he retired from the field. In the end the pessimism of Lincoln proved unfounded. Union successes in the autumn, combined with the political mistakes of his opponents, helped turn the tide of victory. Above all, however, Lincoln had won the confidence of the masses of the plain people, and it is doubtful if his re-election was ever in danger.

The campaign began in earnest when a group of Radical Republicans met on May 31, wrote a platform in which they condemned Lincoln as "politically, militarily and financially a failure," and nominated their early standard-bearer, John C. Frémont. Their following was never large, and in September Frémont withdrew from the campaign.[12] Early in June the regular Republicans met at Baltimore. Their strategy was to attach the War Democrats, and this they did by stressing the preservation of the Union and nominating for the vice-presidency Andrew Johnson, a War Democrat who was then military governor of Tennessee. Lincoln's renomination was almost unanimous, and he expressed his own satisfaction by implying that the convention had decided that it was better not to "swap horses while crossing the river." Hoping to profit from Union reverses, the Democrats

---

[12] Lincoln rightly gauged the strength of this group. When news reached him of the convention, he expressed his feelings by reading to his cabinet *Samuel,* XXII, 2: "And every one that was in distress and every one that was in debt, and every one that was discontented, gathered themselves unto him; and he became a captain over them; and there were with him about four hundred men."

delayed their convention until August 29. Governor Seymour of New York, a "peace Democrat," who had opposed many of Lincoln's policies, was permanent chairman, while the dominant member of the platform committee was Clement L. Vallandigham, whose bitter opposition to the war had led to his arrest and banishment to the Confederacy.[13] This sort of leadship did the Democrats little good, and their platform was no better. Declaring the war a failure and asserting that "humanity, liberty, and the public welfare demand that immediate efforts be made for a cessation of hostilities," they demanded peace on the "basis of the Federal Union of the states." Their nominee, General McClellan, was probably the strongest candidate they could have found, and he accepted after virtually repudiating the platform. The results of the election demonstrated clearly the fact that the North was committed to a continuation of the war until the Union was restored. Lincoln won a plurality of nearly half a million and carried all but three states, Kentucky, Delaware, and New Jersey.[14]

J. F. Rhodes, *A History of the Civil War,* Chaps. I–VI, VIII–X, XIII, XIV, gives a compact and understandable account of military operations. C. and M. Beard, *The Rise of American Civilization,* Chap. XVIII, is interpretative. Probably the best single-volume account of these years is J. G. Randall, *The Civil War and Reconstruction.* For the war itself see Chaps. VIII–XXV, XXIX. On politics read W. E. Binkley, *American Political Parties,* Chap. X. Excellent appraisals of Lincoln during the war are by the Englishman, Lord Charnwood, *Abraham Lincoln,* Chaps. VII, XI, and by N. W. Stephenson, *Lincoln,* Chaps. XV–XXXIV. On Grant as a general, see L. A. Coolidge, *Ulysses S. Grant,* Chaps. IX–XXII, and on Lee, D. S. Freeman, *R. E. Lee,* Vol. IV, Chap. XI. The everyday life of the common soldier is told in the monumental F. A. Shannon, *The Organization and Administration of the Union Army, 1861–1865,* Vol. I, 195–255.

[13] He later went to Canada and from there directed his campaign in 1863 for the governorship of Ohio. Badly defeated, he returned in 1864 to take an active part in the presidential campaign.

[14] The electoral votes were: Lincoln, 212; McClellan, 21. The popular vote, according to Stanwood, was: Lincoln, 2,330,552; McClellan, 1,835,935.

NATIONALISM AND SECTIONALISM

Chapter XXI

BEHIND THE LINES

The blockade was the real destroyer of the South.

NATHANIEL W. STEPHENSON

The national resources, then, are unexhausted, and, as we believe, inexhaustible. The public purpose to re-establish and maintain the national authority is unchanged, and, as we believe, unchangeable.

ABRAHAM LINCOLN (December 6, 1864)

FINANCING THE WAR

In the long run the determining factor in modern warfare is the economic strength of the contending forces, and the barometer of economic strength is the success or failure of the financial operations of the governments. This is clearly seen in the Civil War, when the developing prosperity of the North created wealth more rapidly than it was destroyed, while in the beleaguered South economic destruction gradually paralyzed both military and financial operations. In concrete terms, the North had relatively little difficulty in financing the war, while the South fought desperately a losing financial battle. As is customary during war, both governments sought to meet added expenditures by increasing existing taxes, levying new ones, and floating loans, thus paying part of the war expenditures as they were incurred and shifting the rest to the shoulders of future generations. In addition, both North and South resorted to fiat money, in the last analysis but another form of taxation.

The financing of the Civil War is an extremely important aspect of American history not alone because of its influence upon the existing conflict but because of its lasting effect, an effect that had its ramifications for decades in the social, economic, and political life of the nation. Since 1789 the principal method of financing the federal government had been by means of a tariff, and Congress naturally turned to this source. The Republican Party had already committed itself to an increase, and even before

Lincoln's inauguration a new tariff, framed largely by J. S. Morrill and designed to supplant the low rates of 1857 with a schedule as high as that of the Walker tariff of 1846, had passed the Senate March 2, 1861.[1] The Morrill tariff, which raised the rates to an average of about 25 per cent, proved inadequate for war needs, and each successive Congress pushed up the rates until the average level in 1864 was around 47 per cent. Not only was Congress interested in revenue, but there was continual pressure from war industries demanding protection and from manufacturers clamoring for higher rates to offset the rapidly rising excise taxes. Of the war tariffs those of 1862 and 1864 were the most important. The latter, says Taussig, "was in many ways crude and ill-considered; it established protective duties more extreme than had been ventured on in any previous tariff act in our history," yet "five days in all were given by the two houses to this act, which was in its effects one of the most important financial measures ever passed in the United States."[2] Nevertheless, this tariff, crudely drawn and recklessly passed, remained for three decades the basis of the American protective system. Compared with the rates of 1857, the duties of 1864 constituted a revolution in American economic policy.

Of less significance, because they were repealed after the war, were the increases in the excise taxes and the imposition of an income tax. Every merchant and every housewife became quickly cognizant of the numerous internal taxes placed upon manufactured articles and business transactions during the conflict. The method of distributing these excises was later likened by David A. Wells, Special Commissioner of Revenue, to that of the Irishman at Donnybrook Fair: "Whenever you see a head, hit it; whenever you see a commodity, tax it." A tax on incomes was levied for the first time in our history in 1861, when 3 per cent was imposed on incomes above $800. This was increased in 1862 and 1865 until incomes between $600 and $5000 were taxed at 5 per cent and those over $5000 at 10 per cent.[3]

More important than taxation in the immediate financing of the war by the North was the policy of borrowing. During the period of actual fighting the government obtained about four times as much from loans as from all other sources put together. The public debt reached its highest point on September 1, 1865, when it amounted to $2,846,000,000.[4] It consisted of loans bearing at least five different rates of interest and maturing at nineteen

[1] F. W. Taussig, *Tariff History of the United States,* seventh edition, 167–168.
[2] *Ibid.*
[3] Approximately $1,280,000,000 from internal duties and $910,000,000 from the tariff were obtained between 1861 and 1865, while the income tax yielded about $347,000,000 before it was abolished in 1872.
[4] The public debt was $74,985,000 when Lincoln took over the administration.

different periods of time. They were floated through designated agents, the most famous being Jay Cooke, "the financier of the Civil War," who, at the end of the conflict, had established himself as the leading banker of the country.

As the war progressed, it became imperative to widen the market for United States bonds, and this was an important cause of the National Bank Act of 1863, probably the most important financial legislation of the Civil War. With the destruction of the second Bank of the United States and the creation of the independent treasury, the federal government had retired from any connection with or supervision of the nation's banking system. The result had been far from favorable. By 1862 there were some 1600 banks established under the varying laws and privileges of twenty-nine states, whose 7000 or more different banknotes varied in value with the soundness of the banks of issue. The ease of counterfeiting and the difficulty of carrying on business under such a situation are easy to imagine. Under the National Bank Act of 1863 the federal government was authorized to grant charters to groups of not less than five stockholders (the amount of the capital stock being graduated for cities of different sizes), who were required to subscribe not less than one third of their capital for federal bonds. These bonds might be deposited with the Secretary of the Treasury, who would issue national banknotes up to 90 per cent of the face of the bonds. These banknotes were receivable for all government dues except imports and were guaranteed by the government.[5] Owing to the strict regulations, charters were taken out slowly, and to encourage applications an act of 1865 put a 10-per-cent tax on state banknote issues. The net result was to establish a new experiment in federal control, a new banking system for the nation, and a new and important type of currency, and at the same time to eliminate the state banknotes. Incidentally, it helped to consolidate the powerful financial interests behind the government.

In addition to taxes and loans, the government by various acts beginning in 1862 authorized the issue of $450,000,000 of paper money "on the credit of the United States." For the issuing of these "greenbacks," as they were called, there was perhaps an excuse: specie payment had been suspended, and there was a scanty supply of monetary medium. Nevertheless, the greenbacks, which had no metallic backing, declined in value and contributed to the price inflation during the war. Over $433,160,000 was in circulation in 1865, besides over $20,000,000 in fractional paper currency.

---

[5] The inducement held out to capitalists to organize national banks was the double interest that might be obtained: that on the bonds they bought and that on the banknotes they lent. As long as the treasury gave them in banknotes but 90 per cent of the face of the bond, however, this advantage was not very great.

So effectively had Gresham's law worked during the war days that even fractional coins disappeared, and the government had been forced to issue paper in fractional denominations.

Except for the protective tariff, which was forbidden under the Confederate constitution, the government of the Confederacy resorted to all the methods of finance used by the Northern government and in addition discovered some new ones. Loans through bond issues of various types were floated, some of the most important being the "produce loans." These began in May, 1861, when $100,000,000 of 8-per-cent twenty-year bonds was floated, which might be sold for specie or exchanged for produce. The war had hardly started when Secretary of the Treasury Memminger suggested a "war tax" in the form of a direct tax of one half of one per cent on all property except Confederate bonds and money. Under the Confederate constitution this tax was optional among the states and was usually met by state bonds issued to defray the levy. In 1863 the Confederate Congress passed a law providing for a tax of one tenth on agricultural products and authorized any officer of the army within certain limits to seize such products. Specie in the southern branch of the United States mint was confiscated, as was the property of alien enemies and the debts owed by Southerners to Northerners, but the chief method of war financing was the issue of fiat paper money. How much of this was printed even the Confederate government probably did not know, but it is estimated to have been around one billion dollars. What value these paper notes may have once commanded had largely evaporated by 1864. "Before the war," said one Southerner, "I went to market with the money in my pocket, and brought back my purchases in a basket; now to take the money in the basket and bring the things home in my pocket." [6]

Considering the difficulties under which the Confederacy labored, its general financial operations were extraordinarily successful. Nevertheless, the financial situation had pretty generally broken down by 1864. In the last analysis the crux of the situation depended upon foreign credits to obtain both money and supplies. The credits were obtainable in return for exports, especially cotton and tobacco, but the naval blockade made it increasingly difficult to export large quantities to Europe. The textile mills of New England and Europe depended for their cotton upon the South, and Southern statesmen believed that the influence of King Cotton would be the determining factor in the struggle. It was certainly an important element in the result, but not in the way that was expected. In the hope that Great Britain would interfere in the war to keep open her supply of raw cotton, the Confederacy at first put an embargo on cotton exports and

6 Quoted by G. C. Eggleston, *A Rebel's Recollections*, 84.

urged producers to hold back their crop. This might conceivably have brought results but for counteracting factors. The heavy crops of the fifties had built up a surplus of raw cotton that enabled the mills to run at least on part time. By the time the cotton famine actually came, Northern workers had found employment in other industries, while the antislavery sentiment in Great Britain had been so strengthened by Lincoln's Emancipation Proclamation that the autocratic pro-Southern government found it inexpedient to interfere.

Furthermore, other economic factors also operated to keep Great Britain neutral. Short wheat crops in England from 1860 to 1862 had brought heavy purchases from the United States and led British statesmen to point out that any move to bring in cotton would operate to hold back wheat. The threat of a boycott on wheat appears to have originated with Secretary Seward and to have been pushed in England by Northern sympathizers. Whether the need of American wheat actually kept Great Britain neutral it is difficult to say. It is the belief of the most recent student of Civil War diplomacy that it was not so much wheat *per se* that kept Great Britain neutral as the desire for war profits.[7] Great Britain could obtain plenty of wheat elsewhere; she bought it from the United States (1) because it was cheaper and more convenient to purchase it here, and (2) because she could exchange arms and munitions for it. Certainly Britain's economic interests, for the moment at least, were more closely identified with the North than with the South.

It is impossible to determine the cost of war in terms of human sacrifice and suffering. Estimates of financial loss and expenditures, however, can be made. David A. Wells estimated in 1869 that the total expenditure of the federal government in the eight and a quarter years of the war and postwar period was about $4,172,000,000. To this he added $923,000,000 as the increased cost over normal expenditures and debt to the northern states; $1,200,000,000 as the loss to the northern states from the diversion and suspension of industry and the reduction of the American marine and carrying trade; and $2,700,000,000 as the direct expenditures and loss of property by the Confederate states. "These estimates which are believed to be moderate and reasonable," he said, "show an aggregate destruction of wealth or diversion of industry, which would have produced wealth in the United States since 1861, approximating *nine* thousand *millions* of dollars. What does it measure? It is substantially a thousand millions a year for nine years; or, at the wages of five hundred dollars a year, the labor of two millions of men exerted continuously during the whole of that period. It is three times as much as the slave property of the country was ever worth.

[7] F. W. Owsley, *King Cotton Diplomacy*, 567 ff.

It is a sum which at interest would yield to the end of time twice as much as the annual slave product of the South in its best estate." [8] To this estimate billions were to be later added in pensions, and the South was to be subjected to the misery and humiliation of "reconstruction."

LIFE IN THE NORTH

Economic life in the North during the war was one of extraordinary expansion and prosperity. Quite naturally those industries dealing with munitions and war supplies were the first to feel the stimulus, particularly woolens and metal goods, but eventually the prosperity spread to practically every type of manufacturing. Cotton-manufacturing alone, because of the reduced supply of raw material, suffered a decline. Expansion in certain industries, particularly in ready-made clothing, had been made possible by the invention of the sewing machine, first put on the market by Elias Howe in 1849, and by the application of the sewing machine to leather through the patent of L. R. Blake and Gordon McKay. The rapid expansion of industrial life brought in its wake a considerable development of city-building, particularly in the munition centers. "On every street and avenue," said the Chicago *Tribune* of October 8, 1863, "one sees new buildings going up, immense stone, brick, and iron business blocks, marble palaces and new residences, everywhere the grading of streets, the building of sewers, the laying of water and gas pipes, are all in progress at the same time."

With industrial expansion went the expansion of transportation and mining. While Union armies in the South were tearing up rails and destroying bridges, far-sighted entrepreneurs in the North were rapidly adding to the railroad mileage. The most famous of the railroads chartered during the war was the Union Pacific, construction of which did not begin in earnest, however, until after the conflict (page 404). Of the railroads built during the war the longest was the Atlantic and Great Western, later part of the Erie system, which ran from Salamanca, New York, to Cincinnati, Ohio, and was important in linking New York and St. Louis by a one-gauge railroad. It was during the war that St. Louis was connected by rail with Kansas City. Important also was the effort of Massachusetts to obtain her part of the western trade, when, in 1863, she took up the unfinished work on the Hoosac tunnel and pushed to completion the connection between Boston and Albany. In all, about 23,000 miles of railroad were constructed during the sixties, and a large proportion of this was either laid or planned during the war. The building of railroads and the

[8] Report of the Special Commissioner of the Revenue, 1869, page vi, Ex. Doc. No. 27, House of Representatives, 41st Congress, Second Session.

manufacture of munitions naturally stimulated such basic mineral products as coal and iron.

Extractive industry grew more important with the discovery in 1859 of the famous Comstock lode of gold and silver in Nevada, which, with other mines, yielded during the war at least $8,000,000 of the precious metals and stimulated a movement of prospectors and immigrants into the mountain states. Far more important than the precious metals was the inauguration of a new industry in 1859 with the discovery of oil on the Drake farm at Titusville, Venango County, in northwestern Pennsylvania. High-grade mineral oil quickly displaced whale and other animal oils for lighting and lubrication and set in motion forces destined profoundly to modify our social and economic life. The region around Oil Creek, Pennsylvania, rapidly took on the aspect of a western boom town as thousands of wells were bored, and production as early as 1862 mounted to 128,000,000 gallons.

Amazing as was the expansion in manufacturing, it was duplicated in certain branches of agriculture. The wheat crop increased; more hogs were marketed than ever before, and wool-production rose from 40,000,000 to 140,000,000 pounds. How agricultural production increased while tens of thousands of farmers were drawn into military service or lured to the Far West can be explained only by the rapid introduction of new farm machinery, particularly the reapers of McCormick and Hussey, and by the settlement of large numbers of immigrants, drawn to the frontier by the Homestead Act of 1862. Stimulation of agricultural production came from the increased war-time needs, the heavy demand from European nations, where the harvest for three years had been poor, and, of course, the high prices. The latter were due both to increased demand and to currency inflation. Just as during the World War, so also during the days of civil conflict, the American farmer experienced an era of artificial expansion and prosperity that was later to bring disaster and political unrest.

No one would deny that the Civil War, in ending the long controversy over the relative power of the state and federal governments, had important political effects. Its economic results, however, were far more significant. Not alone did it put an end to chattel slavery and artificially stimulate agriculture to its eventual disaster, but it enormously speeded the development of American capitalism. The War of 1812 brought the introduction of the factory system, and the Civil War tremendously speeded the Industrial Revolution. With this Industrial Revolution came not only the rapid expansion of industry but the age of big business and the early stages of capitalistic consolidation. From this point of view the Civil War ushered in a new economic era. Concentration of capital and consolidation of business went hand in hand. Before the war the millionaires of the nation might have been counted on one hand; at its conclusion there were scores. And why not? Railroads that had never declared a dividend before the war were now paying 8 or 9 per cent. Dividends of from 30 to 40 per cent were common in textiles, while munitions and food-manufacturing concerns were paying even more. Stocks soared to many times their former value. That these war-time profits were often made in the most indefensible manner, particularly by those who sold to the government, there can be no doubt. The habit of the woolen manufacturers of palming off shoddy in place of virgin wool gave to the whole tribe of war millionaires and profiteers the descriptive term, "shoddy aristocracy." Among the classic examples of incredible war profiteering was the loan made by J. P. Morgan to finance the purchase from the United States government of 5000 defective and condemned carbines for $17,486, which were then resold to the government through General Frémont in Missouri for $109,912. When the defective carbines began shooting off the thumbs of the soldiers using them, the consignment was rejected. Thereupon the sellers presented to the government a claim for $58,175 (half of the shipment having already been paid for in good faith) and actually collected the money.

As if this were not a sufficiently rapid method of accumulating wealth, the nation, or at least the wealthy portion of it, turned itself without reserve to speculation. While stock values doubled and tripled, transactions during 1863 in the stock exchange totaled nearly a billion and a half dollars. A "frenzied throng of eager speculators," reported an observer in 1864, crowded the city exchanges and their approaches. "Streets are blocked up by a mass so frenzied by the general passion for gain that almost all regard for personal safety and respect for personal propriety seems lost. . . . The number of brokers has more than quadrupled in a few months, such has been the enormous increase in stock-jobbing. Their aggregate business, in the city of New York alone, has risen from twenty-five to more than a hundred millions a day." It is not surprising that in such a situation the lust for riches found in the varying fortunes of the Union arms the most lucrative opportunities to speculate in greenbacks and army supplies. As a contemporary observer suggested, there was a fortune in Wall Street for everyone "who is not a natural idiot."

However the wealth may have come, the new capitalists were thoroughly alive to their power and to further possibilities for gain. While street railways proceeded in construction and transcontinental railroads pressed in the legislatures for long-term franchises, the larger roads already established began to consolidate and to absorb the minor lines. In 1866 the Western Union acquired its last important rivals, and the telegraph system was a virtual monopoly. Throughout industrial life there began that process of consolidation that was destined to be such an important characteristic of the decades to follow.

The easy gains from speculation and war profiteering naturally led to a riot of extravagance and pursuit of pleasure unprecedented as yet in America. Athletic and other spectacles were liberally patronized, race tracks were crowded, and the theaters played to packed houses. Vice was rampant, and merchants found the readiest sale for the most expensive clothing, furnishings, and jewelry. In disgust the New York *Independent* lamented in 1864:

> Who at the North would ever think of war, if he had not a friend in the army, or did not read the newspapers? Go into Broadway, and we will show you what is meant by the word "extravagance." Ask Stewart about the demand for camel's hair shawls, and he will say "monstrous." Ask Tiffany what kind of diamonds and pearls are called for. He will answer "the prodigious," "as near hen's-egg size as possible," "price no object." What kind of carpetings are now wanted? None but extra. . . . And as for horses the medium-priced five-hundred-dollar kind are all out of the market. A good pair of "fast ones," "all right," will go for a thousand dollars sooner than a basket of strawberries will sell for four cents.

It is hardly surprising that under such conditions the more realistic preferred the easy profits of the marketplace to the rigors and dangers of army life. Few indeed were the masters of industry and capital of subsequent years who had seen service in the army; many of the robber barons of the new industrial feudalism got their start in the hectic days of war. The amazing thing is that the system of volunteer enlistments proved as successful as it did. Up to 1863 fully 800,000 had joined the Union forces before the system broke down. In that year came the Draft Act of March 3, which divided the nation into enrollment districts, apportioned a quota for each district, which, when not filled by volunteers, was to be secured by a public drawing from the list of names of the district. While this might be fairer than the volunteer system, it was open to many abuses, for a drafted man might be exempted upon furnishing a substitute or paying $300. While the North as a whole accepted this act, the opposition to the exemption features and the belief that politics played a part in the enforcement led to spasmodic outbreaks against it. Riots in New York (July, 1863) destroyed $1,500,000 of property and resulted in the killing or wounding of over 1000 persons. Early efforts to stimulate volunteer enlistments by bounties and later efforts by drafted men to purchase substitutes introduced a mercenary aspect to army service and encouraged desertion. "Bounty-jumping" on the part of men who received pay for enlistment, then deserted, changed their names, and enlisted again developed almost to the status of a profession. One man was discovered who had jumped the bounty thirty-two times.[9]

[9] A reasonable estimate of northern desertions would be a little over 300,000. F. A. Shannon, *Organization and Administration of the Union Army*, II, 179.

While capital increased in power during the war years, the position of labor became relatively weaker. Although war demands and inflation pushed prices up by an average of 100 per cent, wages, as always in such a situation, lagged behind. While wages, particularly in the war industries, tended eventually to adjust themselves to prices, it appears that real wages at the end of the war stood at about a third less than in 1860. As usual, it was the salaried professional classes, clergymen, teachers, government employees, and others who suffered most. The failure of real wages to keep pace with the cost of living is explainable in part by the systematic importation of cheap European labor, by the use of Negro strikebreakers and by the employment of labor-saving machinery, all of which helped to counteract the gap in labor ranks made by enlistments and the increased demand for labor. As the weakened position of labor became obvious during the last two years of the war, strikes became frequent, and renewed efforts toward organization became common. At least ten national unions came into existence between 1863 and 1866, including the first of the great railroad brotherhoods, the Brotherhood of Locomotive Engineers (1863), and this movement toward organization continued even more rapidly in the late sixties.

To describe life in the North as simply a careless riot of extravagance would be to give but part of the picture. The war ended with 1,052,038 men in the Union army; there was hardly a Northern family that escaped personal war experience, and there was hardly a hamlet, however remote it might be, without soldier graves to decorate. The same self-sacrifice that the masses always display in such circumstances and the same inevitable suffering were evident again. Besides local ministrations to soldiers' families, important sanitary and welfare work in the army, now done by the Red Cross and other organizations, was then accomplished through the United States Sanitary Commission and the United States Christian Commission. The Sanitary Commission, approved by the government and supported by private donations and the proceeds of huge "sanitary fairs," supplemented the medical department of the army by providing medicines, bandages, convalescent homes, and nurses, and aided morale by providing food, clothing, and tobacco, by maintaining headquarters in the cities for traveling soldiers, by publishing a hospital directory, and by contributing in many other ways. The Christian Commission did much the same sort of thing, but was particularly interested in the spiritual welfare of the soldiers. The contribution of these welfare workers, of whom Clara Barton was perhaps the most famous, only the common soldier could adequately appreciate.

The generosity of private individuals was not limited to war needs but spread out into other channels, particularly education. At least fifteen colleges were founded during the sixties. Despite the strain of war, the federal government found time to pass the most important single piece of educational legislation in our history, the Morrill Act of 1862. Introduced by Justin S. Morrill in 1857, vetoed by Buchanan, and again passed during the Lincoln administration, the Morrill Act authorized a donation to each state of 30,000 acres of public land for each of its senators and congressmen, the income from which was to be devoted to mechanical and agricultural colleges, with provision for military training. Through its medium sixty-nine "land-grant colleges" have arisen.

WAR TIME IN THE CONFEDERACY

From the point of view of administration, the Confederate government found itself in an impossible situation. Based on the theory of state sovereignty, it found itself compelled to carry on a conflict in which the highest form of efficiency and integration directed by an all-powerful central authority was essential. Extraordinary war-time powers, it is true, were conferred upon the Confederate government. The Conscription Act, signed by Davis April 16, 1862, almost a year before forced service was resorted to in the North, made white males from eighteen to thirty-five (later forty-five) eligible for three years' service. About the same time came the first of a series of acts suspending the writ of *habeas corpus*. Davis stood consistently for the strong centralization of military authority in his hands, and during the larger part of the war he carried his Congress with him.

Despite the heroic resistance of the South and its apparent unity, the Confederate government was beset with difficulties from the start. In the first place, the sentiment for secession was far from unanimous. Many political leaders, in fact, had strongly opposed secession. Some, like Alexander H. Stephens, had followed their states; others, like Andrew Johnson, had not. In the Alleghenies slavery had never achieved a strong foothold, and here was to be found a region of Unionist sentiment penetrating like a peninsula into a sea of slavery. The chief Unionist strongholds of the South were in western North Carolina, northern Alabama, and eastern Tennessee, but some Unionists were to be found in every state. During the course of the struggle nearly 300,000 white Union soldiers were enrolled from the Confederacy. Besides having a very real Unionist group, the Confederacy was handicapped by internal dissensions of various kinds, which expressed themselves chiefly in a personal opposition to Davis and his government quite as bitter as anything that Lincoln experienced. This originated in part from a conflict between the small farmer and the planter aristocracy, in part from the old conflict between state and federal authority, in part from the tension of a long war and impending defeat and the natural tendency to blame the situation on the government, and finally from the personality of Davis and his advisers.

The situation in which Davis found himself was in many ways a curious one. A West-Pointer and a colonel in the Mexican War, he had a natural bent for a military career and no desire whatsoever for the presidency. Considering himself a military expert, he attempted, not always with wisdom, to direct the Southern war, until in the desperation of defeat Congress created (January, 1865) the office of commanding general, which Davis bestowed upon Lee. In that important realm of statesmanship involving the skillful handling of men, a realm in which Lincoln was so adept, Davis was weakest. From the beginning he lost the ardent personal support of many of the strongest secession leaders. Yancey, who had contributed perhaps more than any other single person to bringing about secession, was sent immediately on a fruitless mission to England. Rhett, without cabinet portfolio, became eventually the leader of the opposition. Toombs, the first Secretary of State, resigned in the summer of 1861. With the exception of Attorney General Benjamin, the cabinet was composed of mediocrities and never evoked popular enthusiasm. In spite of much opposition to Benjamin, Davis not only retained him, but promoted him to the portfolio of the State Department. Davis was rigid, dogmatic, without humor, and handicapped by physical wretchedness, but he was far from being the high-handed tyrant pictured by his enemies, and he was without doubt a statesman of great ability.

The key to Southern defeat rests in the last analysis upon the economic breakdown. While the war accentuated existing economic tendencies in the North, it turned the economic life of the South upside down. That civilization, based upon the production and exportation of staple agricultural products and the importation of manufactured goods, collapsed before the "anaconda policy" of the North. Land and slaves, the chief form of Southern wealth, had to be shifted from export staples to foodstuffs, a difficult and wasteful process, and eventually to manufacturing. Free importation of manufactured goods was prevented by the Union navy, and the South resorted to large-scale blockade-running. Considering the small amount of maritime activity in the pre-war South, the skill and success of Southern blockade-runners were amazing. Arms, ammunition, clothing, medicines, and various luxuries came from Europe to various ports in the West Indies, where they were picked up by the lead-colored, low-built steamers that ran them into Wilmington, Charleston, Savannah, Mobile, and Galveston. In spite of frequent captures by the Union navy, blockade-running was so profitable that it found no lack of financial support. "Fifty or sixty millions of dollars," complained the president of a manufacturers' convention in Augusta in 1864, "have gone into blockade running, while scarcely a new dollar has gone into manufacturing." [10] Much traffic was at first carried overland from Mexico, but the capture of Vicksburg and the patrol of the Mississippi by federal gunboats speedily ended the trans-Mississippi commerce. The enormous profits obtained by running luxuries through the blockade often proved too much for patriotism, and the Confederate government in 1864 was forced to forbid the importation of wines, spirits, laces, carpets, furniture, and jewelry, and to insist that a certain amount of space on incoming and outgoing boats be reserved for government use.

To overcome the effects of a one-sided civilization, every effort was made to encourage existing iron and textile factories and to create new ones. The Confederate government itself established or took over factories producing whisky, salt, and munitions of various kinds, and these operations were sufficiently successful to take care of the ordinary military needs. Except for war industries, there was but slight development in manufacturing, and those who had formerly purchased manufactured goods from Europe or the North were forced to bring out again the spinning wheel and the hand loom and revert to the earlier days of home industry. As a matter of fact, the Confederacy in the war years made tremendous progress toward establishing a self-sufficing economy. The weakest link in the economic chain was the transportation system. As it wore out or was destroyed by Union soldiers, it increasingly failed in the vital function of distributing foodstuffs and industrial products.

Two factors dominated the social life in the South during the war, the blockade and the invasion of enemy armies. They not only upset the economic system, destroyed transportation, and brought privation and suffering, but colored in an infinite variety of ways the thought and life of the people. Currency inflation, war profiteering, and economic disintegration bred speculation until it was quite as rampant and even more demoralizing than in the North. "The passion for speculation," complained Davis bitterly in 1863, "has seduced citizens of all classes from a determined prosecution of the war to a sordid effort to amass money." While luxuries were often obtainable by the wealthy, there was at times an actual scarcity of food in the cities, and there were bread riots in Atlanta, Mobile, and other places. Profiteering, speculation, and actual hunger did more than anything else to weaken the morale of the South, but there were other influences. Exemptions from the draft (page 365), such as the "Fifteen Slave" Act, exempting one overseer for each plantation where there were fifteen slaves, the exemption of civil officials, and the possibility for a time of hiring substitutes gave rise to the feeling that the conflict was

---

[10] Quoted by Rhodes, *History of the United States,* V, 396, from the Augusta *Chronicle* of May 26, 1864.

"a rich man's war and a poor man's fight." These factors, in combination with war weariness and the failure of the Confederate authorities to take care of the civilian population, eventually brought widespread desertion, estimated at some 200,000 men. These deserters, forced oftentimes to maintain themselves in armed bands, engendered lawlessness. In sharp contrast to this was the heroic devotion of the women, who turned with self-sacrificing industry to unaccustomed tasks, responsibilities, and dangers. For decades Southern statesmen had conjured up the bugbear of slave insurrection, but, when the opportunity arrived, the Negro proved his peaceful devotion. "One of the strange things in this eventful history," says Rhodes, "is the peaceful labor of three and one-half million slaves whose presence in the South was the cause of the war and whose freedom was fought for after September, 1862, by northern soldiers." [11]

THE EUROPEAN FRONT

Interference by European nations in the American civil conflict might quite effectively have changed the course of events. As the ruling classes in England and France were generally sympathetic toward the South, it was the objective of the Confederacy to bring about such interference and of the North to prevent it. The trump card of the Confederacy was the foreign demand for cotton, but important as this was, it failed to win the game (page 358). The Confederate government was no sooner organized than a commission was sent to Europe. It was soon succeeded by two special commissioners, James M. Mason and John Slidell, sent to England and France respectively. Their best efforts won only the recognition of Southern belligerency and some secret and illegal aid. Slidell prevailed upon the French firm of Erlanger & Company to float a Confederate loan of $15,000,000 secured by cotton, but as $5,000,000 was spent on vessels never delivered, $6,000,000 to "bull" the market for the bonds, and another million in semiannual drawings to redeem them, the loan was unsuccessful as a source of revenue and of but slight value as a political demonstration. Napoleon III, who ordinarily followed the lead of England in his dealings with the Confederacy, took the initiative in 1862 when he suggested to England and Russia that they insist upon a six months' armistice. When both nations declined to participate, this came to nothing.

Although the relations of the North with the British government were strained more than once to the breaking point, the main objective was achieved. Great Britain officially maintained a position of neutrality, and France followed. Great Britain's proclamation of neutrality recognizing Southern belligerency was bitterly resented in the North, but she could

[11] J. F. Rhodes, *History of the Civil War, 1861–1865*, 381.

hardly do otherwise under the circumstances. Such a proclamation did not afford recognition of independence nor did it commit her to the reception of diplomatic agents.

The first serious clash between the two nations occurred November 7, 1861, when the United States man-of-war *San Jacinto,* Captain Wilkes commanding, overhauled the British mail steamer *Trent,* and removed Mason and Slidell, the Confederate commissioners bound for Europe. Although Great Britain, during the Napoleonic wars, had repeatedly stopped neutral ships and forcibly removed individuals, she now demanded the surrender of the prisoners in words that practically threatened war, and commenced military preparations for such an event. In the North the action of Wilkes aroused great enthusiasm, but war with England at the time was unthinkable. The commissioners were released, with Secretary Seward pointing out that in so doing we were simply following a policy for which we had long contended.

Another problem of neutral rights, which had been a source of much controversy during the Napoleonic wars, the doctrine of ultimate destination, arose again. In the earlier conflict Great Britain had insisted that the "broken voyage" did not neutralize contraband, while the United States had taken the opposite position. During the Civil War, however, this country reversed itself, seized British ships bound to the West Indies or Mexico and laden with munitions obviously destined eventually for the Confederacy. The British government acquiesced and swallowed its own medicine, but the same problem was to arise again during the World War to plague the United States.

More fruitful of hard feeling between the two nations was Britain's violation of her role as a neutral in allowing the Confederates to build in her shipyards vessels destined to prey upon Northern commerce. Such action not only was specifically forbidden by British law but violated the primary obligation of a neutral to prevent her ports from being used as a base of operations against a nation at war. Despite the protests of the able American ambassador, Charles Francis Adams, the *Florida* and the *Alabama* were built in Great Britain and allowed to escape. Britain's defense that the mere building of a ship in her yards did not make her responsible for its subsequent career was under the circumstances somewhat specious. When Adams, with reference to the possible sailing of another such ship, warned the British foreign minister, Russell, that "It would be superfluous in me to point out to your lordship that this is war," the British government saw the point, and the practice stopped. For the direct damages caused by the *Florida* and the *Alabama* Great Britain was to make eventual restitution (page 504), but there could be no adequate recompense for the indirect blow to the American merchant marine.

In France the wily Napoleon would have been only too glad to lend aid to the Confederacy, but he did not dare do so alone, and his hands were tied by his adventure in Mexico. In the hope of bolstering his tottering throne, he had conceived the grandiose scheme of establishing a French colonial empire in America, a scheme that he thought would win the support of ardent nationalists seeking glory, of French bourgeois in search of commerce, and of the Catholic party, which was anxious to safeguard its church from the attacks of Mexican revolutionists. Beginning as a joint project to collect debts owed to Great Britain, Spain, and France, it developed into the establishment of a Mexican empire ruled over by a puppet emperor, Archduke Maximilian of Austria, and supported by French armies. Demands of Secretary Seward that the French evacuate Mexico and the refusal of the United States government to recognize Maximilian made it unwise, if not practically impossible, for the Mexican government to receive a minister from the Confederate states. With this the last faint hope in the Confederacy of foreign intervention failed.

The story is summarized in H. U. Faulkner, *American Economic History*, Chap. XVII, emphasizing the economic, and told more fully in A. C. Cole, *The Irrepressible Conflict*, Chaps. XIII–XV (History of American Life), in J. F. Rhodes, *A History of the United States*, Vol. V, Chaps. XXVII, XXVIII, and in J. G. Randall, *The Civil War and Reconstruction*, Chaps. XXVII–XXIX. Intellectual reactions are in Merle Curti, *The Growth of American Thought*, Chap. XVIII. The most nearly complete study of the North is E. D. Fite, *Social and Industrial Conditions in the North During the Civil War*, particularly Chaps. IX–XI. See also D. R. Dewey, *Financial History of the United States*, Chaps. XII, XIII. Probably the best description of life in the South is N. W. Stephenson, *Day of the Confederacy* (Chronicles of America). For foreign affairs see S. F. Bemis, *A Diplomatic History of the United States*, Chap. XXI and T. A. Bailey, *A Diplomatic History of the United States*, Chaps. XXI, XXII. E. D. Adams, *Great Britain and the American Civil War*, Vol. II, Chap. XVIII, interprets the British attitude. For sources, see F. Flügel and H. U. Faulkner, *Readings in the Economic and Social History of the United States*, 447–472, and H. S. Commager, *Documents of American History*, Vol. I, 389–450.

NATIONALISM AND SECTIONALISM

Chapter XXII

THE TRAGIC ERA

*The true doctrine of reconstruction is, that
defeated rebels have no civil nor political rights,
which loyal men are bound to respect, and that
all loyal men, without regard to race or color, are
entitled to equal rights as citizens.*

RESOLUTION AT A FANEUIL
HALL MEETING (1866)

*Tyranny and despotism can be exercised by
many more rigorously, more vigorously, and
more severely than by one.*

ANDREW JOHNSON

PROBLEMS OF PEACE

The war for Southern independence had solved two important questions: Negro chattel slavery was ended, and the ultimate supremacy of
the federal government was established. But, like most wars, it created
more problems than it solved. Its greatest effect, perhaps, was the stimulation that it gave to economic processes in the North, and with this came
the rising power of capitalism. Politically, the conflict between the states
marked the shift in power from the slaveholding oligarchy of the South
to the rising plutocracy of the North.

Hardly less significant for the moment was the tremendous economic
destruction suffered by the South. To the terrific economic loss amounting
to billions of dollars was added the necessity of shifting from slave to free
labor and from the large plantation to the small farm. The problem of the
future was a pressing one, particularly for the 4,000,000 Negroes whose
sudden freedom had separated them from their moorings and set them
adrift in an economic world that held for them little hope. Unlike the
peasants of Russia and France, where freedom from serfdom did not mean
loss of land, the Negroes of America found themselves utterly separated
from their earlier means of livelihood. Thousands of them, enjoying their
new-found freedom, wandered about the country believing that "the year

371

of jubulee" had arrived when the government would split the land and give to each one "forty acres and a mule." It is hardly surprising that under such circumstances Southern planters, ruined and desperate, retaliated by passing the "Black Codes," state laws designed to reduce the Negro to a position of serfdom. Although the Civil War did not create the racial problem in the South, it accentuated an existing one in many ways. While the South was swept by economic demoralization and the North was shifting from agriculture to industry, the West was expanding and rapidly creating new regional problems, which were quickly to have their effect upon the economic and political life of the nation.

As far as the South was concerned, the problems of reconstruction were primarily social and economic. It was its tragedy and that of the nation as a whole that the great problem of the economic rehabilitation was subordinated to that of establishing Republican political supremacy. Complicated as are the reasons for this unfortunate result, it is possible to disentangle them. The Union Party that elected Lincoln in 1864 was a composite of old antislavery Republicans of 1860, War Democrats who would support Lincoln in maintaining the Union, old-time Whigs interested in the tariff, internal improvements, and sound money, and other groups. As this coalition inevitably disintegrated at the end of the conflict, the Republican faction moved aggressively to save their party and, if possible, maintain it in power. They comprised in their leadership some of the ablest and likewise some of the most unscrupulous leaders in both branches of Congress. Behind them were northern industrialists who would consolidate business and maintain the protective tariff, financiers who would put a stop to the inflation brought on by the war, and railroad promoters who had already begun to tap the public treasury. Such men had no desire to see southern planters back in Congress co-operating with western farmers and bringing their influence to bear upon such problems as currency, banking, taxation, tariff, and monopoly practice. In addition, of course, there were well-meaning enthusiasts of the Sumner type, who believed that the most momentous issue at the moment was the freedom and protection of the black man and that only in the Republican Party was his future safe. The effort to establish Republican supremacy was strengthened, of course, by the attempt of Andrew Johnson to build a national party based upon a moderate policy toward the South. If the Northern Democracy should coalesce with the politically reconstructed Southern states, there was a strong likelihood that Republican supremacy in the federal government would end. The policy of the Republican Party, therefore, was to prevent the Southern states from returning to the Union under Democratic control. To forestall this event, many Southerners were disfranchised, Negroes were given the vote, and under military supervision a Republican Party based on Negro votes was created, which for almost a decade controlled the South and ensured Republican supremacy in the federal government.

The whole problem of Southern reconstruction was complicated by the assassination of Lincoln. This is undoubtedly the chief significance of the passing of the great leader. When Lincoln succumbed on the morning of April 15, 1865, to the assassin's bullet, the South in her most tragic moment lost her best and most powerful friend. Lincoln was essentially a conservative and cautious statesman, kindly by nature and utterly free from any vindictiveness that would have led him to sanction punitive measures toward the South. "I hope there will be no persecution," he said, "no bloody work after the war is over. No one need expect me to take any part in hanging or killing these men. . . . We must extinguish our resentments if we expect harmony and union." That these were not mere words is amply demonstrated by his Proclamation of Amnesty and Reconstruction, issued December 8, 1863, in which he offered pardon to all except designated classes [1] provided they would take the oath of allegiance and accept the recent laws and proclamation respecting slavery, and proclaimed that, when the number taking the oath of allegiance amounted to 10 per cent of the voting population of 1860, the state government might be organized and receive executive recognition. Lincoln's "10-per-cent plan," although quite generally approved in the North, aroused immediate opposition on the part of the Radical Republicans, who had already clashed with the President on the conduct of the war. Their answer was the Wade-Davis Bill of July 2, 1864, which authorized re-establishment of civil government when half of the citizens had taken the oath of allegiance, but debarred from voting or holding office all who had fought with the Confederacy. Feeling that this was too severe, Lincoln pocket-vetoed the bill. The Wade-Davis Bill and its veto, nevertheless, marked a definite break between Lincoln and the Radical Republicans, which undoubtedly would have grown deeper if the President had lived. The motives behind the Wade-Davis Bill seem to have been primarily three, and they were the same that later accentuated the conflict between Johnson and Congress: a wish to curtail the extraordinary war powers of the President, a desire to punish the South, and an anxiety to prevent the increase in Democratic power by the return of the seceded states.

CONGRESSIONAL RECONSTRUCTION

Shocked as was the nation by the assassination of Lincoln, the leaders of the Radical Republicans could hardly stifle a sigh of relief. The President's

[1] Former Confederate civil and diplomatic officers, those who had resigned federal civil and military positions to serve the Confederacy, and Confederate officers above the rank of colonel in the army and lieutenant in the navy.

policy of moderation and reconciliation was no part of their plan, and in his successor, Andrew Johnson, they hoped to find a more pliant tool. Johnson indeed had "breathed fire and hemp" when denouncing treason and calling for the punishment of traitors, but his attitude emanated from his hatred of treason and his bitterness toward the aristocracy of the South rather than from any desire to enfranchise the blacks or strengthen the Republican Party. Sprung from the poor whites of the South, Johnson had grown up in Tennessee, where he had pushed forward in the rough school of border-state politics. He was a tailor by trade, and it was not until he had reached adult life that his wife introduced him to the rudiments of an education. Possessed of much sheer intellectual force, oratorical ability, and unquestioned courage, Johnson soon passed from state politics to the federal House and Senate. A representative of the poor whites, so ably described by Helper and Olmsted, he was possessed by the fierce democracy of the frontier and loyalty to the Union. In Tennessee he had led the opposition to secession, and Lincoln had made him military governor of the state. When, in 1864, the Republicans attempted to appeal to all Unionists on a national ticket, the War Democrat, Andrew Johnson, was given second place. As honest and sincere as Lincoln, he lacked the latter's breadth of view, tolerance, and political finesse. Whether Lincoln could have carried his Congress with him in the dark days of reconstruction is doubtful; certainly the unbending and tactless Johnson could not.

When Johnson became President April 15, 1865, he retained Lincoln's cabinet and after a few weeks' delay determined to follow Lincoln's policy of reconstruction. He recognized the three state governments set up under the "10-per-cent plan"—Louisiana, Arkansas, and Tennessee—and also the rump government in Virginia maintained during the war. On May 29 he issued two proclamations, one of amnesty and the other providing a mode of political reconstruction for North Carolina. The former was virtually the same as that issued by Lincoln on December 8, 1863, except that Johnson excluded other groups from taking the oath, in particular all persons possessing $20,000 or more. All in the excluded groups might apply to the President for clemency. Under the Lincoln-Johnson policy all the states had held elections and, with the exception of Texas (where the convention met the following spring), had assembled constitutional conventions before the end of October, 1865. Through the temporary governors whom he had appointed, Johnson made known to these constitutional conventions that his policy included official recognition of the results of the war. As a consequence, each of the states rescinded the ordinances of secession, abolished slavery, and, with the exception of South Carolina, repudiated the Confederate debt. Johnson also urged these states to join in the ratification of the thirteenth amendment, which had passed Congress

on January 31, 1865; all but Mississippi did so. When Congress convened
in December, 1865, the situation was as follows: Johnson had recognized
the Lincoln governments in the four states of Louisiana, Arkansas, Tennessee, and Virginia and had himself set up governments in North Carolina, South Carolina, Georgia, Florida, Alabama, Mississippi, and Texas.
With the necessary aid of these states the thirteenth amendment had been
adopted (December 18, 1865), and all of them except Texas had elected
representatives and senators, who were now seeking admission to Congress.

For the Radicals in Congress this reconstruction was altogether too rapid.
Dominated by the motives already discussed and led by such men as
Thaddeus Stevens in the House and Charles Sumner in the Senate, this
group succeeded in preventing either body from receiving the newly elected
representatives. Their next move was the creation of a joint committee of
fifteen, ostensibly to investigate the claims of the southern states for recognition, but actually to devise a congressional scheme of reconstruction that
might become the program of the Radicals in Congress. As we have already
pointed out, the dominating influence behind the new Radical Republican
bloc was the rising capitalism of the North. As quite often happens, however, the leaders were dominated by quite different motives. Thaddeus
Stevens, far from being the vindictive villain painted by his enemies, was a
brilliant politician and a relentless foe whose political career was largely
given over to battling for the rights of the poor. Sumner, his health broken
by the cowardly attack of Brooks, had a one-track mind that saw in the
Negro question the only matter of importance. Behind these two men other
politicians with perhaps less worthy motives quickly coalesced. In the ensuing game of politics the South unfortunately played into the hands of
this group. Seeking, for example, her ablest men, she recalled to power
many prominent Confederate leaders. The sight of these men seeking admission to Congress so soon after the war was needlessly irritating and
made it easy to misinterpret the attitude of the South. More disastrous were
the "Black Codes," already mentioned, which so restricted the social and
economic rights of the Negro as virtually to reduce him to serfdom. These
codes, along with serious race riots in the South during the spring and
summer of 1866, went far to convince the North that the South, as far as
the Negro was concerned, had no intention of abiding by the result of the
war. Unwittingly, perhaps, the southern states had played into the hands
of the Radicals, and the latter were quick to take advantage.

The first skirmish in the battle between the President and Congress came
in February, 1866, when Johnson vetoed a bill extending the life and widening the scope of the Freedmen's Bureau and giving the President power to
extend military authority in any state that discriminated against the Negroes. The Freedmen's Bureau had been a protective institution to aid and

guide the Negro in the transition from slavery to freedom. Johnson vetoed the bill on the ground that the bureau was expensive and unnecessary and the powers granted to him unconstitutional. His veto, which was sustained, may have sprung from the most unselfish and patriotic motives, but the Freedmen's Bureau was hardly the issue upon which to commence the battle.[2] In answer to the "Black Codes," Congress in March passed the Civil Rights Bill, the authorization for which was based upon the second section of the thirteenth amendment. It declared Negroes citizens of the United States, granted them equal civil rights, and placed cases arising under this act in the federal courts. Vetoed by Johnson, this act was passed over his veto on April 15.

On the last day of April the Joint Committee on Reconstruction made its report. Declaring that the recently organized governments of the southern states had no legal standing, and asserting that the South was attempting to undo the results of the war, the report insisted that the privilege of statehood be denied until certain guarantees be written into the Constitution and agreed to by the South. Specifically, it believed that the main features of the Civil Rights Bill should be incorporated in the Constitution. Acting on this report, Congress approved the fourteenth amendment, June 13, 1866, and it was quite evident that readmission to the Union would be dependent upon acceptance of this amendment.

However one looks at it, the fourteenth amendment is undoubtedly one of the most important parts of the American Constitution. One authority on this period has recently described it as "a shrewdly conceived political platform, especially designed to catch votes in the forthcoming Congressional election of 1866." The Beards speak of the amendment as subduing "the states for all time to the unlimited jurisdiction of the federal Supreme Court," while a recent popular writer speaks of it as "the eternal bulwark of great property rights." Others insist that it wrote *laissez faire* into the Constitution. Ostensibly the four sections of the fourteenth amendment were put into the Constitution to ensure certain results of the war. Section 1 conferred citizenship both state and national upon Negroes, and it forbade any state to abridge the privileges or immunities of citizens or to deprive any person of life, liberty, or property without due process of law. It was the second sentence of section 1, as we shall later point out, that conferred such notable protection upon property rights. Section 2 provided that representatives should be apportioned among the several states according to number of inhabitants, thereby superseding that part of Article I, Section 2, of the Constitution that allowed three fifths of the slaves to be counted for representation, and it further provided for a proportional reduction of

---

[2] A bill continuing the life of the Freedmen's Bureau for two years was passed in July over the President's veto.

representation if the vote was denied to any of the male inhabitants twenty-one years of age and citizens of the United States. The intention of the section was to prevent the South from adding materially to its political power without at the same time granting the franchise to the Negro. It seemed unreasonable to the North that an important political result of the war should be an increase in Southern political power. Section 3 debarred from federal or state office anyone who, having taken the oath of allegiance, had engaged in insurrection, unless pardoned by a two-thirds vote of each house. Section 4 constitutionally validated the public debt incurred in putting down secession, thus winning the support of federal bondholders, while at the same time it repudiated obligations incurred by the seceding states.

While the economic implications of the fourteenth amendment were not apparent to the masses in 1866, the features designed to protect the Negro were clear enough. In a sense the amendment embodied the essential conditions under which Congress in 1866 was willing to readmit the seceded states. Whether or not it was a reasonable solution depended upon one's point of view. In any case Johnson opposed it, and of eleven southern states only Tennessee approved it. Congress accordingly readmitted that state on July 24, in part as a gesture of sincerity toward the South and in part to add two more Republican senators to the next Congress. In the meantime, the whole question of presidential as opposed to congressional reconstruction was carried to the electorate in the fall campaign. Johnson hoped that a coalition of moderate Republicans and Democrats would endorse his policy, but in this he was disappointed. His own injudicious and intemperate attacks upon Congress, in conjunction with the skillful political maneuvers of his opponents, proved his undoing. In almost all the states the Republican Party organization passed into the hands of the Radicals, and the fortieth Congress was completely under their domination.

Failure of the southern states to ratify the fourteenth amendment and the Radical victory in the autumn elections cleared the way for reconstruction on whatever terms Congress might decide. Despite the fact that during the winter of 1866 and 1867 southern legislatures had repealed the most obnoxious parts of the "Black Codes" and that Andrew Johnson was urging upon these legislatures at least a modified Negro suffrage, the last session of the thirty-ninth Congress attacked Johnson and the South with a spirit of vindictiveness and hatred hardly equaled in war time. All was subordinated to the exigencies of party politics. The first two acts on the congressional program were directed against Johnson. The Tenure of Office Act forbade the President to remove civil officers, including cabinet members, except with the consent of the Senate. This act was intended to protect Edwin M. Stanton, Secretary of War, who sympathized with the Radicals and virtually acted as their agent in the cabinet. Another piece of legislation, known as the Army Act and secretly drafted by Stanton, was designed to make the military establishment almost independent of the President.

Having attempted to tie the hands of Johnson, Congress proceeded to lay down the terms of political reconstruction. Under the first Reconstruction Act, passed like the two just mentioned over the President's veto on March 2, 1867, the existing Southern governments were declared inadequate and illegal. The South was divided into five military districts, each under a major general, who might continue the civil officers and courts or replace them by military tribunals if he desired. In each of the states new elections upon the basis of Negro suffrage were to be held, and, when the new legislature had accepted the fourteenth amendment and the state had adopted a new constitution that provided for Negro suffrage and was otherwise acceptable to Congress, it might be readmitted to the Union. Fearful that the South might prefer military rule to reconstruction on the terms set down, Congress by supplementary acts authorized the military commanders to register the voters and supervise the elections, at the same time providing that acceptance of the new constitution by a majority of the registered voters rather than a majority of the possible votes of the state was sufficient. Likewise, the oath of allegiance was made so rigid that almost 200,000 of the most intelligent citizens of the South were disfranchised. As a result of these acts, some 703,000 black and 627,000 white voters were registered, elections were held, new constitutions were adopted, and finally, in 1870, the last of the seceded states returned to the Union.

One final step in the plan of congressional reconstruction remains to be noted—the fifteenth amendment, introduced in Congress in 1867 and ratified the following year, which attempted to ensure to the Negro his right to vote. The chief purpose of all this, as has been pointed out, was to assure Republican supremacy nationally by creating a dominant Republican machine in the South. As often happens in political history, however, real motives are rationalized into fine-spun constitutional theories. While Lincoln and Johnson thought of the Union as something still intact that had been momentarily thrown out of equilibrium by the unsuccessful effort at secession, Sumner was developing his theory that the southern states had committed suicide, and Stevens talked of them as conquered provinces. Fruitless likewise was the discussion as to whether the reconstruction acts were illegal. Six months before the first reconstruction act was passed, Johnson had declared the country at peace, and nearly three months before the act the Supreme Court in the case *ex parte* Milligan (1866) had declared that military tribunals were illegal except where war made civil courts impossible. When, two years later, the constitutionality of the Reconstruction Act seemed likely to be questioned in the case *ex parte* McCardle, involving a Mississippi editor convicted by a military tribunal, Congress interfered and passed an act depriving the Supreme Court of the right to issue a writ of *habeas corpus* or to extend its jurisdiction over cases arising under the reconstruction acts.[3] The Radicals in Congress had no more intention of having their plans frustrated by the Supreme Court than by the President. It was not until the Radicals lost control of Congress that the Supreme Court mustered courage to declare parts of the reconstruction acts unconstitutional.

RECONSTRUCTION IN THE SOUTH

How little this congressional legislation met the real needs of the South is only too obvious. An English traveler picturing the Tennessee valley five years after the war, said that "it consists for the most part of plantations in a state of semi-ruin and plantations of which the ruin is for the present total and complete. . . . The trail of war is visible throughout the valley in burnt-up gin-houses, ruined bridges, mills, and factories . . . and in large tracts of once cultivated land stripped of every vestige of fencing." According to a Northern general, "Window-glass has given way to thin boards, in railway coaches and in the cities. Furniture is marred and broken, and none has been replaced for four years. Dishes are cemented in various styles, and half the pitchers have tin handles. . . . A set of forks with whole tines is a curiosity. Clocks and watches have nearly all stopped." Economic disintegration and poverty were everywhere. For the first two years after the war it was even doubtful if the rich agricultural land of the South would raise enough to keep the population from starvation. In some of the unhealthy communities of the South one fourth to one third of the Negroes, it is believed, died during the first years of readjustment.

Along with the economic collapse came a social revolution equally striking. Pike gives what was undoubtedly an extreme example of the situation in South Carolina:

In the vicinity lived a gentleman whose income when the war broke out was rated at $150,000 a year. Not a vestige of his whole vast estate remains today. Not far distant were the estates of a large proprietor and a well-known family, rich and distinguished for generations. The slaves were gone. The family is gone. A single scion of the house remains, and he peddles tea by the pound and molasses by the quart, on a corner of the old

---

[3] That the Supreme Court had little sympathy with the punitive state and federal laws is also seen in the cases of Cummings *v.* Missouri (1867) and *ex parte* Garland. In these decisions the court invalidated state laws in Missouri and Arkansas that prohibited ex-Confederates from practicing certain professions.

homestead, to the former slaves of the family and thereby earns his liveli-hood.[4]

The impoverishment of the whites, coupled with the freeing of the slaves and the problem of 4,000,000 blacks separated from their former means of livelihood, naturally resulted in some effort by the whites to deal with the Negro problem. Their first effort was the "Black Codes," which were rarely enforced and soon repealed. Congress attempted to deal with the same problem through the Freedman's Bureau. While the Freedmen's Bureau undoubtedly made an important contribution to the welfare of the black man during the early months of his freedom, and there seems little doubt that he needed some outside protection, the work of the bureau was gener-ally unpopular in the South. "The institution," asserts Fleming, "was based upon the assumption that the Negro race must be protected from the white race," and under it the "alienation of the two races began." [5]

But the attempt to protect the Negro through the Freedmen's Bureau was as nothing compared with the efforts under the reconstruction acts quickly to raise his social and political status. As the freeing of the slaves progressed and the Negro turned for direction and leadership from his former master to the federal soldiers and Unionist officials, representatives of the Republican Party pressed in to organize the Negroes. The Union League of America, which in the North was destined in the years to come to develop into conservative clubs of wealthy men, became in the South the political organization into which the Negro was enrolled. As the former Southern leaders were disfranchised, political reconstruction was carried on through the medium of enfranchised Negroes (politically welded by means of the Union League), some Southern whites, commonly called "scala-wags," and Northern fortune-seekers, known as "carpetbaggers" because they were supposed to carry their worldly possessions in a carpetbag. Al-though many of the scalawags were honest, if narrow, men, and not a few of the carpetbaggers possessed real ability, the governments of carpetbag-gers, scalawags, and Negroes set up in the southern states were no more than a parody on government. The legislatures were unusually corrupt, with bribery, fraud, and outright theft the order of the day. Negroes and poor whites who had never paid a penny in direct taxes themselves voted bills in a few years that trebled or quadrupled the debt of their state. The state debt of South Carolina rose from $1,000,000 to $29,000,000 by 1873 and that of Alabama from $7,000,000 to $32,000,000 by 1874. In the South Caro-lina legislature the Negroes outnumbered the whites 88 to 67, and only 22

---

[4] J. S. Pike, a well-known journalist and United States minister to The Hague, 1861–1866, wrote his impressions of reconstruction in *The Prostrate State: South Carolina Under Negro Government* (1874).

[5] W. L. Fleming, *The Sequel of Appomattox*, 116–117.

of the 155 members could read or write. According to the governor, there were two hundred trial judges in that state who could not read. To the burden of corrupt and ignorant government was added the humiliation of seeing the higher political offices taken over by outsiders. In seven states four governors, ten United States senators, and twenty of the thirty-five representatives were carpetbaggers. In behalf of the carpetbag governments one or two things can be said. The new constitutions set up were, in general, an improvement on the old, and many of the laws, particularly those that made the first provision for free compulsory education, marked an important advance. It should also be noted that the postwar years were a period in which political and business ethics throughout the nation sank, perhaps, to their lowest depths in our history. The legislatures and politicians of the North had little to learn from the carpetbag governments of the South.

NATIONAL POLITICS

While the Radical Republicans were organizing to control the southern states, they determined to remove all opposition at the national capital. The Supreme Court had already been deprived of the power of passing on reconstruction cases, and a strong movement had developed to get rid of Johnson. This might be done by impeachment proceedings, but a committee of the House had made a searching examination of his public and private life and had failed to discover a single incident upon which such action might reasonably be taken. Nevertheless, on February 24, 1868, the House of Representatives impeached the President for "high crimes and misdemeanors," and a committee of managers, which included Thaddeus Stevens, Benjamin F. Butler, G. S. Boutwell, and other well-known politicians, was appointed to press the charges. The defense, which was given six days for preparation, was largely conducted by former Attorney General Stanbury, Benjamin R. Curtis, William M. Evarts, and William S. Groesbeck, all distinguished for their legal attainments. As provided by the Constitution, the Senate sat as the jury, with Chief Justice Chase presiding at the trial.

Although there were eleven charges against Johnson, only one, that he had violated the Tenure of Office Act in dismissing Secretary of War Stanton, had in it any substance. Stanton, who represented the Radicals in the cabinet, had long been a thorn in the side of the President. Unable longer to stand his disloyalty, Johnson dismissed him in August, 1867, and placed Grant in temporary charge of the war office. Congress, however, when the suspension was reported to it in December, refused to concur, whereupon Grant surrendered the War Department and Stanton took possession. Johnson persisted, dismissed Stanton a second time, and appointed Lorenzo Thomas Acting Secretary of War. Stanton refused to give up the office and had Thomas arrested for violating the Tenure of Office Act. The case was now in the courts, where Johnson was anxious to have it in order to test the constitutionality of the act, but the Radicals, wishing to avoid this, withdrew the charges. The Tenure of Office Act had provided that the tenure for cabinet members should be limited to "the term of the President by whom they may have been appointed and for one month thereafter." The defense pointed out that Stanton had been appointed by Lincoln in 1862 and simply continued in office without appointment by Johnson and therefore had no protection under the Tenure of Office Act.

As the trial went on, it became increasingly clear to the country that the whole affair was political. While many of the Radical Republicans were quite willing to oust Johnson on this ground, there were a few who refused to vote guilty unless they believed him so. There were others who had no desire to see Benjamin Wade (president *pro tempore* of the Senate) succeed to the presidency. A two-thirds vote was necessary to convict, and Johnson was saved by one vote—35 to 19. To the vote of not guilty cast by the twelve Democratic senators was added that of seven independent Republicans.[6]

Republican tactics during the later part of the Johnson administration were largely influenced by the coming election. The convention of the National Union Republican Party, as it was then called, was held, in fact, during May, while the impeachment trial was still in progress. The unanimous choice of the convention was General Grant, with Schuyler Colfax, Speaker of the House, nominated to run with him. From the point of view of politics, Grant's nomination was perfect. As the ablest of the Union generals, he had won international fame, while his unassuming simplicity had made him popular with the rank and file of the army. His ignorance of the ways of politics and his lack of understanding of the cross currents of public affairs made him an ideal figurehead for the brilliant politicians who directed the affairs of the party. Lacking interest in politics, he had voted in but one presidential election and then had cast his ballot for the Democrat Buchanan. He had become available to the Republicans when he quarreled with Johnson over the Stanton affair and was nominated as the candidate most likely to win. He was the first of a long line of soldier candidates produced by the Civil War. Although the platform handled controversial matters as gingerly as possible, it gave its approval to congressional reconstruction and put itself on record for payment of the war debt in full and for pensions to veterans. "The guarantee by Congress of equal suffrage to all loyal men of the South was demanded," it said, "by every consideration of public safety, of gratitude and of justice, and must be maintained; while

[6] Senators Trumbull, Fessenden, Fowler, Grimes, Henderson, Ross, and Van Winkle.

the question of suffrage in all the loyal states properly belongs to the people of the states."

The Democrats in their convention were split between one group, led by Francis P. Blair, Jr., which would emphasize disapproval of congressional reconstruction, and another, led by George H. Pendleton of Ohio, which would soft-pedal reconstruction and emphasize some other issue, particularly finance. In the end the platform contained the ideas of both groups. It endorsed Johnson's administration, condemned the "so-called" reconstruction acts as "unconstitutional, revolutionary and void," demanded that the states be restored immediately to their rights and that the question of franchise should be left to the states. As a portent of long years of financial controversy, the platform demanded that government bonds be subject to taxation, and that, when possible, bonds should be paid in "lawful money" (greenbacks) rather than in coin. This last inflationary suggestion, known as the "Ohio idea," made its author, Pendleton, a candidate for nomination. Other candidates were Johnson, who felt that the party should endorse his policy by granting him the nomination, and Chief Justice Salmon P. Chase, who never lost hope that he might some day receive the nomination and who was once described by Lincoln as having a mild "insanity on the subject of the presidency." The nomination, however, went to Horatio Seymour, war-time governor of New York, and the second place to Francis P. Blair, Jr., of Missouri. The nomination of Seymour, a conservative on financial matters, was a virtual repudiation of the inflationary plank in the platform and meant that the Democrats entered the campaign a divided party.

To the electorate, wearied over the long Southern controversy, it was Grant's famous phrase in his letter of acceptance, "Let us have peace," that probably carried the greatest weight. He won by an electoral vote of 214 to 80, but his majority in a total popular vote of 5,700,000 was only 300,000. As the newly enfranchised Negroes of the South cast 600,000 votes for him, it is clear that without their help he would have had a minority of the popular vote and quite probably of the electoral vote. While the closeness of the contest gave the Democrats some hope for the future, it confirmed the Republicans in their Southern policy. It also led the Republicans soon after the election to send to the states the fifteenth amendment in the hope of making permanent their gains in the South.

FAILURE OF POLITICAL RECONSTRUCTION

That congressional reconstruction enabled the Republican Party to maintain its control over the federal government in the uncertain days following the war there can be no doubt. In this sense it was successful. In the long run, however, it failed. Not only were ways found to eliminate the Negro from Southern politics and thus restore the supremacy of the whites, but the reaction of the South against the Republican Party, which had been the cause of so much humiliation and misery, was to swing that section into the opposing political camp. With the restoration of white supremacy came inevitably the solid Democratic South. When Grant became President in 1869, four states were not yet "reconstructed"—Virginia, Texas, Mississippi, and Georgia. Georgia had been restored to her proper relationship in the Union, but, because of a trick by which she had eliminated the Negro members of the state legislature, Congress had refused to admit her representatives, and the state had been returned to military rule. By a supplementary reconstruction act, these four states were now required to ratify both the fourteenth and the fifteenth amendment before reconstruction was completed. By 1870 this condition had been complied with, and all the eleven southern states were represented in Congress.

The South might now be reconstructed to the satisfaction of Republican politicians, but there was little in the situation to guarantee permanency. The sudden elimination of the old ruling class from political domination and its forceful replacement by governments of carpetbaggers, scalawags, and Negro ex-slaves created a situation too artificial and too intolerable to last. As the Grant administration progressed, it became increasingly evident that this situation could only be maintained by armed force. Withdraw federal troops, and the artificial structure would collapse. The first and most persistent method of eliminating the Negro from politics was by means of intimidation and force. In the early years this was done through secret societies, the most famous of which were the Ku Klux Klan and the Knights of the White Camelia. By riding around at night in grotesque costumes, it was not difficult to frighten superstitious and ignorant Negroes, and, where this was not sufficient, an occasional flogging or murder served to curtail their political activities and keep them at home on election day. While some defense can be offered for the activities of the Klan, the general effect upon Southern society was harmful. Its activities, while spectacular, were, of course, anything but unusual. They are typical of the extralegal methods that have been used in all ages when the dominant group finds its political position or economic power seriously challenged. Congress answered such efforts to nullify the reconstruction acts by passing enforcement acts and the Ku Klux Act (1870–1871), which laid severe penalties upon anyone conspiring to impede the effects of the fourteenth and fifteenth amendments, gave Congress complete control of congressional elections, and authorized the President to suspend the writ of *habeas corpus* and establish military law in localities where it seemed necessary. As enforcement was in the hands of federal courts, there were many indictments, and in one case Grant declared nine counties of South Carolina in rebellion and placed them under martial law, October, 1871. Grant, who was now completely under the control of the Radical group, made a real effort to enforce these acts, and the Ku Klux Klan eventually disbanded. The final result, however, was nil. By 1876 white supremacy had been virtually restored in all the states except South Carolina and Louisiana, and in those states federal troops alone maintained the carpetbag governments.

As the years went on, the restoration of white rule was aided in a number of ways. The Freedmen's Bureau went out of operation in 1872, and an important protection to the Negro was removed. In the same year Congress passed the Amnesty Act, which restored political privileges to all but a few hundred Confederate veterans and thus brought back into Southern political life a more conservative and responsible type of Southern white. The Supreme Court, which had always been skeptical of congressional reconstruction, now, as opportunity arose, threw out as unconstitutional various parts of the enforcement acts. This culminated in the decision in United States *v.* Harris (1883), a case involving a group of white men who had taken some Negroes from officers of the law and ill-treated them. This seemed certainly a violation of the Ku Klux Act, but the court questioned the constitutionality of the act on the ground that the fourteenth amendment in the words "No State shall make or enforce" had laid restrictions upon the states and not upon individuals. As this was an act of individuals and not of a state, Congress had no power. The same stand was taken shortly after when the court declared the Civil Rights Act of 1875 unconstitutional. This act had attempted to ensure to the Negro equal rights in public conveyances, hotels, and theaters, but the court pointed out that violations of this act had not been committed by the states.

Eventually the Southern whites found numerous ways, legal or illegal, of nullifying not only congressional legislation but also the fourteenth and fifteenth amendments. A poll tax or other taxes automatically eliminated a good proportion of the poverty-stricken Negroes. Where that was not sufficient, a law like that passed by Mississippi, which provided that every voter must be able to read any part of the Constitution or to give an interpretation of it when it was read to him, accomplished the same purpose. This was designed to debar the black illiterates but still allow the white illiterates to vote. An even more forthright method of excluding Negroes, which was later declared unconstitutional by the Supreme Court, was a Louisiana law of 1898, which included the well-known "grandfather clause." Under this act any citizen, regardless of property or educational qualifications, who had voted before January 1, 1867, might still vote, along with his descendants. In some states gerrymandering was used, as, for example, in Mississippi, where one election district composed largely of

Negroes was laid out three hundred miles long and twenty miles wide. Where these devices were inadequate, intimidation could always be used. Such was the futility of congressional reconstruction. Its results accentuated the economic demoralization of the postwar South, prolonged the war-time animosity, strengthened racial feeling, and turned the South into the hands of the Democratic Party for more than half a century. In brief, it accentuated and prolonged the unfortunate effects of the war. Upon the North the effect was also disastrous. By use of popular shibboleths and by "waving the bloody shirt," the Republican Party and its industrial allies focused the attention of the country for over a decade upon reconstruction, prevented the union of Southern and Western agrarians, and so delayed serious consideration of significant economic problems. It was in these years that industrial capitalism developed a dominant economic and political power.

More extended treatments of this period are L. M. Hacker and B. B. Kendrick, *The United States Since 1865*, Chaps. I–III, and W. A. Dunning, *Reconstruction, Political and Economic*, Chaps. I–VII. The most recent general treatment by a specialist on this period is J. G. Randall, *The Civil War and Reconstruction*, Chaps. XXX–XXXV. On the constitutional side read W. A. Dunning, *Essays on the Civil War and Reconstruction*, Chap. II ff. On the early period of the Johnson administration see H. K. Beale, *The Critical Year*, Chaps. I–III. On the social aspect of reconstruction see W. L. Fleming, *The Sequel of Appomattox* (Chronicles of America). and Allan Nevins, *The Emergence of Modern America*, Chap. I (History of American Life); on the impeachment of Johnson, E. P. Oberholtzer, *A History of the United States Since the Civil War*, Vol. II, Chap. X, and Dunning, *Essays on the Civil War and Reconstruction*, 253–305. A rewarding chapter on the political division is in Paul H. Buck, *The Road to Reunion*, IV. For sources consult H. S. Commager, *Documents of American History*, Vol. II, 1–56, 86–88, 96.

THE INDUSTRIAL AGE

Chapter XXIII

INDUSTRIALISM TAKES POSSESSION

The world, after 1865, became a bankers' world.

HENRY ADAMS

The progress of evolution from President Washington to President Grant was alone evidence enough to upset Darwin.

HENRY ADAMS

SIGNIFICANCE OF THE REPUBLICAN VICTORY

To the generation that witnessed the historic surrender at Appomattox Court House, the significant results of the Civil War were the restoration of the Union and the end of chattel slavery. To the historian of more recent years the Civil War also appears significant in that it speeded the overthrow of the landed aristocracy and placed the economic and political power of the nation in the hands of the rising financiers and industrialists. This was accomplished not alone by smashing the economic power of plantation-owners but also by a series of political maneuvers and legislative acts that left the interests of industrial capitalism firmly entrenched.

The political instrument by which this was done in the early years was the Republican Party. Its main planks in 1860 had been free land, a high tariff, and opposition to further extension of slavery. Through the turmoil of a civil war, a conflict caused in part by Republican leaders, these ends had been accomplished. The Morrill tariff, the Homestead Act, and the thirteenth amendment had achieved the first historic mission of the Republican Party. Gaining power in 1860 through a Democratic split, and returned to office in 1864 because of the abnormal war situation and the secession of a great portion of the Democratic Party, the Republicans succeeded in retaining power until 1885 partly by turning the South into a Republican "rotten borough." One important result of this was the creation of a Democratic solid South, which in turn prevented in later years a coalition of the discontented agrarians of the South and West. By the time such a coalition was possible, the hold of industrialism upon national politics was too strong to be broken.

Perhaps the first important legislative milepost marking the journey of industrial and finance capitalism to a position of dominance in America was the Morrill tariff. Passed early in 1861, it reversed the downward trend of the American tariff, which had reached a low point in 1857, and reestablished a very definite policy of high protection. Except for half-hearted attempts at reduction in 1872, 1894, and 1913, high protection h remained a permanent American policy. The Morrill tariff not only marked in dramatic fashion the shift in power from one economic class to another, but presaged a policy of war financing that distinctly favored industrial capitalism. Although heavy taxes were eventually levied to meet the costs of war, it was evident enough that the policy of the administration was to shift the costs as far as possible to future generations. It is true that a small income tax was eventually levied, but it was not high enough seriously to inconvenience the war profiteers and was repealed in 1872. The money raised by bonds was almost four times that obtained by taxes.

The very method of paying for the war as far as possible by loans inevitably allied Northern capitalism with the government, and the National Bank Act of 1863 strengthened this alliance. The National Bank Act not only tapped new sources of credit but dealt a death blow to the notes of the state banks, thus conferring an incalculable boon upon the creditor class of the East. Furthermore, it was quite apparent that the federal government, although it had been forced to resort to fiat money during the war, had every intention of deflating the currency and returning to specie payment as soon as possible after the conclusion of the conflict. Upon transportation, representing at that period perhaps the most important speculative interest of developing capitalism, the Republican Party looked with an almost loving solicitude, granting to the transcontinental railroads, chartered in the sixties, blocks of land as large as a European country and loans to aid construction. Lest the free grant of land under the Homestead Act should inconvenience the industrialist by keeping wages high, the Immigration Act was passed in 1864, which allowed the importation of contract labor.

This type of legislation, indicative of the swing from agrarian to industrial domination, was climaxed in 1868 when the economic results of the war were written into the Constitution in the fourteenth amendment:

> All persons [says the most important section of that amendment] born or naturalized in the United States and subject to the jurisdiction thereof, are citizens of the United States and of the State wherein they reside. No State shall make or enforce any law which shall abridge the privileges or immunities of citizens of the United States; nor shall any State deprive

any person of life, liberty, or property, without due process of law, nor deny to any person within its jurisdiction the equal protection of the laws.

On the face of it the words are a straightforward attempt to protect the civil rights of the newly enfranchised Negro. Such, indeed, was the purpose of one faction of the congressional committee that framed the amendment. There were on the committee, however, some members who were determined to strengthen the federal government and federal courts as against those of the states, this desire being stimulated by fear of attacks of the state governments upon private property. Such apparently was the attitude of John A. Bingham, Republican representative and railroad lawyer from Ohio, and of his colleague, Roscoe Conkling of New York. The latter, arguing some years later in a famous railroad case (San Mateo County *v.* Southern Pacific Railroad Company, 1882), had no hesitancy in pointing out that the framers were interested in property rights as well as the rights of Negroes:

> At the time the Fourteenth Amendment was ratified [said Conkling] individuals and joint stock companies were appealing for congressional and administrative protection against invidious and discriminating state and local taxes. . . . That complaints of oppression in respect of property and other rights made by citizens of the northern states who took up residence in the South were rife in and out of Congress, none of us can forget. . . . Those who devised the Fourteenth Amendment wrought in grave sincerity. . . . They planted in the Constitution a monumental truth to stand four square to whatever wind might blow. That truth is but the golden rule, so entrenched as to curb the many who would do to the few as they would not have the few do to them.

Although Conkling made this statement fourteen years after the amendment was adopted and at a time when he was anxious to give to it this interpretation, there is no reason to believe that he was not telling the truth. Certainly, at the time, there were many who saw its real meaning, and there was very strong opposition to its adoption. As a protection to the civil rights of Negroes the fourteenth amendment has been almost worthless, a part of the Constitution not enforced; as a protection of property it has achieved its great role. So constantly was it used that even the Supreme Court as early as 1877 complained:

> In fact, it would seem, from the character of many of the cases before us, and the arguments made in them, that the clause under consideration is looked upon as a means of bringing to the test of the decision of this court the abstract opinions of every unsuccessful litigant in a State court of the justice of the decision against him, and of the merits of the legislation on which such a decision may be founded.[1]

[1] Davidson *v.* New Orleans, 96 U.S. 97, 104 (1877).

The extent to which many judges appeared to assume that the amendment had written the economic theory of *laissez faire* into the Constitution led Justice Holmes years later to remonstrate, "the Fourteenth Amendment does not enact Mr. Herbert Spencer's Social Statics." At all odds—and this we shall point out again in the next chapter—it was the most effective weapon forged by the rising capitalism of the North to protect and enhance its interests.[2]

GRANT AND HIS ADMINISTRATION

It has been the habit of historians to emphasize two aspects of the Grant administration: the continued efforts of the Radical Republicans to build a political machine in the South by means of Negro suffrage, and the spectacular episodes illustrating the moral debacle that succeeded the idealism of the war years. More important than either of these was the developing strength of Northern industrialism, which was to give the tone to American civilization during the succeeding years. In all this President Grant occupied the role of the innocent bystander. Nominated for the presidency as the most popular man in the North and the one most likely to bring success, he was quite unfitted to lead the nation in a critical period. A great soldier and personally courageous, he was unskilled in politics and utterly lacking in either a political or an economic philosophy. Except for efficient service in the Mexican War, his career until the Civil War had been a succession of discouraging failures. Personally honest, he trusted too much in friends who were not, while his own failure as a farmer and business man gave him an exaggerated respect for those who had accumulated fortunes. He saw no harm in accepting costly gifts from friends who used their positions to despoil the public treasury. With men who loved good whisky, fine cigars, and blooded horses, the luxuries of the day, he was perfectly at home, but he never understood the milieu in which he found himself or appreciated the fact that he was the innocent tool of the worst elements of the political and business world of his time. An unostentatious and silent man who took his own counsel, Grant, when he took advice at all, generally followed that of second-rate men.

Grant's naïve approach to the problems of political office was demonstrated by his cabinet, picked apparently without consultation. For the Department of State he chose an old friend, Elihu Washburn of Illinois, who, fortunately, gave way quickly to Hamilton Fish of New York, the outstanding personality in the administration. To the treasury he ap-

---

[2] Between 1890, when the Supreme Court interpreted the word "person" as applying to corporations, and 1910, the "court rendered 528 decisions on the Fourteenth Amendment and only nineteen concerned the Negro race, while 289 related to corporations." C. C. Regier, *The Era of the Muckrakers*, 7.

pointed the wealthy New York merchant, A. T. Stewart, who was constitutionally debarred and could not serve; he then appointed G. S. Boutwell of Massachusetts, a leader of the Radical Republicans and an influential adviser. A. E. Borie, a rich invalid of Philadelphia, was appointed to the Navy Department but soon resigned. Grant's faithful friend and mentor, John A. Rawlins, was given the War Department. Better appointments were those of J. D. Cox to the Interior and E. Rockwood Hoar to be Attorney General, but eventually Grant forced both to resign.

If Grant's cabinet brought a gasp of dismay, his unfitness for the presidency was even more strikingly demonstrated during the first year by the gold conspiracy culminating on "Black Friday," September 24, 1869, an episode that almost threw the nation into a financial panic. The conspiracy was engineered by Jay Gould and James Fisk, two of the most unscrupulous stock gamblers of the period, whose operations centered on the Erie Railroad, which they controlled. The banks, it will be remembered, had suspended specie payment in 1861, and the available gold supply of the nation was small. The government had from $75,000,000 to $100,000,000, obtained from import duties, and it was accustomed to sell from two to six millions a month, which business men bought to make up foreign trade balances and for other purposes. Foreign buyers of foodstuffs must necessarily purchase American greenbacks, then selling at $1.33 in relation to a gold dollar. If the gold in the nation could be cornered, the value of the greenbacks would decrease, prices of foodstuffs would go up, western farmers would hasten to sell grain, and the freight profits of the Erie would increase. With mounting profits the value of the common stock would also rise, and the latter could be dumped on the unsuspecting public. The problem was to prevent for a time the monthly treasury sales. Fisk and Gould convinced the President that a cessation of sales would help the farmer. Grant wrote to Boutwell suggesting that sales should stop and left for a trip to western Pennsylvania. Immediately the conspirators began buying up gold as rapidly as possible until, on September 24, its price reached 162. By that time the situation was so serious that even Grant comprehended the danger. Boutwell ordered the sale of four million dollars' worth of gold, and that, combined with the fact that Gould began secretly to sell his own gold, broke the corner, and the price of gold collapsed.

The "Black Friday" incident is the classic example of the low business morality of the period and of the unfitness of Grant's leadership, but it is merely one of innumerable similar episodes characteristic of American business life of the period. More significant as an example of the methods by which members of the federal government were implicated in current speculation was the Crédit Mobilier affair. The Crédit Mobilier was a construction company organized by the stockholders of the Union Pacific to build the railroad. As stockholders of the railroad they voted to themselves as stockholders of the construction company contracts at high figures on the theory that it was wise to take what profits would be obtained at once, regardless of the financial condition of the road after it was built. The construction company's device for reaping immediate profits was not at all unusual at the time. In the case of the Union Pacific, however, the railroad was heavily subsidized by the taxpayers through the federal government and was looked upon as a great national project. To prevent a too close scrutiny by Congress, Oakes Ames, congressman from Massachusetts and a leading figure in the Union Pacific, decided to distribute among influential congressmen, "where they will do the most good," some 343 shares in the Crédit Mobilier. "We want more friends in Congress," wrote Ames, and shares were allotted at little or no cost to the Speaker of the House, Schuyler Colfax (later Vice-President), to Representative James A. Garfield (later President), to Senator Henry Wilson (later Vice-President), and to a number of other prominent legislators. Accusations by the New York *Sun* during 1872 brought a congressional investigation, which ruined the political careers of certain politicians but enabled others sanctimoniously to bluff their way out. "When the greatest railroad in the world . . . was finished," said Senator Hoar, "I have seen our national triumph and exaltation turned to bitterness and shame by the unanimous report of three committees of Congress that every step of that mighty enterprise had been taken in fraud."

The second administration of Grant brought further disclosures to shake the faith of the electorate in their public servants. In 1874 Benjamin H. Bristow, who had succeeded Boutwell as Secretary of the Treasury, began to run down rumors that revenue officials were in collusion with distillers to defraud the government of the tax on whisky. When the "Whisky ring" was finally exposed, it was found to implicate a revenue official in St. Louis who had entertained Grant and given him a team of horses and a wagon, and the trail of indictments led to Grant's private secretary, General Babcock. Although Grant at first insisted that "no guilty man escape," he later became convinced that Babcock was being persecuted, asked to be a witness in his behalf, and made conditions so difficult for Bristow that the latter resigned. Babcock, who was acquitted, was given another post, and members of the ring who were convicted were later pardoned by the President. The scandal of the "Whisky ring" had hardly died down before it was discovered that Secretary of War Belknap had received money from an employee of the Indian service for the privilege of retaining an office. When the House voted to impeach the guilty cabinet officer, Grant accepted his resignation, thus saving another friend from merited punishment. These investigations of political corruption undertaken by the Democratic opposition and the better element of his own party Grant viewed as merely political propaganda and an attempt to besmirch his friends of the Radical wing of the party.

While it is undoubtedly true that political and business morality reached a low ebb during the postwar decade, the student should not be misled by the idea that such ethics were in any way limited to this period. The disclosure of the "muckrakers" a half century later demonstrated only too well that such practices were a concomitant of the rapidly expanding industrial order, where easy wealth was to be obtained by the unscrupulous, and where financial success became the great criterion of success in life. Far from being the most significant feature of the Grant era, this corruption was but the surface indication of assumption of power by a new ruling class. It was this class that had rendered powerless Andrew Johnson, lifelong champion of the common man, foe of monopolies, and strong opponent of the granting of public lands to railroads and other business enterprises. His place was taken by Grant and by a clique of Radical Republican politicians, who consciously or unconsciously, as the case might be, represented in the federal government the rising power of a ruthless capitalism.

In the Grant administration Eastern capital gathered in the fruits of the war and prepared for greater conquests. Those who had bought war bonds with depreciated currency saw the first Grant Congress pledge the faith of the United States to pay in coin its bonded indebtedness, and toward the end of his administration (January 14, 1875) the Resumption Act, which called for the return to specie payments on January 1, 1879, increased the wealth and strengthened the position of the mortgage-holders and the creditor class. Manufacturers contemplated with satisfaction the repeal of the internal taxes of the war and the maintenance of high tariffs, while the wealthy were relieved of the income tax imposed by the war. Railroads and other corporations, by land grants or evasion of the homestead acts, continued to absorb the best of the government land. Here we find the fundamental indications of a new era.

REVOLT OF THE LIBERAL REPUBLICANS

Although the full depths of the degradation of the Grant administration had not yet been plumbed by 1872, enough discontent had developed among the liberal element to bring the greatest split that the party experienced until 1912. Nepotism, corruption, inefficiency, misrule, bitter partisan politics—all the political crimes in the catalogue had flourished, a situation that led Senator Grimes, a Republican leader, to call his own party "the most corrupt and debauched political party that ever existed." Failure of the administration to bring peace and reconciliation in the South antagonized liberal Northerners; failure of any real effort at civil-service reform disgusted many; and the maintenance of the high-tariff policy embittered still others. The prevalent discontent first exhibited itself in an important way in Missouri in 1870, when the Liberal Republicans elected B. Gratz Brown governor and Carl Schurz United States Senator. The latter, one of the political refugees of the German revolution of 1848, had been a prominent journalist and a soldier in the Civil War and was now to assume a position of leadership among the better element of the Republican Party. As the discontent grew, a preliminary conference was held at Jefferson City, Missouri, in 1872, and a national convention in Cincinnati soon after. Here were gathered not only Brown and Schurz, but Jacob D. Cox of Ohio, Senator Trumbull of Illinois, Governor Blair of Michigan, Charles Francis Adams, late ambassador to England, Horace Greeley, editor of the New York *Tribune* and many of the best men in public life. As they were backed by some of the most influential journals of the period, their prospects were bright.

The task of the convention was to secure the nomination of someone who would command the allegiance of the Liberal Republicans and the backing of the Democratic Party. For this purpose either Adams or Trumbull would have been satisfactory. The convention made its first mistake in electing Schurz as chairman and thereby removing from the floor the ablest parliamentarian in attendance. Its second mistake was in nominating Horace Greeley as its candidate. The nomination of Greeley was secured by Governor Brown, who, convinced that his interests were being betrayed by Schurz and Blair, appeared on the scene and in a spectacular speech withdrew from the contest and urged the nomination of Greeley as the "man most likely to win." Brown was nominated for the vice-presidency. Nothing could have been more preposterous than the nomination. Although editor of the most influential newspaper of the country, Greeley was unstable, a faddist and a man whose personal appearance and career made him an easy target for cartoonists. As one of the most ardent anti-slavery men in the country and one of the strongest high-tariff advocates, he was of all possible nominees probably the most difficult for the Democrats to swallow. This miracle was accomplished, however, when that party at its Baltimore convention "ate crow" and endorsed both the candidates and the platform of the Liberal Republicans. The platform had emphasized absolute amnesty to the South and "a thorough reform of the civil service," but had sidestepped the tariff issue by referring it to the people in their congressional districts. This disposal of an important issue was in return for Greeley's backing, but its chief effect was to weaken the most significant movement for tariff revision between the Civil War and the late eighties.

The Republican convention was perfunctory except that Henry Wilson of Massachusetts was substituted for Schuyler Colfax as the running mate for President Grant. The platform, which one historian accurately described as "adjectival pomp, mingled with plain buncombe," dwelt largely on the achievements of the party, but urged reform of the civil service. The result of the campaign was never in doubt. Greeley fought mainly on the issue of Southern reconciliation "in the confident trust that the masses of our countrymen North and South are eager to clasp hands across the bloody chasm." Opposed by the conservative financial interests, confronted by politicians who waved the bloody shirt, and pilloried by Nast and other cartoonists in the most vicious manner, Greeley secured the electoral vote of only six states—Texas, Georgia, and the border states of Kentucky, Maryland, Missouri, and Tennessee. "I was the worst beaten man," said Greeley, "who ever ran for high office. And I have been assailed so bitterly that I hardly knew whether I was running for President or the Penitentiary." Superficially, the Liberal Republican movement of 1872 appeared to have accomplished nothing. Actually, it gave an impetus to the General Amnesty Act of 1872, to the passage of the more liberal tariff of that year, and to a healing of the bitterness of the war-time feeling, and it helped to prepare the way for Tilden and Hayes.

DISPUTED ELECTION OF 1876

Despite the revolt of 1872, there was but slight change in the tactics and leadership of the Republican Party. Continued disclosures of corruption in high places, combined with the growing strength of the Southern Democracy, presaged a political overturn in the congressional elections of 1874. This was made practically certain by the panic that struck the business world in 1873, inaugurating a five-year depression, the most serious the nation had yet experienced. Ringing the changes on the corruption of the administration and blaming the Republicans for the depression, the Democrats swept to an easy victory, capturing the House by a large majority, gaining control of a number of uncertain states, such as New York, and proving victorious in such usually Republican strongholds as Ohio, Pennsylvania, and Massachusetts. A few of the worst type of the reconstruction politicians, such as Benjamin F. Butler, actually lost their seats in Congress, to the lasting benefit of the country.

With the Democrats in control of the House, the political atmosphere in Washington distinctly changed. The administration found it no longer possible to inflict military rule upon the South for the benefit of the Republican Party, and corrupt officials of that organization found themselves under the close scrutiny and sometimes rigid investigation of the opposite party. An adverse resolution in the House effectively ended a third-term boom for Grant, and Congress, as usual, became the sounding board for politicians looking toward the next election. Early in 1876 James G. Blaine led the way by an attack on Jefferson Davis that again stirred up the sectional animosity. To the politicians who made capital by "waving the bloody shirt," Blaine loomed as the logical candidate, but his speech also served to uncover the strength of the more sober-minded citizens and in the end did much to prevent his nomination. The liberal independents who had led the revolt in 1872 contented themselves for the moment with a conference, where they passed resolutions reiterating their demands of 1872 and virtually threatening secession again should Blaine be nominated.

When the Republicans met in 1876 to nominate their presidential candidates, they at last saw the handwriting on the wall. They listened to Robert G. Ingersoll in one of his most eloquent speeches describe Blaine as the "plumed knight" who "threw his shivering lance full and fair against the brazen forehead of every traitor to his country," and then turned and nominated Rutherford B. Hayes, a brigadier of the Civil War who had demonstrated his political ability by winning the governorship of Ohio three times against popular Democratic candidates. Although Hayes was not a candidate of the Liberal Republicans, he was a man untouched by personal or political scandal and unconnected with the Washington politics of the Grant administration. The convention passed resolutions commending Grant and wrote a platform advocating the payment of the public debt, civil-service reform, and a protective tariff. The Democrats nominated Governor Samuel J. Tilden of New York, an able, if not always scrupulous, corporation lawyer, who had been a leader in the fight against the Tweed ring in New York and as a reform governor had given the state an efficient and honest administration. Their platform attacked the corruption of the administration and demanded reform in the currency system, in the tariff, and in the civil service, and a scaling down of the public expenses.

On the morning after election the nation as a whole conceded the victory to Tilden. He had carried the doubtful states of New York, New Jersey, and Indiana and had a majority of 250,000 votes over his Republican rival. It was discovered, however, that there was a dispute regarding the returns of the three southern states of South Carolina, Louisiana, and Florida and a technical question concerning one elector in Oregon, which was easily settled. If these electoral votes, numbering twenty in all, were counted for Hayes, he would have one more electoral vote than the 184 conceded to Tilden. Troops were immediately thrown into Florida and "visiting statesmen" (Republican and Democratic politicians) descended upon the capitals of the three disputed states to look after the interests of their party. In all three states there was evidence of fraud and intimidation, but on the face of the returns Hayes had a clear majority in South Carolina and Tilden in Louisiana, with the vote in Florida extremely close. In Florida and South Carolina the returning boards certified the election of the Republicans, but the contest was taken to the courts, and two sets of returns found their way to Washington. In Louisiana the board of canvassers threw out enough Tilden votes to give the victory to the Republicans, but the Democratic electors met and also forwarded a certificate giving the state to Tilden. Although the returning boards in the three states were undoubtedly venal and the board in Florida twice offered to sell the vote of the state to the Democrats, it is doubtful if outright bribery was used. Nevertheless, pressure of many kinds was exerted, the air was rife with cries of fraud and corruption, and the tension became strained as the Democrats realized the strong possibility of the election's being "stolen" from their grasp. More than one felt like Colonel Henry Watterson, who threatened to lead a hundred thousand Kentuckians to Washington to see that justice was done to Tilden.

With conflicting returns coming from the disputed states, the decision was thrown back on Congress, which found little aid in the Constitution. That document directed that "the President of the Senate shall, in the presence of the Senate and House of Representatives, open all certificates, and the votes shall then be counted," but it failed to designate who should count them or which votes should be counted. A joint committee of the House and Senate finally offered a compromise scheme—the setting up of an electoral commission composed of five representatives, five senators, and five justices of the Supreme Court, whose decisions were to stand unless rejected by both houses voting separately. By an understanding the senators and representatives were divided equally between the two parties, while two Democratic and two Republican justices (indirectly designated by the act) were to nominate a fifth who was expected to be an independent. It was obvious that the decision on the election would rest with the fifth judge, who, it was expected, would be David Davis. Justice Davis, however, who had political ambitions and no desire to accept the thankless task, escaped when the Democrats of the Illinois legislature foolishly combined with the independents and elected him to the Senate. With Davis gone, the last hope of the Democrats faded. Only Republicans were left on the Supreme Court, and Joseph P. Bradley became the fifth judge. By a strict party vote of 8 to 7 all the disputed electoral votes were counted for Hayes.[3]

Bitterly disappointed, the Democrats unsuccessfully attempted a filibuster to prevent the counting of the votes by March 4. In the meantime,

[3] New material on the disputed Hayes-Tilden election is to be found in a secret memorandum prepared by Abram S. Hewitt, Chairman of the Democratic National Committee, and described in Allan Nevins, *Abram S. Hewitt* (1936), 320 ff.

friends of Hayes met with the Democrats at the "Wormley conferences" and promised that, if the Democrats allowed the count to be completed, Hayes would cease to support by federal arms the Republican governments in Louisiana and South Carolina. This deal was made without express authority from Hayes, but the President, immediately after inauguration, investigated the situation and withdrew the federal troops from the two states. Without military support the Republican carpetbag governments collapsed, and the political reconstruction of the South was ended. In his program of conciliation toward the South, Hayes appointed the independent leader of the 1872 revolt, Carl Schurz, as Secretary of the Interior; William M. Evarts, defender of Johnson at the impeachment trial, as Secretary of State; and David M. Key, a former Confederate soldier, as Postmaster General. By a compromise in a disputed election the Republican Party continued to control the executive branch of the government, but it is evident that the election of 1876 marked the end of Republican domination of the South.

C. and M. Beard, *The Rise of American Civilization*, Chap. XVIII, is illuminating. On the 1868 campaign, E. P. Oberholtzer, *A History of the United States Since the Civil War*, Vol. II, Chap. XI, and, on the 1872 campaign, Vol. III, Chap. I, is adequate. The campaign of 1876 is summarized also in Oberholtzer, *op. cit.*, Vol. III, Chap. XXI, and at greater length in H. J. Eckenrode, *Rutherford B. Hayes*, Chaps. VI–X. Interpretation and narrative are combined in J. G. Randall, *The Civil War and Reconstruction*, Chaps. XXXVI, XXXVII. Also see Commager, *Documents of American History*, Vol. II, 56–86, 95.

THE INDUSTRIAL AGE

Chapter XXIV

THE TRIUMPH OF THE INDUSTRIAL REVOLUTION

> *When the historian of the future writes the
> history of the nineteenth century he will doubtless
> assign to the period embraced by the life of the
> generation terminating in 1885, a place of im-
> portance, considered in its relations to the interests
> of humanity, second to but very few, and perhaps
> to none, of the many similar epochs of time in any
> of the centuries that have preceded it.*
>
> DAVID A. WELLS (1889)

STEEL, MEAT, AND OIL

Writing in 1889, David A. Wells declared that "the recital of the economic experiences and industrial conditions of the generation next preceding is very much akin to a recurrence to ancient history." [1] Indeed, America
between the forties and the eighties had developed from a nation dependent
largely upon water transportation to one boasting the finest railway system
in the world, from a nation using iron almost exclusively where strong
metal was required to one whose factories produced huge quantities of
steel, and from a nation whose industrial life was carried on largely in the
household or shop to one that had turned definitely to factory production
and was rapidly assuming the leading position among the industrial nations of the world. In fact, the census taken in the year that Wells wrote
showed for the first time the value of manufactured products far in excess
of agricultural, a clear indication of the America that was to be. Speeded by
the Homestead Act, the building of railroads, and the discovery of minerals
in the Rockies, American settlements, which in the forties had hardly
passed the Missouri, had now spread out until by the nineties they extended
from the Atlantic to the Pacific, while population had grown from 17,000,000
in 1840 to 76,000,000 in 1900.

The old America was a nation of farmers, artisans, and small-scale business men, transporting their goods by wagons, river steamers, or canal
boats; the new America still had its millions of farmers, but it was now

[1] David A. Wells, *Recent Economic Changes*, 65.

more and more characterized by its industrial proletariat massed in cities, its capitalists and big business men, its consolidation of industry, its enormous factories, and its far-flung railroad system. The number of industrial wage-earners had grown from 957,000 in 1849 to 4,252,000 in 1889, and the railway mileage from less that 3000 in 1840 to 167,000 in 1890, while in the volume and value of factory-made goods the United States had jumped from fourth place among the nations in 1860 to first rank in 1894, when her factory production amounted to more than that of Great Britain and Germany combined. In 1840 but 8.5 per cent of the population lived in 44 cities of 8000 or over; in 1890 over 32 per cent were congregated in 547 cities. From an essentially agricultural nation the United States was changing into a nation of industrial cities.

The secret of this transformation to a new America was, of course, the Industrial Revolution, essential characteristics of which were the shift from

ECONOMIC GROWTH 1859–1929			
YEAR	POPULATION	VALUE OF AGRICUL-TURAL PRODUCTS IN DOLLARS	VALUE OF MANU-FACTURED PRODUCTS IN DOLLARS
1859	31,443,000		1,886,000,000
1879	50,155,000	2,213,000,000	5,370,000,000
1899	75,994,000	4,717,000,000	11,407,000,000
1919	105,710,000	23,783,000,000	62,418,000,000
1929	122,775,000	12,575,000,000 [2]	70,435,000,000

hand to machine production and the movement of manufacturing from the home or small shop to the factory. Gaining its first impetus from the closing of European trade during the era of the embargo and nonintercourse acts and the War of 1812, the Industrial Revolution developed in the succeeding decades through the expansion of domestic markets, the improvement of transportation facilities, and the aid of a protective tariff. Already well established, the factory system was given a tremendous impetus by the Civil War, with its almost insatiable demand for woolens and munitions and by the abnormal demand for food, which, coupled with scarcity of labor, trebled the output of farm machinery and laid the foundations of the meat-packing industry. Stimulated by westward expansion, the rehabilitation of the South, and the rapid increase in population, the demand for manufactured products continued to expand in the years following the war. As before the Civil War, industry was also stimulated by an abundance

2 This table has not been continued in recent years by the *Statistical Abstract*, but the figure $12,575,000,000, the gross income of agricultural products for 1929, is close enough to complete the table.

of agricultural commodities, upon which many important industries are based, by expanding transportation facilities, by the protective tariff, and, in its later phases, by the development of a foreign market. Likewise, new inventions produced new industries, which found a market through the development of large-scale advertising and sales campaigns. Centered in the early decades chiefly in the Northeast, manufacturing pushed westward as it followed population and the sources of raw material.

In the great industrial advance of the postwar period, steel was the key industry. Up to the sixties that metal, because of the expense of manufacture, was used only for the finest and most costly articles. In the fifties two men, William Kelly, an American, and Henry Bessemer, an Englishman, discovered a method of eliminating foreign substances by forcing a cold blast of air through the molten pig iron, after which such quantities of carbon and other elements might be introduced as would make the desired quality of steel. When the patent rights of the two were reconciled in 1866, the age of steel became a reality. The manufacture of that precious metal, which had formerly taken three months, was reduced to half an hour, and steel, or at least a crude form of it, became as cheap as iron. A dozen important Bessemer works were founded in the early seventies, including the Cambria Works at Johnstown, Pennsylvania (1871), the Bethlehem Works at Bethlehem, Pennsylvania (1873), and the J. Edgar Thomson Steel Works near Pittsburgh. Between 1860 and 1880 the number of establishments manufacturing iron and steel increased from 402 to 1000, capitalization from $23,343,000 to $230,972,000, the value of the product from $36,537,000 to $296,558,000, and the employees from 22,000 to 141,000. More important than the increase illustrated by these figures was the fact that most of this increase represented steel rather than iron production, a development of tremendous social and economic significance in the fields of transportation, engineering, and building. Without steel, says Nevins, "the huge crops of the Middle West and the growing volume of manufactured goods from the Mississippi Valley could never have been carried." Without low-cost steel it would be hard to envisage the age of the automobile, the airplane, and the skyscraper.

While steel was undoubtedly basic in the development of the American Industrial Revolution, there were similar advances in practically every branch of industry. Particularly to be noted in the war and postwar years were the development of the meat-packing industry and the widespread use of petroleum. The former was made possible by the rapidly extending ranchers' frontier, the spread of the railway network throughout the cattle country, the invention of refrigeration, the wider use of canning, and the appearance of able entrepreneurs. These factors meant a great increase in the production and export of meat products, and it presaged the new

America of apartment-house dwellers, delicatessen stores, and package groceries. During most of the period since the Civil War, slaughtering and meat-packing has ranked first among American industries in the value of products. Its great figures were Philip D. Armour, who gained his experience during the war and later with his brothers founded Armour and Company at Chicago; Nelson Morris, a young Bavarian Jew who had risen to importance through war contracts; and Gustavus F. Swift, a Cape Cod Yankee who first saw the advantage of dressing the meat in the West and sending it eastward in refrigeration cars.

More spectacular than the development of the meat-packing industry was the sudden expansion of the petroleum business. Up to the sixties oils for lighting and lubrication had been obtained chiefly from whales and other animals, with the commercial beginnings on a small scale of oil extraction from coal. For years medical quacks had taken the oil oozing out of the ground in western Pennsylvania and sold it to the simple-minded as a cure for almost all known diseases. One of them, Samuel Kier, having discovered that it might be used for lubrication and lighting, began to refine and sell it. A certain G. H. Bissell, attracted by an advertisement of Kier's medicine, had it analyzed at Yale. Convinced of its usefulness, he organized a company for production, leased land in northwestern Pennsylvania, and sent Edwin Drake to sink a well. When, in August, 1859, "Drake's Folly," as the near-by farmers called it, began to run twenty-five barrels a day, the oil industry was born. Western Pennsylvania quickly took on the appearance of a boom country as derricks cut the skyline in all directions and towns and cities sprang up like magic. Country roads suddenly became crowded highways as struggling teamsters hauled the oil to market. It was the wildest and most hectic era in the history of oil, when men made fortunes overnight and regions rose and declined within a few months. Pithole City, for example, which did not exist in 1865, grew within a few months to a city of 15,000, which did a postal business greater than any other city in the state but Philadelphia, only to revert a few years later to an open wheat field. The first pipe line came in 1865, and the first tank car came a little later, as refineries began to mass around Pittsburgh and Cleveland. Oil, which in 1859 was only a quack medicine, was universally used a decade later for lubrication and lighting.

These three industries, steel, meat-packing, and oil, stand out, it is true, in the forefront of American industrial development in the postwar years. But more than that, they typify an expanding industrial civilization, which was rapidly pushing agriculture into second place and creating huge cities of slums and palaces, of millionaires and exploited proletariat. They indicate the coming of the new America, the child of industrial capitalism, buoyant, optimistic, creative, but at the same time greedy, ruthless, and quick to grasp the opportunities lying everywhere at hand. The America of the seventies, eighties, and nineties represents the first flush of an expanding capitalist society, the period of ruthless aggression and exploitation, not yet mellowed by social legislation or softened by a developing culture.

A CONTRACTING WORLD

If the Industrial Revolution was based upon machine production and the factory system, its development was made possible only by a simultaneous expansion of the means of communication, which facilitated the exchange on a larger scale and in more rapid fashion of the products of the new factories. In the early stage, as in later years, improvements in communication rested primarily upon steam and electricity. When Robert Fulton, in 1807, demonstrated the practicability of the steamboat, and George Stephenson in England, in 1829, successfully harnessed the steam engine to wheels revolving on rails, the consummation of the Industrial Revolution was made possible. It was speeded by the discovery of the electromagnetic telegraph by Samuel F. B. Morse in 1832, the successful operation of the first telegraph in 1844, and the laying of the first successful Atlantic cable by Cyrus W. Field in 1866. By 1847 the chief cities of the East and Middle West were connected by telegraph wires, which were pushed across the continent to San Francisco in 1861, when 50,000 miles of telegraph lines were in operation. When Alexander Graham Bell, in 1870, first heard the voice of his assistant, Thomas A. Watson, coming over a line from Cambridgeport to Boston, a new era in communication history was born. The telephone was the sensation of the Philadelphia Centennial Exposition of 1876, and by 1880 there were 50,000 telephone receivers in use, the number increasing to 1,700,000 in 1890. By the latter year electric power also had demonstrated its usefulness in transportation, and in the next two decades electric "trolleys" supplanted the horse car on the street railways of the cities.

Upon the Mississippi and its tributaries the steamboat had played its great role in the internal transportation history of the United States, but by 1880 its day was done. The place of the steamboat in distance transportation had been taken by the railroads, which were able not alone to follow the natural routes of transportation but also to expand in all directions. It was here that man won his first great victory over nature. "The railway," commented the English traveler, Sterling, in 1857, "is the soul of western civilization." Beginning with a few short lines in the thirties and forties, connecting rivers or canals, railway mileage had grown to 30,000 in 1860, to 93,000 in 1880, and to 167,000 in 1890.

In the history of railroad expansion the two outstanding achievements were the penetration of the Allegheny passes and the conquest of the Great

Plains; the first had been accomplished by 1860, the second in the decades following the Civil War. The trans-Allegheny and the transcontinental lines formed the essential skeleton of the American system, the remaining lines being largely extensions or ramifications. The railroads that had reached the Lakes and the Ohio valley by 1860, the roads that were to develop into the great systems known as the Baltimore and Ohio, the Pennsylvania, the Erie, and the New York Central, were then but successions of tiny roads, often with different gauges, which necessitated frequent transfers of passengers and freight—slow, uncertain, expensive, and inconvenient. With the exception of the Erie, which almost until the twentieth century was controlled by a succession of unscrupulous speculators, the great roads of the East were characterized in the decades following the war by a program of expansion, consolidation, and improvements. The latter consisted among other things in establishing a uniform gauge for the tracks, the substitution of steel for iron rails, the double-tracking of the main routes, and the introduction of heavier cars, block signals, air brakes, dining cars, and Pullman sleepers.

While the railroads of the Northeast and Middle West were largely concerned with expansion and improvements, the South was occupied in rehabilitating the roads that had deteriorated or been destroyed by the war. But this prosaic and necessary task was hardly noted in the spectacular achievements that characterized the construction of the great transcontinental railroads, upon which the eyes of the nation were fixed. It was the lure of Oriental trade and the discovery of gold in California that first awakened the dreams of a transcontinental road, but it was the exigencies of the Civil War that started actual construction. Although surveys had been made, sectional rivalries, complicated by the slavery struggle, had delayed the projects. In 1862 the Union Pacific Railroad Company was finally created by Congress to build a railroad from Nebraska to the eastern boundary of California, while the Central Pacific, a California corporation, undertook to build from the Pacific Coast eastward to meet the Union Pacific. Both were granted a right of way, free use of building materials, grants of twenty square miles of public land for each mile of rail laid, and government loans of $16,000 a mile for construction on the level country, $32,000 for construction in the foothills, and $48,000 for construction through the mountain ranges. Construction hardly got under way seriously until 1867, but after that, stimulated by government subsidies, it was pushed to a triumphant conclusion. Neither hostile Indians nor the severity of the mountain winters was allowed to stand in the way as both companies struggled frantically to push their rails farther in the effort to attain the maximum of government aid. In the later weeks of the work, 20,000 men were laying two miles of track a day. Finally, on May 10, 1869, at Promon-

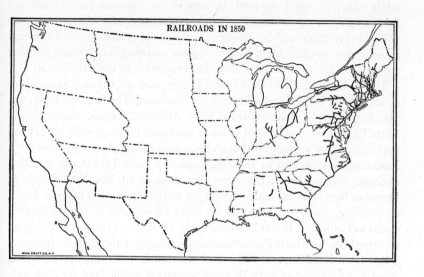

RAILROADS IN 1850

MAN. DRAFT CO., N.Y.

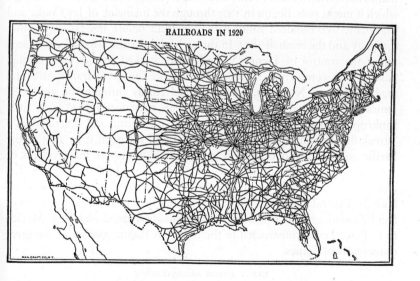

RAILROADS IN 1920

MAN. DRAFT CO., N.Y.

tory Point, Utah, Leland Stanford drove the last spike, of California gold, while telegraph wires received the taps of the hammer and transmitted them to a rejoicing nation. The whole project had been characterized by political corruption and by exorbitant promoters' profits obtained through construction companies, but its achievement was the greatest transportation triumph in American history since the completion of the Erie Canal.

The Union Pacific and the Central Pacific were not the only railroads to be subsidized by Congress. In 1863 the Atchison, Topeka, and Santa Fé, planning to build southwestward from Atchison, Kansas, along the old Santa Fé trail, obtained a land grant of 6400 acres for every mile built. Construction did not begin until 1869 and was soon held up by the panic of 1873. Resuming construction in 1880, the company pushed its tracks to Albuquerque, and finally, in 1881, they met those of the Southern Pacific at Deming, New Mexico, and a new route to the Pacific was opened. Later, by building, purchase, and lease, the Santa Fé was able to run on its own tracks to California. It was also during the Civil War (1864) that Congress chartered the Northern Pacific Railroad, granting it the right to construct a line from Lake Superior westward and north of latitude 40°. Its land grant was to consist of forty alternate sections of public land for each mile within the territories and twenty alternate sections within the states through which it might pass. Begun in 1867 through the financing of Jay Cooke and Company, five hundred miles had been built before the failure of that company and the crash of 1873. In the early eighties the crippled road came under the control of Henry Villard, who, backed by German capital, pushed it to completion in 1883. The last of the great transcontinental roads, the Great Northern, was developed chiefly through the genius of James J. Hill. Interesting several Canadian capitalists (1878) in a little bankrupt railroad, known as the St. Paul and Pacific and described as a "streak of rust running through a desert," Hill extended it by 1893 to the Pacific and quickly developed it as a route to transport the products of American agriculture and industry to the Far East. In the meantime, Leland Stanford, Collis P. Huntington, Charles Crocker, and others who had built the Central Pacific consolidated several little lines running south out of San Francisco and, by extending them through Arizona and New Mexico to El Paso, Texas, constructed in the Southern Pacific another of the great transcontinental lines.

EARLY LABOR ORGANIZATION

While factory production was increasing by leaps and bounds and railroad entrepreneurs were extending their lines at the average rate of 4500 miles a year, labor, the giant upon whose strength and skill all this was based, was beginning to stir. The organization of labor began as soon as the

Industrial Revolution was well under way, but the early efforts had been weak and largely local. Real organization waited upon the massing of labor in large factories in great urban centers and the development of communication facilities whereby labor might be welded together. It also awaited the development of political democracy, which gave to labor political as well as economic power. The harsh working conditions of the early decades showed no improvement as the Industrial Revolution progressed; rather, the prospects of labor grew darker as workers were herded into the unsanitary slums of the growing cities. Long hours, low pay—much of it taken away by the truck system of payments (payments in kind) and by company stores—unsanitary conditions of work, degrading rules in many of the factories, unconscionable exploitation of women and children, absence of labor legislation, and inability to obtain justice in the courts—these were the major evils out of which the labor movement developed. The need of organization was made even more evident with the rising cost of living during the Civil War and with the rapidly increasing power and integration of capital. The inevitable growth of big business and the consolidation of wealth in modern capitalist society, it was quickly seen, could be balanced only by a consolidation of labor.

The early trade-union movement, based upon local crafts or city consolidations, largely disintegrated, it will be remembered, in the panic of 1837. A revival came in the forties and fifties; local craft unions again appeared, at least twenty of which had national organizations by 1860. Greater demand for labor and the rising cost of living during the Civil War provided a new impetus to the revival, and numerous local unions and at least ten more national unions came into existence. Among these was the first of the great railroad brotherhoods, the Brotherhood of Locomotive Engineers, organized in 1863 as the "Brotherhood of the Footboard," which was followed in 1869 by the Brotherhood of Locomotive Firemen. With numerous local unions and at least thirty-two national trade unions existing in 1870, the movement toward labor consolidation was well established. The next step was to increase the power of labor by uniting these local and national unions in a great organization. Already one notable attempt to bring all labor together had been made under the leadership of W. H. Sylvis in the National Labor Union. Organized in 1866 on the basis of city assemblies of trade unions, it held seven annual conventions and at the height of its power had a membership of 600,000. The National Labor Union, like other strong unions in earlier years, seemed more interested in co-operative and educational enterprises and in exerting pressure upon the government for such things as Chinese exclusion, the establishment of a government bureau of labor, and legislation for the eight-hour day, than in a program of militant trade unionism. Its strength was largely broken by the panic of 1873.

In the meantime, there had appeared an organization destined for a few years to play the leading role in American labor history. Aroused by post-war conditions in the clothing industry, Uriah S. Stevens, a Philadelphia garment worker, and six fellow craftsmen organized in 1869 the Noble Order of the Knights of Labor. Secret at first—even its name was unknown —it grew slowly; its first national convention was not held until 1875, and its membership in 1883 was only 52,000. Then came a sudden spurt that lifted its enrollment within three or four years to a million. In the mean-time, owing to popular distrust and the opposition of the Catholic Church, it had abolished its secrecy. At the height of its power in the middle eighties it seemed destined for great achievements. Professor Ely, writing in 1886, described it as "the most powerful and remarkable labor organization of modern times . . . established on truly remarkable principles which involved either an intuitive perception of the nature of industrial progress, or a wonderful acquaintance with the laws of economic society."[3]

The decline of the Knights of Labor, however, was even more rapid than its rise, and for this many explanations can be offered. Although its membership included craft unions, it was based primarily on the idea of industrial unions rather than craft distinctions. It invited to its ranks all members of the working class, white and black, men and women, skilled and unskilled. Not only was its membership extremely heterogeneous, but its policies were in no way clear-cut, and friction within its ranks was continuous. While it felt "that strikes are deplorable in their effect and contrary to the best interests of the country," it undertook them, often quite inadequately prepared. In the end it was disastrously affected by their failure. Although it refused to organize a political party, it sought by indirect political means to accomplish its aims. Its program was a mixture of straight labor objectives and general reforms—the eight-hour day, taxes on incomes and inheritances, workingmen's compensation, postal savings' banks, appropriation of the unearned increment on land, government ownership of public utilities, and the development of co-operatives. It probably spread its energies over too wide a field, particularly in its enthusiastic promotion of co-operatives, which failed. Overcentralization of power created suspicion in the ranks, the inadequate leadership of Terence V. Powderly weakened the organization, and it bore the brunt of the public opposition to organized labor after the May Day riots and the bombing in Haymarket Square, Chicago, on May 3, 1886. The order had promoted the May Day demonstrations but presumably was quite innocent of the bombing. As conditions within the order became more demoralized, it found itself less able to withstand the weapons that capital was perfecting—the lockout, the blacklist, the "yellow-dog contract," and refusal to arbitrate.

[3] R. T. Ely, *The Labor Movement in America*, 75.

Above all else the Knights of Labor disintegrated because they failed to win the allegiance of the stronger craft unions. Representatives from a number of these crafts met in 1881 and founded an organization that was reorganized in 1886 as the American Federation of Labor. Although its early program embodied such demands as the protective tariff, compulsory education for children, an anticontract immigration law, and the establishment of a national bureau of labor statistics, the trend of the federation's policy was distinctly away from political action to trade unionism pure and simple, with its demand for an eight-hour day, higher wages, and better working conditions. Its early leaders, men like Adolph Strasser of the International Cigar Makers Union, and Samuel Gompers, president, with the exception of one year, from 1882 until his death in 1924, had little faith in political reforms. Setting aside any dreams of a millennium, they directed their strength essentially to the labor front, fighting where opportunity offered for what small gains might be attained at the moment. "We are all practical men," asserted Strasser before a Senate committee in 1883. "We have no ultimate ends. We are going on from day to day. We are fighting only for immediate objectives—objects that can be realized in a few years." [4] Their philosophy and tactics resembled those of the old-line unionism characteristic of the British labor movement during the last half of the nineteenth century.

Although the American Federation of Labor was a loose federation of national and international unions,[5] it contained among its affiliates some industrial unions, such as the United Mine Workers. At the same time, there were important labor organizations, notably the four railroad brotherhoods (the locomotive engineers, the conductors, the firemen, and the trainmen), that never affiliated. Like the Knights of Labor, the federation grew slowly at first, its membership numbering but 100,000 in 1890. By that time, however, it had definitely pushed its rival into the background, and during the next ten years it grew to 548,000. This spectacular advance in the nineties came despite two of the most serious setbacks that American labor has experienced. According to the Bureau of Labor, there was a total of 23,798 strikes between 1881 and 1900, involving 123,442 establishments and 6,610,000 workers, but of all these the most important were probably the Homestead strike of 1892 and the Pullman strike of 1894. They represent in spectacular fashion the rising consciousness of labor in the new industrial order and the bitterness of the struggle between labor and capital. In both of these strikes labor was beaten.

The Homestead strike was a struggle between the Amalgamated Associa-

---

[4] *Report of the Committee of the Senate Upon the Relations Between Capital and Labor,* I, 460.
[5] The term "international" is used for craft organizations having members in Canada.

tion of Iron and Steel Workers, one of the most powerful unions of its day, and the Carnegie Steel Company. It came about over failure to agree upon a wage scale after the introduction of labor-saving machinery at the Homestead, Pennsylvania, plant of the Carnegie company and through the determination of Carnegie and his manager, Henry C. Frick, to fight the power of the Amalgamated to a finish. Frick hired three hundred Pinkerton detectives to guard the mill. As they floated down the river in barges, the steel workers opened fire, and in the battle that followed ten persons were killed. In private warfare labor is often able to fight on equal terms with the employer, but in such warfare violence often takes place and is usually followed, as at Homestead, by the calling in of the National Guard. These soldiers theoretically occupy a neutral position, and are interested only in keeping the peace and protecting property, but their presence ordinarily helps only the employer and means ultimate defeat to the workers. Such was the case at Homestead, where the strike collapsed after six months. The power of the Amalgamated was broken, and for over forty years the steel magnates were able to prevent the organization of labor in the most important industry of the nation.

Quite as significant was the Pullman strike, which marked the entrance of the federal government into the role of strikebreaker and was the occasion for the first important use of the injunction as a weapon against labor. The strike originated over a wage-reduction in the Pullman Palace Car Company at Pullman, Illinois (May 11, 1894), and became of national interest when the American Railway Union, an industrial union created by Eugene V. Debs, voted not to handle Pullman cars and declared a sympathetic strike. The boycott extended to twenty-seven states, but the center was Chicago, where there was some disorder and destruction of property. Although Governor John P. Altgeld had already called out the state militia and asserted that the situation was well in hand, President Cleveland sent federal troops to Chicago to ensure the movement of mail. He based his action on the theory that a federal statute empowered him to use federal troops to execute federal laws. On the ground that the strike was a conspiracy in restraint of trade and so illegal under the Sherman Antitrust Act, Cleveland directed his Attorney General, Richard P. Olney, to apply in the federal courts for an injunction forbidding all persons to interfere in any way with the operation of trains or with workers in the performance of their duties. When Debs and other leaders refused to obey the "blanket injunction," they were arrested and imprisoned for contempt of court. In the face of federal troops and federal injunctions the strike collapsed but it provided a never-to-be-forgotten lesson. Organized labor for the next forty years waged a persistent battle against the use of the injunction in industrial warfare.

THE RULERS OF THE INDUSTRIAL AGE

There is something to be said both for the "great man" theory of history and for the type of history that emphasizes the activities of government. This observation is true, however, only when the dominant personalities and real rulers of an age are accurately determined. The student of American history in the half century following the Civil War is quite devoid of perspective if he fixes his eyes upon the activities at Washington and the career of the politicians who made that city their temporary home. The real rulers of America rarely visited the capital city; their power rested in their direct control, not of votes, but of the nation's wealth as represented in mines, factories, and railroads. Their interest in federal or state governments was concerned only with using these agencies to increase their own economic power or to prevent action that might interfere with their operations. At such moments their agents usually cared effectively for their interests. It is true that most of them supported the Republican Party lavishly, but that was chiefly because the Republicans were most likely to win. In areas where the rival party was supreme that party was supported. The *Realpolitik* of the true baron of the new industrial feudalism was expressed by the railroad magnate who asserted that "in Republican counties he was a Republican, and in Democratic counties he was a Democrat, but everywhere he was for the railroad." The cynical Harriman is reputed to have said that if he wanted state legislation he could buy it, and, if necessary, he could buy Congress and the judiciary as well.

"The United States," wrote a British journalist as late as 1910, "is like an enormously rich country overrun by a horde of robber barons, and very inadequately policed by the central government and by certain local vigilant societies." [6] This was even more true of American civilization in earlier decades, when the barons of the new industrial order were pushing to the front and carving out their respective domains. In the top ranks of the new hierarchy were such men as Jay Gould, William Vanderbilt, Leland Stanford, Collis P. Huntington, James J. Hill, and Edward H. Harriman in railroads; Andrew Carnegie and Henry C. Frick in steel; the Rockefellers, Henry H. Rogers, John D. Archbald, and Stephen V. Harkness in oil; Philip D. Armour and Gustavus F. Swift in meat-packing; William A. Clark, John William Mackay, and the Guggenheims in minerals; and Jay Cooke and James Stillman in banking. Over them all ruled the two potentates, John D. Rockefeller and J. Pierpont Morgan, whose economic interests were rapidly stretching out to include transportation and industry of

[6] William Archer, "The American Cheap Magazine," *Fortnightly Review*, LXXXVII, 950 (1910).

various types and who seemed destined by 1900 to divide the economic resources of the nation between them.

If the historian is to judge American civilization from the careers of its great economic leaders, this country was indeed the land of opportunity. With the exception of J. Pierpont Morgan, whose father was a banker, and William K. Vanderbilt, whose father had already become an important figure in transportation, the barons of finance, industry, and transportation were almost all self-made men. John D. Rockefeller and Jay Gould were sons of obscure New York farmers; James Fisk and Collis P. Huntington began life as Yankee peddlers, Daniel Drew as a cattle drover, and Jay Cooke and James J. Hill as clerks on the frontier. Stanford and Mackay arrived in California with barely a cent in their pockets. John Wanamaker, the merchant prince of the East, began as a humble clerk, and Harriman as an errand boy in a broker's office; Carnegie, the steel magnate, came to America a poor immigrant boy whose first job was in a cotton mill. And so one might go on indefinitely; their youth was one of cold poverty, their life was ended amid riches that would amaze an Oriental potentate. Except in a few eastern cities where some wealth had been accumulated in the hands of older families, the opportunities of a rapidly developing country were open to all, and in the mad scramble some found themselves at the top of the heap. In the formal sense, with the exception of Morgan, there was hardly one of them who had received an education beyond the three Rs. Few Americans of the Civil War period, except those training for the professions, went to college; the new rulers of America were about their business while still in their teens. Carnegie was the son of a Scotch weaver and Mackay of poor Irish immigrants, but in general the new barons were of English-Yankee stock or descendants of New England Yankees. A few of the lesser magnates, such as Albert A Pope, manufacturer of bicycles and automobiles, and William F. Draper, manufacturer of textile machinery, had rendered distinguished service in the war, but there were few of them of military age who had felt called upon to take up arms. When necessary they hired substitutes and spent the golden war years in laying the foundations of their fortunes, not infrequently at the expense of the government and those who enlisted. With an unerring eye on the main chance, they instinctively followed the advice that Judge Mellon of Pittsburgh gave to his son James:

> I had hoped my boy was going to make a smart, intelligent business man and was not such a goose as to be seduced from duty by the declamations of buncombed speeches. It is only greenhorns who enlist. You can learn nothing in the army. . . . In time you will come to understand and believe that a man may be a patriot without risking his own life or sacrificing his health.

The philosophy of the new rulers was fairly simple; it can be summed up in the exclamation of the young Rockefeller, "I'm bound to be rich! Bound to be rich!" Writing of the frontier town of St. Louis, Jay Cooke commented, "Through all the grades I see the all-pervading, all-engrossing anxiety to grow rich. That is the only thing for which men live here." As to the methods by which riches might be attained, there were ordinarily no scruples. In the bitter economic warfare, decency and honesty were lost sight of. For those who were emerging on the top, the economic doctrine of *laissez faire* seemed quite satisfactory, except when something was to be gained by government help. The same men who had no hesitancy in seeking large land grants, high tariffs, or any other type of government "hand-out" bitterly resented any effort to control the wealth that the government donations had helped to create. Their attitude was much like that of James J. Hill, who complained, after the Supreme Court had declared the Northern Securities Company illegal: "It really seems hard when we look back upon what we have done . . . that we should be compelled to fight for our lives against the political adventurers who have never done anything but pose and draw a salary." More forthright was the colorful H. H. Rogers, who once thundered, "We will see Standard Oil in hell before we will let any set of men tell us how to run our business." If the political philosophy of the robber barons was a bit inconsistent, their ethical conceptions seem quite as confused. There were few who would hesitate to bribe a congressman, ruin a competitor by illegal means, or mulct a confiding investor by financial manipulations. "If you have to pay money to have the right thing done," wrote Huntington to his agent during a congressional railroad fight, "it is only just and fair to do it." Most of the barons were ardent upholders of the church and liberal contributors to philanthropy. Drew founded a theological seminary, Wanamaker and Rockefeller taught Sunday schools, and Cooke set aside one tenth of his profits for charitable purposes. Some, like Stanford, founded colleges or universities; others took some established institutions under their wing. Carnegie, the only one who seriously doubted the mission of the church, devoted most of his fortune to founding libraries and promoting peace. The philosophy of these men was but a reflection of their time. It was not, for example, until the nineties that the church in America began to view seriously its own mission in the new industrial order.

LEGAL AIDS

By 1870 the triumph of the Industrial Revolution in the economic world seemed assured, and the results of these economic changes were already making themselves felt in the social and cultural aspects of American life.

There remained only the task of writing the economic philosophy of the barons of the new industrialism into constitutional law. The first step in this process, as suggested in the last chapter, was taken when the fourteenth amendment was written into the Constitution. In brief, the amendment was expected to protect corporations and private business against the attacks and restraining influences of state legislatures. Although the Supreme Court under John Marshall had, by a strict interpretation of that part of the constitution forbidding a state to impair the obligation of contract, given some protection to corporations from attacks by state legislatures, the barons of the new industrial age were not satisfied. The states' rights court under Taney had weakened the position of Marshall, and something more must be done to limit the power of the states. How this was accomplished will be briefly told.

The phrasing of the fourteenth amendment was skillfully designed to do just this. "No state," said the most significant of the sentences, "shall make or enforce any law which shall abridge the privileges or immunities of citizens of the United States; nor shall any state deprive any person of life, liberty or property without due process of law; nor deny to any person within its jurisdiction the equal protection of the laws." As to what were "privileges or immunities," what was "life, liberty or property," what was "equal protection of the laws," and just what the term "person" meant—all these questions were left to judicial determination.

The expectation of the framers that the courts would so interpret the fourteenth amendment as to make it a powerful weapon in defense of private property was justified, although it took some time to develop such an interpretation. The most important cases out of which such an interpretation developed had nothing to do with the emancipated slaves. The first group, known as the slaughter-house cases (1873), were suits to test the validity of a Louisiana law of 1869 designed to protect the health of the people of New Orleans and certain parishes by granting to a corporation a virtual monopoly of the slaughtering business. When the independent butchers attacked this law on the ground that it violated the fourteenth amendment, the court by a five-to-four decision held that the law fell within the police power of the state, that the amendment did not transfer the protection of all fundamental civil rights from the state to the federal authority, but that certain civil rights were left to the jurisdiction of the state, and that the essential purpose of the amendment was to protect the black man. Minority opinions, however, pointed to a future interpretation that would greatly extend the meaning of the amendment and subject almost all state legislation of an economic nature to federal judicial analysis.

As might have been expected, the fate of the fourteenth amendment was fought out over the question of government control of the rapidly growing railroad net. The first of the so-called Granger cases, known as Munn *v.* Illinois (1876), involved the validity of an Illinois law declaring grain elevators to be public warehouses, subjecting them to strict regulation, and establishing maximum charges. The plaintiffs charged that the business was not a public calling and hence did not fall under government regulation, and that the rates fixed violated the due-process clause because they were fixed by the legislature and not by the judiciary. Both of these contentions were denied by the court. "Property," said Chief Justice Waite, "does become clothed with public interest when used in a manner to make it of public consequence. When, therefore, one devotes his property to a use in which the public has an interest, he, in effect, grants to the public an interest in that use, and must submit to be controlled by the public for the common good." As to the contention that the fixing of rates was a judicial matter, the justice asserted categorically that "it has been customary from time immemorial for the legislature to declare what shall be reasonable compensation under such circumstances." "For protection against abuses by legislatures," said Justice Waite, "the people must resort to the polls, not to the courts." The position taken by the court in the Munn case was taken again the same year in the case of Peck *v.* Chicago and Northwestern Railroad Company, when it upheld the right of the state of Wisconsin to fix maximum railroad rates and insisted that such was the business of the legislature rather than of the courts. The same position was again taken by the Supreme Court in the Ruggles case (1883).

·If one may judge from the clear-cut decisions just mentioned, which cover the first fifteen years after the adoption of the fourteenth amendment, it would appear that the Supreme Court was very definitely opposed to extending its jurisdiction over every conceivable type of economic legislation that a state legislature might pass. The personnel of the Supreme Court, however, changes, while private corporations continue to live and press their interests, undismayed by the earlier decisions. The railroads, in one case after another, maintained their position until finally, in 1889, in the Minnesota rate case (Chicago, Milwaukee and St. Paul Railway Company *v.* Minnesota), the court completely reversed itself, and took the ground that an unreasonable rate might deprive one of property without due process of law and that the reasonableness of a rate was, therefore, ultimately a judicial question. The new position was reaffirmed in Reagan *v.* Farmers Loan and Trust Company (1894) and in Smyth *v.* Ames (1898), when the court declared that the principle "must be regarded as settled" that the judiciary might review a rate determined by the legislature, and that it was equally well settled that property affected with a public interest was entitled to a "fair return" on a fair valuation. Later the fourteenth amendment was used in cases involving wages, hours, and conditions of labor as well as in many other fields in which the public welfare, as expressed in an act of a state legislature, came into conflict with the interests of some private property. One thing is evident: by the early nineties big business, the heir of the Industrial Revolution, had, through its ally, the judiciary, so interpreted the amendment that its position seemed impregnable. Whether this position could be maintained was for the future to decide.

For a brief survey, see Edward C. Kirkland, *A History of American Economic Life,* Chap. XI, or H. U. Faulkner, *American Economic History,* Chap. XX. C. and M. Beard, *The Rise of American Civilization,* Chap. XX, is an excellent interpretative chapter. The period from 1878 to 1898 is intelligently interpreted in I. M. Tarbell, *The Nationalizing of Business,* Chaps. IX, X. On railroads of the period, see John Moody, *The Railroad Builders* (Chronicles of America); on labor, N. J. Ware, *The Labor Movement in the United States,* Chaps. I–IV; on the oil industry, John Flynn, *God's Gold,* 105–257 or Paul H. Giddens, *The Birth of the Oil Industry.* Interesting material is in F. Flügel and H. U. Faulkner, *Readings in the Economic and Social History of the United States,* 793–802, 816–835.

THE INDUSTRIAL AGE

Chapter XXV

THE LAST FRONTIER

> *This, then, is the real situation: a people composed of heterogeneous materials, with diverse and conflicting ideals and social interests, having passed from the task of filling up the vacant spaces of the continent, is now thrown back upon itself, and is seeking an equilibrium. The diverse elements are being fused into national unity. The forces of reorganization are turbulent and the nation seems like a witches' kettle.*
>
> FREDERICK JACKSON TURNER

THE TRANS-MISSISSIPPI ADVANCE

More than two centuries elapsed between the founding of the first permanent white settlement within the boundaries of the present United States and the occupation of land as far west as the Mississippi. The settlement of the area between the Mississippi and the Pacific, however, was the work of little more than half a century. The first state (excepting Louisiana) to be carved out of the trans-Mississippi West was Missouri (1821), followed by Arkansas (1836), Texas (1845), Iowa (1846), and California (1850). The rest of this tremendous region was separated into the territories of Oregon (1848), Utah (1850), New Mexico (1850), and Minnesota (1849) or left completely unorganized. By 1850 the westward moving frontier ran from eastern Minnesota south through eastern Nebraska and Kansas and then through Arkansas to Texas. Little occurred during the early fifties to extend the line westward except the creation in 1854 of the territories of Kansas and Nebraska and the artificial stimulation to settlement as proslavery and antislavery men struggled for control in Kansas. Areas of settlement, however, had appeared in California, in Oregon, and in Utah (pages 238 ff.), and these continued to grow during the decade. The intervening territory, America's "last frontier," was largely occupied during the next three decades, and it will be the business of this chapter briefly to trace the story. It was peopled by miners, ranchers, and farmers, who were lured by discoveries of rich deposits of minerals and by the opportunities to exploit free grass and to obtain free land. The process was speeded by favorable land laws, by a rapidly increasing immigration, and particularly by the building of the great transcontinental railroads, the invention of barbed wire, and the quantity production of cheap windmills.

THE MINERAL FRONTIER

Primarily because of their use as money, the precious metals have had an influence on history far out of proportion to their intrinsic value. It was the lure of gold and silver that inspired the conquests of Cortez and Pizarro and led to the first explorations in North America. Not only were the precious metals the most important influence in the early white exploration and settlement of America, but the discovery of these metals affected profoundly the economic history of Europe through their influence upon world prices.[1] The influence of the precious metals, however, was declining until the discovery of gold in California in 1848 brought a sudden influx of population to the western coast. By the late fifties placer mining was giving out in the valleys of California, and the thousands of gold-seekers who had been lured from all quarters of the world were keenly alert for new fields to conquer. Their hopes were realized in 1858 when gold was discovered in the Pikes Peak country and particularly rich deposits of silver near Lake Tahoe, about twenty miles east of the California boundary. Thousands were again set in motion, and for the next decade prospectors swarmed through the region of the Rockies from Canada to Mexico, providing an impetus for the division and subdivision of territories and the creation of the mountain states.

News reached Omaha late in 1858 that gold had been discovered about ninety miles from Pikes Peak in the southwestern part of what was then Kansas territory. Before winter set in, the caravans of gold-seekers were again headed westward, and during the next year mining camps sprang up near the present sites of Denver and Colorado Springs, and elsewhere. The depression following the panic of 1857 undoubtedly provided an added impetus, and by 1860 almost 100,000 miners had arrived. It was soon discovered that there was little placer mining. The precious metals were embedded in quartz and could be secured only by expensive machinery and heavy capital expenditure, and many a gold-seeker who had started westward with the motto "Pikes Peak or Bust" painted gaily on his covered wagon had returned home "Busted by Gosh!" Nevertheless, enough remained to organize the Territory of Jefferson in 1859. Congress, however, deadlocked over the slavery controversy, paid no attention until 1861, when

[1] See, for example, Earl T. Hamilton, *American Treasure and the Price Revolution in Spain 1501–1650* (1934).

it discarded the name of Jefferson and created the Territory of Colorado, carved out of the existing territories of Kansas, Nebraska, Utah, and New Mexico. After a slow growth of a quarter century, statehood was achieved in 1876.

More spectacular and valuable were the simultaneous discoveries made on the extreme western border of the Utah territory in Carson Valley, on one of the main routes to California. The Mormons long maintained a service station in the valley for immigrants, and through this valley for a decade thousands had passed without realizing the great wealth underlying the surface. Discovery of rich pay dirt led to a rush to Carson Valley in the summer of 1859, the creation of the territory of Nevada (1861) out of part of Utah Territory, and the grant of statehood three years later.[2] The most important of these new discoveries was the Comstock lode, which yielded between 1860 and 1890 some $340,000,000 worth of gold and silver. After 1890 the Comstock lode declined rapidly, thus seriously affecting the prosperity of the state, but new discoveries of copper and the precious metals in 1906 and thereafter at Tonopah, Goldfield, and elsewhere brought a fresh influx of population and a new prosperity. The great wealth of the Comstock went not to the early claim-holders, who soon sold out, but to John William Mackay and his associates.[3]

In the year following the great rush to Nevada, gold was discovered on the reservation of the Nez Percé Indians near the juncture of the Clearwater and Snake Rivers in what is now Idaho. In 1861 came the inevitable stampede, and the town of Lewiston sprang up to become the center of the mining operations in that region. The Clearwater mines were followed by discoveries on the Salmon, another tributary of the Snake, and the Boise mines came on the heels of this boom. As thousands of prospectors swarmed over the hills, other discoveries were inevitable. James and Granville Stuart were at work in 1862 in the region of what is now western Montana, where Bannock City became the center of their operations. In the following year new discoveries produced Alder Gulch, Virginia City, and Helena, "the last of the boom towns of the period." This rapid influx of miners brought the creation of Idaho Territory in 1863 from the territories of Washington, Dakota, and Nebraska, followed in 1864 by the creation of the Territory of Montana out of northeastern Idaho, and of Wyoming Territory in 1868 from three existing territories.

---

[2] American literature has been enriched and posterity given an excellent description of the early years of Nevada by the fortunate circumstance that Samuel L. Clemens (Mark Twain) went to Nevada in 1861 as secretary to his brother, Orion Clemens, the territorial secretary, and immortalized his experiences in *Roughing It* (1872).

[3] The great fortune that Mackay took from the Comstock lode he later used to establish the Commercial Cable Company and the Postal Telegraph System in an effort to break the monopoly of the Western Union.

In the meantime, other mining enterprises were being pushed farther south. Ever since the Gadsden purchase of 1853, various companies had been opening up old Spanish mines in New Mexico and prospecting for new ones. This activity, centering in Tucson, was dominated by Confederate sympathizers and subsided temporarily when Colonel J. H. Carleton, in 1862, led a Union regiment from California to New Mexico. Carleton's soldiers, however, were instrumental in opening new placer deposits on the left banks of the Colorado near Bill Williams Creek, which drew away many of the Tucson miners and resulted in the separation of the western part of New Mexico in 1863 and the creation of Arizona Territory.

Within ten years after the discoveries of 1858, the states of the mineral frontier had been laid out. Except for subdividing the Dakotas, the political divisions of the United States were complete. The foundations of the mountain states had been laid by miners, mostly during the Civil War. The evanescent mining towns, nevertheless, which appeared and disappeared as the rumors of discoveries raced up and down the Rockies from Canada to the Mexican border, seemed but an insecure basis upon which to build new commonwealths. The same was true of the population first attracted to the mining camps. Women were few; virtuous women even more rare. The men as a whole were hard-bitten and reckless adventurers, who ranged in type from the serious-minded prospector through the various assortment of parasites who lived on the miners to the "road agents" or highwaymen who preyed upon the traveler. Paxson, historian of the frontier, has well caught the spirit of the typical mining town:

A single street meandering along a valley, with one story huts flanking it in irregular rows, was the typical mining camp. The saloon and the general store, sometimes combined, were its representative institutions. Deep ruts along the streets bore witness to the heavy wheels of the freighters, while horses loosely tied to all available posts at once revealed the regular means of locomotion, and by the careless way they were left about showed that this sort of property was not likely to be stolen. The mining population centering here lived a life of contrasts. The desolation and loneliness of prospecting and working claims alternated with the excitement of coming to town. Few decent beings habitually lived in the towns. The resident population expected to live off the miners, either in way of trade or worse. The bar, the gambling house, the dance hall have been made too common in description to need further account. In the reaction against loneliness, the extremes of drunkenness, debauchery, and murder were only too frequent in these places of amusement.[4]

[4] F. L. Paxson, *The Last American Frontier* (1910), 170–172. By permission of The Macmillan Company, publishers.

THE RANCHERS' FRONTIER

In the normal frontier advance the rancher has preceded the farmer. This may be partly explained by the fact that it takes less capital and effort to exploit the grass than it does to cultivate the land, and that in the early stage of inadequate transportation facilities the only farm commodity that is likely to reach the market is meat on the hoof. Although the ranchers' frontier has always played a part in American history, its most spectacular period was in the two decades after the Civil War. It was then that the cow country reached its fullest expansion—an episode made famous in American history by the paintings of Remington, the activity of Roosevelt, the dime novels and the "pulp" magazines that have circulated for decades among the youth of the land, and the "westerns," which have been an important part of the stock-in-trade of the "movies" since the birth of that form of amusement.

A combination of favorable circumstances led to the sudden spectacular development of the last ranchers' frontier. Primarily it was a fortuitous linking of supply, demand, and facilities for transportation. A reservoir of cattle had developed in Texas during the Civil War, for which there was little market. In the years after the war it was discovered that the short gray grass of the northern plains of Texas would rear cattle to a much greater size than that of the coast range, and it was also accidentally discovered that cattle could live on the northern plains during the winter and that they would fatten there to a size far beyond that of the southern range. A large market existed in Europe and the eastern states, and the contact was made in the late sixties as the transcontinental railroads began rapidly to push into the prairies.[5] The wholesale slaughter of the buffaloes and the removal of the Indians to reservations left a vast region between the hundredth meridian and the Rockies almost free of population except for the Indians—an open country to anyone who cared to exploit it. The technique of the cattle industry during the early years, as a consequence, was to collect the salable cattle on the upper ranges of Texas, drive them north to a railroad point, and fatten them for the market.

The outstanding features of the industry were the round-up and the long drive. Because of its low altitude and warm climate, Texas remained the great breeding ground, while the northern states and territories, with their rich pastures, sweet water, and bracing air, became the best feeding grounds. On the great southern ranges occurred two round-ups during the year, the calf round-up in May, when the young cattle were marked with the owner's

---

[5] The development of the refrigeration car by Gustavus F. Swift in the late seventies was an impetus both to the cattle industry and to the development of slaughterhouses near the source of supply in the great western cities.

brand, and the beef round-up in July or August, when the cattle were again gathered in and the mature or fatted animals, especially the yearling steers, were cut from the herd and driven toward the railroad, the new herd of beef cattle accumulating as the cattle of one round-up after another were added to the herd. On the "long drives" to the railroad it took a week or ten days to break a herd to the trail, but, when once established, it could travel from ten to fifteen miles a day. The trip then became monotonous rather than dangerous unless by some chance the herd should become frightened and attempt to stampede. This was an ever present danger, for the cattle were easily frightened; it is said that the appearance of the full moon, rising between two peaks of a cleft hill and shining red and large into a valley that had previously been quite dark, once started one of the most uncontrollable stampedes on record. It was to prevent this that the cowboys rode round and round the herd "singing to the cattle" in the night and ready to break up any milling that might lead to a stampede. The long drives, which sometimes took many weeks, ordinarily ended at or near some railroad—Abilene, Kansas, on the Kansas Pacific; Dodge City, Kansas, on the newly built Atchison, Topeka, and Santa Fé; Ogallala on the Union Pacific in Southern Nebraska; or Miles City and Glendive on the Northern Pacific.

With a low initial investment cost, a steady market, and high profits, the cattle business, like every other in a similar situation, was soon in an unhealthy and overexpanded condition. The idea of buying a few cattle that would rapidly increase while they fed on government land was too much for the investors and speculators. Large cattle companies were formed in Europe and in the East, and outside capital began to flow rapidly to the Great Plains. How rapidly expansion proceeded is evident from the comment of Granville Stuart, a Montana pioneer.

> It would be impossible to make people not present on the Montana cattle ranges realize the rapid changes that took place on those ranges in two years. In 1880, the country [central and eastern Montana] was practically uninhabited. One could travel for miles without seeing a trapper's bivouac. Thousands of buffalo darkened the rolling plains. There were deer, elk, wolves and coyotes on every hill and in every ravine and thicket. In the whole territory of Montana there were but 250,000 head of cattle, including dairy cattle and work oxen.

> In the fall of 1883, there was not a buffalo remaining on the range, and the antelope, elk, and deer were indeed scarce. In 1880, no one had heard tell of a cowboy in 'this niche of the woods' and Charlie Russell had made no pictures of them; but in the fall of 1883, there were 600,000 herd of cattle on the range. The cowboy . . . had become an institution.[6]

[6] Reprinted by permission of the publishers, The Arthur H. Clark Company, from Granville Stuart's *Forty Years on the Frontier*, II, 187–188.

The normal growth of the market for food and leather drove the prices of cattle upward, and this, combined with the ease of expansion, developed a mania for speculation. Mountain stock-growers, if the live-stock journals are to be believed, were reaping a profit of from 25 to 40 per cent, and the "bovine king" or "cattle baron" became a picturesque figure in the hotels of Chicago and New York as well as on the western prairies. The height was reached in May, 1882, when top prices reached $9.35 a hundred on the Chicago market and when steers ready for fattening brought sometimes as high as $60. By 1885 it was evident that the cattle business had pretty largely ceased to be a frontier industry and had fallen victim to overexpansion. The small local cattleman had been largely eliminated, and the business was in the hands of absentee owners. Furthermore, the speculation and scramble for profits had extended the business far beyond the margin of safety. Herds were being pushed on to the poor grass and overstocked areas, where drought or a hard winter would bring disaster. The boom collapsed in 1885, when cattle dropped to a third or less of their former price. The golden era of the ranchers' frontier was ended, and the cattle industry was forced to retreat and change its methods.

While the collapse of the late eighties was forcing a reorganization of the cattle industry, other influences were at work to bring to a conclusion the ranchers' frontier. The railroads that had made possible the rapid development of the cattle industry also speeded the advent of the farmer, and the farmers' frontier spelled the end of the open range and the long drive. It was the invention of barbed wire, as we shall see, that facilitated the advancing farmers' frontier and in turn helped to change the methods of the cattle industry. As the ranchers witnessed the farmers' frontier eating into the open range, the more far-seeing of them hastened also to enclose land. Much of this enclosure was illegal, the estimates of illegal enclosures in 1888 running as high as 8,000,000 acres, but the increasing attack of both farmers and ranchers upon the public land soon changed the economic position of the West. The end of the open range and of the long drives was also hastened by the appearance of cattle diseases and the quarantine laws passed by northern states against Texan cattle.

Temporary as was the ranchers' frontier, it had some very definite influences upon our history. Above all, it helped to open up for settlement the vast area between the hundredth meridian and the Rockies. The continual clamor of both ranchers and farmers for more land also speeded the opening of Oklahoma to settlement. With the rapid growth of the ranchers' frontier, the packing industry pushed westward to center in Chicago, St. Louis, Kansas City, and Omaha, where it quickly became monopolized in the hands of Armour, Hammond, Morris, and Swift. Improved methods of packing and refrigeration were forced upon the industry by the problem of transportation, while the exportation of meat became of greater importance than ever before. The conflict between the cattlemen on the one hand and the packers and railroads on the other for the profits of the industry was fundamental in the economic and political controversies of the period and in promoting the rising tide of Populism.

THE FARMERS' FRONTIER

Pressing rapidly on the heels of the ranchers' frontier came the vanguard of farmers, who succeeded by 1890 in ending the American frontier. Several factors were responsible for the speed with which the Great Plains were overrun by farmers. First of all were the favorable land laws of the federal government, which encouraged not only *bona fide* settlers but speculation of various kinds. In the second place, the building of the transcontinental railroads facilitated access to the new country, while the railroads themselves encouraged settlement. A third and extremely important cause was the invention and cheapening of barbed wire, which made it possible for the farmer to enclose his land against the depredations of the cattlemen. Among other causes was the realization that the broad western prairies were not arid plains but regions of great agricultural possibilities. Nor should the rapidly increasing immigration be forgotten; for many years a large number of "new Americans," especially Scandinavians, headed for the Great Plains.

The Homestead Act of 1862, as we have seen (page 229), marked the culmination of a long agitation for free land. Its influence upon American development, however, has probably been overemphasized. The Homestead Act played an important but not a determining part in filling up the last frontier. For three quarters of a century the westward movement had progressed steadily under a system whereby the settler had paid for his land, and there is no reason to believe that it would not have continued. Free land simply speeded the occupation of the West and made land speculation easier.

This act, upon which our land policy has since been based, granted a quarter section (160 acres) free to a head of a family or a person over twenty-one who was a citizen of the United States or who had filed his intention to become one. A residence on the land of five years was required, good faith to be evidenced by erection of a house and cultivation of the land. After six months (raised in 1891 to fourteen) the entry might be commuted (purchased before the residence requirement had been fulfilled) by payment of $1.25 an acre. By a number of subsequent amendments the original legislation has been liberalized: by the Timber and Stone Act of 1878, which allowed citizens to purchase 160 acres of lands

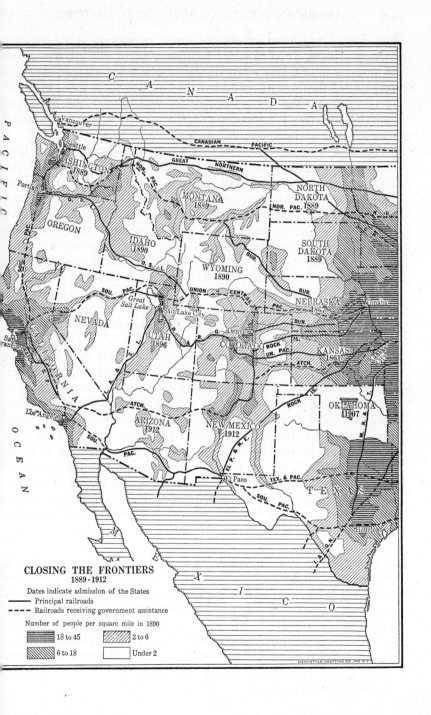

CLOSING THE FRONTIERS
1889-1912

Dates indicate admission of the States
——— Principal railroads
- - - Railroads receiving government assistance

Number of people per square mile in 1890

18 to 45	2 to 6
6 to 18	Under 2

MANHATTAN DRAFTING CO.,INC.,N.Y.

unfit for cultivation but valuable for timber or minerals at not less than $2.50 an acre; by an act of 1909, which provided for enlarged homesteads of 320 acres in arid land where dry farming was necessary; by an act of 1912 cutting the five-year residence requirement to three years; by an act of 1916 allowing 640-acre homesteads for stock-raising; and by various amendments permitting veterans of the Civil and succeeding wars to count their terms of service against the residence requirements.

Liberal as were the land laws, they were constantly evaded, and large areas were brought into private hands without fulfillment of the conditions. More serious was the evasion of the spirit, if not the letter, of the laws. By means of the privilege of commuting, corporations interested in mining, ranching, or lumbering were able through their agents to buy up after six months for as little as $1.25 an acre land worth many times that amount. It is estimated that, between 1881 and 1904, 23 per cent of the land transferred from the government to private individuals was transferred by commuting and that in North Dakota during the first decade of the present century more acres were commuted than were obtained through five years' residence.[7] "Actual inspection of hundreds of commuted homesteads," asserted an agent of the land office, "shows that not one in a hundred is ever occupied as a home after commutation." [8]

So notorious was the evasion of the Homestead Act that Congress in 1879 appointed a commission to examine the land system, but its recommendations were ignored. It was not until the rise of the conservation movement in the early years of the century, when Theodore Roosevelt appointed the Public Land Commission to study the problem, that the public-land system was again critically scrutinized. By that time it was too late to do much about it, for most of the usable land had been taken up. All in all, between 1862 and 1926, the government had issued 1,391,128 patents for approximately 223,159,053 acres of land. The Public Land Commission, commenting upon the Homestead Act, said: "It protects the government, it fills the state with homes, it builds up communities and lessens the chances of social and civil disorder by giving ownership of the soil, in small tracts, to the occupants thereof." This optimistic picture is but partly true. A goodly portion of the public domain went in the end not to the small farmer but to the large corporation through commutation. It is likewise interesting to note that while 223,159,053 acres were patented up to 1926, at least 137,000,000 acres were granted to railroad corporations or to states for railroad purposes.

While it may be true that the policy of free land distribution has lessened the chances of social and civil disorder, the fact remains that the

---

[7] B. H. Hibbard, *A History of the Public Land Policies*, 387.

[8] Quoted in Hibbard, *op. cit.*, 389.

overproduction of agricultural commodities and the overexpansion of the agricultural domain in the decades following the Civil War brought economic distress to the western farmers and made the agricultural states of the West the region of the most acute economic and political discontent. That the policy of free land as laid down by the Homestead Act speeded the settlement of the trans-Mississippi West, there can be no doubt; it also appears evident that it unintentionally promoted fraudulent speculation in public land and stimulated an overproduction of agricultural commodities, timber products, and mineral resources.

"Conditions of immigration have changed," said Benjamin Harrison in a debate on the admission of the Dakotas in 1884. "The immigrant who is seeking a home in the West does not now use as his vehicle a pack-train, a Conestoga wagon, or even a broad horn. The great bulk of the people who have gone into Dakota have gone upon the steam-car, many of them within sight of the home which they were to take up under the homestead laws of the United States . . . whereas in the case of the state of Indiana it was thirty years after admission of that state into the Union before a single line of railroad was built in its territory." [9] Not alone were conditions changed in the sense that a pioneer could ride on a railroad to his new land, but he was encouraged by rival railroads to pioneer on their respective lines. To encourage private capital to build the great transcontinental railroads, lavish land grants had been conferred upon the railroads, which included a right of way and alternate sections on each side of the track, ranging from five sections a mile to as high as forty in the case of the Northern Pacific. Settlements were encouraged by the railroads not alone to ensure future freight and passenger service but also to sell off their generous land grants.[10]

In the effort to gain settlers few methods of propaganda or advertising were neglected by the railroads. Maps and documents descriptive of the country were printed in many languages and widely distributed throughout the United States and Europe. In Europe this was done chiefly through consular officers of the United States, by steamship agents, and often through the railroads' own offices established in the principal foreign cities. In some cases men influential in particular localities were employed to lead bands of immigrants to this country. In the United States propaganda was carried on by newspaper advertisements, by public lectures, and partic-

[9] Forty-eighth Congress, Second Session, *Congressional Record,* Vol. XVI, Part I, 109 (December 9, 1884).

[10] Many of the western states, as well as the railroads, made strenuous efforts to attract immigrants. Minnesota as early as 1868 established an immigration board, printing pamphlets in half a dozen languages, advertising in the Irish press, and maintaining agents in Germany. Wisconsin, Michigan, and Missouri also had immigration boards, and most of the southern states passed laws in the postbellum years to encourage immigration.

ularly by work among veterans' organizations. Transportation costs from the East to the point of settlement were ordinarily reduced to a minimum. To those going to look over the land (holders of "land exploration tickets") reduced rates were given, or credit for their fare was extended to those who subsequently bought land. Free transportation to purchaser and family en route to settle the lands they had taken was ordinarily extended, and all kinds of reductions and financial inducements were made in the actual purchase of land. Some of the more enterprising roads, like the Northern Pacific, actually set up large and comfortable reception houses for the immigrants, equipped with beds, cookstoves, working conveniences, and hospitals, and made arrangements for the purchase of food at cost. The Northern Pacific also experimented with great wheat farms in an effort to induce men with capital to undertake large-scale agriculture. A study of the methods used by these railroads to induce settlements lends force to the opinion of Professor Commons that "the desire to get cheap labor, to take in passenger fares, and to sell land have probably brought more immigrants than the hard conditions of Europe, Asia, and Africa have sent." [11]

Professor Webb, in his significant book, *The Great Plains*,[12] notes how the development of the plains frontier was dependent upon transportation facilities, water supply, and fencing. The solving of the transportation problem really began with the transcontinental railroads. The problem of water on the western plains never can be adequately solved, but the history of America's efforts to find a solution extends from the dug wells of the first pioneers to the tremendous irrigation projects of the federal government culminating at Boulder Dam. "The history of the Great Plains," says Webb, "has been pretty largely dominated by a hunt for water." For the average prairie farmer the supply of water depended on pumping up the ground water by means of a windmill, and the development of the quantity production of small metal windmills went hand in hand with frontier expansion into the Great Plains. The part played by windmills in this region is suggested by a statement made in 1927 by one of the earliest windmill companies.

> As to use, windmills are chiefly used in the United States by the small farmer, dairyman, cattle feeder, and ranchman; and although mills are sold in every state of the Union, comparatively few are sold in the states bordering along the Atlantic and Pacific or south of the Ohio and east of the Mississippi.
>
> From Ohio to Nebraska and from Minnesota to Texas the windmill is in quite general use, and, considering the differences in the use of the land in these states and the stage of development, there is little difference in the

[11] J. R. Commons, *Races and Immigrants in America,* 108.
[12] W. P. Webb, *The Great Plains* (1931).

extent of the use of the windmill. Probably 90 per cent of all of the windmills are used in these states.

There are towns in Texas, Kansas, and Nebraska where practically every
house has a windmill.[13]

Adapted to the almost continuous delivery of small amounts of water, the
windmill was the most important mechanical aid to the occupation of the
Great Plains.

Without the windmill the settlement of the great prairies of the West
might have been indefinitely delayed; without barbed wire the plains
might still be in possession of the cowboy and the roaming herds of cattle.
Up to the sixties the fencing material of the nation was primarily wooden
rails and secondarily rocks or hedge growth. When the frontier line left
the timbered region and came into the prairie, the pioneer found neither
timber nor stone. At first he avoided the open land, although it was often
the most fertile, and remained as long as possible near the wooded areas.
When the pioneer finally struck into the plains, he endeavored frantically
to find substitutes for these old materials. Hedges of various types were
experimented with in the seventies, but they provided no solution. Practical farmers, however, were already turning their attention to the possibilities of barbed wire. Several patents were taken out in the late sixties,
but the first practical barbed wire seems to have been evolved by Joseph F.
Glidden and Jacob Haish, both of Illinois, in 1874 and 1875 respectively.

Although bitter patent suits followed the invention, with eventual control of manufacture largely in the American Steel and Wire Company,
there was little delay in making the product known to the farmers. The
estimated production and sale of barbed wire was but 10,000 pounds in
1874; six years later it was approximately 80,500,000. In 1874 the wire sold
for $20 a hundred pounds, in 1880 for $10; and in 1897 it reached the ab-
normally low mark of $1.80 a hundred. With the coming of barbed wire
the way was opened for a more rapid expansion. "It was not until about
1875," said an old settler in Texas, "that the black lands really became available for agricultural purposes. The development of those lands had lagged
for lack of the means of fencing them at moderate cost. They were so far
from timber as to make rail fences out of the question. The want was supplied by the Glidden barb wire, which beginning about 1875, was shipped
into the state, not by the carload but by the trainload. After that immigrants
ceased to stop in East Texas, and the black lands came into their own." [14]

Barbed wire spelled the doom of the open range and the long drive, and
the cattlemen did not submit tamely to the new invention. For years they
retaliated upon the farmers, descending upon the outlying farms and cut-

[13] Statement of Fairbanks, Morse and Company, quoted by Webb, *op. cit.,* 340–341.
[14] Quoted by Webb, *op. cit.,* 317.

ting the wire to pieces. But it was a losing battle. The range country changed into a big pasture country, and the cattlemen themselves were forced to wire off their own land. This in turn enabled them to improve their breeds. In short, barbed wire revolutionized ranching without destroying it. At the same time it speeded the westward movement. "It was barbed wire," says Webb, "and not the railroads or the homestead law that made it possible for the farmers to resume, or at least accelerate, their march across the prairies and onto the plains. Even the fertile Prairie Plains were but sparsely settled until after the advent of barbed wire." [15]

THE END OF THE FRONTIER

Officially the frontier (technically a region of more than two and less than six people per square mile) came to an end in 1890. In that year the Census Bureau commented as follows: "Up to and including 1880 the country had a frontier of settlement, but at present the unsettled area has been so broken into by isolated bodies of settlement that there can hardly be said to be a frontier line. In the discussion of its extent, its westward movement, etc., it cannot, therefore, any longer have a place in the census reports." As far as the political development of the Far West was concerned, this statement seemed true enough, although it must be admitted that political considerations rather than extent of settlement were often the deciding factor regarding admission to the Union. After Nebraska (1867), no new state was admitted until Colorado in 1876. At that time the House of Representatives was Democratic and, believing that Colorado would be a Democratic state, granted admission. Colorado, however, went Republican in 1876 and cast three votes for Hayes in the disputed election of that year. After that the Democrats regarded dubiously the admission of new states, and there were no more additions to statehood for thirteen years.

By the middle eighties, settlers, following the Northern Pacific, occupied the Dakotas, Montana, and Washington in sufficient numbers to justify statehood, but, with poignant memories of Colorado, Democratic congressmen prevented admission until after the election of 1888. "I have no doubt that if the population of Dakota was not well known to be distinctively Republican," complained Senator Ingalls disgustedly, ". . . that bill to admit the Dakotas would have long ago been acted upon." The Democratic defeat of 1888, however, created a new situation. Knowing that the Republicans would admit the territories clamoring for statehood as soon as they took over power in 1889, the Democrats now hastened to make what political capital could be obtained from favoring admission and by the

15 Webb, *op. cit.,* 317.

"Omnibus Bill," signed by Cleveland in February, 1889, North Dakota, South Dakota, Montana, and Washington were added to the sisterhood of states. Very shortly after the Republicans again obtained possession of the government, they added Idaho and Wyoming, in 1890. But four more states were still to come in. Utah, after the Mormon church had abolished polygamy in 1890, and at least a quarter of a century after its population warranted statehood, was admitted in 1896. Oklahoma had been chiefly an Indian reservation until 1889, but the pressure of white settlers was too much, and the government finally gave in. At noon on April 22, at the sound of the bugle, Oklahoma was officially opened, and settlers by the thousands raced in to occupy the better land. Within a year Oklahoma's population numbered 259,000, but statehood was not conferred until 1907. Some efforts were made, 1905–1908, to bring Arizona and New Mexico in as a single state, but opposition of the inhabitants of Arizona prevented it. Further delays were caused by President Taft's opposition to a clause in the Arizona constitution providing for the recall of judges. The temporary removal of this provision brought statehood to both territories in 1912.

The existence for three centuries of a frontier of unoccupied land to which the westward moving settlers might go, as we have observed before, has undoubtedly been one of the most important influences that have molded American civilization. It was the frontier that more than anything else differentiated the underlying economic conditions in the United States from those of western Europe, that determined the predominance of the extractive industries, the lines of manufacturing development, and the content and direction of foreign trade. It was the influence of the frontier that molded our banking and currency systems and determined the course of transportation development. The influence of the frontier upon our economic life is clear enough, but its effects upon social and political development are equally important. It has gone far to determine the psychology and philosophy of the American people.

If the predominating influence of the frontier is granted, as it is by most historians, its disappearance necessarily marked the end of an era. Undoubtedly, the end of a condition in which new land and new resources are being constantly opened to exploitation will have its effect upon methods and types of manufacturing, upon prices of commodities, wages of labor, social life, and cultural patterns. To predict with any degree of accuracy just what these effects will be is impossible in our present complicated civilization. Nevertheless, it should be noted, in the first place, that, although the frontier is technically ended, many of its conditions still exist. Good free land is gone, but inferior land with modern scientific agriculture may be made to produce adequate yields. There is still an abundance of cheap land available, and there is still the possibility of finding free land on the Canadian frontier. Since the depression of 1929 hundreds of thousands of people have moved back on to farms; it is still possible for the poor man to escape to the land.

In any consideration of the influence of the frontier it is extremely important that the student keep in mind the fact that other influences have also contributed powerfully to the making of modern America. Some recent historians have rejected Turner's thesis as to the overpowering influence of the frontier and have maintained that America is the child of modern industrialism and capitalism rather than of the frontier. The expanding frontier itself, insist these critics, was largely the result of the expanding needs of western Europe as that part of the world was changed by the Industrial Revolution. In other words, the intellectual, cultural, and economic patterns of modern America have been molded not alone by the agricultural frontier but by the forces of the Industrial Revolution and modern capitalism as they arose in Europe and finally came to America.

C. and M. Beard, *The Rise of American Civilization,* Chap. XIX, is an excellent introductory chapter. F. L. Paxson, *A History of the American Frontier,* Chaps. L–LIX, covers this period. E. Hough, *The Passing of the Frontier* (Chronicles of America), is a well-written summary. The most significant writing on this subject is W. P. Webb, *The Great Plains,* Chaps VI–VIII. For the cow country of the Northwest read E. S. Osgood, *The Day of the Cattlemen,* Chaps. IV, V. The colonization work of the railroads is discussed in J. B. Hedges, *Henry Villard and the Railways of the Northwest,* Chap. VI. F. Flügel and H. U. Faulkner, *Readings in the Economic and Social History of the United States,* 473–476, 750–764, gives the Homestead Act, the government description of the last frontier, and other material.

THE INDUSTRIAL AGE

Chapter XXVI

THE AGRARIAN REVOLT

There are three great crops raised in Nebraska. One is a crop of corn, one a crop of freight rates, and one a crop of interest. One is produced by farmers who by sweat and toil farm the land. The other two are produced by men who sit in their offices and behind their bank counters and farm the farmers.

Farmers' Alliance (August 23, 1890)

THE REVOLUTION IN AGRICULTURE

The transformation experienced by American agriculture in the half century following 1860 was quite as significant for the future of America as the simultaneous revolution in industry. Of the changes that particularly strike the historian, changes so momentous as to constitute an agricultural revolution, four were of outstanding importance: the overthrow of the slave system, the end of the frontier, the introduction of labor-saving machinery, and the subordination of agriculture to industry. The abolition of slavery, in conjunction with the Civil War, ruined the plantation-owner. His wealth had hitherto been almost entirely invested in land and slaves, and without slaves his land was of little value. Without capital to rehabilitate his plantation or to pay wages to labor, he broke up his plantation into small holdings and rented them to Negroes or poor whites on a share basis. From a region where commercial staples were raised on large plantations, the South was transformed into a land of tenant farms and share-croppers. For this new system little could be said except that for the moment it solved the problem of a livelihood for the freedmen and provided an opportunity for the plantation-owner to do something with his land. It was a system characterized by waste, inefficiency, and human exploitation.

As the system of share-cropping quickly developed, the tenant farmer found himself in the condition of peonage, perpetually in debt to plantation-owner or local storekeeper, who supplied him with land, tools, seed, and supplies and took a lien on the future crop. By the end of the century perhaps a fourth of the Negro farmers had raised themselves from the status of peons and had come to own their farms, although often under a heavy mortgage. The smashing of the plantation system was of some aid to the middle-class farmer and poor white of the South, who were thus enabled to increase their holdings. At the same time, the breakdown of the gap between the wealthy slave-owner and the small farmer had a political as well as an economic significance. While the acreage per farm in the South decreased in the years following the Civil War, the number of freeholds increased. The higher planting class, in so far as it has survived at all, has generally deserted agriculture for the city and found an outlet for its talent in banking, transportation, industry, and other enterprises connected with the postwar economic development of the South.

To agricultural expansion and the significance of the end of the frontier some attention has already been given. In amazement at the tremendous industrial advance that has characterized the United States since the Civil War, it is quite easy to miss a similar expansion in agriculture. In 1860 the entire population of the nation was but 30 million, while in 1910 there were at least 50 million living on farms or in villages largely supported by agriculture. During this half century the number of farms tripled from two million to six million, while over 500 million acres were added to cultivation, an area almost as large as western Europe. With the closing of the frontier this expansion eventually slowed up, but in the meantime it had brought overproduction and, in conjunction with other causes, an agrarian distress that was chronic for a quarter century after the Civil War.

No phase of the agricultural revolution was more significant than that which pertained to the scientific and technical changes. Although numerous improvements in agricultural tools and numerous experiments in scientific crop-rotation and cattle-breeding had been made, agriculture as late as 1860 was essentially primitive. In the next few decades the picture quickly changed. The revolutionizing of agricultural machinery began with planting tools, particularly the plow, which was perfected by 1869 when James Oliver produced his chilled-steel plow. Essential progress in wheat-production, however, was dependent upon harvesting machinery, for the amount of grain that can be raised depends primarily upon the amount that can be harvested between the time when the grain is ripe and the time when it spoils. Progress here began with the invention of the Hussey and McCormick reapers, patented in 1833 and 1834 respectively, but not widely used until the sixties. These reapers, which cut the grain and raked off the straw, almost doubled the amount of wheat that could be harvested in a given time. Improvements on the original reaper were quickly made; C. W. and W. W. Marsh in 1858 patented the Marsh harvester, which again doubled the existing speed, and in 1878 John F. Appleby invented a twine

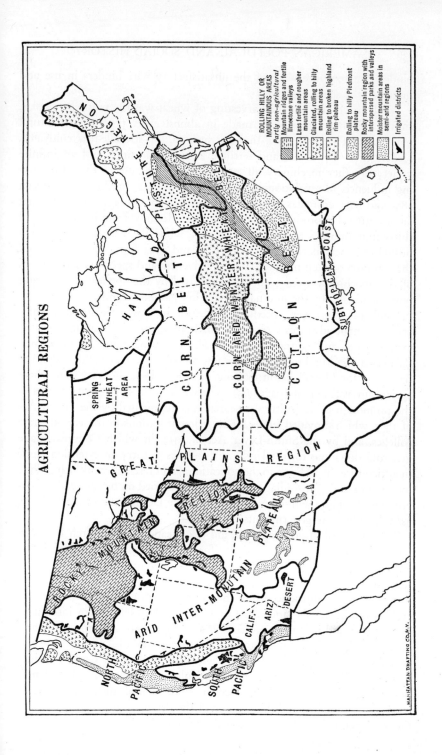

AGRICULTURAL REGIONS

ROLLING HILLY OR
MOUNTAINOUS AREAS
Partly non-agricultural

Mountain ridges and fertile
limestone valleys

Less fertile and rougher
mountain areas

Glaciated, rolling to hilly
mountain areas

Rolling to broken highland
rim plateau

Rolling to hilly Piedmont
plateau

Rocky mountain region with
interspersed parks and valleys

Moister mountain areas in
semi-arid regions

Irrigated districts

MANHATTAN DRAFTING CO., N. Y.

binder that took the place of the unsatisfactory wire binders in use and increased the speed eightfold.

While machinery for the harvesting of wheat was the most spectacular, similar advances were being made in almost every type of agricultural machinery. The disk plow, the disk harrow, the straddle-row cultivator, seeders that sow, cover, and fertilize at the same time, and an infinite variety of other machinery all tended, chiefly because of their time-saving influence, to revolutionize methods and increase production. Between 1855 and 1894, estimates an agricultural expert, the average time of human labor required to produce one bushel of corn declined from four hours and thirty-four minutes to forty-one minutes, while the time required for a bushel of wheat declined between 1830 and 1894 from three hours and three minutes to ten minutes. The effectiveness and speed of certain types of this machinery were eventually increased by the application of steam power and later by the internal-combustion gasoline engine.

While inventors were speeding production by new agricultural machinery, important advances were being made in scientific agriculture. To the experimental and educational work already being done by gentlemen farmers, agricultural societies, and a few schools, there were added after the passage of the Morrill Act in 1862 one or more colleges in every state where agriculture was taught (page 365). The work of the land-grant colleges in the promotion of agricultural research was augmented by the Hatch Act of 1887, which provided funds for experiment stations in the various state colleges, and by the Smith-Lever Act of 1914, in which Congress made generous donations for the land-grant colleges to carry on extension work in agriculture. In addition to the educational and research work being done by the state colleges, similar activity is being carried on by the federal government through the numerous bureaus of the Department of Agriculture, as well as by state governments.

The sum total of governmental aid to education and research has been large. The Bureau of Entomology, for example, has directed the battle against many pests, including the corn-borer, the Japanese beetle, the Mediterranean fruit fly, and the gypsy-moth, while the Bureau of Plant Industry alone has introduced into this country 30,000 new plants. The federal government, ever since the Carey Act of 1894, has shown interest in reclamation and irrigation projects, at first by encouraging the states and later by building itself huge dams for the storage and distribution of water. Inventions, research, education, reclamation—these have been the chief instrumentalities that have speeded agricultural production, released millions of men for other work, allowed the cultivation of much land hitherto considered unusable, and taken some of the drudgery from farm life. On the other hand, the cost of new machinery and scientific methods has made of the farm a more strictly capitalistic enterprise and consequently an enterprise more difficult for the man without capital to enter. It has increased both tenant farming and the landless proletariat and has also contributed to the overproduction of agricultural commodities.

While technical methods of agricultural production were experiencing epoch-making changes, the position of agriculture in the structure of American economic life was undergoing transformation. In brief, American agriculture was being subordinated to the interests of industry and was profoundly affected by the development of world capitalist society. As western Europe and the seaboard states turned definitely to manufacturing in the decades following the Industrial Revolution, the American farmer turned where possible to commercial agriculture. As the teeming populations of the rapidly growing cities were forced to draw their foodstuffs from a greater distance, the old-fashioned self-sufficing farm largely disappeared. The signal, in a sense, was given in 1846, when Great Britain, finally deciding that she must obtain her food outside her own country, turned her back upon the mercantilism of her early empire and repealed the "corn laws." It was then that the American farmer began to play a new role—as producer of foodstuffs for the expanding industrial population of western Europe. Without his food the full effects of industrial development could not have been felt, and from this point of view McCormick's reaper as much as Hargreaves's spinning jenny may have been a determining factor in the Industrial Revolution.

In this new role agriculture was approved and aided by the American industrialist, who found in agricultural exports a means whereby the adverse balances of trade might be paid. While American industry and transportation were being developed in part by European loans, American agriculture provided the exports to pay for the loans. All this speeded the development of both American agriculture and American industry. All might go well until competition from elsewhere produced overproduction and the economic world collapsed into one of its periodic fits of illness. This is what happened. Rapid expansion in the United States, combined with a similar expansion in other underdeveloped agricultural countries, brought overproduction, a decline in prices, and agricultural distress. This situation, which in general lasted from the end of the Civil War to the late nineties, was accentuated by the periodic economic crises that curtailed the market for agricultural commodities. Such was the inevitable result of the shift from the self-sufficing farm to commercial agriculture. While this change was in progress, American industry was increasing in strength even more rapidly than agriculture (page 400). Its representatives began to dominate the federal government and to determine the economic policies that were generally pursued in the half century after the Civil War. In brief, national policies with regard to tariff, currency, transportation, and other aspects of our economic life favored industry rather than agriculture.

THE GRANGER MOVEMENT

American history in the period between the Civil War and the end of the century can be understood only in terms of a developing industrial capitalism, the subordination of agriculture, and the revolt of the agrarian interests against the new condition. In retrospect this is easy enough to see; the farmers of the period, however, but vaguely understood the causes of their troubles. Briefly, the agrarian distress was caused by an overproduction of agricultural commodities at a time when prices were declining not only because of overproduction but also because of a contracting currency and a tightening in the world's gold supply. Stimulated by the boom period of the Civil War, by currency inflation, and by the Homestead Act, the frontier line had pushed rapidly westward. In spite of the large areas of fresh agricultural land, the pressure of vast numbers of settlers soon pushed up the price of land. Although the profits of agriculture were small, the rising value of lands, combined with the necessity to purchase new and expensive machinery, encouraged the farmers to borrow heavily, until, by 1900, over 40 per cent of Middle Western farms were covered by mortgages. The interest on these mortgages, contracted with eastern money-lenders, averaged from 7 to 10 per cent, but, when various service charges were added, the total interest ran much higher. Until well after 1900 the farmer was the particular victim of the loan shark.

Borrowing even at high rates may not be ruinous in an era of advancing prices. Such was not the case during the postwar decades. Even before the devastating panic of 1873, agricultural prices had commenced their downward trend, a trend that, with respites in certain years, continued until the middle nineties. A mortgage contracted when wheat was a dollar, corn 50 cents, or cotton 12 cents was unbearable when wheat dropped to 50 cents, corn to 25 cents, or cotton to 6 cents, for it was impossible for the farmer to double his labor and the area under cultivation. While the prices of the commodities that the farmer sold were declining, the prices of the manufactured commodities that he bought, protected by high tariffs and business consolidation, showed no similar trend. In many cases, particularly in railroad freight rates, the opposite was true. The farmer of the period after the Civil War understood but vaguely, if at all, the significance of the new day, but he was quick to discern the danger to his own interests in the abuses of the railroads, in the results of industrial monopoly, and in the policy of currency contraction. Here was something tangible that he could fight, and it was along this front that the battle was waged.

Although the debtor farmer, from the close of the Civil War, persistently opposed currency deflation, the first great agrarian battle of this period was directed against the railroads. The early years of the railroad were characterized by the one great desire, that they be built at whatever sacrifice and cost. As time went on, however, and the abuses of unregulated expansion and competition developed, the attitude of the public became more critical. The railroads were, indeed, open to serious charges. They had been built at exorbitant expense by such construction companies as the Crédit Mobilier (page 391) and had fallen later into the hands of financial manipulators who milked them of their profits and piled up a capitalization of watered stock upon which they endeavored to pay dividends through high freight rates and passenger fares. Bitter warfare at competitive points led to discrimination of various kinds among shippers, particularly in the form of rebates, and in charging more for a short haul under monopoly conditions than for a long haul under stiff competition. This abuse bore heavily upon the farmer, who had no choice as to the railroad that would carry his products to the market, and the railroads were quick to make the farmer pay for the losses that they might sustain in carrying industrial freight between competitive points. The efforts of the railroads to save themselves by pooling arrangements only served to heighten the wrath of the farmers. Lack of any feeling of responsibility to the public, coupled with unfair discrimination, was accompanied by a widespread policy of political corruption, which extended from the government of the smallest town to the halls of Congress. The lavish distribution of free passes was but the mildest form of public debauchery. Charles Francis Adams, Jr., himself a railroad president, put it tersely when he wrote, "The system was indeed fairly honeycombed with jobbery and corruption." [1]

Although the farmers as a class felt the railroad abuses most acutely, agitation for control of the railroads was in no way limited to the agricultural classes. The city shipper also could be ruined by rate discrimination, and the fate of a whole community could be determined by it. It was, nevertheless, in the agricultural states of the Middle West that the agitation first became effective, and, as it happened, largely through the efforts of farmers' organizations. Agricultural organizations have existed in the United States since the latter part of the eighteenth century, but their efforts were almost entirely local until after the Civil War. The first great national organization was the Patrons of Husbandry, founded in 1867 by Oliver Hudson Kelley, formerly a clerk in the Bureau of Agriculture, who, after a trip through the South, became convinced that a social and educational organization among the farmers was necessary to promote progressive agricultural methods. The Patrons of Husbandry filled a real

[1] C. F. Adams, Jr., *The Railroad Problem*, 126.

need and by 1875 had grown to include some 20,000 "Granges" or local lodges and a membership of at least 750,000. In its early years its strength was centered in the Middle West. "We are not enemies of the railroads . . . or of any corporation," asserted the National Grange in 1874, and "we wage no aggressive warfare against any other interest whatever." Nevertheless, the Granges gave to the irate farmers a chance to meet with one another in an organization to air their grievances, and the influence of the society was considered so powerful that the first state laws to regulate common carriers were popularly termed "Granger laws" and the legal cases arising therefrom "Granger cases."

With agrarian discontent now mobilized and led by farmers' organizations, legislation was inevitable. It began in Illinois, where the legislature, in 1869, passed an act limiting the railroads to "just, reasonable and uniform rates," and where the new state constitution (1870) instructed the legislature to "pass laws to correct abuses and to prevent unjust discrimination and extortion in the rates of freight and passenger tariffs." By a series of legislative enactments during the next three years, Illinois set up a board of railway warehouse commissioners, provided for maximum passenger and freight charges, regulated warehouses, and provided a general railway incorporation act. The same years saw similar acts in Minnesota, Iowa, and Wisconsin, and a great impetus was given throughout the country to the movement for railroad-regulation. Some of this early "Granger legislation" was extreme, unscientific, and possibly confiscatory, but it struck at certain outstanding evils: unreasonable rates, discriminations between persons and places, pooling agreements and consolidations, and the granting of free passes. It set in motion the movement for railroad-regulation and marked out the essential objectives. "Several of the principal features of American railroad legislation," says Professor Buck, "can be looked upon as primarily Granger in the origin." [2]

THE COMING OF FEDERAL REGULATION

The opposition of the railroads to the Granger legislation was aggressive and persistent. They attacked it as a violation of the fourteenth amendment, even questioning the power of the state to regulate public utilities. They insisted that state regulation was a violation of the power of Congress, granted by the Constitution, to regulate interstate commerce, and they asserted vigorously that the reasonableness of a rate was a judicial and not a legislative question. Pressing these contentions year after year in the courts, the railroads finally broke the power of state legislation and made federal regulation inevitable.

[2] S. J. Buck, *The Granger Movement*, 205.

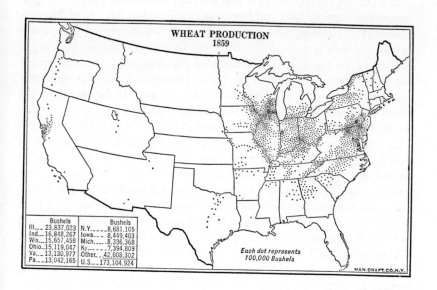

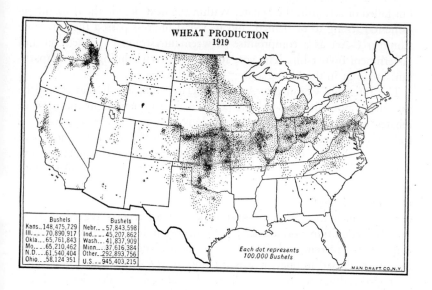

In an earlier chapter we have told the story of how the right of the government to regulate rates and fares was established in the case of Munn *v.* Illinois (1876) and in that of Peik *v.* Chicago and Northwestern Railway (1876) and then how the Supreme Court, more than a decade later in the Minnesota rate case (1889), succumbed to the railroads' contention (reversing its previous position) that the reasonableness of a rate was ultimately a judicial rather than a legislative question (page 415). In the meantime, the effectiveness of state regulation was further impaired by the decision in the Wabash case (Wabash, St. Louis and Pacific Railway *v.* Illinois, 1886). This involved an Illinois law forbidding a greater charge for a short haul than for a long haul, and the court now held that a state could exercise no control over transportation beyond its limits. "That species of regulation," said the court, "is one which must be . . . of a general and national character, and can not be safely and wisely remitted to local rules and local regulations." After this there could be little doubt that further development of railroad-regulation would be through federal rather than state agencies.

Years before the Wabash decision had made federal regulation inevitable, the demand for national action had developed. A Senate committee, reporting in 1874, had urged government construction of transportation facilities for the purpose of offering competition to the railroads, and in 1878 a bill aiming at the worst of the railroad abuses had passed the House but failed of action in the Senate. Within the next decade the demand became too strong to be denied, and in 1887 Congress passed the Interstate Commerce Act as a compromise between unrestrained competition and government ownership. The vote for it was overwhelming and nonpartisan: 219 to 41 in the House and 37 to 12 in the Senate.

The Interstate Commerce Act (1) declared that all charges should be just and reasonable; (2) forbade personal discriminations in the form of rebates or otherwise and discriminations between localities, classes of freight, or connecting lines; (3) forbade a greater charge for a short haul than for a long; (4) forbade pooling and traffic agreements; and (5) ordered that all rates should be publicly posted and that no advance might be made except after ten days' notice. The enforcement of the act was placed in the hands of the Interstate Commerce Commission of five members, to which the railroads must make annual reports regarding their financial condition and rates. The commission had the power to hear complaints and render decisions in the form of orders to the carriers. If the roads refused to obey, it was the duty of the commission to institute court proceedings to force compliance. For almost two decades the Interstate Commerce Act represented an ideal rather than a consummation. Opposition of the railroads, constant and widespread violation, court decisions that stripped the commission of what little power it had, and the inability of the commission to enforce its decisions except through long, costly, and uncertain litigation soon made it evident that the act had failed · in its purpose of providing adequate federal regulation. The commission became little more than a fact-finding body. The significance of the act rests chiefly in the fact that it inaugurated the policy of federal regulation of railroads.

THE CURRENCY PROBLEM

Although railroad abuses contributed to the woes of agriculture by reducing the margin of profit, the primary difficulty was the declining prices of agricultural commodities. While overproduction was the essential cause, the postwar deflation was an important factor. To understand the battle over currency that was waged steadily from the end of the Civil War to the historic campaign of 1896, it is necessary to review briefly the earlier history of currency. In 1792, it will be remembered, Congress, upon the advice of Hamilton (page 251), adopted a system of free and unlimited coinage of gold and silver at a ratio of 15:1. While 15:1 was an accurate ratio in 1792, the increase in the world's production of silver lowered the price of that metal, with the result that silver was overvalued at the legal ratio and gold, under the working of Gresham's law, disappeared from circulation. In an effort to bring back gold and achieve a more accurate ratio, Congress in 1834 changed the ratio from 15:1 to 15.98:1, or approximately 16:1, by reducing the content of the gold dollar to 23.22 grains of pure gold. Under the new ratio gold was overvalued, and it became even more so after the new discoveries of that metal in California in 1848. As a consequence, the silver dollar disappeared, and the government kept fractional silver in circulation only by debasing it in 1853. So many years had elapsed since silver had been presented at the mint for the coinage of dollars that Congress in 1873 dropped the silver dollar from the list of coins that might be minted.

In the meantime, the destruction of the second Bank of the United States eliminated its notes from circulation; American currency at the opening of the Civil War, therefore, consisted of gold, subsidiary coins, and the notes of the state banks,[3] the value of the latter depending on the standing of the individual bank. In December, 1861, the banks, followed shortly by the federal government, suspended specie payments, thus eliminating gold from circulation. Partly to fill the gap in the currency and partly to help pay for the war, the government by a succession of acts authorized the printing of $450,000,000 of legal-tender paper money, known as greenbacks, and receivable for all debts public and private except payment of customs duties and interest on the public debt (page 357). They had no backing

---

[3] Such banks, of course, operated under state charters.

except the credit of the government, and their value in terms of gold fluctuated with the prospects of Northern victory, declining by 1864 to less than fifty cents. In addition to the greenbacks, the Civil War introduced another type of currency in the form of national-bank notes. In the hope of creating a standarized paper currency, of driving out the innumerable varieties of state banknotes, of creating a powerful financial interest behind the government, and of creating a wider market for United States bonds, Congress in 1863 established the national banks (page 357). Before many years the national-bank notes (which the government issued on the credit of its bonds) became a leading element in the American currency system.

The Civil War boom, in conjunction with suspension of specie payment and the introduction of fiat money, produced a rapid economic expansion and drove prices skyward. The end of the war reversed the tendency and, by bringing hardship to those in debt, made the problem of currency a major economic and political issue for three decades. Throughout this period the general attitude of successive administrations was to favor "sound money" even if it meant deflation and to oppose the rising demand for an easing of the currency situation. Inflation may have injured the creditor class in the years of the Civil War, but the situation was now reversed, and the demand for a currency inflation that would restore money to the value at which debts had been contracted was insistent.

No one presented the issue with more convincing clarity than did Senator Jones of Nevada, speaking in the Senate in May, 1890:

> Any serious enhancement in the value of the unit of money between the time of making a contract or incurring a debt and the date of fulfillment or maturity always works hardship and frequently ruin to the contractor or debtor.
>
> Three-fourths of the business enterprises of this country are conducted on borrowed capital. Three-fourths of the homes and farms that stand in the name of the actual occupants have been bought on time, and a very large proportion of them are mortgaged for the payment of some part of the purchase money.
>
> Under the operation of a shrinkage in the volume of money, this enormous mass of borrowers, at the maturity of their respective debts, though nominally paying no more than the amount borrowed, with interest, are, in reality, in the amount of the principal alone, returning a percentage of value greater than they received, more than in equity they contracted to pay and oftentimes more, in substance, than they profited by the loan. To the man of business this percentage in many cases constitutes the difference between success and failure. Thus a shrinkage in the volume of money is a prolific source of bankruptcy and ruin.[4]

[4] Fifty-first Congress, First Session, *Congressional Record,* Vol. XXI, Part II, appendix, 239.

GREENBACKS AND SILVER

The immediate problems involving currency after the Civil War were primarily three: the constitutional status of the greenbacks, the question whether the existing issues should be enlarged or contracted, and the question whether specie payment should be resumed. The first issue came before the Supreme Court in Hepburn *v.* Griswold (1870), when the court ruled that the Constitution gave Congress no power to make paper money legal tender for debts contracted before the law was passed. A review of the case by the court with a changed personnel in Knox *v.* Lee (1871) reversed the earlier decision and made the greenbacks legal tender for contracts made before or after they had been issued. The question as to the volume of greenbacks developed quickly when, in 1866, the treasury was authorized to retire them. In the presidential campaign of 1868 the Democrats inserted in their platform the "Ohio idea," a plan to increase the circulation of legal-tender notes by providing that all United States bonds, except where there was a specific agreement to the contrary, should be paid in legal tender.

The failure of the greenback advocates in this campaign only served to stiffen the fight, and a few years later a political party, the Greenback Party, was formed, which reached the climax of its strength in 1878. Its presidential candidate, Peter Cooper, polled but 81,000 votes in 1876, but in the congressional elections of 1878 the Greenback candidates won a million votes, chiefly among the farmers, and elected numerous state officials and fifteen representatives to Congress. Even this was no true indication of their real strength, for both major parties were shot through with inflationary sentiment. Their standard-bearer in 1880 was General James B. Weaver, a brilliant orator, a sound thinker, and one of the ablest men to appear in public life during these years. After a strenuous campaign he polled but 308,000 votes, and after that the Greenback Party declined rapidly, merging in 1884 with the Antimonopolists. While the Greenback Party urged various reforms, its chief interest was in currency inflation, the platform of 1878 denouncing "the limiting of the legal-tender quality of greenbacks, the changing of currency-bonds into coin bonds, the demonetization of the silver dollar, the excepting of bonds from taxation, the contraction of the circulating medium, the proposed forced resumption of specie payment, and the prodigal waste of public lands."

Though the Greenbackers lost their fight for a larger volume of greenbacks, they finally succeeded in 1878 in preventing further contraction, and the amount of greenbacks then outstanding, $346,681,016, is the amount circulating today. The final result was in the nature of a compromise, and it virtually ended the effort to inflate by means of greenbacks. The opposition of the Greenbackers and others to the resumption of specie payment, however, failed utterly. The Republicans, defeated in the congressional elections of 1874, hastened in the following year to pass the Resumption Act calling for the restoration of specie payments on January 1, 1879. The act, quite naturally, was bitterly opposed, for it meant a further deflation of prices as greenbacks were brought to a par with gold, but the opposition could never muster sufficient strength to repeal the act. With the resumption of specie payment the nation, after an interlude of eighteen years, found itself again with a currency based upon hard money.

The greenback compromise and the resumption of specie payments in no way ended the demand for inflation. The battle simply shifted to the silver front, where it remained for two decades. The dropping of the silver dollar in 1873, which had been accomplished with but slight comment and but little opposition, had occurred, curiously enough, simultaneously with the beginning of a long decline in the price of silver. This decline was chiefly due to the discovery of new deposits in the West at a time when the market was being seriously curtailed by the monetary policies of the European nations. Germany in 1871 and Holland and the Scandinavian countries from 1873 to 1875 adopted the gold standard, while the Latin Monetary Union (France, Switzerland, Belgium, Italy, and Greece) ended free coinage of silver and limited the coinage of that metal. In the middle of the nineteenth century England and Portugal were the only European gold-standard countries; by 1880 there was not a mint in Europe open to the free coinage of silver, and every nation had gone on the gold standard. As a result, the bullion value of 371¼ grains of pure silver (contents of the United States silver dollar), which was over $1.02 in 1873, fell to 88.6 cents by 1880, 52.3 cents by 1896, and 48 cents by 1900.

As the price of silver declined, it became evident that, if free and un-limited coinage at the old ratio of 16:1 could be restored, a flood of silver would be presented at the mints. After enough silver had been coined, gold would be driven out (Gresham's law), and the nation would go on a silver basis, with a resulting inflation of prices. Such was the dream of the inflationists, who now denounced the elimination of the silver dollar as the "crime of 1873" and clamored for a restoration of free and unlimited coinage of gold and silver at the old ratio of 16:1. In this, of course, they were aided and abetted by the silver-mining interests, who provided most of the financial backing for the campaigns. Beginning in 1876, a succession of bills looking toward a remonetization of silver was introduced in Congress, backed particularly by the debtor agricultural states of the South and West and by the silver-producing regions. The bill that finally passed in 1878 was introduced by Representative Richard P. ("Silver Dick") Bland of Missouri and originally called for free and unlimited coinage at 16:1. In the Senate the bill was changed from free and unlimited to a limited coinage, the Secretary of the Treasury being instructed to purchase not less than $2,000,000 or more than $4,000,000 worth of silver a month and coin it into silver dollars. In both houses the bill passed by a majority of over two to one. That the masses were in favor of inflation there seems to be no doubt. Said the chairman of the resolutions committee of a mass meeting in Chicago, "We would in this manner arouse the slumbering consciousness of the President and his advisers to some apprehension of the fact that there is a thunderstorm brewing in the West, and that unless they have a care, somebody is likely to be hit by the lightning of public indignation, unless they concede the just demands of the people." [5] Despite this warning, Hayes vetoed the bill, but it was quickly passed over his veto.

Although it was a compromise that satisfied few, the Bland-Allison Act nevertheless remained in force for twelve years, and under its operation 378,166,000 silver dollars were coined. This was a considerable amount of silver, but, to the surprise of many, the large government purchases failed to raise the price of that metal, to stay declining commodity prices, or to drive out gold through the workings of Gresham's law. The failure to drive out gold was not due alone to the limited amount of silver injected into the currency system. While silver dollars were being added to the monetary supply, banknote circulation was contracting as Civil War bonds were paid off. Furthermore, the ordinary monetary needs of business were increasing.

Silver advocates considered the Bland-Allison Act merely an opening wedge, and agitation continued throughout the next decade to liberalize it. This agitation was strengthened by the declining price of silver and of agricultural commodities and was supported by the numerous farmers' organizations that appeared during the eighties in the South and West to take the place of the declining Granges. In the South these farmers' organizations coalesced into the National Farmers' Alliance and Industrial Union, which, by 1889, was reaching for a union with a similar National Farmers' Alliance in the Northwest. This stirring of the farmers brought into being in the same year various independent or populist parties, which conducted a spirited campaign in 1890, electing nine representatives and two senators and pledging twice that number of Republican and Democratic congressmen to their principles. Encouraged by their success in 1890, the National People's or Populist Party was launched in 1891.

Before the elections of 1890, however, inflationists had written a new currency law upon the statute books. This was the Sherman Silver Purchase Act of 1890, which required the treasury to purchase 4,500,000 ounces of silver bullion each month, for which treasury notes having full legal-tender value were to be given in payment. This amount not only absorbed

[5] Quoted by C. R. Williams, *Life of Rutherford B. Hayes,* II, 120.

practically the entire output of American mines but doubled the amount of silver being injected each month into the currency system. From the point of view of the opponents of inflation, there was nothing good about the bill except that it provided for purchase by weight rather than by value, so that, no matter how long silver might drop in value, only a stated amount could be purchased. The act was in part the result of political jobbery; it resulted from a deal whereby Eastern Republicans supported it in return for Western Republican backing of the McKinley tariff passed in the same year.

The amount of silver called for in the Sherman Silver Purchase Act was quite enough, as was evident three years later, to drive out gold and inflate prices, but as yet this was not clear to the debt-burdened farmers, and in the following years the inflationary movement reached its climax. Despite the fact that the Sherman Act absorbed all American silver, the price of that metal continued to decline, a situation that stirred silver-miners and silver politicians to renewed activity at the same time that the agricultural situation spurred on the development of the Populist Party. Meeting in national convention in July of 1892, some 1300 delegates nominated the former Greenbacker, James B. Weaver of Iowa, as their presidential candidate and adopted a (for those days) radical program.

> We meet [said the preamble of one of the most remarkable and moving documents in American political history] in the midst of a nation brought to the verge of moral, political and material ruin. Corruption dominates the ballot-box, the legislatures, the Congress, and touches even the ermine of the bench. The people are demoralized. . . .The newspapers are largely subsidized or muzzled, public opinion silenced, business prostrated, homes covered with mortgages, labor impoverished, and the land concentrating in the hands of capitalists. The urban workmen are denied the right to organize for self-protection, a hireling standing army unrecognized by our laws, is established to shoot them down, and they are rapidly degenerating into European conditions. The fruits of the toil of millions are boldly stolen to build up colossal fortunes for a few, unprecedented in the history of mankind; and the possessors of these in turn, despise the Republic and endanger liberty. From the same prolific womb of governmental injustice we breed the two great classes—tramps and millionaires.

Continuing with a withering attack, they stated their platform: free and unlimited coinage of silver at a ratio of 16:1; a graduated income tax; postal savings banks; government operation of railroads, telephones, and telegraphs; direct election of United States senators; the secret ballot; and the initiative and referendum. Of all these demands, inflation through silver was closest to their hearts.

With the panic of 1893 the battle over silver became even more acute.

Like every other panic, that of 1893 represented the climax of a business cycle produced by overexpansion. President Cleveland, however, convinced that it was due wholly to the fear of business men that the gold standard was endangered, called Congress into special session and demanded the repeal of the Sherman Silver Purchase Act. The act had been in force only three years, and only $155,931,002 had been purchased, but it was enough to start Gresham's law to work. Congress, after weeks of debate, repealed the act, and Cleveland, by means of bond sales, succeeded in keeping sufficient gold in the treasury to prevent the currency from shifting to a silver standard. For this Cleveland was hailed as a hero by the creditor East, but to the inflationist of the West and South, who for two decades had struggled to bring inflation in just this way, he was a traitor and a villain. Hot with wrath, the Western and Southern Democrats threw over the leadership of Cleveland in 1896, coalesced with the Populist Party, nominated William Jennings Bryan on a platform of 16:1, and gathered their forces for a mighty effort.

Introductory chapters on the farmers' uprising are C. and M. Beard, *The Rise of American Civilization,* Chap. XXII, and H. U. Faulkner, *American Economic History,* Chap. XXV. The story of the Granger movement is briefly told in S. J. Buck, *The Agrarian Crusade* (Chronicles of America), and more fully in his *The Granger Movement,* Chaps. I, IX. On the Populist movement see S. J. Buck, *The Agrarian Crusade,* and J. D. Hicks, *The Populist Revolt,* Chaps. VIII–XIII. Aspects of the financial history are in D. R. Dewey, *Financial History of the United States,* Chaps. XII–XIX. Source material is in F. Flügel and H. U. Faulkner, *Readings in the Economic and Social History of the United States,* 741–750, and H. S. Commager, *Documents of American History,* Vol. II, 91–94, 97–99, 113–116, 118–124, 129–138, 142–152.

Chapter XXVII

POLITICAL HISTORY, 1876–1896

Nowhere in the modern world have economic issues exercised so potent an influence on politics. . . . Nowhere has party organization been developed to such dangerous perfection.

JAMES BRYCE

POLITICAL BACKGROUND

From 1861, when Abraham Lincoln took office, to 1913 (with the exception of the two administrations of Cleveland), the Republican Party had control of the executive branch of the government. This power, which was obtained in the first instance by a split in the Democratic Party over the slavery issue, was maintained through the Civil War by the withdrawal of Southern Democrats and the demoralization of Northern Democrats. It was perpetuated during the reconstruction period by the disfranchisement of Southern leaders and the enfranchisement of the blacks. Even after the close of political reconstruction the party maintained its prestige as the savior of the Union. As early as 1860 the Republican Party had tied itself closely to Northern industrialists, and this union became stronger in the war and postwar years as it sponsored protective tariffs, aided railroads, opposed inflation, and became the political instrument of the rising industrial capitalism. Supported by manufacturers and skilled laborers in the East, by the farmer who had profited from the homestead acts, by the veteran who had fought in the Union army, and by the crusader who had cast his vote against the extension of slavery and would continue to protect the freedman, the Republican power was maintained by the prestige of success and by a closely knit political machine supported by the moneyed interests of the time. It was, moreover, the "respectable party" of the period, but how tenuous was its claim to such an attribute is illustrated only too well by the scandals of the Grant administration. Its weakness, in fact, was its long, continuous occupation of office and the low political and business morality of many of its leaders, which laid it open to the constant attacks of its opponents. It was this that developed a strong independent or "mugwump" element in the party—men who refused to be bound by strict party discipline, who insisted upon a high standard of political morality, and who differed with the dominant element in regard to such matters as the Southern policy and the maintenance of a high protective tariff.

The Democratic Party, despite its failure to win the presidential office until the campaign of 1884, was far from being as weak as might superficially appear. It developed real opposition during the war, forcing the Republicans to nominate for the vice-presidency in 1864 Andrew Johnson, a War Democrat. A large group of independent Republicans had joined with the Democrats in 1872, and in 1876, despite the legal enfranchisement of the blacks, the Democrats had actually polled the greater number of votes. Beginning with the forty-fourth Congress in 1875, there was a period of twenty-two years in which, except for short intervals in 1881 and 1889, they controlled at least one branch of the federal legislature. The role of the Democratic Party, therefore, in the three decades after the war, was primarily one of opposition and criticism. During most of the period there was no clear-cut issue to divide the parties. Except for the reconstruction issue, which was over by 1877, and a brief period in the late eighties and early nineties when Cleveland forced his party to take a stand on the tariff, there was little of fundamental difference between them. Even on the tariff, when it came to a "show-down," it was found that the Democratic Party harbored many high-protectionists. On railroad control, on antitrust legislation, on the currency, and, in fact, on all the great important economic questions, the battles transcended party lines.

It is true that the Democrats harked back to the principles of Jefferson and Jackson, professed faith in the common man, opposed extension of federal authority, and talked about economy in government, but in the milieu of postwar conditions this was hardly of prime significance. The essential similarity that existed during most of these years between the two major parties was well expressed by Lord Bryce:

> . . . neither party has any clean-cut principles, any distinct tenets. Both have tradition. Both claim to have tendencies. Both have certainly war cries, organizations, interests, enlisted in their support. But those interests are in the main the interests of getting or keeping the patronage of government. Tenets and policies, points of political doctrine and points of political practice have all but vanished. . . . The American parties now continue to exist, because they have existed. The mill has been constructed, and its machinery goes on turning, even if there is no grist to grind. . . . An eminent journalist remarked to me in 1908 that the two parties were like two bottles. Each bore a label denoting the kind of liquor it contained, but each was empty.[1]

[1] James Bryce, *The American Commonwealth* (revised edition, 1912), II, 21, 24, 29.

Since the major parties displayed but minor differences, it is necessary to examine the third parties to discover essential conflicts, and even here the picture is confused. The Prohibition Party, which presented its first candidates in a presidential election in 1872, stood for an issue that was hardly fundamental politically or economically. The National Greenback Party (Greenback Labor Party in 1878) had a radical tinge, but its essential demand was inflation through paper money, and faith in this solution was shared by many prominent Republicans and Democrats, who nevertheless stayed in their own parties. The Populist Party, on the other hand, had in it the makings of a real party of protest against existing tendencies, expressed, for example, in its demand for government ownership of railroads, telegraphs, and telephones, but its primary demand was for inflation through silver, and this demand was so widely held that the Democrats adopted it in 1896. The taking over by the major parties of popular third-party planks has, indeed, been so usual that one finds here an explanation for the weakness and brief existence of many third parties and for the continual strength of the old major organizations. With the exception of the short-lived Populist Party, no minor party challenged in any fundamental way the existing economic order until the founding of the Socialist Labor Party in 1892 and the Social Democratic Party in 1898. The former never developed beyond the status of a tiny protesting group; the latter grew steadily in the years from 1900 to 1914. Both will be discussed in a later chapter.

Although there was but slight difference in the philosophy and program of the two major parties, both displayed great skill in establishing discipline and organization. To the existing permanent national committee, which looked after the general welfare of the party, particularly in national campaigns, was added a congressional committee to work in congressional elections. Office-holders formed the skeleton of the political machinery, individuals who acted as key men in their respective localities and who were regularly levied upon for the sinews of war. In this way the government itself helped to finance and perpetuate the party in power. Outside financial help came from business big and little, which hoped to gain economically by the perpetuation in office of one group or the substitution of another. The masses were kept in line by the organization of political clubs, by mass demonstrations, which often took the form of torch-light processions, and by propaganda of all kinds. The actual buying of votes was common enough, particularly in the days before the secret ballot was introduced. How this might work in a doubtful state like Indiana is illustrated by a letter apparently written by the treasurer of the National Republican Committee, who instructed the leaders in that state to "divide the floaters into blocks of five and put a trusted man with the necessary funds in charge of these five, and make him responsible that none get away, and that all vote our ticket."

Closely knit political organizations of this type made it difficult for men of independence to achieve public office, and lawmaking bodies, municipal, state, and even federal, did little more than carry out the will of the machine, and the will of the machine was the will of the boss, a professional politician who might or might not hold political office. With a substitution of names the picture that Elihu Root drew of New York might apply with equal truth during these years to almost any state in the Union:

> From the days of Fenton, and Conkling, and Arthur, and Cornell, and Platt, from the days of David B. Hill, down to the present time, the government of the state has presented two different lines of activity, one of the constitutional and statutory officers of the state, and the other of the party leaders,—they call them party bosses. They call the system—I do not coin the phrase, I adopt it because it carries its own meaning—the system they call "invisible government." For I do not remember how many years, Mr. Conkling was the supreme ruler in this state; the governor did not count, the legislatures did not count; comptrollers and secretaries of state and what not, did not count. It was what Mr. Conkling said; and in a great outburst of public rage he was pulled down.
>
> Then Mr. Platt ruled the state; for nigh upon twenty years he ruled it. It was not the governor; it was not the legislature; it was not any elected officers; it was Mr. Platt. And the capitol was not here [in Albany]; it was at 49 Broadway; with Mr. Platt and his lieutenants. It makes no difference what name you give, whether you call it Fenton or Conkling or Cornell or Arthur or Platt, or by the names of men now living. The ruler of the state during the greater part of the forty years of my acquaintance with the state government has not been any man authorized by the constitution or by the law.[2]

The vast power of the machine, combined with the necessity of large funds to support this type of politics, not only called for large contributions from office-holders and business interests looking for franchises and other favors that legislatures might grant, but also stimulated graft of all kinds. The tie-up of local political machines with the vice interests of the underworld was notorious, as was the corruption of legislators, who repeatedly "sold out" the interests of the community to franchise-grabbing corporations. Low as was the political morality of the time, there were many political leaders who were scrupulously honest, and the citizens were not generally callous or indifferent; the picture of corrupt politics stirred the better element of the voters to intermittent protests and occasional house-cleanings.

[2] Elihu Root, *Addresses on Government and Citizenship*, 202.

National politics were on a somewhat higher level than municipal and state, but left much to be desired. In the federal government students of politics watched with interest the decline in the power of the President after the death of Lincoln, and the rise in the prestige of the Senate. If there ever had been the nicely balanced power envisaged by the Fathers, it was rarely apparent between 1860 and the end of the century, although Hayes and Cleveland fought to maintain the importance of the presidential office, and the House of Representatives, under the guidance of Speaker Thomas B. Reed in the session 1889–1891, reasserted its power for a brief period.

THE ADMINISTRATION OF HAYES

After eight years of the Grant administration and the bitterness engendered by the disputed election (pages 395–398), the nation greeted the advent of Hayes with a sigh of relief—at least, such was the sentiment of all but the professional politicians. With the latter, both Republican and Democratic, Hayes's relations became quickly strained, and his administration was a four-year period of political turmoil. Methodical, conscientious, independent, and adhering scrupulously to the highest standards of private and public morality, he introduced a chilling note into the free and easy atmosphere of federal politics. Republican politicians did not like his cabinet, partly because he had not found places for their friends and partly because they were opposed to the Southerner, Key, and the reformer, Carl Schurz (page 398). Confirmation of these cabinet members was delayed until it became obvious that the nation supported Hayes, but the Senate retaliated in succeeding months by rejecting fifty-one nominations, a larger number than had yet been rejected by a Senate of the same political faith as the President. The withdrawal of federal troops from the South and the collapse of the carpetbag governments in South Carolina and Louisiana further embittered old-time Republican politicians (the "Stalwarts," as they proudly called themselves), who looked upon this as a rank betrayal of their party.

Even worse, from the point of view of the politician, were the mild efforts of Hayes toward civil-service reform. In June he issued an executive order forbidding United States officeholders to take part in the management of political organizations and to contribute to assessments for political purposes. This order struck at the root of the existing system and was such a radical departure that Hayes failed to enforce it. That he was in earnest, however, in his belief in reform was evidenced by his willingness to fight out the issue with Congress relative to conditions in the New York Custom House. A commission to investigate, appointed by Secretary Sherman, found inefficiency, neglect, a superfluity of workers, and the appointment of officials subordinated to the needs of the local political machine. Reforms recommended by the commission were ordered by the administration. When Chester A. Arthur, collector of the port and prominent in New York politics (later President of the United States), and Alonzo B. Cornell, naval officer and chairman of the state and national Republican committees, refused to carry out the reforms, Hayes suspended them. Led by Senator Conkling of New York, the Senate refused for a time to confirm the nomination of their successors, but eventually capitulated.

While Hayes was rapidly losing the support of the Republican "Stalwarts" in Congress, the Democrats lost no opportunity to make the situation more difficult. The House, under Democratic control, appointed a committee (Potter Committee) to investigate the legality of Hayes's title to the presidency. The Democratic majority reported that he had not been legally elected, the Republican minority that he had been. In the meantime, the Republican Senate had appointed a similar committee, which subpoenaed 30,000 Western Union telegrams that had been sent during the election. The deciphering of the Democratic telegrams showed efforts at bribery, which so damaged their cause that the investigation injured rather than helped them. Hayes's last Congress (the forty-sixth) had Democratic majorities in both houses, which were intent upon repealing the "force bills" passed during the reconstruction years to ensure federal supervision of Southern elections. Not having a sufficient majority to pass them over the President's veto, the Democrats resorted to tacking "riders" on to appropriation bills in the hope that the President would accept the "riders" rather than lose the bills. Taking the position that this was an effort to "place the Executive under the coercive dictation of a bare majority of the two houses of Congress" and a "mode of evading the Constitutional provision as to the President's participation in legislation," Hayes vetoed the appropriation acts containing the "riders" and eventually won the fight. The policy of Hayes in this struggle restored to some degree the standing of the executive, and it was generally approved even by many who believed that the time had come to repeal the "force acts."

The most important piece of legislation during the Hayes administration was the Bland-Allison Act discussed in the last chapter. Hayes vetoed it on the ground that "it authorizes what I think is dishonest," but he carried it out loyally when it was passed over his veto. The fact that party lines broke down on this bill illustrates the subordination of politics to economics and the lack of a clear-cut difference between the parties on economic problems. In the domestic scene the outstanding event of the four years was the great railroad strike of 1877, which Hayes saw only as a disorder to be repressed by federal troops. Hayes, in fact, had little, if any, conception of the social and economic implications of either the drive for inflation or the labor uprising of 1877, but neither did other political leaders of his time. Limited as was his economic outlook, Hayes on the whole gave to the nation an honest, courageous, and progressive administration and did much to rehabilitate the Republican Party in the mind of the independent voter.

GARFIELD AND ARTHUR

The Hayes administration was hardly under way before political leaders of both parties were laying plans for the election of 1880. Regretfully contemplating the happy years of the Grant administration, many of the "Stalwart" bosses urged another term for Grant, arguing that the two-term precedent applied only to consecutive terms. In this group were Senators Platt and Conkling of New York, Don Cameron of Pennsylvania, and General Logan of Illinois, who whipped a majority of their delegations into line for Grant. Other political leaders, who were opposed to the third term, picked the magnetic and popular James G. Blaine of Maine as the man most likely to beat Grant. Independents favored Senator George G. Edmunds of Vermont or John Sherman of Ohio. The plot of the Grant cohorts to nominate their candidate by enforcing the unit rule in voting was foiled by a combination of opponents, and, when it was found impossible to get a majority for either Grant or Blaine, the Blaine and Sherman forces joined in the thirty-sixth ballot to nominate a compromise "dark horse" candidate, James A. Garfield of Ohio. As a sop to the Grant adherents, who had held their 306 votes intact throughout the convention, the nomination for the vice-presidency went to Chester A. Arthur. The platform contained strong planks for aid to veterans and exclusion of the Chinese, an evasive sentence on the tariff, and a reluctant advocacy of civil-service reform—a typical platform of the day, carefully avoiding fundamentals. Despite the fact that Tilden's crown of martyrdom had been somewhat tarnished by election exposures, he could have had the Democratic nomination. Upon his refusal the Democrats, anxious to emphasize their loyalty, nominated Winfield S. Hancock, a Union general of sterling character but without political experience. Their platform bitterly denounced the "great fraud" of 1876 but otherwise resembled that of the Republicans. The Greenbackers nominated James B. Weaver (page 445).

Lack of issues made the campaign of 1880 an apathetic one. Garfield won by a popular plurality of less than 9500 votes in a total of about nine million but by an electoral vote of 214 to 155. He carried all the states in the North and West except New Jersey, Nevada, and part (five electoral votes) of California. Although Garfield had been a prominent member of the House of Representatives since 1863, it is not easy to estimate his stature as a statesman. A skillful orator, a man endowed with commanding presence and great intellectual power, he represented well the American ideal of a self-made man. Born of New England parentage in a log cabin in Ohio, he had worked his way upward as canal boy, carpenter, and teacher; he had attended Williams College and found himself at the age of twenty-six president of Hiram Eclectic Institute. A distinguished volunteer officer in the Civil War, he was mustered out in 1863 with the rank of major general. Elected to Congress, he served as chairman of important House committees and was minority leader in the House during the Hayes administration. Upon his friends, who were many, he left the impression of a vacillating politician and a person without great moral force. His short period as President, nevertheless, revealed Garfield's strength of will in fighting a factional political battle to a finish.

As a compromise candidate Garfield made every effort at the beginning to reconcile the various factions, but, when this became impossible, he threw over the "Stalwarts" of New York and cast in his lot with the "Half-Breeds." The announcement of his cabinet [3] alienated Conkling, and, when Garfield nominated W. H. Robertson, leader of the anti-Conkling Republicans in New York, as Collector of the Port of New York, the fight was precipitated. When the Senate held up confirmation, Garfield withdrew all nominations except that of Robertson, thus serving notice upon senators that their own candidates would have to wait upon the settlement of this case. This pressure was too strong, and the two New York senators, Conkling and Platt, realizing that they could not prevent confirmation, resigned their seats and returned to Albany for vindication.[4] While this battle was raging, Postmaster General James set about investigating charges of graft connected with the letting of contracts for the carrying of mail over the so-called "star routes," stage lines chiefly in the Far West, and involving Second Assistant Postmaster Brady, ex-Senator S. W. Dorsey, secretary of the Republican National Committee, and other politicians. Although the investigations and trials continued until 1883, when only one conviction of a minor individual was obtained, the political atmosphere in Washington became increasingly tense.

On July 2, as Garfield was setting out for a class reunion at Williams College, he was shot by a disappointed office-seeker, who exclaimed, "I am a Stalwart and I want Arthur to become President." After a courageous

[3] In it were James G. Blaine, Secretary of State (bitterly disliked by the Conkling faction); William Windom of Minnesota, Secretary of the Treasury (opposed in the East); R. T. Lincoln of Illinois, Secretary of War (son of the former President); Wayne McVeagh of Pennsylvania, Attorney General (leader of the anti-Grant men in Pennsylvania); T. L. James of New York, Postmaster General (a civil-service reformer).

[4] Although Vice-President Arthur also repaired to Albany to urge their re-election, the New York legislature upheld Garfield. Conkling retired to private life, but Platt became the boss of the New York Republican machine and sixteen years later returned to the Senate.

battle for life, Garfield passed away on September 19, and Chester A. Arthur became President. The exclamation of a friend, which Platt quotes in his *Autobiography*, " 'Chet' Arthur President of the United States! Good God!," expressed adequately the feelings of most sober citizens. But Arthur, pet of the New York machine, who represented in the minds of many the most objectionable type of contemporary politician, rose to the occasion. Those who expected that his administration would revert to the worst days of Grant were pleasantly disappointed. His administration, in fact, was progressive and is notable for civil-service reform and for the first real effort after the Civil War to reform the tariff, and Arthur himself showed independence in vetoing a particularly obnoxious River and Harbors Bill and the first Chinese exclusion act. His administration, declared the *Nation* in 1884, "will not suffer by comparison with any of its predecessors since Lincoln's. Indeed it is above the average of post-bellum respectability."

The assassination of Garfield undoubtedly speeded civil-service reform. Agitation for it had been continuous, and both major parties had at least given it lip service. The Civil War provided some impetus, and Thomas A. Jenkes, member of Congress from Rhode Island and "father of civil-service reform" in this country, had introduced bills in 1865 and thereafter providing for appointment on the basis of ability. Grant showed some interest, and in 1871 a rider was attached to an appropriation bill, authorizing the President to prescribe rules for the admission of persons into the civil service and allowing him to appoint a commission to put the reform into effect. George W. Curtis, for many years editor of *Harper's Weekly*, was made chairman, and rules were formulated. Grant failed to back the commission, Curtis resigned in disgust, and Congress let the appropriation lapse. The movement was, of course, stimulated by the incredibly poor appointments of the Grant administration and by the fact that Hayes and his Secretary of the Interior, Schurz, were both sincere believers in this type of reform. Although Hayes did not enforce his executive order forbidding assessments of officeholders, he did do battle with the New York machine over the spoils system and the inefficiency in the New York Custom House. Garfield was but a mild reformer whose death did more to advance the movement than anything he had done during his life. The chief executives, overwhelmed by the importunities of hordes of office-seekers, were ordinarily sympathetic to civil-service reform. Professional politicians, on the other hand, almost always opposed it, insisting that only through the spoils system could political parties be maintained and pointing to the supposed danger of developing an aristocratic class of government officeholders. Believers in this reform organized the New York Civil Service Reform Association in 1877 and the National Civil Service Reform League in 1881.

President Arthur, to the great surprise of many, came out unequivocally for reform in his first message of December, 1881, and in his second message a year later stated that, if the bill then pending should be passed, he would sign it. Severe Republican reversals in 1882 and the strong prospect of a Democratic victory in 1884 undoubtedly influenced many Republicans to favor a civil-service-reform act, while the Democrats who had long advocated this reform could hardly oppose it. The act, signed in January, 1883, bore the name of Senator G. H. Pendleton but had been largely written by Dorman B. Eaton, a pioneer worker for this cause. The Pendleton Act provided for a bipartisan commission of three, who should prepare and enforce rules governing the appointment of officials by open competitive examinations; it prohibited political assessments and removals for political reasons. The system was to be inaugurated in the departments at Washington and in customs houses and post offices having a staff of more than fifty employees, but the "classified list" might be enlarged at the discretion of the President. Eaton was made chairman of the new commission, and during Arthur's administration about 15,600 positions, approximating 12 per cent of the total offices, were placed on the list. Succeeding Presidents, notably Cleveland, Roosevelt, and Taft, added certain offices to the list, which with the rapid growth of the government service had increased the government employees under civil-service rules to 467,000 by 1932 or 83 per cent of the entire number.

Except for the Pendleton Act, congressional activity under Arthur was chiefly concerned with the problem of taxation. A treasury surplus made action imperative. The result was a decrease in internal-revenue taxes and a slight reduction in tariff rates. The history of tariff legislation and of foreign affairs under this administration will be discussed in later chapters.

THE DEMOCRATIC VICTORY OF 1884

Passing over Arthur and ignoring the candidates of the independents, the Republicans at their convention of 1884 nominated James G. Blaine of Maine for the presidency and General John A. Logan, an Illinois Stalwart, for the vice-presidency. Endowed with a commanding presence, a magnetic personality, a gift for brilliant oratory, and an intuitive talent for political leadership, Blaine had many claims to the nomination. He had been elected to Congress in 1862 and had been Speaker from 1869 to 1874 and Secretary of State for a brief period under Garfield. His long feud with the New York "Stalwarts" impaired his position in that state, but his chief weakness was his willingness to use his political power for personal financial advancement, which was typical enough at the time but lost him the support of many independent voters.

Taking advantage of these vulnerable points, the Democrats nominated Governor Grover Cleveland of New York on the second ballot and T. A. Hendricks of Ohio for vice-president. Then in his late forties, Cleveland had had an exceptionally short political career. Born at Caldwell, New Jersey, the son of a Presbyterian minister, he had gone as a young man to Buffalo, where he won a respected position in the legal profession, served a term as sheriff of Erie County, and was elected mayor of the city in 1881 by the reform element. A factional quarrel among the leaders of the Democratic machine in New York, combined with the reputation that he achieved as mayor of Buffalo, won him the nomination and election to the governorship of the state. Although conservative in outlook, without imagination or personal charm, and with little understanding of the fundamental economic or social problems of his age, Cleveland acquired great political strength, which rested on his absolute integrity in an age of loose political morality. He was gifted with a strong intellect and independence of mind, but his most appealing characteristic was his desperate earnestness to do what he believed to be right. Having thought a problem through and having reached a decision, he could not be swerved by any thought of political future or of whom he might antagonize. He was known as the "veto mayor" and the "veto governor," and in the latter office he soon won the enmity of Tammany Hall. He was loved by the younger Democrats, said General Bragg in seconding Cleveland's nomination, for his "judgement and iron will" but "most for the enemies he has made."

Two minor parties entered the election—a coalition of Antimonopolists and Greenbackers, who nominated Governor Benjamin Butler of Massachusetts, and the Prohibitionists, who nominated John P. St. John. Because of the closeness of the election their activities may have exerted some influence. With little difference in the party platforms, the campaign soon degenerated into one of personalities. Blaine was attacked on the ground of political corruption, his opponents emphasizing particularly his connection with the defunct Little Rock and Fort Smith Railroad, an Arkansas land-grant railroad that had received aid from Congress and whose worthless bonds Blaine had sold among his friends. Cleveland was assailed as the father of an illegitimate child. It had all the characteristics, says Beard, of a pot-house quarrel, and in the words of Andrew D. White was "the vilest political campaign ever waged." Two episodes at the end of the campaign hurt Blaine. Returning to New York at the conclusion of a long speaking tour, Blaine was greeted by a delegation of New York clergymen, whose spokesman, Burchard by name, characterized the Democratic Party as the party of "Rum, Romanism and Rebellion." Blaine failed to repudiate this slur, and many Irish voters were alienated. That night his wealthy backers in New York gave him a dinner at Delmonico's, which laid him open to the charge that he was the rich man's candidate. As the election in the end depended upon the doubtful state of New York, which went to Cleveland by a margin of 1149 votes, any one of a number of influences may have been the deciding factor.[5] The popular vote showed a plurality for Cleveland of about 23,000 in a total of 10,000,000. Above all, it was probably the support of the independents that elected Cleveland.

Cleveland's administration, as the first Democratic one since the Civil War, was received by old-time Republicans as a major catastrophe. Conservatives, however, had nothing to fear. In his political and economic philosophy Cleveland differed hardly at all from Republican Presidents who preceded and followed him. The reforms that he advocated—improvement of the civil service, reduction of the tariff, repeal of the Bland-Allison Act, rehabilitation of the navy, safeguarding of the public land, and protection of the Indians—had also been urged by Hayes and Arthur. The one major piece of legislation of his first term, the Interstate Commerce Act of 1887, was the result of a decade of agitation and was nonpartisan (page 442). If the Cleveland administration differed in any way from others, it was in the scrupulous care with which the chief executive guarded the public treasury and in the greater participation of the South in the affairs of the national government. Politically, the administration proved that the national welfare was quite as safe in the hands of the Democratic as in that of the Republican Party. At the same time Cleveland's insistence upon a tariff reduction, in his famous message of 1887, was a great boon to American politics in forcing both parties to take a definite and opposing stand on at least one major issue. Although Cleveland was easily the dominating personality in the administration, his cabinet was up to the average. Thomas F. Bayard (Delaware), Secretary of State, represented the best of his party and was a satisfactory appointment in every respect; William C. Whitney, a wealthy anti-Tammany reformer of New York, did much to rebuild the navy and was probably as good a Secretary of the Navy as the country has ever had. L. Q. C. Lamar (Mississippi), one of the two Southern cabinet members,

---

[5] A transparency carried in a Democratic victory parade summed these up:

The *World*	Says	the	Independents	Did It.
The *Tribune*	"	"	Stalwarts	Did It.
The *Sun*	"		Burchard	Did It.
Blaine	"		St. John	Did It.

Theodore Roosevelt Says it was the Soft Soap Dinner.
We say Blaine's Character Did It.
But we Don't Care What Did It.
    It's Done.

as Secretary of the Interior, showed unusual interest in protecting the public lands; A. H. Garland (Arkansas), Attorney General, was one of the ablest statesmen of the New South. Daniel Manning (New York) in the treasury satisfied the conservative business interests.

The fact that Cleveland had a Republican Senate during his administration was partly responsible for the lack of much important legislation. Certain acts, however, should be mentioned. After a fight with the Senate over the President's right to remove officeholders, the remainder of the Tenure of Office Act (page 337) was repealed. The Presidential Succession Act provided for a succession of cabinet members in case of the death of President and Vice-President, and the Electoral Count Act definitely placed upon the states the responsibility of deciding disputes regarding presidential electors. The demand of settlers for the 250,000 square miles of land set aside for Indian reservations resulted in the Dawes Act of 1887, which conferred citizenship and ownership of a plot of land (160 acres to heads of families, 80 acres to single adults and orphans, and 40 acres to each dependent child) upon Indians who would renounce tribal allegiance, the remainder of the land to be held in trust by the government for the Indians with the power to open it for settlement upon adequate payment to the Indians. In 1889 the Dakotas, Montana, and Washington entered the Union (page 430), and in the same year the Department of Agriculture was established.

Cleveland was a sincere civil-service reformer, and during his first administration about 7000 offices were added to the classified list. In his second administration 42,500 were added, bringing the percentage of government officeholders under civil-service rules in 1897 to 45 per cent. Nevertheless, Cleveland substituted Democrats for Republicans when terms on the unclassified list ran out, and he also removed many Republicans. He evidently went as far on the road to reform as he thought practical, but the net result was to displease ardent reformers and to alienate many leaders in his own party. Cleveland likewise soon aroused opposition among the majority of veterans by the scrupulous care with which he scrutinized pension applications. The policy established after the Civil War was to grant pensions to veterans disabled by wounds or disease contracted in the service. To veterans' organizations and pension lawyers growing fat by pressing soldiers' claims, this policy seemed too conservative, and agitation was continuous to liberalize the laws. The result was an act of 1879 that allowed arrears of pensions to be paid from the date of injury. As the average payment of arrears was about $1000, the number of applications grew tremendously, and human ingenuity was taxed to the limit to invent excuses for pensions. When the Bureau of Pensions seemed too slow in granting claims, or rejected them, members of Congress introduced special or "private" bills to cover the cases, which were passed without question. Many of these bills Cleveland examined in detail, and of the 2042 passed during his first four years he vetoed 233, often exposing in sarcastic language the preposterous claims upon which they were based. His belief that pensions should represent a national roll of honor rather than be a means of plundering the treasury was likewise expressed in his veto of the Dependent Pension Bill of 1887, which provided for a pension of $12 a month to every veteran who had served three months and was now disabled, whether or not he had received any injury in the service, and a similar amount to widows of such veterans. Another storm was aroused over Cleveland's order, which he later rescinded, to return to the former Confederate states the battle flags captured by Union soldiers.[6]

THE RETURN OF THE REPUBLICANS

Hardly an act of Cleveland's first administration won him any popular acclaim; his policies, on the contrary, had antagonized veterans, alienated party leaders, and aroused the opposition of protected industry and agrarian inflationists. Furthermore, the Tammany machine of New York was against him. His rugged independence and conscientious concern for the public interest, however, commanded the respect of the common man, and there was no one in 1888 seriously to dispute his leadership. He was renominated by acclamation on the first ballot, with A. G. Thurman of Ohio as his running mate and on a platform that endorsed his tariff message of 1887. Upon Blaine's refusal to run, the Republicans nominated General Benjamin Harrison (grandson of President William Henry Harrison), a corporation lawyer from the doubtful state of Indiana, whose term in the Senate had been without distinction. He was, however, thoroughly acceptable to conservative business interests, as was the vice-presidential nominee, Levi P. Morton, a New York banker. Replying to Cleveland's tariff message of 1887, the Republican platform emphasized adherence to a protective tariff, but threw in some other planks advocating a liberal pension policy, the control of oppressive corporations, and civil-service reform.[7]

For the first time in years the two major parties could come to grips on an important issue, and the American people got their first real education in the tariff question. Quite naturally the Republican leaders exacted

---

[6] This was done in 1905 by a Republican administration.

[7] Minor parties included the United Labor Party, the Union Labor Party, and the Prohibition Party, all of which suggested reforms that, though later adopted, played no important part in this campaign.

heavy campaign contributions from the protected interests. This money, strategically expended, combined with a deal whereby Tammany knifed Cleveland in return for Republican support of its candidate for governor (David B. Hill), lost Cleveland the two doubtful states of Indiana and New York and with them the election. In an unusually heavy vote Cleveland polled 100,000 more than Harrison but lost the electoral count by 233 to 168.

The election of 1888 brought to the Republicans not only the presidency but also, for the first time since 1875, control of both houses of Congress. Their majority in the fifty-first Congress, however, was exceedingly small and was obtained in part by the admission in February, 1889, of the "omnibus states" (page 430). Such a thin majority, combined with the fact that Cleveland's popular vote had actually exceeded that of Harrison, behooved the Republican Party to move cautiously, but this was exactly what it did not do. The two chief posts in the cabinet went to James G. Blaine, Secretary of State, and William Windom, Secretary of the Treasury, both of whom had served in a similar capacity under Garfield. John Wanamaker, the merchant prince of Philadelphia, who had done yeoman service in filling the Republican campaign chest, was Postmaster General. In earlier years Harrison had sneered at civil-service reform, but as President he faithfully observed the Pendleton Act. During his last two years he enlarged the classified list and appointed Theodore Roosevelt to the Civil Service Commission. In general, however, the Republicans, particularly in the Post Office Department, cleared out their opponents so efficiently that civil-service reformers felt that the movement had collapsed. The First Assistant Postmaster General pointed with pride to the fact that he had removed one Democrat for every three minutes during his first year in office.

The reaction of the bosses of the Republican Party to the policies of Cleveland was illustrated not alone in the wholesale operation of the "spoils system" but also in their attitude toward the public treasury. Under Arthur and Cleveland the treasury had accumulated a surplus, and both Presidents had suggested a reduction of the tariff. Committed to a high tariff, the Republicans were determined to take care of the surplus in other ways. One method was greater liberality to the veterans. "It is no time," said Harrison, "to weigh the claims of old soldiers on apothecary's scales," and, acting on this theory, he appointed Corporal James Tanner as Commissioner of Pensions. Tanner may not have been responsible, as alleged, for the oft quoted remark, "God help the surplus," but his administration was so liberal that even Harrison finally dismissed him. Nevertheless, the Republicans sponsored a Dependent Pension Bill similar to that vetoed by Cleveland, and such a bill became law in 1890.

In addition to the Dependent Pension bill, the fifty-first Congress passed three notable pieces of legislation in 1890: the Sherman Silver Purchase Act, already described (page 447), and the McKinley tariff and the Sherman Antitrust Act, both of which will be discussed in Chapter XXIX. The first two were forced through by the party in power; the last-mentioned act was nonpartisan. The Republican majority in Congress was so slight during the first two years of the Harrison administration that party legislation was whipped through only by means of the autocratic methods adopted by Thomas B. Reed of Maine, Speaker of the House. To prevent filibustering, he directed the clerk to count all in the room as present and at the same time refused to entertain motions that were obviously dilatory. This, in addition to his power as member of the Rules Committee to nominate the chairmen of committees, made it possible for him to dominate legislation. The Democrats protested vociferously against the tactics of "Czar" Reed, but followed the same procedure in the next Congress when they again had a majority. Reed's methods tended in the long run to weaken the influence of individual congressmen. For the moment they increased the power of the lower house.

The aggressive program of the Harrison administration ended with the election of 1890. The Republicans, who had mistakenly interpreted the results of 1888 as a mandate to raise the tariff, found themselves on the defensive in the midterm election. For the second time in our history a campaign was fought over the tariff, and in this case there could be no doubt as to the decision. Although the McKinley tariff had been signed scarcely a month before the November elections, its effect upon the cost of commodities was already apparent. In a wave of protest the voters increased the Democratic representation in the lower house from 159 to 235 and reduced the Republicans from 166 to 88, while the Republican majority in the Senate was cut from fourteen to six.

With the two houses under the control of opposite parties, there was little to do during the next two years but prepare for the coming election. Blaine resigned from the cabinet three days before the nominating convention to put himself in line for the nomination, but the convention on the first ballot nominated Harrison for a second term by a vote of 535 to Blaine's 183. The platform endorsed the McKinley tariff and compromised on the silver issue. The Democratic machine politicians tried to forestall the nomination of Cleveland, but his popularity with the masses, combined with the disapproval of the McKinley tariff, made him the logical choice. He was nominated on the first ballot with Adlai E. Stevenson of Illinois, a politician of the old school, as the candidate for vice-president. The platform denounced the McKinley tariff as the "culminating atrocity of class legislation" and, interestingly enough considering the Democratic stand four years later, came out strongly for "sound money," characterizing the silver legislation of 1890 as "a cowardly makeshift." The campaign was notable as marking the appearance of a strong third party, the Populists, in a presidential campaign and the first appearance of socialism in a national campaign in the form of the Socialist Labor Party.

"It is a funny thing," remarked Cleveland of himself, "for a man to be running for the presidency with all the politicians against him." While the politicians were not particularly opposed to Harrison, he aroused little enthusiasm among them. The campaign, as a result, was rather lifeless. For the third consecutive campaign the tariff was the chief issue, and Cleveland won by an electoral vote of 277 to 145 for Harrison and 22 for the Populist, General Weaver.[8] "The people," as Senator Cullom truthfully wrote to Harrison, "sat down on the McKinley Tariff Bill two years ago and they have never gotten up." Here we find the chief explanation for the Republican defeat. Among minor issues was the Homestead strike in the summer of 1892, a bitter struggle over the reduction of wages in the highly protected steel industry, which helped to swing the labor vote to the Democratic candidates.

CLEVELAND A SECOND TIME

The panic of 1893 and the depression that followed dominated the second administration of Cleveland. Believing quite erroneously that the silver legislation was the cause of the panic, Cleveland called Congress into special session and secured a repeal of the act, after which he saved the gold standard by repeated sales of gold bonds to the Morgan and other New York banks. This thoroughly alienated the inflationist group, of the South and West, while the efforts of the administration to break the Pullman strike of 1894, by calling out federal troops and securing an injunction against the strike leaders, lost him the support of labor (page 410). The efforts of the Democrats to lower the tariff in the Wilson-Gorman Act of 1894 was a fiasco. The result of all this was a complete demoralization of the Democratic Party in the elections of 1894, when the Republicans obtained a large majority in the House and a safe control in the Senate. Democrats also deserted in droves to the Populist Party, helping to send to Washington seven Populist representatives and six senators. Under these conditions the last two years of Cleveland were devoid of important legislative accomplishment. The President and his conservative cabinet held the lines of battle against the onslaught of dis-

---

[8] Cleveland got 5,556,543 votes to Harrison's 5,175,582 and Weaver's 1,040,886. Weaver carried Colorado, Kansas, Idaho, and Nevada, with one electoral vote each in Oregon and South Dakota.

satisfied inflationary congressmen of both parties, whose activities were consequently largely limited to speeches and preparation for 1896. In his cabinet were the able John G. Carlisle, Secretary of the Treasury, who saw eye to eye with Cleveland on financial policies, and Richard Olney, whose advice was the dominant influence in Cleveland's monetary policy, his tactics in the Pullman strike, and his conduct of foreign policy. In his second administration Cleveland made progress in civil-service reform and won the endorsement of the conservative business interests by saving the gold standard and crushing the Pullman strike. With the rank and file, on the other hand, his popularity was gone, and as a political leader his day was done.

C. and M. Beard, *The Rise of American Civilization,* Chap. XXIII, is a good introductory chapter. For the Hayes administration, see H. I. Eckenrode, *Rutherford B. Hayes,* Chaps. X, XI; for Garfield's campaign and presidency, R. G. Caldwell, *James A. Garfield,* Chaps. XIV, XV; for Arthur's administration, J. F. Rhodes, *A History of the United States from Hayes to McKinley,* Chaps., VII–IX; for Cleveland's campaign, Allan Nevins, *Grover Cleveland,* Chaps. XI, XXIV, XXVII; for Harrison's administration, Rhodes, *op. cit.,* Chaps. XIV–XVII. For sources consult H. S. Commager, *Documents of American History,* Vol. II, 104–106, 109–113, 120–121, 138–142.

THE INDUSTRIAL AGE

Chapter XXVIII

THE GILDED AGE

The association of poverty with progress is the great enigma of our times.

HENRY GEORGE

We leave the Republic in 1890 at the very climax of prosperity—its past marvelous; its present equally so; its future full as ever of golden promise.

ANDREW CARNEGIE

THE URBAN TREND

The dominant factor in American history during the last third of the nineteenth century was the industrialization of the nation. Certain economic, political, and legal aspects of this revolution have already been emphasized (Chapters XXIII and XXIV). There remain to be discussed the effects of industrialization upon the life of the people. Of these effects the first and most important was undoubtedly the speeding of urbanization, which was evident in all sections save those where the pioneer farmer was for the first time opening the land to cultivation. Between 1860 and 1900 the number of cities of 8000 or more population increased from 141 to 547 and the population living in them from over 5,000,000 to over 25,000,000, while the percentage of people in such cities almost doubled from 16.1 to 32. By the latter date one out of every three Americans lived in such cities. The lure of the city played upon every conceivable emotion; the loneliness of country life, the drudgery of farm work, the lack of opportunities in an expanding economic world all played their part. Fundamentally, however, manufacturing was rapidly moving from the home to the factory, and the population followed. Only the first processes of production remained on the farm, and even there conditions were being continually modified by new machinery.

It was in the Northeast, particularly in New England, that the rural decline was most in evidence. Three fifths of the area of Connecticut, three fourths of Vermont, and nearly two thirds of New Hampshire and

Maine, for example, decreased in population during the eighties. In that decade 932 townships out of 1502 in all New England showed a decline in population. Competition of western land and the lure of the near-by cities had long been affecting the New England countryside, but it was not until some years after the Civil War that the deserted farm became a characteristic of every rural New England township. As farmhouses fell into disrepair and cleared fields relapsed into tangled underbrush, the small workshop also disappeared. "The proportion of abandoned wagon shops, saw mills, and other mechanical businesses," commented one observer, "has far outstripped the abandonment of farms." What was far worse for the rural sections, however, was the fact that those who remained were likely to be the less enterprising, the less venturesome, and the more conservative. In many regions the best stock almost disappeared. Eventually some of these areas were resuscitated by dairying, truck farming, and other types of agriculture, and the better land replenished by immigrant farmers, but for the time being the rural exodus was startling. Nevertheless, the North Atlantic states as a whole showed during the eighties a 20-per-cent increase in the number of inhabitants, an increase predominantly in the cities and fostered by migration from the country districts and by European immigrants, who tended, as in earlier decades, to concentrate in the more densely populated eastern centers.

Although the cityward trend of population in the Middle West, particularly in the north-central states, was clearly revealed by the census, the effects were far less devastating than in New England. It was largely a drawing off of unnecessary rural population; the more fertile land of the West ensured operation of the farms, with a tendency to shift to commercial agriculture. With the more venturesome people departing for the West or the cities and with the agricultural situation improving, the farmers who remained tended to become more conservative in their economic and political views. The exodus, nevertheless, was striking. While every Middle Western state increased in population and every large city during the eighties advanced by leaps and bounds, over half of the townships of Ohio and Illinois declined in population. Chicago, for example, grew from 500,000 to over a million during that decade, while Detroit, Milwaukee, Cleveland, and other cities grew from 60 to 80 per cent. As in the East, this increase in city population was due both to migration from rural regions and to immigration from Europe. While Scandinavians and Germans settled in the country as well as in the cities, the larger part of the 900,000 immigrants who found their way to the Middle West in this decade congregated in urban centers.

Although some factories existed in the South in the days before the Civil War, the Industrial Revolution had made but little progress in that section. In the first two decades after the war the South continued to be primarily agricultural and to specialize in such staples as cotton and tobacco. Lack of capital, however, tended rapidly to break up the large plantations into small farms, where the old crops were raised by white or colored tenant farmers or share-croppers, who sometimes advanced in the economic scale but more often sank to a state of peonage through the atrocious credit system in vogue. One result was the addition of 2,500,000 farms in the South between 1865 and 1900.

This break-up of the large plantation worked by slaves and the substitution for it of the system of share-cropping were tremendously important in the social and political life of the South. It had little influence, however, on the trend toward urbanization. That came from the doubling of the railroad system between 1878 and 1890, from the wide movement to erect cotton factories, from the success in the manufacture of tobacco products and in the exploitation of coal, iron, and, later, water power. Perhaps the manufacture of tobacco by the Duke family at Durham, North Carolina, was the harbinger of the new industrial South, but tobacco manufacture was soon to sink into insignificance before the rapidly developing textiles. The cry of "bring the mills to the cotton" was taken up with a driving enthusiasm that doubled, in the eighties, the number of spindles and looms. In 1880 there were less than 500,000 spindles in North Carolina, South Carolina, and Georgia, while there were over 8,500,000 in New England. A quarter of a century later over half of the raw cotton was manufactured in the South. Proximity of coal, iron, and limestone in Virginia, Tennessee, and Alabama brought also a development of the iron industry. The center was Alabama, where the tons produced increased from 347,000 in 1880 to 2,710,000 in 1929, and where Birmingham, soon to be one of the great iron centers of the world, grew from 3000 in 1880 to 260,000 in 1930. The South found new wealth in cotton-seed products and lumber and, with the coming of electricity, in the water power of the Appalachians. While the urban trend was noticeable in the South, manufacturing was generally on too small a scale suddenly to create many large cities.

WAYS OF LIVING

Despite the rapid urbanization of America, the United States as late as 1900 was still primarily an agricultural nation. Over half of the people lived on farms or villages supported by agriculture, one third of those gainfully employed gave agriculture as their occupation, and over 60 per cent of our exports came from the farms. The rural elements felt last and least the revolutionary changes that were affecting the manner of American life. The Industrial Revolution, of course, brought improved farm machinery and emphasized commercial agriculture. The village store and the mail-order house supplied to prosperous farmers many commodities heretofore manufactured on the farm, while the work of the kitchen was further lightened by new cooking utensils, particularly by the introduction of aluminum, and by such new household appliances as the practical flat-iron with a detachable handle. On the whole, however, farm life, as it always had been, was mainly a life of hard physical drudgery from sun-rise to sunset, whether on the rocky hillside farm of New England or on the broad Dakota prairies. Relaxation came in ways that had changed but little through the years—the church picnic, the husking bee, the county fair, the country dance, the trip to town. For the long hours and hard labor of agricultural life there was the compensation of independence and the expectation of a more prosperous future, an expectation, however, that was frequently frustrated by low prices, poor markets, and the inevitable mortgage.

It was the city dweller whose manner of living was chiefly affected dur-ing the eighties and nineties. In the hectic changes that characterized the city, life became so colorful, so variegated, and, withal, so artificial, that it has been fittingly termed "the gilded age." [1] In these checkerboard cities, chaotically growing, and revealing the wide variation in wealth and living conditions, was mirrored the changing America. At one extreme were the masses of workers, mostly immigrants who dwelt in "jerry-built" wooden or brick tenements—square miles of them—without suf-ficient air, adequate sanitation, or heat, where high rents caused over-crowding and prepared the way for vice and disease. Here the ingenuity of exploiting profit-takers condemned millions of human beings to living conditions often worse than those they had left behind in Europe. From these wretched tenements went forth the mass of workers to labor for wages below any conceivable decent standard of living. Even this was not sufficient, and in many cases work was brought home, where the entire family might labor for a miserable pittance.

At the top of the social and economic structure were the captains of transportation and industry. Already by 1900, it was estimated, one tenth of the population owned nine tenths of the wealth, and the handful of millionaires of 1860 had grown to 3800. The brownstone houses or near-by suburban mansions of these recipients of sudden wealth, built in every style known to man, were often the scene of vulgar display. While the more civilized imported art galleries and donated fortunes for education or charity, others taxed their ingenuity to conceive new and more useless

[1] It was Mark Twain and Charles Dudley Warner who wrote *The Gilded Age* (1873) and unwittingly gave to this period a permanent name.

forms of expenditure. Some pieced out at fashionable summer resorts their year of expensive social entertainment; others made the grand tour of Europe, where their display of wealth amazed the Old World but at the same time gave a deceptive picture of American civilization. Nor was it long before some of this wealth moved to Europe as scions of titled aristocracy found in the daughters of American millionaires an easy method of replenishing their fortunes. Whatever was sensational in the doings of this class was speedily handed on to the common man in the recently born "yellow press."

More typical of American culture of the Gilded Age was the life of the middle class—the clerks, the shopkeepers, the minor executives, and the professional people. Dwelling in modest homes and comfortable apartments, they were usually able to maintain a standard of living equal to, if not better than, that of their parents, to educate their children, and to strive for a higher status. Their thick upholstered furniture, heavy draperies, marble-topped tables, and living rooms cluttered with "whatnots" and bric-a-brac collected from the ends of the earth, seem a bit ridiculous today, but they represented comfort and dignity to that generation. It was this class that benefited most from new improvements in living—the telephone, invented in the seventies, the electric light, patented in 1880, the Welsbach gas burner, widely used after 1890. In going to work they profited from the new age of bridge-building inaugurated with the completion of Roebling's Brooklyn Bridge in 1883, and from the development of the electric trolley car in the nineties, and the building of elevated railroads. They were the gainers by improved city paving, by the development of better sewage-disposal, by new municipal water plants and better-organized fire departments with improved apparatus. Except for the very wealthy, they were the first to gain from all mechanical devices that made life easier and from improved educational and cultural facilities, which came first in the cities.

If it was the middle class of the cities that profited most from the improvements in living, it was the women of this group who were the chief beneficiaries. It was they who were to profit from the simpler diet and more sensible house furnishings that were being suggested and from the more sensible clothing that a few pioneers had the courage to introduce. For the first time women in large numbers moved from the home to the world of industry and business. Not alone were they to be found in the factory, but now in the office, the store, and even the professions. The number of female breadwinners rose from 2,500,000 in 1880 to 4,500,000 in 1890 and over 5,300,000 in 1900. While many women found a new freedom and economic independence in work outside the home, others found time to devote their attention to the numerous women's clubs that sprang up like mushrooms. Although these clubs were of an infinite variety and served many purposes, their chief reason for existence was cultural. In 1889 they were united into a great national organization, the General Federation of Women's Clubs.

While some women wasted their new-found freedom in the futile round of useless club activity, others sought further to improve the lot of their sex through political suffrage. Under the leadership of Susan B. Anthony and Elizabeth Cady Stanton, agitation was kept up from the seventies on. Two groups of workers were united in 1890 under the National American Woman Suffrage Association, which pushed the cause in state and national legislatures. Despite much noble effort, there were but four states at the close of the century—Wyoming, Colorado, Utah, and Idaho—that recognized woman as the political equal of man. In education greater progress could be shown. By the end of the seventies most of the state universities had opened their gates to women. In the meantime, women's colleges on a par with the best for men had been founded—Vassar, opened in 1865 by a rich brewer of Poughkeepsie; Mount Holyoke, transformed from a girls' seminary into a college; Smith, founded in 1871 through the vision of a country minister and the wealth of a village spinster; and Wellesley, created in 1875 by the liberality of a Boston lawyer. Women's colleges were added to the great universities, Barnard at Columbia in 1889 and Radcliffe at Harvard in 1894. More significant than this was the fact that the secondary schools as well as the elementary were being "manned" by women.

THE CULTURAL LEVEL

If the cultural level can be gauged by the status of America's most cherished institution, the public school, the latter part of the century showed a significant advance. The 7,000,000 pupils enrolled in the public schools in 1870 increased to 15,500,000 in 1900, the 300 public high schools of 1860 to over 6000, and the twelve state normal schools of 1860 to 175. At the end of the century there were almost 500 colleges, about double the number in 1860. Illiteracy declined from 17 per cent in 1880 to less than 11 per cent in 1900. Two facts were obvious: educational facilities were increasing more rapidly than population, and the more prosperous sections had assumed the responsibility of providing free public-school education beyond the elementary grades. This was accompanied by a willingness to lengthen the school term and to enforce the statutes requiring attendance. By 1900 at least ten states provided for free textbooks.

The advance, however, was not to be measured only in quantitative terms. There was likewise a qualitative advance. While education was undoubtedly plagued by many educational "crazes," there was a distinct improvement. As the ideals of Pestalozzi and Herbart were brought to America, the use of the hickory stick declined; teachers realized that a better method of education was to appeal to a student's interests and thus lead rather than drive him into new fields of knowledge. Education became less a matter of sheer memory as the student was changed from a passive recipient to an active seeker of knowledge. The more sensitive communities went so far as to forbid corporal punishment. Throughout the system there was a real effort to carry education beyond the "three Rs" and make it contribute to a richer life. Courses in drawing, music, and nature study were frequently added. With the addition of courses in the household and manual arts the curriculum became more practical, and eventually an extra year was added to the high school. At the other end of the educational ladder the wide introduction of kindergartens was a notable advance. It would be easy, of course, to shade in the darker aspects of the American educational picture—low salaries of teachers, their inadequate preparation, the low standing of the profession, the backwardness of many sections, particularly in the South, and the inadequate standards of the rapidly growing parochial schools. More significant for a true understanding were the rapid and general advance throughout the nation and the improvement of the educational system. This applied also to the colleges, public and privately endowed, which became more responsive to the new age of science, more liberal in their rules regarding choice of studies, and more nearly adequate in their graduate work, as many Americans trained in the methods of German universities brought back to their native land the refinements of foreign scholarship and research.

Deficiencies of childhood education were to some extent removed by an unparalleled expansion of public libraries and a notable development of Chautauquas. Except in a few eastern cities, tax-supported free libraries were rare in 1860. By the end of the century, however, eighteen states had authorized the use of taxing powers for this purpose, and the number of free circulating libraries of three hundred or more volumes numbered over 9000. Andrew Carnegie was already pouring millions into this form of education, while the Astor, Lenox, and Tilden collections were combined in New York to form the nucleus of what was soon to be one of the great libraries of the world. While every progressive city was establishing its public library, ingenious librarians, notably William F. Poole, Charles A. Cutter, and Melvil Dewey, were devising schemes for cataloguing that made these collections easily available.

During the years after 1880 an unusual number of adults were stimulated in some form or other by the activities of the Chautauquas. In 1874, through the influence of Lewis Miller, an Ohio manufacturer, and John H. Vincent, a Methodist clergyman, a training school for Sunday-school teachers was set up at Lake Chautauqua, New York. Its activities soon expanded to all types of courses, and before long its activities were emulated by a host of Chautauquas or summer schools throughout the country. Some had permanent abodes and lasted all summer; others met under a tent for a week or so. On their circuits appeared eventually the most famous of the educational, political, and artistic talents of the nation. In the winter their activities were extended by lecture courses in the larger towns and by courses of study often based upon textbooks written specifically for the Chautauqua courses. The whole movement represented an effort at adult education that bridged the gap from the lyceum movement of the middle period to the summer schools and extension courses of the great universities of the twentieth century.

More important than Chautauquas, libraries, or even the public school in determining the cultural level of the adult masses were the newspapers and magazines. Between 1880 and 1900 the number of newspapers and their subscribers increased twice as rapidly as population; America as never before became a nation of newspaper-readers. The tendencies of the American press during these years, therefore, are of great significance. Most important of all, perhaps, is the fact that newspapers became less and less vehicles for the personal views of the editors and more and more commercial ventures supported by advertisers and to a less degree by the pennies of the masses. To obtain advertising, the circulation must be large, and to obtain a large circulation the newspaper must have a wide appeal. The news must be up to the minute and presented in terse style, and there must be material of interest to every member of the family. The demand for better news-coverage resulted during the nineties in the establishment of the Associated Press service under the management of Melville E. Stone (1892) and of the Scripps-McRae Press Association (1897). Efforts to widen the appeal of the newspapers were more successful after 1884, when S. S. McClure formed the first American company for the purpose of syndicating feature material to appeal to men, women, and children. The development of Associated Press news and syndicated feature articles, combined with the commercialization of the press, gave to the newspapers a sameness throughout the country. The dominating editorial personalities of the war and postwar period—Raymond of the *Times,* Greeley of the *Tribune,* Bennett of the *Herald,* Bryant of the *Evening Post,* and the second Samuel Bowles of the Springfield *Republican*—had passed from the scene by 1880. Their peers thereafter were few; as a rule editorial policy was dominated by the owner, and editorials were anonymously produced according to the owner's whims.[2]

The most striking tendency during the last years of the century was that toward "yellow journalism." Its originator in America was Joseph Pulitzer, an immigrant of Jewish-Hungarian parentage, who, after a newspaper apprenticeship under Carl Schurz, acquired in 1878 the St. Louis *Post-Dispatch* and in 1883 the then almost defunct New York *World*. Emphasizing sensational news and adding political cartoons and feature articles of various types, including a colored supplement to the Sunday edition, with comics for children, Pulitzer quickly pushed his circulation from 14,000 to hundreds of thousands. Pulitzer and his Sunday editor, Morrill Goddard, set the style and the pace; others quickly imitated. While the Scripps brothers commenced the construction of a chain of live newspapers in the Middle West, William Randolph Hearst, son of a wealthy Californian, invaded New York in 1895 with the purchase of the *Morning Journal*. Hearst beat Pulitzer at his own game. The result was that journalism in the late nineties and the early years of the new century, as typified, in the expanding mass of Hearst papers, sank to its lowest depths. Yellow journalism had one good feature in that it forced all papers to improve their appearance. Numerous inventions helped in this—the Mergenthaler linotype machine (1885), faster presses, color printing, and better methods of reproducing pictures. To aid the reporter there were the telephone (1876), the typewriter, practical by 1878, and the fountain pen (1882). Fortunately, the father of "yellow journalism" was a liberal and a humanitarian, whose efforts, as he himself said, were "dedicated to the cause of the people rather than that of the purse-potentates," and the New York *World* under Pulitzer and Frank I. Cobb kept up a continual crusade against various public evils, remaining for a half century the most independent and brilliantly edited paper in the East.

Like the newspapers, the magazines were eventually influenced by the desire for mass appeal and large-scale advertising. The field, however, until the end of the century, was dominated by the distinguished, dignified, and at the same time well-illustrated *Harper's, Scribner's,* and *Century*. Although the editorial policies of the three were about the same and changed little throughout the years, the three-cornered rivalry kept all of them on the alert to engage the best talent available. Despite the preeminent position of these magazines, the *Atlantic Monthly,* the *North American Review,* and the *Forum,* which catered to much the same intellectual level, managed to hold their readers. While the prestige of these famous monthlies was hardly diminished, the number of magazine-readers was considerably enlarged by the coming of the more popular magazine. Outstanding among these was the *Ladies' Home Journal,* founded in 1883 and successfully edited in the nineties and thereafter by Edward W. Bok. Neutral on political and economic questions, it was brightly edited and did much to raise the cultural level of middle-class American women; its wide circulation was undoubtedly due in part to its low price of ten cents. In 1893 Samuel S. McClure founded *McClure's* and set the price at fifteen cents. When *Munsey's* and the *Cosmopolitan* lowered their price to ten cents and were followed almost immediately by *McClure's,* the era of the cheap magazine began. The cheap magazine caught more readers and greater advertising, and the resulting profits made it possible for the owners to compete successfully for available talent. In closer touch with the common man, the cheaper magazine was necessarily less pedantic and more humane, and it was soon to drift naturally and easily into the muckraking of the Roosevelt period.

The widening market for magazines, the passing by Congress of the international-copyright law in 1891, and above all the regional differences and the innumerable cross currents of American life, were all a stimulation to creative genius in the world of literature. The originality of the New England school of the middle period had largely exhausted itself by the end of the Civil War, but, as the century drew to a close, a renascence in literature and the arts was apparent. If the variegated literary product of the period can be characterized by any single phrase, perhaps the struggle between romanticism and realism might serve the purpose. That the social and economic problems of the Gilded Age were of a nature to call forth the highest literary genius, there can be no doubt; that few authors came to grips with it, is a tragedy. Warner and Twain, in *The Gilded Age* (1873), wrote a satire of American life without approaching the fundamentals that made such a picture possible; Henry Adams, in *Democracy* (1882) and *The Education of Henry Adams* (1907), denounced party loyalty, the spoils system, and the low order of politics, without suggesting a remedy; William Dean Howells constructed excellent novels of American social life, but in the end retired to a long and cloistered editorship of the *Atlantic,* where he soon lost touch with the American scene. John Hay, in one of the first important novels involving the class struggle, *The Bread-Winners* (1884), aptly characterized as "the first polemic in American fiction in defense of Property," soon found a more congenial field in diplomacy. Hamlin Garland, author of unforgettable novels of the struggles and seeming futility of frontier life, eventually retired to a conservative literary career.

One of the most important groups of writers of this period was the "local-color school of fiction," which attempted to catch in various sections the changing life of America. Notable among this group were Edward Eggleston, the scene of whose work was Indiana, George W. Cable and Lafcadio Hearn, who wrote of New Orleans, Bret Harte of the Far West, Mark Twain of the Mississippi, and Sarah Orne Jewett and others of New England. A host of local-colorists exploited the South, over-romanticizing and oversentimentalizing the life of the prewar days. Of these only one, Joel Chandler Harris, who preserved the folklore of the Negro in his Uncle Remus tales, made any permanent contribution. Unfortunately for the authors, it was romantic sentimentality that the readers clamored for, and in the end this is what they usually got. Local-color fiction was probably largely an escape from urban realities. So, in a sense, were the many novels that pictured a happier and more intelligent society of the future, such books as Edward Bellamy's *Looking Backward* (1888) and Howells's *A Traveler from Altruria* (1894). Some authors preferred to desert the cruder American scene for the older civilizations. Henry James in England soon lost touch with the realities of American life, and F. Marion Crawford in Italy completely deserted them. Hearn unsuccessfully sought relief in Martinique and Japan.

Not all the work was dominated by romanticism and escape. Mark Twain, in *The Prince and the Pauper* (1881) and *A Connecticut Yankee in King Arthur's Court* (1889), challenged the romantic trend of his day. Harold Frederic, in his portrayals of village life, particularly in *The Damnation of Theron Ware* (1896), made a real contribution to the progress of realism. Stephen Crane, in *Maggie* (1892) and *The Red Badge of Courage* (1895), did even more. There were others, like Garland, who at some time or other worked in patterns of realism. For the moment, however, this group made little headway and was submerged at the opening of the century in the rococo romanticism of the historical novels.

In poetry the Gilded Age had less to show than in prose. Whitman, buoyant and optimistic and struggling to comprehend the life and destiny of America, passed from the scene in 1892, having made but little impression upon his own generation. The polite poets who cluttered the popular magazines with their inane wares simply bridged the gap for a greater school to appear some decades later. Secluded from the world, but endowed with high artistic genius, were the Southern poet, Sidney Lanier, and the New England poetess, Emily Dickinson. The masses read the farm and city ballads of Will Carlton, the rural poetry of James Whitcomb Riley, and the delightful rhymes of Eugene Field.

Discussion of literature has so far been confined to the output that aspired to literary value. Unfortunately for American taste, the masses were more likely to read the impossible romances of Bertha M. Clay and Laura Jean Libby [3] and the "Old Sleuth" stories of H. P. Halsey, while Horatio Alger, Jr., and W. T. Adams (Oliver Optic) spurred on the youth by tales of worldly success. Nevertheless, this period, particularly the eighties, marked a real renascence, one critic asserting that "the decade 1880–1890 produced more good novels than any other American decade."

In the other arts also a renascence was apparent. The younger artists, breaking away from hampering tradition, painted with a boldness and originality that commanded attention in Europe as well as in America. The most famous, perhaps, were John S. Sargent, primarily a portrait-painter, and James A. McNeill Whistler, whose art encompassed many types of subjects, men who spent most of their time in Europe, where they found a ready market. Greater than either as a portraitist was the realist, Thomas Eakins, whose failure to attract enthusiasm for his work is an enlightening commentary both on the progress of the arts in America and on the viewpoint of the Gilded Age. More characteristic of American art was the painting of landscapes, which, under the brushes of such men as George Innis, Childe Hassam, and J. A. Weir, reached high excellence. Quite as notable were the memorable seascapes of Winslow Homer and Albert P. Ryder. Significant also was the illustration of books and magazines, which at the end of the century reached its highest point. Illustrators of the type of A. B. Frost, E. W. Kemble, Frederic Remington, Howard Pyle, E. A. Abbey, and Joseph Pennell gave to this work a dignity that was soon to decline before the drawing-room heroes and beautiful girls of less talented artists.

In sculpture and architecture America was likewise to see a revival. Postwar America had been content to decorate its parks with standardized war monuments, which were usually without distinction or artistic merit. Indoors, artistic aspirations in sculpture usually went no higher than the genre groups of John Rogers, which adorned the marble-topped tables of thousands of parlors. But with the work of Saint-Gaudens, MacMonnies, French, and Barnard, American sculpture entered upon a golden age. The bronze statutes of Civil War heroes now took on a spirit of realism, while the younger sculptors turned quickly to other themes.

The realism of a new age was also making itself felt in architecture, but it was a slow process. American architecture undoubtedly sank to its lowest depths in the years of Grant and Hayes. The classic revival of the early middle period had long since spent itself, and the Gothic revival had degenerated into overdecorated and overornamented buildings, littered with jigsaw trimmings, and topped by ugly mansard roofs fitted

---

[3] Both of these names were pseudonyms.

with useless gables and towers. In the cities the highest achievements in living quarters were "old-law tenements" and depressing mansions with brownstone fronts. As American architects trained in the schools of France returned to their native land, architecture achieved a higher level. Henry Hobson Richardson and Richard Morris Hunt, with frequent commissions for public buildings in a rapidly growing nation, revived the structural styles of Romanesque and Renaissance, while others again took up the classic style. Fortunately, the architectural improvement was gradually carried over into private dwellings; the houses designed by Richardson, Hunt, and their followers seem too heavy and stately for their needs, but any move toward simplicity was an advance over the gingerbread atrocities of the Grant era. In the World's Fair of 1893 came the architectural climax of the period, but in this creation of marvelous beauty there was little that was indigenous to American civilization. In one structure, however, the Transportation Building, largely designed by Louis Sullivan, where a conscious effort was made to adapt form to function, there was a refreshing gust of realism. The future, in fact, was with the Chicago school, Sullivan, Daniel Burnham, John W. Root, and others, who were experimenting with steel structures and skyscrapers and other buildings in which utility was stressed as well as beauty.

THE AGE OF SCIENCE

The influence of the Industrial Revolution and the impetus from Darwin's revolutionary hypothesis were the twin forces behind the scientific development of the last half of the nineteenth century. In this country advancing science was encouraged by the practical needs of a rapidly expanding economic life and by increased facilities for scientific research. As in earlier decades, America's chief contribution was on the practical side. The decade 1840–1850 had seen 6480 patents issued; the number in the decade 1890–1900 was 221,500. It was the age when Americans gave to the world the self-binding reaper and innumerable other improvements in agricultural machinery, the first transatlantic cable, the typewriter, new typesetting and printing machinery, the railway air brake and the refrigerator car and electric railways, the duplex telegraph and the telephone, the motion picture, the electric light, and a practical motor car. The story of this scientific advance has been told many times, but it cannot be too often emphasized that here lies the background of the social and economic life of the people. Whatever claim politicians, statesmen, soldiers, and diplomatists may have upon the attention of the student of history, it is upon the inventors, scientists, and industrial entrepreneurs that we must fix our attention if we are to understand a changing civilization. Men like J. F. Appleby (farm machinery), Alexander Graham Bell (telephone), George Eastman (photography), Thomas A. Edison (electricity), Langley and the Wrights (airplanes), and Henry Ford and others (automobiles) are quite as important for the historian as Cleveland or Roosevelt.

Of all lines of scientific advancement, none was more significant than that in electricity. Although the telegraph was invented in the thirties and the first transatlantic cable laid in 1866, it was not until the last quarter of the century that the electrical age really dawned. Its chief results have been in the creation and transportation of energy. In communication the advance has been steady from Bell's telephone of 1876 to Marconi's wireless of 1901 and the development of radio in the 1920s. The substitution of electricity for animal power or steam on street-car lines and railroads has been significant. Electricity has made easier the development of the automobile and airplane. Edison's electric light solved the problem of illumination, and, as scientists discovered how to manufacture electricity from water power and to transport it over long distances, there seemed to be no limit to its possible applications.

Considering the allurements of practical science and the financial rewards derived therefrom, the amount of work in scientific theory done in scholastic laboratories by scholars is significant of the finer aspects of this period. Beginning with the Columbia School of Mines in 1849 and the Massachusetts Institute of Technology and Worcester Polytechnic in 1865, the opportunities for scientific education and research were rapidly enlarged as other engineering schools were founded and as the universities added scientific courses and schools to their curriculum. At the same time national associations were organized to help pool the knowledge gained by research and to stimulate to greater efforts. In practically every branch of science there appeared great leaders. J. Willard Gibbs of Yale, in his researches in thermodynamics, influenced almost every branch of physics and "provided the theoretical basis for the new science of physical chemistry." [4] Simon Newcomb of Johns Hopkins, who recomputed the elements of the solar system, was recognized throughout the world as a pre-eminent astronomer. A notable school of geologists, basing their work on the evolutionary theory, made important contributions to the history of land-formation and by the study of fossil remains to the science of paleontology. Biological research was advanced by noted scholars, and psychology, which had heretofore been hampered as a branch of philosophy, now took on new life as an experimental science. G. Stanley Hall

[4] A. M. Schlesinger, *The Rise of the City,* 232.

founded Clark University and established there a famous school of experimental psychology, while William James did yeoman service for the same cause at Harvard.

Even in the social sciences there was a quick movement toward realism as the shoals of scholars returning from the German universities began to build from minute and thorough investigations new concepts of economics, history, and sociology. R. T. Ely, John R. Commons, Thorstein Veblen, and others, encouraged by Francis A. Walker, began to part company with classical economy as historical and statistical research opened a new vista. When Frederick Jackson Turner read in 1893 his paper on "The Significance of the Frontier in American History," he made it indisputably evident to all that American history must be viewed from the economic and physiographic viewpoints as well as from those of politics and diplomacy. In the meantime the work of Eggleston and the monumental volumes of McMaster were pointing the way to social history and to the life of the common man. Henry Adams, in the first five chapters of his *History of the United States,* also gave a striking example of the new history. On every hand there was evidence that eventually the student might gain a knowledge of his nation's history. With John W. Burgess, Woodrow Wilson, and F. J. Goodnow, realism also crept into political science, while the rise of sociology, through the work of Lester F. Ward, Franklin H. Giddings, William G. Sumner, and others, gave evidence that college students eventually must come to grips with a scientific study of society.

Upon no phase of American life was the effect of science more disturbing than upon religion. The evolutionary philosophy of Darwin and Spencer, popularized in America by John Fiske, E. L. Youmans, founder of the *Popular Science Monthly,* and others, brought a conflict the reverberations of which have not yet subsided. As the findings of Darwin were subjecting the Bible to the most minute and critical study, theologians and religious leaders were bound to reconsider the whole question of orthodox religion. Some repudiated Darwinian principles as utterly destructive of the Bible and all real religion; others sought to recast their faith by reconciling science and religion, asserting that one might accept the first without sacrificing any of the essentials of Christianity. The effect upon American religion was bound to be far-reaching. In the long run it tended to minimize the differences between sects and to give encouragement to those who would discard theological controversies and lay emphasis upon the immediate problems of the machine age. Broadcast by the stirring words of such English clergymen as Kingsley and Maurice, the "social gospel" reached this country. After the manner of Toynbee Hall in London, Hull House in Chicago and the Henry Street Settlement in

New York pointed the way until by the end of the century many city churches, whose leaders were dominated by the new religion, were striving to make of their churches social, recreational, and intellectual centers. While older preachers still thundered damnation for the erring and salvation by grace, many of the younger men talked of "Christian Socialism" and began critically to eye the economic order.

THE PEOPLE AT PLAY

The history of American recreation for the half century after 1870 is largely a story of urban amusement. The rural population had little time or energy left over for recreation, and what there was changed little through the years. In the towns and cities, however, increasing wealth gave to the wealthy an opportunity for amusement; the summer vacation and the shortening work day did the same for the middle and working classes. The urbanization of America affected the recreational life of the people in at least three important ways: first, the desire of the wealthy and middle classes to recapture the opportunities for exercise that an earlier age had enjoyed in the open country; second, the increasing professionalization of sports as the poorer classes, who had neither time, opportunity, nor money personally to participate, took their recreation in watching others perform; and third, the development of indoor amusement.

In answer to this demand for exercise, gymnasiums appeared in the cities, and tennis courts were thickly sprinkled over the suburban regions. Late in the 1870s golf was introduced, and by the end of the century country clubs with golf links were to be found where the wealthy congregated. The eighties and nineties were the "dude era" of golf; it was during the first decades of the new century that the game was rapidly taken up by the middle class. Wider in its appeal and enthusiastically followed by all classes was bicycling, a form of exercise that was to have an important influence upon the movement for better roads. At the height of its popularity "wheeling" was challenged by the automobile, but a decade was to pass before the motorcar was much more than a "plaything of the rich." At the turn of the century probably more adult Americans played croquet than any other game, but it was too leisurely to hold the allegiance of an intense and hurried generation.

For those who had neither the time nor the money for personal participation, there developed a rapid extension of professional athletics. Undoubtedly baseball held the premier position among American sports. Small-town America had been nurtured on baseball, and it was early professionalized; the National League, which aimed to make professional baseball respectable, was founded in 1876. Although many minor or "bush" leagues prospered, the National League succeeded until the nineties in crushing any rival that threatened to become national in scope. When the Western League, organized in 1893, became the American League in 1900 and began a bitter and successful war against the older organization, the monopoly of the National was broken, and baseball "fans" by the million were now able to follow their favorites in both leagues as the teams of each gave daily battle in the leading cities of the country and at the end of the season fought for the world title. Boxing, which commanded the support of large numbers, was always essentially professional, as was horse racing, which grew rapidly during these years. Although tennis, track, and other outdoor sports struggled with fair success to maintain an amateur standing, the line between professional and amateur was often so faint as to be almost indistinguishable. In college sport intercollegiate athletics developed teams of star performers, while the great majority of students were simply onlookers, and professional coaches and star athletes supported by scholarships gave to intercollegiate sport a tinge of professionalism. Real efforts to reform college sport were made in the early years of the new century but with only indifferent success.

One form of outdoor recreation developed widely in these years was the amusement park. The trolley lines, with their normal traffic curtailed on Sunday, sought increased income by sponsoring amusement parks. Some could show little more than a trolley station and a pavilion; others, like Coney Island, boasted every type of amusement. On a larger scale and with an educational interest were the series of expositions that began with the Columbian Exposition in Chicago in 1893 and the Trans-Mississippi Exposition in 1898. These gave to millions of Americans an opportunity and an excuse to extend their recreation to regions far from home.

Even more characteristic of indoor than of outdoor recreation was the amusement provided by stars and professionals rather than by wide-scale mass participation. The recreational facilities provided by the Y.M.C.A. and the Y.W.C.A. did something to counteract this, but the theater, particularly in the winter, provided the chief recreation for the urban masses. Increasingly the themes utilized by the theater turned to American scenes with American actors in the leading roles. In the eighties and nineties plays depicting rural life—Denman Thompson's *The Old Homestead,* Lottie Parker's *Way Down East,* and James A. Herne's *Shore Acres*—vied in popularity with such Civil War plays as Bronson Howard's *Shenandoah* and David Belasco's *The Heart of Maryland.* The production in 1878 of Gilbert and Sullivan's *Pinafore* brought quickly into favor the comic opera, which was given further stimulus in 1886 by the phenomenal success of the operetta *Erminie* and a little later by the charming operas of Reginald De Koven and Victor Herbert. Undoubtedly the most important development during these years in the field of indoor amusement was the incipient moving picture. Animated picture films were projected as early as 1894 and 1895, but it was not until well after the turn of the century that the moving picture became the leading form of cheap indoor amusement.

Students as yet have given but little attention to the causes and implication of the tremendous growth of secret fraternal organizations that took place in the decades following the Civil War. Patterned in general after the ancient Masonic order, they took the form in the college world of Greek-letter fraternities and in the world at large of scores of secret organizations. Their membership, which amounted to over 6,000,000 in 1900 and 15,600,000 in 1914, was made up essentially of artisans, shopkeepers, and the smaller professional men, drawn for all sorts of reasons to the Odd Fellows, the Freemasons, the Knights of Pythias, the United Woodmen, and the "animal orders" of Moose, Elks, Owls, and Eagles, or to one or more of the innumerable similar organizations. Escape from the drabness of life through the medium of gorgeous uniforms and mystic ceremonies undoubtedly made them popular, as well as the recreational facilities and the sick and death benefits—to say nothing of the business, professional, and political contacts that they offered. Their tremendous vogue was to be weakened in later years by the "movies," the automobile, and the radio, but for the half century following 1870 they occupied a leading place in the recreational life of the people.

Two brilliant chapters that catch the spirit and significance of the Gilded Age are C. and M. Beard, *The Rise of American Civilization*, Chap. XXV, and L. M. Hacker and B. B. Kendrick, *The United States Since 1865*, Chap. XIII. On the earlier part of this period, see Allan Nevins, *The Emergence of Modern America*, Chaps. VIII–X, XII, and on the later period A. M. Schlesinger, *The Rise of the City*, Chaps. IV–XI (both in the History of American Life). Intellectual trends are summarized and interpreted in Merle Curti, *The Growth of American Thought*, Chaps. XX–XXII, and in Vernon L. Parrington, *Main Currents in American Thought*, Vol. III. See the bibliography at the back of this book for titles on the many topics of this chapter.

Chapter XXIX

LINES OF ECONOMIC BATTLE

A small number of men are obtaining the power to forbid any but themselves to supply the people with fire in nearly every form known to modern life and industry, from matches to locomotives and electricity. They control our hard coal and much of the soft, and stoves, furnaces, and steam and hot-water heaters; the governors on steam-boilers and the boilers; gas and gas-fixtures; natural gas and gas-pipes; electric lighting, and all the appurtenances. You cannot free yourself by changing from electricity to gas, or from the gas of the city to the gas of the fields. If you fly from kerosene to candles, you are still under the ban.

HENRY DEMAREST LLOYD

CONSOLIDATION OF BUSINESS

For almost a quarter of a century following the Civil War, American politics, except for the protests of minor parties, failed to come to grips with the fundamental problems of American civilization. Essentially, these problems evolved from the Industrial Revolution, which had created a new America, and the most important among them were the plight of the farmer, the growing power and consolidation of industrial capitalism, and the position of labor in the new industrial order. By the late eighties, however, these problems could no longer be avoided, and on the political front conflicting philosophies and economic interests were fought out over the policies to be followed with reference to currency, tariff, labor, and the public control of transportation and industrial monopolies. Some attention has already been given to currency, to labor, and to the efforts to control transportation. It will be the purpose of this chapter to discuss more fully the questions of industrial consolidation and tariff so that a broad economic background may be presented for the epic struggle of 1896.

With the growth in America of population, of markets, of adequate transportation facilities, and of a realization of the savings to be effected by large-scale production, the development of big business was inevitable. In the sixty years from 1850 to 1910, the average manufacturing plant multiplied its capital more than thirty-nine times, the number of its wage-earners nearly seven times, and the value of its output more than nineteen times. This normal development was not in itself necessarily dangerous to the general welfare; quite the contrary, it was often distinctly advantageous to the consumer. The danger lay in the consolidation of industry to an extent that competition was throttled and a condition of monopoly created. The danger of monopoly was well understood, and custom or common law had long attempted to limit monopolies to those created or controlled by the government. Thus the coining of money was a monopoly of the government, the right to the sole use by a private individual or company of a new invention was a monopoly granted by the government, and the right of the public to control a monopoly such as a railroad was hardly questioned. The problem that developed in the decades after the Civil War arose out of a situation in which industrial units were uniting in some form or other to create monopolies not granted by the government and as yet not under public control. Briefly stated the problem was as follows: (1) should the public allow the development of monopolies unhindered and uncontrolled, (2) should it allow them to develop subject to government control, or (3) should it prevent the development of monopoly and attempt to maintain competition? The first was unthinkable, the second seemed unwise, and the third, in line with age-old precedent, seemed to most the natural thing to do.

The effort to prevent monopolies was also consistent with the teachings of the classical economists, who conceived the ideal state as one in which free competition reigned supreme. "Competition is the life of trade" was a favorite maxim. The effect of unbridled competition on the producers, however, was to drive some into bankruptcy and others to seek safety in consolidation. Practically all the witnesses appearing before the Industrial Commission in 1899 testified that "competition so vigorous that profits of nearly all competing establishments were destroyed" [1] was the driving force behind business consolidation. In every type of business, new and old, bitter competition left in its train the wreckage of what had earlier been prosperous concerns. Even railroads, which enjoyed a virtual monopoly over at least part of their short history, were almost ruined where competition existed. The golden age of the small business lasted until the panic of 1873; after that American business sought by various methods—pools, trusts, holding companies, mergers, and "community of interest"—to escape ruinous competition and achieve greater profits.

The earliest means of avoiding competition was by "pooling," a device

[1] *Preliminary Report of the Industrial Commission,* 9.

by which the members of the pool sought to control prices by apportioning in some way the available business. Such agreements can be traced back in the cordage industry to 1861, but the important period of pooling was in the fifteen years after the panic of 1873, when pools were resorted to in the salt, whisky, coal, and other industries. They were particularly popular among the railroads, which sought to save themselves by apportioning freight and fixing rates. Although pools in one form or another persisted for many years, they were specifically declared illegal in railroads by the Interstate Commerce Act of 1887 and were rapidly superseded during the decade 1887–1897 by a new device known as the "trust," a term that came to be popularly used in later years to designate a monopoly of any kind. A trust, strictly speaking, was a form of organization in which the stockholders under a trust agreement turned over to a group of trustees a controlling portion of the stock of a company to be administered by the trustees. Unlike a pool, this was no confederation, but an actual consolidation of interests.

If the stockholders of the principal units of an industry turned over their stock to a single group of trustees, a monopoly might be created. Such a monopoly was actually achieved by the Standard Oil Company through trust agreements in 1879 and 1882, when 90 per cent of the refining capacity of the country was consolidated in a single trust. So successful was the Standard Oil Trust that other industries hastened to follow, the most important of which were the American Cottonseed Oil Trust (1884), National Linseed Oil Trust (1885), National Lead Trust (1887), Distillers' and Cattle Feeders' Trust (Whisky Trust, 1887), Sugar Refineries Company (1887), and National Cordage Company (1887).

The ease with which a monopoly could be created by a trust agreement aroused, as we shall see, an immediate reaction in the form of state and federal antitrust laws, which brought the dissolution of the Standard Oil Company by the Ohio courts in 1892. This, with the depression of 1893, held up further consolidation under the trust form, and, when the consolidation movement commenced again in the period 1897–1904, the form adopted was the holding company. A holding company is an organization formed to hold a sufficient proportion of the stock of another company to enable it to control the operations of that company. Thus, the board of directors of the holding company, with a controlling share of the stock of a number of units in the same industry, may dominate the policies of them all. Under the leadership again of the Standard Oil Company, and encouraged by the complacent corporation laws of a number of states, particularly New Jersey, West Virginia, Delaware, and Maine, almost all the important industries of the period were reorganized into holding companies. Certain of these holding companies, such as the Standard Oil Company of New Jersey and the Northern Securities Company, obviously created monopolistic conditions and were dissolved by the Supreme Court. Others, such as the United States Steel Company, which for all practical purposes have established monopoly situations, managed to survive court action. Today almost all important industries have in them huge holding corporations. Some of them are virtually monopolies; others are not. Whether or not, it has made little difference in the long run. The inevitable integration of capital has often created a "community of interest" that has produced a situation similar to monopoly. In like manner business has often accomplished the same end by such devices as the trade association.

These last remarks anticipate the story. We are here primarily interested in the early agitation against monopolies and the early antitrust legislation. There can be no doubt that the early reaction of Americans to monopolies was distinctly hostile. There existed a deep-seated antipathy to them, inherited from the old common-law conception, an antipathy that was strengthened by the ruthless policies of big business and by the exposures and denunciations of the public press. It was obvious even to the most superficial observer that both the producer of raw materials and the consumer of the finished product were almost helpless before a strong monopoly. Even labor saw the dangerous implications of a situation in which the control of the machines was being consolidated into the hands of great corporations without a simultaneous consolidation of its own ranks. The political debauchery practiced by big business was rightfully regarded as a national menace, and the fear of it was well expressed by the Michigan Supreme Court: "Indeed, it is doubtful if free government can long exist in a country where such enormous amounts of money are allowed to be accumulated in the vaults of corporations, to be used at discretion in controlling the property and business of the country against the interest of the public, for the personal gain and aggrandizement of a few individuals." [2] To the argument that large-scale production decreased costs, the consumer could only say that he had benefited little if at all. Another decade and economists were able to show that by combination business had increased its margin of profit but the consumer had gained little. After an exhaustive investigation the Industrial Commission came to the conclusion in 1902 "that in most cases the combination has exerted an appreciable power over prices and in practically all cases it has increased the margin between raw materials and finished products. Since there is reason to believe that the cost of production over a period of years has lessened, the conclusion is inevitable that the combinations have been able to increase their profits." [3]

[2] Richardson *v.* Buhl *et al.*, 77 Michigan State Reports, 658.
[3] *Final Report of the Industrial Commission*, XIX, 621.

If any date is to be picked for the start of a strong antimonopoly movement in this country, it might be 1879, the date of the publication of Henry George's *Progress and Poverty*. His insistence that the woes of modern civilization were largely due to a monopoly of land stirred his generation profoundly, particularly those who had seen the passing of the frontier. Edward Bellamy's *Looking Backward* (1887), of which a million copies were sold, pictured a sane and plentiful life under a socialistic economy and thus threw into invidious comparison the chaotic life of competitive capitalism. Henry Demarest Lloyd and other journalists were commencing their attacks in the public press. Lloyd's book, *Wealth Against Commonwealth* (1894), did not appear until the first outburst of antitrust legislation had been passed, but it remains the most powerful indictment of monopoly ever written. Opposition to monopolies soon expressed itself politically. As early as 1872 both major parties opposed further land grants to railroads; the Greenbackers in 1880, the Antimonopolists in 1884, and finally all four of the chief parties in 1888 (Republican, Democratic, Prohibitionist, and Union Labor) called for government action to prevent monopolies.[4]

Although the common law frowned upon conspiracies in restraint of trade, specific statute law on this subject hardly existed in the states. In the federal government there was neither common nor statute law to govern the practice of courts. The common law was somewhat indefinite and hardly went beyond declaring conspiracies invalid when they were proved. It was to bring this whole problem upon a more definite basis that agitation for state and federal legislation began. Investigations by the federal House and by state legislatures preceded action, but, when the movement once started, the progress of legislation was rapid. By the end of 1890 at least twenty-seven states and territories had passed laws against monopolies, while fifteen states had incorporated provisions in their constitutions.

Antitrust bills were presented in Congress in 1888, but the famous Sherman Antitrust Act was not passed until 1890.[5] The general principles of the act are contained in the first two of the eight sections:

> Sec. 1. Every contract, combination in the form of trust or otherwise, or conspiracy, in restraint of trade or commerce among the several states, is hereby declared to be illegal. . . .
> Sec. 2. Every person who shall monopolize or attempt to monopolize any

[4] Opposition to monopolies, of course, can be found long before this period. At least one party before the Civil War, the Equal Rights Party (Locofocos), which emerged in 1835 and was significant in New York state politics, included this in its principles.

[5] The name is a misnomer. It was written not by Sherman but by the Judiciary Committee, of which Senator Edmunds of Vermont was chairman. Edmunds himself wrote five of the eight sections.

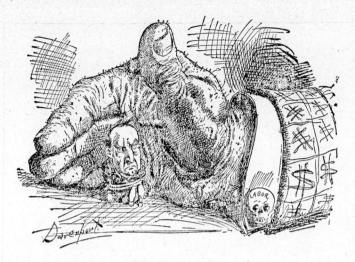

A Man Well in Hand.

A WHOLE SHOW IN HIMSELF

Election Cartoons, 1896

("A Man Well in Hand" by permission of the *New York Evening Journal;* "A Whole Show in Himself" by permission of Frank A. Munsey Company.)

UNCLE SAM—THAT'S A LIVE WIRE, GENTLEMEN!

IS THIS WHAT WE WANT?

IMPERIALISM CARTOONS

("That's a Live Wire, Gentlemen!" by permission of Frank A. Munsey Company;
"Is This What We Want?" by permission of the Press Publishing Company.)

part of the trade or commerce among the several states, or with foreign nations, shall be deemed guilty of a misdemeanor.

For violation fines and imprisonment were provided, with the provision that the injured person might recover three times the amount of the damages. The Attorney General was instructed to institute proceedings.

No measure has surpassed the Sherman Antitrust Act in popularity. Only one day was given to its discussion in the Senate, and but one vote was cast against it in the two houses of Congress. Apparently the nation believed in the act and wanted it enforced. Nevertheless, very little effort was made to enforce it until the days of Theodore Roosevelt, and, as far as business was concerned, it was essentially futile. The political weakness of the Harrison administration after 1890, the close affiliations of Cleveland with Wall Street, and the domination of the McKinley administration by big business prevented aggressive action; only eighteen suits were instigated under the act down to 1901, and these were generally unsuccessful. A decade and a half after the Sherman Act was passed, there were few who would dispute Professor Jenks's statement that "a study of these statutes and of the decisions of our courts of last resort which have been made under them will show that they have had little, practically no effect, as regards the trend of our industrial development." [6]

While the Sherman Act may have had little if any effect upon the trend of business consolidation, it has had some influence upon the labor movement. Senator Sherman, sensing the possibility that the act might be used for another than the obvious purpose, sent to the committee that framed the bill a proviso that labor and farmers' organizations be excluded from the operation of the act. The proviso was not included because the senators felt it unnecessary. Four years later Attorney General Olney suggested the act to Cleveland as a means of fighting the Pullman strike of 1894. Later it was used to prevent labor from conducting interstate boycotts against the products of manufacturers whom they believed unfair.

THE TARIFF ISSUE

To many antimonopolists it was the tariff that was primarily responsible for the development of industrial monopolies. As we have already noted, the climax of the early protective-tariff movement was reached in 1828 in the so-called "tariff of abominations" (page 256). The strong opposition of the South, climaxed by the attempted nullification of South Carolina, was followed by a period of lower tariffs. Although the protective feature was never lost sight of, the trend, except for the brief period 1842–1846,

[6] J. W. Jenks, *The Trust Problem* (revised edition, 1905), 218.

was downward. With the tariff of 1857 the nation approached as near to a free-trade basis as had existed since 1816. This period of lower tariffs was due in part to the long control of the federal government by the Democratic Party, dominated by the Southern wing. Their power was broken by the victory of the Republican Party in 1860, and with the Morrill Act of 1861 a new period of high tariffs was inaugurated. The Republicans, hoping to attract the old high-tariff Whigs, had advocated in their platform of 1860 an increase in rates; and the Morrill Act followed their victory. This act was not passed as a war measure, but it contributed to precipitating the conflict. War having started, the rates were raised at every session of Congress, with wholesale advances in 1862 and 1864. Not only did the government need revenue, but the manufacturers not unreasonably demanded more protection to balance the vast system of internal taxes that had been levied upon many commodities. By the end of the war the average level was about 47 per cent, and these tariffs, crudely conceived and hastily drawn, remained the basis for many years of the American system (page 356).

With the exception of the short period after the panic of 1857, the years 1846–1861 had been characterized by great prosperity, and there had been practically no demand on the part of manufacturers for the Morrill tariff. Having tasted the sweets of protection, however, they were loath to relinquish them, and, being better organized to fight reduction, they were able to maintain them. Their fighting position was greatly strengthened by the fact that the two major parties up to 1888 were in substantial agreement on the tariff issue. The exorbitantly high tariffs resulting from the war, however, did not go unchallenged. With the passing of the emergency and the realization of their unscientific nature, a strong movement developed for reduction. This was led by such men as David A. Wells, Special Commissioner of the Revenue, Secretary of the Treasury McCulloch, and Carl Schurz, and was promoted by the recently founded American Free Trade League, which included in its membership many respected leaders of public opinion. The first break came in an act of 1870, which aimed to reduce taxation but resulted only in a lowering of the rates on such purely revenue articles as tea, coffee, wines, and sugar, and hardly touched the problem of protection. With the growth of the Liberal Republican movement in 1872, which drew to itself most of the tariff reformers, the party in power hastened to protect itself just before election by reducing the rates by an average of 10 per cent. A decline of revenue resulting from the panic of 1873 gave an excuse for restoring the duties of 1875.

There was some discussion of tariff revision in the campaign of 1880, but it was the surplus of $100,000,000 in the treasury during 1881 and 1882 that brought some action. In view of this surplus, President Arthur, in his first message, urged a reduction of the internal taxes and a revision of the tariff. Congress replied by authorizing the appointment of a tariff commission. This commission, entirely protectionist in its make-up and headed by the secretary of the National Association of Wool Manufacturers, recommended reductions that in some cases ran as high as 50 per cent. The average reduction recommended was about 25 per cent, which, considering the personnel of the commission, is a remarkable commentary on the existing tariff. The response of Congress was to lower the general tariff rate about 5 per cent but to repeal most of the internal taxes remaining from the Civil War days. Real revision, as usual, was prevented by wholesale lobbying and by the clever maneuvers of strong protectionist congressmen, who referred the measure to a conference committee of both houses containing an overwhelming majority of high-protectionists.

It was Grover Cleveland who forced the two major parties to take a definite stand on the tariff question and who was responsible for placing it squarely before the voters. Disturbed by the mounting treasury surplus, which had climbed to over $500,000,000 by June 30, 1885, and convinced that the way out led through tariff reduction, Cleveland devoted his entire message of 1887 to the problem. The existing tariff law he characterized as a "vicious, inequitable, and illogical source of unnecessary taxation," which "ought to be at once revised and amended," but pointed out clearly that he was not advocating free trade. "Our progress toward a wise conclusion," he insisted, "will not be improved by dwelling upon the theories of protection and free trade. This savors too much of bandying epithets. It is a *condition* which confronts us, not a theory. . . . The question of free trade is absolutely irrelevant. . . ." Fearing the effect of this message upon the next election,[7] many Democrats greeted it coldly, but the great majority rallied to the President. Under the direction of Roger Q. Mills, chairman of the Ways and Means Committee, and John G. Carlisle, Speaker of the House, the Democrats introduced in 1888 a bill "to prevent the accumulation of surplus revenue by reducing the excessive and unjust rates of taxation." Led by William McKinley and Thomas B. Reed, the Republicans made a spirited attack on the Mills Bill, and in the "great tariff debate of 1888" the public had an opportunity to hear a full discussion of the problem. The Mills Bill passed the House by practically a straight party

[7] Much light is thrown on Cleveland's character by his reply to a group of tariff reformers who had urged him, because of the political danger, to delay his tariff message until after the coming presidential elections. "Do you not think," he said, "that the people of the United States are entitled to some instruction on this subject?" Worthy of note is another remark, "What is the use of being elected or re-elected unless you stand for something?" Robert McElroy, *Cleveland*, I, 264.

vote, 162–147, but was not pressed for passage in the Republican Senate. To show the type of revision that might be expected from the Republicans, Senators Allison and Aldrich also prepared a bill, but it was buried by the Ways and Means Committee of the House.

Although Cleveland received the greater popular vote in the election of 1888, fought chiefly over the tariff issue, Harrison won the presidency and carried with him both houses of Congress. Acting on the assumption that they had received a mandate from the nation to revise the tariff upward the Republicans in 1890 pushed through the McKinley tariff. Described as the "climax of protection," the McKinley Act raised the average level to almost 50 per cent, placing quite unnecessary protection upon agricultural products and extremely high rates on the finer grades of woolens, cottons, linens, and clothing, and on iron, steel, glass, and tin plate. To take care of the treasury surplus, the duties on sugar were removed, but at the same time a bounty of two cents a pound was granted to domestic producers. As a gesture toward the growing American exports, and at the insistence of Secretary of State Blaine, the President was given the power to raise the duties on certain commodities if he believed other nations were levying discriminatory duties against American goods. The reaction of the voter to the McKinley tariff in the election of 1890 was swift and decisive. In a veritable landslide the Republican majority in the House was overthrown, and the majority in the Senate was cut down. In 1892, the third consecutive election in which the tariff was the chief issue, Cleveland was elected for a second time and in this instance with a Democratic majority in both houses (page 466).

If any American party ever had a clear mandate, it would appear that the Democrats had such a one when they took over the government in 1893. The Wilson Bill, as it emerged from the House, was an honest effort toward tariff reduction, but by the time it passed the Senate it was hardly recognizable. Democratic senators, many of whom were antagonistic to Cleveland and all of whom were quick to insist on protection to the industries of their own states, largely rewrote the tariff. In the end, it lowered the average to a little less than 40 per cent and put wool, copper, and lumber on the free list. Coal, iron, and sugar, which the House had put on the free list, were protected by duties in the Senate. To all true tariff-reformers, the Wilson-Gorman Act of 1894 was a bitter disappointment. Cleveland denounced it as a piece of party perfidy and dishonor, but allowed it to become a law without his signature. It did much to demoralize and weaken the party that sponsored it. To take care of the prospective decline in income resulting from lowered rates, the Democrats added to the bill an income tax of 2 per cent on incomes over $4000, but the Supreme Court declared it unconstitutional in 1895.

THE GATHERING OF THE FORCES

As the nation entered the last decade of the century, the prospects were reasonably bright. The postwar deflation, accentuated by the panic of 1873, seemed to be temporarily halted. For the farmers, 1890 was the most prosperous year they had experienced for a long period. Federal regulation of railroads had been inaugurated in 1887, and the thrifty administration of Cleveland, combined with industrial prosperity, had piled up a large treasury surplus, which presaged a reduction of taxation. The popular Sherman Antitrust Act of 1890 went far to lift from the masses the fear of big business, while the Sherman Silver Purchase Act of the same year was a move toward inflation that might ultimately help the debtor. True, the McKinley tariff was unpopular, but with the election of Cleveland that measure was doomed. Many reforms, long agitated, appeared to have been finally achieved.

The bright prospects of 1890, however, quickly faded. It was soon evident that the great demand for agricultural products in 1890 was due to poor crops abroad, and the prices of wheat, corn, and cotton resumed their downward course. For the moment the inflationary silver act appeared to be futile. Europe suffered a serious depression in 1890, which eventually affected adversely American exporters and at the same time caused a liquidation of American securities held abroad and an export of gold from this country. The extravagances of the Harrison administration had depleted the federal treasury, and the hoped-for reduction in taxation had ended only in a higher tariff. The failure of labor in the spectacular Homestead strike of 1892 was a distinct blow to the organized workers. To the more intelligent observers it was soon apparent that in their existing form little could be expected from either the Interstate Commerce Act or the Sherman Antitrust Act. To increase the disillusionment came the panic of 1893. Most conservative business leaders attributed the panic to the Sherman Silver Purchase Act and the fear that the nation would go off the gold standard; Republican politicians stressed business men's fear of the impending tariff reductions; the Democrats countered by attributing the catastrophe to Republican legislation, particularly the McKinley tariff, and to the extravagant policy of the Harrison administration. Any or all of these may have been contributing causes; the primary factor, as we see it now, was the overexpansion of transportation facilities and industrial production, accompanied by unconscionable stock-manipulation and reckless speculation. It marked the end of a business cycle and, as usual, was preceded by a similar depression abroad.

Whatever may have been the causes, the effects were devastating. Over six hundred banks failed in the single year 1893, and seventy-four railroad corporations operating more than 30,000 miles of railroad went into the hands of receivers. To Cleveland, whose economic knowledge was, to say the least, somewhat limited, there was only one cause for all this— the silver legislation of 1890. Calling Congress in special session, he demanded its immediate repeal. Despite bitter opposition from agrarian inflationists such as Bland and Bryan, repeal quickly passed the House by 239 to 108. In the Senate, however, the battle lasted for almost three months before Cleveland was victorious. There party lines were utterly smashed; including pairs, 22 Democrats and 26 Republicans favored repeal, with 22 Democrats, 12 Republicans, and 3 Populists opposed.

Having secured repeal of the Sherman Silver Purchase Act, Cleveland set himself to save the gold standard. When the gold reserve fell below the $100,000,000 mark, the treasury sold four issues of bonds between January, 1894, and January, 1896, the first three to the bankers and the fourth to the public. The difficulty of maintaining the gold standard when bankers presented paper to the treasury for gold and then turned back the gold for bonds is obvious, and Cleveland's persistence against the endless chain was highly commended by those who believed with him. The disappointment of the inflationists, on the other hand, with victory almost within their grasp, can easily be imagined. To intensify their resentment was the fact that Cleveland had saved the gold standard by selling his third issue of bonds to J. Pierpont Morgan, August Belmont, and the Rothschilds on terms by which the government obtained $65,116,244 and the syndicate netted for itself a fat profit of $7,500,000. Cleveland's currency policy presented a blank wall to the inflationists and hopelessly split his party.

While the agrarian South and West were embittered over the repeal of the silver legislation, organized labor likewise felt the opposition of the federal government. Cleveland's use of the Sherman Antitrust Act to break the Pullman strike of 1894 and his questionable, if not unconstitutional, sending of federal troops to Illinois against the courageous opposition of Governor John P. Altgeld [8] placed the administration definitely on the side of capital (page 410). The tariff fiasco of 1894 shattered the hope of all honest tariff-reformers. The fate of the income-tax part of the Wilson-Gorman Act left conservative capitalism the victor on all fronts. An income tax, it will be remembered (page 494), had been levied during the Civil War, and its constitutionality had been subsequently upheld by the Supreme Court (Springer v. United States). Nevertheless, the question of the constitutionality was again brought to the Supreme Court in the case of Pollock v. Farmers' Loan and Trust Company. Attacked by eminent counsel on the ground that it was socialistic, that it was class legislation violating the rights of property, that it imposed undue burdens upon cer-

[8] See the Constitution, Article IV, Section 4.

tain sections, and that it was a direct tax that could be levied only in proportion to population (Article I, Section 9), the tax was eventually held invalid by a vote of 5 to 4.[9] The conduct of the court throughout the proceedings had been vacillating, and the opinion of the majority, delivered by Justice Field, was plainly marked by class prejudice. After this decision there were few who could doubt that learned judges as well as the common man might be dominated by economic traditions. With the exception of the period following the Dred Scott decision, it is doubtful if the prestige of the Supreme Court ever sank lower.

THE CRITICAL ELECTION

The panic of 1893 alone was enough to bring a political reversal, but when to this were added the disappointment, disillusion, and resentment occasioned by Cleveland's financial policy, the Democratic Party had little to hope for in 1894. In the congressional elections of that year the Republicans won the House by a tremendous majority (248 to 104) and recovered a slight lead in the Senate, where the Populists now held the balance of power. In that year the Populists polled 1,471,600 votes, an increase of 42 per cent over 1892, and elected seven congressmen and six senators. With the Democratic Party thoroughly demoralized, the Republicans viewed the prospects for 1896 with confidence. Few even of their most astute politicians realized the task that confronted them.

When the Republican convention met in June of 1896, the nomination of William McKinley was a foregone conclusion and was effected on the first ballot. For the vice-presidency Garret A. Hobart of New Jersey received the nomination. The easy victory of McKinley was due primarily to the efforts of a Cleveland capitalist, Marcus Alonzo Hanna, who had relinquished his business career the year before to push the political fortunes of his friend. Hanna soon became symbolic of the capitalist of his day who used politics to serve the needs of big business, and he was cartooned in the opposition press with a low-browed bulldog face and his waistcoat covered with dollar signs. As a matter of fact, Hanna was a realist in politics and business, certainly no worse than the typical politician and big business man of his era. He sincerely believed that the salvation of his country lay in the election of McKinley, the return of the Republican Party, and a close alliance between business and politics. His lack of hypocrisy won for him wide respect, and during his years in the Senate he attained the stature of real statesmanship.

[9] The case was heard twice. Justice Jackson had been ill during the first hearing, and the decision was 4 to 4. Upon a rehearing Jackson voted to uphold the act, but another justice changed his mind and voted against it.

Hanna's primary object at the convention was the nomination of Mc-Kinley. Both men were ardent protectionists, and a strong protective plank was written into the platform. Neither was interested primarily in currency. McKinley had voted for both the Bland-Allison Act and the Sherman Silver Purchase Act, and Hanna, like many other prominent men in Ohio, tended toward bimetallism. When Hanna realized that the convention was dominated by gold-standard Easterners, he sacrificed his own position, swung McKinley to gold, and allowed the "sound money" men to write the platform—holding them off just long enough to make them feel they had won a great victory for which in return they must support McKinley.[10] In the meantime, Hanna had tried to conciliate the silver Republicans, but without success. When the gold plank was presented, Senator Henry M. Teller of Colorado moved to substitute one calling for the free and unlimited coinage of gold and silver at the ratio 16:1. When this was rejected, thirty-three delegates followed Teller from the hall.

Whatever hopes the Democratic Party had in 1896 were dependent upon capturing the agrarian discontent in the West and South. To do this it was necessary to repudiate the gold-standard Cleveland Democrats of the East and somehow absorb the rising Populist movement. This the Democratic Party succeeded in doing, but it was not quite enough. When its convention met, the South and West were in the saddle. They wrote the platform, which demanded the free coinage of both metals at 16:1, condemned the bond issues of Cleveland, denounced the system of national-bank notes, the McKinley tariff, and the interference of the federal government in local affairs, demanded laws to protect the interests of labor, and called for a more equitable system of taxation. The platform was unique in repudiating practically every domestic policy that its own party administration had followed for four years, and it was a direct call to the masses of the country to do battle against plutocracy. The defense of the Cleveland administration by Senator Hill of New York and Governor Russell of Massachusetts was greeted with resentment, and the report of the minority of the platform committee was downed by a sectional vote.

It was in the debate over the platform that the party found its leader and its candidate for three presidential elections. William Jennings Bryan (1860-1925), born in Illinois, had moved as a young man to Nebraska,

[10] The Republican currency plank as finally adopted by a majority of approximately 8 to 1 was as follows: "We are unalterably opposed to every measure calculated to debase our currency or impair the credit of our country. We are, therefore, opposed to the free coinage of silver except by international agreement with the leading nations of the world, which we pledge ourselves to promote, and until such agreement can be obtained the existing gold standard must be preserved. All our silver and paper currency must be maintained at parity with gold, and we favor all measures designed to maintain inviolably the obligations of the United States and all our money, whether coin or paper, at the present standard, the standard of the most enlightened nations of the earth."

where an unremunerative law practice turned his mind to politics. Nominated for Congress in a strongly Republican district, he was carried in on the Democratic landslide of 1890 and re-elected two years later. He was an unsuccessful candidate for the Senate in 1894 and spent the next two years as editor of the Omaha *World-Herald,* a newspaper subsidized by the silver interests. In Congress Bryan's oratorical abilities, as displayed in powerful speeches against the McKinley tariff and Cleveland's currency policy, won him quick recognition, and his speaking trips in the South and West made him well known in those sections. For two years Bryan had been preparing for this moment, urging his candidacy upon his friends and polishing his speech before many a country audience. Whatever Bryan was or was not, he was an orator of consummate power, who could give voice to the unspoken thoughts of the multitude and play at will upon their emotions. He did both at the convention, and, when the stirring peroration ended, twenty thousand people were cheering wildly.

Having behind us the producing masses of this nation and the world [he concluded], supported by the commercial interests, the laboring interests, and the toilers everywhere, we will answer their demand for a gold standard by saying to them: you shall not press down upon the brow of labor this crown of thorns, you shall not crucify mankind upon a cross of gold.

Bryan's cross-of-gold speech made his nomination inevitable. In the radical wing of the Democratic Party, which had taken possession of the convention, Governor John P. Altgeld was the strongest personality, but his German birth disqualified him for the nomination. Considering the platform, "Silver Dick" Bland was perhaps the logical candidate, and there were many who dallied with the idea of nominating H. M. Teller, the Republican silver senator. But the sentiment was obviously for Bryan, and he was nominated on the fifth ballot. Arthur Sewell of Maine, a bank president and shipbuilder, received the vice-presidential nomination. With their principal demand now incorporated in the Democratic platform, the Populists, rather than split the radical strength, also nominated Bryan, but presented for the vice-presidency Thomas E. Watson. The Prohibition, the National,[11] and the Socialist-Labor Parties also offered candidates, but the only minor party to play a significant role was a group of seceding gold Democrats, inspired by Cleveland and largely financed by Republicans, who nominated candidates and split the Democratic strength in several critical states.

---

[11] The Prohibitionists in 1896 split into two groups, those who would stress a single issue, and the minority (National Party), who included planks for free silver, an income tax, and government ownership of railroads and telegraphs.

"I am a tariff man standing on a tariff platform," declared McKinley at the beginning of the campaign. "This money question is unduly prominent. In thirty days you won't hear anything about it." "In thirty days," replied Judge Day, "you won't hear of anything else." Day was correct; but the battle cries of "gold standard" and "16 to 1" were but symbols of a more fundamental conflict. On the one side were the great interests vested in finance, industry, and transportation, the "money power" of the new capitalism, which had developed rapidly in the three decades following the Civil War; on the other were the agrarians of the West and South and the "common people" of all sections who sensed the significance of the battle. The campaign, said Tom Johnson, was "the first great protest of the American people against monopoly—the first great struggle of the masses of our country against the privileged classes." After forty years the historian with equal accuracy may say that it was the last such uprising, unless the campaigns of 1912 and 1932 might be so considered.

The Republican campaign tactics, as directed by Hanna, were in no way original, but they were extremely effective. McKinley remained at home and from his front porch delivered carefully prepared speeches to hand-picked delegations sent to Canton, Ohio, by special trains. With the moneyed interests recovered from their initial fright, Hanna extracted at least $4,000,000 for the National Committee alone, which he used for "educational" propaganda—120,000,000 pamphlets, 1400 campaign speakers, bands, parades, and so on. Mortgage-holders terrorized farmers with threats of foreclosure, and manufacturers frightened laborers with threats to close their factories if Bryan was elected. Denunciation and ridicule were heaped upon Bryan. Gold Democrats and Republicans vied in manufacturing opprobrious epithets. He was the "Baby Demosthenes," a "political fakir," a "slobbering demagogue," and the "boy orator of the Platte." To his own followers, however, Bryan was the "Silver Knight of the West," that "Homer Bryan" that Vachel Lindsay sang of many years later. For him no front-porch speeches. Equipped with a paltry campaign fund of less than $300,000, Bryan invaded the enemy's territory, delivered his speech of acceptance in New York City, and toured twenty-nine states, talking directly to five million people. Except on the money issue, Bryan was an economic conservative, but his affiliations in the campaign with the Populists effectively scared the conservatives, who ordinarily comprise the great majority. Money, propaganda, and every known political tactic, fair or foul, finally wore down the opposition, and the Republicans were victorious by a popular vote of 7,035,638 to 6,467,946 and by an electoral vote of 271 to 176. Bryan carried most of the West and South but lost Kentucky and California by a few votes. In these states the gold Democrats were chiefly responsible for his defeat.

The significance of the election is clear enough. The Democratic Party, by going radical, had pushed the Republican Party into a more conservative position, and this party, dominated by the propertied classes and generally committed in theory to economic *laissez faire,* was again in the saddle. What looked like a political and economic revolution of major proportions had been quelled. As the nation turned into a new century and swung again into the upgrade of a new business cycle, its destinies were to be formulated under the aegis of conservative capitalism. No one has expressed this more clearly than the poet, Vachel Lindsay:

> Boy Bryan's defeat
> Defeat of western silver.
> Defeat of the wheat.
> Victory of letterfiles
> And plutocrats in miles
> With dollar signs upon their coats,
> Diamond watchchains on their vests
> And spats on their feet.
> Victory of custodians,
> Plymouth Rock,
> And all that inbred landlord stock.
> Victory of the neat.[12]

A brief account of business consolidation is in H. R. Seager and G. A. Gulick, Jr., *Trust and Corporation Problems,* Chap. V. Ida M. Tarbell, *The Nationalizing of Business,* Chaps. I–VII, XI–XV, is clear and well written. On the tariff, see F. W. Taussig, *A Tariff History of the United States,* Chaps. V, VI, and Allan Nevins, *Grover Cleveland,* Chaps. XVII, XXI, XXII, XXXI. The popular uprising preceding the 1896 campaign is well handled in S. J. Buck, *The Agrarian Crusade,* and J. D. Hicks, *The Populist Revolt,* Chaps. III–VIII. On the campaign of 1896, see Nevins, *op. cit.,* Chap. XXXVI; C. S. Olcott, *The Life of William McKinley,* Vol. II, 293–326; and Paxton Hibben, *The Peerless Leader: William Jennings Bryan,* Chaps. XV–XVII.

[12] From Vachel Lindsay, "Bryan, Bryan, Bryan, Bryan," *Collected Poems* (1923), p. 103. By permission of The Macmillan Company, publishers.

Chapter XXX

PRELIMINARIES TO IMPERIALISM

The Hawaiian pear is now fully ripe and this is the golden hour for the United States to pluck it.

J. L. STEVENS, UNITED STATES MINISTER TO HAWAII (1893)

FOREIGN AFFAIRS FROM JOHNSON TO CLEVELAND

It has been the habit of historians to deprecate American foreign policy during the three decades after the Civil War on the ground that it was indefinite and planless and that it was dominated by inexperienced politicians. Both criticisms can be exaggerated. Although reversals of policy are sometimes apparent, there is a thread of continuity during this period that is unmistakable. The years immediately following the war were concerned with liquidating the difficulties with Great Britain and France that had developed throughout the conflict. Toward Latin America there was an evident intention of maintaining the Monroe Doctrine, of assuming leadership in affairs of the western hemisphere, and in the later years of promoting a closer relationship with the nations to the south. While no strong effort was made in the Pacific to extend American interests, there developed a very definite policy of protecting those interests that existed. Except for the years when Seward dominated the Department of State, there was little desire for territorial expansion; on the contrary, our policy was to promote commercial expansion without annexation. With the inevitable expansion of American economic interests, however, this policy broke down, but it was left to the next generation to enter actively upon the dubious course of economic and political imperialism. American foreign trade reached a total of a billion dollars by 1872, and, as the value gradually doubled in the next thirty years, it exercised an increasing influence upon diplomacy.

Certain adventures in diplomacy were failures and some were managed with little skill, but during most of the period the Department of State was directed by capable men. William H. Seward, who continued in office under Johnson, was an aggressive statesman and an ardent imperialist, who upheld the Monroe Doctrine and acquired Alaska. Hamilton Fish, who served under Grant, may have lacked the brilliance of some of his predecessors, but his persistence and sensible diplomacy represented a high-water mark in the conduct of our foreign affairs. William M. Evarts, Secretary under Hayes, was a distinguished and capable lawyer; Blaine, who served briefly under Garfield and again under Harrison, was erratic in his diplomacy, but he made a notable contribution in reviving and advocating the doctrine of Pan-Americanism. Mediocrity characterized the Department of State under Frelinghuysen (Secretary under Arthur), but the years of Thomas F. Bayard (Cleveland's first administration) were marked by a distinct improvement. Although lacking in finesse, American diplomacy was successful during the last two years of Cleveland's second administration under Richard Olney. While brilliant politicians and statesmen succeeded one another at the head of the department, the long service of less famous but no less able men gave to American diplomacy a continuity and strength that should not be forgotten. Outstanding among these men were Alvey A. Adee, a member of the department for fifty-four years and at one time *ad interim* Secretary of State; J. W. Foster, minister to Mexico, Russia, and Spain, Secretary of State 1892–1893, and representative of the United States in various international disputes, and John Bassett Moore, connected with the Department of State off and on from 1885 until after the World War.

CIVIL WAR LIABILITIES

The victory of the North in the Civil War strengthened greatly the diplomatic position of the United States. In the first place, it was now possible to move aggressively against the extension of French imperialism in Mexico. During the Civil War the United States government could do little more than protest against the establishment of a puppet emperor in Mexico supported by French troops (page 370). After the end of the struggle Sheridan was sent to Texas with orders to mobilize a powerful force along the Rio Grande, and Seward, in the fall of 1865, informed the French government that the United States would not tolerate the maintenance of a foreign army in Mexico designed to coerce the Mexican people. France responded with a promise to withdraw the army if the United States would recognize Maximilian. This Seward refused, having already sent Sherman on a mission to Juarez, the revolutionary leader, a gesture that virtually recognized the latter. Napoleon saw that the game was up and withdrew his troops by May of 1867. With French support withdrawn, the empire collapsed like a house of cards, and the hapless Maximilian was captured and executed. The result of the Mexican diplomacy was an important victory for the United States and the Monroe Doctrine.

While it was obvious enough that France had sympathized with the South and had used the situation to embark on the Mexican adventure, the resentment of the North against Great Britain was far more bitter. The sympathy of the British government toward the South, the Mason and Slidell incident, and Britain's violation of neutrality in permitting Southern cruisers to be built in her shipyards all rankled deeply. Nor was the feeling improved by the refusal of Earl Russell to arbitrate the *Alabama* claims. On this side of the water the agitation of Irish-American citizens, culminating in the Fenian invasion of Canada in 1865, greatly irritated the British people, as did the exaggerated claims for "indirect" damages proposed by Sumner and other anti-British politicians. There were, in fact, a number of questions pending between the two governments that needed settlement: the Civil War claims, the problem of naturalization,[1] the boundary between Oregon and British Columbia, and the North Atlantic fisheries.

With the retirement of Palmerston and Russell there appeared more willingness on the part of the British government to arbitrate the issues in dispute. Reverdy Johnson, who followed Adams as minister at St. James's, signed a convention (Johnson-Clarendon convention) with Great Britain providing for the arbitration of these questions, but it was rejected by the United States Senate. After two more years of patient negotiations the treaty of Washington was signed in 1871 and accepted by the Senate. "This treaty," says John Bassett Moore, "provided for four distinct arbitrations, the largest number ever established under a single convention, and by reason of this fact as well as the magnitude of the questions submitted, was undoubtedly the greatest treaty of arbitration that the world has ever seen." The four problems to be arbitrated were the North Atlantic fisheries, the Puget Sound boundary line, the *Alabama* claims, and other financial claims between British citizens and the United States. A separate commission or arbitrator was to act on each of these problems. As a sop to American feelings, Great Britain had expressed in the treaty of Washington "the regret felt by Her Majesty's Government for the escape under whatever circumstances, of the *Alabama* and other vessels from British control and for the depredations committed by those vessels."

Under these circumstances the negotiations proceeded. An agreement on the fisheries was eventually patched up to last for ten years, but no final settlement was reached until 1910. The boundary-line dispute was referred to the German Emperor, who decided in favor of the United States,

---

[1] An agreement was reached with respect to this problem in 1870, which met implicitly the American position that one nation must faithfully recognize naturalization acquired under the laws of another nation.

and his decision is the existing boundary line. For the claims other than the *Alabama* claims, British citizens were awarded $1,929,819, while American claims were disallowed. The *Alabama* claims, which received the greatest amount of public attention, were referred to a court of five, one each from Italy, Switzerland, Brazil, Great Britain, and the United States. The United States was represented by Charles Francis Adams, while Caleb Cushing, William M. Evarts, and Morrison R. Waite acted as counsel. The introduction by the United States of the question of indirect claims almost ended the possibility of successful arbitration, but, after the court excluded such claims, a decision was reached. The court, with the English judge dissenting on almost every point, decided that Great Britain had failed to exercise due diligence in maintaining her neutrality and awarded to the United States $15,500,000 in gold. The arbitrations resulting from the Washington treaty went far to improve the existing relations between the United States and Great Britain and were a real triumph in the promotion of international amity.

ALASKA

A great many reasons have been offered to explain the sale of Alaska to the United States—the imperialism of Seward, the desire of the United States to repay Russia for her friendliness during the Civil War, the belief in Russia that in case of a war with Great Britain she would lose the territory, the desire of American economic interests (ice, furs, and telegraphs) to obtain concessions. As a matter of fact, Alaska was a burden and expense to Russia, and she was quite willing to get rid of it. That, combined with Seward's enthusiasm for expansion, explains the purchase. The American people neither knew nor cared about it, and the appropriation for the purchase went through the House only after the Russian government had bribed certain congressmen. The price for "Seward's ice box," as it was called, was $7,200,000.

For at least three decades the chief value that Alaska had for the outside world was the annual yield of furs obtained from the seals on the Pribilof Islands. Each spring this largest herd of seals in the world returned from their winter cruise to the Pribilof Islands to bear their young, and here under proper supervision a certain proportion of the males might be slaughtered without destroying the herd. Following the earlier policy of Russia, the United States declared the islands a government preserve and leased the privilege of obtaining the seals to a private company. When outsiders endangered the existence of the herd by indiscriminate killing on the seas, the United States declared that the Bering Sea was under her exclusive jurisdiction (*mare clausum*) and in 1886 seized three British vessels for catching seals in that area. An attempt to reach an international agreement to protect the seals failed because of Canadian opposition, and renewed seizures in 1889 brought further protests and the submission of the question to arbitration. The arbitrators in 1892 denied the American contention of exclusive jurisdiction over Bering Sea outside the three-mile limit and required the United States to pay an indemnity. They drafted a set of regulations to safeguard the seals, which remained in force for five years. It was not until 1911 that a convention was signed by Great Britain, Russia, Japan, and the United States, which finally disposed of the issue by forbidding pelagic sealing north of latitude 30° (North) except within the territorial jurisdiction of any of these powers, that is, within the three-mile limit.

The second diplomatic controversy with Great Britain over Alaska likewise had an economic background. When the United States acquired Alaska in 1867, the boundaries were those agreed upon by Russia and Great Britain in a treaty of 1825. This treaty provided that the boundary between Alaska and British Columbia should be ten marine leagues from the ocean but failed to note whether the line was to be measured from the outer islands or follow the sinuosities of the shore line. The matter was of no significance until the discovery of gold in the Yukon in 1896; then difficulties arose as to jurisdiction. In 1903 the dispute was referred to a mixed commission composed of three Americans, two Canadians, and Lord Alverstone, the English Chief Justice. As Alverstone consistently upheld the American contentions, the arbitration (if such it can be called) was a victory for the United States.

THE UNITED STATES IN THE PACIFIC AREA

American interest in the Far East goes back to the voyages of the Salem and New York merchantmen in the 1780s, which sought in China to compensate for the trade losses sustained in the West Indies (page 116). Despite a considerable development of this trade, it was limited until the Opium War of 1842 to the single city of Canton. When Great Britain, as a result of that war, forced China to open other ports to her, Commodore Kearney, an American naval officer who happened to be in the Far East, secured without instructions from Washington an extention of trading privileges to Americans on the same basis. At Kearney's solicitation the United States sent Caleb Cushing to China, and in 1844 he made the first treaty with that nation, a treaty that obtained for the United States the status of the "most favored nation" and established the doctrine of "extraterritoriality." Cushing's insistence that the United States wanted no territory and that customs duties fixed by treaty should be collected by China was in such contrast to the policy of European nations that a basis of friendly relations was established between the two countries, which has continued to the present day. The friendly relations established by Cushing were cemented by Anson Burlingame, a New Englander sent by Abraham Lincoln in 1861 as ambassador to China. Burlingame was a man of ability, enthusiasm, and tact, who so won the esteem of the Chinese government that, when he resigned from the American service after six years, the Chinese government prevailed upon him to head a Chinese mission to the nations of Europe. It was while passing through the United States on this mission that he drew up with Secretary Seward the famous Burlingame treaty (1868). This treaty stipulated the territorial integrity of China, recognized the right of China to regulate its internal trade not affected by treaty, secured exemption from persecution or disability on account of religion, recognized the right of voluntary immigration, and pledged the privilege of residence and travel in either country on the basis of the most favored nation.

Before a decade had passed, however, the idealistic relations set up by the Burlingame treaty broke down before the exigencies of labor opposition, race prejudice, and political opportunism. From the time when gold had been discovered, Chinese laborers had emigrated in large numbers to the Pacific coast, where they had done much of the rough work of the new country and had been especially useful in the building of the first railroads. With the panic of 1873 and the drought of 1876, the attitude toward Chinese laborers changed. Dennis Kearney and other labor leaders, seeking to protect white labor, held meetings on the sand lots of San Francisco and whipped up the anti-Chinese sentiment to the point of frenzy and violence. Both major parties in their platforms of 1876 demanded action, and Congress passed an act limiting Chinese immigration and calling upon the President to inform the Chinese government that the terms of the Burlingame treaty referring to immigration would not hold after January 1, 1879. Doubting the congressional power to abrogate a treaty and pointing out the fact that such abrogation would leave Americans in China unprotected, Hayes vetoed the bill. In 1880 a commission, headed by James B. Angell, succeeded in modifying the existing treaty to enable the United State to "regulate, limit or suspend" immigration. Congress then passed an act suspending Chinese immigration for twenty years. Arthur vetoed this as a violation of the treaty on the ground that the term of twenty years meant prohibition rather than suspension. Congress then passed a ten-year exclusion bill, which he signed.

The expedition of Commodore Matthew C. Perry to Japan in 1854 and the part played by the United States in the opening of Japan to outside trade has already been recounted (page 315). Townsend Harris, our first representative in Japan, was a diplomat of great ability, whose chief problem was to maintain the gains that had been made against the antiforeign legislation. The treaties that the United States had made were with the shogun, who represented at that time the actual power in Japan. The antiforeign element opposed the shogun and eventually overthrew him, but the mikado, who then assumed the actual power, turned against the antiforeign group, accepted the open-door policy, and proceeded with the modernization of Japan. It was during this controversy in 1865 that one of the antiforeign nobles fired upon an American vessel trying to get through the Straits of Shimonoseki. The nations with commercial interests in Japan (Great Britain, Holland, France, and the United States) sent a joint expedition, which demolished the forts and burned the town of the belligerent noble, after which they demanded either an indemnity or the opening of further ports. At the time the mikado decided to pay the indemnity, but the incident speeded the opening of Japan.

From then until the end of the Russo-Japanese War, relations between Japan and the United States were on the whole uneventful and cordial. The return of our part of the Shimonoseki indemnity (about three quarters of a million dollars) was a gesture of good will that Japan reciprocated in many ways. It was not until the twentieth century, when the problem of Japanese immigration and the opposition of Japan to the "open-door policy" in China developed, that relations between that nation and the United States became strained.

HAWAII

Of great importance to the United States from the point of view of commercial and naval strategy were the Hawaiian Islands. From the earliest days of American trade in the Pacific, Yankee whalers and traders had stopped at these beautiful islands to replenish their stores and collect sandlewood for the Chinese market. Missionaries came in the twenties, introducing various aspects of Western civilization, and they were followed by permanent white settlers. With the discovery of gold in California, Hawaii found a ready market for sugar and other foodstuffs, and from that time on her economic relations with the United States became increasingly intimate. Only opposition in the United States prevented annexation in the fifties and the ratification of reciprocity treaties in 1855 and 1867. The demand for reciprocity, of course, emanated chiefly from American sugargrowers who had settled in the islands and who were anxious to export their product to this country free of duty. Such a treaty was eventually consummated in 1875 with the added stipulation that no part of the territory of Hawaii might be leased or disposed of to any other country. The treaty of 1875 was for seven years, but in 1884 an extension of reciprocity was arranged in return for the grant of Pearl Harbor for a naval base.

The treaty of 1875 was undoubtedly one of the most important events in Hawaiian history, for the stimulation that it gave to trade led inevitably to annexation. One result was a spectacular increase in the export of sugar to the United States, from 18,000,000 pounds in 1875 to 260,000,000 in 1890, a development that profoundly affected many phases of the economic and social structure of Hawaiian society. The native population, for example, was declining rapidly, and the sugar-planters, in search of labor, imported 10,000 Portuguese and 20,000 Chinese and Japanese. By 1900 the native Hawaiians had sunk to less than one fifth of the population; at the same time Americans were rapidly absorbing the major portion of Hawaiian wealth. By the early nineties almost two thirds of the private lands were owned by Americans and Europeans, who also leased the greater part of the crown lands. Of the wealth invested in sugar plantations, Americans owned three fourths.

This notable period of Hawaiian prosperity was suddenly ended by the McKinley tariff of 1890, which put sugar on the free list, thus encouraging Cuban sugar but at the same time protecting the domestic producer by paying a bounty of two cents upon sugar produced in the United States (page 494). The effect was to cut the price of Hawaiian sugar in half and to stimulate again the movement for annexation, which offered to Hawaiian capitalists their only hope. The economic difficulties were further complicated by the political situation. King Kalakaua, puppet of the American settlers, died in 1891 and was succeeded by his sister, Liliuokalani, jealous of her prerogatives and opposed to foreign domination. Caught in this situation, the foreign capitalists organized for protection, secured the support of the American minister, J. L. Stevens, and, in the presence of a detachment of United States marines, overthrew the Hawaiian monarchy. A provisional government was established under American protection and a commission sent to Washington to frame a treaty of annexation. Before the Senate could act, Harrison's administration came to an end, and Cleveland became President. Suspecting that the revolution had been effected only by the aid of Stevens and the marines, Cleveland withdrew the treaty and sent a commissioner to Hawaii to investigate. The report confirmed Cleveland's suspicions, and he instructed the new minister to press for a restoration of the monarchy with an amnesty to the revolutionists. The provisional government under Sanford B. Dole, instead of following Cleveland's wishes, proclaimed a republic, which Cleveland immediately recognized. In the meantime, both houses of Congress had gone on record as opposed to intervention in Hawaiian affairs, while Japan protested against our annexation. Thus the situation rested until war with Spain changed the spirit of Congress and brought a joint resolution for annexation. This McKinley signed on July 7, 1898.

SAMOA

Just as American trading interests eventually brought American control in Hawaii, so they first called attention to Samoa. A coaling station and a port of call on the route to Australia would be advantageous to the growing American commerce, and the excellent port of Pagopago in the Samoan Islands was ideal. The story of Samoa is that of a long and complicated succession of internal troubles fostered and aggravated by the intrigues of foreign agents and the rivalries of foreign powers. It is hardly worth recounting except as an illustration of how imperialism sometimes functions in its early stages. As early as 1850, British, American, and German traders had been active, and in 1872 an American naval officer made an agreement with a native chieftain giving to the United States exclusive trading privileges in the port of Pagopago. This failed to win the approval of the American government, but similar provisions were incorporated in a treaty in 1878, while the British and Germans secured like concessions for other parts of the islands. For the next ten years consuls of the three nations inspired native uprisings and intrigued for power, but their actions were repeatedly disavowed by their home governments.

By 1886 the tension became so great that Secretary Bayard suggested that the three nations concerned hold a conference over the Samoan situation. While the conference was in session, a new revolution broke out, Germany assumed control of the situation, and the United States and Great Britain hurried warships to the scene to protect their interests. While the warships of the three nations glared at one another off the far-away island of Apia, a terrific storm descended, destroying all the ships but the English war vessel *Calliope,* which put to sea in the face of the hurricane and escaped. Shortly thereafter Bismarck called another conference, which set up a complicated triple protectorate with Germany in the preponderating position. This was in the nature of an entangling alliance foreign to American tradition, and Cleveland in his second administration insisted that the Samoan question be reopened. No change in status took place, however, until 1899, when the apparent inability of the natives to rule themselves gave the interested nations an excuse for taking over the islands. The United States obtained the island of Tutuila with the harbor of Pagopago and Germany the remainder, while Great Britain withdrew entirely.

LATIN AMERICA

The great interest in territorial expansion southward subsided temporarily with the overthrow of the agricultural imperialists in the Civil War; it did not revive until industrial and financial imperialism again gave an impetus. In two cases when expansion was favored by the administration and could easily have been effected, consummation was blocked by the Senate. The first of these concerned the Danish West Indies. The lack of a coaling station in the West Indies had hindered American operations during the Civil War, and Seward, with his appetite for territory whetted by the purchase of Alaska, hit upon these islands as the next objective in his program of expansion. The Danes in 1867 finally consented to sell, if treaty complications with France could be cleared away and if the inhabitants of St. Thomas and St. John approved by plebiscite. The cession was overwhelmingly approved by the inhabitants, a price was fixed, and the Danish parliament approved, but annexation was blocked by the United States Senate.

The opposition of Congress to the Johnson administration undoubtedly influenced the rejection of the treaty with Denmark, and it also played a part in the objections to the annexation of Santo Domingo. In 1868 President Baez, the dictator then in power, suggested that, because of the chaotic condition of the country and its declining industry, the United States assume a protectorate over Santo Domingo as a first step toward annexation. The administration favored the proposal, but a resolution introduced in Congress authorizing such a move was tabled. The idea of annexing a part of the second largest and richest island in the West Indies intrigued Grant even more than Johnson, and soon after his accession to office he sent one of his private secretaries, Orville E. Babcock, to the island to inquire into the situation. Babcock came back with a protocol for a treaty of annexation, which Grant made known to his astonished cabinet. When the cabinet showed little interest, Grant went ahead just the same, authorizing his agents to sign a treaty of annexation and a convention for the lease of Samaná Bay in case the treaty should fail.

Referred to a Senate committee, the treaty was adversely reported, and, in spite of personal and political pressure brought to bear by the President, the Senate turned it down. Grant was nothing if not persistent. He returned to the matter in his message of December, 1870, asking for a commission to investigate the situation on the island. Congress complied, and an able commission was appointed,[2] which returned with a report favorable to annexation. Congress, nevertheless, took no action. Considering the fact that we eventually assumed a protectorate over Santo Domingo in 1905 and purchased the Danish West Indies in 1917 at a price much higher than that set in 1867, many students of American imperialism have regretted that the earlier opportunity was neglected. Others believe that the Senate acted then with more wisdom than in later years.

[2] It consisted of ex-Senator Wade, Andrew D. White, and Samuel G. Howe (educator and philanthropist), with the Negro, Frederick Douglass, as secretary.

That the United States was not interested in southern expansion during the seventies and eighties was demonstrated again in 1882 when President Salomon of Haiti offered to cede an island to the United States and this country declined. To the offer Secretary Frelinghuysen answered that "the policy of this government, as declared on many occasions in the past, has tended toward avoidance of possessions disconnected with the main continent." Even Cuba, the "Pearl of the Antilles," upon which Southern statesmen in antebellum days had cast longing eyes, now concerned the United States chiefly in her role as a neutral during the Cuban revolution. Against the inefficient and autocratic rule of Spain the Cubans rose in revolution in 1868, and for the next ten years the struggle was carried on with barbarous cruelty. Since Cuban exiles used the United States as a base for shipping munitions to their compatriots, relations between this country and Spain at times became strained. The most famous occasion was in 1873, when the filibustering ship *Virginius,* owned by Cubans and illegally flying the American flag, and with her crew composed chiefly of Englishmen and Americans, was captured and fifty-three of her passengers and crew shot. Feeling in this country ran high, and the government demanded the punishment of the officers, a salute to our flag, and an indemnity. Spain easily proved that the vessel was not American, and the salute was waived, but an indemnity was obtained. Two years later Secretary Fish cabled to our representatives in Europe a communication regarding Cuba that closed with these words:

> In the absence of any prospect of a termination of war or of any change in the manner in which it is conducted on either side, he [President Grant] feels that the time is at hand when it may be the duty of other governments to intervene, solely with a view of bringing to an end a disastrous conflict and restoring peace to the island of Cuba.

Nothing came of this, and in 1878 the ten years' war came to an end with concessions by Spain and promises of better conditions. Seventeen years of comparative peace followed, but "it was the apathy of exhaustion rather than the tranquillity of satisfied hopes." [3]

With one or two exceptions, these years were characterized by the development of friendly relations with Latin America. The bitterness engendered by the Mexican War was softened, and upon more than one occasion the United States was called upon to mediate or arbitrate disputes that had arisen among our southern neighbors. The long friction with Mexico subsided when Porfirio Diaz became dictator in 1876 and, in subsequent years, became exceedingly generous in granting concessions to American capital. The most outstanding effort to create better relations was

[3] G. H. Stuart, *Latin America and the United States,* 159.

indicated by James G. Blaine's revival of "Pan-Americanism." A man of spirit and imagination, Blaine envisioned a day when the American nations might settle their disputes by peaceful means and enter into closer economic bonds. While Secretary of State for a brief period under Garfield, he was laying plans for a congress of the independent nations of the western hemisphere when Garfield's death ended the project for the moment. Frelinghuysen canceled the plans, but Blaine never relinquished his idea, and, when he again became Secretary of State in 1889, such a congress met in Washington. Blaine's motives were primarily commercial, and the first Pan-American conference discussed such projects as the creation of a customs union, uniform systems of weights, measures, and coinage, and the promotion of better systems of communication. Its chief contribution was the establishment of an International Bureau of American Republics, which later changed its name to the Pan American Union and is now housed in a magnificent building, the gift of Andrew Carnegie. It has helped to promote friendly relations, has acted as a clearing house for information, and has promoted at least ten subsequent conferences. These conferences until recent years [4] confined themselves largely to discussions, recommendations, and the promotion of the co-operative spirit. The Second World War has given to recent conferences a greater significance.

THE VENEZUELA BOUNDARY

Since the years when Secretary Seward had brought pressure to force the withdrawal of the French from Mexico, no important controversy involved the Monroe Doctrine until Cleveland in 1895 stepped into the long-standing boundary dispute between Venezuela and the British colony of Guiana. When gold was discovered in the disputed territory, the situation became acute. Venezuela repeatedly demanded that the line be arbitrated, and finally, upon Great Britain's refusal, severed diplomatic relations and appealed (1887) to the United States. When Cleveland returned to the presidency in 1893, he took up the matter aggressively, convinced that Great Britain was unjustly ignoring the rights of a weaker nation. After the offices of the United States had been offered and refused, Cleveland through Secretary Olney addressed to Great Britain a note that for its truculence and swaggering tone is probably without parallel in diplomatic history. After reviewing the situation and drawing an invidious comparison between monarchical Europe and the free institutions of America, the note continued:

> Today the United States is practically sovereign on this continent, and its fiat is law upon the subjects to which it confines its interposition. Why?

[4] R. G. Adams, *The Foreign Policy of the United States*, 311.

It is not because of the pure friendship or good will felt for it. It is not simply by reason of its high character as a civilized state, nor because wisdom and justice and equity are the invariable characteristics of the dealings of the United States. It is because, in addition to all other grounds, its infinite resources combined with its isolated position render it master of the situation and practically invulnerable as against any and all other powers.

The note went on to say that, while the United States did not take it upon herself to decide which party was right, she did maintain that "it is certainly within its right to demand that the truth shall be ascertained."

Salisbury, the British minister, did not answer for more than four months and then pointed out that the Monroe Doctrine was not a part of international law and that in any case it had not been violated, and he vigorously denied the assumption of power implied by the United States in the note. Arbitration was refused. Cleveland submitted this correspondence to Congress, asked for an appropriation to conduct an independent investigation, and closed his message with these words:

When such report is made and accepted it will, in my opinion, be the duty of the United States to resist . . . the appropriation by Great Britain of any lands or . . . territory which after investigation we have determined of right belongs to Venezuela.

In making these recommendations I am fully alive to the responsibility incurred and keenly realize all the consequences that may follow.

I am, nevertheless, firm in my conviction that while it is a grievous thing to contemplate the two great English-speaking peoples as being otherwise than friendly . . . there is no calamity . . . which equals that which follows a supine submission to wrong and injustice. . . .

There could be no mistaking the meaning of these words, and the more responsible men in both countries threw their influence upon the side of moderation and peace. Congress appropriated $100,000, a commission set to work, and both Great Britain and Venezuela offered to put all information at its disposal. Its work, however, was never finished, for Great Britain now agreed to arbitrate, and a treaty to that effect was drawn up. In the end, Great Britain obtained most of the land in dispute, but Venezuela was awarded the mouth of the Orinoco River. The whole Venezuelan incident added to the prestige of the United States among Latin-American nations, showing as it did our willingness to go to great lengths to protect their interests against a European nation. On the other hand, the loose talk in the Olney note about the United States being "practically sovereign on this continent," where "its fiat is law," was hardly welcomed in Latin America. While Great Britain did not recognize the Monroe Doctrine as international law, it was in fact enforced against her. The willingness of the United States to revive the doctrine, to enforce it, and even to extend its original meaning represents the significance of the incident. The critical situation that this incident developed led to the signing of a treaty in 1897 between the United States and Great Britain, providing for the future settlement of disputes by arbitration. Jealous of its power and suspicious of England, the Senate rejected the treaty.

Despite the lack of finesse displayed in the Venezuela incident, American diplomacy between the Civil War and the Spanish-American War was ably handled. France was eliminated from Mexico; Great Britain found it wise to pay claims for her violation of neutrality during the Civil War, and other differences with that nation were ironed out. Russian possessions in North America were wisely purchased, but at the same time there was no evidence of a desire to absorb any and every piece of territory available. Although Congress refused to annex either the Virgin Islands or Santo Domingo, the government showed its intention to maintain, if not extend, the Monroe Doctrine. A growing aggressiveness, which in some cases amounted almost to a "chip-on-the-shoulder" attitude, was sometimes apparent, but only in Hawaii was there a clear-cut case of the economic imperialism that was soon to dominate our foreign policy. Even here, however, it was to take the stimulation of a foreign war to bring about annexation.

On the difficulties with Great Britain after the Civil War read S. F. Bemis, *A Diplomatic History of the United States,* Chap. XXIII, or Allan Nevins, *Hamilton Fish,* Chaps. XVIII–XXIII, both representing the most recent scholarship. On our early relations with the nations of the Pacific area, see P. J. Treat, *Japan and the United States,* Chaps. I–VI, Tyler Dennett, *Americans in Eastern Asia,* Chaps. XIV–XXII. On Samoa and Hawaii, W. F. Fletcher, *American Foreign Relations,* Vol. II, Chaps. XXVII, XXVIII, is adequate. They are discussed more briefly in Bemis, *op. cit.,* Chap. XXV. On the Venezuelan dispute see Allan Nevins, *Grover Cleveland,* Chap. XXXIV. Results of the most recent research is gathered together in T. A. Bailey, *A Diplomatic History of the American People,* Chaps. XXIV–XXIX. Many sources are in H. S. Commager, *Documents of American History,* Vol. II, 42–43, 67–68, 150–155, 170–173.

A WORLD POWER

Chapter XXXI

ECONOMIC IMPERIALISM

The Philippines are ours forever. . . . And just beyond the Philippines are China's illimitable markets. We will not retreat from either. We will not repudiate our duty in the archipelago. We will not abandon our opportunity in the Orient. We will not renounce our part in the mission of our race, trustee, under God, of the civilization of the world.

ALBERT J. BEVERIDGE

We assert that no nation can long endure half republic and half empire and we warn the American people that imperialism abroad will lead quickly and inevitably to despotism at home.

DEMOCRATIC PLATFORM OF 1900

THE ADVENT OF THE NEW IMPERIALISM

The overthrow of the agrarian Democracy in the epic conflict of 1896 opened the way for an even more aggressive development of American capitalism. In our domestic economic life, as we shall see, this was characterized by a new wave of business consolidation, by a revival of the high-tariff system [1] and by the preservation of the gold standard. In foreign affairs it was marked by a rapid expansion of investments in economically backward nations and by the establishment of an overseas colonial empire. As far as territorial expansion was concerned, the acquisitions of 1898 merely followed a habit that had characterized our entire national existence. The difference between the expansion before and that after the Spanish-American War lay essentially in the motive. The "old imperial-

---

[1] Although the Wilson-Gorman tariff had been satisfactory as a revenue-producer and gave reasonable protection to most interests, McKinley called the fifty-fourth Congress into special session to revise the tariff. The Wilson-Gorman Act was speedily wiped from the statute books and the Dingley tariff substituted (July, 1897). Somewhat lower than the McKinley tariff, it was more protective than the Wilson-Gorman. Wool and hides, for example, were removed from the free list. The coincidence of returning prosperity with the passing of the Dingley Act enabled Republicans to associate economic prosperity with high protection.

ism" was interested in the acquisition of land primarily as a new region for settlement, and in the case of the United States the principal economic motive was agricultural rather than commercial or financial. Here we find some explanation for the purchase of Louisiana, the acquisition of Florida, the annexation of Texas, the conquest of the Southwest, and the occupation of Oregon.

The "new imperialism," on the other hand, was not concerned with settlement. The annexation of Puerto Rico, the Philippines, Hawaii, and Guam, the establishment of protectorates over Panama, Haiti, Santo Domingo, and Nicaragua, and the purchase of the Virgin Islands were consummated either for purposes of naval strategy or for the promotion of American financial imperialism. The new imperialism was the natural result of the Industrial Revolution; mechanical inventions so speeded the production of commodities that new markets had to be found abroad if industrial expansion was to continue. At the same time, it was often necessary to develop new sources of raw materials and, if possible, to control them. Quite as important was the need to open new markets for capital. Wealth in the industrial era tended to concentrate in the hands of the owners of new machinery. As this wealth accumulated and the market for capital investment grew more restricted at home, financiers were forced to go far afield to discover new opportunities for profitable investment. One result of financial imperialism, however, must be noted—it has the tendency to kill the goose that lays the golden egg. Seeking high interest rates, the owner of capital invests his money in factories, mines, railroads, and other facilities in less developed countries, until eventually these regions are able not only to take care of their own needs but also quite often to cancel their debts and themselves enter into the competition for world markets. This is exactly what happened in the United States. For three centuries this country had been a market for both the manufactured goods and the surplus capital of Europe. European investments (mostly British) in the United States, which were estimated at about $400,000,000 in 1860, had grown to $2,000,000,000 by 1880 and $3,-000,000,000 by 1900. As late as 1910 the total European investment in this country amounted to $6,000,000,000.

By 1898,[*] however, the situation was rapidly changing. Although the United States at the turn of the century was still heavily in debt to outside investors, she was now producing an economic surplus and was herself beginning to invest abroad. One reasonable estimate puts the foreign investments of the United States at this time at $500,000,000, almost all of which, it is significant to note, were in North or South America.[2] This is not to

[2] N. T. Bacon in the *Yale Review*, IX, 265–285; also given in Robert Dunn, *American Foreign Investments*, 2. The distribution was as follows: Canada, $150,000,000; Mexico, $185,-

imply that the sudden emergence of an American colonial empire was caused alone by the fact that the United States had reached a stage in economic maturity when such a step was natural. This factor may have been fundamental, but there were many other causes. This is particularly true of the war with Spain. In 1898 American investments in Cuba amounted to $50,000,000, and the trade between that island and the United States reached $100,000,000 annually in the early nineties. Nevertheless, it was the people as a whole, rather than big business, who demanded the war. When the war was ended and the problem of a colonial empire presented itself, advocates of economic imperialism were more vocal.

PRELIMINARIES TO WAR

Inefficient, corrupt, and dictatorial as the Spanish rule in Cuba undoubtedly was, the Cuban revolution of 1895 seems to have been stimulated primarily by economic depression rather than by political discontent. By the nineties Cuban economic life was essentially based upon sugar. In Europe the development of beet sugar had forced Cuba to depend largely upon the American market for her outlet, and this market was dominated by the sugar trust, which had a predominant influence upon the price of raw sugar. Despite these handicaps, the period from 1890 to 1894 was one of real prosperity for Cuba. For this the McKinley tariff of 1890, which removed the duty on raw sugar (page 494), and a reciprocity treaty in the following year were responsible. How closely Cuba's economic life was bound to the United States was clearly seen in 1894, when the Wilson-Gorman Act restored a 40-per-cent duty on raw sugar, which automatically ended the reciprocity treaty and plunged Cuba into a bitter depression. Many plantation-owners discharged their workers and ceased operations. In the unhappy island the cost of living advanced as the price of sugar declined.

When disorders broke out in 1895, Cuban capital was won to the revolution. By this time American capital invested in sugar and tobacco plantations and iron mines was also sufficiently large to be concerned with the outcome. From then until the United States entered the war, the complaint of the destruction of American property was continually at the forefront of the negotiations. "The wholesale destruction of property on the Island," wrote Olney to the Spanish minister in Washington in 1896, "is utterly destroying American investments that should be of immense value and is utterly impoverishing American citizens." Ambassador Woodford later pointed out

000,000; Cuba, $50,000,000; other Latin-American countries, $55,000,000; Europe, $10,-000,000; China and Japan, $5,000,000; life-insurance guarantee investments in Russia and elsewhere, $45,000,000.

at Madrid "that we raise in the United States about one-tenth of the sugar we consume; that we must purchase from abroad the remaining nine-tenths; that before the present Civil War we drew much of our supply from Cuba and so sold to Cuba in return flour, meat, and manufactures; that all this commerce is practically destroyed." American property in Cuba was naturally imperiled by the method of carrying on warfare. The Spanish expeditionary force numbered 200,000 men, a force too large for the revolutionists to cope with in open warfare. Their policy, therefore, was to resort to guerrilla tactics, and to hasten the economic collapse of Cuba by levying assessments on plantation-owners and by destroying the plantations that continued to function. These tactics, it was hoped, might eventually involve the United States. General Valeriano Weyler, who became governor of Cuba in 1896, met the tactics of the revolutionists by gathering the rural population into "reconcentration" camps, where thousands died of hunger and disease.

Despite destruction of American property and the interference with trade caused by the revolution, the war between this country and Spain was primarily a "newspaper man's war" rather than one promoted by big business. In the United States the cause of the Cuban revolution found wide sympathy. The agitation of the Cuban exiles was taken up by the "yellow press," particularly by Pulitzer's New York *World* and by the Hearst newspapers, which painted in lurid colors the cruelties of Spanish misrule. The telegram that Hearst is alleged to have sent to the artist Remington in Cuba, "You furnish the pictures and I'll furnish the war," may never have been sent, but it expresses clearly enough the war-making intent of certain American newspapers. Two incidents tended particularly to inflame the American mind against Spain. The first was the publication on February 9 of a stolen private letter from the Spanish Minister, de Lôme, to a friend in Cuba, which referred to McKinley as "weak and a bidder for the admiration of the crowd, besides being a would-be politician who tries to leave a door open behind himself while keeping on good terms with the jingoes of his party." De Lôme resigned, and the incident was officially closed, but its effect was unfortunate.

More serious was the blowing up of the *Maine* in the harbor of Havana on the evening of February 15 with the loss of two officers and 258 members of the crew. Dispatched to Havana a few days earlier at the request of the American consul, the *Maine* had been received with every mark of courtesy and good will. As to how the tragedy occurred, no answer has ever been found. An American naval court of inquiry reported that the immediate cause was the explosion of a submarine mine; a Spanish investigation reported that the explosion originated within the vessel. If from the outside, was the explosion accidental, was it set off by insurgents anxious to embroil the United States, or was it done by Spain? However one looked at it, the latter explanation was the most improbable, but it was the one that the masses accepted, and "Remember the *Maine*" became the war cry of the conflict that followed. After the destruction of the *Maine* the chance of avoiding war was slim. By this time not only the "yellow press" was clamoring for war, but also politicians who realized that such a step would be popular.

Likewise, many of the intellectuals of the type of Roosevelt, Lodge, Hay, and Whitelaw Reid of the New York *Tribune* had become enamored with the philosophy of Captain Mahan and were playing with the idea that America's manifest destiny might logically lead her into the paths of imperialism. Advocacy of expansion in the Caribbean and the Pacific, freely expressed in congressional debates and in the public press, in conjunction with a naval development that had gone on under Democratic and Republican administrations alike since the early eighties, made easier a declaration of war and a policy of imperialism at its conclusion.[3] In a reaction from the grinding economic battles of the nineties, the masses warmed to the prospect of new adventure, particularly to the idea of helping an oppressed people win its freedom.

Despite all this, the war with Spain was unnecessary and might have been avoided. The responsibility seems to have ultimately rested upon the vacillating McKinley, who allowed his own desire for peace to be thwarted by jingo politicians of both parties. At the end of March, McKinley sent an ultimatum to Spain, demanding the revocation of the "reconcentration" policy and an armistice until October 1. The revocation was issued immediately, and instructions were sent to the governor general, ordering such an armistice on April 9. Woodford, American ambassador at Madrid, communicated to Washington on April 3:

> The Spanish minister for foreign affairs assures me that Spain will go as far and as fast as she can. . . . I know that the Queen and her ministry sincerely desire peace and that the Spanish people desire peace, and if you can still give me time . . . I am sure that before next October I will get peace in Cuba, with justice to Cuba and protection to our great American interests.

Cabling on April 10, he again reiterated that Spain was "loyally ready to go, as fast and as far as it can," and that a final settlement before August 1 could be obtained on one of the following bases: "Either such autonomy as the insurgents may agree to accept, or recognition by Spain of the independence of the island, or cession of the island to the United States."

[3] J. W. Pratt, "The 'Large Policy' of 1898," *Mississippi Valley Historical Review*, XIX, No. 2, pp. 219–242 (September, 1932).

Practically all that McKinley had asked for had been granted by Spain with assurances that she would go the limit to maintain peace. The President, nevertheless, without giving Congress the facts about the message of April 10, and with full knowledge that his action could only mean war, placed the issue before Congress with the words: "With this last overture in the direction of immediate peace [referring to the ultimatum of March 27–29] and its disappointing reception by Spain the Executive is brought to the end of his effort. . . . The issue is now with Congress." After some days of debate as to the wording of the resolution, Congress on April 19 voted recognition of Cuban independence, authorized the use of armed forces to make this effective, but pledged itself by the Teller Resolution "to leave the government and control of the Island to its people." McKinley's signature the following day made war a reality. It was formally declared on April 25.

WAR WITH SPAIN

There can be no question as to the popularity throughout the nation of the war with Spain. Fortunately for the jingoists, it was so short that the people hardly had time to tire of it. The war lasted just 115 days and was a series of unchecked successes. In accounting for the sudden and overwhelming defeat of Spain, the historian notes an unstable political situation in that country, an inefficient government, lack of adequate preparation, and the fact that the conflict was fought far from the home base. More important, since the war was essentially a naval conflict, were the superior strength of the American navy and the confidence and skill of its personnel. Since the early eighties every effort had been made to strengthen this branch, and by 1896 it had reached a high state of efficiency. Under the inspiration of Theodore Roosevelt, who acted as Assistant Secretary of the Navy in the months preceding the conflict, preparations had been speeded.[4]

Unlike the Navy, the War Department was quite unprepared for the emergency. Secretary Alger, who headed this branch, was a Michigan politician who regarded the army chiefly as an opportunity for political patronage. Alger had given repeated assurances that the army was prepared and had repeatedly urged upon McKinley the advisability of war. Instead of being prepared, however, it was woefully lacking in all that was necessary to carry on a war. The regular army of 18,000 men was widely scattered in the frontier posts of the West. To draw these troops in, to double the size of the regular force, and to mobilize, equip, and train 200,000 volunteers was quite beyond the ability of the War Department. It was not until

---

[4] The Secretary of the Navy from 1897 to 1902 was John Davis Long, former governor of Massachusetts and congressman, whose tactful, calm, and efficient administration of the department contributed to the navy's war record as much as Roosevelt's impetuous enthusiasm.

June 14 that the first contingent embarked from Tampa, Florida, for Cuba, and, when they left, they were clad in winter uniforms without adequate hospital equipment, proper food, or medical provision against malaria, typhoid, scurvy, and dysentery. The inadequacy of the War Department was not due to Congress, which had voted in March $50,000,000 for war preparation, had authorized in June a bond issue of $200,000,000, and had voted an increase in the internal-revenue taxes and added stamp taxes on many commercial transactions.

The American plans of campaign called for the destruction of the Spanish fleet and the occupation of the Spanish possessions in the Far East and the Caribbean. Two months before war was declared, Roosevelt had telegraphed to Commodore Dewey:

> Secret and confidential. Order the squadron, except Monacacy, to Hong Kong. Keep full of coal. In the event of declaration of war your duty will be to see that the Spanish squadron does not leave the Asiatic coast, and then offensive operations in Philippine Islands.

Five days after war was officially declared, Dewey with his six ships had reached Manila Bay. Disregarding the possibility of mines, he steamed through the narrow channel into the bay on the night of April 30 and at daybreak commenced the attack. The Spanish fleet of two cruisers, five gunboats, and some smaller craft, drawn up in crescent formation, awaited the attack. Five times the American fleet steamed past the Spanish squadron, pouring into it a deadly fire. By noon the Spanish ships were smoking ruins, and the shore batteries had been silenced. Besides her fleet, Spain had lost 167 killed and 214 wounded. Not a single American ship had been damaged and but seven men slightly wounded. While the nation went wild with excitement over this extraordinary victory, Dewey established a blockade of Manila Bay while he waited for the arrival of troops to complete the conquest of the Philippines. During the two months that intervened, England, France, Germany, and Japan sent battleships to Manila to observe the blockade, and during this time some misunderstandings arose between Dewey and the German admiral, Von Diedrichs, over the rules of neutrality. This and the fact that Germany had made some efforts to prevent the war gave rise to the supposition that that nation was anxious to make trouble. That Von Diedrichs acted arrogantly there is no doubt, but there is also no external or internal evidence that can be deduced from the German archives to show that Germany's observance of neutrality during the conflict was not scrupulously correct or that Von Diedrichs was in any way interested in making trouble for Dewey.

The first contingent of American troops arrived in the Philippines on June 30 and was gradually augmented until General Merritt had 10,700 under his command. In co-operation with the Philippine insurgents under Emilio Aguinaldo, a joint attack of naval forces and American infantry was launched against Manila. The city speedily surrendered, August 13, one day after the peace protocol had been signed.

While Dewey was steaming toward the Philippines, the Atlantic fleet under Admiral Sampson and Commodore Schley was throwing a blockade around Cuba. In the meantime, the Spanish admiral, Cervera, had left the Cape Verde Islands on April 29 for an unknown destination. Although American naval officers were certain that Cervera would head for Cuba, and made plans accordingly, the mystery of his whereabouts for some days spread consternation along the Atlantic coast. Word finally came that Cervera had eluded the American fleet and on May 19 had slipped into Santiago harbor. Here the American fleet, consisting of four first-class battleships, one second-class battleship, two cruisers, and several yachts, had gathered by June 1 and commenced the blockade.

With Cervera bottled securely in Santiago harbor, the navy settled back to await the arrival of the American expeditionary force. Amid incredible confusion the army, numbering a little less than 17,000 men and commanded by General Shafter, put out from Tampa on June 14 and began to disembark on June 22 some fifteen miles east of Santiago. Fighting began immediately, but it was not until July 1 that a general attack was ordered on the heights commanding the city—San Juan Hill, Kettle Hill, and El Caney. These points were bravely defended, and it took twelve hours of spirited fighting before they were in the possession of the American army. The American losses on July 1 were 112 officers and 1460 men killed, wounded, and missing. While Shafter, convinced that his force was too small to capture Santiago, dug in to await reinforcements, the Spanish commander, Governor General Blanco, equally convinced that Santiago was doomed, ordered Admiral Cervera to make a dash for freedom. This he did, and, shortly after nine o'clock on the morning of July 3, the Spanish fleet steamed out of Santiago harbor and turned westward. Hardly prepared for such a bold move, the American ships got steam up as quickly as possible, closed in on Cervera's fleet, and in a running fight destroyed or drove on to the beach all the Spanish ships.[5] At 1:15 the *Cristóbal Colón,* the last of Cervera's squadron, struck her colors. In one short morning the power of the Spanish empire had been utterly broken, and the continuation of the war was but a matter of days. Santiago surrendered on July 17, and General Miles, now in command of the army, departed for the

[5] The brilliance of the victory was marred by a long controversy between Sampson and Schley as to the relative credit belonging to each. Sampson, when the battle commenced, was on shore holding a council of war with Shafter, and Schley was in nominal command. As a matter of fact, the battle was a captains' fight, and the victory was due to no particular strategy, but primarily to the superior marksmanship of the American bluejacket.

conquest of Puerto Rico. It was hardly a conquest, for the expedition was received with enthusiasm by the population, and Miles was in control of most of the island when the protocol for peace was signed on August 12. Mr. Dooley, famous humorist of the time, described the expedition as "Gin'ral Miles' Gran' Picnic an' Moonlight Excursion."

The day following the surrender of Santiago, Spain requested the French ambassador at Washington to arrange the preliminary terms for the cessation of hostilities. In the negotiations, which terminated on August 12, Spain agreed: (1) to the immediate evacuation of Cuba and the relinquishment of Cuban sovereignty; (2) to the cession of Puerto Rico and an island in the Ladrones as an indemnity; (3) the occupation by the United States of "the city, bay and harbor of Manila pending the conclusion of a treaty of peace which shall determine the control, disposition, and government of the Philippines." The American peace commission, which opened negotiations in Paris on October 1, was composed of William R. Day, who had resigned as Secretary of State to head the commission; C. K. Davis, chairman of the Senate Committee on Foreign Relations; W. P. Frye, President *pro tempore* of the Senate; Senator George Gray; and Whitelaw Reid, editor of the New York *Tribune;* John Bassett Moore was secretary. The decisions of the commission, of course, were dictated from Washington, but, unlike the commission that Wilson took to Paris in 1919, this one was made up of powerful senators and molders of public opinion.

Two primary questions confronted the negotiators, the Cuban debt and the future of the Philippines. For a month Spain fought in vain to saddle the Cuban debt upon either Cuba or the American people. With this disposed of, the more important question of the Philippines was taken up. Annexation, it was evident, involved the subjection of an alien race in a remote tropical clime; it meant a definite embarkation upon the uncertain path of imperialism, the taking up of the "white man's burden," a new departure for the American people. The administration was at first uncertain, but McKinley, with his ear to the ground, was convinced that the majority of voters were in favor of territorial expansion, and instructions were sent to demand the cession of the entire archipelago. To a group of Methodist clergymen McKinley gave his own explanation for his decision. To give the islands back to Spain, he said, "would be cowardly and dishonorable"; to turn them over to France or Germany "would be bad business and discreditable"; to leave the islands to themselves would be impossible, for the islanders were incapable of self-government, so "there was nothing left for us to do but to take them all, and to educate the Filipinos, and to uplift and civilize and Christianize them, and by

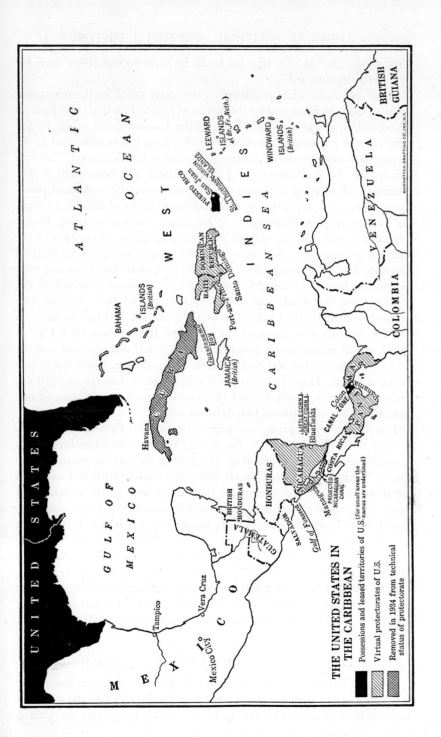

THE UNITED STATES IN THE CARIBBEAN

Possessions and leased territories of U.S. (for small areas the U.S. names are underlined)

Virtual protectorates of U.S.

Removed in 1934 from technical status of protectorate

UNITED STATES

GULF OF MEXICO

Tampico

Vera Cruz

Mexico City

M E X I C O

GUATEMALA

SALVADOR

Gulf of Fonseca

BRITISH HONDURAS

HONDURAS

NICARAGUA

Map PROPOSED NICARAGUAN CANAL

LITTLE CORN I.
GREAT CORN I.
Bluefields

COSTA RICA

PANAMA

Colon
CANAL ZONE
Panama

BAHAMA ISLANDS (British)

Havana

Guantanamo Bay

JAMAICA (British)

C A R I B B E A N S E A

A T L A N T I C O C E A N

W E S T I N D I E S

HAITI
Port-au-Prince

DOMINICAN REPUBLIC
Santo Domingo

PUERTO RICO
San Juan

St. Thomas
VIRGIN ISLANDS (Br., Fr., Neth.)

LEEWARD ISLANDS

WINDWARD ISLANDS (British)

COLOMBIA

VENEZUELA

BRITISH GUIANA

MANHATTAN DRAFTING CO., INC., N.Y.

God's grace do the very best we could by them as our fellow men for whom Christ also died."

At all events, the chief provisions of the treaty called for the relinquishment of Cuba by Spain and for the cession of Puerto Rico and other Spanish West Indies, of the island of Guam in the Ladrones, and of the Philippines on the payment of $20,000,000. By the time it was submitted to the Senate in January, however, a strong opposition had developed. This was headed by the Anti-Imperialist League, which had been cradled at a Faneuil Hall meeting in Boston and whose membership contained prominent citizens of all political parties and many walks of life. Establishing its headquarters in Washington, it circulated petitions opposing Philippine annexation and maintained a ceaseless agitation. Opposition in the country at large came from the tobacco, beet-sugar, and other agricultural interests fearful of competition, from labor leaders like Gompers who feared the menace of cheap Oriental labor, from many who looked dubiously upon the whole imperialist experiment, and from idealists who refused to abandon the Declaration of Independence and had no stomach for the forceful subjugation of the islanders. Big business, on the other hand, sensed in annexation new fields for economic conquest and saw the Philippines as the key to Oriental trade. In the Senate, where the debate lasted a month, Hoar, Pettigrew, and other senators bitterly attacked the treaty, and it was finally ratified (February 6) only by a margin of one vote more than the required two-thirds majority.

Bryan, who was a strong anti-imperialist, advised Democratic senators to vote for ratification on the theory that the war should be brought to a conclusion and the question of imperialism be later submitted to the voters. Whether Bryan influenced many votes is doubtful, but as far as he could he made imperialism the paramount issue of the campaign of 1900. Although a significant and influential minority in the country opposed imperialism, the issue for the masses was too remote to stir them deeply. Flushed with an easy victory over Spain, intrigued with the thought of unlimited economic expansion, and prepared by Christian teachings to accept the "white man's burden," the average voter had no quarrel with the administration leaders for annexing Puerto Rico and the Philippines. Certainly, after the campaign of 1900, there was little likelihood that the McKinley administration would retreat from the position it had taken.

CUBA

It was in Cuba that the United States learned the significant lesson that it is quite unnecessary to annex territory in order to enjoy the financial rewards of imperialism. By the Teller Resolution (page 521) the United

States had disclaimed any intention to exercise sovereignty or control over that distracted island. American soldiers, nevertheless, maintained control of Cuba from the conclusion of hostilities in August, 1898, until May, 1902. Under General Leonard Wood their stay had been productive of much good. The cities had been cleaned, sanitary measures undertaken, stable government established. The United States Army Medical Corps, through the brilliant work of Walter Reed and his colleagues, had at last discovered the cause of yellow fever and accomplished one of the great marvels of experimental medicine.

Before American troops were withdrawn, however, it became evident that the United States had no intention of relinquishing its control over Cuba. Ignoring the Teller Resolution, Senator Platt presented a rider to the Army Appropriation Bill of March 2, 1901, which was subsequently made part of a treaty between Cuba and the United States and incorporated in the constitution of Cuba. The Platt Amendment provided that the government of Cuba should not enter into any treaty or compact with a foreign power that might impair her independence, that Cuba should not assume any public debt for which the ordinary revenues were inadequate, that Cuba consent to the intervention of the United States "for the preservation of Cuban independence, the maintenance of a government adequate for the protection of life, property, and individual liberty," and that Cuba lease or sell to the United States land sufficient for coaling or naval stations. Against certain sections of the Platt Amendment the Cubans protested loudly but without success. Cuba was forced to agree, and under the sanction of this amendment the United States established two naval stations and has repeatedly intervened to protect American economic interests.

The first of these interventions came in 1906, when an insurrection broke out in protest against the fraudulent re-election of President Estrada Palma. After repeated appeals from Frank Steinhart, American consul general at Havana and the leading financial figure in Cuba, Roosevelt dispatched Secretary of War Taft to the island to investigate. The result was American occupation from September, 1906, until January, 1909, under the governorship of Charles E. Magoon. The Magoon regime not only left Cuba heavily in debt but opened the island wide to American contractors and concession-seekers. It was a disastrous experience for Cuba. The next landing of troops took place in 1912 as the result of a Negro revolution against the Gómez regime, which had been depriving that race of political rights. The United States, ever on the alert to safeguard the Cuban government from revolutionists and protect American investments, rushed marines to Nipe Bay, where the United Fruit Company had large plantations and the Spanish-American Iron Company (subsidiary of

Bethlehem Steel) had mines and mills. With the collapse of the revolution the American troops were withdrawn. In 1917 came the next intervention, this time to quiet a revolution that had broken out against the fraudulent re-election of President Menocal, a representative of conservative business and *persona grata* to the United States. The possibility that the United States might enter the World War made it particularly desirable that Cuba be kept quiet, and the revolutionists were quickly informed that no government based on revolution would be recognized by the United States. Marines were landed, and Menocal was returned to office as a result of the liberals' refusal to participate in the election. When the Menocal government declared war on Germany, it was maintained in office by United States marines, who for this purpose were conveniently kept in the island until 1921.

By the middle twenties there was little of value in Cuba that had not been taken over by American financial interests, and this ownership was largely concentrated in the National City Bank of New York, which directly controlled the General Sugar Company, the Consolidated Railways, the immense sugar holdings of the Cuba Company, and many other Cuban corporations, and through its twenty-four branch banks financed the native sugar-planters. In 1923 J. P. Morgan and Company loaned the Cuban government $50,000,000, and Cuban taxpayers as well as Cuban business fell under the domination of American bankers. By 1928 one estimate [6] placed American investments in Cuba at $1,150,000,000, of which $600,000,000 was in sugar, $115,000,000 in public utilities, $120,000,000 in rails, $50,000,000 in mines, $20,000,000 in tobacco, $110,000,000 in government securities, and the rest distributed among hotel, mercantile, industrial, and other interests. Under the impetus of American investments Cuba had become a land of great sugar and tobacco plantations, owned abroad and worked by a landless Cuban proletariat, whose prosperity was almost entirely dependent upon the American market, which in turn was dependent upon the American tariff. The economic domination was strengthened under the tyrannical President Machado, a puppet of the National City Bank, whose execrable regime was maintained in power from 1925 to 1933 through the backing of the United States government. From all this it is evident that Cuban wealth has fallen under American control and that Cuban political life from 1898 until 1934, and to some extent thereafter, has been largely directed from Washington. The result has been the impoverishment, degradation, and exploitation of the Cuban people. "Cuba," said one historian, "is no more independent than Long Island," and the history of her subjection presents a gloomy record.

[6] L. H. Jenks, *Our Cuban Colony,* 299 ff. Other estimates give higher figures.

PUERTO RICO

The history of Puerto Rico since American annexation in 1898 bears some resemblance to that of Cuba. There have been a notable advance in the sanitary and educational facilities of the island, improvement of transportation facilities, and construction of public works. It was in Puerto Rico that Major Bailey K. Ashford of the medical corps began the experiments that resulted in an understanding of the causes of the anemia brought on by the hookworm. The wealth of the island has increased, but, as in Cuba, that wealth has come under control of American capital, the land has been consolidated into large sugar and tobacco plantations, and the small farmer has been reduced to the status of a landless proletarian. The island is now essentially a two-crop country dependent upon the American market, and, when the market for these commodities collapses, as it did in 1929, the economic situation becomes intolerable. In 1930 at least 60 per cent of the population was unemployed. Cursed by absentee landlordism, dependent upon American capital and markets, and with the prices of manufactured commodities kept high by the American tariff, the economic condition of the Puerto Rican peasant is probably worse than under Spain.

Economic distress has accentuated political unrest. The Foraker Act of 1900 established civil government and placed it in the hands of a governor and executive council of eleven (six of whom were to be Americans), appointed by the President, and a popularly elected house of delegates. In 1917 Puerto Ricans were made citizens of the United States and given the right to elect an upper house, with the President reserving the right to veto bills and appoint the governor and certain other officials. This extension of political rights undoubtedly improved the political situation, but the economic conditions of recent years have strengthened the demand for complete home rule. Only by full autonomy can Puerto Ricans deal with the tariff and other economic questions. A petition from the Puerto Rican legislature for home rule in 1928, however, was denied by President Coolidge.

THE PHILIPPINES

"The Pacific Ocean is in our hands now," exulted Whitelaw Reid. "Practically we own more than half the coast on this side, dominate the rest, and have midway stations in the Sandwich and Aleutian Islands. To extend now the authority of the United States over the great Philippine Archipelago is to fence in the China Sea and secure an almost equally commanding position on the other side of the Pacific—doubling our control of it and of the fabulous trade the Twentieth Century will see it bear. Rightly used, it enables the United States to convert the Pacific Ocean into an American lake." This roseate dream of the imperialists, it is hardly necessary to say, was never consummated. From the beginning the Philippines have been a burden rather than an asset. The Filipinos had co-operated with the American forces in overthrowing Spanish rule, but they were equally opposed to domination by the United States. It took 60,000 men three years to put down the native rebellion, and the cost was almost as great as that of the Spanish-American War. The backbone of the insurrection was finally broken by General Funston's sensational capture of the native leader, Aguinaldo, but this first disagreeable concomitant of imperialism, accompanied as it was by tales of American cruelty, disillusioned many regarding the divine mission of the United States in the islands. The United States, in fact, found herself at the end of the Spanish-American War occupying the same position in the Philippine Islands that Spain had occupied in Cuba before the war. It was a direct exchange of roles.

While the subjugation of the islands was in progress, McKinley appointed, in 1899, a commission headed by President Schurman of Cornell to study conditions in the island, and the following year President Roosevelt sent a second commission, headed by William Howard Taft, to organize a civil government. Such a government was established in 1901 with the central control in the hands of an American governor and executive council. To the council three natives were later added, while a beginning of home rule appeared in the franchise regulations of municipal elections. The skillful work of the Taft commission was found good by Congress, which ratified it by the Philippine Act of July 1, 1902, and further provided that two years after the taking of a census a Philippine legislature should be established, the lower house of which was to be elective and the upper house to be composed of the Philippine Commission. The census was completed in 1905 and the first elections held in 1907, and thus, eight years after American occupation began, partial home rule was granted. In the United States the Democratic Party, since 1900, had been committed to eventual Philippine independence. When that party assumed office in 1913, however, it failed to live up to its promises, but in the Jones Act of 1916 it made the upper house of the Philippine legislature an elective body. Except for the veto power of the governor and the provision that an American was to head the Department of Instruction and Health, the government of the island was turned over to the natives. Agitation for complete independence, nevertheless, continued.

In the meantime, some efforts were made to tie more closely the economic bonds between the United States and her colony. In the tariff of 1902, a 25-per-cent reduction was allowed on goods imported from the Philippines; in 1909 free trade was allowed except for the limitation of duty-free imports upon sugar, tobacco, and hemp, and in 1913 unrestricted free trade was finally established. Despite the fact that the annual trade between the United States and the Philippines had grown by 1930 to over $200,000,000, the Philippines as an experiment in economic imperialism had been a disappointment. Not more than $160,000,000 of American capital had been invested in the islands, and more than three fourths of this amount was in government securities and public utilities. Furthermore, the great hope that the islands would act as a stimulus to Oriental trade had not been realized. On the other hand, the United States had assumed the "white man's burden" seriously and had spent large sums on sanitation, education, and public works, to say nothing of increased naval and military expenditures to protect the islands. Financially, the Philippines had been a heavy loss to the American people. Philippine products were also competing actively with those raised in America, another fact that helped to strengthen the movement for independence that culminated in the Tydings-McDuffie Act of 1934 (page 646).

THE CONSTITUTIONAL ASPECT

While governments were set up in the new possessions, the inevitable constitutional problems appeared. Since Puerto Rico and the Philippines were outside the continental United States and inhabited by an alien people, the President and Congress appeared to consider them outside the jurisdiction of the Constitution and laws. As a consequence, they disregarded the experience of over a century and proceeded to set up a system of administration resembling that of the British Empire in the colonial period. The constitutional status of those possessions and of their inhabitants remained for the Supreme Court to decide, and the question, to use the popular phase of the day, as to "whether the Constitution followed the flag," was one of more than academic importance.

Fundamentally, the "insular cases" attempted to settle two questions: (1) whether the United States had the right to acquire and rule a subject state, and (2) just what was the constitutional status of these regions. The first question was settled in De Lima v. Bidwell (1901), a case involving the question whether duties on Puerto Rican sugar under the Dingley tariff were legally collected. By a 5-to-4 decision the court held that Puerto Rico was not a foreign country in any respect, that the Dingley tariff did not apply, and that the duties must be refunded. The case of Downes v. Bidwell had to deal with the legality of a 15-per-cent tariff on Puerto Rican goods imposed in the Foraker Act of 1900 (page 529). By another 5-to-4 decision the court held that Puerto Rico was a territory of the United States but not part of it and that Congress had a right to legislate and govern

a territory as it saw fit, and that the Foraker Act was therefore constitutional. In other words, the Constitution did not follow the flag; the status
and rights of territories acquired were subject to the will of Congress.
From the point of view of practical administration, these decisions were
reasonable and perhaps inevitable. Constitutionally, however, they cleared
the way for almost any type of imperialism.

Brief introductions are H. U. Faulkner, *American Economic History,* Chap. XXVI:
B. H. Williams, *Economic Foreign Policy of the United States,* Chap. I; and
S. F. Bemis, *A Diplomatic History of the United States,* Chap. XXXVIII. Excellent
on the preliminaries to the Spanish-American War are L. H. Jenks, *Our Cuban
Colony,* Chaps. I–IV; Walter Millis, *The Martial Spirit,* Chap. IV; J. F. Rhodes, *The
McKinley and Roosevelt Administrations,* Chap. III; and, above all, J. W. Pratt, *Ex-
pansionists of 1898,* Chaps. VI, VII. On the war itself read Millis, *op. cit.,* Chaps.
VI–XII. The subsequent history of Cuba is covered in Jenks, *op. cit.,* Chaps. V–XVI;
of Puerto Rico in B. W. and J. W. Diffie, *Porto Rico: A Broken Pledge,* Chaps. III–X;
and of the Philippines in Bemis, *op. cit.,* Chap. XXVI. Also see H. S. Commager,
Documents of American History, Vol. II, 181–198.

A WORLD POWER

Chapter XXXII

EXPANDING IMPERIALISM

*In Monroe's time, the only way to take a part
of South America was to take land. Now finance
has new ways of its own.*

WALTER HINES PAGE

VENEZUELA AND THE DRAGO DOCTRINE

With the acquisition of Puerto Rico and the establishment of a protectorate over Cuba, American coils quickly tightened around the Caribbean. In this policy of expansion two influences were predominant. In the first place was the desire to build and safeguard an interoceanic canal, and in the second, the necessity of establishing a "Pax Americana" that would allow the unhampered exploitation of this region by American economic interests. In the attainment of these ends an efficient technique was developed, which resulted, as we shall see, in the establishment of new protectorates over Panama, Santo Domingo, Haiti, and Nicaragua, in the purchase of the Danish West Indies, and in the gradual elimination of European economic exploitation from those regions that we had decided to make our own. It resulted incidentally in a wide extension of the Monroe Doctrine and in a strong reaction in Latin America against the domineering policy of the United States. In the end this aggressive policy overreached itself, and a strategic retreat was necessary, but in the buoyant years from McKinley to Harding the policy of imperialistic expansion in the Caribbean was followed alike by Republican and by Democratic administrations.

Our increasing sensitiveness with respect to the Caribbean was clearly emphasized at the time of the second Venezuelan incident. In retaliation for the losses sustained by their nationals during a civil war and the failure of the Venezuelan government under the dictator Castro to meet the interest on the foreign debt, Great Britain, Germany, and Italy withdrew their legations, seized Venezuelan gunboats, and blockaded the ports of that nation (December, 1902). With the consent of Castro and the urging of our Department of State, the three European nations consented to arbitrate. In a letter written almost fourteen years later,[1] Roosevelt asserted that he forced arbitration by threatening to send Dewey and his fleet to prevent Germany from forcibly taking possession of Venezuelan territory. With the exception of a statement by Dewey that he had received orders to move the Atlantic fleet, no evidence to substantiate Roosevelt's boast has been uncovered. That the United States government, however, made its position quite clear during this incident, there can be no doubt. European nations, it held, had a perfect right to protect the lives and property of their nationals, but any effort to obtain territory in Latin America would be resisted by the United States.

, While the Latin-American nations were appreciative of that part of the Monroe Doctrine that opposed the annexation of territory by European nations, they repudiated the assumption that a nation might interfere to collect debts. In a communication to our Department of State, Luis Drago, Argentine Minister of Foreign Affairs, clearly enunciated this point of view. Pointing out that "the collection of loans by military means implies territorial occupation to make them effective, and territorial occupation signifies the suppression or subordination of the governments of the countries upon which it is imposed," Drago insisted that the principle that the Argentine Republic "would like to see recognized is: that the public debt can not occasion armed intervention nor even the actual occupation of the territory of American nations by a European power." The "Drago Doctrine" enunciated a theory sound in international law and wise in practice, and upon more than one occasion the United States government has endorsed it. In practice, however, it has not always been the guiding policy of this country.

PANAMA

One of the first fruits of the Spanish War was a revived interest in the Panama Canal. The spectacular voyage of the *Oregon* from the Pacific to join the Atlantic fleet had demonstrated the military necessity of a canal, and, now that the United States was a power in the Caribbean, it seemed intolerable that such a waterway should ever come under the control of another nation. The interest of the United States in such a canal project goes back to 1846, when a treaty with New Granada gave to this country the right of free transit across the isthmus of Panama, and the United States in return guaranteed the neutrality of the isthmus and freedom of transit as well as the rights of sovereignty and property of New Granada therein. Interest in the isthmus was soon stimulated by the discovery of gold in California, and in 1850 the United States and Great Britain, by

[1] J. B. Bishop, *Theodore Roosevelt and His Times*, I, 222–224, and W. R. Thayer, *The Life and Letters of John Hay*, II, 286–288.

the Clayton-Bulwer treaty, agreed among other things that neither nation would seek any exclusive control over a canal built in Nicaragua. If the United States was to build an interoceanic canal, the first step, obviously enough, was to end the Clayton-Bulwer agreement. This was done in 1901 by the Hay-Pauncefote treaty, which gave to this country the power to build and police the canal, but on the condition that it should be open to the merchant vessels and warships of all nations, in war and peace, without discrimination or inequality of tolls.

In the meantime, a French company under de Lesseps had, during the eighties and nineties, made a futile effort to construct a canal. Its failure and the impending end of its lease, combined with the anxiety of the United States to take up the project, brought matters to a head. Some doubt had earlier existed as to the merits of the Nicaragua and Panama routes; three American commissions had recommended the former, and sentiment was generally favorable to the northern canal. At the critical juncture Phillippe Bunau-Varilla, formerly chief engineer under de Lesseps, but now a resident and citizen of Panama, appeared in Washington and lobbied so successfully that he won over both Hanna and Roosevelt. In one of his ablest speeches Hanna convinced the Senate of the superiority of the southern route, and the Spooner Amendment to the pending canal bill provided for a canal across the isthmus if satisfactory titles could be obtained from the New Panama Canal Company for $40,000,000 and control of the necessary territory from Colombia. Otherwise the President "might fall back to the Nicaragua route." The French company saw the light and agreed to sell at the fixed price, and the Hay-Herran convention (1903) was drawn up between Colombia and the United States, by which the latter agreed to a payment of $10,000,000 and $250,000 a year after nine years for what amounted to a perpetual lease of a strip wide enough to build the canal. The treaty passed the United States Senate but failed of ratification in Colombia. Popular disapproval, a feeling that the compensation was too low, and possibly a desire to procrastinate until the French lease ran out in 1904 and thus to obtain an additional $40,000,000, all contributed. The disgust of Roosevelt and the Department of State over this unexpected delay, the fear on the part of the people of Panama that they might lose the benefits of a canal, and the underground machinations of Bunau-Varilla were the chief ingredients out of which a revolution was soon concocted.

After conferences with American officials, leaders of the revolutionary party determined to risk the enterprise. It was on October 31 that the United States minister at Bogotá notified Hay that the Colombian Senate had adjourned without ratifying the treaty. On November 2, one day before the revolution was scheduled to take place, the acting Secretary of the

Navy telegraphed to the commander of the *Nashville* at Colón, "Prevent landing of armed force, either government or insurgent with hostile intent." More detailed instructions were sent to three other vessels. At 3:40 P. M., November 3, Acting Secretary of State Loomis wired Ehrman, American consul at Panama, "Uprising on isthmus reported. Keep Department promptly and fully informed," to which Ehrman at 8:15 replied, "No uprising yet. Reported will be in the night. Situation is critical." Two hours later Ehrman telegraphed, "Uprising occurred tonight; no bloodshed. Army and Navy officials taken prisoners. Government will be organized tonight." At 11:18 on the same night Ehrman was directed by Loomis to act promptly in preventing Colombian soldiers from moving from Colón to Panama. In brief, the United States had interfered by military force to prevent the Colombian government from putting down a rebellion.

On November 6, three days after the revolution, Ambassador Beaupre telegraphed that the Colombian government would ratify the Hay-Herran treaty if the United States would assist in preserving Colombian sovereignty over the isthmus. If the actions of the American government on November 3 had been consummated, as was claimed, under the excuse of the treaty of 1846, this offer and request could hardly be denied. The United States, however, had decided otherwise. On the same day Loomis instructed Ehrman, "when you are satisfied that *de facto* government, republican in form, and without substantial opposition from its own people, has been established in the State at Panama, you will enter into relations with it as the responsible government of the territory." Immediately Ehrman advised that Bunau-Varilla had been appointed minister. The latter was officially received by Roosevelt on November 13, and five days later, November 18, Hay and Bunau-Varilla signed a treaty by which the United States agreed to pay $10,000,000 down and $250,000 a year after nine years for the perpetual lease of a ten-mile zone across the isthmus. Within fifteen days (November 3 to November 18) there had been consummated the revolution, recognition by the United States, and the treaty that made possible the canal, incidentally establishing under the treaty a protectorate over Panama.

All parties are agreed on the importance of the American help. Without American warships there probably would have been no revolution, certainly no successful one, and without American guarantee Panama would not exist. "From the morning of the second of November," says Bunau-Varilla, "all of the inhabitants of Colón were looking towards Kingston, hoping for the appearance of the ship symbolizing American protection," and, when it actually came, he says, "without one word having been uttered the revolution was accomplished in the hearts of all." In his message of January 4, 1904, Roosevelt asserted that "no one connected with this Government had any part in preparing, inciting, or encouraging the late revolution on the Isthmus of Panama, and . . . save from the reports of our military and naval officers . . . no one connected with this Government had any previous knowledge of the revolution except such as was accessible to any person of ordinary intelligence who read the newspapers and kept up a current acquaintance with public affairs." This statement, while characteristically Rooseveltian, is hardly convincing. More accurate is his reported statement made in a speech at Berkeley, California, in March, 1911:

> I am interested in the Panama Canal because I started it. If I had followed traditional conservative methods I would have submitted a dignified state paper of probably two hundred pages to the Congress and the debate would be going on yet, but I took the Canal Zone and let the Congress debate, and while the debate goes on, the canal does also.

Whatever may be the conclusion regarding the ethics of this affair, the efficiency with which it was executed commands admiration.[2]

While the means were anything but justified, the end has proved an unqualified good. A canal commission of seven, appointed under the chairmanship of Rear Admiral John G. Walker, commenced its work in the spring of 1904. It was the duty of the commission not only to organize the building of a canal but to conduct the civil government of the Canal Zone, and, most important of all, to make the region habitable for white men. The first two years were spent largely in the preliminary work of sanitation, and the remarkable work done under the supervision of Colonel W. C. Gorgas remains one of the most famous efforts at preventive medicine that history records. A second commission was appointed in 1905, and a further reorganization was effected in 1907, when the whole project was placed in the hands of the Engineer Corps of the United States Army, with Lieutenant Colonel George W. Goethals as chairman and Colonel Gorgas as chief medical officer. Including fortifications and later payment to Colombia, the cost of the canal was approximately $600,000,000.

SANTO DOMINGO

The most populous of the West Indian islands and the richest in natural resources is Haiti, which is divided between the little republic of Santo Domingo on the east and Haiti on the west. The island has a further

---

[2] During the Wilson administration the United States in a treaty offered to pay Colombia $25,000,000 in recompense for what had happened in 1903, as well as to smooth the way for American oil men and other concession-seekers. The United States Senate ratified the treaty in 1921. S. F. Bemis, *A Diplomatic History of the United States*, 517–518.

significance because of its strategic position on the trade routes leading to the Panama Canal. From its first independence in 1844 until the definite assumption of an American protectorate in 1907, the career of Santo Domingo had been one of perpetual storm and incessant revolutions. In this kaleidoscope of revolutions and dictators, foreign debts had inevitably accumulated. In 1892 and 1893 an American concern, the San Domingo Improvement Company, by buying the debt of £170,000 sterling from a Dutch company, got its hands on a portion of the debt, with the under-standing that it was to be allowed to collect the customs and turn a portion of them over to the Dominican government. This arrangement the Dominican government repudiated in 1901, whereupon the company appealed to the United States government. In the negotiations that followed, the Dominican government finally offered to purchase the American claims for $4,500,000, the payments to be secured by customs receipts, with the right of the United States to send a financial agent upon failure to pay. A protocol to this effect was signed in 1903.

Upon the failure of Santo Domingo to make any payments, an American financial agent took over the customs house of Puerto Plata in 1904. Foreign nations, fearing discriminations in favor of American debtors, became aroused, and France threatened to seize the customs house of Santo Domingo City. To ward off interference, Roosevelt forced the Dominican government to sign a treaty in 1905 that would both clear up the financial difficulties and at the same time place that nation under the protection of the United States. Although Roosevelt appeared quite willing to reduce Santo Domingo to a protectorate of the United States and even to police it, he had no desire to annex the country. "I have about the same desire to annex it," he insisted, "as a gorged boa-constrictor might have to swallow a porcupine wrong end to." The Senate, not so anxious to rush in, failed to ratify the treaty, and Roosevelt put it in force by an "executive agreement." Ratification of a similar treaty, however, was secured in 1907, under which a new loan for $20,000,000 was to liquidate the old debts, a general receiver of customs was to be appointed by the United States to collect and apportion the customs receipts, and, until the existing debt was paid, the public debt was not to be increased except by consent of the United States. Kuhn, Loeb and Company took the $20,000,-000 loan, and in 1914 the National City Bank floated a second.

Interference in political life commenced in 1912, when Taft forced the resignation of a president, and culminated with the invasion of the marines in 1916. From that year until 1924, when the marines were withdrawn, Santo Domingo remained under a military government conducted by United States officers. Revolutionary movements were ruthlessly suppressed, and a Dominican constabulary was established to maintain order.

Roads were built, the sanitation improved, and the educational system reconstructed. Although the Dominicans might differ radically among one another, they were agreed on one thing—the desirability of ending American occupation. This was finally achieved under a convention that validated executive orders and contracts made under the military government and extended the treaty of 1907 during the life of the existing bond issues. Actually, it meant an indefinite control of Dominican finances by the United States, with the power of intervention. In the meantime, a subsidiary of the National City Bank had obtained almost complete control of the financial life of the country, and at least one third of the sugar industry was owned by American capital.

The intervention in Santo Domingo is also significant because it provided the occasion for a wide extension of the Monroe Doctrine. In defending his Dominican policy, Roosevelt enunciated in a message to Congress (1904) a theory that has since become known as the "Roosevelt corollary to the Monroe Doctrine."

> If a nation [said Roosevelt] shows that it knows how to act with reasonable efficiency and decency in social and political matters, if it keeps order and pays its obligations, it need fear no interference from the United States. Chronic wrongdoing, or an impotence which results in a general loosening of the ties of civilized society, may in America, as elsewhere, ultimately require intervention by some civilized nation, and in the Western Hemisphere the adherence of the United States to the Monroe Doctrine may force the United States, however reluctantly, in flagrant cases of such wrongdoing or impotence, to the exercise of an international police power.

Here was the Monroe Doctrine carried to its logical conclusion. If the premise is admitted that one nation may interfere in the affairs of another to preserve property and collect debts, the United States must assume this duty or allow European nations to do it. As European intervention would endanger the Monroe Doctrine, the duty of policeman must be assumed by the United States. There were two very practical objections to the policy enunciated by the Roosevelt corollary. While Europe might be quite willing that the United States assume the disagreeable duty of collecting debts and maintaining the peace, it was quite possible that the task of policing Latin America might become too onerous for the United States. In the second place, Latin America might resent, as she did, the self-righteous assumption by the United States of the right to determine when intervention should take place. While glad to be protected from Europe, the Latin-American nations asked quite logically how they were to be protected from the United States. To them the Roosevelt corollary seemed a doctrine of brazen imperialism. It took the American people two decades to realize the impracticability of the Roosevelt corollary and to commence a retreat from the preposterous policy that it enunciated.

HAITI AND NICARAGUA

In Santo Domingo the United States worked out a general technique of economic imperialism, which was followed in Haiti and Nicaragua. Although the political history of the Negro republic of Haiti had been quite as stormy as that of Santo Domingo, her government had been careful to pay her debts, and no American citizen appears to have been injured in life or property. The National Bank of Haiti, founded by French capital, had in 1881 been entrusted with the administration of the Haitian treasury. Upon its reorganization in 1910, Secretary of State Knox, an ardent advocate of "dollar diplomacy," insisted upon the injection of American capital, and four New York banks became subscribers. In 1914 and 1915, because of political disturbances, the United States government suggested several times the establishment of a relationship between the two nations after the manner of the Dominican treaty of 1907, but was repeatedly refused. A state approximating political anarchy having been reached, marines landed on December 10, 1914, and removed $500,000 from the National Bank of Haiti, and on July 28, 1915, military occupation was inaugurated. After thorough intimidation a puppet president and puppet legislators, elected under supervision of the marines, ratified, November 11, 1915, a treaty by which the United States was to appoint a general receiver of customs to collect the tariffs and a financial adviser to tell the Haitian government how to spend its money. Haiti promised not to increase her public debt without consent of the United States and to create an efficient constabulary, to be officered in the first instance by Americans. By other provisions Haiti agreed not to surrender any of her territory to any other power nor to make any treaty or contract that might impair her independence. The United States was given authority to intervene for the preservation of Haitian independence or for the protection of life, property, and individual liberty, and provisions were made for the development of the nation's resources by the United States. The treaty was for ten years but later was extended to twenty.

Under this treaty Haiti became very definitely a protectorate of the United States, with American officials directing the government under the protective force of the marines. The results were those that ordinarily follow American occupation. The finances were put on an orderly basis, and the educational, sanitary, and transportation systems were tremendously improved. Rebellions were crushed, and peace was brought to the distracted island. On the other side of the shield was also to be found the familiar picture. Loss of political independence was followed by wholesale American economic penetration and exploitation. Native opposition to American control was continuous and was intensified by the revival of the *corvée* (a law requiring forced labor on the roads), by the tactlessness of American officers, and by the ruthlessness, if not cruelty, with which revolts were put down. Some 1500 Haitians, for example, lost their lives in the Caco revolt of 1918. These points were all brought out in an investigation made by a Senate committee in 1922. By this time criticism of American occupation of the island had become so intense in the United States as well as in Haiti that some reorganization was necessary. The rigor of American control was somewhat relaxed, and some of the worst abuses were ended. Weary of the role of policeman, President Hoover sent a commission in 1930 to study the Haitian problem, and in the following year most of the marines were withdrawn, and the Haitianization of the services was pushed rapidly. By agreements in 1933 American control was ended except for an American fiscal representative to direct the customs service and supervise other aspects of Haitian finance. After nineteen years of occupation, the last marines departed on August 15, 1934.

The occupation of Santo Domingo and Haiti was followed in 1917 by the purchase from Denmark of the Virgin Islands (St. Thomas, St. John, St. Croix) for $25,000,000. Since these islands are on one of the routes to the Panama Canal, naval strategists considered them important, and they were governed until 1931 by a naval officer. In that year the islands were turned over to the Department of the Interior, and civil government was established. American ownership brought little, if any, advantage to the islanders, and their prosperity and population have declined. Prohibition in the United States ended for a time their famous rum business (except bay rum), and the development of oil-burning ships decreased the importance of the excellent harbor of St. Thomas as a coaling station.

Control of Santo Domingo and Haiti and the purchase of the Danish West Indies secured control of the strategic routes from Europe to the Panama Canal. Meanwhile came the inevitable spread of American power in Central America. Nicaragua was the first of the Central American states to fall a victim to American economic penetration, and her possession of a second route for an interoceanic canal was the primary cause. American interest was definitely drawn to Nicaragua in 1907, when, because of an impending Central American war, the United States brought pressure upon the five nations there to erect a Central American court to compose their differences. Two years later (1909) a revolution broke out against President José Santos Zelaya, apparently financed by Adolfo Diaz, a local official of an American mining concern. Using as an excuse the execution by Zelaya of two American filibusters who had joined the revolution, the

United States broke off relations with Zelaya, supported the revolution, and since that time has dominated the political life of the nation.

Actual occupation by the marines began during a revolution in 1912, and, with the exception of a brief period in 1925, continued until 1933. In 1911 the Knox-Castrillo convention, providing for a Nicaraguan loan and American control of customs, was signed but failed to pass the United States Senate. Nothing daunted, Brown Brothers and J. and W. Seligman, under the benign eye of the Department of State, made a private agreement with the Nicaraguan authorities by which in return for a small loan the New York financiers were to have 51 per cent of the stock of the National Bank, Nicaragua was to reform her currency, and the loan was to be secured by a lien on customs, the latter to be collected by an American, nominated by the banks and approved by the American Department of State. Under the pressure of Secretary Knox these loan contracts were approved by the Nicaraguan Senate. Other loans have been made, and, under the protecting guns of American marines, United States bankers have tightened their grip not only on the customs, but on the internal taxes, the National Bank, and the railways. The main objective, as far as the American government was concerned, was achieved in 1916, when, against the protests of Costa Rica and Salvador, the Byran-Chamorro treaty gave the United States for the sum of $3,000,000 the right to construct a canal through Nicaragua and a ninety-nine-year lease on the Great Corn and Little Corn Islands, and a naval base on the Gulf of Fonseca.

With American marines walking the streets of Managua, the conservative party maintained control of the government under reasonably peaceful conditions from 1917 until 1925. A liberal *coup d'état* in that year overthrew the conservative government, precipitating the worst period of revolutionary activity in Nicaraguan history. President Coolidge, insisting that the United States intervene to protect American life and property, to safeguard canal rights, to prevent foreign interference, and to uphold a Central American treaty made in 1923 between the five Central American nations, in which they had agreed not to recognize governments set up in an extraconstitutional manner, sent Henry L. Stimson to Nicaragua to find a formula to compose the differences between the factions. The agreement reached called for a general peace and the surrender of arms by all factions, the supervision of the 1928 and subsequent elections by Americans, the organization of a Nicaraguan constabulary officered by Americans, and a temporary occupation by a sufficient force of American marines to secure the enforcement of the peace terms. This program was carried out with the exception that Sandino, one of the liberal revolutionary leaders, continued revolutionary activities until 1933, when he and his followers were granted public lands upon which to establish an agricultural colony. A month earlier (January 2, 1933) the last of the marines were withdrawn.

MEXICO

It was one thing to ride roughshod over the impotent republics of the Caribbean and Central America, but quite another to deal with a large and wealthy nation like Mexico. In 1877 the government of Mexico came under the control of a strong-armed dictator, Porfirio Diaz, who, backed by the landed aristocracy, held control for more than a quarter century. While the power of Diaz and his group was primarily based upon the exploitation of agriculture through the system of peonage, Diaz throughout these years encouraged the investment of foreign capital. As Mexico was endowed with rich natural resources and cheap labor to exploit them, foreign capital needed no second invitation. American investors, it was estimated, had placed as early as 1902 some $500,000,000 in Mexican plantations, mines, railroads, and other industries, an amount that more than doubled in the next ten years, owing chiefly to the rapid development of the Mexican oil fields. By 1910 about 80 per cent of the investments in Mexican railroads were in American hands, and 70 per cent of the oil output was handled by American concerns.

The despotism of the aged Diaz was finally overthrown in 1911, when Francisco Madero, Jr., and a band of sincere liberals headed a revolution to end the ruthless exploitation of the peasants and to protect the natural resources from foreign concession-seekers. While it is difficult to trace the influence of foreign interests in the revolutionary turmoil that ensued, certain facts seem evident. Diaz, in his later years, apparently regretted the rapid penetration of American oil interests and sought to neutralize this by encouraging British oil men to invest heavily. As a consequence, it is believed, Madero was encouraged, if not financed in part, by American oil interests. At any rate, Madero was immediately recognized by the United States, and in March, 1912, President Taft prohibited the purchase of munitions in the United States by factions opposing the Madero government. Madero hung on until February, 1913, when Victoriano Huerta, a counterrevolutionist representing the Diaz group, overthrew the government, had Madero assassinated, and assumed power. Huerta was recognized by twenty-six European governments and by Japan but not by the United States. President Wilson, shocked by the brutal assassination of Madero, refused recognition with the words, "we can have no sympathy with those who seize the power of government to advance their own political interest or ambition."

Wilson called his Mexican policy "watchful waiting," but "watchful action" would have better described it. Determining to eliminate Huerta, he purchased England's desertion of the Mexican dictator by promising to repeal the discriminatory canal tolls, then lifted the embargo on arms, in February, 1914, and in April found an excuse to occupy Vera Cruz. The capture of Vera Cruz cost the lives of eighteen American marines and two hundred Mexican men, women, and children, but it ended the career of Huerta. With revenue and supplies cut off, he fled from the scene, and the forces of Venustiano Carranza entered Mexico City. Another year of turmoil, and the United States, followed by other nations, recognized Carranza. The troubles of neither nation, however, were over. Francisco Villa, a disappointed rival of Carranza, took up arms against his chief and complicated the situation by crossing the border in March, 1916, raiding Columbus, New Mexico, and killing a number of American citizens. The outcry of patriots, politicians, and oil men against "watchful waiting" was too loud to be ignored, and Wilson ordered General Pershing to lead a punitive expedition into Mexico to capture Villa. Pershing spent nine months in Mexico and came back without Villa. Our impending entrance into the European war ended the possibility of further intervention.

Since 1917 the diplomatic problems of the two nations have swung chiefly around the economic interests of American investors as affected by the Mexican constitution of that year. Under the influence of the liberal Obregón faction, a constitution was promulgated that nationalized church property, secularized the schools, promised varied legislation, and declared that the soil and subsoil of Mexico belonged to the Mexican people. In the future only Mexicans might acquire ownership of Mexican land, except that the nation might grant the same right to foreigners on condition that they agree "to be considered Mexicans in respect to such property, and accordingly not to envoke the protection of their governments to the same, under penalty, in case of breach, of forfeiture." Under no condition might a foreigner acquire land within 100 kilometers from the frontier or 50 from the coast. Although this was not retroactive, it was bitterly opposed by American investors, who almost succeeded in precipitating war in 1919.

The conservative Carranza was overthrown by Obregón in 1920, and, when it became evident that the great majority of Americans had little interest in interfering in Mexico for the benefit of oil, the administration became more conciliatory. Diplomatic relations, withheld since the revolution of 1920, were again established in 1923, and after some years of tension President Coolidge sent Dwight W. Morrow, a partner of J. P. Morgan and Company, as ambassador. Despite Mexican suspicions regarding Morrow's financial affiliations, his tact and common sense quickly won the friendship of the Mexicans, Difficulties over land laws and oil leases were eventually straightened out, and relations between the two nations for the first time in many years became satisfactory. While Wilson's policy was somewhat confusing, the Mexicans have eventually realized that the general policy of this country toward their nation is one of conciliation and hands off. Although the anticlerical activity of the Mexican government has aroused animosity among Catholics in the United States, this has been counteracted by the recent interest and rising appreciation in this country of Mexican art and culture as Americans in increasing numbers visit their neighbor to the south.

THE FAR EAST

As far as the United States had any policy in the Far East during the nineteenth century, it was the desire to keep the field open for free and equal commercial opportunities for all nations, so that the United States might not be excluded. This policy was continued and more definitely enunciated in the new century as the result of the Industrial Revolution at home and of three important developments in the Far East. The first was the annexation of the Philippines, which made the United States a power in that part of the world; the second was the phenomenal emergence of Japan as a great nation; and the third was the imperialistic designs of Japan and the great European nations upon the integrity of China. Certain European nations since 1840 and Japan in more recent years had cast covetous eyes upon the resources of China and had struggled to increase their influence in that nation. During the last decade of the century a new wave of imperialism encompassed China when England, France, Russia, and Germany secured long-term leases of important Chinese ports, under which spheres of political and economic influence were being established. Japan joined in the imperialistic scramble after her war with China in 1894-1895, when she annexed Formosa and made Korea a sphere of Japanese influence.

American dreams of commercial expansion and economic penetration were quite obviously imperiled by the territorial disintegration of China. It might have been quite easy in 1899 to form an alliance with Japan and Great Britain to preserve the "open door" in China, but the American policy of isolation prevented this step. As a consequence, the United States acted alone. In September of that year Secretary John Hay addressed his famous "open door" note to the great powers, requesting each to make a declaration to the effect that (1) it would not interfere with any treaty port or vested interest in its sphere of influence, (2) it would allow the Chinese tariff to continue and to be collected by Chinese officials without discrimination against any foreigners, and (3) it would not discriminate against other nations in port dues or railroad rates. Only Great Britain answered favorably, but Hay, ignoring the evasive replies of the others, announced that in view of the favorable reception of his proposals they would be regarded "as final and definitive."

It was one thing to write notes and another to have them taken seriously. Since 1899 the preservation of the political integrity of China and the maintenance of the open door have been the essential policy of the United States in the Far East, but, despite the exertion of almost every pressure short of war, this policy in the long run has failed. When China herself reacted against foreign aggression and in the Boxer Rebellion of 1900 attacked the British legation at Peking, the United States participated in a joint expedition to rescue the survivors. This invasion of China gave Hay an opportunity to reaffirm the open door policy and to insist that the affair should not be used as an excuse to violate China's territorial integrity. For the moment American policy seemed successful. The other nations agreed and contented themselves with an indemnity. America's share was $24,-440,700, which was almost twice the amount of American claims. The excess debt was later (1908) canceled by Congress,[3] and the amount has been used by China to send Chinese students to American universities.

Within four years the United States was again playing an important role in Asiatic affairs, this time in helping to bring to a conclusion the Russo-Japanese War of 1904–1905. After a series of striking victories, Japan, approaching the end of her resources, asked Roosevelt to intervene. Without constitutional authority Roosevelt (according to his own story) warned France and Germany that, if either one of them interfered in behalf of Russia, the United States would aid Japan.[4] Then he persuaded both Russia and Japan to undertake negotiations for peace, which culminated in the treaty signed at Portsmouth, New Hampshire, in April, 1905.

Relations between Japan and the United States, which had been exceedingly cordial during the Russo-Japanese War, soon became strained. The average Japanese, ignorant of the secret diplomacy, held the United States responsible for the failure of Japan to obtain greater rewards from her victory. This feeling was accentuated by the agitation in the West against Japanese immigration and by the famous order of the San Francisco school board to segregate Japanese children in a special school. This difficult situation was somewhat eased by the "gentlemen's agreement" of 1907, in which the Japanese government agreed not to issue passports

[3] The amount was $11,961,000. In 1924 Congress remitted further the amount that was then still due, $6,137,500. Thus, in all, about three fourths of the original indemnity was remitted.

[4] Letter of Roosevelt to Sir Cecil Spring-Rice, dated July 24, 1905, and quoted by Tyler Dennett, The Russo-Japanese War, 2. No verification of Roosevelt's own statement has yet been discovered.

to skilled and unskilled laborers desiring to go to the United States, and by the Root-Takahira agreement of 1908, in which both nations promised to respect each other's territorial possessions in the Pacific, to support Chinese independence, and to uphold the open door. The fundamental difficulty between the two nations, however, lay in the aggressive imperialism of Japan, which brought the annexation of Korea in 1910, the taking over of the German interests after the World War in 1919, and the subsequent occupation of Manchuria. By 1919 Japan was the paramount imperialistic power in the Far East, and Hay's open door policy was all but ignored.

Except for an increase in exports to China from $16,724,000 in 1900 to $138,455,000 in 1920, American economic penetration has not been notably successful. This failure has been in no small degree due to the opposition of Japan, and herein lies the real difficulty between the two nations. American interests won an initial victory in 1898, when the China Development Company (a New Jersey Corporation) obtained a concession to build a railroad, but it did not push the enterprise. Beginning in 1905, Edward H. Harriman, dominated by his dream of a round-the-world railroad, attempted to obtain a joint Japanese-American control of the South Manchurian railroad. Japan dropped this plan and (with Russia) blocked his efforts to build a parallel line. Undiscouraged by this, American bankers, backed aggressively by the Department of State and supported by a personal telegram from Taft to the Prince Regent of China, obtained participation in a Chinese loan of $30,000,000 to build the Hukuang railroad. Flushed by this success, Americans entered aggressively into a six-power consortium for a large reorganization loan to China after the Chinese Revolution of 1911. "Dollar diplomacy is justified at last," wrote Willard Straight, agent of the Morgan bankers and guiding hand in the negotiations, but the six-power loan was never consummated. Insisting that this loan would "touch very nearly the administrative independence of China itself" and would be "obnoxious to the principles upon which the government of our people rests," Woodrow Wilson opposed it. Soon after came the World War with its significant effect upon the Far East.

American imperialism reached its highest point in the first administration of Woodrow Wilson. Under Republicans and Democrats alike, American economic interests had been aggressively pushed in the Caribbean region and protected in the Far East. "Dollar diplomacy" had been the guiding motive in our foreign relations. The result had been the establishment of protectorates over Cuba, Haiti, Santo Domingo, Nicaragua, and Panama, domination of Central America, annexation of Puerto Rico, purchase of the Virgin Islands, acquisition by treaty of the Great Corn and Little Corn Islands, and provision for naval stations at Guantánamo, Cuba, at Mole St. Nicolas, Haiti, at Samaná Bay, Santo Domingo, and in the Gulf of Fonseca. In brief, the Caribbean had become an American lake, and the United States had established her first sphere of influence. In the Far East the story had been different. The acquisition of the Philippines had not been followed by heavy American investments; nor had the islands proved a stepping stone to Oriental trade. Although efforts were made to maintain equal economic opportunities in China, the combined pressure of European and Japanese imperialism was too much. Wilson's refusal to sanction American particpation in the six-power loan marked the first retreat from the "dollar diplomacy" of Knox and Taft, just as his refusal in the later months of his second administration to interfere in Mexico in behalf of American oil interests marked the beginning of a retreat in Latin America.

In H. C. Hill, *Roosevelt and the Caribbean,* Chap. V, the Venezuelan incident is ably presented. Our Caribbean policy is covered in S. F. Bemis, *A Diplomatic History of the United States,* Chaps. XXVIII, XIX. On Panama see particularly J. F. Rippy, *The Capitalists and Colombia,* Chaps. II–V and T. A. Bailey, *A Diplomatic History of the American People,* Chap. XXXII; on Santo Domingo, M. M. Knight, *The Americans in Santo Domingo,* Chaps. I–IX; on Central America, G. H. Stuart, *Latin America and the United States,* 4th ed., Chaps. XIII–XIV. For Mexico see Bemis, *op. cit.,* Chap. XXX, and G. H. Stuart, *op. cit.,* Chaps. VI–VII. On the Far East see Bemis, *op. cit.,* Chaps. XXXV, XXXVI, XL and Bailey, *op. cit.,* Chap. XXXIV, 577–581. Source material is in F. Flügel and H. U. Faulkner, *Readings in the Economic and Social History of the United States,* 877–910, and H. S. Commager, *Documents of American History,* Vol. II, 190–192, 203–206, 209–215, 225, 232–256, 267–274, 292–294.

A WORLD POWER

Chapter XXXIII

THE AGE OF BIG BUSINESS

*In recent times absentee ownership has come to
be the main and immediate controlling interest
in the life of civilized man.*

THORSTEIN VEBLEN

*The central government in its policy toward
the large corporations must adopt one of two
courses. Either it must discriminate in their favor
or it must discriminate against them. The third
alternative—that of being what is called "impartial"—has no real existence.*

HERBERT CROLY

POLITICS

Aggressive American imperialism at the turn of the century was but the
reflection of an expanding economic life that was carrying the American
republic to new heights of productive capacity. The dark months following the panic of 1893 had passed, and prosperity had returned in full measure. With McKinley in the White House, with Hanna, the personification
of American business, directing the fortunes of the Republican Party, and
with Congress packed with the representatives and agents of big business,
hardly a cloud flecked the bright sky of *laissez-faire* capitalism. As the
first McKinley administration drew triumphantly to a close, there was no
question as to McKinley's renomination and but slight doubt as to his
re-election. His nomination, in fact, was unanimous, and interest in the
convention, contrary to precedent, centered in the nomination of the candidate for the vice-presidency. Two years earlier the Republican machine
in New York state, in order to ensure victory, had nominated Theodore
Roosevelt for governor, but he had proved too independent, and Senator
Platt, in the hope of removing him from New York and pushing him
upstairs into political oblivion, now headed the movement for his nomination. Despite the opposition of Hanna, the lukewarm approval of
McKinley, and the reluctance of Roosevelt himself, such a demand arose
that his nomination also was unanimous. Dwelling with pride upon the

prosperity of the past four years and defending the foreign policy of the administration, the platform pledged the party to the gold standard and the protective tariff. For the workers it pledged protection against contract and convict labor and promised restriction of immigration; for the liberals it opposed combinations designed to create monopolies.

Still affected by the split over the currency issue, the Democrats had as yet developed no leader who could reconcile the two factions, and Bryan was unanimously nominated for the presidency, with Adlai E. Stevenson, who had served with Cleveland and who was entirely innocent of "radicalism," for the vice-presidency. Imperialism, their platform insisted, was the "paramount issue," but monopolies were also roundly denounced, and the Dingley tariff was assailed as a "trust-breeding" measure. The platform pledged an enlargement of the Interstate Commerce Act, denounced government by injunction, and advocated a Nicaraguan canal. From the earlier Populist platforms they picked the plank advocating the direct election of United States senators and, upon the insistence of Bryan, inserted a demand for "free silver." [1] Some fire was injected into the campaign by the speaking tours of Bryan and Roosevelt and by the fact that certain prominent anti-imperialist Republicans deserted their party to endorse Bryan. The result, however, was hardly in doubt. Prosperity and the efficient management of Hanna brought the expected victory. McKinley obtained a plurality of 860,000 in a total vote of over 13,700,000 and won by an electoral vote of 292 to 155. Again the American people had repudiated free silver and the radicalism of Populism and had endorsed territorial expansion.

The blissful security brought by this easy victory was not to last long. Scarcely six months after his second inauguration, the kindly McKinley, while attending the Pan-American Exposition at Buffalo, was shot by a demented anarchist (September 6). Eight days later he died, and Theodore Roosevelt, young, vigorous, outspoken, and independent, became President of the United States. To the elder statesmen who had enjoyed the serenity of the McKinley regime, the accession of Roosevelt was a shock. Nor were their misgivings without foundation. The most dynamic and colorful personality to enter the White House since the days of Jackson, Roosevelt's conception of the presidency was quite opposite to that of his predecessor, McKinley, or his successor, Taft. Except where his powers were specifically limited by the Constitution, he assumed that they existed, and, in his own words, he "caused to be done many things not previously done by the President" and "greatly broaden[ed] the use of executive

---

[1] The Populist party split, one group endorsing Bryan, while the middle-of-the-road faction nominated their own candidates. A most important event in third-party history was the appearance of the Social Democratic Party, which nominated Eugene V. Debs (page 591).

power." A born leader, a skillful politician, and a man of incredible energy, Roosevelt inevitably occupied the center of whatever activity he entered. With unerring sense, moreover, he caught the aspirations of the common man and dramatized them in his own personality.

With the possible exception of the younger Adams, it is doubtful if any President had entered the White House with a richer or more varied experience than Roosevelt had crammed into the twenty years since his graduation from Harvard. Eighteen months after graduation he was elected to the New York legislature. A sojourn in the cow lands of Dakota was followed by his candidacy for mayor of New York, by a period as Civil Service Commissioner under Harrison, as Police Commissioner of New York, Assistant Secretary of the Navy under McKinley, Colonel of the "Rough Riders," Governor of New York, and Vice-President. And during these years he had also found time to write enough biography and history to win a place in the world of literature. A personification of the "strenuous life" that he urged upon all, and endowed with a restless energy, Roosevelt found it difficult to practice the cautious restraint of the ordinary politician, and he was constantly committing himself in vigorous language to projects that he often failed fully to support. His railroad legislation, his prosecutions of the trusts, and his efforts in behalf of pure foods and conservation gave a foundation for the reputation that he established as a progressive leader, even if it did not convince the more uncompromising progressives of the La Follette type. As the glamour of Roosevelt's personality has somewhat dimmed, historians are inclined to accept the elder Senator La Follette's critical estimate:

> While Mr. Roosevelt was President, his public utterances through state papers, addresses, and the press were highly colored with rhetorical radicalism. His administrative policies as set forth in his recommendations to Congress were vigorously and picturesquely presented, but characterized by an absence of definite economic conception. One trait was always pronounced. His most savage assault upon special interests was invariably offset with an equally drastic attack upon those who were seeking to reform abuses. These were indiscriminately classed as demagogues and dangerous persons. In this way he sought to win approval, both from the radicals and the conservatives. This cannonading, first in one direction and then in another, filled the air with noise and smoke, which confused and obscured the line of action, but when the battle cloud drifted by and quiet was restored, it was always a matter of surprise that so little had really been accomplished. . . . He smeared the issue, but caught the imagination of the younger men of the country by his dash and mock heroics. Taft cooperated with Cannon and Aldrich on legislation. Roosevelt cooperated with Aldrich and Cannon on legislation. Neither President took issue with the reactionary bosses of the Senate upon any legislation of national importance.

Correct as La Follette's estimate undoubtedly is, the fact remains that many of Roosevelt's presidential policies were progressive and forward-looking. Bryan, La Follette, Debs, and the Populists may have raised the standard of revolt, but Roosevelt, when he saw reform was popular, gave to it a publicity and a leadership of which he alone was capable. He originated little, but no politician was ever quicker to pick up and make his own the popular issues raised by others. An ardent nationalist and an aggressive imperialist, Roosevelt, furthermore, gave to American foreign policy a tone of vigor that raised the nation to a prominent place in international diplomacy.

INDUSTRIAL COMBINATIONS

The dynamic personality of Roosevelt so filled the public eye during the decade after his accession to the presidency that it is difficult to evaluate his influence. With the exception of the Hepburn Railroad Act (to be discussed later), the results of his activity upon national legislation were rather meager. His efforts to control or prevent monopoly, though spectacular, affected in no fundamental way the development of American economic life. It is true that the full effects of his activities were not felt until after his administration, but the fact remains that the consolidation of business and the concentration of the money power went on with little interruption during his years in office. When the second great period of business consolidation came to an end about 1904, it was not primarily because of Roosevelt's drive against monopolies, but because there was little left to consolidate.

Despite the outcry against monopolies that had resulted in the Sherman Antitrust Act of 1890 (page 490), the consolidation movement up to 1897 had not reached great proportions. At that time there were but twelve important combinations, and their total capitalization was well under $1,-000,000,000. It was in the half dozen years after 1896 that the great wave of industrial consolidation took place, making it the outstanding feature of American economic life at the opening of the new century. It was stimulated by the almost uninterrupted agricultural and industrial prosperity from 1896 to 1902, by the confidence inspired by the conservative victories of 1896 and 1900, and by the favorable foreign-trade balances, which reached such proportions that Europeans began to talk of the "American invasion." It was also stimulated by the complacent corporation laws of some of the states, particularly New Jersey, West Virginia, Delaware, and Maine, which permitted the organization of pure finance corporations under a general statute and endowed with the widest powers.

Whatever the causes, consolidation went on rapidly. John Moody's *Truth about the Trusts,* a comprehensive survey published in 1904, listed

318 "greater" or "lesser" industrial trusts representing mergers of nearly 5300 distinct plants with a capitalization of over $7,000,000,000. Of these, 82, with a capitalization of $1,196,700,000, were organized before January 1, 1898, and 236, with a capitalization of over $6,000,000,000, between that date and January 1, 1904. In the latter group were six of the greater trusts —the Amalgamated Copper Company (organized 1899), the American Smelting and Refining Company (1899), the Consolidated Tobacco Company (1901), the International Mercantile Marine Company (1902), the Standard Oil Company (1899), and the United States Steel Corporation (1901). These six, along with the American Sugar Refining Company (1891), had a capitalization of over $2,500,000,000, and, with a single exception, all were formed after 1898 and all were incorporated under New Jersey laws. Along with this consolidation was the continued tendency toward concentration. By 1914 establishments doing an annual business of over $100,000 numbered less than one eighth of the total, but they employed over three fourths of the wage-earners and turned out in value more than four fifths of the products. Nearly half of the products, in fact, came from 14 per cent of the concerns, which had an annual output of over $1,000,000 each.

The climax of this consolidation movement came in 1901 with the organization of the United States Steel Corporation. An erratic, uncertain, and highly competitive business, the manufacture of steel by 1900 was dominated by Andrew Carnegie and the newly organized Carnegie Steel Corporation, which not only held the leading position in the production of crude and semifinished steel but commanded large reserves of ore and coke as well as transportation companies. Carnegie, now interested in literary ventures and schemes of philanthropy, was anxious to retire, but the value of his properties was so great that they could be disposed of only through a monster consolidation. The project was so stupendous that only the immense financial power of J. Pierpont Morgan seemed large enough to swing it, and upon Morgan Carnegie concentrated his efforts. It was not without reason that Carnegie had won the reputation of the supersalesman of his day, and his tactics in this situation were to scare his competitors into buying him out. Morgan had already interested himself in the steel business by reorganizing the Federal Steel Company and investing heavily in other concerns. Believing the psychological moment had arrived, Carnegie announced plans for an extension of his business that would have brought ruinous competition upon the steel interests of Morgan and other magnates. As he began to put these plans into operation, panic-stricken millionaires hastened to Morgan, and in the end a consolidation was effected that included the Carnegie companies. Carnegie took $447,000,000 in bonds as his part of the transaction and retired to build libraries and en-dow foundations, while Morgan and his lawyer, Elbert H. Gary, built up a structure with a capitalization of $1,402,847,000, of which $510,206,000 represented preferred stock, $508,227,000 common stock, and the remainder bonds. As the tangible value of the property was estimated by the Commissioner of Corporations at $682,000,000, it is obvious that all the common stock and from one to two fifths of the preferred represented water. This type of financial structure is noted because it is typical of the methods used in the business consolidations effected during these years. When the consolidations prospered and the water was soaked up, the rewards for the organizers, who ordinarily took large blocks of stock as their payment, were enormous. Such was the case with most of the consolidations, for they dominated their respective fields and were in a position to profit from the rapid industrial expansion of the nation.

In 1903 the consolidation movement rapidly slowed down. For six years the market had been crammed with issues of new securities, until speculators and investors could no longer absorb them. Morgan called them "undigested securities," and Hill, with more realism, "indigestible securities." The overexpansion and speculation resulted in a brief depression in 1903, which further curtailed the market, while the sudden activity of the administration served also to discourage the movement. Roosevelt, in his first message to Congress (December, 1901), gave clear expression to his attitude toward big business. While opposed to "crude and ill-considered legislation," he noted "a widespread conviction . . . that the great corporations were in certain of their tendencies harmful to the public welfare" and urged that they should be "not prohibited, but supervised and within reasonable limits controlled." He also advocated that the cabinet be enlarged by a Secretary of Commerce and Industries, who should interest himself in industry and labor. That the President took his own message seriously was demonstrated in the following year when his Attorney General, Philander C. Knox, instituted proceedings under the Sherman Antitrust Act against the Northern Securities Company, a railroad holding company organized by Harriman, Hill, and Morgan to control transportation in the Northwest.[2] On a campaign speaking tour in the same year (1902), he attacked the trusts, and in 1903 Congress passed three acts to control big business: (1) the Expediting Act to give preference to federal suits brought under the Interstate Commerce Act and the Sherman Antitrust Act; (2) the Elkins Antirebate Act to eliminate one of the worst of

[2] The formation of the Northern Securities Company followed a spectacular battle between the railroad giants. Harriman and Hill, for control of transportation in the Northwest, a battle that was climaxed by a Wall Street struggle in April, 1901, when Harriman's efforts to gain control of the Northern Pacific sent the stock of that railroad skyrocketing to $1000 a share. When the battle proved a stalemate, the contesting parties decided to erect a monopoly and divide the spoils.

the railroad abuses; and (3) the creation of the Department of Commerce and Labor, with a subsidiary Bureau of Corporations, to make "diligent investigation into the organization, conduct and management of corporations." An effort was made in the Pure Food Act of 1906 to give the public some protection against harmful foods and drugs, and a more comprehensive act in 1908 aimed to bring the meat-packing business under supervision. All told, the Roosevelt administration instituted sixteen civil and eighteen criminal suits in an effort to enforce the Sherman Act, and Taft was even more aggressive in his efforts to enforce it.

Most of the suits against monopolies started by Roosevelt were decided in the Taft administration, but the dissolution of the Northern Securities Company in 1904 and the pending suits undoubtedly disturbed the financial world. "Wall Street," asserted one newspaper, "is paralyzed at the thought that a President of the United States should sink so low as to enforce the law." But Wall Street was unduly disturbed. Contrary to popular belief, Roosevelt was hardly a "trust-buster." If the consolidation movement slowed up, it was primarily attributable to other reasons, and Roosevelt's activities had no detrimental effect upon the earnings of the large corporations. In fact, 1905 and 1906 were years of great prosperity, and the panic of 1907 was due essentially to overexpansion and reckless speculation rather than to any governmental interference in big business. It was essentially a "bankers' panic" and largely limited to the financial centers. Business men, however, were inclined to attribute it to the meddlesome activities of Roosevelt. "Hail Caesar," cried the New York *Sun,* "we who are about to bust salute thee."

As with most panics, the chief result of 1907 was to speed the concentration of wealth and power. The small speculators and capitalists, unable to weather the storm, were sunk, and their holdings were gathered in by the larger interests. The most notable example was the purchase of the Tennessee Coal, Iron and Railroad Company by the United States Steel Corporation. The Tennessee Company was so closely connected with New York financial interests that its collapse would have greatly accentuated the panic. A delegation from the Morgan interests interviewed Roosevelt on the advisability of purchase. The President stated that he "felt it no public duty . . . to interpose objections," and the United States Steel Corporation, already controlling 50 per cent of the steel production, became stronger than ever. The panic of 1907, as we shall see, by emphasizing the defects of the currency system and the weakness of the banking structure, speeded the movement for currency and banking reform. It led in the first instance to the appointment of the Aldrich Commission to study banking, to the promise by both parties of banking reform in the campaign of 1912, and finally to the Federal Reserve Act.

THE REVOLUTION IN TRANSPORTATION .

The building and operation of railroads was the first large-scale business that developed in this country. With the completion of the transcontinental lines in the eighties a skeleton system had been laid down, and it was the business of the next generation to supplement and tie together the main routes. Seventy thousand miles were built during the eighties, which brought the total mileage in 1890 to 167,000. The panic of 1893 held up development, but in the prosperous years following 1898 construction averaged 5000 miles a year. In 1900 there were 198,964 railroad miles in operation, in 1910 there were 249,992, and in 1920 some 263,821. The relatively small increase between 1910 and 1920 and the fact that between 1916 and 1920 more mileage was abandoned than built was striking evidence that the great days of railroad expansion had ended. The precarious condition of the railroads, accentuated by rising costs during the World War, the competition of trolley cars and motor traffic, and the approach to the saturation point account largely for the halt in railroad construction. Despite the tremendous industrial expansion, railroads in 1920, valued by the Interstate Commerce Commission at $18,900,000,000, represented one tenth of the total wealth of the nation, employed 1,700,000 persons, and with their stocks and bonds represented the most important single group of securities in the financial world.

Railroads in America were the typical flower of economic *laissez faire*. Built rapidly and chaotically, they had often reaped huge rewards and as often almost perished from extreme competition. Conscienceless in their relations with the public and in their debauchery of public servants, they had by their methods produced an uprising in the eighties and an effort by state and federal legislation to eliminate the worst abuses. This legislation, as we have noted, failed in its purpose (page 442), and the railroads entered the twentieth century more integrated and powerful than ever and with legislative control little more than a mockery. The abolition of pooling by the Interstate Commerce Act of 1887, in fact, had spurred the movement toward consolidation. With little cessation up to 1904, the larger railroads, by purchase, by lease, by ownership of a majority of the stock, had tied in many smaller competing lines. In many cases this operated to increase efficiency and was to the public benefit; in others, by eliminating competition, it merely increased the power of the railroads to the detriment of the public. So far had railroad consolidation progressed that in 1906 it was estimated that 176,000 miles of the 228,000 in operation were divided among seventeen systems, of which the five most important were the Vanderbilt (21,333 miles), handling the traffic in New York and along the Great Lakes; the Pennsylvania (20,370), serving the middle Atlantic and running west to the Mississippi; the Hill system (21,303), dominating the routes in the Northwest; the Morgan roads (17,810), controlling the Erie, the transportation of New England, and a large proportion of the southern lines; and the Gould system (16,902), serving the southern transcontinental routes. But integration went much further than this, for these groups were often linked by interlocking directors and "community of interest." As late as 1921 La Follette, with elaborate diagrams, showed how twenty-five directors linked together 82 per cent of the transportation and how the railroads were closely allied with the leading equipment companies.

Against the continued abuses and the overweening power of the railroads a new revolt could not long be delayed. Roosevelt took the leadership in the demand for new legislation; La Follette, Cummings, and other senators kept up an incessant fight in Congress, and the people were aroused by attacks in the popular magazines. Tangible legislative results began in 1903 with the Elkins Act, which in clear-cut phrases attempted to eliminate rebating. Despite powerful pressure from the railroad lobby, the revolt continued in 1906 with the Hepburn Act, which enlarged the Interstate Commerce Commission from five to seven members, extended its jurisdiction to include express and sleeping-car companies, pipe lines, switches, spurs, tracks, and terminal facilities, and empowered it to determine just and reasonable rates and to order the companies to adhere to them. It forbade free passes and made it illegal for the railroads to carry commodities that they had themselves produced, and it instructed the commission to prescribe methods of bookkeeping that the railroads must adopt. Rates must be published thirty days before change. The Hepburn Act not only obviated the faults of the act of 1887 but also made the Interstate Commerce Commission a powerful and responsible body. It inaugurated a real regulation. The essential reason was that under the new act the commission had the power to fix rates, which the railroads must obey unless saved by court decision. The fact that now the railroads rather than the commission had to initiate court action made all the difference in the world. The weakness of the act, in the mind of La Follette, was its failure to give the commission power to evaluate the railroads. Such a power was necessary, he argued, before a "reasonable rate" could be determined, and such power was eventually granted in 1913.

Undoubtedly, the Hepburn Act was the most important piece of economic legislation of the Roosevelt administration. Federal regulation now became an important characteristic of American railroad history, and it was strengthened in succeeding years. In 1910 the Mann-Elkins Act clarified the short-and-long-haul clause of the earlier act, granted the commission power to suspend for six months the operation of a new scale of rates, and set up a special Commerce Court to hear railroad cases.[3] Entrance into the difficult field of labor relations began with the Erdman Act of 1898, which provided for the voluntary settlement of railroad disputes, and by the Adamson Eight-hour Act of 1916.

During these years when steam railroads were reaching the limit of their expansive power and the technique of public control was being improved, they were forced to face the competition of new forms of transportation. The most important in the years before the World War was the electric trolley car. It was in 1884 that the first overhead trolley line was built in Kansas City. Expansion was slow during the experimental years, but after 1890 inventors and entrepreneurs turned to the development of electric street railways with the same enthusiasm that an earlier generation had shown for steam railroads. From 1902 to 1907 the annual increase of track averaged 2000 miles, falling to half that amount in the next five years. In the cities electric power was soon applied to the elevated systems, and it made possible the construction of subways. Although the most important function of the electric railway has been the handling of city traffic, it soon spread into the suburbs and eventually linked the communities in the more thickly populated sections. In the golden age of the electric trolley it was possible to travel for hundreds of miles without stepping into a steam railroad train. This new competition the railroads met by reducing fares, by improving service, by entering themselves into the field of electric railroads, and finally by commencing the electrification of their own tracks. As early as 1906 the New York Central began operation by electricity from the Grand Central in New York City, and two years later the New York, New Haven and Hartford inaugurated complete electric passenger service from the same terminal to Stamford, Connecticut.

While electric railroads were inaugurating a new era in city transportation, the appearance of the internal-combustion engine driven by gasoline presaged the bitterest competition for both steam and electric railroads. For a century inventors had experimented with the "horseless carriage," and as early as 1877 the American, George B. Selden, had propelled a vehicle by a gasoline engine. It was not until the turn of the century, however, that mechanics of the type of Charles E. Duryea, Ransom E. Olds, Elwood Haynes, and Henry Ford began to market such contraptions for general sale. In the early years experimenters drove the "horseless carriage" with steam, electricity, carbonic acid gas, and alcohol, but they concentrated eventually upon the gasoline engine. For years the automobile was primarily the "plaything of the rich," but by 1914 the price range was within the reach of the upper middle class. In that year production of

---

[3] Convinced that the Commerce Court was biased in favor of the railroads, Congress failed in 1912 to appropriate funds for its maintenance, thus ending its career.

automobiles reached 569,000, and the number of vehicles registered was over 1,258,000. Up to that time the competition offered by the automobile to established forms of transportation was not significant; the great expansion of motor traffic was to come in the next fifteen years. In the meantime, however, the automobile had speeded a renascence of road-building reminiscent of a similar era a hundred years earlier (page 246). The bicycle craze of the nineties and the introduction of rural free delivery in 1896 had started the movement, but it was the automobile that made the construction and maintenance of the chief highways a state rather than a local function, that introduced new types of road construction, and that literally turned the United States into a "nation on wheels."

Of no practical use at the time but destined before many years to develop into an important means of transportation was the airplane. There were few in 1900 who believed in the possibility of a practical heavier-than-air machine. Among these was the Smithsonian scientist, Samuel P. Langley, who correctly mastered the theory, but whose machine in 1903 failed to ascend on a trial flight over the Potomac. More successful were the efforts of two mechanics from Dayton, Ohio, Orville and Wilbur Wright, who in the same year, at Kitty Hawk on the Carolina coast, accomplished the first successful flight wth a heavier-than-air machine carrying a man. Until the World War the development of airplanes was in an experimental stage, but by 1914 they were sufficiently practical to be an important instrument in warfare. Their commercial development was to come in the twenties.

Despite the development of new and old forms of transportation, this generation found time also to turn its attention to a revival of waterways. Except on the Great Lakes, inland waterway transportation had been on the wane since 1880. The difficulty of the railroads in handling transportation during boom years, the desire to reduce railroad rates by establishing competition, the dramatic building of the Panama Canal, and the successful operation of inland waterways in Europe all helped to stir up interest. The organized agitation in sections that would benefit caught the ear of Roosevelt, and the President, impelled in part by his interest in conservation, appointed in 1909 an Inland Waterways Commission to survey the possibilities. The chief results of this wave of interest were the building of the Cape Cod Canal, the reconstruction and enlargement of the old Erie Canal, the canalization of the Ohio River, and the completion of the first link in the proposed "Lakes-to-Gulf Deep Waterway." The flow of federal and state money into many of these projects has brought in some sections a revival of inland waterway transportation, but the results as a whole have failed to measure up to the hopes of the proponents of these schemes.

Although some progress had been made in enlarging transportation facilities with the revival of canals, and a beginning had been made in motor transportation and in the building of airplanes, the railroads at the end of the second decade of the century were still far and away the most important means for the movement of passengers and freight. The problems of the railroads, however, were increasing. Not only were they forced to meet new competition—competition financed, in the case of the canals at least, by public funds—but their profits were being controlled by the gradual extension of government regulation of rates, fares, and hours of labor. What was more important, this control was destined in the years to come to be even more widely extended.

CONSOLIDATION OF CAPITAL

Consolidations in industry and transportation were both a cause and a result of a similar concentration of capital. It is the very essence of capitalist economy that its profits should accumulate in the hands of the owners of the machinery of production and transportation. As these profits become larger than is necessary for the personal needs of the owner or the expansion of his business, they seek investment elsewhere, which investments, if successful, produce additional profits for additional investment. The desire for higher profits encourages consolidations, and the process of concentration is speeded by periods of depression, when the stronger, abler, or luckier capitalist is able to eliminate or absorb his weaker competitor.

In the mad scramble for the nation's wealth two dominating influences had emerged—the Rockefeller and the Morgan interests. The shrewd architects of the oil monopoly soon found their profits far in excess of the needs of their own expanded industry and sought outlets for their capital in copper, railroads, public utilities, and important industrial products. Their financial operations centered in the City Bank of New York, soon to be known as the National City Bank, which took the leadership in American financial imperialism and became for a time the largest bank in the world. Only the financiers headed by J. P. Morgan could rival the power of the Rockefellers. The small private banking house of J. P. Morgan had specialized in the reorganization of railroads, many of which it controlled, but its domination eventually extended to a powerful banking chain including the National Bank of Commerce, the First National, and the Chase National, into such insurance companies as the "big three"—the Mutual, the Equitable, and the New York Life—and into industrials, with the United States Steel Corporation as its crowning achievement.

Nor were these two financial interests necessarily rivals. Occasionally gigantic battles were staged, but cross investments and interlocking directorates rapidly drew them together. Around the Morgan-Rockefeller interests, wrote John Moody in 1904,

> or what must ultimately become one greater group, all other smaller groups of capitalists congregate. They are all allied and intertwined by their various mutual interests. For instance, the Pennsylvania Railroad interests are on the one hand allied with the Vanderbilts and on the other with the Rockefellers. The Vanderbilts are closely allied with the Morgan group, and both the Pennsylvania and the Vanderbilt interests have recently become the dominating factors in the Reading system, a former Morgan road and the most important part of the anthracite coal combine which has always been dominated by the Morgan people. . . . Viewed as a whole, we find the dominating influences in the Trust to be made up of an intricate network of large and small capitalists, many allied to one another by ties of more or less importance, but all being appendages to or parts of the greater groups, which are themselves dependent on and allied with the two mammoth, or Rockefeller and Morgan groups. These two mammoth groups jointly . . . constitute the heart of the business and commercial life of the nation.[4]

The significance of this concentration of financial power was not lost upon the more thoughtful observers, and the charge was frequently made that a "money trust" existed as well as monopolies in industry. It was contended, in brief, that only by sufferance of these interests could large amounts of money be borrowed. The wave of antitrust agitation that swept over the nation in the first decade of the century eventually resulted in a congressional investigation of the "money trust," and the report of the Pujo Committee (1913) confirmed the general belief. The committee insisted that through consolidations of potentially competitive banks and trust companies, through interlocking directorates and stockholdings, through the influence of powerful banking houses on railroads, insurance companies, and industrial concerns, and through partnership arrangements between the leading banking houses in the purchase of security issues, a dangerous control of money and credit had been effected and competition in the money market largely eliminated. The monopoly, the committee insisted, was largely in the hands of J. P. Morgan and Company, the First National Bank of New York, and the National City Bank, which controlled through seven subsidiary banks some $2,000,000,000. Four allied financial institutions in New York, it appeared, held thirty-four directorships in various concerns whose aggregate resources were $22,245,000,000.

If by a "money trust" [reported the committee] is meant an established and well defined identity and community of interest between a few leaders

4 John Moody, *The Truth about the Trusts*, 493.

of finance which has been created and is held together through stock holdings, interlocking directorates, and other forms of domination over banks, trust companies, railroads, public service, and industrial corporations, and which has resulted in a vast and growing concentration of control of money and credit in the hands of a comparatively few men— your committee has no hesitation in asserting as a result of its investigation that this condition, largely developed within the past five years, exists in this country today.[5]

Although builders of this tremendous power denied its existence, the situation was clear enough. The committee in its report made a number of recommendations to improve the situation along the line of banking reform, decentralization of credit control, and supervision of the stock market, which were incorporated, as we shall see, in subsequent legislation.[6] These reforms, as we shall also see, have had little if any effect upon the continued concentration of capital.

THE CONSOLIDATION OF LABOR

To meet the industrial and financial concentration, labor likewise strove to integrate and consolidate its power. Its success at the turn of the century was in no small degree attributable to the firm foundations that had been laboriously laid during the late eighties and early nineties by Gompers and his associates (page 409). The membership of the American Federation of Labor was only 278,000 in 1898, but its growth in the next few years was phenomenal. In 1900 the membership was 548,000, and in 1904 it was 1,676,000; growth then slowed up, the membership in 1914 numbering 2,000,000. The years from 1898 to 1904, in fact, were undoubtedly the most successful in the history of the organization. "It was the harvest," as Gompers put it, "of the years of organizing work which were beginning to bear fruit." Not only did membership increase rapidly, but great progress was made in achieving recognition from employers. The National Civic Federation (organized in 1901), the first president of which was Marcus A. Hanna, devoted itself in its early years to the promotion of better relations between capital and labor and the adoption of the trade agreement. It was, as one labor historian describes it, "a honeymoon period of capital and labor."

Middle-class liberal organizations also came to the aid of labor—the National Consumers League (organized 1898), the National Child Labor

---

[5] *Report of the Committee Appointed to Investigate the Concentration of Control of Money and Credit, Sixty-second Congress, Third Session,* 130.

[6] Federal Reserve Act, 1913; Clayton Antitrust Act, 1914; Securities Act, 1933; and Securities Exchange Act, 1934.

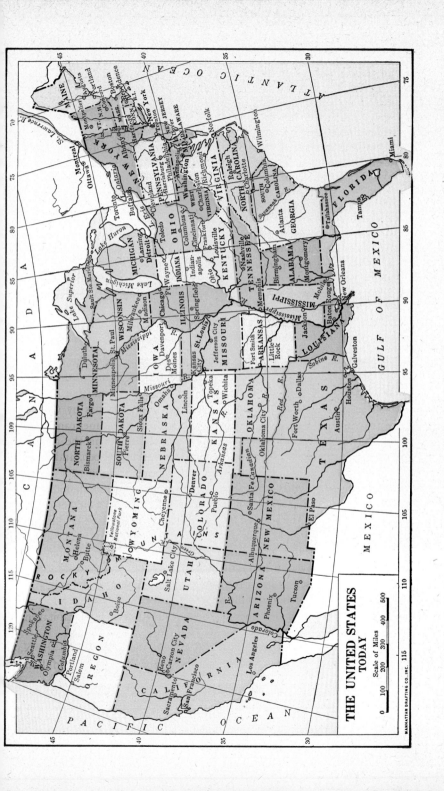

THE UNITED STATES
TODAY

Scale of Miles

0   100   200   300   400   500

MANHATTAN DRAFTING CO., INC.

Committee (1904), and the American Association for Labor Legislation (1906). Committed to collective bargaining and social legislation, these organizations played their part in conjunction with organized labor in the promotion of social legislation. Such legislation had been slow in coming; it was 1912 before Congress insisted upon an eight-hour day for government contract work, 1913 before the Department of Labor was created in the cabinet, 1914 before an attempt was made to exempt labor from prosecution under the Sherman Antitrust Act, 1915 before the La Follette Act sought to ensure decent conditions for American seamen, and 1916 before an eight-hour law was passed for interstate railroad employees. In the states, however, more progress was made. Acting under the police power, more than two thirds of the states passed child-labor legislation fixing a minimum age limit for work, limiting the hours of labor, prohibiting certain employments as dangerous to health, and fixing educational requirements that must be met before children could be released for labor. Congress in 1907 appropriated $150,000 for an investigation of child labor and in 1912 created the Children's Bureau. Legislation to protect women from long hours and from labor conditions detrimental to health was placed on the statute books, and a beginning toward better wage standards was made in 1912 and 1913, when nine states passed minimum wage laws.

Although it was more difficult to obtain legislation safeguarding conditions of work for men, probably the greatest victory achieved in social legislation during the prewar years applied directly to them. The theory long held in Europe that responsibility for occupational accidents should rest upon the industry rather than upon the individual was finally accepted in this country. Beginning with Maryland in 1902, several states passed insurance laws with compensation features, which, however, were declared unconstitutional. By constitutional amendments and carefully framed laws, judicial opposition was eventually overcome, and between 1911 and 1921 all but six of the states and the District of Columbia had workmen's compensation laws.

Great as were the gains recorded during these years by organized labor, scarcely 10 per cent of the wage-earners were organized in 1914. The gains achieved had come only after severe and persistent struggle and in the face of public indifference, antagonism of employers' associations representing the massed power of capital, and opposition of the judiciary. To make the struggle more difficult, there were the factional fights over policies within the unions themselves. In its struggle upward the chief weapon of labor has been the strike. In the quarter century 1881–1905, according to government estimates, there had been 36,757 strikes, of which over half had occurred in the last eight years. Nor was there any cessation in the use of this powerful weapon. Perhaps the most spectacular of the strikes during these years was that in 1902 of the recently organized United Mine Workers in the Anthracite coal regions of Pennsylvania. On the one side were the miners, demanding a reduction of hours from ten to nine, a 20-per-cent increase in wages, payment according to the weight of the coal mined, and recognition of the union. On the other were the coal operators, controlled by the eight railroads that tapped the anthracite region, which were in turn dominated by Morgan and the most powerful capitalists of the time. Under the capable leadership of John Mitchell, 150,000 striking miners held their ranks firm from May to October, while offering repeatedly to arbitrate their grievances.

As autumn approached with an impending coal famine, Roosevelt determined to take a hand. He first sent Hanna to Wall Street in an effort to bring peace, but without avail. Then followed on October 3 a stormy but futile conference at Washington between the miners and the operators. The latter would concede nothing and demanded that the strike be crushed by invoking the Sherman Act and by military intervention—the method used by Cleveland at the time of the Pullman strike. Roosevelt had not the slightest intention of crushing the strike for the benefit of the operators. Rather he had made up his mind to operate the mines with federal troops during the emergency while a committee headed by Cleveland investigated the situation. When the President's intentions were made clear to Morgan, the operators capitulated, and the miners returned to work pending arbitration by a commission appointed by the President. The arbitral award granted the miners a 10-per-cent increase in wages, a shorter work day, and a union check-weighman at the scales. It took two more strikes, 1912 and 1916, before they won the eight-hour day and union recognition. The finesse shown by the President in handling the coal strike and his obvious desire to ensure justice for labor, capital, and the consumer won widespread approbation. It raised him to the pinnacle of popularity and made inevitable his election in 1904.

Gains to labor through the coal strike of 1902 were attained partly through the courageous interference of the federal government. More indicative of the power of labor at its best was the victory attained after two short strikes in New York City, when, in 1910, the manufacture of women's clothing was transformed from an oppressively sweated and chaotic industry to one strongly organized, with machinery of arbitration to take care of subsequent disputes. The strikes were also significant in showing the rise of women workers in the trade-union movement and their fighting capacity in time of trouble. That labor had far to go, however, was strikingly demonstrated at the close of the prewar years, when the United Mine Workers struck in Colorado for recognition, higher wages, and the enforcement of the state labor laws. The best efforts of

President Wilson failed to induce John D. Rockefeller, Jr., and other mine-owners to arbitrate, and the friction was climaxed on April 20, 1914, when a pitched battle at Ludlow caused the burning of the tent colony of strikers and the death of six men, two women, and eleven children. With federal troops dispatched to the scene and the mines operated by strikebreakers, the strike collapsed. The episode illustrated but too clearly the slight advance that had been made in handling the crucial problem of industrial warfare.

The spearhead of the opposition to organized labor was the National Association of Manufacturers (founded 1895) and its satellite, the American Anti-Boycott Association (1902). The latter financed court action against labor, notably the cases against the Danbury hatters' boycott and that against the boycott of the Buck Stove and Range Company of St. Louis. In an effort to establish a closed shop the Hatters' Union attempted a nation-wide boycott of the products of D. E. Loewe and Company of Danbury, Connecticut. The boycott was attacked as a violation of the Sherman Antitrust Act. The case dragged through the courts for fourteen years, the result being a complete victory for the plaintiff and the decision that an interstate boycott was illegal.[7] More exasperating to organized labor was the court action involving the boycott supported by the American Federation of Labor against the Buck Stove and Range Company. The company obtained an injunction from the Supreme Court of the District of Columbia forbidding the officers and members of the federation not only from including the plaintiff's products in the "We Don't Patronize" list in their official publication but also from referring to the dispute in print or by word of mouth. This incredible injunction was obeyed as far as the unfair list was concerned, but otherwise ignored, and Gompers, Mitchell, and Frank Morrison (secretary of the federation) were sentenced to imprisonment. New complications developed, the sentences were not served, and the case was eventually outlawed in 1914 under the statute of limitations. Unfortunately, however, all efforts of labor to test the injunction as involving the constitutional guarantees of free speech, free press, and peaceable assemblage were avoided by the courts.

Employers, however, hardly needed a special organization to fight their battles in court. The judiciary, grounded in eighteenth-century legal philosophy, ignorant of industrial conditions, and by their nature conservative and closely allied with the owning classes, presented the chief obstacle to social legislation and to the progress of the labor movement. Social legislation was ordinarily passed on the theory that the police power of the state warranted legislative interference to promote the general welfare; the

---

[7] In 1914 Congress, in the Clayton Antitrust Act, exempted labor unions from prosecution under the antitrust laws, but this effort was largely negated by the Supreme Court (page 604).

courts, on the other hand, resting on the fifth and fourteenth amendments, have thrown out such laws as a violation of liberty, as an infringement of contract, or as class legislation, and have sought to confine the police power very narrowly to health, safety, and morals. At some time or other practically every type of legislation designed to protect the worker has fallen under the ban of the courts. The early climax was probably reached in 1905, when the United States Supreme Court declared that the Lochner ten-hour law for bakers in New York state had "reached and passed the limit of the police power," and when, in 1907, the New York court nullified a law prohibiting night work for women. Fortunately the judiciary responds eventually to public opinion, and during the next ten years the Supreme Court reversed itself on the constitutionality of such laws. In the war and postwar years the courts, in another period of reaction, as we shall see, invalidated the labor provisions of the Clayton Act, narrowly restricted picketing, upheld the "yellow-dog" contract,[8] held minimum-wage laws for women unconstitutional, and continued to break strikes by the free use of injunctions.

Organized labor was confronted not alone by opposition from without but by internal friction. This involved chiefly the question of political tactics and that of labor organization. Against the conservative policy of Gompers—a policy of holding the balance of power, of rewarding friends and punishing enemies—others urged the formation of a labor party in the European fashion. The latter group represented the left wing, and, when they found themselves unsuccessful, some turned their backs on organized labor and affiliated with the Socialist Labor Party, while others stayed in the organized labor movement attempting to convert it to political action through the medium of the Socialist Party (page 591). More serious for the moment was the conflict between the theory of organization by craft unions, a policy strictly adhered to by Gompers and the dominant faction, and that of organization by industrial unions, that is, by organization in which all workers in an industry should be in the same union. The idea of industrial unions had flourished during the period of the Knights of Labor, and it was to revive again as the Industrial Revolution continued to produce labor-saving machinery and displace the hand labor of many of the crafts.

Revival of industrial unionism took definite shape in 1905, when representatives of various industrial unions, led by Eugene V. Debs, the popular leader of the Socialist Party, Daniel De Leon, leader of the Socialist Labor group, William D. Haywood, and others, met in Chicago and organized the Industrial Workers of the World. Their purpose was "one great industrial union, embracing all industries, providing for craft autonomy

---

[8] A contract by which an employee agrees not to join a union during his term of service.

locally, industrial autonomy internationally, and wage class unity generally." "It must be founded on the class struggle," said their manifesto, "and its general administration must be conducted in harmony with the recognition of the irrepressible conflict between the capitalist class and the working class."

Although the membership of the I. W. W. probably never exceeded 75,-000, the militancy of its members and the strength of its leadership gave it a prominence out of proportion to its numerical strength. It kept the lumberjacks of the Northwest in a state of unrest, and its leaders ably conducted the spectacular strikes at Lawrence, Massachusetts, in 1912 and Paterson, New Jersey, in 1913. Its revolutionary propaganda gave to its opponents an opportunity ruthlessly to crush it during the war years, but it had fulfilled a valuable function. It gave the conservative unions a lesson in labor militancy, spurred the organization of the unskilled workers, and kept alive the practical theory of industrial unionism. Two decades later there were serious students of the labor problem who were convinced that the salvation of organized labor lay in the direction of the labor tactics pointed out by the I. W. W.

For a more complete introduction to the topics of this chapter see H. U. Faulkner, *The Quest for Social Justice,* Chaps. II, III, VI (History of American Life). More detail on the economic is in H. U. Faulkner, *American Economic History,* Chaps. XXI–XXIII. In H. F. Pringle, *Theodore Roosevelt,* Chaps. XI–XIV, is a discussion of Roosevelt and big business. On labor see L. L. Lorwin, *The American Federation of Labor,* Chaps. III–V; on consolidation, H. R. Seager and C. A. Gulick, Jr., *Trust and Corporation Problems,* Chap. V, and John Moody, *Masters of Capital* (Chronicles of America). For source material consult H. S. Commager, *Documents of American History,* Vol. II, 215–225, 235–239, 258–262, 287–288, and F. Flügel and H. U. Faulkner, *Readings in the Economic and Social History of the United States,* Chaps. XIV, XV, XVIII.

Chapter XXXIV

THE ERA OF REFORM

*There is everywhere in the social frame an
outward unrest, which as usual is the sign of
fundamental changes within.*

GOLDWIN SMITH in the *Forum* (1890)

*Let us agitate, organize and move forward,
casting aside timidity and insisting that the Republic shall no longer lag behind the march of
progress.*

BENJAMIN O. FLOWER in the *Arena* (1900)

*I hail as a benefactor every writer or speaker,
every man who, on the platform, or in book,
magazine, or newspaper, with merciless severity
makes such attack, provided always that he in
turn remembers that the attack is of use only if
it is absolutely truthful.*

THEODORE ROOSEVELT (1906)

AMERICA AT THE TURN OF THE CENTURY

By 1900 most of the characteristics of modern America were clearly discernible. Industrialization was rapidly concentrating the American people in urban areas, and this process went on without cessation in the new
century (page 468).[1] Of the population increase during the next decade
(16,000,000) seven tenths was in towns of 2500 or over. Two geographic
sections, New England and the eastern north-central states, in fact, showed
an absolute decrease in rural population. By 1930 the percentage of urban
population (2500 or more) had grown to 56.8 and the population in cities
of 8000 or more to 49.1. The urbanization of America, as we have emphasized, was caused essentially by the Industrial Revolution, which by
1894 had raised the United States to the leading position among the industrial nations of the world. By the end of that decade the United States

[1] The population recorded in 1900 was 75,994,575.

produced in value of manufactured products twice as much as Great Britain and half as much as all Europe together.

Industrialization and urbanization were, then, the outstanding new characteristics of American civilization, and their effects upon American life were profound. The cityward trend of population was speeded by new agricultural machinery, which made possible the production of the same amount of food with less labor, and by the superior opportunities offered in the city to the talented boys from rural regions. Sociologists were quick to point out the fact that the depletion of rural regions was not merely numerical but also physical and moral, as the more enterprising stock moved out. Thus economic, social, and even political problems of infinite variety and complexity were produced. The rural decline, it should be noted, came despite the almost unprecedented agricultural prosperity of the years 1896–1919 and despite the increasing attractions of rural life. The end of the frontier slowed perceptibly the rapid agricultural expansion and gave opportunity for intensive improvements. The introduction of rural free delivery in 1896, the rapid improvement of roads after the coming of automobiles, the speedier transportation that brought the rural regions into closer contact with urban advantages, the development of electric power in the household and on the farm, all tended toward the equalization of farm and city life, and these tendencies were to continue in the succeeding years.

In the cities the problems of chaotic growth were evident on all sides. Only rarely were efforts made intelligently to control city growth, to prevent overcrowding, and to provide for parks and recreational facilities. Building laws were antiquated, sanitation was backward, and overcrowding was common, especially in the slums where the masses of immigrants congregated, and where life was a continual battle against the filth, disease, and vice engendered by such conditions. In sharp relief and indicative of the maldistribution of wealth were the ostentatious palaces in city and country of the barons of the new industrial order. Rapidly the farmer was ceasing to be the typical American; rather he was giving place to the middle-class city man, the clerk, the shopkeeper, the salesman, the small executive. In turn the mode of life of the typical American was inevitably changed by the exigencies of the small city apartment.

While America was changing its ways of living, a fundamental modification was taking place in its racial composition. Obviously, all Americans are immigrants or the descendants of immigrants, and from 1820, when the first immigration records were kept, until 1898, over 17,000,000 aliens had come to the United States. Essentially this immigration had been from the northwestern area of Europe—the British Isles, Germany, and the Scandinavian peninsula. The white population of the United States, therefore, was primarily made up of the so-called Teutonic races. The end of the frontier, declining economic opportunities in America, and improved conditions in western Europe slowed up this immigration, and by 1896 the source was shifting to southern and eastern Europe, Austria-Hungary, Italy, and Russian Poland. In actual numbers this immigration during the early years of the twentieth century reached a height never before achieved and in relation to the total population was greater than at any time since the forties. Between 1903 and 1914 there were but two years in which the immigration fell below 700,000, and in six of these years it rose beyond the million mark. The census of 1910 showed 13,500,000 foreign-born inhabitants of the United States (one seventh of the whole), while an equal number were native whites of foreign parentage. Two sections, New England and the middle Atlantic states, showed a majority of the population composed of foreign-born white or of native white of foreign or mixed parentage.

At least two major problems with many ramifications were presented by this deluge of immigrants. Speaking generally, the economic and cultural level of the "new immigration" with its accompanying depressed standard of living was lower than that of the old. Skilled workers were fewer, and the percentage of illiteracy was large. Of those over fourteen who arrived between 1899 and 1909, nearly 27 per cent were illiterate; of the largest single group, the South Italians, over half could not read or write. Unable to speak English, at least two thirds congregated in the cities among their own people, where assimilation was difficult and where they were easily subjected to political and economic exploitation. A second problem concerned itself with that of racial assimilation. Since the immigrants were segregated among their own people, a considerable proportion of them of Jewish stock and at least a quarter planning to return to their native land, intermarriage with the older stock was retarded. America, the great "melting pot" of which Israel Zangwill so eloquently wrote, seemed to many no longer capable of melting its newcomers into a homogeneous whole.

This fear was, of course, greatly exaggerated; it was evident enough that what one sociologist called the "great dilution" was still rapidly going on. The America of the future would be a mixture of all the races of Europe, not merely of those of its western fringe. The change in the racial complexion was also speeded by the decline in the birth rate of the older American stock. The early advocates of "birth control" had been ruthlessly silenced, but the limitation of families continued, and it was noticed that the immigrant women of the second generation followed the example of their native sisters in curtailing the size of their families. Nor did the denunciations of "race suicide," of which Roosevelt's were the loudest, make any perceptible difference. The causes were social and economic; among them were the difficulties of raising a family under urban conditions, and a decided resistance to lowering the standard of living. Actually it was "class suicide," rather than "race suicide," for the decline in birth rate was limited chiefly to the "well-to-do."

On the west coast a special phase of immigration troubled the inhabitants in the years after 1900. Although the Chinese continued to slip in after the Exclusion Act of 1882, their number was not large. The Japanese, on the other hand, who had numbered but 2000 in 1890, increased to 24,000 by 1900 and 72,000 by 1910. In proportion to the total population this number was very small, but the superior industry of the Japanese and his lower standard of living brought him into competition with white labor and the small farmer and developed agitation for exclusion similar to that which arose against the Chinese in the seventies. The Asiatic Exclusion League was formed in 1905, and the issue assumed international importance the next year when the San Francisco board of education ordered the segregation of Chinese and Japanese children in a separate school (page 546).

Relations with other colored races concerned primarily those that were already here. It is possible that there were as many Indians in 1900 as when the white man first invaded the continent, but their condition was far different. Desperately poor, scourged by the white man's diseases, and easily exploited by the dominant race, they were in an unenviable situation. The Dawes Act of 1887 had been a concession both to humanitarians and to the greed of the white man for land. That act sought to break down the system of communal living by apportioning the land among the Indians. They were to become citizens of the United States but at the same time were denied the right to mortgage or sell their land for twenty-five years. From 1887 until 1906, when new legislation was passed, the government disposed of 75,000,000 acres, about three fifths of the whole.[2] Of this over 50,000,000 was acquired by the government to be sold to white settlers. Experience proved that twenty-five years was a period so long as to discourage the Indian from taking his allotment, and in 1906 the Burke Act empowered the Secretary of the Interior to grant full property rights to deserving individuals without waiting for the expiration of the full period, but at the same time it postponed citizenship until such ownership was granted. During the next two decades more than half of the Indians achieved citizenship, and at least half of their children were attending public schools. Their economic welfare improved somewhat, and as there is little racial feeling between Indian and white, intermarriage and racial dilution continued.

[2] This was land over and above what the Indians needed under the Dawes Act; it was land sold to the United States government, the proceeds of which were to constitute a tribal fund to be administered in the interests of the Indians.

Of tremendous importance to the future of America were the relations between the Negro and white races. In 1850 Negroes had represented 15.7 per cent of the population. Although the number of Negroes had actually doubled by 1900, the proportion had fallen to 10.7. In Mississippi and South Carolina the Negro still comprised more than 50 per cent of the population and in Florida, Georgia, and Alabama more than 40 per cent. Failure of congressional reconstruction had reduced the Negro to political impotency and economic peonage, while the struggle upward from slavery was made even more difficult by segregation laws, by a closely drawn color line, by such extralegal methods of dealing with Negro crime as lynching, and by Negro-baiting politicians who used this means to consolidate their power among poor and middle-class whites. Except in the steel mills of Birmingham, the industrialization of the South had been of little benefit to the Negro. Although the Negro showed a strong tendency to migrate to the city, his chief role continued to be that of the tenant cotton farmer. If viewed superficially in 1900, the future of the race seemed dark indeed.

Despite overwhelming difficulties, however, the Negro race had moved forward and was to continue to make progress. Illiteracy declined from 44.5 per cent in 1900 to 30.4 in 1910; the number of Negro-owned farms increased during the same years by almost a fifth, and there was a steady accretion of Negroes to the ranks of the skilled workers and professional class. Nor was the race without capable leaders in its upward movement. Booker T. Washington, born in slavery, but one of the greatest men produced by the South since the Civil War, represented the conservative leadership. Founding in 1881 the Normal and Industrial Institute at Tuskegee, Alabama, he urged his race to seek salvation through education and hard work. "The race, like the individual, that makes itself indispensable," said he, "has solved most of its problems." Fundamental as was this program, it failed to satisfy the young and talented Negroes of a new generation, who chafed against the prevalent racial and economic discrimination. Led by W. E. B. Du Bois and demanding equality of opportunity and equality before the law, this group carried on a steady campaign of propaganda.

America in 1900 was still the land of opportunity. Individuals shifted rapidly from one economic class to another, and even immigrant boys rose to fame and fortune. In comparison with Europe the standard of living was high, but a cold examination of facts gave little cause for rejoicing. According to the census of 1900, only in occasional groups did workers receive as much as $18 a week; two thirds of the male workers over sixteen years of age received less than $12.50. The average wage was less than $2 a day, with only the highly paid skilled workmen receiving $3. Labor students agreed that at least two thirds of the adult male workers failed to obtain $600 a year, a figure that more than one economist put as the "extreme low limit" of a living wage for a family. That the great majority of American workmen lived on the margin of existence was evident; Robert Hunter, after intensive study, insisted that not less than 10,000,000 persons in the United States lived in poverty. Nor were conditions to improve in the next few years. Economists in 1914 found themselves in agreement on at least two points: that few adult workers earned wages high enough to ensure a decent minimum standard of living, and that real wages had declined from 1900 to 1914. This situation hardly approximated the dreams that immigrant agents had conjured in the minds of America-bound immigrants.

Quite as disturbing were the facts concerning the distribution of wealth. Spahr's careful study, published in 1896, revealed that seven eighths of the families held but one eighth of the wealth, while 1 per cent of the families owned more than the remaining 99 per cent.[3] Studies of probated estates made a decade later bore out these conclusions. Estates probated in five Wisconsin counties in 1900, including both Milwaukee and rural communities, revealed the fact that the poorest two thirds of the population owned from 5 to 6 per cent of the wealth and the poorest four fifths scarcely 10 per cent, while the richest 1 per cent owned half. As these findings were buttressed by similar studies made during three different periods in Massachusetts, the conclusion is inescapable that fully 80 per cent of the people lived on the margin of existence, while the wealth of the nation was largely owned by the remaining 20 per cent.

THE MUCKRAKERS

As periods of prosperity and depression alternate under capitalist economy, so we have eras of reform and reaction. Certainly nothing characterized the America of the first fifteen years of the present century more than a reforming zeal, a quest for social justice that would remake the old America. That such an era of reform was long overdue can hardly be doubted when the student attempts to construct a picture of conditions at the turn of the century. Chaotic growth and expansion, dominated by individualism and *laissez faire*, had fostered a money madness and a worship of the god Success that left their imprint upon all phases of social, economic, and political life. Some inadequate hints have been given in previous pages of the darker side of American civilization as it developed in the decades after the Civil War—inequality of wealth, wide prevalence of poverty, racial discrimination, domination of politics, religion, education, and the courts by big business, unconscionable exploitation of natural resources, carelessness of human life, economic exploitation of women and

---

[3] C. B. Spahr, *The Present Distribution of Wealth in the United States*, 69.

children, the degradation of democracy. *Laissez faire* applied to a nation fabulously rich in natural resources had brought a spectacular economic development, but at a price far too dear measured in terms of human welfare.

Why the uprising against the old order should have taken place at this particular time can only be conjectured. The economic strain of the eighties and nineties, with their bitter battles over railroads, monopolies, and the tariff, undoubtedly helped shake the naïve faith of the masses in the beneficence of *laissez faire*. The rapid business consolidation at the turn of the century brought home to the nation the great power of a conscious capitalism and the increasing helplessness of labor and the consumer. The end of the frontier slowed up expansion and gave the nation an opportunity to take stock of its resources. In part the uprising came through a fortuitous combination of reforming politicians, brilliant muckraking journalists, and a people ready for a change in policy. Like all important historical movements, the decline of *laissez faire* and the rise of progressivism and reform did not burst suddenly upon the country. Its origins can be seen in the realistic tone beginning to creep into the literature of the eighties and nineties in such famous books of protest as Lloyd's *Wealth Against Commonwealth* (1894), in a few articles in the magazines, and in the restless stirrings of the more realistic and socially conscious people of the type of Henry George, Edward Bellamy, Henry Demarest Lloyd, and Eugene V. Debs.

Of all the influences that spread the reforming zeal of that generation, none were more potent than the popular magazines. In 1900 only one high-class magazine, the *Arena,* founded by Benjamin O. Flower, "the editorial dean of democracy," consistently agitated for reform.[4] The great magazines of the nineties—*Harper's, Scribner's,* and the *Century*—were "models of the sedate, exclusive and not wholly indigenous culture of the latter part of the nineteenth century." The same was to some extent true of the *Atlantic* and the *North American Review.* More popular magazines, however, such as the *Ladies' Home Journal* (1883) the *Cosmopolitan* (1886), the *Forum* and *Munsey's* (1889), *Pearson's* and *Everybody's* (1899), were feeling their way to success by lower prices and by more closely satisfying the demand of the masses (page 477). Low price increased their circulation enormously just at the time when many of them began to print articles of exposure.

Although articles of protest had been appearing for some years, the "era of the muckrake" may be said to have begun late in 1902, when Lincoln

---

[4] The *Arena* was edited successively by Benjamin O. Flower, 1889–1896; Charles Clark Ridpath, 1896–1898; Paul Tyner, 1898–1899; John Emery McLean, 1899–1904; and by Flower again, 1904–1909.

Steffens, on the staff of *McClure's*, happened to learn of the flagrant municipal corruption in St. Louis and published an account of it under the title, "Tweed Days in St. Louis," the first of Steffens's brilliant exposures of municipal politics. The same number contained the announcement of Ida Tarbell's forthcoming series on the Standard Oil Company. It was largely a coincidence that Steffens, Miss Tarbell, Ray Stannard Baker, and others happened to be on *McClure's* and to commence their famous articles at this time. The sensational success of these articles and the mounting circulation of *McClure's* soon brought its competitors into the field, and by 1904 *Everybody's, Hampton's, Pearson's,* the *Cosmopolitan,* and many others were in the thick of the battle. In 1906 Steffens, Miss Tarbell, and Ray Stannard Baker took over the *American* and made it a leader in the movement of exposure.

Although some of the literature of the muckrake was ephemeral and sensational, an extraordinarily large amount of it was done with conscientious accuracy, and it provides an invaluable commentary on the life of the period. Filled as it was with what might seem the most libelous material, it is significant that no major suit was ever sustained against author or publisher. To list the most important of the articles would be difficult, for the muckrakers prodded into every phase of our civilization—political corruption state and national, big business, child labor, vice, religion, the newspapers, fake advertising, and impure food, to name but a few. Some mention, however, should be made of the meticulously accurate articles of Steffens on municipal corruption, Miss Tarbell's scholarly work on the history of the Standard Oil Company, Burton J. Hendrick's story of the life-insurance scandals, Ray Stannard Baker's noteworthy contributions to the railroad and Negro problems, Charles Edward Russell's articles on the beef trust, George Kibbe Turner's on vice in New York and Chicago, Samuel Hopkins Adams's on patent medicine and fraudulent advertising, and, of course, the most luridly sensational of them all—David Graham Phillips's scathing attacks on the United States Senate (*The Treason of the Senate*) and Thomas W. Lawson's on the ways of big business (*Frenzied Finance*). Nor should the work of the novelists in this ferment of social revolt be forgotten. Frank Norris in his *The Octopus* (1901) pictured the struggle between the farmers and the railroads and in *The Pit* (1903) wrote an epic of grain speculation on the Chicago exchange. Winston Churchill turned from romance to attacks on the railroads and on corrupt politics, David Graham Phillips exposed the shortcomings of American society, and Jack London attacked the capitalism of the new century. Upton Sinclair's *The Jungle* (1906), dealing with the stockyards, was perhaps the most powerful in its immediate effects.

The attack on existing abuses that began late in 1902, says one student, "became militant in 1903 . . . and sensational in 1904 and 1905." While it was at its height in 1906, Roosevelt likened some of the more sensational writers to the man with the muckrake in Bunyan's *Pilgrim's Progress,* "who could look no way but downwards with the muckrake in his hands." The term "muckrakers," aptly applied to a few, was quite unjustly applied to all. Declining in 1908, muckraking was revived by the failure of the Republican Party to reform the tariff and continued as part of the Progressive movement that culminated in 1912. The virtual disappearance of muckraking in the decade after 1912 was probably due to a natural conservative reaction, to a belief that many conditions had been righted, to the destruction or purchase of certain of the liberal magazines by big business, to the fact that congressional investigating committees were taking over from the journalists the role of muckraking, and to the absorption of the nation in the World War. The muckrakers seem to have been rather directly responsible for certain definite reforms—the pure food and drug acts, the Meat Inspection Act, the reforms in life insurance, the improvement of advertising. Their chief contribution, of course, was to deepen and strengthen the whole reform movement, and in this way their influence must have been felt in a myriad of ways. Optimistically, *Everybody's* in 1909 summarized what it believed the movement had accomplished:

> Wall Street cannot gull the public as it once did. Insurance is on a sounder basis. Banking is adding new safeguards. Advertising is nearly honest. Rebating is unsafe. Food and drug adulteration are dangerous. Human life is more respected by common carriers. The hour of the old time political boss is struck. States and municipalities are insisting upon clean administrators. The people are naming their own candidates. Independent voters, and that means thinking men, are legion. The children are having their day in court. Protection is offered to the weak against the gambling shark and saloon. Our public resources are being conserved. The public health is being considered. New standards of life have been raised up. The money God totters. Patriotism, manhood, brotherhood are exalted. It is a new era. A new world. Good signs, don't you think? And what has brought it about? Muckraking. Bless your heart, just plain muckraking. By magazine writers and newspapers and preachers and public men and Roosevelt.

The historian can only comment that these were at least the objectives, if not the attainments, of this great era of reform.

THE QUEST FOR SOCIAL JUSTICE

The reforms that marked the first fifteen years of the present century were in part an effort to catch up with a changing civilization. This was particularly true in the case of women, who by 1900 were feeling the full effect of the Industrial Revolution. More and more were the traditional occupations of the housewife—the manufacture of textiles, the making of clothing, the canning and preservation of food, the laundering of clothes—finding their way to the shop or factory, where women followed to carry on the work. This, of course, was but a continuation of a tendency that had been going on since the early days of the Industrial Revolution. More significant in the new century was the rapidity with which women entered commercial life as saleswomen and stenographers and such occupations or professions as nursing, social work, and teaching. The entrance of women into industry, commerce, and the professions increased their economic independence, and this inevitably raised their general status. In innumerable ways it was to affect the social history of the new century. Economic independence made for later marriages, fewer children, and more frequent divorces. It often meant a family life in which both father and mother worked outside the home, leaving the education of the children to teachers and outside agencies. In the field of labor it brought women into competition with men, thereby tending to keep down the wages of both sexes. The notoriously low wages that women accepted were in part due to the fact that their work was often optional, that it was frequently a stop-gap until marriage rather than a career, and that women were more difficult to organize into trade unions. At all events, their independence was not purchased without a price. Their exploitation brought a reaction in the form of social legislation to lower hours, to improve conditions of work, and even to establish a minimum wage.

As in the early years of the Industrial Revolution, the entrance of women into the economic life was accompanied by a flow of population from rural to urban sections. Growth of cities, desertion by women of the home for the factory and office, improvements in transportation and home equipment made possible by electricity were quickly changing the larger cities from aggregations of independent homes to rows of massive apartment houses. The alteration, commented one observer in 1904, "is so great and so swift as to force itself upon us with somewhat of a shock," and with many others she protested against seeing the American home "lifted clear off the ground—yardless, cellarless, stairless, even kitchenless." Under such conditions habits of life inevitably changed. More and more recreation was found outside the home; for many the city apartment was little more than a place to sleep in. As the kitchen grew smaller and the sedentary occupations of city life required less food, dietary habits changed. The groaning boards of an earlier day disappeared. Prepared foods purchased in packages from a near-by grocery served for breakfast, a sandwich and a drink satisfied the noonday hunger, and finally the only meal of importance for many was the evening meal. With children no longer an economic asset, families became smaller.

Dietary changes of this type naturally decreased the household drudgery. So also did the gas stove, the electric light, the telephone, and other electric equipment such as the vacuum cleaner, the electric iron, and the washing machine, which found their way into an increasingly large number of homes. The small apartment equipped with labor-saving machinery gave women more leisure, and some of it was contributed to the welfare of their various communities. Women's clubs developed rapidly; the General Federation of Women's Clubs, which had been founded in 1889, had 1,000,000 members by 1914, and these clubs, which in their early days had been largely literary, were increasingly turning their attention to economic and social problems. "We have no platform," said the president of the federation at the tenth biennial convention in 1910, "unless it is the care of women and children, and the home, the latter meaning the four walls of the city as well as the four walls of brick and mortar," and it was noted that in many communities the women's club was the only organization devoted to civic improvement. All this contributed to the many reforms that were actively pushed in these years—better building codes to improve the slum districts, improvements in the sanitary laws to control disease, the drive on legalized and organized prostitution—and, of course, it gave a tremendous impetus toward political enfranchisement.

Even more indicative of the reform spirit of the new century was the attention given to the welfare of children. Children under sixteen engaged in gainful occupations numbered in 1900 at least 1,700,000. Although 60 per cent were agricultural workers, conditions even here were often deleterious. The worst conditions were in the factories, but the wave of child-labor legislation beginning in 1905 tended greatly to improve the situation. Less success was obtained, however, through federal legislation. In the hope of bringing the more backward sections into line, legislation was introduced into Congress as early as 1907 to exclude from interstate commerce goods from mines and factories employing children under fourteen years of age. Finally passed in 1916, it was speedily declared unconstitutional. An attempt to accomplish the same object in 1919 by the imposition of a 10-per-cent tax on the net profits of factories employing children under fourteen met a similar fate.[5]

While child-labor legislation struggled against the cupidity of exploiting manufacturers and often of parents, against a Constitution written for an agricultural and commercial age, and against a conservative judiciary, important advances were made in other directions. Especially should be noted

[5] Hammer v. Dagenhart, 247 U.S. 251 (1918); Bailey v. Drexel Furniture Company, 259 U.S. 20 (1922).

THE NEW REIGN OF TERROR.

Talk About the French Revolution!

(By permission of the *New York Evening Journal*)

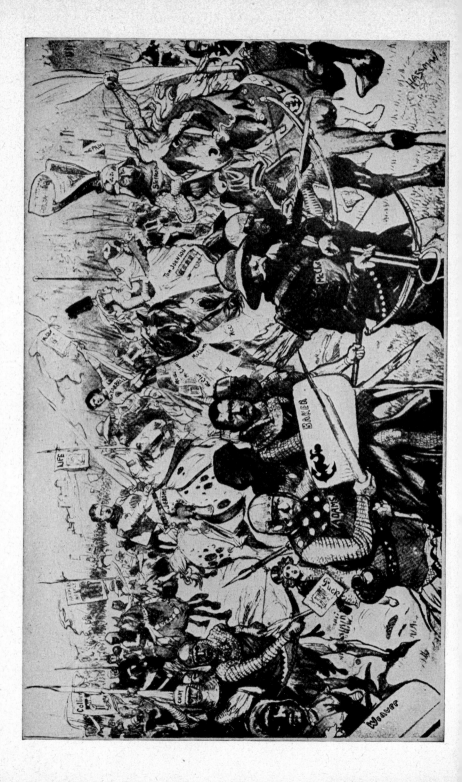

the decline in infant mortality. In certain states in 1900 it was found that 160 infants died out of every thousand and that the death rate for children under five was one in every twenty. Experts asserted that 50 per cent of this mortality was preventable. So great was the advance during the next decade that the census for the registration area in 1911 showed a decline of 22 per cent in the death rate of children under one year and a decline of 27 per cent for those under five. This was accomplished in numerous ways: tenement-house legislation, improved city sanitation, better inspection and the supervision of the milk supply, establishment of low-cost milk depots for poor families, the development of the system of visiting nurses, day nurseries, and city playgrounds. These notable humanitarian efforts had begun in the later nineties, but it was in the new century that they expanded rapidly. The new century also saw increased interest in the needs of the older children, as exemplified in the founding and growth of such organizations as the Boy Scouts of America (1910), the Campfire Girls (1912), and the Girl Scouts (1912). Some attention, based upon scientific penology, was also given to the defective and delinquent child by means of the establishment of juvenile courts, a movement greatly stimulated by the writing and lectures of Judge Ben B. Lindsey. Important likewise was the introduction of medical inspection in schools. Massachusetts in 1906 was the first state to introduce it in all its schools, but so rapidly did the movement spread that by 1912 seven states had passed mandatory laws and ten permissive laws, while in two others and the District of Columbia medical inspection was carried on under rules promulgated by the boards of health.

Education likewise felt the pressure of the changing spirit of these years. The early belief that education was the hope of democracy was not relinquished; rather it was emphasized by John Dewey and his disciples, who argued that the aim of education was not mere knowledge but social efficiency. In other words, education must go beyond book learning and include play, use of tools, contact with nature, and the development of personal expression. To buttress the realistic conceptions of Dewey came great psychologists, G. Stanley Hall, Edward L. Thorndike, and others, who subjected older concepts of education to the acid test of the laboratory. The result was a changing education to meet the needs of the new day. Vocational training, including courses in agriculture, industry, trade, and commerce, were introduced into the high school and the grades. In many cities high schools of commerce and the mechanic arts were established. This meant a turning from the older subjects, with the result that Greek, astronomy, and geology tended to drop from the curriculum. The high school, in fact, which in the nineteenth century had been primarily a preparation for college, became, with increased enrollment, a preparation for life. The traditional division of grades also tended to break up as the high school extended downward into the junior high school and upward into the junior college.

Education also was the recipient of many improvements in material equipment made possible by the machine age. The coming of the automobile, followed by the building of better roads, made possible the elimination of many of the small rural schoolhouses and their consolidation into larger fireproof buildings, furnished with modern equipment and presided over by better-trained teachers. It was well that this was so, for the system of public education in the United States expanded with almost incredible speed. Pupils registered in public schools almost doubled from 1900 to 1928 (15,500,000 to 29,000,000); between 1890 and 1918 one public high school was established for every day of the calendar year, with the result that the number of students attending high school increased from 500,000 in 1900 to 4,000,000 in 1928. College attendance likewise increased more than five times during the first three decades of the century, until fully one eighth of the nation's population between eighteen and twenty-one were in college. In the nineteenth century a grammar-school education had been considered the right of every child; in the twentieth century most children aspired at least to a high-school education. This, of course, meant mass education, and the problem of adequately caring for the masses of students swarming at the gates of high schools and colleges became a leading problem for the twentieth-century educator.

CULTURAL PATTERNS

Religion, like every other phase of cultural life, could hardly escape the influence both of the Industrial Revolution and of the era of reform. At least three tendencies during these years are easily discernible: a trend toward church unity, a further liberalization of theology, and a strong movement toward socialized religion. For the trend toward unity the urbanization of America was in part responsible. Depleted country districts that in earlier years had supported several churches could now comfortably maintain but one, and Protestant denominations found it possible to minimize their differences and consolidate their resources. The tendency was furthered when various branches of the same church, which in earlier years had been split by doctrinal differences or by the slavery controversy, found it possible to reconcile their differences. Furthermore, the Protestant denominations, which for many years had co-operated in such organizations as the Young Men's and Young Women's Christian Associations, now felt it possible in 1905 to found the Federal Council of the Churches of Christ in America. The ratification of the constitution of the Federal

Council three years later found thirty-three evangelical bodies representing 17,000,000 members tied loosely into an organization whose business it was to study problems vital to American Protestantism and make recommendations to its constituent churches. Fortunately dominated by socially minded leaders, it has always been in advance of the mass of church members and has helped to direct American Protestantism along progressive channels.

Important in minimizing the differences between sects had been the liberalization of theology, which had received such a tremendous impetus from the new swing. By 1900 modernism was well in the ascendancy among the intellectuals of the Protestant denominations and was particularly strong in the theological seminaries. It went hand in hand with the insistence by the leaders of the new generation that the church lay aside its theological controversies and direct its efforts toward an amelioration of the intolerable conditions existing in the social order (page 482). It might be all right to talk of the life to come, but it was more important, they insisted, to ensure a decent and happy existence here below. In the theological seminaries, courses in sociology were introduced to supplement the conventional curriculum; in the actual work of the church the "social gospel" promoted "institutionalized churches," that is, churches that supported all types of philanthropic enterprises and organized charities. It was also noticeable that churches and church leaders were more ready to take a definite stand on social and economic questions of a controversial nature. Thus the Methodist Episcopal Church asserted in 1908 "that the organization of labor is not only the right of laborers and conducive to their welfare, but is incidentally of great benefit to society at large," while the Federal Council in the same year urged the protection of the worker from dangerous machinery and occupational disease, abolition of child labor, the end of the sweating system, the reduction of hours, the six-day week, workers' compensation, old-age insurance, and "the most equitable division of labor than can be devised."

If statistics of membership are to be taken seriously, it can hardly be asserted that either the growth of modernism or the social gospel had decreased the vitality of organized religion. As a social and intellectual factor the church may have declined in certain Protestant sections of the Northeast, but in the rural West and South its role was undiminished. Between 1900 and 1914 church membership, according to church statistics, increased by 16,000,000. While all the churches shared, the Roman Catholic, benefiting from the large immigration from Italy, Austria-Hungary, and other Catholic countries, gained the most members. The accretion of membership went hand in hand with a continued enlargement of the scope of educational and philanthropic interests of the churches, as seen in schools, colleges, hospitals, and relief organizations, and it continued despite increasing competition from the golf course, the automobile, and other recreational interests that now beckoned to the churchgoer on the Sabbath.

In designing the cultural pattern of the new century, at least as far as the masses were concerned, no instrument was more important than the newspaper. The high-speed power press, the linotype, the typewriter, and the telephone had all appeared before 1900, but it was after that date that their full influence was to be felt. With each succeeding year new inventions, such as the printing telegraph machine and the motor truck, were to contribute to speed in the collection and dissemination of news. Of nineteenth-century origin also was "yellow journalism," with its appeal to the sensational and its inevitable degradation of public taste. To strengthen popular appeal, the newspapers tended increasingly to assume many of the characteristics of a magazine. The nineteenth-century newspaper was essentially a medium for the dissemination of news and of the political and other views of the editor. With the decline of personal journalism the twentieth-century newspaper became essentially a money-making business. While news was collected more efficiently than ever through the Associated Press and other agencies, new features were added. Enterprising journals now carried a financial page, a sporting page, a theatrical page, a women's page, comic strips and bedtime stories for the children, "advice to the lovelorn," columns of humorous comment on the passing show, and other features to widen interest and increase circulation. Although the excellence of the features was determined by the flair of the individual journalist, the fact that news was gathered by associations, features distributed by syndicates, and in some cases strings of newspapers controlled by one person—all this tended to standardize the reading of the masses.

The newspapers still continued to provide the chief reading matter for most of the people, but their leadership in formulating public opinion was being shaken by the popular magazines. The conservative and polite literary magazine of the type of *Harper's, Scribner's,* the *Century* and the *Atlantic* found itself pushed into the background as the low-priced popular publication, of which *McClure's* was pre-eminent, entered aggressively into the field of political and economic muckraking. As muckraking declined and the popular magazines fell under the sway of big business, they relinquished their leadership in the arena of public affairs and, like the *Saturday Evening Post,* became essentially mediums for recreational reading. Their influence on political and economic questions, where any was exerted, was essentially conservative.

Like the magazines, literature and art reflected the speed, the mechanization, and the interests of the period. Improved processes of typesetting and binding decreased the price of the novel, while authors, responding to the increasing tempo, reduced its size to 150,000 or 200,000 words. Before this period few American novels achieved a circulation of 100,000; by 1900 such sales were common. The dominant note in American fiction at the opening of the century was romanticism, as exemplified in the tremendous vogue of the historical novel.[6] Whether this came from a burst of patriotism accompanying the Spanish-American War, from a revived interest in American history, from a desire to escape from the grinding economic conflicts of the nineties, or from all three it is difficult to determine, but historical fiction, with an occasional rural novel, caught the popular fancy.

It was indeed fortunate for American letters that not all the literary talent was absorbed in the literature of escape. The realistic school of Tolstoy and Zola had won some converts during the Gilded Age, and a few of the younger generation, such men as Frank Norris, Upton Sinclair, Jack London, Robert Herrick, and David Graham Phillips, joined their ranks. Even some of the romanticists, influenced by the era of the muckrake, turned briefly from historical fiction. The ablest of the realists during these years was Theodore Dreiser, but his uncompromising handling of sex and his powerful novels of men and women fighting futilely against circumstances too strong to surmount won him little recognition in the prewar days. Poetry in 1900, like fiction, was dominated by romanticism, tempered somewhat by the rural dialect poets, Will Carleton and James Whitcomb Riley. Already a new note had been struck by Edwin Markham in "The Man With the Hoe" (1898); within a decade and a half an amazing change had taken place. Now the stage was occupied by the realists: Edwin Arlington Robinson with his honest portrayal of life, Vachel Lindsay interpreting the Middle West with his ragtime boomings, Carl Sandburg with his virile poems of Chicago, Robert Frost with his sketches of New England, and Amy Lowell with her revolutionary pioneering in *vers libre*.

More accurately perhaps than even fiction or poetry did the theater mirror the cross currents of American life. The romanticism of the early years was reflected on the stage by historical plays and particularly by musical comedies with scenes set in some far-off land. As time went on, the stage also occasionally attempted the "problem play" and in its own way attempted some muckraking. Although the American stage, in such actors as Mrs. Fiske, John Drew, the Barrymores, David Warfield, Mrs. Leslie Carter, Otis Skinner, and others, had as great artists as it had ever had, the theater was all but ruined by the advent of big-business methods, which, in line with current tendencies, sought to consolidate theatrical properties and monopolize the talent of artists. Against this there developed the

---

[6] Outstanding examples are S. Weir Mitchell's *Hugh Wynne* (1898), Winston Churchill's *Richard Carvel* (1899) and *The Crisis* (1901), and Mary Johnston's *To Have and to Hold* (1900).

hope of the municipal theater and the "little-theater" movement. The first failed, but the latter proved a stimulating influence, and in the end rival interests prevented the utter degradation of the American drama.

Many of the best theatrical productions of these years were European importations. The European influence, however, was much more important in music and art. Although a few Americans were playing with the idea of Negro and Indian music, the masses were chiefly concerned with the popular songs of the street and the melodies from musical comedies. The chief advance in music was in the spread of symphony orchestras in the larger cities and efforts to establish permanent opera companies outside New York. In painting, Americans continued to follow the modes of Europe, with a distinct tendency toward realism. Architecturally, Americans made distinct contributions in the construction of skyscrapers and of factory and office buildings, but undoubtedly the greatest flowering of American art was in sculpture. Men like Ward, Saint-Gaudens, Barnard, MacMonnies, Taft, the Borglums, and many others brought American sculpture almost overnight to a place on a par with the best in the world. In the first ten years of the century America produced more first-grade sculpture than during its entire previous history.

More significant by far in the social history of the world were the contributions that America continued to make in the realm of science. As in earlier years, such contributions, as might be expected in a new and rapidly expanding nation, were primarily of a practical rather than a theoretical nature. Thus the telephone, the telegraph, the radio, and the airplane were largely developed by American inventors, as well as many other such practical applications of electricity as the trolley car, the electric light, and household electrical equipment. Though many inventors continued to emulate Goodyear, Bell, Edison, and the Wright brothers, whose inventions were largely the result of individual efforts individually financed, the tendency was now to group engineers and inventors in well-equipped laboratories supported by large industries, where research and invention became institutionalized and directed toward the interests of a particular business. Nevertheless, college professors, government scientists, and individual research workers and inventors were widening the world's knowledge in the many fields of science—knowledge that was rapidly remaking cultural and social patterns.

In no field of science was greater advance made in America than in preventive and curative medicine, aided by new discoveries in chemistry, physics, entomology, bacteriology, and other sciences. As in other fields of science, a discussion of these contributions would mean a book in itself. Note has already been made of the work of Walter Reed and his associates in Cuba on yellow fever and of Bailey K. Ashford on causes of anemia in Puerto Rico. Ashford's work was followed up in this country by Charles W. Stiles, whose efforts went far toward the eradication of the hookworm in the American South. Great impetus was given by Edward L. Trudeau to the control of tuberculosis by his demonstrations of the curative value of outdoor living and proper diet. In the field of food chemistry, the work begun in the early years of the century by W. O. Atwater was carried to important results years later by the discovery and classification of vitamins by such pioneers as Thomas B. Osborne, L. B. Mendel, Henry C. Sherman, and E. V. McCollum. Through the work of these and many others the average life span was extended almost ten years between 1901 and 1927.

The best single chapters are C. and M. Beard, *The Rise of American Civilization*, Chap. XXVII, and L. M. Hacker and B. B. Kendrick, *The United States Since 1865*, Chap. XXII. A longer survey is H. U. Faulkner, *The Quest for Social Justice*, Chaps. I, V, VII–XIII (History of American Life). John Chamberlain, *Farewell to Reform*, Chaps. III–VIII, is interpretative. On the agitation for reform, see C. C. Regier, *The Era of the Muckrakers*, particularly Chap. XV, and, on the "Muckrakers" themselves, Louis Filler, *Crusaders for American Liberalism*. Read also Merle Curti, *The Growth of American Thought*, Chaps. XXIV–XXV.

A WORLD POWER

Chapter XXXV

THE NEW DEMOCRACY

> *I earnestly commend to your careful considera-*
> *tion the laws in recent years as adopted by the*
> *State of Oregon, whose effect has been to bring*
> *government back to the people and to protect it*
> *from the control of the representatives of selfish*
> *and special interests.*
>
> WOODROW WILSON (1910)

> *There was room on that platform [Progres-*
> *sive] for anyone who had seen Peter Pan and*
> *believed in fairies.*
>
> DONALD RICHBERG

> *The Socialist party declares that the capitalist*
> *system has outgrown its historical function, and*
> *has become utterly incapable of meeting the prob-*
> *lems now confronting society.*
>
> SOCIALIST PARTY PLATFORM (1912)

POLITICAL REFORM

To no small extent politics is but a reflection of the civilization of a people, and, like other phases of American civilization, political life also felt
the impelling drive for reform. Several factors had contributed to the
decline of American political life in the last half of the nineteenth century.
The reckless war-time spending, coupled with the emotional let-down of
the postwar years, had softened the moral fiber of politicians. In the rapid
economic growth of the nation, the great prizes of wealth and power were
to be found in the world of business, and the most talented of American
youth deserted politics for business, leaving government to professional
politicians. In the bitter struggle for the nation's resources, the ethics of
business and politics declined rapidly as big business and professional
politicians worked together to take from the people the wealth of the
nation. Public indifference, which took such a situation for granted, made
it possible.

The low estate into which government had fallen was particularly evident in municipal and state government but was also reflected in national politics. The discouraging picture of municipal government that Bryce had described in the eighties was still authentic twenty years later. As Lincoln Steffens went from city to city, he found the same conditions—a political machine headed by a "boss" (who often held no office himself), allied on the one hand with the underworld and on the other with franchise-grabbing public utilities. The primary object of these machines seemed to be the perpetuation of power and the robbing of the citizenry rather than the maintenance of efficient government. Only when conditions became intolerable was there revolt. Then some temporary relief was to be found in the administration of such men as Seth Low in New York, Tom Johnson in Cleveland, or Mark Fagen in Jersey City. State governments were little better, for they too were dominated by the boss and the machine, which ordinarily stood ready to do the bidding of big business. A reform wave in Ohio in 1905 purified to some extent the state legislature and elected as one of the representatives Frederic C. Howe. His description of the last day of the session might apply to the legislature of many a state:

> Enmities were forgotten and by a tacit agreement each member was permitted to call up some bill that bore his name and if it was not too controversial it was permitted to pass. Thus members had something to show their constituents. These last hours were pandemonium. Many of the law-makers were drunk. . . . Scores of bills went through by gentlemen's agreement. Nobody knew what they contained and nobody cared. . . . I came away from the legislature with scant respect for the laws of the land. I had seen how they were made. Some were frankly bought and paid for. . . . Only occasionally were bills in the public interest forced through by the pressure of public opinion, and they were so crippled with amendments that they were of little value.[1]

The effort, as Woodrow Wilson put it, "to bring government back to the people and to protect it from the control of the representatives of selfish and special interests" took several forms: the election of reform candidates, the introduction of more efficient methods of government, the passing of laws for better control of the special interests, and the development of a new technique of democracy. The leadership in reform, which had come from the rural districts in the age of Populism, now passed to the cities. Without leadership reform could make but little progress, but this came with a new generation of public servants anxious to carry out the desires of the more public-spirited voters. Pioneers in the movement for better city government were Hazen S. Pingree of Detroit, Samuel M. ("Golden

[1] F. C. Howe, *Confessions of a Reformer* (1925), 165–166. By permission Charles Scribner's Sons.

Rule") Jones of Toledo, and Tom L. Johnson of Cleveland, whose battles against old-time political machines and vested interests won them the mayoralty of their respective cities and resulted in many municipal reforms. Johnson, in the opinion of Steffens, was the "best mayor of the best governed city in the United States." Typical of the new leaders in state politics were Robert M. La Follette, who became governor of Wisconsin in 1902, and Woodrow Wilson, who became governor of New Jersey in 1910.

Of the various schemes to introduce more efficiency in government, none were more interesting than the effort through the commission form of government and the city-manager plan to rescue the municipal governments from grafting politicians and special interests. When Galveston, in 1900, was visited by a terrific storm and tidal wave, which drowned one seventh of the population and destroyed one third of the property, the citizens threw aside the existing unwieldy form of government and put their reconstruction in the hands of a commission of five. So successful did this prove to be that the system was made permanent under a new charter in 1901. These five elected commissioners, sitting in open meeting, were to vote city ordinances, determine appointments, award contracts, and carry on other city business. As the success of the Galveston experiment was demonstrated, Houston in 1905, Des Moines in 1907, and many other cities in the next few years adopted some form of the commission plan. Variations soon appeared, particularly the city-manager plan first introduced at Dayton after the flood of 1913. It sought through a single paid individual, supervised by an elected commission, to run the affairs of the city as a president and board of directors might conduct a business. Efforts at reform in city government necessitated new charters or new state legislation, which made the battle for city home rule an important phase of the political reform movement during the early years of the century.

Any method of restoring democracy, it was hoped, would contribute to the more efficient control of special interests. Specifically, the effort was furthered by laws strengthening the railroad commissions and setting up other commissions to handle new public utilities. La Follette and his Wisconsin legislature were pioneers in this work, and it was climaxed when Wilson's legislature in New Jersey passed a strong public-utilities law, a corrupt-practices act governing campaign methods and expenditures, and a badly needed antitrust act. To many, however, the great hope for the restoration of popular rule lay in the initiative, the referendum, the recall, and the direct primary. The initiative would enable the people to initiate legislation; by the referendum they could force legislators to refer legislation back to the voter for ultimate confirmation or rejection; by the recall they could displace unsatisfactory public servants. The direct primary, it was hoped, would give the voter as well as the machine an opportunity to choose candidates. This new technique of democracy originated chiefly in Europe, but so much of it was tried out in this country first in Oregon that the whole movement came to be known as the "Oregon system." Its adoption in Oregon was due largely to the efforts of William S. U'Ren, a quiet, self-effacing individual, whose name today is almost forgotten but whose influence upon American political development was important.

In national political reform these years were concerned chiefly with the movements for the direct election of United States senators and for woman suffrage. Although the Senate contained many men of great ability, it had by 1905 lost the confidence of the voters. Chosen by state legislatures, dominated by machine bosses and big business, too many senators represented special interests rather than the public welfare. Bryce had asserted in 1888 that "some, an increasing number, are senators because they are rich; a few are rich because they are senators," and the Senate came to be known as a "rich man's club." Since the senators themselves were naturally reluctant to change the constitutional provision regarding their own election, the voters took matters in their own hands and by 1912 had devised methods of circumventing the Constitution and choosing the persons they wanted. As an increasing number of men elected by new methods took their seats in the Senate, that body succumbed to public pressure; the seventeenth amendment passed both houses in 1912 and on May 31, 1913, became part of the Constitution. The seventeenth amendment may not have greatly improved the caliber of the Senate, but it brought the membership in closer touch with the electorate.

Another reform long overdue was the active participation of women in the political life of the nation. Partial suffrage for specific purposes existed in many states, but in 1900 only four, Wyoming, Colorado, Utah, and Idaho, had granted full political rights. Since 1890, when two organizations advocating woman suffrage had combined into the National American Woman Suffrage Association, the agitation, under the leadership of Carrie Chapman Catt and Anna Howard Shaw, had become more active. It was not until 1910, however, that the movement was given a new impetus by the addition of Washington to the states granting woman suffrage. Six more were added by 1914, but this progress seemed too slow for the more ardent advocates, and a campaign was started to secure an amendment to the Constitution. In this they gained but little help at first from the major parties. Roosevelt, when asked to recommend such a step to Congress, advised a delegation of women workers to "go, get another state," but in the election of 1912, as leader of the Progressive Party, he reversed himself and advocated national action. Taft and Wilson both sidestepped the issue in 1912, but Wilson was eventually forced to commit himself. The more militant suffragists, under the leadership of Alice Paul, organized the Congressional Union, paraded the streets of Washington, picketed the White House, and gave the politicians no rest until action resulted. Both major parties endorsed equal suffrage in 1916. Wilson, in 1918, appealed to Congress for federal action, and in the next year Congress passed the woman-suffrage amendment (nineteenth), which was ratified during the midst of the campaign of 1920.

LEFT-WING POLITICS

The social and economic reforms of the early years of the century were in line with socialist ideals and in turn they gave an impetus to the development of the Socialist Party. Socialism in its various forms was not a new phenomenon in American history. During the second quarter of the nineteenth century, as we have noted (page 268), numerous experiments in utopian socialism had been attempted. Short-lived and essentially non-political as were these experiments, they gave for many years a utopian tinge to American socialism. In the years after the continental revolutions of 1848, many German refugees and tens of thousands of German workmen sought here the political freedom that they had failed to attain at home. Many of these German immigrants brought to America the new ideas of Marx and effected a union of utopian and scientific socialism. The General German Workingmen's Association became in 1869 a section of the First International, and for a brief period after 1872 the headquarters of Marx's First International were located in New York. But socialism in America during the last half of the century was largely limited to German immigrants, although the ground for a wider appeal was being laid by such reformers as Edward Bellamy and Henry Demarest Lloyd and in such progressive movements as that of the Populist Party, whose platforms contained socialist demands. The Workingmen's Association became politically active in 1876 when it organized the Workingmen's Party of the United States with a Marxist program and changed its name in the following year to the Socialist Labor Party of North America.

The Socialist Labor Party never attained real strength, and its chief significance was in inaugurating political socialism in this country. It nominated its first presidential ticket in 1892, when it polled 21,512 votes in six states, and reached its maximum power with 82,204 votes in the congressional elections of 1898. It was weakened in its early years by the growth of anarchism and in its later years by a factional split over trade-union tactics, which eventually reduced the party to utter impotency. Believing the trade-union movement represented a less developed form of class consciousness than the political organization, it sought to obtain union endorsement of candidates of the Socialist Labor Party and to convince the unions that socialist principles should be a condition of membership. This was particularly true after Daniel De Leon had become the leader and had literally transformed the party into a personal organ. De Leon's failure to capture either the Knights of Labor or the American Federation of Labor led him in 1896 to start a rival organization, the Socialist Trade and Labor Alliance, which had a brief existence in New York City.

While De Leon was in conflict with the trade unions, a new socialist movement had developed in the West under the leadership of Eugene V. Debs and Victor L. Berger, who in 1898 organized the Social Democratic Party of America. In the election of 1900 the faction of the Socialist Labor Party that opposed De Leon joined the Social Democratic Party in nominating candidates, and in the following year a unity convention of these two groups founded the Socialist Party. While the strength of the Socialist Labor Party declined, the Socialist Party grew rapidly in the prewar years. Its presidential vote of 97,730 in 1900 grew to 402,321 in 1904, to 420,820 in 1908, and to 897,011 in 1912. Some thirteen dailies (English and foreign-language) and two hundred weeklies carried party news and propaganda, with the result that an increasing number of local Socialist candidates were elected to office. In 1910 Milwaukee elected Emil Seidel to the mayoralty and Victor Berger to Congress. While intellectual leadership was furnished by Berger, Morris Hillquit, and other American intellectuals who joined the party, the presidential standard-bearer during these years was the beloved Eugene V. Debs, whose warm human qualities, oratorical ability, and utter sincerity were the great tower of strength of the party. Although the party won thousands of the more socially minded bourgeois, its greatest strength was among labor, and it maintained a persistent fight against Gompers and old-line unionism in an effort to swing trade unionism to the socialist cause.

NATIONAL POLITICS

By the time the election of 1904 rolled around, Roosevelt was riding high on the popularity he had won by his successful handling of the anthracite coal strike and by his campaign against monopolies. The death of Hanna eliminated the only possible opposition, and Roosevelt was nominated by acclamation, with Charles W. Fairbanks of Indiana, an old-guard machine politician, as his running mate. The only live thing about the convention, remarked one delegate, was a picture of the late Mark Hanna hung above the stage. The platform was largely a recitation of Republican achievement and a colorless commitment to the usual planks. Turning from the "peerless leader," the Democrats nominated Judge Alton B. Parker of New

York, a conservative, gold-standard Democrat of the Cleveland school. Except for denunciation of the Roosevelt administration, their platform was about as colorless and indefinite as that of the Republicans. The sudden reversal that made a conservative New York judge the standard-bearer of the erstwhile radical Democrats, while the progressive Roosevelt was endorsed by the old-guard Republicans and financed by big business, must have been a bit confusing to the voter. The result, however, was never in doubt; it was an overwhelming victory for Roosevelt by an electoral vote of 336 to 140.[2]

Roosevelt's overwhelming victory in 1904 undoubtedly strengthened his hand and enabled him to push his policies with greater effectiveness than during his first three years. What these policies were was now clearly evident. As ardently as McKinley or any old-guard Republican, Roosevelt supported the high tariff, the gold standard, and imperialism. Where he differed from his predecessor was in his efforts to enforce the Sherman Antitrust Act and the Interstate Commerce Act and in his firm belief that the federal government might interfere aggressively to protect the people as a whole from the depredations of a few. *Laissez faire* was no part of his philosophy. He always had a long list of reforms that in succession he insisted were of the greatest importance, but the fact that he favored so many mitigated against carrying any to a logical conclusion. Nevertheless, his second administration was notable for the passing of the Hepburn Act (1906), the Meat Inspection and Pure Food and Drug Act (1906), an employers' liability law for railroads (1906, declared unconstitutional in 1908, and later re-enacted), an act limiting the hours of railroad employees (1907), and an aggressive campaign to conserve natural resources and make them more useful. Actual construction of the Panama Canal began in May, 1904, and was vigorously pushed throughout the next four years. The strong foreign policy of the first administration was continued during the second, accompanied by a strengthening of the army and the navy. While aggressive imperialism was demonstrated in forcing a protectorate upon Santo Domingo, some recognition of the growing peace movement was evident in the "gentlemen's agreement" with Japan (page 546) and in our participation in the second Hague Conference (1907).

Although Roosevelt undoubtedly had a majority of the voters with him, his career as a reformer had not been an easy one. Many of his bills had been killed in committee; others had failed to pass. Conservative senators fought his policies, and Speaker Joseph G. Cannon led the opposition in

---

[2] The popular vote was Roosevelt 7,628,834 and Parker 5,084,491. The Socialist, Debs, polled 402,321 and the Populist, Thomas E. Watson, 117,183. The votes of the Socialist Labor and Prohibition Parties were negligible.

the House. As Roosevelt's term came to an end, there was naturally much talk regarding his successor. In the elation of victory Roosevelt had announced on the night of his election in 1904 that "under no circumstances will I be a candidate for or accept another nomination." Although, as he himself truly said, he could "have had the Republican nomination with practical unanimity by simply raising one finger," he adhered to his resolution. He had, however, no intention of resigning active influence upon the office, and was determined to select his successor. The one man in the Senate most clearly identified with the Roosevelt policies was La Follette, but the Wisconsin progressive was not entirely in Roosevelt's confidence. Passing over favorite sons who were too conservative, Roosevelt finally chose his personal friend and official associate, William Howard Taft, as the ideal man to carry on his policies.

By judicious employment of publicity and federal patronage, Taft was easily nominated on the first ballot. The platform was long and verbose, chiefly concerned with praising the Roosevelt administration and promising a continuation of his policies. Its most important parts were those that recommended an amendment to the Sherman Antitrust Act giving more publicity to corporate methods and more control to the federal government, favored the regulation of the issuance of injunctions by the federal courts, and promised a revision of the tariff "immediately after the inauguration by a special session of Congress." A minority platform report, urged by La Follette, which contained several really progressive planks, was quickly squelched as a "socialistic" document. The Democratic fiasco under Parker and the Eastern conservatives threw that party back into the hands of Bryan and the progressives. For him the Denver convention was a personal triumph; with little opposition he obtained the nomination and wrote the platform. In striking contrast to that of the Republicans, the Democratic platform was amazingly explicit. Among the methods to prevent the evils of private monopoly it advocated laws to prevent interlocking directorates in competing companies, a federal license for a corporation engaged in interstate commerce "before it shall be permitted to control as much as 25 per cent of the product . . . , the license to protect the public from watered stock" and to prohibit any company from controlling more than 50 per cent of the product, and laws forcing such concerns to sell to all purchasers on the same terms. Almost equally explicit were its propositions with respect to railroads.

Although certain of Bryan's specific suggestions were later incorporated in the legislation of the Wilson administration, they were, of course, denounced as impractical and socialistic. Be that as it may, the voter preferred the Roosevelt brand of liberalism to that of Bryan, and Taft, heir to the

Roosevelt policies, was victorious by an electoral vote of 321 to 162.[3] Bryan polled 1,300,000 more votes than Parker four years earlier, but, like Parker, he failed to carry the pivotal states of New York, New Jersey, Indiana, and Ohio. Hope for the party in the future must come from a new leader who could win support from both factions and gather votes from the outside.

THE TAFT ADMINISTRATION

In a less progressive era Taft might have made an ideal President. By temperament he was kindly, judicious, slow to act. Although he had few of the qualities that arouse enthusiasm, he was personally popular. If his economic philosophy is to be judged from the record of legislative achievement during his administration, it must be pronounced quite as liberal as that of Roosevelt. The full strength of the Rooseveltian liberalism, however, had passed him, and his misfortune was to allow himself to be maneuvered on to the conservative side of certain controversies. Political ineptitude was in part to blame for his troubles; certainly his reputation as a reactionary during these years was hardly warranted. His political philosophy, however, was more conservative than his economic; to him the domain of the executive included only those powers specifically granted. The President, he believed, was to be a balance wheel rather than the main spring from which all government action originated.

Politically, the Taft administration is significant in that it marked the disintegration of the Republican Party, just as the second administration of Cleveland had brought a similar disintegration in the Democratic ranks. Although the background was somewhat different, the fundamental cause was similar—a break between the liberals and the conservatives. Roosevelt's political skill and his own immense popularity had prevented such a split during his administration. Furthermore, progressivism did not reach full tide until the days of Taft. By that time enough progressives had found their way into Congress to keep up an incessant battle for reform, and with the dominating figure of Roosevelt removed, the activities of the redoubtable La Follette and his colleagues, Dolliver, Cummins, Beveridge, Bristow, and others, loomed larger in party politics. From the very beginning of the Taft administration friction within the party developed. To progressives his cabinet was a disappointment. Only two members of the Roosevelt cabinet were retained, and the fact that a majority were corporation lawyers hardly presaged an aggressively liberal administration.

The first business of the administration was to carry out its pledge of

[3] The popular vote was 7,677,788 to 6,407,982, with Debs, the Socialist, polling 420,890; Chapin, the Prohibitionist, 252,511; Hisgen, Independent Party, 83,651; Watson, Populist, 29,-146; Gilhaus, Socialist Labor, 14,021.

tariff revision, politically a ticklish and dangerous business. The McKinley tariff of 1890, it will be remembered, resulted in a Republican defeat, while the unfortunate Wilson-Gorman Act of 1894 had done much to discredit the Democrats. Roosevelt had carefully avoided the tariff issue, but now the Dingley Act, which had been on the statute books for ten years, was due for revision. The Republican platform had promised "revision" but had neglected to say whether up or down. Nevertheless, the House, under the leadership of Sereno E. Payne, prepared a new tariff with the revisions generally downward. In the Senate, under the leadership of Nelson W. Aldrich, 847 amendments were tacked on, which were generally higher, and this despite the relentless opposition of La Follette and the progressives. When the Payne-Aldrich Act was finally passed (1909), it was discovered that of the 2024 items in the Dingley tariff, 654 were decreased, 220 increased, and 1150 left unchanged. Hides were put on the free list, but the duties on cotton and woolens were increased. The bill called for the creation of a special customs court to hear appeals in customs cases and a tariff commission to study the tariff scientifically. Taft admitted that the woolen schedule was not good and in the later stages of the bill made a slight effort to temper the high protection. Later, in a speech, he said that "on the whole . . . the Payne tariff bill is the best tariff bill the Republican Party ever passed." This might quite easily have been true, but there was nevertheless a rather general dissatisfaction with it throughout the country and a feeling that the Republican machine had not fulfilled its pledge, a dissatisfaction carefully nurtured by liberal Republicans and Democrats alike.

Before the Payne-Aldrich Bill was disposed of, a controversy over conservation seemed to place the Taft administration in a position of opposition to the Roosevelt policies. Conservation had been one of the primary policies of the Roosevelt administration. Influenced by such men as Frederick Haynes Newell, government engineer, and Gifford Pinchot, the first great exponent of scientific forestry in America, Roosevelt embarked on an aggressive policy of conservation. An old act of 1891, which allowed the President to set aside parts of the public lands as forest reserves, was revived, and Roosevelt withdrew for reservations 148,000,000 acres as against his predecessors' 45,000,000. To take care of this land, he induced Congress to create a forestry service, over which he placed his friend Pinchot. To promote irrigation, he favored the Newlands Reclamation Act (1902), which provided for the setting aside of the proceeds from the sale of arid and semiarid lands in sixteen designated western states and their use to create a fund for irrigation work. He appointed the Inland Waterways Commission to study this problem and at its suggestion called a governor's conference on conservation that led directly to conservation commissions in numerous states. All in all, Roosevelt did much to counteract the ruthless exploitation of public resources and turn the nation's attention to the need of conservation.

Taft also was a firm believer in conservation, but he questioned the legality of Roosevelt's withdrawals by simple executive order and returned large areas to public entry, at the same time asking and obtaining from Congress authority to withdraw what land seemed necessary for the public welfare. In January, 1910, he submitted to Congress a definite conservation program, which included a modernization of the land laws, especially along the line of separating the title to the surface from the title to underlying minerals, and the disposal of the minerals by lease rather than by sale. Congress not only acted favorably upon this but also passed the Appalachian Forest Reserve Act, setting aside two million dollars a year until June 30, 1915, for the purchase and upkeep of lands lying near the headwaters of navigable streams.

Taft's trouble with the conservationists arose over the fraudulent patenting of the so-called Cunningham coal claims in Alaska. One L. B. Glavis, investigating these patents for the government, charged that Secretary of the Interior Ballinger,[4] who formerly had acted in the capacity of legal adviser to the Cunningham claimants, was now trying to smother the investigation and push through the patents. Glavis appealed to Pinchot, and Pinchot not only lent his aid in bringing the matter before the President but joined in the public attack upon Ballinger and his policies. Taft dismissed Glavis and Pinchot from the service and exonerated Ballinger. The matter, however, soon became a public issue, debated in the press and kept alive by a congressional investigation. Taft's unqualified approval of Ballinger did much to obscure his own real contributions to conservation and to widen the split in his own party.

That the insurgents were rapidly getting out of hand was demonstrated in March, 1910, when the liberal Republicans in the House, co-operating with the Democrats, overthrew the power of Speaker Joseph G. (Uncle Joe) Cannon and modified the system that gave the Speaker such tremendous power. The Speaker's influence came from his right to appoint all committees and their chairmen and from his own chairmanship of the Committee on Rules, which determined procedure and made special rules. While this system had the advantage of expediting business and of placing responsibility, it concentrated legislative power in too small a group. In an effort to make the Speaker merely the presiding officer, the House succeeded in replacing the old Committee on Rules by a larger one elected by the House and in eliminating the Speaker from this committee.

---

[4] Taft had dropped Roosevelt's Secretary of the Interior, James A. Garfield, an enthusiastic conservationist, and appointed in his place R. A. Ballinger, a corporation lawyer.

The overthrow of Cannon was an excellent index of the sentiment of the nation. In the fall elections the Democrats not only elected governors in Massachusetts, Connecticut, New York, Indiana, and other states but secured an overwhelming control of the House, which in the next session numbered 227 Democrats, 163 Republicans, and 1 Socialist (Berger). The Republican majority in the Senate was reduced from 28 to 10. In addition, new insurgent Republicans from the West came to join the dissenting ranks.

With the sixty-second Congress controlled by Democrats and insurgent Republicans who were at odds with the Republican President, an orderly legislative session seemed unlikely. Much of the time was spent in attacking the high rates of the Payne-Aldrich tariff, and with unexpected ease Congress in 1911 passed three tariff bills: a farmers' free list, placing agricultural implements, boots and shoes, wire fence, and other commodities on the free list; an act revising downward duties on wool and woolen manufactures (Schedule K), and an act reducing the tariff on cottons, chemicals, metals, paints, and other commodities. Taft immediately vetoed all three on the ground that the Tariff Commission set up under the Payne-Aldrich Act had not yet assembled the data upon which the tariff might be scientifically reduced. The following year Congress passed two more tariff bills, one reducing the duties on iron and steel and the other on woolens. Taft again vetoed both, this time because the Tariff Commission had gathered data for a scientific revision, which Congress had not used.

Although opposed to tariff-reduction when carried out by the old-fashioned methods that Congress was attempting, the President was strongly in favor of reciprocity with Canada. Such an agreement was concluded, calling for a free list of more than a hundred articles and reductions on more than four hundred more. The bill passed the Democratic House and eventually the Senate also, but only after insurgent Republicans had bitterly opposed it on the ground that it would hurt the farmers and help manufacturers. In the United States the reciprocity measure served only to widen the breach in the Republican Party; in Canada it aroused a reactionary nationalism, which in a general election threw out the Liberal Party and elected the Conservatives committed to a repudiation of reciprocity.

Despite the apparent conservatism of the Taft administration, the four years 1909–1913 witnessed much progressive legislation. The impetus given by the previous administrations undoubtedly made some of it inevitable, but it was essentially a reaction to popular demand during a reform period. In justice to Taft, however, it should be said that he strongly supported this legislation. Particularly notable were acts authorizing the establishment of a postal-savings system in 1910 and the parcels post in 1912. The first was bitterly opposed by the private banks and the second by the express companies and country merchants, but both were progressive reforms long overdue. Other legislation included the establishment of the Economy and Efficiency Commission to point out improvements in the functioning of governmental bodies, the laws already noted regarding conservation of natural resources, and the Mann-Elkins Act empowering the Interstate Commerce Commission to suspend for ten months any proposed change in rates to allow time for investigation, and the establishment of the Commerce Court to hear railroad cases. The Department of Commerce and Labor was separated into two departments, and the Children's Bureau was set up in the new Department of Labor. In answer to Democratic criticisms, acts were passed in 1910 and 1911 requiring publicity of the sources and expenditures of money used in federal campaigns. More important, perhaps, than all these was the ratification of the sixteenth amendment. An income-tax clause had been added to the Payne-Aldrich tariff, but grave doubts as to its constitutionality led Taft to urge that it be deleted and the matter put in the form of a constitutional amendment. This was done, and ratification came in 1913.

Although Taft pushed the prosecution of monopolies under the Sherman Antitrust Act quite as vigorously as had Roosevelt, it was evident by 1913 that neither had made any real contribution to a solution of the problem of consolidation or monopoly, unless failure to achieve much through the courts after a decade of effort was a contribution by showing how little could be done. By 1913 the whole problem was more complicated than ever. The Standard Oil and the American Tobacco monopolies, it is true, were technically dissolved, but it was soon evident that their dissolution made little practical difference in these particular industries. The Supreme Court, which in the Trans-Missouri Freight case decision (1897) had refused to see any difference between reasonable and unreasonable combinations in restraint of trade, now treated the nation to an *obiter dictum* when in two decisions in 1911 it professed to see a difference and insisted that the only restraint intended by the law was of trade that monopolized or intended to monopolize. This "rule of reason," which attempted to differentiate between "good trusts" and "bad trusts," was highly satisfactory to big business, but it made the whole question of the legal status of monopolies more difficult.

THE RETURN OF THE DEMOCRATS

Like most "middle-of-the-roaders," Taft was able to please neither the right nor the left. To the conservatives he was an apostle of the revolutionary Roosevelt, who supported dangerous and radical legislation; to the progressives he was a traitor to the policies of Roosevelt and a tool of the moneyed interests. Concerned over the rising opposition and anxious to consolidate his party before the approaching congressional election, Taft in the spring of 1910 made known that he would no longer refuse patronage to the insurgents. But the olive branch was rejected, and, after the results of the election were known, the insurgents, or the Progressives, as they now began to call themselves, hastened to consolidate their forces. In January, 1911, the National Progressive Republican League was formed at the residence of La Follette; it endorsed progressive measures and criticized the failure of the Taft administration to secure satisfactory legislation on the tariff, trusts, banking, and conservation. Four months later a group of Progressive Republicans met with Senator Bourne of Oregon and decided that they must agree upon one man to oppose Taft. Many at that time assured La Follette that they would support him. The Wisconsin senator easily had the best claims to Progressive support, and in October the National Conference of Progressive Republicans at Chicago endorsed him.

The role of the Progressives in the coming campaign, however, would be largely determined by the attitude of Roosevelt, and many prominent Progressives had withheld their support from La Follette in the hope that Roosevelt would head the movement. Returning from his long African hunting trip in June, 1910, Roosevelt plunged immediately into New York state politics by supporting the Progressive wing of the Republicans in the fall campaign in opposition to the regulars backed by the Taft administration. This, in conjunction with a famous speech on the "new nationalism," delivered in August at Osawatomie, Kansas, placed him unmistakably with the insurgents. There he advocated federal regulation of trusts, tariff revision, conservation, a graduated income tax, direct primaries, recall of elective officers, labor legislation, and an adjustment of state and federal relations that there might be no neutral ground to serve as a refuge for lawbreakers. This position was reiterated in subsequent speeches and in editorials in the *Outlook*.

With Roosevelt now committed to progressivism and with the liberal Republican politicians scenting victory in the air, pressure was brought upon him to seek the presidential nomination. In February, 1912, seven Republican governors issued a statement (prepared by Roosevelt) asserting that the requirements of good government demanded his candidacy. Roosevelt answered a few days later with the statement, "I will accept the nomination for President if it is tendered to me, and I will adhere to this decision until the convention has expressed its preference." This announcement killed the La Follette boom everywhere except in Wisconsin, and Roosevelt embarked upon an aggressive campaign for delegates in those states having presidential preferential primaries. In a spirited campaign he won in all but Massachusetts, Wisconsin, and Georgia, capturing 278 delegates to 68 for Taft and 36 for La Follette. On the basis of this, Roosevelt insisted that he was undeniably the overwhelming choice of the Republican Party, and all reasonable criteria would seem to point that way. The will of the people, if such it was, had little influence upon the convention. By the same steam-roller methods with which Roosevelt had four years earlier secured the nomination of Taft, the latter now crushed the aspirations of Roosevelt. Administration delegates, hand-picked from the South, gave Taft a large nucleus to start with, and the National Committee and the Committee on Credentials saw to it that disputes were decided in favor of the regular Republican machine. When Roosevelt saw that the convention was in the hands of his opponents, he issued a scorching blast and urged his followers to participate no longer in the voting.

Before the convention broke up, Roosevelt was offered by his followers a nomination on a dissenting ticket, and he accepted on condition that a new party be formed. In conformity with this wish, a call was issued for a nominating convention in August. "I feel like a bull moose," said Roosevelt on arriving in Chicago for the convention, and the head of a moose became the symbol of the new Progressive Party. The enthusiasm of the delegates was boundless. "They fully believed," says Stanwood, "that they were entering upon a movement for the regeneration and emancipation of the American people, and the renovation and purification of American life." "We stand at Armageddon, and we battle for the Lord," shouted Roosevelt as he concluded his keynote speech to a convention that in its fervor resembled an old-fashioned religious revival. The vice-presidential nomination went to Hiram Johnson of California.

Laboring under no illusions that they were battling for the Lord, the Democratic politicians in the meantime had foregathered at Baltimore. The schism in the Republican ranks made victory more than likely, and there was no dearth of candidates, particularly from the crop of Democratic govenors elected in 1910. The leading candidates were Champ Clark, Speaker of the sixty-second Congress, and Governor Woodrow Wilson of New Jersey. In the end the nomination went to Wilson on the forty-sixth ballot chiefly because Bryan deserted Clark and supported the New Jersey governor after Tammany Hall had turned to Clark. The nomination for Vice-President went to Thomas R. Marshall of Indiana.

For the average voter 1912 represented a golden era. Reform was in the air. The Democratic platform emphasized tariff revision and control of monopolies but also favored valuation of railroads, currency legislation, anti-injunction laws, and presidential primaries. The Progressive Party had a long list of political and social reforms, which represented the most important of the measures that social and political reformers had evolved during the past decade. More radical than the Progressives were the Socialists, who again nominated Eugene V. Debs. Declaring that "the capitalist system has outgrown its historical function, and has become utterly incapable of meeting the problems now confronting society," and denouncing "this outgrown system as incompetent and corrupt and the source of unspeakable misery and suffering to the whole working class," the platform called for collective ownership of the important means of production and distribution and for a list of reforms during the transition period that included most of those supported by the Progressive Party and many more. Even the Republican platform took on a tinge of liberalism. With platforms of this nature and with three of the four leading candidates crusaders for reform, it appeared for once that the voter could hardly lose. The Republican split threw the election to Wilson with an electoral vote of 435 to 88 for Roosevelt and 8 for Taft.[5] The latter carried only Vermont and Utah. In terms of the popular vote, Wilson was a minority President. There can be no question, however, that the majority of the voters in 1912 desired reform, and in the sense that Wilson was a progressive he represented the popular will.

THE NEW FREEDOM

The new President was born at Staunton, Virginia, in 1856, of "Scotch-Irish" Presbyterian ancestry, and was educated at Princeton and the Johns Hopkins. After a distinguished career as a teacher of political science, as an author of works on American government and history, and as president of Princeton University, he entered politics as governor of New Jersey. Intellectually, his interests were largely limited to government and politics, and his ideas stemmed from the liberal school of nineteenth-century British politics. "He was an orator," says a recent historian, "rather than a thinker, a preacher rather than a philosopher." Nevertheless, he had a penetrating intelligence and an ability to organize his ideas and present them with clarity and smoothness that made him a successful college lecturer and later an excellent political campaigner. Beliefs with Wilson took on the form of moral precepts, and he pursued them with all the stubbornness of his race.

Until 1910 Wilson's knowledge of government was largely academic. Suddenly thrown into the milieu of practical politics, he adapted himself with amazing facility, assumed an undisputed leadership, and successfully drove through a program of reform legislation. His political philosophy, like most of his ideas, was definite enough. He believed thoroughly in

[5] Wilson got 6,293,000 votes; Roosevelt, 4,119,507; Taft 3,484,956; Debs, 901,873; Chapin (Prohibitionist), 207,829; Reimer (Socialist Labor), 29,259.

democracy, in the rule of the people, and in the theory that the chief executive, as the elected representative of the people, was commissioned by them to carry out the program upon which he was elected. It was the business of the executive, like that of a parliamentary prime minister, aggressively to take the responsibility of real leadership. It was only in this way, he believed, that the unofficial leaders or bosses could be eliminated. It was the philosophy of men like Jackson and Roosevelt, and with a conscientious determination he assumed this role. His economic philosophy was that of the classical economists, a philosophy, perhaps, of the classroom rather than of the world as it was. Repudiating the socialist conception of public ownership and little interested in the theory of public control advocated by the Progressives, he would restore the older method of free economic competition. "I am for big business," he said, "but not for the trusts." "American industry," he said again, "is not free, as it once was free; American enterprise is not free; the man with only a little capital is finding it harder to get into the field, more and more impossible to compete with the big fellow. Why? Because the laws of the country do not prevent the strong from crushing the weak." This was the "new freedom" that he emphasized, and, he continued, "We propose to prevent private monopoly by law, to see to it that the methods by which monopolies have been built up are impossible." Today this sounds like the last call of the nineteenth-century economic individualism, and, in pursuit of it, Wilson soon found that laws alone were of little avail. Inevitably he was forced to the method of public control and under the stress of war time to the socialist ideal of government operation and ownership.

Between Cleveland and Wilson sixteen years had elapsed, and during that period the Democrats had maintained an incessant barrage of criticism against successive Republican administrations. It was now inevitable that the legislation that they had advocated would be attempted, particularly with a leader of the type of Wilson. Immediately after inauguration the President called a special session of Congress to revise the tariff, and, breaking the precedent established by Jefferson, he appeared personally before it to urge a vigorous reduction. While suggesting duties on luxuries and on goods not produced in the United States, Wilson urged that the basis of the tariff revision be an equalization of the cost of production in the United States and abroad, which would produce a "competitive tariff." Such a bill, which put iron, steel, raw wool, sugar (the latter in 1916), and certain agricultural products on the free list and made big reductions on manufactured cottons and woolens, but raised the rates on chemicals, had already been prepared. It passed the House overwhelmingly and the Senate by a rather close vote and then only after the President had vigorously rebuked the lobby. While a great majority of the items had been reduced and an honest effort had been made to get away from indiscriminate and wholesale protection to a competitive basis, the Underwood-Simmons tariff of 1913 was still essentially protective. That policy had not been deserted. To compensate for reduced revenues, an income tax, now made legal by the sixteenth amendment, was added. Incomes from $3000 (married men $4000) to $20,000 were taxed 1 per cent, with additional taxes on those from $20,000 to $500,000, after which the rate became 6 per cent. It was thus modestly that the taxation of incomes under the new amendment began.

With the tariff bill well under way, but before it had passed, Wilson again appeared before Congress with plans for a revamping of the banking system. The system of national banks, established during the Civil War (page 357), by introducing safer banking facilities and a standard banknote based on the credit of the federal government, had marked a long step forward. Experience, however, had revealed certain weaknesses, in particular the cumbersome transfer system, the decentralization of credit, and the inelasticity of the banknote issues, dependent as they were on government bonds. These weaknesses were especially evident during the panic of 1907. In the following year the Aldrich-Vreeland Act was passed, which made temporary provision for banking reforms until a more permanent measure could be passed, and the National Monetary Commission was set up to make an intensive study of the banking situation. Both parties in 1912 were committed to some type of banking reform, and the general lines that these reforms would take were already fairly evident.

The consummation of the agitation for banking reform came with the Federal Reserve Act (Owen-Glass Act) of December 23, 1913. While the technical details of the banking structure set up by this act fall in the province of more specialized treatments, it may be noted briefly that the chief defects of the old national-bank system were somewhat alleviated. The country was divided into twelve districts in each of which a federal reserve bank was to be set up and owned by the national banks in the district, which were required to join the system. These federal reserve banks were to do no direct banking with individuals or business houses but to act simply as agents of the member banks of the district, to purchase and sell bills of exchange, grant loans to member banks, issue federal-reserve notes, and perform similar banking operations. To supervise them there was the Federal Reserve Board at Washington consisting of the Secretary of the Treasury, the Comptroller of the Treasury, and six members nominated by the President. Their business was to initiate, unify, and carry out general policies. By this system, it was hoped, greater integration and centralization might be achieved. Under the act two new types of currency were provided: the federal-reserve-bank notes issued, like the old national-bank notes, on the security of government bonds and intended gradually to supplement the national-bank notes and the federal-reserve notes issued on the security of short-term commercial paper. It was these notes that were expected to expand and contract with the needs of business and thus introduce a needed elasticity into the currency system. The structure of the Federal Reserve Board was strongly opposed by the banking industry as subject to political control, but the system as a whole was soon conceded to be a distinct improvement on the old system. Nevertheless, it left much to be desired, and an effort was subsequently made to obviate by legislation defects revealed in the boom years of the twenties and the depression years of the thirties (page 689).

The Underwood-Simmons tariff and the Federal Reserve Act were considered by the President an integral part of his program to achieve the "new freedom." The high tariff was the "mother of trusts," and business, it was believed, had again been brought to a competitive basis. The former national-bank system had tended to give a currency monopoly to the great bankers; this had been remedied by the new banking act. Now came the problem of curbing or destroying industrial monopoly, and this the President believed might be achieved by making the Sherman Act more specific. In consequence, Congress in 1914 passed the Clayton Antitrust Act. It forbade discrimination in price between purchasers when such discrimination lessened competition or tended to create monopoly, and it outlawed the "tying" agreements under which manufacturers sometimes sold to dealers under conditions requiring the latter not to handle the products of competitors. It forbade corporations to acquire stock in another concern if the effect was to lessen competition, and it forbade interlocking directorates in competing concerns doing an interstate business whose capital, surplus, and undivided profits aggregated more than a million and in banks with deposits, surplus, or undivided profits exceeding $5,000,000. Labor unions and farmers' organizations were specifically exempted from prosecution under the antitrust acts.[6] Five days earlier Congress had created the Federal Trade Commission, whose business was to investigate persons and corporations (except banks and interstate carriers) subject to the antitrust laws, make reports to Congress, issue orders to these concerns to desist from illegal practices, and, if necessary, institute court action to enforce the laws. Its functions with reference to business and the antitrust acts were not unlike those of the Interstate Commerce Commission in the early days of that organization.

[6] This was done presumably to enable these groups to deal on more nearly even terms with big business. The exemption was also made because the Sherman Antitrust Act had been used up to this time more effectively against labor unions than against industrial trusts. Likewise, the political strength of workers and farmers undoubtedly played a part.

With the passing of these acts the reform wave that had gathered force for over a decade reached its crest. Before it spent its force, however, it brought other legislation. Acts were passed providing for the development of Alaska, the Newlands Act for arbitration of railway labor disputes, legislation for federal aid in constructing state highways, the creation of federal farm loan banks to improve credit facilities for the farmers, the La Follette Seamen's Act to ensure decent working conditions on American merchant ships, and the enlargement of self-government in Puerto Rico and the Philippines. Some advancement in civil-service reform was taken in 1917 (in part reversed by Harding) when postmasters of the second and third class were put under civil-service examinations. Just how far the reform spirit would have taken the administration if left unhampered no one can say. Unfortunately, foreign complications of a serious nature began early to occupy and increasingly absorb the attention of the administration. First came the troubles with Mexico (page 543), and then in August, 1914, the World War. After 1914 domestic reform assumed a less important place; after our entrance into the war in 1917 it practically ceased.

H. U. Faulkner, *The Quest for Social Justice,* Chap. IV, is a brief survey. Particularly good on the Progressive movement is B. P. DeWitt, *The Progressive Movement,* Chap. I–V. See also F. E. Haynes, *Social Politics in the United States,* Chaps. VIII, IX. On the Taft administration read C. A. Beard, *Contemporary American History,* Chaps. XI, XII, or, a more nearly complete treatment, F. A. Ogg, *National Progress,* Chaps. I–X. On the election of 1912 see James Kerney, *Political Education of Woodrow Wilson,* Chaps. XIV–XVI, and W. E. Dodd, *Woodrow Wilson and His Work,* Chap. V. On Wilson's first administration F. L. Paxson, *Pre-War Years, 1913–1917,* Chaps. I–VIII, is sympathetic to the Wilson administration but is reasonably objective.

Chapter XXXVI

THE WORLD WAR

> *It is not improbable that the only way of maintaining our present preeminent trade position . . . is by declaring war on Germany. . . . If we should adopt this policy, an excellent plan would be for our government to make a large investment in a Franco-British loan. Another plan would be to guarantee such a loan.*
>
> AMBASSADOR WALTER HINES PAGE
> (telegram to Wilson, March 5, 1917)

> *But the right is more precious than peace, and we shall fight for the things which we have always carried nearest our hearts. . . . The world must be made safe for democracy.*
>
> WOODROW WILSON (April 2, 1917)

THE WAR COMES TO EUROPE

To the United States, setting her house in order after a decade of reform agitation, the World War came as a shock. Except among a few students of history and diplomacy, there was slight comprehension of the forces that had impelled the world toward a major tragedy, and the war-time propaganda, which placed upon Germany the entire blame, did little to clarify the issues. Now that two decades have passed, it is possible more accurately to determine the major causes of this great catastrophe. First of all were imperialistic rivalries. As the nations of western Europe became industrialized, they sought an outlet for manufactured goods in the less developed regions of the world. Great Britain had obtained the lion's share, but in the decade after 1870 other nations moved aggressively to obtain what was left. Behind this imperialistic rivalry were France seeking to restore her national spirit after her defeat in 1870; Germany, with an amazing industrial development and with the most powerful army in the world, demanding "a place in the sun"; Russia in search of an ice-free port on the Pacific; and Japan looking for markets to support her teeming population; while smaller nations sought to pick up the crumbs of imperialism let fall from the feast of their more powerful neighbors. In this scramble for markets and territories Africa had been carved up into colonies and protectorates, and there was every indication that the same fate awaited Asia.

While colonial rivalries kept the chancelleries of Europe on the *qui vive* and precipitated numerous diplomatic crises, serious European rivalries were a continuous menace to peace. France had never been reconciled to the separation of Alsace-Lorraine, and the more warlike of her statesmen awaited only the right moment to regain the lost provinces; Russia, without an outlet to the Mediterranean, had her eyes fixed on Constantinople and sought to dominate the Balkans. Italy, since her unification, would extend her boundaries to include Italian-speaking peoples to the north and east; Austria-Hungary, cut off from expansion to the west, looked upon the Balkans as a normal region for expansion and thus came in conflict with Russia. Obviously there was enough tinder here for a dozen conflagrations, and it is amazing that, with the exception of the Balkans, Europe maintained peace over a long period. For this period of peace Germany was primarily responsible. Wedged in between hostile nations and anxious to maintain the *status quo* in Europe, she constructed in 1882 the Triple Alliance with Austria-Hungary and Italy. To protect herself, France achieved an alliance with Russia in the early nineties and a close understanding with Great Britain, while the latter attempted to iron out her conflicting imperialistic rivalries with Russia and Japan.

With Europe indulging in an orgy of militarism, imperialism, and nationalism, it was unlikely that this balance of power could be indefinitely maintained. It was finally upset in the Balkans, where racial hatreds and nationalist strivings were complicated by the conflicting ambitions of Austria and Russia. One of the Serbian intrigues against Austria, encouraged by Russia, came to a head on June 28, 1914, when Archduke Francis Ferdinand, heir to the Austrian throne, was assassinated while visiting the city of Sarajevo in the Austrian province of Bosnia. Given a free hand by Germany, Austria was determined to punish Serbia, and Russia, similarly encouraged by France, mobilized for the defense of her fellow Slavs. Mobilization, in the eyes of Germany, was tantamount to war, and, when Russia refused to order demobilization, Germany declared war (August 1). Two days later she declared war on France, and, when the German army invaded Belgium, Great Britain entered the war (August 4). Before many months all Europe, with the exception of Spain, Holland, Switzerland, Denmark, and the Scandinavian peninsula, was involved. Forsaking the Triple Alliance, Italy remained neutral until 1915, when she joined the Allies, followed by Rumania and Portugal (1916) and Greece (1917).

Turkey (1914) and Bulgaria (1915) were brought into the war on the side of the Central Powers.[1]

WHY WE FOUGHT

Amazed at the blundering diplomacy that had made possible such a war, and confused as to the issues, the United States, following a century-old tradition, took an official position of neutrality. In an appeal to the American people, "drawn from many nations, and chiefly from the nations at war," President Wilson urged neutrality "in fact as well as in name during these days that try men's souls." But the world was too small for this to be more than a pious hope. At least four major influences were at work eventually to break down neutrality: (1) the heterogeneous character of the American population, (2) the increasing economic interest of the United States in the war, (3) the superior propaganda facilities of the allied Powers, and (4) the violations of neutral rights by the belligerents.

Of particular interest to politicians, propagandists, and national leaders was the reaction of the foreign-born population to the war. While the older stock had emanated largely from the British Isles, at least 9,000,000 of the American population had been born in Germany or had one parent born there. About one third of our population was foreign-born or of foreign-born parentage. Upon that group particularly propagandists worked, but in the end the influence of foreign-born groups was of far less importance than other factors in determining the road that the United States was to follow.

Of greater significance was the increasing economic stake of this country in the Allied cause. The most pronounced early effect of the war upon America was a tremendous economic stimulation. This is of particular importance because the nation in the spring and summer of 1913 appeared to be sinking into the downward swing of an economic cycle, a trend that was quickly reversed by the European war. Just as during the Napoleonic wars a hundred years earlier, Europe was too busily engaged in destruction to provide sufficient raw materials, and the United States became a source of all types of commodities, particularly foodstuffs and munitions. The value of wheat exports, for example, rose from $39,000,000 in 1913 to $300,000,000 in 1917 and the value of munition exports from $5,-000,000 to $803,000,000. Production of cotton, foodstuffs, and minerals jumped forward, while the value of the exports of domestic merchandise almost tripled. The excess value of exports over imports for the year ending June 30, 1914, was $435,800,000; for that ending in 1917, $3,567,800,000. All this meant a sudden and widespread prosperity. The United States

[1] Japan, with her eye on German possessions in Asia, declared war on Germany August 23, 1914.

profited enormously during the early years of the war, and her profits came almost entirely from the Allied Powers. As Great Britain tightened the blockade around Germany and extended the contraband list, it became increasingly difficult to export to the Central Powers. While American exports gravitated inevitably to Britain and her allies, these exports, owing to the diminutive size of the American merchant marine and the fact that Germany's great merchant marine had been driven from the seas, were more than ever dependent upon British ships.

In another important way American economic life was changed by the World War and her interests tied more closely with those of the Triple Entente. To finance the large-scale purchases, Europe shipped during the war close to a billion dollars in gold to the United States, and private citizens in Europe disposed of American securities to the value of two billion dollars. When the war broke out, foreign investments in the United States were estimated at over $5,000,000,000, while American investments abroad amounted to at least $2,500,000,000, leaving this country a debtor to Europe by over $2,500,000,000.

Although Secretary of State Bryan held to the view that "money is the worst of all contrabands" and that loans to belligerent powers were "inconsistent with the spirit of neutrality," the administration very early conveyed the impression that it would not oppose short-term credits that American bankers might extend to the belligerents, and a year later (August, 1915) that it would not oppose loans floated here. The charge has often been made that this attitude was influenced by the desire to maintain economic prosperity in the United States, but the position of the administration was perfectly legal and in line with every precedent of international law. Any other position at the time was hardly to be expected.[2] Beginning with the Anglo-French loan in October, 1915, private loans to the Entente Powers were floated here to the extent of some $1,500,000,000. After we entered the war, the United States government extended credits to European governments amounting to over $10,500,000,000. From a debtor nation the United States almost over night emerged as the great creditor nation of the world. It is of more than passing significance that while the Allies floated here $1,500,000,000 in loans, Germany borrowed but $35,000,000, of which only $27,000,000 was outstanding when we entered the war.

While economic interests were tying the United States more closely to the Allied nations, organized propaganda was effectively used. Propa-

[2] The whole attitude of the Wilson administration on the question of war loans was opened up early in 1936 by a Senate committee investigating the munitions industry, headed by Gerald P. Nye. Opposing views may be examined in C. A. Beard, "Solving Domestic Crisis by War," *New Republic,* LXXXVI, No. 111, 127–129 (March 11, 1936), and Newton D. Baker, *Foreign Affairs,* XV, No. 1, 1–86 (October, 1936).

ganda agencies, both of the Triple Entente and of the Central Powers, exerted themselves to the utmost to influence public opinion, but in this the Entente were far more successful. "Entente propaganda in the United States," wrote Professor Hayes, "was even more general than that of the Teutons; it was also more adroit, more sympathetic, and more conformable to American prejudices and American wishes." [3] Above all, it was more successful because Great Britain, through control of the cables and strict censorship, was able to color the news that reached America. Honest, unbiased news largely disappeared from American papers after August, 1914. With this great advantage to start with, propaganda was adroitly pushed through weekly reviews of the war distributed to hundreds of newspapers, moving pictures, articles in newspapers and magazines (written when possible by sympathetic Americans), contacts with influential men in all professions, speeches, debates, and lectures by American citizens—in brief, by every known method of influencing public opinion. While the British talked of saving the world from barbarism and the French played up their contributions to American independence, famous men like James Bryce, highly respected in America, lent their names to the most incredible stories of German atrocities. Against the skillful Allied propaganda the blundering efforts of Germany to subsidize the American press and influence American opinion made little progress and were eventually utterly discredited when, in 1915, President Wilson demanded the recall of the Austrian ambassador, Dumba, and the German attachés, von Papen and Boy-Ed. These men had exceeded their official rights in pushing German interests in war time and were without doubt involved in plots to sabotage the production of munitions for the Allies.

That the presentation of the Entente case was far more efficient than that of the German there can be no question. This does not mean, however, that the United States was thus tricked into the war on one side. It undoubtedly helped to build up sympathy for the Entente Powers and hostility toward Germany, but the continual blunders in the policy of the Central Powers were quite sufficient to accomplish that without other aid. Furthermore, the traditions and culture of the American people were largely based on those of Great Britain; language, literature, and legal and constitutional institutions stemmed from the British Isles. If this country was to enter the war at all—and there were many influences that appeared to be driving her inevitably into that course—the choice she made as to sides was the natural one. Most Americans felt very definitely that they were fighting on the side of civilization and liberal institutions, an attitude enunciated by leaders in all walks of life and an attitude effectively and repeatedly expressed by Woodrow Wilson.

[3] C. J. H. Hayes, *A Brief History of the Great War*, 208.

THE PROBLEM OF NEUTRALITY RIGHTS

While economic interest and effective propaganda provided the background for American sympathy with the Allies, the immediate cause of our participation in the war was the violation of neutral rights by Germany. Until Germany began her submarine warfare, however, the violator of neutral rights was chiefly Great Britain. Whatever existing rules of international law there may have been were speedily disregarded by the British government. By blockading neutral countries and discriminating between neutrals the British navy established an illegal blockade, extended the list of contraband articles to suit her needs, extended the right of search on the high seas, compelled neutral ships to put into British ports for search, tampered with American mail and mail from neutral countries destined for the United States, and refused passage to German exports designed for American industry. The doctrine of the continuous voyage, which the United States had insisted on during the Civil War, was revived and greatly extended.

Against these violations the Department of State vigorously protested, but, as no pressure was brought to bear, with little effect. Answers to American notes were long delayed, and Great Britain refused to yield a point. Failure of the American government to press the case of American rights is not difficult to understand. To some extent it may have been due to the rising pro-Ally sentiment, which would have made it politically inexpedient in view of the coming election. Considering American sympathy toward the Entente and the economic relations with the Allied group, it would have been difficult in any case for the government to push the controversy much farther. Any likelihood that the British government might take American protests seriously was further discountenanced by the pro-Ally sympathies of Secretary of State Lansing and of the President's adviser, Colonel House, and by the United States ambassador to Great Britain, Walter Hines Page, an intense Anglophile who believed Great Britain should be allowed to "save the world" without protest as to her methods.

As in the Napoleonic wars a century earlier, victory in the World War rested upon control of the seas. Unless Germany could break the British blockade and obtain access to neutral goods, her cause was doomed. With her fleet bottled up by the superior English navy, she took the only course open, that of breaking the blockade by submarine warfare. On February 4, 1915, she issued a proclamation that the waters around the British Isles were a "war zone" and threatened to sink at sight "every merchant ship . . . even if it is impossible to avert dangers which threaten the crews and passengers," pointing out that the frail structure of submarines made it impossible to visit and search and to care for the safety of crew and passengers. Refusing to recognize that modern naval warfare modified in any way the international law regarding merchantmen, President Wilson informed the German government that it would be held "to a strict accountability" for any acts jeopardizing the property or lives of American citizens. Despite this warning, the submarine warfare was pushed. The American ship *Gulflight* was torpedoed on May 1 with the loss of two American lives, and on May 7 the British passenger ship *Lusitania* was sunk with the loss of 1198 lives, including 128 Americans. Germany's defense for this act was that the *Lusitania* was armed, carried munitions, and was an auxiliary cruiser of the British navy. These allegations except the one that the ship carried munitions, were not satisfactorily proved and in any case were no extenuation in the mind of Wilson. In the last of three notes (July 21) to the German government, Wilson asserted that a repetition of such an act would be regarded as "deliberately unfriendly," and, when two more American lives were lost by the sinking of the British ship *Arabic* (August 17), Ambassador von Bernstorff pledged (September 1): "Liners will not be sunk by our submarines without warning and without safety of the lives of non-combatants, provided that the liners do not try to escape or offer resistance."

Even after the *Lusitania* incident, desire for war with Germany was not widespread. Bryan resigned from the Department of State rather than sign the last two notes to Germany on the ground that they might lead to war. In Congress Representatives McLemore and Senator Gore introduced resolutions to warn Americans from traveling on armed ships, and it was only after a struggle that Wilson's followers defeated the McLemore resolution and prevented a vote on the Gore resolution. On March 24, 1916, a German submarine torpedoed the French passenger ship *Sussex,* with the loss of three American lives. Wilson issued an ultimatum (April 19) that, unless this type of warfare ceased, diplomatic relations with the German Empire would be severed. When, on May 4, the German government backed down and officially reiterated her former pledge, the danger of immediate war passed.

"HE KEPT US OUT OF WAR"

There is much evidence to point to the fact that Wilson early in 1916 was seriously considering America's entrance into the war on the Entente side, but that he was determined, before any such action, to make an effort to bring about peace. While his confidential agent, Colonel House, sounded out the belligerent governments on the possibilities of a negotiated peace, the presidential campaign approached, pushing all else for the moment into the background. Early in June the Republicans, in an effort to catch both conservatives and progressives, nominated for the presidency Charles Evans Hughes, then Associate Justice of the Supreme Court. His running mate was Fairbanks of Indiana. The Progressive Party again nominated Roosevelt, but the erstwhile Bull Moose leader, insisting that the defeat of Wilson outweighed all other considerations and that Hughes should be supported by all "progressive-minded and patriotic men," declined to run. The Democrats nominated Wilson and Marshall by acclamation.

Essentially, the campaign was dominated by the European situation. The Republican platform denounced the Underwood tariff and the Democratic program of taxation, but it put its chief emphasis upon foreign affairs, bitterly criticizing Wilson's handling of the Mexican situation, stressing military preparedness, and pledging "an honest neutrality between the belligerents." The Democrats, pointing with pride to their domestic legislation and to the maintenance of peace, "stood pat" on their record. As became the "outs," the Republicans attacked Wilson's foreign policy as "shifty" and "vacillating" and made much of his "surrender" to organized labor in September, when, in the face of a nation-wide railroad strike, he urged Congress to pass the Adamson Eight Hour Act. While the Republicans sought to win the ardent pro-Ally Americans by denouncing Wilson's failure to safeguard American lives on the high seas, they also labored among certain "hyphenated" groups who resented Wilson's attitude toward Germany's submarine policy. This effort to "drum up both sides of the street" handicapped their leader, who could not be prodded into definite statements as to whether, for example, he would declare war on Mexico or break off diplomatic relations with Germany. Hughes's failure to meet Hiram Johnson and reconcile the Progressives of California probably cost him that state and with it the election.

While Wilson enunciated his political philosophy to delegations who journeyed to his summer home, Bryan and other orators toured the West, emphasizing above all else the slogan, "He kept us out of war." Wilson's appeal to the progressive voter was undoubtedly greater than that of Hughes, but above all else his victory in 1916 was chiefly due to his maintenance of peace in a world that had gone mad. Although he carried only New Hampshire and Ohio in the northern and eastern industrial states, he won the South, the border states, and all the trans-Mississippi West except South Dakota and Oregon. A majority of the popular vote brought with it also control of both houses of Congress.[4]

---

[4] The electoral vote was 277 to 254 and the popular vote 9,129,000 to 8,538,200. The result was at first uncertain and awaited the returns of California. The Socialist candidate, Allan L. Benson, nominated on a mail referendum, polled a vote of 585,000.

With the election out of the way, Wilson turned to the problem of bringing about peace. His European agents were hopeful in the autumn that a move on his part might result in something tangible, but the President delayed until December 18, when he issued a circular note to the warring nations asking for a statement of their war aims, hoping that this might open the way to peace negotiations. Germany immediately offered to negotiate but did not state her terms until January 29, 1917. Great Britain's demands were submitted on January 10, and on January 22 Wilson in an address to the Senate made a final plea for peace in which he offered certain principles upon which a lasting peace could be effected. These efforts proved of no avail; the Allied governments were now convinced that the war must be fought to a finish, and Germany, on January 31, 1917, announced that on the following day unrestricted submarine warfare would be resumed.[5]

The German announcement was followed four days later by the severance of diplomatic relations. When the President, however, attempted to institute armed neutrality by obtaining a congressional appropriation to arm merchant ships, a filibuster prevented passage of the act. Nevertheless, in an old act the President found authorization for arming American ships. Events during the next two months shifted American opinion sufficiently to make a declaration of war possible. The publication of an intercepted note from the German foreign secretary, Dr. Alfred Zimmermann, to the German ambassador in Mexico aroused great resentment. In case of war between the United States and Germany the ambassador was to induce Mexico to make war upon the United States by the promise of Texas, New Mexico, and Arizona, and to invite the Mexican president to urge Japan to abandon the Allies and form an alliance with Germany. The Russian revolution in March, which overthrew the old autocratic regime and introduced a parliamentary government, aroused the enthusiasm of liberals and won many of them to the idea of intervention on the side of the Allies. Most important, however, was the toll of the German submarines, which during February and March took eight American vessels and forty-eight American lives.

Calling into special session the sixty-fifth Congress, Wilson on April 2, in a memorable address, demanded a declaration of war. "Our motives," he insisted, "will not be revenge or the victorious assertion of the physical might of the nation, but only the vindication of right. . . . The world must be made safe for democracy." The Senate on April 4, by a vote of 86 to 6, declared a state of war existing between the United States

---

[5] Except that one American ship a week plainly marked and carrying no contraband might cross in each direction.

and Germany, and two days later the House concurred by a vote of 373 to 50.[6]

On the part of the masses the declaration of war was greeted with sober resignation rather than with light-hearted enthusiasm. With war a reality, however, the nation girded itself to a mighty effort, which was soon to turn the tide of battle. Allied fortunes in 1917 were at a low ebb. Their financial credit had reached a breaking point, food was becoming scarce, the depredations of German submarines were rapidly depleting the Allied merchant marine, and a defeatist attitude was growing, particularly in France. Russia as a military power had been crushed, and the Central Powers were ready to concentrate their strength upon the western front. German leaders professed to believe that the United States would make no contributions to the Allied cause greater than had already been made, but in this they quite misjudged the potential strength of the nation and the intention of Wilson to use it to the utmost.

Profiting from three years of Allied experience, machinery was quickly set up to co-ordinate resources and speed production of war supplies. The Council of National Defense had already been established in 1916 by act of Congress; it consisted of the Secretaries of War, Navy, Interior, Commerce, and Labor, who were assisted by an advisory council of seven experts and by subordinate committees such as those on shipping, inland waterways, coal-production, aircraft-production, and munitions. To this was added in July, 1917, the War Industries Board to co-operate in regulating and promoting production of war materials along with the distribution of credit, fuel materials, and labor. A few weeks later the War Trade Board was created to supervise commerce and foreign-trade regulations, and, in April, 1918, the War Finance Corporation to distribute credit to war industries. Wide governmental control over production and conservation of food was conferred in August, 1917, by the Food Control Act, which forbade hoarding, willful destruction, and discrimination in sale and distribution and gave the President power to purchase, store, and sell certain commodities and to regulate prices. Under the stimulus of the United States Food Administration, production of food was greatly increased, while domestic consumption of wheat and meat was cut to 70 per cent of normal through the method of wheatless and meatless days and the rationing of such commodities. Under the same act the Fuel Ad-

[6] Diplomatic relations with Austria-Hungary were terminated April 8 but war was not declared until December 7. Diplomatic relations were terminated with Turkey April 20 but war was not declared against either Turkey or Bulgaria.

ministration was set up, which set prices, regulated distribution, and promulgated a program of fuel-conservation.

To speed production and cut domestic consumption was one thing; to transport the products was an even more difficult problem. The elimination of the German merchant marine and the curtailment of Allied shipping had already made clear the inadequacy of the American merchant marine, and Congress in 1916 passed the Ship Purchase Act establishing the United States Shipping Board with power to purchase, lease, build, and operate vessels during and for five years after the war. This was now reorganized (April, 1917) into the United States Emergency Fleet Corporation, which embarked on an immense program of construction. At an expenditure of approximately $1,000,000,000, it not only succeeded in building ships faster than the enemy could destroy them but raised the tonnage of American vessels engaged in foreign trade from 2,191,000 in 1916 to over 11,000,000 in 1921. Under the stimulation of the Emergency Fleet Corporation, the number of shipyards increased from 61 in 1917 to 341 by the end of the war and the number of workmen from 45,000 to 380,000.

On land the problem was not to create transportation facilities but to use better those that existed. The financial condition of American railroads at the outbreak of the war was far from strong. War stimulation brought prosperity in 1915 and 1916, but the added profits were largely negated by rising prices and wage expenditures made necessary by the Adamson Act. Railroad management co-operated wholeheartedly with the government, but the necessity of a central control for more efficient handling of the transportation of materials and troops eventually became so evident that in December, 1917, the President issued a proclamation providing for government operation, and Congress, on March 21, 1918, passed the Railroad Control Act, which stated the terms under which the government operation would be carried on. William G. McAdoo was made director general, rates were raised to bring income in line with rising prices, and regional organizations were established to supplement the work of the central administration.

Mobilization of the labor resources of the nation was effected with remarkable success. Despite the fact that immigration was more than cut in half as a result of the war and that about 4,800,000 men were drawn into the army and navy, production was speeded throughout the entire period of the war. Samuel Gompers and the American Federation of Labor supported the war enthusiastically, removing restrictions and regulations that seemed inimical to efficiency, while the War Labor Board, the War Policies Board, and the Railroad Wage Commission determined government policies regarding hours, wages, and working conditions and did much to iron out industrial disputes and curtail labor disturbances. Although the gap was in part filled by women, who flocked into industry as never before, it was impossible to avoid a shortage of labor. The result was a universal increase in wages, so large in some cases that many workers for the first time perhaps were able to purchase luxuries. To many this seemed preposterous, and the myth of the "silk-shirted worker" grew rapidly. The cost of living, however, increased with wages, and it is doubtful if real wages increased appreciably for most workers during the war.

That the cost of the conflict to the United States would be extremely large was evident enough, for it was clear that this country must finance both herself and the Allies. Including the $10,500,000,000 loaned to the Allied governments, the direct cost of the war was approximately $35,-000,000,000, an amount close to three times the total expenditure of the government during the first hundred years of its existence and over $1,-000,000 an hour for the twenty-five months following the declaration of war. Yet this was raised with comparative ease. About one third was obtained through taxation and the rest by loans. Refusing to raise the rates of the Underwood tariff, the Democratic Congress, beginning with the War Revenue Act (October 3, 1917), increased the rates of the income and inheritance taxes, levied an excess-profits tax on business, increased the excises on tobacco and liquors, levied taxes on instruments, documents, luxuries, amusements, and facilities furnished by public utilities. As a result, the federal income from taxes, which had amounted to $779,000,000 [7] in 1916, was pushed up to $4,648,000,000. Through four "Liberty Loans," and a final "Victory Loan," all of which were heavily oversubscribed, the government raised over $21,435,000,000, while another $1,000,000,000 was added through war saving certificates of five dollars and war saving stamps of twenty-five cents.

On the whole, the success of the government in mobilizing the resources of the nation cannot be questioned. Production of food and munitions of all types was immensely speeded. As a result of the shipbuilding program, half of the American army and all our military supplies were transported on American ships. Whatever criticisms may have been levied against government operation of railroads during war time, the government not only succeeded in its primary object of more efficient transportation of troops and supplies but also spent large sums in improving and modernizing railroad equipment. An intelligent handling of the labor problem brought results, while the financing of the war, although it tended to promote inflation, was phenomenally successful. On the other hand, the program for large-scale aircraft-production was a failure. The American ar-

[7] Fiscal year ending June 30.

tillerymen, likewise, were forced to rely upon French and English guns, and it was not until toward the end of the war that American rifles in sufficient numbers could be produced and shipped abroad for our own troops.

Considering the heterogeneous character of the American people, their dislike of restraint, and the early lack of enthusiasm for entering the war, the skill with which the government throttled opposition, regimented the nation to the task at hand, and whipped up the war spirit was not the least among its triumphs. In this the chief influence was Wilson himself, whose ability to express the war aims in terms of high idealism not only won him the support of his countrymen but made him the spokesman of the Allies. To Wilson it was a "war for humanity," a "war to make the world safe for democracy," "a war to end war"—a conflict not with the German people, but with their autocratic rulers. In the cold disillusionment of postwar perspective, this may sound incredible, but to the people of those days it gave to American participation the atmosphere of a great crusade. In this the President was effectively supported by a large-scale propaganda machine (Committee of Public Information), which distributed posters and literature, fed newspapers with the proper material, and aroused the nation with "four-minute speakers." The Allied propaganda was now given an American slant. To seal the public mind against doubt as to the purpose of the war or the wisdom of the methods by which it was prosecuted, the Espionage Act (June 15, 1917) was passed, imposing severe penalties for advocating treason, for resistance to the laws, for refusal to perform military duty, and for obstructing the draft, and lest any possible obstruction or criticism might escape under this act, the Sedition Act, far wider in scope (May 6, 1918), was passed. Considering the almost negligible opposition to war, once it had been declared, and the whole-hearted co-operation of the nation, the hysterical intensity with which government agencies tracked down suspects and the ruthless severity with which they prosecuted them revealed, to say the least, that war administration and democratic principles are apt to be far apart.[8] In the maze of regulatory war-time boards, commissions, and corporations set up by federal and state governments, Wilson's slogan of the "new freedom" passed into the limbo of forgotten shibboleths, of interest only to historians.

---

[8] Debs, four times candidate for the presidency on the Socialist ticket, was sentenced to ten years in jail for a speech delivered at Canton, Ohio. Congressman Victor Berger was sentenced to twenty years, and his paper, the *Milwaukee Leader,* was denied use of the mails. Conscientious objectors to military service on religious grounds were assigned to noncombatant service or otherwise disposed of. Some 450, who for political or other reasons refused military service, were sentenced to military prisons.

THE WAR COMES TO AMERICA

Twenty-three Months of Tension
(By permission of the *New York Herald-Tribune* and *The New York Times*)

By Oscar Cesare in the New York Evening Post.

"BONDS—WHICH?"

TRIUMPHAL ENTRY INTO NORMALCY

WORLD WAR CARTOONS

THE GREAT CRUSADE

Under the stimulation of the preparedness propaganda, the National Defense Act of 1916 had called for an increase over a period of five years of the regular army to 223,000 and of the National Guard to 450,000. With the advent of war this number was clearly inadequate. The current belief that American participation would be chiefly in the form of financial aid and contribution of war supplies was now quickly dispelled as Entente spokesmen made it clear that exhaustion of Allied man power made necessary a large American army. Although resort to the draft had been taken by both Union and Confederate governments during the Civil War, it was contrary to American tradition and was strongly opposed in Congress. Upon the demand of the administration, however, Congress passed the Selective Service Act (May 18, 1917), making liable to military service all male citizens between twenty-one and thirty years old (with certain exceptions), and subsequent legislation extended the age limits to eighteen and forty-five years inclusive. In June, 9,586,000 were registered before 4557 local boards, and in September the first 500,000 were called. In the meantime, reserve officers had been hurriedly trained, and thirty-two cantonments had been set up to receive the troops. Altogether 24,234,000 were registered, of whom 2,810,296 were called into the service. Including the national army (selective service men), the national guard, the regular army, and the navy, about 4,800,000 men were in uniform during the war. Of the army, 2,086,000 soldiers reached France, and 1,390,000 saw active service at the front. In command of this huge army was General John J. Pershing, who had directed the expedition into Mexico in 1916 and who was dispatched in June, 1917, to establish American headquarters in France.

Better prepared than the army was the navy, which had been continually increased in size and kept at a high state of efficiency since the Spanish-American War. Under the command of Admiral William S. Sims it co-operated with the British navy in blockading Germany, in maintaining a ceaseless war against submarines, and in laying a barrage of 56,000 mines across the North Sea to cut off the emergence of German submarines. Its most valuable work, however, was in conveying merchant vessels and troop ships, and so efficient was this work that not a single American transport was lost on the eastward voyage during the nineteen months of the war.

The first year of American participation was largely devoted to the raising and training of an army for the large-scale operations planned for the spring of 1918. Pershing had no sooner appraised the situation in

France than he recommended an army of 3,000,000 men, one third of which should be ready for the spring offensive. "It is evident," he communicated, "that a force of 1,000,000 men is the smallest unit which in modern war will be a complete, well-balanced and independent fighting unit." Backed to the limit by the administration, Pershing turned a deaf ear to the Allied demands that the American soldiers be distributed among the British and French divisions, and insisted that they operate as a unit. Although Pershing may have been influenced in part by considerations of personal and national prestige, his point of view was probably sound. Breaking up the American forces would have seriously injured their morale, while an integrated and powerful army contributed fundamentally to turning the tide of war.

If the American army was to act as a unit, it must finally be given a sector in which to operate. With the British defending the channel ports and the French defending Paris in the middle section, the Americans quite naturally were assigned to the line in eastern France west of the Vosges. To prepare for such operations was a tremendous task. To avoid taxing the already overcrowded facilities of the northern ports, docks, warehouses, and debarkation camps had to be constructed at Brest and in the more southern harbors of St. Nazaire and Bordeaux; railroad lines must be improved or constructed to maintain an unhindered movement of troops and supplies. Veteran troops had to be retrained in the new type of trench warfare characteristic of the World War, while raw troops must be hardened and trained.

Except for the large-scale preparations being made by the American army, the cause of the Allies never seemed darker than in the spring of 1918. The Russian revolution, followed by the treaty of Brest-Litovsk (December 1, 1917) and the withdrawal of Russia from the war, had released 500,000 German troops for the western front. An Austrian offensive in November had wrecked the Italian army; the French morale was at its low point. Taking advantage of these factors and in the hope that a major offensive might end the war, the Germans launched on March 2 a crashing attack against the British lines north of Amiens. Between that date and July 18, five major assaults drove back the Entente lines, netting 150,000 prisoners and 3000 square miles of territory. The terrific German blows resulted in a unified Allied command under Marshal Ferdinand Foch and a willingness by Pershing to postpone his plan of an American army operating as a unit in its own sector. American troops were rushed to the aid of the French and made important contributions in checking the German advance. In a successful assault in Cantigny (May 28) the First Division demonstrated beyond doubt the fighting qualities of the American soldiers. Relieving a French division northwest of Château-

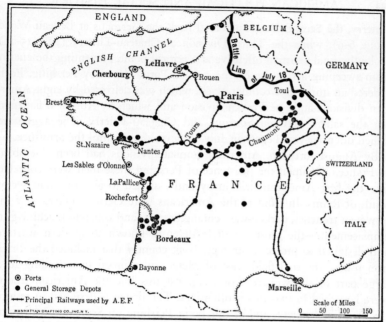

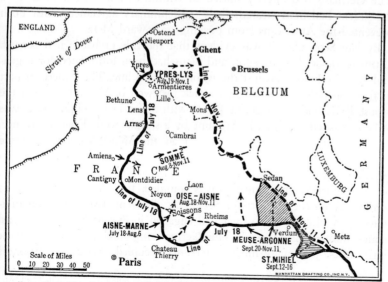

THE AMERICAN ARMY IN FRANCE

Thierry, the Second Division forced back the Germans at Belleau Wood (June 6–9), while the Third Division at Château-Thierry (July 15–18) broke the final German offensive at a critical point, preventing the enemy from sweeping across the Marne toward Paris. Urged by Pershing, Foch ordered an immediate counterattack, which was delivered by eight American divisions and one French division and which by August 6 flattened out the salient between Soissons and Château-Thierry. The aggressive Allied offensive that began on July 18 never ceased until the armistice.

By August forty-five American combat divisions had been assembled in France, and upon the insistence of Pershing these men were collected into the first American field army and assigned to an important sector south of Reims. In front of the Americans were German defenses of interwoven trenches, barbed-wire entanglements, and concrete machine-gun emplacements—the most elaborate defenses known to modern warfare and designed to protect a strategic back country that included the Briey iron mines, the coal fields east of Metz, and railroad lines leading to a large part of the western front. Against this line the American troops were launched in two major offensives. The first was designed to reduce the St. Mihiel salient, and at this point Pershing on September 12 began the attack with some 550,000 Americans supported by 48,000 French colonials and several hundred British and French tanks and airplanes. The Germans had already started to withdraw, and within three days the salient had been cleared. Only a preliminary agreement with Foch prevented the Americans from pushing on toward Metz.

By late September it was evident that the tide of battle had turned. Ultimate victory was in sight, and plans had been formulated for a general Allied offensive against the whole German line. The American part in these operations was to be an attack just west of Verdun between the Meuse River and the Argonne forest, with Sedan as the objective. It was to be supported west of the Argonne by a simultaneous French advance. Along a 24-mile sector, on September 26, the Meuse-Argonne offensive was launched, and continued with but little intermission for forty-seven days. Stiffening German resistance was finally broken down, and, when on November 11 the armistice was sounded, the American army was converging on the outskirts of Sedan. In all twenty-two American divisions numbering 1,200,000 men had engaged in this operation, with casualties numbering 120,000.[9] The German line had been driven back thirty miles, 560 square miles of territory occupied, and 28,000 prisoners

---

[9] In round numbers the American losses in the war were as follows: 49,000 killed in battle; 236,000 wounded; 57,000 dead of disease and 6500 of other causes. Of the 2,086,000 American soldiers who reached Europe, 1,390,000 saw active service at the front. In October they held 101 miles of front, 23 per cent of the Allied line.

taken. In the meantime, the German defense had been cracking along the whole line, and their army was in retreat from the North Sea to the Argonne forest.

Even before the last Allied offensive had started, it was evident to the German government that the cause of the Central Powers was lost. Bulgaria signed an armistice on September 20, and Austria had asked for terms. To propitiate the Allies, the Kaiser had appointed the liberal Prince Maximilian of Baden as chancellor and democratized the government by making the chancellor responsible to the Reichstag. On October 4 the new chancellor communicated to Wilson that his government desired to open peace negotiations on the basis of the Fourteen Points, which Wilson had already proposed in a message to Congress (January 8) as "the only basis of peace." Having convinced himself that the German government was in earnest and that it would accept the terms of an armistice as determined by Allied military command, Wilson turned the correspondence over to the Allied governments on October 23. On November 5 the terms of the armistice were made known: evacuation of all conquered territory, surrender of most of the German navy, surrender of all territory west of the Rhine, with the bridgeheads at Cologne, Coblenz, and Mainz, and the erection of a neutral zone east of the Rhine. By this time revolutions had convulsed Austria-Hungary and were sweeping into Germany. With thrones tottering on all sides and Berlin in the hands of the revolutionists, the Kaiser abdicated (November 9) and the next day fled to Holland. At eleven o'clock on the morning of November 11 Germany accepted the terms of the armistice and the World War came to an end.

THE PEACEMAKERS

Ostensibly the terms of peace were to be based on the famous Fourteen Points, which Wilson had enunciated in his message to Congress. These were: (1) open covenants of peace openly arrived at; (2) freedom of the seas in peace and war except as they "may be closed in whole or in part by international action"; (3) removal of economic barriers between nations; (4) reduction of national armaments; (5) impartial adjustment of territorial claims. The next eight points had to do chiefly with territorial adjustments: (6) evacuation of Russia; (7) evacuation and restoration of Belgium; (8) restoration of France and the return to her of Alsace-Lorraine; (9) readjustment of Italian frontiers along recognized lines of nationality; (10) independent development for the peoples of Austria-Hungary; (11) reconstruction of the Balkan states along racial lines, and access to the sea for Serbia; (12) self-determination for the peoples of the

Turkish Empire; (13) independence for Poland and an outlet to the sea; and (14) a "general association of nations" to be formed, under specific covenants, for the purpose of affording mutual guarantees of political independence and territorial integrity to great and small nations alike."

That the United States might play an important part in the making of peace was undoubtedly one of the impelling reasons behind Wilson's determination to enter the war, and it helps to explain why he threw precedents aside and personally participated in the conferences. In addition to a host of experts who had been working for months on the problem, the President chose as his colleagues on the peace commission Robert Lansing, Secretary of State; Edward M. House, his confidential diplomatic agent; General Tasker H. Bliss, one of the ablest of the American army officers; and Henry White, a Republican who had served in various diplomatic posts.

As the idealistic spokesman of the Allies, Wilson with his Fourteen Points represented the hopes of millions of common men that the world might be reconstructed on a basis of sanity and justice. His arrival in France in December, 1918, was the signal for an outburst of popular enthusiasm such as the world has seldom seen. When the peace conference met a month later, however, the stage was quite different. Instead of "open covenants openly arrived at," the terms of peace were to be made by an inner council of ten—in reality by the representatives of the four important Allied nations: Lloyd George of England, Clemenceau of France, Orlando of Italy, and President Wilson. The Allied representatives had two main objectives—the weakening beyond repair of the military power of Germany and the attainment of various objectives that had been promised in numerous secret treaties. Before hard-bitten politicians demanding revenge and insisting on the commitments of secret treaties, the idealism of the Fourteen Points had little chance. Wilson's great hope was the League of Nations, but on the part of many Allied representatives he found only lukewarm support. In the face of these obstacles and with his prestige somewhat dimmed by the Democratic defeat in the congressional elections of 1918, Wilson was forced time and again to give way. In the end he saved some parts, particularly the League of Nations, and through this medium he hoped that some of the injustices of the treaty might be remedied.

In the famous Hall of Mirrors in the palace of Louis XIV, Germany under protest signed the treaty of Versailles on June 28, 1919. Forced to assume the sole guilt of the war, Germany was required to cede Alsace-Lorraine to France and other territories to Denmark, Belgium, and Poland, to allow Allied occupation of strategic points for fifteen years, to reduce her army to 100,000 men, and over a period of years to pay reparations to the limit of her ability, the amount to be determined each year by the victors. The treaty of Versailles marked the complete military and economic collapse of the German Empire, and it was followed by treaties with other nations that territorially created a new Europe. The treaty of Versailles directly concerned the United States in at least two ways: reparations, of which the United States was entitled to a share and which later were to become entangled in the whole question of war debts, and the League of Nations incorporated as an integral part of the Treaty. It was the question of American adherence to the League that determined in this country the fate of the treaty.

Briefly stated, the purpose of the League of Nations was to prevent war by formulating plans for a general reduction of armament, by providing for machinery for mediation and arbitration, and by obtaining pledges from the members to respect the territorial integrity and political independence of other members of the League and to submit disputes to arbitration. The League was to be conducted through an assembly in which all member nations were to be represented, a council with five permanent members (France, Great Britain, Italy, Japan, and the United States) and four elected, a permanent secretariat at Geneva and the Permanent Court of International Justice (World Court) to arbitrate disputes involving legal rights as distinguished from political interests. The League was the culmination of decades of peace agitation and was considered by its proponents as probably the most valuable result of the war. That the majority of Americans sympathized with its purpose there can be no doubt. On the other hand, there was evident an increasing opposition to America's adherence. Some of it was political, and some was inspired by dislike of the methods by which Wilson was trying to force acceptance, but most of it was an honest opposition to the project. It was argued that the British Empire might dominate the League, that through it the United States might become involved in European wars, and that it was intended to perpetuate the injustices of the Versailles treaty. Above all, however, the fate of the League was determined by the natural reaction that followed the war. The unselfish idealism of war days could hardly last; the great adventure was over, and, the sooner we were separated from the entanglements of Europe, the better.

In the Senate the treaty had a long and stormy career. During the peace conference Wilson had paid a brief visit to America to explain the League to members of Congress; he took back with him, from such men as Root, Taft, and Hughes, suggestions for changes that would better safeguard the interests of the United States and that with some difficulty were incorporated in the covenant. Among these was a recognition of the Monroe Doctrine. When the President finally returned from the conference, he was met by a demand from a group of senators that the League be separated from the treaty and considered after peace had been made. Refusing this, Wilson submitted the treaty to the Senate on July 10, and, when bitter opposition led by Senator Henry Cabot Lodge demanded amendments and reservations, he decided to take the issue directly to the people. A sick man when he started on his trip, Wilson collapsed on September 26 as a result of a paralytic stroke. The Senate, after debating the treaty for weeks, voted fifteen reservations, then voted down the treaty with the reservations (November 19), and some days later defeated it again without reservations. A final effort to pass the treaty in March, 1920, again failed. By a joint resolution Congress then declared the war with Germany at an end, but Wilson vetoed the resolution. The issue was then referred to the electorate in the presidential campaign of 1920. A Republican victory brought a new joint resolution (July, 1921) ending the war, and this was signed by President Harding. Later, separate peace treaties were signed with Germany, Austria, and Hungary and ratified by the Senate.

A brief economic summary is H. U. Faulkner, *American Economic History*, Chap. XXVII, and an excellent general chapter is C. and M. Beard, *The Rise of American Civilization*, Chap. XXVIII. On the causes of American participation, read C. H. Grattan, *Why We Fought*, Chaps. II, III; J. D. Squires, *British Propaganda at Home and in the United States*, Chaps. III, IV; Walter Millis, *Road to War*, Chaps. IX–XII; and C. C. Tansill, *America Goes to War*, Chaps. II–IV. P. W. Slosson, *The Great Crusade and After*, Chaps. I, II, pictures social conditions during the war, and F. L. Paxson, *Pre-War Years*, Chaps. XIII–XXII, is a general history of the years 1913–1917. For the economic side see A. D. Noyes, *War Period of American Finance*, Chaps. II–V, and G. B. Clarkson, *Industrial America in the World War*, Chaps. XII–XXX. A brief picture of the diplomatic relations is in S. F. Bemis, *A Diplomatic History of the United States*, Chap. XXXII, and a more extended treatment is in T. A. Bailey, *A Diplomatic History of the American People*, Chaps. XXXVII–XL. Our part in making the Versailles Treaty is told in T. A. Bailey, *Woodrow Wilson and the Lost Peace*. Also see H. S. Commager, *Documents of American History*, Vol. II, 276–277, 282–285, 290–292, 305–313, 325–326, 329–332, 338–342, 352–353.

A WORLD POWER

Chapter XXXVII

POLITICS AND DIPLOMACY

*America's present need is not heroics but heal-
ing; not nostrums but normalcy; not revolution,
but restoration . . . not surgery but serenity.*

WARREN G. HARDING (1920)

THE RETURN TO NORMALCY

Tired of adventures in Europe and pinched by the postwar economic let-
down, the American people in 1920 were ready for a political change. The
chieftains of the Republican Party knew this well enough, and there was
a mad scramble for the presidential nomination. Of the many candidates,
former Governor Frank O. Lowden of Illinois represented the conservative wing of the party, General Leonard Wood supposedly carried on the
Roosevelt tradition, and Hiram Johnson of California bore the hopes of
the more radical element of the party. By strong and well-financed campaigns a considerable enthusiasm was worked up for Lowden and Wood,
with the result that they appeared at the convention with a voting strength
so nearly equal that neither obtained the nomination. When the party
leaders sensed the deadlock, they turned to Warren Gamaliel Harding,
Senator from Ohio, whose candidacy had been quietly but cleverly pushed
by Harry M. Daugherty. The nomination for the vice-presidency went
to Governor Calvin Coolidge of Massachusetts, whose emphatic telegram
to Gompers at the time of the Boston police strike had served both to
cover up his own equivocal conduct (page 631) and to win him national
fame. The party platform was a wholesale denunciation of Wilson's foreign and domestic policy and at the same time endorsed in perfunctory
fashion conservation, a strong national defense, immigration-restriction, a
protective tariff, and child-labor legislation. Government ownership or
operation of railroads was condemned. Opposed to Wilson's League, the
platform promised an "agreement with the other nations of the world as
shall meet fully the duty of America to civilization and humanity in accordance with American ideals and without surrendering the right of the
American people to exercise its judgment and power in favor of justice
and peace."

With their peace treaty beaten in the Senate and their great leader physically stricken, the Democrats looked forward gloomily to the election. Defending their policies, nevertheless, domestic and foreign, they stood by their guns, promising a continued support of the Democratic tariff, declaring that "labor is not a commodity," endorsing woman suffrage, maternity and infancy pension legislation, a child-labor law, and independence for the Philippines. The treaty of Versailles, including the League, they insisted, ought to be ratified "without reservations which would impair its essential integrity." Except for its plank on foreign affairs, the Democratic platform was obviously more liberal than the party had been during its preceding two years, when the administration had broken strikes and violated civil liberties without hesitation, a fact that many liberals did not forget. Governor James M. Cox of Ohio received the presidential nomination on the forty-fourth ballot and with him Assistant Secretary of the Navy Franklin D. Roosevelt. Of the minor parties should be noted the Socialists, who for the fifth time nominated Eugene V. Debs, then imprisoned in the Atlanta penitentiary for having delivered an antiwar speech, and the Farmer-Laborites, who nominated Parley P. Christensen of Utah and urged public ownership of mines, railroads, and national resources, social legislation, and a lifting of the blockade against Russia.

Indefinite as the Republicans might be with respect to the League, it was obvious enough that the only important issue separating the two parties was their attitude on this problem. But the election did not really swing on this point. The overwhelming vote cast for Harding, suggests one political writer, was in reality a vote against Wilson, already "the symbol both of the war we had begun to think of with disillusion, and of the peace we had come to think of with cynicism." [1] Along with this was the ardent, if futile, hope that we might return to the world of the pre-war era, or, as Harding expressed it, to "normalcy." [2] Harding himself was a small-town newspaper-owner of mediocre talents, a party hack whose career in the Senate had been without distinction. He had neither the understanding nor the quality of leadership necessary to guide the nation through the critical reconstruction period. From one point of view alone could much be said for Harding's fitness; the new President was a handsome, urbane, conscientious, patient, and self-effacing gentleman who exercised a soothing effect upon the frayed-out nerves of the generation of postwar politicians. Republican senators, tired of presidential dictation, had nominated one of their own, a man with whom they could work.

[1] Mark Sullivan, *Our Times,* Vol. VI, p. 111.

[2] The popular vote was: Harding, 16,152,000; Cox, 9,147,000; Debs, 919,800; Christensen, 265,400. Harding received 404 electoral votes to Cox's 127.

The Harding administration will be known in history chiefly for the famous Washington conference on far-eastern affairs (page 642) and for the scandals in various administrative departments of the government. In the latter respect the Harding administration has been correctly likened to that of Grant. In both cases war was followed by a moral debacle, and in both cases political corruption flourished in local and national governments. Typical of the former was the "wide-open" city of Chicago during the administration of William H. Thompson, where "racketeers" and gunmen figuratively held the city by the throat. Reminiscent of the Tweed Ring of the 1860s was the city of New York in the 1920s under Tammany domination. Here the situation became so bad that various investigations were set afoot, culminating in one conducted by a Joint Committee of the State Legislature under the direction of Samuel Seabury. These investigations disclosed a picture of carelessness and corruption permeating the city government from top to bottom; they discovered not a few politicians who had degenerated into a position of little more than errand boys for gangsters and "racketeers," and certain lower courts that had become, as Seabury put it, but a "hideous caricature which parades as justice." When the trail of corruption appeared to lead to Mayor James J. Walker himself the chief executive of the great metropolis resigned rather than face public hearings on his conduct.

As in the Grant administration, the nation was injured by unfortunate appointments to important federal offices. Harding, as a matter of fact, had made a conscientious effort to construct a good cabinet. Except for the inevitable appointments of his campaign manager Harry M. Daugherty to the Department of Justice and of the chairman of the Republican National Committee, Will H. Hays, to be Postmaster General, the cabinet was favorably received. Charles E. Hughes as Secretary of State, Andrew W. Mellon as Secretary of the Treasury, and Herbert Hoover as Secretary of Commerce were considered unusually strong appointments.[3] They turned out to be the men whose policies dominated the decade.

Few men have been more heartlessly betrayed by their friends than Harding. Rumors of corruption in the Veterans' Bureau had led to the ousting of the director, Charles R. Forbes, early in 1923. Later he was indicted and sent to jail, when it was discovered that one fourth of the billion dollars appropriated for veterans had been wasted or stolen during his term in office. Thomas W. Miller, Alien Property Custodian, was later (1927) found guilty of defrauding the government in the sale of alien property and was given a jail sentence, but Daugherty, who was

---

[3] Other cabinet members were J. W. Weeks (Massachusetts), Secretary of War; Edwin Denby (Michigan), Navy; Albert B. Fall (New Mexico), Interior; H. G. Wallace (Iowa), Agriculture; and J. J. Davis (Pennsylvania), Labor.

tried on the same charge, escaped. It was soon believed by those in a position to know that the Prohibition Enforcement Bureau of the Treasury Department was the most corrupt organization in Washington and that large-scale violators of the Volstead Act were frequently given protection by the Department of Justice under the control of Attorney General Daugherty.

Better known, perhaps, because the sorry story was dragged through the courts for years, was the scandal connected with the government oil reserves. By an executive order in 1912 President Taft had created in the Elk Hills district of California an oil reserve for naval emergency, and in 1915 President Wilson had similarly created another naval reserve at Teapot Dome, Wyoming. At the behest of Secretary of the Interior Fall and with the approval of Secretary of the Navy Denby, Harding, in May, 1921, signed an executive order transferring these oil reserves from the Department of the Navy to that of the Interior. It was not long before Fall leased the Elk Hills reserve to his friend, Edward L. Doheny, and in the next year the Teapot Dome field to another friend, Harry F. Sinclair. Suspicion regarding these transactions led to a Senate investigation under the direction of Thomas J. Walsh, to the indictment in 1924 of Fall, Doheny, and Sinclair for bribery and conspiracy to defraud, and to the conclusive proof that Fall had received a "loan" without security or interest of $100,000 from Doheny and larger amounts from Sinclair. These disclosures led to the resignation of Denby, the fine and imprisonment of Fall, and the return of the oil reserves to the United States government, which failed, however, to convict Doheny and Sinclair, the major actors in the drama.

Although the Washington Conference and political corruption may have taken the limelight, it should not be forgotten that the policies of the government for the entire decade were laid down during the Harding administration. The Emergency tariff and the Fordney-McCumber tariff set the nation back on the road to high protection, where it had been before the Democratic interlude. Reduction of taxation, particularly of a type favoring the higher income brackets, and economy in government were constant administration demands. As to allied debts, a policy of wholesale reduction was established, but insistence upon payment of the remainder. For the veterans Congress adopted a policy of care for the disabled, while Harding, Coolidge, and Hoover maintained opposition to a bonus. Price-fixing of agricultural products set up during the war was discontinued, but almost all other types of agricultural aid were favored. The long fight for adequate immigration restrictions culminated in the quota system. Real efforts were made to restore the merchant marine to private control, while aid to interstate road building was continued. It is true that these domestic economic policies were formulated by Hoover and Mellon just as our foreign policies were those of Hughes. Nevertheless, Harding loyally supported them.

Worn out by two and a half years in office and harassed by betrayals of many of his friends, well known to insiders but not yet disclosed to the public, Harding suddenly passed away in San Francisco on August 2, 1923. Before daybreak the next morning Calvin Coolidge was sworn into office by his father, a notary public, at the family farmhouse in Plymouth, Vermont.

THE COOLIDGE ERA

Even more than his predecessor, Coolidge was the product of machine politics. A native of Vermont and a graduate of Amherst, Coolidge had studied law in Northampton, Massachusetts, but in lieu of legal practice had sought a career in politics. By closely adhering to the dictates of the machine, he had pushed his way up through local and state politics to find himself governor of the state in 1919. His opportunity came in September of that year at the time of the Boston police strike. Avoiding any action that might have prevented the strike, he remained in the background until the critical stage was over; then he dramatically ordered the state militia into Boston and sent to Gompers his telegram, "there is no right to strike against the public safety by anybody, anywhere, any time." The police strike made Coolidge Vice-President.

A tight-lipped and tight-fisted Yankee, Calvin Coolidge connoted in the minds of many the homely virtues of thrift and industry that a spendthrift age liked to remember but not to practice. Quite as much the representative of big business as Harding, the new President could be depended on to run the government cheaply, while big business without fear of interference could indulge in the most amazing spectacle of high-handed speculation and ruthless economic exploitation that the nation had ever experienced. Above all, by again introducing into the federal government an atmosphere of cautious respectability, the Republican Party was able to recover somewhat its standing among those who had looked askance upon the free and easy ways of the Harding years. The period of the Coolidge administration was one of almost uninterrupted prosperity. The public debt declined by a third, the standard of living rose, and optimism reigned. In such an era there was little for the politician to do but sit tight and ride his luck. This was the policy of Coolidge.

The new President began, however, by offering to Congress in December, 1923, a program of legislation bequeathed to him by his predecessor. This program Congress ignored but passed instead a Civil War pension and a World War bonus bill. The bonus bill, which provided for adjusted service certificates in the form of twenty-year endowment policies based on length of service, was vetoed by Coolidge but immediately passed over his veto. Except for the bonus, the main business of the sixty-eighth Congress was investigating the scandals of the Harding administration, which was but one way, as far as the Democrats were concerned, of preparing for the coming campaign. The failure of Congress to pass legislation sponsored by the administration and its keen interest in investigating corruption in the administration were due in part to the strong block of progressives in both houses, who frequently combined with the Democrats to outnumber the administration forces. For the coming campaign the Republican position was slightly improved by the resignation in March, 1924, of Denby and the elimination of Daugherty.

There was little in the Republican convention to indicate a lively campaign. Except for a few cast for La Follette and Hiram Johnson, Coolidge received all the votes and was nominated on the first ballot. The vice-presidential nomination was offered to Lowden and upon his refusal was given to Charles G. Dawes, a Chicago banker and politician who had recently become famous in international finance as the chairman of the reparations committee that had suggested the so-called "Dawes plan" (page 645). The Republican platform stressed economy, tax-reduction, a high tariff, a strong merchant marine, liberality to veterans, and aid to agriculture, and favored the World Court and limitation of armaments. When, the day after the convention adjourned, Senator La Follette declared that the Republican Party had turned its back upon the farmer, there were not a few who interpreted this statement of the veteran liberal as more than a gesture.

The Democrats found it extremely difficult to agree either upon a set of principles or upon a candidate. A resolution condemning the Ku Klux Klan was defeated by a small majority, but a strong plank endorsing the League was overwhelmingly beaten. Embittered by long conflict over these two issues, the voting on candidates continued for 103 ballots before a choice could be made. The candidates with the greatest strength were William G. McAdoo, son-in-law of Wilson and upholder of his policies, supported by the drys, the Protestants, and the rural democracy; Governor Alfred E. Smith of New York, Catholic, wet, and representative of the urban democracy; and Senator Oscar W. Underwood of Alabama, representative of the best traditions of Southern politics. McAdoo and Smith fought each other to a standstill, and the nomination finally went to a compromise candidate, John W. Davis, a native of West Virginia but at the time a Wall Street lawyer who favored joining the League and enforcing the eighteenth amendment. With him was nominated a liberal Westerner, Governor Charles Bryan of Nebraska, brother of William J. Bryan. The platform quite naturally bore down heavily upon the scandals and corruption of Republican rule and stressed a scientific tariff and tax-reduction. Looking toward labor, the Democratic Party asserted again that "labor is not a commodity" and, with its eye upon the agricultural vote, demanded an improvement in the condition of the farmers, condemned monopolies, urged readjustments of railway rates on heavy commodities, particularly agricultural, and endorsed the immediate operation of Muscle Shoals at full capacity and the construction of deep waterways from the Great Lakes to the Gulf and to the Atlantic. While favoring the ideals of the League, the platform suggested that the question of entrance be submitted to a referendum.

What might have been an utterly lifeless campaign was given some spirit by the entrance of a Progressive Party under the leadership of the veteran liberal, Robert La Follette. The failure of agriculture to recover after the depression of 1920–1921 had again put the western farmer in a fighting mood, while organized labor, disillusioned by the indifference, if not hostility, of the federal government, was seeking a method of fighting back. Building on the discontent of farmer and laborer, the Conference for Progressive Political Action met early in 1922 to plan for action. At a fourth meeting, in July, 1924, it offered to nominate La Follette on his own platform. The Wisconsin senator accepted, chose as his running mate Senator Burton K. Wheeler (Democrat) of Montana, and wrote the platform. The latter was a typical liberal document of the Roosevelt-La Follette era, dominated by the fear of monopoly and filled with promises of many excellent reforms. "The great issue before the American people today," it said, "is the control of government and industry by private monopoly." Perhaps the two most interesting changes it advocated were public ownership of railroads and abolition of the right of the Supreme Court to nullify acts of Congress.

The La Follette ticket was sponsored not only by the railroad brotherhoods but also by the executive council of the American Federation of Labor. For the first and only time in its history the A. F. of L. officially endorsed a presidential candidate, an action motivated by La Follette's attractive labor record as well as by the growing discontent among the ranks of labor. The Socialist Party, weakened by the withdrawal of the right wing during the war and of the left wing in the postwar years, and hoping that this effort might mean the origin of an American Labor party, also backed the La Follette ticket. Endorsed also by the Farmer-Labor Party, the Progressive movement of 1924 seemed to have a sound foundation for a powerful liberal party. Despite an active canvass, however, its campaign failed to catch the imagination of the voter. Obviously there was little to choose between the platforms or the political philosophies of the candidates of the two major parties; between them there were no real issues. The Progressives, nevertheless, handicapped by a rising prosperity and sabotaged by labor leaders affiliated with the old parties, had little chance. Coolidge's strength in the eastern and middle-western states gave him an easy victory; Davis carried only the solid South and Oklahoma. La Follette captured the electoral vote of Wisconsin alone, but ran ahead of Davis in eleven western and far-western states.[4]

The next four years, 1925–1929, will go down in history as a period of remarkable economic activity (which was generally considered prosperity) reflected in practically every phase of production except agriculture and a few industries, such as coal and textiles, where specific conditions had brought overproduction. Under such conditions little that was new in legislative policy was likely to develop. The Republicans "stood pat" on immigration-restriction, tax-reduction, mild enforcement of prohibition, and refusal to join the League or the World Court. Quite willing to favor farming constituencies by "conservative" agricultural relief, the administration refused to countenance "radical" reform, which might involve price-fixing, and Coolidge twice vetoed McNary-Haugen bills with scathing denunciations (page 685). Throughout its career the Coolidge administration stressed (if it did not always practice) government economy and succeeded in substantially reducing the debt.

Failure to enact outstanding legislation was not due to the prevailing prosperity alone; the political complexion of Congress was in part responsible. The sixty-ninth Congress elected in 1924 had given the Republicans a large majority in both houses, but in the dominant party were many younger progressives upon whom party loyalty rested lightly. The elections of 1926 eliminated the old-guard majority in the Senate, giving the insurgents the balance of power. As a consequence, the La Follette insurgents, who had been read out of the party in 1924, were now welcomed back, but it made little difference in the general situation. Throughout the twenties the two major parties showed very slight differences, and the votes in Congress tended to be dominated by geographic and economic influences rather than by party policy or principles, a tendency that was climaxed in the next presidential election by the break-up of the solid South. For the moment it appeared as if the Democratic Party had forsaken its historic role as an opposition party.

The great vogue that Coolidge enjoyed throughout the country, however, did not extend to Congress. His program of legislation was ignored, and Congress, without leadership from the administration, went its own way. In unprecedented fashion it even turned down a cabinet appoint-

[4] The popular vote was 15,725,000 for Coolidge; 8,386,500 for Davis; and 4,822,900 for La Follette. Of the electoral vote Coolidge obtained 382, Davis 136, and La Follette 13.

ment.[5] Old leaders were passing away,[6] and a younger school of politicians not yet broken to political subserviency had taken their places. Under the circumstances Coolidge stood by and allowed the governmental machine to proceed under its own momentum.

Despite his unimpressive record and the fact that he had served six years, Coolidge in all probability could have obtained the presidential nomination again in 1928. His intentions he kept to himself until August, 1927, when he issued to the press the brief statement, "I do not choose to run for President in 1928." His silence had held back other candidates, but the door was now open, and numerous politicians entered the lists. Before the preprimary campaign was well under way it was evident that Herbert Hoover, Secretary of Commerce under two administrations and opponent of the McNary-Haugen bills, was the leading candidate. His only real opponent was ex-Governor Lowden, whose endorsement of the McNary-Haugen legislation won him some support in the agricultural states. Lowden's best efforts, however, failed to prevent the nomination of Hoover on the first ballot. Senator Charles Curtis of Kansas was nominated for the vice-presidency. The Republican platform consisted mainly of praise of the domestic and foreign policy of the Coolidge administration interspersed with noncommittal or indefinite statements regarding serious domestic problems. While pledging the party to none of the congressional schemes of agricultural aid, the platform recounted Republican legislation designed to aid distressed agriculture and promised more of the same type.

The Democratic nomination was as much of a foregone conclusion as had been that of the Republican Party. Animosities engendered by the 1924 convention had subsided, while the reputation of Alfred E. Smith, governor of New York, had grown. Following a terrific arraignment of Republican corruption in the keynote speech of Claude G. Bowers, the convention nominated Smith on the first ballot, with Senator Joseph T. Robinson of Arkansas to run with him. Except for the denunciation of Republican policies, the Democratic platform differed little from that of their opponents and was even less forthright. Like the Republican, it promised enforcement of the eighteenth amendment and agricultural reform, but proposals for the latter were almost as indefinite as those of the Republicans. On tariff it promised adequate protection based on "actual differences between

[5] This was the appointment of Charles B. Warren to be Attorney General after Harlan F. Stone had been appointed to the Supreme Court. The failure of Warren to receive ratification brought to the post John G. Sargent of Vermont. Gradually the Harding cabinet changed. Hughes resigned from the Department of State and was followed by Frank B. Kellogg; the death of H. G. Wallace brought William M. Jardine to the Department of Agriculture; the resignation of Weeks from the War Department was followed by the appointment of Dwight F. Davis; Curtis D. Wilbur followed Denby in the Navy.

[6] For example, Lodge and Wilson died in 1924, Bryan, La Follette, Cannon, and Cummins in 1925.

the cost of production at home and abroad, with adequate safeguard for the wage of the American laborer," whatever all that may have meant.

The lack of difference between the two major parties was even more evident as the campaign progressed and as the Democrats insisted that they intended no revolutionary change in the tariff. On prohibition both parties promised enforcement. In foreign relations the Republicans appealed to internationalists by promising adherence to the World Court, while the Democrats, anxious not to antagonize those opposed to adherence to the League, suggested that the issue be referred to the people. The death of La Follette, the withdrawal of labor and Socialist support, and above all the general prosperity had smashed the Progressive Party. The Socialists nominated Norman Thomas, a former Presbyterian minister and a brilliant journalist and orator, and the Workers Party (Communist) nominated William Z. Foster, leader of the famous steel strike of 1919, but neither candidate made much impression in the boom months of 1928. Except for the utterly different types of personality represented by the two major candidates, there would have been little reason for the campaign.

Born on an Iowa farm and orphaned in his youth, Hoover graduated from Stanford University and rapidly accumulated a fortune as a mining engineer and financial promoter. He had become famous during the war as head of the Belgian relief work and had served eight years as Secretary of Commerce. An efficient administrator, he was without experience or ability in politics. His economic and political philosophy was that of the Manchester liberals of a century earlier, modified slightly to meet the ideas of industrial and financial imperialists. His opponent, on the contrary, had had little formal schooling and was provincial in his experience. Sprung from the "Sidewalks of New York" and favorite of Tammany Hall, Smith had had an almost entirely political career, culminating in four terms as governor of New York. Realistic in his politics and warmly personal in his approach, Smith was unsurpassed in his knowledge of the machinery of American government and in his ability to handle political friends and foes. His economics was that of a mild liberal. Personally he was "wet" and a Catholic.

Although there was little difference in the official position of the two major parties, there was considerable conflict within the ranks of both. It is not surprising that under the circumstances the election turned upon the divergent views and personalities of the candidates. Smith, repudiating his party platform on prohibition, urged referring the question to the states, and persistently hammered at the Republican Party for its corruption, its failure to develop a program for farm relief, and its inactivity in the face of the rapidly growing menace of public-utility monopoly. The Republican candidate accepted prohibition as "a great social and economic experiment, noble in motive and far reaching in purpose," and based his campaign chiefly on the policy of continuing Coolidge prosperity. "The slogan of progress," said Hoover, "is changing from the full dinner pail to the full garage." Smith's religion and his stand on prohibition weakened him badly in the rural South and West and account for the fact that for the first time since the Civil War the "solid South" was completely smashed.[7] He carried but eight states, Arkansas, Louisiana, Mississippi, Alabama, Georgia, South Carolina, Massachusetts, and Rhode Island.[8] This overwhelming presidential victory was carried over into the seventy-first Congress, where the Republicans secured a large majority in both houses.

Blessed by an extraordinary prosperity and favored by an overwhelming majority in Congress, Hoover began his administration under the most auspicious circumstances.[9] If "the engineer in politics," however, had any idea that the general government was to proceed in the smooth, cold, and scientific manner in which the Department of Commerce had functioned during his administration, he was doomed to speedy disillusionment. Calling his Congress into special session, he pointed out the need of "legislation to effect further agricultural relief and legislation for limited changes in the tariff." After fighting for weeks with Congress over the type of farm relief, he finally signed, in June, 1929, the Agricultural Marketing Act, after the debenture scheme and other "radical" innovations had been deleted (page 685). Hoover's recommendation of tariff-revision, which appears to have emanated chiefly from concern over the plight of agriculture, ran an even stormier course, finally resulting in a new tariff in June, 1930, which passed the Senate by a margin of two votes. By that time its original purpose, if it had any, had been largely lost sight of, and its increased duties on manufactured goods brought the active opposition of the progressive bloc of senators from the farm states, who voted against it. On the ground that a raising of the tariff would further curtail a declining foreign commerce, over a thousand economists urged the President to veto the bill, but without avail. The Hawley-Smoot tariff, which marked the apex of American protectionism, was probably as unwise and inopportune as the economists had asserted; at any rate, it apparently did nothing to improve the economic situation (page 684).

Whether the Agricultural Marketing Act or the Hawley-Smoot tariff

[7] Harding carried Tennessee in 1920.

[8] The popular vote was: Hoover, 21,385,000; Smith, 14,981,000; Thomas, 267,800; Foster, 48,000. The electoral vote was 444 to 87.

[9] Of the earlier cabinet, Hoover kept Andrew W. Mellon in the Treasury and James J. Davis in the Department of Labor. Excepting Henry L. Stimson, Secretary of State, the rest of the cabinet were hardly known and were essentially political appointees. Mellon retired from the Treasury in February, 1932, and was sent as ambassador to Great Britain. He was succeeded by Ogden L. Mills.

had anything constructive to contribute to American economic life, it is impossible to tell. The administration of Hoover, like that of Van Buren a century earlier, was dominated by one factor, the economic collapse that descended upon the nation in September of 1929, a preliminary to years of depression. If the administration expected that either piece of legislation would soften the blow, it was disappointed. In the last two years of the Hoover administration some legislation was pushed through to ease the economic distress. The most important was the act of January, 1932, creating the Reconstruction Finance Corporation with a capital of $500,-000,000 and power to incur debts to three times that amount. Designed originally to render aid in financing agriculture, commerce, and industry, its scope was soon enlarged to authorize the loan of large amounts to states, cities, and other governmental agencies for self-liquidating public projects and direct relief. The Republican method under Hoover seemed designed to help big business at the top in the hope that such aid would stimulate better conditions and that prosperity would trickle down to the masses. This legislation failed utterly to stay the depression, and the administration, which had begun under sunny skies, ended in the most terrific economic storm that had yet rocked the nation.

In the meantime, Hoover had taken the first steps toward a more nearly adequate enforcement of the laws by appointing in 1929 the National Law Enforcement Commission headed by George W. Wickersham. To first survey the field in a scientific manner was an excellent procedure, but it was of little avail if the findings were not used. When the administration discovered that the commission questioned certain aspects of prohibition enforcement, the report was ignored. As the depression got under way, the progressive Republicans became even more hostile toward Hoover than toward Coolidge. This antagonism came to a head early in 1930, when Charles Evans Hughes was nominated to the office of Chief Justice of the Supreme Court to succeed William H. Taft. In the minds of progressives Hughes's affiliations with large corporations hardly fitted him for such a position, but they could not prevent confirmation. They were more successful, however, in rejecting a certain North Carolina judge noted for his anti-Negro and antilabor bias, who had been nominated to the Supreme Court to succeed Edward T. Sanford. A much better nomination, that of Owen J. Roberts of Philadelphia, was confirmed.[10] Congress, it was clear, had become restless long before the campaign of 1930 changed the situation. Only one American President, James Monroe, ever survived politically a real business depression, and Monroe was probably saved by

[10] On January 12, 1932, the great liberal jurist, Oliver Wendell Holmes, resigned at the age of 90. His successor, Benjamin N. Cardozo of New York, one of Hoover's best appointments, was confirmed without opposition.

the fact that no strong political party existed to oppose him. Hoover was no exception to the rule. The congressional elections of 1930 turned the weak minority of House Democrats into a majority and in the Senate left the Republicans with the slimmest kind of majority. Under such conditions not much legislation of importance was likely to take form.

The depression was already three years old when the presidential campaign approached, with nothing in sight that might dispel the economic gloom. Under the circumstances the Republican Party was decidedly on the defensive. Little opposition to Hoover developed in the primaries, and, when the convention assembled, he was nominated on the first ballot. Any other course would have been a repudiation of his administration. Among the Democrats a more spirited contest developed. Smith was anxious to run again, and the Speaker of the House, John N. Garner, the candidate of the Hearst press and the McAdoo faction, had strong backing. The leading candidate, however, was Franklin Delano Roosevelt, governor of New York, a liberal Democrat of the Smith type but without the handicaps that made Smith's candidacy four years earlier so unpopular. He received the nomination on the fourth ballot after McAdoo and Hearst switched their support to him, and Garner was chosen to run with him. Hopeful that the faith of the American workers in the beneficence of capitalism might be shaken after three years of suffering, the Socialists again nominated Norman Thomas. The Communists nominated William Z. Foster, and the Prohibitionists, sensing the impending doom of the "noble experiment," also chose candidates.

As in all the campaigns since the World War, the platforms of the two major parties were much alike. The chief differences were in the length of the documents and the method of handling prohibition. The Democrats, calling their platform "a covenant with the people," compressed their oft-times meaningless phrases into some 1400 words; the brevity of the document made it likely that a fair proportion of the voters would read it. Regarding prohibition, both parties saw the handwriting on the wall; the Democrats declared flatly for repeal of the eighteenth amendment and the Republicans for its revision. The Democratic plank seemed more definite and forthright, but actually both pointed to the same objective, control returned to the states with federal protection for those states that desired to remain dry. Both piously objected to a return of the saloon.

Actually, the campaign was dominated by one fundamental factor—the depression. The tactics of Hoover and his lieutenants were to convince the voters that the Republicans had accomplished all that could be safely done and that a Democratic victory would mean only a greater economic collapse. Roosevelt, in a series of speeches, gave his views, usually in general terms, on important economic problems of the day, always conveying the impression that existing economic policies needed changing and that a change would bring economic improvement. Political prognosticators and straw votes foretold the final result. Hoover, who had carried forty states in 1928, captured only six in 1932, with 59 electoral votes. Roosevelt carried 42 states with 472 electoral votes.[11] As overwhelmingly victorious were the Democrats in the congressional and state elections. Twenty-nine of the thirty-four governors-elect belonged to that party and twenty-eight of the thirty-five Senators-elect. In the House, with 313 seats, they held an overwhelming majority. For the first time since the sixty-fifth Congress (1917–1919), the Democratic Party had control of both the legislative and the executive branch. If they possessed any real program to meet a major economic catastrophe, their opportunity had come.

CROSS CURRENTS IN DIPLOMACY

The repudiation of the League of Nations by the American people in the campaign of 1920 was a clear indication of their desire to return to an earlier policy of isolation in matters of foreign policy. Understandable as this reaction was, such a policy was becoming increasingly difficult as American economic interests developed in other parts of the world. It is now quite apparent that one of the important influences of the World War upon American development was the impetus that it gave to American economic imperialism. Until 1914 the United States had been a debtor nation; her economic development had in part been financed with a continued flow of investment funds from Europe. In that year foreign investments in this country were estimated at between four and five billion dollars. The situation, however, was beginning to change. By the opening of the century American capital was seeking investment abroad (page 517), and by 1914 estimates put American foreign investments at around $2,500,-000,000. The United States was still a debtor nation to the amount of between $2,500,000,000 and $3,000,000,000, but this condition was quickly changed by the European war. Pressed for funds, Europeans dumped American investments to the amount of $2,000,000,000 on the market, while European governments succeeded in floating loans to the amount of $1,500,-000,000. In addition to these were the loans amounting to approximately $10,350,000,000 that the United States government made to the Allied governments during the war or shortly thereafter.

In brief, the World War quickly changed the United States from a debtor nation to a creditor nation. Economically exhausted by the war, Europe relinquished to the United States her position as the source of

[11] Of the popular votes Roosevelt secured approximately 22,800,000; Hoover 15,760,000; and Thomas, 880,000.

world capital, and during the twenties the United States was called upon to finance the economic reconstruction of Europe as well as to provide capital for other parts of the world. As a result, American investments abroad by the early thirties had piled up to the astounding figure of around $18,000,000,000, in addition to the government loans already mentioned. Significant also is the fact that only half of this money loaned abroad was in the form of public and private securities. The other half was in "direct investments" made by American corporations in industrial, mining, public utility, agricultural, petroleum, and other economic enterprises. A good proportion of this investment had been stimulated by the desire of American manufacturers to avoid the high tariff walls of the postwar period. A part of it represented wealth accruing to Americans through a favorable balance of trade that had been left in Europe. Along with all this was a rapid development of foreign commerce, which was four and a half times as great in 1929 as in 1900.

Rapid expansion of foreign investment was bound inevitably to have its effect upon American foreign policy. Primarily, its influence was to modify or soften the policy of isolation that had dominated the attitude of the American people since the days of Washington and Jefferson. Support for this changing policy came on the one hand from internationalists of various types, liberals and idealists anxious to eliminate friction and prevent war, and on the other from the bankers who wanted protection for invested funds and an opportunity for foreign nations to pay their debts. Some support also came from industrialists eager to extend their markets and from farmers anxious to regain markets that had been lost. In any case, there was a shift in policy during the twenties amounting almost to a "diplomatic revolution." Superficially, the postwar years appear to be characterized by a reactionary nationalism without parallel in our history; actually, the United States was making real progress in breaking down its policy of isolation.

In illustration of this changing policy one may call in review almost every phase of postwar diplomacy. Although the American people repudiated in 1920 the League of Nations and Harding called it "as dead as slavery," the United States participated officially or unofficially in so many of the League's activities that it was suggested that this country was sneaking into the League by the back door. By 1930 the United States had taken part in more than forty League conferences, all presumably nonpolitical. The United States did not join the World Court, but all administrations since Wilson, both Republican and Democratic, have favored such action.[12] The Senate went so far as to vote favorably upon adherence to the

---

[12] Several distinguished American citizens have served, nevertheless, as judges of the World Court—John Bassett Moore, Charles Evans Hughes, Frank B. Kellogg, and Manley O. Hudson.

court, but with five reservations. The other members of the court were willing to accept four of the reservations, but the United States, nevertheless, did not join. In 1919 the statutes of the World Court were so amended as to meet all objections of the United States, but up to 1935 no further action by this country was taken. In January of that year—and after the Senate Foreign Relations Committee had favorably reported it—a bill favoring American participation in the World Court was rejected by the Senate.

Although the United States did not join either the League or the World Court, its influence was exerted toward peace. This is evident, for example, in the Briand-Kellogg pact. In 1927, on the tenth anniversary of America's entry into the World War, Aristide Briand suggested that France and the United States join in an agreement to outlaw war in any disputes that might arise in the future between the two nations. Urged on by peace advocates in this country, Secretary of State Kellogg not only accepted the idea but suggested that other nations be invited formally to renounce war and sign a general multilateral treaty. The result was that the United States and fourteen other nations, in 1928, signed such a treaty condemning recourse to war for the solution of international controversies, renouncing it as an instrument of national policy, and agreeing that the settlement or solution of all disputes shall never be sought except by pacific means. Later most of the nations of the world subscribed to the pact. It was a gesture in the right direction, but, unfortunately, as Kellogg suggested, "the only enforcement behind the pact is the public opinion of the people."

In another way the United States made an effort, at least, to contribute to world peace. Whatever stability there may have been in the Far East had been completely upset by the World War. Furthermore, the aggressive imperialism of Japan was endangering the open-door policy of the United States and creating an international situation of extreme delicacy. In the hope of stabilizing conditions in the Far East and of making some contribution to the ideal of world peace, President Harding, under the whip of a Senate resolution proposed by Borah, extended in the summer of 1921 invitations to Great Britain, France, Italy, and Japan for a conference at Washington to discuss limitations of armaments,[13] and to Belgium, Holland, Portugal, and China, along with the powers first named, to discuss the problem of the Pacific and the Far East. On both of these problems something, at least for the moment, was accomplished. The five great nations agreed to scrap capital ships beyond a certain number and

---

[13] It was not inappropriate for the United States to make this move toward a reduction of armament, for American navalism, as seen in increasing naval armaments, had been a constant factor in this country for half a century.

for a period of ten years to renew their capital ships on a specified ratio of 5-5-3-1⅔-1⅔; that is, Great Britain and the United States were each to have 525,000 tons; Japan 315,000; France and Italy each 175,000. Unfortunately, no agreement could be reached on cruisers, destroyers, submarines, and other auxiliary craft. Discussion of the Far Eastern situation resulted in several treaties. One of them was a four-power treaty signed by the United States, Great Britain, Japan, and France—significant because it ended the old British-Japanese alliance—by which each nation agreed to respect the rights of the others in their insular possessions in the Pacific and to submit all controversies to diplomacy. Another treaty, signed by all nine powers, promised to respect the territorial integrity of China and the open door. The same powers signed another treaty, establishing the principles of China's control over her own tariff, while, in a special treaty between China and Japan, the latter agreed to turn over to China the former German rights in the Shantung peninsula.

The Washington conference was hailed as a great milestone on the way to peace. It appeared to have halted the race of Naval armaments and to have thwarted Japanese ambitions to dominate the Far East. How weak was the structure set up by the Washington Conference, however, was soon apparent. First of all it failed to establish a ratio for auxiliary ships, and there ensued a race between the powers to strengthen these branches. The result was President Coolidge's invitation to the four great powers, in 1927, to another conference to widen the scope of limitations. As only Japan and Great Britain accepted, the resulting conference at Geneva failed to accomplish anything. Two years later Great Britain took the initiative and invited the signatories of the Washington treaty to meet at London. At the London conference of 1930 the five nations agreed to extend the holiday on capital ships until 1936, Great Britain agreed to accept naval parity with the United States, and limits were set up within which a system of ratios was established for auxiliary craft. The fact that the new naval ratio (10–10–7, except that in submarines Japan and the United States were to be on an equality) allowed a building up rather than a scaling down was a step backward. It portended increased expenditures for naval armaments, which in subsequent years were to be realized.

The effort at naval limitation begun so bravely at Washington in 1921 finally collapsed with the failure at the second London conference in 1936. This conference, made necessary by Japan's announcement in December, 1934, that she would not abide by the London agreement beyond 1936, was rendered largely futile by Japan's early withdrawal on the ground that her "honor" would not permit her to abide by the 5-5-3 ratio. In the end, Great Britain, France, and the United States signed a "qualitative" treaty to run until 1942, which provided that none of the signatories should build or acquire ships of various classes beyond a certain weight [14] or armed with guns beyond a certain caliber. There was no "quantitative" limit; any of the nations could build as many ships as it wanted. Thus the bright hopes of 1921 faded.

Typical of the cross currents of American foreign policy during these years was the handling of the war-debt problem. While strong nationalists and isolationists bitterly denounced the European nations for failure to meet their obligations, and the United States government took the official position that these debts were legal and just obligations that must be paid, there was in actual practice a willingness to modify these obligations to such an extent that it amounted to cancellation of a large part. While in theory we took one point of view, in practice we followed another. After America's entrance into the World War the United States government, as we have noted, had loaned to the Allied governments somewhat over $10,350,000,000. Inability or reluctance on the part of European nations to meet these obligations led Congress to set up machinery in 1922, in the shape of the World War Foreign Debt Commission, to discuss with the debtor nations plans for refunding. As a result, refunding agreements, by which the total debt was refunded at $11,500,000,000 to be paid over a period of sixty-two years, were made between 1923 and 1930 with fifteen of the twenty debtor nations. The principle followed was ability of the respective nations to pay. Thus rates of interest varied from 0.4 per cent for Italy to 1.6 per cent for France and 3.3 per cent for Great Britain, and the amount of debt reduction varied from 25 per cent for Great Britain to 52 per cent for France and 75 per cent for Italy.

Despite these substantial reductions, there was a widespread belief in Europe that the United States should cancel the entire debts as part of her contribution to the war. It was pointed out, moreover, by the European debtors that the money borrowed had never left the United States, but had been used here to purchase supplies and had contributed to the amazing business enjoyed in this country. Likewise Europeans asserted that there was not enough gold in Europe to pay the debts, and that what gold existed was necessary to support the currencies. In the United States there were many who felt that the money, even if it could be collected, was hardly worth the hate and resentment that it had stimulated in Europe. The bitterness engendered against the United States by the war debts and the difficulty of paying them were increased by the fact that the Allied nations found it impossible to collect the German indemnities. A commission had originally fixed the bill of German reparations at $33,000,000,000. When the

[14] The limits were: capital ships, 35,000 tons; aircraft carriers, 23,000; class A cruisers, 10,000; class B cruisers, 8000; destroyers, 3000; submarines, 2000. No capital ship was to have guns of over 16 inches, no submarine guns of more than 5.1 inches.

Germans in 1922 failed to keep up their payments on this staggering figure, the French occupied the Ruhr (1923). An Allied committee of experts, headed by Charles G. Dawes, thereupon (1924) scaled down the annual payments, and for four years the Germans attempted to follow the new payments.

When the Dawes Plan broke down, another committee, under the chairmanship of Owen D. Young, offered a new plan, which reduced the German debt and provided that a part of the reparations might be canceled if the United States would reduce the debts owed to her by the Allies. To handle the reparations, a Bank for International Settlements was established. That part of the Young Plan that linked German reparations with Allied war debts to the United States was opposed to the policy of the American government and was not recognized. That such a connection existed, however, was evident enough in 1931. When Germany defaulted again in that year, President Hoover, to forestall a world economic collapse, declared a moratorium for one year on Allied debts. At the end of the year the various debtor nations, led by France, refused to resume payments. Eventually only Finland felt the obligation to continue payments. Although the United States refused to change her position on the validity of these debts, most Americans by 1935 realized that their complete payment was unlikely. There was, nevertheless, much resentment here because the Allied governments spent vast sums on rearmament while they were unwilling to pay their debts for the last war. In fairness to the debtor nations, however, it might be said that the existing high tariffs, curtailing the international movement of commodities, made the payment of international debts extremely difficult.

RETREAT FROM IMPERIALISM

Reversal of an aggressive foreign policy and a willingness to conciliate are even more strikingly displayed in our policy toward Latin America than in that toward Europe. The climax of American imperialism in Latin America seems to have been reached in the capture of Veracruz (1914), the military occupation of Haiti (beginning 1915), Pershing's invasion of Mexico (1916), and the acquisition of the Virgin Islands (1917). Since then there has been a steady retreat. The military dictatorship of American marines that had been imposed on Santo Domingo in 1916 was ended in 1924. The marines, who had been in Nicaragua since 1912, with the exception of a brief period in 1925, were withdrawn in 1933. In similar manner military occupation of Haiti, which had been continuous since 1915, was ended in 1934. It is true that withdrawal did not take place without some effort to safeguard the purposes for which military occupation had been undertaken. Thus Santo Domingo agreed that the bond issues of 1918 and 1922 were irrevocable obligations, that the treaty of 1907 should remain in force during the life of the bond issues, and that a general receiver of customs should remain during this period. Haiti agreed to submit to a limited control of her finances until the outstanding bond issues should mature in 1942 and 1943. The same arrangements obtained in Nicaragua, where an American collector of customs and a high commission controlled by the United States remain to handle financial matters and protect foreign bondholders.

The ending of the military occupation of Santo Domingo, Haiti, and Nicaragua, with guarantees that financial obligation be met, is not in itself particularly significant. In conjunction with other events, however, it illustrates a definite tendency. Military withdrawals took place under the Coolidge and Hoover administrations. President Roosevelt announced that his foreign policy was that of the "good neighbor" and in 1934 signed with Cuba a treaty abrogating the famous Platt Amendment, which had reduced Cuba to the position of a protectorate of the United States.[15] With regard to Mexico, there were continuous efforts to improve relations throughout the twenties and early thirties and an unwillingness to interfere in behalf of American investors or American Catholics disturbed by the treatment of their church. The explanation for this change of front is not difficult to find. In the first place Theodore Roosevelt's corollary to the Monroe Doctrine, which would make the United States the policeman of Latin America and the collector of the debts owed to American citizens, was no longer practical. Too many Latin-American states were disturbed by revolutions, and too many had defaulted on their bond issues, for any one nation to police them all. In the second place, American industrialists were desperately anxious to extend their foreign markets, and this could not be done without building a spirit of good will among our southern neighbors. Finally, it was beginning to dawn on the American people that colonies and dependencies were more likely to be a source of trouble and financial loss than of gain. In brief, imperialism, as far as Latin America was concerned, had turned sour, and there was no appetite for further adventures. In the case of Cuba the abrogation of the Platt Amendment came only after the United States had won the enmity of a large portion of the Cuban population by virtually upholding for years the dictatorship of the hated Machado. The end of the Platt Amendment may have been only a gesture, since Cuban wealth is still largely owned by Americans and Cuban prosperity is largely dependent upon American tariff policy,

[15] See above, page 527. Similarly, negotiations were begun in 1934 and a treaty ratified in 1939 with Panama changing Panama's status from that of a protectorate of the United States to that of a more or less independent nation.

but it was a gesture that helped this country to regain in some measure the good will of the Cuban people.

More astonishing than the reversal of policy in the Caribbean has been that in the Far East. The open-door policy with respect to Chinese trade and exploitation was flouted time and again by Japan. While the United States still considered it basic in her Far Eastern diplomacy, it was obvious during the twenties and thirties that she had no intention of carrying her advocacy beyond words. This was particularly true after the European powers having interests in the Far East showed an unwillingness to co-operate with this country in an effort to stay the hand of Japan. Evidence of this was seen in 1931 at the time of the Japanese invasion of Manchuria, when the United States vigorously reminded Japan of her treaty obligations and asserted that "It [United States] does not intend to recognize any situation, treaty, or agreement which may be brought about contrary to the covenants and obligations of the Pact of Paris." When the United States took the leadership in 1932 in opposition to the Japanese invasion of Shanghai, she met with a similar unwillingness on the part of European nations to co-operate.

Toward the Philippines there was a distinct cooling of interest. These islands, which American imperialists had pictured as the stepping stone to "China's illimitable markets," were actually relinquished in 1935. The Filipinos, it will be recalled, never took kindly to American rule, and American authority was established only after a native rebellion had been ruthlessly crushed (page 530). Civil government was established over most of the islands in 1901, and, generally speaking, they had been governed wisely. Sanitation had been improved, transportation facilities constructed, and an educational system established. Notwithstanding these very tangible blessings of American rule, the Filipinos continued to agitate for independence. Furthermore, the Democratic Party, which had opposed annexation, continued through the years to encourage the hope of independence and gradually extended the suffrage and modified the government until the islanders enjoyed virtual home rule.

It was not the agitation of the Filipinos nor the promises of the Democrats that eventually changed the Philippines from a colony to a protectorate, but rather the desire of American farmers—growers of cane and beet sugar, tobacco, and coconut—to eliminate competition. The agricultural bloc, in 1933, in conjunction with anti-imperialist Democrats, passed over President Hoover's veto a bill to establish a protectorate, but both houses of the Philippine legislature voted it down. The matter was revived under Roosevelt, and a modified bill was enacted (Tydings-McDuffie Act), which was accepted by the Filipinos. The act provided for a ten-year period in which the Philippines would be in effect an American protectorate. The islands were to have a Philippine executive, but American naval bases were to be maintained. Philippine immigrants were effectively debarred from this country, and Philippine imports were to pay the regular American tariffs. In return for nominal independence, the Filipinos had to face the loss of the American market, a staggering price to pay.[16] They also had to face the possible loss of independence from the aggressive imperialism of Japan. That this was a real danger had already been amply demonstrated by the Japanese invasion of Manchuria in September, 1931, followed by the establishment of the puppet government of Manchukuo. Secretary of State Stimson condemned the procedure as a violation of the Nine-Power Treaty, the Kellogg Pact, and the open-door policy, and refused to recognize the new state ("Stimson Doctrine"). The League of Nations likewise passed resolutions that it would not recognize any situation, treaty, or arrangement brought about by means contrary to the Covenant of the League or the Kellogg Pact, and sent a commission to investigate the situation. Japan resigned from the League and, since nothing was done to oust her from Manchuria, kept control of that region.

In the years after the First World War, American foreign policy with respect to Europe undoubtedly reacted toward isolation, but it was by no means a policy of intransigence. There were a scaling down of war debts and finally a moratorium, agreements on naval armaments, co-operation with the League, and the signing of peace pacts. In 1933 a policy of fifteen years was reversed by the resumption of diplomatic relations with Russia. Even the high-tariff policy restored under Harding showed signs of intelligent modification by Roosevelt. As a contribution to peace in the Far East, the United States brought into being the Washington conference with its resulting treaties and some fourteen years later decided to withdraw from the Philippine Islands. In Latin America the policy was a steady withdrawal from the absurd lengths to which "dollar diplomacy" under Roosevelt, Taft, and Wilson had carried us. While these were all gains in the direction of world peace and improved international relations, the outlook in many other respects was far from bright. By the middle thirties it was evident to all that the Briand-Kellogg pact, as well as the rest of the machinery erected in Europe to prevent war, was of little use. International agreements on naval limitations had broken down, and with each succeeding year the United States was piling up larger armaments. For direct military and naval purposes the seventy-fourth Congress in 1935 passed an annual budget of

---

[16] In 1900 the United States took 12 per cent of the exports of the Philippines; in 1934 it took 87 per cent. One crop, sugar, comprising 60 per cent of Philippine exports, was practically all taken by the United States.

over $800,000,000, which, with funds that the army and navy might obtain through the Works Relief Act, brought the total to be spent for the year on national defense at well over $1,000,000,000. This was approximately four times the expenditure of 1913. The military expenditures of other nations were also growing by leaps and bounds, and, as the decade drew to a conclusion, the prospects of world peace grew ever darker.

Brief surveys are in C. and M. Beard, *The Rise of American Civilization*, Chap. XXIX, and in L. M. Hacker and B. B. Kendrick, *The United States Since 1865*, Chaps. XXVIII, XXIX. No full-length political history of the 1920s has yet been written, but there is much on the early years in Mark Sullivan, *Our Times*, Vol. VI, Chaps. I–XV. On diplomacy, read S. F. Bemis, *A Diplomatic History of the United States*, Chaps. XXXIV–XL, and T. A. Bailey, *A Diplomatic History of the American People*, Chaps. XLI–XLIV. See also H. S. Commager, *Documents of American History*, Vol. II, 361–365, 371–372, 374–377, 381–384, 399–402, 405–406.

Chapter XXXVIII

LIFE IN THE POSTWAR DECADE

The business of America is business.

CALVIN COOLIDGE

The principles (habits of thought) which govern knowledge and belief, law and morals, have accordingly lagged behind, as contrasted with the forward drive in industry and the resulting workaday conditions of living.

THORSTEIN VEBLEN

PROSPERITY AND REACTION

Except for a decided reaction from the liberalism of the prewar years, American life and culture in the twenties were largely a continuation of those tendencies already evident. Though in actual numbers the growth of population was greater than in any previous decade in our history, it was evident that in relation to total population there was a slowing down. There was no decline, however, in the speed of urbanization. While the total population increased by approximately 17,000,000 from 1920 to 1930, the population on farms declined from 31,614,000 to 30,169,000. Despite this decline in rural population, there was an actual increase in agricultural production, made possible by the introduction of farm machinery. One cause of the decline of rural population was the prosperity of industry, which lured to the city hundreds of thousands each year. To the city dweller of these years it was quite unnecessary to search statistics to prove the development of urban civilization. Under his eyes he saw rising toward the sky huge apartment blocks and towering office buildings, many of them, it is true, merely filling the shortage occasioned by the war. Although the suburbs showed a similar rapid development, congestion within the city limits increased.

Certainly in the urban regions the atmosphere of the twenties was one of optimism and hope. For most Americans employment was steady and money wages were increasing. Though there was some debate on the

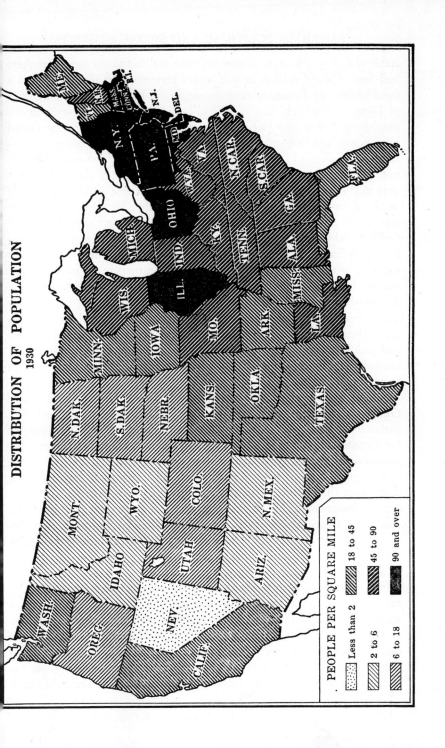

DISTRIBUTION OF POPULATION
1930

PEOPLE PER SQUARE MILE

Less than 2
2 to 6
6 to 18
18 to 45
45 to 90
90 and over

status of real wages, most economists were inclined to the view that there had been a slight decline in real wages between 1900 and 1914 [1] and a considerable rise during the next decade. In this they followed the findings of Douglas, who held that there had been a gain of 19 per cent in the purchasing power of a full week's work in 1926 over that of the period 1890 to 1899 and that most groups of manual workers had enjoyed a substantial increase in real wages in the decade following the war, although nonmanual workers, excepting teachers, experienced a decline.[2] Whatever may have been the advance in real wages, there could be no doubt as to an improvement in the standard of living. By whatever criterion one might choose—health and mortality statistics, increase in hospital facilities, school attendance, variety of goods and services sold to consumers, reduction in hours of labor—the story was the same. This seemed true despite the fact that the share of the wage-earners in the total national income increased but slightly, if at all, after 1900. Notwithstanding the depressed condition of agriculture, which weighed down the farmer with added financial burden, there were changing aspects of rural life that also raised the living standard of many farmers. Automobiles, improved roads, and radios broke down an erstwhile isolation, improved machinery decreased the drudgery, and better schools afforded greater opportunities to rural children.

Although there was an undoubted gain in the standard of living, conditions were far from satisfactory. In 1921 and 1922 the United States Department of Labor worked out a "minimum health and decency budget" for incomes sufficient, as it said, to purchase the minimum quantity of commodities "necessary to maintain a family of five at a level of health and decency" for one year. As estimated for ten cities, it varied from a little more than $2000 to somewhat above $2500, yet studies of wage-earners' incomes quickly revealed the fact that more than nine tenths of American wage-earners failed to achieve such a minimum. Income-tax statistics for 1920, a typical year, showed that 83 per cent of those over ten years of age gainfully employed did not receive an income amounting to $1000. Even more sobering was the fact that the lives of few wage-earners were adequately covered by insurance, that there was practically no security of employment, and that after 1920 there was an actual increase in child labor. In June, 1924, the National Child Labor Committee estimated that 2,000,000 boys and girls under fifteen were at work, the majority as farm laborers. It was not so much the actual conditions, however, that influenced the psychology of the average American; it was his feeling that conditions were improving and that the future held out a

[1] H. U. Faulkner, *The Quest for Social Justice*, 23–24.
[2] P. H. Douglas, *Real Wages in the United States 1890–1926*, Chap. XXII.

real hope. Savings-bank accounts increased nearly fourfold, from 11 to 43 millions, between 1914 and 1925, and the amount deposited increased from 8 to 23 billions; the number of building and loan policies increased in ten years from 3,103,935 to 8,554,352 in 1924. At that time over 11,000,000 families owned their own homes. While a good proportion of this prosperity was enjoyed by the middle class, there is plenty of evidence of large wage-earner participation. The latter group in some cases were even buying shares of stock (page 676).

Of the influences potent during the postwar years, it was the motorcar above everything else that gave tone to the period. By the middle twenties ownership was no longer a class distinction; practically the whole nation had now joined the brotherhood of automobile-owners. With the end of the frontier Americans had begun to settle down, but the motorcar revived the migrating tendency and undoubtedly stimulated the booms in California and Florida. With tourist camps, wayside inns, tea rooms, and gas stations littering the highways, America became a nation on wheels. Not only was the range of social and business contacts immensely enlarged and facilitated, but the whole tempo of civilization was speeded. Although the automobile tended to break down provincialism, it also helped to promote standardization. Science never contributed a more useful tool to mankind, but not all its effects were beneficial. There was rapid growth of highway accidents, making travel a dangerous occupation, and there were the facilities that the automobile provided for organized and unorganized crime.

Probably no element in the population gained more from the rising standard of living than women. Particularly, they profited from the invention of new household appliances, such as oil furnaces, vacuum cleaners, and electric stoves and refrigerators, and from the simple and more sanitary home furnishings. They profited also from the simpler and lighter diet that became fashionable. Such changes in ways of living were in part the cause and in part the result of the continued migration of women from the home to the office and factory; the number of women engaged in gainful occupation increased by more than half a million between 1910 and 1920. Relative to the increase in population, this was by no means startling, but it was significant in that the decade showed a decline in the number of women in the traditional occupations and a large increase in many lines hitherto largely occupied by men. Such occupations as those of stenographer and secondary-school teacher, which at one time had been masculine, were now almost entirely given over to women. Although the successful invasion of many occupations by women was in part due to the lower wages that they would accept, the eventual results were salutary. During these years of rapid economic expansion, men found work in other lines, while women found in their jobs an economic independence that was reflected in many ways. The census of 1920 showed eight and one half million women and girls over ten years of age "gainfully employed," of whom almost one in four was married.

The newly found economic independence enjoyed by millions of women, along with other effects of full-time work, undoubtedly influenced the decline in the birth rate. It was also a factor in the increase of divorce; the annual ratio of divorces to marriages rose between 1914 and 1928 from one in ten to one in six. By the latter year the divorce rate in the United States was probably higher than anywhere else in the world, with the possible exception of Russia. It was the growing economic power of women as well as the persistent agitation of such able leaders as Elizabeth Cady Stanton, Susan B. Anthony, Carrie Chapman Catt, and Anna Howard Shaw that finally won for them the suffrage by the proclamation of the nineteenth amendment in August, 1920 (page 589). Although a handful of women participated actively in the political life of the next decade, any dream that woman suffrage would bring a millennium in American political and social life was quickly dispelled. The effect of the nineteenth amendment during the first twenty years after ratification appeared slight.

While America enjoyed an advance in material prosperity, she suffered from a decade of spiritual reaction, which worked itself out in many and devious ways. It was in part a normal reaction from the reform years that preceded the war (Chapter XXXIV), in part a reaction from the frenzy of the "great crusade," and in part a nostalgic desire to return to an era that had gone forever. Harding's hope for an impossible return to "normalcy" was a key to the decade. In economics the spirit of the age was seen in a renewed glorification of *laissez faire,* illustrated by the refusal of Congress to countenance continued government operation of railroads, merchant shipping, or airmail service, and by Coolidge's veto of government operation of Muscle Shoals. In religion it was to be seen in the revival of "fundamentalism," the climax of which came in antievolution laws in Tennessee (1925), Mississippi (1926), and Arkansas (1928). The Tennessee law, which made it "unlawful for any teacher in any of the . . . public schools of the state, to teach any theory that denies the story of the divine creation of man as taught in the Bible," was given world-wide publicity in the famous trial in 1925 of a school teacher, J. T. Scopes. The almost incredible spectacle of the great Democratic leader, Bryan, and the famous liberal lawyer, Clarence Darrow, trying to settle the validity of the Biblical story of creation in a trial of an unknown teacher in an obscure Tennessee town brought home to millions all over the world the current status of religious belief.

Quite as typical of the reaction was the sharp decline of the liberal humanitarian movement of the prewar days. Not only was there a slowing down of social legislation, but the judiciary, led by the Supreme Court, began again to invalidate social legislation already passed.[3] Advocates of compulsory unemployment insurance or old-age pensions were voices crying in a wilderness. The victory of materialism in many phases of our civilization was as discouraging as the rise of rampant nationalism. Americans interested in preserving the liberal American constitutional tradition of free speech and free assemblage were appalled at the legal and extra-legal methods used to attack liberals, radicals, or "reds," methods that were not only countenanced but participated in by state and federal governments. Typical of this were the breaking of strikes by government authorities (the general strike in Seattle by Mayor Ole Hanson, 1919, and the bituminous-coal strike in the same year by the federal government); the transportation of alien communists (the *Buford* to Russia 1919); the suppression of periodicals by the Post Office Department (the *Masses,* the Milwaukee *Leader,* and others in 1917); terrorization by governmental officials in the raiding of meetings and in arrests and searches without warrants (raid by the New York Assembly Lusk Committee on the Rand School, 1919); use of third-degree methods on radicals; murders and floggings by extralegal agencies, of which those by the Ku Klux Klan were perhaps the most notorious; antisyndicalist laws in some of the states to make it illegal to belong to certain radical organizations; and even the debarring from Congress of Victor Berger, legally elected Socialist from Milwaukee, and of five Socialist assemblymen from the New York legislature on the ground that they could not loyally enforce the Constitution.

Symbolic to many of the tone of the reactionary twenties was the case of Nicola Sacco, a shoe worker, and Bartolomeo Vanzetti, a fish peddler, Italian anarchists accused of murdering a shoe-factory paymaster at South Braintree, Massachusetts, in April, 1920. The evidence upon which they were convicted seemed so inadequate, the judge who presided over the court and the jury seemed so biased, that liberals and radicals throughout the world, to say nothing of many conservatives, looked upon the trial as an example of how innocent men might be railroaded to death because they were radicals. Men and women who were convinced of the innocence of the charge came to their assistance and kept the case open for seven years but under Massachusetts law were unable to secure a retrial. The Massachusetts governor, under liberal pressure, asked a committee of three promi-

---

[3] The decision in Bailey *v.* Drexel Furniture Company, 259 U.S. 20 (1922), declared unconstitutional a federal act that imposed a 10-per-cent tax on the net profits of factories employing children under fourteen years of age. In Atkins *v.* Children's Hospital, 261 U.S. 525 (1923), a minimum-wage law for women in the District of Columbia was declared unconstitutional. For other examples of Supreme Court reaction, see below, pages 675–676.

nent citizens, headed by A. Lawrence Lowell, president of Harvard, to go over the evidence. When this committee reported that it saw no reason for changing the verdict, the men were executed. For liberals throughout the world the day of execution (August 27, 1927) was one of mourning, while demonstrations of protest in many distant lands attested the intense feeling aroused by the case.

RESURGENT NATIONALISM

Even a brief survey of American politics and diplomacy during the post-war years (page 627) makes it evident enough that one characteristic of that era was a return to the strong isolationism of earlier years. Refusal to sign the Versailles treaty, to accept a mandate over Armenia, to conclude a proposed defensive alliance with France and Great Britain, to join the League of Nations or even the World Court, was a certain indication of this. The war left in America a feeling that was more than mere resentment against being involved in the troubles of Europe. On the part of many there was an earnest and sincere desire that such a catastrophe must not occur again, and it was partly as a gesture toward this group that the Harding administration called the Washington conference and the Coolidge administration sponsored the Briand-Kellogg pact.

Nationalism in the United States, however, took other forms than a mere anxiety to avoid European entanglements. Some of it was resentment at European criticisms. Americans were undoubtedly amazed at the changed attitude of our former allies. In 1918 the United States was the "savior of the world"; in 1920 it was "Uncle Shylock." Americans naturally resented being pictured as a nation of crass materialists whose interest was chiefly in amassing greater wealth. Some of the reactionary nationalism was, of course, a hang-over from the war, a distrust of the loyalty of aliens. Some of it was undoubtedly stimulated by conservative economic interests, who bitterly opposed the Russian experiment and prevented until 1933 the re-establishment of diplomatic relations with Soviet Russia.

Whatever may have been the numerous causes of the resurgent nationalism, it found vent in various forms. Politicians of the type of Mayor William H. Thompson of Chicago and Mayor John F. Hylan of New York found a popular policy in denouncing writers of American-history textbooks for alleged pro-British sympathy and in carrying on heresy hunts in history and social-science textbooks. These investigations disclosed some curious theories as to the function of history in the public schools and made textbook-writers more careful to mention heroes of Irish and German extraction who had played a part in American history; otherwise they had little effect. More serious was the so-called "antiradical legislation," making illegal meetings of radicals, display of revolutionary emblems, and membership in organizations advocating radical political or economic changes. Criminal syndicalist laws of one kind or another were passed in thirty-two states.

One of the most striking and at the same time one of the most unfortunate aspects of nationalism that appeared during the decade was a revival of "Know-Nothingism," which took the form of a sudden reappearance of the Ku Klux Klan. The Klan of the postwar years had little in common with that of the Civil War reconstruction period except the name. Its new slogan was "native, white, Protestant" supremacy and it was directed against the Jew, the Catholic, and alien influences wherever it saw them rather than against the Negro. Moreover, its great strongholds were not in the older South but rather in the Middle West, in Texas, Arkansas, Oklahoma, northern Louisiana, and Oregon. Revived in 1915, the Klan grew but slowly until 1920, when it took a sudden spurt. Feeding on ignorance, fear, and superstition, the Klan grew until by 1925 it had a membership of from four to five million. Revelations of dastardly crimes committed under the guise of Klan activity and of the personal and political corruption of certain Klan leaders quickly turned decent people against it, and its membership and influence declined as quickly as they had grown.

To one effect of nationalism the historian can turn with pleasure—the great revival of interest in American history. The fifty-volume series, *The Chronicles of America* (1918–1921), *The Pageant of America* (15 volumes, 1926–1929), *The Dictionary of American Biography* (20 volumes, 1928–1936), and *A History of American Life* (12 volumes, 1927–), were all important co-operative works illustrating in a spectacular way this tendency. The decade also saw a burst of activity that brought new biographies of most of the important figures in American history, while the contributions of scores of secondary figures were for the first time adequately studied. Of even more importance, perhaps, was the fact that these biographies were presented with a realism and a striving for scientific truth that opened invitingly many new avenues of historical research. Significant also was the consideration that the authors of the postwar decade gave to social history. Along with the production of historical and biographical works came a wider popular interest in American history, displayed in important moving pictures of great American epics, in an interest in American colonial architecture, furniture, and all types of Americana, and in the restoration or preservation of early buildings or historic shrines—such places, to name but two examples, as Jefferson's Monticello estate and the Wayside Inn at Sudbury, Massachuestts. This reached its climax, perhaps, in the restoration of Williamsburg, Virginia, to its colonial appearance by John D. Rockefeller, Jr.

Of all the evidences of nationalism, none was more striking than the changed attitude toward immigration. The deluge after 1895 of immigrants from southern and eastern Europe, however, presented difficult problems of amalgamation and stimulated a movement for restriction. Various groups appeared who would radically cut down immigration: dwellers on the Pacific coast fearful of the "yellow peril," students of population who feared a racial deterioration, many patriotic citizens who believed that the influx of foreigners was so great as to prevent rapid "Americanization" and imperil the preservation of American traditions, and, finally, organized labor, who would protect their jobs and the American standard of living against cheap foreign labor. The fear of a new burst of immigration as a result of the war strengthened the position of all these groups. Except for a handful of liberals and radicals, almost the only group still favoring easy immigration laws were the employers, who were still anxious for a continued supply of cheap labor, but their position was weakened by the fact that the nation was experiencing the unique phenomenon of widespread prosperity with considerable unemployment. Even in the boom years of the twenties the average number of unemployed ran well above a million and a half, while in the recession years of 1921, 1922, 1924, and 1927 unemployment estimates ran between two and four millions.

Influenced chiefly by organized labor, Congress had moved toward immigration restriction as early as 1882, when Chinese immigration was finally prohibited. By the same act certain undesirable classes were excluded. Spurred on by the Knights of Labor, Congress enacted laws in 1885 and 1891 prohibiting the bringing over of contract labor, and in the 1891 act a head tax of fifty cents was imposed. Under the same act the office of Commissioner General of Immigration was created, and for the first time complete control of the immigration processes was placed in the hands of the federal government. By legislation in 1891, 1893, 1907, and 1917, the policy was developed to exclude immigrants morally, mentally, or physically unfit, those afflicted with physical or mental disease, anarchists, vagrants, paupers, and contract labor, while steamship lines were forbidden to encourage or solicit immigrants, were made liable to fine for bringing immigrants illegally, and were made responsible for returning them. In an effort to find a short cut, immigration restrictionists early hit upon the idea of a literacy test. Acts incorporating such a test were vetoed by Cleveland, Taft, and Wilson, chiefly on the ground that a literacy test was ineffective and an inadequate method of separating desirable from undesirable immigrants. In 1917 Congress finally passed the literacy test over Wilson's veto.

As a method of restricting immigration, the literacy test was an utter failure. In 1921 over 805,000 immigrants were admitted, while under all the excludable groups only 14,000 were returned. Congress, as a consequence, passed in that year the Emergency Quota Act, which limited immigration in any year to 3 per cent of the number of each nationality in the United States according to the census of 1910. The act was to be for one year and applied to all countries except those in the western hemisphere. In 1922 it was re-enacted with some changes for two more years. Two objectives were obviously in the minds of the framers of the 1921 legislation, a general restriction of immigration and a selective restriction that would limit immigration from southern and eastern Europe while encouraging that from northern and western Europe. The act certainly cut down the total amount, but it failed to restore the old flow from northern and western Europe. Furthermore, it failed to satisfy ardent restrictionists. In 1924, accordingly, a new act was passed, which established a quota of 2 per cent of the number of any nationality residing here in 1890, with the exception of Canada, Mexico, and the independent nations of South America, and, of course, with the exception of merchants, travelers, seamen, and officials. The act threw a gratuitous insult at a proud nation by excluding the Japanese rather than putting them on a quota basis. It also provided that the numerical quota scheme of 2 per cent should remain in force only until 1927, when a "national origins" quota should be substituted. The real origin of the American people as constituted in 1920 was to be ascertained by government experts, upon whose findings immigration was to be apportioned among the nationalities, with the total immigration limited to 150,000 a year. Because of the impossibility of determining the origin of the American people with any degree of accuracy, Congress postponed the operation of the new quota scheme until 1929.

By 1930 it was evident enough that the purpose of the restrictionists had been accomplished. In the fiscal year 1930–1931 but 48,500 were admitted, with the apportionment for 1930 as follows: northern and western Europe, 40.2 per cent; southern and eastern Europe, 20.8; Asia, 1.9; Canada and Newfoundland, 27.0; Mexico, 5.2; West Indies, 2.2; other countries, 2.7. As the economic scene in America darkened, there were actually more aliens who returned to their native land than immigrants who came here. It was evident that America intended no longer to be the haven for the oppressed of all nations, and efforts to soften the law to safeguard the victims of political persecution failed. The most significant feature of the administration of the law was the extraordinary power given to administrative officials. Under the law prospective immigrants likely to become public charges might be debarred. By arbitrarily fixing at one time the possession of $1000 as the measuring stick, officials were able to debar the larger proportion of immigrants who were otherwise quite eligible for admission. It also gave them determining power regarding admission of immigrants from the western hemisphere. While something can be said for a law that allows immigration to be regulated according to the need for labor in this country, the delegation of such power to immigration officials is open to question.

To the postwar generation no aspect of social life was of more absorbing interest than the prohibition experiment. Contrary to the belief of many who should have known better, there was nothing sudden about its advent. For at least a century the movement for temperance, and even for prohibition, had advanced and receded (page 266). As late as 1900 its success, measured by legislation, was not especially encouraging to its promoters. In that year only Kansas, Maine, North Dakota, New Hampshire, and Vermont were legally dry, and the last two were to revert to local option in 1903. This situation, however, was no true reflection of the real strength of the movement. By the turn of the century the leading propaganda organization and the pressure groups that were later to have so much influence were already active, and an increasing number of Americans were beginning to look upon the use of liquor as an unqualified evil that must be radically restrained if not abolished.

The chief count against alcoholic beverages was the growing conviction that their consumption was physically harmful and economically wasteful, that the liquor industry was a prolific source of political corruption, and that the saloon was the ally of every evil influence. While prohibition was winning the increasing support of employers who demanded sober workmen and social reformers who believed it essential in any warfare on prostitution, disease, and poverty, the chief strength of the movement came from organized religion. Each of the leading denominations had its temperance society, but of these undoubtedly the Temperance Society of the Methodist Episcopal Church was the most powerful. Quite as important were the undenominational societies, particularly the Women's Christian Temperance Union and the American Anti-Saloon League. The support of both of these organizations came so largely from religious denominations, however, that they represented the church in action. The W. C. T. U. by 1900 already boasted of 10,000 local branches and a half million members and had already begun its pressure upon state legislatures to provide for antialcoholic propaganda in the public schools. Founded in 1893, the American Anti-Saloon League became the most aggressive of the prohibition organizations. Well supported by public subscription and ably led by men who knew every trick of the political game, it soon forced politicians to recognize its power. In brief, its objects were to convince the American people that the drinking of alcohol was morally wrong and to organize the sentiment of rural Protestantism to ban the liquor traffic by political means. In both these objectives it was amazingly successful.

Against the onslaughts of the prohibition forces the organized liquor traffic fought back, but despite its political power and tremendous financial resources it was unable to withstand the fighting tactics of the prohibition organizations. By the opening of the World War it appeared that rural America, at least, had determined to go dry. The revival of prohibition sentiment came first in the South; Georgia took state-wide action in 1907, Alabama in 1907 (wet again, 1911–1915), Mississippi and North Carolina in 1908, West Virginia in 1912, Virginia in 1914, and Arkansas and South Carolina in 1915. In the meantime, the movement had swung to the Middle and Far West, where Arizona, Colorado, Oregon, and Washington voted dry in 1914, and the legislatures of Idaho and Utah by statute hoped to dry their respective states by 1916. Where state-wide prohibition did not exist, legislative provision had been made for local option, and by means of this most rural sections had closed their saloons. By 1916 almost half the population and three fourths of the area of the nation had attempted prohibition. The cities remained the last stronghold of alcoholic beverages, for here were congregated the large proportion of more recently arrived immigrants, who never dreamed that alcoholic beverages were morally wrong, who were generally out of the reach of antialcoholic propaganda, and who were dumfounded at the idea that anyone should want to withhold from them a commodity that they had always used.

When it became obvious that the cities were not likely to be "dried" by state legislation or local option, prohibition forces turned to federal legislation. Their first victory was the Webb-Kenyon Act, which prohibited the shipment of intoxicating liquors into any state, territory, or district where they were intended to be used in violation of the local law. Passed over the veto of President Taft, in March, 1913, its constitutionality was upheld (1917) by the Supreme Court. In December of that year (1913) the prohibition forces presented their first resolution in Congress providing for national prohibition by constitutional amendment. It was not until 1917, however, that such a resolution passed both houses and was sent to the states for ratification. In a little more than a year three fourths of the states had ratified it; [4] it was proclaimed in January, 1919, and went into force on January 16, 1920. Already enforcement legislation, known as the Volstead Act, had been passed over President Wilson's veto on October 28, 1919; it defined alcoholic beverages as any that contained more than 0.5 per cent alcohol and imposed severe regulations upon the manufacture and

[4] The eighteenth amendment was eventually ratified by all the states but Connecticut and Rhode Island. There was no compensation for loss of property.

distribution of alcoholic products. Undoubtedly, the desire to conserve grains during war time had speeded the consummation of federal prohibition.

Despite the long agitation for prohibition, it now seems evident in the light of subsequent events that the nation was hardly ready for it. It is doubtful if any federal law was ever more unpopular or more consistently, intentionally, and widely violated. People who had used alcoholic beverages as a matter of course were outraged and, as soon as they had collected their wits, began to make beer and wine at home. Others resented what they considered to be a violation by the government of their personal liberty. Either for this reason or because it now seemed smart to drink, many began to use alcoholic beverages for the first time in their lives. It suddenly became the fashionable thing to serve liquor, and, in the face of such a change in the folkways of the people, it was impossible to maintain respect for the law.

In addition to what appeared to be a fundamental change in the attitude of the population, several other factors militated against the success of the experiment. In the first place, the manufacture of alcoholic drinks is a comparatively simple process and can easily be done at home and beyond the eye of the law. In the second place, the tremendous profits in the illicit manufacture and sale of alcoholic beverages built up a powerful underworld element that reduced the illicit manufacture, distribution, and sale of alcoholic beverages to a science at the same time that it shocked the nation by the crimes that it committed and by its debauchery of enforcement officials. The speakeasy, night club, and roadhouse had taken the place of the saloon. The debate as to whether prohibition increased or lessened crime was waged hotly and kept before the nation some of the evil effects of prohibition. A third influence tending to the failure of the experiment was the sabotage of enforcement by local officials in wet communities, and a fourth was the inefficiency of federal enforcement efforts. Enforcement and its personnel were at first largely a football of politics, and the operation was primarily a function of the Internal Revenue Bureau of the Treasury Department, although actually it spread over many departments of the government. By the time the prohibition bureau had been put upon a merit basis and the confusion in enforcement straightened out by greater centralization, the tide against prohibition had risen too high to be stopped. Congress, which had initially passed the prohibition amendment and the Volstead Act in part to be free of a politically annoying issue, showed little interest in appropriating funds sufficient to dry up the nation—in case it could be dried. By the end of the decade it was evident that any effort adequately to enforce the amendment would cost more than Congress was willing to appropriate.

The changing attitude toward prohibition was revealed in the national campaign of 1928, when the Democratic candidate, Alfred E. Smith, favored a return of the liquor problem to the states. So unsatisfactory was the situation that President Hoover appointed the Law Enforcement Commission (Wickersham Commission) to study the question along with other problems of law enforcement. Its report, submitted in January, 1931, opposed repeal of the eighteenth amendment but admitted from the evidence that enforcement had broken down. While all the old arguments against repeal still held, including perhaps the most important of all— that alcohol was an anachronism in an age of high-powered motor vehicles —it was evident by the campaign of 1932 that prohibition was doomed. The Democrats, in fact, went so far as to demand outright repeal of the eighteenth amendment. The Republicans, on the other hand, demanded "revision"—submission of the question to the states in the form of an amendment, which, if ratified, would return liquor control to the states with federal protection of the dry states. This solution was virtually that suggested by the Democrats in 1928 and greeted at the time by Republicans with supercilious scorn.

The overwhelming victory of the Democrats presaged quick action. The special session of Congress called immediately after the inauguration modified the Volstead Act by permitting the manufacture and sale of beer and wine having an alcoholic content of not more than 3.2 per cent by weight or 4 per cent by volume, but forbidding interstate transportation into those states prohibiting manufacture and sale. Already in the closing days of the Hoover administration, Congress had sent to the states an amendment repealing the eighteenth amendment, and with the ratification of this (1933) the whole matter, as far as the federal government was concerned, was put back about where it had been in 1919. The rapidity of repeal, however, caught the states unprepared, and the variety of liquor control that followed was almost as wide as the number of states.

CULTURE IN THE JAZZ AGE

Although postwar students of American civilization were prone to criticize adversely the trend toward standardization, certain undeniable contributions were made during these years in raising the cultural level of the nation. Perhaps the most important was in the field of education. "The outstanding achievement of the American school during the period from 1914 to 1928," says one historian, "was to make secondary education almost as universal as the previous hundred years had made primary education." [5] Stated concretely, this meant that the number of high-school students had grown from 1,500,000 in 1914 to nearly 4,000,000 in 1926, at

[5] P. W. Slosson, *The Great Crusade and After*, 320.

which time practically half of all children of high-school age were enrolled in either public or private schools. It also meant that the cost of education in this country doubled between 1920 and 1926.[6] This was due not alone to the rapid increase of students but also to the additions to the curriculum and to an expansion in the conception of the facilities necessary to an education. The old-fashioned schoolroom with its modest equipment was no longer considered sufficient. The new high-school buildings erected throughout the nation had laboratories, gymnasiums, auditoriums, theaters, swimming pools, playgrounds, athletic fields, lunch-rooms and sometimes even libraries. Although the curriculum of the high schools, dominated as it was by the requirements for college entrance, remained much as it had been, there were, nevertheless, additions, particularly in the direction of vocational training. In some cities where the pressure of students and the cost of equipment rose more rapidly than they could be met, a solution was sought in the unsatisfactory "platoon system," by which an effort was made to educate the students by relays.

Almost as spectacular as the high-school expansion was the deluge of students seeking admission to colleges. College enrollment rose from 266,-654 in 1910 to 462,445 in 1920, to 868,793 in 1928, and to over a million in 1935. By the middle twenties the average American had begun to believe that youth had as much right to a college education as to a high-school training. Not only so, but parents expected that the institutions of higher learning would add indefinitely to their courses to provide training for business and every conceivable type of vocation. While the state universities strove desperately to meet the increasing flood of students by rapidly increasing their facilities, the privately endowed colleges and universities attempted to protect themselves by doubling tuition fees, raising entrance requirements, establishing quotas of various types, and at the same time making strenuous efforts to obtain increased endowments. To do all these things and at the same time maintain standards was no easy task, but on the whole, it was creditably performed. Some colleges and universities even found time to carry on interesting pedagogical experiments, as, for example, the elimination of formal class instruction and alternation of class instruction with outside practical work of some type. Critics of American college education pointed to antiquated curricula, standardization of product, and domination by capital because of the necessity of seeking the financial aid of wealthy men.[7] Although some of this criticism was exaggerated, there was a basis for much of it. Despite the fact that many millions after 1915

---

[6] It was estimated at $2,744,000,000 for the school year 1925–1926, about one half of the world total expended for education.

[7] Notably J. E. Kirkpatrick, *The American College and Its Rulers* (1926); T. B. Veblen, *The Higher Learning in America* (1918); and Upton Sinclair, *The Goose Step* (1923).

were given by private donors to education, notably by Milton S. Hershey (education of orphans), George Eastman (the Massachusetts Institute of Technology and the University of Rochester), James B. Duke (Duke University), Edward M. Harkness (Yale University), the Rockefeller Foundation, the Carnegie Corporation, and the Guggenheim Memorial Foundation, outside influence resulting in flagrant violations of academic freedom were not numerous. Probably the most detrimental influence affecting the college came from alumni interested in athletic rather than educational standing.

In the other great popular educational forces, the newspapers and magazines, the postwar tendencies were much like those of earlier decades. Personal journalism of the old-fashioned kind declined, except in the feature columns, which flourished as never before. More and more the newspapers became primarily business ventures, and their function as molders of public opinion was largely subordinated to advertising and to the interests of advertisers. The increasing cost of newsprint forced most of the metropolitan papers to raise the price from two cents to three, but even this in no way met the cost of production. Publishers became more and more dependent on advertisers if they would stay in business, to say nothing of making money. To attract advertising, circulation must be increased, and to increase circulation it was necessary to enlarge the paper and to cater through feature sections to every member of the family. The strain was too much for many papers, and there was a speeding up of consolidation. Many famous papers went out of business or were merged with others, as, for example, in the merging of the New York *Herald* and the New York *Tribune* and the union of the New York *World* and the New York *Telegram*. In the decade of 1914–1924 the newspapers of New York were reduced from seventeen to eleven; during a period of fifteen years the morning papers in Chicago dropped from seven to five and in Detroit from three to one. In certain respects this trend was unfortunate, for in many a small city where opposing political groups had maintained papers that provided some intellectual competition, there was now only one, and American newspapers with their syndicated news and feature articles began to take on an unwonted sameness. Although the number of newspapers in the nation declined by 2000 between 1914 and 1929, the "chain newspapers" prospered; this was particularly true of the Hearst chain, which specialized in "yellow journalism," and the Scripps-Howard group, which attempted to maintain a tradition of liberalism. Perhaps the most unfortunate development of the decade was the "tabloid," a small paper that specialized in pictures and in stories involving sensational murders and sex. Through them public taste was degraded for the sole motive of financial gain.

Similar trends were to be seen in magazine publishing. Despite increased advertising, the monthly magazines were forced to double their prices and increase their size. At the same time those popular monthlies, which in the first decade of the century had indulged in the crusading fervor of the muckrakers, were now safely back on the beaten track, providing light fiction and success stories of individuals who found themselves on the upper rung of the ladder during the days of "Coolidge prosperity." The older and more "respectable" monthlies—*Harper's, Century* (until 1930), *Scribner's*—kept alive by changing their format and tackling more seriously the problems of the day. Even the staid *Atlantic* made slight concessions. The more radical weeklies, on the other hand, such as the *Nation,* the *New Republic,* and the *New Masses,* failed to attract any large number of the old liberal group. While certain of the old weeklies, such as *Harper's* and the *Independent,* had disappeared, the *Literary Digest* and the newly founded *Time* developed large circulations by a lively summarization of the news. Excellent monthlies or quarterlies summarizing current events, such as *Current History* and *Foreign Affairs* (founded 1922), were at the disposal of the intelligent reader, but the majority of Americans undoubtedly read such magazines as *Liberty* and the *Saturday Evening Post* or one or more of a group of fiction magazines known in the trade as the "pulps," magazines specializing in Western tales and "confessions" or other types of sex stories. Among the magazines they were the counterpart of the "tabloid" in newspapers.

Although the cultural level, as in preceding generations, was as yet still largely determined by the schools and the press, two new agencies, the motion picture and the radio, had entered to share in an important way in the molding of American civilization. By the end of the decade close to 23,000 motion-picture houses with an aggregate seating capacity of over 11,000,000 were playing to over 100,000,000 admissions a week, while the industry was grinding out some five hundred feature pictures a year in addition to many hundreds of "shorts." The flagging interest of many in moving pictures was revived in 1929 and 1930 by the sudden introduction of talking pictures, which gave the industry new popularity and importance. The influence of the "movies," which had come to be a chief recreation for all classes, in shaping attitudes and social values, while impossible to gauge with any accuracy, was undoubtedly tremendous by that time.

The same observation applies with equal force to the radio. An amusement that had been largely confined to the tinkerings of amateur electricians interested in wireless quickly developed into a great amusement industry after WWJ in Detroit, in August, 1920, and KDKA in East Pittsburgh, in November of that year, started commercial broadcasting in this country. Unlike the nations of Europe, where broadcasting is usually a government monopoly with receiving sets subject to taxation, the United States let the industry develop during its early years with little or no restriction. Aided by intense competition, it grew rapidly but at the same time chaotically. In March, 1927, Congress established the Federal Radio Commission, which endeavored to bring some order out of this chaos. Since broadcasting had developed in the United States largely as a private commercial business, it was chiefly supported by advertisers. By 1936 advertisers were pouring $100,000,000 a year for time rental alone into eight networks comprising 561 stations, and it was inevitable that the programs that reached the 26,000,000 radios would be of the type that would appeal to the mass level of intelligence, mainly popular music of various kinds and light comedy.

Despite the influence of the motion picture and the radio, shifting objectives in the world of literature and the arts also set the postwar generation apart from that which preceded it. Reaction against sentimentality and romanticism, heralded by such pioneer realists as Norris, Sinclair, and Dreiser (page 583), now luxuriated in the era of postwar disillusionment. The dominating figure was still Theodore Dreiser, whose *An American Tragedy* (1925) symbolized the new era. The most widely read novelist of the period was undoubtedly Sinclair Lewis, who in a series of powerful social satires, characterized by overpowering detail and intimate knowledge of American life, held up to ridicule much that was false and vulgar in contemporary morals. Reaction in a variety of ways against the inanity and futility of many aspects of modern bourgeois civilization also can be seen in the symbolic irony of James Branch Cabell and in the fiction of many of the younger novelists, such as Ernest Hemingway, John Dos Passos, Sherwood Anderson, and William Faulkner. What the generation could do in fine literary craftsmanship was exemplified in the fiction of Willa Cather.

More remarkable perhaps than the fiction was the renascence of poetry that appeared in the second decade of the century and carried over into the postwar years. The poetry of Edgar Lee Masters, Vachel Lindsay, Carl Sandburg, Edwin Arlington Robinson, Robert Frost, Amy Lowell, and Edna St. Vincent Millay ran the gamut from the most harsh and bitter realism through the newer forms of free verse to an emphasis upon the most exquisite type of sheer beauty. No such outburst had appeared since the middle of the nineteenth century. In the world of art, realism, combined with a willingness to experiment with new forms, dominated the work of the younger painters. Looking back upon the portrait-painters of the preceding generation, the younger artists took their cue from Eakins rather than from Sargent, while others, as they scanned the art of Europe, preferred to follow the school of Matisse and Cézanne rather than the more conventional painters. The same trend was observable in mural painting, where the greatest influence, however, came from the two Mexican artists, Rivera and Orozco. American sculpture, which had enjoyed a golden age in the first two decades of the century (page 584), declined in amount and significance. As starkly realistic as any form of art was the drama, which, under the leadership of Eugene O'Neill, Maxwell Anderson, and Robert E. Sherwood, reached in the twenties and thirties the highest development in this country. American architecture, influenced by such pioneers as Louis Sullivan and Frank Lloyd Wright, with their theory that form should follow function, also reached its greatest flowering. While American musicians have made some effort to work with Negro and Indian music, no indigenous school of music, except for this, has developed. America's contribution, if such it can be called, had been in developing a syncopated ragtime for a nervous, hectic, and rapid style of dancing popular in the rapidly moving life of the new century. Ragtime developed into jazz, "the folk music of the machine age," as one famous orchestra leader called it, and the decade of the twenties has been often called the "jazz age."

Although notable work was done in many forms of literature and art, future historians will probably think of the postwar years as an age dominated by industrialism and science. "The business of America," said Coolidge, "is business," and most Americans agreed. Their concern was with the extension and operation of the economic processes. In their moments of relaxation the typical American talked about the booming stock market, drove his automobile an incredible number of miles, witnessed baseball games, played golf, or went to the moving pictures. It is not surprising that in such an age sport became largely professionalized and that that important new form of art, the motion picture, was largely prostituted to the search for profits. In an age so dominated by the economic motive, it is amazing that the arts flourished as they did.

Hand in hand with business went an expansion in the activities of science and research. As in earlier years, American contribution to science was largely in its application to the everyday needs of life, as, for example, in the application of electricity to a multiplicity of uses. This practical and opportunistic attack upon the frontiers of knowledge was undoubtedly speeded by the fact that much of the research was no longer carried on in the laboratory of the individual worker but was supported in research laboratories by hundreds of industries. But it is amazing to note, nevertheless, the extent of scientific research unselfishly carried on merely to extend the world's knowledge. Thousands of college professors in their own little laboratories and scores of scientists in the endowed laboratories of foundations were pushing the realm of knowledge in an ever widening radius. Of the six Nobel prize awards to Americans up to 1930, three had gone to research in physics, one in chemistry, and two in medicine.[8] From the colleges and foundations went a continual stream of expeditions to probe the secrets of the animal, vegetable, and mineral resources of the world— of the sky above, the world beneath, the waters under the world. There was no field of scientific knowledge in which Americans did not make notable additions during these years.

Unfortunately, less progress was being made in the field of human relations, but even here some advance could be seen. Frederick Jackson Turner and Charles A. Beard had given to American historians a realistic conception of American history and a hint as to how it should be interpreted. Beard and others had taken the lead among political scientists in insisting upon a realistic study of government, which had resulted in much practical improvement in municipal administration. Economists in large numbers were deserting theory for a study of economic institutions as they actually existed, and sociologists were giving their attention to such problems as race relations and propaganda and to other important fields. There was hope by the early thirties, but absolutely no certainty, that science, if given a chance, might save civilization from the chaos and destruction into which rampant nationalism, racial hatreds, imperialism, and the bitter competition for economic profits were fast driving it.

C. and M. Beard, *The Rise of American Civilization,* Chap. XXX, provides an introductory survey, as does L. M. Hacker and B. B. Kendrick, *The United States Since 1865,* Chap. XXXIV. P. W. Slosson, *The Great Crusade and After,* Chaps. III–XV (History of American Life), is a scholarly and well-written account of the social life. A popular but accurate picture is Frederick L. Allen, *Only Yesterday.* Interesting comments on American social conditions by a Frenchman are in André Siegfried, *America Comes of Age,* Part I. On the American mind in the twenties read Merle Curti, *The Growth of American Thought,* Chap. XXVII. Any chapter in R. S. and H. M. Lynd, *Middletown,* a study of a typical small American city, will give the student a good picture of the particular phase of life with which the chapter deals. On the prohibition movement see P. H. Odegard, *Pressure Politics,* Chaps. III–VI, and Charles Merz, *The Dry Decade.*

[8] A. A. Michelson, 1907, Robert A. Millikan, 1923, and Arthur H. Compton, 1927, in physics; Alexis Carrel, 1912, and Karl Landsteiner, 1930, in medicine; Theodore W. Richards, 1914, in chemistry.

Chapter XXXIX

CAPITALISM AT FULL TIDE

Acceleration rather than structural change is the key to an understanding of our recent economic developments. Gradually the fact emerged during the course of this survey that the distinctive character of the years from 1922 to 1929 owes less to fundamental change than to intensified activity.

Recent Economic Changes

THE BOOM YEARS

The artificial prosperity of the war years, in which almost every phase of agriculture, transportation, and industry had participated, was followed by an inevitable collapse. The decline, however, did not set in until the late spring of 1920 and did not reach its most acute stage until the later months of 1921. Contraction of orders, followed by reduction of wages and widespread unemployment, and accentuated by a "buyers' strike," resulted in deflation, industrial stagnation, and a curtailment of foreign trade; the number of those actively employed declined by one third and wage rates by the same proportion. No phase of our economic life suffered more than agriculture. Between the high of 1919 and the low of 1921 the prices of most farm commodities were cut in half. The same in general was true of retail prices. In 1921 all the elements were present to point to a long and severe economic depression. Not only was the United States suffering from deflation and economic stagnation, but the rest of the world was in the same condition. Impoverished by the war, crushed under staggering debts, and handicapped by unfavorable exchange rates, the warring nations of Europe were in no condition to resume even normal peace-time purchases from the United States.

Instead of having a long-drawn-out depression, however, the United States quickly recovered, and certain sections and large groups enjoyed during the twenties an unexpected era of prosperity. The postwar depression was short, and by the end of 1922 many industries, including the railroads, were again recording capacity business. Some reasons for this recovery and for the boom years that followed may be suggested. In the first place, the deflation had been sudden and thorough. Industry found itself at the bottom of the business cycle and adjusted itself to peace conditions in a short time, and both industry and the consumer were possessed of resources to commence the upward climb. Furthermore, the foreign market for American commodities was temporarily resuscitated by loans abroad, amounting during the twenties to over $7,000,000,000. As long as these loans could be maintained, American goods could be sold.

Of all the elements tending toward economic prosperity, undoubtedly the most important was the existence of new or relatively new industries for whose products there was a persistent demand. The automobile industry, which grew phenomenally during the decade, created, it is estimated, some 4,000,000 jobs and indirectly supported between sixteen and twenty million people, thus taking care approximately of the population increase of the twenties. Stimulated directly by this unusual growth of the automobile industry was the boom in road-building. An average of two billion dollars a year was spent on roads, providing employment and in turn stimulating many of the heavy industries. Industry was helped also by the development of the radio and by many household electrical appliances that quickly assumed the status of necessities rather than of luxuries. Since most of these commodities were too expensive to be purchased outright by the average wage-earner, installment buying was developed beyond anything yet seen. From 60 to 80 per cent of all automobiles were bought on installments, and there was hardly a commodity of any size that could not be purchased "on time." In the later years of the decade fully 15 per cent of all goods were sold in this manner.

Every American boom period has been characterized by large-scale land speculation. That of the twenties was no exception. Instead of displaying itself on the frontier, however, it took the form of speculation in city real estate and in a phenomenal construction of city buildings. Building-construction in 120 cities reached the high point of $3,399,000,000 in 1925, almost four times the amount expended in 1916, the highest amount in the prewar years, while total building-construction in 1925 amounted to over $6,000,000,000. Some of this construction was the result of failure to build in the war years, but much of it represented the speculation of the period. Besides automobiles, roads, and building-construction, which provided employment for wage-earners and an outlet for capital, other reasons may be suggested for the prosperity of the twenties. Science made its numerous contributions. While population, for example, increased 12 per cent between 1920 and 1928, the productivity of the average worker increased 25 per cent and the national wealth by at least twenty billions. It was this increased productivity more than anything else which impressed economists. "Since 1921," said Wesley C. Mitchell in reviewing the work of the

Committee on Recent Economic Changes, "Americans have applied intelligence to the day's work more effectively than ever before. . . . The old process of putting science into industry has been followed more intensively than before; it has been supplemented by tentative efforts to put science into business management, trade-union policy and Government administration." [1]

Undoubtedly this increased productivity and efficiency go far to explain the economic boom of the 1920s. Though in reality there was little that was new in this—it was an acceleration rather than any structural change in our economic life—nevertheless, this acceleration brought increased prosperity in which labor as well as capital participated. Although the relative share of the national wealth that went to the wage-earners probably did not increase, there is no doubt that the real wages of certain groups of workers did advance, and this was reflected in savings-bank accounts, insurance policies, and home-ownership, as well as in the purchase of consumers' commodities.

The economic prosperity of the twenties unfortunately was far from universal. Agriculture, as we shall see, never recovered from the postwar depression. Coal-mining never regained its prewar prosperity; the textile and leather industries failed to respond to the prevailing industrial boom. While the middle Atlantic, the eastern north-central, and the Pacific states were prosperous, the South, the Middle West, and those parts of the mountain sections dependent upon agriculture failed to share in the good times. Those parts of New England dependent on leather and textiles likewise suffered. Nevertheless, the rapidity with which industrial America recovered from the war so amazed Europeans that they came to America in droves to study the remarkable phenomenon, and many American economists, forgetting the lessons that might have been derived from freshman courses in economics or history, talked happily of the dawn of a "new economic era," in which panics and depressions would be forever banished.

BIG BUSINESS IN THE TWENTIES

The reform wave that swept the country during the first decade of the century had culminated in the Federal Reserve Act, the Clayton Antitrust Act, and the creation of the Federal Trade Commission. This legislation, it was hoped, would prevent monopoly, restore competition, and create a more rational control of the nation's finances. As the twenties drew to a close, however, it was obvious that this legislation had failed to accomplish its objects. Business consolidation, which had been rapid in the period 1897–1904 (page 552) and then had slowed down, began with renewed

[1] *Recent Economic Changes*, 862.

vigor in the years after the war. While the new era of consolidation was felt in practically every line of business, it was particularly notable in those new industries that had developed since the early era of consolidation—automobiles, chemicals, aluminum, moving pictures, radios, and utilities.

Of the consolidation that took place in this decade, the most spectacular and the most significant was undoubtedly in the public utilities. In the whole utility field but twenty-two mergers were recorded in 1919, but in 1926 the number was over 1000. More than 3700 utility companies disappeared during the years 1919–1927, including many municipally owned concerns. So far had this gone by 1930 that it was estimated that one half of the electric power generated by the larger power companies was controlled by three great holding groups—the United Corporation, the Electric Bond and Share Company, and the Insull group—that two thirds of the electrical energy was controlled by six groups and over 90 per cent by fifteen groups. So far had this progressed and so indisputable was the evidence as presented by the Federal Trade Commission, that it was quite obvious that many of the consolidations were merely holding companies superimposed upon one another for no purpose but to allow small groups to control vast properties and draw unconscionable profits from the consumer. As the nation was gradually aroused to the seriousness of the situation, the so-called "power trust" became a political issue, and efforts were made during the Roosevelt administration, as we shall see, to abolish unnecessary holding companies and establish effective federal regulation.

Among other industries infected by the new mania for consolidation were the manufacture and distribution of package goods (General Foods Corporation), communication facilities (International Telephone and Telegraph Corporation), banking in the innumerable mergers that finally made the Chase National Bank the largest in the world and in the development of chain banking on the Pacific coast. Notable also was the consolidation of retail units, particularly in the drug, tobacco, and grocery fields. By the middle twenties the typical small merchant was feeling the competition of powerful corporations, just as the small manufacturer in earlier decades had felt the heavy hand of large consolidated units. Even the two great mail-order houses began to establish retail outlets in the urban centers. How far the development of chain-store retailing might go was not yet clear, but some of the economic and sociological effects were evident to all. Disturbed by the consolidation of capital, congressional investigators had warned the nation in 1913 of the existence of a "money trust" (page 561), but the two succeeding decades showed no cessation in the tendency for wealth to consolidate. A careful survey in 1930 showed that the two hundred largest corporations controlled nearly half of all nonbanking corporate wealth (probably 38 per cent of all business wealth), received 43.2 per cent of the income of all nonbanking corporations, and were controlled by approximately 2000 individuals.

Despite three decades of state and federal legislation designed specifically to prevent monopoly and maintain competitive conditions, consolidation in the twenties proceeded with but slight interference. For this tendency there were many reasons. Overexpansion of business during the war years resulted in a period of bitter competition, which again stimulated mergers. The prosperity and optimism of the twenties made it easy to float stock and bond issues and to take care of the financial operations necessary for new organizations. It was evident, also, that the attitude of the public was changing. Distrust of big business was not so evident. Whether it was an appreciation of the inevitability of consolidation in a capitalist system, the inability of antitrust legislation to prevent it, or the prosperity of the country that made the public less quick to scent the dangers, it is hard to tell. Certainly, the wider distribution of stocks and bonds of the larger corporations must have helped to break down the opposition, as well as the speculative spirit that prevailed during the decade. Before the World War the ordinary individual had never seen a stock certificate or bond, to say nothing of actually owning one. In the twenties such ownership became common, and while the value of stocks mounted and while interest and dividends were paid, it did not take much propaganda to change the attitude of the public, at least momentarily, toward big business.

Failure of the antitrust legislation to be effective was due not alone to economic tendencies but also to failure on the part of the judicial and executive branches to support it. When the Supreme Court, in 1920, refused to dissolve the United States Steel Corporation, on the ground that neither size, short of monopoly, nor the possession of potential power to restrain trade was necessarily a violation of the antitrust acts, it seemed clear enough that big business had nothing to fear from the courts. Any hope that monopoly might be restrained by an extension of the principle of public interest to cover the activities of various industries was prevented by decisions such as those holding that gasoline-stations, employment agencies, and ticket-brokers were not public-interest enterprises. The Supreme Court even put its stamp of approval upon trade associations, whose activities in reality were often but a camouflaged method of creating monopoly conditions. It is difficult to find a single judicial decision during the decade antagonistic to business consolidation. Moreover, neither the Coolidge nor the Hoover administration paid much attention to the antitrust laws. The Department of Commerce under Hoover prided itself on encouraging co-operation rather than competition on the part of business, while Coolidge packed the Federal Trade Commission with men hostile to the antitrust acts in an apparent effort to prevent their enforcement. In the meantime, big business was developing by means of holding companies, investment trusts, voting trusts, and nonvoting stock, to say nothing of the old devices of interlocking stockholding and directorates, a technique for the creation of "combinations and trusts—vertical, horizontal and circular—with vaster ramifications, with greater resources than any combinations that have hitherto appeared." [2]

LABOR IN RETREAT

While the nation was swept with a wave of business consolidation and the position of capital was strengthened, the power of organized labor declined. At the height of its power in 1920, organized labor comprised probably not more than 10 per cent of the wage-earners, but in general this small percentage represented in intelligence, skill, and income the vanguard of the labor movement. In brief, it *was* the American labor movement, and its history provides a reasonable index of the status of American labor. Of the various labor organizations the American Federation of Labor was the largest and most important (page 409). It had registered great gains during the war years, when its average membership had doubled (from 2,020, 671 in 1914 to 4,078,740 in 1920), and it had become a recognized element in the national life. Its decline in membership to 2,532,261 in 1932, while in part a result of the depression of 1921 and 1922 and in part a reaction from the rapid expansion of the war period, was caused by many other factors and marked a decline in power and prestige.

Above all else, labor in the twenties had to contend against the "spirit of the times." The reform wave of the prewar years, culminating in the sacrifice and idealism of the war days, had spent itself, to be succeeded by a decade of reaction. The claims of labor evoked little sympathy in a world longing for "normalcy" and intent upon amassing rapid wealth. The Wilson administration, which in war time had sought the aid of labor, turned against it in 1919, when the Attorney General smashed a bituminous-coal strike by means of an injunction obtained under the Lever Fuel and Food Act and in the same year helped to break a railroad shopmen's strike. The judiciary, which had tended in the prewar years to recognize human as well as property rights, faced about and in numerous decisions restricted or eliminated many of the hard-won gains of labor. Federal child-labor laws were declared unconstitutional by the Supreme Court in 1918 and 1922, and a minimum-wage law for women fell under the ban of the court in 1923. The court even upheld a decision making it illegal to try to organize employees who had signed a "yellow dog contract"; it cut the heart out of the protection that Congress intended to give labor in the Clayton Act by declaring a secondary boycott illegal, and it even permitted a suit

[2] H. W. Laidler, *Concentration of Control in American Industry*, 11.

against an unincorporated union for violation of the antitrust acts. One judge went so far as to question the legality of a labor union *per se* as a conspiracy in restraint of trade. With utter disregard of the Clayton Act, judges freely granted injunctions in labor disputes, at the same time making little or no effort to safeguard the constitutional rights of labor. The judicial abuse of the injunction went so far that anti-injunction bills became the chief legislative objective of organized labor, and finally, in 1932, a Federal Anti-Injunction Act was passed, again prohibiting injunctions in federal courts as well as the use of "yellow dog contracts."

In a period of reaction it could hardly be expected that the general run of employers would fail to take advantage of the situation. Led by the National Association of Manufacturers, the National Metal Trades Association, and the League for Industrial Rights (formerly the American Anti-Boycott Association, which financed many legal battles against labor), and aided in many places by the local chambers of commerce, an intensive open-shop drive was inaugurated. It was aided to a greater extent, perhaps, than ever before by the old technique of the labor spy, the strikebreaker, and the *agent provocateur*. Propaganda that placed the onus of high prices upon labor and pictured every labor leader as a racketeer went far to alienate the middle class. More dangerous was the development under the instigation of the employer of the company union. Not more than a dozen plants of any importance had company unions in 1917; ten years later there were hundreds, with an estimated membership of over 1,400,000. They were particularly evident in the railways after the collapse of the shopmen's strike, in the metal trades, and in the electrical industries.

Harder to combat than these, said militant trade unionists, were the various schemes of stock-ownership, pension plans, and welfare projects, which may have in some places improved the status of the worker but oftentimes were a substitute for wage increases and in the end broke down the independence of the worker. Led by powerful companies in the utility, steel, oil, and railroad industries, and encouraged by installment buying, the number of employee stockholders grew to well over a million. Less than 2 per cent of the stock in the companies where employee stock-ownership was pushed most agressively ever got into the hands of the wage-earners, but the psychological effect in breaking down class consciousness was undoubtedly tremendous. Another method of winning the loyalty of the worker to the company rather than to the union was the establishment of insurance and pension schemes. By 1927 group insurance had been written to cover some 4,700,000 workers, and pension schemes included 4,000,000 more; most of this had been established during the previous fifteen years. It would take pages merely to list the various methods of promoting plant loyalty, which run all the way from sponsoring a baseball team to the presentation of a gold watch upon the completion of 25 years' nonstrike service. Organized labor, thoroughly cognizant of the implications of all this, has demanded its compensation in wages and has insisted upon taking care itself of its own insurance and welfare. In the twenties it fought a losing battle, but the succeeding depression greatly curtailed the welfare schemes and deflated the glory of stock ownership.

For part of its decline in prestige and power labor had only itself to blame. Its leadership was inadequate, unable to respond to new conditions or to develop a new technique. Policies that may have suited the prewar years no longer fitted the times. Gompers, who had dominated the labor movement for three decades, died in 1924, but his policies were continued. While strong unions like the bituminous-coal workers were disintegrating, the federation failed to organize the textile workers of the South and those in the new mass-production industries, particularly steel, automobiles, rubber, and radio. By failing to throw itself whole-heartedly into the steel strike of 1919, it not only contributed to the defeat of labor but also missed the opportunity of re-establishing itself in the steel industry. Its tradition of craft as against industrial unionism hampered its efforts to organize the new industries, and its antired campaigns weakened the influence of the more aggressive members, who urged a more militant policy. In fact, the long battle during the twenties between the "progressive" and "conservative" factions in the labor movement tended as much as anything else to stalemate efforts toward organization. Some gains in membership were made in the "service" occupations and among government employees, but on the whole the decade was one of almost uninterrupted defeat and retreat.

RECENT TRANSPORTATION CHANGES

No decade in our history has seen more significant changes in transportation than that which followed the World War, and of these changes the rapid extension of the use of the automobile was probably the most important. Practical automobiles had been constructed as early as 1893, but for another decade the whole industry was in an experimental stage (page 558).

The horseless carriage had caught the imagination of the nation, and in the decade that preceded the World War the automobile ceased to be the plaything of the rich or the obsession of tinkering mechanics, and its use was extended to the upper middle class. It was during the twenties that the use and ownership of the motor car were extended to the masses, and this extension was undoubtedly due chiefly to the influence of the greatest figure in the automobile industry, Henry Ford, who by mass production and continued price reductions made this possible. As late as 1914 the production of automobiles was about 569,000, the number of vehicles registered only 1,258,000, and the capital invested 407,730,000; in 1929 the production was 5,180,033, the number registered over 26,501,000, and the total value of the product over $3,722,000,000. In that year there was one automobile to every five persons in the country.

Of the tremendous social and economic effects of the automobile, some hint has already been given (page 653). Among these none has been more important than the impetus given to road-building. By 1915 the movement for improved roads was well under way; the states through the highway commissions that had been set up were more and more taking over from towns and counties the responsibility of caring for the more important roads and were beginning to lay plans for long-term programs. During the next fifteen years the federal government stepped in, and through the Rural Post Roads Act of 1916, supplemented by legislation in 1919 and 1924, reverted to its earlier policy of aiding states to build primary interstate roads and secondary connecting links, the states contributing an amount equal to that given by the federal government. With federal aid some 127,000 miles of road had been built by 1935. It was estimated that in the late twenties the annual amount spent by all government agencies on roads was somewhere between two and three billion dollars. Nevertheless, there was still much to be done. Of the 3,000,000 miles of roads in the United States, only 23 per cent in 1936 were better than dirt roads.

Although the development of air transportation has been almost as spectacular as that of the automobile, it is still one of the less important of the forms of transportation. Despite the impetus given by the World War, development in the United States until 1927 was slow. Then came a sudden spurt. The spectacular flights of Lindbergh and others turned men's minds to the conquest of the air; technical improvements were rapidly making air transportation safer; the prosperity of the twenties made capital available, and heavy government subsidies gave encouragement. The federal government, which in 1918 had established an experimental air-mail service, allowed the Post Office to develop it upon a satisfactory basis until 1925, when Congress virtually ordered the Post Office Department to turn the mail service over to private contractors. Heavy mail subsidies, in conjunction with the fact that the army and navy purchase even in times of peace more than one third of the airplanes manufactured in this country, have provided the structure upon which the manufacture and use of airplanes have been developed. Federal subsidy of air transportation, it should be remembered, just as its subsidy of the Merchant Marine, was essentially for purposes of national defense.

During the five years 1927–1931 the advance of air transportation was spectacular. The depression eventually cut in half the number of airplanes manufactured and delayed somewhat the development of commercial air transportation. Unlike most other industries, however, air transportation, measured in passengers carried, declined but slightly as a result of the economic collapse. Technical improvements, greater speed combined with greater reliability and safety, and reduced fares have all tended to keep alive the interest of the traveling public. The airplane has already won an assured place in the carrying of mail and long-distance transportation of passengers. Except in these fields, it is as yet not a serious competitor with other forms of transportation.

While new methods of transportation were developing rapidly, the relative position of railroads declined. By 1900 the railroads had become the outstanding and virtually unrivaled agency of distance transportation. Since then more than 60,000 miles have been added to the American railroad system, but the significant changes since 1900 in railroad facilities are represented by extensions in other than first trackage and in operating improvements. A new wave of railroad legislation, beginning with the Hepburn Act of 1906 and culminating in government operation during the World War, brought effective public regulation (page 557). The return of the railroads to their private owners on March 1, 1920, was the occasion for even wider public control in the Transportation Act of 1920 (Esch-Cummins Act) than had existed previous to the World War. There had been much agitation for a continuation of government operation, particularly by organized railroad labor, which advocated the "Plumb plan," a scheme that called for the government purchase of the railroads and their operation by a board of directors upon which the public, operating officers, and employees should be equally represented. Such a solution was too drastic in the postwar reaction, but the Transportation Act of 1920 did extend government regulation, especially by giving the Interstate Commerce Commission (now enlarged to eleven members) the power to regulate capital structure. Other features of the act were the extensions of the power of the commission to prescribe minimum as well as maximum rates and to divide the nation into rate districts, where rates were to be prescribed that "under honest, efficient and economical management" would give a "fair return" upon the aggregate value of the railroad property. The carriers were ordered to turn back to the Interstate Commerce Commission one half of the excess earnings above 6 per cent, which was to be used as a revolving fund for the benefit of the weaker railroads. Shifting its attitude from that of promoting unlimited competition, Congress authorized the commission to work out plans for the consolidation of railroads into not less than twenty nor more than thirty-five systems. The creation also of a Railroad Labor Board was a half-hearted effort to prevent strikes and stabilize the labor aspect of the industry, the chief significance of which was that it presaged similar efforts in the future.

The Transportation Act of 1920 is significant as providing the law under which the railroads operated during one of the most critical decades of their history. Although the act as a whole was a wise extension of government powers, certain parts of it proved unworkable. The Railroad Labor Board, powerless to enforce its decisions, was abolished in 1926; [3] the bitter opposition of the more prosperous railroads to the "recapture clause," combined with the attitude of the Supreme Court in the O'Fallon decision, [4] made it impossible to recover excess profits from the railroads and led the Interstate Commerce Commission in 1930 to ask Congress to modify the act. Finally, the difficulties of working out a plan of railroad consolidation that would promote efficiency and at the same time maintain competition proved so difficult that it was not until December, 1929, that the commission first offered a tentative scheme of twenty-one systems.

Despite terrific competition from private automobiles and passenger busses, the railroads as a whole carried on successfully during the twenties. The total return on investment from class I railroads from 1921 to 1927 has been estimated at only 4.3 per cent, but the more prosperous and better-managed earned large profits. A glance at the following table, in fact, will show a healthy increase in freight revenue and a willingness on the part of the public to invest in railroads and of railroad management to increase facilities. Class I railroads or their subsidiaries, during the eight years 1921–1927, spent for extensions, additions, and betterments close to $6,000,000,000. On the other hand, there was a continued decline, except for one year (1923), of the number of passengers carried, while passenger miles decreased from 47,369,906,000 in 1920 to 26,875,642,000 in 1930 and 22,651,334,000 in 1940. A closer study of passenger statistics shows that commutation traffic grew during the decade and that long-distance travel about held its own, the marked decline coming within the middle ranges. Even before the

Railroads During the 1920s

Year	Investment in Road and Equipment (in millions)	Freight Revenue (in millions)	Passenger Revenue (in millions)	Passengers Carried (in thousands)	Taxes (in millions)
1920	19,849	4,421	1,305	1,269,913	289
1925	23,231	4,648	1,065	901,963	366
1929	25,465	4,899	876	786,432	403

[3] Succeeded by an even more powerless body, the Board of Mediation, established in 1926 by the Railroad Labor Act (Watson-Parker Act).

[4] St. Louis and O'Fallon Railway Company v. United States, 279 U.S. 461 (1929).

collapse of 1929 more than one railroad was questioning the advisability of maintaining passenger traffic.

The revival of interest in internal waterways that occurred in the early years of the century has continued to the present day. The incomparable system of inland waterway facilities with which this country is blessed has undoubtedly helped keep the interest alive, as well as the belief that water transportation is cheaper than that on land. The dreams of river and lake towns have contributed, but probably the greatest impetus since the World War has come from the agrarian distress and the belief on the part of the farmers that water transportation would cut freight charges sufficiently to expand the foreign market. Agitation in the Middle West has brought to consummation the Lakes to the Gulf Deep Waterway project, but the dream of a St. Lawrence Ship Canal has not yet been realized. This project, which would mean a system of deep waterways from the Great Lakes to the Atlantic and would include schemes for important hydro-electric developments, was endorsed by the Canadian parliament and by Presidents Hoover and Roosevelt, but the Senate in 1934 refused to ratify an enabling treaty. On the ground that the project was necessary for long-range defense needs of both nations, it was revived in 1941 in the form of an agreement (requiring only a majority approval of Congress) between Canada and the United States. Since its inception the St. Lawrence seaway and power program has been opposed by private utilities, by the railroads as unnecessary for transportation needs, and by the State of New York, which has spent in recent years over $200,000,000 on the Barge Canal, a competing route. It has also been discounted by many economists in the belief that the savings would not be as large as expected.

One more aspect of the American transportation problem during the 1920s, namely, that of the merchant marine, remains to be noted. When the World War ended, the United States Shipping Board and the Emergency Fleet Corporation owned over 1500 ships with a gross tonnage of over 9,000,000. Faced with the problem of what to do with this vast tonnage, Congress in the Merchant Marine Act of 1920 (Jones Act) laid down the policy (1) that the federal government get out of the shipping business as soon as possible, but (2) that an American merchant marine be kept on the seas, and (3) that it be maintained by various types of indirect subsidies. The methods of subsidization as enlarged and liberalized by the Merchant Marine Act of 1929 consisted mainly in selling government-built ships at a small fraction of their cost, in loaning money on favorable terms, and in paying far more for carrying mail than the service was worth. By following this policy the government succeeded in retiring from the freight and passenger business on the Pacific by 1928 and from the passenger business on the Atlantic by 1929. It also succeeded in maintaining an American merchant marine on the seas which by the end of the decade was still the second-largest in the world. From the point of view of vessels with modern construction and equipment, however, it was rapidly falling behind.

THE DECLINE OF AGRICULTURE

The years from 1897 to 1919 represented one of the few periods of prosperity enjoyed by the American farmer. The hard and discouraging years of the seventies, eighties, and nineties had temporarily passed, and a succession of good harvests after 1897, combined with rising prices, enabled the farmer to pay his debts, enlarge his operations, and improve his facilities. Demand for agricultural products appeared to be catching up with the supply, while new discoveries of gold in Alaska and elsewhere aided in inflating prices. Furthermore, the rapid extension of the agricultural area was slowing down. While the farming area had increased by at least 15,000-000 acres annually for the thirty years prior to 1900, the increase for the next decade was only 4,000,000 acres a year. Technically, the frontier had come to an end.

Quite naturally the farmer, who had been living since the panic of 1873 on the ragged edge of financial insolvency, looked forward with renewed hope. Between 1900 and 1910 the prices of agricultural products increased by nearly half, while the value of farm property doubled. Under such circumstances the sod houses of Nebraska and the Dakotas quickly gave way to comfortable homes and spacious barns. Only one great obstacle seemed to prevent full prosperity: high interest rates, or, in other words, difficulty in obtaining credit. There was, indeed, a real need for banking institutions designed to meet the peculiar needs of the farmer, but it was not until 1916 that the federal government seriously faced the problem. In that year the Wilson administration pushed through the Federal Farm Loan Act, establishing in twelve cities federal land banks, which were to lend money to groups of farmers (National Farm Loan Associations) on the security of farm mortgages, the money for the loans to be obtained from the sale of bonds secured by these mortgages. Also joint-stock land banks were established to deal directly with the individual farmer. With these banks an important beginning, at least, was made in attacking the problem of agricultural credits.

The favorable tendencies just described were accentuated during the World War. Assured of high profits and urged on by the government, farmers expanded their production to the limit, contributing in no small degree to the Allied victory. With the conclusion of the war came the inevitable collapse; the prices received by farmers for cotton, wheat, hogs, and

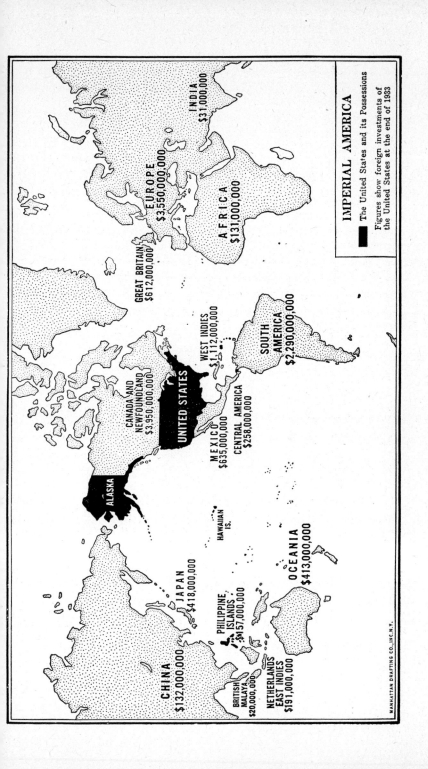

IMPERIAL AMERICA

■ The United States and its Possessions

Figures show foreign investments of
the United States at the end of 1933

CANADA AND
NEWFOUNDLAND
$3,950,000,000

UNITED STATES

ALASKA

MEXICO
$635,000,000

CENTRAL AMERICA
$258,000,000

WEST INDIES
$1,112,000,000

SOUTH
AMERICA
$2,290,000,000

GREAT BRITAIN
$612,000,000

EUROPE
$3,550,000,000

INDIA
$31,000,000

AFRICA
$131,000,000

CHINA
$132,000,000

JAPAN
$418,000,000

PHILIPPINE
ISLANDS
$157,000,000

BRITISH
MALAYA
$20,000,000

NETHERLANDS
EAST INDIES
$191,000,000

HAWAIIAN
IS.

OCEANIA
$413,000,000

MANHATTAN DRAFTING CO., INC., N.Y.

cattle in 1921 were but half those of 1919, while the price of corn was but a third. Although there was some recovery during the years 1923 to 1926, the decline was again resumed and was speeded by the depression of 1929. Just as in the years following the Civil War, the farmers were again affected by two primary factors: overproduction of agricultural goods and a deflation in prices. Among the many influences leading to overproduction and price deflation, the following must be counted: the cessation of war demands, the greater competition in the world markets of Canada, Australia, Argentina, Russia, and other relatively new regions, which had also speeded production during the war years, the impoverishment of Europe and unsettled political conditions there, and the unfavorable effects of the high American tariffs, which made it difficult for the nations of Europe to exchange manufactured goods for agricultural products. Nor should the effect on the world's trade of our status as a creditor nation be forgotten. To pay back the interest and principal on loans made by American investors, foreign peoples were compelled to increase the exportable surpluses, and agricultural commodities lent themselves most easily to this type of expansion.

Among the domestic factors that operated against agricultural prosperity have been dietary and style changes, an immigration policy which helped to raise the cost of labor, higher freight rates, and increased handling and storage costs. To make the situation more difficult, the post-war depression struck American agriculture in a transition period. Modernization of equipment was in full swing as horses were being exchanged for automobiles and tractors. In the livestock industry a program of pure breeding and disease-control was under way, and everywhere the farmers were pushing ahead to a better standard of living. All this was stopped by the depression, and, to make matters worse, taxes continued to mount while agricultural prices collapsed. As is usually the case, there was no drop in the prices of manufactured goods comparable to that experienced by agricultural commodities.

Under such circumstances it is not surprising to find that the bankruptcy rate per 1000 farms jumped from 0.21 in 1920 to slightly over 1.20 for the years 1924–1926 and that farm-mortgage indebtedness increased almost $2,000,000,000 between 1920 and 1929. Agricultural land values were utterly demoralized, government experts estimating a decline from $79,000,000,000 in 1920 to $58,000,000,000 in 1927, a figure that was to sink even lower with the depression beginning in 1929. For the nation as a whole the percentage of farms operated by tenants rose from 38 in 1920 to 42 in 1930, and the estimates five years later were over 50 per cent. When to this is added the increased mortgage burden carried by farmers, it is not surprising that many students were wondering whether the American farmer was destined to sink to the status of the European peasant. Industrial prosperity and agricultural decline, in conjunction with the introduction of improved machinery, brought a decline of population on farms from 31,614,000 in 1920 to 30,169,000 in 1930, with a net movement from the farms for the decade of about 600,000 each year. This decline came despite a population increase for the nation as a whole of over 17,000,000.

Every depression has had its political reverberations, and it was hardly to be expected that the long depression in agriculture would not receive government attention, particularly since agriculture under our system of government is strongly represented in the Senate and representatives from agricultural states ordinarily ignore party lines to coalesce in support of farm legislation. In general, the demand of the farmers during the twenties was for governmental aid and protection that would put them on a par with more favored economic interests. The legislation that sprang from this demand contemplated greater tariff protection, better credit facilities, and the creation of machinery to raise prices artificially. As a whole, it was characterized by a new emphasis. Up to the World War agricultural legislation had been concerned chiefly with production; in the postwar years the emphasis has been largely upon marketing.

So anxious were the Republicans to rid themselves of the Underwood tariff that a special session of Congress in 1921 rushed through an emergency tariff (May 27) and a year later a more permanent measure, the Fordney-McCumber tariff (September, 1922). Fear of a deluge of cheap European goods, a desire to protect new war industries, and an anxiety to propitiate the farmers were behind this legislation. The Fordney-McCumber Act as well as the Hawley-Smoot tariff of 1930 put heavy duties on agricultural commodities. Some of the rates undoubtedly helped to protect certain commodities, but the primary problem of the farmers was to regain and extend their foreign market and this could be done only by lowering duties on manufactured goods. As these three tariff measures had done quite the opposite, it is probable that the farmer on the whole was injured rather than helped by the legislation. On the other hand, the acts designed to extend better credit facilities were an undoubted benefit. They included the War Finance Corporation, revived in 1921 to finance the exportation of agricultural products through emergency credits, and the Agricultural Credits Act of 1923, which set up a federal intermediate credit bank in each federal land-bank district to extend credit for periods intermediate between the usual short-term commercial loan and the long-term obligations secured by land. Essentially they were banker's banks which were to loan on notes, drafts, and other agricultural security already discounted by other banks or credit associations.

Legislation of this type, while it might be helpful, hardly got at the root

Psychology of the 20's.

some
5 m. people had jobs in some way
dep. upon B'ness (1 out of 9 persons
gainfully employed in U.S.

Gov't spent $ 10 $ for h'way construction
during 20's.

By 1928 —
giving direct employment to 5%
of all ind. workers + paying 6%
of all ind. wages.

Stim. gasoline, leather,
plate glass, rubber, steel, paint,
+ cement ind.

created 1000's of jobs —
mechanics, chauffeurs + filling-
station attendants.

Welfare capitalism
1st wages consid above average,
paternalistic attitude toward employees,
stubborn opposition to trade unionism.

Prosperity of 20's by no means fictitious —
much solid economic achievement

1. For most Americans, employment was
steady & wages increasing.
   Usually pay remained substantially higher
   than before war.
   Prices were high, but wages & salaries
   in certain marked exceptions were well up
   level.
   Good prices rose propo. less than
   wages.

2. Improvement in Standard of living
   - Health & mortality statistics
   increase in hosp. facilities
   school attendance
   variety of goods & services sold to cons.
   reduction in hours of labor.

3. Increased efficiency thru. scientific
   management & improved machines
   made human labor more prod. than
   ever before.

MUCH OF PROSPERITY of Pd reflected
RAPID GROWTH OF NEW INDUSTRIES.

MOST 4. → Growth of Auto. Ind. — most imp. single
factor in creating prosp. of 20's.
ASTONISHING
IN DEGREE → he motorcar above everything else
OF EXPANSION gave tone to the Pd.
   1. By middle 20's. ownership no
   longer a class distinction

helped
bring down 2. Range of social & b'ness control
payments? immensely enlarged — Mobility
   3. tempo of civilization speeded.

REGISTERED AUTOS
   1920 — 8 million
   1929 — 23 million (1. car for
   6 inhab.)

In 1908 — Ford set out to sell his car
at price wh. ave. middle class Am. coul.
meet

of the trouble, and the more radical members of the congressional "farm bloc," prodded by farm leaders throughout the country, turned to the enactment of bills that would artificially raise prices. The principle first advocated was the creation of a gigantic government corporation that should purchase certain of the chief agricultural products at a price that would yield a fair profit, then sell the surplus abroad at what it would bring, the loss on the foreign sales to be distributed among the farmers in the form of an equalization fee. Thus the final price to the farmer would be the domestic price minus the equalization fee. This plan was incorporated in the McNary-Haugen bills passed by Congress in 1927 and 1928 but vetoed by President Coolidge. With both parties in the campaign of 1928 seeking agricultural support by promising legislation, action could not long be delayed. It came in the Agricultural Marketing Act of 1929, by which Congress appropriated $500,000,000 to be lent by the Federal Farm Board to co-operative associations to promote orderly marketing and stabilize prices. The board not only encouraged marketing co-operatives but also created stabilization corporations, which went into the market and made large purchases of grain and cotton. It was ironical to find a government under the leadership of Herbert Hoover, who preached the doctrine of "rugged individualism," attempting to save the farmers by encouraging marketing co-operatives and by entering the commodity markets to upset the normal flow of goods and the price structures. Ironical or not, it might have helped but for the depression, which engulfed the nation the year that the act was passed. Under the circumstances the act accomplished little.

ECONOMIC COLLAPSE

The twenties began with a depression and ended with one, but the intervening years had been so active and prosperous that many, forgetting the normal swing of business cycles in a capitalist economy, had predicted an indefinite continuation. Such observers failed to recognize certain fundamental flaws in the economic structure, which worked to undermine the rather widespread prosperity. In the first place, certain industries, notably coal-mining, textiles, shipbuilding, railroad equipment, and leather manufactures had never fully revived after the postwar depression. Even more important was the failure of agriculture to recover.

In the industries that did show a relative prosperity in the boom years, there were factors destined eventually to undermine their structure. Although the decade showed a considerable increase in real wages, it was evident that the proportion of total income in industries going into profits was relatively greater than that going into salaries and wages. As a result, wealth was piling up where it would be used chiefly for further industrial expansion rather than where it might be used for consumers' goods. It was also evident that employment was not keeping pace with the growth of either population or capital equipment. Even in the boom years unemployment ran over a million and a half. Overexpansion in certain industries and failure of others to recover, accompanied by considerable unemployment and by a maldistribution of the profits of industry, tended to bring collapse. To these influences must be added the economic situation abroad. Impoverished by the war, suffering from a long-continued depression, cursed by a revival of intense nationalism, Europe was in no condition to buy heavily from the United States. Purchases might be made if we would loan them money or take goods in exchange. Loans for a time were made, but eventually dwindled, while normal trade was increasingly curtailed by the Fordney-McCumber (1922) and Hawley-Smoot (1930) tariffs. The tendency in the twenties for the world's gold to move to the United States raised prices here and further injured foreign trade.

As the boom cycle swung toward its apex, it was, as usual, accompanied by a frenzy of speculation. Unprecedented, however, in American history was the extent of popular participation in this mania of speculation. The inevitable end came with the stockmarket crash of October 29, 1929, followed by an economic decline that continued with but little interruption until the spring of 1933. Some idea of its extent is seen from the figures of the United States Bureau of Labor Statistics. Using 1926 as a base year with an index figure of 100, the average of wholesale prices declined from an average of 95.3 in 1929 to 65.9 in 1933, employment from 97.5 to 64.6, and payrolls from 100.5 to 44. Exports declined in value from $5,241,000,000 to $1,611,000,000 and imports from $4,399,000,000 to $1,323,000,000. That the depression was the most severe in our history, economists were generally agreed, but there was no unanimity as to the reasons. Among the many factors suggested as contributing to its length and severity must be counted the weakness of the American banking structure, with its series of credit crises; the collapse of the foreign market, accompanied by the unsettlement of European currencies; increasing European competition, helped by the migration of American industries abroad to escape tariff walls; the growing rigidity of the price system, due to increased business consolidation; the growing concentration of wealth and income; and, finally, the difficulty of putting the unemployed back to work with the rapid development of labor-saving machinery. In no previous depression had the American nation faced the same combination of adverse factors, and the efforts of the Hoover administration to halt the economic debacle appeared to be without effect (page 638). In such a situation the political overturn of 1932 was to be expected.

H. U. Faulkner, *American Economic History* (5th ed.), Chap. XXVIII, is a longer summary. Among the most recent significant treatments of consolidation are H. W. Laidler, *Concentration of Control in American Industry*, Chap. XXIII, and A. A. Berle, Jr., and G. C. Means, *The Modern Corporation and Private Property*, Chaps. II–V. The decline of labor is clearly told in L. L. Lorwin, *The American Federation of Labor*, Chaps. VIII–XI. H. G. Moulton *et al.*, *The American Transportation Problem*, Chaps. XXI–XXXI, is a thorough study of postwar conditions. J. D. Black, *Agricultural Reform in the United States*, Part I, is perhaps the best study of agriculture during the twenties. A shorter discussion is Chester C. Davis, "The Development of Agricultural Policy Since the End of the World War," *Yearbook of Agriculture, 1940*, 297–326. Also examine H. S. Commager, *Documents of American History*, Vol. II, 345–347, 353–358, 367–372, 384–386, 390–393, 402–405, 406–408, 412–417.

Chapter XL

ROOSEVELT AND THE NEW DEAL

*What we seek is balance in our economic sys-
tem—balance between agriculture and industry
and balance between the wage earner, the employer and the consumer. We seek also balance
that our internal markets be kept rich and large,
and that our trade with other nations be increased on both sides of the ledger.*

FRANKLIN D. ROOSEVELT
March 5, 1934

*Our purpose was not only to provide work in
all sections for all parts of the population, but to
enable them all to share in the benefits to be obtained from the works so long as bricks and
mortar shall endure. As far as it was humanly
possible, the Government has followed the policy
that among American citizens there should be no
forgotten men and no forgotten races. It is a wise
and truly American policy. We shall continue
faithfully to observe it.*

FRANKLIN D. ROOSEVELT
Address at Howard University,
October 26, 1936

MEETING THE EMERGENCY

The conditions that faced Franklin D. Roosevelt when he took the oath
of office on March 4, 1933,[1] were unprecedented in American history. General business had sunk to 60 per cent of normal, while commodity prices
in January had declined to the low point up to that time of the depression. In November of the preceding year American exports had sunk to the
lowest monthly total in thirty years, with little prospect of improvement.
Estimates of the number of unemployed ran from 13,000,000 to 17,000,000.

[1] This was the last inauguration to take place on March 4. On February 6, 1933, the
Secretary of State proclaimed the adoption of the twentieth amendment, long advocated by
Senator George Norris of Nebraska, which abolished the "lame-duck" sessions and pro-
vided for the inauguration of the President on January 20 rather than March 4.

Nothing illustrated more strikingly the depth of the economic depression than the collapse of the nation's credit structure. Over 1400 banks had failed during 1932, with the banking situation approaching a climax in the early months of 1933. On February 14 the leading banks in Detroit closed their doors, and the state of Michigan declared an eight-day banking moratorium, an action quickly followed elsewhere until by March 2 at least twenty-one states besides the District of Columbia either had declared moratoria or were allowing their banks to operate under special regulations. On inauguration day both New York and Illinois declared bank holidays, an action that was immediately followed by the closing of the stock and commodity exchanges.

Under such circumstances the pronouncements and policies of the new President were awaited with tense expectancy. His brief inaugural address cautioned against unreasoning fear, denounced "the rulers of the exchange of mankind's goods" and the "unscrupulous money changers," pledged a special session of Congress, and intimated that if necessary he would ask for extraordinary powers to deal with the emergency. There must be "a strict supervision of all banking and credits and investments," he insisted, and "an end of speculation with other people's money." Calling for action to deal with agriculture and unemployment, he declared, "Our greatest primary task is to put people to work."

That these were not mere words was quickly evident. He immediately called a special session of Congress to pass emergency relief legislation and on March 5 declared a nation-wide bank moratorium, at the same time placing an embargo on the withdrawal and transportation of gold and silver. By the time Congress met on March 9, the Emergency Banking Act had been prepared, which confirmed the actions already taken by the President and gave him emergency powers to regulate transactions in credit, currency, gold, silver, and foreign exchange. The Secretary of the Treasury was empowered to call in all gold and gold certificates and the Comptroller to appoint a conservator for any national bank in difficulty or needing reorganization. The act provided that members of the Federal Reserve System might open under license and sought to strengthen the position of these banks by empowering the Reconstruction Finance Corporation to purchase or receive as collateral for loans the preferred stock of the banks. Under these regulations the bank moratorium came to an end on March 13, much to the relief of millions who had been trying to carry on a normal economic life with inadequate currency.

Other legislation quickly followed. An economy act, the first and apparently the last effort of the first Roosevelt administration to balance the budget, gave the President broad power to establish a new pension system and to reduce salaries of all federal employees up to 15 per cent for the fiscal year ending June 30, 1934. In anticipation of the repeal of the eighteenth amendment, a beer and wine act was passed, permitting states to allow the manufacture and sale of malt and vinous liquors having an alcoholic content of not more than 3.2 per cent by weight. As a first attack on unemployment, the President was authorized to establish the Civilian Conservation Corps to construct works of a public nature in connection with reforestation, flood and fire control, and similar projects, an act that enabled the government quickly to absorb over 300,000 of the younger unemployed.

These were but the first guns in a four-year battle waged against unemployment, insecurity, and economic distress, a battle that quickly brought a score or more of important legislative acts, which came to be known as the "New Deal," and an intricate and confusing maze of administrative agencies to carry them into effect. It was, in effect, an effort toward a planned economy. This legislation, as we shall see, extended greatly the government's supervision over, control of, and participation in the economic life of the nation, a development that naturally brought much opposition and criticism from exponents of economic *laissez faire*. The large administrative agencies that were set up, it was pointed out, had greatly enlarged the Washington bureaucracy. The unprecedented peacetime powers given the President, it was insisted, were developing a dictatorship, while the interference in the economic life of people, it was charged, was unconstitutional. On the part of the masses of people, however, the reception of the new legislation was sympathetic. The emergency was great, unusual action was necessary, and experiments, it was felt, must be given an opportunity to prove themselves before they were condemned. Many felt that the New Deal was America's way of meeting an economic situation that Europeans had met in a less fortunate fashion. The cabinet that the President picked [2] to aid him in carrying out the New Deal was not received with great enthusiasm but proved in the end reasonably effective and up to the level of the average cabinet. Its work was strengthened

[2] Cordell Hull, Tennessee, Secretary of State, succeeded in 1945 by Edward R. Stettinius, Jr.; W. H. Woodin, Pennsylvania, Secretary of the Treasury, succeeded in 1933 by Henry Morgenthau, Jr., New York; George H. Dern, Utah, Secretary of War, succeeded in 1936 by H. H. Woodring, Kansas, and in 1940 by Henry L. Stimson, New York; Homer S. Cummings, Connecticut, Attorney General, succeeded in 1939 by Frank Murphy, in 1940 by Robert H. Jackson, in 1941 by Francis Biddle, and in 1945 by Tom C. Clark; Claude A. Swanson, Virginia, Secretary of the Navy, succeeded in 1940 by Franklin Knox, and in 1944 by James Forrestal; James A. Farley, New York, Postmaster General, succeeded in 1940 by Frank C. Walker and in 1945 by Robert E. Hannegan; Harold Ickes, Illinois, Secretary of the Interior; Henry A. Wallace, Iowa, Secretary of Agriculture, succeeded in 1940 by Claude R. Wickard and in 1945 by Clinton P. Anderson; Daniel C. Roper, South Carolina, Secretary of Commerce, succeeded in 1938 by Harry L. Hopkins, in 1940 by Jesse Jones, and in 1945 by Henry A. Wallace; Frances Perkins, New York, Secretary of Labor, succeeded in 1945 by Lewis B. Schwellenbach. Of the original cabinet only Harold Ickes and Frances Perkins remained at the beginning of Roosevelt's fourth administration. Later Henry Wallace rejoined the cabinet.

by the careful selection of undersecretaries and New Deal administrators, many of them college professors and experts, who soon became known as the "brain trust." [3]

DEALING WITH AGRICULTURE

One of the most complex and difficult problems faced by the administration was the long-drawn-out depression in agriculture that had baffled Republican administrations from Harding to Hoover. This problem was attacked in the Farm Relief and Inflation Act (Agricultural Adjustment Act) passed in May, the first of the major New Deal acts. Based on the theory that the distress of the farmer was due to overproduction, the act sought to raise prices and bring back prosperity by eliminating the surplus. Specifically this and subsequent acts sought to restore the farmer's purchasing power to the position it had enjoyed during the prewar period, from August, 1909, to July, 1914, a time when it was believed the prices farmers paid were in balance with prices received. To accomplish this object the Agricultural Adjustment Administration (AAA) was set up, which might: (1) grant to cotton-growers, who would reduce their acreage by at least 30 per cent, options to purchase from the Federal Farm Board an amount of cotton corresponding to the amount they had agreed not to raise, which options the holders might sell if the price of cotton went up; (2) grant "rental" or benefit payments to farmers for acreage temporarily taken out of cultivation; and (3) authorize and encourage marketing agreements to eliminate waste and provide for more scientific distribution. To finance this curtailment program taxes were to be levied upon the processors of agricultural products. During the first year the AAA concentrated chiefly upon reduction of the cotton, wheat, corn, and hog production and after a year's trial Congress considered the experiment sufficiently successful to pass in 1934 two additional acts, which extended the program to include beef and dairy cattle, peanuts, rye, barley, flax, grain sorghums, sugar beets, and sugar cane, and to strengthen the tobacco and cotton curtailment by special acts.

No part of the New Deal program aroused more criticism than that pertaining to agriculture. The destruction and curtailment of foodstuffs at a time when millions lacked sufficient food seemed difficult to justify. Furthermore, the processing taxes were quickly shifted by the manufacturer to the consumer; this, combined with curtailment of production, brought a rapid increase of prices to the ultimate user. The general rise of prices

[3] Notably Assistant Secretary of State Raymond Moley (resigned, August 27, 1933), Assistant Secretary of Agriculture Rexford G. Tugwell (resigned, 1936), Assistant Secretary of State Adolf Berle, Jr. (1938–1944), and Roswell McGill, Assistant Secretary of the Treasury (1938–1939).

tended to keep the farmer's dollar about where it had been before. The farmers, having been paid for curtailing one product, sometimes turned to the production of others, while curtailment in America stimulated production of similar commodities abroad. But whatever may have been the disadvantages of the program of crop curtailment, on the whole the benefits to the farmer appeared substantial. By the opening of 1935 the AAA pointed to the fact that the purchasing power of units of farm products in 1934 had averaged 73 per cent of the prewar level, as compared with 55 per cent at the low point of March, 1933, that the purchasing power of farmers' net income in 1934 was nearly 80 per cent of the prewar level as compared to 52 per cent in 1932, and that the farmers' per capita share of the national income in 1934 was 80 per cent of the prewar level as compared with 60 per cent in 1932. While this improvement quite obviously may not have been due solely to the government program, it marked an important gain.

The AAA had operated a little over two years and a half when the Supreme Court, on January 6, 1936, declared certain parts of the Farm Relief and Inflation Act unconstitutional (page 706). The possibility that this might happen had already led the administration to search for other methods of agricultural relief. The devastating drought of 1934, followed by the dust storms of the spring of 1935, had called the attention of the nation in no uncertain fashion to the tragic results of soil-destruction. The need for meeting this problem had already been recognized to a small degree by the creation in 1933 of the Soil Erosion Service and by the enactment of the Soil Erosion Act (April 27, 1935), which created the Soil Conservation Service under the Secretary of Agriculture to conduct soil-erosion surveys, carry out preventive measures, and enter into agreements with, or provide financial aid to, any agency whereby lands might be acquired by purchase, by condemnation, or otherwise, to protect land resources against soil-erosion. After the AAA decision Congress greatly enlarged the scope of the work by passing the Soil Conservation and Domestic Allotment Act (February 29, 1936), appropriating $500,000,000 for the preservation and improvement of soil fertility, the promotion of the economic use and conservation of land, diminution of wasteful and unscientific soil exploitation, and protection of rivers and harbors against soil-erosion. Direct aid might be given to co-operating farmers for two years, after which aid was to be extended only to states that had adopted authorizing legislation and a conservation plan acceptable to the Secretary of Agriculture.

The agricultural program of the government was wider than the mere raising of prices through crop curtailment. It involved, as we shall see, a general increase in prices through inflation and a program of financial aid to the farmers to help them in production and in refinancing their obligations. The Farm Relief and Inflation Act, for example, authorized the Federal Land Banks to issue $2,000,000,000 in 4-per-cent bonds to refinance farm mortgages at an interest rate not to exceed 4½ per cent. In 1934 Congress passed the Farm Mortgage Refinancing Act (January 31), which created the Federal Farm Mortgage Corporation to extend further aid in refinancing farm debts. It passed the Farm Mortgage Foreclosure Act (June 12) to make possible the extension of loans to farmers to enable them to recover properties already foreclosed, and finally it enacted the Frazier-Lemke Bankruptcy Bill (June 28), providing that in cases of bankruptcy the farmer might demand an appraisal and then repurchase his property over a period of six years with interest at 1 per cent. If either creditor or mortgagee objected to the settlement, the farmer might retain the property for a period of five years at a reasonable rental with bankruptcy proceedings halted. Declared unconstitutional by the Supreme Court (page 705), the Frazier-Lemke Act was repassed with the period of five years cut to three, a change which satisfied the Court. This series of agricultural acts tended to halt the flood of mortgage foreclosures and to ease the financial situation that had long confronted the farmer, and incidentally operated in the long run also to benefit insurance companies and banks, which were the chief holders of farm mortgages. Early in the administration, Congress, by the Farm Credit Act (June 16, 1933), had authorized the grouping of the numerous agricultural credit facilities into four divisions, under the Farm Credit Administration, dealing with land banks, production credit, intermediate credit, and co-operative credit. In the first year and a quarter of its existence the FCA made 1,400,000 loans totaling almost $2,000,000,000. "Lending this money," declared the governor of the FCA as early as October 31, 1934, "has practically meant the stoppage of foreclosures, which were at their peak when the Farm Credit Administration was organized."

The description of the agricultural legislation just given by no means exhausts the direct and indirect efforts made by the federal government to improve the lot of the farmers. There was the Federal Surplus Commodities Corporation to distribute surplus farm produce among state relief organizations. There was the much criticized resettlement project of moving farmers from submarginal lands and settling them on subsistence homesteads or in semirural villages. There were the flood-control projects, the subsidizing of interstate highways, and the large amounts allotted for rural electrification. There were also the efforts to help the farmer by reciprocal tariffs and in many other ways. In fact, it would be difficult to think of any method for aiding the farmer which was not tried during Roosevelt's first administration. That the sum total of all of these efforts was of benefit to the farmer could hardly be denied. The gross income of the farmers increased notably during the thirties. By 1936, however, at least two facts about the agricultural situation were becoming evident. In the first place, it was the large farmer rather than the small one who was chiefly benefiting. In the second place, the efforts of the federal government to help the farmer save his land had taken the government into the business of land mortgages on an unprecedented scale. By the end of 1937, it is estimated, probably half of the agricultural long-term paper was held by governmental agencies. At the same time private finance agencies were largely abandoning the field.

CURRENCY AND BANKING UNDER THE NEW DEAL

Essentially the financial program of the first Roosevelt administration appears to have been twofold: the raising of prices through inflation and the eradication of the chief evils in American banking, particularly in the Federal Reserve system. The first objective developed from the plight of the debtor, particularly the farmer, always adversely affected by an economic depression. The almost continuous demand for inflation, growing stronger, of course, during periods of economic depression, had been an outstanding characteristic of American economic history. The move toward inflation, resulting from the depression of 1929, began with the Emergency Banking Act of March 9, 1933 (page 689), and was continued on the following day by an executive order halting the export of gold except when licensed by the treasury, on April 5 by a similar order forbidding the hoarding of gold and gold certificates, and on April 19 by one forbidding the export of gold. The last order was interpreted as taking the nation off the gold standard and was made more definite by the Gold Repeal Joint Resolution of June 5, which canceled gold clauses in debts public and private and made them payable in legal tender. Already a broad legal base for inflation had been laid in the Farm Relief and Inflation Act, which gave the President power, if he so desired, to expand the credits of the Federal Reserve Banks up to $3,000,000,000; to issue United States notes solely on the credit of the United States up to $3,000,000,000, these notes to be used only to retire federal obligations but to be legal tender for all debts, public and private; to devalue the gold dollar up to 50 per cent, and to accept silver up to $200,000,000 for six months at a price not exceeding 50 cents an ounce from foreign governments in payment of war debts. Most of the old methods of inflation demanded by Greenbackers and Populists, as well as new ones, were all combined here in one act.

A temporary rise in prices in the late spring and early summer of 1933 halted momentarily the movement for inflation, but, when the price index sank in the early autumn, agitation was renewed. On October 22 the government announced that it would purchase newly mined gold from the

American mines and shortly thereafter that it would buy foreign gold at a price determined by the RFC. Instead of the old legal price of $20.67 an ounce the new price was $31.36, which was finally increased to $34.45. In December the same policy was extended to silver when the treasury was ordered to purchase all silver mined in the United States at $64\frac{1}{2}$ cents an ounce, a price $21\frac{1}{2}$ cents higher than that existing in the open market at the time. Not satisfied with the situation and desiring a more clear-cut authorization, the President asked Congress in January for specific power to devalue the dollar between 40 and 50 per cent in terms of its former gold content, to manage the dollar within these limits, to impound in the treasury the gold held in the Federal Reserve Banks, to assure to the government whatever profits might accrue from devaluation, and to use $2,000,000,000 of the profits as a fund to stabilize the dollar. This authority having been granted, the President, in February, 1934, officially fixed the value of the dollar at 59.06 per cent of its former (1900) value. The procedure by which the inflation was carried out was quite simple. The government merely kept its gold in the treasury and allowed paper to circulate in its place. It offered to buy gold, but, when it did so, simply exchanged for the gold more paper dollars than it had previously when the dollar contained more gold.

In inaugurating this plan the President had said that his objective was "to make possible the payment of public and private debts at more nearly the price level at which they had been incurred" and that he was "moving toward a managed currency." In the particular method that he pursued he appeared to have been influenced by a school of economists who hold that the price level of commodities is closely influenced by the gold content of the monetary medium. That such a relationship existed no one would deny, but as a short-cut to inflation it proved disappointing. While the gold content of the dollar had been reduced by law 40.94 per cent, prices after three months had risen only 22 per cent, and it was impossible to know what part of this increase was due to added taxes and improved economic conditions and what to monetary inflation. The fact that nine tenths of the nation's business is conducted on credit rather than by currency probably offers the chief explanation for the lag of prices. At all events, this lag served to turn the inflationary efforts of the government from currency to credit, and, except for some silver legislation in June, 1934, it ceased tinkering with the currency.[4] Efforts to repair the credit structure of the nation

---

[4] The Silver Purchase Act of 1934 announced that our national policy was to increase the use of silver in the country's monetary stock "with the ultimate objective of maintaining one-fourth of the monetary value of such stocks in silver." It authorized the President to nationalize silver and to buy it at his own discretion. Although considerable amounts were purchased from Mexico at great loss, the effort to make it one fourth of the monetary stock was never seriously undertaken. The silver legislation was largely a business of propitiating senators from the silver states.

had begun under Hoover in the establishment of the RFC and the Home Loan Banks and were continued under Roosevelt in such legislation as the Loans to Industry Act and the Home Owners' Loan Act. This policy of improving the credit structure was a major feature of all the banking legislation.

The second great objective in the financial policy of the Roosevelt administration, the improvement of the banking system, began in earnest with the Glass-Steagall Act of June, 1933. Probably the most important and certainly the most widely discussed parts of the act were those that separated security affiliates from the parent banks of the Federal Reserve system and those that set up the Federal Deposit Insurance Corporation to provide insurance on deposits for member banks of the Federal Reserve system and for state banks that desired to participate.[5] Other parts of the act restricted the use of Federal Reserve Bank credit for speculative purposes, restrained such banks from dealing in foreign securities, and made it illegal for private banks to act both as banks of deposit and as underwriters and promoters of securities, but it broadened the power of national banks by allowing them to establish branch banks in those states allowing branch banking.

Supplementary banking legislation was passed in 1935, when very important changes were made in the direction of greater federal power over money and credit. The Federal Reserve Board was reorganized into a seven-member board with the elimination of the Secretary of the Treasury and the Comptroller from ex-officio membership. A Federal Open Market Committee, consisting of the seven members of the Federal Reserve Board (now called the Board of Governors) and five elected representatives of the twelve regional banks, was established; it was to have power to control credit fluctuations by purchasing and selling government obligations in the open market and, if necessary, to check speculation by doubling the required percentage of reserves.

Included in the financial program of the government was the establishment of some sort of federal supervision over the stock exchanges, a supervision made imperative by the chaotic speculation and unscrupulous manipulation that had characterized the exchanges in the years preceding the crash of 1929. The Sale of Securities Act in 1933 sought to protect investors by requiring the filing with the Federal Trade Commission of certain information regarding new securities sold in interstate commerce, and provided that, even after permission had been granted by the commission,

---

[5] This act provided for total insurance of deposits up to $10,000 and partial insurance on amounts above that figure, but these provisions were not to go into effect until 1934. As an interim measure deposits up to $2500 were insured. This temporary provision was extended to 1935 when the original insurance features of the 1933 act were discarded and a limit of $5000 was set to the amount insured.

the sellers of securities were still liable in civil or criminal suits for untrue statements. Severe criticism by industrialists and stockbrokers led Congress in the Securities and Exchange Act (June, 1934) to back down from the advanced position of the previous year and to weaken the liability of underwriters. The new act, however, established a bipartisan Securities and Exchange Commission to administer the act, required the licensing of all stock exchanges and registration with full information of all listed securities, defined the functions of dealers and brokers, banned manipulation to establish artificial prices, provided for regulation of margins and brokers' credit by the commission and the Federal Reserve Board, and set up initial standards of credit. While no informed person expected that this legislation would affect a millennium, many believed that it might eliminate some of the worst evils of stock-market speculation. Regulation of a similar type was extended over commodity exchanges by the Commodity Exchange Act of 1936.

INDUSTRY AND THE NEW DEAL

Perhaps no piece of legislation during these years was more revolutionary in its implications than the National Industrial Recovery Act (June, 1933), a two-year emergency measure for the purpose of providing employment and stimulating industry. This objective, it was hoped, might be attained, in the first place, by a bond issue of $3,300,000,000 to finance the construction of federal, state, and local projects (for which taxes were provided), and, in the second place, by granting wide powers to the President to promote self-regulation of industry under federal supervision. This might be done by curtailing overproduction, increasing wages, shortening hours of labor, and raising prices. To accomplish it the President was authorized to work out codes of fair competition, which industry was expected to accept voluntarily but which might be forced upon it through a system of licensing. Four years of depression with bitter competition had driven wage levels far below a standard of decent subsistence and the price of commodities often below the cost of production. If industry could be temporarily freed from the threat of prosecution under the antitrust laws, and if each branch of industry could formulate codes of fair competition involving agreements concerning wages, prices, and sales methods, it was hoped that cutthroat competition might be softened and an improvement in economic conditions result. The NIRA was a definite move away from *laissez faire* and "rugged individualism" and a step toward co-operation and economic planning.

To carry into effect the provisions of the NIRA a National Recovery Administration (NRA) was set up with General Hugh S. Johnson as administrator. With a corps of assistants and in conjunction with representatives of industry and labor, he formulated codes, which, after public hearings, were finally promulgated over the President's signature. As there were several thousand industries eligible for codification, the codes were somewhat hurriedly drawn with the expectation of subsequent amendment. Until the separate codes could be formulated, the President in July proposed a blanket code on hours and wages, known as the President's Reemployment Agreement, which banned child labor, set a working week of thirty-six hours for industrial workers and forty hours for white-collar workers, with minimum wages for industry of 40 cents an hour and for white-collar workers of $12 and $15 a week, depending on the size of the community. Any employer willing to adhere to the blanket agreement was to receive the symbol of the Blue Eagle. With parades and mass meetings to whip up enthusiasm in this war on depression, the NRA was inaugurated. At the end of a year some four hundred codes had been adopted, hearings had been completed on three hundred more, and at least 20,000,000 workers, it was estimated, had been brought under the codes.

Although adherents of the NIRA were enthusiastic as to its results, criticism came from many directions. Certain industrialists disliked its philosophy and believed it was unnecessary; many small industrialists felt that the codes and their administration favored the large manufacturer; labor insisted that in many cases the employer was evading the spirit, if not the letter, of the labor provisions. To check on the effects of the NRA a National Recovery Review Board under the chairmanship of Clarence Darrow had been set up early in 1934. After examining certain of the codes and their operation, the Board reported that the NRA was fostering monopoly and oppressing small industrialists, distributors, and consumers. The barrage of criticism culminated finally in the nation-wide textile strike of September, 1934, the resignation of General Johnson, and a reorganization of the NRA. After the Supreme Court decision (May, 1935) in the Schechter case (page 705) the NRA for all practical purposes came to an end. What the controversial NIRA contributed toward recovery it is impossible to determine. Labor under Section 7a had been given the right to organize and be represented by delegates of its own choosing. Since this gave an impetus to labor organization, and since the codes eliminated child labor and raised wages in the sweated trades, labor considered the destruction of the NRA a severe blow. Industry (not legally, but in fact) had been temporarily relieved from the operation of the antitrust acts, something for which they had clamored for many years. Only the consumer appeared to have gained nothing. Except for labor, however, the end of the NRA was looked upon by the average person with surprising indifference. Interestingly enough, it was Section 7a, later used as the basis of the National Labor Relations Act, that turned out to be the most lasting part of the NIRA.[6]

No American industry was subjected to more forthright criticism than the public utilities. The previous decade had witnessed rapid consolidation, the erection of one holding company on top of another, and the creation of a financial structure that camouflaged earnings, misled the investing public and resulted in the maintenance of unnecessarily high prices (page 673). A rising tide of protest was evident before the economic collapse; with the coming of the depression federal legislation to supplement the inadequate state supervision was inevitable. The first act, the Muscle Shoals and Tennessee Valley Development Act (1933), envisaged more than utilities regulation.[7] It was, in fact, a great experiment in regional planning. It created a board of three, known as the Tennessee Valley Authority, which was to maintain and operate properties owned by the government at Muscle Shoals, Alabama, in the interest of national defense and the development of agriculture and industry in the Tennessee valley. As it had power to build dams and power plants and develop a program of flood-control, reforestation, prevention of soil erosion, and manufacture of nitrogen products for fertilizer and explosives, it affected many interests. In the realm of the manufacture, distribution, and sale of electric power, it was very definitely intended to act as a "yardstick" by which private utilities might be judged, and the chief opposition to the TVA came from this group. Despite bitter opposition, the government continued the policy of power-development under public control, even lending money to cities to build public plants to drive down the rates of private industry.

Major legislation with respect to public utilities, however, did not come for two years. The Utilities Holding Company Act (1935), more bitterly fought than any other piece of New Deal legislation, sought to eliminate some of the worst evils that had developed during the chaotic twenties. Among other things, it granted the Federal Power Commission authority to regulate rates and business practices of utilities doing an interstate business, prohibited holding companies beyond the second degree, required federal sanction for the issuance of securities, acquisition of properties, and the handling of other kinds of business, and provided that after three years holding companies must limit their operations to single integrated systems [8] and to business directly connected with the supply of power

---

[6] It may also be considered a precedent for the Fair Labor Standards Act of 1938 (page 717).

[7] During the First World War the federal government built a large dam at Muscle Shoals on the Tennessee River to manufacture chemicals for explosives. After the war many people, led by Senator Norris of Nebraska, urged that the government continue operation to manufacture fertilizer for farmers. Others urged that the government sell the manufacturing plant to private operators. This was the background of the long controversy leading to the TVA.

[8] Exceptions might be made by the Securities and Exchange Commission.

service to consumers. The tremendous pressure brought to bear on Congress during the passage of this act and the charges and countercharges made led to investigations of lobbying by both the House and the Senate.

LABOR AND THE NEW DEAL

As usual during a depression, no element of the population suffered more acutely than the wage-earner, and there was evidence enough in the early thirties of the detrimental effects of this particular depression. Wages, as usual, had decreased more rapidly than prices; there was an increase in industrial accidents, reflecting a let-up in safety and accident-prevention activities, and there was an increase in sweatshops and in the overworking of women and children. Above all were the millions of unemployed—a problem that must be faced. Whatever permanent labor legislation might be enacted, relief of various kinds had to be immediately extended. Essentially, the policy quickly developed by the federal government was to afford relief through various useful projects by which the unemployed might find work. This policy, it was hoped, not only would relieve unemployment but would, by the spending of large amounts of money for wages and construction materials, prime the pump of economic prosperity.

This program began with the Emergency Relief Act (May 12, 1933), which created the Federal Emergency Relief Administration and authorized the RFC to make available to it $500,000,000 for emergency relief to the states. It was followed a month later by Title II of the NIRA, which set up the Public Works Administration under the direction of the Secretary of the Interior with $3,300,000,000 to promote construction in the public interest. To broaden the work of the PWA and to care for unemployed outside the construction industry, the Civil Works Administration was set up late in 1933 with appropriations from the PWA and the FERA. The CWA was eventually demobilized, but similar efforts were continued by the FERA and other bodies. Despite the efforts of the PWA, small progress seemed to be made toward absorbing the millions of unemployed. In an effort to speed re-employment Congress in 1935 appropriated $4,880,000,000 for a second public-works program, and the President by executive order established the Works Progress Administration (later called Work Projects Administration) to co-ordinate the entire works program. This was done in part to initiate various types of work outside the category of public works.

The WPA continued until the increased economic activity produced by the Second World War made it unnecessary. During the seven years from 1935 to 1942, when Congress ordered it liquidated, the WPA spent about $10,500,000,000, plus $2,700,000,000 contributed by sponsors, chiefly local governments. It never solved entirely the unemployment problem, but at the height of its activity it provided jobs for 3,000,000. At one time or another it employed 8,500,000,000 persons. Among the many things accomplished by the WPA were the construction of 122,000 public buildings, 664,000 miles of new roads, 77,000 new bridges, 285 new airports, and 24,000 miles of storm and water sewers, and the repair of thousands of existing facilities. Besides this it built parks, playgrounds, reservoirs, and innumerable other things that were greatly needed. Not only did the WPA provide jobs for skilled and unskilled workers in the various building projects, but it helped white-collar workers, including teachers, actors, artists, and writers. It also stretched out through the National Youth Administration to aid high school and college students to obtain an education.

To labor the most important part of the New Deal was Section 7a of the NIRA, which granted to labor the "right to organize and bargain collectively free from interference, restraint or coercion by employers." No employee as a condition of employment might be required to join a company union or refrain from joining a labor organization of his own choosing. The impetus given by this act resulted in widespread organization activities and, during the first year, in an increase of over 1,000,000 in the membership of labor unions. Organization was particularly rapid among bituminous coal-miners, where unionism was revived, and in the clothing industry. Of particular interest was the growth of "federal unions," industrial unions based on the shop rather than the craft, for which the American Federation of Labor granted during the first year of the NRA a total of 1368 charters to 800,000 workers. The high hopes of 1933, however, had faded by the spring of 1934, as labor met strengthened opposition on the part of employers, widespread evasion of the codes set up under the NIRA, and the failure of the government effectively to enforce the labor provisions of the act and of the codes.

The natural result of this situation was a rapid increase of strikes during the later part of 1933 and during 1934, culminating in September, 1934, in a nation-wide textile strike, called by the United Textile Workers, which involved some 450,000 workers. The wave of industrial conflict that swept the country resulted in government action. The national and local compliance boards set up under the NIRA, swamped with complaints, proved inadequate, and in 1933 the National Labor Board was established to enforce the labor provisions of the act. Even the NLB, with its nineteen regional boards, was quite ineffective, and rising discontent brought its abolition. Under the authority of Public Resolution No. 44 (June 19, 1934) the President established the nonpartisan National Labor Relations Board, which, it was hoped, might accomplish more. In the meantime threatened or actual strikes had led the President to appoint boards of arbitration and adjustment to take care of labor troubles among the longshoremen, the automobile workers, the steel workers, and, some months later, the textile industry. Despite the challenging by many employers of the constitutionality of the labor provisions of the NIRA, Congress, after the invalidation of that act by the Supreme Court, sought to make the labor provisions permanent by the National Labor Relations Act (July 5, 1935). Not only were the earlier provisions re-enacted but the act made permanent the National Labor Relations Board. Similar labor provisions, it should be noted, were also incorporated in the Guffey-Snyder Coal Act (1935), passed in an effort to stabilize the chaotic soft-coal industry, and setting up a "little NRA" in that industry. The National Labor Relations Act, as it turned out, has done more to strengthen the legal rights of labor than any other single piece of federal legislation.

The preceding discussion is far from including all the legislation passed during the first Roosevelt administration in behalf of labor. A system of federal labor exchanges was established in 1933; a Railroad Retirement Act (1935), which took the place of an earlier act declared unconstitutional, provided for retirement annuities for railroad workers; a special act provided machinery for settling disputes in the air-transport industry; and legislation (Walsh-Healey Government Contracts Act) required the government to place contracts only with concerns paying prevailing wages and meeting the stipulations regarding fair labor conditions. Most important of all, perhaps, was the Social Security Act (1935). Among its many benefits to labor were (1) the effort to provide a system of old-age pensions to aged needy persons by federal grants equal to the amounts appropriated by the states, (2) a scheme for contributory old-age pensions to be paid for by an income tax on employees and a payroll tax on employers, and (3) an effort to encourage the development of a federal-state system of unemployment insurance through laws passed by the states, the money to be obtained through a payroll-excise tax paid to the federal treasury solely by the employers.

Social-security legislation of this type had made little progress in this country during the predepression years, but the demand after 1930 for old-age and unemployment insurance became too strong to withstand. Besides unemployment and old-age insurance, the Social Security Act carried appropriations to take care of needy dependent children; for the promotion of the health of mothers and children in areas suffering severe economic distress; for medical, surgical, and corrective services for crippled children; for the vocational rebuilding of the physically disabled and aid for the needy blind; and, finally, for adequate public health services. This type of work was to be done by the states through grants from the federal government.

SOCIAL, POLITICAL, AND CONSTITUTIONAL ASPECTS

The preceding effort to describe the more important features of the so-called New Deal legislation makes it evident that this legislation encompassed a great many phases of our economic, social, and political life. Certain of the acts were designed primarily to hasten economic recovery, others to remedy abuses. Much of the legislation was sorely needed, some of it was long overdue, and there were few in the nation prepared to condemn it *in toto*. Many who might condemn certain legislative acts favored other parts of the program. By many, however, the general philosophy and tendency of the New Deal were considered foreign to American traditions and were attacked with vehemence. The general charge was frequently made, for example, that it was breaking down "free enterprise" and moving toward socialism. That the New Deal extended government supervision, control, and activity in the economic life of the nation, and that it was reaching toward a "planned economy," there could be no doubt, but the charge that it contemplated fundamental change in the economic system was hardly warranted by the facts. The fundamentals of capitalist economy —private ownership of the means of production and distribution and the profit system—were maintained. In the case of agriculture this was carried to the extent of promoting scarcity rather than plenty in order to increase prices and profits. It was repeatedly maintained by leaders of the New Deal that they were engaged in saving capitalist economy by attempting to eliminate some of its major evils such as exploitation and insecurity.

Nevertheless, it was clear enough that the New Deal considerably extended federal supervision over the nation's economic life and that it was actually participating in it. But this was not new. It had started quite definitely with the Interstate Commerce Act of 1887 and the Sherman Antitrust Act of 1890, and had been in progress for forty years. Indeed, it had been given considerable impetus in the Hoover administration by the Agricultural Marketing Act, by the establishment of the Reconstruction Finance Corporation, and in various other ways.[9] The new element in the New Deal was the acceleration of the decline of *laissez faire,* and the acceleration was indeed rapid. As a recent historian has put it:

> Our state has become transformed—almost overnight. Formerly it concerned itself almost exclusively with civil administration and national defense, and when it intervened in other realms it for the most part acted in the capacity of umpire between equals. . . . Today, however, the state is

[9] This point of view is developed more fully in H. U. Faulkner, "Antecedents of New Deal Liberalism," *Social Education,* III, 153–160 (March, 1939).

operating to defend the underprivileged, to increase the national income, and to effect a more equitable distribution of that income among the various categories of producers. To achieve these ends not only has the American state taken on the whole job of assuring social security, but it has also become a participant in and an initiator of business enterprise. Our state, in short, has become the capitalist state, where only yesterday it was the *laissez-faire,* or passive, state; it constructs and operates plants; it buys and sells goods and services, lends money, warehouses commodities, moves ships and operates railroads. In one sense, the state is seeking to erect safeguards for the underprivileged against exploitation; in another it is competing with and replacing private enterprise—without, however, parting company with capitalist relations.[10]

Essentially, the New Deal sought to prevent the disintegration of the existing economic system by establishing some sort of balance among economic groups—a balance between agriculture and industry and a balance between the wage-earner, the employer, and the consumer. Such appeared to be the objective of the New Deal. Whether such an objective was practically possible and, if so, even advisable, was, of course, a matter of opinion. In any case, there was much dissent.

While the economic and social implications of the New Deal obviously commanded the greatest attention, political scientists were also quick to sense changes in the political system. The tremendous increase in the number of government employees made necessary by the New Deal activities led many to look with alarm upon the growth of bureaucracy in American government. Others contemplated with dismay the wide powers granted by Congress to the President or to his subordinates, which allowed them to promulgate rules and procedures that seemed to set up important lawmaking bodies outside Congress. Others saw in the widespread extension of federal supervision a continuing decline in the role of the states in the American political system. At the same time constitutional lawyers pondered over the legality of the new legislation and its effect upon the development of American constitutional law.

Considering the circumstances, it was to be expected that the constitutionality of the important phases of the New Deal legislation would be attacked and that the nation would look forward with more than ordinary interest to the attitude of the Supreme Court. Congress and the administration defended the legality of the legislation on the grounds that it was necessary to meet an emergency and that it was authorized under a reasonable interpretation of the general-welfare clause and, more specifically, under the powers of Congress to tax and to regulate interstate commerce. It was not until January, 1935, that the deliberate machinery of the Supreme

[10] Louis Hacker, *American Problems of Today,* vii.

Court began to grind out opinions on the important federal legislation. The first came on January 7, when the court by an eight-to-one decision nullified Section 9c of the NIRA, which had authorized the President to ban transportation across state lines of oil produced in excess of state quotas. The section was held illegal because Congress, in not laying down proper rules to guide the President, had delegated to him unwarranted powers.[11]

More important was the five-to-four decision (February 18) that upheld certain of the inflationary acts of the administration. Three questions were involved: (1) whether Congress could set aside the obligation incorporated in many private contracts to pay interest and principal in gold or some other type of coin or currency, (2) whether the holder of a federal gold certificate was entitled to payment in accordance with terms of the gold obligation or its equivalent, and (3) whether the holder of a Liberty Bond was entitled to payment in gold. On the first question the government was upheld. On the second question the plaintiff was refused access to the Court of Claims because, summarized Chief Justice Hughes, "We hold that the plaintiff has shown no actual damage and hence that the Court of Claims could not entertain the suit." On the third question, said Hughes, "We hold that the Joint Resolution of June 5, 1933, so far as it attempted to override the obligation of the United States created by the bond in suit, is invalid. It went beyond the Constitutional authority of Congress." The practical result of the entire decision, however, was virtually to give the government a free hand in its currency legislation.

In May came other important decisions. The Railroad Retirement Act, in a five-to-four decision, was invalidated because, in the opinion of the majority, it violated the due-process clause "by taking the property of one and bestowing it upon another" and because it was a misuse of the interstate-commerce power. A similar fate (May 27) befell the Frazier-Lemke Act when the court in a unanimous decision ruled that the legislation violated the provision of the fifth amendment that declares private property shall not be taken for public use without just compensation.[12] On the same day and also by a unanimous decision the NIRA was doomed when the court held that the code-making provisions were an invalid transfer of legislative power from Congress to the President and that in this case (Schechter case) the attempt to regulate industry in the manner prescribed was an improper use of the interstate-commerce power. There is "no warrant," said the court, "for the argument that the poultry handled by the defendants at their slaughterhouse markets was in 'current' or 'flow' of interstate commerce."

Another severe blow was administered some months later (January 6,

---

[11] Congress, by the "Hot Oil" Act (February, 1935), attempted to meet this objection.
[12] See above, page 693, for the result of this decision.

1936), when, in a six-to-three decision, the court demolished the Agricultural Adjustment Act, declaring the act invaded the reserved rights of the states and was an improper use of the taxing power. By a unanimous decision a few days later the court ordered $200,000,000 of impounded processing taxes to be refunded to the rice-processors and left in doubt the status of other farm taxes already levied on processors. The majority decision against the AAA (Hoosac Mills Case) so definitely forecast the invalidation of other New Deal legislation that it was no surprise when the court (May 18), in a decision involving the Guffey-Snyder Coal Act, held that the tax levied on coal sales was a penalty rather than a tax and that the wages and hours regulations were an infringement of states' rights. On the other hand, the administration won a victory when the court, by an eight-to-one decision (February 18, 1936), ruled that Wilson Dam at Muscle Shoals was constitutionally constructed and that the TVA might sell its surplus power. While the test was limited to this narrow field, the ruling was on one of the most hotly contested powers exercised by the TVA, and gave encouragement to those believing in this important experiment.

Not since the income-tax decision of 1895 had the Supreme Court been the object of such close scrutiny and such bitter criticism as was invoked by many of the decisions just mentioned. Pointing to the fact that certain of the judges could always be found against the New Deal legislation while others usually favored it, many believed that economic and social opinions rather than constitutional law were the determining factor. Learned justices seemed to be able to find law and precedents for either point of view. Old demands that larger majorities be required to invalidate state or federal legislation were revived, and there was a persistent demand for a constitutional amendment giving Congress power to pass social legislation. To many, such an amendment seemed particularly necessary when it became evident that the effort to extend federal control over the economic life of the nation, a control that had been gradually developed under the powers to tax and to regulate interstate commerce, now seemed definitely blocked.[13]

FOREIGN AFFAIRS DURING ROOSEVELT'S FIRST ADMINISTRATION

Attention has already been called to the fact that the Roosevelt policy with respect to foreign relations had been essentially that followed by his

[13] In its platform of 1936 the Democratic Party favored a constitutional amendment if necessary to carry out the New Deal program; the Republican Party avoided the issue, but Governor Landon reserved the right to favor an amendment to permit the states to regulate hours and wages if the statutory method was ineffective. In practice both parties dodged during the campaign the issue of a constitutional amendment. During his second term, as we shall see (pages 712–715), Roosevelt preferred to influence the Supreme Court in other ways.

predecessors during the decade of the twenties (page 646). The "good neighbor" policy toward other nations on the American continent, most strikingly illustrated by the abrogation of the Platt Amendment in a new treaty with Cuba in 1934, had been foretold by President Roosevelt's statement a year earlier that the "definite policy of the United States from now on is one opposed to armed intervention" and by a clear declaration at the Seventh Pan-American Conference at Montevideo (1933) against the intervention of any state of the American continent in the internal affairs of another state. This policy of pursuing friendly relations, which appeared to doom Theodore Roosevelt's corollary to the Monroe Doctrine (page 539), was further demonstrated by the President's visit in 1936 to the Inter-American Conference for the Maintenance of Peace at Buenos Aires. That the crude and high-handed methods of the old-fashioned imperialism were no longer to be followed was strikingly demonstrated not alone by our relations with Latin America but also by our projected withdrawal from the Philippines (page 647). Certainly by 1936 Latin America was gradually being won to the conviction that Roosevelt and Secretary of State Hull were utterly sincere in their gestures of friendship.

Toward Europe our policy was more confused. Efforts toward greater harmony and better relations were evident in the recognition of Russia (1933) after a sixteen-year policy of nonrecognition, in American advocacy of reduced armaments, and in the signing of reciprocal trade agreements to modify the highly nationalistic tariff walls that characterized the years after the First World War. On the other hand, the administration struck a rather strong nationalistic note at the London Economic Conference in 1933 by refusing to discuss the question of war debts or to co-operate in any policy of currency-stabilization at that time. Discouraging to many was the rejection by the Senate (1935) of American participation in the World Court after such a move had been favorably reported by the Senate Foreign Relations Committee. Strong isolationist sentiment, whipped up by anti-British bias, brought defeat by a vote of 52 to 36, seven less than the required two-thirds majority.

America's efforts to promote limitation of armaments, which had begun with the Washington Conference of 1922, were practically ended, at least for the time being, by the failure of the London Naval Limitations Conference (1935–1936). Japan's notification that she would not be bound after December 31, 1936, by the Washington naval treaty, the rapid rearmament of Europe led by the fascist nations, and the Vinson Naval Parity Act (1934), which sponsored an aggressive building program in this country, all helped to doom the London conference. In line with the world-wide extension of armaments, the United States in 1935 and 1936 voted the largest peace-time military budgets up to that time in her history.

While the United States was increasing her army and navy to unprecedented peace-time strength, some efforts were being made to maintain neutrality in the face of an impending European war. A reconsideration of the problems of neutrality had been forced upon the nation by the work of the Senate Munitions Investigation Committee under the chairmanship of Senator Gerald P. Nye, and the interest thus aroused resulted in three neutrality acts between 1935 and 1937. These acts, in addition to requiring all persons engaged in the manufacture of munitions of war to register with the Secretary of State and to export only under a license, provided that, when the President proclaimed the existence of a state of war (involving either foreign belligerents or factions in a civil war), it would be unlawful to export arms, munitions, or implements of war to the belligerent states or to neutral states for transshipment to, or use of, a belligerent country, and it directed the President to enumerate definitely such arms, munitions, and implements. When a state of war was proclaimed, it became unlawful to purchase, sell, or exchange bonds, securities, or other obligations of a government at war, issued after the date of proclamation, or to lend or extend credit to any such government or any person active in its behalf, although the President might make exceptions for ordinary commercial credits. The carrying of arms to belligerents and the transshipment of them was forbidden to American vessels, and American citizens were warned that they might travel on belligerent vessels only at their own risk. The neutrality acts were an effort to profit from experience and so avoid the complications which apparently had brought this country into the First World War. To do so the nation had to retreat from her long-cherished policy of "freedom of the seas," a policy which had helped to involve her in two wars.[14] The neutrality acts marked the full tide of American isolationism.

The Roosevelt administration made a real effort to ease international strains through reciprocal trade agreements. Although the administration made no effort to effect a thorough-going revision of the Hawley-Smoot Act passed in the preceding administration, it did ask of Congress, and was granted by the Trade Agreements Act of 1934, the power for three years to negotiate trade agreements with foreign governments and to raise or lower tariffs by not more than 50 per cent.[15] Pushed enthusiastically by Secretary of State Hull, who thoroughly believed that economic recovery was dependent upon a revival of foreign trade, at least twenty-seven such treaties had been signed by May, 1943. Although this method of tariff reduction seemed slow and piecemeal, it was actually more far-reaching than appeared. It was provided that the benefits of each agreement were

---

[14] See pages 136–145, 150, 157–173, 608 ff.
[15] Renewed for three years in 1937 and 1940 and for two years in 1943.

to extend under the most-favored-nation principle to all nations not discriminating against the United States. Because of the volume of trade between the two countries, the treaty with Canada (1935, renewed in 1938) was the most important. Concessions by Canada included a reduction on the duties of 180 commodities and a guarantee of the lowest rates for any non-British country on 767 items of the Canadian schedule, while the United States on her part made large reductions, particularly on agricultural products, lumber, and whiskies. Obviously, a reduction of tariffs might injure certain American interests, but the general and long-term effect, the administration believed, would be satisfactory. In any case, the treaties were followed by increased foreign trade with the nations with which they had been signed, although some of this increase may have been, and probably was, due to other causes, including improved economic conditions. More important, perhaps, was the influence of the reciprocal tariffs in reversing a world-wide tendency that in the previous fifteen years had pushed tariff walls higher and higher.

Although the administration was lukewarm toward the neutrality acts, the nation hoped that they might help in keeping us out of a future European war. The recognition of Russia was approved by most as an acknowledgment of a situation which had been virtually recognized *de facto* for some years. The trade-agreement policy was considered by most to be an intelligent effort to deal with a difficult and complicated problem, too often a football of party politics. Few doubted the soundness of the "good neighbor policy" toward Latin America. Despite the breakdown of the London conference and the whole effort toward limitation of armaments, the nation as a whole applauded Roosevelt's foreign policy as making definite progress toward sounder international relations. That forces destined to break down all efforts at peace—forces over which this nation had little or no control—were already making themselves felt, was a fact which the average American, isolated from the conflicts of other continents, had as yet but slight realization.

For the New Deal through the first Roosevelt administration, L. M. Hacker, *American Problems of Today,* Chaps. VII–X, is interpretative and descriptive. More spirited is the survey in Charles and Mary Beard, *America in Midpassage,* Chaps. III–VI. C. A. Beard and G. H. F. Smith, *The Old Deal and the New Deal,* is an excellent summary, as is Basil Rauch, *The History of the New Deal, 1933–1938.* The NRA is described in detail in L. S. Lyon *et al., The National Recovery Administration,* Chaps. I–X, and interpreted by its one-time administrator, Donald Richberg, *The Rainbow,* Chaps. IX–XII. For labor see Lyon, *op. cit.,* Chaps. XI–XV. Leo Pasvolsky, *Current Monetary Issues,* particularly in Chap. VI, contains an excellent account of currency. Foreign policy is summarized in T. A. Bailey, *A Diplomatic History of the American People,* Chap. XLIV. For sources, see H. S. Commager, *Documents of American History,* Vol. II, 417–445.

Chapter XLI

THE DECLINE OF REFORM

Our national policy in foreign affairs has been based on a decent respect for the rights and dignity of all nations. By an impressive expression of the public will and without regard to partisanship we are committed to all-inclusive national defense; to full support of all of those resolute peoples, everywhere, who are resisting aggression and are thereby keeping war away from our hemisphere; to the proposition that principles of morality and considerations for our security will never permit us to acquiesce in a peace dictated by aggressors and sponsored by appeasers.

FRANKLIN D. ROOSEVELT
Message to Congress
January 6, 1941

THE ELECTION OF 1936

As far as one could judge from election returns, the New Deal grew steadily in popular approval during the first four years. It met its first test in the midterm elections of 1934 and emerged with an easy victory. Assured of popular support and aided by a returning prosperity, the Democrats approached with confidence the election of 1936. Ignoring a handful of die-hard conservatives, the Democratic Party renominated Roosevelt and Garner, pledged a continuation of the New Deal policy, and wrote the usual platform laudatory of their accomplishments.

The Republicans were handicapped not only by widespread approval of the Roosevelt policies but also by the repudiation in 1934 of some of their old leaders and the fact that many of their present leaders were sympathetic with certain parts of the New Deal. The only hope, it was felt, was to turn from their former leadership, and on the first ballot at their convention they nominated Alfred M. Landon, governor of Kansas. A man of limited and provincial experience, Landon had been an acceptable governor during a trying period and had recently been pushed into public prominence by the Hearst press and sympathetic Republican papers. For second place the convention chose Franklin Knox, publisher of the Chicago *Daily News,* a former Theodore Roosevelt Progressive, but now acceptable to "Old Guard" Republicans.

Voters seeking guidance from the platforms of the two major parties found them amazingly alike. Both stood for federal regulation of business, both would enforce and strengthen antitrust legislation, both advocated sound currency and a balanced budget, both stood for peace and against foreign alliances, and both went on record for old-age security, help to the unemployed, and aid to agriculture. For labor both insisted on the right of collective bargaining and social legislation. The difficulty of the Republicans was well illustrated by their tariff plank, which promised to repeal the Trade Agreements Act, but, at the same time, pledged a policy of "bargaining for foreign markets." If there was a difference it was found in the fact that the two parties had reversed their historic roles. The Republicans appeared to be standing for states' rights and strict construction, and the Democrats for an enlarged federal conception and a loose construction of the basic law. In any event the platforms (as is not unusual) were largely ignored in the campaign.

Republican campaign strategy was to attack the New Deal as regimentation and socialism, to demand a stable currency and curtailment of the national debt, and to criticize many specific measures of the Roosevelt administration. The administration defended its record and pointed to returning prosperity, and in a final campaign speech Roosevelt promised to continue his social-welfare legislation. The influence of the minor parties was negligible; it was evident that the mass of liberal and radical voters had deserted the left-wing candidates for Roosevelt. Only the Union Party, headed by Representative William Lemke, exerted any real influence, and this only in a few local situations.[1] In a tremendous landslide the Democrats were returned to power. The electoral vote was 528 to 8, with Landon carrying only Maine and Vermont, and the popular vote approximately 27,477,000 to 16,680,000.[2] The Democrats also won substantial increases in both the Senate and the House. The new Senate after January 1 would have 75 Democrats, 17 Republicans, 2 Farmer-Laborites, 1 Progressive, and

---

[1] Lemke's backing came chiefly from the National Union for Social Justice, an organization founded by the Reverend Charles L. Coughlin, a Detroit priest, famous for his radio speeches. In addition to rather vague and general demands for social justice, the chief demand of this organization was for a change in the banking system that would return to the federal government the sole power to create currency. The Union Party disintegrated soon after the election.

[2] Of the minor parties the approximate votes follow:

William Lemke and T. C. O'Brien, Union	882,479
Norman Thomas and George Nelson, Socialist	187,720
Earl Browder and James W. Ford, Communist	80,159
D. L. Colvin and C. A. Watson, Prohibitionist	37,847
John Aiken and E. F. Teichert, Socialist Labor	12,777

1 Independent. The House would contain 334 Democrats, 89 Republicans, 7 Progressives, and 5 Farmer-Laborites. So overwhelming, in fact, was the Democratic victory that wise politicians were aware that this unwieldy Congressional majority might easily break into warring factions. Such a landslide evidently was not due, as some contended, merely to the support of left-wing voters or to the recipients of government aid. It went much deeper. It was probably due to a general approval of New Deal efforts, a feeling that Roosevelt was more receptive to the challenge of a rapidly changing economic order, a belief that he sensed and sympathized with the aspirations of the common man, and a fear that Republican victory meant reaction. After this vindication many supporters felt that Roosevelt should devote himself to consolidating the substantial gains already made rather than to forcing further reforms at the same rapid rate. More ardent New Dealers, on the other hand, felt that the election gave a mandate to the administration to continue its policies of the past few years. Whether Roosevelt would or could do this was the moot question as he entered his second term.

THE SUPREME COURT

In the mind of the President, the great obstruction to reform was not the essential conservatism of Congress but what he believed to be the reactionary views of a majority of the Supreme Court.[3] Had it not already ruined his program of dealing with agriculture and industry by invalidating the AAA, the NIRA, and other acts co-ordinated with them? True, the currency program and the TVA were as yet virtually intact, but the legislation governing these might still be impaired. Then there was the whole New Deal policy regarding labor. The court had avoided the labor aspect when it declared the NIRA unconstitutional, but the Guffey-Snyder Coal Act (the "Little NIRA") had been thrown out in part because the court believed the wages and hours regulations to be an infringement of states' rights. In his last dramatic speech during the campaign Roosevelt had hurled defiance at his foes and pledged a continued fight for the aims of the New Deal. If the election actually gave him a mandate to continue the battle, the Supreme Court, he believed, must be brought into line.

Presidential and even Congressional attacks upon the Supreme Court, it should be noted, were by no means unknown during times of stress. Jefferson had bitterly attacked the court, and his Congress had impeached (but not convicted) one of the associate justices (page 154). Jackson had

---

[3] The Supreme Court at this time consisted of Chief Justice Charles E. Hughes and Associate Justices Louis D. Brandeis, Pierce Butler, Benjamin N. Cardozo, James C. McReynolds, Owen J. Roberts, Harlan F. Stone, George Sutherland, and Willis Van Devanter.

expressed his opinion of that body in no uncertain words (pages 193, 195). Lincoln and the Republican Party had refused to accept the decision of the court in the Dred Scott case, and Congress during the Reconstruction period had stripped the Supreme Court of appellate jurisdiction over cases involving the right of *habeas corpus*. As opposition to the court increased, there was much discussion as to the best manner of dealing with the situation, and many plans were proposed. Some believed that Congress could cut the knot by a simple enactment requiring a majority of six or seven justices to invalidate a statute; others advocated a constitutional amendment to do this or one which would enlarge the powers of Congress concerning social and economic legislation. Before any specific plan could solidify into definite action, the President in a special message to Congress on February 5 offered his own solution. It was, in brief, a new law which would empower the President to appoint a new federal judge when any judge failed to retire within six months after reaching the age of 70. The number of federal judges who could be appointed was limited to fifty, and of these but six could be added to the Supreme Court. This would make it possible to increase the Supreme Court to fifteen members.

In his message the President emphasized the necessity for a "constant infusion of new blood" to deal with the complexities of modern life. "Little by little, new facts," he insisted, "become blurred through old glasses fitted, as it were, for the needs of another generation; older men, assuming that the scene is the same as it was in the past, cease to explore or inquire into the present or the future." If the assumption of the President was correct, the existing court, with six of the nine justices over 70 years of age and five past 74, was inadequate. Whether it was correct or not, bitter opposition immediately developed, and the battle over the Supreme Court occupied most of the attention of Congress during the entire session, to the virtual exclusion of other problems. As the debate grew more bitter, the President in a "fireside chat" on March 10 criticized the increasing tendency of the court to act as a policy-making body and a third house of Congress rather than as a judicial body willing to give the statutes the benefit of reasonable doubt. His purpose, he claimed, was simply to re-establish the court as an independent body.

Although disappointed because the President had not proposed a more straightforward and fundamental "reform," many of his followers, nevertheless, rallied to the support of the measure. They backed his arguments in the "fireside chat" and insisted that he was merely "unpacking" rather than "packing" the court. They pointed to the absurdity of invalidating fundamental reforms by five-to-four decisions and insisted that the government must be brought up to date to meet the needs of changing times. The method, they held, was perfectly legal, and in this they were upheld by many constitutional lawyers. The opponents attacked the bill as one which, in the words of the Senate Committee on the Judiciary, was a "dangerous abandonment of constitutional principle," a subjugation of the courts to the will of Congress and the President, and an effort thereby to "destroy the independence of the judiciary, the only certain shield of individual rights." In the battle the President was opposed almost unanimously by Republicans, by many conservative Southern Democrats opposed to New Deal legislation, and by other Democrats who were sincerely worried over the integrity of the judiciary. Overjoyed to see the solid phalanx of Democrats disintegrating under opposition to the bill, the Republicans stood aside and allowed the leadership of the opposition to be taken by Democratic Senators Edward E. Burke, Joseph O'Mahoney, Carter Glass, and others.

Except for a letter to the Senate Committee on the Judiciary from Chief Justice Hughes to the effect that the Supreme Court was "fully abreast of its work," that august body, the main center of attack, maintained complete silence. Nevertheless, something had apparently happened to it, at least to some of its members. On March 29 the same court which a year previously had invalidated a minimum-wage law of the state of New York now upheld a minimum-wage act of the state of Washington. The acts were slightly different, but the principle was the same. Justice Roberts had changed his vote. On April 12, by a similar five-to-four decision, the court upheld the Wagner Labor Relations Act, a keystone of New Deal policy. On May 24, in three decisions (two of which were by five-to-four majorities), the court upheld various aspects of the Social Security Act. These decisions, of course, gave renewed strength to the opponents of the President's proposal. After all, they pointed out, even the "nine old men" were not oblivious to the need of a new approach to social problems. Further to weaken the proposal came the resignation of Justice Van Devanter on June 2. This gave the President a chance to appoint someone whose ideas were more in line with New Deal policy and helped to prove that some solution could be found without going as far as the President had wished. These developments all contributed to the slashing denunciation of the bill which the Senate Judiciary Committee released in June by the narrow margin of one vote.

The sudden death shortly afterward of Democratic Senate Leader Joseph T. Robinson, who had been in charge of the bill, so disrupted administration forces that Roosevelt gave up the battle. The controversy, however, produced some legislation. In March Congress enacted a bill permitting Supreme Court justices who had reached the age of 70 to retire on full pay. In August the Judicial Procedure Reform Act allowed the Attorney General to intervene in suits involving the constitutionality of Acts of

New Deal Government Activities

Top—Wilson Dam, Now Operated as a Part of TVA Development. *Center*—A New School in Rhode Island built with PWA Funds. *Bottom*—Slum Clearance, Philadelphia, Pennsylvania. One of the Courts in the Juniata Housing Project constructed for the American Federation of Hosiery Workers with a PWA housing loan. (Photographs by Ewing Galloway, N. Y.)

MODERN LIFE

Top—China Clipper (Pan American Airways Photo). *Left center*—The Forty-Story Philadelphia Savings Fund Building. The south side is bricked up almost solidly; the other three sides are nearly all glass. (Photograph by Ewing Galloway, N. Y.) *Right center*—Control room in NBC Studios, New York. (Photograph by Sydney Desfor.) *Bottom*—Modern Streamlined Train. (Hendrich-Blessing Studio, Chicago.)

Congress, provided that such suits be appealed directly to the Supreme Court, and declared that the issuance of lower court injunctions against Acts of Congress must be approved by a court of three judges, including at least one from the Circuit Court of Appeals. On these points, at least, there could be little difference of opinion on the necessity of reform.

Thus ended the most severe conflict over the judiciary since the days of Jefferson. But the story of the Supreme Court during the Roosevelt administration was by no means finished. In August the President sent to the Senate the nomination of Senator Hugo L. Black to take the place of Justice Van Devanter. The pronounced liberality of Senator Black's economic views aroused the conservatives, who used what machinery there was to delay consideration. It was also charged at the time that Black had been a member of the Ku Klux Klan. Although his friends denied it, Black remained silent. Senatorial courtesy in the end prevailed, and he was confirmed by a vote of 63 to 16. About a month after his confirmation a series of syndicated newspaper articles produced proof of an earlier connection of Justice Black with the Klan. Black met the attack in a radio speech admitting earlier membership but denying recent connection, pledged his faith in religious and racial toleration, and warned the nation against a revival of intolerance. In January, 1938, Justice Sutherland retired; the President nominated Solicitor General Stanley Reed to succeed him, and the latter was confirmed without a dissenting voice. Another vacancy occurred in July with the death of Justice Cardozo, who was succeeded by Felix Frankfurter. The resignation of Justice Brandeis in March, 1939, brought the appointment of William O. Douglas, and the death of Pierce Butler in November of the same year brought the nomination of Attorney General Frank Murphy. Between August, 1937, and January, 1940, Roosevelt had an opportunity to appoint five new justices, Black, Reed, Frankfurter, Douglas, and Murphy—a majority of the court.[4]

ECONOMIC AND SOCIAL LEGISLATION

Whether or not the first session of the Seventy-fifth Congress would have interpreted the tremendous Democratic victory of 1936 as a mandate to pursue further the New Deal policies, it is impossible to say. Bogged down by the Supreme Court controversy, it did little during its seven months' session except pass routine bills and debate the court issue. Some effort was made to bolster up agricultural relief until a new and compre-

---

[4] In 1941 Chief Justice Hughes and Associate Justice McReynolds resigned. Justice Stone was made Chief Justice and the two vacancies were filled by James F. Byrnes and Robert Jackson. Justice Byrnes resigned in 1942 to head the office of Economic Stabilization and was succeeded by Wiley B. Rutledge, Jr.

hensive farm bill could be passed which would satisfy the Supreme Court. The most encouraging of this minor farm legislation was the Farm-Tenant Act providing funds for the Secretary of Agriculture to make loans to tenant farmers at 3 per cent and to purchase farms and equipment. Congress managed to weaken the antitrust acts by amending the Sherman Antitrust Act to allow manufacturers and their distributors to fix prices on identical or trade-marked articles sold by retailers. At the President's request it extended the life of the Civilian Conservation Corps for another three years. Undoubtedly the most important legislation of the session was the Wagner-Steagall Housing Act, passed to aid unemployment and "to remedy the unsafe and unsatisfactory housing conditions and the acute shortage of decent, safe and sanitary dwellings for families of low income in rural and urban communities." A United States Housing Authority under the Department of the Interior was set up, and $500,000,000 was made available. Loans were to have an interest of not over 4 per cent, and a period of 60 years was allowed for maturity. In this way the federal government entered a new field and assumed a new responsibility.

With the Democratic Party split wide open on the court issue, the prospects for co-operation on a major program of legislation were hardly encouraging. Roosevelt, nevertheless, called Congress into special session in November and presented a definite four-point program. The first was a comprehensive farm bill which would prevent overproduction and at the same time keep in mind the needs of the consumer, something to take the place of the former AAA. The second was a wages and hours bill which would "protect workers unable to protect themselves from excessively low wages and excessively long hours." The third was government reorganization along the lines of modern business administrative practice in the interest of efficiency and economy, a need which Presidents from Theodore Roosevelt on had pointed out. Finally, there was the request for conservation and more regional planning along the lines of the TVA. The program as presented by the President was challenging and important, but the legislation which it involved was highly technical and controversial. At any rate, the special session failed to do more than make a preliminary exploration of the various items. Later sessions did something with all the proposals except the request to expand regional planning.

It was not only the disintegration of the Democratic ranks, coupled with the controversial and technical character of the legislation, which prevented immediate action, but also the depression which settled on the nation during the second half of the year. The interest of Congress shifted from the proposed legislation to economic conditions and to the possibility of aiding business rather than to a wages and hours bill or to regional planning. The decline of economic activity, in fact, was so sudden and severe as to change temporarily the whole complexion of governmental activity. The President gave much time to conferences with business and labor leaders in an effort to get their opinions as to the causes and cure of the economic recession. Even the much neglected "little businessman" was called to a Washington conference. The result of all this seemed to add up to little or nothing. If one could judge from the speeches of high government officials, the cause of the depression was the existence of monopolies and trusts. But monopolies and trusts had long served as a "whipping boy" upon which to place the blame for many ills. Actually the government did little except to ease credit conditions and hope that the situation would improve. One thing was certain, and that was that large relief appropriations must be continued and that any hope of balancing the budget was gone. In the meantime the Republicans were in a position to blame the depression on the New Deal policies just as the Democrats five years earlier had blamed the depression of the Hoover administration on lack of adequate legislation.

When the third session of the Seventy-fifth Congress met in January, 1938, Roosevelt again urged agricultural legislation, a wages and hours bill, a government-reorganization bill, and tax revision without impairing federal income. He insisted that the "misuse of the powers of capital" must be ended "or the capitalist system will destroy itself through its own abuses." This point he followed up by a special message on April 29 in which he presented statistics to show the growing concentration of wealth and capital and the decline of competition. He asked for an appropriation of $520,000 for an inquiry by a special committee, which Congress granted. The session ended in a burst of legislation. The Housing Act of 1937 was amended to encourage small home building. The Revenue Act of 1938, which the President allowed to become law without his signature, sought to propitiate big business by modifying the taxes on undistributed profits and on capital gains. At least one great objective of the President was obtained in a wages and hours act, known as the Fair Labor Standards Act. This act, which represented a broad extension of federal control of industry, had been killed in the special session by a coalition of Southern Democrats and Northern Republicans. Somewhat modified, it was now pushed through by liberals and Northern conservatives of both parties who believed that Northern industry would be in a better position if Southern competitors were forced to pay the same minimum wages. In brief, the act covered labor engaged in interstate commerce or production of goods for interstate commerce. Maximum working hours were to be 44 hours a week for the first year, 42 for the second, and 40 thereafter. Minimum wages were to start at 25 cents an hour and be increased to 40 cents over a period of seven years. Certain exemptions were allowed, and elaborate machinery set up to enforce the act. While this act held out encouragement to low wage-earners for a brighter future, the minimums even after seven years bore little relation to a decent American standard of living.

With a midterm election impending, it was impossible to delay longer a general agricultural act. Profiting from six years' legislative experience and secure in the belief that the new Supreme Court would uphold new agricultural legislation, Congress enacted the Agricultural Adjustment Act of 1938, popularly known as the "Second AAA." One Senator disgustedly described the act as the "most completely conglomerate mess of involved language which was ever perpetrated upon a free people." That the 104-page act was complicated, no one could deny. Its objectives, however, were clear enough. Its primary aim, like that of earlier acts, was to maintain the prices of certain agricultural products at a level in relation to the cost of the commodities bought by farmers in 1909–1914 (page 691). It did this by preserving old experiments and adding new ones. Each year the Secretary of Agriculture was to determine a "parity price" and quotas for each commodity. Methods were established to induce the farmers to keep within these quotas, and the government agreed to recompense the farmers if the actual selling price should fall too far below the "parity price." The act at the same time preserved the objectives of the Soil Conservation and Allotment Act of 1936. New features included the establishment of crop insurance for wheat farmers and the policy of maintaining an "ever-normal granary." The latter looked forward to maintaining adequate supplies by fixing marketing quotas in years of bumper crops large enough to take care of lean years. The act applied not only to wheat and corn but to cotton, rice, and tobacco, thus winning the support of Congressmen from both the Middle West and the South.

With the conclusion of the Seventy-fifth Congress, virtually all the economic and social program of the New Deal had been completed. The Seventy-sixth Congress, meeting in 1939 and 1940, gave most of its attention, particularly in the latter year, to international problems and the needs of American defense. It did, however, pass one important piece of domestic legislation (Wheeler-Lea Transportation Act) when it expanded the powers of the Interstate Commerce Commission. The commission was now given jurisdiction over rates which resulted in undue advantage between persons, localities, ports, or gateways into regions, over services performed within terminal areas, and over water carriers operating in the coastwise, inland, and intercoastal trade. On the other hand, the commission was relieved of the necessity of proposing railroad consolidations, but retained the power to approve any consolidation proposed by the carriers.

Just as the reform era of the early years of the century petered out when men turned their attention to the First World War, so the reform program of the New Deal ended with the Second World War. In the midterm elections of 1938 Roosevelt declared his opposition to a "moratorium on reform which, in effect, is reaction itself." But the tide of world events was against him.

LABOR

With the exception of the Fair Labor Standards Act (page 717) and amendments liberalizing the old-age benefits under the Social Security Act, the New Deal program with respect to labor was largely completed during the first Roosevelt administration. Perhaps the greatest contribution made during the second term was to preserve the National Labor Relations Act against strong attacks. Manufacturers criticized the act as one-sided and unfair—employers could not institute proceedings, and were forbidden even to talk with employees about labor organization—while the A. F. of L. attacked the National Labor Relations Board as biased in favor of industrial unions. That the act was one-sided in the sense that it was purposely passed to protect workers in their efforts to organize and bargain collectively with employers was obvious enough. Its intent was to establish a more equal balance of power. That its decisions were biased in favor of the C.I.O. was hard to prove. If one thing was evident, it was that the board under the chairmanship of J. Warren Madden was performing an extremely difficult and complicated task and enforcing the law as effectively as one could expect under the circumstances. Investigations of the board's activities by the Senate Committee on Labor and by a special House committee backed by all the forces opposed to the act failed to accomplish much up to the end of 1940 except to convince the President that a reappointment of Madden might fail of confirmation. Madden was succeeded in 1940 by Professor Harry A. Millis of the University of Chicago.[5]

While the National Labor Relations Act and other legislation gave government encouragement and protection to organized labor, progress in organization itself depended on other factors. First of all was the need of regaining middle-class sympathy and approval. This sympathy, which had been largely shaken in the twenties (page 676), was to a considerable extent regained in the thirties. With the depression came the feeling that

[5] In discussing federal labor legislation it is easy to forget the fact that labor is also affected by legislation in the separate states. State legislation, in turn, is often encouraged or retarded by what happens in Congress or the Supreme Court. For example, by the middle of 1937 all forty-eight states, with Alaska, Hawaii, and the District of Columbia, had passed unemployment compensation laws in order to participate in the Social Security Act benefits. By the end of 1938 all the states, with Alaska, Hawaii, and Puerto Rico, had old-age pension laws. A Supreme Court decision made it possible by the end of 1938 for twenty-five states, the District of Columbia, and Puerto Rico to pass minimum-wage laws. Several states, including New York and Pennsylvania, also passed labor-relation laws patterned after the federal law.

labor had suffered severely and needed greater protection. Of great help also was the activity of the Senate Committee on Education and Labor, under the chairmanship of Robert M. La Follette, which received special instructions to investigate "violations of the rights of free speech and assembly and undue interference with the right of labor to organize and bargain collectively." As this committee spread on the record and newspapers carried the stories of the use of labor spies, tear gas, and deadly weapons by supposedly reputable employers, and of the abridgment of the constitutional rights of free speech and assemblage in company-owned towns and regions, the general public for the first time realized the difficulties under which labor worked in its efforts toward organization.

In the second place, Supreme Court backing of labor legislation was necessary. This came, unexpectedly to many, on April 12, 1937, in the middle of the battle over the Supreme Court, when that body upheld the constitutionality of the National Labor Relations Act in five cases. In general, these cases concerned the problem whether certain industries, including steel and men's clothing, affected interstate commerce sufficiently to be covered by the act. With the exception of the Fansteel decision in 1939, which virtually outlawed sit-down strikes, the court during succeeding months not only approved by implication the constitutionality of the act but time and again upheld the procedure and the decisions of the National Labor Relations Board. This protection of the board was extended in 1940 even to protection against the lower courts when by a unanimous decision the Supreme Court held that "the findings of the board, as to the fact, if supported by evidence, shall be . . . conclusive." A significant victory both for the board and for labor unions came on January 6, 1941, when the court in the H. J. Heinz Company case supported the board's decision that a company must sign a written agreement with a union after both sides had arrived at an oral understanding.

Finally, the success of labor organization depended in the last analysis on the ability of labor to help itself by taking advantage of the means which the government had placed in its hands. The American Federation of Labor, which had built up a membership of over 4,000,000 in 1920, had declined to 2,532,261 in 1932. Technological improvements which had eliminated or weakened many of the old crafts, failure to organize the new mass industries, inadequate leadership, and loss of dues-paying members as a result of the depression, had been some of the causes for this (pages 675-677). Could organized labor in its weakened condition take advantage of its new opportunities? Labor made the effort, and, all things considered, made rapid progress. Organizing machinery, grown almost rusty, was put into commission, old leaders were put in the field, and younger men who showed any talent were urged to action. With the claim that unions were now not only protected by the federal government but encouraged by Roosevelt himself, the movement for organization grew rapidly. By 1944 organized labor had a membership of over 13,000,000. The A. F. of L. claimed 6,800,000; the C.I.O., over 5,000,000; the United Mine Workers, 500,000; the Railroad Brotherhoods, 400,000; and thousands of others were scattered in various independent unions.

It soon became clear to many labor leaders that ultimate success for the labor movement could be achieved only by organization of the "mass" industries—steel, for example, where organization had once existed and had been crushed, automobiles, rubber, radio, aluminum, cement, and other industries hitherto unorganized. It was also clear, at least to leaders of existing industrial unions, that this must be done, if it was to be effective, through industrial or "vertical" unions. Vertical organization in the mass industries was approved by the A. F. of L. Convention in 1934. Despite this approval, industrial unionists found it impossible at the 1935 convention to secure industrial charters for newly organized unions of radio, automobile, and rubber workers. Convinced that the A. F. of L. had no interest in vertical organization, John L. Lewis, president of the United Mine Workers, called a meeting of leaders of industrial unions and organized the Committee for Industrial Organization. This group, composed of eight unions affiliated with the A. F. of L., proposed to organize industrial unions in the mass-production industries independently of help from the A. F. of L.

Upon refusal to disband as ordered by the Executive Committee of the A. F. of L., ten C.I.O. unions were suspended from membership in the A. F. of L. in 1936.[6] Nevertheless, the C.I.O. pushed a campaign of organization aggressively. Their first objective was steel, but the movement for organization spread so rapidly that, contrary to expectations, the first major battle was fought in the automobile industry. Following spectacular strikes early in 1937 in the Chrysler and General Motors Corporations, the C.I.O. effected compromise settlements which recognized the C.I.O. as the bargaining agency for its own members—a result which brought union recognition to virtually all the major units in the automobile industry with the exception of the Ford Motor Company. The latter fell in line in 1941. During the strike wave of 1936 and 1937 labor frequently resorted to the "sitdown" technique—refusal to work and at the same time refusal to leave the factory. The "sit-down" was new to American labor struggles and

[6] United Mine Workers of America; Amalgamated Clothing Workers of America; International Ladies' Garment Workers Union; United Textile Workers of America; Oil Field, Gas Well, and Refinery Workers of America; International Union of Mine, Mill, and Smelter Workers; Federation of Flat Glass Workers of America; Amalgamated Association of Iron, Steel, and Tin Workers; United Automobile Workers of America; United Rubber Workers of America.

aroused widespread criticism. In the end it turned out to be a passing phase and was banned as unconstitutional both by state courts and by the Supreme Court.

As the battle shifted to the steel industry, the United States Steel Corporation, to the surprise of all, changed its lifelong policy of opposition to organized labor and signed agreements with the C.I.O. Smaller companies followed the lead, but certain of the independents refused. This led to bitter but unsuccessful strikes and to the first major reverse of the C.I.O., but subsequently even "Little Steel" recognized the unions. The C.I.O., nevertheless, continued its aggressive campaign, spreading into many industries and making numerous efforts to organize white-collar workers. It also entered politics, particularly in New York State, where two of its strongest unions, the Amalgamated Clothing Workers under the leadership of Sidney Hillman and the International Ladies Garment Workers Union,[7] led by David Dubinsky, organized the American Labor Party, which played a prominent part in the campaign of 1936 and in subsequent elections in New York State. The United Mine Workers also aggressively backed candidates and contributed $500,000 to the Democratic campaign of that year. Untiring organizational efforts and aggressive tactics, combined with able leadership, quickly brought to the C.I.O. large additions in membership.

Aroused by the success of the C.I.O., the A. F. of L. greatly increased its activity and its membership. Both the C.I.O. and the A. F. of L. were often trying to organize in the same field and each accused the other of "stealing" members. There were times when the two organizations supported opposing political candidates and took different points of view on the advisability of certain labor legislation. This disunion obviously weakened labor, and numerous efforts were made, sometimes inspired by the President himself, to heal the breach. All efforts up to 1945, however, failed, in part because of the bitterness engendered by the long conflict, the unyielding attitude taken by some of the leaders, and the conflict of groups for power. Unity seemed less likely after 1938 when the Committee for Industrial Organization changed its name to Congress of Industrial Organizations, adopted a constitution, and took on a more permanent form. It seemed even less likely when John L. Lewis resigned from the presidency in 1940 and two years later led his United Mine Workers out of the C.I.O. Philip Murray, who had earlier led the drive to organize the steel workers, succeeded him as head of the C.I.O.

---

[7] Withdrew from the C.I.O. in 1939 and later rejoined the A. F. of L. When the "left wing" groups gained control of the American Labor Party in 1944, Dubinsky and his followers withdrew to found the Liberal Party. Both parties were active in the campaign of that year.

INTERNATIONAL PROBLEMS

While America busied herself with economic rehabilitation and New Deal experiments, the clouds on the international horizon were rapidly darkening. The period between the First and Second World Wars has been called a "long armistice." In reality it was a period of revolutions, civil wars, and minor international conflicts. The First World War left central Europe with a legacy of political and economic disorganization, impoverishment, and discontent. The defeated nations believed that they had been unjustly treated in the peace treaties, and there was wide dissatisfaction with the boundary lines established by the Treaty of Versailles. All this was fertile ground on which ambitious and unscrupulous politicians could rise to power and establish dictatorships by preaching racial and religious hatred. Having established themselves in power, they maintained it by persecuting political, racial, and religious minorities, developing armed might, and holding forth to their deluded peoples dreams of conquest and empire. Then they developed a specious prosperity by large-scale rearmament and preparations for war.

Mussolini set the pattern in Italy after 1922 when he assumed dictatorial power, abolished democratic government and civil liberties, and stamped out opposition. Having built up his army and navy, he embarked on the conquest of Ethiopia in 1935, telling his people that it was the beginning of a new Italian empire like that of ancient Rome. Two years earlier Hitler had gained control of Germany, overthrown the republic, and begun his career of incredibly cruel persecution of Jews, Catholics, and believers in democratic institutions. Like Mussolini, he began to rebuild his armed forces in preparation for foreign conquests. Imitating these "sawdust Caesars," ambitious rulers and rising politicians in certain minor countries of Europe, such as Spain and Rumania, set up dictatorships modeled after the Fascist regime in Italy and the Nazi rule in Germany. All this was a portent of things to come, and the civil war in Spain, ending with a dictatorship under Franco in 1939, proved to be the curtain-raiser of the Second World War in Europe.

Disillusioned with the results of the First World War, and fully occupied with economic prosperity, most Americans gave little attention to the problems of Europe during the 1920's. During the 1930's, however, those problems could hardly be ignored. The collapse of democracy in central Europe, the conquest of Ethiopia, the Spanish revolution, and the rapid rearmament of Germany all indicated serious possibilities for the future, at least to those who were far-seeing enough to understand the implications. The first effect upon the American people, however, was to strengthen the feeling of isolation and the desire to avoid European complications which might lead to a second world war. This led in 1934 to the Johnson Debt Default Act, which forbade foreign governments in default of their debts to the United States to market securities in this country. In the following year the Senate rejected our entry into the World Court. Then came, as we have seen (page 708), the series of neutrality acts, which were extended in 1937 as a result of the Franco revolution in Spain to cover civil wars. With these acts American isolationism reached its climax.

While European dictators were setting the stage for a second world war, American foreign policy followed broadly the lines laid down in the early years of the Roosevelt administration. The hope of increasing foreign commerce and improving international relations through trade agreements was aggressively continued (page 707). The good neighbor policy toward Latin America was conscientiously followed. The furore over the expropriation of American oil properties by Mexico in 1938 was kept in the sphere of diplomacy, and relations with that country improved. At the eighth Pan-American Conference at Lima in 1938 resolutions were passed endorsing the trade agreement policy and the settlement of international problems by peaceful means. Another resolution opposed intervention of one state in the internal affairs of another (an official abrogation by the United States of the Roosevelt corollary to the Monroe Doctrine), and a declaration was passed against racial and religious persecution and against the political activities of alien minorities in the interest of their home countries.

Dangerous as was the situation in Europe, the foreign policy of the United States in the late thirties was more directly concerned with the Far East. Japan, it will be remembered (page 648), conquered Manchuria in 1931, but this country, following the "Stimson Doctrine," had not recognized the puppet government in Manchukuo. Japan, now firmly under the control of the war lords, again invaded China in 1937. This was simply a renewal of a policy of conquest and annexation begun in 1895 when she took Formosa after an earlier war with China. The United States held that the invasion of China was a violation of the Nine-Power Treaty and of the "open door" policy. Japan's position, as maintained from the start and explicitly stated in a note of November, 1938, was that "Japan is directing her energy to the establishment of a new order based on genuine international justice throughout East Asia. . . . It is the firm conviction of the Japanese Government that, in the face of the new situation fast developing in East Asia, any attempt to apply to the conditions of today inapplicable ideas and principles of the past would neither contribute toward establishment of real peace in East Asia nor solve immediate issues." Japan also asserted on numerous occasions that there was no desire on her part to interfere with the "open door," although her daily actions belied this position.

The United States found herself in a difficult position indeed. Her policy in the Far East as it had developed for almost forty years was to support both the "open door" policy and the political integrity of China. Japan had repeatedly ignored the latter, and had violated her pledges to respect at least the "open door" policy. We could maintain such a policy only by a victorious war against Japan, and there was nothing to indicate at the time that this country would support such a war. The average person could see neither political nor economic interests great enough to warrant it.[8] In such a situation the United States could do little but protest and give some aid to China. Since Japan had invaded China without declaring war (she called it an "incident"), President Roosevelt refused to recognize officially the existence of war, and thus avoided applying the Neutrality Act. He did this presumably on the theory that such a policy would help China more than Japan, for Japan largely manufactured her own munitions and China had to import them. It is difficult to say whether he was correct in this belief, for Japan was largely dependent upon the United States as a market for her silk and as a source of scrap iron, high-grade gasoline, and other necessities of war. In any event we continued for some three years to send these commodities to Japan, at the same time bolstering China with loans.

Although the United States protested more than once over the infringements of American rights in China, the most serious incident occurred in December, 1937, when the American gunboat *Panay* was bombed and machine-gunned near Nanking. The United States government obtained apologies, indemnities, and a promise that no such incident would happen again. On July 26, 1939, the United States announced to Japan her intention, six months from that date, to end the American-Japanese trade treaty. This would free us to take any action regarding trade without treaty violation. The situation became increasingly tense after the opening of the European war and the collapse of France and Holland in 1940. The United States immediately made it clear that she would consider any Japanese action to absorb European colonies in the Far East as a violation of the Four-Power Treaty of 1922 (page 643). On her side Japan, in September, 1940, announced an alliance with Germany and Italy, a treaty in which the three powers pledged political, economic, and military assistance to one another if one of them was attacked by a power at that time not involved in the European war or the Chinese-Japanese conflict. This triple alliance of the dictator powers was directed primarily against the United States, and was so understood. This country replied by another loan to China, by a

[8] The value of American exports to China in 1936, the year before the war broke out, was $46,819,000; imports, $74,340,000. American investments in China at their high point in 1930 (including over $43,000,000 in missions) was approximately $239,895,000. The figures for Japanese trade with the United States in 1936 were: exports, $204,312,000; imports, $171,720,000.

complete embargo on shipments of steel and scrap iron to any place outside the western hemisphere except Great Britain, and by requesting that all Americans in the Far East, if possible, return home. Having discovered that the United States had not been intimidated by the triple alliance, Japan softened the truculent statements of her official spokesmen, and assured the world that the tripartite pact was not directed against the United States. So the situation rested at the end of 1940.

While American relations with Japan deteriorated, the European phase of the Second World War began. By 1938 Hitler felt strong enough to begin his policy of military aggression, and in March he coolly annexed Austria. In September of that year, with the assent of France and England, he added the Sudetenland, the German-inhabited section of Czechoslovakia. In 1939 he took over the rest of Czechoslovakia and forced the Lithuanians to give up Memel. The amazement in America at this rapid turn of events was as nothing in comparison with that created by the signing on August 23, 1939, of a nonaggression pact between Germany and Russia, two nations whose ideologies and ambitions appeared to have little in common. The immediate effect of the treaty was to free Germany from the danger of an attack from the east and allowed her to invade Poland on September 1. In collaboration with Russia, Poland was quickly crushed and divided between the two invading nations. Two days after the invasion of Poland, Great Britain and France, convinced that appeasement was worthless, declared war on Germany. Except for an unprovoked attack by Russia on Finland and the defeat of the smaller nation, the war was quiescent during the winter. But it was no "phony war," as some were beginning to believe. Suddenly, in April, Germany invaded Denmark and conquered Norway, and in May and June ruthlessly crushed Holland, Belgium, and France. As in the case of Poland, the invasion of Denmark, Norway, Holland, and Belgium was unprovoked and in most cases in violation of solemn treaties.

During these months the American government had followed its long-established policy of working for peace, but when war came it had established a strict legal neutrality. During the Czech crisis, Roosevelt had called the attention of both Germany and Czechoslovakia to their obligations under the Kellogg-Briand Pact, had appealed for peace to both Hitler and President Beneš, and had made a personal appeal to Mussolini in behalf of peace. In a similar manner, at the time of the Polish crisis, Roosevelt addressed notes to Hitler, President Moscicki, and Victor Emmanuel of Italy, this time making specific suggestions as to means of avoiding war. When Italy hung on the verge of war in 1940, Roosevelt offered to transmit any demands which Italy desired to make and to seek assurances that any concessions made at the moment would be made good at the end of the war. In the spring of 1940 the President sent Undersecretary of State Sumner Welles on a tour of the belligerent capitals to obtain pertinent information which might be useful in the establishment of peace.

AMERICA PREPARES FOR WAR

As the clouds of war darkened in Asia and Europe, the Roosevelt administration was by no means indifferent to the coming danger or inactive in preparing for it. In a notable speech in October, 1937, the President made his position clear. Likening war to a disease in which a quarantine must be set up, he declared that peace-loving nations must make a "concerted effort in opposition" to nations breaking treaties and ignoring "human instincts." "We are determined to keep out of war," said the President, "yet we cannot insure ourselves against the disastrous effects of war and the danger of involvement." Shortly afterward he wrote that "whether we like it or not we are part of a large world of other nations and peoples. As such we owe some measure of co-operation and even leadership in maintaining standards of conduct helpful to the ultimate goal of general peace." With words such as these Roosevelt began definitely as early as the middle of 1937 to take the leadership in developing sentiment to aid the victims of aggression.

The next year he issued a definite warning when he pledged that, in case Japan or Germany should attack the British Empire, "the people of the United States will not stand idly by if . . . Canadian soil is threatened." At the same time he left no grounds for doubt as to the opposition of the United States to the Axis policies. The American ambassador to Germany was recalled in 1938 and did not return. The President also urged increased armaments. In a special message to Congress in January, 1938, he insisted that our national defense was, "in the light of increasing armaments of other nations, inadequate for purposes of national security," and asked for a 20-per-cent increase in authorization for the navy. Congress responded with a regular military appropriation of over a billion dollars, with another $1,156,000,000 in a special naval appropriation, the largest peacetime naval program in our history. Appropriations in 1939 were also large, with special attention given to the air force.

When the European war broke out, all aspects of the defense program were speeded up. To promote greater unity of action in the face of the European crisis, the United States sent a call for a consultative meeting of foreign ministers of the American states, to be held at Panama in September, 1939. Here the representatives renewed the declaration of solidarity of the Lima conference and issued a general declaration of neutrality, setting forth standards of conduct to be followed by American states as neutrals. Finally the conference issued the Declaration of Panama, asserting that belligerent activities should not take place in waters adjacent to the American continents. This declaration, however, went unrecognized and unheeded by the belligerents. Following this new policy of hemisphere collaboration, the Pan-American Conference at Havana, in July, 1940, proposed a treaty (to go into effect when two thirds of the American states had ratified it) setting up an Inter-American Commission of Territorial Administration to take over and administer any territory respecting which there is "some transfer or intent to transfer sovereignty." This commission, as things turned out, was never needed, but it was a well-timed warning to the Axis powers to keep out of the western hemisphere. Also in 1940 an agreement was concluded with Canada for a joint defense board of the two nations to study defense problems affecting the northern part of North America. Another important step in hemisphere defense was taken when the President, on September 3, 1940, made known an agreement which he had reached with Great Britain to exchange fifty "over-age" destroyers for the right to lease naval and air bases in British possessions in the western hemisphere. These destroyers, of doubtful value to us, were of immediate and vital need to Britain; the bases were essential for our defense. Those we obtained in Newfoundland and Bermuda, announced the President, were "gifts generously given and gladly received"; the others, to be located in the Bahamas, Jamaica, St. Lucia, Trinidad, Antigua, and British Guiana, were in exchange for the destroyers.

Two days after France and Great Britain declared war, the President issued (September 5, 1939) the usual proclamation of neutrality and then a second proclamation necessitated under the Neutrality Act of 1936, embargoing the shipment of arms, munitions, airplanes, and airplane parts to belligerents, banning the travel of Americans on belligerent ships, and delimiting the war zone. The following year, as Germany conquered Denmark, Norway, Belgium, and Holland, he "froze" the credits of these nations in the United States in order to protect American property in the invaded countries. Shortly after war broke out in Europe, Roosevelt called Congress into special session to modify the Neutrality Act. In line with his often expressed belief and in line also with the growing sentiment of the nation, he believed that the arms embargo should be repealed so that all aid short of war might be extended to Great Britain and France. There was also a growing belief in America that England was fighting our battle as well as her own and that aid to Britain was a cheap price to pay for defense against Germany. Opponents of repeal argued that such action would favor only one side, and, by involving us in an economic way with that side, would eventually drag the nation into war as it had done twenty-two years earlier. Isolationist opposition was stiff, but after a month of debate Congress acceded to the President's wish. The new act, passed on November 3, repealed the arms embargo, but insisted that all sales to combatants must be on a cash basis with delivery on their own ships (cash-and-carry plan), except sales to their territories far distant from the war zone. The act retained the prohibition of loans to warring powers, of travel by Americans on belligerent ships, and of the sailing of American ships into combat zones.

The difficulty of repealing the arms embargo as well as securing a few months later a Lend-Lease Act made clear the continued strong isolationist sentiment and the extreme reluctance to be drawn into the European conflict. Ignoring the fact that these might be defense measures against an impending conflict, isolationists saw them only as acts which would lead us inevitably into an unnecessary war. Congressional spokesmen for this point of view included Senators Nye and Wheeler and Representative Hamilton Fish. Throughout the country opposition was strengthened by the America First Committee and its leading spokesman, Charles A. Lindbergh, as well as by the Hearst press and the Chicago *Tribune*. For one reason or another various smaller groups added their opposition: Father Coughlin's Christian Front and other organizations imbued with a fascist ideology, and the Communist Party, which insisted that the conflict was an "imperialist war." On the other hand, various committees were organized to promote both measures, the most important of which were the Non-Partisan Committee for Peace through the Revision of the Neutrality Law and the Committee to Defend America by Aiding the Allies, both under the leadership of the influential Kansas editor William Allen White. Both committees exerted strong influence in revising the Neutrality Act and securing lend-lease.

By the end of 1940 the President was convinced that Britain had approached the end of her ability to purchase munitions under the cash-and-carry plan and that new means must be found to aid her without the necessity of repealing either the Johnson Act or the Neutrality Act. When the Seventy-seventh Congress met in January, 1941, Roosevelt reiterated his defiance of dictators and denunciation of appeasers and asked for what he called "all-out aid" to the embattled democracies. The act presented a few days later asked for power to lend or lease to such nations any equipment the use of which the President believed would be in the interest of American defense. Isolationists, who believed that it was an immediate step toward war, opposed it, as did many who believed that in its original form it conferred too great a power on the President. After two months' debate it was finally passed and signed (March 11), but with certain amendments. The President's lend-lease powers were to terminate by June 30, 1943, unless Congress by concurrent resolution ended them before that date; a limit of $1,300,000,000 was placed on the valuation of the aid to be given out of existing supplies for which appropriations had already been made; and, finally, Congress kept control of the purse strings by limiting expenditures "to the extent to which funds are made available . . . by Congress." The day after Roosevelt signed the historic lend-lease bill he asked Congress for $7,000,000,000 to implement the act. With but slight opposition and in less than two weeks Congress granted his request. By renewal of the law and subsequent appropriations lend-lease was extended to June 30, 1945. Total lend-lease aid by July, 1944, amounted to $29,660,000,000. As the President truly said, "the United Nations' fighting partnership had been made far stronger by lend-lease and reverse lend-lease."

In the meantime military and naval preparedness was pushed. In 1940 total appropriations for national defense reached the astounding total of over $17,692,000,000, and the President's budget message for 1941 asked for $10,881,000,000 more for the same purpose. Congress in 1940 committed itself to a two-ocean navy and for the first time in our history to a system of compulsory peacetime conscription. The act called for the registration of all male citizens (or those who had declared their intention of becoming citizens) between the ages of 21 and 36 and made these liable for a training period limited to twelve months and for service in the western hemisphere and in the possessions of the United States, including the Philippines. The minimum number in training was to be 695,990 and the maximum at one time to be 900,000. In addition to this, Congress raised the enlisted strength of the army to 375,000, the navy to 170,000, the Marine Corps to 34,000, and the National Guard, which the President was empowered to call for a year's active service, to 346,130 men. Congress also authorized 25,000 planes for the army and 10,000 for the navy, the construction of 292 combat vessels and 57 auxiliary ships for a two-ocean navy, and supplies to equip an army of 2,000,000 men.

This was a tremendous program for a nation not geared to wartime production and it got under way with discouraging slowness. To provide greater co-ordination and efficiency the President appointed an advisory commission of experts headed by four men: William S. Knudsen, in charge of general production; Sidney Hillman, in charge of labor relations; and the Secretaries of War and the Navy. To give the defense effort a non-partisan character the President in June, 1940, offered the Secretaryship of War to Henry L. Stimson, who had served in the Republican cabinets of Taft and Hoover, and the Secretaryship of the Navy to Franklin Knox, Republican candidate for Vice-President in 1936. The move for preparedness may have come a little late, as some Republicans later contended, but, once started, it had every appearance of being a thorough-going effort. In any event, the President realized more keenly the need of preparedness than the nation as a whole and to Roosevelt must go the chief credit for what preparation this country achieved.

In the midterm elections of 1938 the Democratic Party sustained its first major reversal since 1932. The Republicans gained eighty-one seats in the House, eight in the Senate, and fifteen state governorships. It was clear that the Democratic setback was more than a customary midterm reversal. Democrats attributed it to the depression of late 1937 and early 1938; Republicans saw in it a disillusionment of liberals with the New Deal and a widespread desertion of progressives from the Democratic camp. In any event, the Republicans for the first time in six years played an important role in the two houses of Congress.

The paucity of important domestic legislation, however, was by no means wholly due either to Republican success or to a more even distribution of New Deal and anti-New Deal forces. Since much of the New Deal program had already been passed, there was a normal slowing up. More important, of course, was the fact that Congressional attention was shifted after August, 1939, from domestic problems to foreign affairs. The new Congress, nevertheless, found time to legislate on two political problems, government organization and political corruption. Both efficiency and economy demanded a simplification and a reorganization of governmental agencies. Roosevelt described the situation as a "higgledy-piggledy patchwork of duplicate responsibilities and overlapping powers" and in 1936 had urged the Seventy-fifth Congress to take action. Three years later Congress authorized the President to appoint six special administrative assistants to perform, such duties as he might prescribe. Acting under these powers, Roosevelt quickly grouped twenty-three boards and corporations under three great units—the Federal Works Agency, the Federal Loan Agency, and the Federal Security Agency—and subsequently consolidated other governmental units.

During the 1938 campaign rumors circulated widely that certain government officials in the relief agencies were using their power to influence or intimidate voters. The opportunity for this type of political corruption in the vast relief and spending organizations under the New Deal was obviously great, and both parties combined in 1939 to pass the Hatch Political Activity Act. The act among other things made it unlawful for any person employed by the federal government to use his official authority to influence an election either by granting or withholding favors and for any person to solicit or receive political contributions from any person receiving compensation, employment, or other benefit from Congress. A second Hatch Act in 1940 extended the provisions of the earlier act to cover state and local employees (about 300,000 at the time) whose activities were supported in whole or in part by the federal government. It also forbade any political committee to receive contributions or make expenditures aggregating more than $3,000,000 in any one year or for any individual to contribute to such committee more than $5000 during the same period of time. Except for a few politicians there was general agreement that the Hatch Acts aimed at much-needed reforms. When the campaign of 1940 ended, however, it seemed evident that the spirit of the legislation if not the letter had been widely evaded.

It was clear after the fall of France that the foreign situation would play a larger part in the campaign of 1940 than it had played in any previous campaign since 1916. Although Roosevelt refused to commit himself definitely on the question of a third term, he early intimated that the serious international crisis might induce him to throw over precedent and tradition and run again. No one doubted his ability to obtain the nomination if he desired it, and only two of the Democratic candidates for the nomination, Postmaster General Farley and Vice-President Garner, had the temerity even to enter seriously the preferential primaries. Wherever they did so, they were snowed under by Roosevelt despite the fact that the President had not yet even announced that he was a candidate. During the early months of the year the leading candidates for the Republican nomination were Thomas E. Dewey, well known as the "racket-busting" district attorney in New York City, Senator Arthur H. Vandenberg of Michigan, and Senator Robert H. Taft of Ohio. It was only in the latter part of the campaign that Wendell Willkie, President of Commonwealth and Southern, and hitherto famous chiefly as the most persistent and vocal opponent of the TVA experiment, became a leading contender. During the preconvention campaign the Republicans found themselves in the same position as Landon in 1936—unable to attack the New Deal as a whole because millions of Republican voters believed in much of it, and therefore reduced to criticism of specific details of legislation. In any case the totalitarian victories culminating in the fall of France made the candidates' attitude on America's relation to the European war more immediately important than their position on domestic problems. Roosevelt's policy of preparedness and aid to Britain was well known. Of the Republicans, Willkie's position seemed closest to Roosevelt's.

When the Republican convention met at Philadelphia, it was any man's victory. Dewey up to that time had been the favorite of various polls and had the largest block of votes pledged to him. It was evident, however, that there was a swelling public demand for a candidate independent of organization affiliations but at the same time with a personality vivid enough to attract support. Such a candidate was Willkie, and, in a sudden uprising against the old guard of the party, the convention, backed by widespread popular demand, nominated him on the sixth ballot. For the vice-presidential candidate it turned to Charles L. McNary of Oregon, Senate Republican leader and well known for two decades as spokesman of the farmers and coauthor of the McNary-Haugen bills (page 685). The combination of a New York public utility lawyer and an Oregon farmer was considered a strong one. In their platform the Republicans supported defense but opposed involvement in foreign wars. They pledged a revision of the tax system, elimination of "waste, discrimination, and politics from relief," and the encouragement of "a healthy, confident, and growing private enterprise." On labor the platform promised extension of social security and supported collective bargaining but demanded revisions of the National Labor Relations Act. Its plank on agriculture seemed to support most of the methods already used by the Democrats. It criticized the methods of making the reciprocal trade agreements but made no promise to repeal them. It promised enforcement of the antitrust act, advocated a constitutional amendment outlawing a third term, and favored withdrawal of "the President's arbitrary authority to manipulate the currency."

It was not until July 16, the second day of the Democratic convention meeting in Chicago, that Roosevelt broke his long silence on the third term, and announced through the chairman that he "never had and has not today any desire or purpose to continue in the office of the President," and that "all the delegates to this convention are free to vote for any candidate." Since the President had virtually prevented other possible candidates from campaigning by reserving this statement until the convention, and since he had not prevented his name's being used in the primaries, his statement had no effect. The most powerful political bosses of the party were at Chicago to renominate him, and he was chosen on the first ballot. At the evident dictation of the President, the party machine secured the nomination of Secretary of Agriculture Henry A. Wallace for the vice-presidency, a nomination made in part to checkmate the influence of the Republican nomination of McNary in the agricultural states. The Democratic platform, like the Republican, promised adequate defense and no participation in foreign wars. The army, it said, would not be sent to fight outside the Americas, "except in case of attack." It promised an extension of social security, a continuation of the principles of the National Labor Relations Act, and an increase in slum clearance and low-cost housing construction, and it defended government ownership of public utilities.

Superficially, the platforms of the major parties seemed much the same, but there was a real contrast in their approach to American problems as a whole. Except in agriculture, the Republicans showed a distinct nostalgia for *laissez faire* in governmental attitude toward economic life; the Democrats would continue their wide application of government power. The left-wing third parties saw the major issue in foreign affairs. The Socialist Party nominated Norman Thomas for the fourth time, and affirmed the party's opposition to war and aid to belligerents. The Communists nominated Earl Browder and centered their campaign on opposition to participation in war and militarization at home. The Prohibition Party, showing signs of increased activity, nominated the well-known statistician Roger Babson. The role of the third parties in 1940, however, was negligible. The Socialist Party, for example, polled fewer votes than it had polled in any election since 1900.

As in 1936, the Republicans were handicapped by their inability to take a strong stand in opposition to the principle of much New Deal legislation and were reduced to criticism of details. On agriculture Willkie seemed to accept the broad policy of the Agricultural Adjustment Act although he reserved the right to re-examine specific programs. He committed himself to free collective bargaining, to the Wages and Hours Act, and to social security. He even back-watered somewhat on public ownership of utilities. On foreign policy he stood for strong defense and favored economic assistance to China and aid to England short of war—exactly as Roosevelt did. In the end the major effort of the Republicans was based on the assertion that the domestic policies of the Democratic administration were breaking down the American tradition of free economic competition, that the New Deal had failed to solve the problems of agriculture and unemployment and had not brought back prosperity, and, finally, that the foreign policy of Roosevelt would lead us inevitably into a European war.

Although the leading polls predicted a Roosevelt victory by a small margin, the result was dubious until the end. Efforts to predict the result were made more difficult by the radio speech of John L. Lewis, President of the C.I.O., shortly before election, in which he urged his followers to vote for Willkie. The Lewis speech took on particular significance because the trend against Roosevelt in the agricultural states of the Middle West was marked, and the result of the election would be determined by the vote in the great industrial states of the Northeast. The results, as predicted, showed the greatest Republican gains in the midwestern and Great Lakes states, the greatest Democratic gains in New England. Willkie carried ten states—Colorado, Kansas, Iowa, Indiana, Maine, Michigan, Nebraska, North Dakota, South Dakota, and Utah. The electoral vote was 449 to 82 and the popular vote of the major parties 27,245,000 to 22,333,000.[9] Despite

---

[9] Inability of the Communist and Socialist parties to get on the ballot of certain states undoubtedly reduced the size of their votes. The approximate vote of the minor candidates follows:

Norman Thomas and Maynard Kreuger, Socialist	116,976
Roger Babson and Edgar V. Moorman, Prohibitionist	58,678
Earl Browder and James W. Ford, Communist	49,028
John W. Aiken and Aaron M. Orange, Socialist Labor	14,861

the overwhelming victory in the electoral count, Roosevelt received less than 55 per cent of the vote. Willkie had surpassed the Republican vote of 1936 by approximately 5,500,000; Roosevelt's vote was slightly less than in the previous election. If there was anything certain regarding the returns, it was that Roosevelt had lost in the rural and agricultural regions but had retained the labor vote in the industrial sections. Presumably the latter was due to his record of social legislation and his promise to retain the social gains of his administration. In other words, the result of the election appeared to have rested essentially upon a domestic issue. As the smoke of the election battle cleared away, however, it seemed clear that the fate of the nation during the next four years would be essentially determined not by the domestic scene but the international situation. Whatever this fate might be and whatever policies the nation might adopt rested not upon one political party, but alike upon Republicans and Democrats.

For the election of 1936 and the first two years of the second Roosevelt administration read Charles A. and Mary R. Beard, *America in Midpassage*, Vol. I, Chaps. VII–VIII. In the same volume Chaps. IX–X give a critical appraisal of Roosevelt's foreign policy. C. A. Beard and G. H. E. Smith, *The Old Deal and the New Deal*, summarizes both domestic and foreign policies to 1940. J. R. Walsh, *The C.I.O., Industrial Unionism in Action*, Chaps I–VI, covers the early history of the C.I.O. T. A. Bailey, *A Diplomatic History of the American People* (2nd ed.), Chap. XLIV, carries the story to late 1939. Walter Johnson, *The Battle Against Isolation*, discusses American attitudes toward the European war. Allan Nevins and Louis Hacker, eds., *The United States and Its Place in World Affairs*, Chaps. XIV–XXXIV, gives the world background, as does C. G. Haines and R. J. S. Hoffman, *Origins and Background of the Second World War*, Chaps. V, XII, XV.

A WORLD POWER

Chapter XLII

AMERICA GOES TO WAR

> *By this declaration we reaffirm our faith in
> the principles of the Atlantic Charter, our pledge
> in the Declaration of the United Nations and our
> determination to build, in cooperation with other
> peace-loving nations, world order under law,
> dedicated to peace, security, freedom and the
> general well-being of all mankind.*
>
> CRIMEA CHARTER

THE END OF NEUTRALITY

It was evident by the spring of 1941 that both the American government and the great majority of the American people had forsaken neutrality both in thought and in act. They had definitely placed themselves on the side of the nations fighting Germany, Italy, and their satellites. Both the Neutrality Act and the Johnson Debt Default Act remained on the statute books, but for all practical purposes they had been nullified by the Lend-Lease Acts. Moreover, as the weeks went by, other items of legislation, official speeches, and government action made increasingly clear the policy of the United States. Our government, for example, on March 30, seized Italian and German merchant ships and arrested their crews under provisions of the Espionage Act of 1917 and three months later closed the German and Italian consulates and expelled Axis agents from the country. On April 10 an arrangement was concluded with the Danish minister to the United States authorizing the United States to take over the protection of Greenland during the war. On July 7 President Roosevelt announced that, in accordance with an understanding reached with Iceland, forces of the United States had arrived in that country to supplement and eventually to replace the British troops there. These moves were to strengthen hemisphere defense and to keep the sea lanes open.

Once committed to aid the enemies of Hitler through lend-lease, the United States government was determined that the commodities should reach their destination. As severe losses to the British merchant marine began to endanger lend-lease delivery, the President on May 28 reasserted the early American doctrine of "freedom of the seas" (forsaken under the Neutrality Acts) and promised aid. "The delivery of needed supplies to Britain," he declared, "is imperative. This can be done; it must be done; it will be done." These words were accompanied with a proclamation of "unlimited emergency" in which the President called upon "all loyal citizens to place the nation's needs first in mind and in action to the end that we may mobilize and have ready for instant defensive use all of the physical powers, all of the moral strength, and all of the material resources of the nation." From this time on, American destroyers were aiding in the convoy of lend-lease material. Large air and naval forces patrolled the Atlantic, and the President in September ordered the navy to destroy on sight any German or Italian submarines or raiders entering waters "the protection of which is necessary for American defense."

To strengthen our position on the sea and to legalize our activities, President Roosevelt asked Congress on October 9 to modify the Neutrality Act in order to allow the arming of merchant ships and to permit American merchant ships to sail into combat zones and belligerent ports. Point was given to the first part of this request by the fact that at least eleven American-owned ships were sunk by German or Italian submarines between November 9, 1940, and October 19, 1941, with the apparent loss of ninety-four men. In addition, three American destroyers were attacked: the *Greer*, fired upon but not hit on September 4, 1941; the *Kearney*, struck and damaged by a torpedo off Iceland on October 17, with ten men injured and eleven missing; the *Reuben James*, sunk on October 30 while convoying in the North Atlantic, with the loss of half her crew. In reply to the President's request and under the impetus of these attacks the House repealed the clause forbidding the arming of merchant ships. The Senate, after long debate, but finally stirred to action by the sinking of the *Reuben James*, voted also to allow American merchant ships to sail into combat zones and belligerent ports. The House accepted this addition (November 13) only after bitter opposition and by a close vote of 212 to 194.

In the meantime the Second World War entered a new phase. Despite the nonaggression pact of 1939 and subsequent agreements, friction between Germany and Russia became increasingly acute as Germany strengthened her influence in the Baltic region and extended her power in the Balkan states. Only Russia stood between Hitler and complete control over the continent of Europe. Determined to crush his great continental rival, Hitler invaded Russia on June 22, 1941. The German armies swept across the plains of Russia, but were finally halted in December at the suburbs of Moscow by the bitter northern winter and the stubborn Russian defense. At the outset Washington denounced the invasion and offered to extend to Russia the benefits of the Lend-Lease Act. In August the President and

Prime Minister Churchill issued a joint message to Joseph Stalin, promising the maximum of supplies possible. Shortly afterward an American mission to Moscow worked out the details.

Undoubtedly the widening of the area of war was one influence which led to the meeting between Prime Minister Churchill and President Roosevelt on the high seas in mid-August. Here the two leaders issued a joint statement of eight common principles as a basis for peace:

1. No territorial or other aggrandizement by the United States or Britain.
2. Territorial changes only through self-determination.
3. "All peoples" have a right to choose their own forms of government; those forcibly deprived of the right should have it restored.
4. Free international trade.
5. World-wide co-operation to secure "improved labor standards, economic adjustments and social security."
6. After the final destruction of the Nazi tyranny, assurance of a secure peace, of "freedom from fear and want."
7. Freedom of the seas.
8. "Abandonment of the use of force," disarming of aggressor nations, and the lightening of "the crushing burdens of armaments."

This statement, which came to be known as the Atlantic Charter, had for the time being no official standing; it was simply a statement of principles issued by the leaders of the two nations. It was, however, later subscribed to by the twenty-six nations that signed the United Nations Declaration on January 1, 1942, as well as by those that signed later. Though often ignored in subsequent years, the Atlantic Charter has significance as the first peace program issued by responsible government leaders during the Second World War. Neither as inclusive nor as specific as Wilson's famous Fourteen Points, the Atlantic Charter was, nevertheless, a noble statement of objectives upon which to fight a war. President Roosevelt in his Congressional message of January 6 had already expressed his hope of a postwar world founded upon four essential freedoms: freedom of speech and expression, freedom of religion, freedom from want, and freedom from fear. If the average American had as yet any program for a postwar world —beyond the utter defeat of the Axis powers—it was probably a combination of the "four freedoms" and the Atlantic Charter.

Although most Americans, particularly those on the east coast, were primarily concerned with Europe, it was events in the Far East that led directly to our entrance into the Second World War. For years American policy in the Far East had been to check Japan, but at the same time to prevent a spread of the Asiatic conflict. It was clear by 1941 that this policy had failed as Japan aggressively pushed her plans for a "new order" in eastern Asia. Following her alliance in September, 1940, with Germany and Italy (page 725), Japan signed, on April 13, 1941, a neutrality pact with Russia which apparently strengthened her position in Manchuria and cleared the way for a more aggressive prosecution of the Chinese war. It also helped to clear the way for the occupation of Indo-China. Vichy, over-awed by the Axis, professed to believe that Indo-China was in danger of British attack and consented to this "military co-operation." The United States replied on July 24 by freezing Japanese assets in the United States and on August 1 by ending the export of aviation gasoline to Japan. Great Britain quickly followed our lead by abrogating her commercial treaties with Japan.

It was soon clear that Japan's invasion of Indo-China was merely a prelim-inary to an advance into Thailand and other regions. On August 17 the United States warned Japan that "any further steps in pursuance of a pol-icy or program of military domination by force or threat of force of neigh-boring countries" would compel the United States "to take immediately any and all steps . . . necessary toward safeguarding the legitimate rights and interests of the United States and American nationals. . . ." The Brit-ish government took the same position and announced shortly afterward that a break between Japan and the United States would cause the British to "range ourselves unhesitatingly at the side of the United States." On November 10 Prime Minister Churchill stated that in case of war between Japan and the United States a British declaration would follow "within the hour."

As relations between the two nations deteriorated, Japan, through her ambassador, Admiral Nomura, requested resumption of conversations looking toward a peaceful settlement of Far Eastern problems. The policies of the two nations, however, were so far apart that these conversations made little progress even after Japan in early November sent a special envoy, Saburu Kurusu, to take charge of the negotiations in Washington. The negotiations came to a climax on November 20 when Japan presented a new proposal which called for the supplying by the United States to Japan of as much oil as Japan might require, a suspension of freezing measures, and a discontinuance by the United States of aid to China. Since this proposal made no provision for abandonment by Japan of her warlike operations or aims, it offered no basis for a peaceful settlement. The United States replied on November 26 with a clear-cut plan which included a multilateral nonaggression treaty for all nations in eastern Asia, a trade agreement based upon reciprocal most-favored-nation treatment, and other economic concessions and advantages. During these conversations the Pres-ident, learning of new contingents of Japanese troops bound for Indo-China, asked the meaning of these movements. Japan answered that the reason for them was fear of Chinese aggression. On December 6 the President sent a personal appeal in the interest of peace to Emperor Hirohito.

The answer, delivered personally to Secretary Hull on December 7 by Ambassador Nomura and Special Envoy Kurusu, asserted that the Japanese government had striven for peace and "always maintained an attitude of fairness and moderation, and did its best to reach a settlement." The American government, on the other hand, "always holding fast to theories in disregard of realities, and refusing to yield an inch on its impractical principles, caused undue delay in the negotiation." The United States, said the note, by trying to impose its own "selfish views upon others," had prevented any solution. "Obviously," continued the note, "it is the intention of the American Government to conspire with Great Britain and other countries to obstruct Japan's efforts toward the establishment of peace through the creation of a new order in East Asia, and especially to preserve Anglo-American rights and interests by keeping Japan and China at war." As Secretary Hull read these words, his eyes blazed. Turning to the Japanese envoys, he said, "I have never seen a document that was more crowded with infamous falsehoods and distortions—infamous falsehoods and distortions on a scale so huge that I never imagined until today that any Government on this planet was capable of uttering them."

An hour before the Japanese representatives delivered this message Japan began her war on the United States by a surprise attack on Pearl Harbor. This was followed immediately by attacks on Guam, Wake Island, the Philippines, and other American bases in the Pacific and upon British Hong Kong and Malaya. The next day (December 8) Japan formally declared war on this country and Great Britain. The treacherous and unexpected attack on Pearl Harbor was a costly blow to the United States; it destroyed most of the aircraft on the ground, destroyed or disabled eight warships and other vessels in the harbor, and killed or wounded over 4500 men. Its military effect was to prevent the United States from taking the offensive in the Pacific for more than six months and to give Japan a free hand during that time to attack the British and Dutch colonies in the Far East.

Perhaps its most important effect, however, was to unite the American people over night into a single opposition against the aggressor nations. On Monday, December 8, President Roosevelt appeared before Congress and asked for a declaration of war on Japan. The vote for war in the House was 388 to 1 and in the Senate 82 to 0. On December 10 Germany and Italy announced a state of war existing with the United States, and on the following day Congress without a dissenting voice declared war upon those nations. Six months later (June 5, 1942) the United States declared war on Bulgaria, Hungary, and Rumania, satellite nations of Germany. Great

Britain followed the United States with a declaration of war on Japan. Other nations or their governments in exile followed.[1]

The first problem faced by the nation was to raise the armed forces to a strength capable of fighting the Axis powers on land and sea and to equip them adequately for the task. The Draft Act of 1940 (page 730), which made all male citizens between 21 and 36 liable to twelve months' service in the western hemisphere or the possessions of the United States, was extended the next year to include all from 20 to 44 inclusive and gave the President power to lengthen the period of service. After war had been declared, restrictions as to where these men might serve were removed, and the draft was extended downward to include youths of 18 and 19.[2] By the end of 1944 the armed forces numbered approximately 11,800,000; there were 8,000,000 in the army and 3,800,000 in the navy. These included 200,000 women in the army, navy, marine, and coast guard reserves. The mere training of these men and women was a tremendous task which required the facilities of hundreds of training camps and colleges, as well as thousands of expert instructors. The Second World War was much more mechanized than any previous conflict and required more extended and more technical training. The ability of the army and navy to do this job was an important contribution to ultimate victory.

To care for the great increase in the needs of the army and navy, Congress voted huge sums. Early in February, 1945, the Treasury announced that the war so far had cost $238,000,000,000 and estimated that the cost up to June 30, 1946, would be $357,900,000,000. During 1944 the war cost the American people about $250,000,000 a day or almost $175,000 a minute. This is almost four times the cost of the First World War at its height. Excise and income taxes were increased steeply, and the latter were extended

[1] On January 2, 1942, the following twenty-six nations at war with one or more of the Axis powers signed a "Declaration of the United Nations," agreeing not to make a separate armistice or peace and to employ full military and economic resources against the enemy each was fighting: United States, United Kingdom of Great Britain and Northern Ireland, U.S.S.R., China, Australia, Belgium, Canada, Costa Rica, Cuba, Czechoslovakia, Dominican Republic, El Salvador, Greece, Guatemala, Haiti, Honduras, India, Luxembourg, Netherlands, New Zealand, Nicaragua, Norway, Panama, Poland, North Africa, Yugoslavia. Later Mexico, the Philippines, Ethiopia, Iraq, Brazil, Bolivia, Iran, Colombia, and Liberia also signed. France and Denmark, without signing, were considered members. Eight other nations, without declaring war, had severed relations with one or more of the Axis powers. Germany's satellites, Rumania, Hungary, Bulgaria, Croatia, and Slovakia, declared war against one or more of the United Nations. Finland was at war with Great Britain and Russia. Japan and her puppet states, Manchukuo and Burma, were not at war with Russia. Early in 1945 Turkey, Egypt, Argentina, Syria, Saudi Arabia, and Lebanon declared war on Germany.

[2] Exceptions were allowed for ministers, conscientious objectors, and important government officials, and deferments were allowed for those holding key jobs in defense industries.

downward to include virtually all wage-earners. Taxes, however, took care of less than half the current cost of the war (46 per cent in 1944), and the government attempted to meet the rest by selling war stamps and bonds. Six war-loan drives (all oversubscribed) brought in over $100,000,000,000 by the end of 1944, in addition to other billions purchased regularly by individuals, organizations, and banks. The government was particularly eager to sell war bonds, not alone to obtain funds for carrying on the war, but also to ward off inflation by absorbing in this way any excess buying power which the people might have.

It was one thing to vote money and call men into the armed service and quite another and more difficult task to produce the equipment to fight a global war. Somehow America had to retool and transform industry as quickly as possible into war production, control the production and use of raw materials, and allocate capital and labor. More than that, it had to expand industrial capacity to take care of the huge demand for particular commodities. It also had to establish an authority which could direct and control this revolution in the economic life of the nation and integrate the needs of the military and civilian population.

A beginning was made in May, 1940, when the President established a Council of National Defense composed of six members of his cabinet, aided by an Advisory Commission of experts. Its business was to obtain raw materials, supervise production, handle labor problems, manage farm products, supervise transportation, control prices, and deal with consumer problems. Most of the work of the Advisory Commission was later consolidated in the Office of Production Management. But the OPM was far from satisfactory, and after further experimentation it was abolished in January, 1942, and succeeded by the War Production Board. At the head of the WPB the President placed Donald Nelson, a Chicago business executive, with final authority for the production and distribution of raw materials and finished products and their allocation among military and civilian needs. In addition to the chairman, the WPB included the Vice-President, the Secretaries of War and the Navy, Federal Loan Administrator Jesse Jones, and Price Administrator Leon Henderson. These were the commanding generals in the battle of production during the early years of the war.[3]

So rapid was the conversion of American industry to the war effort that within six months after Pearl Harbor the problem of production was largely solved. The United States, said Mr. Nelson toward the end of May, "is actually doing things today which were unthinkable a year ago. It is executing programs which sounded utterly fantastic no more than six

[3] Donald Nelson resigned in September, 1944, and was succeeded by Julius A. Krug. Leon Henderson resigned as Price Administrator in 1943 and was succeeded first by Prentiss Brown and later by Chester Bowles. Jesse Jones resigned in 1945 and was succeeded by John W. Snyder.

months ago." The record established during the first six months of the war was continued. Each year of the war, production increased over the previous year, and this despite a growing shortage of manpower. Annual steel production was stepped up from 52,799,000 tons in 1939 to 96,369,000 in 1944, when the United States produced over 50 per cent of the world's supply. In 1944 American manufacturers built 96,369 airplanes. Thousands of factories turned from the production of peacetime products to the manufacture of materials for war. The great automobile industry, for example, converted itself almost entirely to the manufacture of airplanes and engines, tanks, guns, trucks, jeeps, and other products for army, navy, and lend-lease. What this meant specifically was revealed by General Brehon Somervell when he spoke to the National Association of Manufacturers in December, 1944. At the time of Pearl Harbor, he said, "most of our present army was in civilian clothes. We possessed exactly 1,157 planes suitable for combat, and almost the same number of usable tanks. . . . [Since then] you have made 187,000 planes, 68,000 tanks, 1,800,000 trucks, 2,800,000 medium and big guns, 15,000,000 machine guns and rifles, 43,000,000,000 rounds of ammunition, 43,400,000 bombs, 196,000,000 uniforms and 98,000,-000 pairs of shoes." By that time 50 per cent of American productive capacity was engaged in the war effort. It was estimated at the end of July, 1944, that the combined war production of the United States, Canada, and the British Empire had reached a level four times as high as that of the Axis powers. So well, in fact, was production going by the late summer of 1944 that the WPB began to order cut-backs in war production and to allow some resumption of civilian-goods production in areas where local labor was available.

Not only did manufacturing achieve miracles, but notable records were made in other economic areas. Mineral production as a whole reached a new level in 1944, "particularly noteworthy," said Secretary Ickes, "because the nation skimmed much of the 'cream' from its mineral resources during the First World War." This performance included new records of production for bituminous coal and petroleum. Despite a decrease in farm population of over 4,700,000 in the four years 1941–1944, agricultural production increased each year in an effort to meet the expanding needs of the armed forces, the civilians, and lend-lease. Innumerable amateur farmers also helped to enlarge the overall agricultural production by planting "victory gardens." Quite as notable as any civilian efforts was that achieved by the transportation facilities, particularly the railroads. Whereas in the First World War the government had found it necessary to take over and operate the railroads, in the Second World War privately operated railroads managed to do a superb job under the supervision of the Office of Defense Transportation. Railroads reported that they had moved two and a half times the number of ton miles of freight in 1944 as they had in 1939 and four and a half times the passenger traffic. This enormous load was handled with virtually the same number of locomotives as in 1939 and with but a nominal increase in cars.

Despite the unusual records of manufacturers, miners, farmers, and transportation workers, the unusual war demands inevitably resulted in chronic shortages of certain commodities at various times, particularly for civilians. By 1942 the chief problem was not processing so much as obtaining raw materials. The first great shortage, that of aluminum, brought the government into action with a government-owned but privately operated expansion program which increased production at least four times over prewar years. By the middle of 1942 the aluminum shortage for war needs had vanished, but other shortages had appeared in iron, ships, rubber, gasoline, fuel oil, and other commodities. Nation-wide drives to recover scrap metal improved the production of steel. A successful expansion of shipbuilding facilities overcame the loss of 600 ships sunk by enemy submarines by the end of 1942. No sooner was the submarine menace under control than the increased needs of 5,000,000 soldiers overseas again strained the shipping facilities, despite the fact that we were building sixteen times as many ships in 1944 as in 1941.

So it was with gasoline, fuel oil, and rubber. Before the war most of the oil that reached the Atlantic coast had come north from the Gulf ports by tankers. German submarines practically ended this form of transportation. The government built huge pipelines from the Middle West to get this oil to the coast, but by the time this had been done the demand of the armies in Europe prevented increased amounts from going to civilians. Quite different from the aggressive efficiency with which the government handled the shortages in aluminum, shipping, and oil was the muddling slowness in meeting the rubber shortage. After Japan's conquest of the East Indies had cut off the rubber supply of the United States, existing rubber stocks were frozen and tires rationed. Gasoline rationing was also started (May, 1942), in part to save rubber. Although the desperate situation was clear to everyone, it was six months after Pearl Harbor before government agencies had actually organized a synthetic-rubber program. The delay seems to have been caused chiefly by the farm blocs' insistence that the rubber be manufactured from agricultural products as well as from oil. Action came only after the President had appointed a special committee headed by Bernard M. Baruch to investigate the problem and later a National Rubber Conservation Director to put the program into action. In mid-1944 the Rubber Director resigned, asserting that synthetic-rubber production was running at the rate of 836,000 tons a year compared with prewar imports of crude rubber ranging from 550,000 to 650,000 tons a year. This was a bright picture, but it meant little to civilian motorists, for military needs had expanded as rapidly as production. Much of this expansion was subsidized by the government. The Reconstruction Plant Corporation, acting through the Defense Plant Corporation, had made available for conversion or construction about $11,000,000,000 by the end of 1943. This included the building of sixty synthetic-rubber plants, six long-distance pipelines, and many new factories.

Since there were not enough raw materials for both war and civilian needs, the government was forced to establish a system of priorities and rationing. Early in 1942 the OPA began to ration automobiles, tires, tubes, and other commodities. In May it began to ration gasoline on the eastern seacoast, and on December 1 it extended its control over gasoline to the entire nation. In the meantime fuel oil had been rationed. Long before this, local shortages had begun to appear in meat, butter, canned goods, and other foodstuffs. A definite rationing system began in May, when civilians registered for stamp books necessary for the purchase of sugar. In November rationing was extended to coffee. The nation was not surprised, therefore, when Secretary of Agriculture Wickard announced late in December that rationing would be imposed early in 1943 on many types of processed foods needed particularly by the armed forces.

By the end of 1943 approximately 95 per cent of the food, gasoline, fuel oil, coal, shoes, and tires and many other essential goods were on the ration list for civilians. The situation was by no means static; the OPA could ease or tighten restrictions as shortages ceased or grew more acute. Rationing was essential to the war effort, and the great masses of patriotic Americans loyally supported it. It was accompanied, as we shall see, by government price-fixing. Unfortunately a small minority attempted to evade these regulations, and a "black market," particularly in gasoline and meats, existed at various times and places, which the OPA found itself inadequately equipped entirely to eradicate.

One shortage which seemed likely to continue as long as the war was that of manpower. While approximately 12,000,000 men were eventually drawn into the armed services, the tremendous war effort demanded additional millions for war industries. Probably not more than 500,000 persons were employed in war industries in 1939; three years later the number was 20,000,000. The nation's wage-earners rose from 45,500,000 in 1939 to 54,000,000 in 1944. The shift of millions of wage-earners to war industry and the addition of millions of new wage-earners created many problems: the learning of new jobs, the training of apprentices, competition between industries for skilled mechanics, scarcity of labor in one section with an abundance in another, and the drafting of skilled labor for the armed services.

These and other problems led the President in April, 1942, to create a War Manpower Commission with Paul V. McNutt as chairman. It was authorized "to establish basic national policies to assure the most effective mobilization and maximum utilization of the nation's manpower in the prosecution of the war." For a short time the WMC was given dictatorial power over the nation's manpower, including control over the Selective Service System, but this was later withdrawn. With the help of the WMC the acute labor shortage in the war industries was largely solved. The drafting of essential workers was deferred, and millions of new war workers were recruited among women who had not been working outside the home, and among older men, boys under draft age, and workers in nonessential industries. The President, however, considered the shortage still bad enough to justify his asking, in his message of January, 1944, for a "national service law" which "will make available for war production or for any other essential services every able-bodied adult in the nation," and he repeated the request in 1945. Congress, however, did not comply.

On the whole, organized labor gave every possible support to the government's war effort and to attempts to overcome the manpower shortage. When the war started, Philip Murray of the C.I.O. and William Green of the A. F. of L. joined with the Railway Brotherhoods in pledging a no-strike policy. This pledge was generally kept as far as the responsible leaders were concerned, although there were sometimes unauthorized or outlaw strikes. In many of these cases the workers were ordered back to their jobs by their union officials. In view of the difficulties bound to arise over the increased cost of living and the innumerable adjustments to war conditions, the President created, in January, 1942, a twelve-man War Labor Board. It had equal representation from management, labor, and the public and was given final jurisdiction over labor disputes and wage adjustments.

A notable exception to labor's no-strike policy was John L. Lewis and his United Mine Workers, who refused to allow the WLB to settle a wage dispute and went out on strike in the spring of 1943. This forced the government to take over 3000 bituminous mines in twenty-six states and led Congress to pass the Smith-Connally Act over the President's veto, making it a criminal offense to instigate or assist a strike in a government-seized industry. In October the miners went out a second time, and again the government assumed control; but this time the miners won their demand for larger pay by agreeing to work longer hours. In 1945 the anthracite miners voted to strike, and the government again took over the mines. An increase in pay ended the walkout. Threat of a railway strike in December, 1943 led the government to take over operation of the railways for three weeks while the wage disputes were adjusted. Even with the miners' strikes counted, the number of man-hours lost in this way was but a fraction of one per cent of the total working time. Considering the extra strain of wartime production, the longer hours of work, and the increased cost of living, the record was unusually good.

The greatest failure of the federal government during the First World War had been its inability to control prices, which increased 100 per cent. Hoping to prevent a repetition of such increases, President Roosevelt in 1940 set up an agency to stabilize prices and in 1941 established it as the Office of Price Administration. No government agency had a more difficult job. It was expected to fix fair maximum rents in defense areas and fair maximum prices on thousands of commodities at all stages of their distribution. It was also expected, through the WLB, to keep wages and the prices of commodities in some kind of equilibrium. Moreover, it had to regulate the dealings of millions of buyers and sellers in a scarcity market in which innumerable influences were at work to break the price ceilings. This task the OPA was expected to accomplish in spite of strong opposition by various groups, an inadequate personnel to enforce its orders, and until Congress legislated in 1942, extremely vague powers.

Chief opponents of the administration policy of stabilization were farmers who wanted no ceilings on agricultural products and laborers who wanted higher wages. The policy of the administration was to set top prices for agricultural commodities but to recompense the farmers for higher costs of production through subsidies. This was finally accomplished over the opposition of the "farm bloc." This group was strong enough in 1944 to pass legislation to end price ceilings by removing subsidies, but it failed to carry the bill over the President's veto, and the subsidies were renewed. The policy of the government with regard to wages, as laid down by the War Labor Board in January, 1942, was to limit increases in straight-time wage rates to 15 per cent above the level of January 1, 1941, a policy known as the "Little Steel formula." Labor leaders sought to modify or set aside the Little Steel formula on the ground that the cost of living had increased much more than 15 per cent. They bitterly criticized the wage and cost-of-living indices of the Bureau of Labor Statistics, upon which the Little Steel formula was presumably based, and presented figures prepared by their own economists to prove the need of higher wages. The Bureau of Labor figures actually showed a rise in the cost of living of over 25 per cent from 1939 to 1945, but a majority of the War Labor Board, insisting that the "take home pay" of the average wage-earner had risen at least as much, refused to change the formula. However, the WLB softened its policy by allowing vacation pay and increased wages for overtime, and by other means.

Whether its figures were exact or not, there could be no doubt that the government had warded off the catastrophe of a runaway inflation. It had thereby done much to save from ruin those who lived on fixed salaries or other fixed income, and it had saved tens of billions of dollars in the cost of the war. Convinced that the policy was sound, the President late in 1942 established the Office of Economic Stabilization (first under former Justice James F. Byrnes, later under Fred M. Vinson and William H. Davis) to aid the OPA and the WLB and to supervise all efforts to stabilize the nation's economy. This policy of centralized overall supervision was carried further in 1943 when Byrnes was made chairman of the Office of War Mobilization, which was created to direct and integrate all agencies (including the WPB) concerned in the nation's internal war efforts.[4]

No discussion of the home front would be complete without noting the numerous volunteer activities of the average citizen. Through the Office of Civilian Defense millions of men and women secured special training as air-raid wardens, airplane-spotters, auxiliary policemen and firemen, hospital orderlies, and nurses' aids. Civilians acted as pilots in the Civil Air Patrol. Many gave their time to the arduous duties on draft and ration boards; 3,000,000 volunteers wrapped bandages and did other work for the Red Cross. Men, women, and children collected scrap metal, paper, and other commodities, sold war bonds and stamps, and collected money for the United Service Organizations and other war funds. In some way or other almost everyone made his contribution to the war effort.

THE PACIFIC WAR

The sneak attack of the Japanese on Pearl Harbor (December 7, 1941) succeeded beyond expectation. It released the Japanese from danger of a flank assault by the American fleet and left them free for a smashing attack upon the Philippines and Singapore. Their position was strengthened three days later when the Japanese air force destroyed two of the largest British warships near Singapore and left the United Nations with but slight naval strength in the Far East. The grand strategy of the Japanese was quickly evident. Before the end of the year they had captured the United States islands of Guam and Wake, the British colony of Hong Kong on the coast of China, and had swept through Thailand and invaded the Philippines, Burma, and Malaya. The great British naval base of Singapore fell on February 15, 1942, and left the Japanese free to concentrate upon the British and Dutch West Indies. Before the end of March they had overrun the Celebes, Borneo, Sumatra, Java, and the Solomon Is-

---

[4] This was changed in October, 1944, to the Office of War Mobilization and Reconversion, to take care of the multitudinous problems of reconversion, contract settlement, retraining, and unemployment.

lands and had invaded New Guinea. By that time they were within bombing distance of northern Australia. During the four months after Pearl
Harbor the Japanese had conquered a vast empire rich in tin, rubber, oil,
and other commodities needed in modern warfare, and at the same time
had broken the power of the United Nations in eastern Asia. The conquest
had been rapid but by no means unopposed. Small contingents of the British, Dutch, and American navies, aided by airplanes, fought the Japanese
invaders in a five-day battle in the Macassar Straits in January, again off the
island of Bali in February, and a few days later in the battle of the Java Sea.
These three battles inflicted severe losses upon the Japanese invaders but
merely delayed their advance.

In the meantime the small American and Philippine armies were holding
on tenaciously in the Philippines under the command of General Douglas
MacArthur. A few hours after Pearl Harbor squadrons of Japanese bombers swept over the Philippines and wrecked a large part of the American
air strength. With but slight opposition from the weakened American air
force, the Japanese invaded the Philippines three days after Pearl Harbor
and captured Manila on January 2. Lacking adequate aid on the sea and
in the air, MacArthur concentrated his 15,000 Americans and 40,000 Philippine troops for a last stand on the mountainous Bataan Peninsula and on
the fortified island of Corregidor at the entrance of Manila Bay. Ordered
by his government to leave, MacArthur escaped to Australia early in March,
entrusting the command to General Jonathan W. Wainwright. From
early January until April 9 the American and Philippine armies fought off
the overwhelming Japanese forces on Bataan before Wainwright ordered
a surrender. Wainwright himself, with a smaller force, retreated to Corregidor, where he hung on against constant attack until May 6. Cut off from
any help from their homeland, and engaged in a battle that was hopeless
from the start, the heroic defenders of Bataan and Corregidor held back the
might of the Japanese Empire for six months.

Badly handicapped by the severe losses at Pearl Harbor, the United
States could do little more for five months than fight a defensive battle. The
main strategy was to hold the defense line running from Dutch Harbor in
the Aleutians to Midway, Hawaii, and Samoa in the south, and behind this
defense to keep open the supply line to Australia and the South Pacific. The
Japanese strategy was a further advance to the south to engulf Australia
and eastward to attack the Hawaiians. The tide finally turned on May 4
when a Japanese effort to break the southern supply line brought on a naval
battle in the Coral Sea northeast of Australia. A four-day battle inflicted
heavy losses upon two Japanese fleets and ended their advance toward the
south. A month later (June 3–6) American reconnaissance planes spotted a
Japanese fleet approaching Midway Island, bent on smashing the main

American defense line. In the battle which followed planes from Midway and naval carriers inflicted a staggering defeat on the Japanese fleet. The battles of the Coral Sea and Midway marked a radical departure in naval warfare. In both engagements, the opposing fleets neither saw one another nor exchanged gunfire. The fighting was done entirely by airplanes. Although the Japanese landed troops shortly after the battle of Midway on Attu and Kiska among the Aleutian Islands of Alaska (recaptured 1943), Hawaii was never again in danger of attack by a Japanese fleet.

After Coral Sea and Midway the United States was ready to take the offensive. The turn began on August 5 with a combined sea and air attack on Guadalcanal in the Solomons and the landing of American troops. To the Japanese the Solomons were important as a jumping-off place for an attack on Australia and other Allied territory to the south. To the United Nations they were necessary both for defense and as a point of departure for the northward movement against Japan. Japan was thoroughly aware of the strategic importance of the Solomons and made repeated efforts to reinforce her garrison and regain the lost territory. The struggle came to a climax in the great naval battle off Guadalcanal (November 13–15). Here the American fleet, under William F. Halsey, Jr., turned back the Japanese with severe losses. The battle of the Solomons, described as the "greatest naval battle since Jutland," differed from the Coral Sea and Midway engagements in that the battleships were in direct firing contact with one another.

Although the Japanese were defeated in three major naval battles and in numerous minor engagements, they maintained a desperate resistance in the islands of the South Pacific. It was not until February, 1943, that they were finally driven out of Guadalcanal. At the end of 1943 the United Nations were just completing the conquest of the Solomons and beginning the occupation of Bougainville and New Britain. For two years American and Australian troops had fought bitterly in the jungles of New Guinea to dislodge the Japanese, but the enemy still held bases on the northern coast. This progress seemed slow indeed for two years of hard fighting.

In November, 1943, however, the situation changed rapidly when American forces landed on Tarawa and Makin in the Gilbert Islands. At this point Admiral Chester W. Nimitz, in charge of the Pacific fleet, and General MacArthur decided that the attack on Japan would be through the islands of the Central Pacific. In February, 1944, they struck Kwajalein in the center of the Marshalls, the first Japanese territory to be captured by the Allies. In June they moved north to the Marianas, where they conquered Saipan and later recaptured Guam. American troops at Saipan met the bitterest resistance they had yet encountered in any island invasion. Before it was conquered, Americans suffered 15,000 casualties, 2300 of them killed. But Saipan was of major importance; from it the B-29's could begin the bombing of Japan, and American troops could make the next island-hop to the Philippines. After Saipan the entire Pacific strategy developed rapidly.

When MacArthur escaped from Bataan to Australia in March, 1942, he made the statement: "I came through and I shall return." The promise was kept on October 20, 1944, when MacArthur's invasion force, commanded by General Walter Krueger, landed on Leyte in the Philippines. Japan tried desperately to prevent this move. Her fleet emerged but met the worst defeat it had yet suffered. Again and again Japan tried unsuccessfully to reinforce the Leyte garrison. By mid-January Leyte was conquered, and the American force moved on to the island of Mindoro. On January 9, 1945, came the invasion of Luzon. The American force landed at Lingayen Bay north of Manila, the point where the Japanese more than three years before had invaded the Philippines. Before February had ended, American troops had captured Manila and ousted the Japanese from Bataan and Corregidor, the rocky island fortress in the mouth of Manila Bay. While Krueger's troops gradually completed the conquest of the Philippines, another task force struck at Iwo Jima, more bitterly defended than even Saipan. The next objective was Okinawa, also stubbornly defended. The capture of Iwo Jima, only 750 miles from Tokyo, and Okinawa, only 330 miles from Kyushu, made the systematic bombing of Japan relatively easy. Large-scale bombing of Japan's important centers of war production became a matter of almost daily routine. Moreover, possession of the Philippines and Okinawa largely cut off the newly won empire in the East Indies from the Japanese mainland and prepared the way for the next Allied move against Japan. With the end of the European war in May, 1945, the United States and Great Britain were in a position to greatly intensify the Pacific War.

While American forces were moving northward through the Pacific islands on the long road to Tokyo, other American troops, in conjunction with British and Indian forces, were protecting India from Japanese invasion along the Burma frontier. Successful in this, they found it difficult to drive the Japanese from Burma itself. It was not until January, 1945, that they succeeded in forcing the enemy far enough to the east to open part of the old Burma Road, the supply route to Chiang Kai-shek's Chinese armies. In the meantime, however, American air men had succeeded in flying small quantities of supplies across the mountains from India to China, enough to give some encouragement to the Chinese and to keep a small American air force operating against the Japanese in China. Finally, in May, 1945, British Imperial troops captured Rangoon, ousted the Japanese from Burma, and freed the entire Burma road. The success of the Burma campaign ended the danger of a further Japanese advance in India.

THE EUROPEAN WAR

Left with the major responsibility of defense against the Japanese, the United States during 1942 devoted her greatest strength to the Pacific war. As far as Europe was concerned, the best that we could do was to aid our allies through lend-lease and make preparations for eventual military co-operation in strength. What units of the navy and air force could be spared from the Pacific area were used chiefly in the Atlantic for convoy duty and in combating the submarine menace. In both activities notable success was achieved. In co-operation with the British navy, improved techniques of detecting submarines and of convoying troops and supplies were developed. During 1942 the Allies lost 1859 ships (422 of the American merchant marine), but by the end of the year they had greatly reduced the losses. A year later the Germans were losing more U-boats than the Allies were losing merchant ships. Lend-lease in 1942 was pushed aggressively; in conjunction with the British we sent the Russians 3000 planes, 4000 tanks, and 30,000 trucks. Similarly, thousands of planes, tanks, and trucks went to the British fighting the Germans in North Africa. Expansion of the army was speeded; by the end of 1942 it had grown to 5,000,000 men, of whom 1,200,000 were overseas. Those in the British Isles, under General Dwight D. Eisenhower, were already intensively training for the invasion of Europe. An American air force was established in England to lend aid to the brave air men who had defended their island for almost three years. American bombers made their first raid over Germany on July 4.

Where Americans would launch their first attack was disclosed on November 7 when British and American troops, aided by sea and air power, landed at Casablanca on the Atlantic coast of French Morocco and at Oran and Algiers on the Mediterranean coast of Algeria. The expeditionary force to North Africa consisted of 850 vessels—500 transports protected by 350 naval vessels—the longest overseas movement of troops in history up to that time. The French offered resistance at first but quickly capitulated, renounced the Vichy government of France, and co-operated with the Allies. Just as the invasion of Guadalcanal ended the purely defensive stage of American strategy in the Pacific, so the invasion of Africa marked the beginning of the American offensive on the Atlantic front. Churchill aptly described the African invasion as the "end of the beginning." In January, 1943, President Roosevelt flew to Casablanca to discuss war strategy with Churchill, and there they announced that war would be terminated with the Axis only on a basis of "unconditional surrender."

The purpose of the invasion was to drive the Axis forces out of Africa in preparation for the invasion of Europe. For many months the British, based on Cairo, had fought the Germans and Italians back and forth across the deserts of Egypt and Libya. By early 1943 General Bernard Montgomery's British army had driven Field Marshal Rommel's German and Italian forces backward from Egypt into Tunisia. Now the Americans advanced eastward from Algeria to catch the enemy in an east-west nutcracker. Beginning in early February, the Allies kept up a severe and almost continuous attack until they had driven the Germans and Italians northward to the Tunisian seacoast and forced the surrender of Tunis and Bizerte on May 7. Defeated on land and harassed without let-up by a superior air power, the German and Italian armies remaining in Africa were beaten into surrender.

Less than two months after that surrender the Allies were ready for the invasion of Sicily. An immense fleet of over 3000 transports and landing barges, accompanied by warships, bombers, and fighting planes, set out on July 9. The landing was made without difficulty—the Americans under General Patton on the southern coast and the British on the southeast corner—but it took the Allies more than a month to smash the Germans and drive them out of Sicily. The Sicilian campaign was well executed and brought important results. Mussolini fled to the protection of Hitler, and the Italian government surrendered unconditionally September 8. The surrender of Italy brought with it possession of most of the Italian fleet. The capture of Sicily and the later invasion of Italy lessened the menace of air and submarine attacks in the Mediterranean and opened up the Allied route to the East through the Mediterranean Sea. It also gave us air fields in Italy from which Allied planes could bomb Nazi-held southern Europe.

The day after Italy announced her surrender Lieutenant General Mark Clark's Fifth Army, accompanied by British divisions, crossed the straits and established a toehold at Salerno on the Italian mainland. The main British army landed at Taranto inside the Italian heel and moved up the east coast of Italy. French contingents took up a position between the Americans and the British. The mountainous terrain of Italy lent itself to defense, and the Germans, throwing fresh divisions into Italy, elected to contest every foot of ground. The fight had been bitter at the Salerno beachhead, and it continued so as the Allies fought their way northward through the Italian hills. The end of the year found the Allies north of Naples but still far from Rome. In the hope of speeding the Italian campaign, a second American invading force landed (January 27, 1944) behind the German lines at Anzio about thirty miles south of Rome. The Germans tried desperately to oust the invaders but failed. Nevertheless, Rome did not fall until June 6. At the end of the year the Allied line stretched approximately from Pisa on the west to Mezzano on the east.

While British, French, and American forces were driving the Germans

WAR ON THE PACIFIC

Top—Amphibious craft loaded with troops heads for the beach at the invasion of Okinawa, April 1, 1945. (Official U. S. Navy Photo from Acme.)

Bottom—Marines waiting for the order to advance after landing on the beach at Iwo Jima. (U. S. Marine Corps from Acme.)

CROSSING THE RHINE

Jeeps and tanks of the 87th Division, United States Third Army, roll over a pontoon bridge erected by Army engineers. (Signal Corps photo from Acme.)

northward in Italy, Roosevelt, Churchill, and Stalin met at Teheran [5] late in November, 1943, to plan the strategy of the European war. There, said the final communiqué, "we have reached complete agreement as to the scope and timing of the operations to be undertaken from the east, west and south"; and it added, "no power on earth can prevent our destroying the German armies by land, their U-boats by sea, and their war plants from the air. Our attack will be relentless and increasing." That these were not mere words became clear enough in 1944.

When the Germans attacked Russia in 1941, their objectives were the capture of Moscow, Leningrad, and the Ukraine. They failed to win Moscow and Leningrad, but occupied the Ukraine. Their strategy in 1942 was to concentrate their power in a mighty drive southeast into the Crimea and the Caucasus. The heroic defense of Stalingrad, followed by the capture of the German army besieging that city (January, 1943), and a counteroffensive ended the German drive. Russia's counteroffensive in 1943 canceled the German gains of 1942. The Allied plan of 1944 included continued pressure upon the German lines in Italy, a new Russian offensive in the east, and an invasion of France by British and American forces.

Under the direction of General Eisenhower, supreme allied commander, arms were collected in Great Britain and troops trained in 1943 and early 1944. Throughout this period the British and American air forces had methodically bombed German war factories, oil plants, and transportation lines and anything else that might be useful in war, and these attacks were intensified in the weeks before D-day. After almost two years of thorough preparation, all was ready. On June 6 the sky was alive with 11,000 Allied planes, and the English Channel swarmed with 4000 ships. Early that day the invasion force hit the shores of Normandy, quickly secured a beachhead, and within twenty-four hours poured 250,000 men on to the Cherbourg peninsula. The port of Cherbourg was captured late in June, and a month later the Allied troops broke through the German lines at St. Lô and swarmed out of the Cherbourg peninsula on to the plains of Brittany. Amerians now sped across northern France behind the rapidly retreating Germans to free Paris (August 25).

Ten days earlier a new Allied invasion, mainly American and French troops from Italy and Africa, landed on the south coast of France between Marseilles and Nice and proceeded to move northward to make contact with the Allied troops advancing from Normandy. By early December the

[5] Shortly before, Roosevelt and Churchill had conferred at Cairo with Chiang Kai-shek. There they issued a declaration that, as a result of Allied victory, Japan would be stripped of all the islands which she had seized since 1914. All the territories stolen from China, such as Manchuria, Formosa, and the Pescadores, would be restored to the Republic of China, and Korea would become a free and independent state.

Germans had been driven almost entirely from France and Belgium, and the Allied lines stretched along the German border from Switzerland to the Netherlands. In several places the Allies had reached German soil. The Germans, however, were not yet beaten. They struck back in mid-December in a dramatic counteroffensive in Belgium and Luxembourg, which carried their armies fifty-one miles westward, almost to the Meuse river. The Battle of the Bulge lasted more than a month before the German salient was flattened and the Allies were ready to invade Germany.

Two days before the port of Cherbourg fell to the American invaders, Russia launched her great 1944 offensive. She swept the Germans out of White Russia and the eastern half of Poland, knocked Rumania out of the war in August and Bulgaria in September,[6] forced the Germans to withdraw from most of Yugoslavia, and then swung up the Danube to attack Budapest. In September she forced the capitulation of Finland. In the meantime the Russian advance forced the Germans to withdraw from Greece and made possible the invasion by a British army. On the northern sector of the Russian line the offensive was renewed with tremendous vigor early in January, 1945. A northern army struck northward from Poland into German East Prussia, a central army took Warsaw and advanced directly west toward Berlin, and a southern army overran the industrial and mining area of German Silesia to outflank Berlin from the south. After a period of consolidating gains, the offensive was renewed in late March, resulting in the capture of Vienna on April 13 and a direct attack on Berlin.

By the end of January the Allied armies in western Europe, two thirds of which were American, were ready for the final campaign. At the north was Field Marshal Alexander's Twenty-first Army Group, composed of Canadian and British troops and also, at the beginning of the offensive, of William H. Simpson's Ninth American Army (later transferred to Bradley's Twelfth Army Group). In the center was General Omar N. Bradley's American Twelfth Army Group, composed of the First Army under Courtney H. Hodges, the Third Army under George S. Patton, and the Fifteenth under Leonard T. Gerow. At the south was the Sixth Army Group of Jacob L. Devers, which included the American Seventh Army of Alexander M. Patch and the French troops. During February the Allies broke through the German "West Wall" defenses, breached the Roer river line, and poured on to the Cologne plain. American troops first reached the Rhine on March 2; the First Army captured Cologne on March 6 and crossed the Rhine over the captured bridge at Remagen on March 8. By the end of that month all the Allied armies had crossed the river.

During April the Allied armies pocketed twenty-one Nazi divisions in

---

[6] Rumania withdrew from the Axis on August 23, 1944, and signed an armistice on September 13; Bulgaria signed an armistice on October 28, and Finland on September 19.

the Ruhr basin and then swept eastward over Germany. On April 18 Patton's Third Army reached Czechoslovakia, thus cutting pre-Munich Germany in two. In the meantime American troops had reached the Elbe at Magdeburg (April 11), but had paused to allow the Russians to capture Berlin. As Allied armies swept into Germany, the Italian campaign was stepped up, and on May 2 all German troops in northern Italy and in southern and western Austria surrendered unconditionally. Mussolini, who had done more than any other to bring Italy to her unfortunate plight, was captured and executed by Italian partisans. With the Russian army in Berlin and with British, French, and American troops rapidly overrunning Germany, the end of the war could be only a few days off. On May 7 the German government, now headed by Admiral Doenitz after the reported death of Hitler, surrendered unconditionally to the Allied armies of General Eisenhower. A second dramatic ceremony of unconditional surrender was enacted two days later under Russian auspices in the ruined city of Berlin. The great drama of German military might which began with the invasion of Poland on August 1, 1939, ended with utter defeat and humiliation and with the occupation of Germany by the Allied powers. The United States occupational force (the Fifteenth Army) took over 14,000 square miles to administer, a region including the Saar basin, the Rhine valley, and the western part of the Ruhr basin.

THE ELECTION OF 1944

With MacArthur's troops back in the Philippines and Eisenhower's armies fighting along the western frontier of Germany, the American people for the third time in their history cast their votes in a wartime presidential election.[7] For the first time in their history they gave some attention to the possibility of voting by the armed forces. Months before candidates were chosen or platforms written, the question of how many of the 11,800,000 men and women in the armed forces would vote, and for whom, was a live issue. The problem, as the President saw it, was to make it as easy as possible for them to vote, particularly the 5,000,000 overseas. Congress rejected a plan favored by the President for a single federal ballot and also another plan leaving the entire matter up to the states. Under pressure for some action Congress finally, in March, passed a bill permitting service men overseas to use a federal ballot provided (1) that they applied for, and failed to receive, a state ballot, and (2) that the governors of their home states certified that the federal ballot was acceptable under state law. The President described the bill as wholly inadequate but allowed it to become law without

---

[7] The first time was in 1812 when James Madison was re-elected; the second in 1864 when Abraham Lincoln was returned to office.

his signature. In the end twenty states accepted the federal ballot, but few members of the armed forces used it, most of them preferring and obtaining a state ballot.

The Republicans, who had gained strength in the Congressional elections of 1942, considered their prospects brighter than for many years. As a result there was no dearth of candidates. They included Wendell L. Willkie, unsuccessful standard-bearer in 1940; Governor Thomas E. Dewey of New York, a leading contender for the nomination in 1940; and Governor John W. Bricker of Ohio. Minor strength developed for General Douglas MacArthur and for Lieutenant Commander Harold E. Stassen, who had resigned the governorship of Minnesota to accept a commission in the navy. Willkie waged an aggressive campaign for his thesis that the Republicans should take a stronger stand in favor of internationalism. He chose the Wisconsin primaries as a testing ground for his principles, and, when he failed to win a single delegate, retired from the field. MacArthur eliminated himself by stating that agitation for a military man was "detrimental to the war effort" and that he would not accept the nomination. By the time the Republican convention met, the nomination was virtually decided. Bricker had fought an aggressive campaign, but Republican leaders were insistent that Dewey would have the best chance of defeating Roosevelt and were prepared to nominate him. When Bricker saw the overwhelming trend of the convention, he voluntarily withdrew from the race. Dewey, who had never admitted that he was a candidate, was nominated on the first ballot, with only one vote—for MacArthur—cast against him. Bricker was given second place on the ticket.

On domestic issues the Republican platform stressed encouragement of private enterprise in reconversion, lower taxes, "states' rights," and the subjection of reciprocal trade agreements to approval by Congress. Though critical of federal power and bitter against the New Deal, it appeared to support the New Deal policies regarding agriculture and labor, confining itself to criticism of minor policies and methods of administration. All this was much like the stand in 1936 and 1940. The crux of the platform necessarily rested on foreign policy. The party, it was said, sought peace, freedom, and security "through organized international cooperation and not by joining a world state." The platform did, however, "favor responsible participation by the United States in post-war cooperative organization among sovereign nations to prevent military aggression and to attain permanent peace with organized justice in a free world." "Such organization," said the platform, "should develop effective cooperative means to direct peace forces to prevent or repel military aggression. Pending this we pledge continuing collaboration with the United Nations to assure these ultimate objectives."

Like Dewey, President Roosevelt was not a formal candidate, although both had allowed their names to be entered in state primaries. Not until a week before the convention did he make known that he would accept the nomination. "But if the people command me to continue in this office and in this war," said he, "I have as little right to withdraw as the soldier has to leave his post of battle." Since the Roosevelt leaders came to the convention with a majority of the delegates, he was nominated on the first ballot.[8] The chief interest in the convention turned out to be the nomination for the vice-presidency. Evidently believing that the liberalism of Vice-President Henry A. Wallace would be a political liability in the coming campaign, Roosevelt allowed the party bosses to substitute Senator Harry S. Truman of Missouri, who was nominated on the second ballot. Chief interest in the Democratic platform centered in the statements of foreign policy. These included support of the Atlantic Charter, the "four freedoms," and the Good Neighbor policy, and a pledge "to join with other United Nations in the establishment of an international organization based on the principles of the sovereign equality of all peace-loving states," an organization "with power to employ armed forces when necessary to prevent aggression and preserve peace." On the home front the platform pledged political equality for racial and religious minorities, extension of social security, aid to business and agriculture, and "faith in competitive private enterprise, free from control of monopolies, cartels, or other arbitrary private or public authority."

Since the party platforms were not fundamentally different, the campaign largely followed the traditional lines—the "outs" leveled criticism at anything that seemed vulnerable, and the party in power defended its record. Republicans asserted that the Roosevelt administration had failed to restore real prosperity after the depression but instead had stifled business and free enterprise. After twelve years in office, they said, the Democratic administration had grown tired, quarrelsome, and incompetent; it was time for a change. For dealing with the problems of peace at home and abroad, a new leadership which could work effectively with Congress was necessary. Both Dewey and Bricker insisted that the Communists were capturing the Democratic Party. Answering these criticisms and charges, the Democrats insisted that the social philosophy and experience of the New Deal were necessary to meet the transition to a peacetime economy. On foreign affairs they asserted that they had an organization that was winning the war and gaining experience in dealing with our allies, and that they were better prepared to make the peace and deal with postwar international problems than the Republicans with their traditional isolationism.

The campaign was unique in many ways. Not only was it a wartime

[8] Roosevelt received 1086 votes; Senator Harry D. Byrd, 89; James A. Farley, 1.

election, but it was the first time that a president had sought a fourth term and the first time a major party had nominated the same person four times. Never before had such a large number of votes been cast outside the country, and never before had so many civilians shifted their place of residence between elections. Moreover, this was the first time that a large section of labor had organized to participate aggressively in a campaign, except through a third party. This had been done effectively through the Political Action Committee sponsored by the Congress of Industrial Organizations. Many of these factors tended to confuse predictions of an election generally conceded to be close. Final returns showed Roosevelt the victor by a popular vote of 25,602,505 to 22,006,278 and an electoral vote of 432 to 99.[9] Dewey carried twelve states: Maine, Vermont, Ohio, Indiana, Wisconsin, Iowa, North Dakota, South Dakota, Nebraska, Kansas, Wyoming, and Colorado. About 2,800,000 votes were cast by the armed forces, a substantial majority of which, it is estimated, went for Roosevelt. His victory is attributed to a belief that international co-operation and future peace could be more safely entrusted to him than to his opponent, a reluctance to change leadership during a war, a continued support of the New Deal, and the active support of organized labor. The defeat of certain extreme isolationists seemed to indicate a desire that the United States play a more active role in international affairs.

PROBLEMS OF THE POSTWAR WORLD

During the first two years of our participation in the war the energies of the nation were devoted largely to the battle of production, to the building and training of a large army and navy, and to combat operations in the Pacific and Mediterranean areas. With the successful invasion of France it was evident that the tide of war had turned and that the problems of peace could no longer be evaded. Congress began in the spring of 1944 with the Servicemen's Aid Act, the so-called "G.I. Bill of Rights." This was an omnibus veterans' aid measure providing for hospitalization, education and vocational training, loans for homes, farms, and businesses, aid in obtaining employment, and unemployment benefits. As a first step authorization was given for the construction of additional hospital facilities costing $500,000,000. Rough estimates put the cost of the whole program at well over $3,000,000,000. Provision had already been made for a special mustering-out bonus of from $100 to $300.

[9] The traditional third parties (Socialist, Socialist Labor, and Prohibition) played a minor role and received a negligible vote. The Communist Party dissolved and offered no candidate under the party label. Two parties operating chiefly in New York City, the American Labor Party and the Liberal Party, supported Roosevelt and polled over 800,000 votes, enough to overcome Dewey's upstate lead.

In the autumn Congress turned to the problem of reconversion and the handling of surplus property. The War Mobilization and Reconversion Act established an Office of War Mobilization and Reconversion (page 748) to co-ordinate all activities of the various agencies dealing with such problems of reconversion as contract-settlement and surplus-property disposal, employment and vocational training, unemployment compensation, and the building of public works. It also set up a special three-man board for the purpose of disposing of an estimated $100,000,000,000 in surplus war property in the form of war plants, surplus agricultural commodities, stockpiles, and surplus land. The greatest domestic problems which faced the nation as the war drew to a close were the rapid conversion from war production to peace production and the provision of jobs for war workers and 12,000,000 returning veterans. There was much talk during the campaign and the succeeding months about the needs of providing 60,000,000 jobs in the postwar period. Except for the legislation just mentioned and the plans of private business for quick conversion, little had been done.

Experience in the First World War had made it perfectly clear that the time for planning international economic and political co-operation was during the war and not after its conclusion. A start toward this was made in November, 1943, when forty-four nations established a United Nations Relief and Rehabilitation Administration. Its purpose was to provide the people of liberated countries with food, clothing, and shelter and to supply seeds, agricultural implements, and other needs to aid in the restoration of agricultural and industrial production. The need for this was already clear from experience in North Africa, Sicily, and Italy.

Efforts to stabilize international relations were made in July, 1944, at the Bretton Woods National Monetary Conference attended by forty-four nations. Its specific job was to reach tentative agreements on plans to stabilize world currencies and set up a bank to finance economic reconstruction. Another object was to modify the type of trade barriers which have often been a contributing cause of wars. The conference finally hurdled a maze of technical and political differences, and proposed, in the first place, an International Monetary Fund of $8,800,000,000, to be furnished by the subscriber nations on a quota determined by ability to contribute. Nations needing funds to deal in foreign currency might obtain them under regulations which would prevent the wild speculation that was common in the days after the First World War and also prevent the strong government controls that had blocked free international trade and engendered friction in the 1930s. In the second place, the conference proposed a Bank for Reconstruction and Development, with a capitalization of $9,100,000,000, to aid in reconstruction after the war. All this was merely a plan which the various governments must agree to.

Another effort late in the year to plan for the postwar world was made by the International Aviation Conference, called together by the United States and attended by most of the nations except Russia. The conference proposed a permanent International Civil Aviation Organization and reached technical agreements on such matters as airport facilities, weather reports, and signaling devices. The United States offered five "freedoms of the air": (1) the right of innocent passage across designated routes of any nation; (2) the right to land on any nation's soil for technical reasons, such as refueling; (3) the right to carry traffic from the home country to any point in the world; (4) the right to bring through traffic back home from any point in the world; (5) the right of free competition for traffic throughout the world. Not all the nations accepted all points, but it was decided that those nations which did not might exchange airline privileges through bilateral agreements.

The monetary and aviation conferences were outstanding examples of international postwar economic planning. More important in the minds of most people, however, was the possibility of some type of organization that would maintain international peace and security. In the late summer of 1944 representatives from the United States, Russia, Great Britain, and China met at Dumbarton Oaks in Washington and agreed on a general plan. They proposed an international organization composed of (1) an Assembly of representatives of all peace-loving nations based on the principle of sovereign equality, (2) a Security Council of representatives of the United States, Great Britain, Russia, China, France, and six others selected by the Assembly for terms of two years, and (3) an International Court of Justice to adjudicate justiciable questions. Provisions were also suggested for a permanent Secretariat and for an Economic and Social Council, the latter to "facilitate solutions of international economic, social and other humanitarian problems and promote respect of human rights and fundamental freedoms." The Dumbarton Oaks proposals, like those of Bretton Woods, were merely tentative and required acceptance by the various governments. They seemed destined, however, to form the framework of whatever world organization is eventually adopted.

That Dumbarton Oaks would not be in vain was made clear early in November, 1945. At Yalta, on the Crimean peninsula, Roosevelt, Churchill, and Stalin again met to plan the military strategy for the final defeat of Germany and to plan for the postwar world. The demand for unconditional surrender, made by Roosevelt and Churchill at Casablanca, was affirmed. The powers agreed each to occupy a separate zone of defeated Germany and asserted their "inflexible purpose to destroy German militarism and nazism and to assure that Germany will never again be able to disturb the peace of the world." "We are determined," said the Crimea pledge, "to disarm and disband all German armed forces; to break up for all time the German General Staff . . . remove or destroy all German military equipment; eliminate or control all German industry that could be used for military production; bring all criminals to just and swift punishment and exact reparation in kind for the destruction wrought by the Germans. . . ." The powers pledged their aid in the economic and political rehabilitation of liberated Europe on the basis of the Atlantic Charter. An attempt to solve the Polish problem was made by proposing a new provisional government "on a broader democratic basis, with the eastern boundary approximately at the Curzon line," but with "substantial" accessions of territory to the north and west.[10] At the same time plans were made for regular meetings of the foreign secretaries of Great Britain, Russia, and the United States.

"We are resolved," said the representatives of these nations, "upon the earliest possible establishment with our allies of a general international organization to maintain peace and security." Pointing out that the foundations for such an organization had been laid at Dumbarton Oaks, they announced that a conference of the United Nations would be called to meet at San Francisco on April 25, 1945, to prepare a charter.[11] The wholehearted agreement of the three great nations at the Crimea Conference, the firmness of their tone, and the definiteness of their proposals resolved the confusion of millions of the Allied peoples and gave new hope to a warweary world. Yalta strengthened and consolidated the Allied might during the last months of the European war.

Whether the program laid down at Yalta would be fulfilled depended entirely upon the determination, sincerity, and good will of the great nations in co-operating to establish a peaceful world. Under the best of circumstances this would be difficult. It was made more so by the sudden death on April 12 of Franklin D. Roosevelt, America's great war leader and one of the architects of the Yalta program. He did not live long enough to see either the meeting of the security conference for which he had planned or the victory in Europe to which he had contributed so much. Roosevelt's death may have complicated the making of the peace, but it

[10] The "Curzon line" was originally drawn in 1919 by an Allied commission headed by Viscount Curzon, but not accepted by the Polish nation. It ran from East Prussia on the north through the cities of Grodnow, Brest-Litovsk, and Sokol to Czechoslovakia on the south. It gave the western Ukraine and White Russia to the Soviet Union and was the approximate line of the German-Russian partition of Poland of 1939.

[11] The American delegation to the San Francisco Conference, chosen on a two-party basis, included the following: Secretary of State Edward R. Stettinius, Jr.; Former Secretary of State Cordell Hull; Senator Tom Connally and Representative Sol Bloom, chairmen of their respective foreign relations committees; Senator Arthur Vandenberg and Representative Charles A. Eaton, ranking minority members of the same committees; Dean Virginia Gildersleeve of Barnard College; and Commander Harold Stassen, former Governor of Minnesota.

strengthened the determination of the nation under the leadership of President Harry S. Truman to press the Pacific war to a successful conclusion, to lay the foundations for a just peace, and to establish a practical security council to prevent future wars.

The best brief histories of the military operations are found in the annual numbers of the *American Annual* and the *New International Year Book*. On the diplomatic background see *Peace and War: United States Foreign Policy, 1931–1941,* issued by the State Department in January, 1943, and Forrest Davis and E. K. Lindley, *How War Came: An American White Paper from the Fall of France to Pearl Harbor* (1942). The story of lend-lease is in Edward R. Stettinius, Jr., *Lend Lease: Weapon of Victory* (1944). The problems of world peace are discussed in Herbert Hoover and Hugh Gibson, *Problems of Lasting Peace,* Chaps. X–XIV; Sumner Welles, *The Time for Decision,* Chaps. VII–XII; and Wendell L. Willkie, *One World.*

GENERAL BIBLIOGRAPHY

I. THE BACKGROUND OF COLONIZATION

BIBLIOGRAPHICAL NOTE. The literature of American history is extremely large and is growing rapidly; it is possible in these bibliographies to list only the more significant books. More exhaustive bibliographies must be sought in specialized treatments. Helpful to students is Edward Channing, A. B. Hart and F. J. Turner, *Guide to the Study and Reading of American History* (rev. ed., 1912). Fortunately a new edition of this work is in preparation. More exhaustive are the annual volumes sponsored by the American Historical Association and prepared by Grace G. Griffin, *Writings on American History* (1906–   ). A short cut to the sources and secondary works on American biography may be found in Allen Johnson and Dumas Malone, eds., *Dictionary of American Biography* (20 vols., 1928–1937) at the end of the separate biographies. This work has not only availed itself of the best contemporary scholarship but among its more than 13,600 biographies are many Americans important in economic and social history not customarily treated in the older dictionaries. Students interested in social and economic history should likewise not neglect the *Encyclopaedia of the Social Sciences* (15 vols., 1930–1935). The student will also find J. T. Adams and R. V. Coleman, eds., *Dictionary of American History* (5 vols., 1940) a valuable short cut to important information.

The results of American historical research have become so extended that it has become practically impossible, except in brief surveys like the present book, for a single individual to write a lengthy history of the United States. The last and probably the most successful effort is that of Edward Channing, *History of the United States* (6 vols., 1905–1925), although the story is carried only to the close of the Civil War. Dependable because of its meticulous scholarship, the work broadens in its later volumes to include a greater proportion of economic and social history. Of the efforts to interpret American history and civilization that of Charles and Mary Beard, *The Rise of American Civilization* (2 vols., 1927), Vol. III, *America in Mid-passage* (1939), is easily the most distinguished. Louis M. Hacker, *The Triumph of American Capitalism* (1940), covering mainly the period to 1865, is a brilliant economic interpretation.

Increasingly historians have been forced to resort to co-operative efforts when a broad period is to be covered. Attention should be called to four notable series: Albert B. Hart, ed., *The American Nation* (28 vols., 1904–1916), mostly written more than a quarter century ago and in part superseded by later scholarship; Allen Johnson, ed., *Chronicles of America* (50 vols., 1918–1921), short and popular accounts of various phases, and Arthur M. Schlesinger and Dixon Ryan Fox, eds., *History of American Life* (12 vols., 1927–   ), an effort to recount the social history of America. A successful co-operative attempt to promote visual education in American history is R. H. Gabriel, ed., *The Pageant of America* (15 vols., 1925–1929).

For certain phases of American history the following are recommended. Economic: E. C. Kirkland, *A History of American Economic Life* (rev. ed., 1939); H. U. Faulkner, *American Economic History* (5th ed., 1943). Financial: D. R. Dewey, *Financial History of the United States* (12th ed., 1935); W. J. Shultz and M. R. Caine, *Financial Development of the United States* (1937). Diplomatic: S. F. Bemis, *A Diplomatic History of the United States* (rev. ed., 1942); T. A. Bailey, *A Diplomatic History of the American People* (2nd ed., 1942). Constitutional: A. C. McLaughlin, *A Constitutional History of the United States* (1935); H. C. Hockett, *A Constitutional History of the United States* (2 vols., 1939), Vol. I on 1776–1826 and Vol. II on 1826–1876.

Short collections of source materials easily available to the student include William Macdonald, *Documentary Source Book of American History* (3rd ed., 1928), almost entirely constitutional; H. S. Commager, ed., *Documents of American History* (1935), chiefly political and constitutional; A. B. Hart, ed., *American History Told by Contemporaries* (5 vols., 1897–1929); and H. S. Commager and Allan Nevins, eds., *The Heritage of America* (1939), the last two collections containing much social history. The source books on economic history are G. S. Callender, *Selections from the Economic History of the United States, 1765–1860* (1909), with excellent introductory essays; E. L. Bogart and C. M. Thompson, *Readings in the Economic History of the United States* (1916); and F. Flügel and H. U. Faulkner, *Readings in the Economic and Social History of the United States* (1929).

For those who desire a more complete list or a more extended criticism of American historiography the following should be consulted: W. T. Hutchinson, ed., *The Marcus W. Jernegan Essays in American Historiography* (1937); Michael Kraus, *A History of American History* (1937); and those parts having to do with America in H. E. Barnes, *A History of Historical Writing* (1937).

EUROPE ON THE EVE OF EXPANSION. For the European background E. P. Cheyney, *European Background of American History* (1904), American Nation Series, is still valuable. For general accounts of the late Middle Ages see G. C. Sellery and A. C. Krey, *Medieval Foundations of Western Civilization* (1929); J. W. Thompson, *Economic and Social History of Europe in the Later Middle Ages, 1300–1530* (1931); Carl Stephenson, *Mediaeval History* (1935); E. P. Cheyney, *The Dawn of a New Era* (1936); E. Lipson, *The Economic History of England* (3 vols., 1915–1931); and the early chapters of Curtis Nettels, *The Roots of American Civilization* (1938). Detailed discussions of various aspects of the Middle Ages can be found in the *Cambridge Medieval History.*

THE COMMERCIAL REVOLUTION. For a brief general account see Clive Day, *History of Commerce* (rev. ed., 1923) and for a more detailed story W. C. Abbott, *Expansion of Europe* (2 vols., 1918). Readable accounts of discovery and exploration include J. P. O. Martin, *The Golden Age of Prince Henry the Navigator* (1914); Joseph Jacobs, *Story of Geographical Discovery* (1904); and J. N. L. Baker, *History of Geographical Discovery and Exploration* (1932). Monumental is W. Cunningham, *The Growth of English Industry and Commerce* (5th ed., 3 vols., 1910–1912), but more usable are H. E. Egerton, *A Short History of English Colonial Policy* (2nd ed., 1909); W. H. Woodward, *A Short History of the British Empire, 1510–1911* (3rd ed., 1912); and C. P. Lucas, *Beginnings of English Overseas Enterprise* (1917). An illuminating interpretation of the old imperialism which will repay reading is J. R. Seeley, *The Expansion of England* (1888). On Columbus the old work of C. R. Markham, *Life of Columbus* (1892) is still standard. Leading sources are in Cecil Jane, ed., *Select Documents Illustrating the Four Voyages of Columbus* (1930–1933) with an essay on Columbus. The present situation in scholarship regarding Columbus is reviewed in C. E. Nowell, "The Columbus Question," *Am. Hist. Rev.,* XLIV, No. 4, 802–822 (July, 1939).

THE GEOGRAPHIC BACKGROUND. The physiographic influence upon American history has been brought out in A. P. Brigham, *Geographic Influences in American History* (1903); Ellen C. Semple, *American History and Its Geographic Conditions* (1903) and *The Influence of Geographic Environment* (1911); and A. B. Hulbert, *Soil and Its Influence Upon the History of the United States* (1930). Elementary surveys of the products and resources of this country are to be found in Livingston Farrand, *Basis of American History* (1904), American Nation Series, and in Ellsworth Huntington, *The Red Man's Continent* (1919), Chronicles of America, while a more detailed study is in C. R. Van Hise, *Conservation of Natural Resources in the United States* (rev. ed., 1930). Suggestive to a student of geography is E. Huntington and S. W. Cushing, *Principles of Human Geography* (2d ed., 1922). Valuable material is in C. C. Colby, *Source Book for the Economic Geography of North America* (1921).

THE ROLE OF THE INDIAN. The literature on this subject is rather specialized and most of it hardly fits the need of the average student. D. G. Brinton, *The American Race* (1901) is a brief but clear introduction. Somewhat older but valuable is J. T. Short, *The North Americans of Antiquity* (1880). The best of the recent books is E. R. Embree, *Indians of the Americas* (1939). A popular treatment of some of the most interesting of the Indians is Paul Radin, *The Story of the American Indian* (1927). In Francis E. Leupp, *The Indian and His Problem* (1910) is a clear statement of recent conditions, while administration is exhaustively treated by Lewis Meriam and others, *The Problem of Indian Administration* (1928).

II. THE SETTLEMENT OF AMERICA

THE SPANISH SETTLEMENTS. The competent textbook, M. W. Williams, *The People and Politics of Latin America* (1930) provides an adequate introduction to Spanish America. Brief and popular is I. B. Richman, *The Spanish Conquerors* (1919) in the Chronicles of America. One of the best volumes in the Chronicles is H. E. Bolton, *The Spanish Borderlands* (1921). A subject of never-failing interest is covered in C. H. Haring, *The Buccaneers in the West Indies* (1910) and P. A. Means, *The Spanish Main* (1935). William R. Shepherd, *Latin America* (1914) is particularly good on the transplanting of Spanish culture, and William S. Robertson, *History of the Latin American Nations* (rev. ed., 1932) provides a survey of later history. H. I. Priestley, *The Coming of the White Man* (1929) is a competent study of the social and economic phases of Spanish American civilization. Specialized features of the economic life are well treated in C. H. Haring, *Trade and Navigation Between Spain and the Indies in the Time of the Hapsburgs* (1918) and L. B. Simpson, *The Encomienda in New Spain* (1929). The classic volumes of W. H. Prescott on Mexico and Peru still make thrilling reading for the student.

THE FRENCH IN AMERICA. The most recent and probably the best brief survey is that of Carl Wittke, *History of Canada* (rev. ed., 1933). W. B. Munro, *Crusaders of New France* (1918) and H. I. Priestley, *The Coming of the White Man* (1929) deal briefly with the colonial period, while C. W. Colby, *Canadian Types of the Old Regime* (1908) studies typical leaders in various fields. A. L. Burt, *The Old Province of Quebec* (1933) is a recent important and scholarly contribution. The famous volumes of Francis Parkman will repay any student.

THE DUTCH AND THE SWEDES. On the Dutch in New York see J. R. Brodhead, *History of New York* (2 vols., 1871); John Fiske, *Dutch and Quaker Colonies* (2 vols., 1899); T. A. Janvier, *The Dutch Founding of New York* (1903); J. H. Innes, *New Amsterdam and Its People* (1902); A. C. Flick, ed., *History of the State of New*

York (1933); and M. W. Goodwin, *Dutch and English on the Hudson* (1919), Chronicles of America. The role of the Swede is handled in Amandus Johnson, *The Swedish Settlements on the Delaware* (1911); J. T. Scharf, *History of Delaware, 1609–1688* (2 vols., 1888); and Francis Vincent, *History of Delaware* (1870). See also H. I. Priestley, *op. cit.*

THE COMING OF THE ENGLISH. Since colonial history for many years was the primary field of historical exploitation in this country, the bibliography is tremendous. Of the single volumes that of Curtis Nettels, *The Roots of American Civilization* (1938) is the most original, emphasizing the economic phase. O. P. Chitwood, *A History of Colonial America* (1931) is also a satisfactory textbook. M. W. Jernegan, *The American Colonies, 1492–1750* (1929) is a very skillful interweaving of economic, social and political history. Other notable one-volume accounts include C. M. Andrews, *The Colonial Period* (1912) in the Home University Library; Carl Becker, *The Beginnings of the American People* (1915); C. M. Andrews, *The Fathers of New England* (1919), Chronicles of America; J. T. Adams, *The Founding of New England* (1921); T. J. Wertenbaker, *The First Americans* (1927); and J. T. Adams, *Provincial America* (1927), the last two in the History of American Life Series and dealing particularly with the everyday life of the people.

The first great co-operative historical project in this country was that of Justin Winsor, *Narrative and Critical History of America* (8 vols., 1884–1889), still valuable for its excellent bibliographical knowledge on sources and authorities. The early volumes of the American Nation Series are also still usable. E. M. Avery, *History of the United States and Its People from Their Earliest Records to the Present Time* (7 vols., 1904–1910) actually carries the narrative only to 1806 but is valuable for its interesting illustrations and facsimiles. This nation's first great historian was George Bancroft, whose *History of the United States from the Discovery of the Continent* carries the story to 1789 and was published between 1834 and 1882. While highly nationalistic and partisan and resting on the theory that God had ordained the British settlements to pioneer in world democracy, the volumes are based on much study of the sources, are heavily documented and in many parts written with much spirit. The historical writings of John Fiske in some 12 volumes are distinguished for charm of style and picturesque narrative but are not always dependable for accuracy and fairness. John A. Doyle, *English Colonies in America* (5 vols., 1882–1907) is the work of a careful English scholar. The most important contributions to the history of the continental American colonies are the volumes of Herbert L. Osgood, *American Colonies in the Seventeenth Century* (3 vols., 1904–1907) and *American Colonies in the Eighteenth Century* (4 vols., 1924–1925), largely political, constitutional and military. The work of Charles M. Andrews, while heavily weighted with political and constitutional narrative, deals also with economic and social material. His work of many years is now being co-ordinated in *The Colonial Period of American History* (1934–   ).

III. COLONIAL DEVELOPMENT

THE EXPANSION OF NEW ENGLAND. In addition to the works of Bancroft, Osgood, Doyle, Winsor and Channing cited in the bibliography of the last chapter the following are suggested: L. K. Mathews, *The Expansion of New England* (1909); R. H. Akagi, *The Town Proprietors of the New England Colonies* (1924); Florence M. Woodard, *The Town Proprietors in Vermont* (1936); Edward Eggleston, *The Beginners of a Nation* (1897); S. E. Morison, *Builders of the Bay Colony* (1930); Brooks Adams, *The Emancipation of Massachusetts* (1887), critical of the Puritan common-

THE VANQUISHED AND THE VICTORS

Top—German Delegation Preparing to Sign Surrender Document at General Eisenhower's Headquarters May 7, 1945. *Left to right*: Major Wilhelm Oxenius, aide to General Jodl; Colonel General Gustav Jodl, Chief of Staff, German Army; and General Admiral Hans Georg Friedeberg. Major General Kenneth W. D. Strong of the United States Army stands behind General Jodl. (Acme Newspictures, Inc.)

Bottom—Allied Army Leaders at Meeting in Berlin. Field Marshal Sir Bernard L. Montgomery, Great Britain; General Dwight D. Eisenhower, United States; Marshal Gregory K. Zhukoff, Russia; and General de Lattre de Tassigny, France. (Associated Press Wirephoto.)

THE "BIG THREE" AT YALTA

Prime Minister Winston Churchill, President Franklin D. Roosevelt and Premier Joseph Stalin. Standing in the rear (*left to right*) are Admiral Sir Andrew Cunningham, Admiral Ernest King, Air Marshal Portal, Admiral William D. Leahy and other high-ranking allied officers. (Acme Newspictures, Inc.)

wealth; C. F. Adams, *Three Episodes of Massachusetts History* (1893), illuminating studies of important developments; and A. B. Hart, ed., *Commonwealth History of Massachusetts* (5 vols., 1927–1930). One of the most famous books ever written in America and an important source is William Bradford, *History of Plymouth Plantation*, an account of the colony by a man who was governor for many years. On the other New England colonies see G. L. Clark, *A History of Connecticut* (1914); I. B. Richman, *Rhode Island: Its Making and Its Meaning* (2 vols., 1902); S. M. Brockunier, *The Irrepressible Democrat, Roger Williams* (1940). W. H. Fry, *New Hampshire as a Royal Province* (1908); and L. C. Hatch, ed., *Maine, A History* (5 vols., 1919).

THE PROPRIETARY COLONIES. On Maryland M. P. Andrews, *History of Maryland— Province and State* (1929); J. T. Scharf, *History of Maryland* (3 vols., 1879); and N. D. Mereness, *Maryland as a Proprietary Province* (1901) will be found adequate. A concise treatment is J. M. Gambrill, *Leading Events of Maryland History* (rev. ed., 1917). The works of S. G. Fisher are excellent on Pennsylvania: *The Quaker Colonies* (1919) dealing also with Delaware, *The Making of Pennsylvania* (1896), and *Pennsylvania, Colony and Commonwealth* (1897). Of particular value for its economic and social emphasis is T. J. Wertenbaker, *The Founding of American Civilization: The Middle Colonies* (1938). An excellent recent biography is W. I. Hull, *William Penn: A Topical Biography* (1937). Two scholarly books on South Carolina are Edward McCrady, *South Carolina Under Royal Government, 1719–1776* (1899) and W. R. Smith, *South Carolina as a Royal Province* (1903). On Georgia, James R. McCain, *Georgia as a Proprietary Province* (1917); E. M. Coulter, *Short History of Georgia* (1933); A. A. Ettinger, *James Edward Oglethorpe* (1936); and V. W. Crane, *Southern Frontier, 1670–1732* (1928).

POLITICAL FOUNDATIONS. Particularly to be recommended on the political and constitutional aspects of colonial life are J. F. Sly, *Town Government in Massachusetts, 1620–1930* (1930); R. H. Akagi, *The Town Proprietors of the New England Colonies* (1924); Viola F. Barnes, *The Dominion of New England* (1923); E. B. Greene, *The Provincial Governor* (1898); W. R. Shepherd, *History of Proprietary Government in Pennsylvania*, Columbia University Studies in History, Economics and Public Law (1896); W. T. Root, *Relations of Pennsylvania with the British Government, 1696–1765* (1912); P. A. Bruce, *Institutional History of Virginia in the Seventeenth Century* (2 vols., 1910); P. S. Reinsch, *English Common Law in the Early American Colonies* (University of Wisconsin Bulletin, No. 31); and L. W. Labaree, *Royal Government in America* (1930). Many valuable monographs on various aspects of government will be found in the Johns Hopkins University Studies.

THE GROWTH OF RELIGIOUS LIBERTY. Among the books on American religion which throw light on this particular subject are W. W. Sweet, *The Story of Religions in America* (1930); A. L. Cross, *The Anglican Episcopate and the American Colonies* (1902); S. H. Cobb, *The Rise of Religious Liberty in America* (1902); E. F. Humphrey, *Nationalism and Religion in America, 1774–1789* (1924); and E. S. Bates, *American Faith* (1940).

IV. COLONIAL LIFE

THE PEOPLE. The latest treatments of colonial population are E. B. Greene and V. D. Harrington, *American Population before the First Federal Census* (1932) and S. H. Sutherland, *Population Distribution in Colonial America* (1936). Although limited in its scope, the first serious effort to determine the race and nationality of colonial population was done by the Twelfth Census in *A Century of Population*

Growth, 1790–1900 (1909). See also F. B. Dexter, "Estimates of Population in the American Colonies" in American Antiquarian Society *Proceedings*, V, 22–50. Some attention to the composition of Virginian society is given in T. J. Wertenbaker, *Patrician and Plebeian in Virginia* (1910). The part played by various nationalities has been emphasized, if not exaggerated, in a number of books: G. D. Bernheim, *German Settlements in North and South Carolina* (1872); Oscar Kuhns, *The German and Swiss Settlements of Colonial Pennsylvania* (1901); C. A. Hanna, *The Scotch-Irish* (1902); A. B. Faust, *The German Element in the United States* (1909); and H. J. Ford, *The Scotch-Irish in America* (1915). In an effort to deflate what they consider the "Scotch-Irish Myth" the American Irish Historical Society has published much on the contributions of the Irish. Of particular interest is M. J. O'Brien, *A Hidden Phase of American History* (1919). See also his *Pioneer Irish in New England* (1937). On the Negro race see U. B. Phillips, *American Negro Slavery* (1918). The volume of Lee M. Friedman, *Early American Jews* (1934) is fragmentary. On colonial immigration see the early chapters in M. L. Hanson, *The Atlantic Migration 1607–1860* (1940) and Carl Wittke, *We Who Built America* (1940).

COLONIAL ECONOMY. Several excellent studies are now available on colonial agriculture, particularly Lyman Carrier, *The Beginnings of American Agriculture* (1923); P. W. Bidwell and J. I. Falconer, *History of Agriculture in the Northern United States Before 1860* (1925); and L. C. Gray, *History of Agriculture in the Southern United States to 1860* (2 vols., 1933), the last two being products of the Carnegie Institution. See also Joseph Schafer, *The Social History of American Agriculture* (1936). Of special value are T. J. Wertenbaker, *The Planters of Colonial Virginia* (1922) and A. O. Craven, *Soil Exhaustion As a Factor in the Agricultural History of Virginia and Maryland, 1606–1860* (1926). Source material may be found in E. L. Bogart and C. M. Thompson, *Readings in the Economic History of the United States* (1915) and in L. B. Schmidt and E. D. Ross, *Readings in the Economic History of American Agriculture* (1925).

The outstanding work on colonial industry is V. S. Clark, *History of Manufactures in the United States, 1607–1860* (1916). See also Malcolm Keir, *Manufacturing* (1928) and R. M. Tryon, *Household Manufactures in the United States, 1640–1860* (1917). Specialized scholarly works of value include Kathleen Bruce, *Virginia Iron Manufacture in the Slave Era* (1931) and A. C. Bining, *British Regulation of the Colonial Iron Industry* (1933). Curtis Nettels, "The Menace of Colonial Manufacturing," *New England Quarterly*, IV, 230–269 is an important article. The main features of colonial commerce are discussed in Clive Day, *History of Commerce of the United States* (1925), a brief treatment, and in E. R. Johnson, T. W. Van Metre, G. G. Heubner and D. S. Hanchett, *History of Domestic and Foreign Commerce of the United States* (2 vols., 1915). Specialized but valuable is C. C. Crittenden, *The Commerce of North Carolina 1763–1789* (1936). H. A. Innis, *The Cod Fisheries: The History of an International Economy* (1940) is excellent on the colonial period. As an introduction to the theory of colonial trade read the article on mercantilism in the *Encyclopaedia of the Social Sciences* and Louis Hacker, *Triumph of American Capitalism*, Chaps. III–VIII. A standard volume is Gustav Schmoller, *The Mercantile System and Its Historical Significance* (1896). English colonial policy is exhaustively treated by George Louis Beer in *Origins of British Colonial Policy, 1578–1660* (1908); *British Colonial Policy, 1754–1765* (1907); and *The Old Colonial System* (1913). On the condition of white labor see Edward Eggleston, *The Transit of Civilization* (1901); E. I. McCormac, *White Servitude in Maryland* (1904); J. C. Ballagh, *White Servitude in Virginia* (1895); J. S. Bassett, *Servitude and Slavery in the*

Colony of North Carolina (1896), the last three in the Johns Hopkins Studies; and C. A. Herrick, *White Servitude in Pennsylvania* (1926). See also A. E. Smith, "The Transportation of Convicts to the American Colonies in the Seventeenth Century," *American Historical Review,* XXXIX, No. 2 (Jan., 1934). Colonial Negro slavery is handled in U. B. Phillips, *op. cit.,* in W. E. B. DuBois, *The Suppression of the American Slave Trade* (1896), and in many other works.

EVERYDAY LIFE. The everyday life of our ancestors has long been of interest. In addition to C. M. Andrews, *Colonial Folkways* (1919), Chronicles of America, the student should read T. J. Wertenbaker, *The First Americans, 1607–1690* (1927) and J. T. Adams, *Provincial Society, 1690–1763* (1927) in the History of American Life. The many books of Mrs. Alice Morse Earle are invaluable. See also W. B. Weeden, *Economic and Social History of New England* (2 vols., 1891); A. W. Calhoun, *Social History of the American Family* (3 vols., 1917–1919); S. G. Fisher, *Men, Women and Manners in Colonial Times* (2 vols., 1898); Elizabeth A. Dexter, *Colonial Women of Affairs* (1924); and P. A. Bruce, *Social Life in Virginia in the Seventeenth Century* (1907). An important study of urban life in America up to 1742 is Carl Bridenbaugh, *Cities in the Wilderness* (1938). Harold R. Shurtleff, *The Log Cabin Myth* (1939) attempts to refute the idea that log cabins were the early dwellings in English colonial America. In Carl Van Doren, *Benjamin Franklin* (1938) the student will find the most competent life of the great colonial. Perry Miller, *The New England Mind* (1939) is an able study.

V. THE BATTLE FOR EMPIRE

THE SIGNIFICANCE OF THE FRONTIER. The literature of the frontier has been collected by F. J. Turner and Frederick Merk, *List of References on the History of the West* (rev. ed., 1922). Also valuable is E. E. Edwards, "References on the Significance of the Frontier in American History," U. S. Dept. of Agriculture, Biographical Contributions, No. 25 (Oct., 1935). For the emphasis given to the frontier, historians are indebted to Frederick Jackson Turner, a few of whose brilliant essays have been collected in *The Frontier in American History* (1921) and *Significance of Sections in American History* (1933). See also *The Early Writings of Frederick Jackson Turner* (1938) with an able introductory essay by Fulmer Mood. F. L. Paxson, *History of the American Frontier, 1763–1893* (1924) and Dan E. Clark, *The West in American History* (1937) are efforts to integrate the story. The most brilliant work on the frontier in recent years is W. P. Webb, *The Great Plains* (1931), dealing with the trans-Mississippi region. See also the illuminating essay of M. E. Curti, "The Section and the Frontier in American History," *Methods in the Social Sciences* (1931). The Turnerian thesis has recently been under some fire, particularly by L. M. Hacker in the pamphlet "The Farmer Is Doomed" (1933); in the *Nation,* Vol. 137, pp. 109–110 (July 26, 1933) and in *The Triumph of American Capitalism,* Chap. XV. It is criticized in D. R. Fox, ed., *Sources of Culture in the Middle West* (1934) and same author, *Ideas in Motion* (1935). See particularly G. W. Pierson, "The Frontier and Frontiersmen of Turner's Essays," *Pennsylvania Magazine,* LXIV, 449–478 (Oct., 1940). Excellent readings are in I. F. Woestemeyer and J. M. Gambrill, *The Westward Movement* (1939).

THE EARLY WESTWARD MOVEMENT. The most significant material on this subject will be found in Chap. II, "The First Official Frontier of Massachusetts Bay," and III, "The Old West," of Turner, *The Frontier in American History.* See also L. K. Mathews, *The Expansion of New England* (1909); R. H. Akagi, *The Town Pro-*

prietors of the New England Colonies (1924); Archibald Henderson, *The Conquest of the Old Southwest* (1920); K. P. Bailey, *The Ohio Company of Virginia and the Westward Movement 1748–1792* (1939); S. J. and E. H. Buck, *The Planting of Civilization in Western Pennsylvania* (1939); W. S. Lister, *The Transylvania Company* (1935); T. P. Abernethy, *Western Lands and the American Revolution* (1937), a significant study; C. L. Skinner, *Pioneers of the Old Southwest* (1919); and H. E. Bolton, *The Spanish Borderlands* (1921). For the geographic background Ellen C. Semple, *American History and Its Geographic Conditions* (1903) is helpful. Biographies of important figures are John Bakeless, *Daniel Boone* (1939); C. S. Driver, *John Sevier* (1932) and L. K. Koontz, *Robert Dinwiddie* (1941).

IMPERIAL RIVALRY. On this subject, C. W. Alvord, *The Mississippi Valley in British Politics* (2 vols., 1917), scholarly and penetrating, is essential. A good general account is in Channing and a more detailed discussion in Osgood. Francis Parkman's famous volumes combine style, brilliance and scholarship. G. M. Wrong, *The Conquest of Canada* (1918), Chronicles of America, and his *Rise and Fall of New France* (2 vols., 1928) are dependable. Particularly valuable is V. W. Crane, *The Southern Frontier, 1670–1732* (1929). F. E. Whitton, *Wolfe and North America* (1929) is an interesting biography.

VI. THE CLASH OF INTERESTS

THE ECONOMIC BACKGROUND. On mercantilism see the works cited in Chapter IV; also Ugo Rabbeno, *The American Commercial Policy* (2nd ed., 1895) and H. E. Egerton, *A Short History of British Colonial Policy* (2nd ed., 1909). The student is again referred to the standard works on this subject by George Louis Beer: *Origins of the British Colonial Policy, 1578–1660* (1908); *British Colonial Policy, 1754–1765* (1907); and *The Old Colonial System* (1913). A new and significant study is L. A. Harper, *The English Navigation Laws: A Seventeenth Century Experiment in Social Engineering* (1939), emphasizing the influence of the acts on British shipbuilding. The role of the colonial merchant in bringing on the Revolution is described in W. S. McClellan, *Smuggling in the American Colonies* (1912) and A. M. Schlesinger, *The Colonial Merchants and the American Revolution* (1918), Columbia University Studies. A briefer summary is in Schlesinger, *New Viewpoints in American History*, Chap. VII. See also V. D. Harrington, *New York Merchant on the Eve of the Revolution*, Columbia University Studies, 404 (1935) and L. Sellers, *Charleston Business on the Eve of the Revolution* (1934). In Louis M. Hacker, "The First American Revolution," *Columbia University Quarterly*, XXVII, No. 3 (Sept., 1935) the theses of Channing, Andrews, and Van Tyne are questioned when the point is brilliantly developed that the Revolution resulted from the constricted economic opportunities for colonial merchant capitalism. See also his *Triumph of American Capitalism*, XI, XII.

THE END OF "SALUTARY NEGLECT." In addition to the books just cited the student should read C. W. Alvord, *The Mississippi Valley in British Politics* (2 vols., 1917) as well as other material on the British background such as R. Coupland, *The American Revolution and the British Empire* (1930) and G. O. Trevelyan, *The American Revolution* (4 vols., 1899–1912), scholarly and written in excellent style, but somewhat biased from the Whig point of view. W. E. Lunt, *History of England* (1928), Chap. XXX gives a brief but clear account of British politics. Among the books giving clear pictures of conditions in America are J. T. Adams, *Revolutionary New England* (1923); C. L. Becker, *The Eve of the Revolution* (1918), Chronicles of

America; G. E. Howard, *Preliminaries of the Revolution* (1905), American Nation Series; and above all the brilliant chapter in the Beards, *Rise of American Civilization*. For the intellectual background see V. L. Parrington, *The Colonial Mind, 1620–1800* (1927), Vol. I in *Main Currents of American Thought* and also Michael Kraus, *Inter-Colonial Aspects of American Culture on the Eve of the Revolution with Special Reference to the Northern Towns* (1928). The volume by the Englishman, H. E. Egerton, *Causes and Character of the American Revolution* (1923), is an excellent restatement.

THE POLITICAL ASPECT OF THE REVOLUTION. Bancroft's strongly biased volumes, like most older treatments, are mainly political; C. H. Van Tyne, *The Causes of the War of Independence* (1922) is also political. C. M. Andrews, *The Colonial Back-ground of the American Revolution* (1924) is the considered effort of the greatest living colonialist. In C. H. McIlwain, *The American Revolution* (1923) will be found a recent constitutional interpretation. The various political theories on the Revolu-tion are summarized in C. E. Merriam, *History of American Political Theories* (2nd ed., 1920). Among the biographies of the early revolutionary leaders are William Tudor, *The Life of James Otis* (1823); M. C. Tyler, *Patrick Henry* (1899); George Morgan, *The True Patrick Henry* (1907); R. V. Harlow, *Samuel Adams* (1923); and John C. Miller, *Sam Adams, Pioneer in Propaganda* (1936).

THE CLIMAX APPROACHES. On all aspects S. E. Morison, *Sources and Documents Illustrating the American Revolution and the Formation of the Federal Constitution, 1764–1788* (1923) will be found useful. Most of the books already cited deal with the years 1775 and 1776. Specialized studies include Allen French, *The First Year of the American Revolution* (1934) and *The Day of Concord and Lexington* (1925) and G. W. Graham, *The Mecklenburg Declaration of Independence* (1905).

VII. REVOLUTION

THE DIE IS CAST. The most satisfactory study of the Declaration is probably Carl Becker, *The Declaration of Independence* (1922). See also H. Friedenwald, *The Declaration of Independence* (1904) and J. H. Hazelton, *The Declaration of Inde-pendence: Its History* (1906). Of the many biographies of Jefferson two recent ones, A. J. Nock, *Thomas Jefferson* (1926), emphasizing his economic views, and F. W. Hirst, *Life and Letters of Thomas Jefferson* (1926), emphasizing political theories, are both excellent. M. D. Conway, *The Life of Thomas Paine* (2 vols., 1892) is standard.

WHIGS AND TORIES. A brief consideration of the internal political and social con-flicts is in J. F. Jameson, *The American Revolution Considered as a Social Move-ment* (1926) and more detailed discussions in A. C. Flick, *Loyalism in New York* (1901); I. S. Harrell, *Loyalism in Virginia* (1926); C. H. Van Tyne, *Loyalists in the American Revolution* (1902); J. H. Stark, *Loyalists of Massachusetts* (1910); Lewis Einstein, *Divided Loyalties* (1933); and A. G. Bradley, *Colonial Americans in Exile* (1932).

THE ORDEAL OF BATTLE. Intensely patriotic but biased is the account of George Bancroft. Channing's third volume is scholarly and C. H. Van Tyne, *War of In-dependence* (1929) is perhaps the most satisfactory account up to 1778. Among the best studies of the Revolution are those by G. O. Trevelyan, *The American Rev-olution* (4 vols., 1899–1912), and W. E. H. Lecky, *The American Revolution,* a part of his larger work entitled *History of England in the Eighteenth Century.* Many old ideas are deflated in S. G. Fisher, *The Struggle for American Independence* (2 vols.,

1908). For the experience of a critically important state see A. C. Flick, ed., *History of the State of New York* (1933), Vols. 3-4. On the military history see J. W. Fortescue, *History of the British Army* (Vol. III, 1902), competent on military operations but otherwise biased; C. F. Adams, *Studies Military and Diplomatic* (1911); L. C. Hatch, *The Administration of the American Revolutionary Army* (1904); C. K. Bolton, *The Private Soldier Under Washington* (1902); E. E. Curtis, *The Organization of the British Army in the American Revolution* (1926); and T. S. Anderson, *The Command of the Howe Brothers During the American Revolution* (1936). On naval operations see A. T. Mahan, *Major Operations of the Navies in the War of American Independence* (1913); C. O. Paullin, *The Navy in the American Revolution* (1906); G. W. Allen, *A Naval History of the American Revolution* (2 vols., 1913); and, for a brief discussion, H. and M. Sprout, *The Rise of American Naval Power, 1776–1918* (1939). A recent interesting article is R. G. Adams, "A View of Cornwallis' Surrender at Yorktown," *Am. Hist. Rev.,* XXXVII, 25–49. On diplomacy the standard work is S. F. Bemis, *The Diplomacy of the American Revolution* (1935), but A. B. Darling, *Our Rising Empire* (1940) is an important summary. See also E. S. Corwin, *French Policy and the American Alliance of 1778* (1916); B. Faÿ, *The Revolutionary Spirit in France* (1927); F. Wharton, *Revolutionary Diplomatic Correspondence* (5 vols., 1889); and J. B. Perkins, *France in the American Revolution* (1911). The reactions on the British Empire are described in R. Coupland, *The American Revolution and the British Empire* (1930). Among the biographies of naval or military leaders the following are suggested: P. Russell, *John Paul Jones* (1927); Brand Whitlock, *Lafayette* (2 vols., 1929); Rupert Hughes, *Life of Washington* (3 vols., 1925–1930); W. E. Woodward, *George Washington* (1926); J. C. Fitzpatrick, *George Washington Himself* (1933); N. W. Stephenson and W. H. Dunn, *George Washington* (1940); G. W. Greene, *Nathanael Greene* (3 vols., 1890); J. A. James, *Life of George Rogers Clark* (1928); and Jean-Edmund Weelen, *Rochambeau, Father and Son* (1936), with the American diary of the Vicomte de Rochambeau.

ECONOMIC AND SOCIAL ASPECTS. Brief but valuable is J. F. Jameson, *The American Revolution Considered as a Social Movement* (1926). Some material on this phase is in Allan Nevins, *The American States During and After the Revolution* (1924). On manufacturing see V. Clark, *History of Manufactures of the United States 1607–1860* and W. B. Weeden, *Economic and Social History of New England 1620–1789* (2 vols., 1890) and on commerce E. R. Johnson *et al., History of Domestic and Foreign Commerce of the United States* (2 vols., 1915). On financial history consult D. R. Dewey, *Financial History of the United States* (12th ed., 1935); W. J. Shultz and M. R. Caine, *Financial Development of the United States,* Chap. III; W. G. Sumner, *Finance and Financiers of the American Revolution* (2 vols., 1891); C. J. Bullock, *Finances of the United States* (1895); E. P. Oberholtzer, *Life of Robert Morris* (1903); and C. E. Russell, *Haym Salomon and the Revolution* (1930). See also R. V. Harlow, "Aspects of Revolutionary Finance," *Am. Hist. Rev.,* XXXV, 46–68 (Oct., 1929). One of the most valuable recent economic studies of this period is Robert A. East, *Business Enterprise in the American Revolutionary Era* (1938). Religious aspects are dealt with in A. M. Baldwin, *New England Clergy in the American Revolution* (1928) and E. F. Humphrey, *Nationalism and Religion in America 1774–1789* (1924).

VIII. A NEW NATION

THE SCARS OF WAR. The works already cited in the last chapter covering economic and social history are useful on this phase: W. B. Weeden, *Economic and Social*

History of New England; Victor Clark, *History of Manufactures in the United States;* J. F. Jameson, *The American Revolution Considered as a Social Movement;* D. R. Dewey, *Financial History of the United States;* W. R. Shultz and M. R. Caine, *Financial Development of the United States;* and C. J. Bullock, *Finances of the United States, 1775–1789.* See also Channing, *History of the United States,* Vol. III and H. J. Carman, *Social and Economic History of the United States* (2 vols., 1930–1932), Vol. I. John Fiske, *The Critical Period* (1888) is interestingly written, but overemphasizes the darker aspects. Brief but sound is G. S. Callender, *Selections From the Economic History of the United States,* pp. 122–177.

THE "CRITICAL PERIOD" AND THE ARTICLES OF CONFEDERATION. Fiske, *op. cit.* is a good introduction. George Bancroft, *History of the Formation of the Constitution* (2 vols., 1882) is old and exaggerates the situation but is still valuable. Dry reading but very useful is Allan Nevins, *The American States During and After the Revolution, 1775–1789* (1924). See also A. C. McLaughlin, *The Confederation and the Constitution* (1905); J. P. Warren, "The Confederation and Shays' Rebellion," *Am. Hist. Rev.,* XI, No. 1 (1905); and W. A. Dyer, "Embattled Farmers," *New England Quarterly,* IV, 460–481 (July, 1931). Two standard and famous histories of the middle period begin after the Revolution: John B. McMaster, *History of the People of the United States* (8 vols., 1883–1913), emphasizing social history, resting particularly upon newspaper sources, and a mine of information, and James Schouler, *History of the United States of America* (7 vols., 1880–1913), essentially political. On foreign affairs see A. B. Darling, *Our Rising Empire 1763–1803* (1940).

DRAFTING A CONSTITUTION. On the Constitution Max Farrand, *Records of the Federal Convention* (3 vols., 1911) is essential. His other books, *The Fathers of the Constitution* (1921), Chronicles of America, and *Framing the Constitution* (1913), are enlightening as coming from the pen of an expert. A. C. McLaughlin, *op. cit.,* and his *A Constitutional History of the United States* (1935) are important treatments by a specialist. Charles A. Beard, *An Economic Interpretation of the Constitution* (1913) has influenced all subsequent studies of this document. R. L. Schuyler, *The Constitution of the United States* (1923) is an interesting interpretation. Two excellent studies of the "Father of the Constitution" which develop his political philosophy are A. E. Smith, *James Madison* (1937) and E. M. Burns, *James Madison, Philosopher of the Constitution* (1938). A fine study of one of the ablest opponents of ratification is Helen Hill, *George Mason, Constitutionalist* (1938). Another critic whose career was distinguished is ably treated in E. W. Spaulding, *George Clinton, Critic of the Constitution* (1938). On the reaction in the states consult O. G. Libby, *Geographical Distribution of the Vote of the Thirteen States on the Constitution* (University of Wisconsin Bulletin, 1894); F. G. Bates, *Rhode Island and the Formation of the Union* (Columbia University Studies, 1898); S. B. Harding, *The Contest Over the Ratification of the Constitution in the State of Massachusetts* (1896); C. H. Ambler, *Sectionalism in Virginia from 1776 to 1861* (1910); J. B. McMaster and F. D. Stone, *Pennsylvania and the Federal Constitution* (1888); E. Wilder Spaulding, *New York in the Critical Period* (1932); and L. Trenholme, *Ratification of the Federal Constitution in North Carolina* (1932).

IX. FEDERALIST DOMINATION

STARTING THE MACHINERY. For the political history see McMaster, Schouler, Channing and J. S. Bassett, *The Federalist System* (1906), American Nation Series. Particularly enlightening is Charles A. Beard, *Economic Origins of the Jeffersonian De-*

mocracy (1915) and *The American Party Battle* (1928). In E. S. Maclay, ed., *Journal of William Maclay* (1890) will be found the reactions of a Republican senator to the financial program of the Federalist government. For the economic history consult D. R. Dewey, *op. cit.;* W. J. Schultz and M. R. Caine, *op. cit.;* A. B. Hepburn, *History of Coinage and Currency in the United States* (rev. ed., 1915); J. L. Loughlin, *History of Bimetallism in the United States* (4th ed., 1897); David K. Watson, *History of American Coinage* (1897); W. G. Sumner, *History of Banking in the United States* (1896); P. W. L. Ashley, *Modern Tariff History* (3rd ed., 1920); and F. W. Taussig, *Tariff History of the United States* (7th ed., 1923). Hamilton's famous reports may be found in *American State Papers, Finance,* Vol. I. On specific political aspects the following are important: C. A. Beard, *The Supreme Court and the Constitution* (1912); Gaillard Hunt, *The Department of State* (1914); H. B. Larned, *The President's Cabinet* (1912); L. Rogers, *The American Senate* (1926); G. H. Haynes, *The Senate of the United States: Its History and Practice* (2 vols., 1938); D. S. Alexander, *History and Procedure of the House of Representatives* (1916); R. V. Harlow, *A History of Legislative Methods Before 1825* (1917); and C. E. Merriam, *History of American Political Theories* (2nd ed., 1920). For a history of the Attorney General's office see Homer Cummings and Carl McFarland, *Federal Justice* (1937). The writings of the leading statesmen are all important. Among the best of the biographies are those of Hughes, Woodward, Stephenson, and P. L. Ford on Washington; those by Nock, Hirst, and Chinard on Jefferson; by F. S. Oliver, W. G. Sumner, and J. T. Morse on Hamilton; by Gaillard Hunt, A. E. Smith, and E. M. Burns on Madison; by Morse, Chinard, and C. F. Adams (Vol. I of the *Works*) on John Adams; by Bernard Faÿ and Carl Van Doren on Franklin; and by Monaghan on Jay. Claude Bowers, *Hamilton and Jefferson* (1925) is brilliantly written but strongly biased in favor of Jefferson.

FOREIGN COMPLICATIONS. Brief accounts will be found in such books as R. G. Adams, *History of the Foreign Policy of the United States* (1924); C. R. Fish, *American Diplomacy* (2nd ed., 1916); J. H. Latané, *A History of American Foreign Policy* (rev. ed., 1934); T. A. Bailey, *A Diplomatic History of the American People* (1939); above all, A. B. Darling, *Our Rising Empire 1763–1803* (1940) and S. F. Bemis, *A Diplomatic History of the United States* (1936). Invaluable are S. F. Bemis, *Jay's Treaty* (1923) and *Pinckney's Treaty* (1926) and A. P. Whitaker, *Spanish-American Frontier* (1927). Consult also B. W. Bond, *The Monroe Mission to France* (1907); C. D. Hazen, *Contemporary American Opinion of the French Revolution* (1897); and the two brilliant studies by F. J. Turner, "The Policy of France Toward the Mississippi Valley in the Period of Washington and Adams," *Am. Hist. Rev.,* X, 249 and "The Diplomatic Contest for the Mississippi Valley," *Atlantic Monthly,* XCIII, 676, 807. C. M. Thomas, *American Neutrality in 1793* (1931), Columbia University Studies, No. 350 is a valuable study.

ADAMS AND THE DOWNFALL OF FEDERALISM. Most of the bibliography already cited in this chapter covers the administration of Adams as well as Washington. The student particularly should consult Beard's *Economic Origins of the Jeffersonian Democracy.* In addition are E. D. Warfield, *The Kentucky Resolutions of 1798* (2nd ed., 1894); F. M. Anderson, "Enforcement of the Alien and Sedition Acts," *Am. Hist. Assoc. Reports* (1912) and "Contemporary Opinion of the Virginia and Kentucky Resolutions," *Am. Hist. Rev.,* V, 45 and 225. L. D. Baldwin, *Whiskey Rebels* (1939) is the first adequate account of the Whisky Rebellion.

X. JEFFERSONIAN REPUBLICANISM

JEFFERSON AND HIS PHILOSOPHY. Besides the biographies of Chinard, Nock, and Hirst already cited see Allen Johnson, *Jefferson and His Colleagues* (1921), Chronicles of America; Carl Becker, *The Declaration of Independence* (1922); C. E. Merriam, Jr., "The Political Theory of Jefferson," *Political Science Quarterly*, XVII (1902), 24–45; C. A. Beard, *Economic Origins of the Jeffersonian Democracy* (1915); R. J. Honeywell, *The Educational Work of Thomas Jefferson* (1931); J. S. Williams, *Thomas Jefferson, His Permanent Influence on American Institutions* (1913); Claude Bowers, *Jefferson in Power* (1936); G. Chinard, "Jefferson and the Physiocrats," *University of California Chronicle*, XXXIII (1931), 18–31; C. S. Thomas, "Jefferson and the Judiciary," *Constitutional Review*, X (1926), 67–76; and the article by Carl Becker in the *Encyclopaedia of the Social Sciences*.

REPUBLICANISM AT THE HELM. In addition to the standard works by Channing, McMaster and Schouler the student should acquaint himself with the famous work of Henry Adams, *A History of the United States from 1801 to 1817* (9 vols., 1889–1891), an extremely able study of the period of the Jeffersonian Republicans with particular emphasis upon diplomatic history—somewhat critical of Jefferson. His biographies of *Albert Gallatin* (1879) and *John Randolph* (1882) are also important. In Edward Channing, *The Jeffersonian System* (1906), American Nation Series, is a briefer but fair appraisal. A specialized study is D. H. Gilpatrick, *Jeffersonian Democracy in North Carolina, 1789–1816* (1931), Columbia University Studies, No. 344.

THE WEST AND THE LOUISIANA PURCHASE. Besides the great work of Adams specialized treatments will be found in such books as J. K. Hosmer, *History of the Louisiana Purchase* (1902); F. A. Ogg, *Opening of the Mississippi* (1904); I. J. Cox, *Early Exploration of Louisiana* (1906); T. Marshall, *History of the Western Boundary of the Louisiana Purchase* (1914); and E. S. Brown, *Constitutional History of the Louisiana Purchase* (1920). On Florida read I. J. Cox, *West Florida Controversy 1789–1813* (1918).

THE TURN OF JEFFERSON'S FORTUNES. On Jefferson's controversy with the Supreme Court see C. S. Thomas, "Jefferson and the Judiciary," *Constitutional Review*, X (1926), 67–76 and A. J. Beveridge, *Life of John Marshall* (4 vols., 1916–1919), one of the greatest American biographies—unsympathetic to Jefferson. On Burr see W. F. McCaleb, *The Aaron Burr Conspiracy* (1913); S. H. Wandell and M. Minnigerode, *Aaron Burr* (1925); Nathan Schachner, *Aaron Burr* (1937), an able defense of Burr; and I. J. Cox, "General Wilkinson and His Later Intrigues with the Spaniards," *Am. Hist. Rev.*, XIX, 794–812. J. R. Jacobs, *Tarnished Warrior: Major General James Wilkinson* (1938) is the first adequate biography.

ECONOMIC BOYCOTT. In addition to the general histories of this period and such surveys of American foreign relations as those of Latané, Fish, R. G. Adams, Sears, Bailey, Darling, and Bemis, consult such specialized treatments as W. W. Jennings, *The American Embargo* (1921) and L. M. Sears, *Jefferson and the Embargo* (1927). The nature of the trade interfered with is studied in N. S. Buck, *The Development of the Organization of Anglo-American Trade 1800–1850* (1925).

XI. RESURGENT NATIONALISM

AGRARIAN IMPERIALISM. On the European background: F. E. Melvin, *Napoleon's Navigation System* (1919); E. F. Hecksher, *The Continental System* (1922); and

H. W. V. Temperley, *George Canning* (1905). Probably the best discussion of the causes of the War of 1812 is J. W. Pratt, *Expansionists of 1812* (1925). His failure to emphasize sufficiently the agrarian distress is rectified in G. R. Taylor, "Agrarian Discontent in the Mississippi Valley Preceding the War of 1812," *Journal of Political Economy*, XXXIX, No. 4, 471–505 (1931). See also C. B. Coleman, "The Ohio Valley in the Preliminaries of the War of 1812," *Mississippi Valley Hist. Rev.*, VII, 39–50 (June, 1920); J. F. Zimmerman, *Impressment of American Seamen* (Columbia University Studies, 1925); W. W. Jennings, *The American Embargo* (1921); L. M. Sears, *Jefferson and the Embargo* (1927) and T. C. Smith, "War Guilt of 1812," *Mass. Hist. Soc. Proceedings*, LXIV, 319 ff.

THE "SECOND WAR OF INDEPENDENCE." Besides the general histories—Adams, McMaster, Schouler, etc.—see K. C. Babcock, *Rise of American Nationality, 1811–1819* (1906); J. W. Fortescue, *History of the British Army* (Vols. VIII–X, 1917–1920), an English account; and C. P. Lucas, *Canadian War of 1812* (1906). On the naval aspect, A. T. Mahan, *Sea Power in Its Relation to the War of 1812* (2 vols., 1905) is the best interpretation. Brief accounts are R. D. Paine, *The Fight for a Free Sea* (1920), Chronicles of America, and H. and M. Sprout, *The Rise of American Naval Power, 1776–1918* (1939); and a longer one is Theodore Roosevelt, *Naval War of 1812* (1882). The work of the privateers is told in E. S. Maclay, *A History of American Privateers* (1924) and G. Coggeshall, *History of American Privateers and Letters of Marque During Our War with England in the Years 1812, 1813 and 1814* (1856). On the opposition to the war see J. T. Adams, *New England in the Republic* (1926); S. E. Morison, *Maritime History of Massachusetts, 1783–1860* (1921); S. E. Morison, *Life and Letters of Harrison Gray Otis* (2 vols., 1913); Henry Adams, *Documents Relating to New England Federalism* (1877); C. R. Brown, *Northern Confederacy According to the Plans of "Essex Junto," 1796–1814* (1915); and E. P. Powell, *Nullification and Secession in the United States* (1898). On the peace treaty: Henry Adams, *Life of Albert Gallatin;* J. Q. Adams, *Memoirs;* C. E. Hill, *Leading American Treaties* (1922); and F. A. Updike, *The Diplomacy of the War of 1812* (1914). For brief accounts see Bemis or Bailey.

REPUBLICAN NATIONALISM AND THE ERA OF GOOD FEELING. F. J. Turner, *Rise of the New West* (1906), one of the best of the American Nation Series, is still a sound account. As the domestic issues of these years were chiefly economic, the student is referred to Faulkner, *American Economic History* (4th ed., 1938); E. C. Kirkland, *A History of American Economic Life* (rev. ed., 1939); F. W. Taussig, *Tariff History of the United States* (8th ed., 1931); E. Stanwood, *American Tariff Controversies in the Nineteenth Century* (1903); D. R. Dewey, *Financial History of the United States* (12th ed., 1935); R. C. H. Catterall, *Second Bank of the United States* (1903); and A. B. Hulbert, *Paths of Inland Commerce* (1920), Chronicles of America. Biographies of the statesmen of this period include D. C. Gilman, *James Monroe* (rev. ed., 1898); Carl Schurz, *Henry Clay* (2 vols., 1909); Bernard Mayo, *Henry Clay, Spokesman of the New West* (1937), which covers the story to 1812; G. G. Van Dusen, *Life of Henry Clay* (1937), the best one-volume biography; W. M. Meigs, *John Caldwell Calhoun* (2 vols., 1917); J. S. Bassett, *Andrew Jackson* (2 vols., 1916); Marquis James, *Andrew Jackson: the Border Captain* (1933) and *Andrew Jackson: Portrait of a President* (1937); and Claude Fuess, *Daniel Webster* (2 vols., 1930). Nationalism as displayed in the development of constitutional law is developed fully in the monumental A. J. Beveridge, *Life of John Marshall* and in C. Warren, *The Supreme Court in United States History* (3 vols., 1922), and more briefly in E. S. Corwin, *John Marshall and the Constitution* (1919). Critical of the court is G. Myers, *History of the*

Supreme Court (1912). An able specialized study is B. F. Wright, *The Contract Clause of the Constitution* (1938).

MONROE AND HIS DOCTRINE. On the origins W. F. Reddaway, *The Monroe Doctrine* (1924) is the most adequate, and on its development and effect Dexter Perkins, *The Monroe Doctrine, 1823–1826* (1927), *The Monroe Doctrine, 1826–1867* (1933), and *The Monroe Doctrine, 1867–1907* (1938). Other important treatises include H. W. V. Temperley, *Foreign Policy of Canning* (1925); C. K. Webster, *Foreign Policy of Castlereagh, 1815–1822* (1925); J. F. Rippy, *Rivalry of the United States and Great Britain for Latin America* (1929); and W. C. Ford, "John Q. Adams and the Monroe Doctrine," *Am. Hist. Rev.,* VII, 676–695 (July, 1902) and VIII, 29–52 (Oct., 1902). Essential for an understanding of the subject is C. C. Griffen, *The United States and the Disruption of the Spanish Empire, 1810–1822* (1937).

XII. JACKSONIAN DEMOCRACY

THE ERA OF HARD FEELING. The administration of John Quincy Adams can be followed in Channing, McMaster, Schouler, and H. E. Von Holst, *The Constitutional and Political History of the United States* (8 vols., 1876–1892), a study of the forces tending to disintegrate the nation. See also Von Holst, *John C. Calhoun* (1882), a fair study by a man who opposed Calhoun's principles. The best sources on the Adams administration are C. F. Adams, ed., *Memoirs of John Quincy Adams* (12 vols., 1874–1877) and W. C. Ford, ed., *Writings* (7 vols., 1913–1917). See also J. T. Morse, *John Quincy Adams* (1909) and C. F. Adams, *John Quincy Adams* (1902).

THE ASCENDANCY OF KING ANDREW. Besides the general works cited above two excellent brief accounts are William Macdonald, *Jacksonian Democracy* (1906), American Nation Series, and F. A. Ogg, *The Reign of Andrew Jackson* (1919), Chronicles of America. Claude G. Bowers, *The Party Battles of the Jackson Period* (1922) concentrates on the spectacular. The political development is interpreted in M. Ostrogorski, *Democracy and the Organization of Political Parties* (2 vols., 1902). Probably the most valuable single volume on the period is F. J. Turner, *The United States, 1830–1850* (1935). The biographies are important: J. S. Bassett, *Andrew Jackson;* Marquis James, *Andrew Jackson* (2 vols., 1933–37); G. Hunt, *John C. Calhoun;* Von Holst, *John C. Calhoun;* T. D. Jervey, *Robert Y. Hayne and His Times* (1909); W. M. Meigs, *Thomas Hart Benton* (1904); Carl Schurz, *Henry Clay* (2 vols., 1887); Bernard Mayo, *Henry Clay, Spokesman of the New West* (1937); G. G. Van Dusen, *Life of Henry Clay* (1937); C. Fuess, *Daniel Webster* (1930); E. M. Shepard, *Martin Van Buren* (1899); and D. T. Lynch, *An Epoch and a Man* (1929). T. H. Benton, *Thirty Years' View* (2 vols., 1854–1856), a history of the times by an active participant, is valuable. In the same category is Martin Van Buren's *Autobiography* (1920).

THE END OF THE BANK. Most of the books already cited deal with this phase. In addition see D. R. Dewey, *Financial History of the United States;* R. C. H. Catterall, *The Second Bank of the United States;* R. C. McGrane, *Correspondence of Nicholas Biddle* (1919); S. Tyler, *Roger B. Taney* (1872); B. C. Steiner, *Life of Roger Brooke Taney* (1922); and C. B. Swisher, *Roger B. Taney* (1935), a definitive biography. The political aspect is covered in S. R. Gammon, Jr., *The Presidential Campaign of 1832,* Johns Hopkins Studies, XL, No. 1 (1922).

THE TARIFF AND NULLIFICATION. For the political theory C. E. Merriam, *History of American Political Theories* (new ed., 1920) is excellent. Specialized scholarly studies include C. S. Boucher, *The Nullification Controversy in South Carolina* (1916);

D. F. Houston, *Critical Study of Nullification in South Carolina* (1896); and J. G. Van Deusen, *Basis of Disunion in South Carolina* (1928). See also Taussig, Stanwood and other writers on the tariff.

OTHER ISSUES. Other aspects of Jackson's administration are touched on in R. C. McGrane, *The Panic of 1837* (1924); U. B. Phillips, "Georgia and State Rights," *Am. Hist. Assoc. Reports* (1901); F. L. Benns, *The American Struggle for the West India Carrying Trade, 1815–1830,* Indiana University Studies (1923). For other aspects of foreign policy see books by Bemis, Foster, Bailey, or Fish. See also the biographies of Van Buren, Livingston, and McLane in S. F. Bemis, ed., *American Secretaries of State.*

VAN BUREN AND THE PANIC OF 1837. The general histories cover the campaign of 1836. For Van Buren see his *Autobiography* (1920) and the lives by E. M. Shepard and D. T. Lynch. On the economic aspect: McGrane, *Panic of 1837;* D. R. Dewey, *State Banking Before the Civil War* (1910); E. G. Bourne, *The History of the Surplus Revenue of 1837* (1885); and David Kinley, *The Independent Treasury of the United States and Its Relation to the Banks of the Country* (1910). Also read Samuel Resneck, "The Social History of an American Depression, 1837–1843," *Am. Hist. Rev.,* XL, No. 4, 662–687 (July, 1935).

XIII. AMERICAN LIFE AT THE BEGINNING OF THE NINETEENTH CENTURY

TOWN AND COUNTRY. Among the first and still among the best efforts to deal with the social history of the early republic are McMaster, *History of the People of the United States,* Vol. I, Chap. I and Henry Adams, *History of the United States,* Vol. I, Chaps. I–VI. Also of value are Gaillard Hunt, *Life in America One Hundred Years Ago* (1914) and A. H. Wharton, *Social Life in the Early Republic* (1902). Other material may be found in J. T. Adams, *New England in the Republic, 1776–1850* (1926); P. W. Bidwell, "Rural Economy in New England at the Beginning of the Nineteenth Century," *Transactions of the Conn. Acad. of Arts and Sciences,* XX (1916); R. J. Purcell, *Connecticut in Transition 1775–1818* (1918); and A. W. Calhoun, *A Social History of the American Family from Colonial Times to the Present* (3 vols., 1916–1919). Sources on social history, not always reliable, are to be found in the writings of foreign travelers. The best studies of their contributions are in Henry T. Tuckerman, *America and Her Commentators, with a Critical Sketch of Travel in the United States* (1864) and Jane L. Mesick, *The English Traveller in America, 1785–1833,* Columbia University Studies in English and Comparative Literature (1922). In Allan Nevins, *American Social History as Recorded by British Travellers* (1923) are interesting excerpts.

TRAVEL AND COMMUNICATION. For early travel the most valuable is Seymour Dunbar, *History of Travel in America* (4 vols., 1915), illustrated with rare prints. A conventional but scholarly history is Caroline McGill *et al., History of Transportation in the United States* (1917), a study by the Carnegie Institution. Helpful for its illustrations is Malcolm Keir, *The March of Commerce* (1927). Again the accounts of travelers are important. See Tuckerman and Nevins listed above.

EDUCATION AND THE ARTS. Perhaps the most satisfactory textbook is E. P. Cubberley, *Public Education in the United States* (1919). Suggestive studies are A. O. Hansen, *Liberalism and American Education in the Eighteenth Century* (1926); E. H. Reisner, *Nationalism and Education Since 1789* (1922); H. G. Good, *Benjamin Rush and His Services to American Education* (1918); and particularly M. E. Curti,

The Social Ideas of American Educators (1935), Chaps. 1 and 2, fully annotated with complete bibliographies. Studies of important colleges include P. A. Bruce, *History of the University of Virginia* (5 vols., 1920–1922) and S. E. Morison, *The Founding of Harvard College* (1935) and *Harvard College in the Seventeenth Century* (2 vols., 1936). See also R. J. Honeywell, *The Educational Work of Thomas Jefferson* (1931) and Dumas Malone, *Public Life of Thomas Cooper* (1926). For art see C. H. Coffin, *The Story of American Painting* (1907). For architecture: T. F. Hamlin, *The American Spirit in Architecture* (1926), Pageant of America; H. B. Major, *The Domestic Architecture of the Early American Republic* (1926); Fiske Kimball, *Domestic Architecture of the Colonies and the Early Republic* (1922) and *Thomas Jefferson, Architect* (1916).

THE PROFESSIONS. Arthur Hornblow, *A History of the Theatre in America from Its Beginnings to the Present Time* (2 vols., 1919); A. H. Quinn, *A History of the American Drama from the Beginning to the Civil War* (1923); F. L. Mott, *A History of American Magazines, 1741–1850* (3 vols., 1930–1938); F. R. Packard, *History of Medicine in the United States* (2nd ed., 2 vols., 1931); H. B. Shafer, *The American Medical Profession, 1783–1850* (1936), Columbia University Studies, No. 417; J. T. Flexner, *Doctors on Horseback: Pioneers of American Medicine* (1937), an account of several early American physicians; Charles Warren, *History of the Harvard Law School and of Early Legal Conditions in America* (3 vols., 1909).

THE CLERGY AND RELIGION. There are still many gaps to be filled in the history of American religion. Henry K. Rowe, *The History of Religion in the United States* (1924) is brief but suggestive. Also brief but excellent, J. A. Faulkner, *The Methodists* (1903) and H. E. Luccock and Paul Hutchinson, *The Story of Methodism* (1926). See also the work of W. W. Sweet, particularly the sources he is editing, *Religion on the Frontier* (1931–   ). Williston Walker, *A History of the Congregational Church in the United States* (1894) is old but thorough. Suggestive contributions are Philip Schaff, "Church and State in the United States," *Am. Hist. Assoc. Papers,* II, 385–543 and E. F. Humphrey, *Nationalism and Religion in America, 1774–1789* (1924). For two important leaders see Peter Guilday, *The Life and Times of John Carroll, Archbishop of Baltimore 1735–1815* (1922) and E. S. Tipple, *Francis Asbury, The Prophet of the Long Road* (1916).

XIV. AMERICA MOVES WESTWARD

THE INFLUENCE OF THE WESTWARD MOVEMENT. The student is again referred to the works of Frederick Jackson Turner, F. L. Paxson, D. E. Clark, and W. P. Webb and to the comments in the bibliography of Chapter V.

THE DEVELOPMENT OF A LAND POLICY. P. J. Treat, *The National Land System* (1910); R. G. Wellington, *The Political and Sectional Influence of the Public Lands, 1828–1842* (1914); G. M. Stephenson, *The Political History of the Public Lands from 1840 to 1862* (1917); and B. H. Hibbard, *A History of the Public Land Policies* (1924). A. M. Sokolski, *The Great American Land Bubble* (1932) is a popular account. Old but invaluable for its detail is Thomas Donaldson, *The Public Domain, Its History With Statistics* (1884). See also Lewis Haney, *A Congressional History of Railways in the United States* (1910).

THE SETTLEMENT OF THE OLD NORTHWEST. Brief accounts are in McMaster and Channing. Also see E. E. Sparks, *The Expansion of the American People* (1900); F. J. Turner, *Rise of the New West* (1906) and *The United States 1830–1850* (1935); F. L. Paxson, *History of the American Frontier* (1924); and L. K. Mathews, *Ex-*

pansion of New England (1909). A good brief account of the settlement of western New York is Paul D. Evans' chapter in A. C. Flick, ed., *History of the State of New York*, Vol. VI (1934). The most recent and most valuable on its region is Beverley W. Bond, Jr., *The Civilization of the Old Northwest* (1934). There are many accounts of travelers which are invaluable, among which should be noted: F. E. Trollope, *Domestic Manners of the Americans* (2 vols., 1932), bitterly anti-American; Harriet Martineau, *Society in America* (1837); Fredreka Bremmer, *Homes of the New World* (2 vols., 1853); J. W. Monette, *History of the Discovery and Settlement of the Valley of the Mississippi* (1846); Timothy Flint, *Recollections of the Last Ten Years* (1826) and *History and Geography of the Mississippi Valley* (1832); J. M. Peck, *Guide for Emigrants to the West* (1837); R. G. Thwaites, ed., *Journals of Lewis and Clark* (1904-1905); *Early Western Travels* (32 vols., 1904-1907); Basil Hall, *Travels in North America in the Years 1827-1828* (3 vols., 1829); and J. S. Buckingham, *The Eastern and Western States of America* (3 vols., 1842).

THE SETTLEMENT OF THE OLD SOUTHWEST. Most of the books of travels listed under the last section contain material on the Old Southwest. See also C. L. Skinner, *Pioneers of the Old Southwest* (1919), Chronicles of America, and U. B. Phillips, "Origin and Growth of the Southern Black Belts," *Am. Hist. Rev.*, IX, 798 ff.

THE MAKING OF AN AMERICAN COMMUNITY. Consult the bibliography under the first four sections of this chapter. Also Morris Birkbeck, *Notes on a Journey in America* (1818).

THE TRANS-MISSISSIPPI WEST. Emphasizing the influence of firearms, barbed wire, and water, W. P. Webb, *The Great Plains* (1931) is an original and significant approach. Katherine Coman, *Economic Beginnings of the Far West* (2 vols., 1912) is an important contribution and C. Goodwin, *The Trans-Mississippi West* (1922) is a straightforward account. See also F. L. Paxson, *History of the American Frontier* (1924) and *The Last American Frontier* (1910) and Dan E. Clark, *The West in American History* (1937). The volumes in the Chronicles of America by Hough, Skinner, and White are both interesting and useful. On Utah: M. R. Werner, *Brigham Young* (1925); J. H. Evans, *Charles Coulson Rich, Pioneer Builder of the West* (1936), a biography of a great Mormon leader; Reva Stanley, *A Biography of Perley P. Pratt* (1937), another important Mormon; and L. H. Greer, *Utah and the Nation* (1929). On Oregon: J. Schafer, *History of the Pacific Northwest* (1905) and C. J. Brosnan, *Jason Lee, Prophet of the New Oregon* (1932). On California: S. E. White, *The Forty Niners* (1918); Walter Colton, *Three Years in California* (1850); R. H. Dana, *Two Years Before the Mast* (1840); and Julian Dana, *Sutter of California*, the most nearly complete of the biographies. Allan Nevins, *Frémont, Pathmaker of the West* (1939) gives important information on the background of California's settlement.

XV. THE INDUSTRIAL REVOLUTION

THE COMING OF THE FACTORY SYSTEM. On the English background C. R. Fay, *Great Britain from Adam Smith to the Present Day* (1928) and Arthur Redford, *The Economic History of England, 1760-1860* (1931) are excellent. The standard work on American manufacturing is V. S. Clark, *History of Manufactures in the United States, 1607-1860* (new ed., 1929), but much detailed information can be found in two old books: J. L. Bishop, *History of American Manufactures from 1608-1860* (3 vols., 1866) and A. S. Bolles, *Industrial History of the United States* (1878). While few adequate histories of specific industries have been written, the following will be found helpful: Broadus Mitchell, *The Rise of Cotton Mills in the South*

(1921) and his *William Gregg, Factory Master of the Old South* (1928); M. T. Copeland, *The Cotton Manufacturing Industry in the United States* (1912); Caroline F. Ware, *The Early New England Cotton Manufacture* (1931); A. H. Cole, *The American Wool Manufacture* (2 vols., 1926); C. B. Kuhlmann, *Development of the Flour-Milling Industry in the United States* (1929); L. H. Weeks, *A History of Paper Manufacturing in the United States, 1690–1916* (1916); Kathleen Bruce, *Virginia Iron Manufacture in the Slave Era* (1931); and Blanche E. Hazard, "Organization of the Boot and Shoe Industry in Massachusetts Before 1875," *Quarterly Journal of Economics*, XXVII (Feb., 1913). On inventions see W. Kaempffert, *History of American Inventions* (2 vols., 1924). Although limited to one city, Vera Shlakman, *Economic History of a Factory Town: A Study of Chicopee, Massachusetts*, Smith College Studies in History, XX, Nos. 1–4, covers many phases of the Industrial Revolution and is an important study. The same is true of C. M. Green, *Holyoke, Massachusetts* (1939) and M. T. Parker, *Lowell: A Study in Industrial Development* (1940).

THE EXPANSION OF TRANSPORTATION. General accounts include the invaluable Seymour Dunbar, *History of Travel in America* (4 vols., 1915); B. H. Meyer (ed.) but written by C. E. MacGill *et al.*, *History of Transportation in the United States Before 1860* (1917); Malcolm Keir, *The March of Commerce* (1927), Pageant of America; and A. B. Hulbert, *Paths of Inland Commerce* (1920), Chronicles of America. R. G. Albion, *The Rise of New York Port* (1939) is an able study of America's most important commercial center. On turnpikes: T. B. Searight, *The Old Pike* (1894); A. B. Hulbert, *The Old National Pike* (1901) and *Historic Highways* (15 vols., 1902–1905). River steamboating: F. E. Dayton, *Steamboat Days* (1925); G. L. Eskew, *The Pageant of the Packets* (1929); and L. D. Baldwin, "Shipbuilding on the Western Waters," *Miss. Valley Hist. Rev.*, XX, 29–44 (June, 1933). Canals: Hulbert, *Historic Highways*, Vols. XIII–XIV; A. F. Harlow, *Old Towpaths* (1926); W. F. Dunaway, *History of the James River and Kanawha Company* (1922); C. L. Jones, *Economic History of the Anthracite Tidewater Canals* (1908); G. W. Ward, *The Early Development of the Chesapeake and Ohio Canal Project* (1889); E. L. Bogart, *Internal Improvement and State Debts in Ohio* (1924); J. W. Putnam, *The Illinois and Michigan Canal* (1908); and N. E. Whitford, *History of the Canal System of the State of New York* (2 vols., 1906). Railroads: C. E. Carter, *When Railroads Were New* (1909); Slason Thompson, *A Short History of American Railways* (1925); T. W. Van Metre, *Principles of Railway Transportation* (1922); U. B. Phillips, *History of Transportation in the Eastern Cotton Belt to 1860* (1908); Thelma Kistler, *The Rise of Railroads in the Connecticut River Valley*, Smith College Studies in History, XXIII, Nos. 1–4 (1938); Edward Hungerford, *The Story of the Baltimore and Ohio Railroad 1827–1927* (2 vols., 1928); H. W. Shotter, *The Growth and Development of the Pennsylvania Railroad* (1927); and F. W. Stevens, *The Beginnings of the New York Central Railroad* (1926). The story of the express companies is well told in A. F. Harlow, *Old Waybills* (1934). In W. J. Lane, *From Indian Trail to Iron Horse* (1939) is a story of the development of transportation in New Jersey from 1620 to 1860.

FINANCING THE INDUSTRIAL REVOLUTION. On money, banks, and the tariff consult D. R. Dewey, *Financial History of the United States* (12th ed., 1935); A. B. Hepburn, *History of Coinage and Currency in the United States* (rev. ed., 1915); W. G. Sumner, *History of Banking in the United States* (1896); Charles A. Conant, *History of Modern Banks of Issue* (rev. ed., 1915); F. W. Taussig, *Tariff History of the United States* (8th ed., 1931); Edward Stanwood, *American Tariff Controversies in the Nineteenth Century* (1903); and P. Ashley, *Modern Tariff History* (3rd ed., 1920).

THE HUMAN ELEMENT. Very little work has been done on the early American inventors and entrepreneurs, but short biographies of most of them are in the *Dictionary of American Biography*. In K. W. Porter, *The Jacksons and the Lees* (2 vols., 1937) there is an excellent picture, chiefly through sources, of the merchant capitalist of the early national period. The same author has done a definitive biography of *John Jacob Astor: Business Man* (2 vols., 1931). W. T. Hutchinson, *Cyrus Hall McCormick* (2 vols., 1930–35) is also a first-class biography. For source material on labor see the *Documentary History of American Industrial Society*. An account of some length is J. R. Commons *et al.*, *History of Labour in the United States* (2 vols., 1918), and briefer accounts are in G. S. Watkins, *An Introduction to the Study of the Labor Problem* (1922) and Mary Beard, *A Short History of the American Labor Movement* (1920). Important for this period is Norman Ware, *The Industrial Worker, 1840–1860* (1924).

XVI. THE MARCH OF THE HUMAN MIND

THE HUMANITARIAN REVOLT. Essential for this chapter are C. R. Fish, *Rise of the Common Man* (1927) and A. C. Cole, *The Irrepressible Conflict* (1934) in the History of American Life Series, both equipped with extensive annotations and bibliographies. Extremely suggestive are the observations of the French traveler A. de Tocqueville, *Democracy in America* (English tr., new ed., 2 vols., 1898). On prison reform see L. N. Robinson, *Penology in the United States* (1921); O. F. Lewis, *The Development of American Prisons and Prison Customs, 1776–1845* (1922); Harry Elmer Barnes, *History of Penal Reformatory and Correctional Institutions in New Jersey* (1918), *Progress of American Penology* (1922), and *The Evolution of Penology in Pennsylvania* (1927). On the blind, W. H. Illingworth, *History of the Education of the Blind* (1910) and on prohibition, J. A. Krout, *The Origins of Prohibition* (1925). On the better treatment of the insane read F. Tiffany, *Life of Dorothea Lynde Dix* (1890) or H. E. Marshall, *Dorothea Dix, Forgotten Samaritan* (1937).

EXPERIMENTS IN LIVING. Brief introductions are in Morris Hillquit, *History of Socialism in the United States* (1910) and Harry Laidler, *History of Socialist Thought* (1927). There are more detailed studies in J. H. Noyes, *History of American Socialisms* (1870); Charles Nordhoff, *The Communistic Societies of the United States from Personal Visit and Observation* (1875); and W. A. Hinds, *American Communities and Cooperative Commonwealths* (2nd ed., 1908). On specific communities: Albert Shaw, *Icaria: A Chapter in the History of Communism* (1884); B. M. H. Shambaugh, *Amana That Was and Amana That Is* (1932); G. W. Noyes, ed., *Religious Experiences of John Humphrey Noyes, Founder of the Oneida Community* (1923); and O. B. Frothingham, *George Ripley* (1882), which tells of Brook Farm.

EDUCATION FOR THE MASSES. Brief résumés of education for the middle period are in C. F. Thwing, *A History of Higher Education in America* (1906); Z. G. Dexter, *History of Education in the United States* (1911); S. C. Parker, *History of Modern Elementary Education* (1912); and E. P. Cubberley, *Public Education in the United States* (1925). For the philosophy of education as influenced by the economic background read the brilliant study of M. E. Curti, *The Social Ideas of American Educators* (1935). Other interesting books are O. A. Bennett, *History of Manual and Industrial Education up to 1870* (1926); C. G. Woodson, *The Education of the Negro Prior to 1861* (1915); and E. M. Coulter, *College Days in the Old South* (1928). On the beginnings of higher education for women read A. C. Cole, *A Hundred Years of Mount Holyoke College* (1940).

THE GROWTH OF DEMOCRACY. See McMaster, Vol. II, Chap. 17 and Vol. V, Chap. I and C. E. Merriam, *A History of American Political Theories* (1903). On early woman suffrage: C. C. Catt and N. R. Shuler, *Woman Suffrage and Politics* (1923); F. H. Howe, ed., *Julia Ward Howe and the Woman Suffrage Movement* (1913); W. R. Waterman, *Frances Wright* (1924); E. C. Stanton, S. B. Anthony, M. J. Gage, and I. H. Harper, *History of Woman Suffrage* (6 vols., 1881–1922); and I. H. Harper, *Life and Work of Susan B. Anthony* (3 vols., 1899–1908).

THE GOLDEN DAY. Among the extensive bibliography the following are of a somewhat general nature: Lewis Mumford, *The Golden Day* (1926) and *Sticks and Stones: A Study of American Architecture and Civilization* (1924); V. L. Parrington, *Main Currents in American Thought* (3 vols., 1927–1930); Van Wyck Brooks, *The Flowering of New England* (1936); R. H. Gabriel, *The Course of American Democratic Thought* (1940); L. C. Elson, *The History of American Music* (1904); T. F. Hamlin, *The American Spirit in Architecture* (1926), Pageant of America; F. L. Mott, *A History of American Magazines 1741–1850* (1930); Lorado Taft, *A History of American Sculpture* (1924); and S. T. Williams, *The American Spirit in Letters* (1926). In Newton Arvin, *Hawthorne* (1929) and Lewis Mumford, *Herman Melville* (1929) two great men are discussed in distinguished fashion.

XVII. THE OLD SOUTH

SOUTHERN DEVELOPMENT. Nowhere can the student obtain a better picture of the antebellum South than in U. B. Phillips, *Life and Labor in the Old South* (1929) and W. E. Dodd, *The Cotton Kingdom* (1929), Chronicles of America, both written in charming style but based on long study and research. Brief syntheses are E. G. Hawk, *Economic History of the South* (1934) and W. B. Hesseltine, *A History of the South* (1936), while more detailed studies of various phases are L. C. Gray, *History of Agriculture in the Southern United States to 1860* (2 vols., 1933); M. B. Hammond, *The Cotton Industry* (1897); M. Jacobstein, *The Tobacco Industry in the United States,* Columbia U. Studies, XXVI, No. 3 (1907); J. C. Robert, *The Tobacco Kingdom: Plantation, Market, and Factory in Virginia and North Carolina, 1800–1860* (1938); and A. O. Craven, *Soil Exhaustion as a Factor in the Agricultural History of Virginia and Maryland, 1660–1860* (1925). Important contemporary studies throwing light on this subject are Daniel R. Goodloe, *An Inquiry into the Causes Which Retard the Southern States* (1848); T. R. Kettell, *Southern Wealth and Northern Profits* (1861); and H. R. Helper, *The Impending Crisis of the South* (1857).

THE PLANTER ARISTOCRACY. Most of the books listed under the various sections of this chapter throw light on the planter aristocracy, particularly those of Phillips and Dodd. See also A. C. Cole, *The Irrepressible Conflict* (1930) in the History of American Life Series and G. S. Johnson, *A Social History of the Sea Islands* (1925). Many books of reminiscences of the Old South have been written, e. g., V. V. Clayton, *Black and White Under the Old Regime* (1899) and Susan D. Smedes, *Memorials of a Southern Planter* (4th ed., 1900), but more detached in its point of view is Francis P. Gaines, *The Southern Plantation, a Study in the Development and Accuracy of a Tradition* (1924). A valuable survey is R. S. Cotterill, *The Old South* (1936). On this and other sections Minnie C. Boyd, *Alabama in the Fifties* (1931), Columbia University Studies, No. 353 is helpful.

THE PLAIN PEOPLE. Most writers, both contemporary and subsequent, have been interested in either the aristocrat or the slave. Fortunately this was not true of

Frederick L. Olmsted, the most indefatigable traveler in the South. Interested in agriculture in the middle- and poorer-class white, his books, *Journey in the Seaboard Slave States* (1856), *A Journey Through Texas* (1857), *A Journey in the Back Country* (1860), and *Journeys and Explorations in the Cotton Kingdom* (1861), comprise the most valuable observations on these classes. His work is critically appraised in Broadus Mitchell, *Frederick Law Olmsted: A Critic of the Old South,* Johns Hopkins Studies, XLII, No. 2 (1924).

THE SLAVE SYSTEM. Of the many books on slavery the following are scholarly and dependable: U. B. Phillips, *American Negro Slavery* (1918), *Life and Labor in the Old South* (1929), and his two volumes of sources in the *Documentary History of American Industrial Society* (1910); Benjamin Brawley, *A Short History of the American Negro* (1919), by a Negro; Frederic Bancroft, *Slave Trading in the Old South* (1931); C. S. Sydnor, *Slavery in Mississippi* (1933); and R. B. Flanders, *Plantation Slavery in Georgia* (1933). Also valuable is J. S. Bassett, *The Southern Plantation Overseer as Revealed in His Letters* (1925), a study based on letters to President James K. Polk by his plantation overseers. Of the contemporary material, of which there is a large amount, none is more interesting (with the exception of Olmsted) than J. E. Cairns, *The Slave Power* (2nd ed., 1863), a study by an English economist; J. S. Buckingham, *The Slave States of America* (1842) by an intelligent English traveler; H. R. Helper, *The Impending Crisis in the South* (1857), a bitter and somewhat exaggerated arraignment of the system by a middle-class Southerner, and a famous defense entitled *The Pro-Slavery Argument* (1852), by several well-known Southern authors.

THE POLITICAL SOUTH. Arthur C. Cole, *The Whig Party in the South* (1913) is detailed with an inclusive bibliography. Also valuable are R. R. Russel, *Economic Aspects of Southern Sectionalism, 1840–1861,* University of Illinois Studies, XI, Nos. 1–2 (1923); J. G. Van Deusen, *Economic Basis of Disunion in South Carolina,* Columbia U. Studies (1928); S. J. Folmsbee, *Sectionalism and Internal Improvements in Tennessee History* (1939); R. H. Shyrock, *Georgia and the Union in 1850* (1926); and N. W. Stephenson, "Southern Nationalism in South Carolina in 1851," *Am. Hist. Rev.,* XXXVI, 314–335 (Jan., 1931). See also bibliography under Chapters XVIII and XIX.

XVIII. AGRICULTURAL IMPERIALISM

HARRISON AND TYLER. This administration is covered in Channing, McMaster, and Schouler as well as in Stanwood, *History of the Presidency.* The financial aspect is treated in Dewey, *Financial History of the United States.* For Harrison read his sketch in the *Dictionary of American Biography;* D. B. Goebel, *William H. Harrison, a Political Biography* (1926); and Freeman Cleaves, *Old Tippecanoe* (1939); for Tyler see L. G. Tyler, *Letters and Times of the Tylers* (3rd ed., 1896) or the more recent and better-balanced O. P. Chitwood, *John Tyler, Champion of the Old South* (1939). In this and later sections the biographies of important men are essential: Schurz, *Henry Clay;* Van Dusen, *Life of Henry Clay;* Fuess, *Webster;* Hunt, *John C. Calhoun,* etc. Albert K. Weinberg, *Manifest Destiny* (1935) provides an adequate treatment of the philosophy of expansion. J. R. Poage, *Henry Clay and the Whig Party* (1936) is a study of American politics from 1840 to 1852.

CANADIAN BOUNDARY LINE. On this topic the following are helpful: R. W. Mowat, *The Diplomatic Relations of Great Britain and the United States* (1925); J. S. Reeves, *American Diplomacy Under Tyler and Polk* (1907); H. S. Burrage, *Maine in the Northeastern Boundary Controversy* (1919); W. A. Dunning, *The British Empire and the United States* (1914); P. E. Corbett, *The Settlement of Canadian-American Disputes* (1937); J. M. Callahan, *American Foreign Policy in Canadian Relations* (1937); L. B. Shippee, *Canadian-American Relations, 1849–1874* (1939); Fuess, *Daniel Webster;* and the general histories of foreign relations such as Bemis and Bailey.

TEXAS AND THE CAMPAIGN OF 1844. Consult E. D. Adams, *British Interests and Activities in Texas, 1838–1840* (1910); G. L. Rives, *The United States and Mexico, 1821–1848* (2 vols., 1913); J. F. Rippy, *United States and Mexico* (2nd ed., 1931); E. C. Barker, *Mexico and Texas, 1821–1835* (1928); and J. H. Smith, *The Annexation of Texas* (1911). The following biographies are essential: E. C. Barker, *Life of Stephen F. Austin* (1925) and E. I. McCormac, *James K. Polk* (1922). Of the American Presidents only J. Q. Adams, J. K. Polk, and R. B. Hayes kept extensive diaries; Polk's is exceedingly valuable and fortunately an abbreviated edition has been published by Allan Nevins with an able biographical sketch of Polk.

MANIFEST DESTINY. In addition to the books listed in the last section the following are valuable on the preliminaries of the Mexican War: E. D. Adams, *British Interests and Activities in Texas* (1910) and E. C. Barker, ed., *Diplomatic Correspondence of the Republic of Texas* (1907). On the war itself J. H. Smith, *The War with Mexico* (2 vols., 1919) is the standard work. Brief but well and vividly written is N. W. Stephenson, *Texas and the Mexican War* (1921), Chronicles of America. See also H. I. Priestley, *The Mexican Nation: a History* (1923) and for the social reactions in this country C. R. Fish, *The Rise of the Common Man* (1927). C. W. Elliott, *Winfield Scott: The Soldier and the Man* (1937) is a definitive biography. Nevins, *Frémont* is valuable on the California phase.

THE WILMOT PROVISO AND THE ELECTION OF 1848. On the proviso, C. B. Going, *David Wilmot, Free Soiler* (1924) is exhaustive. For the election of 1848 consult A. C. McLaughlin, *Lewis Cass* (1899); O. O. Howard, *General Taylor* (1892); Brainard Dyer, "Zachary Taylor and the Election of 1848," *Pacific Historical Review,* IX, 173–182 (June, 1940); T. C. Smith, *The Liberty and Free Soil Parties in the Northwest* (1897); A. C. Cole, *Whig Party in the South* (1912); as well as Schouler, Vol. V; Channing, Vol. VI; and McMaster, Vol. VII.

COMPROMISE OF 1850 AND THE CAMPAIGN OF 1852. Channing, McMaster, Schouler, and Von Holst cover this story. In addition J. F. Rhodes, *History of the United States from the Compromise of 1850* (7 vols., 1893–1906; new ed., 7 vols., 1928) is available. Rhodes's monumental work is the result of great industry and is still valuable but must be used by students with care as it has been subjected to continued attacks by Southern historians on the ground of failure to understand the South and by the newer historians because it takes little account of the tremendous economic forces of the period. Other books are J. Macy, *The Anti-Slavery Crusade* (1919) and *Political Parties in the United States* (1924); R. H. Shryock, *Georgia and the Union in 1850* (1926); T. C. Smith, *The Liberty and Free Soil Parties in the Northwest* (1897) and *Parties and Slavery* (1906); A. C. Cole, *The Whig Party in the South* (1912); and R. F. Nichols, *The Democratic Machine, 1850–1854* (1923). Most important is R. F. Nichols, *Franklin Pierce* (1931). Two recent studies of the slavery controversy are D. L. Dumond, *Anti-slavery Origins of the Civil War in the United States* (1939) and A. Y. Lloyd, *The Slavery Controversy, 1831–1860* (1939).

MORE MANIFEST DESTINY. On the Far East: C. M. Fuess, *Caleb Cushing* (2 vols., 1913); W. E. Griffis, *Townshend Harris* (1895); P. J. Treat, *Diplomatic Relations Between the United States and Japan, 1853–1895* (2 vols., 1932); Tyler Dennett, *Americans in Eastern Asia* (1922); and F. R. Dulles, *The Old China Trade* (1930). On

Latin America: A. A. Ettinger, *The Mission to Spain of Pierre Soulé* (1932); M. W. Williams, *Anglo-American Isthmian Diplomacy, 1815–1915* (1916); W. O. Scroggs, *Filibusters and Financiers* (1916); G. H. Stuart, *Latin America and the United States* (1922); L. M. Sears, *John Slidell* (1925); J. F. Rippy, *Joel R. Poinsett* (1935); P. N. Garber, *The Gadsden Treaty* (1923); and the articles in *American Secretaries of State* on Buchanan, Clayton, and Marcy. C. W. Ramsdell, "The National Limits of Slavery Expansion," *Miss. Valley Hist. Rev.,* XVI, 151–171 (Sept., 1929) discusses the mixed motives behind the desire for Cuba.

XIX. THE IRREPRESSIBLE CONFLICT

THE PROSPEROUS FIFTIES. The economic history of this decade must be pieced together from the various books on industry, transportation, agriculture, and finance listed under Chapters XIV, XV, and XVII. A. C. Cole, *The Irrepressible Conflict,* Chap. I is an excellent summary, as are the early chapters in J. G. Randall, *The Civil War and Reconstruction* (1937).

UPSETTING THE COMPROMISES. Many early historians, of whom Rhodes was the outstanding, attribute the Kansas-Nebraska Bill to the ambitions of Douglas for the presidency. In P. O. Ray, *The Repeal of the Missouri Compromise* (1909) the point is developed that it was the fulfillment of a campaign pledge of Senator Atchison of Missouri. In F. H. Hodder, "The Genesis of the Kansas-Nebraska Act," *Wis. Hist. Soc. Proceeds.,* LX, 69–86 and in "The Railroad Background of the Kansas-Nebraska Act," *Miss. Valley Hist. Rev.,* XXX, 3–22 the view is held that it was due to sectional rivalry over the terminus of a Pacific railroad. Allen Johnson, *Stephen A. Douglas* (1908) adds the further suggestion that Douglas was anxious to give the Democratic Party an outstanding principle upon which to stand. The part played by Douglas is told in great detail in George F. Milton, *Stephen A. Douglas* (1934), an outstanding biography.

SLAVERY IN THE TERRITORIES. On this episode see C. Robinson, *The Kansas Conflict* (2nd ed., 1898); L. W. Spring, *Kansas, the Prelude of the War for the Union* (1885); Eli Thayer, *The Kansas Crusade* (1889); and O. G. Villard, *John Brown 1800–1859* (1910). See also R. V. Harlow, "The Rise and Fall of the Kansas Aid Movement," *Am. Hist. Rev.,* XLI, 1–25 (Oct., 1935). H. S. Commager's recent life of *Theodore Parker* (1936) contains material on the antislavery crusade. See also R. V. Harlow, *Garrit Smith, Philanthropist and Reformer* (1939). The Dred Scott case is discussed in Charles Warren, *The Supreme Court in United States History* (2 vols., 1932); in B. C. Steiner, *Life of Roger Brooke Taney* (1922); in F. H. Hodder, "Some Phases of the Dred Scott Case," *Miss. Valley Hist. Rev.,* XVI, 3–22 (June, 1929); and in E. S. Curtis, "The Dred Scott Decision in the Light of Contemporary Legal Doctrine," *Am. Hist. Rev.,* XVII, 52–69 (Oct., 1911).

PRE–CIVIL-WAR POLITICS. In addition to the large general histories consult C. H. Ambler, *Sectionalism in Virginia from 1776–1861* (1910); G. T. Carpenter, *The South as a Conscious Minority 1789–1861* (1930); F. Curtis, *The Republican Party* (2 vols., 1904); Jesse Macy, *The Anti-Slavery Crusade* (1917) and *Political Parties in the United States, 1846–1861* (1900); W. S. Meyers, *The Republican Party* (1928); R. R. Russel, *Economic Aspects of Southern Sectionalism, 1840–1861* (1922); J. C. Sitterson, *Secession Movement in North Carolina* (1939); T. C. Smith, *The Liberty and Free Soil Parties in the Northwest* (1897) and *Parties and Slavery* (1906); and E. Stanwood, *A History of the Presidency* (2 vols., 1916). On Know-Nothingism and its origins read R. A. Billington, *The Protestant Crusade* (1938). To understand this subject it is necessary to dip into the biographies of the prominent statesmen. In addition to the excellent biographies of Douglas by Allen Johnson and G. F. Milton and of Pierce by Roy F. Nichols, the following are important: Frederic Bancroft, *The Life of William H. Seward* (2 vols., 1900); A. O. Craven, *Edward Ruffin, Southerner* (1932); W. E. Dodd, *Jefferson Davis* (1907); R. McElroy, *Jefferson Davis, the Unreal and the Real* (2 vols., 1937); P. S. Flippin, *Herschel V. Johnson of Georgia* (1931); A. B. Hart, *Salmon Portland Chase* (1899); M. Story, *Charles Sumner* (1900); G. H. Haynes, *Charles Sumner* (1909); W. A. Linn, *Horace Greeley* (1903); Louis Pendleton, *Alexander H. Stephens* (1908); U. B. Phillips, *The Life of Robert Toombs* (1913); L. A. White, *Robert Barnwell Rhett* (1931); J. A. Woodburn, *Life of Thaddeus Stevens* (1913); and A. B. Miller, *Thaddeus Stevens* (1939), the latter somewhat appreciative.

1860 AND SECESSION. Special studies of this period in addition to the many listed above are P. G. Auchampaugh, *James Buchanan and His Cabinet on the Eve of Secession* (1926); D. L. Dumond, *The Secession Movement, 1860–1861* (1931); Mary Scrugham, *The Peaceable Americans, 1860–1861,* Columbia University Studies, XCVI, No. 3 (1921); E. D. Fite, *The Presidential Campaign of 1860* (1911); and W. E. Dodd, "The Fight for the Northwest, 1860," *Am. Hist. Rev.,* XVI, 774–788 (July, 1911). One scholar's interpretation of secession is in E. M. Coulter, ed., *The Course of the South to Secession, An Interpretation by Ulrich Bonnell Phillips* (1939). Another is C. R. Fish, *The American Civil War: An Interpretation* (1940). Avery Craven, *The Repressible Conflict, 1830–1861* (1939) believes that the war was not inevitable. See also G. T. Curtis, *Life of James Buchanan* (2 vols., 1883); A. J. Beveridge, *Abraham Lincoln* (2 vols., 1928), which carries the story to 1858; N. W. Stephenson, *Lincoln* (1922); Carl Sandburg, *Abraham Lincoln: The Prairie Years* (2 vols., 1926); and A. C. Cole, *The Irrepressible Conflict* (1934).

XX. CLASH OF ECONOMIC SECTIONS

RESORT TO ARMS. See the bibliography under the last two sections of the previous chapter.

STRATEGY POLITICAL AND MILITARY—THE WESTERN WAR—WAR IN THE EAST. The best military history is J. C. Ropes and W. R. Livermore, *The Story of the Civil War* (4 vols., 1895–1913). J. F. Rhodes tells the story in some detail in his *History of the United States,* Vols. III and IV and has condensed the account in *History of the Civil War* (1917). See also T. A. Dodge, *A Bird's Eye View of Our Civil War* (rev. ed., 1897); J. K. Hosmer, *The Appeal to Arms* (1907); William Wood, *Captains of the Civil War* (1921), Chronicles of America; and W. B. Wood and J. E. Edmunds, *A History of the Civil War in the United States* (1905). J. G. Randall, *The Civil War and Reconstruction* (1937) is also an excellent condensation. The two books of N. W. Stephenson, *Abraham Lincoln and the Union* and *The Day of the Confederacy,* both in the Chronicles of America, are fascinating reading. Important on this subject is A. Howard Meneely, *The War Department, 1861* (1928), Columbia University Studies, No. 300. On the border states see E. C. Smith, *The Borderland in the Civil War* (1927) and in more detail J. C. McGregor, *The Disruption of Virginia* (1922) and E. M. Coulter, *The Civil War and Readjustment in Kentucky* (1926). On naval operations: D. D. Porter, *The Naval History of the Civil War* (1886); J. T. Scharf, *History of the Confederate States Navy* (1886); F. B. C. Bradlee, *Blockade Running During the Civil War and the Effect of Land and Water Transportation on the Confederacy* (1925); A. T. Mahan, *Admiral Farragut* (1892); H. W.

Briggs, *The Doctrine of the Continuous Voyage* (1926); and J. P. Baxter, 3rd., *The Introduction of the Ironclad Warship* (1933). The memoirs of the military chieftains are important: U. S. Grant, *Personal Memoirs* (2 vols., 1885–1886); W. T. Sherman, *Memoirs* (2 vols., 1886); G. B. McClellan, *McClellan's Own Story* (1887); and P. H. Sheridan, *Personal Memoirs* (1888). See also Jefferson Davis, *Rise and Fall of the Confederate Government* (2 vols., 1881) and J. E. Johnston, *Narrative of Military Operations* (1874). The best lives of Lee are Sir F. Maurice, *Robert E. Lee the Soldier* (1925) and D. S. Freeman, *R. E. Lee* (4 vols., 1934–1935), the latter a monumental and definitive work. A recent appraisal of one of the abler Confederate soldiers is H. J. Eckenrode and Bryan Conrad, *James Longstreet, Lee's War Horse* (1936). On Grant: L. A. Coolidge, *Ulysses S. Grant* (1917), a conventional treatment, and W. E. Woodward, *Meet General Grant* (1928), popular. J. G. Nicolay and J. Hay, *Abraham Lincoln: A History* (10 vols., 1890) gives Lincoln's war record in detail, while N. W. Stephenson, *Lincoln* (1922) handles this phase intelligently. Carl Sandburg, *Abraham Lincoln: The War Years* (4 vols., 1939) is the greatest wartime study of the emancipator. On the Hampden Roads Conference see E. C. Kirkland, *Peacemakers of 1864* (1927).

POLITICS DURING THE WAR. Besides Rhodes, McMaster and Schouler see N. W. Stephenson, "Lincoln and the Sense of Nationality in the North," *Am. Hist. Assoc. Report* (1919); E. J. Benton, "Movement for Peace Without Victory During the Civil War," *West. Res. Hist. Soc. Collections* (1918); E. C. Kirkland, *The Peacemakers of 1864* (1927); and J. G. Randall, *Constitutional Problems Under Lincoln* (1926). In B. J. Hendrick, *Statesmen of the Lost Cause* (1939) is a vivid treatment of Davis and his cabinet. Stewart Mitchell, *Horatio Seymour of New York* (1938) is full on New York politics during wartime.

XXI. BEHIND THE LINES

FINANCING THE WAR. On the financial history of the North D. R. Dewey, *Financial History of the United States* is a good brief account. On special features see W. C. Mitchell, *History of the Greenbacks* (1903); D. C. Barrett, *The Greenbacks and the Resumption of Specie Payments, 1862–1879* (1931); and A. M. Davis, *The Origin of the National Banking System* (1910). E. P. Oberholtzer, *Jay Cooke, Financier of the Civil War* (2 vols., 1907) and Henrietta Larson, *Jay Cooke, Private Banker* (1936) are adequate biographies. On the Northern Secretary of the Treasury see J. W. Shuckers, *The Life of Salmon P. Chase* (1874). On Southern finances consult J. C. Schwab, *The Confederate States of America, 1861–1365: A Financial and Industrial History* (1901); J. L. Sellers, "An Interpretation of Civil War Finance," *Am. Hist. Rev.*, XXX, 282–297 (Jan., 1925); and H. D. Capers, *The Life and Times of C. G. Memminger* (1894).

LIFE IN THE NORTH. Of the general histories McMaster is particularly good on this phase. The most valuable single work is E. D. Fite, *Social and Industrial Conditions in the North During the Civil War* (1910). There are excellent chapters on both Union and Confederacy in J. G. Randall, *The Civil War and Reconstruction* (1937). See also C. A. Dana, *Recollections of the Civil War* (1898); Gideon Welles, *Diary;* C. J. Stillé, *A History of the United States Sanitary Commission* (1866); L. P. Brockett and M. C. Vaughan, *Woman's Work in the Civil War* (1867); E. Lonn, *Desertion During the Civil War* (1928); and F. A. Shannon, *The Organization and Administration of the Union Army* (2 vols., 1928). No student should fail to read A. C. Cole,

The Irrepressible Conflict (1934) as an excellent synthesis of the social history of the time.

WAR TIME IN THE CONFEDERACY. In addition to Cole, *The Irrepressible Conflict,* Stephenson, *The Day of the Confederacy* and Rhodes, Vol. V, already cited, the following are useful: H. J. Eckenrode, *Jefferson Davis, President of the South* (1930); Mary B. Chestnut, *Diary from Dixie* (1905); J. B. Jones, *A Rebel War Clerk's Diary* (2 vols., 1866); W. H. Russell, *My Diary North and South* (1863); and B. H. Wise, *The End of an Era* (1899). On the military and political phase: A. B. Moore, *Conscription and Conflict in the Confederacy* (1924) and F. L. Owsley, *State Rights in the Confederacy* (1925). In C. H. Wesley, *The Collapse of the Confederacy* (1937) the collapse is attributed to internal breakdown of morale.

THE EUROPEAN FRONT. On the part played by cotton see F. L. Owsley, *King Cotton Diplomacy* (1931); J. A. B. Scherer, *Cotton as a World Power, a Study in the Economic Interpretation of History* (1916); and L. B. Schmidt, "The Influence of Wheat and Cotton on Anglo-American Relations During the Civil War," *Iowa Journal of History and Politics,* XVI, 400–439 (July, 1918). Particularly on Great Britain see C. F. Adams, *Charles Francis Adams* (1900); E. D. Adams, *Great Britain and the American Civil War* (1925); and D. Jordan and E. J. Pratt, *Europe and the American Civil War* (1931). On other phases see J. M. Callahan, *The Diplomatic History of the Southern Confederacy* (1901); J. Bigelow, *France and the Confederate Navy* (1888); L. M. Sears, *John Slidell* (1925); and Bancroft, *William H. Seward.* The diplomatic story is summarized in Bemis and Bailey.

XXII. THE TRAGIC ERA

PROBLEMS OF PEACE AND CONGRESSIONAL RECONSTRUCTION. The notable history of Rhodes continues during this period but is chiefly political. Better rounded is E. P. Oberholtzer, *A History of the United States Since the Civil War* (5 vols., 1917–1937), stressing the economic and social history. J. G. Randall, *The Civil War and Reconstruction* (1937) is a usable summary. Allan Nevins, *The Emergence of Modern America* (1927) is the best introduction to the social history of the period and contains a full bibliography. The first person seriously to develop the reconstruction as a period for serious historical research was William A. Dunning. His *Reconstruction, Political and Economic* (1907) is one of the best of the American Nation Series and his *Essays on the Civil War and Reconstruction* (1904) remains perhaps the best introduction to the constitutional problems. His students have carried on the work in specialized fields. Howard Beale's article "Reconstruction" in the *Encyclopaedia of the Social Sciences* is a synthesis of the latest research on this field. His article "On Rewriting Reconstruction History," *Am. Hist. Rev.,* XLV, 807–827 (July, 1940) is an excellent statement of the present status of reconstruction historiography. See also C. H. McCarthy, *Lincoln's Plan of Reconstruction* (1901). C. G. Bowers, *The Tragic Era* (1929) is badly biased. G. F. Milton, *The Age of Hate* (1930) is scholarly and more satisfactory. Valuable is B. B. Kendrick, *Journal of the Joint Committee of Fifteen on Reconstruction* (1914).

RECONSTRUCTION IN THE SOUTH. A brief but excellent introduction is W. L. Fleming, *The Sequel to Appomattox* (1919), Chronicles of America. There has been much specialized work on this field of which the following are the most important: E. M. Coulter, *The Civil War and Reconstruction in Kentucky* (1926); W. W. Davis, *Civil War and Reconstruction in Florida* (1913); H. J. Eckenrode, *The Political History of Virginia During Reconstruction* (1904); W. J. Fertig, *Secession and Reconstruction in Tennessee* (1898); J. R. Ficklen, *History of Reconstruction in Louisiana to 1869* (1910); W. L. Fleming, *The Civil War and Reconstruction in Alabama* (1905) and *Documentary History of Reconstruction* (2 vols., 1906–1907); J. W. Garner, *Reconstruction in Mississippi* (1901); J. G. de R. Hamilton, *Reconstruction in North Carolina* (1914); P. S. Pierce, *The Freedmen's Bureau* (1904); C. W. Ramsdell, *Reconstruction in Texas* (1910); F. B. Simpkin and R. H. Woody, *South Carolina During Reconstruction* (1932); T. S. Staples, *Reconstruction in Arkansas* (1923); and C. M. Thompson, *Reconstruction in Georgia* (1915). See also A. A. Taylor, *The Negro in South Carolina During Reconstruction* (1924); J. C. Lester and D. L. Wilson, *Ku Klux Klan; Its Origin, Growth, and Disbandment* (1905); and S. F. Horn, *Invisible Empire: The Story of the Ku Klux Klan, 1866–1871* (1939), the most detailed narrative of the Klan, but biased in favor of that organization.

NATIONAL POLITICS. This topic is covered in Rhodes, Oberholtzer, and Dunning, in Stanwood, *History of the Presidency* (new ed., 2 vols., 1928) and in the following books dealing particularly with Andrew Johnson: Howard Beale, *The Critical Year* (1930); G. F. Milton, *The Age of Hate* (1930); D. M. DeWitt, *The Impeachment and Trial of Andrew Johnson* (1903); L. P. Stryker, *Andrew Johnson: A Study in Courage* (1929); and R. W. Winston, *Andrew Johnson, Plebeian and Patriot* (1928). See also J. A. Woodburn, *Life of Thaddeus Stevens* (1913) or preferably A. B. Miller, *Thaddeus Stevens* (1939).

XXIII. INDUSTRIALISM TAKES POSSESSION

SIGNIFICANCE OF THE REPUBLICAN VICTORY. The interpretation of the political and economic development of these years is nowhere better explained than in Charles and Mary Beard, *Rise of American Civilization,* Chap. XVIII. See also Beale, *The Critical Year* and his article "Reconstruction" in *Encyclopaedia of the Social Sciences.* On the victory of Grant see Charles H. Coleman, *The Election of 1868* (1933), Columbia University Studies, No. 392. On the fourteenth amendment consult C. A. Beard, *The Supreme Court and the Constitution* (1912); J. R. Commons, *Legal Foundations of Capitalism* (1924); H. E. Flack, *The Adoption of the Fourteenth Amendment* (1908); Gustavus Myers, *History of the Supreme Court of the United States* (1912); and C. Warren, *Supreme Court in United States History* (rev. ed., 2 vols., 1926). Also the article by H. J. Graham, " 'The Conspiracy Theory' of the Fourteenth Amendment," *Yale Law Journal,* XLVII (1938), 371–403 and XLVIII (1938), 171–194.

GRANT AND HIS ADMINISTRATION. The conventional biography of L. A. Coolidge, *Ulysses S. Grant* (1917), or the more modern biography, W. E. Woodward, *Meet General Grant* (1927) may be read with profit. W. B. Hesseltine, *Ulysses S. Grant Politician* (1935) is the most satisfactory on the later years. Rhodes and Oberholtzer develop the scandals in some detail while James Bryce, *The American Commonwealth* does the same for the Tweed Ring in New York City. On special phases see J. B. Crawford, *The Crédit Mobilier of America* (1880); C. F. Adams, *Chapters of Erie* (1886); D. T. Lynch, *Boss Tweed: The Story of a Grim Generation* (1928); and A. B. Paine, *Thomas Nast, His Period and His Pictures* (1904). No one has criticized this period more bitterly than Henry Adams, *Education of Henry Adams* (1918). The most recent and one of the most illuminating volumes on these years is Allan Nevins, *Hamilton Fish; the Inner History of the Grant Administration* (1936).

REVOLT OF THE LIBERAL REPUBLICANS. Besides Rhodes and Oberholtzer see E. D.

Ross, *Liberal Republican Movement* (1919); Carl Schurz, *Reminiscences* (3 vols., 1908); and Don C. Seitz, *Horace Greeley: Founder of the New York Tribune* (1926). Consult also W. E. Smith, *The Francis Preston Blair Family in Politics* (2 vols., 1933). DISPUTED ELECTION OF 1876. P. L. Haworth, *The Hayes-Tilden Election* (rev. ed., 1927) is the standard discussion. Both C. R. Williams, *Life of Rutherford B. Hayes* (2 vols., 1914) and H. J. Eckenrode, *Rutherford B. Hayes* (1930) are sympathetic biographies. John Bigelow, *Samuel J. Tilden* (2 vols., 1895) is detailed on the campaign. A. C. Flick, *Samuel Jones Tilden: A Study in Political Sagacity* (1939) is a definitive biography. See also Allan Nevins, *Abram S. Hewitt: With Some Account of Peter Cooper* (1935) for new information from the Hewitt papers. P. H. Buck, *The Road to Reunion* (1937) is a brilliant study of the decline of Civil War animosities.

XXIV. THE TRIUMPH OF THE INDUSTRIAL REVOLUTION

STEEL, MEAT AND OIL. Among the general books which might head this chapter are H. U. Faulkner, *American Economic History* (4th ed., 1938); Edward C. Kirkland, *A History of American Economic Life* (rev. ed., 1939); B. J. Hendrick, *Age of Big Business* (1919), Chronicles of America; W. Kaempffert, ed., *Popular History of American Invention* (2 vols., 1924); D. A. Wells, *Recent Economic Changes* (1889), an attempt to describe the Industrial Revolution by a contemporary; and Ida M. Tarbell, *The Nationalizing of Business* (1936), History of American Life Series. On steel see H. N. Casson, *Romance of Steel* (1907) or J. Russell Smith, *Story of Iron and Steel* (1908) and the biographies of the steel masters listed below under the section "Rulers of the Industrial Age." On meat-packing see R. A. Clemen, *The American Livestock and Meat Industry* (1923) and J. H. Collins, *The Story of Canned Foods* (1924). On oil, Ida M. Tarbell, *History of the Standard Oil Company* (2 vols., 1904) is an excellent, if not always detached, account. An excellent specialized account of the discovery and early years is P. H. Giddens, *The Birth of the Oil Industry* (1938). J. T. Flynn, *God's Gold* (1931) is both a first-class biography of Rockefeller and an account of the rise of the oil industry. The most recent and most detailed biography is that of Allan Nevins, *John D. Rockefeller* (2 vols., 1940).

A CONTRACTING WORLD. E. R. Johnson and T. W. Van Metre, *Principles of Railroad Transportation* (1921) is a good introduction and John Moody, *Railroad Builders* (1919), Chronicles of America, is a brief but well-written account of some of the early railroads. More detailed are R. E. Riegel, *Story of the Western Railways* (1926) and, of course, the histories of specific railroads mentioned in this chapter: C. F. Adams, Jr., *Chapters of Erie* (1886); S. Daggett, *Chapters on the History of the Southern Pacific* (1922); J. B. Hedges, *Henry Villard and the Railways of the Northwest* (1930); F. V. Smalley, *History of the Northern Pacific Railroad* (1883); and Nelson Trottman, *History of the Union Pacific* (1923). See also L. H. Haney, *Congressional History of Railways* (2 vols., 1910). Additional bibliography will be found under Chapter XXXIII.

EARLY LABOR ORGANIZATION. There are several excellent introductory texts to labor problems, those by G. C. Groat, F. T. Carlton, G. S. Watkins, C. R. Dougherty. Mary R. Beard, *Short History of the American Labor Movement* (rev. ed., 1925) and Selig Perlman, *History of Trade Unionism in the United States* (1922) are valuable but brief. In more detail is J. R. Commons *et al., History of Labor in the United States* (4 vols., 1918–1935). On the Knights of Labor: R. T. Ely, *Labor Movement in America* (1886), a contemporary study; T. V. Powderly, *Thirty Years of Labor* (1889), by one who was long grand master; H. J. Carman, Henry David, P. N.

Guthrie, eds., *The Path I Trod* (1940), an autobiography of Powderly from his own writings; and N. J. Ware, *Labor Movement in the United States, 1860–1895* (1929), chiefly concerned with the K. of L. On the A. F. of L. see Samuel Gompers, *Seventy Years of Life and Labor* (2 vols., 1925) and L. L. Lorwin, *The American Federation of Labor* (1933), the first adequate effort to appraise this organization. On the Pullman strike see Louis Adamic, *Dynamite: The Story of Class Violence in America* (1931); W. R. Browne, *Altgeld of Illinois, 1847–1902* (1924); Harry Barnard, *"Eagle Forgotten": The Life of John Peter Altgeld* (1938); and Grover Cleveland, *Presidential Problems* (1904), Chap. II, the latter a presidential defense. For the Haymarket riot see Henry David, *A History of the Haymarket Affair* (1936).

THE RULERS OF THE INDUSTRIAL AGE. Of the business leaders mentioned in this chapter a number have full-length biographies. The steelmasters: B. J. Hendrick, *Life of Andrew Carnegie* (2 vols., 1932), official, but detailed and carefully done; Andrew Carnegie, *Autobiography* (1920); George Harvey, *Henry Frick, The Man* (1928); Ida M. Tarbell, *Life of Elbert H. Gary* (1928), eulogistic. The bankers: Carl Hovey, *The Life of J. Pierpont Morgan* (1912); Lewis Corey, *The House of Morgan* (1930); and Harvey O'Connor, *Mellon's Millions* (1933), the last two extremely critical but based on sound research. Two lives of Stillman have appeared but neither is of much value. On the oil men: J. T. Flynn, *God's Gold* (1931) not only is excellent on Rockefeller but contains material on other oil magnates. For the railroad magnates see J. G. Pyle, *Life of J. J. Hill* (2 vols., 1917); George Kennan, *E. H. Harriman* (2 vols., 1922); J. B. Hedges, *Henry Villard and the Railways of the Northwest* (1930); and G. T. Clark, *Leland Stanford* (1931). Oscar Lewis, *The Big Four* (1938) is a colorful account of Stanford, Huntington, Hopkins and Crocker. G. Myers, *History of the Great American Fortunes* (1909–1910) is critical and salutary to counteract the official biographies. The *Dictionary of American Biography* contains biographies of all the leaders listed in this chapter and the *Encyclopaedia of the Social Sciences* appraises some of them.

LEGAL AIDS. See the books listed under the first section (Significance of the Republican Victory) of Chapter XXIII; also B. R. Tremble, *Chief Justice Waite: Defender of the Public Interest* (1938).

XXV. THE LAST FRONTIER

THE TRANS-MISSISSIPPI ADVANCE. The best bibliographical introduction to any period of frontier history is F. J. Turner and F. Merk, *List of References on the History of the West* (rev. ed., 1922). Undoubtedly the most significant treatment of this phase is W. P. Webb, *The Great Plains* (1931). Other general treatments include Katharine Coman, *Economic Beginnings of the Far West* (2 vols., 1912); F. L. Paxson, *The Last American Frontier* (1910); F. L. Paxson, *History of the American Frontier* (1924); Cardinal Goodwin, *The Trans-Mississippi West* (1922); W. J. Ghent, *The Early Far West: A Narrative Outline, 1540–1850* (1931); R. E. Riegel, *America Moves West* (1930); C. C. Rister, *The Southwestern Frontier, 1865–1881* (1928); and Dan E. Clark, *The West in American History* (1937).

THE MINERAL FRONTIER. On this phase the old book of C. H. Shinn, *Story of the Mine* (1896) recounts the early days of Nevada; Mark Twain, *Roughing It* (1873) gives an intimate picture of the boom days of the Comstock Lode as does E. Lord, *Comstock Mining and Miners* (monograph of the U. S. Geological Survey, IV, 1883). S. E. White, *The Forty Niners* (1920), Chronicles of America, tells vividly the history of early California and the same story is developed in R. G. Cleland, *California:*

the American Period (1922); W. J. Trimble, *The Mining Advance into the Inland Empire*, University of Wisconsin Bulletin, No. 638 (1914) tells of the development of the mining frontier while T. A. Rickard, *A History of American Mining* (1932) provides a valuable introduction.

THE RANCHERS' FRONTIER. Considerable interest and much first-class research has been expended in this field in the past ten years, producing such excellent works as E. S. Osgood, *The Day of the Cattleman* (1929), concerned chiefly with Montana; E. E. Dale, *The Range Cattle Industry* (1930); O. B. Peake, *The Colorado Range Cattle Industry* (1937); and W. P. Webb, *The Great Plains* (1931). Of great value also are P. A. Rollins, *The Cowboy* (1922); E. D. Branch, *The Cowboy and His Interpreters* (1926); and R. M. Wright, *Dodge City the Cowboy Capital* (1913). J. J. McCoy, *Historic Sketches of the Cattle Trade of the West and Southwest* (1940) is a contemporary account written in 1874. Emerson Hough, *The Passing of the Frontier* (1918), Chronicles of America, is a popular summary; the same author's *The Story of the Cowboy* (2 vols., 1897) was perhaps the first serious study of the cow country. For those interested in folksongs, John A. Lomax, *Cowboy Songs* (1910). There has been much periodical literature on this subject, of which much of the best has appeared in the *Mississippi Valley Historical Review*, e. g., E. E. Dale, "The Ranchman's Last Frontier" (June, 1923); Louis Pelzer, "A Cattlemen's Commonwealth on the Western Range" (June, 1926); R. S. Fletcher, "End of the Open Range in Eastern Montana" (Sept., 1929); and Harold Briggs, "The Development and Decline of Open Range Ranching in the Northwest" (March, 1934).

THE FARMERS' FRONTIER. On the public lands see G. T. DuBois and G. S. Mathews, *Galusha A. Grow, Father of the Homestead Act* (1917); G. M. Stephenson, *The Political History of the Public Lands from 1840 to 1862* (1917); B. H. Hibbard, *A History of Public Land Policies* (1924); and T. Donaldson, *Public Domain* (1881). Three recent articles add to an understanding of this act: F. A. Shannon, "The Homestead Act and the Labor Surplus," P. W. Gates, "The Homestead Law in an Incongruous Land System," both in the *American Hist. Rev.*, XLI, No. 4 (July, 1936); and R. M. Robbins, "The Public Domain in the Era of Exploitation, 1862–1901," *Agricultural History*, XIII, 97–108 (April, 1939). In Carter Goodrich and Sol Davison, "The Wage Earner in the Westward Movement," *Pol. Sci. Quart.*, L, 161–185 (June, 1935) and LI, 61–116 (March, 1936), the safety-valve theory is questioned. It is defended in Joseph Schafer, "Concerning the Frontier as a Safety Valve," *Pol. Sci. Quart.*, LII, 407–420 (Sept., 1937) and "Was the West a Safety Valve for Labor?", *Miss. Valley Hist. Rev.*, XXIV, 299–314 (Dec., 1937). See also Carter Goodrich and Sol Davison, "The Frontier as a Safety Valve: A Rejoinder," *Pol. Sci. Quart.*, LIII, 268–271 (June, 1938) and Murray Kane, "Some Considerations on the Safety Valve Doctrine," *Miss. Valley Hist. Rev.*, XXIII, 169–188 (Sept., 1936). On the influence of railroads in colonization see J. B. Hedges, "The Colonization Work of the Northern Pacific," *Miss. Valley Hist. Rev.* (Dec., 1926) and *Henry Villard and the Railways of the Northwest* (1930). On the influence of water supply and fencing the only adequate treatment is in W. P. Webb, *The Great Plains* (1931). The story of barbed wire is well summarized in E. W. Hayter, "Barbed Wire Fencing—a Prairie Invention," *Agricultural History*, XIII, 180–207 (Oct., 1939). See also Everett Dick, *The Sod House Frontier, 1844–1890* (1937) and *Vanguards of the Frontier* (1941), and H. E. Briggs, *Frontiers of the Northwest* (1940).

THE END OF THE FRONTIER. C. W. Wright, "The Disappearance of Free Land in Our Economic Development," *American Economic Review*, XVI, No. 1, Supplement (March, 1926), reprinted in Flügel and Faulkner, *Readings*, 758–764.

XXVI. THE AGRARIAN REVOLT

THE REVOLUTION IN AGRICULTURE. No adequate history of American agriculture since 1860 has yet been written. An introduction to the literature, however, can be found in L. B. Schmidt, *Topical Studies and References in the Economic History of American Agriculture* (rev. ed., 1923) and E. E. Edwards, "References on the History of Agriculture in the United States," U. S. Dept. of Agriculture, Bureau of Agricultural Economics, 1934. Two books of readings are E. G. Nourse, *Agricultural Economics* (1916) and L. B. Schmidt and E. D. Ross, *Readings in the Economic History of American Agriculture* (1925). Among other helpful books are P. P. Brooks, *The Agrarian Revolution in Georgia, 1865–1912* (1914); H. N. Casson, *The Romance of the Reaper* (1908); Leo Rogin, *The Introduction of Farm Machinery in Its Relation to the Productivity of Labor in the Agriculture of the United States* (1931); W. T. Hutchinson, *Cyrus Hall McCormick* (2 vols., 1930–1935); and Joseph Schafer, *The Social History of American Agriculture* (1936).

THE GRANGER MOVEMENT. The standard volume is S. J. Buck, *The Granger Movement* (1913); a shorter summary is his *The Agrarian Crusade* (1920), Chronicles of America. Also essential are F. E. Haynes, *Social Politics in the United States* (1924) and Nathan Fine, *Labor and Farmer Parties in the United States, 1828–1928* (1928).

THE COMING OF FEDERAL REGULATION. In addition to the books listed in the last section see L. H. Haney, *A Congressional History of Railroads in the United States, 1850–1887* (1910); I. F. Sharfman, *The Interstate Commerce Commission* (4 vols., 1931–1937); and the reports of the "Hepburn Committee," N. Y. State Assembly Document, No. 38 (1880) and of the "Cullom Committee," Senate Reports, 49th Cong., First Session, No. 2356 (2 vols.).

THE CURRENCY PROBLEM—GREENBACKS AND SILVER. F. L. McVey, *The Populist Movement* (1896); S. J. Buck, *The Agrarian Crusade* (1920); and J. D. Hicks, *The Populist Revolt* (1931) tell the political story. On the more technical economic aspect: Davis R. Dewey, *Financial History of the United States* (12th ed., 1935); A. B. Hepburn, *History of Coinage and Currency in the United States* (rev. ed., 1915); A. D. Noyes, *Forty Years of American Finance* (1909); W. C. Mitchell, *A History of the Greenbacks* (1903); J. L. Laughlin, *History of Bimetallism in the United States* (4th ed., 1897); and Don C. Barrett, *The Greenbacks and the Resumption of Specie Payments, 1862–1879* (1931). Excerpts from the reports of the Treasury Department are in Flügel and Faulkner, *Readings*, while Cleveland tells his own part in maintaining the gold standard in *Presidential Problems* (1904).

XXVII. POLITICAL HISTORY, 1876–1896

POLITICAL BACKGROUND. On this topic consult again Rhodes, Oberholtzer, Stanwood; H. T. Peck, *Twenty Years of the Republic, 1885–1905* (1906); James Bryce, *The American Commonwealth* (new ed., 2 vols., 1922–1923); E. E. Robinson, *The Evolution of American Political Parties* (1924); Nathan Fine, *Labor and Farmer Parties in the United States, 1828–1928* (1928); F. E. Haynes, *Social Politics in the United States* (1924). Valuable on this period is Allan Nevins, *Abram S. Hewitt: With Some Account of Peter Cooper* (1935).

THE ADMINISTRATION OF HAYES. In addition to the books listed above see J. W. Burgess, *Administration of President Hayes* (1916); C. R. Williams, *Life of Rutherford B. Hayes* (2 vols., 1914); and H. J. Eckenrode, *Rutherford B. Hayes* (1930).

GARFIELD AND ARTHUR. Besides the books listed under the last two sections see

T. C. Smith, *Life and Letters of James A. Garfield* (2 vols., 1925); G. F. Howe, *Chester A. Arthur* (1934); R. G. Caldwell, *James A. Garfield* (1931); and A. R. Conkling, *Life and Letters of Roscoe Conkling* (1889). Civil-service reform may be followed in Rollo Ogden, *Life and Letters of Edwin Lawrence Godkin* (2 vols., 1907); Edward Cary, *George William Curtis* (1894); C. R. Fish, *Civil Service and the Patronage* (1904); D. H. Smith, *United States Civil Service Commission* (1928); and F. M. Stewart, *National Civil Service Reform League* (1928).

THE DEMOCRATIC VICTORY OF 1884. Most of the books already cited for this chapter touch on this election. The standard volume is H. C. Thomas, *Return of the Democratic Party to Power in 1884* (1919). Robert McElroy, *Grover Cleveland* (2 vols., 1923) is highly eulogistic; Allan Nevins, *Grover Cleveland* (1932) is better balanced. The most thorough life of Blaine is D. S. Muzzey, *James G. Blaine* (1934). On pensions see W. H. Glasson, *Federal Military Pensions in the United States* (1918). This period is particularly rich in memoirs and reminiscences, among the most valuable of which are James G. Blaine, *Twenty Years in Congress* (1884); G. F. Hoar, *Autobiography of Seventy Years* (2 vols., 1903); Hugh McCulloch, *Men and Measures of Half a Century* (1888); T. C. Platt, *Autobiography* (1910); Carl Schurz, *Reminiscences* (3 vols., 1908); and John Sherman, *Recollections of Forty Years* (2 vols., 1895).

THE RETURN OF THE REPUBLICANS. No first-class life of Harrison has yet appeared. The best of the campaign biographies is Lew Wallace, *Life of Gen. Ben Harrison* (1886). See short sketch in *Dictionary of American Biography*. On the other hand Reed has been adequately dealt with: S. B. McCall, *The Life of Thomas Brackett Reed* (1914) and W. A. Robinson, *Thomas B. Reed: Parliamentarian* (1930).

CLEVELAND A SECOND TIME. Besides books already listed see Grover Cleveland, *Presidential Problems* (1904), his own discussion of the problems which he met; Matilda Gresham, *Life of Walter Quinton Gresham* (2 vols., 1920); and J. A. Barnes, *John G. Carlisle* (1931). Biographies of other statesmen of the period include F. H. Gillett, *George Frisbie Hoar* (1934); C. M. Fuess, *Carl Schurz* (1932); and T. E. Burton, *John Sherman* (1906).

XXVIII. THE GILDED AGE

THE URBAN TREND. Perhaps the best single chapter on this period is Charles and Mary Beard, *The Rise of American Civilization,* Chap. XXV. Also rewarding is L. M. Hacker and B. B. Kendrick, *The United States Since 1865,* Chap. XIII. The first important efforts to synthesize the social history of these years are Allan Nevins, *The Emergence of Modern America* (1927) and A. M. Schlesinger, *The Rise of the City* (1933), History of American Life Series, containing detailed annotations and bibliographies. The Schlesinger volume is supplemented by Ida M. Tarbell, *The Nationalizing of Business* (1936), a volume in the same series and on the same period but covering primarily the economic aspect. D. A. Wells, *Recent Economic Changes* (1889) gives the views of a contemporary who sees an important economic revolution taking place. Thomas Beer, *The Mauve Decade* (1926) is an impressionistic account of the nineties. On the urban trend, besides Schlesinger see A. F. Weber, *The Growth of Cities in the Nineteenth Century* (1899), Columbia University Studies, and Josiah Strong, *The Twentieth Century City* (1898).

WAYS OF LIVING. Except for Nevins, Schlesinger and the Lynds, *Middletown* (1929), the picture of life in the eighties and nineties must be reconstructed from many sources. Books which deal with various aspects of the period can be found in the footnotes and bibliographies of the first two books named. On the status of women see Edith Abbott, *Women in Industry* (1910); Thomas Woody, *A History of Women's Education in the United States* (2 vols., 1929); J. C. Croly, *The History of the Women's Club Movement in America* (1898); and J. L. Wilson, *The Legal and Political Status of Women in the United States* (1912).

THE CULTURAL LEVEL. See E. P. Cubberley, *Public Education in the United States* (1925), most satisfactory general textbook; F. C. Moore, *Fifty Years of American Education* (1917); E. E. Slosson, *American Spirit in Education* (1921), Chronicles of America. More specialized are Woody, *op. cit.;* S. C. Parker, *History of Modern Elementary Education* (1912); E. W. Knight, *Public Education in the South* (1922); C. F. Thwing, *A History of Higher Education in America* (1906); and Merle Curti, *The Social Ideas of American Educators* (1935). On libraries see S. S. Green, *The Public Library Movement in the United States, 1853–1893* (1913) and on Chautauqua, J. H. Hurlbut, *The Story of Chautauqua* (1921) and H. A. Orchard, *Fifty Years of Chautauqua* (1923). On other topics in this chapter consult W. G. Bleyer, *Main Currents in American Journalism* (1927); J. M. Lee, *History of Journalism in the United States* (1923); A. Tassin, *The Magazine in America* (1916); Don C. Seitz, *Joseph Pulitzer, His Life and Letters* (1924); V. L. Parrington, *Beginnings of Critical Realism in America, 1860–1920* (*Main Currents in American Thought,* Vol. III); *Cambridge History of American Literature;* Bliss Perry, *American Spirit in Literature* (1921); Van Wyck Brooks, *New England: Indian Summer* (1940), brilliant and fascinating literary criticism; Newton Arvin, *Whitman* (1938); S. Isham, *History of American Painting* (new ed. by Royal Cortissoz, 1936); Suzanne La Follette, *Art in America* (1929); Lorado Taft, *History of American Sculpture* (new ed., 1930); and F. Kimball, *American Architecture* (1928).

THE AGE OF SCIENCE. W. Kaempffert, *History of American Inventions* (2 vols., 1924); L. L. Woodruff, ed., *The Development of the Sciences* (1923); E. S. Dana *et al., A Century of Science in America* (1918); John Fiske, *A Century of Science* (1900); J. W. Draper, *History of the Conflict Between Religion and Science* (1875); J. Y. Simpson, *Landmarks in the Struggle Between Science and Religion* (1925); A. D. White, *History of the Warfare of Science with Theology in Christendom* (2 vols., 1896); H. E. Barnes, ed., *History and Prospects of the Social Sciences* (1925) and his *The New History and the Social Studies* (1925).

THE PEOPLE AT PLAY. A. H. Quinn, *History of American Drama from the Civil War to the Present Day* (rev. ed., 1935); Arthur Hornblow, *A History of the Theatre in America* (2 vols., 1919); Carl Wittke, *Tombo and Bones: A History of the American Minstrel Stage* (1930); and J. A. Krout, *Annals of American Sport* (1929), Pageant of America. The best history of American recreation is F. R. Dulles, *America Learns to Play* (1940).

XXIX. LINES OF ECONOMIC BATTLE

CONSOLIDATION OF BUSINESS. On the early trust movement the *Preliminary Report of the Industrial Commission on Trusts and Industrial Combinations,* Vol. I of the Commission's Report (1900) and *Final Report of the Industrial Commission,* Vol. XIX of the Commission's Report (1902) are invaluable. Excellent textbooks are J. W. Jenks and W. E. Clark, *The Trust Problem* (5th ed., 1929); Eliot Jones, *The Trust Problem in the United States* (1921); and H. R. Seager and C. A. Gulick, Jr., *Trust and Corporation Problems* (1929). An early book summarizing the situation at the turn of the century is John Moody, *The Truth About the Trusts* (1904). His

Masters of Capital (1919), Chronicles of America, is interesting reading. Important for these early years are H. D. Lloyd, *Wealth Against Commonwealth* (1894); C. Lloyd, *Life of Henry Demarest Lloyd* (2 vols., 1912); A. H. Walker, *History of the Sherman Law* (1910); Ida M. Tarbell, *History of the Standard Oil Company* (2 vols., 1904); and J. T. Flynn, *God's Gold* (1931). Bibliographies in Chapters XXXIII and XXXIX will supplement this list for later periods.

THE TARIFF ISSUE. Consult P. Ashley, *Modern Tariff History* (3rd ed., 1920); Edward Stanwood, *American Tariff Controversies in the Nineteenth Century* (1903); F. W. Taussig, *Some Aspects of the Tariff Question* (1915) and *Tariff History of the United States* (8th ed., 1931). Also examine R. McElroy, *Grover Cleveland;* Allan Nevins, *Grover Cleveland;* J. A. Barnes, *John J. Carlisle;* and C. S. Olcott, *William McKinley* (2 vols., 1906).

THE GATHERING OF THE FORCES. The economic background is examined and the political story told in S. J. Buck, *Agrarian Crusade* (1921), Chronicles of America; J. D. Hicks, *The Populist Revolt* (1931); Nathan Fine, *Labor and Farmer Parties in the United States* (1928); F. E. Haynes, *Third Party Movements Since the Civil War* (1916), *Social Politics in the United States* (1924) and *James Baird Weaver* (1919). More specialized are A. M. Arnett, *Populist Movement in Georgia* (1922); F. B. Simkins, *Tillman Movement in South Carolina* (1926); B. B. Kendrick, "Agrarian Discontent in the South, 1880–1890," *Am. Hist. Assoc. Rep.* (1920); Hallie Farmer, "Economic Background of Frontier Populism," *Miss. Valley Hist. Rev.* (March, 1924); and C. R. Miller, "Background of Populism in Kansas," *Ibid.* (March, 1925). For labor see histories of labor and D. L. McMurry, *Coxey's Army* (1929). On the financial situation: W. J. Lauck, *The Causes of the Panic of 1893* (1907) and F. P. Weberg, *The Background of the Panic of 1893* (1929).

THE CRITICAL ELECTION. Rhodes, Peck and other historians cover the election of 1896 but further information is to be found in the biographies: Thomas Beer, *Hanna* (1929); Herbert Croly, *Marcus Alonzo Hanna* (1912), an excellent biography; Paxton Hibben, *The Peerless Leader: William Jennings Bryan* (1929); and M. R. Werner, *Bryan* (1929), the last two mildly satirical. J. C. Long, *Bryan, The Great Commoner* (1928) is more appreciative, while W. J. Bryan, *The First Battle* (1896) is the great leader's own account of the campaign. C. S. Olcott, *William McKinley* (2 vols., 1916) has value but is exceedingly uncritical. C. V. Woodward, *Tom Watson, Agrarian Rebel* (1938) is essential for a study of Southern Populism. An important article is Harvey Wish, "John Peter Altgeld and the Background of the Campaign of 1896," *Miss. Valley Hist. Rev., XXIV*, 503–518 (March, 1938).

XXX. PRELIMINARIES TO IMPERIALISM

FOREIGN AFFAIRS FROM JOHNSON TO CLEVELAND. This period is covered in R. G. Adams, *History of the Foreign Policy of the United States* (1924); W. F. Johnson, *American Foreign Relations* (2 vols., 1916); J. H. Latané, *History of American Foreign Policy* (rev. ed., 1934); L. M. Sears, *History of American Foreign Relations* (1927); S. F. Bemis, *A Diplomatic History of the United States* (1936); and T. A. Bailey, *A Diplomatic History of the American People* (1940).

CLEARING UP THE CIVIL WAR LIABILITIES. Besides the general histories of foreign relations just cited the following deal more specifically with this topic: W. A. Dunning, *The British Empire and the United States* (1914); R. W. Mowat, *Diplomatic Relations of Great Britain and the United States* (1925); and Allan Nevins, *Hamilton Fish* (1936). Consult also L. B. Shippee, *Canadian American Relations, 1849–1874*

(1939) and Brainard Dyer, *The Public Career of William M. Evarts* (1933).

ALASKA. J. M. Callahan, *Alaska Purchase and American-Canadian Relations* (1908) is a careful examination, and Jeannette P. Nichols, *Alaska* (1924) gives a well-rounded story. V. J. Farrar, *The Annexation of Russian America to the United States* (1937) adds new material.

THE UNITED STATES IN THE PACIFIC AREA. For the earlier period the following are the most important: J. M. Callahan, *American Relations in the Pacific and in the Far East, 1784–1900* (1901); Tyler Dennett, *Americans in Eastern Asia* (1922); John W. Foster, *American Diplomacy in the Orient* (1903); T. F. Millard, *America and the Far Eastern Question* (1909); P. J. Treat, *Japan and the United States, 1853–1921* (2nd ed., 1928) and *The Diplomatic Relations Between the United States and Japan, 1866–1895* (1932).

HAWAII. C. H. Burroughs, *Annexation of Hawaii* (1912); J. E. Carpenter, *America in Hawaii* (1899); Tyler Dennett, *Americans in Eastern Asia;* G. F. Hoar, *Autobiography;* and R. F. Pettigrew, *Course of Empire* (1920), the last two giving the reactions of anti-imperialist senators. More recent treatments are J. W. Pratt, *Expansionists of 1898* (1936) and R. S. Kuykendall, *The Hawaiian Kingdom, 1778–1854* (1938).

SAMOA. Besides the general books, R. L. Stevenson, *A Footnote to History: Eight Years of Trouble in Samoa* (1891) is interesting. Also J. W. Foster, *op. cit.* and G. H. Ryden, *The Foreign Policy of the United States in Relation to Samoa* (1933).

LATIN AMERICA—THE VENEZUELA BOUNDARY. Standard books include J. H. Latané, *United States and Latin America* (1920); W. S. Robertson, *Hispanic American Relations with the United States* (1923); G. H. Stuart, *Latin America and the United States* (rev. ed., 1928); and J. F. Rippy, *Latin America in World Politics* (rev. ed., 1931). On the part played by American leaders: Alice F. Tyler, *The Foreign Policy of James G. Blaine* (1927); Allan Nevins, *Grover Cleveland;* Henry James, *Richard Olney and His Public Service* (1923). For Cleveland's own account see Grover Cleveland, *Presidential Problems* (1904). See C. C. Tansill, *The United States and Santo Domingo, 1798–1873* (1938) for the most complete and accurate account.

XXXI. ECONOMIC IMPERIALISM

THE ADVENT OF THE NEW IMPERIALISM. On the beginnings of American imperialism some material is available in P. T. Moon, *Imperialism and World Politics* (1926); Scott Nearing and Joseph Freeman, *Dollar Diplomacy* (1925); R. W. Dunn, *American Foreign Investments* (1926); B. H. Williams, *Economic Foreign Policy of the United States* (1929) and *American Diplomacy* (1936); and L. H. Jenks, *Our Cuban Colony* (1929); Chaps. I–II. Essential is Albert K. Weinberg, *Manifest Destiny: A Study of Nationalist Expansion in American History* (1935). Dexter Perkins, *The Monroe Doctrine, 1867–1907* (1938) should not be neglected.

PRELIMINARIES TO WAR. F. E. Chadwick, *Relations of the United States and Spain* (3 vols., 1909–1911) is exhaustive but J. F. Rhodes, *The McKinley and Roosevelt Administrations* (1922) contains an excellent brief résumé of the diplomatic history. Walter Millis, *The Martial Spirit: A Study of Our War with Spain* (1931) covers this aspect as does Jenks, *op. cit.* An illuminating résumé of American foreign policy is in J. B. Moore, *Four Phases of American Development, Federalism-Democracy-Imperialism-Expansion* (1912). See also H. E. Flack, *Spanish-American Diplomatic Relations Preceding the War of 1898,* Johns Hopkins Studies, XXIV (1906) and E. J. Benton, *International Law and Diplomacy of the Spanish American War* (1908).

The career of Root, who became Secretary of War in 1899, is told in distinguished fashion by P. C. Jessup, *Elihu Root* (2 vols., 1938).

WAR WITH SPAIN. Walter Millis, *The Martial Spirit* is the best one-volume account. For the work of the navy see George Dewey, *Autobiography* (1913); J. D. Long, *New American Navy* (1913), by the Secretary of the Navy; and A. T. Mahan, *Lessons of the War with Spain* (1899). For the army: Nelson A. Miles, *Serving the Republic* (1911); R. A. Alger, *Spanish-American War* (1901), by the Secretary of War; and Theodore Roosevelt, *Rough Riders* (1899). Also on foreign relations consult R. A. Reuter, *Anglo-American Relations During the Spanish-American War* (1924) and L. B. Shippee, "Germany and the Spanish-American War," *Am. Hist. Rev.*, XX, 754-777 (July, 1925).

CUBA. Leland H. Jenks, *Our Cuban Colony: A Study in Sugar* (1928) is the best single volume as far as it carries the story. Carleton Beals, *The Crime of Cuba* (1933), highly colored but accurate, carries the story to the eve of the 1933 revolution. Harry F. Guggenheim, *The United States and Cuba* (1934) is a defense of the American domination by the ambassador of the United States during a part of the Machado regime. The most valuable in recent years is Foreign Policy Association, *Problems of the New Cuba* (1935). D. A. Lockmiller, *Magoon in Cuba: A History of the Second Intervention, 1906-1909* (1938) defends the Magoon administration.

PUERTO RICO. B. W. and J. W. Diffie, *Porto Rico: A Broken Pledge* (1931) is extremely critical of American occupation. Victor S. Clark and others, *Porto Rico and Its Problems* (1930) is a scientific and intelligent survey.

THE PHILIPPINES. Among the excellent books on the Philippines are D. C. Worcester, *The Philippines Past and Present* (2 vols., 1914); C. B. Elliott, *The Philippines* (2 vols., 1917); F. B. Harrison, *The Corner-stone of Philippine Independence* (1922), by an anti-imperialistic governor-general; and J. S. Reyes, *Legislative History of America's Economic Policy Toward the Philippines* (1923).

XXXII. EXPANDING IMPERIALISM

VENEZUELA AND THE DRAGO DOCTRINE. H. C. Hill, *Roosevelt and the Caribbean* (1927) has the best discussion of the Venezuelan incident. On the Drago Doctrine see article "Calvo and Drago Doctrines," *Encyclopaedia of the Social Sciences*.

PANAMA. On Panama see Nearing and Freeman, *Dollar Diplomacy* (1925); Philippe Bunau-Varilla, *Panama, Its Creation, Destruction and Resurrection* (1913) by the archconspirator of the affair; J. B. Bishop, *The Panama Gateway* (1913); E. R. Johnson, *The Panama Canal and Commerce* (1916); M. W. Williams, *Anglo-American Isthmian Diplomacy, 1815-1915* (1916); J. F. Rippy, *The Capitalists and Colombia* (1931); and D. C. Miner, *The Fight for the Panama Route* (1940). In W. L. McCain, *The United States and the Republic of Panama* (1937) is a full story of our relations with that country.

SANTO DOMINGO. Brief accounts are in Nearing and Freeman, *op. cit.* and in Dana G. Munro, *The United States in the Caribbean Area* (1934). The best single volume is M. M. Knight, *The Americans in Santo Domingo* (1928). See also U. S. Senate Select Committee, *Inquiry into Occupation and Administration of Haiti and Santo Domingo* (67 Cong., 1922) and Carl Kelsey, "American Intervention in Haiti and Santo Domingo," *Am. Acad. Polit. and Social Science, Annals,* C, 109-202.

HAITI AND NICARAGUA. In addition to the books just cited under Santo Domingo see Carleton Beals, *Banana Gold* (1932); C. D. Kepner and J. H. Southill, *The Banana Empire* (1935) and C. D. Kepner, *Social Aspects of the Banana Industry*

(1936), Columbia University Studies, No. 414, both scholarly investigations; A. C. Millspaugh, *Haiti Under American Control, 1915–1930*, World Peace Foundation (1931); "American Occupation of Haiti," *Foreign Policy Reports*, V, Nos. 19–20 (1929); "Caribbean Situation: Cuba and Haiti," *Foreign Policy Reports*, IX, No. 8 (1933); and "Caribbean Situation: Nicaragua and Salvador," *Foreign Policy Reports*, IX, No. 13 (1933).

MEXICO. To understand the relations between the United States and Mexico it is necessary to comprehend the Mexican scene. Two books showing a real understanding of Mexican civilization and tradition are Carleton Beals, *Mexican Maze* (1931) and Ernest Gruening, *Mexico and Its Heritage* (1928). American relations with Mexico are adequately handled in C. W. Hackett, *Mexican Revolution and the United States, 1910–1926* (1926) and J. F. Rippy, *The United States and Mexico* (rev. ed., 1931).

THE FAR EAST. Tyler Dennett, *Americans in Eastern Asia* (1922) covers the history to 1901 and should be supplemented with M. J. Bau, *The Open Door Doctrine with Relation to China* (1923) and Tyler Dennett, *John Hay* (1933). P. J. Treat, *Japan and the United States, 1853–1921* (2nd ed., 1928) is an authoritative study. More detailed is his *Diplomatic Relations between the United States and Japan, 1865–1905* (1938). See also the excellent volume by A. W. Griswold, *The Far Eastern Policy of the United States* (1938). On dollar diplomacy in the Far East see H. K. Norton, *China and the Powers* (1927); J. W. Overlach, *Foreign Financial Control in China* (1919); and H. D. Croly, *Willard Straight* (1924), a biography of the agent of the Morgan bankers in China.

XXXIII. THE AGE OF BIG BUSINESS

POLITICS. J. F. Rhodes, *The McKinley and Roosevelt Administrations* (1912) is interesting, but fails to evaluate underlying economic forces and is not up to his earlier work. In Mark Sullivan, *Our Times*, Vols. II and III many aspects of social history are developed as well as political history. On Roosevelt the student should read his *Autobiography* (1913) and Henry F. Pringle, *Theodore Roosevelt* (1931), the best balanced biography. J. B. Bishop, *Theodore Roosevelt and His Times* (2 vols., 1920) is an authorized biography and W. R. Thayer, *Theodore Roosevelt: An Intimate Biography* (1919) is written by a friend and admirer. Also valuable for the period is *La Follette's Autobiography* (1913); Champ Clark, *My Quarter Century of American Politics* (1920); N. W. Stephenson, *Nelson W. Aldrich: A Leader in American Politics* (1930); and H. S. Duffy, *William Howard Taft* (1930). H. F. Pringle, *The Life and Times of William Howard Taft* (2 vols., 1939) is a definitive biography.

INDUSTRIAL COMBINATIONS. In addition to the standard works listed under Chapter XXIX the student is referred to H. R. Mussey, *Combination in the Mining Industry* (1905); Abraham Berglund, *The United States Steel Corporation*, Columbia University Studies (1907); H. L. Wilgus, *Story of the United States Steel Corporation* (1901); *Report of the Commissioner of Corporations on the Steel Industry* (1911); and Scott Nearing, *Anthracite: An Instance of Natural Resource Monopoly* (1915). See also W. H. Taft, *The Anti-Trust Act and the Supreme Court* (1914) and D. M. Keezer and Stacy May, *The Public Control of Business* (1930).

THE REVOLUTION IN TRANSPORTATION. In addition to the books listed under Chapter XXIV the following are valuable on railroads: Slason Thompson, *History of American Railroads* (1925); W. Z. Ripley, *Railroads, Rates and Regulations* (1912) and *Railroads; Finance and Organization* (1915); and C. R. Fish, *The Restoration of the Southern Railroads* (1919), U. of Wisconsin Studies. On waterways A. F. Harlow, *Old Towpaths* (1926) is a fascinating story of the rise and decline of canal transportation. A standard economic study is H. G. Moulton, *Waterways vs. Railways* (1912). In a recent scholarly study Mildred H. Hartsough, *From Canoe to Steel Barge on the Upper Mississippi* (1934) traces the transportation changes on the Mississippi. On automobiles see R. C. Epstein, *The Automobile Industry* (1928) and H. L. Barber, *The Story of the Automobile* (1927). On airplanes E. Hodgins and F. A. Magoun, *Sky High* (1929) and *A History of Aircraft* (1931) tell the general story while P. T. David, *The Economics of Air Mail Transportation* (1934) is an excellent specialized study.

CONSOLIDATION OF CAPITAL. On the so-called money trust the best source is *Report of the Committee Pursuant to House Resolutions 429 and 504 to Investigate the Concentration of the Control of Money and Credit* (1913), known as the Report of the Pujo Committee. Helpful are John Moody, *Masters of Capital* (1919); L. P. Brandeis, *Other People's Money* (1914); F. L. Allen, *The Lords of Creation* (1935); and Lewis Corey, *House of Morgan* (1930). On the more recent period, Harry Laidler, *Concentration of Control in American Industry* (1931) and A. A. Berle, Jr., and G. C. Means, *The Modern Corporation and Private Property* (1932).

CONSOLIDATION OF LABOR. Of the many books the following are suggested: J. R. Commons *et al.*, *History of Labour in the United States* (1918); Selig Perlman and Philip Taft, *History of Labor in the United States, 1896–1932, Labor Movements* (1935); Don D. Lescohier and Elizabeth Brandeis, *History of Labor in the United States, 1896–1932, Working Conditions, Labor Legislation* (1935); N. J. Ware, *The Labor Movement in the United States* (1929), chiefly about the Knights of Labor; Leo Wolman, *Growth of American Trade Unions 1880–1923* (1924); L. L. Lorwin, *The American Federation of·Labor* (1933); C. H. Wesley, *Negro Labor in the United States* (1927); Samuel Gompers, *Seventy Years of Life and Labor* (2 vols., 1925); P. F. Brisenden, *The I. W. W., A Study of American Syndicalism* (1919) and J. S. Gambs, *The Decline of the I. W. W.* (1932), both in the Columbia University Studies.

XXXIV. THE ERA OF REFORM

AMERICA AT THE TURN OF THE CENTURY. The topics in this chapter are covered in greater detail in H. U. Faulkner, *The Quest for Social Justice* (1931), History of American Life Series, which contains extensive bibliographies. On various aspects of American social history about 1900 see E. G. Murphy, *The Problem of the Present South* (1904); R. S. Baker, *Following the Color Line* (1908); R. L. Garis, *Immigration Restriction* (1927); C. B. Spahr, *The Present Distribution of Wealth in the United States* (1896); J. A. Ryan, *A Living Wage* (1906); Robert Hunter, *Poverty* (1904); P. H. Douglas, *Real Wages in the United States, 1890–1926* (1930); and J. A. Riis, *A Ten Years' War* (1900).

THE MUCKRAKERS. On this topic C. E. Regier, *The Era of the Muckrakers* (1932) is an excellent introduction to the subject. Louis Filler, *Crusaders for American Liberalism* (1939) is a more complete picture of the reform movement as it functioned in the literature of exposure. See also John Chamberlain, *Farewell to Reform* (1932) and B. P. DeWitt, *Progressive Democracy* (1915). Two famous muckrakers tell of their experiences: Charles Edward Russell, *Bare Hands and Stone Walls* (1933) and Lincoln Steffens, *Autobiography of Lincoln Steffens* (2 vols., 1931). Valuable on social reform are two other autobiographies: F. C. Howe, *Confessions of a Reformer* (1925) and Morris Hillquit, *Loose Leaves from a Busy Life* (1934).

THE QUEST FOR SOCIAL JUSTICE. Jessie Taft, *The Woman Movement from the Point of View of Social Consciousness* (1915); Mary I. Wood, *The History of the General Federation of Women's Clubs* (1912); Thomas Woody, *A History of Woman's Education in the United States* (2 vols., 1929); A. E. Hacker, *A Short History of Woman's Rights* (2nd ed., 1914); Alice Henry, *The Trade Union Woman* (1915); Rheta C. Dorr, *What Eight Million Women Want* (1910); Edith Abbott, *Women in Industry* (1910); and J. R. Commons and J. B. Andrews, *Principles of Labor Legislation* (1920). In G. B. Mangold, *Problems of Child Welfare* (1914) most aspects of this topic are discussed. A specialized study is L. H. Gulick and L. P. Ayres, *Medical Inspection of Schools* (1913). On education: E. P. Cubberley, *Public Education in the United States* (1919) and I. L. Kandel, ed., *Twenty-Five Years of American Education* (1924). Critical of American colleges are Thorstein Veblen, *The Higher Learning in America* (1918) and Upton Sinclair, *The Goose Step* (1923).

CULTURAL PATTERNS. On religion: H. K. Rowe, *The History of Religion in the United States* (1924); C. S. McFarland, *The Progress of Church Federation* (1917); G. B. Smith, ed., *Religious Thought in the Last Quarter Century* (1927); Walter Rauschenbusch, *Christianity and the Social Crisis* (1907); and H. U. Faulkner, "American Christianity and the World of Everyday" in *Essays in Intellectual History,* dedicated to J. H. Robinson (1929), Chap. VIII. For newspapers consult W. G. Bleyer, *Main Currents in the History of American Journalism* (1927) and J. M. Lee, *History of American Journalism* (1917). On literature see *The Cambridge History of American Literature* (4 vols., 1917-1921); F. L. Pattee, *The New American Literature* (1930); Carl and Mark Van Doren, *American and British Literature Since 1900* (1925); and Louis Untermeyer, *American Poetry Since 1900* (1923). On art: Samuel Isham, *The History of American Painting* (new ed. by Royal Cortissoz in 1936); Frank Weitenkampf, *American Graphic Art* (1912); and Lorado Taft, *History of American Sculpture* (rev. ed., 1924).

XXXV. THE NEW DEMOCRACY

POLITICAL REFORM. While no full-length picture of these years has yet been drawn, the story of political reform may be pieced together from numerous volumes including the following: H. U. Faulkner, *Quest for Social Justice* (1931); B. P. DeWitt, *The Progressive Movement* (1915); F. E. Haynes, *Social Politics in the United States* (1924); W. B. Munro, *The Initiative, Referendum and Recall* (1912); J. D. Barnett, *The Operation of the Initiative, Referendum and Recall in Oregon* (1915); C. A. Beard and B. E. Shultz, *Documents on the Initiative, Referendum and Recall* (1912); F. C. Howe, *Wisconsin, An Experiment in Democracy* (1912); C. A. Beard, *American Government and Politics* (rev. ed., 1931); Tso-Shuen Chang, *History and Analysis of the Commission and City-Manager Plans of Municipal Government in the United States* (1918); and C. D. Thompson, *Public Ownership* (1925), the most complete summary. On woman suffrage the most usable volume is Carrie C. Catt and Nettie R. Shuler, *Woman Suffrage and Politics* (1926) and the most complete is Elizabeth C. Stanton, Matilda J. Gage and Ida H. Harper, eds., *The History of Woman Suffrage* (6 vols., 1881-1922). See also Ida H. Harper, *Life of Susan B. Anthony* (3 vols., 1908). On the philosophy of the movement: C. E. Merriam, *American Political Ideas, 1867-*

1917 (1920); Herbert Croly, *The Promise of American Life* (1909); W. E. Weyl, *The New Democracy* (1912); and Walter Lippman, *Preface to Politics* (1914) and *Drift and Mastery* (1914). Among the important biographies are Fremont Older, *My Own Story* (1919); Brand Whitlock, *Forty Years of It* (1913); Tom Johnson, *My Story* (1911); R. M. La Follette, *La Follette's Autobiography* (1913); F. C. Howe, *Confessions of a Reformer* (1925); Lincoln Steffens, *Autobiography of Lincoln Steffens* (2 vols., 1931); C. E. Russell, *Bare Hands and Stone Walls* (1933); and Morris Hill-quit, *Loose Leaves from a Busy Life* (1934).

LEFT-WING POLITICS. Nathan Fine, *Labor and Farmer Parties in the United States* (1928); F. E. Haynes, *Social Politics in the United States* (1924); Morris Hillquit, *History of Socialism in the United States* (5th ed., 1910) and his *Loose Leaves from a Busy Life* (1934); and Harry W. Laidler, *A History of Socialist Thought* (1927).

NATIONAL POLITICS—THE TAFT ADMINISTRATION. See bibliography under "Politics" in Chapter XXXIII and that under "Political Reform" and "Left-Wing Politics" in this chapter. The best single account is H. F. Pringle, *The Life and Times of William Howard Taft* (2 vols., 1939).

THE RETURN OF THE DEMOCRATS. The literature on Woodrow Wilson is already large. The biography of R. S. Baker, *Life and Letters of Woodrow Wilson,* of which six volumes had appeared by 1937, is the authorized life; it is by far the most detailed and is quite objective, particularly in the later volumes. Among others are W. E. Dodd, *Woodrow Wilson and His Work* (1921), a favorable picture by a recognized historian; J. Kerney, *The Political Education of Woodrow Wilson* (1926), particularly good on Wilson's connection with New Jersey politics; William Allen White, *Woodrow Wilson: the Man, His Times and His Task* (1924), an effort at a psychological interpretation; and J. P. Tumulty, *Woodrow Wilson as I Knew Him* (1925), by his private secretary. On the election of 1912: W. J. Bryan, *A Tale of Two Conventions* (1912); C. Clark, *My Quarter Century of American Politics* (1920); W. F. McCombs, *Making Woodrow Wilson President* (1921); B. P. DeWitt, *Progressive Movement* (1915); and Donald Richberg, *Tents of the Mighty* (1930).

THE NEW FREEDOM. In addition to the works on Wilson cited above read Woodrow Wilson, *The New Freedom* (1913), campaign speeches giving his own philosophy; H. H. Kohlsaat, *From McKinley to Harding* (1923); D. F. Houston, *Eight Years with Wilson's Cabinet* (1926). On the tariff see bibliography under "The Tariff Issue," Chapter XXIX. On the antitrust legislation see bibliography under "Consolidation of Business," Chapter XXIX; Edward Berman, *Labor and the Sherman Act* (1930); and G. C. Henderson, *The Federal Trade Commission* (1924). There are now exhaustive works on the Federal Reserve System: E. W. Kemmerer, *The A B C of the Federal Reserve System* (1916); H. Parker Willis, *The Federal Reserve System* (1923); P. M. Warburg, *The Federal Reserve System* (2 vols., 1930), complete history and criticism; S. E. Harris, *Twenty Years of the Federal Reserve Policy* (2 vols., 1933), exhaustive; and J. L. Laughlin, *The Federal Reserve Act, Its Origins and Problems* (1933), best on the history of the act.

XXXVI. THE WORLD WAR

THE WAR COMES TO EUROPE. One of the ablest interpretations of the development of modern Europe is Harry Elmer Barnes, *World Politics and Modern Civilization* (1930). His *Genesis of the World War* (rev. ed., 1929) is the most brilliant and convincing statement of the revisionist point of view. In S. B. Fay, *Origins of the*

World War (rev. ed., 2 vols., 1930) the student will find a meticulous examination of the prewar diplomacy; B. E. Schmitt, *Coming of the War* (2 vols., 1930) develops the conventional interpretation.

WHY WE FOUGHT. There is much research yet to be done on this topic, but the following will open up the subject: H. E. Barnes, *Genesis of the World War,* Chap. IX; C. Hartley Grattan, *Why We Fought* (1929); H. D. Lasswell, *Propaganda Technique in the World War* (1927); J. D. Squires, *British Propaganda at Home and in the United States 1914–1917* (1935); Walter Millis, *The Road to War* (1935); and C. C. Tansill, *America Goes to War* (1936). See also that part of R. S. Baker, *Life and Letters of Woodrow Wilson* bearing on this subject. In T. A. Bailey, "The Sinking of the Lusitania," *Am. Hist. Rev.,* XLI, 54–73 (1935) there is the most recent research on this subject. Also consult the diplomatic histories of Bailey and Bemis for the results of recent scholarship. A conventional interpretation is in Newton D. Baker, "Why We Went to War," *Foreign Affairs,* XV, No. 1, 1–86 (Oct., 1936). A valuable discussion of the first Wilson administration is in F. L. Paxson, *Pre-War Years 1913–1917* (1936). See also his *America at War, 1917–1918* (1939). An important study is Harley Notter, *The Origin of the Foreign Policy of Woodrow Wilson* (1937).

THE PROBLEM OF NEUTRALITY RIGHTS. In addition to the books already cited see J. B. Scott, *A Survey of International Relations Between the United States and Germany, August 1, 1914–April 6, 1917* (1917); Charles Seymour, ed., *Intimate Papers of Colonel House* (4 vols., 1926–1928); B. J. Hendrick, *Life and Letters of W. H. Page* (3 vols., 1922–1925); W. J. Bryan, *Memoirs* (1925); M. E. Curti, *Bryan and World Peace* (1931), Smith College Studies in History; M. E. Curti, *Peace or War* (1936); J. von Bernstorff, *My Three Years in America* (1920) and *Memoirs* (1936); J. Kenworthy and G. Young, *Freedom of the Seas* (1928); and Alice M. Morrissey, *The American Defense of Neutral Rights* (1939).

"HE KEPT US OUT OF WAR." For this see the books on Wilson cited in the last two sections of Chapter XXXV and those already cited in this chapter.

MOBILIZING RESOURCES. The following are reasonably complete: B. Crowell and R. F. Wilson, *How America Went to War* (6 vols., 1921); W. F. Willoughby, *Government Organization in War Time and After* (1919); G. B. Clarkson, *Industrial America in the World War* (1923); E. L. Bogart, *War Costs and Their Financing* (1921); C. R. Van Hise, *Conservation and Regulation in the United States During the World War* (1927); and George Creel, *How We Advertised America* (1920). In Preston Slosson, *The Great Crusade and After: 1914–1928* (1930) there is a discussion of the life of the people during war time. See also Mark Sullivan, *Our Times,* Vol. V. Zechariah Chafee, Jr., *Freedom of Speech* (1921) tells what happened to civil liberties during the war. Also see J. R. Mock and Cedric Larson, *Words That Won the War: The Story of the Committee on Public Information, 1917–1919* (1939).

THE GREAT CRUSADE. On the military campaigns see J. J. Pershing, *Final Report to the Secretary of War* (1919) and his *My Experiences in the World War* (2 vols., 1931); U. S. War Dept., *War with Germany: A Statistical Summary* (1919) written by L. P. Ayres; also R. J. Beamish and F. A. March, *America's Part in the World War* (1919); Frederick Palmer, *America in France* (1919) and his *Newton D. Baker* (2 vols., 1931); W. S. Sims and B. J. Hendrick, *The Victory at Sea* (1920); and W. S. Graves, *America's Siberian Adventure, 1918–1920* (1931). A serviceable summary is C. J. H. Hayes, *Brief History of the Great War* (1928).

THE PEACEMAKERS. R. S. Baker, *Woodrow Wilson and World Settlement* (3 vols., 1922); Robert Lansing, *Peace Negotiations: A Personal Narrative* (1921);

E. M. House and C. Seymour, *What Really Happened at Paris* (1921); Allan Nevins, *Henry White: Thirty Years of American Diplomacy* (1930). See also B. M. Baruch, *The Making of the Reparation and Economic Sections of the Treaty* (1920); D. F. Fleming, *The United States and the League of Nations, 1918–1920* (1932) and his *The United States and World Organization 1920–1933* (1938). For a brilliant British interpretation: J. M. Keynes, *Economic Consequences of the Peace* (1920). In H. C. Lodge, *The Senate and the League of Nations* (1925) is a defense of the Senate's repudiation of the treaty.

XXXVII. POLITICS AND DIPLOMACY

THE RETURN TO NORMALCY. As the student approaches the present it becomes increasingly difficult to find well-balanced history. He must in part construct his own history from the facts contained in such summaries as the *New International Year Book* (1908–   ); the *Americana Annual* (1923–   ); the *American Year Book* (1910–1919; 1925–   ); and the *American Labor Year-Book* (1916–   ). See also current periodicals, particularly *Current History, Foreign Affairs, Time, Nation* and *New Republic*. No better synthesis can be found than in the later chapters of C. and M. Beard, *Rise of American Civilization* (new ed., 1933) and *America in Midpassage* (1939). Excellent also are D. L. Dumond, *From Roosevelt to Roosevelt* (1937) and Louis M. Hacker, *American Problems of Today* (1938). The political and legislative history of the twenties is summarized in J. C. Malin, *The United States After the World War* (1930). In Mark Sullivan, *Our Times: The United States, 1900–1925,* Vol. VI, *The Twenties* (1935) and in S. H. Adams, *Incredible Era* (1939) are the most complete discussions of the campaign of 1920. The last-named book leaves much to be desired but is the best life of Harding which has appeared.

THE COOLIDGE ERA. Besides the historians cited above the student should read William Allen White, *A Puritan in Babylon* (1939), an interpretative study of the decade, and Claude M. Fuess, *Calvin Coolidge, the Man from Vermont* (1940), less objective than the White book but more informative. Harvey O'Connor, *Mellon's Millions* is a caustic appraisal. For Hoover and his administration see Will Irwin, *Herbert Hoover, A Reminiscent Biography* (1928); W. S. Meyers and W. H. Newton, *The Hoover Administration* (1936); R. L. Wilbur and A. H. Hyde, *The Hoover Policies* (1937); H. F. Pringle, *Alfred E. Smith: A Critical Study* (1927); A. E. Smith, *Up to Now* (1929), an autobiography; Anonymous, *Washington Merry-Go-Round* (1931); Arthur Capper, *The Agricultural Bloc* (1922); and C. E. Russell, *Story of the Non-Partisan League* (1920). R. V. Peel and T. C. Donnelly, *The Campaign of 1928* (1931) is an adequate analysis, while Nathan Fine, *Labor and Farmer Parties in the United States 1828–1928* (1928) covers most of the third parties. On political corruption, federal and municipal, see M. E. Ravage, *The Story of Teapot Dome* (1924); M. R. Werner, *Privileged Characters* (1935); W. B. and J. B. Northrop, *The Insolence of Office* (1932); Norman Thomas and Paul Blanshard, *What's the Matter with New York* (1932); Lloyd Lewis and H. J. Smith, *Chicago: The History of Its Reputation* (1929); and C. E. Merriam, *Chicago* (1929).

CROSS CURRENTS IN DIPLOMACY—RETREAT FROM IMPERIALISM. On most phases of international relations since 1920 the reports and special studies of the World Peace Foundation and the Foreign Policy Association are invaluable. Also follow the magazine *Foreign Affairs*. General interpretations are R. L. Buell, *International Relations* (rev. ed., 1931) and Quincy Wright, ed., *Interpretations of American Foreign Policy* (1930). On the League, J. S. Bassett, *The League of Nations* (1928) is excellent up to that year. On the Washington Conference: R. L. Buell, *The Washington Conference* (1922) and Yamato Ichihashi, *Washington Conference and After* (1928). On the Briand-Kellogg pact, D. H. Miller, *Peace Pact of Paris* (1928). See also M. E. Curti, *Peace or War* (1936), an excellent history of the peace movement in the United States. On war debts see C. Bergman, *History of Reparations* (1927) and the Foreign Policy Association Reports; on America's attitude toward the League, D. F. Fleming, *The United States and World Organization 1920–1933* (1938).

XXXVIII. LIFE IN THE POSTWAR DECADE

PROSPERITY AND REACTION. The most detailed survey of American social conditions during the twenties is the report of the President's Reseach Committee on Social Trends, *Recent Social Trends* (2 vols., 1933). An able integration of postwar social history is P. W. Slosson, *The Great Crusade and After: 1914–1928* (1930), Vol. XII in A History of American Life Series. The later volumes of Mark Sullivan, *Our Times* (6 vols., 1926–1935) deal with the social life of the period, as does the sprightly volume of Frederick L. Allen, *Only Yesterday* (1931). In Robert S. Lynd and Helen M. Lynd, *Middletown* (1929) will be found a careful and brilliant study of contemporary American culture as exhibited in a typical small midwestern city (Muncie, Indiana). A background for the social life of this period is H. U. Faulkner, *The Quest for Social Justice* (1931). All of these books deal with the influence of the automobile, the changing status of women and other tendencies suggested in this chapter. On the standard of living consult Paul Douglas, *Real Wages in the United States 1890–1926* (1930), and the chapters in *Recent Economic Changes* (1929) by Leo Wolman, "Consumption and the Standards of Living" Vol. I, pp. 13–78 and by Morris A. Copeland, "The National Income and Its Distribution" Vol. II, pp. 757–839. On the spiritual and intellectual reaction the following are helpful: Zechariah Chafee, Jr., *Freedom of Speech* (1920); J. M. Mecklin, *The Ku Klux Klan; a Study of the American Mind* (1924); E. S. Bates, *This Land of Liberty* (1930); Walter Lippmann, *American Inquisitors* (1928); Bessie L. Pierce, *Public Opinion and the Teaching of History in the United States* (1926); and A. G. Hays, *Let Freedom Ring* (1928), a story of the activities of the American Civil Liberties Union. The publications of the American Civil Liberties Union provide excellent material for a study of this subject. On the Sacco-Vanzetti case Jeannette Marks, *Thirteen Days* (1929) tells of the last-minute efforts to stay the execution; Felix Frankfurter, *The Case of Sacco and Vanzetti* (1927) is a legal analysis by a competent student. O. K. Fraenkel, *The Sacco-Vanzetti Case* (1931) is both a history and a source book.

RESURGENT NATIONALISM. Many phases of the reactionary aspect of this development may be traced in the books just cited in the previous topic. On the recent developments in American historical scholarship the volume by H. E. Barnes, *The New History and the Social Studies* (1925) is the most thorough study. It is more briefly done in H. E. Barnes, ed., *The History and Prospects of the Social Sciences* (1925). Of the many books on immigration the following are suggested: J. R. Commons, *Races and Immigrants in America* (1907); J. W. Jenks and W. J. Lauck, *The Immigration Problem* (1917); G. M. Stephenson, *History of American Immigration, 1820–1924* (1926); and R. L. Garis, *Immigration Restriction* (1927).

THE PROHIBITION EXPERIMENT. Brief accounts are in Faulkner and Slosson and more detailed studies in E. H. Cherrington, *Evolution of Prohibition in the United States* (1920), by a leader of the drys; Peter Odegard, *Pressure Politics, the Story of the Anti-*

Saloon League (1928), a scholarly study; Charles Merz, *The Dry Decade* (1931), a popular picture; and the famous report of the Wickersham Committee, *Report on the Enforcement of the Prohibition Laws of the United States* [71st Congress, 3rd session, House Doc. 722 (1931)].

CULTURE IN THE JAZZ AGE. See bibliography under "Cultural Patterns" in Chapter XXXIV; also Slosson, *The Great Crusade and After* and his bibliographies. Important interpretations of American civilization include E. H. Gruening, ed., *These United States* (2 vols., 1923–24); H. E. Stearns, ed., *Civilization in the United States: An Inquiry by Thirty Americans* (1922); and J. T. Adams, *Our Business Civilization* (1929). On education, see D. R. Fox, *Quarter Century of Learning* (1931) and I. L. Kandel, ed., *Twenty-Five Years of American Education* (1924).

XXXIX. CAPITALISM AT FULL TIDE

THE BOOM YEARS. Perhaps the most detailed study of the economic life of the twenties was made by the Committee on Recent Economic Changes of the President's Conference on Unemployment, *Recent Economic Changes* (2 vols., 1927). Other general studies of value are R. G. Tugwell, *Industry's Coming of Age* (1927); E. D. Durand, *American Industry and Commerce* (1930); and E. R. A. Seligman, *The Economics of Installment Selling* (2 vols., 1927), the last a study of American marketing methods. L. M. Hacker, *American Problems of Today* (1938) is a good summary, while Stuart Chase, *Prosperity, Fact or Myth* (1929) and *Men and Machines* (1929) are good interpretations.

BIG BUSINESS IN THE TWENTIES. D. M. Keezer and Stacy May, *Public Control of Business* (1930); F. A. Fetter, *The Masquerade of Monopoly* (1931); J. L. Bonbright and G. C. Means, *The Holding Company* (1932); H. W. Laidler, *Concentration in American Industry* (1931); A. A. Berle, Jr., and G. C. Means, *The Modern Corporation and Private Property* (1932); C. D. Thompson, *Confessions of the Power Trust —A Review of the Findings of the Federal Trade Commission* (1932); and H. S. Raushenbush and H. W. Laidler, *Power Control* (1929). Some of the methods of high finance are described in W. Z. Ripley, *Main Street and Wall Street* (1927).

LABOR IN RETREAT. In addition to the bibliography on income and standards of living in the last chapter, see C. A. Dougherty, *Labor Problems in American Industry* (1933); L. L. Lorwin, *The American Federation of Labor* (1933); R. W. Dunn, *The Americanization of Labor* (1927); Leo Huberman, *The Labor Spy Racket* (1937); G. James *et al., Profit Sharing and Stock Ownership for Employees* (1926); R. F. Foerster and E. H. Dietel, *Employee Stock Ownership in the United States* (1926); and Abraham Epstein, *The Problem of Old Age Pensions in Industry* (1926). Selig Perlman and Philip Taft, *History of Labor in the United States 1896–1932* (1935) is a standard discussion. Norman Thomas, *Human Exploitation in the United States* (1934) gives some indication as to why labor organizes.

RECENT TRANSPORTATION CHANGES. In addition to the volumes cited in Chapter XXXIII under the topic "The Revolution in Transportation" see the studies on recent transportation in *Recent Economic Changes* and *Recent Social Trends;* H. G. Moulton and associates, *The American Transportation Problem* (1933), invaluable; D. P. Locklen, *Railroad Regulation Since 1920* (1928); Rogers McVeagh, *The Transportation Act, 1920* (1923); H. G. Moulton, C. G. Morgan and A. L. Lee, *The St. Lawrence Navigation and Power Project* (1929), scholarly and critical; Tom Ireland, *The Great Lakes-St. Lawrence Deep Waterway to the Sea* (1934), enthusiastically favorable; National Industrial Conference Board, *The American Merchant Marine Problem* (1929); and D. H. Smith and P. V. Betters, *The United States Shipping Board* (1931).

THE DECLINE OF AGRICULTURE. The chapter by E. G. Nourse in *Recent Economic Changes* is an excellent introduction. In addition see J. D. Black, *Agricultural Reform in the United States* (1929); Wilson Gee, *Place of Agriculture in Our Life* (1930) and *American Farm Policy* (1934); E. R. A. Seligman, *The Economics of Farm Relief* (1929); and the National Industrial Conference Board, *The Agricultural Problem in the United States* (1926). The *Yearbook of the Department of Agriculture* for these years is valuable source material. Stuart Chase, *Rich Land, Poor Land* (1936) is an excellent popularization of the story of wasteful agriculture.

ECONOMIC IMPERIALISM. Detailed bibliographies are given in Chapters XXX–XXXII. Attention is again called to P. T. Moon, *Imperialism and World Politics* (1926); Scott Nearing and Joseph Freeman, *Dollar Diplomacy* (1925); R. W. Dunn, *American Foreign Investments* (1926); B. H. Williams, *Economic Foreign Policy of the United States* (1929); Max Winkler, *Investments of United States Capital in Latin America* (World Peace Foundation, 1929) and *Foreign Bonds, An Autopsy* (1933); and C. F. Remer, *Foreign Investments in China* (1933). An extremely important aspect of imperialism is discussed in Ludwell Denny, *We Fight for Oil* (1928).

ECONOMIC COLLAPSE. On the background of the economic collapse *Recent Social Trends* and *Recent Economic Changes* are again suggested as well as F. C. Mills, *Economic Tendencies in the United States* (1932). Of the recent writing on the causes of the depression probably the best are J. M. Clark, *Strategic Factors in Business Cycles* (1934) and W. C. Schluter, *Economic Cycles and Crises* (1933).

XL. ROOSEVELT AND THE NEW DEAL

MEETING THE EMERGENCY. As far as it goes, the most satisfactory summary of the Roosevelt policies is L. M. Hacker, *American Problems of Today* (1938), an interpretation. Also excellent are Charles and Mary Beard, *America in Midpassage* (1939) and C. A. Beard and G. H. E. Smith, *The Old Deal and the New Deal* (1940) and Basil Rauch, *The History of the New Deal, 1933–1938* (1944). Early descriptions include E. K. Lindley, *The Roosevelt Revolution* (1933) and J. D. Magee *et al., The National Recovery Program* (rev. ed., 1934). Sympathetic to the New Deal is B. L. Landis, *The Third American Revolution* (1933); C. A. Beard and G. H. E. Smith, *The Future Comes* (1933); and S. C. Wallace, *The New Deal in Action* (1934). Critical are William Macdonald, *The Menace of Recovery* (1934); D. V. Brown *et al., The Economics of the Recovery Program* (1933); L. P. Ayres, *The Economics of Recovery* (1933); and the Columbia University Commission, *Economic Reconstruction* (1934). Criticism from the left will be found in Norman Thomas, *The Choice Before Us* (1934) and *Human Exploitation in the United States* (1934), and in Harry Laidler, *A Program for Modern America* (1936). Appraisals by the New Dealers themselves will be found in R. G. Tugwell, *Industrial Discipline and Governmental Acts* (1933) and *The Battle for Democracy* (1935) and A. A. Berle, Jr., *et al., America's Recovery Program* (1934). An important appraisal from an ex-New Dealer is Raymond Moley, *After Seven Years* (1939). An excellent study of the economic aspects is Dale Yoder and G. R. Davies, *Depression and Recovery* (1934). For a British appraisal read Editors of the Economist, *The New Deal* (1937). For sources see F. D. Roosevelt, *The Public Papers and Addresses of Franklin D. Roosevelt* (5 vols., 1938), edited and collected by Samuel I. Rosenman.

DEALING WITH AGRICULTURE. The issue is drawn by the Secretary of Agriculture in H. A. Wallace, *America Must Choose* (1934). A sympathetic description is Wilson Gee, *American Farm Policy* (1934).

CURRENCY AND BANKING UNDER THE NEW DEAL. Numerous articles on this phase will be found in the economic journals, particularly the *American Economic Review*, which should be carefully followed. There are several excellent books: Leo Pasvolsky, *Current Monetary Issues* (1933); J. I. Bogen and M. Nadler, *The Banking Crisis* (1933); and the National Industrial Conference Board, *New Monetary System of the United States* (1934).

INDUSTRY AND THE NEW DEAL. Exhaustive on this phase is The Brookings Institution, *The National Recovery Administration* (1935), a co-operative effort of six authors. A vivid description of the career of the NRA by its first administrator is H. S. Johnson, *The Blue Eagle from Egg to Earth* (1935).

LABOR AND THE NEW DEAL. Ordway Tead and H. C. Metcalf, *Labor Relations Under the Recovery Act* (1933); C. R. Dougherty, *Labor Under the NRA* (1934); and Emanuel Stein *et al.*, *Labor and the New Deal* (1934). In Samuel Yellen, *American Labor Struggles* (1936), Chap. X is an account of the longshoremen's strike. For a background of the social security legislation see Eveline M. Burns, *Toward Social Security* (1936); Paul H. Douglas, *Social Security in the United States* (1937); and Maxwell Stewart, *Social Security* (1937).

SOCIAL, POLITICAL, AND CONSTITUTIONAL ASPECTS. Efforts at interpretation include Lewis Corey, *The Decline of American Capitalism* (1934); George Soule, *A Planned Society* (1934), *The Coming American Revolution* (1934) and *The Future of Liberty* (1936); Lewis Mumford, *Technics and Civilization* (1934); Donald R. Richberg, *The Rainbow* (1936); and Stuart Chase, *Government in Business* (1935).

FOREIGN AFFAIRS. For detail see National Industrial Conference Board, *A Picture of World Economic Conditions, 1829–1932* (7 vols., 1928–1932) and Council on Foreign Relations, *The United States in World Affairs, 1931–1933* (5 vols., 1932–1935). America's position in world affairs is graphically portrayed in J. T. Shotwell, *On the Rim of the Abyss* (1936). Roosevelt's foreign policy is summarized in T. A. Bailey, *A Diplomatic History of the American People* (1940). On Latin America see Samuel F. Bemis, *The Latin American Policy of the United States* (1943).

XLI. THE DECLINE OF REFORM

THE ELECTION OF 1936. On this and subsequent sections of this chapter *The Public Papers and Addresses of Franklin D. Roosevelt* (5 vols., 1938) are indispensable, including as they do many editorial comments of the President himself. The ablest single chapter is in Charles A. and Mary R. Beard, *America in Midpassage,* Vol. I, Chap. VII. Alfred M. Landon, *America at the Crossroads* (1936) gives the views of the Republican candidate.

THE SUPREME COURT. An excellent brief account is C. A. and M. R. Beard, *op. cit.,* Chap. VIII. A popular account of the battle is in Joseph Alsop, Jr., and Turner Catledge, *The 168 Days* (1938), and a philosophical and legalistic discussion in R. H. Jackson, *The Struggle for Judicial Supremacy* (1941).

ECONOMIC AND SOCIAL LEGISLATION. C. A. Beard and G. H. E. Smith, *The Old Deal and the New Deal* (1940) integrates the legislation of the first two terms. R. L. Dewey, "Transportation Act of 1940," *Am. Ec. Rev.,* XXXI, 15–26 is helpful on the most important railroad legislation since 1920.

LABOR. The conflict between the A. F. of L. and the C.I.O. is told in Edward

Levinson, *Labor on the March* (1938) and J. Raymond Walsh, *C.I.O., Industrial Unions in Action* (1937), both sympathetic with the C.I.O. A background is given in R. R. R. Brooks, *When Labor Organizes* (1938). The same author in *Unions of Their Own Choosing* (1938) writes on the work of the National Labor Relations Board.

FOREIGN AFFAIRS. American foreign policy is critically appraised in C. A. Beard, *A Foreign Policy for America* (1940) and C. A. and M. R. Beard, *America in Mid-passage*, Chaps. IX–X. On neutrality: Allen W. Dulles and H. F. Armstrong, *Can America Stay Neutral?* (1939) and Edward Borchard and W. P. Lage, *Neutrality for the United States* (1940), Part II. On Latin America see the following: *Foreign Policy Reports:* C. H. Thompson, "Results of the Lima Conference," XV, No. 1 (March 15, 1939); H. J. Trueblood, "Progress of Pan-American Cooperation," XV, No. 23 (Sept. 15, 1940); and same author, "The Havana Conference of 1940," XVI, No. 13 (Sept. 15, 1940). On the Far East see also *Foreign Policy Reports:* T. A. Bisson, "America's Dilemma in the Far East," XVI, No. 8 (July 1, 1940). On the trade agreements: D. H. Porter, "Six Years of American Tariff Bargaining," *Foreign Policy Reports*, XVI, No. 3 (April 15, 1940) and F. B. Sayre, *The Way Forward: the American Trade Agreement Policy* (1939). Indispensable are *Documents on American Foreign Relations* by various editors, 5 vols., covering Jan. 1938–June, 1943 (World Peace Foundation, 1939–44). Latin American relations are interpreted in S. F. Bemis, *The Latin American Policy of the United States* (1943). American attitudes are discussed in Walter Johnson, *Battle Against Isolation* (1944). On the European Background read Dwight E. Lee, *Ten Years: The World on the Way to War, 1930–1940* (1942) and Frederick L. Schurman, *Design for Power* (1941).

THE ELECTION OF 1936. Wendell Willkie, *This is Wendell Willkie* (1940) is a collection of speeches. In a supplement to the *New Republic*, Vol. 103, No. 10 (Sept. 2, 1940), there is an extremely critical appraisal of Willkie, and in J. T. Flynn, *Country Squire in the White House* a similar appraisal of Roosevelt.

XLII. AMERICA GOES TO WAR

Peace and War: United States Foreign Policy, 1931–1941 (1942) is the official State Department account of the diplomatic background of the war. A brief account of military operations will be found in the annual numbers of the *Americana Annual* and the *New International Year Book*. A longer account is in Edgar McInnis, *The War* (4 vols., 1940–44), a volume devoted to each of the first four years of the war. Some official accounts have appeared, such as *Target: Germany, the Army Air Force's Official Story of the VIIIth Bomber Command's First Year over Europe* (1943). Many eye-witness accounts written chiefly by journalists on special phases have appeared, such as Richard Tregaskis, *Guadalcanal Diary* (1943) and *Invasion Diary* (1944), covering Sicily and Italy; Wes Gallegher, *Back Door to Berlin* (1943), on the conquest of Africa; J. M. Brown, *Many a Watchful Night* (1944), on the invasion of Normandy; and Robert Corse, *Lifeline* (1943), on the merchant marine.

Discussion of the problems of world peace include Herbert Hoover and Hugh Gibson, *Problems of Lasting Peace* (1942); Wendell Willkie, *One World* (1943); and Sumner Welles, *The Time for Decision* (1944).

INDEX